Tamara

The SAGE
Handbook of
African American
Education

EDITORIAL BOARD

The SAGE
Handbook of
African American
Education

Linda C. Tillman

The University of North Carolina at Chapel Hill

Editor

Los Angeles • London • New Delhi • Singapore

For information:

SAGE Publications, Inc.
2455 Teller Road
Thousand Oaks, California 91320
E-mail: order@sagepub.com

SAGE Publications Ltd.
1 Oliver's Yard
55 City Road
London EC1Y 1SP
United Kingdom

SAGE Publications India Pvt. Ltd.
B 1/I 1 Mohan Cooperative Industrial Area
Mathura Road, New Delhi 110 044
India

SAGE Publications Asia-Pacific Pte. Ltd.
33 Pekin Street #02-01
Far East Square
Singapore 048763

Printed in the United States of America

Library of Congress Cataloging-in-Publication Data

The SAGE handbook of African American education/[edited by] Linda C. Tillman.
    p. cm.
Includes bibliographical references and indexes.
ISBN 978–1-4129–3743–6 (cloth)
    1. African Americans—Education—Handbooks, manuals, etc. 2. African American teachers—Handbooks, manuals, etc. I. Tillman, Linda C. II. Title: Handbook of African American education.

LC2717.S34 2009
371.829′96073—dc22   2008001112

Printed on acid-free paper

08   09   10   11   12   10   9   8   7   6   5   4   3   2   1

Acquiring Editor:	Diane McDaniel
Editorial Assistant:	Leah Mori
Production Editor:	Sarah K. Quesenberry
Copy Editor:	QuADS
Proofreader:	Victoria Reed-Castro
Indexer:	Will Ragsdale
Typesetter:	C&M Digitals (P) Ltd.
Cover Designer:	Candice Harman
Marketing Manager:	Christy Guilbault

CONTENTS

"Bringing the gifts that my ancestors gave, I am the dream and the hope of the slave."

This book is dedicated to the memory of

Buck and Caroline Clark

William H. and Carrie L. Nivins Tillman

Eddie L. Tillman

Dennis H. Tillman

Daryl R. Tillman

Raphael A. Fair

Deborah Ann Blue

Richard W. Simmons

Ursel White Lewis

PREFACE

Our children, if respected, and if exposed to good teaching, have the genius to master any content, even alien content.

The single most worrisome change for the African community and its children is the loss of our community's influence over the education and socialization of our children. This is the precise struggle that we began in earnest in 1865, out of enslavement, with many ensuing episodes that mark the continuing struggle, including the early period of the 50s and 60s desegregation documented by Charles V. Hamilton.

Certainly it is the task of educational researchers to illuminate whatever the essential realities are, hegemony and success in spite of it, and where possible, to communicate findings in a clear way to those who need the data and interpretations.

Our acute problem is this: How do we gain sufficient influence and leverage to change the course for our children? How can research and evaluation be used to change our trajectory, reframe the problem, and guide us to valid solutions?

—Asa G. Hilliard III (Nana Baffour Amankwatia II) (2007)

It is my pleasure to serve as the general editor for the *Handbook of African American Education*. I am also grateful for the opportunity to honor the memory and work of the late Dr. Asa G. Hilliard III whose words begin this preface. These quotes were part of Asa's W. E. B. Du Bois Distinguished lecture for the AERA Research Focus on Black Education Special Interest Group in April 2007. As I worked on the completion of this volume, Asa's words seemed to reflect much of the intent and purpose of a *Handbook of African American Education*. I offer them as a "libation" to the publication of this volume.

Additionally, I want to recognize the citizens of New Orleans, Louisiana, who were affected by Hurricane Katrina in 2005, and especially the African American students, teachers, and administrators in the New Orleans Public Schools (NOPS) system. As a former faculty member at the University of New Orleans and a resident of the lower ninth ward, I observed the educational environment for the majority of African American children in New Orleans prior to the onslaught of Katrina. Before Katrina, African American children in the NOPS were underserved and undereducated. As a faculty member, I trained future NOPS principals and worked in schools where I investigated problems that plagued the district: shortages of certified teachers, underfunding, violence, and the warehousing of students in deteriorating and unsafe buildings. Today, New Orleans' public educational system is a patchwork of several different minisystems and is plagued by high absenteeism among students and teachers, low student enrollments, a shortage of teachers and administrators, and parents who are largely uninformed about the specifics of how to access public education for their children. Indeed more than 2 years after Katrina, the NOPS system continues to struggle to educate its majority African American student population. Thus, in many ways Katrina exacerbated the already dismal educational conditions for children in the NOPS. Additionally, Irvine and Foster (1996) have noted that access to Catholic education has provided many African Americans with an alternative to public education. This was particularly the case in New Orleans where significant numbers of African American students attended Catholic schools before Katrina. In the aftermath of Katrina, many Catholic schools have not reopened or are struggling to remain fiscally solvent. Thus, Katrina not only caused the loss of lives, homes, hospitals, businesses, and university programs, and altered the cultural norms of the city, it also resulted in a tremendous social injustice—the denial of an education to many African American children. As we continue to work on behalf of Black children, we must not forget the specific circumstances of those students affected by Hurricane Katrina.

This volume of work represents the collective efforts of many individuals whose knowledge, expertise, and vision helped to move this *Handbook* from an idea to a reality. The intellectual contributions of these scholars to this effort were not surprising to me. Indeed, many African American scholars have devoted their life's work to researching and writing about the education of Black people in this country. Their scholarship has influenced and encouraged me to ask important and often complex questions about the state of Black education at the K–12 and postsecondary levels. Among those questions are the following: What do we know about the education of Black people? What challenges do Black people face in the U.S. educational system? What must be done to improve the educational outcomes and life chances of every Black child? In what ways can educational researchers, practitioners, parents, and policymakers work to change conditions and deficit perspectives that affect these outcomes? While the answers to these questions may appear to be simple, the condition of many urban school systems and the academic achievement levels of many Black children in urban, suburban, and rural districts would suggest that we have yet to provide answers that will lead to a socially just educational system for *all* Black children.

HISTORICAL PERSPECTIVES

The impetus for this *Handbook* came not only from my recognition of the extensive historical contributions that have been made by African American scholars, but also from my admiration of those Black folk who, despite what appeared to be insurmountable odds, fought to gain access to education for themselves and their children. The early struggles to gain access to, and control of, their own education can be seen in the collective and individual efforts of many African Americans who articulated a philosophy of Black education (Booker T. Washington, Carter G. Woodson, W. E. B. Du Bois, Anna Julia Cooper), and those who worked to establish programs and institutions that would provide an education for Blacks (the Common School Movement, Sabbath Schools, Bethune Cookman College, Freedom Schools).

Numerous Black postsecondary institutions such as Bethune Cookman College had close affiliations with the Black church. Black church denominations played a significant role in this struggle and were in the forefront of educating African Americans during and after slavery. For example, when the African Methodist Episcopal Church opened Wilberforce University, it became the first university owned and operated by Blacks. In a discussion of the church's leadership, Tillman (2004) wrote,

> In 1826, Daniel Payne, an African Methodist Episcopal Bishop started a school in Charleston, South Carolina, for free Black children and adult slaves. The school was closed in 1834 when Whites became fearful that free Blacks might have access to and be influenced by abolitionist literature. The South Carolina legislature passed a law that prohibited free Blacks from keeping any school or other place of instruction for teaching any slave or free person of color to read or write. Payne left Charleston and moved north where, because of his leadership as a principal and a minister, he became one of the most influential minister-educators in the Black community. He later founded Wilberforce College (now Wilberforce University) in Xenia, Ohio, the oldest college of the African Methodist Episcopal Church. (p. 107)

Anderson (1988) wrote that the Zion School, established in 1865, was another example of how Blacks took control of their own education. The school was one of the first all-Black schools in the south and was led by an all-Black teaching and administrative staff. Pre- and post-*Brown* exemplars of educational institutions and organizations that were established for African Americans include the Piney Woods School, an interdenominational Christian school founded by Laurence C. Jones almost 100 years ago in rural Mississippi; the Council of Independent Black Institutions founded in 1972; the University of Islam Schools, which are owned and operated by the Nation of Islam; and the Westside Preparatory School of Chicago, founded by Marva Collins in 1975. The work of Carol D. Lee and Haki Madhubuti, who along with others founded the New Concept Development Center (NCDC) of Chicago, is particularly noteworthy. The Center opened in 1972 at the height of the Black Power and Black Arts movements, and the founders envisioned operating a school that would provide resources and leadership from within, rather than from outside of the Black community. Lee (in press) in a discussion of the Center wrote,

> Over the past 35 years, New Concept Development Center (NCDC) of Chicago, Illinois, along with other independent Black institutions (IBIs) across the country, has strived to educate and socialize African American children to assume their future roles as political, intellectual, spiritual and economic leaders in their communities and the world. Its vision is one in which Black people are self-reliant, productive, self-defining, and firmly rooted in family and community—a vision NCDC's founders and staff hope will be impossible for its students to lose.

The NCDC began as a Saturday school program that provided educational support to Black children aged 2 to 12 and has expanded to include three African-centered charter schools under the umbrella of the Betty Shabazz International Charter Schools. Lee noted that alumni of the Center have graduated from historically Black colleges and universities as well as predominantly White institutions, including Stanford, Northwestern, and Princeton. One of the charter schools, the Betty Shabazz International Charter School, has been identified as a school of distinction within the Chicago Public Schools system.

These and numerous other exemplars are representative of the commitment of African American scholars, parents, teachers, administrators, and community members to establish educational institutions and programs that foster high expectations and provide a safe and nurturing learning environment for their children. These exemplars also illustrate how the self-defined knowledge of African Americans is placed at the center, rather than on the margins of teaching and learning as well as educational discourse, practice, and policy (Tillman, 2002).

CONTEMPORARY PERSPECTIVES

Current discourse and practice regarding the education of African Americans in this country is often framed in deficit perspectives about underqualified teachers, ineffective leadership and administration, poor student test scores, underfunded school districts, and a lack of parental involvement. Additionally, media accounts frequently detail the plight of Black males: their disproportionate numbers in special education, high dropout rates, poor college-going rates, and the likelihood that they will end up in prison. In her discussion of the state of Black education, Joyce Elaine King (2005) wrote,

> "Excellence, Superior Quality, Perfection, Knowledge, Critical Examination": these highly valued terms are unlikely to be used by researchers, educators, students, parents, or policy decision makers anywhere in the world. Indeed, for most Black students, particularly those attending dysfunctional, resource-starved schools in the United States, a leader among "civilized" nations, Black education is synonymous with underachievement and academic failure. (p. xxi)

King's analysis should be of concern to us because as policymakers continue to debate about standards, accountability, and the distribution of resources to schools, many of our African American children are being held hostage in these dysfunctional, resource-starved school systems.

A plethora of contemporary issues directly affect the leadership, participation, and academic achievement of African Americans in the U.S. educational system. For example, the U.S. Supreme Court recently ruled against voluntary integration plans in K-12 public schools in Seattle, Washington, and Louisville, Kentucky (*Parents Involved in Community Schools v. Seattle School District*, 2007). These plans were designed to prevent racial segregation in schools by allowing a student's race to be considered in making school assignments. How will the Court's decision ultimately affect African Americans' access to equitable education not only in Seattle and Louisville, but across this country? The declining numbers of Black teachers, principals, and superintendents is also a concern. Who will replace those Black teachers and administrators who leave the profession and retire? Teacher training programs like those that were found at Cheney State Teachers College (Pennsylvania), Bluefield State Teachers College (West Virginia), and Morris Brown College (Georgia) no longer exist, and it is difficult to find teacher education programs that are educating a critical mass of African American teachers. Additionally, when will we begin to view teaching as a profession, and how will we improve working conditions in schools so that more African Americans will choose careers in teaching and administration?

At the state and federal level, the uncertainty of the impact of the No Child Left Behind Act on the educational outcomes of Black children continues to be debated in educational and policy circles. While the Act is intended to benefit African Americans and students in other subgroups, it is not clear whether significant numbers of Black children have benefited from the Act's emphasis on standards and accountability. As the late Dr. Asa G. Hilliard III noted in his W. E. B. Du Bois Distinguished Lecture (2007),

> We are well into the NCLB initiative, and I cannot see how we could call the results achieved as anything more than a miserable failure. Since NCLB, United States academic achievement is actually down, expectations are down, and promises for the future may soon be down as well. (p. 17)

With a reauthorization of the Act, we can only hope that the revised Act will address the issues that Dr. Hilliard identified and will benefit all African American students.

Space does not permit me to discuss all the issues that negatively affect the participation and education of African Americans in U.S. society. However, it is clear from these examples that there is much work to be done as we attempt to articulate an agenda for Black education for students in urban, suburban, and rural schools as well as those in charter, private, and alternative settings.

THE PURPOSE OF THE *HANDBOOK*

The publication of this *Handbook* coincides with the growing interest in the theory, research, practice, and stories of African American scholars and leaders with respect to their status in education. For example, a recent publication titled *Beyond the Big House: African American Educators in Teacher Education* (2005), edited by Gloria Ladson-Billings includes the stories of seven nationally recognized African American teacher educators. Their stories represent "a reconceptualization of the process of teacher preparation from a unique and long-overdue perspective" (book advertisement).

A major purpose of this *Handbook* is to articulate the perspectives of African American scholar/leaders and policymakers about issues affecting the education, participation, and leadership of African Americans in U.S. society. Thus, the content of the *Handbook* is intended to promote inquiry and dialogue, and the development of questions and ideas that focus on critical practice, theory, and research about African Americans in the U.S. educational system. The *Handbook* addresses six major areas: Historical Perspectives on the Education of African Americans; The Landscape of Teaching and Learning for African Americans in U.S. Schooling; African Americans in PK-12 Educational Leadership; African Americans in Higher Education; Current Issues: Theory and Research on the Participation of African Americans in U.S. Education; and African Americans Shaping Educational Policy.

Ladson-Billings (2005) noted that the scholarship on Black education is often criticized for being too narrow (subtext: It's too Black). Yet we know from the work of a very long list of distinguished African American scholar/leaders that African Americans have a long and rich history of excellence at the PK-12 and postsecondary levels in teaching, leading, learning, parental involvement, policymaking, and attending and graduating from postsecondary institutions. The work of these and other scholars has had a significant influence on the field of education and has caused us to be more thoughtful in our research, teaching, and scholarship as we wrestle with current realities and attempt to pose solutions. Indeed, the contributors to this *Handbook* represent a critical mass of African Americans who excel as scholars and policymakers in a variety of educational, private, and public arenas. Thus, it is in the context of this long and rich history of excellence that we present this volume of scholarship that builds on previous work and sets forth a new agenda for researching, writing, and theorizing about the education of African Americans.

This *Handbook* focuses on a specific racial group—African Americans. This focus is intentional on my part; that is, I wanted to "center" the cultural frames of reference, experiences, challenges, and successes with respect to the education of African Americans. Thus, I have purposely chosen not to use the more general term *women and minorities*. As Williams (2005) noted, focusing on Black people allows one to "see important elements that have been overlooked" (p. 5) in previous theory and research. Furthermore, the work in this *Handbook* is also intended to present counternarratives to theory and research on African Americans that fail to capture the broad spectrum of experiences within African American culture. Indeed, African Americans are not a monolithic group; rather, they are poor, middle-income, and wealthy Americans; attend public, private, and charter schools; have high and low standardized test scores; attend public, historically Black, predominantly White, and Ivy League postsecondary institutions; and espouse a variety of cultural norms and values. Thus, the authors present their work from an "assets-oriented perspective" incorporating the range of African American experiences.

The work in the *Handbook* is also cross-disciplinary and is intended to reach a wide audience that includes educational researchers, teachers, leaders, policymakers, and students in undergraduate and graduate-level programs. Within this cross-disciplinary context, several key themes are evident across the chapters: the African American struggle for and achievement of academic excellence; the imperative for strategic, proactive responses to socially unjust conditions facing many African American students, teachers, parents, and leaders; the imperative for providing counternarratives to deficit perspectives on teaching, learning, leading, and community activism for African Americans; and the imperative to implement policies and practices that include rather than exclude African American children. Finally, the scholarship in this *Handbook* gives voice to empowering, race-focused research.

ORGANIZATION OF THE *HANDBOOK*

The *Handbook* is divided into six sections followed by an epilogue. Section I of the *Handbook* presents historical perspectives on the education of African Americans in the United States. The work in this section establishes the context for the political and philosophical struggle for education, as well as the ways in which African American educators were successful in creating and maintaining educational systems that served as a catalyst for future efforts. Historical perspectives on the participation and leadership of African Americans in U.S. education, particularly in the pre-*Brown* era, is a central topic guiding the content of this section. Adah Ward Randolph examines the history of Black education during the antebellum and postantebellum periods in Columbus, Ohio, while Derrick Alridge discusses the educational ideas of selected African American educators and argues for the place of African American educational thought within the larger African American intellectual tradition. Next, V. P. Franklin provides an extensive account of the educational agendas of African American educators and leaders and their contributions to the African American community. Turning to the education of Black women, Linda Perkins examines how Black women struggled to gain access to postgraduate education, 1921 to 1948. In the last chapter in this section, Michael Fultz provides a historical perspective of the ascension and decline of Black teacher groups and associations in the 19th and 20th centuries.

The chapters in Section II of the *Handbook* explore the various dimensions of the participation of Black teachers, Black students, and Black parents in PK-12 education. Teaching and learning are emphasized in these chapters, and authors highlight critical factors that affect teacher competence and the social, emotional, and academic success of African American students. In the first chapter, Peter Murrell offers an alternative to the current discourse on the Black-White achievement gap by looking at social identification, cultural practices, and issues of agency. Next, Yolanda Majors and Sana Ansari focus on classroom community participation structures and consider how African American students' cultural socialization informs their communication, conflict resolution, and literary skills. The next two chapters focus on teachers and teacher practices. H. Richard Milner provides a review of the literature on curricular, instructional, and policy mandates relative to teacher education and argues for a more proactive approach in teacher education to address racist practices and policies, and Mari Roberts and Jacqueline Jordan Irvine discuss teachers' culturally relevant caring practices. The section concludes with the work of Cheryl Fields-Smith who reviews the literature on African American parental involvement and argues that African American parents care about and are very much involved in their children's education.

In Section III of the *Handbook,* the authors are concerned with factors that affect the leadership capacity of African Americans in PK-12 education. Linda C. Tillman reviews the literature on African Americans in the principalship pre- and post-*Brown v. Board of Education* and posits a framework for Black principal leadership, and Robert Cooper and Will Jordan present findings from a study of African Americans enrolled in an urban leadership preparation program. Turning her attention to Black female principals, Tondra Loder-Jackson adds to the scholarly literature on the advancement and experiences of African American women principals using findings from a life history study of Birmingham, Alabama, educators born during the pre– and post–Civil Rights era. In the last two chapters, Mark Gooden discusses the convergence of race, law, and school leadership, while Kay Lovelace Taylor and Linda C. Tillman present findings from a study of African Americans in the superintendency.

Chapters in Section IV of the *Handbook* shift to investigations of the status of African Americans in postsecondary education. Eddie Comeaux and Walter Allen address the decline in the admission of students of African descent in the University of California system since 1996. Jon Yasin adds to the growing body of literature on the influence of hip hop culture on education and discusses hip hop culture and higher education. Next, William Smith analyzes the racial climate for African American students on predominantly White campuses, and Kofi Lomotey and Sessi Aboh examine the topic of historically Black colleges and universities (HBCUs). In the last chapter, Lynette Danley, Roderic Land, and Kofi Lomotey offer a perspective on African American graduate students who are preparing for careers in academia.

Section V of the *Handbook* focuses on current issues affecting the participation of African Americans in U.S. education. In the first chapter, Marvin Lynn and Thurman Bridges connect critical race theory to critical race studies in education as a means for discussing the importance of race in the education of African American children. James Moore and Delilah Owens discuss issues that inhibit positive educational outcomes for African American students, focus on the roles of teachers and counselors, and identify factors contributing to underachievement, such as low expectations, negative self-image, social ills, and cultural dissonance. Next, Carol Malloy and Richard Noble present findings from a study of four charter schools and offer some reasons why African American parents choose charter schools over traditional public schools for their children. The last two chapters focus on two critical areas—African Americans in special education and the education of Black males. Gwendolyn Cartledge and Charles Dukes discuss issues affecting African Americans in special education, and James Earl Davis presents common features of African American male culture and analyzes the dissonance between their culture and traditional schooling.

The final section of the *Handbook* focuses on education policy aimed at improving educational outcomes for African American students. Jennifer Beaumont presents the personal histories of

African American policymakers who have worked to implement policies that benefit African American students and their communities, and Eric Cooper examines the outcomes of a school reform model that uses student strengths as a launching point for movement toward high intellectual performance. Next, Sabrina Hope King and Nancy Cardwell analyze collaborations among a range of stakeholders that are internal and external to public schools in one community. Sheilah Vance provides a legal perspective of the impact of equity in school finance in school districts serving predominantly African American student populations. In the last chapter, Jessica Gordon Nembhard discusses the role of African American Studies Departments in helping college-level students to have a deeper understanding of the economic power within their communities and how to develop entrepreneurial knowledge and skills.

The *Handbook* concludes with an epilogue by Joyce Elaine King. In this provocative essay King presents a post-Katrina analysis of the state of Black education, and cautions us that in the aftermath of Katrina, African Americans still face many complex challenges in the highly contested educational arena.

The scholarship in this *Handbook* does not represent the complete range of issues that affect the participation and leadership of African Americans in U.S. education. However, the authors do address important issues that affect African American teachers, students, and administrators in PK-12 and postsecondary institutions. Additionally, they address the role that educational policy plays in shaping the futures of African American students. Yet there is much more work to be done, and future research and policy initiatives must focus on other equally important issues that include providing educational opportunities for African American students in alternative settings (prisons, juvenile detention centers, etc.), investigating the educational environments of the large number of African American children who live in poverty in the South, investigating the educational environments of schools that have been identified as dropout factories, articulating an early-childhood agenda for Black children, and improving access to and graduation rates from postsecondary education. We hope that you will join us in continuing this work.

REFERENCES

Anderson, J. D. (1988). *The education of Blacks in the South, 1860–1935*. Chapel Hill: University of North Carolina Press.

Hilliard, A. G., III. (2007, April). *Shaping research for global African educational excellence: It is now or never.* W. E. B. Du Bois distinguished lecture, Research Focus on Black Education SIG, presented at the Annual Meeting of the American Educational Research Association, Chicago.

Irvine, J. J., & Foster, M. (Eds.). (1996). *Growing up African American in Catholic schools.* New York: Teachers College Press.

King, J. E. (2005). Preface. In J. E. King (Ed.), *Black education: A transformative research and action agenda for the new century* (pp. xxi–xxx). Mahwah, NJ: Lawrence Erlbaum.

Ladson-Billings, G. (2005). *Beyond the Big House: African American educators on teacher education.* New York: Teachers College Press.

Lee, C. D. (in press). Profile of an independent Black institution: African-centered education at work. In C. Payne & C. Strickland (Eds.), *Teach freedom: The African American tradition of education for liberation.* New York: Teachers College Press.

Parents Involved in Community Schools v. Seattle School District No. 1 et al., No. 05–908 (on certiorari to the U.S. Court of Appeals, 9th Cir. June 8, 2007).

Tillman, L. C. (2002). Culturally sensitive research approaches: An African American perspective. *Educational Researcher, 31*(9), 3–12.

Tillman, L. C. (2004). African American principals and the legacy of *Brown. Review of Research in Education, 28,* 101–146.

Williams, H. A. (2005). *African American education in slavery and freedom: Self-taught.* Chapel Hill: University of North Carolina Press.

INTRODUCTION

GLORIA LADSON-BILLINGS

When I first agreed to take on the responsibility of writing an introduction for this *Handbook,* I had no idea what I was signing on to. When the manuscripts began arriving, I was taken aback by their sheer volume. The sound track that erupted in my mind was an old Sunday School song that starts out, "So high, you can't get over it; so low you can't get under it; so wide you can't get around it; you must come in at the door!" However, when I began to think seriously about what the volume was designed to do and its scope, I thought that, indeed, such a task should result in something high, low, and wide. The editors and authors have taken on the challenge of writing about a monumental work in a most critical moment. It is a big work that somehow often is seen in just the opposite light.

Almost every African American scholar I know who has dedicated his or her career to some aspect of African American life and culture has heard the comment, "Your work is interesting, but it's too narrow." Indeed, when I worked on my book, *Beyond the Big House: African American Educators on Teacher Education* (2005) I was able to comb through the transcripts of the participants and unearth this as a theme I entitled, "Your work is too narrow, but really it's too Black!" I find that sentiment of "narrow work" particularly curious in the academy. First, academics are trained to be specialists. To be successful, they must focus their work on very specific and "narrow" domains. I have colleagues in mathematics education who have dedicated their entire careers to studying mathematical functions—not all of mathematics—just mathematical functions. I have colleagues in anthropology who study one traditional community in a rural village in Central America. Neither of these colleagues has had their work described as "too narrow." Indeed, they are rewarded and acclaimed as "experts" in their fields. So what is it about studying African Americans, and in this case, African American education, that makes it too narrow?

The second part of my thematic assertion—it's too Black—is probably salient to the question posed above. Something about the focus on African Americans makes American culture in the United States very fearful. I would argue that this fear is integrally linked to the complex history and life experiences of African Americans in this society. The very same people who might champion efforts toward "multicultural" education bristle at a focus on African Americans and their education. Clearly, in this introduction I will not have the opportunity to fully unpack and analyze the pathology of race and racism in this culture. However, I will, as a critical race theorist, argue that as long as race matters (West, 1993), blackness and everything associated with it will be opposed and construed as serving special interests.

The first tenet of critical race theory (CRT) is that racism is normal, not aberrant (Delgado & Stefancic, 1999). Although we strive to make negative racial interactions seem abnormal and idiosyncratic, the patterns of Black life indicate that such experiences are a regular part of life in this society. While it is true that certain status characteristics—gender, social class, perceived academic ability, color, and so on—may mitigate some effects of racism, they cannot fully explain how race functions. For example, an expensively dressed middle-aged African American woman can walk into a department store and have no trouble browsing the store racks and purchasing something. However, that same woman might come in the same store a week later wearing her jeans and a T-shirt. This time, her shopping experience may seem quite different. Instead of receiving good service, she may feel that she is under surveillance or be constantly passed over by the store personnel. Of course, one might argue that the difference in the service was linked to the woman's social class, and it would be difficult to disentangle the effects of race versus class in this instance. However, when Black people regularly accumulate these experiences or what CRT scholars call, "micro-aggressions" (Solorzano, Ceja, & Yosso, 2000), they begin to recognize race, not class, as the common feature of the experience.

In one of my own CRT moments (Ladson-Billings, 1998) I was seated, reading the newspaper in the concierge lounge of a major hotel after having given a "distinguished lecture." A White gentleman peered into the room and asked, "What time I was going to begin serving?" He could not have made an assessment based on my class because I was dressed in business clothes. However, one might make the argument that he made his assessment based on gender. Again, we can mentally track these incidents and weigh which attribute is at work. A different CRT moment example is a clearer indicator. A colleague who serves as a university provost tells of the time at a professional conference when he was standing in front of a hotel awaiting his automobile from valet parking. While standing there a White man drove up, jumped out, and handed my friend his keys!

So, if race matters in the realm of the mundane, how might it matter specifically in the realm of the educational histories, patterns, and experiences of African Americans? This is one of the insights that this volume provides. That African Americans do have different experiences in and with education is not news to most African Americans. It *is* news to a broader public that assumes that time and social efforts have either eliminated or alleviated barriers and obstacles of previous years. This volume looks at both macro- and microlevel experiences of African Americans in education. It includes the history, teaching and learning, leaders and leadership, higher education, theory and research, and educational policy. In the latter part of this introduction, I want to address briefly each of these categories that represent the sections of the *Handbook*.

The history of African American education is, in itself, a huge undertaking. It, like each of these sections, is worthy of a volume all its own. Let me start with a declaration that there has never been a time when African Americans were not involved with education—of themselves and their children. Even in the midst of chattel slavery, African Americans were engaged in education. What education meant to African Americans early on was different from what it meant for White Americans. For African Americans, education was so deeply linked to freedom and life that it became a driving quest for generations from the time of *Maafa*[1] to the modern Civil Rights Movement.[2] Despite the threat of death, enslaved Africans found ways to educate themselves. This history includes institution building—from grade schools to colleges, from churches to civic organizations— all designed to share in the education of a people. The history of African American education includes the history of Black teachers and their distinctly different treatment by state and local officials. This history may help us understand the current shortage of Black teachers and the pipeline challenges.

Section II of the *Handbook* focuses on teaching and learning. I have spent much of my intellectual energy on this topic. Despite the literature's emphasis on generic models of teaching and wholly psychologized notions of learning, research on African American teaching and learning by African American scholars has offered us some new ways of thinking about students, their families, their culture, and pedagogy. This work has challenged the literature of cultural deficiency and disadvantage. Instead of designing interventions to compensate for perceived social, cultural, and intellectual lacks, the work of scholars like Delpit (1996), Foster (1996), Ladson-Billings (1994), Murrell (2001), and others focused on the strengths and resilience of African American students, their families, and communities as well as the insights that many Black teachers might have about these assets.

Section III of this volume looks at leaders and leadership. Our historical and cultural amnesia and myopia have caused us to drop African American leaders from the public consciousness. It is only when we get either heroic isolates or educational intimidators (e.g., Joe Clark of "Lean on Mean" fame) that we see examples of African American leaders. We have forgotten the work of school leaders in the many segregated schools that existed throughout the nation. After some southern schools were forced by court order to desegregate, many African American school leaders were demoted or fired. Scholars in educational leadership raise questions about the kinds of schools and districts African American leaders are hired to lead. Like their counterparts in big cities, many African American school leaders have the experience of being assigned to "broken" systems with the expectation that they will miraculously "fix" them.

Section IV draws our attention to African American higher education. This topic covers everything from our proud legacy of Historically Black Colleges and Universities (HBCUs) to our participation in predominantly White institutions (PWIs). Despite economic hardship, limited endowments, and dwindling enrollments, HBCUs continue to serve as an important "port of entry" for many first-generation collegians as well as legacy students. But not all African Americans attend HBCUs. A significant number of the Black college-going population attends PWIs. Once Black students arrive on these campuses, issues of admission and affirmative action, along with campus climate, continue to be an important source of research inquiry. Another component of our thinking about higher education for African Americans concerns the recruitment and retention of African American faculty. At PWIs the small number of African American faculty has a major impact on the success of African American students and their sense of belonging and participation on these campuses. African American faculty members continue to suffer isolation and alienation in their careers. As new faculty, they often lack the mentoring that would lead to tenure and promotion. Additionally, African American faculty members often are discouraged from pursuing research agendas that directly focus on African Americans.

In the next section, the volume focuses on theory and research. Thus, the question of epistemology and methodology is relevant. A huge challenge in African American education research is epistemological. What we know and how we know it remains contested (Ladson-Billings, 2000). African American educational researchers are developing work in frameworks that transcend traditions. Their work may move beyond positivists-functionalists paradigms that reflect the hegemony of dominant discourses and move toward culture-centered perspectives (King, 1995). Thus, the idea that knowing might be affected by race, culture, and social standpoint can have currency in research on African American education. Also, how you actually get at the knowledge imbedded in African American communities presents some exciting possibilities. While traditional work on African American education has relied on the fidelity of extant institutions and their functionaries—schools, community centers, teachers, social workers, police officers—African American researchers may be willing to probe and explore other venues—beauty shops, churches, peer groups, and other informal networks.

In Section VI of the volume, there is a look at the role of African Americans in shaping educational policy. While this may be thought of as a more macrolevel set of questions, we know that policy often starts at microlevels and migrate up to the macro where it influences large numbers of students and shapes thinking. For example, a school principal or group of parents might decide that students should wear school uniforms. Before long, this idea makes its way to the district level, and there is a policy decision that all students must wear school uniforms. Similarly, policy functions in the opposite direction, that is, district, state, or national policies affect the individual classrooms and students. Laws such as the reauthorization of Title I (now known as "No Child Left Behind") create a set of challenges for individual schools, teachers, or students. Or, debates and decisions about increasing diversity on a college campus (e.g., state propositions, initiatives, and court rulings) have direct impact on the college access and opportunity. Work at this level is important in shaping the contours of education for African Americans.

While I have tried to outline the issues this volume tackles, I saved for the last the bigger challenge of epistemology and essence this work evokes. Vincent Harding (1970) argued that the study of African Americans by African Americans has moved through three distinct and significant phases. The first phase is what Harding terms *Negro History*. This is an epistemological stance that insisted that African Americans made contributions to the master narrative. Thus, the chronology, periodicity, and perspectives of European Americans remained unchallenged but African Americans made attempts to insert themselves into that history. Negro Historians worked hard to demonstrate that Black people "did it too!" Discussions of the Revolutionary War now were to include Crispus Attucks, James Forten, and Phyllis Wheatley. Discussions of abolition and resistance to slavery were broadened to include Black participation. Civil Rights efforts expanded to include Black initiative.

The second epistemological phase described by Harding (1970) is the Black History phase. Here, Harding argued, Black scholars begin to carve out a separate and distinct history of their experiences to be studied in opposition to the master narrative of American History. This distinct history created its own sense of chronology (where our history begins) and periodicity (what eras and time periods are bounded by which events), and perspectives. Thus, scholars raised questions such as the relationship of African Americans' story to the dominant story. Were we fighting for freedom just as Whites were fighting for freedom or were we prisoners of war who actually were seeking the kind of reparation that was due to any people in captivity? Were we participating in a "parallel" history, or were we experiencing and creating a separate and distinct history in the midst of oppression? Black History argues for the latter. According to Harding (1970), "Black History suggests that we are the name (that nobody knew); we are the wound (that nobody saw or saw but refused to heal); we are the letters of judgment growing fuller every moment. Black History is an attempt to read them clear" (p. 20).

Harding (1970) further asserted, "Black History cannot help but be politically oriented for it tends toward the total redefinition of an experience which was highly political. . . . And it recognizes that all histories of peoples participate in politics and are shaped by political and ideological views" (p. 21).

The third phase of the Black intellectual experience is what Harding (1970) described as the "Black Studies" Movement. This epistemic phase argues that history as a discipline is too limited to fully capture the robust nature of the African American experience. Instead, we need to look at, along with history, the literature, art, music, dance, psychology, sociology, philosophy, and anthropology of the Black Experience. Thus, a synthetic new field called Black Studies not only changed the way to approach the experiences of African Americans, it also changed the way scholars in most of the humanities and social sciences thought about their work. This epistemic rupture opened the academy to Women's Studies, Chicano/Latino Studies, Asian American Studies, Native American Studies, and a host of other scholarly disciplines.

Sylvia Wynter (2006) challenged us to see the relationship between the "epistemology of knowledge and the liberation of people" (p. 113). Somewhere in our sojourn here in the Americas we began to think the map (scholarly productivity, academic position, intellectual reputation) was the territory (improved academic achievement, intellectual integrity, liberation). Harding (1970) said,

> We should not be terrified by our history, or our future. Instead, we move, becoming participants in the search for a new Black Body, a full body which will receive and give love to all who need it. And in this body we may be granted the grace to become the builders of a new land whose place and shape and time are still unclear. It is nothing we have known here in America. It is nothing we have been promised here. Black History tells us that. But it also tells us that we build, and we begin with an entirely new understanding of ourselves and our surrounding—Black Studies, Black creativity, Black hope. (p. 29)

This volume is an important step in moving us back to the first order of business.

NOTES

1. *Maafa* is the term used to describe the horror of capture, incarceration, middle passage, seasoning, and slavery that Africans experienced in the Americas. Like the notion of holocaust, it speaks to the specific.

2. I call the period between 1950 and 1970 the modern Civil Rights Movement to underscore the fact that African Americans have *always* been involved in Civil Rights struggle.

REFERENCES

Delgado, R., & Stefancic, J. (Eds.). (1999). *Critical race theory: The cutting edge* (2nd ed.). Philadelphia: Temple University Press.

Delpit, L. (1996). *Other peoples' children: Culture and conflict in the classroom.* New York: New Press.

Foster, M. (1996). *Black teachers on teaching.* New York: New Press.

Harding, V. (1970). *Beyond chaos: Black history and the search for the new land* (Black Paper No. 2). Atlanta, GA: Institute of the Black World.

King, J. E. (1995). Culture centered knowledge: Black studies, curriculum transformation, and social action. In J. A. Banks & C. M. Banks (Eds.), *Handbook of research on multicultural education* (pp. 265–290). New York: Macmillan.

Ladson-Billings, G. (1994). *The dreamkeepers: Successful teachers of African American children.* San Francisco: Jossey-Bass.

Ladson-Billings, G. (1998). Just what is critical race theory and what's it doing in a *nice* field like education. *International Journal of Qualitative Studies in Education, 11,* 7–24.

Ladson-Billings, G. (2000). Racialized discourses and ethnic epistemologies. In N. Denzin & Y. Lincoln (Eds.), *Handbook of qualitative research* (2nd ed., pp. 257–277). Thousand Oaks, CA: Sage.

Ladson-Billings, G. (2005). *Beyond the big house: African American educators on teacher education.* New York: Teachers College Press.

Murrell, P. (2001). *The community teacher: A new framework for effective teaching.* New York: Teachers College Press.

Solorzano, D., Ceja, M., & Yosso, T. (2000). Critical race theory, racial microaggressions, and campus racial climate: The experiences of African American college students. *Journal of Negro Education, 69,* 60–73.

West, C. (1993). *Race matters.* New York: Vintage Books.

Wynter, S. (2006). On how we mistook the map for the territory, and re-imprisoned ourselves in our unbearable wrongness of being, of désêtre. In L. R. Gordon & J. A. Gordon (Eds.), *Not only the master's tools: African American studies in theory and practice* (pp. 107–169). Boulder, CO: Paradigm.

ACKNOWLEDGMENTS

The publication of this *Handbook* would not have been possible without the support of many individuals. My family has been a constant source of support during this process. I want to especially thank my mother, Susan Tillman Washington, who, during her illness, encouraged me to continue working on the *Handbook*. I also want to thank the members of my church family who continue to provide me with their unselfish nurturing and support. I am deeply grateful to my ancestors for their legacy of love, commitment, and accomplishment.

The publication of this *Handbook* was a team effort, and I would like to thank those individuals who assisted me with the details of editing a volume of work of this magnitude, including Jane Gorey. Fenwick English, my colleague at the University of North Carolina at Chapel Hill and the members of the editorial board were instrumental in helping me conceptualize the proposal for the *Handbook*. Many thanks to my editorial team at SAGE Publications, Diane McDaniel, Leah Mori, and Sarah Quesenberry for their guidance and professionalism. A very special thanks to section editors Derrick Alridge, V. P. Franklin, Jacqueline Jordan Irvine, Kofi Lomotey, Gwendolyn Cartledge, and Jennifer Beaumont for all their hard work in identifying authors, reading manuscripts, and offering me advice. Additionally, this endeavor would not have been possible without the efforts of the authors whose work is featured in this volume. They represent a critical mass of African American scholar/leaders whose scholarship will have a lasting impact on the field of educational research and education policy. I would also like to thank those persons who served as external reviewers and offered constructive and important feedback to the authors.

A. J. Angulo, *Winthrop University*

Frank Brown, *University of North Carolina-Chapel Hill*

M. Christopher Brown II, *University of Nevada-Las Vegas*

Melanie Carter, *Howard University*

Norvella Carter, *Texas A&M University*

Colleen A. Clay, *York College, City University of New York*

Cheryl Cozart, *George Mason University*

Beverly Cross, *University of Memphis*

Amanda Datnow, *University of California-Los Angeles*

Carla Edlefson, *Ashland University*

David Embrick, *Loyola University-Chicago*

Maisha Fisher, *Emory University*

Lamont Flowers, *Clemson University*

Len Foster, *Washington State University*

James W. Fraser, *New York University*

Fred Frelow, Director, *Woodrow Wilson National Fellowship Foundation*

Micheal Froning, *University of Alabama*

Vivian Gadsen, *University of Pennsylvania*

Lin Goodwin Teachers College, *Columbia University*

Margaret Grogan, *University of Missouri-Columbia*

Paula Groves Price, *Washington State University*

Janice E. Hale, *Wayne State University*

Malik Henfield, *University of Iowa*

Richard Hunter, *University of Illinois-Urbana Champaign*

Barbara Jackson, *Fordham University*

Stephen Jacobson, *State University of New York at Buffalo*

Joseph O. Jewel, *Texas A&M University*

Barbara Jones, *Alabama A&M University*

Cathy Kea, *North Carolina A & T University*

Carol Lee, *Northwestern University*

Dan Levine, Professor Emeritus, *University of Nebraska*

Kristin Lewis, *Drexel University*

Kofi Lomotey, *Fisk University*

Jerome Morris, *University of Georgia*

Marjorie Orellana, *University of California-Los Angeles*

Yoon Pak, *University of Illinois-Urbana Champaign*

Laurence Parker, *University of Illinois-Urbana Champaign*

Diane Pollard, Professor Emeritus, *University of Wisconsin-Milwaukee*

Christopher Span, *University of Illinois-Urbana Champaign*

Lee Stiff, *North Carolina State University*

David Omotoso Stovall, *University of Illinois-Chicago*

Stanley Trent, *University of Virginia*

Sherrise Truesdale, *Minnesota State University at Mankato*

Gerald White-Davis, *Medgar Evers College, City University of New York*

Dwayne Wright, *Cleveland State University*

Linda Valli, *University of Maryland-College Park*

Finally, I would like to thank my colleagues in the American Educational Research Association's Research Focus on Black Education Special Interest Group, the University Council for Educational Administration, and Division A of the American Educational Research Association who encouraged and supported me in this effort. Last, but certainly not the least, I want to acknowledge the support of the Barbara L. Jackson Scholars of the University Council for Educational Administration, who are our next generation of scholar/leaders.

—Linda C. Tillman, Ph.D.
March 2008

SECTION I

THE EDUCATION OF BLACK FOLK

Historical Perspectives

INTRODUCTION

Derrick P. Alridge

V. P. Franklin

The history of African American education is one of struggle and triumph. It is a history of African-descended people aggressively pursuing quality education and schooling to improve their social, economic, and political conditions in the face of seemingly insurmountable obstacles. More specifically, the history of African American education is also one of agency and self-determination in which African Americans sought to develop, operate, and control their own educational institutions and programs.

Throughout the 20th century, historians of African American education documented this rich history of agency and self-determination in bringing about education and schooling for African-descended people and their children. For instance, historian Carter G. Woodson (1919) showed that prior to Emancipation and the end of the Civil War, African Americans sought to improve their social and economic status by gaining an education and starting their own schools, even when it was illegal or dangerous to do so. Historian and activist W. E. B. Du Bois (1935/1995) proposed that Black educational agency during Reconstruction led to free public education in the South in the late 1860s and 1870s. Educator Anna Julia Cooper (1892/1988) argued that educated Black women played a critical role in Black racial uplift.

Woodson, Du Bois, and Cooper understood the importance of knowing the history of African American education and believed that history could help Americans better understand the education of Black folk in the present. As "race men" and "race women," they did not have the luxury of constructing philosophical or historical treatises disconnected from the contemporary realities facing African Americans in public and private schooling. Instead, they offered meticulous and historically and philosophically grounded educational studies based on thorough research of the Black experience. They offered history with a purpose that shed light on the past and the present, and pointed the way to a brighter future.

From the 1930s to the 1950s, Horace Mann Bond was a prominent historian of African American education who also believed that the study of history was key to understanding contemporary educational issues facing African Americans. In his seminal works, *The Education of the Negro in the American Social Order* (1934) and *Negro Education in Alabama: A Study in Cotton and Steel* (1939/1994), Bond attempted to show how social and economic factors affected the public schooling made available to Black children. In addition, in numerous articles in the *Journal of Negro Education* and other scholarly and popular publications, Bond examined the socioeconomic factors that helped to explain issues and trends related to African Americans and intelligence testing, academic achievement, and curriculum development.

More recently, during the 1970s and 1980s, historians of African American education carried on the tradition of Du Bois, Woodson, Cooper, and Bond by producing exemplary scholarly works that reflected contemporary problems and issues. For example, in the late 1970s in the aftermath of the Civil Rights Movement, V. P. Franklin and James D. Anderson (1978) explored the issue of self-determination and agency in Black education. The articles in *New Perspectives on Black Educational History* documented the historic agency of African Americans in developing their own schooling and community-based educational programs. It is evident that the authors were addressing the need for a similar type of self-determinist activity among African Americans in a variety of educational arenas in the post–Civil Rights Era.

As questions about curriculum change for African Americans emerged in the 1970s, Donald Spivey (1978) addressed the history of the vocational and industrial curriculum for Black southerners and raised important questions about the most appropriate types of schooling needed in the late 1970s and early 1980s. At the high point of academic discourse on Black feminism in the 1980s, Linda Perkins (1987) addressed the history of Black women's education in her explication of Fanny Jackson Coppin's work as principal of the Institute for Colored Youth in Philadelphia, Pennsylvania, in the late 19th century. Perkins's book illuminated Black women's persistence and roles in providing quality schooling for Black children, while offering a model for the establishment of exemplary educational programs for African American youth.

Today, as a plethora of social reforms and educational issues confront African Americans and their education, such as the "No Child Left Behind" legislation, increased use of standardized testing, and academic underachievement, historians can play an important role in uncovering the history that sheds light on these contemporary concerns. The historians writing in *this Handbook* seek to address a variety of historical issues that resonate in the African American community today. These issues include Black educational leadership, graduate education, the training and working conditions for Black teachers, and the overall struggle to provide quality education. While the chapters here are richly documented and historically contextualized, they also have great relevance for our understanding of the current conditions.

When Professor Linda Tillman asked us to serve as the coeditors for the history section of *The Handbook*, we were delighted by the opportunity to establish the overall historical context for the volume. We were also pleased with the broad leeway that Professor Tillman granted us in selecting contributors to this section. We purposefully chose historians who had established reputations and whose work also reflected contemporary concerns in African American education.

In the opening chapter, "To Gain and to Lose: The African American Struggle for Education in Columbus, Ohio, 1831–1882," Adah Randolph explores African Americans' quest for education in the 19th century from the antebellum through postbellum eras. Randolph's contribution is significant because she examines a sometimes overlooked period and locale in the development of Black education. Of equal importance, Randolph's chapter provides an excellent account of how, under great social pressure, African Americans persisted and often triumphed in gaining control of their own schooling. Randolph's chapter is a testament to the resolve and determination of African Americans to obtain access to public and private schooling, even under the most difficult conditions. In the chapter "African American Educators and the Black Intellectual Tradition," Derrick P. Alridge illuminates the theoretical and practical ideas of African American educators of the late 19th and early 20th centuries. These educators took the lead in proposing viable educational strategies and philosophies for African Americans. Ultimately, Alridge is concerned with the place of African American educational thought within the larger Black intellectual tradition. His purpose is to document their legacy and to encourage educators and researchers to use the ideas and perspectives of African American educators historically in assessing contemporary alternatives put forward for improving the schooling made available to African American children and adults. In the third chapter, "'They Rose or Fell Together': African American Educators and Community Leadership, 1795–1954," V. P. Franklin delves into the educational agendas of African American educators and leaders from the era of slavery to the emergence of the modern Civil Rights Movement. His chapter explores Black educators as leaders and their significant contributions to the overall advancement of African American communities. In this chapter, Franklin offers models of exemplary community leadership that might be emulated by African American educators and others seeking to advance Black social and educational interests and priorities today.

Linda M. Perkins examines "The History of Black Women Graduate Students, 1921–1948" and describes Black women's struggle for advanced training and education during the interwar years. Her chapter details the sacrifices that African American women were often forced to make in their quest for postgraduate and professional education. This chapter recounts the trials and tribulations as well as successes that may inspire and sustain Black women in their pursuit of graduate and professional education in the 21st century.

The last chapter in this section, "Caught Between a Rock and a Hard Place: The Dissolution of Black State Teachers Associations, 1954–1970," by Michael Fultz describes the rise and fall of Black teachers' groups and associations in the 20th century. The chapter provides an in-depth examination of the employment conditions for Black teachers, the role that Black teachers' associations played in supporting Black educators, and the subsequent displacement of Black teachers following the official desegregation of southern public education. This chapter places in historical context the current shortage of Black teachers and administrators at the elementary and secondary school levels in school districts throughout the United States.

Ultimately, the intention of the contributors to this section of the *Handbook* has been to provide historical analyses and interpretations that will help students and scholars understand the relevant connections between the past and present in African American education. As modern day griots, we see the need to tell the story of the development of African American education historically so that we can better understand present circumstances and plan for the future. And most important, like our forebears, we seek to endow the African American educational experience with significant meaning and purpose.

REFERENCES

Bond, H. M. (1934). *The education of the Negro in the social order*. New York: Prentice Hall.

Bond, H. M. (1994). *Negro education in Alabama: A study of cotton and steel*. Tuscaloosa: University of Alabama Press. (Original work published 1939)

Cooper, A. J. (1988). *A voice from the south*. New York: Oxford University Press. (Original work published 1892)

Du Bois, W. E. B. (1995). *Black Reconstruction in America, 1860–1880*. New York: Simon & Schuster. (Original work published 1935)

Franklin, V. P., & Anderson, J. D. (1978). *New perspectives in Black educational history*. Boston: G. K. Hall.

Perkins, L. M. (1987). *Fanny Jackson Coppin and the Institute for Colored Youth, 1837–1902*. New York: Garland.

Spivey, D. (1978). *Schooling for the new slavery, 1865–1915*. Westport, CT: Greenwood Press.

Woodson, C. G. (1919). *The education of the Negro prior to 1861*. New York: A & B Publishers.

1

To Gain and to Lose

The Loving School and the African American Struggle for Education in Columbus, Ohio, 1831–1882

ADAH WARD RANDOLPH

Many Americans believe that 19th-century free African Americans had access to education. History, however, informs us that first African Americans combined resources to provide an education for their youth, and then they fought for access to public education as the system of common schools developed in the United States. Often after gaining access to public education, African Americans were assigned to segregated schooling. In other words, they gained access to public education only to lose control over the kind of education their children would receive. African Americans believed that education would advance the economic, social, and political aims of the community. However, African American community members were not always in agreement over whether segregated or desegregated education would be best for their children. In 1849, the *Roberts* decision was the first legal push for equitable and desegregated education for African Americans in the United States. The African American community in Boston, however, had been divided over the issue. Thus, the 19th-century educational movement in the urban North is the focus of this chapter with particular focus on Columbus, Ohio, as an example of how African Americans gained access to public schooling, then sought equitable means of education through desegregation, and the costs associated with the desegregation movement in the 19th-century urban North. Moreover, this chapter will examine the laws of many northern states, the leaders who fought for education, and the results of their fight to advance the African American community through education.

COMMON SCHOOLS AND COMMON LAWS: FOR WHITES ONLY IN THE URBAN NORTH

The 19th century was a period in history characterized by many different movements and events that determined the political, social, economic, and educational rights of U.S. citizens. While the 19th century was a time of great change in this country, one of the most important movements during the antebellum period that affected all Americans was the common school movement. As the United States grew and moved westward, many states provided tax-supported means for a common school education in their state constitutions as a vehicle for assimilating all children into a common ethos and culture (Douglas, 2005; Tyack, 1974; Woodson, 1919/1968). For example in Ohio, the first constitution viewed education as "essentially necessary to good government" (Douglas, 2005, p. 14). Speaking to an audience at his alma mater, Oberlin College in 1874, John Mercer Langston argued that "a common school should be one to which all citizens may send their children, not by favor, but by right" (Langston as cited in Daley, 2006, p. 51). Langston went on to argue that

> the object of the common school is two-fold: In the first place it should bring to every child, especially the poor child, a reasonable degree of elementary education. In the second place it should furnish a common education, one similar and equal to all pupils attending it. Thus furnished, our sons enter upon business or professional walks with an equal start in life. Such education the Government owes to all classes of the people. (Daley, 2006, p. 52)

Free African Americans and even enslaved Africans viewed education as a means to improve their life chances, secure their full citizenship rights, and tear down the wall of discrimination they faced. Throughout the 19th century, however, African Americans often found themselves left behind in the common school movement through discriminatory legal statues (Douglas, 2005; Litwack, 1961; Williams, 2005; Woodson, 1919/1968). As common schools appeared across the American landscape, particularly in urban areas, African Americans were legally denied the benefits that these schools promised. Many state constitutions excluded, ignored, or segregated African Americans in the developing system of common schools. While the majority of African people were enslaved, throughout the country there were free Blacks in New England, the Midwest, and Western states who sought to attain their rights and privileges as tax-paying American citizens through the benefits of the public common schools. However, African American access to education varied across and within all the states in the United States.

In New England and some Mid-Atlantic states, including Massachusetts, New York, New Jersey, and Connecticut, segregated education was provided for some African American youth. Throughout the antebellum period, many of the midwestern states, including Illinois, Indiana, Iowa, and Ohio excluded African American children from the common schools. By the close of the Civil War, most states in the North provided segregated education for African Americans. Consequently, over the course of the 19th century, many northern states traversed through a similar pattern related to the education of African American children: exclusion, segregation, and desegregation (Douglas, 2005; Tyack, 1974; Ward, 1993; Wilkerson, 1963). In turn, African Americans demonstrated a pattern of resistance, protest, and liberation as a response to systematic efforts to deny their children access to tax-supported equitable education. A closer look at the forces that created these contending patterns is exemplified through the struggle for education in the northern urban city of Columbus, Ohio.

BLACK EDUCATION IN OHIO: COLUMBUS, THE STATE CAPITAL

In a 1942 edition of the *Journal of Negro History*, sociologist J. S. Himes argued, "Public education of Negro children in Columbus was for many years a major center of struggle" (p. 138). Because of this struggle, Himes concluded that African Americans "won the right to send their children to un-segregated schools a good while before the end of the last century" (p. 138). The schools of Columbus, however, were segregated through de facto means (Ward Randolph, 1996). Himes was correct in his contention that the African American community *had* struggled and won the battle to end de jure segregation. The 19th-century movement for educational access by African Americans had been a long battle—a battle that first dismantled exclusion and then segregation.

From 1804 to 1853, Ohio law ignored, excluded, or provided segregated education for African American children (Douglas, 2005; Taylor, 2005; Ward, 1993). While Ohio was a free state, the settlers of the state held differing views about the rights and privileges of African American people. As schools developed in the state, many Whites who held anti-Black views, particularly in the southern portion of the state, sought to hinder African American advancement and even entrance into Ohio (Gerber, 1976; Griffler, 2004; Taylor, 2005). The myriad sentiments about African American inclusion and attitudes toward their advancement led to continual change in school law during this period. In Columbus, even while there was a more liberal sentiment about the inclusion of African Americans in social, political, and economic arenas, exclusion and later segregation became the norm for African American schooling for most of the 19th century. Consequently, African Americans joined forces to first create educational institutions (Franklin & Savage, 2004; Woodson, 1919/1968). For example, as early as 1831, Blacks created schools in Columbus. By 1849, African Americans had created two private and two secular public schools in Columbus (Ward, 1993).

After educational institutions were created by African Americans, they were absorbed by the growing White public educational structure. The four Black schools that had been supported through religious and secular resources from St. Paul A. M. E. Church, St. Mark A. M. E. Church, the School Fund Society, and the Black Columbusonians School Fund Association were all placed under the direction of the Columbus Board of Education (BOE). Additionally, after Boards of Education took over the administration of Black schools, they often provided inadequate resources for Black youth in segregated facilities. The Black community had collectively established four schools in different locations in Columbus, but the BOE only provided one school in a house, and they did not permit the admittance of Black children into other schools. For example, when Anna Booker sought to attend the North School building in 1854, she was denied admittance (Ward, 1993). Thus, while African Americans had a right to attend the schools developed during the common school movement, their access was limited and often segregated. Consequently, African Americans sought to provide the best possible education within a segregated school system. Such was the case in Boston, New York, Philadelphia, Cincinnati, and Columbus. After continually receiving fewer educational resources than their White counterparts from Boards of Education who controlled fund distribution for Black and White schools, many African American communities faced the difficult decision of dismantling the segregated schools in hopes of securing the same educational benefits as White children through a desegregated system of schooling. Often this push for desegregated education resulted in the loss of control by members of the Black community as well as a loss of Black teachers.

Prior to their inclusion into the public schools in Columbus, African Americans had established separate schools through the Black Columbusonians School Fund Association and through the work of the St. Paul A. M. E. Church. Both organizations secured funds to provide public and private schools for African American youth before Columbus established its system of public education in 1845. When the school law of Ohio changed in 1849, the schools created and maintained by the African American community were reorganized and placed under the control of the Columbus BOE. By 1854, there were four public schools for African American youth in the Columbus system. The BOE had promised the African American community better school facilities, and while it controlled the means of education for Black youth, it did not provide the better-equipped educational facilities it had promised to the Black community (Ward, 1993). From 1854 to 1871, African Americans focused their efforts primarily on attaining equitable segregated educational facilities for their children.

SEEKING BETTER EDUCATIONAL RESOURCES: THE PUSH FOR INCLUSION

From 1804 to 1853, Ohio school laws excluded, and later included, Blacks in the developing school system. Before the Civil War, Columbus had the largest percentage of African American residents in the Midwest other than Indianapolis (Mark, 1928). After the Civil War, the Black population increased steadily in Columbus. The Columbus BOE incorporated the separate Black schools under their jurisdiction in 1853. By 1869, African American citizens of Columbus met in mass to send a petition to the state legislature demanding control of the Columbus "colored" schools and protested the inequitable de jure segregated facilities. Black residents of Columbus were motivated to request that the BOE improve the inadequate facilities provided for Black children in light of their increased population over the past 10 years. Members of the Black community held different views on the best approach to educating Black children. Some Blacks wanted the BOE to retain control, while others wanted Black control of the all-Black schools, similar to the system of schooling in Cincinnati, Ohio (Dabney, 1926/1988; Seifert, 1978; Taylor, 2005).

Reverend James Preston Poindexter, a native of Virginia and a barber by trade, became a leading spokesperson for African American rights in Columbus (Franklin, 1990; Minor, 1947). In a letter to the *Journal* on April 6, 1869, Poindexter questioned the Columbus BOE's plan to renovate an already dilapidated building as an all-Black school. He wrote, "To compel our little ones, residents in the south end, to travel to the north end, and then to crowd them into such a building as that will be when altered, is not to carry out the school law" (Ward, 1993, p. 36). Poindexter asserted that the Columbus BOE had not correctly administered the school law as it pertained to African American youth. Poindexter further declared that the BOE had not given African American children their fair share of the school fund entitled to them under the law. This being the case, Poindexter pointed out three facts: (1) that Black children were entitled to their full share of the monies collected for their education through taxation, (2) that the number of Black children had constituted 1/20 of all the children in the city, and (3) that the accommodations furnished to Black and White children were inequitable (Ward, 1993). Poindexter's letter explicated the state of Black education in Columbus. Subsequent research that compared White and Black schools indicated that the White schools received more educational resources, as was the case in all northern communities that provided segregated schools for African American youth (Douglas, 2005; Mark, 1928; Mason, 1917; Wilkerson, 1963). The Columbus BOE did not respond to Poindexter and a year later, it had still not provided adequate schools for African American youth given their increase in the population. Consequently, Poindexter charged the BOE with placing African American children "in a *pen* at the north end of the city— an old shanty" (Ward, 1993, p. 37). Poindexter threatened the BOE with the three primary means by which African Americans dismantled segregation during this period: moral suasion, court action, and legislative change (Douglas, 2005). In 1870, after the adoption of the Fifteenth Amendment, Poindexter like other Black leaders was part of a "dynamic school crusade" (McAfee, 1998, p. 20) that sought to institutionalize their vision of the purpose and power of education for African Americans through constant petitions and protests. Proverbs 29:18 reads, "When there is no vision, the people perish." The vision of Poindexter and his contemporaries "reflected the optimism of a post-emancipation reform culture that regarded education as crucial to group advancement" (Gaines, 1996, p. 21). During this period, White resistance to "racially integrated public schooling remained strong" (McAfee, 1998, p. 156). Additionally, McAfee noted that reconstruction changes in Northern state education laws that promised racial equity and fairness in education were never materialized. Key decisions in state laws, however, occurred because of the protest of African Americans like the Reverend James Poindexter.

In May of 1871, the BOE assigned the old North building erected in 1847 at the corner of Third and Long Street as the "colored" school. The North building was originally for White students who later abandoned it because of its dilapidated conditions and health risks. Still, the BOE intended to use it for educating African American children. School board members and a contingent of African American men, including Poindexter, W. H. Roney, an African American teacher, Jeremiah Freeland, a past conductor on the Underground Railroad in Columbus, and John Ward, a janitor of the old City Hall as well as a member of the Underground Railroad, suggested that the school be named the Loving School, after school board member, Dr. Starling Loving. Dr. Loving represented the Eighth Ward that consisted mostly of African Americans, and he had always fought for equal rights for African Americans in Columbus. He, after a health inspection, had previously condemned the building and was opposed to its reconstruction, citing the unfitness of the old North building. He stated, "The locality was unhealthy, the building was a disgrace to the city and would be as long as it should stay. And if it was unhealthy for white children it was for colored children too" (Ward, 1993, p. 38). The BOE proceeded with its renovation. Loving's assertion that even with renovations the school would not meet the needs of Black children would be a primary reason for future protest by the Black community. In voting against the use of the old North building, Loving had continued to champion the equitable rights of African American citizens he represented in the Eighth Ward. African Americans, however, won a partial victory when the Loving School opened.

DE JURE SEGREGATION IN THE URBAN NORTH: THE LOVING SCHOOL, 1871–1882

In 1871, the push by African Americans for better school facilities culminated in the opening of the renovated old North building, now named the Loving School. The Loving School was located in the majority Black Eighth Ward on the East side of Columbus, Ohio. All the Black children in Columbus were required to attend Loving; however, a sizable number of Black students did not live in the Eighth Ward or on the East side of town. Rather, Black youth lived in all the wards in the city except the Eleventh Ward. Table 1.1 indicates the distribution of Black children by ward (Gerber, 1976; Ward, 1993).

The location of the Loving School ultimately created transportation problems for a significant number of the Black population who did not live in the Eighth Ward near the school. In fact, only 212 Black children resided in the Eighth Ward as indicated in Table 1.1. Black children outside the Eighth Ward were required to walk to Loving to attend school. For children living in the Eighth Ward, however, the Loving School although segregated was now their only choice in the public tax-supported education system (Douglas, 2005; Litwack, 1961; Ward, 1993).

After the Loving School was renovated, it housed seven grades and had 117 students. The two-story Loving School had eight rooms, could seat 246 pupils, and was heated by stoves. The teaching staff was primarily African American with one White teacher who was temporarily employed. During its first year, the Loving staff consisted of seven teachers, including one who acted as principal. The first group of educators at Loving had to contend with many oppressive

conditions, yet they contributed to the early education of the Black children of Columbus, Ohio (Ward, 1993).

When the Columbus BOE reorganized the school system in the early 1870s, in addition to opening Loving, it opened a brand new school for White children, the Sullivant School, one of the finest schools in the state. While the Sullivant School represented the finest educational advancement for White children that money could purchase, Loving did not. When the BOE gained control of the Black schools, Blacks expected parity with their White counterparts according to their share of the tax dollars, but they quickly surmised that equity would not be granted in the Columbus school system. For example, the Sullivant School was new and provided the White children who attended it the best books, desks, playground, and school facilities available. The Loving School was not new, but a renovated and formerly condemned building previously used by the White community (Ward, 1993). The opening of Loving was chronicled in *The Ohio Educational Monthly*. White observers were mindful to point out that with the opening of Loving, "the colored schools have been removed from the miserable alley rookeries, which have long disgraced the city" (Ward, 1993, p. 44). The "alley rookeries" the observer referred to were the fledging Black schools organized by the Columbus BOE between 1853 and 1871. The alley rookeries did not provide the promised equitable educational resources such as books to Black children.

James S. Waring, a former teacher from Springfield, Ohio, who had taught in the "alley rookeries," became the principal of Loving. Waring was born in Fredricktown, Virginia, to David and Maria Waring who migrated to Bethlehem township, Coshocton County, in 1829. They were part of the continual migration of free African Americans who migrated from Virginia to Ohio (Jackson, 1942). When Waring was 24 years old, he was admitted to Oberlin College (Waite, 2002). He taught in Springfield,

TABLE 1.1   Distribution of African American Children by Ward (1871–1872)

Ward	1	2	3	4	5	6	7	8	9	10	11	Total
Black student population	32	33	26	77	72	9	2	212	14	10	—	487

SOURCE: The Annual Report of the Columbus Board of Education, 1871–1872, p. 106 (cited in Ward, 1993, p. 39).

Ohio, from 1855 until 1863, when he was hired in Columbus. His wife Malvina was also a teacher at Loving. One of their children, Everett J. Waring, would eventually join his father as a teacher at the school.

The Loving School was staffed primarily by African Americans who met the city's qualifications for teaching in the school system. While the standard for teacher employment prior to 1870s was a high school diploma or less, James Waring possessed 15 years of experience and an education from Oberlin College (Ward, 1993). Historians of education have contended that African American teachers were often less qualified than their White counterparts. However, this was not the case of Waring and the corps of teachers at Loving. They were as well educated, and in some cases more educated, than their White counterparts. The majority of staff at Loving were African Americans from Ohio who had been educated in Ohio public and private normal teacher institutions. As noted earlier, James S. Waring was the principal. In addition, Maria L. Baker, Mary L. Robinson, Hattie Woodson, Harriet W. Welch, Sarah G. Jones, and Maggie E. Porter were the teachers. They had been educated in Oberlin College, Wilberforce University, and Cincinnati and Columbus public schools (Waite, 2002). To qualify as teachers in Columbus Public Schools, Waring and his staff were required to submit a letter of application to the Chairman of the Committee on Teachers. In addition, they were required to possess a certificate from the Board of the City School examiners verifying their qualification for the position for which they were applying, as well as a letter attesting to their sound moral character. No applicant below the age of 17 could be appointed. All the teachers employed at the Loving School met these qualifications and taught either primary or grammar school (Ward, 1993).

After much lamentation from Dr. Loving, the BOE decided to compensate African American and White teachers equally. Thus, the teachers' salaries did not depend on race. As the principal, Waring received a salary of $1,250 per year, and teachers' salaries ranged from $550 to $600 dollars a year and were based on their qualifications and previous teaching experience (Ward, 1993). While economic compensation was equal regardless of race, other factors did prevail at Loving School that did not exist at the White schools

such as poor facilities, a high student-teacher ratio, and overcrowding. Because Columbus maintained a segregated school system, Loving remained the only school that employed African American teachers, and it made it difficult for Black teachers to find teaching jobs.

Opening the Loving School did not provide educational access to all African American children as had been promised by the BOE when it assumed control of the system of African American separate public schools. Consequently, African American citizens increased their agitation over their educational rights. In the 1872 *Ohio Educational Monthly*, an observer described the condition of African American schooling in Columbus and elsewhere and the subsequent actions taken by African Americans to secure equal education in the following statement:

> The colored people in various sections of the State are demanding school privileges, and where separate schools are not provided for them, they are rightly demanding admission to the public schools. This is bitterly opposed in many districts, the colored children are abused, and, in one or two instances, the schools have been closed. In several cases the lower courts have been resorted to but with different results. The question has finally been brought before the Supreme Court by a petition for a writ of mandamus to compel the school directors in Norwich township, Franklin county, to admit colored youth to all the school rights and privileges enjoyed by white youth. The school law provides for a separate school for colored youth "when the whole number, by enumeration, exceeds twenty, and when such schools will afford them, as far as practicable, the advantages and privileges of a common school education." When the number of colored children is less than twenty, the board is required to set apart and expend each year their pro rata share of the school funds for their education. But how? This provision has been a disgraceful fraud from its first enactment: for, under a show of justice, it has robbed colored youth of all school privileges. When a separate school for colored youth is not established and maintained, the only way in which they can be provided with school advantages is to admit them to the public schools, and this is done in hundreds of school districts in the State. (Ward, 1993, pp. 48–49)

At the culmination of the first year of the Loving School, Ohioans faced stronger demands from African American citizens to obtain their children's educational rights and privileges, even while some cities and towns allowed African American children to attend mixed schools. The actual number of African American children attending mixed schools was low because of the treatment they received in the schools, and because of economic hardships, many Black children attended school for short periods of time. The majority of Black children, especially those who lived in rural areas or on the outskirts of the city, received little, if any, education (Douglas, 2005; Mason, 1917; Ward Randolph, 2004).

When Loving was opened, a Visiting Committee (VC) was appointed to oversee the management of the school. As noted earlier, members of the Black community had differing perspectives about the most effective ways to control what they thought would be a system of segregated Black schools. One constituency favored BOE control of the schools, while the other group favored African American control over the Black schools. The BOE's appointment of a VC was the compromise between the two positions, whereby the BOE retained control but appointed a board of prominent African American citizens as an auxiliary organization responsible for evaluating the actual administration of Loving. But there was no system of Black schools. The BOE established only one school to meet the needs of all African American children in the city: the Loving School.

The VC consisted of African American men, including Reverend Poindexter, J. C. Underwood, J. Litchford, Willis Mitchell, J. Dickey, and F. B. Roney. During Loving's first year, the VC reported to the school board on discipline in the school. According to the VC,

> the commands of the teachers were kind, yet firm: the obedience of the pupils, cheerful and prompt. We were delighted at the fact that, in dealing with the most stupid of the little ones, no signs of irritation were exhibited, but greater patience, attended with that persistence of effort and fullness of illustration which assures success whenever attainable. (Ward, 1993, p. 50)

Although the VC used derogatory language to describe the academic levels of the students at the time of their observation, they praised the teachers for their ability to work with the students given the conditions of overcrowding, poor facilities, and limited resources to assure success. The VC considered the teaching *conditions* under which learning was taking place at Loving to be excessively cruel. The school only had six teachers excluding Waring and almost 200 students. The student to teacher ratio required the teachers, particularly Sarah Jones the primary teacher, to teach more than one recitation to different groups of children and Waring to perform double duty as an administrator *and* a teacher. In spite of these conditions, by the end of the second school year, Loving had promoted 108 students, and only 43 children failed out of 151 students examined: a success rate of 72%.

During the same school year, the *Ohio State Journal* reported a need for a school for Black children in the Montgomery district. The superintendent recommended "the establishment of a school at the Montgomery school house" (Ward, 1993, p. 50). Twenty-nine African American students lived in the area, which was a great distance from Loving. The BOE did not build a school for Black children, and if Black children were to be educated, they would have to travel to Loving. Thus, distance continued to be an impediment to the education of Black children. Parents and community members continued to agitate over the existence of only one school to meet the educational needs of all the Black children in Columbus. The physical condition of the building such as holes in the ceiling and walls also posed problems not only to the students but also to the teachers. This was a common problem in the tax-supported common schools provided for African American youth (Douglas, 2005).

In the 1871–1872 report submitted by the VC to the BOE concerning the operation of the Loving School, it also emphasized that Loving needed repairs, although it had been renovated at a cost of $6,215.00. The VC observed "openings in the roof of the building, left there when it was remodeled for the colored children into which large quantities of rain and snow fall, greatly to the detriment of the building and discomfort of its occupants" (Ward, 1993, p. 51). The VC further pointed out numerous other maintenance problems with the building, such as malfunctioning sewers, no washstands, no hose for washing, no furniture or carpet in the visitor's room, and finally, no play facilities such as those afforded to all other schools. The gentlemen reminded the BOE about Loving's previous reputation—having caused more illness than any other school building in the city. Despite the report, the BOE made no repairs to the school. The VC's evaluations captured a picture of the actual teaching and learning conditions for the students and teachers at the Loving School. No other school in the district had physical conditions similar to those of the "colored" school. But even under these conditions, the African American teachers at Loving worked to educate the hearts and minds of their students.

The 1873–1874 school year at Loving began with the same number of teachers: six. Only 44% of their students were promoted that year, an abysmal record, and the number of children attending Loving on a daily basis dropped to an average of 86.3%. The Loving School was educating barely 20% of the Black children in Columbus. The attendance and promotion problems were not due to the ineffectiveness of the teachers. The VC was pleased with Waring and "his corps of lady teachers, each of whom seems to vie with the other in good instruction, discipline and direction to their pupils" (Ward, 1993, p. 52). The teaching staff at Loving changed except for Waring, the veteran of the "alley rookeries," who was the proverbial rock in a weary land. During the 1874–1875 school year, four new recruits joined the teaching staff. The high teacher turnover in addition to the deplorable environmental conditions suggest oppressive work demands, dissatisfaction with the Columbus system of education, and teacher burnout as some of the likely causes of the low teacher-retention rate. However, during this year, Loving experienced its greatest success rate in promotions—92%—and the VC reported its satisfaction with the "increased progress of the scholars in the different grades . . . in their respective studies, and with the thorough knowledge that the teachers have of the course of instruction" (Ward, 1993, p. 54). They witnessed the mastery of knowledge provided by the principal and teachers, and the subsequent mastery of students in arithmetic, history, grammar, physical geography, and physics.

The curriculum at Loving was identical to that provided to White students throughout the school system. The curriculum differed from the ideological framework of the time that questioned not only the ability of African Americans to learn but also their ability to teach (Franklin, 1990; Fredrickson, 1971). The purpose of education for African Americans was often discussed and debated (Anderson, 1988; Kliebard, 1999; Watkins, 2001). Historian Kevin Gaines (1996) argued that, "Blacks had their own objectives for education" (p. 33). Furthermore, Anderson (1988) noted that in northern urban schools, and in the developing southern system of African American education, "the prevailing philosophies of black education and the subjects taught in black schools were not geared to reproduce the caste distinctions or the racially segmented labor desired by . . . white industrialists" (p. 28). Loving's curriculum represented opportunities for Black youth. Historians of education have often focused on the inequitable physical and fiscal resources provided to all-Black schools, and the ideological stances of the architects of Black education toward a manual or vocational curriculum (Anderson, 1988; Douglas, 2005; Kliebard, 1999). However, they have failed to assess the actual schooling processes of all-Black schools to elucidate their accomplishments, despite the inequitable fiscal and physical conditions in these schools. Loving exemplified a classical curriculum rather than a vocational curriculum, which consisted of arithmetic, history, grammar, physical geography, and physics. Thus, even while students at the Loving School were not provided with the same conditions for learning as White students, teachers were effective and students did learn. Throughout the history of the Loving School, the VC continually acknowledged the effectiveness of Loving's teachers and administration in implementing the curriculum. Waring and his teaching staff demonstrated through sound pedagogical means that Black children were educable through a liberal curriculum, despite the prevailing beliefs of the era to the contrary.

Change appeared to be a constant at Loving. During the 1874–1875 school years, two key events would alter the teaching staff of Loving: the exclusion of married women from the teaching force and the opening of the Normal School. The result of the first event was the termination of the primary teacher, Mrs. Sarah G. Jones, because she was married. The result of the second event was that in the future Black teachers who would teach at Loving would come from the city's public schools and the Normal School rather than from Oberlin College and Wilberforce University (Waite, 2002). From 1877 to 1881, teachers who were hired at Loving all came from the Columbus School system. To be admitted to the Normal School, applicants had to be prepared to do high school work and be 16 years old. From its beginning, a small number of African Americans attended the Normal School. The first Black graduates of the Normal School were granted 3-year certificates, and their names appeared in the 1876–1877 Annual report. Both the African Americans graduates were male (Ward, 1993). One other incident that affected the operation of the Loving School was the hiring of Virginia Copeland as the assistant principal. Born in Virginia, Ms. Copeland appeared to have been the first teacher from the South to work at the Loving School.

A new issue, school finances, was raised in the VC's report regarding the employment of African American teachers and the conditions of Loving. After the usual praise of the "very efficient corps of teachers," the VC indicated through their appraisal that many of the grades had very small classes. If more Black teachers were hired, the per capita costs of instruction at Loving would be higher than that in the White schools. Although the employment of more African American teachers would raise the cost of operating Loving, the hiring of more African American teachers was warranted. Twenty "colored" applicants had taken the required Board of Examiners' test for teacher certification from 1876 to 1881, and often became substitute or replacement teachers at Loving (Ward, 1993). Although the Columbus BOE claimed it did not have enough resources to add additional staff to Loving, there existed in Columbus a pool of qualified teachers from which to recruit. The BOE did not hire more teachers for Loving during the first 5 years of the school's history, even while it would have greatly enhanced the education of the children by reducing the high student-teacher ratio and allowing for single grade classes. Only seven Black teachers would ever work at Loving during any particular school year.

The VC never missed an opportunity to highlight that the long distances African American youth had to travel was a detriment to their education. The information presented in the 1876–1877 VC report supported earlier conclusions about why the majority of Black youth did not attend the Loving school—distance. But the school also needed repairs that dated back to the first VC report, and the committee continued its complaints concerning the condition of the school building. The VC called attention to the ability of people on the street to gaze into the girls' toilet. In a vice-ridden area, African American girls were not afforded privacy in the most personal of matters. Clearly, the BOE had not granted the prior requests of the VC regarding needed improvements to the physical structure of the school, ignored Dr. Loving's contention concerning the environment in which Loving School was located as "unhealthy," and did not attempt to provide additional schooling for African American youth who did not live within reasonable distances of the school. Hence, one would have to wonder about the benefit of the VC if the BOE did not adhere to its recommendations. The number of African American children in Columbus in 1876–1877 was 550. Of the 385 students who were registered, 256 attended the Loving School. The next few years would prove critical to the continued existence of Loving.

As changes occurred in Loving, the African American community also experienced changes as it wrestled within over the future of segregated schools. When James S. Waring died in 1878, his son Everett became principal of Loving, and Virginia Copeland retained her assistant principal position. Waring would remain in this position for only a short time. Mr. Sparrow, Ms. Green, and Ms. Roden remained as teachers while Ella H. Wilmot, and Emma J. Hall, an 1879 graduate of Columbus High School, became new recruits. Loving remained the only tax-supported school for African Americans in the Columbus community. Changes would occur in Columbus' system of education as it related to African American access to educational facilities.

The President of the School Board, Henry Olnhausen, in his December 15, 1879, address argued that African American children were "well cared for in respect to their educational wants" (Ward, 1993, p. 59). Olnhausen further argued that the opening of certain schools such as the Second Avenue, Douglas, and East Friend Street Schools accommodated the educational needs of Black children who lived at a distance from Loving. Olnhausen maintained that

Loving was in excellent condition, and its curriculum and organization were the same as those of the other schools. The VC disagreed with his assertion regarding the physical upkeep of Loving. Still, Olnhausen argued that the BOE had provided exemplary educational resources for African Americans:

> The colored population has but recently raised from a state of slavery to one of manhood and citizenship, and the new state upon which they have entered imposes upon them duties and obligations which they are expected to meet and fulfill. Education and instruction must qualify them for these new relations and duties. It give [sic] me pleasure to state that the members of the Board, actuated by a kind and humane spirit, have always cheerfully provided for all reasonable wants and accommodations for the colored children. (Ward, 1993, p. 60)

The Columbus BOE had only recently permitted African American children to attend other schools besides Loving, and only after Black parents whose children lived great distances from Loving protested and warned of litigation. The majority of African American students were still forced to attend Loving, and those who attended other schools such the East Friend Street School faced protests by the White community (Ward, 1993).

Regardless of Olnhausen's paternalistic reasoning, Black leaders did not agree with his analyses of the condition of African American education in Columbus (Watkins, 2001). The VC now consisted of African American men and women who comprehended the massive importance of education in the lives of African American youth. They argued that they would

> decide what measure and policies are for the best interest of the whole people; therefore we ought to know something of the great moral, religious, and educational interests which will be effected directly or indirectly by the amount of our information. (Ward, 1993, p. 61)

The VC understood its role and its importance and changed its tone from one of informing to one of demanding changes in the Loving School. The members sought self-determination for the education of their children and themselves. More important, while the VC was a small committee,

it was connected with the larger African American community not just in Columbus but throughout the state. As the committee's tone changed from complacency to action, Poindexter and others questioned the efficacy of segregated schools as they began to agitate against the Black Laws in the state and segregated schools. Poindexter and his allies sought to project their vision of the purposes and benefits of equitable education for African American children.

Two, Four, Six, Eight, We Must Desegregate: Competing Heads, Hearts, and Minds

Rev. James Preston Poindexter and other Black leaders in Ohio, including William S. Scarborough, sought to dismantle segregated education in Ohio. They sought full access to the schools in Columbus and pushed for mixed-race schools throughout the system (Franklin, 1990). Efforts to desegregate the Columbus Public Schools would lead to the closure of the all-Black Loving School. Several factors were prominent in the demise of the Loving School: (a) protest by the Black population of Ohio for the end to segregated schools, (b) the financial strain of a dual-school system, and (c) the poor building facilities and low-income neighborhood of the Loving School. When Loving opened, the Columbus School Board had knowingly placed Black children and teachers in a dilapidated building—a previously condemned building by standards of health and safety. Although the BOE renovated the building, the building was not equal to the standards of the buildings where White children were being educated (i.e., the Sullivant School). In its reports, the VC criticized the physical structure of the building, particularly after 1878, and eventually sought another location for the school. Loving was located in an area known as the "Bad Lands," populated by poor Blacks and Whites (Gerber, 1976; Ward, 1993). The BOE never altered its position regarding the suitability of Loving for the education of African American youth, and it continually overlooked the physical condition of the school because by the end of the decade, it faced another crisis in the White schools: overcrowding due to the increase in European immigration to the city. During this same time, African American protests against the Black Laws in Ohio had increased. Besides Poindexter and Scarborough, the president of Wilberforce University, J. S. Tyler and Benjamin W. Arnett initiated a move to repeal the Black Laws (Ward, 1993). Black Laws were instituted to curtail the entrance of Blacks into Ohio. They required Blacks to post a good behavior bond of $500, register with the local magistrate, and provide a certificate of freedom. Black Laws excluded Black involvement in political, civil, and educational matters by denying African Americans the right to vote, serve on a jury, or attend schools with Whites (Ward, 1993). Poindexter and his comrades advocated for the end of de jure segregated schools, the last vestige of the Black Laws. However, many residents of the African American community disagreed with Poindexter and his colleagues. In 1878, Rev. Poindexter addressed some of the general objections posed by those Blacks who disagreed with plans to desegregate schools. Some of these objections centered on whether or not African American children could learn from White teachers, the loss of Black teaching positions, and the loss of income that would occur in the Black community. While Poindexter dismissed many of these assertions, he did address the loss of income due to the displacement of African American teachers that would occur if the schools were desegregated. He believed that because of the "good to our people of mixed schools" those African American teachers "assent to the sacrifice here proposed, as one righteous to be made" (Ward, 1993, p. 66) to place African American children on equal footing with their White counterparts.

One could argue that Poindexter's experience with the BOE led him to believe that the only avenue for attaining equitable school facilities for Black children would be the demise of the segregated system. He had been instrumental in securing better segregated schooling resources for the Black community. It appears, however, that Poindexter was no longer willing to settle for segregated education. Poindexter altered his vision of Black education. He argued for "mixed" schools primarily because he believed that as long as Loving remained a segregated school, Black children would never receive equitable educational facilities despite the work of exemplary Black teachers. In subsequent correspondence appearing in the local paper, Poindexter

continued to argue that Black teachers would voluntarily sacrifice their jobs and salary once they comprehended the benefit to their race of "integrated" schools (Ward, 1993, pp. 66–67). Poindexter espoused that "uplift of the race" superseded the needs of the few. Poindexter, J. S. Tyler, and others had become staunch integrationists who believed that Black youth would only obtain an education equal to that of Whites if they were in the same classrooms. This ideological debate existed in Boston and in other African American communities where there were segregated schools (Douglas, 2005; Franklin & Savage, 2004; Litwack, 1961; Taylor, 2005). Poindexter, by trying to gain equitable education for Black children, embraced the common ideology of the period concerning the inferiority of Blacks. He posed the following analysis: "The white child imbibes the false idea that the color of his skin makes him the colored child's superior, while the colored grows sour under the weight of invidious distinctions made between him and the white child" (Ward, 1993, p. 67). Poindexter, a Republican, believed in integration as a tool to eliminate racism and to better prepare Black children for competition with Whites. In other words, he believed that desegregation would guarantee full citizenship rights for Blacks. Thus, Poindexter and his colleagues had a two-point plan: fight for better facilities for Black youth and teachers and simultaneously agitate for the demise of segregated schooling. Again, Poindexter contended that African American teachers would willingly sacrifice their positions in the name of racial uplift. Others, however, including African American teachers and principals, disagreed with Poindexter and represented the opposing opinion—to maintain segregated schools in the Black community. Many, including James and Everett Waring, the previous and current principal of Loving School, disagreed with Poindexter and were unwilling to sacrifice Black teachers or Black children.

Solomon Day of Dayton, Ohio, and E. J. Waring and his father contended that Black teacher displacement would occur if desegregation occurred. Day, Waring, and other African Americans feared the loss of employment among African American teachers, the resulting decrease of economic resources in the Black communities, and the psychological and potential educational damage to African American children under the tutelage of European American teachers. Day only wanted school "integration" if it meant that Black teachers would also be included in the schools (Gerber, 1976). A prime reason for the conflicting views among African American leaders was the movement of racial uplift. According to historian Kevin Gaines (1996) in *Uplifting the Race*, "Black spokespersons believed in uplift and education. The sticking point of debate was over precisely what sort of education would be made available to Blacks" (p. 40). Some African American Ohioans viewed the sacrifice of Black teachers as necessary for the whole of the race. Waring, the principal of Loving, was not willing to sacrifice Black children or teachers. He believed that schools based on race during a transitional period produced grandeur results (Gerber, 1976).

At the end of the 1881–1882 academic year, R. W. Stevenson, the Superintendent reported, "The number of colored youth of legal school age, according to the census of 1881, was 605. Separate schools for all grades, except the High School, were provided for them" (Ward, 1993, p. 69). Stevenson's report chronicled the historical process of how Columbus schools did and did not provide educational opportunities to Black children and employment opportunities for Black educators. Earlier in 1878, the very heated debates on mixed schools prompted this subsequent response from Superintendent Stevenson:

> The step had to be taken sooner or later. The recent decisions of the courts, in this state and others, had put the question in such a shape that it became only a matter of choice with the Board, as to whether they would admit the colored children to the schools voluntarily or by compulsion. (Ward, 1993, p. 70)

Thus, the BOE's 1881 decision to finally "integrate" before being forced to do so by law was not because of benevolence but due to social, economic, and political pressures. After the completion of the 1881–1882 school year, the student population of Columbus schools was "integrated." However, teachers, as Waring and Day feared, were displaced and were not included in the desegregated schools of Columbus. Others who could see what the future of "integrated" schools meant increased their protest against the repeal of the separate school law. If the schools had not been desegregated, the BOE would have

had to build another segregated building in another part of the city to educate Black children. The BOE did not want to continue to incur the financial burden of a dual system of education. While it had already purchased a lot for another all-Black school, after their decision to provide mixed schools, the lot and the Loving School were sold (Ward, 1993). Thus, economics played a major role in the reasoning behind the BOE's decision to admit Black youth to the White schools.

Black teachers had lobbied against the closing of separate schools (Gerber, 1976; Ward, 1993), and they were not hired when Columbus "integrated" its schools. And even while the City Board of Examiners reported a total of six "colored" applications during 1881–1882 (one male and five females), these teachers would not find employment in Columbus. Loving had been the only venue of employment for Black teachers. African American educators had no place in the mixed system. African American leaders had fought for "integration" or assimilation into society through education. Because of Poindexter and others, Columbus succeeded in desegregating schools earlier than mandated by the 1887 school law. Although Columbus "integrated" its school population prior to the repeal of the separate school law in 1887, the teachers of African descent did pay the price that Solomon Day prophesied (Erickson, 1959; Ward, 1993).

The argument for segregated schools versus desegregated schools ended for most cities and towns in Ohio with the passage of the school law in 1887. African Americans petitioned the Assembly from 1875 until the bill was passed in 1887. They favored repeal of the Black Laws based on the arguments that would later be used in the *Brown v. Board of Education* case in 1954. The last remnants of the Black Laws ended on February 22, 1887, when House Bill No. 84:34, the Arnett bill, was passed unanimously. Still, in some parts of the state segregated schools were continued despite the new law (Erickson, 1959). Columbus, unlike Cincinnati and other cities in Ohio, however, had "integrated" its schools earlier, in 1882 when it closed the Loving School.

CONCLUSION: TO GAIN AND TO LOSE

In the 19th century, the African American struggle for education was more like a river that ebbs and flows. At times the current was strong and a great deal was accomplished during the inclusion movement in African American northern communities where African Americans agitated, petitioned, and litigated their right to access the developing tax-supported common school movement. On the other hand, the tide sometimes brought with it debris as racist and discontented Whites controlled not only access to public education for African Americans but also the resources and means for gaining an education in separate, segregated and desegregated, schools. In the more than 50 years since the *Brown* decision, many have questioned what has been gained by the desegregation of the schools. John Mercer Langston argued, "Two separate school systems . . . cannot educate these classes to live harmoniously together meeting the responsibilities and discharging the duties imposed by a common government in the interest of a common county" (Langston as cited in Daley, 2006, p. 52). Yet has the government ever fully sought to have African Americans fully partake in all the rights and privileges of American citizenry? Our history informs us that it has been a struggle. And that struggle to seek education has depended on not only the context in which the education occurred but also who the leaders of the community were; the social, political, and economic resources of the community; and more important, White Americans' views about the purpose of education in the lives of African Americans. Whereas African American access to education resembled a pattern of separate, segregated and desegregated, or mixed schools throughout the 19th century, a closer examination of one community, Columbus, Ohio, elucidates how the struggle for equitable education for African Americans had many contending factors within and outside the Black community.

In Columbus, the pattern of education for African Americans consisted of self-supported separate education, exclusion, inclusion through segregation, and later desegregated education. Over these different and parallel movements, both the African American and White communities held varied views about the purpose of the common schools in the lives of African Americans. African Americans during this period believed in the potential of education to ameliorate discrimination; assist in the development of resourses for social, political, and economic advancement; and facilitate the community's acquisition of its full citizenship rights as American citizens. These views propelled leaders of the African American community in Columbus to contest exclusion as the common schools developed in the city. Whereas African Americans in Columbus and elsewhere often gained access to the common tax-supported schools, they often lost the ability to affect the quality of educational facilities and resources provided to African American schools as they were assigned to segregated schools. Moreover, as they gained access to legally desegregated schools, they often lost one of the most valuable resources economically and intellectually in the African American community: African American teachers. While some believed that this was a willing sacrifice, others did not. In sum, the African American movement for education in 19th-century urban America can best be captured in the following quote by Frederick Douglass:

> The whole history of the progress of human liberty shows that all concessions yet made to her august claims have been born of earnest struggle. The conflict has been exciting, agitating, all-absorbing, and for the time being, putting all other tumults to silence. It must do this or it does nothing. If there is no struggle there is no progress. (Douglass as cited in Meltzer, 1995, p. 105)

The 19th-century struggle for education in the urban North was a struggle for the "progress of human liberty." It was a struggle with gains and losses. In the end, however, it resulted in progress.

African Americans in Columbus won their fight to secure equal representation through taxation when their children were given the Loving School. Consequently, the decision of the Columbus BOE to renovate Loving School in 1871 represented a partial victory for activists such as Reverend James Preston Poindexter. Loving, however, was plagued by a number of difficulties during its existence, including its physical inadequacies, the financial strain of the dual-school system, protests of Blacks against segregated schools, and the growing political pressure throughout the state to repeal the separate school law. Additionally, African American movements to establish even more and better school facilities and to desegregate the schools coincided. In Columbus, African Americans succeeded in garnering the admittance of Black youth to the high school in 1874 and the enrollment of Black children in some elementary schools. The Columbus school system represented a semisegregated educational system. The existence of Loving and other such schools throughout the urban North supports the assessment that African Americans even in the free North fought against de jure laws and racism to secure educational means for their children during the common school movement. Often students of history and particularly students of education contend that racism in education only existed in the South. This chapter provided a detailed analysis of the actual conditions of one 19th-century African American segregated school in the urban North. It examined the challenges encountered by African Americans, the qualifications of African American teachers, the effectiveness of African American teachers, the actual conditions of a segregated school including its structure and curriculum, and the role and the context that African American leadership played in securing and maintaining access to schools in the urban northern community of Columbus, Ohio, as an exemplar of similar circumstances in other northern cities. From this analysis, we understand that African Americans in these areas were not readily welcomed into the developing school system but had to agitate, litigate, and protest to obtain their share of tax-supported education in communities such as Columbus. Even after securing access, however, African Americans did not receive equal educational opportunity. The case of the Columbus public schools informs us that regardless of where Black people were they had to agitate, protest, and fight for their human and civil rights as Americans.

Consequently, from 1849 to 1882, in Columbus, like other urban areas during this period, African Americans, although sometimes divided, sought full access to the common schools through a desegregation movement. The movement included contending forces in the Black community, including African American teachers, principals, and preachers. The major roadblock to the inclusion of African Americans was the law and its continual change during the antebellum, postbellum, and Reconstruction periods, and the attitudes and beliefs of White Americans about the rights and role of Blacks in the U.S. society. While Whites' ideological beliefs concerning the educability of African American people varied, African Americans continued to believe in their right and ability to gain an education whether enslaved or free (Douglas, 2005; Williams, 2005). They believed so much in the equalizing powers of education that many communities, including Columbus, sacrificed African American teachers to secure desegregated schools. None of the choices that African Americans were forced to make were easy ones, nor did they envision that their protests and petitions would forever alter the circumstances under which African American children would be educated.

REFERENCES

Anderson, J. D. (1988). *The education of Blacks in the South: 1860–1935.* Chapel Hill: University of North Carolina Press.

Brown v. Board of Education, 347 U.S. 483 (1954).

Dabney, W. P. (1988). *Cincinnati's colored citizens: Historical, sociological and biographical.* Cincinnati, OH: One Book Store. (Original work published 1926)

Daley, J. (2006). *Great speeches by African Americans: Frederick Douglass, Sojourner Truth, Dr. Martin Luther King, Jr., Barack Obama, and others.* Mineola, NY: Dover.

Douglas, D. M. (2005). *Jim Crow moves North: The battle over northern school segregation, 1865–1954.* New York: Cambridge University Press.

Erickson, L. E. (1959). *The color line in Ohio public schools, 1829–1890.* Doctoral dissertation, The Ohio State University, Columbus.

Franklin, V. P. (1990). "They rose and fell together:" African American educators and community leadership, 1795–1954. *Journal of Education, 172*(3), 30–64.

Franklin, V. P., & Savage, C. J. (2004). *Cultural capital and black education: African American communities and the funding of black schooling, 1865 to the present.* Greenwich, CT: Information Age.

Fredrickson, G. M. (1971). *The Black image in the White mind.* Middletown, CT: Wesleyan University Press.

Gaines, K. K. (1996). *Uplifting the race: Black leadership, politics, and culture in the twentieth century.* Chapel Hill: University of North Carolina Press.

Gerber, D. A. (1976). *Black Ohio and the color line, 1860–1915.* Urbana: University of Illinois Press.

Griffler, K. P. (2004). *Front line of freedom: African Americans and the forging of the underground railroad in the Ohio valley.* Lexington: University Press of Kentucky.

Himes, J. S. (1942). Forty years of Negro life in Columbus, Ohio. *Journal of Negro History, 27*(2), 133–154.

Jackson, L. P. (1942). *Free Negro labor and property holding in Virginia, 1830–1860.* New York: D. Appleton Century.

Kliebard, H. M. (1999). *Schooled to work: Vocationalism and the American curriculum, 1876–1946.* New York: Teachers College Press.

Litwack, L. F. (1961). *North of slavery: The Negro in the free states, 1790–1860.* Chicago: University of Chicago Press.

Mark, M. L. (1928). *Negroes in Columbus.* Columbus: Ohio State University Press.

Mason, M. (1917). *The policy of segregation of the Negro in the public schools of Ohio, Indiana, and Illinois.* Master's thesis, The University of Chicago, Chicago.

McAfee, W. M. (1998). *Religion, race and reconstruction: The public school in the politics of the 1870s.* New York: State University of New York Press.

Meltzer, M. (1995). *Frederick Douglass: In his own words.* San Diego, CA: Harcourt Brace.

Minor, R. C. (1947). *James Preston Poindexter: Elder statesman of Columbus.* Columbus: Ohio State Archaeological and Historical Quarterly.

Seifert, M. T. (1978). *Early Black history in the Columbus public schools.* Columbus: Privately Published.

Taylor, N. M. (2005). *Frontiers of freedom: Cincinnati's Black community, 1802–1868.* Athens: Ohio University Press.

Tyack, D. B. (1974). *The one best system: A history of American urban education.* Boston: Harvard University Press.

Waite, C. L. (2002). *Permission to remain amongst us. Education for Blacks in Oberlin, Ohio, 1880–1914.* Westport, CT: Praeger.

Ward, A. L. (1993). *The African American struggle for education in Columbus, Ohio: 1803–1913.* Master's thesis, The Ohio State University, Columbus.

Ward Randolph, A. (1996). *A historical analysis of an urban school: A case study of a northern de facto segregated school, Champion Avenue School: 1910–1996.* Doctoral dissertation, The Ohio State University, Columbus.

Ward Randolph, A. (2004). Owning, controlling and building upon cultural capital: The Albany enterprise academy and black education in southeast Ohio, 1963–1886. In V. P. Franklin & C. J. Savage (Eds.), *Cultural capital and black education: African American communities and the funding of Black schooling, 1865 to the present* (pp. 15–33). Greenwich, CT: Information Age.

Watkins, W. H. (2001). *The White architects of Black education: Ideology and power in America, 1865–1954.* New York: Teachers College Press.

Wilkerson, D. A. (1963). *Public school segregation and integration in the North.* New York: National Association of Intergroup Relations Officials.

Williams, H. A. (2005). *Self-taught: African American education in slavery and freedom.* Chapel Hill: University of North Carolina Press.

Woodson, C. G. (1968). *The education of the Negro prior to 1861.* Salem, NH: Ayer Publishing. (Original work published 1919)

2

AFRICAN AMERICAN EDUCATORS AND THE BLACK INTELLECTUAL TRADITION

DERRICK P. ALRIDGE

S ince Africans arrived on the shores of the Americas nearly four centuries ago, they have held a deep and abiding faith in education as a means of improving their individual and collective social conditions. On slave ships, Africans taught one another the languages of their respective tribes; during slavery many Blacks taught each other how to read and write (Haymes, 2001; Webber, 1978; Williams, 2005). During and after Reconstruction, Blacks established and maintained their own schools, and during the first half of the 20th century, Blacks fought in the courts and protested in the streets for the right to an equal education (Anderson, 1988; Butchart, 1980; Tushnet, 1994).

African American educators have been in the forefront of developing educational agendas for African Americans throughout their quest for education. Through their work as teachers, scholars, intellectuals, and activists, African American educators have left a rich history of ideas about the education of Black peoples. During the first decades of the 20th century, African American educators contributed significantly to a larger burgeoning Black intellectual tradition that addressed the social, economic, and political realities of Black life (Alridge, 2007; Dunn, 1993; Franklin, 1984, 1990; McCluskey, 1997; Meier, 1988; Perkins, 1982).

Despite the plethora of educational ideas expressed by African American educators, historians and philosophers of education have largely overlooked their contributions. For instance, when examining African American educational thought, history and philosophy of education texts typically focus on the well-known debates over vocational and classical education between Booker T. Washington and W. E. B. Du Bois to the exclusion of information about other African American educators. This overemphasis on the Washington and Du Bois debates and the lack of systematic study of the ideas of African American educators hide their contributions as well as the nuances and diversity of views among them. It also prevents us from seeing African American educational thought as a part of a larger Black intellectual tradition.

In this chapter, I briefly examine the educational ideas of Alexander Crummell (1819–1898), Anna Julia Cooper (1858–1964), Booker T. Washington (1856–1915), W. E. B. Du Bois (1868–1963), Carter G. Woodson (1875–1950), Mary McLeod Bethune (1875–1955), and Charles S. Johnson (1893–1956). Collectively, these educators provide a view of the diversity of African American educational thought beyond the binary Washington versus Du Bois and vocational versus classical education paradigms. Examining their ideas is an essential step in moving toward a broader, more accurate understanding of the Black intellectual tradition.[1]

ALEXANDER CRUMMELL, THE EDUCATOR AS CIVILIZATIONIST

One of the most prolific African American educators of the 19th century was Alexander Crummell. Born in New York City in 1819, Crummell studied in the schools of New York and received his college education at Cambridge University from 1849 to 1853. Early in life, Crummell developed a strong sense of self-efficacy, and while in Europe he gained a great appreciation for European ideas, culture, and history (Moses, 1989). For Crummell, Europe represented the kind of civilization African people should emulate. Crummell's reverence for Europe influenced his educational thinking and encouraged him to adopt a civilizationist perspective, identifying highly developed technology, high literacy rates, and adherence to Christianity as the characteristics of advanced civilizations.

Crummell believed that African Americans had the potential to reach higher levels of civilization but that they had not yet received the appropriate education for the mission of race uplift. In one of his earliest speeches on education, titled "The Necessities and Advantages of Education Considered in Relation to Colored Men," Crummell laid out his civilizationist philosophy of education:

> Education is necessary if we wish to make improvement and progress. The human mind was made for improvement and for progress. . . . The higher avenues [above] must be trodden. The abounding treasures within our reach must be seized upon and appropriated. (Crummell, 1844, p. 26)

To reach higher levels of civilization, Crummell believed that Blacks must focus their learning in the sciences, the arts, and modern technology. Without such education, he believed, ignorance and a "dormant intellect" would keep Blacks in a continued state of servitude.

During the 1850s, Crummell accepted a professorship in moral philosophy at the newly established Liberia College in Liberia, a newly formed country in West Africa. While in Liberia, he educated a number of Africans who later assumed leadership positions throughout Africa. He also educated missionaries to work in Liberia (Lance, 1972). Liberia influenced Crummell's educational thought tremendously. Observing the difficulty in establishing a country from the ground up, Crummell realized that any group of people starting anew needed to educate individuals for a variety of occupations in order for the community to flourish. As a result, in addition to classical education, Crummell supported industrial education for Blacks. Speaking before the U.S. House Committee of Education and Labor in 1880, Crummell encouraged committee members to fund training in "skilled labor, in mechanical knowledge, and handicraft" (Crummell, 1992b, p. 209).

Despite his support for providing training in a variety of occupations, however, Crummell repudiated Booker T. Washington's advocacy of industrial education as the sole form of education for Blacks. Industrial education alone, Crummell believed, could not help prepare Blacks for the crucial task of advancing Black society and civilization. He argued that all forms of education, including industrial and vocational training, should include classical and higher education to provide Blacks with a broader vision of life (Crummell, 1992b). According to Crummell, this would enable all Blacks to participate in uplifting their race to higher levels of civilization.

Crummell's civilizationist ideology led him to help found the American Negro Academy (ANA) in 1897. The Academy brought together like-minded, educated Black men for the purpose of "encouragement and assistance of youthful, but hesitant, scholarship, for the stimulation of inventive and artistic powers; and for the promotion of the publication of works of merit" (Moses, 1989, p. 365). The Academy's mission clearly reflected Crummell's belief that men of merit and goodwill should play a role in uplifting the Negro race. Crummell would be joined in his beliefs about race uplift and in his membership in the ANA by his young protégé W. E. B. Du Bois.

At the inaugural meeting of the Academy, Crummell delivered his famous speech titled

"Civilization, the Primal Need of the Race," which illuminated the Christian progressivism in his educational thought (Crummell, 1992a). He noted, "The greatness of peoples springs from their ability to grasp the grand conceptions of being. It is the absorption of a people, of a nation, of a race, in large majestic and abiding things which lifts them up to the skies" (Crummell, 1992a, p. 286). The Black community, Crummell believed, should reach for high levels of civilization; he argued that they could do so most effectively through Christianity (Fullinwider, 1969).

Alexander Crummell was a significant figure in the history of Black education because his ideas predated those of prominent 20th century thinkers with whom we are more familiar. In addition to the vocational/classical education dilemma, Crummell's thought addressed the education of Black women and the role of Black history in the curriculum. Ultimately, he believed that education was the means by which Blacks would uplift themselves to become a great civilization. As a civilizationist, his ideas on education and race uplift would influence the discourse on African American educational thought during the early years of the 20th century.

Anna Julia Cooper, the Victorian Feminist Educator

A contemporary and protégé of Alexander Crummell was teacher Anna Julia Cooper. Cooper was one of a young cadre of Black intellectuals of the early 20th century who saw themselves as the vanguard of the Negro race. Born in North Carolina in 1858, Cooper graduated from St. Augustine's College in Raleigh. During her early years at St. Augustine's, Cooper became fascinated with the influence of education on her own life and prepared herself for a career as an educator. Of her early years as a student at St. Augustine's, Cooper noted,

> When hardly more than kindergarten age it was my good fortune to be selected for a scholarship by Dr. J. Brinton Smith, founder of St. Augustine's Normal School at Raleigh, N.C. . . . in the nucleus he was planning to train as teacher for the Colored people of the South. That school was my world during the formative period, the most critical in any girl's life. Its nurture & admonition

> gave . . . shelter and protection. My lines have fallen in pleasant places & I have a goodly heritage. (quoted in Hutchinson, 1982, p. 19)

One of Cooper's (1892/1988b) earliest articulations of her educational thought was her book of speeches and essays *A Voice From the South.* In this treatise, Cooper argued that Black women were an integral part of the race uplift movement of the late 19th century and must, therefore, obtain higher education to prepare themselves for the mission of race uplift.

Cooper further argued that those Black men obligated to uplift the race, also known as "race men," should support the education of Black women. In expressing her educational philosophy, Cooper espoused a Victorian view of womanhood in which Black women were important to the male-dominated race uplift movement. Like other Victorians, Cooper believed that women and their soft femininity helped balance the crudeness and aggressiveness of men. As such, Black women provided necessary balance in Blacks' struggle for equality. Women's genteel nature, Cooper believed, provided stability for the race uplift movement (Cooper, 1892/1988b).

Cooper's educational ideas may also be observed in her work as a teacher at M Street High School, later known as Dunbar High School, in Washington, D.C. At M Street, Cooper supported both the classical and vocational curricula. Cooper believed that given the variety of abilities possessed by the broad cross-section of students in Washington, both industrial and vocational education should be offered (Hutchinson, 1982).

However, Cooper's passion seemed to lie in further developing classical education at M Street. For instance, while teaching at M Street, Cooper often wrote essays and delivered speeches on the importance of the arts and humanities, focusing much of her attention on teaching students about Black history. Cooper's emphasis on classical education was so successful that many of her students later attended liberal arts institutions such as Oberlin, Harvard, and Dartmouth. Cooper's success in classical education, however, led to her resignation from M Street because school officials, who were socially connected to Booker T. Washington, viewed her emphasis on classical education as an affront to Washington and his advocacy of vocational education (Hutchinson, 1982).

Cooper also critiqued the teacher training of her time. In "The Humor of Teaching," published in *The Crisis* in 1930, she challenged Black teachers not to limit their education to summer classes that focused on new and faddish teaching methodologies. She also asked teachers to extend their thinking beyond a focus on giving exams, depending on lessons plans, and adhering strictly to curriculum guides. Advocating the idea of the teacher as an intellectual, Cooper urged her fellow teachers to seek broader knowledge and ideas that would help them become better educators (Cooper, 1930).

While Cooper was mentored by Crummell and was an acquaintance of Du Bois, she had a precarious relationship with the race men of her era. The patriarchal mindset of these men prevented them from recognizing many of her educational efforts and accomplishments. Given her talents and renown as an author and teacher, it is a travesty that she and other women were not initially invited to become members of the ANA, though years later she would become a member (Alridge, 2007). Cooper believed that Black history should be a critical part of the education of Blacks. In 1921, she received her Ph.D. from the Sorbonne. Her dissertation "The Attitude of France on the Question of Slavery Between 1789 and 1847" reflected her ongoing focus on Black history. In her study, she questioned the commitment of French revolutionists to democracy because of their refusal to address slavery in their calls for liberty (Cooper, 1925/1988a). Cooper also advocated the learning of Black history in the plays that she wrote for her students at M Street High School. Through her scholarship as well as her educational thought, Cooper believed in the importance of educating Blacks about Black history as a means of contributing to race uplift.

Cooper also believed that education should be an integral part of race uplift and self-determination for Blacks (Evans, 2007; Gaines, 1996; Johnson, 2000). In her work for the Colored Social Settlement, she called for education that reached out to the community. Cooper's belief in communal education was further manifested in her work as president of Frelinghuysen University from 1930 to 1940. The university's purpose was to provide education to the adult citizens of Washington, D.C., and Cooper reached out particularly to Black women, encouraging and helping them gain an education as a means of helping themselves (Alridge, 2007).

While Cooper conceptualized Black women's education and leadership within Victorian notions of womanhood, she also aggressively advocated education and leadership roles that empowered Black women. This dialectical position establishes Cooper as both a Victorian and a progenitor of feminism. As a Victorian feminist educator, she successfully merged the ideas of her era and helped lay a foundation for modern-day Black feminism.

Booker T. Washington, the Idealistic Pragmatist

The best-known African American educator of the 20th century is Booker T. Washington. Born into slavery in Franklin County, Virginia, in 1856, Washington learned to read after he was freed at age 9. He later attended Hampton Institute in Virginia, where he came under the influence of General Samuel Armstrong. Armstrong, a teacher and mentor to Washington, stressed the importance of manual labor for Blacks and preached that hard work and spiritual fortitude would help Blacks make a living. According to Armstrong, learning respect for hard labor and mastering a skill should be the foundation of a curriculum for Blacks (Anderson, 1988; Curti, 1974). Armstrong's ideas influenced Washington throughout his life. For instance, in 1911 Washington noted, "[Armstrong] has had a greater influence upon my life than any other person I have ever known, except my mother" (Washington, 1911, p. 53).

In 1881, Washington moved south to help found Tuskegee Institute in Tuskegee, Alabama. Initially Tuskegee had very few resources and even fewer buildings. Washington, therefore, implemented the philosophy of his mentor, Armstrong, calling on students of the newly formed institution to construct the school's buildings, grow food and prepare meals, and take responsibility for the upkeep of the school (Washington, 1911).

Some historians have argued that Washington's educational agenda at Tuskegee epitomized the experiential philosophy that John Dewey advocated years later (Curti, 1974; Moses, 1998). Washington's educational philosophy was grounded in practicality and his belief that Blacks needed to develop discipline, a work ethic, and the vocational skills necessary to earn a living. If Blacks obtained vocational and industrial skills, Washington argued, they could find work and support themselves. Over time, Blacks would build a strong economic infrastructure, leading to respect from Whites and eventually, civil rights. This pragmatic idealist approach comprised the core of Washington's educational philosophy.

Tuskegee was successful in many of its efforts. Washington gained the financial support necessary to build new buildings, hire more faculty, and expand course offerings. A number of Tuskegee graduates became successful teachers, farmers, and businesspeople. Tuskegee, with its work ethic, practicality, and emphasis on self-reliance, represented the concrete manifestation of Washington's educational philosophy.

Despite Washington's advocacy of vocational and industrial education, however, even his views were not absolute. For example, many Tuskegee instructors were themselves classically educated. Moreover, Washington himself pointed out that liberal education had some value within the larger vocational curriculum at Tuskegee.

Margaret Washington Clifford, Washington's granddaughter and a Tuskegee graduate, speaks poignantly about Tuskegee's curriculum. Born in 1921, six years after Washington's death in 1915, Clifford notes that the curriculum had not changed much since Washington's death to the time when she entered the high school at Tuskegee. In an interview, Clifford noted,

> That seal of the National Honor Society represents the fact that [Tuskegee students] had all the courses, all the hours of the Carnegie units necessary for college entrance. You don't get a chapter of the National Honor Society unless you have all of the courses and hours for college credits for college entrance. (M. W. Clifford, personal communication, January 21, 2004)

Despite contemporary presentations of Washington's "accommodationist" educational philosophy, it is important to note that some Whites suspected Washington of having ulterior motives at Tuskegee. For instance, a German immigrant calling himself Ruperth Fehnstoke noted that he was once sympathetic to the "old time Darkey," but had a change of heart after visiting Tuskegee and observing Washington's educational philosophy in action. He stated,

I know from many confidential conversations that almost every student and teacher at the Institute, has but one aspiration, one hope, one prayer that they may eventually be enabled to compel the white man to cringe and do homage to his or her particular sublime majesty. And I know, from the same source-that this idea is being quietly instilled into the minds of the Negro, right here in Tuskegee. (Fehnstoke, 1905, p. 25)[2]

Such comments point to the complexity of Washington himself, as well as to the complex ways in which Whites perceived him. Moreover, during Washington's lifetime some Blacks such as William Monroe Trotter, Du Bois's Harvard classmate and a newspaper editor, were incensed by what they perceived as an "accommodationist" philosophy of education that urged Blacks to wait patiently for their civil rights and dutifully accept work as farmers and laborers.

Despite his influence, Washington did face challenges to his educational philosophy. Much has already been written about Washington's and Du Bois "great debates" on education, so I will not belabor the point here. Shortly after Washington's famous 1895 speech at the Cotton States Exposition in Atlanta, Du Bois wrote a letter to Washington commending him on the effectiveness of his message (Du Bois, 1973). Within weeks, however, Du Bois grew disappointed in what he believed was Washington's acquiescence to White industrialists and the White South. He viewed Washington's philosophy—that Blacks should delay their civil rights to obtain vocational training—as an affront to the Black racial uplift.

By the time of his death in 1915, Washington had grown frustrated with the ineffectiveness of his educational philosophy in bringing about greater cooperation between Blacks and Whites and in tempering White hatred for Blacks. During the early 1900s, lynchings of Blacks in the South escalated (National Association for the Advancement of Colored People, 1919). Consequently, Washington sometimes worked behind the scenes addressing race problems and supported some civil rights advocacy (Lewis, 1993). His educational and social philosophy was enduring and influenced Blacks' ideas about education and civil rights well into the 20th century (West, 2006).

Booker T. Washington was an *idealistic pragmatist* educator who was perhaps overly optimistic about the potential of vocational education to solve the social, economic, and political problems of Black people. By the time of his death, hostility toward Blacks had increased and Blacks were far from obtaining equality. Moreover, many Blacks began to believe that vocational education was not the solution to the Negro problem. Nevertheless, nearly a century after his death, Washington's emphasis on the need for Blacks to gain a practical education and secure skills that would enable them to help themselves still resonates with many Blacks today.

W. E. B. DU BOIS,
THE AFROCENTRIC PRAGMATIST

William Edward Burghardt Du Bois was perhaps the most prolific speaker and writer on the education of African Americans. Born in Great Barrington, Massachusetts, in 1868, Du Bois grew up in an area distanced from the harsh racial tensions of the South. He recalled that there were few Blacks in his community, that he experienced little racism growing up, and that he had a strong sense of himself and his academic abilities (Du Bois, 1968).

After leaving Great Barrington, Du Bois attended Fisk University in Nashville, Tennessee, located in the heart of the Black community. Never before had Du Bois been this close to so many of his people; for the first time he was surrounded by like-minded Blacks of different complexions and of high academic ability. At Fisk, he began to see himself and his classmates as the chosen few who bore the responsibility of uplifting their "lesser brethren" and from this view, his educational philosophy took hold (Du Bois, 1903).

Education, Du Bois believed, should help train Blacks to engage in the struggle for democracy and equality. The battle would be difficult, he realized, and appropriate education would be needed to wage war on Jim Crow, White supremacy, and discrimination. The battle for equality, he believed, would occur in the courts, in classrooms, in science, and in the arts. In each of these venues, Blacks would have to challenge unjust laws and refute prevailing ideas of Black inferiority. To do so effectively, Blacks needed an education that prepared them for intellectual engagement with Whites. As a result, Du Bois

concluded that a classical/liberal education was the most appropriate education for Blacks.

Du Bois, however, was not categorically opposed to vocational or industrial education. He realized that not all Blacks would obtain a classical education or attend college and that a segment of the Black population needed to become skilled laborers, building an economic foundation that would support academic engagement. In the end, however, he believed that classical and liberal education should be a core component of all curricula for Blacks. The purpose of education, he stated, was "not to make a man a carpenter, but to make a carpenter a man."

Du Bois's educational ideas continued to develop during his student years at Harvard University and the University of Berlin. At Harvard and in Berlin, he adopted broader educational ideas than those he held at Fisk. The learned man, he believed, educated in the classics and in the knowledge of modern civilizations, would be the standard-bearer for the Black race. While in Berlin, for instance, he wrote to students at Fisk extolling the benefits of study and travel in Europe, which he believed was the location of the world's greatest civilizations (Du Bois, 1893). During his college years, Du Bois was exposed to the writings of Georg Wilhelm Frederick Hegel. In Hegel's (1801) *The Phenomenology of Mind*, Du Bois found ideas that would help him frame the social and psychological status of Black people living in White-dominated societies such as the United States. From Hegel, Du Bois borrowed the concept of the *dialectic*, which proposed that the conflict between oppositional views would eventually lead to reconciliation.

Du Bois also believed Blacks needed an education that would help them cope with the psychological tensions of being Black in America. In his seminal work *The Souls of Black Folk* (1903), Du Bois argued that Black Americans experienced a "psychic duality" or double-consciousness in which Blacks were potentially torn between their Black identity and their American identity. To successfully navigate the situation, Du Bois believed that Blacks needed to be grounded in a thorough knowledge of Black history and culture. With this grounding, Du Bois believed that Blacks could transcend double-consciousness and more successfully navigate

White society. Du Bois published a number of works on Black history that address the issue of double-consciousness. Some of his most popular books on Black history include, *The Negro* (1915/2002), *Black Folk Then and Now* (1939), *Africa—Its Place in Modern History* (1947), and *The World and Africa* (1947). He also attempted to educate the Black masses through short stories, essays, and pictorials while he was editor of *The Crisis* magazine from 1910 to 1934.

Perhaps Du Bois's most popular tool for teaching Black history was his *Brownies Book,* published from 1920 to 1921. Written for children, the *Brownies Book* consisted of short stories, poems, essays, drawings, and photos that highlighted the accomplishments of Blacks. The purpose of the magazine was to instill in Black children a sense of pride in Black history and culture. Du Bois was an *Afrocentric pragmatist* who believed that education should be grounded in Black history and culture to help Blacks better navigate the larger world (see Rath, 1997). Drawing on Hegel and his own belief in African-centeredness, Du Bois offered a dialectical educational philosophy that he believed would provide Blacks with the skills to flourish in White society and thereby ameliorate the Negro problem.

CARTER G. WOODSON, THE PEOPLE'S HISTORIAN AS EDUCATOR

Carter Godwin Woodson was the most renowned African American historian-educator of the 20th century. Born in New Canton, West Virginia, in 1875, Woodson developed an interest in reading at an early age. Woodson received his bachelor's degree in literature in 1903 from Berea College in Kentucky and his master's degree in 1908 from the University of Chicago. In 1912, he became the second Black student to receive a Ph.D. in history from Harvard. Between his years as a student, Woodson taught in school and served as an administrator in Winona, West Virginia, and in the Philippines.

Like Du Bois, Woodson believed that Blacks lacked an understanding or knowledge of Black history. Moreover, he believed that many Americans, including some Blacks, had negative views of Blacks because of the misinformation provided by revisionist historians who wrote negatively about Black history and social scientists who disseminated theories of Black inferiority. As a historian, Woodson felt that he should play an active role in countering such misinformation (Woodson, 1933/1990). Woodson's belief that Blacks needed to learn about Black history led him to found the Association for the Study of Negro Life and History (ASNLH) in 1915. The organization conducted scientific research on neglected areas of African American life and history. Historians, Woodson believed, should be in the forefront of this endeavor, and he envisioned ASNLH as a major facilitator of such an enterprise. A year later, Woodson and the organization began publishing a scholarly journal titled the *Journal of Negro History.* The journal focused on presenting historical work on the Black experience written by Black and White historians, educators, and independent scholars and was instrumental in building interest and sustaining momentum in the field of African American history and studies.

Woodson's educational thought was similarly reflected in his own scholarly work. His *The Education of the Negro Prior to 1861* (1915) was a meticulous study of the struggle by Blacks to be educated prior to Emancipation. In the book, Woodson chronicled the success of Black communities in establishing schools for themselves. He also argued that educated Blacks were more efficient than uneducated Blacks and were good workers and artisans and excellent managers (Woodson, 1919/1999).

The teaching of African American history was a centerpiece of Woodson's philosophy of education. He, therefore, envisioned ASNLH as an organization organically connected to contemporary issues and problems in the Black community. Guided by this perspective, he believed that the teaching of Black history should be dynamic and relevant and inform our understanding of the present circumstances of Black people and help point to a direction for the future.

Woodson's strong belief in the importance of Black teachers as disseminators of Black history led to the establishment of local branches of ASNLH dedicated to improving the teaching of history among Blacks in local classrooms and communities. This agenda was further advanced in 1937 with ASNLH's establishment of the *Negro History Bulletin,* a publication whose purpose was to provide teachers and students with accessible essays on and primary sources from Black history.

Woodson's crusade to influence curriculum placed him in constant contact with Black teachers. Not only did he speak at schools about Black history, he also made the training of teachers in Black history a critical mission of ASNLH. As such, Woodson was the *people's historian*.

MARY MCLEOD BETHUNE,
THE PEOPLE'S EDUCATOR

Mary McLeod Bethune is known primarily as the founder of Bethune College and a member of Roosevelt's group of Black consultants called the "Black cabinet." However, Bethune was also an educator who seriously contemplated an educational agenda for Black people. Unfortunately, her educational philosophy has been largely overlooked by historians. Born on July 10, 1875, in Maysville, South Carolina, Bethune attended Trinity Presbyterian Mission School at age 10 and enrolled in Scotia Seminary in North Carolina at age 12 (Smith, 1996).

In 1896, Bethune started her career as a teacher at Haines Institute in Augusta, Georgia. At Haines, she came under the guidance of Lucy Craft Laney, who, like Anna Julia Cooper, viewed Black women as caregivers whose primary role was raising children. In this way, Bethune also developed a Victorian notion of Black women as transmitters of knowledge and as standard-bearers for the race. Bethune strongly believed that education was a powerful force in emancipating Blacks mentally and socially in society (McCluskey, 1994).

On October 3, 1904, Bethune founded and opened Daytona Educational and Industrial Institute in Daytona, Florida. The curriculum at Daytona Industrial focused on helping Black girls become economically self-sufficient and providing them with the skills necessary for finding employment and making a living. Bethune also built on Laney's educational philosophy in her advocacy of the "habits of cleanliness, beauty, and thoughtfulness in application to homelife" (McCluskey, 1997, p. 411).

Bethune's educational philosophy was not limited to vocational and domestic training. She was also a proponent of Deweyan progressive education, in which the disciplines could be used to educate students about issues of race in everyday life. In a meeting of the ASNLH, she noted,

> The entire school of progressive education is guided by the great American philosopher John Dewey, whose immortal words, 'Education is life,' have brought us to the realization of 'translating' the materials of history and biography, science and literature into the languages and experiences of the child. (Bethune, 1939, p. 9)

Bethune's advocacy of progressive education grounded in the humanities would eventually become part of the curriculum at Bethune Cookman College. The school offered courses in math, science, English, and foreign languages and eventually became a liberal arts college with strong connections to community life (McCluskey, 1997).

Bethune also strongly believed that Black history should be an integral part of the curriculum for Black children. As such, she called for historians to meticulously research and to present their research to the public to counter the inaccurate and negative information propagated by racist historians. From 1936 to 1951, she served as President of ASNLH where she continued her crusade to use history as a means to empower Black people. Bethune understood the daily struggles of her people and tried to address their struggles on the ground level as an educator. She advocated an educational agenda that focused on Black history and progressive educational ideas for the Black masses. As a result, she was endeared by many in the African American community and epitomized the idea of the *people's educator*.

CHARLES S. JOHNSON, THE
EDUCATOR AND RACE SOCIOLOGIST

Educator and social scientist, Charles Spurgeon Johnson was a leader in facilitating the discourse on race relations. Born in Bristol, Virginia, in 1893, Johnson, like many of his African American contemporaries, experienced first-hand the sting of segregation and closely observed the tenuous relationship between Blacks and Whites as they navigated the peculiar and often complicated social mores of Jim Crow. Reflecting on the early years of his life, he recalled the negative impact Jim Crow had on the psyches of Blacks and Whites, making them distrustful and suspicious of one another (Johnson, n.d.; Sanders, 2005).

Despite the challenges of growing up in a Jim Crow society, Johnson graduated from Wayland Academy in Richmond, Virginia, and received an AB degree from Virginia University in 1916. He later attended the University of Chicago, where he studied with famed sociologist Robert E. Park. Park helped Johnson apply social science methods to the problems of race and racism and provided Johnson with a viable means of addressing his concerns about discrimination.

In 1918, Johnson left Chicago to join the military and served in World War I. On returning to the University of Chicago in 1919, Johnson found himself perplexed by the racial tensions that had escalated in Chicago. In 1919, a race riot broke out in which Johnson himself was nearly attacked. Because of his experience in race relations, he was appointed associate executive secretary to the Chicago Race Relations Committee. In that capacity, he conducted research for and wrote the Commission's report titled, *The Negro in Chicago: A Study of Race Relations and a Race Riot.* The study concluded that Black migration to Chicago created a tense racial environment as Blacks and Whites competed for scarce jobs (Sanders, 2005).

In his study *The Negro in American Civilization: A Study of Negro Life and Race Relations in the Light of Social Research,* Johnson used social science research methods to argue that education could be used to improve African American life and, thus, enhance race relations. Citing census bureau data, he pointed out that while illiteracy among Blacks had decreased significantly between 1880 and 1920, it had decreased at a much slower rate for Blacks than for Whites. In addition, he showed that illiteracy among rural Blacks was double that of urban Blacks. Black illiteracy, he concluded, continued to be an impediment to improving Black life (Johnson, 1930). Further exacerbating the problems of Black education were poorly trained teachers, inadequate school facilities, low teacher salaries, and low academic standards. Johnson believed that education for Blacks would never improve significantly if it relied on state support. He

therefore encouraged the federal government to play a more active financial role in improving Black education. These were only a few of the problems Johnson addressed in his study—problems that he believed must be solved to improve relations between the races (Johnson, 1930). After World War II, Johnson observed that escalating race and class tensions, along with rapid technological advancement, created new challenges for American democracy. To meet these challenges, Johnson believed that school curricula should address real-world problems and actively facilitate the technological, social, and cultural transformation in society. In addition, he believed that education should be flexible and allow for individuals to adjust to societal changes. Johnson noted, "Education does not exist in a vacuum. It is a dynamic process in the context of a culture which is itself dynamic" (Johnson, 1953, p. 23).

Citing Jean Jacques Rousseau as an influence on his thinking, Johnson argued for the transformative power of education and believed that education could improve relationships between disparate groups of people. The teaching of new knowledge about various racial, ethnic, and other groups, he believed, was essential to helping individuals understand the customs and ideas of others. Understanding the cultures of people from different racial and ethnic groups, he surmised, would lead to better race relations, and schools should take the lead in teaching about the diverse peoples of the world (Sanders, 2005).

Johnson operationalized his social and educational philosophy of racial understanding and reconciliation in his work with the Race Relations Institute (RRI) at Fisk University. Established in 1944, the RRI promoted educational workshops and seminars on race, race relations, and racial problems. Responding vigorously to the anti-intellectual climate of the postwar era, the Institute encouraged its participants to question traditional and racist views about various racial and ethnic groups and to search for ways to improve relationships between them (Sanders, 2005). An equally important objective of the RRI was to use social science as a tool to provide objective, empirically based research on race and race relations. In some ways, the RRI was a manifestation of the type of social science institute that Du Bois had called for throughout his life.

By the 1950s, Du Bois was not as optimistic as Johnson about the potential for improving race relations and was suspicious of Johnson's close ties to White philanthropy. Whereas Du Bois had long distrusted White philanthropists' ability to fund Black education without controlling Black decision making, Johnson embraced the support of White philanthropy and was more willing to compromise to gain support for his projects (Gasman, 2002). As a result, Du Bois and Johnson had a somewhat strained relationship. Evidence of this tension may be observed in Johnson's reluctance to include Du Bois in many activities of the RRI and Du Bois's opposition to Johnson's appointment to the presidency of Fisk. Nevertheless, in a letter to a friend, Du Bois acknowledged Johnson's ability to raise funds and even saw the advantages to a Johnson presidency. He stated, "The only thing that we can do now, it seems to me, is to keep still and give him a chance" (Gasman, 2002, p. 512).

Charles S. Johnson and his work with the RRI helped lay a solid educational and social-science-based foundation for the Civil Rights Movement. Throughout the movement, activists and scholars such as Martin Luther King, Jr., Rosa Parks, Septima Clark, and Robert E. Park studied or lectured at the RRI. Johnson's merger of education and social science made significant contributions to both these fields, making him a significant figure in the quest for racial reconciliation and democracy during the postwar era.

Conclusion

The ideas of African American educators of the early 20th century reveal that these educators thought pragmatically and systematically about the role of education in the uplift and advancement of Black people. Collectively, their ideas were grounded in the social, economic, and political experiences of Black people and spoke about the realities of being Black in a White-dominated society. In addition, these educators moved solely beyond the classical versus vocational educational dichotomy to present complex and nuanced educational agendas that readily responded to changing situations and times.

As contemporary scholars of Black education continue to research the problems that plague the education of Black people and explore ways to improve Blacks' education, it is my hope that they will consult African American educators and the Black intellectual tradition. African American educators of the past provide a rich source of ideas relevant to contemporary Black education, particularly because of the persistence of many problems of the past. This chapter represents a broader effort to bring African American educational thought and ideas of the past to light to help provide understanding of contemporary issues in African American education. Providing a brief examination of a few prominent educators of the early 20th century is only one step in this effort.

Notes

1. In recent decades the notion of an Black Intellectual Tradition has come under scrutiny. For instance, in his book, *Color & Culture: Black Writers and the Making of the Modern Intellectual*, historian Ross Posnock (1998) argued against an "identity politics" that promotes the idea of an African American or Black intellectual tradition. For Posnock, such a notion engages a "postmodern politics of difference" that limits knowledge based on racial affiliation. Such a perspective, Posnock posited, is "fixated on racial difference and the question of what and who is authentically black" (p. 3). As such, Posnock engaged Blacks within a cosmopolitan intellectual tradition and attempted to disengage them from notions such as race uplift and the identification of an African American intellectual tradition.

2. See Ruperth Fehnstoke (1905, p. 25). The Bostonian's suspicions were, to a certain extent, warranted. David Levering Lewis, for instance, pointed out that Washington was secretly engaged in activities intended to bring about greater civil rights for Blacks, including garnering legal funds to help test the constitutionality of grandfather and other disenfranchisement clauses in Louisiana and Alabama. See Lewis (1993, p. 258).

References

Alridge, D. P. (2007). Of Victorianism, civilizationism, and progressivism: The educational ideas of Anna Julia Cooper and W. E. B. Du Bois. *History of Education Quarterly, 47*(4), 416–446.

Anderson, J. D. (1988). *The education of blacks in the South, 1860–1935.* Chapel Hill: University of North Carolina Press.

Bethune, M. M. (1939). The adaptation of the history of the Negro to the capacity of the child. *Journal of Negro History, 4*(1), 9.

Butchart, R. E. (1980). *Northern schools, southern Blacks, and Reconstruction: Freedmen's education, 1862-1875.* Westport, CT: Greenwood Press.

Cooper, A. J. (1930, November). The humor of teaching. *The Crisis, 37*(10), 393–394.

Cooper, A. J. (1988a). *Slavery and the French Revolutionists (1788-1805).* Lewistown, New York: Edwin Mellen Press. (Original work published 1925)

Cooper, A. J. (1988b). *A voice from the South.* New York: Oxford University Press. (Original work published 1892)

Crummell, A. (1844). *The necessities and advantages of education considered in relation to colored men.* Alexander Crummell Papers, Schomburg Research Center, New York.

Crummell, A. (1992a). Civilization, the primal need of the race. In W. J. Moses (Ed.), *Destiny and race: Selected writings, 1840–1898* (pp. 280–288). Amherst: University of Massachusetts Press.

Crummell, A. (1992b). Industrial education: How to apply the unclaimed bounty. In W. J. Moses (Ed.), *Destiny and race: Selected writings, 1840–1898* (pp. 206–210). Amherst: University of Massachusetts Press.

Curti, M. (1974). *The social ideas of American educators.* Totowa, NJ: Littlefield, Adams.

Du Bois, W. E. B. (1893). University of Berlin. *The Crisis, 11*(1).

Du Bois, W. E. B. (1903). *The souls of Black folk.* Chicago: A. C. McClurg.

Du Bois, W. E. B. (1968). *The autobiography of W. E. B. DuBois: A soliloquy on viewing my life from the last decade of its first century.* New York: International Publishers.

Du Bois, W. E. B. (1973). Letter to Booker T. Washington. In H. Aptheker (Ed.), *The correspondence of W. E. B. Du Bois: Vol. 1. Selections, 1877-1934.* Amherst: University of Massachusetts Press.

Du Bois, W. E. B. (2002). *The Negro.* Amherst, NY: Humanity Books. (Original work published 1915)

Dunn, F. (1993). The educational philosophies of Washington, Du Bois, and Houston: Laying the foundations for Afrocentrism and multiculturalism. *Journal of Negro Education, 62*(1), 24–34.

Evans, S. Y. (2007). *Black women in the ivory tower, 1850-1954: An intellectual history.* Gainesville: University Press of Florida.

Fehnstoke, R. (1905). *Letters from Tuskegee: Being the confessions of a yankee.* Birmingham, AL: Roberts.

Franklin, V. P. (1984). *Black self-determination: A cultural history of the faith of the fathers.* Westport, CT: Lawrence Hill.

Franklin, V. P. (1990). "They rose or fell together": African American educators and community leadership, 1795–1954. *Journal of Education, 172*(3), 39–64.

Fullinwider, S. P. (1969). *The mind and mood of Black America: 20th century thought.* Homewood Hills, IL: Dorsey Press.

Gaines, K. K. (1996). *Uplifting the race: Black leadership, politics, and culture in the twentieth century.* Chapel Hill: University of North Carolina Press.

Gasman, M. (2002). W. E. B. Du Bois and Charles S. Johnson: Differing views on the role of philanthropy in higher education. *History of Education Quarterly, 42*(4), 493–516.

Haymes, S. N. (2001). Pedagogy and the philosophical anthropology of African American slave culture. *Philosophia Africana, 4*(2), 63–92.

Hutchinson, L. D. (1982). *Anna Julia Cooper: A voice from the South.* Washington, DC: Smithsonian Institution Press.

Johnson, C. (1953). The culture affecting education. In W. Van Til (Ed.), *Forces affecting American education.* (pp. 22–41). Washington, DC: Association for Supervision and Curriculum Development.

Johnson, C. S. (1930). *The Negro in American civilization: A study of Negro life and race relations in the light of social research.* New York: H. Holt.

Johnson, C. S. (n.d.). *A spiritual autobiography.* Charles S. Johnson Papers, Fisk University Special Collections, Nashville, TN.

Johnson, K. A. (2000). *Uplifting the women and the race: The educational philosophies and social activism of Anna Julia Cooper and Nannie Helen Burroughs.* New York: Garland.

Lance, F. J. (1972). *The life and thoughts of Alexander Crummell, a Black minister and educator.* Master's thesis, University of Georgia.

Lewis, D. L. (1993). *W.E.B. Du Bois: Biography of a race, 1868–1919.* New York: Henry Holt.

McCluskey, A. T. (1994). Multiple consciousness in the leadership of Mary McLeod Bethune. *NWSA Journal, 6*(1), 69–81.

McCluskey, A. T. (1997). "We specialize in the wholly impossible": Black women school founders and their mission. *Signs, 22*(2), 403–426.

Meier, A. (1988). *Negro thought in America, 1880–1915: Racial ideologies in the age of Booker T. Washington.* Ann Arbor: University of Michigan Press. (Original work published 1963)

Moses, W. J. (1989). *Alexander Crummell: A study of civilization and discontent.* New York: Oxford University Press.

Moses, W. J. (1998). *Afrotopia: The roots of African American popular history.* Cambridge, UK: Cambridge University Press.

National Association for the Advancement of Colored People. (1919). *Thirty years of lynching in the United States, 1889–1918.* New York: Author.

Perkins, L. M. (1982). Heed life's demands: The educational philosophy of Fanny Jackson Coppin. *Journal of Negro Education, 51*(3), 181–190.

Posnock, R. (1998). *Color & culture: Black writers and the making of the modern intellectual tradition.* Cambridge, MA: Harvard University Press.

Rath, R. C. (1997). Echo and Narcissus: The Afrocentric pragmatism of W. E. B. Du Bois. *Journal of American History, 84*(2), 461–495.

Sanders, K. M. (2005). *"Intelligent and effective direction": The Fisk University Race Relations Institute and the struggle for civil rights, 1944–1969.* New York: Peter Lang.

Smith, E. M. (1996). Mary McLeod Bethune's "Last Will and Testament": A legacy for race vindication. *Journal of Negro History, 81*(1/4), 105–122.

Tushnet, M. V. (1994). *The NAACP's legal strategy against segregated education, 1925–1950.* Chapel Hill: University of North Carolina Press.

Washington, B. T. (1911). *My larger education: Being chapters from my experience.* Garden City: New York.

Webber, T. (1978). *Deep like the rivers: Education in the slave quarter community, 1831–1865.* New York: Norton.

West, M. R. (2006). *The education of Booker T. Washington: American democracy and the idea of race relations.* New York: Columbia University Press.

Williams, H. A. (2005). *Self-taught: African American education in slavery and freedom.* Chapel Hill: University of North Carolina Press.

Woodson, C. G. (1990). *The mis-education of the Negro.* Trenton, NJ: Africa World Press. (Original work published 1933)

Woodson, C. G. (1999). *The education of the Negro prior to 1861.* Brooklyn, NY: A & B Publishers. (Original work published 1919)

3

"They Rose or Fell Together"

African American Educators and Community Leadership, 1795–1954

V. P. Franklin

The prominence of politicians as the leading spokespersons for the African American community in the United States is a relatively recent historical occurrence. Before the civil rights campaigns of the 1950s and 1960s, which brought voting rights to previously disenfranchised Americans, the number of African Americans in elective office was negligible. Indeed, from the 18th century through the 1950s, other African American professionals, especially ministers, journalists, lawyers, and educators, served as the leading spokespersons for the social, political, and economic interests of African Americans in the United States. Together this group of educated professional elites served as an intelligentsia for the African American population. They provided cultural meanings, values, ideals, and objectives drawn both from their extensive training and from the social experiences of the masses and elites of African descent in this society (Cavanaugh, 1983; Franklin, 1992, 1995; Marable, 1985; Wilson, 1980).

While the Black poor and working class, north and south, were actively involved in the creation of cultural values, goals, and practices based on their African background and their experiences in American society, the educated professionals articulated these values and objectives in speeches, sermons, essays, editorials, magazines, and books that were distributed to the public at large. These cultural spokespersons or "intellectuals" not only presented their opinions about the most pressing issues facing the African American population, but they also debated these issues in public forums. Often they organized and led social and political movements to obtain specific cultural objectives. From abolitionism to the recent Civil Rights Movement, African American ministers, journalists, lawyers, business owners, educators, and other professionals provided the leadership for African American communities at the local and national levels (Franklin, 1995).[1]

Historically, the largest group of professionals to provide leadership within the African American community was the educators. While the leadership provided by African American ministers, from Richard Allen in the late 18th century to Martin Luther King, Jr. in the 20th, has been widely discussed and studied, almost no attention has been paid to the role of African American educators. Yet elementary,

---

AUTHOR'S NOTE: This chapter originally appeared in the *Journal of Education, 172*(3), 39–64. Copyright 1990 by the Journal of Education. Reprinted with permission.

secondary, college, and university teachers and administrators served as leaders within Black communities throughout the country (Childs, 1980; Harris, 1987; Hicks, 1977; Swift, 1989; Young, 1977). This chapter will analyze the organized social and political activities of African American educators within educational institutions and outside the classroom. It will examine the leadership that these professional educators provided to campaigns and movements to advance the social, economic, and political circumstances for African Americans.

The experiences of enslaved and free African and African American workers in the United States led them to place a high value on education in general and schooling in particular. Education was valuable not merely as a means for social or economic advancement but as an end in itself. Most African Americans came to believe that although they might acquire (and eventually lose) money, property, civil rights, and social status, once they acquired an education it could not be taken away (Franklin, 1992; Webber, 1978). At the same time, African Americans who acquired literacy or advanced training often recognized an obligation to pass that knowledge on to others within their family, community, and cultural group. This was part of an "ethos of service" that developed among middle- and upper-status African Americans who recognized that their fortune was inextricably tied to that of the entire group. Many ministers, journalists, lawyers, and successful business persons, at one time or another, served as teachers in local public and private schools (Du Bois, 1900; Edwards, 1959; Neverdon-Morton, 1989; Woodson, 1970). Thus, in any survey of African American professionals, the educators would be the largest group, not merely because of numerical strength (though schoolteachers surely outnumbered other professionals), but because so many other professionals spent some time teaching and educating others.

African American Minister Educators in the Early 19th Century

The first Black Episcopal church congregation in the United States is believed to be the African Church founded in Philadelphia in July 1794. Absalom Jones, the rector, provided religious services at the church (later named St. Thomas Episcopal Church), and opened a school in the church building that was open to the entire African American community, not just Episcopalians. Jones served as instructor at the school for many years, even after he became the first African American to be ordained to the Episcopal priesthood in 1804 (George, 1973). Jones's close friend and associate Richard Allen founded Bethel Church in Philadelphia, also in 1794. In 1816, it became the Mother Church for the African Methodist Episcopal (AME) Church, still one of the largest predominantly Black religious denomination in the United States. Richard Allen provided a day school for African American children and adults within the Bethel Church from as early as 1795. The school provided instruction in reading, writing, and arithmetic as well as religion (Raboteau, 1988; Wesley, 1969). Absalom Jones and Richard Allen were undeniably the most important and influential leaders in the Philadelphia Black community during the early decades of the 19th century. Although their prominence stemmed primarily from their positions as pastors of large Black religious congregations, they also saw themselves as educators. They contributed to the community at large through their sponsorship of classes, schools, and other educational programs (Franklin, 1979; Raboteau, 1988; Wesley, 1969).

Richard Allen and Absolom Jones, however, were among the first in a long line of African American minister educators who defined their religious vocation to include establishing schools and other educational programs. Daniel Coker, a contemporary of Jones and Allen, was a former slave who received a classical education from Methodists in Baltimore. After ordination into the Methodist ministry in 1802, Coker taught in the African School opened in the city by the Sharp Street Methodist Episcopal Church. Coker joined the AME denomination after its founding in 1816; he served as principal and teacher at the African Bethel School in Baltimore until 1820, when he sailed for Africa as a Methodist missionary. Reverend Coker pastored and taught in Sierra Leone and Liberia until his death in 1846 (Logan & Winston, 1982; Markwei, 1982).

Throughout the antebellum era, African American minister educators opened schools for the instruction of Black youth and adults in conjunction with their religious institutions. Alexander Twilight graduated from Middlebury College in Vermont in 1823. He studied theology in Plattsburg, New York, and became a licensed

Presbyterian minister. After serving for 5 years as pastor of a small Presbyterian congregation in Brownington, Vermont, Twilight became principal of the Orleans County Grammar School. As principal and headmaster of several schools in Vermont, he came to be regarded as one of the state's outstanding educators. He was so well thought of by fellow citizens that he was elected to the Vermont Assembly as a state representative in 1836. Twilight is believed to be the first African American to serve in a state legislature (Logan & Winston, 1982).

Unlike Allen, Jones, Coker, and Twilight, John Francis Cook, Sr. of Washington, D.C., and Jeremiah Burke Sanderson of San Francisco were educators first, and only later became religious leaders. Cook was born a slave in the District of Columbia, but along with other members of his family, he was purchased and set free by his aunt, Alethia Tanner, in 1830. Cook was apprenticed 5 years with a shoemaker, but he read and studied on his own. After working briefly for the federal government as a messenger, Cook decided to take over a recently defunct private tuition school for Blacks, the Columbian Institute, located in Georgetown. He renamed it the Union Seminary and kept it going until his death in 1855 (Logan & Winston, 1982).

John Cook began studying for the Methodist ministry in 1836, and by 1838 had become pastor of Israel AME Church. He later helped organize the Union Bethel AME Church. When several friends asked to use the Union Seminary to hold a meeting to organize a Black Presbyterian congregation, Cook not only helped them write a church constitution, but he joined the movement and in 1841 became the pastor of the First Colored Presbyterian Church of Washington, D.C. (later 15th Street Presbyterian Church). Subsequently, Cook took an active role in the "National Colored Conventions" initiated by Richard Allen in Philadelphia in 1830 and held regularly throughout the antebellum era in various cities. The purpose of these state and national conventions was to bring local African American leaders and professionals together to debate and discuss activities aimed at abolishing slavery and improving the status of the free Black population in the United States (Bell, 1969; Brown, 1972; McLaughlin, 1967).

Jeremiah Burke Sanderson was born in New Bedford, Massachusetts, in 1821, attending the Black schools in the city and eventually becoming a barber. Like John Cook, Sanderson became involved in the National Colored Conventions, but in 1854 he decided to leave New England and migrate to California. Sanderson first taught in a separate Black public school in Sacramento, but later became principal-teacher in Black public schools in Stockton and San Francisco (Logan & Winston, 1982). During these years (1859–1874), Sanderson also studied for the Methodist ministry and pastored an AME Church in San Francisco, where he was active in organizing several social advancement and religious organizations. On the basis of his reputation as one of the outstanding ministers and educators of the state, Sanderson was asked to join the Republican Party and was elected as a delegate to the state convention in 1874. Tragically, his new political career was cut short by his death the following year in a train accident (Lapp, 1968, 1977; Logan & Winston, 1982).

Perhaps the most distinguished African American minister educator in the 19th century was AME Bishop Daniel Payne. Born in 1811 into the free Black elite of Charleston, South Carolina, Payne was raised by his great aunt. He attended Minor's Moralist Society School and received private tutoring in French, Latin, and Greek. Payne joined the Methodist Episcopal denomination in 1826 and started a school in Charleston for free Black children and adult slaves that became quite a success. Unfortunately, the American Anti-Slavery Society's campaign to educate the southern White population about the horrors of American slavery through pamphlets, newsletters, and other literature drew an angry reaction. A White mob in Charleston attacked the U.S. post office. Fearful that the abolitionist literature would be distributed through free Black schools and educational organizations, the South Carolina legislature passed a law in December 1834 prohibiting free Blacks from keeping "any school or other place of instruction for teaching any slave or free person of color to read or write" (Drago, 1990, p. 30). Daniel Payne's school was closed, and he left South Carolina vowing not to return as long as these anti-Black laws were in effect (Payne, 1888/1969).

Payne headed north and studied theology at the Lutheran Theological Seminary in Gettysburg, Pennsylvania. He was ordained by the Lutheran Church in 1839, but asked to join the AME ministry in 1841. Starting out as an itinerant preacher, Payne quickly moved up the ranks of African Methodism as a result of courage, fortitude, and persistence in establishing religious and educational organizations and enterprises wherever he traveled. In 1852, he was elected a bishop in the AME Church, and from that position Payne went on to become the most influential minister educator in the African American community (Logan & Winston, 1982; Payne, 1888/1969).

In his ministry, Bishop Payne found too great a tolerance among African Americans for illiterate and unlettered preachers. The old "fire and brimstone" cornfield exhorters were acceptable at one time, but they were not the best role models for ministers committed to the religious and social advancement of their people. Payne desired an "educated clergy" for the AME Church, and in the 1850s, he opened several schools and seminaries for the training of young people interested in the Methodist ministry. In 1863, Payne arranged for the purchase of Wilberforce College in Xenia, Ohio, from the Methodist-Episcopal Church. He became president of the new AME institution, a position he retained until 1876, when he became chancellor of Wilberforce University and dean of the theological seminary (Franklin, 2004a; Logan & Winston, 1982; Payne, 1888/1969).

Daniel Payne worked with Abraham Lincoln, Charles Sumner, and Carl Shurz during the Civil War on plans for the emancipation of the slaves. He traveled to London and Paris and represented American Methodism at international ecumenical conferences. He published a well-documented history of the AME Church (1866) and an important textbook *Treatise on Domestic Education* (1885/1971). His autobiography, *Recollections of Seventy Years* (1888/1969), went through numerous editions. Daniel Payne was the most distinguished member of a group of outstanding African American minister educators who contributed to the social, political, and the educational advancement of African Americans in the 19th century (Smith, 1922; Wayman, 1882).

AFRICAN AMERICAN FEMALE EDUCATORS

The patterns of professional and community involvement for African American female educators during the 19th century were basically similar to those of African American men. Culturally, African Americans shared with European Americans the prejudice against "women in the pulpit," and thus there were few (if any) female minister educators in Black communities before the 1890s (Andrews, 1986). But in numerous other ways the professional lives of Black female educators resembled those of Black men. They took leadership positions in social, political, and educational organizations and movements within the community.

Educated African American women opened private venture schools in Philadelphia, New York City, Boston, and smaller cities and towns beginning in the early 1800s. Sarah Mapps Douglass was born into an elite Black family in Philadelphia in 1806 and received private tutoring. After a brief period of teaching in New York City, she returned to Philadelphia in 1832 and opened an academy for Black girls. By 1837, there were more than 40 pupils and according to one report, "all the branches of good and solid female education are taught in Miss Douglass' school, together with many ornamental sciences, calculated to expand the youthful mind, refine the taste, and assist in purifying the heart" (Logan & Winston, 1982; Sterling, 1984, p. 128).

Margaretta Forten, daughter of James and Charlotte Forten, prominent members of the Philadelphia Black community, also maintained a private school in the city for almost 30 years. Sarah Mapps Douglass and Margaretta Forten were leaders in the local antislavery movement, following in the footsteps of their mothers (Grace Mapps Douglass and Charlotte L. Forten), who helped form the Philadelphia Female Anti-Slavery Society in December 1833. In antebellum Philadelphia, several of the leading "antislavery ladies" were Black female educators (Logan & Winston, 1982; Sterling, 1984; Yellin, 1989; Yellin & Van Horne, 1994).

Frances Ellen Watkins Harper, one of the best-known female abolitionists of the 1850s, was born of free parents in Baltimore in 1825. She attended the school for free Blacks opened by her uncle, Rev. William Watkins, and began her teaching career in an AME school in Columbus, Ohio, in 1850. That year she also published her first book of poetry, *Forest Leaves*. Unfortunately, the 1850s witnessed a rapid deterioration in the circumstances for free Blacks throughout the United States following the passage of the Fugitive Slave Act in September 1850 (Campbell, 1970). Many former slaves who had long resided in northern cities were forced to flee for fear that they or some member of their family would be tracked down and reenslaved. In 1854, when Frances Watkins was teaching school in York, Pennsylvania, the Maryland Assembly passed legislation declaring that free Blacks entering the state without legally authorized "freedom papers" were liable to arrest and sale into slavery. This statute enraged Frances Watkins, who would now have difficulty returning home to visit her family. She soon became active in the antislavery movement and eventually gave up her teaching position. She gave speeches throughout the northern states and in Canada espousing the abolitionist cause, and wrote numerous articles for antislavery journals. Following the War, she became involved in the temperance and women's suffrage campaigns while continuing to publish articles, books of poetry, and the novel *Iola Leroy or the Shadows Uplifted* (1892) (Boyd, 1994; Loewenberg & Bogin, 1976, pp. 243–251; Logan & Winston, 1982; Sterling, 1984).

Mary Ann Shadd Cary was another Black educator who responded to the repression of the 1850s by becoming an activist and leader in the antislavery movement. Born in Wilmington, Delaware in 1823, Mary Ann Shadd and her siblings were educated by Quakers at the Price Boarding School in West Chester, Pennsylvania. During the 1840s, she taught in Black schools in West Chester and Norristown, Pennsylvania, in Wilmington, Delaware, and in New York City; but in 1850, the repression associated with the Fugitive Slave Law forced her and her family to emigrate to Windsor, Canada. At first she and her brother, Isaac Shadd, taught in American Missionary Association (AMA)-sponsored religious schools in Chatham, Canada West; but in March 1853 Samuel Ringgold Ward launched his newspaper, *The Provincial Freeman*, and Ms. Shadd became the publishing agent. Because Ward spent most of his time on the antislavery lecture circuit, the running of the newspaper fell on Mary Shadd. Under her editorship, the paper championed the cause of the Black refugees who had come to Canada seeking freedom and self-determination. Although the paper ended publication in 1858, according to some historians, Mary Shadd Cary was "the first colored woman on the North American Continent to Establish and Edit a weekly newspaper" (Logan & Winston, 1982, p. 553; Silverman, 1988; Sterling, 1984).

During the Civil War, Mary Shadd Cary taught briefly in an AMA-sponsored school in Chatham, Canada West, but then returned to the United States in 1863 and became a recruiting agent in Indiana for Black soldiers for the Union Army. Following the War, she taught school in Detroit, but moved to Washington, D.C., in 1869 hoping to gain a position with the federal government. When the position did not come through, she taught in the District public schools and eventually became a principal. In 1870, she entered Howard University Law School, but dropped out later when she was told that she would not be allowed to graduate because of her sex. While teaching and studying in Washington, Mary Shadd Cary continued her involvement in a wide range of activities. She wrote articles for Frederick Douglass's *New National Era*, John Wesley Crowell's *The People's Advocate*, and T. Thomas Fortune's *New York Age*. She traveled throughout the country and lectured on temperance and women's suffrage, and in Washington was one of the leading members of the Bethel Literary and Historical Association. In May 1883, she returned to Howard Law School. After receiving her degree, she set up a successful legal practice (Barden & Butler, 1977; Logan & Winston, 1982; Silverman, 1988).

Whereas Frances Watkins Harper and Mary Shadd Cary were educators who made their greatest contributions to 19th-century African American advancement outside the field of education, Sarah Smith Garnet and Fannie Jackson Coppin were two of the most prominent leaders in their respective communities and their greatest contributions were made as educators. Sarah Smith was born in Queens County, Long Island, New York, in 1831, and because there were no public schools on Long Island at the time, she received her early education from members of her family who were successful farmers. Ms. Smith went on to attend several normal schools in the New York City area and began teaching in the African Free School in Brooklyn. The first African Free School was founded in Manhattan by the New York Manumission Society in 1787, and additional schools were opened in 1820, 1830, and 1831. The schools offered instruction in elementary subjects to boys and girls, and by the 1820s they enrolled more than 600 pupils. In 1834, the African schools were turned over to the New York Public School Society, the local recipient of state public educational funds, and they in effect became the separate Black public schools for New York City. In April 1863, Sarah Smith became the principal of the African School in Brooklyn, the first African American female principal in the New York public school system (Logan & Winston, 1982; Thurston, 1965).

Even before marriage in 1879 to Henry Highland Garnet, prominent Presbyterian minister, lecturer, and Black nationalist leader, Sarah Smith was a leader of the woman's suffrage movement in New York City. She was one of the founders of the Equal Suffrage Club, made up of educated African American women interested in gaining the vote for all women. Sarah Smith Garnet was active in several national women's rights organizations and in 1895 joined in founding the National Association of Colored Women. Her greatest contribution, however, was as a teacher and administrator in the New York City public schools for more than 35 years (Logan & Winston, 1982; McMaster, 1982; Shor, 1977).

Fannie Jackson Coppin, principal of Philadelphia's Institute for Colored Youth (ICY) for more than 35 years, was considered one of the most prominent African American educators of the late 19th century. Born a slave in Washington, D.C., in 1837, Fannie Jackson was purchased for $125 by her aunt, Sarah Clark, when she was 11 years old, and in 1850 was sent to live in New Bedford, Massachusetts, with another aunt, Elizabeth Orr. While there, Fannie worked as a domestic in the home of George Calvert, who recognized her talents and provided her with private tutoring and piano lessons. She entered Rhode Island State Normal School in 1858, completing the course of study in less than 2 years. Aided financially by her aunt Sarah Clark and AME Bishop Daniel Payne, she entered Oberlin College, one of the first American colleges to admit women and African Americans. At Oberlin, she studied Latin, Greek, French, and mathematics, and during her junior year was appointed a pupil-teacher in the college preparatory department. Although some fears were expressed about how students would respond to having a Black teacher, Fannie Jackson was so successful that she had to add classes and ultimately turn away some students. Her classmates elected her class poet and at graduation in July 1865, she was asked to recite her poem "The Grandeur of Our Triumph" (Perkins, 1987, p. 37).

In Philadelphia, the ICY was founded in 1837 through the bequest of Robert Humphries, a Quaker goldsmith. The school began as a trade school for Black orphan boys, but several African American artisans and skilled workers convinced the Quaker Board of Managers that the Black community needed a secondary institution that offered classical training. Gradually, the school expanded its offerings to include academic subjects, and in 1852 the school moved to its own building at Sixth and Lombard Streets in South Philadelphia. Charles Reason, a graduate of the African Free Schools in New York City and an instructor of Greek, Latin, and mathematics at New York Central College in McGrawville, New York, was brought in as principal, and Grace A. Mapps, cousin of Sarah Mapps Douglass and recent graduate of New York Central College, became head of the female department. Under Charles Reason the school's enrollment expanded to well over a hundred students, and in May 1853 Sarah Mapps Douglass's private elementary school was added as the "preparatory department" for the Institute. In November 1856, Reason left the school for personal reasons and became a teacher and principal in the New York City public schools; Ebenezer D. C. Bassett, graduate of Connecticut State Normal School and principal of a public school in New Haven, was named principal. Under Bassett, the ICY not only gained the reputation as "unquestionably the foremost institution of its kind in the country" but also contributed greatly to the social and cultural life of Black Philadelphia through programs and lectures open to the entire community (Logan & Winston, 1982, p. 32; Perkins, 1978).

In 1863, Bassett prevailed on the ICY Board of Managers to revise the school's curriculum to ensure that its graduates would be qualified to become teachers in the separate Black public schools in Philadelphia. The Quaker Managers ultimately agreed and Fannie Jackson was hired in 1865 to oversee the transformation within the female department; Mary Jane Patterson, another Oberlin graduate, was brought in as her assistant. From the beginning of her tenure, Fanny Jackson was extremely successful in raising the quality of instruction and increasing the enrollment in the female department. Then in March 1869, ICY Principal Ebenezer Bassett was appointed by Republican President Ulysses S. Grant to be U.S. Minister to Haiti. The Quaker Managers immediately appointed Fannie Jackson as acting principal. This decision greatly disturbed Octavius Catto, a popular, more experienced, and politically active educator at the Institute. His own story is worth telling. In many ways, O. V. Catto followed the example of Charles Reason, Sarah Mapps Douglass, Ebenezer Bassett, and other African American educators who also served in important leadership positions within antebellum Black advancement organizations (Perkins, 1987).

Octavius V. Catto was the son of Sarah Cain and William T. Catto, pastor of Philadelphia's first African Presbyterian Church. Prominent in local religious affairs, William Catto tutored his young son at home, but he later entered the ICY, where he graduated with distinction in 1858. After graduation, Octavius Catto studied Latin and Greek privately for over a year in Washington, D.C., though he was never enrolled in college. A vacancy on the Institute's staff occurred in September 1859 and Catto was appointed.[2] He worked well and closely with his mentor, Ebenezer Bassett, and during the Civil War, when Bassett made the Institute a recruitment center for Black troops, Catto helped organize and served in the Fifth Brigade of the Pennsylvania National Guard, made up completely of Black soldiers. Although Catto saw no military action, he remained politically active throughout the war (Perkins, 1978; Silcox, 1977).

In October 1864, a National Colored Convention endorsed the creation of a "National Equal Rights League," which would have branches in every state and would work for the attainment of equal civil rights for African Americans in both the North and the South. Octavius Catto was instrumental in the formation of the Pennsylvania State Equal Rights League (PSERL), the local branch of the new national organization. At the February 1865 meeting, one of the major political issues addressed was the decision of public school districts throughout the state not to employ African American educators. In keeping with the predominant social mores of the period, public school officials would not allow African American educators to teach White students. Thus, in school districts throughout the North, no African Americans were hired, even where some schools were predominantly (and even entirely) Black. Given the oftentimes harsh treatment of African American children by instructors in many public schools, the African American community demanded "colored teachers for colored schools." This was what the ICY exemplified. O. V. Catto argued at the Equal Rights Convention, according to its published proceedings, that "the colored man was the best teacher for the colored children [because] ... the colored teacher had the welfare of the race more at heart, knowing that they rose or fell together." Catto believed that when choosing teachers for African American children, "their literary qualifications being sufficient," the African American educators were to be preferred, "not by reason of their complexion, but because they are better qualified by conventional circumstances outside the school-house." African American educators' backgrounds, service, and leadership within the community justified the community's support for "colored teachers for colored schools" (Brown, 1970; Silcox, 1977, pp. 63–64).

O. V. Catto remained active in the Equal Rights League after the Civil War and he helped persuade the state legislature to pass a law in March 1867 desegregating public transportation within the state. By March 1869, when Ebenezer Bassett was appointed Minister to Haiti, Catto had been teaching at the ICY for almost 10 years. He was noticeably upset when the Managers chose Fannie Jackson as acting principal. It has been argued that in the eyes of the Quaker Managers, Catto's militant political positions doomed his pursuit of the principalship (Silcox, 1977). However, the minutes of the ICY Board of Managers meetings revealed that it was Fannie Jackson's superior training at Oberlin College and her success in the female department that led to their decision (Perkins, 1987). Catto decided to remain at the Institute as head of the boys' department. Unfortunately, 2 years later in October 1871, following passage of the Fifteenth Amendment to the U.S. Constitution that allowed Black men to vote in Pennsylvania for the first time since 1838, O. V. Catto was among three Blacks killed during election-day rioting in Philadelphia (Silcox, 1977).[3]

Fannie Jackson was named principal of ICY by the Board of Managers in April 1869. By June 1881, when she married AME minister Levi J. Coppin and became "Mrs. Fannie Jackson Coppin," the ICY had come to be considered one of the best classical secondary schools in the country. It was a major supplier of public school teachers for the segregated public schools in both the North and the South. Its nationally known faculty included Edward Bochet, who received a Ph.D. from Yale University in 1876, the first African American to receive a Ph.D. in physics. The Institute's graduates included physicians, dentists, lawyers, and judges as well as teachers and principals throughout the country. More important, the school continued to serve as a cultural center for the African American community by offering programs, conferences, and lectures on a regular basis (Logan & Winston, 1982; Perkins, 1978, 1987).

Fannie Jackson Coppin also assumed leadership of various organizations and movements within the African American community. She was a member of the Board of Managers for the Home for Aged and Infirmed Colored Persons from 1881 to 1901. The home had been established in 1864 for elderly African American women who were denied admission to other homes for the aged in Philadelphia. Mrs. Coppin was also active in the missionary activities of the AME Church: She was elected president of its Women's Home and Missionary Society and served as a delegate to the Centenary of Missions Convocation in London in 1888. Beginning in 1879, she launched a campaign to improve the industrial training available to African Americans in the city. It began as an "Industrial Fair," organized by Mrs. Coppin in November 1879 to raise money for the AME Church's financially ailing newspaper, the *Christian Recorder*. Ultimately, it led to an industrial education campaign and the opening of an evening school and "Industrial Department" at the Institute where youth and adults could receive instruction in bricklaying, plastering, carpentry, shoemaking, printing, tailoring, stenography, typing, and millinery (Coppin, 1913; Perkins, 1987).

In 1900, Rev. Levi Coppin was elected a bishop in the AME Church and was placed in charge of the church's missionary activities in South Africa. Mrs. Coppin retired from the Institute in 1902 after 37 years of devoted service and joined her husband in Cape Town. There she traveled thousands of miles and organized numerous missionary and temperance societies. The Coppins returned to the United States in 1904, but Mrs. Coppin soon became ill and was forced to remain at home where she completed her autobiography, *Reminiscences of School Life and Hints on Teaching*, published in 1913, the year of her death.

The ICY was closed in Philadelphia after she left in 1902 and removed to a farm 6 miles outside the city in Cheyney, Pennsylvania, where it became an industrial and normal school modeled after Booker T. Washington's Tuskegee Institute.

Under the principalship of Fannie Jackson Coppin, however, the ICY served as a foremost example of the intellectual achievements of African Americans. Even after the closing of the Institute in 1903, Fannie Jackson Coppin's ideals and influences were manifested in the educational and professional achievements of the more than 5,000 students with whom she worked during her almost 40 years of service (Perkins, 1987).

AFRICAN AMERICAN EDUCATORS AND POLITICAL LEADERSHIP

Historians and political scientists have written extensively about the fact that the ministry has historically served as a springboard for African Americans aspiring to political office. The point is usually made that the Black preacher's congregation provides a built-in constituency for launching a political career (Childs, 1980; Hamilton, 1972; Hicks, 1977). The most prominent 19th-century example of this pattern of professional political advancement was Hiram R. Revels, the first African American to serve in the U.S. Senate. Revels was born of free parents in Fayetteville, North Carolina, in 1827, but received his early training in religious schools in Indiana. Ordained by the AME Church in 1845, he pastored congregations in Ohio, Indiana, Tennessee, and Maryland. During the Civil War, he served briefly as a chaplain in the Union Army, but most of his time was spent as an agent for the Freedmen's Bureau in Vicksburg and Jackson, Mississippi. There he helped establish the first schools in the state intended specifically for African Americans. In 1865, Revels broke with the AME Church and joined the Methodist Episcopal Church, North, which was one of the first northern churches to do missionary work among formerly enslaved African Americans during the war (Culver, 1953; Morrow, 1956). After assignments in Leavenworth, Kansas, in Louisville, and in New Orleans, in June 1868 Revels was appointed presiding elder for the Methodist Episcopal Church in Natchez, Mississippi (Logan & Winston, 1982; Thompson, 1982).

During the military occupation and following the onset of Congressional or "Radical Reconstruction," the provisional governor, General Adelbert Ames, had to appoint more than 50 mayors and 220 aldermen in cities and towns throughout Mississippi. As one of the best-educated and most respected African Americans in the state, Hiram Revels was appointed by Governor Ames to the Natchez Board of Aldermen in August 1868. The following year, faction-ridden Republicans in Adams County chose Revels as a compromise candidate for the state senate. In an overwhelmingly Black and Republican district, he won handily. Thirty-five African Americans were elected to the Mississippi state senate that year, composing over one third of that body. In 1870, when the senators addressed the issue of appointing someone to the U.S. Senate to fill out the remaining year on the term of former Confederate President Jefferson Davis, the Black senators put forward Revels, again as a compromise candidate. He was elected on the eighth ballot and served until March 1871 (Thompson, 1982).

During the Reconstruction era, when African American men won the vote, a number of African American educators gained political appointments and used their standing as professionals and community leaders to propel themselves into elective office. This was a new development. There is no record of any African Americans other than the earlier-mentioned Alexander Twilight being elected or appointed to political offices until after the Civil War. Following the war, however, there was a rash of Republican political appointments (Logan & Winston, 1982; Rabinowitz, 1982).

George Boyer Vashon of Washington, D.C., was an educator, lawyer, and one of the first African Americans to receive a high-level federal appointment. The son of abolition activist John Bethune Vashon, George was born in Carlisle, Pennsylvania, in 1824. He studied at private schools, entered Oberlin College at age 16, and in 1844 received the first Bachelor of Arts degree conferred by Oberlin College on an African American. While at Oberlin, he taught school in Chillicothe, Ohio. On graduation, he studied law in Pittsburgh for 4 years under Judge Walter Forward but was not allowed to take the state bar examination because of his race. Disappointed by this discriminatory action, Vashon decided to leave the United States and accepted a position at the College Faustin in Port-au-Prince, Haiti. Before embarking from New York City, however, Vashon took the New York state bar examination and passed; on his return from Haiti in 1850, he settled in Syracuse and began a law practice (Logan & Winston, 1982).

Still committed to teaching, Vashon became a professor of belles lettres and mathematics at New York Central College in 1854. After 3 years, he returned to Pittsburgh and became principal of one of the separate Black public schools. He remained there until 1857, when he became a professor of belles lettres at the city's Avery College. Following the Civil War and the opening of Howard University in Washington, D.C., in 1867, Vashon became the first educator of African descent to be appointed to the faculty. It was while teaching at Howard in 1868 that Vashon accepted his first and only political appointment, as solicitor for the Freedmen's Bureau within the War Department. Vashon worked as a political appointee until 1874 when he moved to Rodney, Mississippi. There he was a professor of law at Alcorn University until his death in 1878 (Cheek & Cheek, 1989; Logan, 1969; Logan & Winston, 1982).

In November 1877, when educator Ebenezer Bassett, former principal of the ICY, left his diplomatic post in Haiti, he was succeeded by another prominent African American educator, John Mercer Langston, a protégé of George Boyer Vashon. John Langston, born in 1829, was the youngest of the four children of a Virginia plantation owner, Captain Robert Quarles, and his servant, Lucy Langston. When both parents died in 1834, the children were taken to live with a friend of his father, Colonel William Gooch, who promised to provide them with an education. John Langston attended the separate public schools in Chillicothe, Ohio, when George Vashon was teaching there. Vashon immediately recognized the boy's potential and helped arrange for him to enter the preparatory department at Oberlin College in 1844. Receiving his B.A. in 1849 and his M.A. degree in 1852, Langston entered the Theology Department, but did not remain. He tried to enter several law schools but was denied admission because of his race; so he studied law privately with Judge Philemon Bliss and was admitted to the Ohio bar in 1854. Langston set up a law practice in and around Oberlin and was active in the anti-slavery movement (Check & Cheek, 1989; Logan & Winston, 1982).

During the Civil War, Langston helped recruit Black soldiers for the Union Army, and afterward he traveled throughout the South as an inspector-general for the Freedmen's Bureau. In January 1869, John Langston moved to

Washington, D.C., and joined his former teacher, George Vashon, on the faculty at Howard University. Together, they organized the Law Department. Langston became the first dean of the Law School, 1870–1873, and served as vice president and acting president between 1873 and 1875. He was also active in the Republican Party and received several political appointments. In 1871, for example, President Ulysses S. Grant appointed him to the Washington, D.C., Board of Public Health; in 1877, President Rutherford B. Hayes appointed Langston as U.S. Consul in Haiti, where he simultaneously served as charge d'affaires for the Dominican Republic (Cheek & Cheek, 1989; Logan & Winston, 1982).

On his return to the United States in 1885, Langston accepted the presidency of Virginia Normal and Collegiate Institute in Petersburg, but when the Democrats gained control of the school's Board of Visitors in December 1887, he resigned and decided to run for the U.S. House of Representatives from the Fourth Congressional District in Virginia. In the election in November 1888, Langston's Democratic opponent won through fraudulent practices at voting sites. Langston challenged the results and was finally granted the seat by a vote of the U.S. House of Representatives on September 23, 1890. Langston ran for the seat again in 1890 but lost. He did serve as a delegate to the Republican national convention in 1892, and that year he was again nominated for Congress, but he refused to run. When he died in 1897, the Colored and Normal School in the Oklahoma Territory founded that year was renamed Langston University in his honor (Cheek & Cheek, 1989).

In the late 19th century, Francis L. Cardozo of South Carolina and Major R. R. Wright, Sr. of Georgia were very prominent African American educators whose accomplishments in the educational arena and within the African American community led to important political appointments. Francis Louis Cardozo was born into Charleston, South Carolina's free Black elite in 1837 and attended a private school for Black children. Apprenticed to a carpenter at age 11, he worked at the trade for 5 years and saved his earnings to pay for a European education. He graduated with honors from the University of Glasgow in 1862, and then studied theology at Presbyterian seminaries in Edinburgh and London (Logan & Winston, 1982).

On his return to the United States in 1864, Cardozo became pastor of the Temple Street Congregational Church in New Haven, Connecticut, but gave up the position when the Congregationalist AMA officials asked him to investigate its schools in his home town, Charleston. Francis's brother, Thomas Cardozo, had been teaching school in Flushing, New York, and in 1864 decided to join the volunteers assisting and teaching the newly freed African Americans in the South. Assigned to Charleston, Thomas Cardozo became the principal of one of the AMA schools and began hiring teachers. Unfortunately, when a rumor reached AMA officials that Thomas Cardozo had been accused of some "sexual impropriety" with a female student in Flushing, Francis Cardozo was sent to Charleston to question his brother about the matter. Thomas Cardozo confirmed the rumor and apologized, but the AMA removed him from his position and replaced him with his brother Francis (Drago, 1990; Perkins, 1984; Richardson, 1986).

Shortly after the end of hostilities, AMA officials decided to concentrate on establishing normal, rather than elementary, schools to provide teachers for the new Black public schools in the South. Avery Institute was founded in Charleston through the efforts of Francis Cardozo and the AMA, with financial help from the estate of Charles Avery in Pittsburgh, Pennsylvania. Cardozo solicited this aid after hearing that the Avery estate was planning to underwrite the building of a Black school in Atlanta. With the additional support of Charleston's free Black elite, Avery Institute opened in the fall of 1867 with eight teachers and 484 students (Drago, 1990; Richardson, 1986).

Francis Cardozo, principal of Avery Institute and one of the best-educated African Americans in South Carolina, also became active in Republican politics. He was elected secretary of state in 1868 and served until 1871, when he resigned to accept a position as professor of Latin at Howard University. However, the governor refused to accept his resignation as secretary of state and Cardozo returned in 1872 to finish out his term. In the fall elections, he won the office of state treasurer and was reelected in 1874 and 1876. He resigned in April 1877 with the downfall of the Republican regime in the state (Burton, 1985; Drago, 1990; Holt, 1977).

Cardozo returned in 1877 to Washington, D.C., where he was given a political appointment in the Department of the Treasury. He remained there until 1884, when he was named principal of the Colored Preparatory High School, later renamed the M Street High School, and still later Paul Laurence Dunbar High School. He served in that capacity until retiring in 1896. As principal, Francis Cardozo set the high academic standards for which this classical high school became nationally known (Logan & Winston, 1982; McLaughlin, 1967).

Although educator Richard Robert Wright, Sr. never gained elective office, he ran for public office several times and received many political appointments. He was one of the most influential African Americans in Georgia's Republican Party (Drago, 1982). Wright was born in slavery in Dalton, Georgia, in 1855, then was moved to Cuthbert, Georgia, by his owner in 1857. His mother, Harriet Wardell, raised him after his father, Richard Wardell, ran away to join the Union Army. Following the War, Harriet Wardell married Alexander Wright, and Richard and his younger brother, Elisha, attended the Walton Springs, Georgia, AMA school, later known as the Storrs School in honor of Ohio abolitionist and Congregational minister Henry M. Storrs. The school had an excellent reputation for its classical curriculum. Richard Wright received national attention when, during a visit by General Oliver O. Howard, Commissioner of the Freedmen's Bureau, to the Storrs School in the fall of 1868, the General asked, "What shall I tell the children of the North about you?" The only response came from Richard, who rose and said, "Tell them we are rising!" The incident eventually was reported in newspapers throughout the country, and inspired the poet and abolitionist John Greenleaf Whittier to write the poem "Howard at Atlanta!" Richard Robert Wright was "the black boy of Atlanta" in that famous work and though his stepfather insisted that he and his brother drop out of school to work for several months, Wright graduated from the Storrs School in 1869 (Haynes, 1952; Logan & Winston, 1982; Patton, 1980, pp. 66–67).

With the support of AMA national officials and a $10,000 grant from the Freedmen's Bureau, Atlanta University was founded in 1869 to provide normal and academic training for African Americans. Richard Robert Wright was among the 82 men and women who were enrolled in the first class. Although Wright was one of the poorest students, he was able to finance his studies by working part-time during the school year, teaching in rural elementary schools during the summers, and through a scholarship he received from the Ladies Benevolent Association of Amherst, New Hampshire. In June 1876, Wright received a B.A. degree as part of Atlanta University's first college graduating class (Bacote, 1969; Patton, 1980).

On graduation, Richard Wright returned to his home town, Cuthbert, Georgia, and became principal of an elementary school. However, because he recognized the need to train more Blacks as teachers, Wright immediately petitioned the AMA for support for opening a normal school in the city. AMA officials agreed and Wright became principal of the Howard Normal School, which he opened in 1876. Wright also became involved in a number of other social, economic, and political activities in the Black community. In October 1876, Wright helped organize the state's first Colored Teachers Association and was elected the president. Wright organized Georgia's first Black county fair in the spring of 1878, and the following year he organized a Farmers Institute to bring the latest information about advancements in agricultural production to rural African Americans. Also that year he began publishing a weekly newspaper, *The Journal of Progress*, which contained economic, political, and religious news relevant to the local African American community (Logan & Winston, 1982; Patton, 1980). Two years later, he became a member of Georgia's Republican Central Committee.

Wright became principal of Georgia's first publicly supported Black high school in 1880 at the request of Augusta's Black community (Bacote, 1969; Patton, 1978, 1980). Blacks in the city had long shown their commitment to education by organizing and maintaining their own schools. When the newly created Richmond County Board of Education began providing secondary education at public expense for White boys and girls, African Americans petitioned the School Board to open a high school for Blacks. But it was only after the Black community made it clear that there were enough students to attend, and they were willing to pay $10 per year tuition, that the School Board agreed to open the Black high school. In October 1880, the Richmond County School Board voted unanimously to appoint Richard Robert Wright as principal of Augusta's new "Colored High School," later named the E. A. Ware High School (Patton, 1978, 1980).

Once in Augusta, Wright did all he could to make the new high school a success. Unfortunately, lack of support from the Richmond County School Board meant that 10 years later he was still the school's only instructor and the average enrollment remained at 32 students. Moreover, the annual flooding of the Savannah River almost destroyed the school building and discouraged many students from attending. This meant that the largest number of Black secondary school students in Augusta in the 1880s attended private church-affiliated schools, whose tuition was sometimes less than the $10 annual fee charged by the public high school (Patton, 1978, 1980).

Despite the problems at Ware High School, Richard Wright continued to provide leadership in many other areas of Black Augusta life. *The Journal of Progress* was moved to Augusta in 1881, and was later reorganized and renamed *The People's Defense*. Wright edited this paper until 1885, when he renamed it the *Weekly Sentinel*, which he continued to publish until 1888. Wright also organized farmers institutes and county fairs, as he had done in Cuthbert, and remained active in what was now the Southwestern Georgia Teachers Association (Patton, 1980). Moreover, throughout the 1880s R. R. Wright was embroiled in the struggle to maintain Black influence within the state Republican Party. He won his party's nomination (but lost the general election) for secretary of state in 1882 and for Congress in 1884. He served as a delegate to the Republican national conventions in 1880, 1884, and 1888 (Logan & Winston, 1982; Patton, 1980).

In August 1890, the U.S. Congress passed the Second Morrill Act, which called for "a just and equitable" sharing of all federal funds by Black and White state land-grant institutions of higher education. According to the U.S. Department of Education officials, Georgia would not receive any Morrill Act funds until a state-supported "Negro institution" of higher education was in operation in the state and eligible for receipt of the federal funds. After much debate and political maneuvering, state officials decided to locate the "Georgia State Industrial College for Negroes" in Savannah. Richard Robert Wright, one of the best known African American educators in the state, was to be the president (Bacote, 1969; Logan & Winston, 1982; Patton, 1980).

During the first 15 of the 30 years Wright was to serve as president of Georgia Industrial College, two of the major issues confronting

him were the African American community's continuing desire for "colored teachers for colored schools" and the opposition of the White Board of Commissioners and other state officials to the inclusion of "classical studies"— Latin, Greek, rhetoric, ancient literature, and history—in the Black college's curriculum. By the early 1890s, Wright believed that the period of White tutelage was coming to an end, and "the Negro teacher naturally and logically [should come] to the front and . . . take charge of the schools for his people." The most appropriate pedagogical methods for training African Americans should be derived from their cultural background; "the environments of the American Negro [made] this peculiar work for colored teachers only" (Wright, 1894, p. 460). The desire of African Americans to run their own educational institutions was acceptable to most White southerners as long as White public school officials, philanthropists, and business executives could exercise ultimate power. Wright's educational philosophy put him at odds with White philanthropists and state educational officials, who favored industrial education for Blacks along the lines advocated by Booker T. Washington (Anderson, 1978, 1988; Meier, 1963; Patton, 1980).

As a graduate of the Storrs School and Atlanta University, R. R. Wright was a classically trained scholar and educator who recognized the need for African American leaders to have the best schooling available in order to work for the advancement of their race. At the same time, Wright also believed that African Americans should exercise their rights as citizens by working in the political arena to further their social and economic interests. These positions and values directly challenged the forces of White supremacy gaining strength in the Redeemed South in the late 1880s and 1890s. This movement led eventually to the disfranchisement of the African American population, the imposition of legal segregation of the races "from cradle to grave," and the solidification of "separate and unequal" public schools for African Americans (Cell, 1982; Fredrickson, 1980; Harlan, 1968; Newby, 1965; Woodward, 1951).

In Georgia, in the 1890s and early 1900s there is evidence not only that state educational officials consistently denied the Black land grant college its fair share of federal funds, but that administrators of the various philanthropic foundations refused to make grants to the college during Wright's administration because of his insistence on providing both classical and industrial education courses for his students. Despite the extreme financial uncertainties, Georgia State Industrial College, later Savannah State College, trained thousands of African American elementary and secondary school teachers who recognized the value and discipline associated with classical study and the practical importance of industrial training. R. R. Wright's educational philosophy was also embodied in the educational objectives of the National Association of Teachers of Colored Children (NATCC), organized in 1904. Wright served as an officer in the national organization that was committed to the improvement of the educational opportunities for African American students and the professional development of African American educators. The NATCC, later the American Teachers Association, served as a national vehicle for addressing the crucial educational issues facing African Americans in the first half of the 20th century (Patton, 1980; Perry, 1975).[4]

AFRICAN AMERICAN EDUCATORS AND ACCOUNTABILITY

The period of ascendancy of Booker T. Washington (1895–1915) coincided with the end of Black political power and influence in this country (Logan, 1965). For example, after 1902 there were virtually no Black elected officials in the South until the coming of the Civil Rights Movement in the 1950s and 1960s. During the intervening years, it was ministers, journalists, independent business owners, lawyers, union officials, and educators who provided leadership within the local and national African American communities. While there were literally thousands of African American educators who provided leadership for African American communities in the North and South during these decades, several became known nationally and internationally. Among the most distinguished were W. E. B. Du Bois, professor of sociology at Atlanta University and one of the founders in 1909 of the National Association for the Advancement of Colored People (NAACP); Kelly Miller, dean of arts and sciences at Howard University and founder in 1921 of the National

Equal Rights League; Alain Locke, professor of philosophy at Howard University and major promoter of the New Negro Literary Movement; Charles S. Johnson, president of Fisk University and leading researcher on race relations; Mary McLeod Bethune, president of Bethune-Cookman College and federal administrator in the New Deal's National Youth Administration; and Benjamin Mays, president of Morehouse College and mentor to Dr. Martin Luther King, Jr., to name only a few (Logan & Winston, 1982).

While maintaining positions as educators and educational administrators, these African American leaders served as spokespersons and representatives of the interests, not merely of those in the educational community, but the African American community as a whole. Through their schooling and professional training they gained important skills and knowledge that they used to serve the needs of the African American population locally and nationally. More important, these African American professionals were willing to take responsibility for the success or failure of the organizations and institutions they led. As was the case with African American educators throughout the 19th century, during the first half of this century African American teachers and administrators in all-Black private and public schools held themselves accountable for the educational outcomes of the children and adults attending their schools (Franklin, 1992; Franklin & Anderson, 1978; Neverdon-Morton, 1989).

The successful campaigns for civil rights and "simple justice" in the 1950s and 1960s led to the enfranchisement of the African American population and the rise to leadership of the Black elected officials (BEOs) (Barker & Walters, 1989; Cavanaugh, 1983; Joint Center for Political Studies, 1989; Landress, 1985; Lawson, 1976, 1985; Nelson & Meranto, 1977). At the same time, with the desegregation of American public education, African American educators and administrators were no longer restricted to segregated Black schools; innumerable employment opportunities opened up for highly skilled teachers and administrators. Unfortunately, in large urban areas, North and South, as BEOs and public school administrators moved into positions of authority within political and educational systems, they still were unable (or unwilling) to intervene to change the social conditions that generated educational failure for

African American children (Scott, 1980). Black politicians asked for votes but were unable to bring jobs to depressed Black neighborhoods and to remove the drugs and criminal element. Black superintendents and principals were appointed to the public school systems, but the educational achievement levels for Black students and others continued to plunge as dropout (and absentee) rates soared (Cole, 1976; Farley & Allen, 1987; Scott, 1980).

During the 1980s and 1990s, as numerous interest groups raised their voices in support of the campaigns to improve the public educational conditions for a "nation at risk," noteworthy for its absence from the chorus of proponents for change was the collective voice of African American educators. Several individual educators, including Marva Collins, Ronald R. Edmonds, and Barbara Sizemore, provided leadership for particular educational projects and programs aimed at improving the educational achievement levels of Black urban children (Collins & Tamarkin, 1982; Edmonds, 1977, 1982; Edmonds & Frederickson, 1979; Sizemore, 1987; Sizemore, Broussard, & Harrigan, 1983). African American educational organizations, such as the Association of Black School Educators, often decried the deteriorating conditions but remained preoccupied with narrowly professional issues such as tenure and promotions. Despite increased information and research on urban schools and programs that achieved educational success for African American students, Black educators and administrators made no collective commitment to educational revitalization within African American communities (Clark, 1983; Hale, 1994, 2001; Hale-Benson, 1986; Silver, 1973; Spencer, Brookins, & Allen, 1985).

This is unfortunate, for the historical record is clear. Throughout the 19th and first half of the 20th centuries, African American educators and administrators not only held themselves accountable for what took place within their educational institutions, but also moved out into the community to provide leadership for organizations and movements aimed at the social, economic, and political advancement of the entire African American population. These educators knew that their progress and advancement as educators and administrators was tied to the overall progress of African Americans as a group. Given the recent failure of the political establishment to improve significantly the situation for African American children in urban public schools, it is time that the African American educators and other professionals assume the leadership role in the revitalization campaigns needed to carry Afro-America into the 21st century (Franklin, 2004b).

NOTES

1. In the larger work I examined the role of African American professionals, including ministers, lawyers, journalists, artists, educators, and politicians, as cultural leaders within the African American community. These spokespersons became members of an emerging African American intelligentsia that articulated a worldview and produced cultural signs, symbols, and meanings for the African American population in the United States (Franklin, 1995).

2. The vacancy occurred because Robert Campbell, who had been teaching natural science in the boys department since 1852, decided to join physician, editor, and author Martin Delany on a trip to West Africa to negotiate for the settlement of free Blacks. Although he returned briefly to the United States in 1863, Campbell returned to West Africa and began an export business. He died in Lagos in 1883 (Blackett, 1986).

3. It should be noted that while O. V. Catto decided to remain at the ICY following the appointment of Fannie Jackson as principal, Mary Jane Patterson, who was hired as Fanny Jackson's assistant in the female department, decided to leave. Linda Perkins (1987) pointed out that

> although Patterson had graduated from Oberlin College three years prior to Fannie Jackson and had taught school before accepting the ICY position, she had been assigned as Fanny Jackson's assistant at a salary $200 less than that of Jackson and Catto. In addition Mary Patterson never received any salary increases during her stay at the Institute. Regardless of her capabilities, she may have felt she was following in the shadow of Fanny Jackson. (pp. 89–90)

Mary Jane Patterson left the Institute in 1869 to become principal of a Black high school in Washington, D.C. (Sterling, 1984).

4. There were of course hundreds of African American educators in the late 19th and early 20th centuries who served as leaders in the communities within which they worked. Although Fannie Jackson

Coppin, Francis L. Cardozo, and Major R. R. Wright, Sr. achieved distinguished records as leaders and educators, they should be considered representative of this much larger group of African American professionals who served the social and educational interests of the entire Black community.

REFERENCES

Anderson, J. (1978). The Hampton model of normal school industrial education, 1868–1900. In V. P. Franklin & J. Anderson (Eds.), *New perspectives on Black educational history* (pp. 61–96). Boston: C. K. Hall.

Anderson, J. (1988). *The education of Blacks in the South, 1860–1935.* Chapel Hill: University of North Carolina Press.

Andrews, W. (1986). *Sisters of the spirit: Three Black women's autobiographies of the nineteenth century.* Bloomington: Indiana University Press.

Bacote, C. (1969). *The story of Atlanta University: A century of service, 1865–1965.* Atlanta, GA: Atlanta University Press.

Barden, J., & Butler, L. (1977). *Shadd: The life and times of Mary Ann Shadd.* Washington, DC: Arlington.

Barker, L., & Walters, R. (1989). Introduction. In L. Barker & R. Walters (Eds.), *Jesse Jackson's 1984 presidential campaign: Challenge and change in American politics* (pp. 3–11). Urbana: University of Illinois Press.

Bell, H. (1969). *A survey of the Negro convention movement, 1830–1861.* New York: Negro Universities Press.

Blackett, R. (1986). *Beating against the barriers: Biographical essays in nineteenth century Afro-American history.* Baton Rouge: Louisiana State University Press.

Boyd, M. J. (1994). *Discarded legacy: Politics and poetics in the life of Frances E. W. Harper, 1825-1911.* Detroit, MI: Wayne State University Press.

Brown, I. (1970). *The Negro in Pennsylvania history.* Harrisburg: Pennsylvania Historical Association.

Brown, L. W. (1972). *Free Negroes in the District of Columbia, 1790–1846.* New York: Oxford University Press.

Burton, O. (1985). *In my father's house are many mansions: Family and community in Edge field, South Carolina.* Chapel Hill: University of North Carolina Press.

Campbell, S. (1970). *The slave catchers: The enforcement of the Fugitive Slave Law, 1850–1860.* Chapel Hill: University of North Carolina Press.

Cavanaugh, T. (1983). *Black elected officials and their constituencies.* Washington, DC: Joint Center for Political Studies.

Cell, J. (1982). *The highest stage of white supremacy.* Durham, NC: Duke University Press.

Cheek, W., & Cheek, A. (1989). *John Mercer Langston and the fight for Black freedom, 1829–65.* Urbana: University of Illinois Press.

Childs, J. (1980). *The political Black minister: A study in Afro-American politics.* Boston: G. K. Hall.

Clark, R. (1983). *Family life and school achievement: Why poor Black children succeed or fail.* Chicago: University of Chicago Press.

Cole, L. (1976). *Blacks in power: A comparative study of Black and white elected officials.* Princeton, NJ: Princeton University Press.

Collins, M., & Tamarkin, C. (1982). *Marva Collins' way.* New York: St. Martin's Press.

Coppin, E. J. (1913). *Reminiscences of school life and hints on teaching.* Philadelphia: AME Book Concern.

Culver, D. (1953). *Negro segregation in the Methodist Church.* New Haven, CT: Yale University Press.

Drago, E. (1982). *Black politicians and Reconstruction in Georgia: A splendid failure.* Baton Rouge: Louisiana State University Press.

Drago, E. (1990). *Initiative, paternalism, and race relations: Charleston's Avery Normal Institute.* Athens: University of Georgia Press.

Du Bois, W. E. B. (1900). *The college-bred Negro.* Atlanta, GA: Atlanta University Press.

Edmonds, R. (1977). Effective schools for the urban poor. *Educational Leadership, 37*(1), 15–27.

Edmonds, R. (1982). Programs for school improvement: An overview. *Educational Leadership, 40*(1), 4–11.

Edmonds, R., & Frederickson, J. (1979). *Search for effective schools: The identification and analysis of city schools that are instructionally effective for poor children.* New York: New York City Public Schools.

Edwards, G. E. (1959). *The Negro professional class.* Glencoe, IL: Free Press.

Farley, R., & Allen, W. (1987). *The color line and the quality of life in America.* Beverly Hills, CA: Russell Sage.

Franklin, V. P. (1979). *The education of Black Philadelphia: A social and educational history of a minority community, 1900–1950.* Philadelphia: University of Pennsylvania Press.

Franklin, V. P. (1992). *Black self-determination: A cultural history of the faith of the fathers.* Brooklyn, NY: Lawrence Hill.

Franklin, V. P. (1995). *Living our stories, telling our truths: Autobiography and the making of the African American intellectual tradition.* New York: Henry Holt.

Franklin, V. P. (2004a). Cultural capital and black higher education: The AME colleges and universities as collective economic enterprises. In V. P. Franklin & C. J. Savage (Eds.), *Cultural capital and black education: African American communities and the funding of black schooling, 1865 to the present* (pp. 35–48). Greenwich, CT: Information Age.

Franklin, V. P. (2004b). Social capital, cultural capital, and the challenge of African American education in the 21st century. In V. P. Franklin & C. J. Savage (Eds.), *Cultural capital and black education: African American communities and the funding of black schooling, 1865 to the present* (pp. 159–172). Greenwich, CT: Information Age.

Franklin, V. P., & Anderson, J. (Eds.). (1978). *New perspectives on Black educational history.* Boston: G. K. Hall.

Fredrickson, G. (1980). *White supremacy: A comparative history of the United States and South Africa.* New York: Oxford University Press.

George, C. (1973). *Segregated sabbaths: Richard Allen and the rise of the independent Black churches, 1760–1840.* New York: Oxford University Press.

Hale, J. E. (1994). *Unbank the fire: Visions for the education of African American children.* Baltimore: Johns Hopkins University Press.

Hale, J. E. (2001). *Learning while black: Creating educational excellence for African American children.* Baltimore: Johns Hopkins University Press.

Hale-Benson, J. E. (1986). *Black children: Their roots, culture, and learning styles.* Baltimore: Johns Hopkins University Press.

Hamilton, C. (1972). *The Black preacher in America.* New York: William Morrow.

Harlan, L. (1968). *Separate and unequal: Public school campaigns and racism in the southern seaboard states, 1901–1915.* New York: Atheneum Press. (Original work published 1958)

Harris, J. (1987). *Black ministers and the laity in the urban church.* Lanham, MD: University Press of America.

Haynes, E. (1952). *Black boy of Atlanta.* Boston: Edinboro.

Hicks, H., Jr. (1977). *Images of the Black preacher.* Valley Forge, PA: Judson Press.

Holt, T. (1977). *Black over white: Negro political leadership in South Carolina during Reconstruction.* Urbana: University of Illinois Press.

Joint Center for Political Studies. (1989). *Black elected officials: A national roster.* Washington, DC: Howard University Press.

Landress, T. (1985). *Jesse Jackson and the politics of race.* Ottawa, IL: Jameson Books.

Lapp, R. (1968). Jeremiah B. Sanderson: Early California leader. *Journal of Negro History, 53*(4), 251–263.

Lapp, R. (1977). *Blacks in Gold Rush California.* New Haven, CT: Yale University Press.

Lawson, S. (1976). *Black ballots: Voting rights in the South, 1944–1969.* New York: Columbia University Press.

Lawson, S. (1985). *In pursuit of power. Southern Blacks and electoral politics, 1965–1982.* New York: Columbia University Press.

Loewenberg, B., & Bogin, R. (Eds.). (1976). *Black women in the nineteenth century: Their words, their thoughts, their feelings.* University Park: Pennsylvania State University Press.

Logan, R. (1965). *The betrayal of the Negro: From Rutherford B. Hayes to Woodrow Wilson.* London: Collier Books.

Logan, R. (1969). *Howard University, 1867–1967.* New York: New York University Press.

Logan, R., & Winston, M. (Eds.). (1982). *Dictionary of American Negro biography.* New York: W. W. Norton.

Marable, M. (1985). *Black American politics: From the Washington marches to Jesse Jackson.* London: Verso Press.

Markwei, M. (1982). The Rev. Daniel Coker of Sierra Leone. In D. Wills & R. Newman (Eds.), *Black apostles at home and abroad: Afro-Americans and the Christian mission from the Revolution to Reconstruction* (pp. 203–210). Boston: G. K. Hall.

McLaughlin, C. (1967). *The secret city: A history of race relations in the nation's capital.* Princeton, NJ: Princeton University Press.

McMaster, R. (1982). Henry Highland Garnet and the African Civilization Society. In D. Wills & R. Newman (Eds.), *Black apostles at home and abroad: Afro Americans and the Christian mission from the Revolution to Reconstruction* (pp. 265–282). Boston: G. K. Hall.

Meier, A. (1963). *Negro thought in America, 1880–1915: Racial ideologies in the age of Booker T Washington.* Ann Arbor: University of Michigan Press.

Morrow, R. (1956). *Northern Methodism and Reconstruction.* East Lansing: Michigan State University Press.

Nelson, W., & Meranto, P. (1977). *Electing Black mayors: Political action in the Black community.* Columbus: Ohio State University Press.

Neverdon-Morton, C. (1989). *Afro-American women of the South and the advancement of the race, 1895–1925.* Knoxville: University of Tennessee Press.

Newby, I. (1965). *Jim Crow's defense: Anti-Negro thought in America, 1900–1930.* Baton Rouge: Louisiana State University Press.

Patton, J. (1978). The Black community of Augusta and the struggle for Ware High School, 1880–1903. In V. P. Franklin & J. Anderson (Eds.), *New perspectives on Black educational history* (pp. 45–60). Boston: G. K. Hall.

Patton, J. (1980). *Major Richard Robert Wright Sr. and Black higher education in Georgia, 1880–1920.* Unpublished Ph.D. dissertation, University of Chicago.

Payne, D. (1969). *Recollections of seventy years.* New York: Arno Press. (Original work published 1888).

Payne, D. (1971). *A treatise on domestic education.* Freeport, NY: Books for Libraries Press. (Original work published 1885)

Perkins, L. (1978). Quaker beneficence and Black control: The Institute for Colored Youth, 1852–1903. In V. P. Franklin & J. Anderson (Eds.), *New perspectives on Black educational history* (pp. 19–43). Boston: G. K. Hall.

Perkins, L. (1984). The Black female American Missionary Association teacher in the South, 1861–1870. In J. Crow & F. Hatley (Eds.), *Black Americans in North Carolina and the South* (pp. 122–136). Chapel Hill: University of North Carolina Press.

Perkins, L. (1987). *Fannie Jackson Coppin and the Institute for Colored Youth, 1865–1902.* New York: Garland.

Perry, T. (1975). *The history of the American Teachers Association.* Washington, DC: National Education Association.

Rabinowitz, H. (Ed.). (1982). *Southern Black leaders during Reconstruction.* Urbana: University of Illinois Press.

Raboteau, A. J. (1988). Richard Allen and the African church movement. In L. Litwack & A. Meier (Eds.), *Black leaders in the nineteenth century* (pp. 1–20). Urbana: University of Illinois Press.

Richardson, I. (1986). *Christian Reconstruction: The American Missionary Association and southern Blacks, 1861–1890.* Athens: University of Georgia Press.

Scott, H. (1980). *The Black superintendent: Messiah or scapegoat?* Washington, DC: Howard University Press.

Shor, J. (1977). *Henry Highland Garnet: A voice of Black radicalism in the nineteenth century.* Westport, CT: Greenwood Press.

Silcox, H. (1977). Nineteenth century Black educator, Octavius V. Catto, 1839–1871. *Pennsylvania History, 44*(3), 51–68.

Silver, C. (1973). *Black teachers in urban schools: The case of Washington, DC.* New York: Praeger.

Silverman, J. (1988). Mary Ann Shadd and the search for equality. In L. Litwack & A. Meier (Eds.), *Black leaders in the nineteenth century* (pp. 87–102). Urbana: University of Illinois Press.

Sizemore, B. (1987). The effective African American school. In G. Noblit & W. Pink (Eds.), *Schooling in social context: Qualitative studies* (pp. 175–202). Norwood, NJ: Ablex.

Sizemore, B., Broussard, C., & Harrigan B. (1983). *An abashing anomaly: Three high achieving predominantly Black elementary schools.* Washington, DC: National Institute of Education.

Smith, C. S. (1922). *A history of the African Methodist Episcopal Church.* Philadelphia: AME Book Concern.

Spencer, M., Brookins, G., & Allen, W. (Eds.). (1985). *Beginnings: The social and affective development of Black children.* Hillsdale, NJ: Erlbaum Associates.

Sterling, D. (Ed.). (1984). *We are your sisters: Black women in the nineteenth century.* New York: W. W. Norton.

Swift, D. (1989). *Black prophets of justice: Activist clergy before the Civil War.* Baton Rouge: Louisiana State University Press.

Thompson, J. (1982). *Hiram R. Revels, 1827–1901: A biography.* New York: Arno Press.

Thurston, E. (1965). Ethiopia unshackled: A brief history of the education of Negro children in New York City. *Bulletin of the New York Public Library, 69*(2), 211–231.

Wayman, A. (1882). *Cyclopedia of African Methodism.* Baltimore: Methodist Episcopal Book Depository.

Webber, T. (1978). *Deep like the rivers: Education in the slave quarter community, 1831–1865.* New York: W. W. Norton.

Wesley, C. (1969). *Richard Allen, apostle of freedom.* Washington, DC: Associated Publishers. (Original work published 1935)

Wilson, J. Q. (1980). *Negro politics: The search for leadership.* New York: Octagon Books. (Original work published 1965)

Woodson, C. G. (1970). *The Negro professional man and his community, with special interest in physicians and lawyers.* New York: Johnson Reprints. (Original work published 1934)

Woodward, C. (1951). *The origins of the New South, 1877–1913.* Baton Rouge: Louisiana State University Press.

Wright, R. R. (1894). The possibilities of Negro teachers. *AME Church Review, 10*(4), 459–470.

Yellin, J. F. (1989). *Women and sisters: The antislavery feminists in American culture.* New Haven, CT: Yale University Press.

Yellin, J. F., & Van Horne, J. (Eds.). (1994). *The abolitionist sisterhood: Women's political culture in antebellum America.* Ithaca, NY: Cornell University Press.

Young, H. J. (1977). *Major Black religious leaders, 1755–1940.* Nashville, TN: Abington.

4

THE HISTORY OF BLACK WOMEN GRADUATE STUDENTS, 1921–1948

LINDA M. PERKINS

A historical examination of African American women's graduate and professional education is a topic that has received little scholarly attention. Although by 1950, Black women earned twice as many baccalaureate degrees in contrast to Black men, very few had an opportunity to attend graduate school. A 1946 survey of African American holders of doctorates and professional degrees noted that only 45 of the 381 Black recipients of doctorates and professional degrees were women. Of the top institutions awarding the Black doctorate holders their baccalaureate degrees, two were male institutions—Lincoln University in Pennsylvania and Morehouse College in Atlanta, Georgia. The other three institutions, Howard University, Fisk University, and Virginia Union were institutions with strong liberal arts and professional schools that enrolled large numbers of men. None of the teacher-training institutions or Black land-grant colleges, where women were primarily concentrated, ranked among the top 20 baccalaureate producing institutions. Overwhelmingly, the African American women who received doctorates were graduates of White undergraduate institutions (Greene, 1946).

This chapter will trace the history of Black women graduate students from the year the first three African American women were awarded doctorates in 1921, to 1948 when the Julius Rosenwald Foundation and the Rockefeller Foundation ceased a 20-year funding program of graduate fellowships to Black students. Although Black women faced numerous obstacles in accessing and completing graduate education (finances, preparation, family obligations), the opportunity to receive financial assistance for graduate school resulted in hundreds of Black women applying for the Rosenwald and Rockefeller fellowships. This chapter will concentrate primarily on Black women doctoral education.

The earliest graduate courses were offered at Yale in 1847 followed by the institution awarding the first Ph.D. in 1861. While colleges in the 19th century awarded master's degrees to anyone who could indicate continuous intellectual activities after earning a baccalaureate, the doctorate was a degree based on the German model of scientific research. During the 1870s, graduate education was expanding throughout the nation and in 1876, the Johns Hopkins University was the first institution of higher education established as a research university (John, 1935).

The awarding of doctoral degrees to African Americans and women began in the late 19th century. The first African American to earn a doctorate was Edward Bouchet who earned his degree from Yale University in physics, in 1876. The first female to earn an American doctorate was a White woman, Helen Magill, who matriculated from Boston University in 1877. However, African American women were the last group among Blacks and women to begin earning the Ph.D.

While African Americans and women of all races had difficulties negotiating within the White male-dominated world of academe, often African American men, by virtue of their maleness had access to institutions and programs that excluded all women. In contrast, White women frequently had access to opportunities and institutions that were inaccessible to all African Americans solely because of race.

Despite the opposition to women's higher education in the early 19th century, by the end of the century, numerous graduate programs were opened to White women. With the opening of these programs to them, White women quickly surpassed African Americans of either gender in earning doctorates. Ironically, however, they often had fewer employment opportunities than their African American counterparts. White women with doctorates were overwhelmingly employed in women's colleges and in smaller numbers in coeducational institutions. African American women with doctorates were able to find ready employment within the African American colleges in a variety of fields (Perkins in Hine, 2005).

Chronicling the difficulties that the first generation of college women encountered in pursuing doctoral work, Margaret Rossiter in an article titled, "Doctorates for American Women, 1868–1907," notes that graduate education in the 19th century was perceived as a "manly accomplishment" (Rossiter, 1982a). Graduate training was viewed by society as not only a "manly accomplishment" but also one reserved for White men only. White women scholars of the late 19th century often had to obtain doctorates from European institutions or were admitted to graduate studies in the United States as "special students" without being awarded degrees. Women of all races and African Americans of both genders were overwhelmingly believed to lack the intellectual capacity to pursue higher education on the level of elite White men. Separate

institutions and fields of study were recommended for both groups. Despite these obstacles, by the late 1890s, with the growth of women's colleges and the need to staff them, many barriers began to fall. Noted institutions such as Yale, Brown, Stanford, Columbia, Pennsylvania, and Chicago opened their doors to women. Rossiter (1982a) reported that, while 25 women had earned doctorates in 1890, within 10 years the number had increased to 204. Yale, Chicago, and Cornell universities accounted for the largest number of women doctorates.

Doctorates for African American men and women came at a much slower pace. Only seven African American men had earned doctorates by 1900. And, in the first decade of the 20th century, only four more could be added to this number. In contrast, in 1920 alone, 93 White women earned Ph.D.'s. This number compared with only 20 African American male doctorates that had been earned from 1867 to 1920. As mentioned earlier, no African American woman earned a doctorate until 1921 and the near universal belief that Blacks should be educated differently than Whites, and the belief that Black aspirations should not parallel those of Whites, kept many aspiring, talented African American men out of doctoral programs. For example, Percy L. Julian who was Phi Beta Kappa and became a chemist of international renown was discouraged from pursuing a doctorate as he sought further study in the field of inorganic chemistry in 1920. One of his major professors was advised when Julian inquired about graduate study,

> Discourage your bright colored lad. We couldn't get him a job when he's done, and it'll only mean frustration. Why don't you find him a teaching job in a Negro college in the South? He doesn't need a Ph.D. for that. (Hamilton, 1975, p. 96)

Julian earned a master's in chemistry from Harvard but went abroad for the doctorate in chemistry, which he earned, from the University of Vienna in 1931 (Hamilton, 1975).

In terms of undergraduate preparation, the issues of class, as well as race, explain the larger number of White women doctorates compared with those of African Americans. Until after World War I, most Black colleges in the South were unaccredited institutions, which focused on primary and secondary work. Hence, students of these institutions were not academically prepared to enter graduate study. The first generation of White women doctorates were financially privileged and had significantly more access to institutions of collegiate status. Although they were excluded from many male institutions of higher education, women's colleges and coeducational colleges were available to them (Astin, 1969). While graduates of the elite Seven Sister Colleges[1] were among the earliest women graduate students, African American women who qualified for these institutions were often not admitted. Helen Horowitz's study of the Seven Sister Colleges noted that only Wellesley College had a policy of nondiscrimination in housing and admissions during the early 20th century. When in 1913, an eruption took place over housing an African American woman at Smith College, the other Seven Sister campuses were polled about their racial policies. Mt Holyoke, Vassar, and Bryn Mawr noted that they did not admit Blacks (Horowitz, 1984).

The barring of African American women students from the Seven Sister Colleges seriously impeded the academic progress of those Black women in the North who were capable and desired to pursue higher education. For example, when Jessie Fauset, an African American woman from a distinguished family in Philadelphia graduated with top honors from Girl's High School in 1900, it was traditional that the top student be awarded a scholarship to Bryn Mawr. Recognizing that Fauset was African American, M. Carey Thomas, Bryn Mawr's president, personally sought funds for a scholarship for Fauset to attend Cornell University (Thomas's alma mater) to assure that Fauset would not apply to Bryn Mawr. Fauset excelled at Cornell and became the first African American Phi Beta Kappa. After Cornell, she studied for a year at the Sorbonne and later earned a master's in French from the University of Pennsylvania (M. Carey Thomas Papers, 1901).

M. Carey Thomas was a prominent example of a talented White woman who had to go abroad to obtain a doctorate. Rejected by Johns Hopkins and other institutions, she earned a doctorate from the University of Zurich in 1883 in philology. Yet the prejudices and stereotypes to which Thomas had been subjected as a woman in no way sensitized her to women who were not upper class and Anglo-Saxon. In an opening address of the 1916 school year to the Bryn Mawr student body, Thomas openly expressed her belief in the intellectual superiority of the White race. She stated,

> If the present intellectual supremacy of the white races is maintained, as I hope that it will be for centuries to come, I believe that it will be because they are the only races that have seriously begun to educate their women. . . . One thing we know beyond doubt and that is that certain races have never yet in the history of the world manifested any continuous mental activity nor any continuous power of organized government. Such are the pure Negroes of Africa, the Indians, the South Sea Islanders, the Turks, etc. . . . (Bryn Mawr College, 1916)

Despite rampant discrimination toward White women in society, the turn of the century was not one noted for interracial sisterhood. In fact, White women were frequently less racially tolerant than White men. W. E. B. Du Bois made this observation in his 1900 study of Black college students, and he reported that it was easier for an African American male to gain entry into a male college than for a Black woman to gain entry into a White woman's college (Du Bois, 1900).

While most women students of any race did not attend Seven Sister Colleges, the role of these institutions in producing a disproportionate number of first generation scholars and academics has been documented. Margaret Rossiter's pioneering work on women scientists clearly documents the importance of these institutions in producing several generations of women scholars. These institutions offered curriculum that corresponded with the leading men's colleges and, hence, well prepared its women students for graduate study (Rossiter, 1982b). The lack of undergraduate preparation was a significant barrier to Black women who desired graduate training.

African Americans in the South were extremely impoverished educationally. As public high schools developed throughout the nation (other than in major southern cities) from the 1880s to the 1930s and were labeled the "people's colleges," few public high schools existed for African Americans. Black institutions of higher education labeled "colleges and universities" often functioned as primary and high schools throughout this period. In 1890, Howard University was the only Black institution of higher education to enroll only college students—a total of 1,053. In contrast, all the seventeen Black land-grant institutions combined in that year enrolled only 52 college-level students. Blacks in the South, particularly in rural areas, did not attend public high schools until after World War II (Anderson, 1988).

Although southern Blacks were at a disadvantage educationally for graduate studies, those who resided outside the region had greater opportunities for primary, secondary, and higher education. In 1833, Oberlin College in Ohio became the first college in the nation to admit both African Americans and women of all races with White male students. Although 90% of African Americans resided in the South prior to Emancipation, a small but significant number of free and freed African Americans were able to obtain an advanced education before and after the Civil War. Alumni records of Oberlin College reveal that more than 400 Black women attended the institution prior to 1910. Of this number, 61 graduated from the literary department, College and Conservatory (Oberlin Alumni Records, 1910).

Prior to foundation support of graduate education, many African American women, primarily schoolteachers, devoted summers that spanned decades in pursuit of graduate degrees. For example, Anna Julia Cooper (Oberlin 1888) began attending summer sessions in 1911 to 1913 in Paris and later the summers of 1914 to 1917 and 1920 to 1921 at Columbia University in pursuit of a doctorate in Romance Languages. In 1925, at the age of 65, Cooper earned a Ph.D. from the Sorbonne, 41 years after she had graduated from Oberlin (Anna Julia Cooper Papers, 1971a).

Cooper spent most of her professional career in Washington, D.C., as principal and Latin teacher at the very prestigious M Street High School, which was later named Dunbar High School in 1915. The Washington, D.C., Black community in general and Dunbar High School in particular with its classically trained faculty played an important role in producing a significant number of Black women academics and scholars (Anna Julia Cooper Papers, 1971b). The first Black women who earned their doctorates in 1921 could trace their roots back to Dunbar High School.

EARLY BLACK WOMEN PH.D.'S

The first African American women to earn doctorates were similar to their White female counterparts in that they were products of educated and privileged families. All these women were products of the Washington, D.C., Black elite. Eva Dykes earned a doctorate in English philology from Radcliffe College; Sadie Tanner Alexander earned a doctorate in economics from the University of Pennsylvania; and Georgianna Simpson earned a doctorate in Germanic Languages from the University of Chicago.

Eva Dykes's father and three uncles were all graduates of Howard University. Dykes graduated from Howard University (the leading Black university in the nation) in 1914. She taught for 1 year and with the encouragement and financial support of one of her uncles, who was a physician, enrolled at Radcliffe College to pursue a master's degree in philology—which was the study of literature and linguistics. As was the case throughout the country, students from Black colleges had to obtain a baccalaureate degree to pursue graduate studies. Thus, Dykes earned an A.B. in 1917 (magna cum laude), an A.M. in 1918, and her doctorate in 1921. Her dissertation was a 600-page thesis on "Pope and His Influence in America From 1715–1850." In addition to the financial support of her uncle, Dykes received financial support from Radcliffe College for five semesters. She returned to her hometown of Washington, D.C., to teach at Dunbar High School (Dykes, 1979).

In an oral interview conducted by Radcliffe College's Black Women's Oral Project, Dykes does not mention anything unusual about being the first African American woman to earn a doctorate from Radcliffe or for that matter to be among the first three Black women to achieve this accomplishment. Her focus was on the educational opportunity she received at Radcliffe. She noted that she had to study Old Gothic at Radcliffe, which she could not study at any other institution (Dykes, 1979).

Sadie Tanner Mossell Alexander also came from a long line of educated family members. Her aunt, Hallie Tanner Johnson, was a physician and founder of the nurse's school and hospital at Tuskegee Institute. Her father, Aaron Mossell, was a graduate of Lincoln University of Pennsylvania and the first Black person to earn a law degree from the University of Pennsylvania (1888). Her uncle, Louis Baxter Moore, was the first African American to earn a Ph.D. from the University of Pennsylvania (1896) and was Dean of Teacher's College at Howard University. Moore was also the first Black member of the Howard faculty to hold a doctorate. Because her aunt and uncle lived in Washington and were a part of the intellectually rich Howard University community, she moved to Washington to attend M Street High School. Mossell noted that Howard played a significant role in her life. She stated, "Speakers from all over the world came to Howard" (Alexander, 1977b). Mossell expected to attend Howard but by the end of the summer of 1916, her mother worked to secure her admission to the University of Pennsylvania and summoned her home to Philadelphia.

Her grandfather paid for Mosell's education at Pennsylvania. Because women could only major in education when Alexander was a student, she enrolled in the School of Education. She had no intentions of becoming a teacher but to follow in her relatives footsteps and obtain a graduate degree. If she had gone to Howard, like Dykes, Mossell would have had to repeat her senior year before going into graduate studies.

Alexander earned her baccalaureate degree in 1918 from the University of Pennsylvania and was awarded a graduate fellowship to the Graduate College at Pennsylvania where she majored in economics and earned a doctorate in 1921. Unable to find employment within the White industry with her economics degree, Alexander worked in a Black insurance company in North Carolina before marrying and returning to Philadelphia. The employment situation remained the same for Mossel (now Alexander) in Pennsylvania, and she decided to return to the University of Pennsylvania to attend Law School and go into practice with her lawyer husband, Raymond Pace Alexander. Alexander graduated in 1927 from Penn's Law School and became the first Black woman to pass the Pennsylvania State Bar (Alexander, 1977b).

Georgianna Simpson was much older than Dykes and Alexander when she obtained her doctorate in 1921. Simpson was also from Washington, D.C., and attended the public and normal schools in the 1870s. She became a teacher in 1885 and subsequently went to Germany to study languages and literature. After she returned from Germany, she joined the faculty of M Street School (later Dunbar High School). Before the turn of the century, Simpson attended summer sessions at Harvard and the University of Chicago. No first person accounts by Simpson exist, and very few records concerning her life have emerged. She earned all three degrees (A.M., M.A., and Ph.D.) from the University of Chicago in Germanic Languages. After leaving Chicago, Simpson taught at Dunbar High School until 1931, when she joined the faculty at Howard University.

THE GENERAL EDUCATION BOARD AND THE JULIUS ROSENWALD FOUNDATIONS

Foundations were central to the funding and control of Black education. The General Education Board (GEB) of the Rockefeller Foundation and the Julius Rosenwald Foundation significantly influenced Black education in the South. The GEB was established in 1902 by the Rockefellers to promote education in the United States without any "distinction of race, sex, or creed." In the early years of its existence, officials of the GEB were very impressed with the philosophy of Black educator Booker T. Washington, the proponent of industrial education. The GEB heavily funded Hampton Institute, Tuskegee Institute, and other schools of the industrial model. Likewise, Julius Rosenwald, who earned his fortune through the mail order store Sears and Roebuck, was also much impressed with Washington and his educational philosophy. In 1917, Rosenwald joined the Board of the Rockefeller Foundation and also established a foundation in his name the same year in Chicago. As a result, both foundations worked in concert in matters concerning Black education in the South (Fosdick, 1962; GEB Papers, 1947).

Although Eva Dykes, Sadie Alexander, and Georgianna Simpson were the first African American women to earn Ph.D.'s, an unknown number of Black women, primarily teachers, attended summer schools in pursuit of graduate degrees. The records of the several hundred African American women who applied to the GEB of the Rockefeller Foundation and the Julius Rosenwald Foundation for graduate fellowships from the 1920s and 1940s reveal that more than half of them had attended summer sessions at their own expense prior to obtaining foundation funds. They attended some of the leading universities in the nation, including Harvard, Columbia, University of Pennsylvania, Cornell, Michigan, Ohio State, Iowa, Minnesota, Wisconsin, Kansas, and the University of Chicago. The funds given by these two foundations were earmarked for the development of Black "leadership" and were restricted primarily to persons 35 years of age or younger. The grants given to women from 1923 to 1929 by the GEB were to study home economics, library science, and general education at Hampton Institute and stipulated that the recipient would return to work in the South.

The impetus for providing funding to African Americans was political, as well as altruistic. Jackson Davis, The GEB Director of Negro Education conducted a study in 1927 titled "Recent Development of Negro Schools and Colleges" in which he noted the increased militancy among Blacks. He pointed out the "buoyant, confident, militant note in Negro poetry and the press" (p. 6). The report continued that African Americans in the South were beginning to be just as outspoken as Northern African Americans on "enforced segregation" and were becoming more "impatient, more aggressive, less inclined to conciliate prejudice and opposition" (p. 6). Davis noted that a growing number of Black colleges had appointed African American men as Presidents and as a result, more Blacks had been appointed to these faculties. In recommending the funding of fellowship to African Americans to graduate schools, he commented, "pressure from the colored group is strong, and it simplifies the matter of social relationships to have an all colored faculty" (Davis, 1927, pp. 13–14).

In 1927, Rosenwald and GEB provided the initial funding to Black women students for study in the fields of nursing, home economics, library science, and general education, and was earmarked for specific colleges—Hampton, Howard, Fisk, and Tuskegee. However, in 1928, the Julius Rosenwald Foundation began awarding fellowships to Blacks for graduate study. Rosenwald targeted students at colleges in Atlanta, Georgia; Howard University and Fisk and Meharry Medical College in Nashville, Tennessee; and Dilliard University in New Orleans as their funding priority. Rosenwald officials noted that they sought to raise these

institutions to the level of White institutions. Rosenwald awards were opened to all fields of study and given to persons between the ages of 24 to 35 (although exceptions could be made to this criterion). Unlike the GEB, Rosenwald did not require applicants to commit themselves to working at a Black institution in the South, although for most applicants, there were few other options.

While Black academics had two sources of funding for advanced study, by the late 1920s, it was clear that given a choice, most preferred the Rosenwald Fellowship. Kenneth Manning in his biography of Ernest Just, an imminent Black zoologist who served on the faculty of Howard University and whose professional survival depended on the largesse of Rosenwald and the GEB noted, "Blacks looked to Rosenwald first, the General Education Board second" for funding (Manning, 1983).

THE EMERGENCE OF THE BLACK WOMAN ACADEMIC

In the 1930s, applications for doctoral study in nontraditional women's fields such as math and the sciences began to appear. A series of lawsuits by the National Association for the Advancement of Colored People challenging the segregation of Blacks in higher education combined with the necessity of more Ph.D.'s on Black college faculties to ensure accreditation propelled the number of African Americans entering graduate school. These lawsuits culminated with the Supreme Court ruling in the *Gaines v. University of Missouri Law School*. Many southern states provided Black students stipends to attend institutions out of state to satisfy the "equal treatment" clause of the 1896 *Plessy v. Fergeson* case. *Gaines* challenged this practice and the Supreme Court ruled in his favor in 1938 (*Missouri ex rel. Gaines v. Canada*, 1938).

The *Gaines* victory increased the number of African Americans applying to graduate and professional schools. One GEB Fellow of the 1930s, Rose Butler Browne who was the first Black woman to graduate from the Harvard School of Education (1937), remembered that after the *Gaines* decision, "Negroes had been pouring into Northern universities to seek advanced degrees. Despite the great depression, money was now available to qualified Negro teachers as never before... they flocked to Teacher's College, Columbia University" (Browne, 1969, pp. 17–18).

Indeed, so many African Americans went to Teacher's College at Columbia that during the summers of the 1930s and 1940s, it was not uncommon for a third of the student body to be Black. According to a 1938 report of the GEB, Columbia University had graduated 121 Black graduate students compared with 81 from the University of Chicago and 66 from Howard University (General Education Board Annual Report, 1938).

The fact that Blacks were being trained to teach in Black colleges resulted in African American women frequently receiving enormous encouragement and support in their graduate programs, even in the male-dominated fields of science and mathematics. For example, Beatrice Yvonne Black, a 1939 Phi Beta Kappa graduate of Smith College, obtained a master's and completed work toward a doctorate in mathematics at Brown University. When the Rosenwald Foundation wrote to the Dean at Brown University to inquire about Black's progress as a student and whether the foundation should continue to fund her, the response was enthusiastic. The Dean noted the dearth of Black mathematicians in the country and stated that Black, as an African American woman, should be more marketable than a "white woman or even a white man." Another professor echoed the Dean in praising Black's ability and also noted her employability. He wrote,

> I am aware of the need for better preparation of the professors of mathematics in Negro colleges. Miss Black will find a position much more easily than would a white woman taking a Ph.D. in mathematics, and she ought to be very useful.
> (Julius Rosenwald Papers, 1941)

Authorities at Yale University expressed the same sentiment as those at Brown University regarding Evelyn Boyd who was also completing a doctorate in mathematics. Like Black, Boyd was a Phi Beta Kappa graduate of Smith College (1945) and also a member of Sigma Xi. The Director of the Graduate Mathematics Program at Yale reported to the Rosenwald Foundation in 1947 that Boyd was "highly gifted" and that the number of Black mathematicians in his estimation would never be large, and Boyd had a definite

future and "serves a definite need in the [Black] community" (Hille, 1947). The enthusiasm for these women was, of course, directly related to the fact that they were not being trained to compete in the White world. Their place had already been determined.

Indeed, unlike many White women who received advanced degrees and were later unemployed or underemployed, most educated Black women did have employment opportunities available to them, albeit within the confines of the Black world. Black colleges readily employed them. Black women faculty were even at the all-male Morehouse College in Atlanta, as well as at leading coeducational institutions of higher education such as Fisk and Howard Universities. Sadie Tanner Alexander was rejected by the many White firms in which she sought employment in 1921 after earning her doctorate in economics. However, she noted in an oral history that she had received teaching offers from Howard, Fisk, and Atlanta Universities—all leading Black institutions (transcript of oral interview, Alexander Papers, 1977a). Anna Julia Cooper, a 1884 Oberlin College graduate who earned a Ph.D. in Romance Languages in 1925 from the Sorbonne at the age of 65 without foundation assistance, responded to a question on a survey of Black college graduates in the 1930s that asked, "length of time between graduation and first employment"; she replied, "not a moment" (Anna Julia Papers, 1971).

Foundation records provide a glimpse into the experiences of African American women as faculty on Black college campuses. For example, the 1938 application of Shirley Graham (later Du Bois) to the Rosenwald Foundation noted that she was the only daughter of a Methodist minister and that she grew up in a home "fiercely devoted to 'service' and 'race pride'" (Graham, 1938). Graham had earned a bachelor's degree from Oberlin in 1934 in music and a master's in music history and criticism in 1935. In addition, she had attended Vassar summer school in 1937, had attended summer schools at Columbia University in the 1920s and 1930s, had earned a certificate in French from the University of Paris in 1930, and had attended the Howard University School of Music from 1927 to 1928. Graham has also studied piano, organ, voice, harmony, and orchestration privately. She became head of the Department of Music at Morgan State College in Baltimore, Maryland, from 1928 to 1931, and later taught at

Tennessee A and I State College (the Black land-grant college) in Nashville from 1935 to 1936. It was while at this institution that Graham applied to the Rosenwald to support her attendance to the Yale School of Drama.

Graham noted in her application her extensive background in the training of art and music. She had studied Greek, architecture, sculpting, and painting and an array of other courses. Graham noted that when she went to Tennessee, her classrooms contained absolutely no equipment or materials for teaching art. She stated that this did not discourage her.

> I had my own "Art Through the Ages," hundreds of prints which I had used at Oberlin, prints and photographs and memories of Paris. Carefully, I prepared my lectures. What brought me up short was the realization, slowly borne on me, that my pupils had no idea what I was talking about. Most of them had come from the rural districts of the Mississippi Valley. Even those who had come from towns or cities had never been inside an art gallery or concert hall. And yet, they wanted to know. I saw hunger for beauty. I laid aside my prints and even my book and lecture notes. We went outdoors and began to study form in the hills and trees and bushes; we learned color by comparing the green of the campus to the blue of the sky, and we saw that sky at sunrise as well as at noon and sunset. Finally, we began copying these things on paper. Out of soap, we carved objects and animals with which they were familiar. I know all this was kindergarten technique, but they did begin to get the feel for the line and form and color. When, by special permission, I was able to take them into an art gallery, they were able to *see*. And, I, myself, recognized new fields opening up before me. I taught the girls line land color in their clothing—how to match and contrast the color of their skin; I showed both boys and girls how green grass and bright flowers transform bare, muddy yards and how cream colored paint would lighten drab, dark rooms. At Oberlin, I had learned to correlate the arts one to another—on this campus, I learned to correlate art with life and every day living. (1938 application, Julius Rosenwald Papers)

Graham's tone within her application reflected deep respect, love, and understanding toward her students. Her description of the lack of resources at Black colleges and the consequences

of segregation and lack of opportunity on the intellectual growth of her students was a story that was to be told many times by other Black professors as well. Graham received the Rosenwald fellowship and attended Yale School of Drama from 1938 to 1941.

Oral histories provide insight into Black women professors' interactions with administrators and their treatment as faculty members. For example, Inabel Burns Lindsay graduated from Howard University in 1920 with honors and was awarded an Urban League Fellowship to attend the New York School of Social Work. Burns recalled that advanced training in Social Work for African Americans was difficult to obtain. She stated that Catholic University and the Catholic School of Social Services in Washington, D.C., were both closed to Blacks when she graduated from Howard. She also stated that it was widely believed that the New York School of Social Work had a quota on the number of African Americans it admitted and that she was one of only three Blacks at the School when she was there. After her year of study in New York, she returned home to St. Joseph, Missouri, to care for her ill mother. Since there were no social services agencies in her hometown, Lindsay taught public school for 1 year. She married and by 1937 had earned a master's degree in social work from the University of Chicago's School of Social Service Administration. She was then invited to Howard University's faculty to assist in establishing a School of Social Work (SSW) and was appointed Director of the Program of Social Services. In 1944, the Howard University Trustees voted to establish an autonomous SSW. In 1945, Lindsay became the first Dean of the School of Social Work at Howard University. She earned a Doctor of Social Work from the School of Social Work in 1952 from the University of Pittsburgh (Lindsay, 1977).

Inabel Lindsay was quite candid in her interview for the Radcliffe's Oral History Project concerning the status of women faculty at Howard University and her experiences on the campus. Mordecai Johnson became Howard University's first African American president in 1929. After his appointment, he recruited many outstanding Black faculty members to the institution, including many women. For example, Johnson brought Eva Dykes, mentioned earlier as one of the first three African American women Ph.D.'s, to Howard's faculty in 1931 in the English Department. Despite the faculty opportunities for

African American women, they were usually paid less and were subjected to gender bias. Lindsay stated that she obtained the job as Dean of the School of Social Work at Howard by default. She stated that Howard was looking for a qualified man because "chauvinistically they wanted a man dean." She stated that when the institution could not find a man to take the job, she was appointed as Acting Dean rather than the permanent Dean. Lindsay also said that most African American men qualified for the job had higher-paying positions in organizations such as the National Urban League and in social service agencies and government. During the search for a Dean, the SSW was being evaluated for accreditation by the Association of Schools of Social Work. The Association alerted Howard officials that it could not become accredited with an Acting Dean. Lindsay also said that she was immediately appointed permanent Dean and served in that position until 1967. She recalled, "I became dean by happenstance." Under her leadership, the SSW grew in size and reputation. Lindsay stated that her goal was to make Howard's SSW a good school of social work and not just a good "Black" school of social work. The SSW's excellence drew White students into the department.

Despite the reputation of the SSW and Lindsay's position as Dean, she stated that President Mordecai Johnson was extremely paternalistic toward her and women faculty in general. She stated that Johnson never referred to her as Dr. Lindsay, Dean Lindsay, or even Mrs. Lindsay, but rather called her "daughter." She stated that she did not believe his attitude was malicious but rather was a reflection of the "culture to which he was accustomed." According to Lindsay, Johnson, an ordained Baptist minister felt that women should be subordinate. She stated that as the only woman on the Dean's Council, she was never expected to contribute any suggestions or to be taken seriously. Sexism was more of a barrier to her professionally than racism because she worked on a Black campus. She noted,

> I was in a predominantly Negro institution, so that race was secondary. Sex, however, was not. There were women on the faculty of course, many of them, very fine outstanding ones who were recognized and accorded to a degree the same academic opportunities of promotion and tenure, although there again I think the bias of sex operated for all women. They didn't get

promoted as readily, nor to as high a rank as a man. But when it came to administration— outside of Home Economics, nursing, or Physical Education, which, of course, had a woman head of the physical education department, women didn't move into the central administration of the University. (Lindsay, 1977, p. 52)

Merze Tate earned a doctorate at Radcliffe College in 1941 and was the first African American woman to earn a degree from Oxford University. Tate taught in Howard's history department beginning in the mid-1940s until her retirement in the late 1970s. In an interview with the author, Tate expressed her outrage at the manner in which she had been treated and underpaid at Howard. She had impressive credentials and, in addition to the aforementioned degrees, had studied in Geneva, the University of Berlin, and Paris. Her situation was not unique, and she indicated that Howard University was not able to get a chapter of AAUW (American Association for University Women) for years because of the inequitable salaries paid to women (L. M. Perkins, personal interview, May 5, 1984).

Lucy Diggs Slowe, the first African American woman Dean at Howard University had severe difficulties with President Johnson concerning gender issues. As Dean of Women, Slowe wanted Howard women students to have more opportunities for leadership on campus and more exposure to a larger number of career options. In an article published in 1933, Slowe criticized Black colleges and their attitudes and treatment of women students. Slowe wrote that Black colleges fostered delayed infancy in its female students with its archaic rules and regulations. She stated that it was not very likely that a woman could see herself as a leader if the college required her to have a chaperone to go shopping. She was also critical of the fundamentalist and conservative religious training that relegated women to an inferior position (Slowe, 1933).

As noted earlier, because Black colleges needed to hire Ph.D.'s to enhance their opportunities for accreditation and to fill faculty openings, well-trained African American women were found on the faculties of most Black college campuses in an array of disciplines. It is probable that salary inequities between similarly trained men and women were the norm on Black college campuses. In the 1919 Annual

Report of the General Education Board on Black colleges, figures were given for the faculties at 12 private institutions. Male salaries ranged from $480 to $2,000, while female salaries ranged from $350 to $950 (1919).

One final example of the mixed-messages received by African American women regarding the use of their talents and aspirations is portrayed in an autobiography of Pauli Murray (1987), *Song in a Weary Throato*. Murray stated that the Dean, Leon A. Ranson, recruited her to the Howard University Law School as a student in 1941. She noted his respect for her intellect and his encouragement. She was drawn to study at Howard because of its stellar faculty and its concentration on preparing civil rights attorneys. Murray stated that although she had been well aware of Jim Crow, on enrolling in Law School at Howard, she met Jane Crow. As Inabel Lindsay had stated, Murray also noted that the racial factor was removed during her studies at Howard, but "the factor of gender was fully exposed." She remembered that the male faculty at Howard was not hostile but actually friendly. Yet they openly joked about women in the classroom. A turning point for Murray was when she was excluded from a "male smoker" given by the Law School to recruit members to a male legal fraternity. When she inquired about membership into the organization, she was shocked when Dean Ranson jokingly told her to start a sorority. She stated,

> The discovery that Ranson and other men I deeply admired because of their dedication to civil rights, men who themselves had suffered racial indignities, could countenance exclusion of women from their professional associations aroused an incipient feminism in me long before I knew the meaning of the term "feminism." (Murray, 1987, p. 184)

In many respects Murray's experience was not unusual. Many successful African American women noted significant Black male encouragement while at the same time noting Black male chauvinism. Inabel Burns Lindsay stated that the reason she went into social work was because a Black male professor at Howard, Dr. E. C. Williams, informed her about the Urban League Scholarship and took the lead in gathering information for her. Like most African American women on Black college campuses, Lindsay had

been an education major, although she never wanted to become a teacher. Her mother had sent all her children to college to become teachers and was quite devastated when she learned that Lindsay was going into something called social work (Lindsay, 1977).

Lindsay (1977) noted the reality of most African American girls of her day as follows:

> In the little Midwestern town where I was born and reared, there was very little else for a Black girl to look forward to other than teaching or working in someone's kitchen. So it was just assumed that I would become a teacher like my brother and sister. (p. 1)

Her mother's view of social work was that her daughter would be working in slums with derelicts. However, years later in reflecting on her career choice, Lindsay noted with gratitude the suggestion of Dr. Williams at Howard that she consider social work. She stated, "I didn't know that there was any professional outlet for a Negro woman except teaching" (p. 51). She also stated that she never knew any women lawyers, doctors, or even librarians when she was growing up (Lindsay, 1977).

Although there was significant competition for fellowships among students from leading Black institutions, such as Howard, Fisk, Spelman, and several others, the competition at smaller, unaccredited or land-grant institutions was not as intense. The Rosenwald Foundation attempted to assist some students from these noncompetitive institutions who showed exceptional promise. However, because awards were usually for a year or less, the recipient usually ended up working on a second bachelor's degree rather than a graduate degree. Such was the case of Naomi Mill Garett in 1944. At the age of 39, she was awarded a fellowship to work toward a doctorate in French at Columbia University. The Rosenwald Foundation waived its upper-age criterion of 35 years due to Garett's outstanding application and references. Garett had earned an A.B. degree from Benedict College in South Carolina in 1927. She attended four summer sessions at Howard University in the 1930s and earned a master's degree from Atlanta University in 1937. At the end of her fellowship year in 1945, Garrett reported to the foundation that Columbia accepted very little of her previous college work. Dismayed she wrote,

Nearly all of the graduate work that I did at Atlanta (where I received my Masters degree) and at Howard University had to be considered as undergraduate hours to give me the number of acceptable credits required for admissions. Thus, I shall have to spend two years in residence here. (Garret file, Rosnewald Papers, 1945, p. 1)

Although the University accepted very few of Garrett's previous college credits, her professors at Columbia praised her academic ability.

The applications of African American women who attended the Seven Sister Colleges or other northern White institutions rose to the top when they applied to either Rosenwald or the GEB. Spelman College, the Black women's college in Atlanta which was endowed by the Rockefeller family and named in honor of Laura Spelman Rockefeller and had a special relationship with the GEB because of this connection, and its graduates, students, and faculty received significant help from the foundation. Recommendations by Florence Read, the president of Spelman from 1927 to 1944, for faculty or students who applied to the GEB virtually assured a fellowship. As a result, Spelman women had a long history of graduate and professional education. The institution regularly compiled statistics of their graduates who had attended graduate schools. One hundred and eleven Spelman alumnae had attended graduate and professional school in the 5-year period from 1947 to 1952 (GEB Papers, 1951).

While these foundations exerted significant control over Black colleges by determining their funding, many of the African American women who obtained fellowships through the Rosenwald and Rockefeller Foundations ended up in the annals of "first" Black achievers—Jane McAllister, first Black woman to earn a doctorate from Teachers College, Columbia (1929); Flemmie Kittrel, first Black woman to earn a doctorate in the field of home economics (Cornell, 1936); Rose Butler Browne, first Black woman to earn a doctorate from the Harvard Graduate School of Education (1937).

The follow-up surveys of the fellowship recipients had a consistent theme of undying gratitude to the foundations. The appreciation was felt not only by those individuals named above who were among the "firsts" but also by the many young African American women who had little

financial means but a great desire to improve their professional status and to be of service to the Black community. Many Black women who received financial aid from the foundations never completed their doctorates due to financial and family constraints. Nevertheless, the women who received assistance for just 1 year repeatedly told the foundation officials how these awards enhanced their lives.

One young woman, Ella Katherine Herrell from Okolona, Mississippi, received a GEB award at the age of 20 in 1929 to attend the University of Illinois School of Library Science. Responding to the question, "How has the fellowship helped you professionally?" she said,

Had it not been for the grant, I would probably be one of the unemployed [during the Depression] for I was not financially able to do it myself, especially so soon after graduation, for I received it the year after my graduation from college. I was on the staff at Fisk at that time, but was untrained and while very interested in the field and wanted it to be my life's work, my salary was very, very small and I was unable to qualify for a higher position. By being permitted to choose the school I wanted to attend, I was able to get contacts, which if I had been forced on my own resources, would probably not have obtained. I was also able to choose one of the best library schools in the country. (Herrell, 1936, follow-up survey card)

Similarly, Sadie Gray Mays, also noted the most frequently mentioned importance of receiving the fellowship—enhancing one's employment opportunities. In response to a similar question to the Rosenwald Foundation, she wrote,

Without the fellowship, the two quarters of work required for the Masters degree would have been difficult, if not impossible. Special training secured would have been harder to obtain. Promotion would have been longer coming and other jobs more difficult to get. (Mays, 1944, p. 1)

Mays had attended the University of Chicago School of Social Work and several summer sessions before receiving a Rosenwald Fellowship. After receiving a master's in social work from the University of Chicago, she joined the faculty of the Atlanta University School of Social Work, was a case worker for the Juvenile Protection Department, and was a faculty member at Howard University School of Social Work (Mays, 1944). Over the 20-year period, Rosenwald awarded 523 fellowships to African American men and women. Slightly more than a third of the fellowships (193) went to women. Not only did these fellowships enhance the recipients' professional opportunities, they also gave them status within their various communities as well. Most Black women college students were not eligible to be considered for these grants because of the types of institutions the foundations targeted for enhancements. However, many African American women who were educated in northern White institutions or the leading Black liberal arts colleges during this period were able to obtain postbaccalaureate degree training at some of the leading graduate institutions in the nation.

CONCLUSION

The number of African American women graduate students and graduates was small compared with White women and African American men by the end of World War II (only 45 Black women out of 381 Black doctorates) and their progress was hampered by race, class, and gender. Nevertheless, the African American women graduate and professional students of the 1920s to 1940s forged new ground and provided the visibility and female role models absent from their own youth. The push by African Americans for self-determination of their own colleges led to professional opportunities for Black women. Many African American women worked and paid their own way to graduate schools by attending numerous summer sessions over a period of years and sometimes decades. Other African American women young enough to benefit from the funds available through the Rosenwald and Rockefeller Foundations, as well as funds from the various institutions that they attended, were able to obtain training that once had been unobtainable and unimaginable, particularly for those in many of the Black colleges.

Numerous Black women academic and professionals have chronicled their challenges as well as their triumphs in the Black Women's Oral History Project conducted by Radcliffe College as well as through their letters and reports to the GEB and the Rosenwald Foundation. These sources enlighten us to the role of not only "Jim Crow," discrimination due to their race, in their quest for higher education and employment, but also the role of "Jane Crow," discrimination due to their gender in their educational and professional pursuits. During the decades between the 1920s and 1950, small number of Black women with doctorates served their race primarily through teaching on the faculties of historically Black colleges and universities. However, the expansion of opportunities after the Civil Rights Movement of the 1960s has dramatically altered the statistics on Black women graduate enrollment and graduation.

While there is a growing gender gap within higher education among all groups except Asians, the gap within the Black community is particularly acute. Despite the slow beginning of Black women's graduate advancement, in 2005, the latest data available on graduation rate note that nearly 65% (64.9) of all doctorates awarded to African Americans were earned by women ("The Gender Gap", 2006).

NOTE

1. These colleges were Smith College, Mount Holyoke College, Barnard College, Radcliffe College, Vassar College, Welleseley College, and Bryn Mawr College.

REFERENCES

Alexander, S. T. M. (1977a). *Alexander family papers.* Philadelphia: University of Pennsylvania Archives.

Alexander, S. T. M. (1977b). *Black women's oral history project.* Cambridge, MA: Radcliffe College Archives.

Anderson, J. D. (1988). *The education of Blacks in the South, 1860–1935.* Chapel Hill: University of North Carolina Press.

Anna Julia Cooper Papers. (1971a). Biographical folder, Moorland-Spingarm Collection, Howard University, Washington, DC.

Anna Julia Cooper Papers. (1971b). Negro College Graduate Questionnaire, Moorland-Spingarn Collection, Howard University Archives, Washington, DC.

Astin, H. (1969). *The woman doctorate in America.* New York: Russell Sage.

Browne, R. B. (1969). *Love my children: An autobiography.* New York: Meredith Press.

Bryn Mawr College. (1916, October 11). *The College News, 2,* 1. Bryn Mawr, PA: Author.

Davis, J. (1927). *Recent developments in Negro schools and colleges.* Unpublished report, Laura Spelman Rockefeller Collections, Rockefeller Archives Center, Sleepy Hollow, NY.

Du Bois, W. E. B. (1900). The college bred-Negro. In *Proceedings of the fifth conference for the study of the Negro problems,* Atlanta University, May 29–30, 1900. Atlanta, GA: Atlanta University Press.

Dykes, E. (1979). *Black women's oral history project.* Cambridge, MA: Radcliffe College Archives.

Fosdick, R. B. (1962). *Adventure in giving: The story of the general education board.* New York: Harper & Row.

The Gender Gap in Black PhD Awards. (2006, December 28). *Journal of Blacks in Higher Education,* p. 1.

General Education Board Annual Report. (1938). Sleepy Hollow, NY: Rockefeller Archives Center.

General Education Board Papers. (1947). Report of the conference of foundation officers with the trustees of the Julius Rosenwald Fund, November 8–9, Rockefeller Archives Center, Sleepy Hollow, NY.

General Education Board Papers. (1951). Roster of Spelman College graduates who have attended graduate and professional schools, Rockefeller Archives, Sleepy Hollow, NY.

Graham, S. (1938). Personal Statement in Shirley Graham File, *Julius Rosenwald Foundation Papers,* Nashville, TN.

Greene, H. (1946). *Holders of doctorates among Negroes.* Boston: Meador.

Hamilton, B. (1975, March). Percy L. Julian fights for his life. *Ebony, 30,* 94–104.

Herrell, E. K. (1936). Follow-up card. *General Education Board Papers,* Rockefeller Archives Center, Sleepy Hollow, NY.

Hille, E. (1947). *Director of graduate studies in mathematics.* New Haven, CT: Yale University. (Undated letter in 1947 reappointment folder, *Julius Rosenwald Papers,* Nashville, TN).

Hine, D. C. (Ed.). (2005). *Black women in America* (2nd ed.). New York: Oxford University Press.

Horowitz, H. (1984). *Alma mater.* New York: Alfred Knopf.

John, W. C. (1935). *Graduate study in universities and colleges in the United States.* Washington, DC: U.S. Office of Education Bulletin.

Julius Rosenwald Papers. (1941). Richardson, R. B. D., Dean, Brown University to George M. Reynolds, Rosenwald Fund, March 21, 1941, Beatrice Yvonne Black Fellowship File, Fisk University, Nashville, TN.

Lindsay, I. B. (1977). *Black women's oral history project.* Cambridge, MA: Radcliffe College Archives.

Manning, K. R. (1983). *Black Apollo of science: The life of Ernest Everett Just.* New York: Oxford University Press.

Mays, S. M. G. (1944). Follow-up questionaire, *Julius Rosenwald Papers,* Fisk University, Nashville, TN.

M. Carey Thomas Papers. (1901). Thomas to Mrs. George Kendrick, Jr. and Registrar of Cornell University, October, Bryn Mawr College Archives, Bryn Mawr, PA.

Missouri ex rel. Gaines v. Canada, 305 U.S. 337 (1938).

Murray, P. (1987). *Song in a weary throat: An American pilgrimage.* New York: Harper & Row.

Oberlin Alumni Records. (1910). Oberlin College, Oberlin College Archives, Oberlin, OH.

Plessy v. Ferguson, 163 U.S. 537 (1896).

Rossiter, M. W. (1982a). Doctorates for American Women, 1868–1907. *History of Education Quarterly, 22,* 59.

Rossiter, M. W. (1982b). *Women scientists in America and struggles and strategies to 1940.* Baltimore: Johns Hopkins University Press.

Slowe, L. D. (1933, Summer). Higher education of Negro women. *Journal of Negro Education, 2,* 352–358.

5

CAUGHT BETWEEN A ROCK AND A HARD PLACE

The Dissolution of Black State Teachers Associations, 1954–1970

MICHAEL FULTZ

In 1954, when the *Brown* decision was rendered, there were 20 Black state teachers associations, concentrated in the de jure segregated South, representing the professional interests of an instructional staff of more than 82,000 African American teachers, principals, and supervisors, and the social aspirations of more than 2.5 million Black children enrolled in their schools ("Biennial Survey of Education in the United States, 1952–54," 1957, p. 77, table 53). By the end of 1970, only two of these associations remained, remnants of a collective organizational history dating back almost a century, hanging on only because the White teachers associations in Louisiana and Mississippi were disaffiliated by the National Education Association (NEA) for their adamant refusal to agree to merger plans with their Black counterparts.

This chapter presents a discussion of the rise and eventual dismantling of these Black teacher groups. It tells a story with a variety of dimensions: (a) the formation of Black teachers associations in the late 19th and the early 20th centuries; (b) the growth and maturation of these organizations through the 1950s; (c) negotiations with the NEA for official recognition; (d) the effects of the *Brown* decision, both in terms of the massive "displacement" of African American educators in the South over the next 20 years through systematic firings, demotions, and discrimination, and in terms of the ideological and social forces that led to the dissolution of the Black state teachers associations through mergers with their White southern counterparts.[1] In its conclusion, the chapter briefly extends its perspective to consider these issues in the context of the broader dismantling of the Black institutional infrastructure of which the teachers associations were integral components.

BEGINNINGS

Apart from sometimes formidable gatherings of local educators and lay citizens who organized the movement for Black education throughout the former slave states in the early Emancipation and

Reconstruction years following the Civil War, and discounting a short-lived Ohio Colored Teachers Association, which held the first of three known annual meetings in Springfield, Ohio, in 1861, the first of the Black state teachers organizations to last into the Civil Rights Era of the 20th century was the Kentucky State Association of Colored Teachers, established in 1877 (Aiken, 1995; "Transactions," 1861). The circumstances leading to the founding of the Kentucky Association were unusual: Its establishment was authorized by an 1874 legislative act, which created public schools for African American children, and the state superintendent of public instruction served as chairman of its initial meeting in Frankfort (Russell, 1946).

More common were the circumstances surrounding the founding of the Georgia Teachers Association (GTA) in 1880, the Colored Teachers State Association of Texas in 1884, the Virginia Teachers Association in 1887, and the South Carolina Teachers Association in 1900. The birth of these organizations hinged on calls for action, dramatic and mundane, initiated by African American educators.

The GTA, for example, was one of several accomplishments of Richard R. Wright, Sr., one of Georgia's leading Black educators for close to 50 years, principal of the state's only public Black high school in the late 19th century (Ware High School in Augusta, founded in 1880) and president of Georgia State Industrial College for Colored Youth (now Savannah State University) from 1891 to 1921. A veteran of teaching in rural Georgia schools since age 15, Wright was valedictorian at Atlanta University's first commencement ceremony in 1876. That same year, in October, Wright organized a Colored Teachers Association for Terrell and Randolph counties, renamed the South-Western Georgia Teachers Association in 1877. A local normal school was soon created. In 1880, growing out of subsequent efforts, the GTA was formed with Wright elected as its first president (Georgia Teachers and Education Association, 1966; Patton, 1980; Walker, 2005).[2]

Both the Virginia Teachers Association (VTA), founded in August 1887, and the West Virginia State Teachers Association (WVSTA), founded in November 1891, grew out of reading circles, a popular form of in-service training in the late 19th century. In fact, the original name of the VTA was the Virginia Teachers Reading Circle, before it was changed 2 years later in 1889.

When elected to lead the Reading Circle, its first president, James Hugo Johnson, a veteran of the Richmond schools, had just finished a 4-week session as the first African American director of a Peabody Institute summer session for Negro teachers in Virginia. In 1888, he was named president of Virginia Normal and Collegiate Institute (now Virginia State University) (Bickley, 1979; Jackson, 1937; Picott, 1975).

In part, the South Carolina State Teachers Association (later, in 1918, the Palmetto Education Association) was organized in reaction to the insulting appointment of White supervisors at summer schools for African American teachers. In 1899, with Senator "Pitchfork" Ben Tillman guiding the reins of resurgent White supremacy, the state of South Carolina sponsored 40 four-week summer schools for White teachers, along with a mere 8 four-week summer sessions for African American teachers. The next year, in 1900, White supervisors took over instruction at the Negro summer schools, ending a tradition of Black leadership dating back to 1881. At one of the summer schools in 1900, on the campus of Benedict College, several participants started the state teachers association to affirm African American capacity and expertise (Potts, 1978).

As Table 5.1 indicates, it was during the 1880s that the Black state teachers movement came to life, with seven associations founded. Four additional organizations were initiated in the 1890s. The formative years spanned almost half a century, from the late 1870s, when public education systems in the South were less than a decade old—and African Americans were beginning to assert their right to public school teaching positions—to the early 1920s, when the chronological outlier among the state groups, the Tennessee State Association of Teachers in Colored Schools, was founded on the campus of the Tennessee Agricultural and Industrial State Normal School in 1923 (Brooks, 1952, 1975; Fultz, 2001). Not coincidentally, Tennessee A&I itself was the outlier among Black land-grant institutions, opening in 1912, long after the region's other Black public colleges had grown from the 1862 and 1890 Morrill Acts.

Although the circumstances surrounding the founding of these Black teacher associations vary, one common theme that cuts through their early histories is the call for greater "professionalism" among African American teachers. This assertion carried a twofold

TABLE 5.1   Black State Teachers Organizations

State	Founding Date
Kentucky	1877
Georgia	1880, 1917; merger, 1922–1923
North Carolina	1881
Alabama	1882
Texas	1884
Missouri	1884
Maryland	1886
Virginia	1887
Florida	1890
West Virginia	1891
Oklahoma	1893 (territorial), 1907
Arkansas	1898
South Carolina	1900
Louisiana	1901
Mississippi	1906
New Jersey	1915
Pennsylvania	1916
Delaware	1918
District of Columbia	1922
Tennessee	1923

agenda. It was simultaneously: (1) a demand for better training so as to carry out what amounted to the sociopolitical obligation of providing for "the education and elevation of our race" ("Transactions," 1861) and (2) recognition that desired outcomes would be more readily achieved through united group organization. This press for greater professionalism was manifest in a variety of ways, often displayed by how the founding and functioning of these groups was intertwined with issues of normal school training and the activities of the Black land-grant colleges. As implied in the discussion above, these interconnections pervade the literature. A few additional examples will suffice.

In Florida, as in Texas, Arkansas, Mississippi, and Tennessee, the president of the state's Black land-grant school was instrumental in the founding of the state teachers group (Dansby, 1956; Patterson, 1981; Thompson, 1973). Meeting at Bethel Baptist Church in Tallahassee immediately following the 1890 summer session at State Normal College for Colored Students (now Florida A&M University), Florida's 3-year old Black public college, Thomas Desaille Tucker, the school's first president, became the

first president of the State Association of Colored Teachers (Porter & Neyland, 1977). In Texas, Prairie View Normal School president L. C. Anderson, and 12 colleagues, convened a meeting on campus in 1884, which resulted in the founding of the Colored Teachers State Association of Texas; by 1937, four of Prairie View's presidents and five faculty members had served as president of the teachers association. The school hosted the teachers group until 1920 (Hollins, 1948; McDaniel, 1977; Montgomery, 1935). In Virginia, meetings for the Virginia Teachers Association were held in conjunction with summer sessions at Virginia Normal in Petersburg from 1888 to 1905, and again from 1907 to 1910 (Jackson, 1937). In Tennessee, the relationship was arguably the closest: Not only was the Tennessee Black teachers group founded in the office of Tennessee A&I's president, William Jasper Hale, it was housed at A&I until its merger with the state's White teachers group in 1967. George W. Gore, the association's executive secretary from its founding, was a Dean at A&I until 1950, when he assumed the presidency of Florida A&M (Brooks, 1975).

Through the 1910s, membership in the Black teacher associations was low, maintained by dedicated pioneers, often in the 100 to 500 range, seldom exceeding 1,000 before the 1920s. Some 91 teachers attended the fourth annual meeting of the Alabama State Teachers Association in 1885; 103 in 1903; 375 in 1909; 1,200 in 1921 (Alabama State Teachers Association, 1903, 1921; "Minutes," 1885; Park, 1910; Proceedings, 1909). In North Carolina, there were 91 members in 1885; 89 in 1901; and then spectacular growth between 1921 and 1924 from 200 to 2,400 members ("Minutes," 1924; North Carolina State Teachers' Educational Association, 1885; Proceedings, 1901). In South Carolina, growth patterns looked like this: 393 members in 1920, 659 in 1923, 1,724 in 1928 (Potts, 1978).

In terms of relative historical development, broadly similar patterns were displayed among White teachers. Nationwide, the movement to establish state teachers associations began around the mid-1840s: There were 17 state organizations organized by 1856, 27 by 1876, the year before the first Black state teachers group was founded. Yet only around 14% to 15% of White educators were enrolled members of state associations in 1907; around 34% in 1916; before jumping to approximately 62% in 1923. In southern states, membership rates in White teacher associations at each of these intervals was typically far lower than in the rest of the nation (Crawford, 1932; Granrud, 1926). In fact, through the 1930s, there were a variety of common structural factors affecting Black and White teachers alike, especially in the South: high turnover among low-wage, modestly educated, largely young, feminized teaching staff, often providing instruction in small, scattered rural school districts, was not conducive to strong organizational affiliations.

In addition, African American teacher organizations faced a unique set of barriers because of entrenched southern racism. Antipathy toward organized African American efforts for self-help was so strong in Louisiana, for example, that in 1927 the president of the Louisiana Colored Teachers Association felt it was prudent to write to parish superintendents to request "that officials of the association be permitted to enter . . . to recruit members" (Middleton, 1984, p. 56). Similarly, in Mississippi in the mid-1920s, both to promote general educational advancement and to recruit local and state memberships in the face of concerted animus, the president of the Mississippi Association of Teachers in Colored Schools organized a "Flying Squadron" of dedicated activists who engaged in a series of in-and-out speaking campaigns across the state. Subsequently, the first of eight Educational Districts within the Mississippi teachers association was organized in the early 1930s (Thompson, 1973).

Generally, it was not until the interwar years of the 1920s to the 1940s that the Black teacher associations attained levels of organizational growth and maturity capable of sustaining social and political influence. During this period, southern Black education began to be established on firmer footing; a new Black educational leadership was emerging as more African American teachers poured into the field and as their collegiate training was notably stronger, demonstrated by dramatic increases in Black teachers' educational credentials (Fultz, 1995). In addition, during this period many of the associations hired full- or part-time executive secretaries to stimulate and coordinate organizational activities. Frequently, these executive secretaries also served as editors of their respective organization's sometimes monthly, often quarterly, "*Bulletins,*" publications that served to dispense research findings, pedagogical expertise, and, increasingly, political news. Overall, Black teachers' social capital was considerably enhanced.

More than anything else, it was the salary equalization drives that started to build in the mid- to late 1930s, continuing strong into the 1940s, which simultaneously boosted memberships and transformed many Black state teachers associations into scarred but determined veterans of the southern school wars. The new climate of the times increasingly validated resort to the courts, an approach considered too risky, and too radical, in earlier years ("Should Negroes," 1935). Plus, the salary equalization lawsuits brought the associations into contact with the National Association for the Advancement of Colored People (NAACP), building connections—and Defense Funds in some instances—both immediate and long-lasting. Moreover, the equalization lawsuits were both harbingers of things to come as well as vivid reminders, if any were needed, of the necessity for group solidarity in the face of furious reactions by an agitated White power structure. In June 1943, for example, in a notorious purge, the Newport News, Virginia, school board summarily fired three of the city's four Black school principals, one of whom was the executive secretary of the VTA, along with several Black teachers, for their activities in the fight for equity. This was one of countless instances throughout the South in which African American plaintiffs and/or their supporters lost their jobs for seeking salary equalization (Picott, 1943, 1975).

THE PYRRHIC VICTORY OF NEA RECOGNITION

But while the salary equalization drives opened new fronts in an escalating educational protest movement, the demands themselves were straightforward claims for interracial equity. Other confrontations with segregation proved to be more ideologically tricky. In fact, in the late 1940s and early 1950s, the demand for African American representation as official voting delegates at NEA national conventions demonstrated the many-sided contradictions that segregation presented for Black teacher associations in the post-WWII period. The issue echoed a long-standing double-bind: "How can negroes (*sic*) organize for social and economic purposes and not by that very organizing draw and invite the drawing of the color line" (Du Bois, 1969, p. 41). The negotiations also verified a new-found influence for a long-time player on the Black educational scene, the American Teachers Association (ATA).

The ATA was founded in 1904 as the National Association of Teachers of Negro Youth. In 1907, then called the National Association of Negro Teachers, it merged with the National Association of Land Grant Presidents to form the National Association of Teachers in Colored Schools (NATCS), the name it retained until 1937 when it became the ATA ("Minutes," 1904; Perry, 1975; Proceedings, 1907). Throughout its early history, the NATCS aspired to become the central umbrella organization representing the interests of African American educators, but like the individual state associations (and perhaps even more so), it struggled with low membership and inadequate finances through the 1930s. The Association's two major achievements came in the mid- to late 1920s, when, under the leadership of W. A. Robinson from North Carolina and H. Councill Trenholm from Alabama, the NATCS (1) spurred the drive that led to the accreditation of African American high schools, colleges, and universities by the regional Association of Colleges and Secondary Schools of the Southern States (Robinson, 1950; Trenholm, 1932, n.d.), and (2) developed a functional relationship with the group that it saw as its fraternal equivalent—and more established model—across the color line, the NEA. In 1926, after initial discussions with NATCS officers, the NEA appointed a Committee on Problems in Colored Schools, reorganized in 1928 as the NEA Committee to Cooperate with the NATCS (Robinson, 1927, 1930; Schultz, 1970).

By the early 1950s, most Black state teachers associations were sophisticated and functional organizations, actively pursuing agendas both professional and political. Memberships were on the rise, and finances were in such relatively good shape that several of the organizations had opened their first real headquarters.[3] In 1951, the NEA-ATA Joint Committee (as the Committee to Cooperate came to be called) won a victory of sorts, when, after several years of discussion, representatives of Black teachers associations were granted the opportunity to become official state-level delegates at NEA national conventions. This was a major breakthrough for the Black groups, which had openly chafed at the

indignity and the Catch-22 consequences of the NEA's refusal to address the exclusionary practices of its White southern affiliates: African American educators were denied membership in the White teacher organizations, and, because the NEA officially recognized only the southern White groups for purposes of allotting delegates, they were also denied the possibility of voting status in the NEA Representative Assembly. With the 1951 agreement, Black teachers associations in 14 states and the District of Columbia were soon sending official delegates to the Representative Assembly proportional to their membership in the NEA ("The Issue of a Pattern," 1946; "The NEA and Its Negro Members," 1950; "Report of the NEA-ATA Joint Committee," 1950; "ATA Recollections," 1957; NEA, 1951, 1954).[4]

But the ATA did not crow over this breakthrough as an unmitigated triumph. While the Joint Committee and other ATA representatives acknowledged that this was a conspicuous step forward for Black teacher organizations in terms of symbolic recognition and actual representation on the national educational scene, they also expressed "dangers as to possible misinterpretation and misuse," which could transform this exploit into exploitation. A 1952 overview presented to the ATA membership through its publication, *The Bulletin,* laid out a number of interrelated misgivings, indicating acute apprehensions. First and foremost, there was "the concern of some state association officers that the temporary expedient not . . . *freeze affiliation of Negro associations as segregated professional groups*" [italics added]. This point was reiterated in several variations: that all interpretations should be avoided that "would seem to imply . . . a parallel and segregated status of NEA Negro members"; that the agreement was to have the limited intent of applying "only for the time necessary and only in the states necessary"; that the agreement was said to be an interpretation, not the modification, of NEA by-laws, thus avoiding an "undesirable record that the NEA was making differentiated legislation for any of its Negro members"; that the NEA should not give the impression that it had established a "Division of Negro Affairs";[5] and, that after the first preliminary discussion (held in 1950), there would be no additional racially separate meetings in which only Black state association presidents would be invited to attend ("The Issue of Representation of NEA Negro Members," 1952, p. 6).

Black educators were right to worry, but in retrospect they were worried for the wrong reasons. Although there was still much to be done, the era of de jure segregation was ending. As events transpired, the pyrrhic victory of winning NEA recognition, combined with both formal mandates and with the "logic of integration" emanating from the *Brown* decision, set the Black state associations on a path that led to merger and the unintended loss of their independence.

The *Brown* Decision and the Dilemmas of Integration

Once the *Brown* decision was rendered, Black educators found themselves trapped on the horns of implacable and inescapable dilemmas, and many knew it from the start. The problems were individual, collective, and organizational. Uniformly, Black teacher groups hailed the *Brown* ruling—the VTA hyperbolically called the decision "comparable to the Magna Carta, the Declaration of Independence, and the Emancipation Proclamation" (Breathett, 1983; "VTA Statement," 1954, p. 14). De jure segregation, with its manifold indignities in the public sphere, had to go. More realistically, however, the VTA statement also recognized the potential problems that the prospect of integration presented, noting that "a major consideration . . . [in implementation] should be the retention of competent teaching personnel irrespective of race" ("VTA Statement," 1954, p. 15). This way of framing the issue became a common phrase in the mid-1950s, often supplemented by data indicating the rising numbers of Black teachers with B.A.s and their extensive classroom experience. It was a measured and mannered way of trying to bring to public attention—and trying to forestall—the looming threat of Black teacher "displacements," the firings, demotions, loss of authority, etc., which would pervade southern states for the next two decades (Fairclough, 2004; Fultz, 2004; Karpinski, 2006). In fact, the likelihood of the displacement of Black educators, especially principals and other administrators, as a result of, or in retaliation for, the integration of public schools was widely recognized even before *Brown* was rendered.

Within 5 years following the *Brown* decision, by 1959, Black state teachers associations in

eight states and the District of Columbia merged with their White counterparts: West Virginia, District of Columbia, Oklahoma, Maryland, Kentucky, Delaware, Missouri, New Jersey, and Pennsylvania ("The State Associations of Negro Teachers," 1959). Thus, as was the case with grade school integration, it was in the border states, where the Black population was neither as large as in the Deep South, nor as traditionally locked into systems of rural agrarian cotton exploitation, that the unification of Black and White teacher organizations first got underway.

In Oklahoma, for example, in late 1955, the 1,500 member, 62-year-old Oklahoma Association of Negro Teachers (OANT) voted to merge with the previously all-White Oklahoma Education Association (OEA). (In October of that year, the OEA opened membership to Negroes.) As OANT president-elect Evelyn Richardson Strong recalled, the vote demonstrated a consensus "that the larger issues of the state, in its efforts to comply with the Supreme Court ruling," could best be served through merger with the OEA (Strong, 1961, p. 247). The onset of troublesome trends of teacher displacements— by October 1955, 127 Negro teachers had lost their jobs—however, meant that the OANT felt it had certain obligations to carry out before organizational deactivation was completed. Specifically, it was determined to show, as Strong commented in an open letter to the membership, that "The Negro teacher is not expendable in Democracy's forward march" (1961, p. 196). Thus, the OANT's vote on merger was to do so as soon as feasible, leaving final determination to its officers. Within a few months, by January 1956, the Association created a $2,800 Legal Defense Fund. In addition, over the next 2 years, the group built up a network for the relocation of displaced Black Oklahoma educators to other parts of the country. At the same time, however, membership of Black teachers in the previously all-White OEA grew, approaching 100% in 1957. By 1958, displacement in Oklahoma had largely peaked and final deactivation of the OANT was completed.

Outside the Border States

In the 11 other southern states with dual NEA affiliates, there was virtually no movement toward organizational unification prior to the mid-1960s. There was certainly no national impetus to unify. After the *Brown* ruling, the NEA spent the remainder of the 1950s taking on escalating internal and external criticism of its reluctance to publicly support the decision; its failure to recognize and condemn the mounting tide of displacements affecting Black teachers in the South; and its policy permitting segregated affiliates (Groff, 1960; Jorgenson, 1959; Lieberman, 1955, 1957; Schultz, 1970).

It was not until 1961 that the NEA passed a resolution endorsing the Brown decision. The debate over this declaration, however, only highlighted the inaction of the NEA with regard to other aspects of a broader civil rights agenda, especially what was being characterized in the Black press as its reluctance to disband its "Jim Crow" affiliates. In contrast, it was increasingly noted that the American Federation of Teachers had outlawed and suspended all of its segregated affiliates in 1956 (Dewing, 1973; Schultz, 1970). Even *Newsweek,* for example, accused the NEA of "shilly-shallying on segregation within its own ranks" (Schultz, 1970, p. 145).

Finally, in 1964, over the objections of NEA executive secretary William Carr and many White southern delegates, the NEA Representative Assembly passed Resolution 12, the basic mandate that would guide the course of affiliate unification over the next several years. Resolution 12 directed all local and state affiliates to remove "restrictive membership requirements" and "to develop plans to effect the complete integration of all local and state affiliates" by July 1, 1966. The NEA Executive Committee was to have "discretionary powers" to take necessary action in cases where affiliates did not comply. Resolution 12 was endorsed by the executive secretaries of the remaining Black state teachers associations in the South, who, through spokesperson J. Rupert Picott of the VTA, noted that without time limits to spur action, there would be "too much deliberation and not enough speed." The era of separate teacher associations was coming to an end.

Two years later, in June 1966, the 62-year-old, 37,000-member NATCS-ATA (representing 11 state and 96 local affiliates) merged with the NEA. As the unification papers were signed, many convention delegates sang the "Battle Hymn of the Republic." The merger had gone relatively smoothly, with the ATA's modest conditions largely met: The NEA was to increase the number of African Americans on staff; establish additional regional offices with integrated personnel; and transfer ATA accounts into a special fund intended to protect and defend the civil rights of Black educators. Unquestionably, the ATA-NEA merger placed additional pressure on the remaining Black state associations.

Over the next year, between 1966 and 1967, dual affiliates in five states merged: Florida (1966), Virginia (1966), Texas (1966), Tennessee (1967), and South Carolina (1967). Between 1968 and 1969, unification was also accomplished in Arkansas (1969), Alabama (1969), and Georgia (1969). North Carolina unified in 1970 after the Black association was briefly suspended. Unification of the state organizations in Mississippi and Louisiana did not take place until 1976 and 1978 respectively. Voting among the Black affiliates was overwhelmingly in favor of merger (more so than among the White groups, when comparisons can be made): in Virginia, the Black group, the VTA, voted 217 to 7 (97%) in favor of merger, the White group's vote was 1,229 to 250 (83%); in Alabama, the ASTA voted 368 to 7 for merger (98%), while the AEA vote was 354 to 155 (70%); in Georgia: the Georgia Teacher and Education Association (GTEA) vote was 389 for, 54 against (88%), GEA, 653 for, 280 against (70%; NEA, 1969; Porter & Neyland, 1977; Talbot, 1981).

It would be a mistake, however, to conclude that the threat of NEA disaffiliation was the most significant factor fostering the mergers. This was undeniably important, but its influence must be considered in combination with other factors as well. First, by the mid-1960s, integrationism was in full swing. A decade had passed since Brown I, and as Picott's remarks indicate, African American patience with *Brown II's* "all deliberate speed" edict was fast becoming frayed. The rise of activist protests characterized by Freedom Rides and sit-ins, on the one hand, and the lawless bullying and braying of "massive resistance" on the other, blended in a unique historical moment. Especially in the aftermath of the widely publicized Birmingham demonstrations in the spring of 1963, the August 1963 March on Washington, and the fall 1963 Birmingham church bombings, proactive integration became a dominant theme in a "civil rights" movement arguably approaching its peak of national influence. Not coincidentally, NEA Resolution 12 was passed within 24 hours of President Johnson's signing of the Civil Rights Act of 1964, national legislation that gave the

U.S. Attorney General statutory authority to initiate and to intervene in school desegregation lawsuits, and also to cut off federal funds in cases of discrimination (Schultz, 1970; U.S. Commission on Civil Rights, 1966). Both Resolution 12 and the Civil Rights Act exhibited the vigorous integrationist perspective of the mid-1960s; both reflected frustration and dissatisfaction with a status quo dominated by southern intransigence; both were unprecedented initiatives promoting not just desegregation, but proactive racial mixing.

In this regard, it is important to recognize that Black educators' push for organizational integration in the mid-1960s was both idealistic and conditional, most often the latter, tied to a variety of then-contemporary considerations. For some Black educators, unification was the attainment of longstanding aspirations. As Thelma Perry (1975), the author of the *History of the American Teachers Association* put it,

> The stated goal of the Negro teachers associations had always been racial equality in education. It was demonstrable fact that this could not occur under the "separate but equal" policy. Hence, the move to integrate teacher groups was in a real sense an implementation of the objectives which Negro teachers had long sought. (p. 336)

For others, the mergers were a "move forward for the wholesome achievement of our accepted American objective," or, alternatively, "the fulfillment of our obligations to our governmental ideology" ("ATA Recollections," 1957, p. 47; quoted in Perry, 1975, p. 327).

More common, however, was this comment by Robert Gregory, president of the Teachers State Association of Texas (TSAT), in his address to the final convention of the Black Texas group, *"Times have compelled us to accept the challenge of change"* [italics added]. Gregory added, "We re-emphasize the point that there does not appear to be any escape from completely desegregated schools in the future" (McDaniel, 1977, p. 83). That is, the combined weight of both historical grievances with segregation and new formal mandates coalesced into a "logic of integration" articulated in various ways, but making the same essential point with regard to the unification of teacher associations:

> Students were going to desegregated schools, and the teachers were already teaching side by side in

desegregated schools. It didn't make sense to have the teacher organizations set a bad example. (Middleton, 1984, p. 128)

> We want integration; therefore, we shouldn't do anything to retard it by continuing segregated professional organizations. (quoted in Speigner, 1956, p. 8)

> The legislation [Civil Rights Act of 1964] made operation of separate state associations untenable; if teachers and pupils were required to integrate, then professional organizations would have to integrate. (McDaniel, 1977, p. 77)

For some Black educators, "The impact of the Civil Rights movement, the sociological changes that are in process and the desire to integrate and be integrated caused [them] . . . to be hesitant about continued membership in a predominantly Negro teachers association" (Talbot, 1981, p. 118). For others, the unification of state affiliates was a protest against Jim Crow, another blow in eradicating de jure segregation. As Samuel Ethridge, the leading African American NEA staff official during the 1960s, noted,

> The rank and file of Black members [in the state associations] . . . looked on the merger as a civil rights achievement in the same way they looked on the right to sit at a lunch counter or to enter the previously all-White universities. (quoted in Middleton, 1984, p. 148)

This was perhaps even more true in the mid-1960s, given the dynamics of the times, than it had been in the mid-1950s, when the mergers began.

These many considerations swirled and blended in personal decisions and local organizational contexts at various points in time. The mid-1960s mergers, for example, displayed certain commonalities. In Florida, what the association's official history describes as "uncertainty after Brown," led first to sharp increases in Black teachers' membership in the Florida State Teachers Association (FSTA), and later, to "precipitous decline." Between 1953 and 1963, membership in the FSTA increased from around 2,500 to 9,704. Then, in a little over a year, membership decreased to around 7,300. The decrease was attributed to several factors, including the decision in 1964 by the White state group, the Florida Education Association (FEA), to drop racial restrictions on membership. In addition, a growing number of Black and White teachers began to favor unification, arguing that it would demonstrate support for desegregation and that a merger might provide a stronger, more broad-based, influence for future state legislation affecting schools (Porter & Neyland, 1977).

An intriguing dimension of the Florida merger, reiterated in several of the state association histories, is the depiction of the executive secretary of the organization as far more cautious about the prospect of merger than the membership at large. Ethridge has made this point as well, noting a general tendency among the "rank and file" in various associations to be "impatient with all of the negotiations and delays" in the unification process (quoted in Middleton, 1984, p. 148). Thus, in Florida, although the group's executive secretary pointedly reminded the membership to "Always keep a fresh horse in the barn . . . because this white horse may not carry a Black man very far; he may throw him," such circumspection had limited effect. In the end, acting on the instructions from its delegate assembly, the FSTA issued a pro-merger communiqué in 1965, noting that, "Current sentiment—eliminating every vestige of separation based on race, creed, or color—signals FSTA to action." In 1966, FSTA delegates overwhelmingly voted in favor of merger, 504 to 11 (Porter & Neyland, 1977, pp. 157–158, 165).

As in Florida, there was a drop in membership in the Black associations in Virginia, Texas, and Tennessee prior to merger, which had the consequent effect of a loss in dues, making their "bargaining power at the conference table . . . weaker and more difficult" (Brooks, 1975, p. 111). These membership losses were not purely volitional. In Virginia and Tennessee, the respective White organizations enacted rules to the effect that membership in the state association was contingent on joining an integrated local unit. The VTA estimated that as more and more White associations dropped membership restrictions—between 1964 and 1966, 99 of 135 VEA county and local units did so—more and more African American teachers signed up with their respective White locals. Thus, over this same 2-year period, the Black state association lost approximately 4,750 members, and $47,500 in dues (Talbot, 1981). In Texas, after the White association removed racial restrictions on memberships in 1963, affiliations in the Black group, the TSAT, dropped by 27%, from 10,036 in

1964–1965 to 7,306 in 1965–1966 (McDaniel, 1977).[6] Thus, bargaining from a weakened position, there were no formal commitments in the merger agreement in Texas that assured Black members shared authority or proportional representation in the unified association. (Similar guarantees in Tennessee and Virginia were modest at best.)

Perhaps serving as an indicator for how short the true heyday of integrationism would be, the six Black associations merging after 1967 tended to be more resolute, more persistent in seeking concessions from their White counterparts, than were the earlier consolidations. They were aided in late 1968 when the NEA Executive Committee created formal "Criteria for Evaluating Merger Plans," an implicit acknowledgment of the shortcomings of prior unification efforts in safeguarding Black concerns (Gray, Reed, & Walton, 1987; NEA, 1969).

In Alabama, more than 25 meetings were held between the Black association, the ASTA, and the White group, the AEA, before unification was accomplished in 1969. The eventual merger plan called for the rotation of top officials and committee assignments during a 6-year interim, and employment without loss of pay for all staff members from both associations. (The AEA had initially sought to fire or demote virtually all the ASTA staff.) The ASTA's Professional Rights and Responsibilities Fund, established in 1959 as a Teacher Welfare Committee and enlarged in 1963–1964 to address the displacement crisis, was to be continued, with the AEA providing a 50% increase in matching funds. The AEA balked, however, and was unwilling to sign off on the merger, if the new unified association had to assume responsibility for the litigation of all pending ASTA civil rights cases. As the ASTA history commented, the "AEA, controlled by superintendents, was not willing to protect the Black teachers discriminated against by some of those same superintendents" (Gray et al., 1987, pp. 264–265). Ultimately, the NEA Executive Committee agreed to assume party-plaintiff status in these cases.

In North Carolina, despite the establishment of a Liaison Committee as early as 1961, concerns about the displacement of Black educators, along with disputes over proportional representation, blocked unification until 1970. In 1969, the North Carolina Teachers Association (NCTA) became the only African American affiliate suspended by the NEA for refusing to approve a merger plan agreed to by its White counterpart.

When the North Carolina Education Association (NCEA) voted to eliminate the word "White" from its constitution in 1965, its leadership believed that this action "would lead to an integrated association similar to those in existence in other states in the South." Officials at the NCTA, on the other hand, articulated an alternative approach, "merger and then integration, rather than the reverse," arguing that from their perspective, merger meant "the blending of the two association gradually by stages," with "certain written in guarantees for membership on official boards, staff, committees, and commissions for a limited period of time." Integration in and of itself, the NCTA argued, would mean the "rapid absorption of the Negro association and the complete loss of its identity and influence" (Murray, 1984, p. 114).

Essentially, things remained at an impasse between the NCTA and the NCEA through 1969. In 1968, the NCTA delegate assembly voted to reject a merger agreement that both a joint Liaison Committee and 80% of the NCEA membership had approved. Criticizing the ambiguous language and lack of specificity in the proposed agreement, the NCTA delegates developed 18 points that they saw as essential to successful merger, including a new name for the association, and *permanent* equal representation on the new Board of Directors and other key committees. Discussion of these points "infuriated NCEA representatives" (Murray, 1984, p. 120). When, in 1969, NCTA officials and delegates reiterated their position by rejecting a fact-finder report that sought to resolve the dispute, the NEA Executive Committee suspended the Black group. (The NCEA had voted to accept the fact-finder report by a vote of 29,188 to 5,344. The NCTA had voted 99 in favor of the report, 72 opposed, and 202 in favor of the group's alternative plan.) Finally, in December 1969, after a special NCTA delegate assembly in which the fact-finder report's 8-year guarantees for proportional representation were discussed (at that point, the NCTA wanted 11-year guarantees and the NCEA wanted only 5-year assurances), the NCTA voted 555 to 22 to accept the plan, with merger slated for the following year. In the end, the North Carolina merger was one of the very few in which the new association did not assume the name of the former all-White group; instead, the North Carolina Association of Educators was born, although it too, as in the vast majority of mergers, took the White group's offices as its headquarters, with the NCTA offices eventually torn down.

The same day the NCTA was suspended at the 1969 NEA convention, delegates also refused to seat representatives from the White affiliates from Louisiana and Mississippi and the Black affiliate from Louisiana. The Black affiliate in Louisiana, the Louisiana Education Association was reinstated before the year was out when, belatedly, it accepted a fact-finder report's conditions for merger. In both Mississippi and Louisiana, however, the White affiliates refused to accept merger plans calling for any degree of rotation in the election of officers and proportional representation on key committees. In both cases, this might have been predicted; in 1966, the White association in Louisiana had been briefly suspended by NEA for being the only affiliate to refuse to remove racial restrictions on membership. In 1970, the NEA Executive Committee disaffiliated both White associations.[7] As noted, unification did not take place in Mississippi until 1976 and not until 1978 in Louisiana.

CONCLUSION

Addressing the ATA annual convention in 1964, ATA president J. Rupert Picott, the longtime executive secretary of the VTA, forcefully commented on the tasks at hand:

> Let all who can hear understand! We must be part of the great march of human beings toward newer understanding in our times. If education is to be the leader, then our mandate is clear. We shall respond to pleas of merger but we decry absorption. ("Resolution Passed," 1965, p. 28)

The spirit of Picott's remarks was often reiterated in the mid-1960s. Black state teachers associations would work within, not against, the integrationist spirit of the times. In doing so, they would work to achieve their long-sought goal of professional equity—and, it was hoped, a more equitable society—seeking to craft reasonable terms for unification with their White counterparts. But, "absorption"—and the word was used often—implying "loss of identity and influence," that "Negro associations and their organization and their leaders [would be] . . . pushed aside as having nothing of value," was explicitly rejected (Gray et al., 1987, p. 241; Murray, 1984, p. 114; NEA, 1964, p. 186; Patterson, 1981, p. 187; Perry, 1975, p. 336).

It is meaningful, then, that in his *History of the Virginia Teachers Association,* Picott pointedly remarked that "the absorption of the Virginia Teachers Association by the Virginia Education Association became an accomplished fact on January 1, 1967." He added, "The absorption . . . removed a power base for black teachers that has not been replaced. The resultant state teachers organization apparently has done very little to perpetuate the black teachers' association legend, memory and/or history" (Picott, 1975, pp. 221–222).

Picott's disheartening assessment of the results—or as he put it, the "nonresults"—of the merger in Virginia represents a common judgment in the histories of the Black teachers associations. In West Virginia, for example, Bickley (1979) has noted that many members of the WVSTA simply assumed that they would attain leadership positions in the new organization; 18 years later, in 1972, African American teachers in West Virginia formed a Black Caucus to address the fact that this had not taken place. Similarly, in Arkansas in 1971, only 2 years after merger, a Black Educators Caucus was formed, succeeded in 1976 by a Minority Affairs Caucus, convening to discuss the notable absence of Black leadership (Patterson, 1981). In South Carolina, the merger agreement was modified in 1971, 1972, and 1975 in attempts to give Black educators additional safeguards in the unified organization (Potts, 1978).

Outcomes in Virginia were particularly egregious, given that the VTA was one of the oldest and arguably one of the strongest of the Black associations, having served as a leader in both the salary equalization and voter registration drives. In a state that had been at the forefront of southern "massive resistance," the VTA had idealistically promoted teacher unification at its annual conventions from the *Brown* decision onward. Yet both Picott and Alfred Talbot, president of the VTA from 1962 to 1964 and chairman of its board of directors from 1964 to 1966, agree that into the 1980s "doubts remain . . . whether the combination of the black and white

teachers associations in Virginia was a significant step forward" (Talbot, 1981, p. 93). According to an evaluation report conducted in 1970, 4 years after the merger, "There was a general feeling among blacks interviewed that the merger did not produce a new organization. Instead, the VEA prevailed and the VTA was 'absorbed.'" Not only were there no African Americans in top management positions or on the sensitive Professional Rights and Responsibilities Commission, most disturbingly, according to the evaluation, "A tour of the VEA building did not lead to a conclusion that there had ever been a statewide teachers organization in Virginia other than the VEA" (quoted in Talbot, 1981, pp. 135–136). In Florida, the official history, coauthored by Gilbert Porter, the executive secretary of the FSTA from 1954 to 1965, verges on bitterness:

> The legal dissolution of the FSTA meant that Black teachers were now forced to seek their interests and goals through the FEA, an organization that had once rejected them and had even gone to court to deny salary equalization. . . . Whatever promise one large association may have held for Blacks in 1966, it was made abundantly clear in the transition that Blacks would witness a drastic erosion of leadership at all levels. Furthermore, the strength in unity had been lost that any minority needs as it fights for its rights and privileges . . . the FSTA membership voluntarily chose to cast its lot with FEA and to seek an uncertain future. (Porter & Neyland, 1977, pp. 166–167)

These assessments must be reconciled with the overwhelmingly positive votes for unification by the Black associations. Were Black teachers simply duped by the lure of integration? Were they pressured into taking "voluntary" actions against their own interests?

Both questions require complex answers. On the one hand, in retrospect, there does seem to have been what might be interpreted as an unwarranted rush for unification prior to 1968. Yet it is also important to highlight several points that mitigate against harsh criticism. First, the *Brown* decision placed Black teachers in an ambivalent position that was seldom publicly discussed since any hint of supporting segregation—even qualified, in terms of the role modeling and socioemotional benefits they provided for Black children—might be seen as giving "ammunition to the enemy." Although many Black teachers, as in Nashville, could support *Brown* while simultaneously working to craft the best possible situation for their students within segregated settings, the tension of doing so mounted as the Civil Rights Movement grew in strength and determination (Ramsey, 2005). This quandary, both personal and ideological, was exacerbated over time as displacements were added to the mix, descending from the border states to the Deep South.

Second, as the Civil Rights Movement burgeoned, as legal and organizational mandates converged, de jure segregation was clearly on its way out and liberal integrationism peaked. Determination and idealism blended with cool assessment. As Vernon McDaniel, executive secretary of the Teachers State Association of Texas at the time of the merger remarked, Black teachers in general "had no illusions" about unification: "There was no hope that single state associations would have the power to transform ultraconservatives . . . into disciples of democracy in human relations" (McDaniel, 1977, p. 111). African American teachers were activated by a variety of considerations: demonstrating "agency" in dismantling caste and Jim Crow; fulfilling long-sought professional and liberal-democratic goals; seeking to attain protection from displacement as well as better personal benefits (such as health care and insurance) (McDaniel, 1977; Porter & Neyland, 1977). Paramount for the vast majority of the associations were attempts to provide legal and social welfare resources to protect their constituents either before unification and/or as part of the merger agreements, and also to ward off the indiscriminate displacements that overarched the period. Although few groups succeeded, as did Texas, in transferring all their assets into a nonprofit trust fund specifically for these purposes, consistently, from Oklahoma in 1955 through Louisiana in 1978, many of the associations sought to prioritize the perspective that

> the right to employment in tax-supported institutions of learning is equally as important as the right to a non-discriminatory form of education. If the former is not insisted upon, it will . . . be a social calamity for Negroes. (Cox, 1951, p. 112)

Thus, even given a certain naiveté, it would be a major ahistorical error to criticize Black teachers

and the Black teachers associations without a keen awareness of the context of the times and the multiple factors at play.

Finally, as McDaniel (1977) also noted, the associations "did not act independently when they terminated their organization[s]. . . . It was the culmination of events with antecedents in a social structure that established separate school systems based upon race and color" (p. 114). In this sense, it is instructive to note that the displacement and dissolution of the Black teachers associations was itself only the most visible aspect of a broader trend: what in retrospect must be considered the unfortunate dismantling of key components of the African American institutional infrastructure that had been developing since the Reconstruction period.

This dimension of the post-*Brown* period has largely escaped attention, and only aspects of what amounts to a panoptic research agenda will be mentioned here. But, as authors such as Frazier (1957), Meier (1963), and Hine (2003) have noted, as a function of class formation, heightened educational achievements, and perceived social imperatives, starting in the 1870s and escalating in the decades around the turn of the 20th century, African American middle class and professional groups began to form various organizations that provided a sense of structure and sociopolitical purpose for Black communities. These included, for example, the National Medical Association, founded in 1895; National Association of Colored Women in 1896; the National Negro Business League in 1900; the NATCS in 1904; National Association of Colored Graduate Nurses (NACGN) in 1908; the NAACP and the National Negro Bar Association in 1909; the National League on Urban Conditions Among Negroes in 1911; and the Association for the Study of Negro Life and History in 1915. Many other groups could be cited, as Black professional organizations proliferated in the first third of the 20th century. As Hine (2003) has commented, "Without the parallel institutions that the black professional class created, successful challenges to white supremacy would not have been possible" (p. 1279).

Yet, as demonstrated in the case of Black teachers associations, in the post-WWII period the drive to eradicate discrimination and de jure segregation gave rise to an integrationist ideology that had profound consequences for a variety of groups within what had become a strong and resilient institutional network. For example, as Hine (1989) has documented in depth, in 1951, after the NACGN had achieved its goal of integration with the American Nurses Association, "They did what no other Black professional or protest organization had ever done: they voluntarily went out of business" (p. x). Various Black state library associations merged with their White counterparts in the 1950s and 1960s (Josey & Shockley, 1977). In 1970, the National Congress of Colored Parents and Teachers, founded in 1926, merged with the National PTA. The Black educational infrastructure was critically altered at a number of local, state, and national levels.[8] In virtually every case, as with state teacher association "displacements," African Americans did not sustain equitable leadership or management responsibilities in the new, "integrated" organizations; social capital diminished; Black voices were not heard.

Born to survive and to persevere the "rocks" of racism and segregation, and later caught up in the ideological entanglements of the "hard place" of integration, for almost a century Black teachers associations served as worthy "watchmen on the wall" seeking to safeguard African American hopes, dreams, and social ambitions ("The Tennessee Negro Education Association," 1940, p. 14). The legacy of their growth, and challenges generated by their dissolution, form a contemporary research agenda in dire need of attention.

Notes

1. Teacher "displacement" refers to dismissals, demotions, forced resignations, "nonhiring," token promotions, lower salaries, less responsibility, and coercion to teach subjects or grade levels other than those for which individuals were certified or had experience. This definition draws from the literature of common practices and policies affecting African American teachers in the 20-year period between the mid-1950s and mid-1970s (Fultz, 2004).

2. Sources do not agree on a specific year when the GTA was founded; all do agree that it was named the Georgia Teachers Association in 1880. In 1923, the GTA would join ranks with the Georgia Association for the Advancement of Education among Negroes to create the Georgia Teachers and Educational Association (GTEA), the standard-bearer for African American educators in the state through the 1960s.

3. Black teachers associations opened new headquarters in Virginia in 1945 (Talbot, 1981), in North and South Carolina in 1947 (Murray, 1984; Potts, 1978), in Georgia in 1952 ("GTEA Purchases," 1952), and in Florida in 1953 (Porter & Neyland, 1977).

4. Prior to this, some Black educators were chosen as "good will token" delegates by a few southern states, some were representatives of local Black associations, and some were observers. There were no restrictions on Negro membership in the state associations in Delaware, Maryland, Missouri, New Jersey, and Pennsylvania.

5. In 1945 or 1946, the ATA rejected a proposal, evidently made by NEA executive secretary Willard Givens in 1944, that the organization become a Department within the NEA ("Editorial Reflections," 1945; "The Issue of a Pattern," 1946; Perry, 1975).

6. As in Florida, where the Black teachers in Dade and Duval counties were among the first to merge, it would be particularly in the urban areas of Virginia (Richmond, Norfolk, Newport News, Roanoke) and Texas (Dallas, Houston, Fort Worth) where the losses in the Black state teachers associations would be especially hard-hitting.

7. In Mississippi, in May 1969, the Black group, the Mississippi Teachers Association, approved a proposed merger plan, 315 to 4 against. In a vote that took place without discussion, the White group rejected the plan, 468 to 60 (NEA, 1969, pp. 442–443).

8. After the announcement of the dissolution of the NACGN in 1951, a prestigious testimonial dinner was held, featuring well-known African American leaders Ralph Bunche and William Hastie as featured speakers. Mabel Staupers, the NACGN's longtime executive secretary, received the NAACP's Spingarn Medal for 1951. However, in 1971, with increasing numbers of Black nurses "beginning to feel that dissolution of the NACGN had been, at best, premature," a National Black Nurses Association was formed (Hine, 1989, p. 191). Similarly, the Black Caucus of the American Library Association was formed in 1971.

References

Aiken, N. (1995). The Ohio Colored Teachers Association. *Report of the Ohio Genealogical Society, 35*, 186–187.

Alabama State Teachers Association. (1903). *Journal of the 22nd Session of the ASTA*, April 8–10, Montgomery, Alabama, 22.

Alabama State Teachers Association. (1921). *Bulletin of the Alabama State Teachers Association, 1920-1921, 53.*

ATA Recollections at Philadelphia. (1957, July). *The Bulletin, 31,* 43.

Bickley, A. (1979). *History of the West Virginia State Teachers' Association.* Washington, DC: National Education Association.

Biennial Survey of Education in the United States, 1952–54. (1957). *Statistical Summary of Education, 1953–54* (chap. 1). Washington, DC: U.S. Department of Health, Education, and Welfare.

Breathett, G. (1983). Black educators and the United States Supreme Court decision of May 17, 1954 (*Brown v. Board of Education*). *Journal of Negro History, 68*, 201–208.

Brooks, G. W. (1952). *A history of the organization, growth, and activities of the Tennessee Negro Education Association from 1923–1951.* Unpublished master's thesis, Tennessee Agricultural and Industrial State University.

Brooks, G. W. (1975). *History of the Tennessee Education Congress, 1923–1967.* Washington, DC: National Education Association.

Cox, O. C. (1951). Vested interests involved in the integration of schools for Negroes. *Journal of Negro Education, 20*, 112–114.

Crawford, A. B. (1932). A critical analysis of the present and significant trends of state education associations of the United States. *Bulletin of the Bureau of School Service, 4*, 12–21.

Dansby, B. B. (1956). A brief historical review of the Mississippi Teachers Association. *Mississippi Educational Journal, 32*, 109–110.

Dewing, R. (1973). The American Federation of Teachers and desegregation. *Journal of Negro Education, 42*, 79–92.

Du Bois, W. E. B. (1969). *The Black North in 1901: A social study.* New York: Arno Press/New York Times.

Editorial Reflections. (1945, September). *The Broadcaster, 18*, 14.

Fairclough, A. (2004). The costs of Brown: Black teachers and school integration. *Journal of American History, 91*, 43–55.

Frazier, E. F. (1957). *The Negro in the United States* (rev. ed.). New York: Macmillan.

Fultz, M. (1995). Teacher training and African American education in the South, 1900–1940. *Journal of Negro Education, 64*, 196–210.

Fultz, M. (2001). Charleston, 1919–1920: The final battle in the emergence of the South's urban African-American teaching corps. *Journal of Urban History, 27*, 633–649.

Fultz, M. (2004). The displacement of Black educators post-Brown: An overview and analysis. *History of Education Quarterly, 44*, 11–45.

Georgia Teachers and Education Association. (1966). *Rising in the sun: A history of the Georgia teachers and education association.* Atlanta, GA: Author.

Granrud, J. (1926). *The organization and objectives of state teachers' associations.* New York: Teachers College.

Gray, J. A., Reed, J. L., & Walton, N. W. (1987). *History of the Alabama State Teachers Association.* Washington, DC: National Education Association.

Groff, P. (1960). The NEA and school desegregation. *Journal of Negro Education, 29*, 181–186.

GTEA Purchases a Home. (1952, October). *GTEA Herald, 20*, 20–21.

Hine, D. C. (1989). *Black women in white: Racial conflict and cooperation in the nursing profession, 1890–1950.* Bloomington: Indiana University Press.

Hine, D. C. (2003). Black professionals and race consciousness: Origins of the Civil Rights Movement, 1890–1950. *Journal of American History, 89*, 1279–1294.

Hollins, A. E. (1948). *The Colored Teachers State Association of Texas as revealed in the Texas press.* Unpublished master's thesis, Prairie View Agricultural and Mechanical College.

The issue of a pattern of NEA-ATA relations. (1946). *The Bulletin, 22*, 11–12.

The issue of representation of NEA Negro members. (1952). *The Bulletin, 28*, 6.

Jackson, L. (1937). *A history of the Virginia State Teachers Association.* Norfolk, VA: Guide.

Jorgenson, L. (1959). The social and economic orientation of the NEA. *Progressive Education, 34*, 98–101.

Josey, E. J., & Shockley, A. A. (1977). *Handbook of Black librarianship.* Littleton, CO: Libraries Unlimited.

Karpinski, C. F. (2006). Bearing the burden of desegregation: Black principals and Brown. *Urban Education, 41*, 237–276.

Lieberman, M. (1955). Segregation's challenge to the NEA. *School and Society, 81*, 167.

Lieberman, M. (1957). Civil rights for the NEA. *School and Society, 85*, 166–169.

McDaniel, V. (1977). *History of the Teachers State Association of Texas.* Washington, DC: National Education Association.

Meier, A. (1963). *Negro thought in America, 1880–1915.* Ann Arbor: University of Michigan Press.

Middleton, E. J. (1984). *History of the Louisiana Education Association.* Washington, DC: National Education Association.

Minutes of the first annual meeting of the National Association of Teachers of Negro Youth. (1904). August 10–12, 1904, Nashville, Tennessee.

Minutes of the fourth annual session of the Alabama State Teachers Association. (1885). April 8–10, 1885, Marion, Alabama.

Minutes of the 44th annual session of the North Carolina Negro Teachers' Association. (1924). November 26–28, 1924, Wilmington, North Carolina.

Montgomery, E. W. (1935). History of state teachers association. *Texas Standard, 9,* 3–4.

Murray, P. E. (1984). *History of the North Carolina Teachers Association.* Washington, DC: National Education Association.

National Education Association. (1928). *Addresses and proceedings of the 66th annual meeting of the National Education Association of the United States.* Washington, DC: Author.

National Education Association. (1950). *Addresses and proceedings of the 88th annual meeting of the National Education Association of the United States.* Washington, DC: Author.

National Education Association. (1951). *Addresses and proceedings of the 89th annual meeting of the National Education Association of the United States.* Washington, DC: Author.

National Education Association. (1952). *Addresses and proceedings of the 90th annual meeting of the National Education Association of the United States.* Washington, DC: Author.

National Education Association. (1954). *NEA handbook, 1954–1955.* Washington, DC: Author.

National Education Association. (1964). *Addresses and proceedings of the 102nd annual meeting of the National Education Association of the United States.* Washington, DC: Author.

National Education Association. (1965). *Addresses and proceedings of the 103rd annual meeting of the National Education Association of the United States.* Washington, DC: Author.

National Education Association. (1966). *Addresses and proceedings of the 104th annual meeting of the National Education Association of the United States.* Washington, DC: Author.

National Education Association. (1967). *Addresses and proceedings of the 105th annual meeting of the National Education Association of the United States.* Washington, DC: Author.

National Education Association. (1968). *Addresses and proceedings of the 106th annual meeting of the National Education Association of the United States.* Washington, DC: Author.

National Education Association. (1969). *Addresses and proceedings of the 107th annual meeting of the National Education Association of the United States.* Washington, DC: Author.

National Education Association. (1970). *Addresses and proceedings of the 108th annual meeting of the National Education Association of the United States.* Washington, DC: Author.

The NEA and its Negro members. (1950). *The Bulletin, 26,* 9.

North Carolina State Teachers' Educational Association. (1885). *Journal of the 4th Annual Meeting of the North Carolina State Teachers' Educational Association,* November 10–11, Raleigh, North Carolina.

Park, R. (1910). Alabama State Teachers' Association. *Southern Workman, 39,* 271–272.

Patterson, T. E. (1981). *History of the Arkansas Teachers Association.* Washington, DC: National Education Association.

Patton, J. O. (1980). Major Richard Robert Wright, Sr. and Black Higher Education in Georgia, 1880–1920. Unpublished doctoral dissertation, University of Chicago.

Perry, T. D. (1975). *History of the American Teachers Association.* Washington, DC: National Education Association.

Picott, J. R. (1943). On the homefront: The Newport News case. *Virginia Education Bulletin, 20,* 6.

Picott, J. R. (1975). *History of the Virginia Teachers Association.* Washington, DC: National Education Association.

Porter, G. L., & Neyland, L. W. (1977). *The history of the Florida State Teachers Association.* Washington, DC: National Education Association.

Potts, J. (1978). *A history of the Palmetto Education Association.* Washington, DC: National Education Association.

Proceedings of the fourth annual session of the NATCS. (1907). August 1–2, 1907, Hampton Institute, Hampton, Virginia.

Proceedings of the 20th annual session of the North Carolina Teachers Association. (1901). June 12–17, 1901, Kittrell College, Kittrell, North Carolina.

Proceedings of the 28th annual session of the ASTA. (1909). April 7–9, 1909, State Normal School, Montgomery, Alabama.

Ramsey, S. (2005). "We will be ready whenever they are": African American teachers' responses to the Brown decision and public school integration in Nashville, Tennessee. *Journal of African American History, 90,* 29–51.

Report of the NEA-ATA Joint Committee. (1950). *The Bulletin, 26,* 17.

Resolution passed by the NEA-ATA joint committee. (1965). *A.T.A. Bulletin, 38,* 28.

Robinson, W. A. (1927). The National Education Association committee on problems in colored schools. *The Bulletin, 7,* 5–6.

Robinson, W. A. (1930). Report of committee to cooperate with National Association of Teachers in Colored Schools. *The Bulletin, 11,* 20–22.

Robinson, W. A. (1950). Some background not to be forgotten. *The Bulletin, 26,* 29.

Russell, H. C. (1946). *The Kentucky Negro Education Association.* Norfolk: Guide Quality Press.

Schultz, M. J. (1970). *The National Education Association and the Black teacher: The integration of a professional organization.* Coral Gables, FL: University of Miami Press.

Should Negroes resort to the courts?—A symposium (The courts and the Negro separate school). (1935). *Journal of Negro Education, 4,* 406–441.

Speigner, T. (1956). The professional responsibility of teachers in this crisis. *Teachers Bulletin: Official Organ of the Palmetto State Teachers' Association, 11,* 8–9.

The State Associations of Negro Teachers. (1959, July). *The Bulletin, 33,* 27.

Strong, E. R. (1961). *Historical development of the Oklahoma Association of Negro Teachers: A study in social change, 1893–1958.* Unpublished doctoral dissertation, University of Oklahoma, Norman.

Talbot, A. K. (1981). *History of the Virginia Teachers Association, 1940–1965.* Unpublished doctoral dissertation, College of William and Mary.

The Tennessee Negro Education Association. (1940, September). *The Broadcaster, 13,* 14.

Thompson, C. D. (1973). *The history of the Mississippi Teachers Association.* Washington, DC: National Education Association.

Transactions of the first annual meeting of the Ohio Colored Teachers Association. (1861). December 25–27, 1861, Springfield, Ohio.

Trenholm, H. C. (1932). The accreditation of the Negro high school. *Journal of Negro Education, 1,* 34–43.

Trenholm, H. C. (n.d.). *Efforts to obtain accrediting for high schools* (H. Councill Trenholm Papers Box 29, Folder 10), Spingarn-Moreland Research Center, Howard University.

U.S. Commission on Civil Rights. (1966). *Survey of school desegregation in the southern and border states, 1965–66.* Washington, DC: Government Printing Office.

VTA statement on school integration. (1954, September). *Virginia Education Bulletin, 34,* 14–17.

Walker, V. S. (2005). Organized resistance and Black educators' quest for school equality, 1878–1938. *Teachers College Record, 107,* 359–363.

SECTION II

THE LANDSCAPE OF TEACHING AND LEARNING FOR AFRICAN AMERICANS IN U.S. SCHOOLING

INTRODUCTION

JACQUELINE JORDAN IRVINE

The transformative power of teaching and learning occurs when students master the content materials and when teachers feel a sense of efficacy about their professional expertise. These classrooms designed for student success are characterized by excitement, confidence, and academic achievement. There is a growing recognition by educational researchers that one of the key variables related to the school achievement of African American students is the teacher. In my own work, I document the critical role that teachers play in the achievement of African American students. Teachers not only influence the achievement and cognitive development of African American students, but they influence their self-concept and attitudes. Because African American children tend to be more teacher-dependent than their other-race peers, they tend to perform poorly in school when they do not like their teachers.

Although teachers play a critical role, the learners are an important part of the instructional process. Teachers are responsible for student learning, but learning is ultimately achieved by students. For example, students' motivation, prior school experiences, gender, attitudes toward learning, self-esteem, competence, and learning preferences contribute to the outcomes of classroom instruction. An important principle in the research on teaching and learning is how students' personal characteristics may facilitate or hinder achievement.

Traditional theories of teaching and learning have fallen short in their explanations of African American students' schooling. These theories often focused on the inheritability of intelligence, the nature versus nurture debate, and behaviorism. More recently, educators have looked to psychologists such as Erikson, Kohlberg, Sternberg, and Gardner for guidance on how learning and teaching occur in the classroom. Again, these theories fail to account for the social and cultural context as well as the complexities of teaching and learning. Pajares (2007) warned that the important questions in education cannot be answered by universal theories. They demand closer attention to cultural issues. He noted that "our students' learning, cognition, and achievement are always situated in a network of sociocultural practices" (p. 37).

African American students' ways of knowing and African American teachers' pedagogy are influenced by their culture and ethnicity. Although it would be unfair to imply that teachers and students are solely a product of their cultural experiences, it would be equally naive to assume that instruction and learning are uncontaminated by cultural variables. Consequently, teachers' and students' race and culture are critical components of their conscious and subconscious selves and hence are manifest in the teaching and learning processes. Culturally responsive teaching recognizes the centrality and significance of teaching and learning and directs attention to effective classroom practices that accept and incorporate cultural traits and behaviors that students bring into the classroom.

How race and culture enter into the classroom depends on a number of complex variables that have often been ignored or dismissed in the literature. I described these complexities (Irvine, 2003) as issues related to the teacher, the students, and the school where the classroom is located.

Teachers bring into their classrooms a host of personal characteristics, attitudes, values, beliefs, and motivations.

It does matter who is being taught—the student. The student's age, developmental level, race and ethnicity, physical and emotional states, prior experiences, interests, family and home life, learning preferences, attitudes about school, and myriad other variables influence the teaching and learning processes. Students are not passive recipients of teaching and have preferences regarding the subject matter that they are taught and the people who teach them.

Teaching and learning take place in schools and communities. Urban, suburban, and rural schools differ from each other. Large and small schools have different climates and teacher-student relationships. Private versus parochial, low-income versus privileged, elementary versus middle, charter versus noncharter are not mere labels for schools. These distinctions matter.

Hence, teaching and learning are complex acts where context and culture are the operative words. The chapters in this section speak to the complexity and the salience of culture and ethnicity. Together they present complex, multilayered explanations for the underperformance of African American students. The authors answer questions such as the following:

- How do identity, race, culture, and ethnicity interact in the schooling experiences of African American students (Peter Murrell)?

- How does cultural socialization inform African American students' communication, conflict resolution, and literary skills (Yolanda Majors and Sana Ansari)?

- What do we know about successful pre- and in-service teacher education programs that prepare educators for urban schools that enroll African American students (H. Richard Milner)?

- How does African American teachers' culturally relevant care influence African American students' school experiences (Mari Roberts and Jacqueline Jordan Irvine)?

- What does the literature reveal about African American parental involvement (Cheryl Fields-Smith)?

Taken together, these chapters offer new perspectives, a variety of solutions, and critical research questions for African American education. Peter Murrell breaks new ground by proposing that research agendas examine the academic underachievement of African American students, not through specious comparisons between Black students and their White and Asian peers, but through an examination of social identification, cultural practices, and issues of agency. His situated-mediated identity theory is a useful framework to consider African American students' learning and the teaching that occurs in school settings.

Yolanda Majors and Sana Ansari's comprehensive and pioneering qualitative study complements Murrell's work. These authors focus on classroom community participation structures that assist African American students shift through often-contentious concerns related to their everyday lived experiences and the literacy tasks they are expected to master. In addition, this chapter focuses on how African American families' racial socialization practices and students' beliefs about their parents and communities operate in the context of school achievement. Majors and Ansari end their chapter with a call for enlightened teacher education programs that dismantles White power and privilege.

H. Richard Milner illuminates Majors and Ansari's teacher education challenge. His comprehensive review of the research literature focuses on curricular, instructional, and policy imperatives that suggest that teacher education programs must place at its center issues of race and culture. Milner poignantly argues for more proactive stances by teacher educators on institutional racist practices and policies and recommends that teacher education programs better prepare teachers to teach African American students in urban schools. Milner notes that teacher care is an important element to be considered in preparation programs.

Mari Ann Roberts and Jacqueline Jordan Irvine spotlight African American teachers' culturally relevant care in their chapter. Current research on the influence of African American teachers on their African American students indicates that not only shared ethnicity but also shared culture has a positive impact on African American students' achievement. The authors examine the reasons why African American teachers are important and explain how African American teacher care and their culturally responsive pedagogy make a difference in the schooling of African American students. Roberts and Irvine believe that the declining numbers of African teachers does not bode well for the school success of African American students.

Cheryl Fields-Smith critiques the extant research by observing that the research on African American parental involvement investigates low-income families and makes inaccurate and incomplete conclusions that Black families are disinterested and disengaged in their children's education. Among her notable and original findings is Fields-Smith's observation that, unknown to many teachers, African American parents design and maintain home-based learning activities that supplement their children's school-based learning.

Finally, the authors in this section have elevated the importance of teaching and learning in the education of African American students. They have emphasized that effective interventions have to be framed by cogent theories and models that recognize the centrality of culture and ethnicity. In addition, future research and policy directives should acknowledge that teaching and learning occur in significant spaces that include students' families, communities, and their own issues of socialization and identity.

REFERENCES

Irvine, J. J. (2003). *Educating teachers for a diverse society: Seeing with the cultural eye.* New York: Teachers College Press.

Pajares, F. (2007). Culturalizing educational psychology. In F. Salili & R. Hoosai (Eds.), *Culture, motivation and learning: A multicultural perspective* (pp. 19–42). Greenwich, CT: Information Age.

6

IDENTITY, AGENCY, AND CULTURE

Black Achievement and Educational Attainment

PETER C. MURRELL JR.

The issue of Black achievement in public schooling has received much attention in the educational research literature on urban education policy and instructional practice in recent times. It continues to be a confounding issue in urban education particularly since the scholarly literature on the topic has tended to frame African American *underachievement* in terms of a deficits perspective, rather than an assets perspective that considers Black *achievement excellence* (Hilliard, 2003). The framing of Black underachievement has most commonly been configured as a problem of an *achievement gap*, by which is meant the performance disparity between groups such as European American students in comparison with African American and Hispanic students, and between economically advantaged versus low-income students. As a result of this framing, a significant portion of research literature in educational policy, sociology of education, and learning theory has attempted to explain why the differential performance exists and what can be done to "close the gap."

Since the early popularization of the term, a number of scholars have decried this simplistic framing by offering more sophisticated critical interpretations of "the gap" showing how it is constituted by a whole host of inequities in resources and opportunity (e.g., Hilliard, 1992; Williams, 1996). These interpretations challenge the tacit assumption that achievement gap phenomenon is solely a matter of differences in the individual intellectual capacity of the compared groups (e.g., Anyon, 2005; Kozol, 2005; Ladson-Billings, 2006; Murrell, 2002; Noguera, 2003). Given the other significant but little-discussed gaps—including the inequality of per-pupil funding, disparities in the quality of teachers, inequity of scholastic resources, and unequal access to educational capital—it can be argued that the popular characterization of America's educational challenge as one of "closing a gap" may actually serve to perpetuate, rather than eliminate, the achievement gap by further camouflaging the historically rooted inequality embedded in the practices, policies, and politics of American education (e.g., Ladson-Billings, 2006; Murrell, 2002).

Given the points raised above, the focus of this chapter is not the on achievement gap but rather on a deeper interpretation of achievement for African American learners—namely, the psychosocial development of African American learners in the context of schooling and the aspects of identity development that are crucial to their school success. We know that race is a significant factor in the schooling success of African American children and youth (Boykin, 1986; Carter, 2003; Fordham,

1996; Howard, 2003; Murrell, 2007; Spencer, 1999; Spencer, Cunningham, & Swanson, 1985; Steele, 1997; Weiler, 2000)—but how? Race influences the development of scholastic potential of African American children even when inequality factors such as teacher quality, equal access to educational resources, and equity of funding are taken out of the equation (Ogbu, 2003; Steele, 1997). Racism in America compromises the developmental integrity of the social and cultural contexts of school life necessary to ensure children's personal and scholastic development. African American learners are particularly vulnerable to the adverse impacts of the ways in which race affects schooling practices and their academic socialization. Given the structural inequality of the wider society as well as the way that structural inequality gets reflected in the daily social and cultural contexts children experience in school, urban educators and theorists need to understand the psychosocial dynamics in the development of academic identities of African American learners.

The framework offered here explains academic achievement as the dynamic interplay between the *racial identity* and *academic identity* development of Black students. In doing so, the framework contradicts the commonly held assumption that the underperformance of African American students, as revealed in achievement gap data, is a consequence of their *disidentification* with education and with schooling. A close read of the research literature on race, ethnicity, culture, and academic performance (see Spencer & Markstrom-Adams, 1990; Stinson, 2007, for reviews) reveals little direct evidence for this assumption. The simplistic "disidentification hypothesis" persists because too little is known about the actual development of academic identity among African American youth in relation to their achievement, their racial identity, and Black culture. Too much of the relevant work on the psychosocial development of African American learners produced by scholars of color has been overlooked (Spencer, 1987; Stevenson, Best, Cassidy, & McCabe, 2003). Only recently has there been research on academic-oriented identity as both a *product* and a *process* of socialization and schooling practices (e.g., O'Connor, 1997, 2001).

The remainder of this chapter will examine and apply what is known about social identification among African American learners to address the question: What does it mean to

be *both* African American and an academic achiever in different school contexts? The discussion uses the situated-mediated identity theory to explain the contribution of identity processes (of both learners and teachers) *and* the contribution of the social-cultural context to the academic performance of African American learners in school settings. The situated-mediated identity theory explains the dual contribution of psychocultural processes (i.e., cultural practices and discourses) and the sociocultural conditions in the social life of schools so that we might better understand the situativity of academic identity for African American students.

IDENTITY AND BLACK ACADEMIC ACHIEVEMENT

The Psychosocial Dimensions of Disidentification

As noted above, a stock explanation of Black academic underachievement is some version of the notion that African American students *disidentify* with schooling. Operating with this assumption, some authors seem to lay blame for lower academic performance with the individual students and the choices they make that lead to their diminished academic attainment (e.g., Fordham & Ogbu, 1986; Lewin, 2000; McWhorter, 2001). Others seem to locate the blame in the bleak prospects for opportunity in the broader social, historical, and political context and the subsequent nihilism felt by young African Americans that diminishes their effort in school (Noguera, 2003; West, 1993). Each account involves a form of *disidentification* to account for underachievement and implies some measure of rejecting values and dispositions vital to academic success. The claim here is that a complete explanation for both academic excellence and underachievement of African American learners cannot solely be based on any one of these three arenas of social identity formation but must comprehensively integrate social identification in the three areas: (1) the individual, (2) the individual's local cultural context of social networks, and (3) the broader societal, political, and cultural context. An explanatory framework must draw on all three. This integration was the attempt of the *cultural ecological theory*, to which this discussion will turn presently.

While the idea of disidentification is important to the explanation of African American achievement, let me explain why it cannot be *the* explanation of underachievement. First, it is not clear what the term *identification* means in the discussion of Black achievement. There are a variety of meanings of the term identification in scholarly literature addressing achievement of African American students. For example, it appears as a *sociological construct* referring to volitional choices young people make about their academic behavior; it appears as a *sociocultural construct* referring to forms they choose to represent themselves; it appears as the *psychological construct* referring to role-identity and the way race, class, and ethnicity have shaped one's personality vis-à-vis schooling. It even appears as a *cultural construct* in reference to the orientations of groups. Hence, since there are a variety of interpretations of what it means to *identify*, disidentification cannot serve as a single unified explanation of identity-mediated achievement—at least until there is a consistent meaning of the term.

A second problem with disidentification as an explanation of school achievement is that it does not make sense to say that a young person *disidentifies* with *education* or *schooling*. Regardless of whether you adopt a cultural, sociocultural, or psychological perspective on identification, an individual can neither *identify* nor *disidentify* with school or with education in general. Social identification is a matter of affiliating with *people*—usually a particular grouping of individuals. "The school" does not qualify as such a grouping. Identification is a process that works with reference to a particular grouping of people and not with abstractions or institutions. In other words, social identity is made with respect to social groups and relationships (Jenkins, 2004; Tilly, 2006). A favorite teacher can serve as a role model for a young person but a school cannot. In a complex social system or institution such as a school, representations are varied, complex, and contradictory in such a way that it simply does not make sense to speak of someone identifying or disidentifying with school.

The third reason why disidentification is not an explanation for underachievement is the most important: There is really no evidence to suggest that African American learners, whether successful or unsuccessful, actually devalue or disown education (Carter, 2005; Perry, Steele, & Hilliard, 2003). Carter (2005) made the case that social and cultural capital does not operate in the simplistic ways put forth by Fordham and Ogbu (1986). She argued that although African American and Latino youth may in fact characterize certain cultural (social-situational) practices as "acting White" that might correspond to "academic behavior," this is by no means based on their academic aspirations, but rather on their social connections and in-group identity. Similarly, Perry (2003), drawing on the work of Boykin and Toms (1985), argued that African American learners have a distinctive social group identity that is at least partly defined by powerful cultural values regarding literacy, learning, and education in African history and culture.

So while social identity is important in achievement, disidentification is not an acceptable explanation for African American underachievement. Social identity is not generic but determined by the individual's social sphere. Social identification occurs in the "local culture"— the crew, posse, the "homies," and so on—that define social identity in the acts of interrelating on an ongoing basis. People, young and old alike, construct their symbolic worlds using the meaning systems immediately and substantially available around them in local cultures, groups, enclaves, etc. they affiliate with (Holland, Lachicotte, Skinner, & Cain, 1998; Murrell, 2007). There are, of course, many local cultures within a school. So to understand social identification of African American learners (or any learners for that matter), it is necessary to understand individuals in relationship to the local cultures they participate in. That is the purpose of the framework presented below.

Beginnings of a Psychosocial Cultural Notion of Identity

One proposition on which there has been consensus over the past 50 years is that schooling experiences of Black learners are comparatively more difficult than for White learners in American society. There is less agreement regarding the explanation of what the psychological and educational impact is on African American learners. Inquiry into African American children's psychosocial development in school settings, and how forms of racism might influence it, was ushered into social science research by the pioneering work of Kenneth B. Clark. The now famous "doll studies" conducted by Kenneth B. Clark and Mamie Phipps Clark were the scientific evidence used to demonstrate the deleterious effects of segregation on Black children in the landmark *Brown v. Board of Education* case in 1954 (Clark & Clark, 1939, 1940). They found that Black children, when given choices, consistently preferred white dolls to brown ones. The Clarks concluded that these doll preferences were due to racial segregation and wrote,

> It is clear that the Negro child, by the age of five, is aware of the fact that to be colored in contemporary American society is a mark of inferior status. . . . The negation of the color, brown, exists in the same complexity of attitudes in which there also exists knowledge of the fact that the child himself must be identified with that which he rejects. *This apparently introduces a fundamental conflict at the very foundations of the ego structure* [italics added]. (p. 350)

The Clarks' work was important because it was the first social science research to seriously examine the relationship between the psychosocial development of Black children and stressors embedded within White social and political contexts that might affect their ability to perform in school. Developmental theorists of the time assumed that the solution to African American children's achievement problems was desegregation and the removal of racial isolation and inequitable educational resources.

While some aspects of the validity of the doll studies methodology have been criticized (Burnett & Sisson, 1995; Vaughan, 1986), this early work nonetheless demonstrated the possibility that self-deprecating racial identification among African American children diminished, and was perhaps diminished by, the quality of their learning experience in school. Although instrumental in the winning of the *Brown v. Board of Education* Supreme Court ruling, the notoriety of the findings may have had an unfortunate side effect. By foregrounding the intrapersonal psychological impacts of racial isolation and racial stigma on African American children, these findings may have lent more credence to an individual deficit model view of Black children in subsequent social science research.

The *deficit model* originally referred to lines of social research that viewed African American children and adults as impaired by the degraded social and economic conditions, in which they were forced to live and hence always inferior in comparison with middle-class European American

norms (Brofennbrenner, 1979). In the case of individual social identity, African American learners were "damaged goods," and this view set a precedent of seeing effects as a matter of psychological damage, as opposed to a matter of the conditions in children's social and cultural environments necessary for healthy psychological development. Subsequent explanations of Black underachievement in the decades to follow were similarly based on this *deficiency perspective*—a "damaged goods" optic that was embodied in the assumption that Black learners developed a diminished self-concept as the result of racial stigma. This optic ushered in a precedent of research that looked at family and sociocultural contexts in deficiency terms (e.g., Coleman et al., 1966; Moynihan, 1965). Hence, rather than focusing on what Black learners were not receiving developmentally and intellectually, the focus was on the imagined ill effects of discrimination on the psyche of African American learners.

Although this later research did begin to pay some regard to the social environment, the "damaged goods" optic with respect to African American learners persisted throughout the 1960s and the 1970s, characterized by a deficiency paradigm termed *cultural deprivation* and *cultural disadvantage*. The working assumption in this paradigm is that decrements in Black learners' school attainment were due to the degraded home and social environment. The common argument in this body of work was that African American youth in low-income city communities were *culturally disadvantaged* and therefore placed at a relative disadvantage in comparison with their White, culturally mainstream peers (Deutsch, 1963; Deutsch, Katz, & Jensen, 1968). According to this perspective, "culturally disadvantaged" students fail because they are not prepared for the high expectations and standards of their middle-class teachers.

This optic in conjunction with the ongoing ideology of Black inferiority in American popular culture occasionally gave traction to the idea that the deprived and degraded status of African Americans results in decrements in intellectual ability that may be passed from one generation to the next. For example, Arthur Jensen (1969) linked the "innate inferiority" deficiency perspective to the "culturally deprived" deficiency perspective in a paper purporting to demonstrate the genetic heritability of intelligence related to racial classification. The impact of his claim that African Americans as a group are genetically less intelligent than White Americans was only somewhat diminished with the discovery that the data from work done by Cyril Burt some decades before had been falsified (The Cyril Burt Affair, 2007). Despite this, the proposition of the heritability of intellectual potential continues to resurface periodically and has most recently *resurfaced* in the publication of the controversial book *The Bell Curve* (Herrnstein & Murray, 1994).

Oppositional Identity and Oppositional Culture

Let us turn again to cultural ecological theory, an important theoretical account aimed at incorporating the historical, social, and cultural contextual factors in school achievement. Two key constructs relevant to social identification here are *oppositional culture* and *oppositional identity* (e.g., Fordham, 1996; Fordham & Ogbu, 1986; Ogbu, 1978, 1985, 2003). The central argument is that ethnic minority students' school performance can be explained as a function of their perceptions of opportunity payoff in educational attainment based on their historical status. According to this theory, émigrés from ethnic-minority groups such as the Japanese, Koreans, Chinese, and West Indians would have a higher expectation that schooling offers opportunity than those of African American, Native American, and Chicano groups. Ogbu's (1978) terms for these groups are voluntary and involuntary minorities, respectively. Voluntary minorities are groups who have, historically, entered American public life under terms of their own choice and volition, whereas African Americans, Native Americans, and Chicanos constitute populations who have been involuntarily incorporated into American society through enslavement, conquest, and colonization. Thus, according to the theory, the latter group's caste-like status is what produces the higher levels of pessimism toward schooling and greater reaction to schools as a mechanism of assimilation and subordination. According to the argument, despite the fact that voluntary minorities have been subjected to exploitation and subordination, as have involuntary minorities, they still tend to perceive schooling more favorably and are more likely to exhibit an effort-optimism than members of involuntary minority groups.

By far, the most controversial element of the Ogbu/Fordham cultural-ecological framework is the ascription of social identity characteristics to entire racial-ethnic groups based on their group status. According to cultural-ecological theory, the explanation for underachievement has to do with a sort of global identification of African American learners. African American underachievement is explained as a consequence of students viewing school success as "acting White" and therefore rejecting behaviors that are necessary for school achievement. On this account, those African American students who are succeeding in school and "acting White" do so at the cost of the derision and sanctions of their peers who position them as "sell outs." The phenomenon supporting this assertion is "camouflaging" where high-achieving African American students keep their successful academic record under wraps. With respect to their identity as Black people, according to this theory, successful African American students become *raceless*—sacrificing racial identity for school success. Those African American students who are less academically successful simply reject those behaviors and markers of the persona of studiousness as "acting White." These African American students are said to adopt an *oppositional identity*—a social identity defined in contradiction to a White persona so as to avoid "acting White" (Fordham, 1996; Fordham & Ogbu, 1986).

Let us look at this account more carefully. I begin by noting that in the educational literature the notion of "opposition" is most often applied to the instance in which lower-achieving Black students are presumed to reject academic culture as "White culture" to the detriment of their academic success (e.g., McWhorter, 2001; Steele, 2000). This overlooks the critical point that within the Ogbu/Fordham paradigm even successful African American students are defined "oppositionally" by virtue of the fact that they are embracing an academic identity of "Whiteness" (academic behavior presumed to be "White behavior") and rejecting behaviors they purportedly attribute to less successful African American student. The point is this: If you are Black in America, you can never fully avoid being positioned in negative ways. The natural and healthy adjustment Black youth make is to resist, contest, and "counter" the negative positionalities (e.g., as less academically talented, lazy, unmotivated) that others impose upon them by improvising their *own* more positive social identities. Thus, the social identities of academically successful African American learners are also defined as a counterpositionality.

This point is important because of the absence of any account of young people's *agency* and capacity to *improvise* their modes of self-expression in a variety of ways and settings. I return to this notion of individual agency in a moment. For now, it is important to note the availability of finer-grained analyses of the contexts in which African American students interact with their peers that have challenged this explanation. The *oppositionality* that Ogbu and Fordham found at Capitol high was likely more a reflection of the stigma of Black inferiority in that particular school context than any feature of a Black academic identity (Perry et al., 2003).

There are in fact a variety of different ways in which African American high achievers interact with different sets of peers (Carter, 2005; Horvat & Lewis, 2003, 2006; O'Connor, 1997, 2001; Stinson, 2007). Hence, *oppositionality* cannot be *the* explanation for Black achievement because it is not a universal, or necessarily common, condition of African American school goers. Moreover, it does not explain achievement excellence. Fortunately, the cultural ecological perspective does not hinge on the idea of oppositionality, freeing us to explore what the limitations are to fashion a better explanatory account. Let us turn to several realizations to consider building on the cultural ecological theory and the notion of oppositionality. The first has to do with the operating conception of *race*.

To begin with, though race is an important factor in American society, it does not operate simply as a categorical designation of behaviors or characteristics. The idea that a racial category connotes ascribable characteristics of individuals in the category is logically and empirically unsupportable. Ascribing racial categorizations of "Black identity" or "Hispanic identity" are therefore not only likely to be gross overgeneralizations, but also lack meaning outside of the context in which they are applied. The cultural variation both between and within these racial categories is too great to be able to ascribe any meaningful characteristics based on race or ethnicity to these groups (Carter, 2005; Conchas, 2006; Gibson, 1997; Mehan, Hubbard, & Villanueva, 1994).

A second point has to do with conceptualization of ethnicity. While racial categorizations of "Black identity" or "Hispanic identity" may serve as descriptions referring to orientations of persons-in-settings, they are unacceptably broad-brush as a meaningful description of the way young people *reference themselves.* These categories have little meaning as indices of self-reference, especially among young people of color who are less and less likely to categorize themselves into a single racial group. For example, according to the 2000 census, nearly 7 million Americans identified themselves as members of more than one race. The 2000 census was the first time that respondents were able to check more than one racial category. Moreover, more than 14 million Hispanic respondents, constituting more than 42% of the respondents, ignored the boxes for Black and White and checked "some other race," indicating perhaps the mixed-race heritage of respondents from the Caribbean, South America, and Central America (La Ferla, 2003). The ethnic-racial-social constructions young people adopt are more complex and nuanced than a simple ethnic categorization. Racial classification in the 21st century is more complex and is not simply a matter of all-or-none, mutually exclusive set of categories.

Hence, we are forced to consider that the social-cultural constructions of self, including racial identification, may be made more through personal experiences and by agency of individuals themselves than by the ascription of ethnic or racial category made by others (Carter, 2005). The situativity of both scholastic performance (Steele, 1997) and social identification (O'Connor, 2001) will vary according to the nature of the discursive setting (including participants and interactants). The social construction of academic identity not only involves individual choice and agency but is also a result of discursive processes over time (Wortham, 2006). For example, Wortham (2006) has shown how the identity development of two African American high school students was shaped by both their evolving positionality in the class and the way they positioned themselves relative to the curricular themes in the class.

For African American youth, *agency* is critical because they have a generally greater need to contest the stigmatizing discourses and images directed at them. Stinson (2007) in his study of successful African American male mathematics students defined agency as the ability to "accommodate, reconfigure, or resist the available sociocultural discourses that surround African American males" (p. 478). African American learners in school contexts are always, to a greater or lesser degree, negatively positioned with regard to the "conventional wisdom" regarding their achievement. That is, because of the popularized notion of an achievement gap, the prevailing stereotype is that if you are Black, you are somehow less academically able. But African American learners also have, to a greater or lesser degree, the capacity to act proactively on the collective meanings and social relationships in a setting (Holland et al., 1998) to maintain the integrity of their social identity.

Finally, identity is not an all-or-none proposition, and neither are Black students' situation-by-situation evaluations of self worth in the day-to-day interactions in school. Both positive and negative self-evaluations may be present in an individual maintaining self-integrity (Stevens, 1997). In other words, the way in which the individual views himself or herself is not solely determined by how that person sees his or her racial membership as a reference group, regardless of whether the group is considered an out-group in the dominant culture (Phinney, Cantu, & Kurtz, 1997). Therefore, approaches that seek to globally link low self-esteem with low academic achievement are flawed (Spencer, 1985; Spencer, Brookins, & Allen, 1985). This is not to say, however, that negative messages and stereotypes about Black people are unimportant in social identity processes of African American learners. Threatening stereotypes—like Black learners are less able—are the content that African American achievers tend to "oppose" as they fashion a social identity. The challenge for educational theory and practice is to get a handle on the dynamics of situational contexts in ways that will help young people do this in school. The challenge for theory is the situativity of social identification. The challenge is to account for the special situativity for African American students and other students of color whose social identity is discursively constructed in school settings that are beset by racially stigmatizing practices and discourses.

Despite a stigmatized status of Blackness in school and society, African American youth may still maintain a strong integrated sense of self-worth, efficacy, and agency. Recent theory has begun to elucidate the relationship between identity and achievement and has attempted to contextualize academic identity in the actual social, cultural, and political fields that young people experience in and out of school (e.g., Flores-Gonzáles, 2002; Nasir & Saxe, 2003; Perry, 2002; Stevens, 2002; Weiler, 2000; Yon, 2000) as well as in the active discursive interactions in cultural settings (e.g., Carbaugh, 1996; Murrell, 2007; Sfard & Prusak, 2005; Wortham, 2001, 2003, 2006). The more specific social-cultural context to examine is the social structure of the school and the structure of social environments. The social structure of the school is co-created by at least two major sets of factors. One set of factors emanates from the institutional policies, procedures, and restrictions (such as tracking, ability grouping, school codes, etc.). The other set of factors is the dynamic social organization of students and teachers—how people sort themselves out in affiliation groups as acts of individual and collective identity. This set of factors often manifests as a set of social categories—jocks, nerds, dopers, preppies, etc. (every generation and setting has their own unique set of terms, but many of the positionalities of the categories can be found in virtually every school setting)—that are differentially positioned to both school authority and to achievement-oriented behaviors.

THEORETICAL FRAMEWORK

As was seen in the previous section, the research literature on identity and Black achievement clearly does suggest that the developmental task of forming an integrated ego-identity is more complicated and therefore more difficult for African American youth. Undoubtedly, there is a greater array of social stressors to the developmental tasks of finding meaning and identity formation for African American youth. One of the more carefully articulated adaptations of this idea is Boykin's triple quandary theory (Boykin, 1986). According to this theory, African Americans have three social identities to negotiate: (1) an African American social identity organized by cultural values shared among the African American community, (2) a "minority" social identity by virtue of being part of the larger group of historically oppressed and marginalized groups in America, and (3) an American social identity organized by shared culturally mainstream core values of middle-class White America, including individualism and competitiveness. In Boykin's theory, comparative decrements in school performance can be explained by the additional stress of having to negotiate three social identities. This experience contrasts with European American peers who do not have to make cultural identity changes to be successful socially and academically (Irvine, 1990). In any event, the likelihood that negative racial self-perceptions and collective perceptions influence school success is greater for African American children and youth (Baker, 1999; Howard, 2003; Murrell, 1999; Phinney et al., 1997; Stevens, 1997). Let us turn now to the issue of how the concept of oppositionality can be further developed to account for achievement of African American learners.

How does *oppositionality* fit? We know that there is *some* aspect of *oppositionality* that must figure into the academic identity development for African American learners. We also know that ethnically and racially situated forms of self-expression are in part the basis for establishing *positionality*—that racial identity is, unavoidably, a component of academic identity formation in African American learners. What we need to account for is *positionality* as a process of social identification and which particular images, meanings, and negative ascriptions young African Americans "oppose" in their schooling experience. To explore what that means, let us further clarify what is meant by positionality.

Put simply, one's *positionality* is a situationally projected social identity. It is the projected social self we strive to project and maintain. It is how we anchor our social identity in the specifics of a given situation or frame. The unique positionalities of African Americans with respect to their school behavior are generally misread and misinterpreted by the adults who teach them and study them. They are misread by researchers who investigate Black achievement and have an inherent assumption that the cultural expressions and dispositions of African American youth toward aspects of school actually represent their dispositions toward academic success. These youth actually modify their self-ascriptions as academically oriented according to peer group situation (Carter, 2003; O'Connor, 1997).

Now, the practices or behaviors young people tag as "acting Black" or "acting White" are situational commentary on practices having to do with how young people position themselves with their affinity groups, adults, and wider society, and not on their core sensibilities about academics. They are not necessarily expressions of academic identity but are more likely situational positionalities according to context (Murrell,

2007). Similarly, Carter (2005) argued that young people of color employ expressions such as "acting White," "acting Black," or "acting Spanish" for *cultural reasons,* not *academic ones.* She stated, "They [young people of color] use their racial and ethnic identities to facilitate in-group solidarity and to assert various cultural symbols of pride and self worth, not as signs of opposition to conventional formulas for success" (p. vi). So the refinement of the theory requires recognition of the difference between *social affiliation* and *academic commitment* as distinct motivations. Failure to see this distinction may result in misreading the motives of young people in school contexts. Among researchers, this misreading takes the form of conflating the cultural expressions and dispositions that African American youth may express toward schooling with what they actually do. The analogous misread by educators often occurs at the point that African American students exhibit low academic performance and their ethnic and racially situated expressions of identity are immediately interpreted as a rejection of academic excellence (Carter, 2005; Murrell, 2007). In any event, it is clear that a more sophisticated rendering of the construct of oppositionality is required to fully account for Black achievement and identity.

The notion of oppositional stance or identity, although not a universal phenomenon among Black students with respect to White school behaviors, still figures importantly in the situational expression of social identity (i.e., positionality) as well as the developmental task of identity formation in the classical Eriksonian sense. Oppositional stance is actually a developmental feature of adolescence. The natural process of youthful opposition to adult meaning systems is called *individuation* and is a normal part of adolescent development. Hence, some degree of acting in opposition to adult authority is to be expected among all young people. Opposition is a situational construct, not a permanent, personality-defining category. But without further refinement, oppositionality as an ascribed feature can only explain failure and underachievement of African American learners—not their success and academic excellence. While oppositionality may, under some circumstances, account for disinvestment and disengagement in school, it does not account for enabling behaviors of scholastic investment and engagement. In other words, oppositionality cannot explain success, because absence of student opposition is not the same as success.

To account for achievement effort, I look to the agency young people exert in the expression of their cultural selves. Projecting a deliberate social self, a *positionality* is an *act of identity*. These acts of identity, especially as exhibited by African American students, do not necessarily indicate or reveal students core values about academics or education. In conjunction with agency, I look to the social-cultural contexts of schooling as canvasses for the projection of social identity. Of particular interest are the ways in which African American students are positioned and repositioned in terms of racially stigmatizing images, discourses, and practices present in the cultural scene. In short, the need is to theorize and understand the formation of *academic identity* among African American youth. An *academic identity* is a form of social identity in which the learner projects, maintains, and improvises an image of self as a learner— usually as an academically able individual because it is rare that a person wants to be known as "not smart." *Academic identities* are socially situated and are mediated by what happens in the social practices of schooling.

Mapping the formation of academic identity among African American learners can be accomplished with the notion of situated identity and its three levels of social identity development: (1) the *intrapersonal* identity development process (i.e., the formation of ego-identity) as theorized by Erikson (1963, 1968), (2) the *interpersonal* identity development process of social identification (i.e., the adoption of a positionality) as theorized by Goffman (1959), and (3) the *transpersonal* identity process of individuals *gaining the agency to improvise* their own expressions of self in dynamic interaction with others who may attempt to ascribe unwanted and ego-degrading projections to the individual (Murrell, 2007).

It is the third level of transpersonal identity processes that is of greatest interest here in unpacking African American achievement. This level of social identification concerns what goes on in the cultural and discourse practices of schools concerning race and the worthiness of African American learners. This is the sphere in which stereotypes make African American learners vulnerable. This vulnerability may be in the formal frames, such as in the instance of stereotype threat (Steele, 1997) as well as in informal

racialized talk that often goes unrecognized through the ongoing discursive practices of schooling (Lewis, 2003). Recent work of several sociologists and educational scholars has demonstrated that cultural racism in the form *discourse practices*—the social practices of communication and everyday human interaction in which culture is most frequently and deeply expressed—is prevalent in school contexts (e.g., Alton-Lee, Nuthall, & Patrick, 1993; Bush, 2004; Lewis, 2003; Pollock, 2004; Tatum, 1997; Van Ausdale & Feagin, 2001; Wortham, 2001, 2003, 2006). The implication is that despite the best efforts of teachers to create a socially and culturally nurturing environment in their classroom, there nonetheless, may be, discursive practices in the school communicating visages of Black inferiority and White privilege that negatively affect African American students and other ethnic minority students.

The Value-Added of the Framework

There are at least two critical factors left out of the complete accounting for academic success for African American learners—both of which involve the development of *agency* and a cultural and social intelligence on how to position oneself in settings complicated by racism and forms of ethnic and cultural stigmatizing in school practices, policy, and pedagogy. One of these critical pieces of the picture is the *agency* young people develop in asserting the integrity of their identity and modes of self-expression, despite the attempts of others to negatively reposition them. The other is the identity work of the adults who work with African American learners.

School success among African American students depends on this agency and the subsequent ability to maintain identity integrity despite a variety of racially and culturally disaffirming discursive practices they experience in school. *Agency* is a critical capacity in the development of academically successful African American youth. The situated-mediated identity theory explanation is that educational attainment is much less a matter of an individual disidentification with school and more a matter of the school context's disidentification with the student.

According to the situated-mediated identity framework, the manner in which school culture misreads or negatively regards the positionalities taken up by young African American students is only part of the story of academic success for some and academic failure for others. The already difficult developmental task of identity formation that all young people must face (Erikson, 1963, 1968) is more complicated and nuanced for African American youth. For African American learners and other learners of African descent in American society, the process of identity formation is further complicated by having to negotiate conditions of racism (Spencer & Markstrom-Adams, 1990).

The situated-mediated identity framework integrates two dimensions of identity development: (1) the critical developmental task of all young people—*identity formation* posited by the bio-psycho-social theory of Erik Erikson and (2) *social identification* as a learner or student. The core proposition of the conceptual framework here is that Black achievement is mediated by the specific forms of social identification experienced by Black youth in the complex intersections of racial, economic, gender, and class privilege in American society. Concurrent with resolving conflicts with ego-identity implications are those conflicts of social identity—struggling with one's sense of place in the immediate daily social settings of school. In other words, identity formation is a more complicated pattern for African American youth and is represented by the *positionalities* (i.e., situated social identities) they take up to make sense of themselves in these complex intersections of race, class, gender, and privilege in a variety of contexts (Boykin, 1986; Murrell, 2007). Their *acts of identity*—that is, their situationally specific forms of social identification in particular contexts—result in positionalities that mediate their school performance as well as their social-emotional development. The concluding section of this chapter examines this process further using the situated-mediated theory.

This brings us to the second factor missing from the academic success/failure equation—the agency and awareness demonstrated by adults in promoting the development and well-being of students. This second factor constitutes the "deep cultural competence" (Murrell, 2005) required of teachers, counselors, parents, and other adults to create a supportive cultural, social, and intellectual environment for learners of color grappling with the formation of their academic identities. Both factors—*agency of adults* and *agency of young people*—must be accounted for simultaneously in our efforts to explain the academic success and failure of African American students in public schooling. To avoid being a degrading force on the development of achievement identities, the adults who work with African American learners must examine their own racialized positionality.

Situated-Mediated Identity Theory

The purpose of the situated-mediated identity framework is to orient both research and practice to the processes of identity that mediate sustained academic engagement, effort, and success optimism. The major components are summarized in Table 6.1.

Situated identity, in simple terms, means that our sense of self, or identity, is not a static, unitary entity but is better thought of as being fluid and situationally expressed. In contrast to the psychological formulation of racial identity as a stable, staged-developed entity (Cross, 1971, 1991; Helms, 1993), this framework posits racial identity formation as a process reflective of, and situated in, social and political-historical struggles. In contemporary developmental theory, identity is a state that is achieved in adolescence and successful identity development is presumed to conclude in adolescence with the achievement of a relatively stable set of values,

TABLE 6.1   Framework for Situated-Mediated Identity Theory

Type of Identity Growth	Type of Social Context	Type of Cultural Practices
Situated identity	Social-cultural community	Primary socialization
Positionality	Social-symbolic community (figured world)	Secondary socialization
Agency	Community of practice activity setting	Improvisational self-determination

SOURCE: From *Race, Culture, and Schooling: Identities of Achievement in Multicultural Urban Schools* by P. Murrell, 2007. Copyright 2007 by Lawrence Erlbaum Associates Inc. Reprinted with permisson.

roles, and self-images that the adolescent arrived at through volitional choices (Erikson, 1963, 1968, 1980). Identity is constructed by the individual as the result of successfully resolving a series of psychodynamic dilemmas (Erikson, 1963, 1968). Situated-mediated identity theory enlarges on the psychobiosocial notion of Erikson's theory by focusing on identity as it is socially mediated and determined by our intentional action—identity is mediated by culture as well as one's own agency (cf. Côté & Levine, 2002). In the situated-mediated framework, identity is our agency in activity—who we are is constituted by what we choose to do and how we choose to invest in that doing.

In this framework, identity is dynamically situated in, and mediated by, the fabric of human networks and social situations individuals participate in (Bakhtin, 1981, 1986; Vygotsky, 1978, 1986). Situated identity is represented in the first column of the first row of Table 6.1. The cultural material available to individuals constructing their identity is a product of historical time, cultural setting, and geographic location. Identity incorporates the historical and cultural development of symbols in the individual but also the legacy of lived social practices and discourses. Social identities are improvised by individuals both at the local culture level (designated as the social symbolic world in Table 6.1) and at the level of activity settings within school (designed as the community of practice in Table 6.1). These are represented by the middle and third rows of Table 6.1, respectively. The degree and success of their self-improvisation depends on their degree of agency.

The developmental levels of social identification are as important to understand as the contexts of local peer culture and school culture, because these contexts "work" together on the individual. The first involves *affiliation*, where a young person expresses or acts with reference to an affinity group. *Affiliation* with a group is the first level of social identification. Young people affiliate with other young people and not with institutions. The second level of social identification is *positionality*, defined earlier. Affiliation often involves the young person appropriating the "cultural material" of the reference group—including forms of talk, behavior, interests, etc., to take on a particular positionality. Taking on cultural forms of the group to represent oneself—exhibiting *positionality*—is the second act of social identification. In this way, identity is anchored to a reference group and the local culture created by the groups' activity. The third level involves *agency*, where the individual uses and *improvises* cultural forms to exhibit the positionality he or she chooses.

IMPLICATIONS FOR TEACHING AND LEARNING

The Situativity of Racial Identity in Academic Identity

Why is this situated identity framework an advance over the contemporary perspectives on racial identity (e.g., Cross, 1971, 1991; Helms, 1993; Tatum, 1997)? It is a way of understanding the dynamic situativity of racial identity in the social contexts that give it reality. The important main idea here is that most African Americans do not walk around with "being Black" in their heads, but rather the sense of racial identity of "being a Black person" is evoked by experience in a situational event. Let me explain this with a couple of personal examples.

As a Black male growing up during the modern Civil Rights movement in the 1960s, I noted (and still notice) whenever I enter an unfamiliar social setting, whether or not there is another Black person in the scene. This is an example of the type of instance (here, an unfamiliar social setting) that will invoke the sensibility of being African American—that "activates," if you will, my racial identity. It is the particular social frame work together with my personal history of being Black that work together to evoke an awareness of being Black. Not only does the situativity of a setting evoke the awareness, but it also evokes particular strategies of coping and self-representation (called positioning) regarding how I want to construe myself as a Black man in this milieu. The situativity of social identity, and awareness of racial identity, are underscored by the fact that, most of the time, in the absence of a race-relevant situational context, I do not walk around with "being Black" in my head. Yet any particular moment and situation can evoke a historically shaped, experientially unique racial identity. And this is not to say that positioning requires an explicit awareness of the race dynamics in a cultural scene.

Let us look at another example more germane to racial identity development that directly involves the methodology of the doll studies. A graphic illustration of the situativity of identity expression is available in an interesting excerpt from an award-winning film by an African American young woman. Kiri Davis's (2006) mini-documentary features an exploration of race and an excerpt in which she replicated a portion of the doll studies methodology with young children. African American children are positioned, one at a time, at a table containing two dolls—one clearly Black and the other White—and asked to express their preference. She asked several questions: (1) "Can you show me the doll you would like best or would like to play with?" (2) "Can you show me the doll that is the nice doll?" (3) "Now, can you show me the doll that looks like you?" In the video, you see a seemly heart-wrenching moment when one of the children indicating that the Black doll was bad and the White doll was nice now indicates that it is the Black doll that looks most like her. The intended effect, indeed the predominant first reaction of my graduate students in human development, is a lament about how awful it is that children see themselves so negatively and how 50 years later we still have not advanced. But if we examine the exchanges closely, we would not automatically infer that the children who responded this way have negative racial identities. Viewed through the lens of the theoretical perspective I am presenting here, we might see instead the importance of situativity in interpreting what these responses really mean developmentally. A closer clinical read of the exchanges between the interviewer and the children suggests an interpretation alternative to one of "negative racial identity."

Consider a developmental analysis using the situated identity framework that would first ask what children's responses about the "niceness" or "badness" of the dolls actually mean in this context. When a child is asked "which is the nice doll" and "which is the bad doll" in a setting that feels like some kind of assessment, what cultural material do you imagine is available to a 5- or 6-year-old child regarding "niceness" and "badness"? Even if the only cultural exposure had were Disney films, this would have been more than enough cultural knowledge needed to accurately infer that light is good and dark is bad. Obviously, there are many more messages in popular media (including children's books) that confirm this relation, which children as young as 1 or 2 years old are exposed to. The responses given by the children might reflect an intelligence of recognizing relations and meanings in the wider social world, especially if the interpretative frame is one of assessment.

A closer analysis might next ask what interpretive frame the children were using to respond to the interviewer's questions. When a child is seated at a desk in front of an adult they do not know well, or at least as well as a parent or family member (e.g., a day care teacher), what does it mean to be asked questions about props (i.e., two dolls) placed in front of them? How responders construe questions depends on what they take to be the framing (Goffman, 1974). There are at least two possible framings for the interaction with children: (1) Is this a test? and (2) Is this a conversation about my preferences? If the assumed frame in the doll studies is the "test" frame, then the children's selections of the White doll in response to the questions would be consistent with what is conventionally interpreted as intelligence, as the children are drawing on the informational material that popular media has made an accurate correlational assessment—namely, the White is good, and Black is bad interpretation frame.

Whether or not one agrees with this interpretation, it is clear that cultural and social situativity are important in interpreting human behavior, especially behavior representing self in a complex social scene. Before one can interpret what is expressed, one needs to know the frame. The implication for understanding the identity development of young people in school settings is then that we are not looking for a *state of being* as much as we are seeking to understand a *process of development*. More concretely, we are looking at development of young people's *agency in doing*—their developing capacity for engaging and negotiating the demands of their lives, particularly schooling. Processes of self-representation are important in identity formation, and identity formation is critical to children's motive structures. A person's identity, in this framework, is never "completed"—but rather is in a process of "becoming," continuously shaped and expressed by how an individual situates himself or herself in the interactional dynamics of social settings. An identity is a work in process, but can be mediated in predictable and positive ways if the social context is constructed in ways supportive of development.

Conclusion

To conclude, let us return to the orienting question: What does it mean to be *both* African American and an academic achiever in different school contexts? To be both African American and a school achiever means that developing a healthy (i.e., ego integrated) racial identity is not an option but a necessity. Unfortunately, this is the developmental task for which African American young people experience the greatest vulnerability from the forms of racism in American public life and public school (Johnson, 2002; Johnston & Nicholls, 1995; Kao, 2000; Murrell, 1999; Neville & Lilly, 2000; Spencer, 2001; Spencer, Brookins, et al., 1985). This in turn means that it is the responsibility of adults to identify and remove these vulnerabilities.

Psychological and emotional well-being is significantly challenged for African American learners in American public schools. Research indicates that the presence of nascent racism is a health concern for African Americans. Racism as social toxin does have health implications for African American learners as well as adults (e.g., Krieger & Sidney, 1996; Landrine & Klonoff, 1996; Nyborg & Curry, 2003). Attenuating the forms of racism that diminish school success is a mental health concern, not just an educational or pedagogical one. So what it means to be an African American achiever is to be one who has developed a means countering the mental health threat posed by both nascent racism and uninspiring school contexts.

Learning attainment and school success is really a whole-being enterprise requiring attention to how the social and cultural climate supports or negates development of African American learners (e.g., Grantham & Ford, 2003; Mercado, 2001; Nir, 2001; Oyserman, Bybee, & Terry; 2003; Rodriguez, Bustamente-Jones, Pang, & Park, 2004; Roth, 2004; Rowley & Moore, 2002).

In closing, what we are called upon to do involves a three-pronged focus on development. One of these prongs involves attention to the social, cultural, and symbolic environment in school settings so that the social toxins of racism and exclusionism do not pose a barrier to the development of young people. The second prong involves an inquiry and interrogation of how young people manage and negotiate the developmental demands of the social, cultural, and symbolic worlds they inhabit, both in school and out. The third prong involves the identity work that adults must in engage in as part of their instructional and professional work with youth of diverse backgrounds. Knowing that social identity of any given young person the result of both individually projected and collective imposed images, teachers (and other adults) need to know more than just the cultural practices and positionings of their students. We need to also be aware of the positionality we project in those interactions with young people and realize that their particular patterns of self-expression, self-representation, and even opposition towards us, may all be anchored to the positionality we chose.

References

Alton-Lee, A., Nuthall, G., & Patrick, J. (1993). Reframing classroom research: A lesson from the private world of children. *Harvard Educational Review, 63*(1), 50–84.

Anyon, J. (2005). *Radical possibilities: Public policy, urban education and a new social movement.* New York: Routledge.

Baker, J. (1999). Teacher-student interaction in urban at-risk classroom: Differential behavior, relationship quality and student satisfaction with school. *Elementary School Journal, 100*(1), 58–70.

Bakhtin, M. M. (1981). *The dialogic imagination: Four essays by M. M. Bakhtin* (M. E. Holquist, Ed., C. Emerson & M. Holquist, Trans.). Austin: University of Texas Press.

Bakhtin, M. M. (1986). *Speech genres and other late essays* (C. Emerson & M. Holquist, Eds., Vern W. McGee, Trans.). Austin: University of Texas Press.

Boykin, A. W. (1986). The triple quandary and the schooling of Afro-American children. In U. Neisser (Ed.), *The school achievement of minority children* (pp. 57–92). Hillsdale, NJ: Lawrence Erlbaum.

Boykin, A. W., & Toms, F. D. (1985). Black child socialization. In H. P. McAdoo & J. L. McAdoo (Eds.), *Black children: Social, educational and parental environments* (pp. 159–17). Beverly Hills, CA: Sage.

Brofennbrenner, U. (1979). Contexts of child rearing: Problems and prospects. *American Psychologist, 34*(10), 844–850.

Brown v. Board of Education, 347 U.S. 483 (1954).

Burnett, M. N., & Sisson, K. (1995). Doll studies revisited: A question of validity. *Journal of Black Psychology, 12,* 19–29.

Bush, M. E. L. (2004). *Breaking the code of good intentions: Everyday forms of whiteness.* New York: Rowman & Littlefield.

Carbaugh, D. (1996). *Situating selves; the communication of social identities in American scenes.* Albany: State University of New York Press.

Carter, P. L. (2003). "Black" cultural capital, status positioning, and schooling conflicts for low-income African American youth. *Social Problems, 50*(1), 136–155.

Carter, P. L. (2005). *Keepin' it real: School success beyond black and white.* New York: Oxford University Press.

Clark, K. B., & Clark, M. K. (1939). The development of consciousness of self and the emergence of racial identity in Negro children. *Journal of Social Psychology, 10,* 591–599.

Clark, K. B., & Clark, M. K. (1940). Skin color as a factor in racial identification of Negro preschool children. *Journal of Social Psychology, 11,* 159–169.

Coleman, J., Campbell, E., Hobson, C., McPartland, J., Mood, A., Weinfeld, F. D., et al. (1966). *Equality of educational opportunity.* Washington, DC: Department of Health, Education and Welfare.

Conchas, G. Q. (2006). *The color of success: Race and high achieving urban youth.* New York: Teachers College Press.

Côté, J. E., & Levine, C. G. (2002). *Identity formation, agency and culture.* Mahwah, NJ: Lawrence Erlbaum.

Cross, W. (1971). Negro-to-Black conversion experiences: Toward a psychology of Black liberation. *Black World, 20*(9), 13–27.

Cross, W. (1991). *Shades of black: Diversity in African American identity.* Philadelphia: Temple University Press.

The Cyril Burt Affair. (2007). Retrieved September 1, 2007, from www.indiana.edu/~intell/burtaffair.shtml

Davis, K. (2006). *A girl like me* [video documentary]. Retrieved September 1, 2006, from http://video.google.com/videoplay?docid=1091431409617440489

Deutsch, M. (1963). The disadvantaged child and the learning process. In A. H. Passow (Ed.), *Education in depressed areas.* New York: Teachers College Press.

Deustch, M., Katz, I., & Jensen, A. R. (Eds.). (1968). *Social class, race, and psychological development.* New York: Holt, Rinehart & Winston.

Erikson, E. H. (1963). *Childhood and society* (2nd ed.). New York: W. W. Norton.

Erikson, E. H. (1968). *Identity, youth, and crisis.* New York: W. W. Norton.

Erikson, E. H. (1980). *Identity and the life cycle* (2nd ed.). New York: W. W. Norton.

Flores-Gonzáles, N. (2002). *School kids/street kids: Identity development in Latino students.* New York: Teachers College Press.

Fordham, S. (1996). *Blacked out! Dilemmas of race identity and success at Capital High.* Chicago: University of Chicago Press.

Fordham, S., & Ogbu, J. (1986). Black students' school success: Coping with the burden of acting white. *The Urban Review, 18,* 176–206.

Gibson, M. A. (1997). Conclusion: Complicating the immigrant/involuntary minority typology. *Anthropology in Education Quarterly, 28*(3), 431–454.

Goffman, E. (1959). *The presentation of self in everyday life.* New York: Anchor.

Goffman, E. (1978). *Frame analysis.* Cambridge, MA: Harvard University Press.

Grantham, T., & Ford, D. (2003). Beyond self-concept and self esteem: Racial identity and gifted African American students. *High School Journal, 87*(1), 18–29.

Helms, J. E. (Ed.). (1993). *Black and white racial identity.* New York: Praeger.

Herrnstein, R. J., & Murray, C. (1994). *Bell curve: Intelligence and class structure in American life.* New York: Free Press.

Hilliard, A. (2003). No mystery: Closing the achievement gap between Africans and Excellence. In T. Perry, C. Steele, & A. G. Hilliard III (Eds.), *Young, gifted, and Black: Promoting high achievement among African American students* (pp. 131–167). Boston: Beacon Press.

Hilliard, A. G., III. (1992). Behavioral style, culture, and teaching and learning. *Journal of Negro Education, 61*(3), 370–377.

Holland, D., Lachicotte, W., Jr., Skinner, D., & Cain, C. (1998). *Identity and agency in cultural worlds.* Cambridge, MA: Harvard University Press.

Horvat, E., & Lewis, K. S. (2003). Reassessing the "Burden of 'Acting White'": The importance of peer groups in managing academic success. *Sociology of Education, 76*(4), 265–280.

Horvat, E., & O'Conner, C. (2006). *Beyond acting white: Reframing the debate on Black student achievement.* New York: Rowman & Littlefield.

Howard, T. (2003). "A tug of war for our minds": African American high school students' perceptions of their academic identities and college aspirations. *High School Journal, 87*(1), 4–17.

Irvine, J. (1990). *Black students and school failure.* Westport, CT: Greenwood Press.

Jenkins, R. (2004). *Social identity* (2nd ed.). New York: Routledge.

Jensen, A. R. (1969). How much can we boost IQ and scholastic achievement? *Harvard Educational Review, 39*, 1–123.

Johnson, R. (2002). Racial identity from an African American perspective. *Journal of Cultural Diversity, 9*(3), 73–78.

Johnston, P., & Nicholls, J. (1995). Voices we want to hear and voices we don't. *Theory Into Practice, 34*(2), 94–100.

Kao, G. (2000). Group images and possible selves among adolescence: Linking stereotypes to expectations by race and ethnicity. *Sociological Forum, 15*(3), 407–430.

Kozol, J. (2005). *The shame of the nation: The restoration of apartheid schooling in America.* New York: Three Rivers Press.

Krieger, N., & Sidney, S. (1996). Racial discrimination and blood pressure: The CARDIA study of young black and white adults. *American Journal of Public Health, 86*, 1370–1378.

Ladson-Billings, G. (2006). From the achievement gap to the education debt: Understanding achievement in U.S. schools. *Educational Researcher, 35*(7), 3–12.

La Ferla, R. (2003, December 28). Generation E.A.: Ethnically ambiguous. *New York Times.*

Landrine, H., & Klonoff, E. A. (1996). The schedule of racist events: A measure of racial discrimination and a study of its negative physical and mental health consequences. *Journal of Black Psychology, 22*, 144–168.

Lewin, T. (2000, June 25). Growing up, growing apart. *New York Times*, sec. 1, p. 1.

Lewis, A. E. (2003). *Race in the schoolyard: Negotiating the color line in classrooms and communities.* New Brunswick, NJ: Rutgers University Press.

McWhorter, J. (2001). *Losing the race: Self-sabotage in Black America.* New York: Perennial.

Mehan, H., Hubbard, L., & Villaneuva, I. (1994). Forming academic identities: Accommodation without assimilation among involuntary minorities. *Anthropology and Education Quarterly, 25*(2), 91–117.

Mercado, C. (2001). The learner: "Race," "ethnicity" and linguistic difference. In V. Richardson (Ed.), *Handbook of research on teaching* (4th ed., pp. 298–330). Washington, DC: American Educational Research Association.

Moynihan, D. P. (1965). *The Negro family: The case for national action.* Washington, DC: U.S. Department of Labor, Office of Planning and Research.

Murrell, P. C., Jr. (1999). Class and race in negotiating identity. In A. Garrod, J. Ward, T. L. Robinson, & R. Kilkenny (Eds.), *Souls looking back: Life stories of growing up Black* (pp. 3–14). New York: Routledge.

Murrell, P. C., Jr. (2002). *African-centered pedagogy: Developing schools of achievement for African American children.* New York: State University of New York Press.

Murrell, P. C., Jr. (2005). *Building professional learning communities of urban educators.* World Conference on Urban Education, Manchester, UK.

Murrell, P. C., Jr. (2007). *Race, culture and schooling: Identities of achievement in multicultural urban schools.* Mahwah, NJ: Lawrence Erlbaum.

Nasir, N. S., & Saxe, G. B. (2003). Ethnic and academic identities: A cultural practice perspective on emerging tensions and their management in the lives of minority students. *Educational Researcher, 32*, 14–18.

Neville, H., & Lilly, R. (2000). The relationship between racial identity cluster profiles and psychological distress among African American college students. *Journal of Multicultural Counseling and Development, 28*, 194–207.

Nir, A. (2001). Planning for tracking: Some implications for students' academic self-efficacy. *Educational Planning, 13*(3), 41–54.

Noguera, P. (2003). *City schools and the American dream: Reclaiming the promise of public education.* New York: Teachers College Press.

Nyborg, V., & Curry, J. (2003). The impact of perceived racism: Psychological symptoms among African American boys. *Journal of Clinical Child and Adolescent Psychology, 32*, 258–266.

O'Connor, C. (1997). Dispositions toward (collective) struggle and educational resilience in the inner city: A case study of six African American high school students. *American Educational Research Journal, 34*(4), 593–629.

O'Connor, C. (2001). Making sense of the complexity of social identity in relation to achievement: A sociological challenge in the new millennium. *Sociology of Education, 74*(extra issue), Current of thought: Sociology of education at the dawn of the 21st century, 159–168.

Ogbu, J. (1978). *Minority education and caste: The American system in cross-cultural perspective.* New York: Academic Press.

Ogbu, J. (1985). A cultural ecology of competence among inner-city Blacks. In M. B. Spencer, G. K. Brookins, & W. R. Allen (Eds.), *Beginnings: The social and affective development of Black children* (pp. 45–66). Mahwah, NJ: Lawrence Erlbaum.

Ogbu, J. (2003). *Black American students in an affluent suburb: A study of academic disengagement.* Mahwah, NJ: Lawrence Erlbaum.

Oyserman, D., Bybee, D., & Terry, K. (2003). Gendered racial identity and involvement with school. *Self and Identity, 2,* 307–324.

Perry, P. (2002). *Shades of white: White kids and racial identities in high school.* Chapel Hill, NC: Duke University Press.

Perry, T., Steele, C., & Hilliard, A. G., III. (Eds.). (2003). *Young, gifted and black: Promoting high academic achievement among African American students.* Boston: Routledge.

Phinney, J., Cantu, C. L., & Kurtz, D. A. (1997). Ethnic and American identity as predictors of self-esteem among African-American, Latino and White adolescents. *Journal of Youth and Adolescence, 26*(2), 165–186.

Pollock, M. (2004). *Colormute: Race talk dilemmas in an American school.* Princeton, NJ: Princeton University Press.

Rodriguez, J., Bustamente-Jones, E., Pang, V., & Park, C. (2004). Promoting academic achievement and identity development among diverse high school students. *High School Journal, 87*(3), 44–53.

Roth, W.-M. (2004). Identity as dialectic: Re/making self in urban school. *Mind, Culture, and Activity, 11*(1), 48–69.

Rowley, S. J., & Moore, J. (2002). Racial identity in context for the gifted African American student. *Roeper Review, 24*(2), 63–67.

Sfard, A., & Prusak, A. (2005). Telling identities: In search of an analytic tool for investigating learning as a culturally shaped activity. *Educational Researcher, 34*(4), 14–22.

Spencer, M. B. (1985). Cultural cognition and social cognition as identity correlates of Black children's personal-social development. In M. B. Spencer, G. K. Brookins, & W. R. Allen, (Eds.), *Beginnings: The social and affective development of Black children* (pp. 215–230). Mahwah, NJ: Lawrence Erlbaum.

Spencer, M. B. (1987). Black children's ethnic identity formation: Risk and resilience of castelike minorities. In J. S. Phinney & M. J. Rotheram (Eds.), *Children's ethnic socialization: Pluralism and development* (pp. 103–116). Newbury Park, CA: Sage.

Spencer, M. B. (1999). Social and cultural influences on school adjustment: The application of an identity-focused cultural ecological perspective. *Educational Psychologist, 34*(1), 43–57.

Spencer, M. B. (2001). Identity and school adjustment: Revisiting the "acting white" theory. *Educational Psychologist, 36*(1), 21–31.

Spencer, M. B., Brookins, G. K., & Allen, W. R. (Eds.). (1985). *Beginnings: The social and affective development of Black children.* Mahwah, NJ: Lawrence Erlbaum.

Spencer, M. B., Cunningham, M., & Swanson, D. P. (1985). Identity as coping: Adolescent African American male's adaptive responses to high-risk environment. In H. W. Harris, H. C. Blue, & E. E. H. Griffith (Eds.), *Racial and ethnic identity: Psychological development and creative expression* (pp. 31–52). New York: Routledge.

Spencer, M. B., & Markstrom-Adams, C. (1990). Identity processes among racial and ethnic minority children in America. *Child Development, 61,* 290–310.

Steele, C. (1997). A threat in the air. How stereotypes shape intellectual identity and performance. *American Psychologist, 52*(6), 613–629.

Steele, S. (2000). A dream deferred: Why the Black-White achievement gap won't close. *American Experimental Quarterly, Spring,* 31–40.

Stevens, J. W. (1997). African female adolescence identity development: A three-dimensional perspective. *Child Welfare, 76*(1), 145–173.

Stevens, J. W. (2002). *Smart and sassy: The strengths of inner-city black girls.* New York: Oxford University Press.

Stevenson, H. C., Jr., Best, G., Cassidy, E. F., & McCabe, D. (2003). Remembering culture: Roots of culturally relevant anger. In H. C. Stevenson (Ed.), *Playing with anger: Teaching coping skills to African American boys through athletics and culture* (pp. 21–87). Westport, CT: Greenwood.

Stinson, D. W. (2007). African American male adolescents, schooling (and mathematics): Deficiency, rejection, and achievement. *Review of Educational research, 76*(40), 477–506.

Tatum, B. (1997). *"Why are all the Black kids sitting together in the cafeteria?" A psychologist explains the development of racial identity.* New York: Kirkus Associates.

Tilly, C. (2006). *Identities, boundaries, and social ties.* Boulder, CO: Paradigm.

Van Ausdale, D., & Feagin, J. R. (2001). *The first R: How children learn race and racism.* New York: Rowman & Littlefield.

Vaughan, G. (1986). Social change and racial identity: Issues in the use of pictures and doll measures. *Psychology, 38*(3), 359–370.

Vygotsky, L. (1978). *Thought and language.* Cambridge, MA: MIT Press.

Vygotsky, L. (1986). *Mind in society: The development of higher psychological processes.* Cambridge, MA: Harvard University Press.

Weiler, J. D. (2000). *Codes and contradictions: Race, gender identity and schooling.* Albany: State University of New York Press.

West, C. (1993). *Race matters.* Boston: Beacon Press.

Williams, B. (1996). *Closing the achievement gap.* Alexandria, VA: Association for Supervision and Curriculum Development.

Wortham, E. F. (2001). *Narratives in action.* New York: Teachers College Press.

Wortham, E. F. (2003). Interactionally situated cognition: A classroom example. *Cognitive Science, 25,* 37–66.

Wortham, E. F. (2006). *Learning identity: The joint emergence of social identification and academic learning.* New York: Cambridge University Press.

Yon, D. (2000). *Elusive culture: Schooling, race, and identity in global times.* Albany: State University of New York Press.

7

CULTURAL COMMUNITY PRACTICES AS URBAN CLASSROOM RESOURCES

Yolanda J. Majors

Sana Ansari

A growing psychological literature supports the importance of racial, ethnic, or cultural socialization for African American youth faced with major social and academic challenges—
especially within distressed urban communities (Bowman & Howard, 1985; Hughes & Chen,
1999; McNeil, 1999; Orellana & Bowman, 2003; Peters, 1985; Rotheram & Phinney, 1987; Spencer,
1983; Spencer, Swanson, & Cunningham, 1991; Stevenson & Davis, 2004). These race-related, quantitative studies, while tending to focus on family networks, provide valuable insight into the processes
through which African American youth acquire salient values, identity, knowledge, and social and
survival competencies. For several decades now, these studies have contributed to how we might come
to understand the nature of positive and negative, direct and indirect influences that are available in
the home lives of African American adolescents, particularly those residing within urban and impoverished communities.

Little qualitative attention, however, has been given to community social spaces[1] and networks outside the family, which offer supportive structures of cultural socialization that shape and frame reasoning. Far less is understood as to how, through participation within such networks, individuals
acquire tools for problem posing and problem solving within academic contexts. For the most part,
research on reasoning has been highly reductionist, both theoretically and methodologically (Kuhn,
1990). These reductionist models do not account for language and culture, but rather attempt to iso-
late reasoning, "focusing on deductive (general to particular, syllogistic reasoning) rather than inductive, (open-ended reasoning that draws general conclusions), for example" (p. 32). As an alternative
to such models, grounded research on reasoning that occurs in cultural community settings takes on
the nuances of the everyday and those complicating factors of problem posing and problem solving
that are a part of being human. From this perspective, and with regard to problem-solving processes
within oral discourses, cultural community practices offer a real-world view of the cognitive tools
individuals within cultures bring to bear on knowledge construction, complex ideas that depend on
linguistic expression, and higher-order thinking and reasoning.

In addition to providing support to thinking, such tools function as part of a transformative framework for education. According to Banks (1998, 2001, 2003), aims of the transformative approach to education are to teach students to think critically and to develop the skills to formulate, document, and justify their conclusions. Such an approach affords students opportunities to engage in critical thinking and to develop more reflective perspectives about what they are learning. The approach pushes students to look critically and reflectively as they examine issues both inside and outside the classroom.

In this chapter, we argue for a new conceptualization about youth socialization, one that (1) goes beyond the traditional focus on quantitative, deductive measurement of racial socialization and parents as the target socialization agent and (2) aims to transform traditional multicultural approaches to education. Such work can offer rich new insights into how urban, African American youth acquire critical reasoning skills that are useful in communication, conflict resolution, resilience, and classroom literacy practice. Furthermore, when practiced in the classroom as a site of critical resistance, such practices become a part of a transformative, equity-minded approach to education and can provide robust learning opportunities that are simultaneously cultural, race conscious, and equity oriented.

This chapter has been organized into three major sections. Because we believe that when leveraged within a classroom cultural socialization practices may provide an alternative space that structures opportunities for students to sort through the real-life dilemmas that they face, as well as work through the academic tasks they are expected to take up, three areas of development are covered in the first section—socialization, literacy, and narrative (Lee, Spencer, & Harpalani, 2003). At the end of the first section, "An Alternative Space for Sorting Through Real-Life Dilemmas," characteristics of community-based cultural socialization practices are outlined to show how these have influenced the present research.

The second section, "Shoptalk as a Framework for Understanding How African American Youth Are Socialized Into Processes of Reasoning," describes a particular program of research in which we are involved within an urban, secondary Language Arts classroom. This work centers on understanding how African American youth are socialized into processes of reasoning where they see alternatives for (and locate alternatives within) decision-making practices, and furthermore, it is grounded within the larger project of equity-based education (Majors & Ansari, 2006). We choose to call this *work* and not research in order to privilege the full engagement that involves a physical, emotional, and mental investment in understanding how students develop through the process of reasoning out particular issues and problems. Such work considers how structures and processes are leveraged *within* and *across* settings. More specifically, the first author's teaching in the classroom revolves around enriching those links between youth cultural socialization, development, and literacy learning. The ultimate purpose of this work is to support students' attempts to think of the possibilities of their own life as well as those around them as they grapple with issues of difference, justice, and community. Furthermore, it is through these processes that students become skilled thinkers in a changing, global society (Langer, 1995).

The third and final section, "Engaging in a Transformative Framework," aims to touch upon important, ongoing issues and challenges for such work in urban education and consequently its implications for teacher education. We argue that the challenge for teacher education is to engage in a transformative framework for preservice teaching students as well. This kind of educational imperative involves challenging the universality of White experience and judgment as the authoritative standard.

AN ALTERNATIVE SPACE FOR SORTING THROUGH REAL-LIFE DILEMMAS

Arnett (1995) defined *socialization* as the process by which people acquire the behaviors through structures of argumentation that promote social and literate development, and knowledge of the social world or culture in which they live. It has been suggested that the central, though not exclusive, responsibility for the transmission of culture and its corresponding values rests with the family (Tyler, Boykin, Boelter, & Dillihunt, 2005). In education, our understanding of the developmental sources and pathways of youth thinking and socialization has expanded in the past two decades. Several features of this knowledge growth are especially salient. First, as in many other areas of developmental and educational sciences, psychology has gained an appreciation for context in the development of adolescent thinking. A second phenomenon, according to Keating and Sasse (1996) is the growing recognition of the effect of noncognitive features of adolescent development on the growth of thinking. For example, the role of social relationships is increasingly seen as central to the understanding of cognitive development throughout the life span, and adolescence is no different in that respect. A third trend is to take account of the essential contextualization and developmental integration by embedding core research questions in more real-world or applied contexts (Keating & Sasse, 1996). One way of capturing the central tendency of these salient features is to identify and explore critical processes during the adolescent years in the very critical ways that are necessary.

Within the psychological debates on racial socialization are three foci, which stand out in the literature: (1) the family as the target socialization agent, (2) coping and resilience to combat stressful situations, and (3) oppositional thinking in response to racist aggression.

Focus on the Family

Rotheram and Phinney (1987) defined *racial socialization* as "the developmental processes by which children acquire the behaviors, perceptions, values, and attitudes of an ethnic group, and come to see themselves and others as members of the group" (p. 11). According to Coard, Wallace, Stevenson, and Brotman (2004), racial socialization also refers to the promotion of psychological and physical health through child rearing in a society where dark skin and/or African features may lead to discrimination and racism, which in turn can lead to detrimental outcomes for African Americans (Peters, 1985) such as high rates and chronicity of behavioral problems, depression, and anxiety. Stevenson, Reed, Bodison, and Bishop (1997) contended that race-related socialization processes include divine, affective-symbolic, and phenomenological strategies that protect youth from discriminatory and psychological antagonistic environments that mediate racism stress and that are related to closer and more protective family relationships. Such traditional perspectives

focus on most structures of socialization as being located within the family.

For example, "African-American parents routinely engage in racial socialization practices as part of their parenting repertoire" (Coard et al., 2004, p. 280). Examples of such practices are offered by Stevenson, Cameron, Herrera-Taylor, and Davis (2002) and they include (a) providing explanation and support for appreciating the spiritual and metaphysical buffers to being Black in a racist world (divine-spiritual justification); (b) providing explanation and support for appreciating the cultural uniqueness of being and behaving Black in a racist world (affective-symbolic-interpersonal justification); and (c) providing explanation and support for appreciating and internalizing the meaning-making experiences of being Black in this world (phenomenological-intrapersonal justification) (p. 85). To our knowledge, there has been little qualitative and empirical evidence documenting such meaning-making experiences outside the family unit. Such research is needed, and across contexts, which externalize these meaning-making processes for practical and empirical purposes.

Stevenson et al. (1997) have focused primarily on the ways in which youth believe in the importance of racial socialization particularly as it extends into family circles. Some of these beliefs include messages about cultural pride, spiritual coping, cultural survival, and racism awareness. They also investigated how these beliefs in youth influence their anger expression and depression and strongly suggest that it is not enough to understand what parents say and do with their children. While the socialization that family circles provide has been a strong emphasis within this particular body of research, it has also fostered a clear dedication to the perspective of the individual youth. According to Stevenson et al., "it is equally important to understand what youth believe separately from the actions of their parents" (p. 203). Hence, the focus of what is under study shifts from that of the *parental practice* toward *youth participation* within practice. Our efforts to view socialization from a cultural standpoint and within community spaces and classrooms get to what the youth under study believe, as well as how those beliefs might play out in productive ways, as youth perspectives and beliefs are informed by the influences, resources, and dangers of the local neighborhood context (Stevenson, 1998).

For example, Rogoff's (1990) model of intent participation (learning through keen observation and listening) is one way of framing these perspectives around the activities in which youth participate. According to Rogoff, Paradise, Arauz, Correa-Chavez, and Angelillo (2003), as in hair salons,

> children, including youth, learn by observing and listening-in on adults and other children. Learning through keen observation and listening, in anticipation of participation seems to be especially valued and emphasized in communities where children have access to learning from informal community involvement. (p. 176)

Combating Stressful Situations

Recent efforts toward improving the psychological empowerment of African American youth have centered on culturally relevant and African-centered activities. These activities include gender-specific health education, rites-of-passage programs, cultural enrichment education, and midnight basketball, to name a few (Stevenson et al., 1997). According to Stevenson et al. (1997), "each intervention has a shared characteristic of promoting the strengths of adolescents with the assumption that the bolstering and buffering of African American racial identity within a hostile societal context is necessary" (p. 203). Intrafamilial activities to promote the racial identity of African American youth have been found to have a moderate relationship to the psychological and academic adjustment of young African Americans (Bowman & Howard, 1985; Spencer, 1983).

Additionally, Boykin and Toms (1985) posited a conceptual framework, specifically with regard to that of racial and cultural socialization that point to three themes of socialization forces that operate on nondominant youth in particular: (a) cultural experiences (i.e., styles, motifs, and patterns of behavior unique to African Americans); (b) mainstream experiences (i.e., influences and values of European American, middle-class culture); and (c) minority experiences (i.e., social, economic, and political forces impinging on racial minorities and leading to a set of coping styles, social outlooks, and defensive positions). Similarly, Thornton, Chatters, Taylor, and Allen (1990) posited a framework

for racial socialization that includes messages related to identity (personal and group), intergroup and interindividual relationships, and social hierarchy. Within this framework, issues such as parental instruction about racism in society, educational struggles, importance of extended family, spiritual and religious awareness, culture and pride, and value issues around child rearing are taken up. In the first author's research within African American community hair salons, instances of cultural socialization have been documented using critical race theory as a framework within what might be messages related to oppositional thinking in response to dominant, mainstream ideologies.

While socializing mechanisms are put in place by family and community networks as a way to enable minority youth to cope with stressful situations, these processes are further useful in helping students engage in oppositional thinking. Consequently, racial and cultural identity can be used as a tool not only to cope with racism but also to engage in a resistance that invokes cultural ways of knowing. The next section highlights the various ways in which cultural identity serve as a tool for empowerment and a discourse of resistance.

Cultural Ways of Knowing as Oppositional Thinking (Reading) in Response to Racist Aggression

Hughes and Chen (1999) categorized racial socialization messages as focusing on (a) an emphasis of cultural heritage and pride, or "cultural socialization"; (b) "preparation for future bias"; (c) "promoting racial mistrust"; and (d) "egalitarianism" (p. 473). They pointed out that these messages can be synergistic, verbal or nonverbal, deliberative or unintended, and proactive or reactive. In their investigations, Stevenson et al. (2002) found that protective factors among African American youth they researched include alertness to discrimination and coping with antagonism. Proactive factors include cultural pride reinforcement and cultural legacy appreciation. Mainstream socialization is seen as neutral and not either protective or reactive practice, but still quite important in understanding the complexity of racial socialization communications.

Such messages are a part of people's cultural ways of knowing, which enable them to deal with, cope, and handle the not-so-invisible aggressions of daily life and the social, economic, structural, and scientific influences that produce them. Cultural ways of knowing and their links with language have been a scientific and artistic fascination for many European and pioneering anthropologists (Golding, 1955; Halliday, 1967; Levy-Bruhl, 1966; Taylor, 1964) who, while on the one hand had little doubt that people from different cultures thought in different ways, also argued that such thought of "savages" was childlike, lacking in abstractions and confused. "The pervasive view was that 'primitive' or cultural thought was pre-logical, animistic, and tolerant of self-contradiction" (Johnson-Laird & Wason, 1977, p. 437). In many ways that view continues to persist and is reflected in our educational systems' tolerance of the status of marginalized youth. Such beliefs are similar in some respects to the *magical* ideas entertained by children as natural and social phenomena, as Piaget established in some of his early studies (Piaget, 1926). However, researchers and anthropologists have gone on to point out that it is a mistake to make judgments about thought processes on the basis of their contents (Boas, 1965; Levi-Strauss, 1966).

One prevalent aim within anthropological studies of the links between language, culture, and thinking has been to identify the source of the mental deficit in primitive thinking, a historical legacy in anthropology. This notion certainly prejudges the issue but is by no means held solely by overtly prejudiced thinkers, though the legacy remains (see Johnson-Laird & Wason, 1977). Many concerned with human psychological development have been genuinely convinced that "primitive mentality" is truly a form of simple mindedness. The grounds for these beliefs include the anthropological evidence about social and natural phenomena, cultural explanations as to why things happen, and erroneous views about their own culture and cognition. It seems to be extremely easy for some psychologists, anthropologists, and educators to establish a deficit in the thinking of people from non-White cultures. It would probably be equally easy for members of that culture or class to reverse the roles. But rather than reverse those roles, what racial and cultural socialization seeks to do is foster ways within African American youth experiences that counter these and other claims about who they and their people are.

Today we are beginning to move away from old notions of "savage thinking." There is increasing concern within the discipline of psychology that our nation's schools are not doing what they should to educate youth (Kuhn, 1991). Some of this concern falls around students' seeming lack of domain-specific knowledge. Additional concern is around students' inability to reason well within and across domains. While the concern has gone to how schools are weak in developing cognitive skills, there is a complete lack of attention to the equally poor job that schools do to develop the social skills of adolescents, especially the kinds of protective skills that nondominant groups need to combat racism in society. Through a wide-angled lens, this grim picture portrays a clear challenge for researchers seeking to enhance their understanding of thinking and learning and educators who wish to cultivate and improve on students' thinking competencies *within* and *across* classrooms.

As such, thinking, learning, and teaching are part of the complex processes of socialization within the classroom. Consequently, it is important to make explicit the socializing mechanisms that are otherwise eclipsed within traditional academic settings. The next section elaborates on these complex processes and the ways in which they are made explicit through academic practices. Using cultural ways of knowing as a starting point for development, the third section draws on cultural socialization as a tool for developing an equity-based curriculum.

SHOPTALK AS A FRAMEWORK FOR UNDERSTANDING HOW AFRICAN AMERICAN YOUTH ARE SOCIALIZED INTO PROCESSES OF REASONING

The first author's interest in racial and cultural socialization processes of youth community experiences as mediated through talk began in 1998, in an urban, African American high school in Chicago. These interests stem from (1) the discourse surrounding the critical problems facing the teaching of "multicultural" education and the appropriation of cultural funds of knowledge in reasoning about complex social problems that students face and (2) the question of how teachers can identify and leverage cultural community practices into curriculum perspectives and instructional approaches for students from different cultural and ethnic backgrounds (Hollins, 1996).

These two issues meet at a critical intersection in urban, U.S. classrooms populated by predominantly students of color and teaching populations that hold diverse perceptions, political beliefs, and attitudes toward culture and learning. The focus of the broader study and intervention in which the first author was involved (Lee, 1992, 1993, 1995, 2007; Lee & Majors, 2003) and on which earlier work is based (Majors, 1999, 2000, 2001a, 2001b) is the domain of responses to literature. Current work builds on the findings of Lee's Cultural Modeling Project[2] intervention and to further the case for the enabling potential of particular kinds of nonnormative discourses within the classroom (see Lee, 2007).

This analysis is significant. It aims to propel classroom teaching and learning forward through the consideration of the culturally and socially embedded norms for attacking problems that students bring into the classroom and, consequently, the consideration of the pedagogical supports that speak to those norms. At the intersection of this movement forward are two challenges. The first involves making explicit the social and cognitive dimensions of the problem-solving task at hand. The second challenge involves the acknowledgment of the multiple and dynamic ways in which teachers and students respond to pedagogical supports that are cultural in nature. Overcoming these challenges involves locating successful ways of fusing literacy teaching and learning with culturally aware and relevant instruction. Whereas these aims are important, this present work attempts to deal with the often overly simplified and highly generalized notion of culture, its complex characteristics that afford opportunities for making sense of not only texts but the world, and how culture—as an aspect of community and meaning making—has continuance in practices outside the immediate home and community.

Our present work in the secondary language arts classroom stems, in part, from Majors's ethnographic investigations of urban and rural African American hair salons across the United States as robust cultural sites for teaching and learning (Majors, 2003, 2004). Findings confirmed that complex problem solving is linked to context, context is linked to identity, and that discourse features that characterize membership within the salon provided opportunities for participation in problem-solving tasks. Preliminary findings also indicate that discourse practices can be used as a scaffold for reasoning in complex problem-solving tasks in language arts classrooms (Majors, 2001a, 2001b, 2002). Salons are traditionally places where co-constructed, community forms of talk—stories, personal narratives, jokes, folklore, and folktales—can be heard. They are also sites in which these genres and African American vernacular English interactional norms are used as resources for the construction of arguments. Within each site, members are socialized, or apprenticed into the broader community by participating in the construction and transmission of knowledge.

Shoptalk,[3] a kind of conversational discourse identified in culturally situated social community settings, socializes adolescents and young adults into routine problem-solving strategies (Majors, 2001a, 2003, 2004, 2007). In short, a young adult participating in Shoptalk might pose a social dilemma with which he or she is dealing, emphasizing its potential consequences. Women and men within the hair salon, through narrations of understanding, would "re-direct" (Scribner, 1984) the initial dilemma in nonthreatening ways that afforded multiple perspectives, often in narrative form, from which to view that dilemma, and how as a consequence the youth come to consider alternative perspectives, take on roles within the argumentation, and take up multiple points of view. Unlike traditional narratives, which position the teller as distanced, removed from the context and unaffected, narrations of understanding told within Shoptalk are reflexive, liberatory, and dialogic, embracing both the local (near to) and distal (far from).

In effect, the routine nature of the talk within the salon, as well as the social histories the women share, act as social supports that potentially, over time, influence prototypical coping responses, particularly for the young women in the salon (Majors, 2007). While very often adolescents and young adults were the impetus of such socializing routines, data show that older adult women were more likely to be involved in these forms of argumentation that afford alternative perspectives. It is the robustness of problem-solving outcomes, which the first author argues, that warrants adapting it to a new setting, namely the classroom. It is from this Shoptalk that Majors has begun to develop a literacy tool for the classroom using videotaped vignettes and transcription of interaction. When used as an instrument for scaffolding within a classroom curriculum, Shoptalk borrowed from the salon and converted into text positioned students (and teachers) to make use of those tacit literate skills and cultural socialization processes.

Enactment of Shoptalk in the classroom draws from an equity-based framework in that it

- Requires critical self-reflection on part of the instructor and the students

- Enables students to examine issues from multiple perspectives

- Encourages teachers to confront their own cultural spaces as sites of ideological development and privileged positions

Consequently, the work in the classroom is a response to a call developed by scholars in the field of critical race theory, teaching, and self-study and answers the *call to work* (Stovall, 2005). Such a call further requires a particular type of engagement centered in a critical perspective on the academy. African American researchers and educators, despite the relative privilege associated with the profession, have distinct experiences with racism that affect their sensibility and judgment. Arguably, these experiences enable African American academics to see the disjuncture between the *narrations of research* and *narrations of understanding*, particularly understanding the reality and complexities of African American youth education. Such a framework, we believe, grounds the consideration of culturally shared strategies for problem solving and coping in order to clarify what constitutes *community-based* and *culturally relevant* socialization practices for problem solving and coping. The development of the curriculum is a space where the particular discourses of equity-based education, socialization, and literacy intersect. The mechanisms for socialization reside within and are developed according to a set of goals that are defined by the transformative, equity-based framework (agency, literacy as liberatory practice, critical thinking, etc.). These curricular goals are integrated by our understanding of literacy and learning.

An equity-based framework is a response, in part, to particular trends in multiculturalism in education. As a subset of ideas and values, multiculturalism is complicit with particular Western epistemological stances that do not demand critical reflection in teaching and learning practices. An equity-based framework responds to a particular trend in multicultural education known as "corporate multiculturalism" (Ansari & Kim, 2005). As such, some key ideas that constitute this discourse of corporate multiculturalism are (1) the ways in which "other" is positioned as powerless, (2) the constitution of "difference" as fashion, and (3) the depoliticization of race, class, sex, and culture. The logic of the marketplace, consequently, has superceded any other considerations.

> It is finally up to an individual's will and intelligence to overcome the restrictions imposed by race, gender and class in order to "make a difference," meaning to become rich. The *homo digitalis* is a living proof. To complement this ideology, a "benevolent" form of multiculturalism has been adopted by corporations and media conglomerates across borders, continents, and virtual space. And our major cultural and educational institutions have followed suit. This global trans-culture artificially softens the otherwise sharp edges of cultural difference, fetishizing them in such a way as to render them desirable. (Gomez-Pena, 2001, p. 12)

As corporate multiculturalism subsumes the larger discourse on difference, it is further exploded by global technologies. The celebration of culture has in turn functioned as a pre-emptory strike against sustained intellectual critique. The treatment of otherness is in large part one of tolerance and management. This "management of difference" is thus constituted as part of a larger agenda of assimilation and enforcement of Western values, paradigms, and ways of thinking. Furthermore, as corporate multiculturalism is a product of the marketplace, it is only relevant to the extent that it is economically beneficial.

Educational institutions do not transcend but rather are intrinsically tied to the movements within corporate multiculturalism (Ansari & Kim, 2005). In consequence, there is an inherent ideological stance on culture that operates within a classroom. Some important initial questions that serve as impetus for change are the following: Who makes decisions on what is learned? Who gets to speak? What is knowledge? While the interest of corporate multiculturalism lies in washing out difference, an equity-based framework is deeply interested in exploring difference and, furthermore, critiquing it.

Part and parcel of this equity-based framework is the focus on critical self-reflection in which students examine issues from various perspectives, which affect their lives. In an attempt to address the discourse of teaching toward multicultural awareness, this approach encourages teachers to confront their own cultural spaces as sites of ideological development and more important, their own privileged positions. Grounded engagement, as a methodological tool, draws attention to the inherent privilege of the researcher and seeks to interrogate that position. An equity-minded agenda calls on critical reflection and resistance to institutionalized notions of self. Consequently, it has been marked by an embrace of reflexivity and the rejection of a "one-size-fits-all approach" to learning and teaching (Majors, 2001a). Thus, in naming self as part of larger contexts that shape it, there emerges a profound understanding of subjectivity and power. We argue that an equity framework, when practiced in a classroom as a site of critical resistance, can provide robust learning practices that are simultaneously race conscious and equity oriented, but there are challenges for teaching and learning.

The implementation of an equity-based curriculum design that attempts to denormalize the dominant-group experience against the backdrop of the experiences of those from underserved diverse populations extends the challenge of how educators respond to the call for race-conscious practices. The site of urgency for this particular exploration in equity-based change is the urban classroom. There are various reasons that make this site especially relevant and, consequently, entail a sense of urgency. One reason, we argue, is that the classroom provides a robust opportunity for exploring issues of implementation, while the notion of equity drives these practices. While equity-based education encourages students to be conversant with an increasingly global and hierarchical societal structure, it is also a significant move forward in taking a step toward the initial promise of multicultural education. This first step, ideally, creates a population of students who in their own communities can model the equity-based framework as a liberatory practice. Furthermore, the urban classroom calls attention to how race and racism enter into our subjectivities and ideological stances. Hence, the classroom and the ensuing curriculum serve as a catalyst for the manifestation of underlying and sometimes repressed assumptions.

As an equity-based framework is invested in rethinking what it means to teach and reinvigorates the notion of liberation and transformation, cultural socialization is invested in using difference as a robust space for learning. The neutralization of race and in consequence, the erasure, so to speak, of cultural epistemologies is what an equity-based framework and cultural socialization seek to resist. Keeping that in mind, the processes of socialization include an analysis of structures of power, participation, and language in discourse as well as social interactions observed. These social interactions include the role of participants, enactments of point of view, the authority of participants as mutually constructed and shared, and finally, what counts as knowledge.

The final section outlines the setting of the study and elaborates on this intersection of literacy, socialization, and equity-based education. Specifically, it illustrates problem-solving strategies that the students used to tackle issues and academic tasks. Furthermore, it makes explicit the socializing strategies that were taken up as a response to particular values, ideas, and cultural paradigms that may have been threatening to them.

ENGAGING IN A TRANSFORMATIVE FRAMEWORK

As in an educational context, discourse in community settings that frame cultural socialization practices offers us a way to externalize the internal thinking strategies that youth engage in and many classroom teachers would like to foster with their students, thus offering not only empirical data for analysis but also useful insights for classroom practice (Kuhn, 1991). The relationship between socialization, literacy, and equity-based education, therefore, is illuminated in the final analysis.

In seeking to understand problem-solving events and practices involving urban youth, and the sites they traverse as they engage in those practices, our starting point was the social (and cultural) practices involved in literacy events. We view those practices as the actions through which critical engagement, ideological stances, and counternarratives are enacted in the classroom, a space that has social, political, ideological, historical, cultural, and literate dimensions.

Participants of these events were African American adolescents between the ages of 15 and 17. The site is a language arts classroom in a small (>500 students) secondary high school in an urban midwestern city. Teacher research and participant observation has taken place across four language arts classes and include 3½ years of course instruction by Majors. All students enrolled in the course participated in the study, across the entire corpus.

The first author's work as a secondary language arts instructor in an urban high school has shown that students will take up similar discourse patterns that involve social reading while engaging in problem-solving strategies. The example that we draw from for this chapter is drawn from a 3-week writing unit discussion (framed around understanding structures of argumentation) that the 10th to 12th graders engaged in—a process of social reading while attempting to take up alternative perspectives in written texts. The written text was a downloaded news release from CNN.com, referring to William Bennett's statement that aborting "every black baby in this country" would reduce the crime rate was a sound argument (CNN.com, September 30, 2005). However, it seemed that before students could take up this written text, there was some heavy engagement in which the students spent a great deal of time representing their own perspectives across three contexts: their own lives, the broader social community, and the textual context in which Bennett's comments were made. In doing so, students were able to use discursive practices familiar to them to engage in strategies for determining what the text was, who was meant to be the reader, and how to best respond to a text that could be disempowering. These discursive practices (e.g., multipartied-overlapping talk, call and response, tonal semantics, narrative sequencing, conversational signifying, indirection) involved both social reading strategies and norms for talk that

were similar to those found within the discourse of the hair salons (Majors, 2007).

The selection of texts and writing activities in the Shoptalk language arts classroom are intended to help students interrogate the word and the world, the text and, relatedly, life's challenges. In the context of taking up complex literary and life texts, both the structure and content of talk play a significant role in framing and creating context and unveiling positionings of speakers (narrators, authors) as social actors, while simultaneously unveiling the ideologies and institutional assumptions inherent in those positionings. Students bring familiarity and various levels of expertise and understanding of this "talk" to generate and unpack complicated readings of texts.

In this unit called *Understanding Structures of Academic Argumentation,* the class spent time unfolding what it meant to construct well-framed, strategic responses to what they were reading, in the form of traditional argument. This unit was designed to provide students with practice in considering alternative points of view, how texts are constructed and read by various audiences, and the implications of those readings on their lives. In this unit, the class considered things that were important to their lives (as African American youth, community members, and thinkers) to make sense of a claim. Specifically, this unit focused on the claim presented by William Bennett in his radio show "Morning in America" on September 28, 2005, in which he stated,

> If you wanted to reduce crime, you could—if that were your sole purpose—you could abort every black baby in this country and your crime rate would go down. That would be an impossibly ridiculous and morally reprehensible thing to do, but your crime rate would go down. (Bennett, 2005)

The first author's instructional goal was that by the end of this unit (introducing students to canonical structures of argumentation) students should have a better understanding of the nature of argument and the routine strategies that are involved in justifying claims and generating counterclaims.

We view the classroom as a site of culture, negotiation, and constructed knowledge where students are allowed initial responses that were emotional and visceral to a text that they deemed threatening to their lives and insulting to their experiences. The socialization aspect of this is how do we, as instructors, help students develop coping mechanisms that enable them to respond intellectually to what they view as threatening? This mirrors what goes on in many mainstream classrooms where students are asked to respond to a text. What is often absent is a push back, or rather a space where perspectives can be interrogated through cultural meanings and norms.

Hence, to propel this interrogation we engaged with the dilemma as an instance of narrative retelling to propel students into academic problem solving. As part of this process, students were asked to lay claim to and identify their own counternarrative responses, while simultaneously recognizing how points of view can be framed and can themselves frame others. Second, we interrogated both narratives, Bennett's and those created by the students in response, enabling the students to begin to draw from their own cultural understandings of language, participation, and power in order to lay the foundations of responding beyond the affective. By taking a political issue and situating that within a hybrid context combining the social and academic through the use of narrative, we attempted to allow students the space to make connections between the claim made by Bennett and how it speaks to their experience in particular ways as members of a particular community. The following written examples of student responses convey their initial reactions in their journals.

Example 1:

"This passage is appalling. How could someone be so selfish? The comment that this man says is very ignorant. He is saying that our ethnic background is the main reason why the crime rate is so high."

Example 2:

"I feel that this man was wrong and that the comment was full of bigotry. He should be ashamed of himself and offer his apology to all African Americans."

Example 3:

"The comments made by Bennett are clearly the result of an ignorant mind reluctant to release his prejudices and misconceptions on another."

Example 4:

"I believe that Bennett is terribly ignorant and insensitive. Bennett's remarks are very hurtful and helps my belief that there is still racism in the worlds."

In the examples cited, students present emotive reactions to a kind of social text (Majors, 2007). In all the examples, the students express horror in addition to making judgments about Bennett's character. However, none appears to address the argument Bennett is making head on. In Example 4, the student appears to find Bennett's comment as being symptomatic of society's racism. As a result, there is an interaction here between audience and speaker, undergirded by a self-awareness of belief systems and values.

Through shared understandings, students were able to see how statements or text, by default, position them as readers and, as in this case, subjects of this text. They are able to see how power operates through language, specifically how they are labeled and represented to a larger audience. However, through the process of socially working through the text, enacting it, and their readings of it, students were able to reposition themselves in relation to that text and to reposition how they responded to it in socially and academically productive ways. This structure allowed students to enact roles as opposed to being positioned within them, with narrative acting as a socializing tool, which in turn helped them cope with this act of being forcefully and succinctly positioned by one glib statement.

Following the journal assignment, we specified the routine strategies (skills) it takes to identify claims within traditional structures of argument by reading the various texts surrounding Bennett's claim. In taking this approach, students confronted their derived understanding of the meaning in Bennett's statement and held it as claim that must, in order to be a true argument, have certain warrants that could establish it as truth. This meant examining various transcripts of the radio broadcast and the ensuing media coverage. The implications of this exercise, we believe, is that it enables students to identify points of view and how those points of view are embedded in belief systems while it also forces students to go beyond the literal meanings of the text. Furthermore, it pushes their thinking away from their initial response, toward a process of interpreting and unpacking the issues implicit within the text. Note the following example:

> Based on what I have collaborated, Bennett's argument is based upon factual evidence from the media when he stated that the crime rate in America will go down if more black babies will be (should) aborted. Bennett is influenced by the facts that the media sends out. For example, the media, such as the news, depict images that only make light of the poverty level and crime in America and how African-American's are the major contributions. He thinks that if more black babies are aborted the crime rate would go down.

In the above example, this student has appropriated the academic language of argument to address particular points. However, he or she does not directly respond to Bennett. Rather he or she problematizes Bennett's claim by addressing larger issues of media sources, power, and representation.

Our focus was not in the reading of the text but in interrogating how that text positioned the author, the reader, and them specifically as African Americans. Hence, the arguments embedded within various texts in this unit become our tools for laying claim to issues around what gets read, who is the reader, and how to talk back to disempowering texts. This begins the process of helping students to move beyond the routine acceptance of a claim, toward identifying alternatives, generating counterclaims, and weighing reasons for and against the claim.

As a third exercise in taking up alternative perspectives, students were told to take the positioning of Bennett and locate potential justifications for his claim, if they could. Students were grouped into pairs and given the task of gathering data to support the hypothesis presented by Bennett. Asked to suspend their own perspectives momentarily and to step into the problem-posing/problem-solving stance of Bennett, students engaged not just in a blank acknowledgment of what was Bennett's claim, but in the processes, routes, through which Bennett traveled to posit his claim. This, we argue, not only encouraged students to take on an alternative, even threatening position beyond its face value, but to participate in a process of inquiry through which evidence (existent or nonexistent) for particular points of view is sought, understood, articulated, and ultimately countered. We believe that this allows for an engagement in culturally

familiar, problem-solving strategies and the sharing of multiple points of view that is productive, both culturally and socially, as well as cognitively beneficial. Hence, students are required to take up epistemological roles within the discourse as they generate readings of texts (both socially constructed oral texts and written texts[4]). These texts, in turn, account for alternative perspectives, which generate proactive "coping" responses to (as opposed to reactive, but sometimes in addition to) socially and academically threatening mechanisms.[5] As such these activities extend beyond the intended participation structure within the classroom. Additionally, these participation structures are enacted through the discourse of Shoptalk that accounts for students' readings of events *and* modes of learning through pedagogical practices that attempt to be culturally responsive, not assumptive. This means that what is encouraged through Shoptalk is the availability of a problem-solving process that anticipates students' contributions of their world views, in relation to what they experience and what they understand, as a part of that problem-solving equation. One aspect of this equation is the overlap that exists between culturally situated strategies and those that are specific to domain-based problem solving.

In the excerpt below, a student points out attitudes that are reflected in the statement Bennett made. He reads the statement not just for what Bennett literally is saying but for the attitudes, values, and ideas instantiated by that claim. Thus, he is attempting to access the non-literal meanings of the text.

> Dear Bennett,
>
> . . . To me your statement was a philosophically insensitive remark made with ignorance of the sensitivity towards a minority ethnic group. What leaves me still skeptical about your statement is your emphasis on the fact that such an inhuman action such as this would work. If you already mentioned that this act would be morally reprehensible why reiterate that it would work? Were you trying to make a quiet stab at African-Americans and enlighten racist individuals (not you of course) with your notion? What also infuriated me was your direct correlation between African-Americans and crime. Though you meant no harm in your comment your hypothesis does not directly reflect your opinion towards minorities. The

timing in which to make this remark was off as well as your decision in expressing this barbaric, thoughtless act.

CONCLUSION: THE CHALLENGE FOR URBAN EDUCATION

There are many ongoing issues and challenges to implementing an equity-based framework, one that (1) requires critical self-reflection on part of the instructor and the students, (2) enables students to examine issues from multiple perspectives, and (3) encourages teachers to confront their own cultural spaces as sites of ideological development and privileged positions.

However, in our conclusion we concentrate on one in particular, teacher education. The classroom and community practices presented in this chapter consider narrations of understanding and view the complex relations within the social construction of that understanding. Work of this kind draws our attention to both the social processes and structures of the kinds of teaching and knowing under study, which give rise to the production of narrations of understanding. Such narrations of understanding draw our attention to the kinds of structures and process of talk through which African American youth, as social historical subjects, can create meanings in their interactions with those narrations (Fairclough, 1992; Wodak & Meyer, 2001). Inherent in this view are the interconnected concepts of power, history, and ideology.

Consequently, narrations of understanding contribute to the kinds of knowing that African American students engage in. This kind of knowing is an active evaluation of some action in events by protagonists, whose actions, thoughts, and feelings are interpreted by members of a community in light of local and distal notions of what is right, wrong, and just. The skill of this kind of knowing involves inferencing, as well as narrative composing and telling skills as a way of fathoming the social and moral meanings of life and everyday events. In this kind of knowing, African American students may see themselves as an othered subject, as they measure themselves according to a discourse of teaching before them, which is informed by White cultural practices, paradigms, and values.

In light of this, it is very important to reevaluate what it means to teach students, particularly those within historically disenfranchised groups.

This leads to particular challenges within the context of teacher education. An equity-based framework, when practiced in a classroom as a site of critical resistance, can provide robust learning practices that are simultaneously race conscious and equity oriented, but there are challenges for teaching and learning.

First and foremost is the challenge of creating a safe space to dialogue about race and racial assumptions, with White, middle-class, and historically privileged preservice teachers. Many preservice teachers may not be willing to talk about their ideas as part of their execution of privilege and willful ignorance. The challenge is to unpack assumptions but, at the same time, create a safe space that allows for transformative conversations. This is part of the socialization process of students in preservice classrooms and an area of research that needs further exploration. Second, an important step toward recognition of historical and political racial injury is to disentangle White privilege. Part and parcel of unpacking privilege is an understanding of how culture, history, and social economy inform individual lives. Because economic and racial privilege allow for and create a sensibility of individual will and the importance of self-motivation, it is a particular challenge to get students to think about individuality within context. An additional challenge in instilling such a curriculum is that as teachers, we must not be afraid of owning and privately and personally addressing issues of voice, written language, and power within ourselves—issues that create and perpetuate biases, issues that obstruct teaching. Jacqueline Jones Royster (1996) reminded us that it is also imperative that we consider the beliefs and values that we hold and that inevitably permit our attitudes and actions in discourse communities to become systematic.

Those of us in teacher education must recognize too that we are indeed preparing a predominantly White teaching force of preservice educators to teach an increasingly culturally and linguistically diverse student body. Implementing strategies of multicultural education and awareness must also entail the recognition of multiple voices that go far beyond that of the White mainstream of which they are a part. Without this recognition, we educators of educators are continuing an ongoing monologue with ourselves as the audience.

While there is an existing dialogue in preservice education, it is limited in its scope and function. Much of this discourse focuses on paying lip service to teaching all students and taking into consideration their cultural contexts; however, there is no ensuing critique of the ways in which the school system and teachers reify racist pedagogy. We believe that not only must we continue the dialogue but that dialogue must be critical and include within it historical and ideological issues, as well as the socializing structures that sustain such ideologies as normative. The challenge here is for the institution and teacher to work to create a useful frame that works with the students' development and simultaneously counters such norms.

An attempt to achieve educational equity through classroom practices in preservice teacher education via an equity-based framework contains an activist dimension. It not only tries to understand the U.S. context of teaching and learning as persistently inequitable and supremacist but tries to change it. It sets out not only to ascertain how the classroom organizes itself along racial lines and hierarchies but to transform it for the better (Delgado & Stefanic, 2000). An important and determining factor in activating this goal is to create a curriculum for preservice educators that allows students to interrogate the inherencies and difficulties of an inequitable educational system and, further, to recognize institutional and cultural privileges that sustain their own power. Moreover, naming Whiteness as a race denormalizes the cultural practices and epistemologies that have come to be the standard in educational curriculum and pedagogy. The danger of not naming race (including Whiteness) only serves to maintain White power and privilege.

As a form of oppositional work, an equity-based framework actively challenges the universality of White experience and judgment as the authoritative standard that binds people of color and normatively measures, directs, controls, and regulates the terms of proper thought, expression, presentation, and behavior. The task of this approach is to identify values and norms that have been disguised and subordinated in the law (Delgado & Stefanic, 2000). To train more caring teachers, we need to develop a cadre of teachers that are racially aware. Racial awareness is contingent on this humanity. In its complexity, the intersection where our students and our own experiences meet serves as a microcosm of society where ideological and historical factors intersect. Hence, it is a space where this framework can be productive, creating conversation, generating

tools, and extending voice. In fact, this is a goal that needs to be aggressively addressed as student populations become increasingly diverse and the student body and the teaching body become more starkly contrasted.

NOTES

1. Exceptions to this would be rites-of-passage programs, cultural enrichment education, and midnight basketball. However, these, like most others, rely heavily on quantitative methods of analysis.

2. Cultural modeling is a conceptual framework to guide the design of English language arts curriculum and pedagogy, particularly in response to literature (Lee, 1997). The design of the curriculum provides students with the opportunity to use the cultural funds of knowledge that they bring into the classroom, including language. Through modeling activities, students examine extended dialogues of African American vernacular English discourse genres such as signifying, rap lyrics, as well as popular videos identified as cultural data sets. The teacher coordinates metacognitive instructional conversations with students to bring to the public floor the strategies they use tacitly in their everyday practice (Lee, 1995, 1997).

3. Shoptalk characterizes a specific genre of conversational discourse. The term focuses on not just the location of talk but also (1) a discourse of shared technical and professional expertise, (2) an interactional and highly dynamic way of talk that includes both stylists and clients, and (3) a transformative medium through which both participants and nonparticipants can interrogate, contest, and make sense of the world. It is often through Shoptalk that the activities of the participants and their subsequent roles within many rural and urban African American hair salons get directed (Majors, 2007).

4. Socially constructed oral and written text are instances of oral or written language in use within specific social (group) discourses and are rehearsed and developed within specific discourse communities such as the African American hair salon.

5. Such mechanisms include institutional and social racism, intergenerational poverty, premature onset of adult responsibilities such as full time employment, responsibility for siblings, domestic responsibilities, and so on.

REFERENCES

Ansari, S., & Kim, J. (2005, November). *Critical multiculturalism: An investigation into the critical in multicultural research at NRC.* Paper presented at the annual conference of the National Reading Conference, Miami, FL.

Arnett, J. J. (1995). Broad and narrow socialization: The family in the context of a cultural theory. *Journal of Marriage and the Family, 57,* 617–628.

Banks, J. A. (1998). Curriculum transformation. In J. A. Banks (Ed.), *An introduction to multicultural education* (2nd ed., pp. 21–34). Boston: Allyn & Bacon.

Banks, J. A. (2001). Citizenship education and diversity: Implications for teacher education. *Journal of Teacher Education, 52,* 5–16.

Banks, J. A. (2003). Teaching literacy for social justice and global citizenship. *Language Arts, 81,* 18–19.

Bennett, W. (2005, September 28). *Morning in America* [Radio broadcast]. Washington, DC: SRN.

Boas, F. (1965). *The mind of primitive man.* New York: Free Press.

Bowman, P. J., & Howard, C. (1985). Race related socialization, motivation, and academic achievement: A study of Black youths in three-generation families. *Journal of the American Academy of Child Psychiatry, 24,* 134–141.

Boykin, A. W., & Toms, F. D. (1985). Black child socialization: A conceptual framework. In H. P. McAdoo & J. L. McAdoo (Eds.), *Black children: Social, educational, and parental environments* (pp. 33–51). Beverly Hills, CA: Sage.

Coard, S. I., Wallace, S. A., Stevenson, H. C., & Brotman, L. M. (2004). Towards culturally relevant interventions: The consideration of racial socialization in parent training with African-American families. *Journal of Child and Family Studies, 13*(3), 277–293.

Delgado, R., & Stefanic, J. (Eds.). (2000). *Critical race theory: The cutting edge* (2nd ed.). Philadelphia: Temple University Press.

Fairclough, N. (1992). *Discourse and social change.* Cambridge, UK: Polity Press.

Golding, W. (1955). *The inheritors.* London: Faber & Faber.

Gomez-Pena, G. (2001). The new global culture: Somewhere between corporate multiculturalism and the mainstream bizarre (a border perspective). *The Drama Review, 45*(1), 7–30.

Halliday, M. A. K. (1967). Linguistic function and literary style: An inquiry into the language of William Golding's *The Inheritors.* In M. A. K. Halliday (Ed.), *Explorations in the functions of language* (pp. 325–360). London: Edward Arnold.

Hollins, E. R. (1996). *Culture in school learning: Revealing the deep meaning.* Mahwah, NJ: Erlbaum.

Hughes, D., & Chen, L. (1999). The nature of parents' race-related communications to children: A developmental perspective. In L. Balter & C. S. Tamis-LeMonda (Eds.), *Child psychology: A handbook of contemporary issues* (pp. 467–490). Philadelphia: Taylor & Francis.

Johnson-Laird, P. N., & Wason, P. C. (Eds.). (1977). *Thinking: Readings in cognitive science.* London: Cambridge University Press.

Keating, D., & Sasse, D. (1996). Cognitive socialization in adolescence: Critical period for a critical habit of mind. In G. R. Adams, R. Montemayor, & T. Gullota (Eds.), *Psychosocial development during adolescence: Progress in developmental contextualism* (Advances in Adolescent Development) (pp. 232–259). New York: Sage.

Kuhn, D. (Ed.). (1990). *Developmental perspectives on teaching and learning thinking skills.* Basel, Switzerland: Karger.

Kuhn, D. (1991). *The skills of argument.* New York: Cambridge University Press.

Langer, J. (1995). *Envisioning literature: Literary understanding and literature instruction.* New York: Teachers College Press.

Lee, C. D. (1992). Literacy, cultural diversity, and instruction. *Education and Urban Society, 24*(2), 279–291.

Lee, C. D. (1993). *Signifying as a scaffold for literary interpretation: The pedagogical implications of an African-American discourse genre.* Urbana, IL: National Council of Teachers of English.

Lee, C. D. (1995). A culturally based cognitive apprenticeship: Teaching African-American high school students' skills in literary interpretation. *Reading Research Quarterly, 30*(4), 608–631.

Lee, C. D. (1997). Bridging home and school literacies: A model of culturally responsive teaching. In J. Flood, S. B. Heath, & D. Lapp (Eds.), *A handbook for literacy educators: Research on teaching the communicative and visual arts* (pp. 330–341). New York: Macmillan.

Lee, C. D. (2007). *Culture, literacy, and learning: Taking bloom in the midst of the whirlwind.* New York: Teachers College Press.

Lee, C. D., & Majors, Y. (2003). Heading up the street: Localized opportunities for shared constructions of knowledge. *Pedagogy, Culture & Society, 11*(1), 49–67.

Lee, C. D., Spencer, M. B., & Harpalani, V. (2003). "Every shut eye ain't sleep": Studying how people live culturally. *Educational Researcher, 32*(5), 6.

Levi-Strauss, C. (1966). *The savage mind.* London: Weidenfeld and Nicolson.

Levy-Bruhl, L. (1966). *How natives think.* New York: Washington Square Press.

Majors, Y. (1999, November). *"Were just playin' school here": When teachers reflect and the challenges of getting beyond reform.* Paper presented at the annual convention of the National Conference of Teachers of English, Denver, CO.

Majors, Y. (2000, November). *"Shut my mouth wide open": Discourse norms from community to school.* Paper presented at the annual convention of the National Council of Teachers of English, Milwaukee, WI.

Majors, Y. (2001a, April). *"That's a hard pill to swallow:" Teacher conceptions and the hidden (truths) of practice.* Paper presented at the annual conference of the American Educational Research Association, Seattle, WA.

Majors, Y. (2001b, April). *When cultural practices become classroom resources: African-American vernacular practices as cultural resources for literacy.* Paper presented at the annual conference of the American Educational Research Association, Seattle, WA.

Majors, Y. (2002). Introduction: The landscape of literacy in seven portraits, portrait III. In B. J. Guzzetti (Ed.), *Literacy in America: An encyclopedia* (pp. xvii–xviii). Santa Barbara, CA: ABC-CLIO.

Majors, Y. (2003). Shoptalk: Teaching and learning in an African-American hair salon. *Mind, Culture and Activity, 10*(4), 289–310.

Majors, Y. (2004). "They thought I was scared of them, but they were scared of me": Constructions of self/other in a Midwestern hair salon. *Anthropology and Education Quarterly, 35*(2), 167–188.

Majors, Y. (2007). Narrations of cross-cultural encounters as interpretative frames for reading word and world. *Discourse and Society, 18*(4), 479–505.

Majors, Y., & Ansari, S. (2006). A multivoiced response to the call for an equity-based framework. *Yearbook of the National Society for the Study of Education, 105*(2), 190–210.

McNeil, D. (1999). *Racial versus ethnic socialization: A family ecology approach.* Unpublished doctoral dissertation, Northwestern University, Evanston, IL.

Orellana, M. F., & Bowman, P. J. (2003). Cultural diversity research on learning and development: Conceptual, methodological and strategic considerations. *Educational Researcher, 32*(5), 26–32.

Peters, M. F. (1985). Racial socialization of young black children. In H. P. McAdoo & J. L. McAdoo (Eds.), *Black children: Social, educational, and parental environments* (pp. 159–173). Beverly Hills, CA: Sage.

Piaget, J. (1926). *The language and thought of the child.* London: Kegan Paul.

Royster, J. J. (1996). When the first voice you hear is not your own. *CCC, 47*(1), 29–40.

Rogoff, B. (1990). *Apprenticeship in thinking: Cognitive development in social context.* New York: Oxford University Press.

Rogoff, B., Paradise, R., Arauz, R. M., Correa-Chavez, M., & Angelillo, C. (2003). Firsthand learning through intent participation. *Annual Review of Psychology, 54,* 175–203.

Rotheram, M. J., & Phinney, J. S. (1987). Introduction: Definitions and perspectives in the study of children's ethnic socialization. In J. S. Phinney & M. J. Rotheram (Eds.), *Children's ethnic socialization: Pluralism and development* (pp. 10–28). Beverly Hills, CA: Sage.

Scribner, S. (1984). Studying working intelligence. In B. Rogoff & J. Lave (Eds.), *Everyday cognition: Its development in social context* (pp. 9–40). Cambridge, MA: Harvard University Press.

Spencer, M. B. (1983). Children's cultural values and parental child rearing strategies. *Developmental Review, 3,* 351–370.

Spencer, M. B., Swanson, D. P., & Cunningham, M. (1991). Ethnicity, ethnic identity and competence formation: Adolescent transition and cultural transformation. *Journal of Negro Education, 60,* 366–387.

Stevenson, H. C. (1998). Theoretical considerations in measuring racial identity and socialization: Extending the self further. In R. Jones (Ed.), *Black psychology* (4th ed., pp. 227–263). Hampton, VA: Cobb & Henry.

Stevenson, H. C., Cameron, R., Herrero-Taylor, T., & Davis, G. (2002). Development of the teenager experience of racial socialization scale: Correlates of race-related socialization frequency from the perspective of Black youth. *Journal of Black Psychology, 28,* 84–106.

Stevenson, H. C., & Davis, G. Y. (2004). Racial socialization. In R. Jones (Ed.), *Black psychology* (4th ed., pp. 176–189). Hampton, VA: Cobb & Henry.

Stevenson, H. C., Reed, J., Bodison, P., & Bishop, A. (1997). Racism stress management: Racial socialization beliefs and the experience of depression and anger in youth. *Youth & Society, 29*(2), 197–222.

Stovall, D. (2005). A challenge to traditional theory: Critical race theory, African-American community organizers and education. *Discourse, 26*(1), 95–108.

Taylor, E. B. (1964). *Researches into the early history of mankind and the development of civilization.* Chicago: University of Chicago Press.

Thornton, M. C., Chatters, L. M., Taylor, R. J., & Allen, W. R. (1990). Socio-demographic and environmental correlates of racial socialization by black parents. *Child Development, 61,* 401–409.

Tyler, K., Boykin, A., Boelter, C., & Dillihunt, M. (2005). Examining mainstream and Afro-Cultural value socialization in African American households. *Journal of Black Psychology, 31,* 291–310.

Wodak, R., & Meyer, M. (Eds.). (2001). *Methods of critical discourse analysis.* London: Sage.

8

PREPARING TEACHERS OF AFRICAN AMERICAN STUDENTS IN URBAN SCHOOLS

H. RICHARD MILNER IV

W hat does it mean to prepare teachers to teach African American[1] students in urban schools? What might the preparation and professional development of these teachers look like? In this chapter, I consider these pressing questions, with special attention placed on educational experiences of African American students. Orfield (2001) maintained, "The number of black and Latino students in the nation's public schools is up 5.8 million, while the number of white students has declined by 5.6 million" (p. 17). The trend in urban schools is even more profound:

> In 1998–1999 there were 26 cities with more than 60,000 students. These cities enrolled 4,715,000 of the nation's 48,392,000 public school students. While about a tenth (9.74%) was enrolled in these districts, the districts served only a minute fraction of the nation's white students and a large share of the blacks and Latinos. (Orfield, 2001, p. 25)

Thus, the need to place attention on the educational experiences of African American students in urban schools is obvious—the preparation of teachers to meet these students' diverse and varied needs should be centrally embedded in and throughout teacher education programs.

I have written this chapter with a sense of urgency because it is critical that teachers are well-educated (and better) prepared to teach African American students in urban schools. The chapter is written to cover the needs and the careers of teachers from the beginning of their preservice program to the end of their teaching. The education of teachers does not end when they graduate from their respective education programs—rather, their learning is—and should be—a lifelong process that must be studied carefully to benefit P-12 and teacher education students. My search of databases for my review of this topic revealed some important conceptual and empirical discussions that related to African American students and to urban education. However, very little of the scholarly literature available that I reviewed had the direct focus of this chapter: preparing teachers of African American students in urban schools. More than a decade ago, Ladson-Billings (1994) wrote, "Almost nothing [no literature] exists on teacher preparation specifically for African American students" (p. 7). This chapter builds on related literature that concerns African American students and urban education, urban class-rooms, and urban schools.

In their literature reviews about African American students and urban education, Ford (1996) and Weiner (2003) discovered that much of the literature painted very negative and inadequate portraits of African Americans and of urban education. Weiner (2003) explained that lack of success in urban schools is often described as a result of "problems in students, their families, their culture, or their communities" (p. 305). To suggest that all, or even most, urban schools, neighborhoods, and people are substandard would be unfairly inaccurate. Some of what is written sends the message that "if it's urban or African American, then it's bad!" Negative descriptors are often used as adjectives to describe students and other individuals in the learning community themselves rather than the institutional, bureaucratic, or systemic situations that are in place and intentionally designed to maintain the status quo. Weiner (2006) wrote, "There are structural and organizational factors, like the school system's size and the centrality of the school bureaucracy"(p. 16) that should be taken into consideration when analyzing urban contexts and situations.

Haberman (2000) explained that "language is not an innocent reflection of how we[2] think. The terms we use control our perceptions, shape our understanding, and lead us to particular proposals for improvement" (p. 203). In teacher education, the language that is used about Black students can also reinforce stereotypes that teachers already bring into the higher education classroom and can also cause capable teachers to turn away from P-12 classrooms with high populations of Black students, urban schools, and Black students in urban schools. Teachers' misperceptions and stereotypes about Black students come from a variety of sources, including their parents, the media, or even isolated negative experiences that they have had with Blacks both inside and outside the classroom. Thus, it is critical for any discussions about Black students, urban education, and teachers to focus not only on powerful classroom situations but also on out of school situations and experiences that have the potential to enable or hinder academic success in the classroom.

Ladson-Billings (1999) explained that the literature has sometimes presented students of color, for instance, as "somehow defective and lacking" (p. 216). In reality, these negative misconceptions are reinforced not only in the classroom but can also be found in the pervasive discourses in the literature concerning Black students and urban schools. A dominant and oppressive perspective is that White people, their beliefs, experiences, and epistemologies (Sheurich & Young, 1997) are often viewed as "the norm" by which others are compared, measured, assessed, and evaluated (Foster, 1999). In terms of practice, African American students in schools on all levels (from pre-K to graduate or professional school) are often placed in remedial courses to "catch up" or "live up" to a norm, for which the model is their White classmates. Research suggests that people of color may experience and represent a different type of "normal" life and that excellence can emerge in multiple and varied forms: People and communities of color from all walks of life can be and are successful (Morris, 2004). In the next section, I discuss central components of urban contexts. That is, how might one define an urban context?

URBAN CONTEXTS

Based on my knowledge and understanding, there is not a static definition of urban education or urban contexts. Scholars define urban education in myriad ways. For instance, some scholars focus on inner-city schools when they refer to urban education. Other scholars may refer to schools in urban (large) metropolitan regions, particularly older cities in the north, when they discuss urban education (cf. Kozol, 1992). Thus, communities can be categorized generally as suburban, rural, or urban. While these contexts have similarities, there are also many differences. For example, suburban schools tend to be relatively homogeneous[3] in terms of socioeconomic status (SES). Compared with their counterparts in other communities, suburban students also tend to score higher on achievement and proficiency tests and tend to pursue postsecondary degrees more often.[4] However, as Ladson-Billings and Tate (1995) explained,

> Although both class and gender can and do intersect race, as stand-alone variables they do not explain all of the educational achievement differences apparent between Whites and students of color. Indeed, there is some evidence to suggest that even when we hold constant for

class, middle-class African-American students do not achieve at the same level as their White counterparts. (p. 51)

In suburban schools, teachers tend to have higher educational credentials, and families tend to be nuclear and more educated. In many respects, urban and rural schools have much in common, particularly where SES is concerned. Both types of schools tend to have high concentrations of students living in poverty, high percentages of single-parent families, the least qualified or credentialed teachers, and the fewest school resources (new school buildings, curricular materials, etc). However, there is a noticeable difference between urban and rural schools in terms of student mobility, size, and diversity, with urban schools and communities tending to be larger, having higher student transience, and having greater ethnic and cultural diversity. These differences in school context—diversity, size, resources, teacher qualifications, and more—cannot be ignored, negated, minimized, or trivialized. Peske and Haycock (2006) explained,

> Classes in high-poverty and high-minority secondary schools are more likely to be taught by "out-of-field teachers"—those without a major or minor in the subject they teach. . . . In secondary schools serving the most minority students, almost one in three classes are assigned to an out-of-field teacher compared to about one in five in low-minority schools. (pp. 2–3)

The literature suggests that more experienced teachers tend to have a more comprehensive repertoire of knowledge where teaching and learning are concerned, and students may experience more opportunities to learn in classrooms with teachers who have been in the profession for more years (cf. Peske & Haycock, 2006).

Reports on high teacher turnover or burnout rates are consistent—teachers often leave urban classrooms—and quickly. Howard (2003) explained some of the issues inherent in teacher attrition, particularly in urban schools:

> Countless numbers of teachers leave because of high levels of stress, unsatisfactory organizational conditions, lack of administrative support, perceived discipline problems, cultural mismatches with students, and a multitude of socio-cultural factors that play out in the classroom everyday. (p. 149)

Howard posed a salient and important question about the effects of teacher attrition in urban schools: Who receives the short end of the teacher shortage when talented teachers leave (or never enter) urban classrooms? And the answer, of course, is the students who are often left with underqualified, undercommitted, and underprepared teachers. Perhaps more than anything, it is the teachers and the teaching that occurs in the urban contexts that can make *a difference* in the education of Black students. It is important to note that I am not suggesting that teaching and teachers are the only factors to consider in improving the educational experiences of African American students in urban schools. Addressing the needs of African American students in urban schools is complex and seriously multifaceted, and there are numerous matters (nuances and idiosyncrasies) to addressing these needs.

For instance, discussions about funding are central to addressing the needs of African American students in urban schools. Wiener and Pristoop (2006) reported that "four states—Illinois, New Hampshire, New York, and Pennsylvania—shortchange their highest poverty districts by more than $1000 per student per year" (p. 6). Roza (2006) explained that "because the traditional role of local property taxes in funding local school districts inherently puts low-wealth and low property value communities at a disadvantage, states should rely more on statewide sources of revenue" (p. 13). While poverty and other negative factors are often used when discussing urban schools, I cannot reiterate enough the point that not all urban schools lack resources or have large numbers of students who struggle with their academics. The scope of the factors that contribute to the needs of African American students in urban schools is far beyond what can be addressed in this chapter. As a result, I focus on what teachers and teaching can do. But why focus on African American students in urban schools?

A FOCUS ON AFRICAN AMERICAN STUDENTS

Why is there such an urgent need to prepare teachers of African American students in urban schools? There is a great need to prepare teachers with increased attention to African

American students in P-12 classrooms because African American students consistently have been misserved and miseducated in P-12 schools and in higher education (Irvine, 1990; Ladson-Billings, 2006; Woodson, 1933). Ladson-Billings (2006) maintained that it is unfair and inconceivable to expect all students to finish their education in the same place because some students—such as African American students—do not begin their education in the same place. In terms of resources, assets, teachers, and policies, the power of Ladson-Billings's position shows up in the learning opportunities and experiences of Black students. Teachers often have low expectations for Black students, and they "teach down" to them, and they often "water down" the curriculum. Black students are grossly underrepresented in gifted education and overrepresented in special education. Teachers in these schools rarely see the brilliance in Black students. They often see difference (i.e., students' conceptions, beliefs, convictions, values, and behaviors that are inconsistent with their own) as wrong. Ford (2006) wrote, "Sadly, I have seen little progress relative to demographic changes—Black and Hispanic students continue to be as underrepresented in gifted programs today as they were 20 years ago" (p. 2).

A report from the Schott Foundation for Public Education (Holzman, 2004) stressed,

In many school districts, up to 70 percent of black boys who enter 9th grade do not graduate four years later with their peers. In most districts, black boys are disproportionately assigned to special education and nearly absent from advanced placement classes. (p. 2)

The Schott Foundation for Public Education places the urgent nature of teaching Black students at the top of the foundation's agenda in *Public Education and Black Male Students: A State Report Card* (Holzman, 2004). In short, the report card revealed that "in 2001/2002 59% of African American males did not receive diplomas with their cohort" (p. 4). Moreover, where education is concerned, the report revealed that "New York City and Chicago, for example, enrolling nearly 10% of the nation's Black male students between them, fail to graduate 70% of those with their peers" (p. 4).

Again, there is a great need to focus on African American students. Skiba, Michael, Nardo, and Peterson (2002) analyzed disciplinary records of 11,001 students in 19 middle schools in a large, urban midwestern public school district during the 1994–1995 academic year. Skiba et al. reported a "differential pattern of treatment, originating at the classroom level, wherein African American students are referred to the office for infractions that are more subjective in interpretation" (p. 317). Different behaviors are often equated with insubordination: teachers often see Black students as deficits rather than as assets. The Skiba et al. (2002) study pointed out that students of color overwhelmingly received harsher punishments for "misbehavior" than did their White counterparts. As an example, the authors described a fistfight at a high school football game in Decatur, Illinois that resulted in the superintendent's recommendation that all seven of the African American students involved be expelled from school for 2 years. Apparently, in the same district, weapons were used in a fight involving White students and less severe punishment was imposed upon those students. Noguera (2003) suggested that policies and procedures in public schools often treat African American students as if they are prisoners, rather than students who are developing, growing, learning, and maturing.

Davis and Jordan (1994) analyzed data from the National Education Longitudinal Study of 1988 administered by the National Center for Educational Statistics. The researchers employed a two-stage, stratified, random sample of 25,000 eighth graders in 1,000 schools across the country. Davis and Jordan reported a connection between discipline and Black male achievement in middle schools. As the researchers explained, "the time teachers spend handling disciplinary problems is time taken away from instruction; Black male achievement suffers as a result" (p. 585). In short, instead of teachers teaching these students, much of their time is spent attempting to discipline the students. Clearly, when students are not in the classroom because of disciplinary approaches and policies that put the students out of the classroom, such as suspension and expulsion, the students are suffering academically. Davis and Jordan explained that these disciplinary actions resulted in student classroom and school disengagement, and the students' achievement suffered because the disciplinary practices served as "disincentives" (p. 586) for these students.

Inherent in such data are questions that focus on why some groups of students—particularly Black students—are punished more severely and more frequently than are others. Admittedly, the answers to the questions about the state, needs, and conditions of Black students in urban schools are enormously complex; there are no cookie-cutter principles to improve the educational experiences of Black students. Still such critiques and analyses are needed if we are to improve the education of all Black students in urban schools as the demographic divide between teachers and students intensifies.

A Demographic Divide

The demographic divide rationale is present in much of the literature that makes a case for the preparation of teachers for diversity (cf. Gay & Howard, 2000; Landsman & Lewis, 2006; Zumwalt & Craig, 2005). Zumwalt and Craig (2005) wrote, "Although the student population is increasingly diverse, 1999–2000 data indicate that public school teachers were predominantly White, non-Hispanic (84%). Of the remaining

proportion, 7.8% were African American, 5.7% Hispanic, 1.6% Asian American, and 0.8% Native American" (National Center for Education Statistics, 2003). Never before have public school teachers in the United States been faced with the challenge of meeting the needs of so many diverse learners, and the teaching force in the United States is increasingly White, monolingual, middle class, and female (Banks & Banks, 2000; Gay & Howard, 2000; Zumwalt & Craig, 2005). Tables 8.1 and 8.2 provide racial demographic data of public school teachers and students.

While there is a demographic divide between teachers and students, students in public schools in the United States are often very segregated in terms of race. In other words, students often attend schools with others of similar ethnic and racial backgrounds. They often attend largely segregated schools, particularly in certain regions of the country and particularly in large urban districts (Orfield, 2001).

The emphasis on and the questions about segregated and desegregated schools should not be ones that focus on desegregation for the sake of desegregation. Perhaps if African American

TABLE 8.1   Teaching Demographics in Public Elementary and Secondary Schools

2003–2004	Elementary Public School	Secondary Public School
White	81.6%	84.2%
Black	8.8%	7.5%
Hispanic	7.0%	5.5%
Asian	1.3%	1.3%
Pacific Island	0.2%	0.2%
American Indian/Alaska Native	0.4%	0.6%
More than one race	0.7%	0.7%

SOURCE: Institute of Education Sciences (n.d.a).

TABLE 8.2   Student Demographics

2003–2005	2003	2004	2005
White	60.5%	59.9%	59.4%
Black	14.9%	14.9%	14.8%
Hispanic	17.7%	18.2%	18.7%
Asian	3.6%	3.7%	3.7%
Pacific Islander	0.2%	0.2%	0.2%
American Indian/Alaska Native	0.9%	0.9%	0.9%
More than one race	2.2%	2.3%	2.3%

SOURCE: Institute of Education Sciences (n.d.b).

students are experiencing optimal learning and educational opportunities in segregated schools, then desegregation may not be necessary. As Siddle-Walker (2000) explained in her historical work, there has been value in segregated spaces where all the students were Black. Moving bodies around to achieve desegregation without changing the essence, the core, the fabric of the educational and institutional system for Black students may not be the answer (Milner & Howard, 2004). Clearly, the push to prepare teachers for diversity is important; the push to prepare teachers for racial, ethnic, cultural, and socioeconomic awareness is, without question, also essential for teacher and P-12 student learning, growth, and improvement. Many teachers will find themselves in classrooms that are not very diverse in terms of racial and ethnic diversity. Many students in urban schools are African American, and teachers must develop the knowledge, skills, attitudes, dispositions, and abilities to teach a diverse group of African American students, a diverse group of White students, or a diverse group of Latino/a students for instance. Thus, while on a large scale, students are increasingly non-White, schools in the United States are increasingly only minimally diverse in terms of racial and ethnic composition (Orfield, 2001).

I am not suggesting that one focus is superior to the other—teachers need to be prepared to teach a wide range of students, all students; however, I argue that the knowledge base and the education of teachers need to shift from a "business as usual" model to more innovative preparation and education that place at the core empirical and conceptual knowledge about the learning and experiences of African American students in P-12 classrooms to help educate teachers. In other words, if we continue to prepare teachers in the same manners in which we have prepared them in the past, Black students will likely find themselves receiving less than optimal learning opportunities, and teachers and schools will continue to fail Black students (Irvine, 1990). It is necessary for us—particularly in teacher education—to rethink teacher education programs and policies if we want to improve the educational experiences of African American students in P-12 schools, and ultimately if we want to improve the experiences of the teachers who will and currently teach African American students in P-12 urban schools. However, the curriculum, policies, and instruction in teacher education programs often resemble those of P-12 contexts (Dixson,

2006). The curriculum is Eurocentric; the policies reflect those in power (viz., White, middle- to upper-class males in suburban contexts); and the instruction is top down and does not consider the ever-present cultural and racial dynamics of the P-12 students, their experiences, and their learning contexts.

The discussion shifts now to a discussion of some of what we know about Black teachers and their teaching of Black students. I focus on Black teachers and their teaching in P-12 classrooms to outline features of successful teaching and teachers of African American students for urban schools. Outlining some of the practices of Black teachers and their success with Black students can be insightful for all teachers interested in teaching Black students. It is also important to note that White teachers (or teachers of any ethnic background) can be successful teachers of Black students (Cooper, 2003; Ladson-Billings, 1994). I focus on Black teachers' experiences and success both pre- and postdesegregation for insights about how all teachers can deepen and broaden their understanding to better meet the needs and situations of Black students at present.

BLACK TEACHERS AND THEIR TEACHING

Much has been written about Black teachers, their experiences, their curriculum development, and their teaching in public school classrooms, both pre- and postdesegregation (Foster, 1997, 1999; Holmes, 1990; Hudson & Holmes, 1994; Irvine & Irvine, 1983; King, 1993; Monroe & Obidah, 2004). This literature is not limited to public schools but also highlights Black teachers' pedagogical style in higher education, namely in teacher education programs (Baszile, 2003; Ladson-Billings, 1996; McGowan, 2000).

In her analyses of valuable African American teachers during segregation, Siddle-Walker (2000) explained that the teachers in her work were

> consistently remembered for their high expectations for student success, for their dedication, and for their demanding teaching style, these [Black] teachers appear to have worked with the assumption that their job was to be certain that children learned the material presented. (pp. 265–266)

Clearly, these teachers worked many hours to help their African American students learn;

although these teachers were teaching their students during segregation, they were also preparing their students for a world of integration (Siddle-Walker, 1996). Moreover, as Tillman (2004) suggested, "These teachers saw potential in their Black students, considered them to be intelligent, and were committed to their success" (p. 282). There was something authentic about these Black teachers and their teaching of Black students. They saw their jobs, roles, and responsibilities to exceed far beyond the hallways of the school or their classroom. They had a mission to teach their students because they realized the risks and consequences in store for their students if they did not teach them and if the students did not learn. An undereducated and underprepared Black student, during a time when society did not want nor expect these students to succeed, could likely lead to obliteration (drug abuse, prison, or even death).

Pang and Gibson (2001) found that "Black educators are far more than physical role models, and they bring diverse family histories, value orientations, and experiences to students in the classroom, attributes often not found in textbooks or viewpoints often omitted" (pp. 260–261). Thus, Black teachers are texts themselves, but text pages of these teachers are inundated with life experiences and histories of racism, sexism, and oppression, along with those of strength, perseverance, and success. Allowing Black students' entry into their rich textual pages seemed to be essential to the learning of Black students. The texts of these teachers are rich and empowering—they have the potential to help students understand and work to change oppression and inequity in the world (Freire, 1998; Wink, 2000). Black teachers have had a meaningful impact on Black students' academic and social success because they often deeply understand Black students' situations and their needs both inside and outside the classroom. For instance, Black teachers lived in the communities of Black students, attended church with their Black students and their families, and even got their hair dressed in the same facilities as their students and related family members.

Successful teachers of Black students maintain high expectations of their students (Siddle-Walker, 1996) and do not pity them but empathize with the students (McAllister & Irvine, 2002), so that students have the best possible chance of mobilizing themselves and empowering their families and communities. Teachers who are committed to improving the lives of their students do not accept mediocrity, and they *encourage and insist* that their students reach their full capacity, mainly because these teachers understand that allowing students to "just get by" can surely leave them in their current situation or even worse. Thus, teachers cannot adopt approaches and instructional models that do not push their students—high expectations, as Siddle-Walker (1996) explained, are necessary to help the students emancipate themselves and to move beyond their current situations.

Irvine and Fraser (1998) described an interaction between a student and teacher below by borrowing James Vasquez's notion, "warm demanders," a description of teachers of color "who provide a tough-minded, no-nonsense, structured, and disciplined classroom environment for kids whom society has psychologically and physically abandoned" (p. 56):

> "That's enough of your nonsense, Darius. Your story does not make sense. I told you time and time again that you must stick to the theme I gave you. Now sit down." Darius, a first grader trying desperately to tell his story, proceeds slowly to his seat with his head hanging low. (Irene Washington, an African American teacher of 23 years, cited in Irvine & Fraser, 1998, p. 56)

An outsider listening and observing the Black teacher's tone and expectations for Darius may frown on the teacher's approach in Irvine and Fraser's study. However, this teacher's approach is grounded in a history and a reality that is steeped in care for the student's best interest. The teacher understood quite deeply the necessity to help Darius learn. She understood the necessity to "talk the talk." There is a sense of urgency not only for Irene to "teach her children well but to save and protect them from the perils of urban street life" (p. 56). Black teachers often have a commitment to and a deep understanding of Black students and their situations and needs because both historically and presently these teachers experience and understand the world in ways similar to their students. For instance, Black teachers know what it means to experience racism and to be discriminated against due to ingrained systems of racism, and they share this and similar commonalities with Black students. Thus, the teachers often have a commitment to the students' communities. Students often do not want to let their teachers down because the teachers are concerned for the students (Foster, 1997). This concern has been described as other mothering (Collins, 1991), and I would add other fathering. The teachers want for their students the best—just as they would want for their own biological children. The students sense this deep level of care from their teachers, and the students do their best work in their teachers' classroom and beyond. They do not want to let their teachers down; they see their teachers as family, and many of the African American students are loyal and very committed to their families.

The question remains how do we transform and reform teacher education programs in ways that prepare teachers to teach African American students in urban schools? What can we learn from Black teachers' teaching and other successful teachers of African American students that can contribute to a discussion about teacher education programs designed to prepare teachers of African American students? The discussion shifts to consider these questions, first by focusing on issues of curriculum and instruction in teacher education and in urban education.

Focus on Curriculum and Instruction

The curriculum and instructional practices in teacher education and the knowledge teachers receive about curriculum and instruction once they leave teacher education are essential. The curriculum can be defined as what students have the opportunity to learn in a particular context; pedagogy can be defined as how the curriculum is taught. The curriculum and pedagogy in teacher education may need to shift to a heightened focus on African American students in urban contexts. Where curricular and instructional matters are concerned, I argue that the teacher education curriculum could be expanded to include a focus on Black students in urban classrooms. For instance, what are some cultural characteristics of African American students? What teaching practices appear to be the most promising for African American students and why? What stakeholders are central to providing optimal learning opportunities for African American students (e.g., parents, policymakers, principals), and how can these stakeholders be used to benefit Black students?

Coupled with these curricular and instructional issues are matters that focus on practicum and student teaching sites and experiences. Teachers in teacher education programs may need to be exposed to teaching sites with populations of African American students in urban contexts—and especially successful, positive with sites with African American students and teachers from any and all racial and ethnic backgrounds. These sites can be seen as a form of the curriculum. Practicum and student teaching sites are texts: they are spaces that can be read, curricular texts that teachers can use as opportunities to learn.

Pedagogically, it is important that teacher educators are prepared to help teacher education students think through the curricula that focus on African American students in urban spaces (materials, information, artifacts, and experiences) so that teachers' experiences do not reinforce the many and pervasive stereotypes that they may have about Black students in urban schools. We certainly cannot assume that teacher educators, themselves, are prepared to work through these issues, so the expertise of the teacher educators covering those issues is critical. It is not enough to send teachers to these sites to work with African American students without a well-developed and planned seminar or course that specifically goes along with the practicum and student teaching experiences. Seminars could be offered along with student teaching and practicum experiences in the particular practicum and/or student teaching site in order to provide students opportunities to digest and work through their many dilemmas and situations as they are experiencing them in the practicum or student teaching experiences. The seminars should not become spaces to complain about situations and experiences. Rather, the seminars can be a place to help teachers develop mindful rationales based on research, theory, and practice. Medina, Morrone, and Anderson's (2005) response "has been the development of a field-based teacher education program that includes a strong commitment to urban education and a dedicated partnership with community schools" (p. 208). More research is needed that focuses on the nature of learning that takes place in field-based sites with African American students as well as the structure, development, and learning of the teachers in the seminars that support the teachers in the field.

I have used Suskind's (1998) *A Hope in the Unseen* with teachers in teacher education courses. Teachers in the courses report new insights and understanding about high-achieving African American students. As is the case with Cedric, an African American student attending an urban school and the main character in Suskind's book, African American students find themselves dealing with situations far beyond their control (lack of resources, for instance)—yet they still persevere *and* achieve. Teachers often admit that they did not realize there are students like Cedric in urban contexts. They are operating from perspectives that have been one-sided. Much of what they have come to understand about schools like Ballou, the urban high school where Cedric attends, is the negative; the teachers come to understand quite well what the students and schools do not have instead of what they actually have. They are operating from deficit perspectives and thoughts. Ford and Grantham (2003) wrote, "Deficit thinking exists when educators hold negative, stereotypic and counterproductive views about culturally diverse students and lower their expectations of these students accordingly" (p. 217).

Methods courses in teacher education should place an emphasis on successful and effective pedagogies for and pedagogues of African American students—approaches that are grounded in research and theory. It is conceivable that when teachers gain perspectives and knowledge about the experiences and the needs of Black students that they are more likely to conceptualize and execute their teaching in ways that better and more effectively meet the needs of Black students. They may be more apt at developing culturally relevant and responsive pedagogy.

Culturally Relevant and Responsive Pedagogy

I have decided to focus now on the pedagogical tenets of culturally relevant teaching because the literature suggests that such pedagogy has the potential to connect with African American students in the P-12 learning context. Ladson-Billings (1994) studied the successful practices of African American students and conceptualized culturally relevant pedagogy. I attempt to draw practical and curricular relevance for

teacher education based on the principles of culturally relevant approaches that were conceptualized from empirical work in P-12 classrooms. Renowned and leading scholars in teacher education have emphasized the importance of developing culturally relevant and responsive classroom curriculum and instruction for students in the P-12 classroom (cf. Foster, 1997; Gay, 2000; Howard, 2001; Ladson-Billings, 1994).

Central to this approach is the notion that teachers develop skills to understand the complexities of students' culture and their ways of experiencing the world. Moreover, the construct suggests that students develop a critical consciousness and that they do not only assume the role of consumers of knowledge. Rather, African American students are empowered to question the status quo and to challenge existing forces that place some groups of people at a disadvantage. Ladson-Billings (1994) further explained that culturally relevant pedagogy

> uses student culture to maintain it and to transcend the negative effects of the dominant culture. The negative effects are brought about, for example, by not seeing one's history, culture, or background represented in textbook or curriculum . . . culturally relevant teaching is a pedagogy that empowers students intellectually, socially, emotionally, and politically by using cultural referents to impart knowledge, skills, and attitudes. (pp. 17–18)

Culturally relevant pedagogy is an approach that helps "students to see the contradictions and inequities that existed in their local community and the larger world" (Ladson-Billings, 1992, p. 382).The real question for teacher education is how do we help teachers become culturally relevant pedagogues? In other words, how do we equip teachers with the intellectual prowess, conceptual understanding, and practical knowledge to become culturally relevant teachers of African American students?

It is not enough for teacher educators to encourage teachers to become culturally relevant teachers. Teacher educators should attempt to model and represent the various tenets of culturally relevant and responsive teaching in their teacher education classrooms. When we think about curricular and instructional relevance and responsiveness, we often think about their importance on the P-12 level. A similar emphasis is needed in the preparation of teachers; that is, relevant curriculum and instruction are needed to prepare teachers to meet the needs of African American students in urban schools. How do we respond to the needs of teachers in teacher education, and how do we develop and implement relevant curriculum and instruction as we prepare them to teach African American students in the urban context? Teacher education programs, classes, and related experiences that have a relevant and responsive nature to them have the potential to meet the needs of teachers who can ultimately meet the needs of African American students in P-12 urban schools.

MODELING AND REPRESENTING

There is a great need to model and represent what teacher educators expect teachers to do in the P-12 classroom with students. It is not enough to *tell* teachers what they should be doing; rather, the true challenge for teacher educators is to model, *show*, and represent what "good" teaching looks like for African American students. In other words, how do we move the theoretical notions around good teaching, such as culturally relevant and responsive pedagogy, into practice? Of course, all the nuances of urban contexts will not be present in the teacher education learning context. However, it is still critical that teachers actually see or observe, based on carefully developed research, the pedagogical possibilities and promise of their work with Black students in urban schools.

Cynthia Dillard (1996) exemplified the power and promise of modeling and representing in teacher education. In her own teaching, research, and writing, she portrays how teacher educators can not only talk (or theorize about) good teaching but can also walk (practice) the theory. For instance, she used reflective journaling to gauge where students in her course were. What issues were her teacher education students grappling with outside the classroom? She also engaged in the journal writing process herself so that students could understand her growth, questions, and needs throughout the semester. There was a level of reciprocity in her approach, and she was able to provide relevant and responsive experiences (pedagogically and curricular) for

her students because she understood where the students were emotionally, socially, and even spiritually on an ongoing basis and vice versa. Moreover, she was coming to terms with her own ways of knowing, living, modeling, and representing in the world and classroom through reflection; the teacher education students were also learning about her as the professor because she shared her personal journal that documented her journey and growth throughout the semester and course with the students. Clearly, attempting to model and represent relevant curricular and instructional approaches is not easy or trivial. It takes hard work and serious understanding of the concepts and ideas of various theories to model good teaching for African American students. The research suggests that an essential step in helping teachers develop the most meaningful teaching for African American students is through a process of teachers' self examination, reflection, and discovery. In other words, as West (1993) declared, it is difficult to work for liberation on behalf of others if one is not emancipated or free himself or herself. Thus, we cannot assume that teacher educators themselves possess the knowledge, skills, sensitivity, or commitment necessary to prepare teachers to teach African American students in urban schools well.

UNDERSTANDING THE SELF IN LEARNING TO TEACH

The literature makes clear the importance of teachers' self-examination and awareness in meeting the needs of students (Zeichner & Liston, 1996). Medina et al. (2005) stressed the importance of helping students "examine their personal notions of urban schools and communities" (p. 208). Woolfolk (1998) wrote that "reflective teachers think back over situations to analyze what they did and why and to consider how they might improve learning for [all] their students" (p. 8). Valli (1997) explained that "reflective teaching emphasizes the importance of teacher inquiry and counteracts a more limited interest in teachers' behavior without considering what is going on in their minds and hearts" (p. 67). Researchers and theorists have attempted to bridge reflective thinking with that of race (Howard, 2001; Milner, 2003) and stressed the importance of teachers' thinking and conceptions in the cultural contexts of learning (Rios, 1996). Moreover, racialized and cultural reflection has been stressed for all teachers, not just White teachers (Tatum, 2001).

Self-reflection is necessary for all teachers—even Black teachers because some teachers of color have internalized, validated, and reified pervasive, counterproductive stereotypes about themselves and others. They have, in a sense, been kidnapped into believing the dominant culture's misconceptions about Black people. Tatum (2001) posited,

> In a race-conscious society, the development of a positive sense of racial/ethnic identity not based on assumed superiority or inferiority is an important task for *both* [italics added] White people and people of color. The development of this positive identity is a lifelong process that often requires *unlearning the misinformation and stereotypes* [italics added] we have internalized not only about others, but also about ourselves. (p. 53)

Teachers could consider reflecting on their own beliefs about Black students as a way to improve their practices with them. For instance,

- Do they believe and know that Black students are capable of excellence in the classroom and beyond? Are they able to recognize the genius and intelligence of Black students?

- Are teachers willing to accept the reality that Black students themselves are not necessarily the problem in the classroom when tensions emerge and that, as teachers, they may need to make some adjustments to meet their Black students' needs?

- What is the nature of their relationships with Black parents and communities?

- In what ways do they expect their students to succeed and achieve? How do they demonstrate this to their students?

A critical look at the self—a deep introspective examination of the intersections of teachers' personal and professional worldview and beliefs may be necessary for optimal instruction with Black students. Teachers who engage in self-reflection realize that excellence begins with the self and rejects the idea that negativity is only outside them.

Clearly, when teachers walk into learning environments with Black students and do not believe that their students are capable of meeting high expectations, do not have or demonstrate a deep level of care for their students, and hold deficit beliefs and perceptions of their Black students, then Black students can be placed at an enormous disadvantage. Successful teachers of African American students know themselves, are willing to confront their biases and misconceptions, and work to provide Black students with meaningful learning opportunities. While understanding the self is important, working to understand African American students' cultural and racialized ways of experiencing and living in the world is also important.

ACQUIRING CULTURAL KNOWLEDGE ABOUT AFRICAN AMERICAN STUDENTS

Many teachers do not enter teacher education courses or programs with any conception of, interest in, or concern about acquiring cultural and racialized knowledge about themselves or others. They adopt color-blind (Johnson, 2002; Lewis, 2001) and culture-blind ideologies (Ford, Moore, & Milner, 2005) wherein the teachers deliberately and often subconsciously do not think about the enormous, central, and profound influences of African American students' race and culture in teaching and learning. Thus, teacher education programs that endeavor to provide teachers with the knowledge base and understanding necessary to teach in urban schools and classrooms with African American students should consider that many teachers will enter the programs without any (or very limited) prior knowledge and understanding of other individuals' race or culture (Bennett, 1995; Cochran-Smith, 1995; Ladson-Billings, 2001).

The results of color-blind and culture-blind beliefs, ideologies, and practices can result in curricula and learning experiences that are often overwhelmingly Euro-centric in content and devoid of the multiple contributions of people from other racial or ethnic backgrounds. Teachers who adopt color-blind and culture-blind ideologies often do not possess the cultural knowledge necessary for pedagogical success with highly diverse students, especially students who are often placed on the margins of learning. Thus, Banks (1995) declared that "both children of color and White children develop a 'White bias' by the time they enter kindergarten" (p. 392), and such bias is perpetuated, nurtured, and sustained quite often in the classroom because of teachers' lack of cultural and racial awareness. The idea is

> some groups of students—because their cultural and racial heritage is more consistent with the culture, norms, and expectations of the school [and their teachers] than are those of other groups of students—have greater opportunities for academic success than do students whose cultures are less consistent with the school [and teachers'] culture. (Banks, 1998, pp. 22–23)

Moreover, the research indicates that when teachers do not "see color," or at least acknowledge that race matters in the teaching and learning process, there may be "ignored discriminatory institutional practices toward students of color such as higher suspension rates for African American males" (Johnson, 2002, p. 154) in conjunction with students of color being overreferred to special education and lower tracked courses in general.

Indeed, it is critical for teachers to acquire affirmative knowledge about Black students. Many Black students are trendsetters; they are giving, kind, bright, athletic, and compassionate. They are often not self-centered. They understand and respect the ties and connections they have to others. For instance, Black students often have very strong ties to their families. They often work part-time jobs and care for their younger siblings. In her qualitative study of eight recently retired African American teachers, Mitchell (1998) reminded us of the insight that teachers can share about students' experiences. The teachers in her study "were critically aware of the experiences of the students, both in and out of school, and of the contexts shaping these experiences" (p. 105). The teachers in the study were able to connect with the students in the urban environments because they understood that what was occurring in school was often a direct result of the students' out of school experiences. There were reasons behind the students' choices in the urban school context. In Mitchell's words,

> [The teachers] recalled situations in which factors outside of the school adversely affected students' behavior. They described students as listless because of hunger and sleepy because they worked at night and on weekends to help support

younger siblings. They described students easily distracted and sometimes belligerent because of unstable living environments. (p. 109)

Thus, these retired teachers understood the connection between the home and school, and they were able to conceptualize how students' feelings had been affected by their home circumstances and situations. The teachers understood that many of their students were doing drugs, living in poverty, and were acting as adults in their homes in terms of bringing in money to support their families. The teachers relied on this knowledge in their decision making with the students. Acquiring knowledge about African American students means that a first step for teachers is not to refer these students to the office when the students do not comply. Because the teachers cared deeply for their students, the teachers refused to place the students' destiny (in a sense) in the hands of another, such as the disciplinary principal. Thus, successful teachers of African American students in urban schools care deeply about their students, and they demonstrate their care with their actions and decisions.

DEVELOPING CARING RELATIONSHIPS

Caring relationships are established, according to Weinstein (1996), by teaching strategies that "draw from a wide range of methods; they are challenging and intensive, flexibly applied, responsive to student obstacles encountered in learning, and vary for time completion" (p. 18). In describing some common characteristics of care among the 13 teachers in his study, Brown (2003) reported,

> These 13 urban teachers create caring classroom communities by showing a genuine interest in each student. They gain student cooperation by being assertive through the use of explicitly stated expectations for appropriate student behavior and academic growth. And these teachers demonstrate mutual respect for students through the use of congruent communication processes. (p. 282)

Quite often, teachers enter urban classrooms secretly afraid of the students because they have never known anyone who "looked, talked, or acted like [students in urban schools]" (Weiner, 1993, p. 119). In short, it is difficult for teachers to care about individuals they fear. Ennis (1996) examined issues of confrontation among 10 urban high schools that enrolled approximately 110,000 students from lower- to middle-class families. Her findings revealed some possible outcomes when teachers feel unsupported by their administrators. Ennis discovered that some 50% of the teachers in the study reported that they did not teach certain content topics "because of the confrontations that such topics generate with specific students" (p. 145). Because these teachers did not want to feel "ganged up on" in their classrooms, students were denied access and opportunities to certain curricular content. The teachers in the study avoided teaching content that "they believed students were disinterested in learning . . . students refused to learn or to participate in learning, or . . . generated discussions that the teachers felt unprepared to moderate" (p. 146). The teachers were, in a sense, granting students permission to fail (Ladson-Billings, 2002) because they were denying students access to important information that may affect their current and future opportunities.

In such classrooms where fear takes precedence over care, teachers give information, ask questions, give directions, give assignments, give tests, assign homework, punish noncompliance, and grade papers (Haberman, 1991). This vicious cycle is tantamount to Ladson-Billings's (1994) and Freire's (1998) notion that students are often passive participants in their own learning, with teachers constantly attempting to pour knowledge (that they feel safe to pour) into "empty vessels." What happens when teachers exhibit fear over care of their students in the P-12 classroom? Students tend to rebel against such teaching by fighting over control with the teacher. Much time is ultimately taken away from the curriculum, teaching, and learning. Students, in a sense, punish teachers by resisting efforts to be controlled (Haberman, 1991). Student resistance takes many forms—clowning in class, interrupting lessons with jokes, acting out to be removed from the class, feigning illness to be removed from the class or excused from assignments, "losing" assignments and forgetting materials (e.g., paper, pencils, forms, books) to avoid work, teasing classmates, and disagreeing with teachers for the sake of disagreement among other distractions.

In Figure 8.1, I attempt to provide a summary of practices, philosophies, and ideologies that can be central to the educational experiences of African American students in urban schools. It is important to note that I conceptualize the information available in the chart from the research reviewed in this chapter as well as from my own research.

CONCLUSIONS AND FUTURE DIRECTIONS

In conclusion, individuals, contexts, and systems on various levels suffer when we do not teach African American students well. Blame is passed along among and between different groups for the situations in which African American students find themselves. Some teachers find themselves miserable in urban schools because they do not have the wide array of knowledge and skills necessary to be successful in these schools, and they blame parents, students, and even their teacher education program. Parents blame teachers and principals for not teaching their children well. Local, state, and federal governments often blame all involved. We should work together to improve the learning and educational experiences of African American students. Besides, the students deserve the best educational opportunities available and engaging "the blame game" likely will not solve the real problems of the human condition.

Irvine's (1988) outline of effective schools, suggested two decades ago, still holds credence in thinking about reforming urban schools and education to meet the needs of African American students: (a) "visionary" leadership; (b) effective, relevant, and responsive instruction (and curriculum); (c) both rigid and flexible bureaucracy (where autonomy and flexibility are welcomed in some instances and strict as well as rigid administration are necessary in other instances—such as disciplinary policies and procedures to keep everyone safe); and (d) partnerships and collaboration with parents and community members. Thus, urban reform, and particularly reform on the classroom level, is necessary and will prove beneficial not only for those attending and working in urban schools but will prove beneficial for all people in a variety of contexts. As the late educational pioneer and scholar Asa Hilliard (1992) explained, "Any reform that benefits those students who

These teachers

Stress the Value and Importance of Learning: Teachers explicitly convey the importance and value of education and learning to students. They help students understand and embrace the reality that one can be smart and intelligent and, at the same time, cool, hip, and "with it."

Immerse Themselves in Students' Life Worlds: Teachers attempt to understand what it means to live in the world of their students through music, sport, film, and pop culture. They incorporate this knowledge and understanding into learning opportunities in the classroom.

Do More With Fewer Resources: Teachers do not allow what they do not have in terms of resources to hinder their effort, goals, and visions for their students. They do whatever it takes to succeed; they never give up.

Reject Deficit Notions: Teachers concentrate on the assets that students bring into the classroom and build on those assets in the learning contexts. They also understand their own assets as teachers and use those as a foundation to bridge learning opportunities in the classrooms.

Understand Equity in Practice: Teachers understand the difference between equality and equity. They work to meet the needs of individual students and realize that their curriculum and instruction may not be the exact same among all students at all times.

Have and Demonstrate High Expectations: Teachers do not water down the curriculum and present unchallenging opportunities for students just because they "feel sorry" for their students. They empathize with and care for their students.

Possess a Collective Vision: Teachers understand that they are working together with their students, their parents, and their community and operate from perspectives of the collective (we, our, us) rather than opponents (them, they, theirs).

Build and Sustain Relationships: Teachers understand that students need to get to know them (keeping in mind professional distance) and that they need to get to know their students. They see their teaching as a family affair and view their students as their own. In other words, they engage in processes of other mothering and other fathering.

Provide Student Entry Into Their Life World: Teachers allow students to learn things about them and make connections to show the commonalities that exist between the students and the teachers. They share their stories with their students and allow students to share theirs with them.

Deal With the (For)ever Presence of Race and Culture: Teachers reject color-blind and culture-blind ideologies. They see themselves and their students as racialized and cultural beings and use these markers as anchors in the learning process.

Perceive Teaching as Mission and Responsibility: Teachers care deeply about their students and develop missions that will allow students to reach their potential.

Develop Critical Consciousness: Teachers critique knowledge and information available. They become conscious fighters against injustice; they speak out against inequity both inside and outside the classroom. They empower students to do the same.

FIGURE 8.1   Features of Successful Teachers and Teaching in Urban Schools

are poorly served always works to the benefit of all" (p. 375).

NOTES

1. The terms *African American* and *Black* will be used interchangeably throughout this chapter.

2. Throughout this chapter, I use the term *we* to include those individuals both inside and outside

teacher education interested in and concerned about the educational experiences, opportunities, and outcomes of African American students.

3. I use the term *homogeneous* loosely here to refer to the reality that suburban schools tend to have less variance than urban schools in terms of socioeconomic status (SES) and ethnic diversity. That is, students tend to come from similar SES levels and to be disproportionately White. Having said this, I acknowledge that there is no such thing as a homogenous classroom—even in classrooms where students

come from the same SES group and share the same ethnic background, the students will have different learning styles, values, beliefs, and behaviors.

4. It is important to note that my categorizations and discussions of different contexts are not definitive. There are, of course, exceptions that must be taken into consideration when discussing any context or group of people. I deliberately qualify the points made in this section with terms such as *tend, often,* and *perhaps.*

References

Banks, J. A. (1995). Multicultural education and curriculum transformation. *Journal of Negro Education, 64*(4), 390–400.

Banks, J. A. (1998). Curriculum transformation. In J. A. Banks (Ed.), *An introduction to multicultural education* (2nd ed., pp. 21–34). Boston: Allyn & Bacon.

Banks, J. A., & Banks, C. A. M. (2000). *Multicultural education: Issues & perspectives* (4th ed.). New York: Wiley.

Baszile, D. T. (2003). Who does she think she is? Growing up nationalist and ending up teaching race in white space. *Journal of Curriculum Theorizing, 19*(3), 25–37.

Bennett, C. I. (1995). *Comprehensive multicultural education: Theory and practice* (3rd ed.). Boston: Allyn & Bacon.

Brown, D. F. (2003). Urban teachers' use of culturally responsive management strategies. *Theory Into Practice, 42*(4), 277–282.

Cochran-Smith, M. (1995). Color blindness and basket making are not the answers: Confronting the dilemmas of race, culture, and language diversity in teacher education. *American Educational Research Journal, 32,* 493–522.

Collins, P. H. (1991). *Black feminist though: Knowledge, conscious, and the politics of empowerment: Perspectives on gender* (Vol. 2). New York: Routledge.

Cooper, P. M. (2003). Effective white teachers of Black children: Teaching within a community. *Journal of Teacher Education, 54*(5), 413–427.

Davis, J. E., & Jordan, W. J. (1994). The effects of school context, structure, and experiences on African American males in middle and high school. *Journal of Negro Education, 63*(4), 570–587.

Dillard, C. B. (1996). Engaging pedagogy: Writing and reflection in multicultural teacher education. *Teacher Education, 8*(1), 13–21.

Dixson, A. D. (2006). What's race got to do with it? Race, racial identity development, and teacher preparation (pp. 19–36). In H. R. Milner &

E. W. Ross (Eds.), *Race, ethnicity, and education: The influences of racial and ethnic identity in education.* Westport, CT: Greenwood/Praeger.

Ennis, C. D. (1996). When avoiding confrontation leads to avoiding content: Disruptive students' impact on curriculum. *Journal of Curriculum and Supervision, 11,* 145–162.

Ford, D. Y. (1996). *Reversing underachievement among gifted Black students: Promising practices and programs.* New York: Teachers College Press.

Ford, D. Y. (2006). Identification of young culturally diverse students for gifted education programs. *Gifted Education Press Quarterly, 20*(1), 2–4.

Ford, D. Y., & Grantham, T. C. (2003). Providing access for gifted culturally diverse students: From deficit thinking to dynamic thinking. *Theory Into Practice, 42*(3), 217–225.

Ford, D. Y., Moore, J. L., & Milner, H. R. (2005). Beyond cultureblindness: A model of culture with implications for gifted education. *Roeper Review, 27*(2), 97–103.

Foster, M. (1997). *Black teachers on teaching.* New York: New Press.

Foster, M. (1999). Race, class, and gender in education research: Surveying the political terrain. *Educational Policy, 13*(1/2), 77–85.

Freire, P. (1998). *Pedagogy of the oppressed.* New York: Continuum.

Gay, G. (2000). *Culturally responsive teaching: Theory, research, and practice.* New York: Teachers College Press.

Gay, G., & Howard, T. (2000). Multicultural teacher education for the 21st century. *The Teacher Educator, 36*(1), 1–16.

Haberman, M. (1991). Pedagogy of poverty versus good teaching. *Phi Delta Kappan, 73*(4), 290–293.

Haberman, M. (2000, November). Urban schools: Day camps or custodial centers? *Phi Delta Kappan, 82*(3), 203–208.

Hilliard, A. G. (1992). Behavioral style, culture, and teaching and learning. *Journal of Negro Education, 61*(3), 370–377.

Holmes, B. J. (1990). New strategies are needed to produce minority teachers. In A. Dorman (Ed.), *Recruiting and retaining minority teachers* [Guest commentary]. Policy Brief No. 8. Oak Brook, IL: North Central Regional Educational Laboratory.

Holzman, M. (2004). *Public education and black male students: A state report card.* The Schott Educational Inequity Index. Cambridge, MA: Schott Foundation for Public Education.

Howard, T. C. (2001). Telling their side of the story: African American students' perceptions of culturally relevant teaching. *Urban Review, 33*(2), 131–149.

Howard, T. C. (2003). Who receives the short end of the shortage? America's teacher shortage and implications for urban schools. *Journal of Curriculum and Supervision, 18*(2), 142–160.

Hudson, M. J., & Holmes, B. J. (1994). Missing teachers, impaired communities: The unanticipated consequences of *Brown v. Board of Education* on the African American teaching force at the precollegiate level. *Journal of Negro Education, 63,* 388–393.

Institute of Education Sciences, National Center for Education Statistics. (n.d.a). *The condition of education.* Retrieved December 6, 2007, from http://nces.ed.gov/programs/coe/2007/section4/table.asp?tableID=721

Institute of Education Sciences, National Center for Education Statistics. (n.d.b). *Digest of education statistics: 2006.* Retrieved December 6, 2007, from http://nces.ed.gov/programs/digest/d06/tables/dt06_016.asp?referrer=list

Irvine, J. J. (1988). Urban schools that work: A summary of relevant factors. *Journal of Negro Education, 57*(3), 236–242.

Irvine, J. J. (1990). *Black students and school failure: Policies, practices and prescriptions.* New York: Greenwood Press.

Irvine, J. J., & Fraser, J. W. (1998, May 13). Warm demanders. *Education Week, 17*(35), 56.

Irvine, R. W., & Irvine, J. J. (1983). The impact of the desegregation process on the education of black students: Key variables. *Journal of Negro Education, 52,* 410–422.

Johnson, L. (2002). "My eyes have been opened" White teachers and racial awareness. *Journal of Teacher Education, 53*(2), 153–167.

King, S. (1993). The limited presence of African-American teachers. *Review of Educational Research, 63*(2), 115–149.

Kozol, J. (1992). *Savage inequalities.* New York: Harper Perennial.

Ladson-Billings, G. (1992). Liberatory consequences of literacy: A case of culturally relevant instruction for African American students. *Journal of Negro Education, 61*(3), 378–391.

Ladson-Billings, G. (1994). *The dreamkeepers: Successful teachers of African American children.* San Francisco: Jossey-Bass.

Ladson-Billings, G. (1996). Silences as weapons: Challenges of a Black professor teaching White students. *Theory Into Practice, 35,* 79–85.

Ladson-Billings, G. (1999). Preparing teachers for diverse student populations: A Critical Race Theory perspective. *Review of Research in Education, 24,* 211–247.

Ladson-Billings, G. (2001). *Crossing over to Canaan: The journey of new teachers in diverse classrooms.* San Francisco: Jossey-Bass.

Ladson-Billings, G. (2002). Permission to fail. In L. Delpit & J. K. Dowdy (Eds.), *The skin that we speak: Thoughts on language and culture in the classroom* (pp. 107–120). New York: New Press.

Ladson-Billings, G. (2006). From the achievement gap to the education debt: Understanding achievement in U.S. schools. *Educational Researcher, 35*(7), 3–12.

Ladson-Billings, G., & Tate, B. (1995). Toward a critical race theory of education. *Teachers College Record, 97*(1), 47–67.

Landsman, J., & Lewis, C. W. (2006). *White teachers/diverse classrooms: A guide to building inclusive schools, promoting high expectations and eliminating racism.* Sterling, VA: Stylus.

Lewis, A. E. (2001). There is no "race" in the schoolyard: Color-blind ideology in an (almost) all White school. *American Educational Research Journal, 38*(4), 781–811.

McAllister, G., & Irvine, J. J. (2002). The role of empathy in teaching culturally diverse students: A qualitative study of teachers' beliefs. *Journal of Teacher Education, 53*(5), 433–443.

McGowan, J. M. (2000). Multicultural teaching: African-American faculty classroom teaching experiences in predominantly White colleges and universities. *Multicultural Education, 8*(2), 19–22.

Medina, M. A., Morrone, A. S., & Anderson, J. A. (2005). Promoting social justice in an urban secondary teacher education program. *Clearing House, 78*(5), 207–212.

Milner, H. R. (2003). Teacher reflection and race in cultural contexts: History, meanings, and methods in teaching. *Theory Into Practice, 42*(3), 173–180.

Milner, H. R., & Howard, T. C. (2004). Black teachers, Black students, Black communities and *Brown:* Perspectives and insights from experts. *Journal of Negro Education, 73*(3), 285–297.

Mitchell, A. (1998). African-American teachers: Unique roles and universal lessons. *Education and Urban Society, 31*(1), 104–122.

Monroe, C. R., & Obidah, J. E. (2004). The influence of cultural synchronization on a teachers perceptions of disruption: A case study of an African-American middle-school classroom. *Journal of Teacher Education, 55*(3), 256–268.

Morris, J. E. (2004). Can anything good come from Nazareth? Race, class, and African American schooling and community in the urban south and Midwest. *American Educational Research Journal, 41*(1), 69–112.

National Center for Education Statistics. (2003). *School and staffing survey, 1999–2000.* Washington, DC: NCES, U.S. Department of Education.

Noguera, P. A. (2003). Schools, prisons, and social implications of punishment: Rethinking disciplinary practices. *Theory Into Practice, 42*(4), 341–350.

Orfield, G. (2001). *Schools more separate: Consequences of a decade of resegregation: The civil rights project.* Cambridge, MA: Harvard University Press.

Pang, V. O., & Gibson, R. (2001). Concepts of democracy and citizenship: Views of African American teachers. *Social Studies, 92*(6), 260–266.

Peske, H. G., & Haycock, K. (2006). *Teaching inequality: How poor and minority students are shortchanged on teacher quality.* A report and recommendations by the Education Trust. Washington, DC: Education Trust.

Rios, F. A. (1996). *Teacher thinking in cultural contexts.* Albany: State University of New York Press.

Roza, M. (2006). *How districts shortchange low-income and minority students.* Washington, DC: Education Trust.

Sheurich, J., & Young, M. (1997). Coloring epistemologies: Are our research epistemologies racially biased? *Educational Researcher 26*(4), 4–16.

Siddle-Walker, V. (1996). *Their highest potential: An African American school community in the segregated south.* Chapel Hill: University of North Carolina Press.

Siddle-Walker, V. (2000). Valued segregated schools for African American children in the South, 1935–1969: A review of common themes and characteristics. *Review of Educational Research, 70*(3), 253–285.

Skiba, R. J., Michael, R. S., Nardo, A. C., & Peterson, R. L. (2002). The color of discipline: Sources of racial and gender disproportionality in school punishment. *Urban Review, 34*(4), 317–342.

Suskind, R. (1998). *A hope in the unseen: An American odyssey from the inner city to the ivy league.* New York: Broadway.

Tatum, B. D. (2001). Professional development: An important partner in antiracist teacher education. In S. H. King & L. A. Castenell (Eds.), *Racism and racial inequality: Implications for teacher education* (pp. 51–58). Washington, DC: AACTE.

Tillman, L. C. (2004). (Un)intended consequences? The impact of the *Brown v. Board of Education* decision on the employment status of black educators. *Education and Urban Society, 36*(3), 280–303.

Valli, L. (1997). Listening to other voices: A description of teacher reflection in the United States. *Peabody Journal of Education, 72*(1), 67–88.

Weiner, L. (1993). *Preparing teachers for urban schools: Lessons from thirty years of school reform.* New York: Teachers College Press.

Weiner, L. (2003). Why is classroom management so vexing for urban teachers? *Theory Into Practice, 42*(4), 305–312.

Weiner, L. (2006). *Urban teaching: The essentials.* New York: Teachers College Press.

Weinstein, R. S. (1996). High standards in a tracked system of schooling: For which students and with what educational support? *Educational Researcher 25*(8), 16–19.

West, C. (1993). *Race matters.* Boston: Beacon Press.

Wiener, R., & Pristoop, E. (2006). *How states shortchange the districts that need the most help.* Washington, DC: Education Trust.

Wink, J. (2000). *Critical pedagogy: Notes from the real world* (2nd ed.). New York: Longman.

Woodson, C. G. (1933). *The mis-education of the Negro.* Washington, DC: Associated Publishers.

Woolfolk, A. (1998). *Educational psychology* (7th ed.). Boston: Allyn & Bacon.

Zeichner, K. M., & Liston, D. P. (1996). *Reflective teaching: An introduction.* Mahwah, NJ: Lawrence Erlbaum.

Zumwalt, K., & Craig, E. (2005). Teachers' characteristics: Research on the demographic profile. In M. C. Smith & K. M. Zeichner (Eds.), *Studying teacher education: The report of the AERA panel on research and teacher education* (pp. 111–156). Mahwah, NJ: Lawrence Erlbaum.

9

AFRICAN AMERICAN TEACHERS' CARING BEHAVIORS

The Difference Makes a Difference

MARI ANN ROBERTS

JACQUELINE JORDAN IRVINE

I was an exceedingly shy, withdrawn, and uneasy student. Yet my teachers somehow made me believe I could learn. And when I could scarcely see for myself any future at all, my teachers told me the future was mine.

—Baldwin (1985, p. 662)

Every teacher leaves a personal imprint or signature. . . . What students are being exposed to is not just subject matter but also an outlook on life.

—Hansen (1995, p. 59)

Do African American students benefit from having teachers who share their ethnic group membership? The research literature summarized in this chapter suggests that effective African American teachers, when compared with their White counterparts, have a more positive influence on their African American students. Irvine (2002) posited that African American teachers' cultural and ethnic experiences and prior socialization affect the manner in which they view their profession and practice their craft. Although it would be unfair to imply that African American teachers are solely a product of their cultural experiences, it would be equally naive to assume that their instructional behaviors and attitudes are uncontaminated by cultural variables such as their work values, opinions, and beliefs; their prior socialization and present experiences; and their race, gender, ethnicity, and social class. Hence, African American teachers' ethnicity and culture are critical components of their conscious and subconscious selves and are manifest in the teaching act. These cultural attributes shape the ways African American teachers view their profession, practice their craft, and impact the academic achievement and social development of their African American students. Consequently, the purpose of this chapter is to explore the role of African American teachers in the schooling of their African American students. Particularly, this chapter focuses on how African American teachers' culturally relevant care influences the school experiences of their African American students.

Topics discussed include the following: (1) the significance of African American teachers in the profession, (2) culturally relevant teacher care, (3) African American students' perception of African American teachers' care, (4) African American teachers' descriptions of their caring behaviors and attitudes, (5) African American teachers and African American students' school achievement, (6) White teachers and African American students, (7) strategies and interventions for the recruitment and retention of African American teachers, and (8) conclusion and areas for future research.

THE SIGNIFICANCE OF AFRICAN AMERICAN TEACHERS IN THE PROFESSION

According to the Center on Educational Policy (2006), 90% of teachers are White and only 6% of teachers are African American. More specifically, the number of African American teachers is continuing to decline as the number of White teachers increases. The American Association of Colleges of Teacher Education (Zumwalt & Craig, 2005) reported that in 1999, 80% of preservice teachers were White women, many who were unfamiliar with the experiences of their culturally diverse students.

The lack of White teachers' awareness of their African American students' culture was explained by Irvine (1990) as lack of cultural synchronization. Unfortunately, African American students' ways of doing and knowing often conflict with and are antithetical to the ways in which schools do and know. The middle-class cultural norms and behaviors of U.S. schools often result in cultural discontinuity or lack of cultural synchronization between the student, his or her community, and the school. This lack of cultural sync becomes evident in instructional situations when teachers misinterpret, denigrate, and dismiss

African American students' language, nonverbal cues, physical movements, learning styles, cognitive approaches, and worldview. When there is a cultural mismatch or cultural incompatibility between students and their school, the inevitable occurs—miscommunication; confrontations between the student, the teacher, and the home; hostility; alienation; diminished self-esteem; and eventual school failure. For example, in the area of language, Padron and Knight (1990) stated, "Language and culture are so inextricably intertwined that it is often difficult to consider one without the other" (p. 177). There are not only obvious differences in minority students' pronunciation, vocabulary, rhythm, pacing, and inflection but also differences in assumptions regarding what is spoken and left unspoken, whether one interrupts, defers to others, or asks direct or indirect questions (Erickson, 1986).

Research by Byers and Byers (1972) provides some help in understanding the cultural and racial implications of synchronization between teacher and student. Byers and Byers investigated nonverbal communication by filming the interaction between a White teacher, two African American, and two White female nursery school students. They found that one of the White girls was more active and successful in getting the teacher's attention. She looked at the teacher 14 times and the teacher reciprocated 8 of these times. On the other hand, a more initiating African American girl looked at the teacher 35 times but caught the teacher's eye only 4 times. The researchers concluded that the African American girl, unlike her White counterpart, timed her glances inappropriately. She made inappropriate moves at crucial times, pulling when she should have pushed or pushing when she should have pulled. The African American girl, unlike the White girl, did not share with the teacher an implicit understanding of cultural nuances, gestures, timing, and verbal and nonverbal cues. The researchers concluded that the White child's interaction and learning with the teacher were productive and enjoyable; the African American child had the opposite experience. This teacher's instructional behaviors signaled a lack of awareness and attention to issues of culture and learning.

This problem of cultural mismatch between teachers and their students of color will exacerbate in the future. Depending on the assumptions made, projections for the number of newly hired public school teachers needed by 2008 to 2009 range from 1.7 million to 2.7 million (Hussar, 2000). These new hires will also be mostly White women and if the past data are instructive, 50% of these new hires will leave their urban school placement within 3 years to be replaced by novice teachers from the same ethnic and cultural background.

The significance of cultural incongruence between African American students and their mostly White teachers becomes apparent in the data on African American student achievement. The consistent gap between the test scores of Black students and their White and Asian counterparts suggests that there is a great deal of progress to be made regarding educational equity. Despite school restructuring and educational reforms, many African American students are failing in school. The most compelling examples of African American students' nonachievement are found in the reported data on standardized test scores. The 2005 National Assessment of Educational Progress (NAEP) data (Center on Educational Policy, 2006) showed 90% of fourth-grade White and Asian students scored at or above the basic level in math, while only 60% of African American fourth graders scored at that level. Similar gaps were found in other subjects. In addition to NAEP data, Talbert-Johnson (2004) reported that the average Scholastic Aptitude Test scores for African Americans is 195 points lower than the average White test takers score. These test score gaps have remained stable over time. Interestingly, these test score gaps exist even when researchers control for social class. In other words, when middle- and upper-middle income African American students are compared with their social class counterparts, the gap persists.

Other negative outcomes related to the failure of schools to educate African American students include excessive discipline of male African American students (Monroe & Obidah, 2003; Talbert-Johnson, 2004) and a disproportionate representation of African American students in special education programs (Blanchett, 2006). Even more disturbing is the fact that many of these African American students have simply given up and dropped out of school (National Center for Educational Statistics, 2004).

It is not surprising that one of the often-cited solutions posited for closing the Black-White test score gap is the recruitment and retention of highly qualified, caring African American teachers. Although much of the literature on the recruitment and retention of African American teachers fails to specify which of their beliefs and behaviors contribute to the achievement of African American students, one of the most often-cited attributes of these African American teachers is their culturally relevant care.

CULTURALLY RELEVANT TEACHER CARE

Teaching is about caring relationships. As Martin (1995) said, teachers turn schoolhouses into school homes where the three c's (care, concern, and connection) are as important as the 3Rs. In an 18-month ethnographic study of four multiethnic schools, researchers concluded that the most consistent and powerful finding related to school achievement for diverse students was this issue of care (Institute for Education in Transformation, 1992). Students said that they liked school and did their best when they thought that teachers cared about them or did special things for them. Students indicated that caring teachers laughed with them, trusted and respected them, and recognized them as individuals. Students did not say that they liked permissive teachers who let them have their way; just the opposite. Students defined caring teachers as those who set limits, provided structure, had high expectations, and pushed them to achieve.

Care has been defined in various ways by researchers. Rogers and Webb (1991) believed that there is no consensus on the definition of care based on experimental and interpretive work, not because there is a lack of understanding about what caring is, but because of researchers' inability to explicitly define and measure the concept. Noddings (2002) explained this predicament. She stated, "The objective of care shifts with the situation and also with the recipient. Two students in the same class are roughly in the same situation, but they may need very different forms of care from their teacher" (p. 20).

One of the most relevant discussions of African American teacher care is found in the historical work of Walker (1993). In her examination of interpersonal caring in segregated African American schools, she defined care as "the direct attention an individual gives to meet the psychological, sociological, and academic needs of another individual or individuals"

(p. 65). Walker and Tompkins (2004) explained that the history of African American caring in segregated schools is both interpersonal and institutional. In these schools, African American teachers' caring roles included counselor, encourager, benefactor, and racial cheerleader. In addition, the segregated schools had caring institutional structures such as extracurricular programs, assembly programs, a curriculum that supported the aspirations and experiences of the African American students, and a homeroom plan that insured a continuing and sustained relationship between teachers and students.

This type of interpersonal and institutional caring has also been documented in historically Black colleges and universities (HBCUs). St. John and Cadray (2004) stated that the "culture of care" (p. 98) is an important tradition in HBCUs and that even White students who attended these institutions found them more caring places than White colleges and universities.

In the area of teacher education, the expanding research literature suggests that care is an integral part of the culturally responsive pedagogical methods and characteristics of African American teachers who purposefully seek positive school outcomes for their African American students (Beauboeuf-Lafontant, 2002; Denbo & Beaulieu, 2002; Irvine, 1999, 2002; Irvine & Fraser, 1998; Monroe & Obidah, 2003; Sizemore, 1981; Walker, 2000; Walker & Snarey, 2004; Ward, 1995; Ware, 2002; Wilder, 2000). The purposeful actions of these teachers often result in a unique kind of culturally relevant teacher care. Culturally relevant teacher care includes the descriptions of Ladson-Billings's (1994) culturally relevant pedagogy, Irvine's (1990) cultural synchronization, and specific behaviors such as "warm demanders" (Vasquez, 1988), "other mothering" (Collins, 1991), and "colortalk" (Thompson, 2004).

AFRICAN AMERICAN STUDENTS' PERCEPTIONS OF AFRICAN AMERICAN TEACHERS' CARE

Evidence suggests that African American students tend to be more dependent on teachers than their other-race peers and tend to perform poorly in school when they do not like their teachers or feel that their teachers do not care for them (Johnson & Prom-Jackson, 1986; Sizemore,

1981; Vasquez, 1988). Ferguson stated, "I did a study of community-based programs in the early 1990s. A teacher at one of the sites said, 'Once these kids know you care, they'll walk through walls for you'" (Sparks, 2003, p. 45).

Consequently, teachers play a critical role in the achievement of African American students (Foster, 1997; Irvine, 1990, 2002; Ladson-Billings, 1994; Stanford, 1998; Walker, 1996). African American students' perceptions of their teachers can have a direct impact on African American students' achievement as well as their social behaviors. Vasquez (1988) discussed the implications of classroom climates for "minority" students. According to Vasquez, teacher care is an important part of a successful classroom environment for students of color because their perceptions of teacher care seem to have a major influence on their performance and behavior. In other words, according to Vasquez, "caring and demanding school environments make kids work hard and learn" (p. 249). The researcher stressed that to provide a caring environment, a teacher must be aware that students of color have a tendency to not separate a person from his or her behaviors, and as a result must have a mutually caring and respectful relationship with a teacher to learn from them. He discussed a type of teacher characterized as a "warm demander" who maintains high standards for students, reaches out to them, and provides assistance to students who need them.

Many themes in Vasquez's (1988) findings were confirmed by Slaughter-Defoe and Carlson (1996) who studied 1,000 African American and 260 Latino third graders' perceptions of school climate. A 24-item questionnaire was used to determine students' perceptions of their relationships with teachers and peers within the school and the classroom. Pertinent to the purpose of this chapter were items on the survey that assessed positive relationships between students and adults in the school. The items focused on students' perceptions of motivating behaviors teachers used, including verbal encouragement of academic performance, fairness, and respect (Slaughter-Defoe & Carlson, 1996). The researchers found that African American children viewed teacher-student relationships as the most important dimension of school climate. Students believed that caring teachers listened to them, were available to comfort and help, and acknowledged their best efforts. Additionally and equally important, the researchers posited that students' ethnic differences strongly influence their perceptions of a positive school climate. Slaughter-Defoe and Carlson concluded that caring teachers were consistently found to be of key importance to the early learning and development of African American students and emphasized that school climate is a multidimensional variable that influences students' perceptions of their teachers and their school.

In Lee's (1999) qualitative ethnography of African American high school students, the participants identified three specific structures and practices that they felt contributed to their poor academic performance. These factors were teacher-centered rather than student-centered classrooms; perceived racism and discrimination from teachers, particularly in assessment; and lack of positive teacher-student interaction and expectations. The students identified negative teacher attributes such as teacher apathy, lack of caring, and negative messages about their perceived academic abilities. Conversely, students also discussed the transformative differences that some caring teachers made in their lives. These students were particularly appreciative of challenging curriculum, high expectations, interactive learning, and close relationships with teachers.

All the low-achieving students in this study felt as if they would improve academically if they had positive relationships with caring teachers. An important implication of Lee's research is the potential that teacher care may promote African American students' success.

Wilder's (2000) study documented how exposure to African American teachers and their instructional practices helped African American students to identify with and feel personally connected to their teachers and the course content that they taught. She conducted in-depth 90-minute interviews over the course of 6 months with 12 respondents aged 18 and 19 and evaluated the students' responses to open-ended questions. The students were selected from a pool of second-semester college freshmen who represented an array of socioeconomic classes and secondary school settings. The students were self-selected volunteers who signed up to participate in her study after hearing the researcher speak at a freshman seminar for incoming African American students. During the course of this study, Wilder found that some of the students had scant knowledge of African American history. Other students lamented about not having African American secondary teachers but remembered and expressed appreciation for those African American teachers in their early schooling.

Wilder's (2000) students highlighted significant ways African American teachers influenced their African American students. Students said that these teachers increased student confidence, provided an opportunity for students to read about African and African American culture, introduced the African American culture and its ties to Africa, and focused on the connections between education and global awareness. The researcher also noted that general descriptions of African American teachers by Black students did not include words that connoted feelings of alienation or marginality.

Howard's (2003) findings from his qualitative study of 20 students in two majority African American high schools are similar to Lee's (1999) work. Student respondents mentioned racism and discrimination and a lack of positive teacher-student relationships as powerful issues that negatively influenced their schooling. Students felt that their teachers were uncaring and generally apathetic toward them. Some students mentioned that many teachers negatively prejudged them because of their race, made them feel as if they knew nothing, and perceived them as lazy underachievers. However, students mentioned that negative teacher attitudes, although demoralizing, ultimately did not prevent them from achieving their academic goals. Carter and Larke (2003) warned that too often teachers, particularly White teachers, are not aware of student views and do not share the same view of an effective teacher and the caring component of school climate. Teachers could benefit from professional development inservices that assist them in understanding the needs of their students.

African American Teachers' Descriptions of their Caring Behaviors and Attitudes

Foster (1997), in an ethnographic study of African American teachers and teaching, interviewed 17 experienced teachers about their perspectives of teaching. Foster's participants had 17 to 66 years of teaching experience and ranged in age from 45 to 85 years. Foster's teachers consciously fashioned philosophies and pedagogies that drew on lessons from their own childhood in African American schools and communities. When remembering their own African American teachers in segregated schools, respondents said their former teachers were caring individuals who commanded respect, were respectful of pupils, and held all students to the highest academic expectations. Foster's teachers said that they demonstrated culturally relevant care for their students by implementing and embodying postures and principles that they admired in their own teachers.

For example, the teachers often addressed or spoke about the students in kinship terms. Even when kinship terms were not used, the teachers' use of cultural metaphors connoted a similar connectedness and common affiliation with students. Foster's (1997) teachers described their role as mentor, coach, supporter, and parent. One teacher in Foster's book thought that relating to students as relatives helped her to establish a special and intimate bond that helped to decrease disciplinary and classroom management problems. The teacher said, "The first thing I do is try to become a mother to all of them. I tell them, as long as you are here with me, I'm your mama until you go back home, and when you go back home, you go to your other mother" (p. 31). She stated that only after this maternal level of affection had been established could she address discipline issues. Foster's work supports the work of Collins's (1991) historical and cultural context of the term, *other-mothers*. Collins documented that in keeping with West African traditions, women care for the children of other women who were unable to provide for their own children. These "other mothers" bolstered African families and communities because their communal care prevented children from being neglected.

Lynn's (2006) article on the culturally relevant practices of three African American male teachers asserted that the caring role of African American teachers was not limited to females. He concluded that his participants saw themselves as "other fathers" who used tough love, discipline, and caring to create a classroom environment that promoted student success.

African American teachers also felt a need to participate in political clarity and "colortalk" with their students (Thompson, 2004). In other words, they did not assume a color-blind approach that ignored or dismissed the realities of racism in society. Black teachers in the literature felt that their care for students should include an overt and active agenda to address racism and structural inequalities in society. The celebrated teacher, Carrie Secret, selected works of literature for her students that "documented the truth about African people" and she used instructional materials that "confronted racism and white supremacy behavior head on" (Perry, Steele, & Hilliard, 2003, p. 153).

Ware (2002) in summarizing the practices and beliefs of African American teachers noted their emphasis on teaching values and character education to their African American students. She noted the work of Henry (1994), King (1991), and Stanford (1995) who described caring African American teachers who used their classrooms as an environment to teach mutual respect and taught students how to treat each other as humans. These teachers saw character education as an "essential foundation for learning." Ware also made the point that African American teachers reported that they occasionally used community language and dialect to engage and connect students to their communities and classroom. The teachers believed that the use of this language signaled to students that they cared about them and respected the communities and families where their students lived.

Ware (2002) emphasized that the Black teachers also taught their students Standard English. For example, Lipman (1995) described a Black male teacher who validated the students' home language but also taught his students Standard English. He would,

> in an expression of cultural solidarity . . .
> sometimes switch to Black vernacular, but in class
> he was a stickler for Standard English discourse,
> correcting his students' oral and written
> grammar and pushing them with a weekly list
> of challenging vocabulary words. (p. 204)

Ware's (2002) summary of African American teachers' caring behaviors literature reveals that "caring is a characteristic that undergirds and explains many of the actions of dedicated and committed Black teachers" (p. 33). Caring, as demonstrated by Black teachers, exceeded the mere declaration that "teachers should care for students." Ware concluded that Black teachers' caring was also demonstrated in more subtle ways, such as creating and maintaining a caring physical classroom environment. One teacher in Lipman's (1995) study worked hard to design and maintain an attractive and clean classroom that was adorned with students' work. The students perceived this classroom as their home at school where they could drop by during lunch hour and before and after school.

The literature reports that African American teachers expressed care for their students by the nature of the discipline they imposed in their classroom. African American teachers' methods of discipline and classroom management are often misunderstood and misinterpreted by uninformed and naive researchers who portray them as insensitive and harsh disciplinarians. To the contrary, many of these teachers reported that their teaching practices were quite the opposite—caring behaviors intended to promote their students academic achievement in school and their survival in a world that often devalues and discriminates against them.

Irvine and Fraser (1998) described the disciplinary practices of a 23-year veteran African American teacher whose passion and mission is suggestive of Vasquez's (1988) "warm demander." The teacher said that her tough-minded, no nonsense, structured, and disciplined classroom environment was motivated out of a peculiar set of negative environmental circumstances and a sense of urgency to not only teach her children well but to save and protect them from the perils of urban street life.

Cooper (2002) emphasized, however, that effective African American teachers of African American students did not appear to be interested in authority for authority's sake. Using Whitehead's (1929) distinction between authoritarianism and authoritativeness, she noted that authoritative teachers have their children's best interests at heart; authoritarians have their own.

Milner's (2006) review of classroom management in urban classes summarized the relationship between teachers' caring behaviors and students' "misbehavior." He said,

> Students recognize when there is unnecessary distance between themselves and their teachers, and the students' actions are shaped by such disconnections. The students often question: "Why should I adhere to this teacher's management desires when she or he does not

really care about me?" In this respect, students see their misbehavior as a way to distance themselves from uncaring and disrespectful teachers, and the cycle seems to continue is spite of teachers' desires to correct student behavior. (p. 503)

AFRICAN AMERICAN TEACHERS AND AFRICAN AMERICAN STUDENTS' SCHOOL ACHIEVEMENT

Although the literature on the influence of African American teachers on the school achievement of their African American students is only beginning to emerge, there are some studies that suggest some positive effects. In an impressive quantitative study, researchers Meier, Stewart, and England (1989) investigated the relationship between the presence of African American teachers and African American students' access to equal education. Specifically, they investigated the question, Does having African American educators have any impact on African American students' school success? The researchers concluded, "The single most important factor for all forms of second generation discrimination is the proportion of African American teachers" (p. 140). In school districts with large proportions of African American teachers, the researchers found that

- fewer African American students were placed in special education classes;
- fewer African Americans were suspended or expelled;
- more African Americans were placed in gifted and talented programs; and,
- more African Americans graduated from high school.

The authors emphatically concluded that "African American teachers are without a doubt the key" to students' academic success (p. 6).

Dee (2004) reanalyzed data from the Tennessee Project STAR and concluded that racial pairing of teachers and students significantly increased the reading and math achievement scores of both African American and White students by approximately three to four percentage points. Interestingly, Dee reported that the race effects were especially strong among poor African American children who attended segregated schools.

Clewell, Puma, and McKay (2005) raised the question, "Does exposure to a same-race teacher increase the reading and mathematics achievement scores of African American and Hispanic students in elementary schools?" The researchers found that Hispanic fourth and sixth grade students with a Hispanic teacher produced higher test score gains in math. In reading, the same effect was noted, but only in the fourth grade. The effect for Black students with Black teachers was somewhat weaker, although fourth grade Black students had significantly higher scores in mathematics when taught by a Black teacher.

Other researchers have found that African American teachers, when compared with their White counterparts, are more successful in increasing student scores in vocabulary and reading comprehension (Hanushek, 1992) and economic literacy (Evans, 1992).

Ehrenberg and Brewer (1995), using an econometric model that accounted for the nonrandom nature of teacher assignment to schools, found that an increase in the percentage of Black teachers in a school resulted in scores gains for Black high school students.

Also of note are findings that conclude that African American teachers influenced African American students' school attendance (Farkas, Grobe, Sheehan, & Shuan, 1990), and these teachers had higher expectations for their African American students than their White counterparts (Irvine, 1990). Other empirical works, such as a study by Hess and Leal (1997), suggested a correlation between the number of teachers of color in a district and college matriculation rates among students of color.

WHITE TEACHERS AND AFRICAN AMERICAN STUDENTS

Documenting effective pedagogical behaviors and attributes of African American teachers does not ignore the fact that some White teachers are excellent instructors for students of color and that some teachers of color are ineffective with culturally diverse students (Ladson-Billings, 1994). All White teachers clearly do not hold negative opinions about African American students and all Black teachers are not effective teachers of Black children. Nevertheless, it is important to acknowledge that the literature reveals that the behaviors of White teachers more often results in limited, negative perceptions of and reactions to African American student behaviors. Irvine (1990) suggested that Black teachers can also fall prey to the trap of negative expectations; however, White teachers are more likely to be out of cultural sync with their African American students, and African American students are more likely to perceive this cultural mismatch as a lack of care (Delpit, 1995).

In comparing Black teachers' culturally specific teaching styles with those of White teachers, Cooper (2002) concluded that Black teachers often exercise authority directly when teaching. Conversely, White teachers often see their role as facilitators and joint constructors of knowledge. Cooper found other differences between African American and White teachers in their perceptions of the purposes of school. Cooper said that White teachers

> tended to see and describe the schools for black children in near conspiratorial terms. In other words, they described schools as places that consciously and deliberately operated to deprive black children of educational opportunities. . . . Many feared the neighborhoods where black children went to school and they went to work. In contrast, Mrs. Valentine, Mrs. Deveraux, and Mrs. Harris, three teachers from the Ladson-Billings study, all spoke of schools in general as something like warrens for black children, places where black culture could be celebrated and transmitted and where survival in the dominant culture could be learned. This is not to say black teachers ignored the realities for black children in schools. Yet they appeared to see potential in their own teaching, and even in the system (when manipulated successfully), that would help children rise above racism and neglect. They voiced the belief that black children could learn despite inadequate material resources and social hostilities. (p. 61)

STRATEGIES AND INTERVENTIONS FOR THE RECRUITMENT AND RETENTION OF AFRICAN AMERICAN TEACHERS

The first point to emphasize in this section is that recruitment of African Americans to teaching is a pipeline issue. In a study, researchers concluded that the reason for the shortage of Blacks in teaching is related to the insufficient number of Black students who graduate from high school with strong academic skills that prepare them for college and teacher education programs (Vegas, Murnane, & Willett, 2001). In other words, African American students are not less attracted to teaching than White students. The problem is that African American students are not taking college preparatory classes and graduating from high schools with the skills necessary to be competent teachers. In the state of Texas, for example, between 1998 and 2001, of those who graduated from high school, nearly two thirds of the African American students did not take a full complement of college prep courses (Carnoy, Loeb, & Smith, 2001).

Regarding specific strategies, African American teachers should be recruited from obvious places: para professionals and high school students in predominately African American schools, community colleges, civil rights and community organizations, Black fraternities and sororities, and Black churches that have Sunday school, day care programs, and after school programs. Other promising strategies include district-level "grow you own" programs with tuition scholarships.

Colleges of education in HBCUs are uniquely poised to lead the nation in designing and implementing programs that produce African American teachers. One third of African American teachers graduate from these institutions (Freeman, 2001). For example, in 1998 more than half of all African American prospective teachers in Missouri, Maryland, Louisiana, Virginia, South Carolina, North Carolina, Delaware, Alabama, and the District of Columbia were trained at HBCUs. Similar to HBCUs, the organization Recruiting New Teachers (2002) has identified successful programs at community colleges where large numbers of students of color matriculate and successfully complete teacher education programs.

Although recruitment is an important and critical strategy for increasing the number of African American teachers, it is not enough. African Americans recruited to teacher education programs need financial assistance and other support systems. African American teacher education students, particularly nontraditional ones, will benefit from child care,

evening classes, tutoring, preparation for certification exams, and counseling.

To retain African American teacher education students, the curricula at teacher education institutions have to be changed. The curriculum has to be revised to increase pre- and in-service teachers' ability to connect pedagogical content knowledge to the prior knowledge and experiences of African American children. Preservice teachers should have ample opportunities for frequent, extended, and authentic in- and out-of-school cultural experiences with African American students, their families, and communities. These issues are particularly needed at teacher education programs at predominantly White institutions.

African American teacher education students have to be trained by stellar teacher educators, specifically African American teacher educators. Colleges of education must become introspective and reflective about how their cultural norms, policies, and formal and informal practices contribute to the absence of African American professors on their campuses and hence contribute to the absence of African American teacher education students. If colleges of education are not able to recruit and retain African American faculty, how will they be able to provide the necessary and beneficial examples of cultural diversity for their teacher education students? Clearly, deans, directors, and chairs must provide the leadership necessary to develop an organizational climate that values diversity and the recruitment and retention of African American faculty and African American teacher education students.

School districts should provide professional development activities for novice and experienced teachers that are designed and implemented by effective African American teachers. Additionally, African American school-based mentors could assist teachers in making connections between theory and practice and help teachers build on their African American students' varied community and home experiences. Tillman's (2005) case study of a first-year African American teacher in an urban school is instructive. She underscored the mentoring role of the principal as a means for enhancing all teachers' professional and personal competence and the principal's role transmitting the school's culture. Finally, Tillman emphasized the principal's transformative leadership that benefited the African American students and connected the school to the students' community.

CONCLUSION AND AREAS FOR FUTURE RESEARCH

This chapter summarized the extant literature on the culturally specific caring behaviors and attitudes of African American teachers with their African American students. This issue is pertinent and relevant for a number of reasons:

1. The literature suggests that African American students' academic performance appears to be related to their personal feelings about their teachers.

2. Effective African American teachers are characterized by their culturally specific caring behaviors and attitudes.

3. African American teachers' culturally relevant caring appears to be related to African American students' school achievement.

4. The number of African American teachers is decreasing and the number of White teachers with limited experiences with students of color is increasing.

New areas of inquiry should continue to investigate the relationship between the presence of teachers of color and measurable variables such as student achievement, school attendance, drop out rates, and participation in extracurricular activities. Additionally, factors contributing to African American students' success that are more difficult to measure quantitatively should be identified. This chapter was devoted to the affective variable of African American teacher care; however, other variables for investigation might include African American teachers' identification with African American culture and their students' community, their nonverbal communication behaviors, their culturally specific behaviors used with their students' parents, and the identification of pre- and in-service training that assisted them in teaching their students.

More research is needed to identify the reasons why African American high school graduates in college preparatory programs choose not to enter the profession. King (1993) ascertained in her work that African Americans do not enter teaching because of the profession's low prestige, low salary, difficult working conditions, inadequate K-12 educational preparation, and the lure of other career opportunities.

An empirical validation of the importance of teacher care remains primarily incomplete. What are the different forms and contexts for the demonstration of teacher care? How does the ethnicity and social class of the student influence teacher care? For example, do Hispanic and Asian students benefit as much from teacher care as African American students?

Finally, no program for increasing the diversity of teachers will be effective if the working conditions of schools remain the same. We cannot expect teachers of any ethnicity to work in schools with minimal teaching resources, low pay, low status, and where they are not treated like professionals. Schools should be transformed into communities where teachers are respected and recognized as professionals. Teachers should be empowered by increasing their participation in decision making, school management, curriculum development, budgeting, staffing, and the design of effective incentive systems.

REFERENCES

Baldwin, J. (1985). *The price of the ticket: Collected non-fiction 1948–1985.* New York: St. Martins.

Beauboeuf-Lafontant, T. (2002). A womanist experience of caring: Understanding the pedagogy of exemplary black women teachers. *Urban Review, 34*(1), 71–86.

Blanchett, W. J. (2006). Disproportionate representation of African American students in special education: Acknowledging the role of White privilege and racism. *Educational Researcher, 35*(6), 24–28.

Byers, P., & Byers, H. (1972). Non-verbal communication in the education of children. In C. Cazden, V. John, & D. Hymes (Eds.), *Function of language in the classroom* (pp. 3–31). New York: Teachers College Press.

Carnoy, M., Loeb, S., & Smith, T. L. (2001). *Do higher state test scores in Texas make for better high school outcomes?* CPRE Research Report Series: RR-047. Philadelphia: Consortium for Policy Research in Education.

Carter, N. P., & Larke, P. J. (2003). Examining INTASC standards through the lens of multicultural education: Meeting the needs of underserved students. In N. Carter (Ed.), *Convergence or divergence: Alignment of standards, assessment and issues of diversity* (pp. 55–70). Washington, DC: American Association of Colleges for Teacher Education.

Center on Educational Policy. (2006). *A public education primer.* Washington, DC: Author.

Clewell, B. C., Puma, M. J., & McKay, S. A. (2005, April). *Does it matter if my teacher looks like me? The impact of teacher race and ethnicity on student academic achievement.* Paper presented at an Invited Presidential Session of the annual meeting of the American Educational Research Association, Montreal, Quebec, Canada.

Collins, P. H. (1991). *Black feminist thought: Knowledge, consciousness, and the politics of empowerment.* New York: Routledge & Kegan Paul.

Cooper, P. M. (2002). Does race matter? A comparison of effective Black and White teachers of African American students. In J. J. Irvine (Ed.), *In search of wholeness: African American teachers and their culturally specific classroom practices* (pp. 47–63). New York: Palgrave.

Dee, T. (2004). Teachers, race, and student achievement in a randomized experiment. *Review of Economics and Statistics, 86*(1), 195–210.

Delpit, L. (1995). *Other people's children: Cultural conflict in the classroom.* New York: New Press.

Denbo, S. J., & Beaulieu, L. M. (Eds.). (2002). *Improving schools for African American students: A reader for educational leaders.* Springfield, IL: Charles C Thomas.

Ehrenberg, R. G., & Brewer, D. J. (1995). Did teacher's verbal ability and race matter in the 1960s? Coleman revisited. *Economics of Education Review, 14*(1), 1–21.

Erickson, F. (1986). Culture difference and science education. *Urban Review, 18*(2), 117–124.

Evans, M. O. (1992). An estimate of race and gender role-model effects in teaching high school. *Journal of Economic Education, 10,* 209–227.

Farkas, G., Grobe, R. P., Sheehan, D., & Shuan, Y. (1990). Cultural resources and school success: Gender, ethnicity, and poverty groups within an urban school district. *American Sociological Review, 55,* 127–142.

Foster, M. (1997). *Black teachers on teaching.* New York: New Press.

Freeman, K. E. (2001). *Just the facts: African American teachers: Educators for the new millennium.* Fairfax, VA: Patterson Research Institute.

Hansen, D. T. (1995). Teaching and the moral life of classrooms. *Journal for a Just and Caring Education, 2,* 59–74.

Hanushek, E. A. (1992). The trade-off between child quantity and quality. *Journal of Political Economy, 100*(1), 84–117.

Henry, A. (1994). The empty shelf and other curricular challenges of teaching children of African descent: Implications for teacher practice. *Urban Education, 29*(3), 298–319.

Hess, F. M., & Leal, D. L. (1997). Minority teachers, minority students, and college matriculation. *Policy Studies Journal, 25,* 235–248.

Howard, T. C. (2003). Culturally relevant pedagogy: Ingredients for critical teacher reflection. *Theory Into Practice, 42*(3), 195–202.

Hussar, W. J. (2000). Predicting the need for newly hired teachers in the United States to 2008–09. *Education Statistics Quarterly, 1*(4), 45–50.

Institute for Education in Transformation. (1992). *Voices from the inside.* Claremont, CA: Claremont Graduate School.

Irvine, J. J. (1990). *Black students and school failure.* Westport, CT: Praeger.

Irvine, J. J. (1999). The education of children whose nightmares come both day and night. *Journal of Negro Education, 68*(3), 244–254.

Irvine, J. J. (2002). *In search of wholeness: African American teachers and their culturally specific classroom practices.* New York: Palgrave.

Irvine, J. J., & Fraser, J. W. (1998). Warm demanders: Do national certification standards leave room for the culturally responsive pedagogy of African-American teachers? *Education Week, 17*(35), 56–57.

Johnson, S. T., & Prom-Jackson, S. (1986). The memorable teacher: Implications for teacher selection. *Journal of Negro Education, 55,* 272–283.

King, J. E. (1991). Unfinished business: Black students' alienation and Black teacher's emancipatory pedagogy. In M. Foster (Ed.), *Qualitative investigations into schools and schooling* (pp. 245–271). New York: AMS Press.

King, S. H. (1993). Why did we choose teaching careers and what will enable us to stay? Insights from one cohort of the African American pool. *Journal of Negro Education, 62*(4), 475–492.

Ladson-Billings, G. (1994). *The dreamkeepers: Successful teachers of African American children.* San Francisco: Jossey-Bass.

Lee, P. W. (1999). In their own voices: An ethnographic study of low-achieving students within the context of school reform. *Urban Education, 34*(2), 214–244.

Lipman, P. (1995). "Bringing out the best in them": The contribution of culturally relevant teachers to educational reform. *Theory Into Practice, 34*(3), 202–208.

Lynn, M. (2006). Education for the community: Exploring the culturally relevant practices of Black male teachers. *Teachers College Record, 108*(12), 2497–2522.

Martin, J. R. (1995). A philosophy of education for the year 2000. *Phi Delta Kappan, 76,* 355–359.

Meier, K. J., Stewart, J., & England, R. E. (1989). *Race, class, and education: The politics of second generation discrimination.* Madison: University of Wisconsin Press.

Milner, H. R. (2006). Classroom management in urban classrooms. In C. M. Evertson & C. S. Weinstein (Eds.), *Handbook of classroom management* (pp. 491–522). Mahwah, NJ: Lawrence Erlbaum.

Monroe, C., & Obidah, J. E. (2003). The influence of cultural synchronization on a teacher's perceptions of disruption. *Journal of Teacher Education, 10*(10), 1–13.

National Center for Educational Statistics. (2004). *Percent of high school dropouts (status dropouts) among persons 16 to 24 years old, by sex and race/ethnicity: Selected years April 1960 to October 2001.* Digest of Education Statistics. Washington, DC: Author. Retrieved June 4, 2005, from http://nces.ed.gov/programs/digest/d03/tables/dt107.asp

Noddings, N. (2002). *Starting at home caring and social policy.* Berkeley: University of California Press.

Padron, Y. N., & Knight, S. L. (1990). Linguistic and cultural influences on classroom instruction. In H. P. Baptiste Jr., H. C. Waxman, J. W. deFelix, and J. E. Anderson (Eds.), *Leadership, equity, and school effectiveness* (pp. 173–185). Newbury Park, CA: Sage.

Perry, T., Steele, C., & Hilliard, A. (2003). *Young, gifted, and Black: Promoting high achievement among African-American students.* Boston: Beacon Press.

Recruiting New Teachers. (2002). *Tapping potential: Community college students and America's recruitment challenge.* Belmont, MA: Author.

Rogers, D., & Webb, J. (1991). The ethic of caring in teacher education. *Journal of Teacher Education, 42*(3), 173–181.

Sizemore, R. W. (1981). Do Black and White students look for the same characteristics in teachers? *Journal of Negro Education, 50,* 48–53.

Slaughter-Defoe, D. T., & Carlson, K. G. (1996). Young African American and Latino children in high poverty urban schools: How they perceive school climate. *Journal of Negro Education, 65*(1), 60–70.

Sparks, D. (2003). We care, therefore they learn: An interview with Ronald Ferguson. *National Staff Development Journal, 24*(4), 42–47.

St. John, E. P., & Cadray, J. P. (2004). Justice and care in postdesegregation urban schools: Rethinking the role of teacher education. In V. S. Walker & J. R. Snarey (Eds.), *Race-ing moral formation* (pp. 93–110). New York: Teachers College Press.

Stanford, G. (1998). African-American teachers' knowledge of teaching: Understanding the influence of their remembered teachers. *Urban Review, 30*(3), 229–243.

Stanford, G. C. (1995, April). *African American pedagogy: Needed perspectives for urban education.* Paper presented at the annual meeting of American Educational Research Association, San Francisco.

Talbert-Johnson, C. (2004). Structural inequality and the achievement gap in urban schools. *Education and Urban Society, 37*(1), 22–36.

Thompson, A. (2004). Caring and colortalk. In V. Siddle Walker & J. Snarey (Eds.), *Race-ing moral formation African American perspectives on care and justice* (pp. 23–37). New York: Teachers College Press.

Tillman, L. C. (2005). Mentoring new teachers: Implications for leadership practice in an urban school. *Educational Administration Quarterly, 41*(4), 609–629.

Vasquez, J. A. (1988). Contexts of learning for minority students. *Educational Forum, 52*(3), 243–253.

Vegas, E., Murnane, R. J., Willett, J. B. (2001). From high school to teaching: Many steps, who makes it? *Teachers College Record, 103*(3), 427–449.

Walker, V. S. (1993). Interpersonal caring in the "good" segregated schooling of African American children: Evidence from the case of Caswell County Training School. *Urban Review, 25*(1), 63–77.

Walker, V. S. (1996). Can institutions care? Evidence from the segregated schooling of African American children. In M. Shujaa (Ed.), *Beyond desegregation: The politics of quality in African American schooling* (pp. 209–226). Thousand Oaks, CA: Corwin Press.

Walker, V. S. (2000). Valued segregated schools for African American children in the south 1935–1969: A review of common themes and characteristics. *Review of Educational Research, 70,* 253–285.

Walker, V. S., & Snarey, J. (Eds.). (2004). *Race-ing moral formation African American perspectives on care and justice.* New York: Teachers College Press.

Walker, V. S., & Tompkins, R. (2004). Caring in the past: The case of a southern segregated African American School. In V. S. Walker & J. R. Snarey (Eds.), *Race-ing moral formation* (pp. 77–92). New York: Teachers College Press.

Ward, J. V. (1995). Cultivating a morality of care in African American adolescents: A culture-based model of violence prevention. *Harvard Educational Review, 65*(2), 175–189.

Ware, F. (2002). Black teachers' perceptions of their professional roles and practices. In J. J. Irvine (Ed.), *In search of wholeness: African American teachers and their culturally specific classroom practices* (pp. 33–45). New York: Palgrave.

Whitehead, A. N. (1929). *The aims of education and other essays.* New York: Macmillan.

Wilder, M. (2000). Increasing African American teachers' presence in American schools: Voices of students who care. *Urban Education, 35*(2), 205–220.

Zumwalt, K., & Craig, E. (2005). Teachers' characteristics: Research on the demographic profile. In M. Cochran-Smith & K. M. Zeichner (Eds.), *Studying teacher education* (pp. 111–156). Mahwah, NJ: Lawrence Erlbaum.

10

AFTER "IT TAKES A VILLAGE"

Mapping the Terrain of Black Parental Involvement in the Post-Brown Era

CHERYL FIELDS-SMITH

The prevailing literature in parental involvement research supports a positive relationship between student success in school and parents' involvement in their children's education. Recently, mandates in educational policy and practice have amplified the calls for parental involvement. Historically, parent's involvement in their children's schooling has served as a mainstay within African American communities (Anderson, 1988; Tillman, 2004; Walker, 1996, 2000). Furthermore, from slavery to segregation, there existed fervor in the pursuit of learning; literacy in particular (Gadsden & Wagner, 1995; Perry, Steele, & Hilliard, 2003). In fact, the close-knit communal bonds found in the depictions of segregated schooling are reminiscent of the notions expressed by the West African proverb, "It takes a village to raise a child."

However, contemporary discourse on the achievement gap frequently problematizes Black families and their communities (Perry et al., 2003), while parental involvement discourse tends to align with White middle-class standards (Gavin & Greenfield, 1998; Graue, Kroeger, & Prager, 2001; Tillman, 2004). Furthermore, school personnel often categorize African American parents as disinterested in their children's education (Boethel, 2003; Chavkin, 1993). The contrast between African American educational history and contemporary perceptions along with the persistent achievement gap warrants further investigation of parental involvement and its context among African American communities. Edwards (as cited by Tillman, 2004, p. 167) posits that the implementation of desegregation placed African American students in a racist schooling context. This chapter explores the ways in which African Americans have continued to pursue and maintain a quality education for their children within this context.

This chapter provides an overview of what can be gleaned from previous literature regarding parental involvement among African American families. In addition, the chapter presents a study by the author with samples of middle- and upper-income African American families that extends the knowledge obtained from previous literature, which focuses primarily on low-income families (Fields-Smith, 2007). Overall, research on parental involvement among African American families has been primarily limited to a focus on low-income communities and comparisons with parents of other ethnicities. In an effort to address these limitations, I designed a study that investigated parental involvement among upper- and middle-income African American families with children in elementary school settings. The chapter ends with suggestions for the future direction of research related to the phenomena of parental involvement among African American families. As in most of the literature, throughout this study the term *parent* will refer to any adult who has assumed responsibility for a child. Therefore, the term parent includes grandparents, aunts, or other relatives as well as an appointed guardian.

REVIEW OF THE LITERATURE

Research on parental involvement among African American families consists mainly of investigations among working class, poor, or otherwise disadvantaged populations. These parents are most likely to be perceived as disinterested in participating in their children's education (Boethel, 2003; Jackson & Remillard, 2005). However, an abundant research base has documented low-income African American parents' concerns for and participation in their children's education. Therefore, this review seeks to debunk the myth of low-income Black parents' disinterest in their children's education.

Based on more than 100 empirically grounded articles, chapters, and books, this review of the literature has been divided into three sections. The first section reviews studies that examined the practices of low-income African American parents. The next section provides a synthesis of literature on parents' beliefs regarding their roles in their children's education. The final section of the literature review highlights the ways in which teachers have been able to effectively influence the involvement of African American, mostly low-income, parents.

Practices of Low-Income African American Parents

Epstein's (1995) typology of parental involvement identified six types of parental activity. These six categories included parenting, communicating, volunteering, engaging in learning at home, collaborating with community, and decision making. Searches for this review resulted in studies that document parental involvement activities among low-income African American parents in each area, except

decision making. The limited availability of research on African American parents' involvement in decision making may be partially explained by the findings of Chavkin and Williams (1993). The authors surveyed 682 African American parents and found that although 83% of the group expressed a desire to participate in school decision making, they reported having very little opportunity to actually be involved in school decision making (such as assisting with school planning, hiring teachers, or selecting curriculum) compared with more traditional roles of attending conferences, helping with homework, and volunteering in the school.

Waggoner and Griffith (1998) interviewed low-income African American parents that served as volunteers in one of four schools attended by their children and school personnel as well. They found that members of the school staff tended to define parent's participation solely from the perspective of the school. The authors wrote, "In interviews at each school, the teachers and principals characterized parent involvement in education as a broad set of activities that occur at and are organized by the school" (p. 71). In comparison, the low-income, Black parent volunteers interviewed conceptualized their participation activities more broadly to include activities at home and at school. They also indicated a viewpoint that being involved benefited their families as well as the school. Furthermore, the study demonstrated that parents who volunteered adapted their home-based practices and parenting to conform to the strategies used by teachers that they observed while they volunteered in the classroom. "Thus, volunteers learned to see their parenting, their children, and other families through the ideological framing of parental involvement in education" (Waggoner & Griffith, 1998, p. 74). Within this compliance, teachers indicated surprise when parents positioned their own ways of being involved without being assigned by school staff. This and similar responses of teachers point to symptoms of a struggle of power between teachers and parents, which has been written about in terms of issues such as parental empowerment and equity in education (de Carvalho, 2001; Fine, 1993).

In their more recent study, Jackson and Remillard (2005) expanded the literature by looking beyond parents' activities to examine the context surrounding the activity including parents' orientation. The study of 10 African American families residing in a low-income community found that each parent served as an advocate for their children's education. Referring to the parents, the authors stated, "They showed evidence of thinking proactively and strategically about their children's futures and the kinds of opportunities they want them to have" (p. 59). Practices that represented advocacy in this study included encouraging their children to develop independence through chore assignments, fostering a value of education, and expressing graduation expectations. Although only three of the 10 parents were able to find time to go to the school on a regular basis, all the parents monitored their children's progress in school. Strategies for monitoring their children's progress included providing homework assistance and obtaining extra work from the teacher.

Parents in Jackson and Remillard's (2005) study also found ways to understand new approaches to math adopted by their children's school. Based on the study, one of the most difficult challenges with the new math program was the teachers' reluctance to send children home with a reference book referred to in the assignments. Parents had to make arrangements with the teacher to promise to return the reference book in order to help their children understand their math assignments.

Finally, the low-income parents in this study also found ways to provide extra learning experiences for their children outside school, and they developed creative methods to practice skills at home. Learning opportunities outside school included trips to the museums, libraries, and even going to the local laundromat. Creative methods for practicing skills usually occurred spontaneously as families went through their daily tasks. Interestingly, the spontaneity of these creative practice activities are reminiscent of the naturalness of instructional strategies found among low-income African American mothers of high-achieving children observed by Scott-Jones (1987). Examples of the creative learning experiences revealed by Jackson and Remillard (2005) include inventing games for counting, using the calendar, and setting the table. Parents also described unique learning opportunities developed during activities such as decorating a Christmas tree and cooking with their children.

Overstreet, Devine, Bevans, and Efreom (2005) examined the factors that predict the school-based involvement of 159 economically disadvantaged, Black parents. Parents in this study had children in elementary grades through high school level. The authors found that parents' educational aspirations, church attendance, community center participation, and their discernment of school receptiveness were each significantly associated with their school-based participation. Results also indicated that church attendance was closely associated with parents' educational aspirations and their discernment of school receptiveness.

In sum, these examples found within the literature provided insight regarding African American parents' participation. As has been documented in the past (Rubin & Billingsley, 1994), the church continues to play a vital role in parents' attempts to educate their children. In fact, church involvement represented the primary form of collaboration with community found in the literature on Black parental involvement. Epstein's (1995) category of communicating masks the forms of advocacy demonstrated by African American parents. Jackson and Remillard (2005) illustrated low-income African American parents' determination to advocate for their children. The literature also indicated that low-income parents' advocacy can foster a seamless connection between home and school given their broad perspective of parental involvement, including home and school-based activities (Waggoner & Griffith, 1998) as well as the manner in which parents sought to make connections between school learning and home-based activities. Low-income African American parents' advocacy also radiated to their parenting roles.

Parents' Beliefs About Their Role

Epstein (1995) developed the overlapping spheres framework for home-school partnerships. Within this framework, home, school, and community exist in interdependent relationships represented by three intersecting circles. The interdependent relationship suggests that for children to succeed in school, families, schools, and communities must assume a shared responsibility for children's education. From the parents' perspective, this framework assumes that parents believe that involvement in their children's education is essential to children's successful outcomes. This assumption reflects a reliance on parents' self-efficacy in connection with their participation in their children's education.

Hoover-Dempsey and Sandler's (1997) seminal work has provided insight into the psychological factors that influence parents' engagement in their children's education. Their review of the literature revealed that parents decided to become involved based on their parenting beliefs, their self-efficacy, and their perception of the school climate. The authors applied role construction theory, which states that parents decide to be involved based on their beliefs regarding their parenting role, child development, child rearing, and the proper home-support role for their children's education.

Parent efficacy represented another major influence on parents' decisions to become involved. Hoover-Dempsey and Sandler (1997) explained parent efficacy by framing the question, "Do parents believe that through their involvement, they can exert a positive influence on children's educational outcomes?" (p. 17). Simply put, parents with high efficacy were more likely to choose high levels of involvement than parents with low efficacy. The present review revealed several examples of these factors among African American parent samples, as well as additional influencing factors.

Drummond and Stipek (2004) explored ethnic comparisons in parents' beliefs regarding their role in particular aspects of their children's education, including homework completion, knowledge of student learning, and the subjects of math and reading. A total of 234 low-income parents, approximately 84 African American, completed questionnaires and interviews for the study. Other ethnicities and races represented in the study included Caucasian, Latino, and Asian parents. Families lived in both rural and urban communities. Drummond and Stipek (2004) found that parents' beliefs regarding their roles in each of these categories of learning did not vary by ethnicity. Low-income parents generally believed that they did not need to assist with homework when their children were doing well in school, or if they felt their children knew more about the subjects of reading or math than they did. Low-income parents in this study also reported that they obtained information about their children's learning through teachers, by going to the school, from their children, or looking at their children's schoolwork. This study

also indicated that parents whose children were in second grade had stronger beliefs in the importance of their involvement than parents whose children were in third grade, which may suggest that as children progress in the grades, parents' beliefs regarding their ability to influence their children's education decrease.

As suggested by Hoover-Dempsey and Sandler (1997), school climate also influenced low-income African American parents' decisions to participate. Smrekar and Cohen-Vogel (2001) suggested, "How parents perceive their role in their children's schooling may be a function of how the school organization treats them" (p. 76). To minimize the influence of school, the authors investigated parental involvement solely from the parents' perspective. Their study focused on low-income, ethnic-minority parents (48% African American, 35% Hispanic, and 17% Pacific Islander or other). Smrekar and Cohen-Vogel (2001) used a random stratified sampling procedure that resulted in a sample of 30 parents of children in one of three classrooms (second, fourth, and sixth grades). The study demonstrated that low-income African American parents may believe in a separation between home and school responsibility for their children's education. For example, parents believed that they were responsible for providing their children moral education while teachers provided academic learning. The authors stated, "The idea that parents ought not interfere with the job of teaching school curricula seems to transcend culture and experience" (p. 90). However, the study also indicated that low-income parents were not intimidated by school personnel despite negative or limited schooling experiences as children.

In sum, the literature on African American parents' decisions to get involved supported the concept of self-efficacy and role construction. For example, parents' decisions to not assist their children with homework when children were doing well in class may be explained by parents' belief in their inability to help children improve on their already successful performance. The distinctions low-income African American parents made between parent responsibility and teacher responsibility conflicts with Epstein's (1995) concept of shared responsibility among home-school partnerships. The idea expressed by parents that may cultivate division between home and school illuminates the need for teachers to assume an initiating stance toward promoting parental involvement.

Influence of Teachers

Teachers can directly influence the engagement of low-income parents. In their study of high versus low teacher encouragement, Gavin and Greenfield (1998) demonstrated that in classrooms of African American students labeled "at risk," teachers who made requests for specific forms of involvement had greater parental involvement than teachers who did not specify the forms of parent engagement they desired. The study measured teachers' encouragement of parental involvement through a questionnaire that assessed parents' responses to teachers' requests for school volunteering and home-school communication. Findings from additional studies support conclusions drawn by Gavin and Greenfield (1998). For example, Drummond and Stipek's (2004) study of low-income parents' beliefs demonstrated that parents valued involvement in their children's learning experiences more when teachers suggested that parents help.

Similarly, parents interviewed by Smrekar and Cohen-Vogel (2001) stated that "if asked, they would find ways to increase their involvement at home and at school" (p. 85). Overall, these studies support the call for teachers to take the initiative to increase parental engagement in their children's learning (Boethel, 2003; Stein & Thorkildsen, 1999).

In her review of 64 studies, Boethel (2003) provided recommendations related to diversity and parental involvement. However, she cautioned that the recommendations should be viewed as tentative because "the research base is so thin" (p. vi). Recommendations included in the report reflect a change in overall perspectives related to parental involvement. For example, Boethel (2003) posited that to foster relationships among families and schools, schools should "honor families' hopes and concerns for their children" (p. vi) and "acknowledge both commonalities and differences among students and families" (p. vi). In addition, the author encouraged the development of explicit school- and districtwide parental involvement policy, which should include prioritizing outreach to families. She also acknowledged the need for school personnel to realize that trust does not happen instantly; rather, trust must be developed over time.

To summarize, the review of literature reveals that dominant perspectives found in the parental involvement discourse may overlook aspects of participation that are critical to understanding the involvement of African American families. Such aspects include the extent to which Black families' parental involvement include various forms of advocacy practices, which would not necessarily be illuminated using Epstein's (1995) six categories of parental involvement activity. Furthermore, the parental involvement literature does not provide a balanced perspective of the diversity found within Black communities, nor does the literature provide an in-depth understanding of the meaning of parental involvement from the perspective of Black families. The study described in the remainder of this chapter contributes to the literature toward these ends.

METHODOLOGY

The study was guided by the following research questions:

1. In what ways are African American parents involved in their children's education at home and at school?

2. In what ways are African American parents involved within and outside the Parent-Teacher Organization (PTO)?

3. What are the self-reported challenges faced by African American parents attempting to be involved in their children's education?

Findings reported in this chapter resulted from interviews with 30 African American parents who represented a variety of backgrounds and varying forms of engagement. A majority (24) of the parents interviewed represented a relatively homogeneous educational level (college, professional, or graduate school) and socioeconomic status (managerial and professional middle class). Conversely, six parents represented working class families with limited educational backgrounds ranging from no college to an associates degree or vocational training. As described in greater detail in Fields-Smith (2007), rather than using numeric measures of income socioeconomic, this study used Zweig's (2004) sociological conceptualizations of class based on the level of autonomy associated with parents' occupations to determine the families' socioeconomic status. Based on this sociological framework, parents with managerial or professional occupations would be assumed to have greater autonomy afforded to them than parents in working-class occupations. However, unlike my previous analysis with a smaller sample (Fields-Smith, 2007) this chapter demonstrates that parents' age and career status may significantly alter occupational autonomy. Parents ranged in age from 32 to 52 years old, and they represented a variety of background experiences, including military, rural, urban, and suburban childhood experiences and included segregated and integrated schooling experiences. The sample includes single, divorced, and married parents. Each parent represented a different family.

Participating families represented five schools located within the same southeastern metropolitan county school district. Four of the five schools were predominantly Black elementary schools. The fifth school represented in the study had a 31% Black student population. Table 10.1 provides additional demographic data associated with each of the schools represented in the study.

Table 10.1 demonstrates that the predominantly Black schools in this study comprise a variety of school types, including two traditional elementary schools, another traditional school that houses a magnet program, and a theme school. Each of these schools have relatively large populations compared with the predominantly White elementary school, which consists of a magnet program for grades four through six only. Interestingly, School B had the largest school population as well as one of the highest percentages of free and reduced lunch students, and yet School B's math and science thematically based curriculum yielded the highest percentage of students meeting or exceeding expectations on standardized tests for reading among the predominantly Black schools.

All data were gathered through extensive interviews with participants. Interview data were transcribed, and the transcripts were reviewed by participants for accuracy. Data were analyzed through a process of coding patterns and identifying themes as described by Creswell (1997). The next section presents a synthesis of the themes found in this study.

FINDINGS

Three major findings of the study will be presented in this section. First, I will report the degree of parents' involvement in PTO. Next, I will present parents' self-reported practices that remain largely unseen by teachers. Finally, I will report the challenges parents faced in their quests to be involved in their children's education. Regardless of their level of involvement within the PTO, each parent represented a family that remained actively involved in their children's education.

Degree of Parents' Involvement in PTO

In this section, I have categorized parents relative to their participation in the PTO within

TABLE 10.1   School Demographics

Type of School	Total (Percentage of Black Students)/Total Population	Total/(Percentage) of Free and Reduced Lunch	Percentage Meeting or Exceeding Reading Test Score Standards
A Traditional	735 (97%)/758	445 (59%)	86%
B Traditional	660 (83%)/798	600 (75%)	81%
C Traditional With Magnet	881 (95%)/925	441 (45%)	86%
D Theme School	1,060 (97%)/1,090	495 (75%)	96%
E Magnet 4th–6th	125 (31%)/414	40 (9.6%)	100%

their children's schools. This created three sub-categories: PTO Leadership, PTO Members, and PTO Inactive. Profiles highlight the similarities and differences that exist among the parents in each category.

PTO Leadership

Being a member of PTO, especially serving in a leadership role, often times pits your interest for your own child with the interest of all the children. PTO is for all of the children. We're here for every one of them, not just for our own.

These words of one parent effectively summarize the attitude expressed by the 17 parents who were serving in a leadership position within their children's school PTO. In fact, for the most part, these parents initially described their practices at the school level, rather than focusing on the ways in which they engaged in their own children's education.

Leadership roles within the PTO varied among the participants. Five parents were currently serving as PTO presidents at the time of their interviews. In addition, four parents interviewed were former PTO presidents. Parents who were not currently serving as president of the organization served on the executive board in other capacities such as chair of a committee or in other officer positions.

Generally, parents who held the highest school-level PTO positions shared several common characteristics. For example, present and past PTO presidents ranged in age from their early 40s to the early 50s. These parents also tended to be in positions or careers that provided them with flexibility in their schedule. For example, of nine PTO presidents, past and present, two parents owned a small business, two were stay-at-home moms, two parents had professional degrees (a lawyer and a psychiatrist), one was a retired school teacher, one was an unemployed executive, and one was a senior executive in a medium-sized corporation. Married PTO leaders shared that they took turns with their spouse serving on the executive board so that their family would have consistent representation at the school level.

Given their educational level and type of employment, PTO leaders were primarily upper- and middle-income family members. One parent, Missy, on the PTO executive board was classified as low-income. Missy became part of the current PTO president's social network when she volunteered regularly during PTO-sponsored activities. As a recently separated mother of three young children, visiting the school during the day was quite a challenge. However, as the chair of the cultural arts committee of the PTO, school day visits were not necessary. Teacher and administrative representatives assist the cultural arts committee with selection of cultural experiences to schedule for school events. Missy could make calls on her days off, prepare updates, and attend monthly meetings in the evenings.

As a PTO executive board member, Missy held similar beliefs as the other PTO leaders regarding the efficacy of a schoolwide impact on their participation in their children's education. PTO leaders consistently acknowledged a dual impact in their involvement as both for the betterment of the school overall as well as to benefit their own children's learning experiences. Interestingly, 14 of the 17 PTO leaders recalled positive childhood experiences during segregated schooling, which may partially explain their "It Takes a Village" mentality toward parental participation. Parents in leadership positions tended to consciously seek these roles in order to have access to school decision making. None of the parents below the age of 37 served in PTO leadership positions.

PTO Membership

In comparison, eight parents reported that they consciously chose to avoid participation on the PTO executive board for several reasons. Parents in this category included four upper-income parents; only one of whom was a stay-at-home mom. The group also included three working-class parents; one who was a stay-at-home mother, and a middle-income, single parent, mother who was a school teacher.

Vicki, a stay-at-home mom, did not choose to participate as a PTO leader in her children's school because she is not in her own words, "the leader type." When asked to define "leader type," Vicki stated that she did not like giving speeches in front of lots of people and that she is basically shy. She described her involvement motivation as, "If there is a need, let me know," and she usually identified needs through the PTO. Two additional parents expressed similar reservations that prevented them from desiring leadership roles within the organization. Parents also avoided leadership roles within the PTO because their families were in transition phases. For example, Sherry shared that she had just returned to work on a part-time basis and that she and her husband had just transferred their child to a new magnet school. Consequently, at the time of the interviews, she had not had time to seek opportunities for involvement in the PTO. Two other parents were in similar positions. Parents also steered clear of PTO leadership roles because they recognized the extra level of commitment required as a member of the executive board. Renee stated,

> The only reason I don't serve as an officer is because I take that role seriously and I know that it is almost like a part-time job. Serving in that role would take away from what I'm trying to do with my own children.

However, the mother of five children found ways to remain involved in the PTO activities.

Like Renee, although the parents in this category evaded leadership roles in the PTO, they still remained highly involved and even provided parental leadership. For example, Jenny and Renee described participation in activist-like roles through their PTO members. Renee used the parent center to research information on programs and grants that would improve her children's school. Once she identified something that would fill a need in the school, she would "rally the troops together and to go for it." She has coordinated efforts that have enabled her children's school to obtain curriculum materials and to establish an African dance class in the elementary school. Similarly, Jenny reported identifying school needs, bringing them to the attention of several other PTO parents, and working toward resolution. Although outside the PTO executive board, these parents were able to position themselves to provide a form of leadership and advocacy for their children's school.

PTO Inactive

Of the 30 parents interviewed, five parents reported that they remained inactive in the PTO. Four of these parents were below the age of 35. Inactive PTO parents included one upper-income parent, who was a noncustodial, single father, and a middle-income, single father, who had custody of his son. The remainder of the parents in the category consisted of three, single, low-income mothers.

For the single mothers, PTO involvement in some ways represented a luxury the family could not afford in terms of time, loss of wages, and effort. Nina and Stephanie worked in major corporations as administrative assistants for 40 hours per week. In addition to their work responsibilities, they had lengthy commutes to work each morning. When they discussed their interactions with the PTO, they described feeling limited in their ability to participate fully. Instead, they both stated that they support the PTO through the fundraiser and other activities such as the fall festival, which was usually held on a weekend. However, attending meetings during the week became a challenge due to work fatigue and lengthy job commutes. Conversely, for Barbara, whom I have written about elsewhere (Fields-Smith, 2006), the decision to not participate in PTO activities was based on the fact that she felt her efforts were not needed. After attending a meeting, Barbara came to the conclusion that she was not needed and she believed the PTO was, "in good hands." Additionally, Gloria, who worked in retail, found it difficult to attend PTO meetings because of her work schedule, which included evenings.

The single fathers in this category participated in very different ways. Scott, a noncustodial father, described his involvement strictly in terms of his daughter's requests. Reflecting on his motivations to participate in activities at school, he remarked, "I would say that when Delia asks me if I would come to something then that's when I would really try to make sure that I could come." On the other hand, Lewis focused his school-based involvement primarily on teachers' requests. He stated, "I think it's very important to be involved. But, kind of like I do at [son's school], you know, I'm going to be there. If you guys need me, let me know. Call me. I'm there for you guys." Similar to parents in the literature, this attitude signals the need for teachers to take the initiative, particularly when it comes to increasing parental involvement at the school.

Despite their lack of involvement in PTO, parents in this category participated in ways that maintained interaction between themselves and their children's teachers. Each of them believed that continued visibility and contact with their children's teachers was critical to their children's success. E-mails, daily drop off or pick ups, and notes in daily agenda planners provided by the school to record homework enabled the parents to maintain a consistent presence with their children's teachers despite their lack of PTO membership. Furthermore, PTO-inactive parents reported that they had supported schoolwide advocacy initiatives such as signing petitions or resolutions to remedy overcrowding on school buses, or to obtain a new gym for their children's school.

Other forms of school-based activities included volunteering in classrooms or in the parent center of the school to do clerical work or even working with small groups of children on academics. Parents' motivations to participate in school-based activities included a desire to improve the schooling experience of other children in the school. However, admittedly parents' desires to serve at the school also satisfied their needs to monitor the school climate and their children's progress. Specifically, school-based participation became a vehicle for parent monitoring by providing access to information regarding their children's performance in relation to other students, the appropriateness of teacher-student interaction, identification of school (and classroom) needs, and knowledge of curriculum content.

To summarize, the highly involved African American parents in this study participated in the PTO to varying degrees ranging from assuming leadership roles to avoiding PTO involvement altogether. Because they believed that their presence in the school communicated their value of education to teachers as well as their children, these parents found meaningful ways to maintain visibility in their children's school. School-based activities served multiple purposes for these parents, including a school improvement function and benefits for their children in particular. Regardless of their degree of involvement in PTO and at school during the school day, parents also participated in learning activities at home, which were largely unseen by their children's teachers.

Invisible Forms of Involvement

While parents expressed a concern for maintaining visibility in the school, they also reported practices related to their children's learning that would not normally be observed by teachers. Invisible forms of engagement found in this study included learning activities both directly and indirectly related to children's schooling experiences. Parents' learning activities at home included academically based actions taken to reinforce, enhance, or surpass their children's schooling experiences. Black parents' participation in home-based engagement with their children ranged from maintaining routines to actual instruction.

Home-based learning activities may have been invisible to teachers, but they were vital to the families represented in this study. Across socioeconomic levels, levels of education, and age, parents most frequently and proudly professed that their most valuable form of home-based engagement were the conversations they held with their children. For example, families reported that they consciously held conversations with their children not only related to schooling, but also aimed at developing their children's critical thinking and decision-making skills. When asked to describe her home-based activities not seen by teachers, Karen immediately responded, "The talks we have at the dinner table that makes them think." She went on to describe conversation starters such as "what would you do if . . . ," which Karen and her husband used to encourage for the moral character development of their children. Similarly other parents in the study held home-based conversations motivated by a desire to not only build their children's character but also provide children with opportunities to practice decision-making skills, to develop critical thinking, and to exercise mental math.

In addition, learning activities at home included varying levels of monitoring and assisting with homework. Parents reflected on occasions when they felt they had to reteach homework concepts using strategies that matched their children's interests, such as using sports themes. Beyond homework, the parents in this study had "extra work," which included store-bought workbooks, particularly in the area of math, that their children were expected to complete on an ongoing basis. When asked why they do these extra learning activities, parents' responses included "to keep their skills up," "so, I know for sure they are learning," "to keep their minds stimulated," and "because the teacher can't do it all." These comments reflect parents' ownership of their children's learning experience.

Other less visible learning experiences included providing access to museums, books, and other community resources related to the topics of study at school. The Internet provided resources for home-based learning extension activities as well. Furthermore, parents engaged in learning activities unseen to most teachers that were not necessarily aligned with school curriculum. These activities included conducting Bible studies, researching context surrounding historical events, studying Black history, learning sign language, and memorizing and reciting poetry. These types of activities were most prevalent among upper-income families and among all the families with children attending the school with a predominantly White student population. Parents stated that the activities reflected their children's interests or content that they believed their children needed, but would not get in school. Parent-led extracurricular activities in the area of Black history often related to a topic of study in school. For example, if the child's teacher taught a lesson on astronomy, parents helped their children conduct research that identified noted Black inventors and scientists in the field to provide a historical and cultural context for what they learned in school. Black parents also used their at-home learning activities to provide a religious context to their children's learning experiences.

Barriers to Involvement

Previous studies have documented well-known barriers to parents' school-based participation. These included child care needs, multiple jobs, and transportation issues (Boethel, 2003). The present study identified two additional explanations for parents' limited involvement at the school that were not regularly discussed in the literature. First, career status or age may influence parental involvement decisions. Mr. Scott, father of two grown sons, and currently PTO president at his fourth grader's school noted, "I'm more involved now than when we were raising our boys because of where I am professionally." At age 51, Mr. Scott had built up a private practice such that he had flexible hours and reasonable control over the number of cases he worked on at one time. Similar situations were expressed by other parents who had adult or older children along with elementary school–age children. Conversations with stay-at-home mothers revealed yet another way in which career status may influence parental involvement. They shared that they were not always stay-at-home parents. Earlier in their marriage, while their husbands held entry-level positions, the mothers had to work either part-time or full-time until there was a level of financial "comfort" where they could stay home with the children. When asked for a referral of a family with young parents, one highly active 50+ father replied, "You have to remember, I'm old enough to be the father to some of these younger parents." He continued, "Parents tend to befriend other parents that are similar to themselves age-wise." Of course, the increased engagement in the learning activities of their younger children may also be explained by parents' increased awareness and maturity and appreciation of the need for parental involvement. Regardless of the explanation, the implications are the same. We should consider to what extent does school parental involvement policy and procedures enable parents to interact across age.

Another barrier to involvement existed among the younger parents. Describing her reasons for minimal involvement in schoolwide social activities, such as PTO-sponsored events, Katie explained,

> I kind of shy away from different things because
> of the type of child she [her daughter] is and I
> know that she's labeled [a behavior problem].
> I think that kind of puts a barrier, not with the
> volunteering because I would do that anyway, but
> as far as getting real connected with a lot of the
> parents and things like that.

Two other parents below the age of 35 reported having a child whose behavior in school became a barrier to being involved at school. For these parents, involvement in PTO may lead to feelings of embarrassment once they were identified and associated with their children's behavior, which frequently did not conform to school expectations. Tammy shared,

> I feel like if I go to the school meetings or other
> events once people find out that I'm (her son)
> mother that because he can be a handful in
> school at times people will assume things
> about me and my household, so why go?

This sentiment suggests that parents of children who have become labeled as behavioral problems may feel alienated from the school. This may be due to their children's poor behavior and even due in part to the teachers' response to that negative behavior. It should be noted that children's challenging behavior in school did not limit parents' involvement outside the school. However, school personnel tend to continually define parental involvement using a school-based framework (Boethel, 2003); therefore, the need for additional understanding of the limitations on parents' school-based participation persists.

DISCUSSION

Combined the review of a literature focused on low-income African American parental involvement and study of middle- to upper-income parents' parental involvement provide insight toward understanding the complexity of Black parents' involvement in their children's education in the postdesegregation era. To overcome issues related to access to decision making and maintaining communication with teachers, African American parents' participation in their children's schooling requires more effort today than in the past. Visibility among school staff, particularly children' teachers, no longer occurs naturally amid closely knit neighborhoods, grocery stores, or even churches. Residential proximity to one another is but one factor contributing to the weakening of the "It takes a village" mentality among African American communities. Despite the challenges of a lack of residential proximity to the teachers in their children's schools, African American parents in this study demonstrated active involvement in their children's education regardless of style of involvement (PTA leadership, PTA member, or non-PTA member).

Parents' self-efficacy and parenting role beliefs markedly influence parents' decisions to be involved in their children's education (Hoover-Dempsey & Sandler, 1997). Simply stated, parental involvement appears to require a modicum of self-efficacy, or beliefs in one's ability to positively influence educational outcomes for one's own children (Hoover-Dempsey & Sandler, 1997). Furthermore, parental involvement requires a belief that being a parent necessarily requires involvement in educational outcomes. This research suggests that parents who have been successful in the educational arena are more likely to develop parental self-efficacy. However, the literature and the present study indicate that low-income Black parents, who frequently have negative schooling experiences, remain determined to be involved in their children's education. This determination may be explained by African American parents' desires to see their children become more successful than they are. Alternatively, even parents whose own educational pursuits have been relatively successful can be reluctant to become involved in their children's schooling within the school setting as exemplified by the Black parent (who was an elementary school teacher), but whose child's nonconforming behavior led to avoidance in school-based activities within her daughter's school. Promoting African American parental involvement at school may require a conscious effort on the part of teachers to build parent self-efficacy. Many scholars have suggested that teachers should initiate parental involvement (Boethel, 2003; Gavin & Greenfield, 1998; Stein & Thorkilden, 1999) which is one way parent self-efficacy can be established and maintained.

Unlike the low-income Black parents described by Waggoner and Griffith (1998), the parents in this study did not indicate that they adapted their home communication and practices to align with teacher behaviors observed while visiting the school. Instead, parents' school-based activities, which not only included volunteering but also participating in decision-making activities, provided access to monitoring their children's schooling experiences. Parents used information gained from their observations to either advocate on behalf of children in the school or to position themselves as architects of their children's schooling supplementing the shortfalls of either curriculum. One possible explanation for this difference is that given their primarily middle- and upper-income status, many of the participating families' home communication and practices were already aligned with, or socially and culturally synchronized to, the expectations and functioning of their children's schools as described by Irvine (1991). The preexistence of alignment between home and school in these areas enabled parents to focus on sociocultural synchronization with regards to additional, and perhaps extraordinary, issues such as identifying areas of opportunity to enhance the content learned in school. Alternatively, parents' use of school-based practices as a monitoring tool could also be reflective of parents' level of self-efficacy in their ability to influence positively their children's educational outcomes. Additionally, Black parents' engagement in learning activities outside teachers' purview suggests that parents adhered to a broad definition of parental involvement similar to the low-income parent volunteers described in Waggoner and Griffith (1998).

FUTURE RESEARCH

This review of the literature and subsequent study indicate that additional research is needed to advance our knowledge about African American parental involvement. In particular, additional investigations are needed to explore variations in parental involvement beliefs and practices within African American communities. To continue toward resolving this issue, additional inquiries should focus on identifying the multiple interpretations of the ideal and expected forms of parental involvement from the perspectives of teachers, parents, and students within the same school community. Studies that compare African American parents' beliefs and practices in various types of schooling compositions (predominantly Black, predominantly White, and integrated) would be helpful toward increased understanding of the role of race in parents' involvement practices. Furthermore, examinations of parental involvement among African American parents of varying ages may reveal intergenerational differences in beliefs regarding shared responsibility between home and school. These types of studies are likely to reveal issues related to equity in parental involvement outcomes, empowerment of parents, and privileges associated with certain forms of parents' involvement. Studies that situate parental involvement at home and at school can reveal parent strategies that effectively overcome these issues.

Research on parental involvement rarely considers parent self-efficacy among African American parents. Continued exploration of parent self-efficacy is needed to determine how and why parent self-efficacy varies by class.

Research applying the framework of parent self-efficacy could also reveal links between school climate and parents' beliefs regarding their ability to positively influence learning outcomes for their children. Such studies may also explore the most effective strategies for teachers and schools to promote parental engagement. Additionally, Colbert (1991) suggested that passivity in African American parents' involvement could be interpreted as parents' overall satisfaction in their children's progress at school. Research on parent self-efficacy among African American parents could also develop understanding of parental involvement from the perspective of seemingly passively involved parents, including the parent of a child identified as a behavior problem. This work may foster strategies to engage the passively involved parent.

In this era of increasing urgency of parental involvement and parental choice, it is imperative that the educational choices of African American parents be examined. For example, research literature on home schooling rarely includes investigations of the home education phenomena among African American families creating a false impression that home schooling is only a White middle-class phenomenon. Periodicals across the country indicate a trend toward increasing participation in home education among Black parents. Research is needed to understand the motivations underlying parents' decisions to home educate or choose other non-traditional methods to educate their children. Given the trends, research on African American parents' educational choices will ultimately document a critical era in Black educational history.

The inability of predominant models and frameworks such as Epstein's (1995) topology of parental involvement activity to fully capture the nature of African American parental involvement suggests the need to develop new models for future research. Several researchers have spurred forward toward meeting this need. Tillman (2004) urged, "Parental involvement must be viewed as relationship building and as a process that occurs over time rather than as a series of isolated events such as PTA meetings, parent-teacher conferences, and discipline hearings" (p. 169). This contradicts Epstein's topology, which emphasizes parental activities. The relationship building stance is critical toward the establishment of trust within the home-school partnership, which has been documented as particularly valued within Black communities (Colbert, 1991; Fields-Smith, 2005; Smrekar & Cohen-Vogel, 2001). Epstein's (1995) home-school partnership model of overlapping spheres assumes shared responsibility between home, school, and community toward the education of children. However, the notion of shared responsibility does not always apply due in part to issues of trust as well as issues of unbalanced power between home and school (Tillman, 2004) and among parents (McGrath & Kuriloff, 1999).

Another factor to be considered toward the development of new models and frameworks of parental involvement is fostering parents' empowerment and abilities to advocate for their children and their schools. The Ecologies of Parental Engagement (EPE) framework presented by Barton, Drake, Perez, St. Louis, and George (2004) provides a "new way to conceptualize parental involvement that frames parents as both authors and agents in schools" (p. 3). Viewing parents as "authors and agents" of their own involvement practices provides an opportunity to broaden the definitions of involvement, thus, moving beyond the school-based focus. The EPE framework also incorporates social capital theory to explore the ways in which parents use their social capital (networks, resources, and knowledge) to effectively bring about desired outcomes for their children. EPE also includes a critical perspective based on critical race theory, which enables researchers to examine issues of power related to macro- and microlevels of parental involvement. Previous models of parental involvement have focused on individual actions or choices; EPE fosters research that explores the interaction between parents and other stakeholders in the education of their children. Barton et al. (2004) stated that using the EPE framework allows researchers to

> understand engagement in relation to many things, not just those things traditionally deemed important in schools. Parental engagement is a desire, an expression, and an attempt by parents to have an impact on what actually transpires around their children in schools and on the kinds of human, social, and material resources that are valued within schools. (p. 11)

Frameworks such as the EPE enable researchers to rethink the value and meaning of parental involvement and ultimately to understand how parents become involved. To date, the EPE framework has been used to gain a better understanding of parental involvement in Latino immigrant communities. Applying the EPE framework, or a similar framework, to research parental involvement among African American communities may reveal additional ways in which African American parents consistently pursue a quality education for their children.

REFERENCES

Anderson, J. (1988). *The education of Blacks in the South, 1860–1935.* Chapel Hill: University of North Carolina Press

Barton, A., Drake, C., Perez, J., St. Louis, K., & George, M. (2004). Ecologies of parental engagement in urban education. *Educational Researcher, 33*(4), 3–12.

Boethel, M. (2003). *Diversity school, family, and community connections* (Annual Synthesis 2003). Austin, Texas: Southwest Educational Development Laboratory.

Chavkin, N. (Ed.). (1993). *Families and schools in a pluralistic society.* Albany: State University of New York Press.

Chavkin, N., & Williams, D. (1993). Minority parents and the elementary school: Attitudes and practices. In N. Chavkin (Ed.), *Families and schools in a pluralistic society* (pp. 73–83). Albany: State University of New York Press.

Colbert, R. (1991). Untapped resource: African American parental perceptions. *Elementary School Guidance & Counseling, 26,* 96–106.

Creswell, J. (1997). *Qualitative inquiry and research design: Choosing among five traditions.* Thousand Oaks, CA: Sage.

de Carvalho, M. (2001). *Rethinking family-school relations: A critique of parental involvement in schooling.* Mahwah, NJ: Lawrence Erlbaum.

Drummond, K. V. & Stipek, D. (2004). Low-income parents' beliefs about their role in children's academic learning. *The Elementary School Journal, 104,* 197–213.

Epstein, J. (1995). School/family/community partnerships: Caring for the children we share. *Phi Delta Kappan, 76,* 701–712.

Fields-Smith, C. (2005). African American parents before and after *Brown. Journal of Curriculum and Supervision, 20,* 129–135.

Fields-Smith, C. (2006). Motivation for participation: Why highly involved African American parents participate in their children's education. *Journal of School Public Relations, 27,* 234–257.

Fields-Smith, C. (2007). Social class and African American parental involvement. In J. Van Galen & G. Noblit (Eds.), *Late to class: Social class and schooling in the new economy. SUNY series: Power, social identity, and education* (pp. 167–202). Albany: State University of New York Press.

Fine, M. (1993). [Ap]parent involvement: Reflections on parents, power, and urban public schools. *Teachers College Record, 94,* 682–729.

Gadsden, V., & Wagner, D. (Eds.). (1995). *Literacy among African-American youth: Issues in learning, teaching, and school.* Cresskill, NJ: Hampton Press.

Gavin, K., & Greenfield, D. (1998). A comparison of levels of involvement for parents with at-risk African American kindergarten children in classrooms with high versus low teacher encouragement. *Journal of Black Psychology, 24,* 403–417.

Graue, M., Kroeger, J., & Prager, D. (2001). A Bakhtinian analysis of particular home-school relations. *American Educational Research Journal, 38,* 467–498.

Hoover-Dempsey, K., & Sandler, H. (1997). Why do parents become involved in their children's education? *Review of Educational Research, 67,* 3–42.

Irvine, J. (1991). *Black students and school failure: Policies, practices, and prescriptions.* Westport, CT: Praeger.

Jackson, K., & Remillard, J. (2005). Rethinking parent involvement: African American mothers construct their roles in the mathematics education of their children. *School Community Journal, 15*(1), 51–73.

McGrath, D., & Kuriloff, P. (1999). 'They're going to tear the doors off this place': Upper-middle-class parent school involvement and the educational opportunities of other people's children. *Educational Policy, 5,* 603–629.

Overstreet, S., Devine, J., Bevans, K., & Efreom, Y. (2005). Predicting parental involvement in children's schooling within an economically disadvantaged African American sample. *Psychology in the Schools, 42,* 101–111.

Perry, T., Steele, C., & Hilliard, A. (2003). *Young gifted and Black: Promoting high achievement among African-American students.* Boston: Beacon Press.

Rubin, R., & Billingsley, A. (1994). The role of the black church in working with black adolescents. *Adolescence, 29,* 251–267.

Scott-Jones, D. (1987). Mothers-as-teacher in the families of high and low-achieving Black first-graders. *Journal of Negro Education, 56,* 21–34.

Smrekar, C., & Cohen-Vogel, L. (2001). The voices of parents: Rethinking the intersection of family and school. *Peabody Journal of Education, 76*(2), 75–100.

Stein, M., & Thorkildsen, R. (1999). *Parental involvement in education: Insight and application from the research.* Bloomington, IN: Phi Delta Kappan International.

Tillman, L. (2004). African American parental involvement in a post-Brown era: Facilitating the academic achievement of African American students. *Journal of School Public Relations, 25,* 161–176.

Waggoner, K., & Griffith, A. (1998). Parent involvement in education: Ideology and experience. *Journal for a Just and Caring Education, 4,* 65–77.

Walker, V. (1996). *Their highest potential: An African American school community in the South.* Chapel Hill: University of North Carolina Press.

Walker, V. (2000). Valued segregation schools for African American children in the south, 1935–1969: A review of common themes and characteristics. *Review of Educational Research, 70,* 253–285.

Zweig, M. (2004). *What's class got to do with it? American society in the twenty-first century.* Ithaca, NY: Cornell University Press.

SECTION III

AFRICAN AMERICAN LEADERS IN PK-12 EDUCATIONAL LEADERSHIP

Introduction

Linda C. Tillman

This section of the *Handbook* presents theoretical and empirical work on African Americans in PK-12 school leadership. A central question guiding the work in this section is, "What factors affect the leadership capacity of African Americans in PK-12 education?" The authors make significant contributions to the literature on African Americans in the principalship and in principal preparation programs, African American women in the principalship, race, law, and school leadership, and African American superintendents in public school districts. These contributions are much needed as there is a paucity of scholarly literature that investigates the history, roles, responsibilities, characteristics, leadership styles, working conditions, and impact on student achievement of African American school leaders. Few studies have investigated the relationship between African American leadership and African American student achievement; however, this is an important topic and there is a need to articulate whether and in what ways same-race affiliation is directly linked to African American student achievement.

In the first chapter in this section, "African American Principals and the Legacy of *Brown*," Linda C. Tillman presents a review of the literature on African Americans in the principalship pre- and post-*Brown v. Board of Education*. Tillman posits a framework for African American principal leadership based on four themes that emerged from the literature: (a) the academic and social development of Black students as a priority; (b) resistance to ideologies and individuals opposed to the education of Black students; (c) the importance of the cultural perspectives of the Black principal; and (d) leadership based on interpersonal caring. Tillman provides a broader lens from which to view Black principal leadership and presents stories of vision, hope, persistence, pride, opportunity, disappointment, racism, sexism, segregation, desegregation, resegregation, and survival. Her chapter focuses on the significance of both the *theory* and the *practice* of African American principals and contributes to an underdeveloped area in the educational leadership/school administration literature—African Americans in the principalship.

In the next chapter, "Leadership Challenges in K-12 Urban Education: Prospective African American Administrators' Views on Educating African American Students and Closing the Achievement Gap," Robert Cooper and Will Jordan present findings from a study of African Americans in principal preparation programs. According to Cooper and Jordan, the current policy framework for school reform is driven by greater accountability for student achievement, which translates into high stakes testing. Thus, in their investigation the authors sought to uncover aspiring principals' receptiveness to "best practice" models of reform, their views about what is needed to improve educational outcomes for African American students, and the connection between beliefs about reform and the degree of implementation. Cooper and Jordan found that African American educators enrolled in an urban leadership preparation program believed that the strategies used to enact transformation in urban schools are largely ineffective and do not always lead to positive changes in teaching and learning. Cooper and Jordan also note that helping aspiring leaders balance the political realities of the urban school context with a lack of support for the type of reforms being implemented is a difficult but necessary function of principal preparation programs. The authors conclude that the tensions experienced by future African American school leaders about notions of best practices and their own understanding of effective teaching and learning for urban students should be paramount in the reform debate if we are to improve the schooling experiences of African American students.

In the chapter by Tondra Loder-Jackson, "The Confluence of Race, Gender, and Generation in the Lives of African American Women Principals," the author adds to the scholarly literature about the advancement of African American women and their experiences within the principalship. Loder-Jackson examined the leadership capacity of African American women from three perspectives: their emergence to the principalship in the post–Civil Rights Era in the face of institutionalized racism and pervasive discrimination; their struggle to integrate the spheres of work and family in the face of persistent institutionalized sexism and despite the hard-won gains of gender equity post–Civil Rights and women's movements; and their distinctive intergenerational outlook on the role that African American women principals play in carrying forth the tradition of activist leadership in the 21st century. Loder-Jackson uses historical literature and prior research on African American women principals, as well as findings from her life history study of Birmingham educators born during the pre– and post–Civil Rights eras to frame her discussion. She emphasizes the importance of examining *generation*, in confluence with race and gender in understanding the leadership capacity of multigenerational African American women principals in the 21st century.

In his chapter, "Race, Law, and Leadership: Exploring the Interest Convergence Dilemma," Mark Gooden argues that race still matters in U.S. society and that the pervasiveness of race can be seen in public education. Gooden posits that in light of this reality, it is not surprising that educating Black children in an environment dominated by White mainstream culture sets up a dilemma. He addresses a central question: How do the concepts of race, law, and school leadership coincide in such matters to better inform educational leaders? Gooden discusses these concepts and how they intersect, defines the construct of interest convergence as well as a related concept called the interest divergence principle, and demonstrates how these principles apply to educational leadership. According to Gooden, as school leaders work to educate all children, they must be willing to examine whether and in what ways race affects their leadership style, the school culture and climate, curriculum and instruction, family involvement, student organizations, accountability, and discipline. Gooden concludes his chapter with some recommendations for practice for educational leaders.

In the last chapter in this section, "African American Superintendents in Public School Districts," Kay Lovelace Taylor and Linda C. Tillman present findings from a study of African Americans in the superintendency. Interviews were conducted with current and former African American superintendents and other individuals who work in search firms and leadership training organizations and serve on school boards. Findings suggest that while the numbers of African American superintendents in public school districts has increased, they continue to be severely underrepresented nationally, the majority of them work in large urban districts that are underfunded and have records of poor student achievement, they are often given unrealistic deadlines to make districtwide improvements, and these superintendents are often viewed as being less capable than their White counterparts. Taylor and Tillman also found that both sitting and future African American school superintendents can benefit from professional development, peer networking, and mentoring. The authors conclude the chapter with recommendations for the preparation, recruitment, and retention of African American superintendents.

The scholarship in this section has placed African American school leadership at the center, rather than on the margins, of the broader discourse on school leadership and the education of African American students. Importantly, this centering of African Americans in school leadership is necessary if educators are to improve the educational outcomes for African American students in a variety of educational contexts, including urban, rural, and suburban districts as well as alternative schools.

11

AFRICAN AMERICAN PRINCIPALS AND THE LEGACY OF *BROWN*

LINDA C. TILLMAN

The year 2004 was filled with celebrations and commemorations of the 50th anniversary of the *Brown v. Board of Education* decision. There were a significant number of conferences that featured experts from education, law, sociology, and civil rights organizations who spoke of promises fulfilled and unfulfilled 50 years after the historic decision. Much of what was written, presented, and discussed during the jubilee year focused on historical accounts of events leading up to *Brown*, court-ordered desegregation efforts, the displacement of Black educators after the *Brown* decision, and the current state of African American education 50 years after this landmark case.[1] Indeed, our thinking has been stimulated about the impact of the *Brown* decision on education today, particularly for African Americans.[2]

One aspect of the *Brown* legacy that is underdeveloped in the literature is the significance of the leadership of African American principals in pre-K-12 education both before and after *Brown*. Pre-*Brown* African American principals were committed to the education of Black children, worked with other Black leaders to establish schools for these children, and worked in all-Black schools, usually in substandard conditions. Post-*Brown* African American principals helped to implement desegregation and educate African American children in the face of resistance. Today these men and women are primarily employed in large, urban school districts and continue to work for the social, emotional, and academic achievement of African American students. Yet many of the historical and contemporary contributions of African American school leaders have not been documented in the traditional literature on educational leadership and administration.[3]

Our knowledge of the contributions of African American school leaders has been enhanced by the work of scholars such as Anderson (1988), Franklin (1984, 1990), Savage (2001), Siddle Walker (1993a, 1993b, 1996, 2003), and Ward Randolph (1997). However, research by and about African Americans in school leadership positions has not become a dominant strand in the scholarship on educational leadership, leaving gaps in terms of an African American perspective (Banks, 1995; Bloom & Erlandson, 2003; Coursen, Mazzarella, Jeffress, & Hadderman, 1989; Dillard, 1995; Tillman, 2007). It is worth noting that, during the commemoration of the 50th anniversary of *Brown*, no special issues were published in the four major educational administration journals identified by Leithwood and Duke (1999)—*Educational Administration Quarterly, Journal of School Leadership, Journal of Educational Administration,* and *Educational Management and Administration*[4]—that focused on the

AUTHOR'S NOTE: An earlier version of this chapter appeared in the *Review of Research in Education, 28,* 101–146. Reprinted with permission of SAGE.

importance of the *Brown* decision to school leadership.

A special issue of *Educational Administration Quarterly*, "Pushing Back Resistance: African American Discourses on School Leadership" (Tillman, 2005b), includes perspectives on *Brown* and its significance to educational leadership. In addition, race and culture as factors in school leadership, topics that have not been extensively discussed in the educational leadership literature, are consistent themes in this special issue. The issues of race and culture in educational leadership are particularly relevant given the increasing number of African American principals and students in pre-K-12 education and the need to investigate issues that may be specific to African Americans in school leadership positions, including same race and cultural affiliation; leadership styles; recruitment, hiring, and retention of African American leaders; instructional supervision; leadership in urban schools;[5] and the relationship between African American school leadership and African American student success. This special issue was the first full issue in *Educational Administration Quarterly* to focus specifically on African Americans in school leadership, and represented an attempt to broaden the discussions on school leadership generally, and to establish a body of work on African Americans in school leadership specifically, in the mainstream school administration literature.[6]

The 1954 *Brown v. Board of Education* decision is significant with respect to African Americans in the principalship for several reasons. First, teachers, principals, and parents were the most important influences in the education of Black children in the pre-*Brown* era of schooling. Thus, discussions about the *Brown* decision and the education of Blacks cannot be held without discussions about the roles played by the central figure in the school: the Black principal. As the research reviewed here will reveal, it was the Black principal who led the closed system of segregated schooling for Blacks, primarily in the South. The Black principal represented the Black community; was regarded as the authority on educational, social, and economic issues; and was responsible for establishing the all-Black school as the cultural symbol of the Black community. Second, the work of Black principals in the post-*Brown* era has contributed to the theory and practice of

educational leadership. As this review will also reveal, the leadership of post-*Brown* African American principals is similar to that of their pre-*Brown* predecessors. Finally, the *Brown* decision is significant with respect to Black principals because one of the goals of the decision was to remedy educational inequities and thus allow Black principals to continue their work under improved social and educational conditions. It is ironic that the *Brown* decision resulted in the firing and demotion of thousands of Black principals, mostly in the southern and border states. As a result, Black principals were often denied the opportunity and authority to act on behalf of Black children in the implementation of desegregation.

Culture appeared to strongly influence the leadership of pre- as well as post-*Brown* African American principals. Tillman (2002) defined *culture* as "a group's individual and collective ways of thinking, believing, and knowing, which includes their shared experiences, consciousness, skills, values, forms of expression, social institutions and behaviors" (p. 4). The research reviewed here reveals that in the closed system of segregated schooling, as well as in post-*Brown* resegregated schools (Orfield & Lee, 2004), Black principals considered the cultural norms of the Black community in their leadership practices. The work of scholars such as Lomotey (1989a, 1993), Dillard (1995), Siddle Walker (1993a, 1996), and Bloom and Erlandson (2003) points to the importance of culture in the leadership of African American principals. For example, Dillard wrote that principals have three cultural management roles: interpreting, representing, and authenticating school culture and relationships. Dillard (1995), citing the conclusions of Mitchell, Ortiz, and Mitchell (1987) in their work on the notion of cultural management, noted that "particularly helpful were their conclusions that background, culture, religion, gender and other identities serve to develop particularized experiential views of schooling and leadership for the school principal" (p. 545). Finally, Dillard noted that "both nurturing and protecting African American children has historically included authoritative and direct ways of interacting, guided specifically by explicit, ethical, social, and *cultural rules and expectations* [italics added]" (p. 551). While the importance of culture, particularly with respect to racial and ethnic group membership, is not fully developed in the traditional educational leadership litera-ture, this review will show that an emphasis on culture as a factor in the leadership of Black principals dates back to the pre-*Brown* era of schooling.

OUTLINE OF THE PRESENT DISCUSSION

The specific focus of this chapter is African American principals in pre-K-12 education in the pre- and post-*Brown* eras. It is not my intent to present a comprehensive review of the broad range of topics in the field of educational leadership. Rather, I have reviewed published research on Blacks in the principalship and identified major themes in the literature. The research is interdisciplinary, including work from the fields of history, sociology, education, and, more specifically, educational leadership/administration. While a great deal of the empir-ical work on Blacks in educational leadership/administration can be found in unpublished dissertations (see, e.g., Hobson-Horton, 2000; Loder, 2002; Shotwell, 1999; Wells, 1991; White, 1995), this review is based on published research and does not include dissertation research on Blacks in the principalship.

The chapter is organized into three sections. In the first section, I discuss historical research on Blacks in the principalship in the pre-*Brown* era and the impact of the *Brown* decision on the dis-placement of Black principals. In the subsequent section, I discuss research on Blacks in the princi-palship in the post-*Brown* era. This work includes case studies, ethnographic research, and an emerging body of research on African American female principals. I conclude the review by sum-marizing major themes across the studies, dis-cussing the impact of the absence of a discourse about race in educational leadership and recom-mending directions for future research.

The presentation and analysis of the research in this review may be considered "different" from what is traditionally offered in "standard" literature reviews in educational research. However, this difference is consistent with the methodological approaches used by some of the researchers whose work is discussed in this review. Several of these authors note that their findings offer a counternarrative to what is writ-ten in traditional educational research (Bloom & Erlandson, 2003; Dillard, 1995; Lomotey,

1989a, 1993; Siddle Walker, 1993a, 1996). These authors rely heavily on the narrative approach and recount participants' stories—stories that, as the authors point out, may not be valued outside these specific racial and cultural experiences. They are stories of vision, hope, persistence, pride, opportunity, disappointment, racism, sexism, segregation, desegregation, resegregation, and survival. The approaches taken by the researchers are intended to place the experiences of African American principals at the center of the inquiry rather than at the margins (Tillman, 2002).

Collectively, the research in this review yielded four consistent themes: (a) resistance to ideologies and individuals opposed to the edu-cation of Black students, (b) the academic and social development of Black students as a prior-ity, (c) the importance of the cultural perspec-tives of the Black principal, and (d) leadership based on interpersonal caring. These themes are not linear. Rather, they overlap, and several themes may be found in a particular study. In addition, the themes cut across the pre- and post-*Brown* eras. Finally, there may be tensions in some of the themes; that is, they are not with-out contradictions and at times may appear to be in conflict within and across the research. A possible limitation of this review is that much of the research focuses on the positive aspects of Blacks in the principalship and "good schools." However, as did Sowell (1976) and Siddle Walker (2003), I chose to highlight scholarship on Black principals in the pre- and post-*Brown* eras that will "expand the narrow lens through which Black leadership has historically been viewed" (Siddle Walker, 2003, p. 59).

HISTORICAL PERSPECTIVES OF THE BLACK PRINCIPALSHIP

The work of Black educators is historically and culturally significant. A tradition of excellence in Black school leadership and an agenda for the education of Blacks date back to the 1860s (Anderson, 1988; Foster, 1997; Franklin, 1990; Pollard, 1997; Savage, 2001; Siddle Walker, 2000, 2001; Watkins, 2001). Black educators helped to build and operate public and private schools, secured funding and other needed resources, worked with the Black community, and served dual but complementary roles as educators and activists for the education of Black children. From a cultural standpoint, the educational philosophies of Black principals generally reflected the collective ethos of Black communities that believed education was the key to enhancing the life chances of their children. Particularly in many small southern towns, the all-Black school was the institution that reinforced community values and served as the community's ultimate cultural symbol (Dempsey & Noblit, 1996).

Thus, even while schools were segregated, they were "valued" by the Black community (Siddle Walker, 2000). Indeed, while separate school systems were the order of the day in the pre-*Brown* era, Black educators taught and nurtured an important segment of the Black community: its children. Henig, Hula, Orr, and Pedescleaux (1999) noted that "by the second half of the twentieth century, black teachers and principals were important role models and respected leaders in their communities. They also comprised a significant proportion of the African-American community's middle-class" (p. 44). Education was one of the few vocations open to middle-class Blacks in the pre-*Brown* era (Foster, 1997; Orfield, 1969; Pollard, 1997; Siddle Walker, 2000, 2001), and, because of their profession, Black principals served as models of "servant leadership."[7] Black principals demonstrated an ethos of service "which obligated those who acquired literacy to transfer this knowledge to others in the Black community" (Savage, 2001, p. 173).

The historical literature on Black principals focuses primarily on two areas: the lives and work of Black principals in the pre-*Brown* era and the employment status of Black principals immediately after the *Brown* decision. The sections to follow discuss research in these two areas.

BLACK PRINCIPALS IN THE PRE-*BROWN* ERA

Much of the scholarship on the lives and work of Black principals who led schools just after slavery into the early 1950s has been written by historians and is typically based on archival research and interviews. The majority of this scholarship has focused on the principal's role in the education of Blacks in the South in the pre-*Brown* era. The tasks of building and maintaining schools for Black children were taken on by

Blacks who assumed leadership roles and functioned as heads or principals of common schools as well as all-Black institutions such as Hampton and Tuskegee institutes (Anderson, 1988; Butchart, 1988; Franklin, 1990; Jones, 2003). For example, Zion School, one of the first all-Black schools in the South, was established in December 1865 and operated with an all-Black teaching and administrative staff (Anderson, 1988). Anderson wrote that Black Southerners were freed during the same time that education for Whites "was transformed into a highly formal and critical social institution" (p. 2). Blacks gained access to education under a different set of circumstances than Whites, for whom education was an entitlement. Anderson described systems of public and private education designed and implemented for and by Black Southerners between 1860 and 1935. Two types of schools established and maintained by ex-slaves were common schools and Sabbath schools. Sabbath schools, for example, were church sponsored, were open in the evening and on weekends, and provided literacy instruction to ex-slaves. According to Anderson, schooling for Blacks in the South was for the most part effective given the segregated context and hostility toward educated Blacks. Indeed, one of the most prominent themes in the history of Black Americans during this era was their persistent struggle to participate in an educational system that would ensure their continued freedom and grant them entrée into a democratic society. Anderson noted,

> The short range purpose of Black education in the post-slavery era was to provide the masses of ex-slaves with basic literacy skills plus the rudiments of citizenship training for participation in a democratic society. The long-range purpose was the intellectual and moral development of a responsible leadership class that would organize the masses and lead them to freedom and equality. (p. 31)

One of the earliest known Black principals was Booker T. Washington, who headed Hampton Institute in Virginia and later Tuskegee Institute in Alabama. Students who attended Hampton and Tuskegee were typically older and had been denied the opportunity to participate in structured education in the years immediately after slavery. Washington was principal during a period of history when the education of ex-slaves was primarily controlled by White philanthropists and industrialists who believed that Blacks should be trained (rather than educated) in skills that would benefit the economic development of the South. As principal, Washington established a manual labor program at Hampton Institute in 1879 (Washington, 1901/1993). The program operated at night after students had worked for 10 hours a day, 6 days a week, 11 months a year for 2 years. The Hampton manual labor program was "designed as an ideological force that would provide instruction suitable for adjusting blacks to a subordinate social role in the emergent New South" (Anderson, 1988, p. 36). Basic skills in reading, writing, and computation were discouraged; rather, Black students received instruction in cooking, sewing, and farming and were taught Christian morals. As the principal, Washington was given a great deal of authority to implement his own vision for educating Blacks, a vision that was consistent with the wishes of the White power structure. He often disagreed with Black leaders and Black educators who fought to provide Blacks with the same type of liberal arts and classical education received by Whites. Washington is credited with designing, implementing, and supervising the education of many Blacks, as well as raising money to modernize two schools that would later become premier all-Black institutions. However, his alliances with wealthy and influential Whites and his willingness to compromise the rights and the future of Blacks make him one of the most controversial figures in the struggle to educate Blacks.

From the 18th century through the 1950s, educated professional elites such as ministers, journalists, and politicians provided leadership in the struggle to educate Blacks (Franklin, 1984, 1990). Throughout the antebellum era, African American minister educators were particularly instrumental in opening schools in the North and the South. As principals or headmasters, these individuals held a strong belief that while Blacks could be stripped of their money, civil rights, and property, the knowledge they acquired through education could not be taken away. Jeremiah Burke Sanderson served as a principal-teacher in all-Black public schools in Stockton and San Francisco, California, from 1859 through 1874. While studying for the ministry, Sanderson became an outstanding educator and advocate for the schooling of Black children. In 1826, Daniel Payne, an African Methodist Episcopal bishop, started a school in Charleston, South Carolina, for free Black children and adult slaves. The school was closed in 1834, when Whites became fearful that free Blacks might have access to and be influenced by abolitionist literature. The South Carolina legislature passed a law that prohibited free Blacks from having "any school or other place of instruction for teaching any slave or free person of color to read or write" (Franklin, 1990, p. 43). Payne left Charleston and moved north, where he became an influential minister educator. He later founded Wilberforce College (now Wilberforce University) in Xenia, Ohio, the oldest college affiliated with the African Methodist Episcopal Church.

The agency of African American teachers and principals in Franklin, Tennessee, between 1890 and 1967 was the subject of research conducted by Savage (2001). In this pre- and post-*Brown* account of the education of Blacks, Savage defined *agency* as "self-reliance, proactive actions, and self-determining philosophies that result from a 'centeredness' within one's community" (p. 172). Savage's research documented the work of African American principals at "four continuously operating African American schools located on the same property in Williamson County just 15 miles south of Nashville, Tennessee" (p. 171). Findings indicated that African American principals "did more with less" (p. 171) with respect to providing an education for Black students. That is, even without money or resources, Black principals operated and maintained schools for Black children. Savage noted that Black principals operationalized agency in three ways: (a) developing resources (acquiring money, materials, and other resources to ensure the success of the school), (b) performing extraordinary services (maneuvering district policies, introducing new curricula and activities, and instilling in Black children resiliency, self-reliance, self-respect, and racial pride), and (c) focusing on the school as the center of the community (transforming schools into the cultural symbol of the Black community). Thus, the concept of *agency* comprised a range of purposeful strategies designed to foster Black self-reliance and empowerment and to resist opposition to the education of Black children.

The eight African American principals in Savage's study were agents of change who served collectively for more than 80 years. While the leadership styles of the principals were somewhat different, Savage found a common theme in their stories: They worked to provide schooling for African American children in the face of hostile conditions. Their passive and direct resistance to overt hostility included working around discriminatory policies (such as lack of resources and efforts to stop the spread of Black schools) and leading significant curricular change (such as adding academic courses to existing manual labor programs). In addition, they had worked to improve the quality of teachers in all-Black schools by recruiting qualified teachers trained in prestigious Black institutions such as Fisk and Tennessee State universities located in nearby Nashville. Educating Black children was the impetus for their actions, and the notion of "doing more with less" was the core of their agency in preparing students for immediate and future success.

African American women also played exemplary roles in the education of Blacks in the pre-*Brown* era (Alston & Jones, 2002; Franklin, 1990; Hine & Thompson, 1998; Jones, 2003; Perkins, 1987). Educated African American women opened schools in the North and the South and served dual roles as teachers and principals. Jeanes Supervisors were females who served as teachers and principals from 1907 through 1967, and their duties included introducing new teaching methods and curricula, organizing in-service teacher training workshops, and serving as assistants to county superintendents of schools. Among the most famous African American female principals who worked in the late 19th and early 20th centuries were Sarah Smith, Mary Shadd Cary, Fannie Jackson Coppin, Anna Julia Cooper, Nannie Helen Burroughs, and Mary MacLeod Bethune. Sarah Smith was named principal of the African School in Brooklyn, New York, in 1863 and was the first African American female principal in the New York public school system. Mary Shadd Cary became a principal in the Washington, D.C., school system in 1869. Fannie Jackson Coppin was the principal of Philadelphia's Institute for Colored Youth from 1869 through 1904 and was one of the most influential Black educators of the late 19th century. Under Coppin's leadership, the institute served as the premier example

of African American intellectual achievement (Perkins, 1987). The institute was considered one of the best secondary schools in the country, and students were exposed to a curriculum that included the classics. It was also considered a training ground for individuals who would teach in the segregated schools of the South. Coppin's vision for excellence in Black education was evidenced in the educational and professional achievements of the more than 5,000 students with whom she worked during her long tenure at the institute. Her efforts represent one of the earliest examples of the link between African American school leadership and African American student achievement.

Anna Julia Cooper, one of the few Blacks to earn a graduate degree in the 19th century, was recruited to teach at the M Street School in Washington, D.C., the city's only Black high school, and became the principal in 1902 (Cooper, 1892/1988). Cooper's tenure at the M Street School was marked by many accomplishments. When she became principal of the school, she was faced with promoting an agenda for Black education that was counter to Booker T. Washington's vocational and industrial program. As noted earlier, Washington's program was viewed by many Whites as the model for educating Blacks, and his philosophy had won the approval of influential Whites who believed in the intellectual inferiority of Blacks. But Cooper fought to build and maintain a curriculum and school culture that prepared students for college and beyond. She defied her White supervisor and prepared M Street students to attend prestigious universities such as Harvard, Brown, Oberlin, and Dartmouth, and under her leadership the school became accredited by Harvard. Her commitment to preparing Black children to attend postsecondary institutions and her refusal to yield to the White power structure and sexist atmosphere in the school and larger community were factors that led to her dismissal as principal. A former student at M Street School noted that Cooper should have expected hostility from males:

> You must also remember that as far as the Negro population of Washington was concerned, we were still a small southern community where a woman's place was in the home. The idea of a woman principal of a high school must account in some part for any reaction Dr. Cooper felt against her. (Washington, 1988, p. xxiii)

According to Franklin (1990), African American female educators participated in similar types of professional and social activities as African American men in the 19th century. However, Cooper's tenure as principal at the M Street School suggests that African American female educators were subjected to various forms of gender discrimination with respect to their supervisory roles. While Cooper was well trained for the principalship, exhibited strong leadership skills, and shared the philosophies of many of her African American male counterparts, the opposition she faced was similar to that experienced by other African American women (e.g., female minister educators) in the pre-*Brown* era.

The historical literature reveals that African American principals were central figures in segregated schooling and the African American community (Anderson, 1988; Franklin, 1990; Pollard, 1997; Savage, 2001; Siddle Walker, 2000, 2001). They served as connections to and liaisons between the school and the community. As principals, they encouraged parents to donate resources to schools, helped raise funds for schools, and served as professional role models for teachers and other staff members. For example, Black principals in the pre-*Brown* era modeled professionalism by attending professional conferences and meetings and earning graduate degrees. They also served as instructional leaders and not only provided a vision and direction for the school staff but also transmitted the goals and ideals of the school to a philanthropic White power structure.

As liaisons to the White community, African American principals often requested funding, resources, and other forms of support for all-Black schools. Black principals enjoyed a significant degree of authority and autonomy that was largely the result of the indifference and neglect of all-White school boards and White superintendents. Whites' lack of interest in the education of Black children (as opposed to training them for manual labor) usually led to the Black principal becoming the ultimate decision maker at the school site. Because segregated schools were primarily closed systems that were important only to Blacks, Black principals could hire and fire teachers, implement programs, and raise money for needed resources. However, these principals had no real power outside the Black community. According to Siddle Walker (2000), they "could consult with the White community, but [they] held little power to make policy decisions" (p. 275). Black principals understood and worked within the existing power dynamics and acted as "middle men."

Understanding the importance of developing an educated Black community, these individuals held themselves accountable for the academic achievement of Black children and adults who attended all-Black public and private schools. Principals in segregated schools "provided counter education to Whites' expectations" (Siddle Walker & Archung, 2003, p. 22) and understood that their own progress was directly linked to the academic, social, economic, and political progress of African Americans as a race.

THE *BROWN* DECISION AND DISPLACEMENT OF BLACK PRINCIPALS

Was the loss of employment for Black principals one of the (un)intended and (un)anticipated consequences (Tillman, 2004b) of desegregation after *Brown*? The *Brown* decision was intended to remedy the inequities of segregated schooling, and, ideally, the decision would provide a more equitable context for Black principals to continue the important work of educating Black children. But the tradition of excellence in African American school leadership was dramatically changed by desegregation, particularly in the South. While some Black principals retained their positions after the historic *Brown v. Board of Education* decision, desegregation had a devastating impact on the closed structure of Black education and thus the professional lives of thousands of Black principals (Ethridge, 1979; Pollard, 1997; Tillman, 2004a, 2004b; Valverde & Brown, 1988; Yeakey, Johnston, & Adkison, 1986).

In his essay "Another Vanishing American: The Black Principal," James (1970) observed that Black principals were "prime victims" of the move from a dual to a unitary system of schooling. Black principals were often the only formally educated Blacks in the community. More important, Black principals had a direct impact on the lives of the students they served; as role models, they provided images that would inspire and motivate Black students. In the post-*Brown* era, displacement of Black principals meant that they were demoted or fired. James noted that, in many instances, Black principals were transferred to central office positions such as coordinators of federal programs or were "given some other title completely foreign to all known educational terminology, a desk, a secretary, no specified responsibilities or authority, and all this with a quiet prayer that [they would] somehow just go away" (p. 20). Because one of the roles of Black principals was to provide a training ground for Black leaders, James lamented that their threatened extinction had dramatic implications for Black leadership in the future. According to James, the loss of Black principals was "catastrophic."

The system of separate, segregated schooling usually favored Black principals (Yeakey et al., 1986). That is, because professional employment opportunities outside this system were almost nonexistent, the maintenance of a segregated system of schooling ensured Black principals a professional role in the lives of Black children and in the Black community. The dismantling of this system interrupted their favored status. According to Yeakey et al.,

> Since racial patterns in most communities, especially those in the South[,] did not countenance blacks supervising whites in any capacity, much less teaching, principals of formerly black schools usually were reassigned as assistants to white principals or as central office supervisors. (p. 122)

The literature on the impact of *Brown* on Black principals is not as prominent as that on Black teachers.[8] Research on the employment status of Black principals is often incorporated into larger studies of Black educators. For example, Ethridge's (1979) study of the employment status of Black educators after the implementation of desegregation focused on teachers, principals, supervisors, and central office personnel. Records on the displacement of Black principals were poorly kept, and Ethridge noted that "the lack of effective data collection throughout the first fourteen years of desegregation will prevent the true impact of the *Brown* decision on Black educators from ever being really known" (p. 222).

Some of the earliest research on the displacement of Black principals was conducted by Hooker (1971), Coffin (1972), Ethridge (1979), Abney (1980), and Valverde and Brown (1988). Hooker's survey of 11 southern states revealed that between 1967 and 1971, the number of

Black principals in states such as North Carolina, Virginia, and Arkansas dropped dramatically. For example, the number of Black principals in North Carolina dropped from 620 to 40.

The years 1954 through 1965 were the most devastating for Black principals (Ethridge, 1979). During the period immediately after the *Brown* decision, Whites believed that Black principals had been ineffective in educating Black children. Expert witnesses who testified during a series of post-desegregation legal proceedings called for the dismantling of all-Black schools and replacing Black principals with Whites. For example, Oklahoma, Missouri, Kentucky, West Virginia, Maryland, and Delaware closed the majority of their all-Black schools between 1954 and 1965, and more than 50% of the Black principals in these states were dismissed. More than 6,000 Black principals were needed to reach equity and parity nationally, and Ethridge concluded that "thousands of educational positions which would have gone to Black people in the South under a segregated system have been lost for them since desegregation" (p. 231).

Abney (1980) speculated that the all-White makeup of Florida school boards as well as control by White superintendents in many of the state's districts figured prominently in the demotion and firing of Black principals. He studied the status of Black principals in Florida during the school years 1964–1965 and 1975–1976 and found that, in 1964–1965, Black principals were employed in each of the 67 school districts in Florida. Ten years later, 27 of these districts had no Black principals, even while the Black school-aged population had increased. Florida added 165 public schools in the 1975–1976 school year but fired or demoted 166 Black principals.

School districts in Florida were also grouped according to the percentage of minorities in the state's general population. Thus, in most instances, when the percentage of minorities in the school population was compared with the percentage of Black school principals, the relative number of Black principals was low. This deficiency was "alarming when one considers the fact that 27 of 67 school districts in Florida do not have a single black public school principal, in spite of a significant number of minority group members in the general and pupil populations" (Abney, 1980, p. 401).[9]

Black principals were being threatened with extinction as a result of desegregation (Fultz, 2004a). Fultz cited a 1971 U.S. Senate Select Committee on Equal Educational Opportunity report revealing that Black principals were being eliminated with "avalanche-like force and tempo" (p. 28). Demotions and firings of Black principals proceeded by four primary means: (a) demoting Black principals to teaching or nonteaching positions, (b) downgrading their schools to lower grade levels, (c) allowing them to retain their title but with no real power, and (d) giving them "paper promotions" to central office positions with no influence. These practices forced Black principals to work almost exclusively in elementary and junior high schools and to work in schools where decision-making authority was allocated to a White assistant. Consequently, Black principals were removed as authority figures at the school-site level. Such practices occurred primarily in southern and rural areas, and Black principals who retained their positions usually worked in urban districts with large populations of Black students.

Patterns of displacement of Black principals also negatively affected the pool of Black teachers who could be mentored for the principalship, effectively eliminating advocates for the recruitment, hiring, and promotion of Black teachers to principal positions (Karpinski, 2004). Demotions and firings of Black principals reflected the deep-seated segregationist ideology of the South, and White Southerners with turn-of-the-century attitudes about Black inferiority would not tolerate Black principals supervising students and teachers in integrated schools. In racially charged communities, displacement of Black principals removed them from having any authority over policy-making and instructional leadership and made it difficult for students, parents, and community members to negotiate with the White power structure. The Georgia Teacher and Education Association (1970; cited in Siddle Walker, 2003) referred to the massive displacement of Black principals as "outer-gration." One of the (un)intended consequences of the *Brown* decision was that Black principals were forced out of the profession (Tillman, 2004b), leading to what Cecelski (1994) has called the "decimation" of Black principals. While there have been modest increases in the number of Black principals since

the early 1970s, they continue to be underrepresented relative to the number of Black students in the population. In the 2003-2004 school year, Black principals represented only 16.4% of all principals nationally (U.S. Equal Employment Opportunity Commission, 2005).

Dempsey and Noblit (1996), in their discussion of school desegregation, noted that

> we acted as if we were ignorant of the fact that desegregation was disproportionately burdening . . . African Americans with the bulk of busing, with the closure of African American schools, and with the demotions and firing of African American educators. (p. 115)

Yet history and research illustrate that displacement of Black principals was one of the negative effects of the *Brown* decision. That is, one of the consequences of the desegregation of America's schools was the loss of Black principals and thus the exclusion of voices and perspectives that were critical to the education of Black children. Not only were positions lost in the numerical sense but, more important, there was a loss of a tradition of excellence, a loss of Black leadership as a cultural symbol in the Black community, and a loss of the expertise of educators who were committed to the education of Black children.

As the research reviewed in this section indicates, the displacement of Black principals had the immediate effect of disrupting the education of Black children and the stability of the Black community. Desegregation placed Black principals, teachers, students, and parents in an unfamiliar space. The racist context of schooling for Blacks became more obvious and more pronounced. Black principals now had no control over the education of their students and no longer served as the liaison between the Black community and the White power structure. While Black principals typically had had no real voice in policy making outside the school itself, the *Brown* decision left them almost completely powerless. Schools were now controlled by Whites, many of whom were resistant to integration. Whites mounted three forms of resistance to integration: (a) States undermined the *Brown* decision by ignoring the mandate and implementing inequitable funding structures; (b) agents of resistance such as White Citizens Councils demonstrated in protest of integration in many southern cities and proposed plans to close all public schools rather than accept integrated schools; and (c) strategies were used to keep Black educators in subordinate positions so that Blacks would have no control or voice in schools (Siddle Walker, 2003).

Several themes are evident in the research on pre-*Brown* principals: the education of Black children as a priority, resistance to ideologies and individuals opposed to the education of Blacks, and the importance of the cultural perspectives of Black principals. Black principals such as Booker T. Washington, Fannie Jackson Coppin, and Daniel Payne were instrumental in establishing schools, garnering resources, and educating Blacks in the period just after slavery. While their individual philosophies may have differed, they shared a collective will to educate Blacks and uplift the race. These Black principals were also agents of change as they fought against theories of inferiority and blatant resistance to the education of Blacks both in their speech and in their actions. In both passive and overt ways, they challenged a White power structure that would deprive Blacks of their right to participate in the free society designed by and for Whites. Racial pride, self-esteem, and self-respect were instilled as a form of passive resistance to theories of inferiority, while the introduction of academic and classical curricula and the recruitment of qualified teachers represented more overt forms of resistance to ideologies and individuals who would keep Blacks in subservient positions.

The cultural perspectives of Black principals were also a consistent theme in the research. Principals were the central figure in the school and the community, and their leadership represented the racial and cultural norms of the Black community and an ethos of service. Their work reflected a cultural heritage of self-determination (Franklin, 1990), a vision for the future of Blacks, and a framework for the work of Black principals who would succeed them. Siddle Walker (2003) emphasized the importance of the cultural perspectives of the Black principal: "The perspective of the Black principal is central to explaining how the segregated Black schools were able to fight the demon of racism by helping Black children believe in what they were capable of achieving" (p. 59).

Some tensions exist in the research on pre-*Brown* Black principals. First, while these principals were dedicated to the uplift of the race, they worked in schools that were never adequately funded and lacked essential resources. Consequently, their leadership was, to a great degree, defined by a constant struggle to access buildings, money, and the other resources necessary to produce an educated class of Blacks. Second, pre-*Brown* educators had differing philosophies regarding the most appropriate education, that is, manual training versus an academic education. This was particularly the case in the debates between leaders such as Booker T. Washington and Anna Julia Cooper. In some ways, these ideological struggles resulted in class distinctions among Blacks. Educators such as Fannie Jackson Coppin and Anna Julia Cooper led elite all-Black schools in the North that produced an educated class of Blacks who would go on to become doctors, lawyers, and teachers. Their leadership represents early evidence of the relationship between principal leadership and student achievement. Conversely, Booker T. Washington led schools in the South that largely produced Blacks who were trained in manual labor skills and who would always work in the Southern economy. Washington's philosophy that Blacks would receive no training that would place them on equal parity with Whites contributed to tensions among Black educators.

Finally, consistent with the time period, most of the pre-*Brown* principals were men. While the contributions of Black female principals are acknowledged in the research, it was expected that the principal would be male and that he would be accorded recognition and respect based on his gender. These expectations suggest that Black women who aspired to the principalship faced a sexist environment. However, the post-*Brown* period would see a gradual shift in the demographics of the principalship, and more Black women would lead schools (particularly at the elementary level) two decades after the *Brown* decision. Despite these tensions, collectively the research indicates that the leadership of African American principals in the pre-*Brown* period offers a framework for discussing the work of post-*Brown* principals.

BLACK PRINCIPALS IN THE POST-*BROWN* ERA

Black principals in the post-*Brown* era faced different types of challenges than their predecessors. In the desegregated schools of the South and North, the roles of Black principals were more complex. Rodgers (1967), in his study of Black high schools, described African American principals as superintendents, supervisors, family counselors, financial advisors, community leaders, employers, and politicians. Scholars conducting research on the education of Blacks in the post-*Brown* era have often focused on the importance of the leadership of Black principals. The research outlined in this section includes ethnographic and case study research on good schools (Lightfoot, 1983; Sowell, 1976), leadership role identity (Lomotey, 1989a, 1993), relationships between segregated schools and the community (Siddle Walker, 1993a, 1996), caring forms of leadership (Lyman, 2000), and African American women in the principalship (Bloom & Erlandson, 2003; Dillard, 1995; Doughty, 1980; Reitzug & Patterson, 1998).[10] As with the themes identified in the literature, these topics overlap. For example, Dillard's research on the leadership of an African American female principal also represents research on a caring leader. The focus of Lightfoot's research is good high schools, but the leadership styles of the principals of these schools are also a consistent theme in her work. Thus, readers will note the overlapping topics in much of the research described in this section.

Sowell (1976) sought to determine the factors that contributed to "black excellence, its sources, and its wider implications for contemporary education and for social policy in general" (p. 7). Sowell studied six all-Black high schools and two all-Black elementary schools. The high schools were selected from Horace Mann's (1970) list of Black high schools with the highest number of alumni with earned doctorates from 1957 through 1962. The two elementary schools in the sample had records of academic achievement.[11] Principals in each of the schools examined were instrumental in students' academic and professional achievement. Two factors were prominent in Sowell's research: a history of educational excellence at each of the schools and strong leaders who were committed to the education of Black children.

Sowell's study is instructive because it offers a historical look at each school: The research not only focused on the prominence of the schools in the pre- and early post-*Brown* periods but also documented their decline after *Brown*. The public schools examined in the study, like the cities in which they were located, were victims of the transformation of urban cities. These cities, which were once centers of educational, economic, and social excellence, were now characterized by crime, poverty, and decay. Their public schools, which once boasted high test scores, numerous academic awards, service to the Black community, and the development of Black professionals, were now being defined by low test scores, locations in decaying neighborhoods, lack of parental support, and discipline problems.

One of the schools, Booker T. Washington High School in Atlanta, Georgia, was illustrative of such changes. The principal at the time of the study noted that the neighborhood surrounding the school was no longer a stable middle-class area but was now considered a neighborhood of lower socioeconomic status, and the school was plagued by poor academic performance, with student test scores below the national average and below those of other high schools in Atlanta. The principal believed that the school needed more than money to address these problems. She talked about the absence of human resources and, particularly, a lack of parental involvement as major problems. Sowell concluded that academic achievement was more than mastery of subject matter; it also included order and respect in the school. More important, the character and the ability of the principal were critical factors in the success of the school and its students.

Sowell's research suggests that the leadership issues facing principals in the pre- and early post-*Brown* periods were similar in some ways and different in others. Leadership in the pre-*Brown* period was defined to a significant degree by de jure segregation, and principals responded primarily to the wishes of the close-knit community of the day. Leadership in the post-*Brown* period evolved amid the changing demographics and dynamics of large urban cities.

Lightfoot (1983) sought to define "good high schools" in case studies of six urban, suburban, and elite schools.[12] Good schools were "described as good by faculty, students, parents, and communities; [they] had distinct reputations as fine institutions with clearly articulated goals and identities" (p. 23). Strong, effective leadership is one of the foundations of the effective schools movement, and the principal, as the instructional leader, sets the tone for the school, decides on instructional strategies, and organizes and distributes school resources (Dantley, 1990; Edmonds, 1979). Lightfoot's (1983) view of good high schools included a broader perspective of "effectiveness" than what is described in the effective schools literature. According to Lightfoot, "goodness" (or effectiveness) cannot be measured on the basis of a single indicator of success such as test scores; rather, it includes "people, structures, relationships, ideology, goals, intellectual substance, motivation, and will" (p. 23). A consistent theme in each of Lightfoot's case studies is the significant role of the principal in the culture of a "good" school. Lightfoot argued that the principal holds the ultimate responsibility for creating the vision, mission, goals, and objectives of the good high school. Furthermore, she emphasized the impact of each principal's leadership philosophy and leadership style on the teachers, students, and community.

One of the schools described in Lightfoot's (1983) study was George Washington Carver Comprehensive High School in Atlanta. Carver was a public school located in a lower socioeconomic neighborhood, and at the time of Lightfoot's study it had "long been known as a dumping ground for Atlanta schools" (p. 11). However, it had begun to make noticeable progress under the leadership of its new African American principal, Norris Hogans, an energetic, passionate individual who was fighting against the negative history of the school and was determined to build a new image of its students, teachers, parents, and staff. Hogans wanted to "undo old perceptions, reverse entrenched habits, and inculcate new behavioral and attitudinal forms" (p. 15). A former elementary school principal, he was selected to "save Carver from total demise" (p. 31). His passion and commitment were considered catalysts for change in a school where change was badly needed.

Hogan's leadership style was considered to be authoritarian. For example, some teachers and students described Hogans as unwilling to negotiate or share power in decisions that affected the entire school community. Yet teachers and students agreed that his philosophy and decisions were critical to achieving positive results. Hogans believed that schools were transformational institutions responsible for providing students with discipline and safety—resources that were often unavailable to them in their homes and communities—and opportunities for meaningful and productive lives at school and in the larger society. Hogans also believed

that schools should demand excellence from students: "I think we don't expect enough from our students. We seem to be content if they score two years below grade level" (Lightfoot, 1983, p. 35). Hogans's belief that students could be successful both academically and professionally led him to address the issue of student achievement in direct ways. He encouraged teachers to set high standards for student achievement and discipline and preached a philosophy that exposure to professions such as business, industry, medicine, and law could be instrumental in developing the aspirations of African American students. Such purposeful exposure to the world of work would link their aspirations to their achievement in the classroom.

In an effort to achieve these goals, Hogans formed the Explorers Program at Carver High. The program was designed for 10th-grade students and included monthly field trips to major businesses and agencies in the Atlanta area. The purpose of the field trips was to teach students how these businesses operated, orient them to careers offered in such businesses, and provide guidance that would help them make informed career choices. Similar to the Boy Scout tradition, which served as an example for the program, the Explorers Program stressed honor, honesty, and rigor—characteristics that Hogans promoted as part of the Carver High School image.

Hogans's vision for the school was an ambitious one given the urban school context of his leadership: He wanted students to experience and benefit from a comprehensive education that would provide them with both technical and academic instruction. He believed that students should be exposed to a threefold curriculum (general, vocational, and academic) that would prepare them for positions as laborers as well as positions in professions such as education and medicine. His philosophy was similar to that of Booker T. Washington, one of his heroes. He believed in the value of vocational and technical training for economic stability, as did Washington; however, he did not share Washington's belief that education and employment opportunities for Blacks should be limited to vocational/manual labor fields.

Teachers, students, and parents at Carver were hopeful that Hogans's leadership would be a significant factor in helping students become "industrious, hard-working citizens" (Lightfoot,

1983, p. 312). Good attendance, a relative lack of discipline problems, a safe and orderly environment, and high employment rates after graduation were viewed as indicators of school success. Under Hogans's leadership, the school had made great strides in each of these areas, and he had led the school through "impressive changes, the progress from terrible to much better" (p. 313). According to Lightfoot, the standards of goodness were being met as a result of Hogans's leadership. While indicators of goodness were evident, Lightfoot also found that there was much more work to be done to achieve other, less measurable standards of goodness such as civility, poise, and ambition, characteristics that students would need in the world outside school.

Lightfoot (1983) noted that "an essential ingredient of good schools is strong, consistent and inspired leadership" (p. 323) and a school culture defined by the vision and purposeful actions of the principal. Hogans was described as a strict authoritarian leader who was both loved and feared by students, teachers, and staff. This description might lead one to assume that Hogans was uncaring and insensitive toward students and the community. However, according to Lightfoot, Hogans was an example of an authoritarian father figure who, above all, had a strong commitment to the social and academic success of Black children. She noted that he embodied three dominant images associated with the literature on school leadership: Principals are disproportionately male, they are usually former coaches or jocks, and they are father figures. Hogans, a Black male was also a former athlete coach, and acted as a father figure.

The post-*Brown* era brought about an emphasis on effective principal leadership as a catalyst for student achievement (see, e.g., Hallinger & Heck, 1996; Murphy, 1988; Witziers, Boskier, & Krüger, 2003). Researchers attempted to define the specific kinds of direct and indirect leadership (Hallinger & Heck, 1996) that established a school culture of success and enhanced student achievement. Some of this research was particularly focused on African American students who had lagged behind their White peers since the advent of school reform efforts, including the standardized testing movement (Anderson, 2003).

Lomotey (1989a) conducted research focusing on the significance of African American principals in the educational success of African American students. Lomotey sought to determine the ways in which the leadership styles of African American principals directly influenced the academic achievement of African American students. The study was conducted in "more successful African-American schools": those that "possess the qualities suggested by the research on principal leadership and academic achievement" (p. 6). Three African American elementary school principals who worked in predominantly African American schools were the subjects of the study. The schools were deemed "more successful" than other African American schools because third and sixth graders scored higher in math and reading on the California Assessment Program over a 2-year period. A central question guided the research: "What kind of leadership do African-American principals exhibit in more successful African American elementary schools?" (p. 6). Data were derived from interviews with teachers and principals and from observations of principals in their daily work. In addition, questionnaires were used to investigate teachers' perceptions of how principals implemented four components of principal leadership that were consistent with the school administration literature: (a) developing goals, (b) harnessing the energy of the staff, (c) facilitating communication, and (d) being involved in instructional management.

Principals in Lomotey's study exhibited more than one leadership style. For example, all the principals placed the education of children as their first priority. However, only two engaged in assertive forms of leadership while establishing a school climate and culture that motivated teachers to focus on the academic achievement of all students. The third principal practiced a more indirect form of leadership and delegated much of the responsibility in each leadership component to support staff. The two principals who engaged in all four components of principal leadership were central figures in the school who performed traditional leadership functions leading to the maintenance of organizational goals. These principals accepted the goals of the organization, facilitated cooperation among staff members, developed and implemented effective communication with their staffs, and actively engaged in curriculum planning, teacher supervision, and student assessment. Lomotey argued that principals who adopt and use all four components of principal leadership help promote the goals of schools: determining how information is disseminated, deciding whose ideas and values are privileged, and controlling the behaviors of others.

The most prominent finding in Lomotey's (1989a) study was that each principal demonstrated a "commitment to the education of African-American children, a compassion for, and understanding of, their students and the communities in which they work, and a confidence in the ability of all African-American children to learn" (p. 131). These principals were committed to the education of African American students and were concerned not only with helping students move successfully from grade to grade but also with enhancing their life chances. They understood that being African American was not enough; they had to exhibit compassion for African American children and their communities. Lomotey posited that because these qualities were shared by each of the principals, this finding

> raises the question of the significance, for African-American principals, of these three characteristics in relation to the four qualities that I sought to explore. It is possible that, given the unique characteristics of these African-American schools (e.g., economic, academic, cultural, and social), these three qualities supersede all others in importance in bringing about success. (p. 131)

Lomotey concluded that principal leadership is critical to the successful schooling of African American students.

In a later study, Lomotey (1993) applied the frameworks from his 1989 study of principals in successful schools to case studies of two African American female elementary principals.[13] Both principals worked in schools that were pilot sites for an African and African American curriculum infusion project. The study focused on the principals' role in facilitating the implementation of the infusion project. In this study, Lomotey referred to the four components of principal leadership as the *bureaucrat/administrator* role identity and the qualities of commitment, confidence, and compassion as the *ethno-humanist* role identity. Specifically, the primary goal of a principal who assumes a bureaucrat/administrator role identity is "schooling": facilitating the

movement of students from grade to grade. The primary goal of a principal who assumes an ethno-humanist role identity is "education": meeting a set of cultural goals.

Findings revealed that both principals exhibited the qualities of commitment, compassion, and confidence and were concerned about education issues related to

> the development of the whole child. As members of the same cultural group, the principals were committed to providing an equitable education to African American children, were confident that these children would excel academically, and showed compassion and understanding for the children and their families. Their goals and actions were purposeful: As leaders, they were committed to ensuring the perpetuation of African-American culture. (Lomotey, 1993, p. 410)

For example, both principals were committed to providing African American students with opportunities to learn about African and African American history and culture. More important, the principals were committed to helping students "develop positive self-concepts and generally to feel good about themselves and their people" (p. 410).

Lomotey (1993) pointed out that while principals are administrators (i.e., they perform various administrative functions), they are also members of distinctive cultural groups, and principals who believe their cultural affiliation is important to their work will make a distinction between their bureaucrat/administrator and ethno-humanist role identities. Lomotey acknowledged that such a distinction could be viewed as conflicting but noted, "Consequently, but not at all unexpectedly, the personal (ethno-humanist) and professional (bureaucrat/administrator) role identities were often intertwined" (p. 410). The principals in this study merged the two identities in their work and balanced "schooling" and "education" to help African American children achieve academic excellence.

Siddle Walker (1993a, 1993b, 1996, 2003) investigated the relationships between segregated African American schools and their communities in the South. Her ethnographic and case study research examined how communities supported schools, how schools supported their communities, and the implications such relationships might have for contemporary school reform efforts. In her award-winning book, *Their Highest Potential: An African American School Community in the Segregated South* (1996), she documented the pre- and post-*Brown* periods of segregated schooling at Caswell County Training School (CCTS) in rural North Carolina. The school educated children from 1934 to 1969, and a central focus of Siddle Walker's investigation was the work of dedicated educators who believed that their jobs extended from the classrooms into the community. A mutually dependent relationship existed between CCTS and the community. The school held itself accountable to the wishes of the Black community, and community members provided financial and other forms of support for the school. Siddle Walker's work represents a counternarrative to earlier work depicting all-Black schools as deficient (see, e.g., Brown, 1960; Clark, 1963; Kluger, 1977). She noted that while such depictions were not completely inaccurate, they often excluded the perspectives of Black principals and in-depth and thoughtful analyses of how they established and maintained schools for Black children. Furthermore, these depictions overlooked "any suggestion that not all education for African-American children during segregation was inferior" (1993a, p. 162).[14]

Siddle Walker (1993a) used terminology similar to that of Lightfoot (1983), describing CCTS as a "good school" on the basis of the school's and the community's belief that it provided a positive social and cultural environment for learning. Siddle Walker acknowledged the inequities as well as the "goodness" of CCTS:

> My description of why CCTS was perceived as a good school is not meant to validate the inequities or minimize the discrimination that existed in this and other segregated schools, where parents were overly burdened to create for themselves the educational facilities and opportunities schools boards often denied them (Anderson, 1988; Bullock, 1967). Rather, I offer this case as representative of the many other southern African-American schools whose communities were also pleased with their schools, but whose histories have been lost and whose value is understood now only by former teachers, principals, parents, and students. (p. 162)

Open-ended interviews were conducted with former teachers, students, parents, and administrators, and themes of goodness in the school-community relationship were explored. In the segregated South, the Black school principal was a key figure in establishing and maintaining standards of goodness. Black principals were committed to the social and academic achievement of students and developed relationships with parents, the broader Black community, and the White establishment to achieve their goals. The segregated school environment often served as a second home for Black students; it was an environment where they were taught, nurtured, supported, and corrected. As the central figure in the school, the African American principal provided vision, leadership, and guidance to students, teachers, and other staff members.

The principal of CCTS was Nicholas Longworth Dillard, highly regarded by the community as well as Black and White educational leaders. As an African American principal in a segregated school environment, Dillard worked to ensure that the school kept its commitment to educating African American children by providing support and encouragement and insisting on high academic standards. Dillard prided himself on being very knowledgeable about educational issues and sought to expose students to a well-educated teaching staff. By 1954, the majority of the teachers at CCTS had earned postgraduate certification. Dillard served as principal of CCTS from 1933 to 1969, and during his tenure he instituted more than 53 "extracurricular clubs and activities to enhance student leadership and development" (Siddle Walker, 1993a, p. 162).

As the principal, Dillard played a critical role in developing the instructional and physical aspects of the school. By 1938, the student population of CCTS had grown to more than 600, and the school was moved to a 10-room building. Later, Dillard would be instrumental in planning, designing, and supervising the construction of a modern 27-room school that opened in 1951. Parents and the community supported the construction of the school by donating almost $8,000 in equipment. This monetary support was evidence of Dillard's positive relationships with parents and the community.

Dillard promoted student achievement primarily in indirect ways. For example, he established an environment that was conducive to student achievement. One strategy for promoting student achievement was to promote parental involvement. Dillard regularly communicated with parents and used activities such as Parent-Teacher Association (PTA) meetings to report to them about the education their children were receiving at CCTS and ways they could help their children. He reinforced the school's expectations for the students and encouraged parents to attend school-related events. In interviews, parents recalled that the success of every student was Dillard's first priority. He conveyed this message to teachers and required them to attend professional development meetings and conferences. Teachers were also required to attend PTA meetings, which provided parents with the opportunity to establish positive relationships with them. As with other accounts of Black principals in segregated schools, Dillard rarely appeared before the White board of education. He was aware that, as an employee, his sphere of authority was primarily confined to the school site. Thus, he prepared parents to make requests for the school before the school board, supporting them in their roles as advocates for Black children. Such actions, while illustrative of indirect forms of principal leadership, were consistent with a time period not yet dominated by an emphasis on school reform.

As the "principal leader of a Black high school" (Siddle Walker, 2003, p. 62), Dillard helped develop a positive relationship with the Black community, and his leadership style is illustrative of the ethic of care in educational leadership (Lomotey, 1989a; Starratt, 1991), where his goals and actions showed in concrete ways that he cared for every student and was committed to their success. Dillard's goals and actions were also consistent with "interpersonal caring" with respect to the successful schooling of African American students (Siddle Walker, 1993b). This interpersonal caring included providing students with psychological, sociological, and academic support.

Students were transferred to integrated schools when court-ordered desegregation closed CCTS in 1969. A parent who attended PTA meetings after desegregation lamented that, in the new school, teachers were rarely present at these meetings, and the meetings were more focused on problems in the school than on the needs of students and what could be done to address them. She noted,

You just didn't see any teachers hardly. What few teachers came said, "you don't just walk up to teachers and ask how your child is doing; you have a conference." They said we were not supposed to ask about any [concerns] about our children [in the presence of] of anyone else. We were used to when we were there at the PTA meeting, we could just talk. (Siddle Walker, 1993a, p. 178)

The racial and cultural mismatch between the Black parents and students and the White principal and majority White teaching staff led to barriers between the school and the community. As noted by Lomotey (1987, 1989a, 1993), same-race affiliation and membership in a distinct cultural group (e.g., African American) are significant factors affecting how principals interact with parents and students. In addition, Lomotey concluded that it is often the case that individuals with similar values, beliefs, and cultural norms (such as teachers, principals, parents, and students) communicate more effectively.

In *How Do They Know You Care? The Principal's Challenge*, Lyman (2000) presented a case study of Kenneth Hinton, the principal of an early childhood education center located in a low-income, racially and ethnically diverse city in the Midwest. Lyman conducted an in-depth qualitative investigation of this caring leader and analyzed his contributions to the school environment. Hinton was chosen for the study because he was well respected and epitomized a caring attitude toward students, teachers, parents, and the community. The framework for the study was based on four perspectives of caring: (a) Caring both *gives* purpose and *is* purpose (Mayeroff, 1971); (b) caring is an ethical orientation (Gilligan, 1982); (c) caring is a relational process involving engrossment, action, and reciprocity (Noddings, 1984); and (d) caring leaders make a difference (Beck, 1994a, 1994b; Dillard, 1995; Lightfoot, 1983, p. 11). According to Lyman, the fourth perspective is informed *by how* leaders make a difference in the lives of students and their families. Thus, it is multifaceted, including the following elements: Caring leaders who protect and nurture are critical to maintaining schools that are good (Lightfoot, 1983); leaders grounded in an ethic of caring transform schools by embracing complexity and making an emotional investment

(Beck, 1994a, 1994b); and caring leaders who advocate for the needs of individual students are critical to students' success, particularly in culturally diverse schools (Dillard, 1995).

As the new principal and director of the recently built early childhood education center, Hinton had supervised much of the construction of the new building, developed the instructional program, hired a new staff, established rapport in the community, and welcomed new students and their families. The school had a racially diverse student population; the majority of the students were African American and White, and a small percentage were Hispanic and Asian. Lyman characterized Hinton as a nonconformist. At times, he challenged the bureaucracy of his school district regarding the most appropriate methods for educating children. He developed his own methods for working with challenging students in his school and worked with his staff to develop innovative programs that would respond to the various social, emotional, and economic needs of students and their families.

Hinton was also compassionate. As an African American male, he had experienced various forms of discrimination in school and in the community. But he was also influenced by an upbringing that stressed a supportive family structure and strong spiritual values, and his experiences led him to engage in acts of compassion that emphasized caring and developing children to their fullest potential. For example, Lyman found that in interviews with school staff and parents they used terms such as *caring, warm, nurturing,* and *loving* to describe Hinton's style of leadership as well as the school environment. As a builder, Hinton was able to build not only physical structures but relationships among key stakeholders: staff, students, parents, and the community. Staff members and members of the community praised Hinton for his ability to build bridges between the races and noted that "his caring for children is clearly not limited to children of color" (Lyman, 2000, p. 31). He served as a role model for students, and his leadership and service extended beyond the walls of the school. Hinton expressed his beliefs about caring in the following statement: "Caring carries with it a loss of class, ethnicity, gender, and religion. If a teacher cares, then these things that separate us through ignorance and fear become

unimportant. Status ceases to matter, and children are simply children" (Lyman, 2000, pp. 116–117).

Hinton's beliefs about caring were an extension of his experiences as a teacher and a learner. His caring leadership style was critical in enhancing student learning and was consistent with Hart and Bredeson's (1996, as cited in Lyman, 2000) assumption that "principals influence student learning outcomes directly and indirectly by what they do, what they believe, and how they use symbols" (p. 219). Hinton was motivated by his desire to "enhance the growth of others and give back to those who helped me" (p. 120). Hinton's decision to "give back" was similar to what Lightfoot (1994) referred to as "giving forward"—the concept that one cannot repay acts of caring but can engage in such acts in the future. Hinton's leadership style was also similar to aspects of Lomotey's (1993) ethnohumanist role identity; that is, he displayed commitment, compassion, and confidence in his interactions with students and their communities. However, unlike the principals in Lomotey's study, Hinton's ethno-humanist role identity was not solely based on same-race/cultural affiliation. Hinton focused his caring leadership on all students. Thus, while same-group racial and cultural membership has been shown to enhance principal-student relationships, Lyman's research suggests that other factors may influence these relationships. Lyman's findings also suggest that, because African Americans also lead mixed-race schools, there is an imperative to practice leadership that will meet the needs of students, teachers, and parents from all racial and ethnic groups represented.

The education of Black students as a priority, interpersonal caring, and resistance were dominant themes in the research on post-*Brown* principals. In some cases, principals were faced with making decisions about how they would continue to educate Black children after desegregation. Nicholas Dillard, the principal of Caswell County Training School had hoped that desegregation would dismantle the inequitable educational structures that had, in many ways, defined his leadership. Yet many of the inequities remained until the school was closed and desegregation was officially implemented. Principals such as Norris Hogans also placed the education of Black students as a priority but had a different vision for educating them. Drawing on the work of his predecessors, Hogans merged historical philosophies with his own vision and implemented a general, vocational, and academic curriculum that would prepare students for the world of work. Collectively, these post-*Brown* principals continued to make the education of Black students a priority and resisted Whites who attempted to undermine the *Brown* decision, teachers who held low expectations for students and who were resistant to change, and in some cases Black parents who, feeling disconnected from the newly integrated school, became less involved in their children's education.

The theme of interpersonal caring was also evident in the research on post-*Brown* principals. Several principals adopted Lomotey's (1993) ethno-humanist role identity and based their leadership on commitment, confidence, and compassion. Such principals were caring and loving and provided academic, social, and psychological support. In research on highly successful and loving elementary schools serving minority and low-income students, Scheurich (1998) found that while principals used the term *caring*, the term *loving* best described environments where principals exhibited extremely supportive attitudes toward students and adults. Scheurich's analysis was consistent with the types of interpersonal caring exhibited by Black principals in the research reviewed here. A tension exists in the research with respect to definitions of goodness in the education of Black students. While researchers sought to describe "good" schools, they also acknowledged that "good" did not necessarily represent a search for perfection. Both Sowell and Siddle Walker found imperfections in good schools. Schools that were once sites of educational excellence now struggled against being defined by external factors such as housing projects, crime, and poor student achievement. Fifty years after the *Brown* decision, schools continue to face these as well as other challenges that affect the quality of schooling for Blacks and thus the leadership capacity of Black principals.

Research on African American Female Principals

The research reviewed in this section focuses on African American female principals in the post-*Brown* period of schooling. There is limited evidence in the post-*Brown* educational leadership literature pointing to the leadership styles, accomplishments, and lives of Black female principals (Allen, Jacobson, & Lomotey, 1995; Benham, 1997; Bloom & Erlandson, 2003; Coursen et al., 1989; Pollard, 1997).[15] Benham (1997) identified several factors that have contributed to the paucity of research on Black women in school leadership. First, the number of Black women in pre-K-12 educational leadership positions, while increasing gradually, is still small relative to the numbers of White men and women and Black men. Thus, it is difficult to identify samples for large-scale studies. Second, a limited number of Black female and male researchers are investigating issues affecting Black school leaders. Further, the absence of a body of research on Black female principals is exacerbated by the fact that theories about women in leadership often refer to women as teacher leaders. Finally, Benham noted that the absence of studies of Black women represents, to a great degree, "an educational leadership discourse and practice that has been structured to impede such treatment" (p. 282). Bloom and Erlandson (2003) concurred with Benham's argument and elaborated on this point in the following statement: "Findings from a minority insider's perspective are regarded as dubious and unlikely to be published in professional journals. Suspect conclusions are summarily ignored or dismissed, seldom becoming a part of administrative leadership theory" (p. 344).

Inclusion of the contributions of African American female principals within predominantly White feminist literature is also problematic. According to Bloom and Erlandson (2003), asking questions about the experiences of African American women from the perspective of a White woman results in two negative outcomes: (a) perpetuating the practice of intellectual and cultural exclusion by creating the appearance of acceptance in women's studies using an ethnic additive model and (b) failing to acknowledge that White women retain White privilege and that women of color do not hold a color of privilege, thereby making African American women's experiences similar in some ways to those of women in general but deviant from the White female norm (p. 344). The result is a privileging of knowledge that often devalues the leadership theory and practice of African American female principals in the educational leadership discourse.

A search of the educational leadership literature reveals an additional challenge in identifying research on Black female principals: Work about these women is often grouped under the topic "women and minorities." Researchers have used this categorization in conducting studies that have included Black female principals (see, e.g., Adkison, 1981; Banks, 1995; Biklen & Brannigan, 1980; Crow & Glascock, 1995; Edson, 1987; Enomoto, Gardiner, & Grogan, 2000; Gardiner, Enomoto, & Grogan, 2000; Jones & Montenegro, 1985; Mertz & McNeely, 1998; Ortiz, 1982; Shakeshaft, 1999; Tonnsen & Truesdale, 1993; Young & McLeod, 2001). However, this research rarely presents detailed portraits of the lives, work, vision, and impact of these principals on the school community and student achievement or discriminatory practices that affect their work. As pointed out by Coursen et al. (1989), "what is true for blacks is not necessarily true for members of other racial minorities and may have nothing to do with women" (p. 87).

In a national survey of Black school administrators, Doughty (1980) found that Black women were most likely to be employed as consultants, supervisors, elementary school principals, and administrative assistants. At the time Doughty conducted her study, Black women in the elementary principalship were more likely to lead in challenging urban districts with predominantly Black student populations. Black women in Doughty's study typically assumed their first leadership position in their middle 40s to early 50s, and were older than Black or White men in such positions. In addition, Doughty's results showed that, after 1966, the percentage of Black women in the principalship decreased relative to the percentage of Black men. Black women were not the specific focus of Doughty's study. However, the findings about these women identified specific challenges and barriers faced by Black female principals and how they adapted to their roles—roles prescribed by their race *and* their gender. Doughty argued that roles associated with race and gender had negative consequences for Black women who aspired to principalship positions and also contributed to the myth of Black women as superhuman, capable of solving every problem and dealing with every crisis:

> The black female school administrator is in a double bind, perhaps even a triple bind. She embodies two negative statuses simultaneously. One is her color, black, and the other is her sex, female, neither of which society values very highly. (p. 165)

Doughty's findings are significant because they focus on the ways in which both race and gender, rather than gender as a single factor, affect the leadership of Black female administrators. For example, at the time of Doughty's study (1972–1973), Black women were usually in supervisory or consultant roles. As principals, they were primarily found in elementary ranks in challenging, predominantly Black schools; they were rarely in the high school principalship, a position reserved for men. Thus, almost two decades after the *Brown* decision, Black women continued to be selected for positions on the basis of their gender. As pointed out by Shakeshaft (1989), women were viewed as *well suited* for teaching, but it was usually the case that men were viewed as *more qualified* to be administrators.

Dillard (1995) conducted a case study of an African American female principal and sought to explore and reinterpret traditional definitions of effective school leadership, particularly in the context of the increasing diversity of schools. A central question guided her research: How do African American women interpret their acts of leadership? As an African American woman, Dillard noted that she approached the research from a critical feminist perspective and was "particularly interested in the inclusion of African American women's realities in the shaping of policy and literature surrounding effective schools and schooling" (p. 543).

Gloria Natham, a caring African American secondary school principal, was the subject of Dillard's research. Natham's school was situated in a metropolitan city that had undergone mandatory districtwide desegregation, and Natham noted that, like many other Black principals, she had been "brought here to clean up this mess and relate to these kids" (Dillard, 1995, p. 545). Natham modeled caring leadership in culturally meaningful ways. Her (re)interpretation of school leadership was a form of "talking back": practicing a style of educational leadership counter to traditional norms. Natham talked back by setting high expectations for students and by holding teachers accountable for helping students reach those expectations. She also talked back by "standing right in their faces" (p. 557), referring to White teachers who held low expectations in regard to the behavior and academic achievement of Black students. She maintained her role as teacher and taught one class each semester. While her decision to teach initially stemmed from her dissatisfaction with the teachers who were being sent to her school, she also taught as a way to reinterpret her role as principal and to be "part of the lives of our kids" (p. 550).

Natham practiced "othermothering" (Case, 1997; Irvine, 1999; Loder, 2005)[16]—consistently nurturing, protecting, and encouraging students and holding herself responsible for their success. Dillard labeled Natham's personal commitment to students as "authentic leadership": leadership grounded in nurturing and protecting children who were not her own. Her authentic leadership also involved establishing credibility with parents and gaining their support in efforts to enhance student achievement. Natham encountered several challenges to her caring style of leadership: racism, uncommitted faculty, lack of support for integration, resistance from veteran teachers, and lack of commitment to the academic success of all children. Despite these challenges, Natham remained committed to educating and caring for her students.

Natham was described as a role model for African American students: "She nurtures . . . and leads by her presence, by her example, by the way she conducts her life and work in putting herself on the line for them" (Dillard, 1995, p. 557). In contrast to Hinton (Lyman, 2000), who did not interpret his caring leadership style as being connected to race, Natham's caring leadership was directly tied to her same-race affiliation with her students and their families, her cultural heritage, and her status as an African American woman. Natham's caring leadership, her talking back, and her commitment to African American students represented overt acts of resistance often viewed as risky, "particularly for African American women working within powerful White male dominated sites such as the high school principalship" (Dillard, 1995, p. 548). Paraphrasing Derrick Bell (1992), Dillard wrote that Natham was an example of a caring African American female principal who served "to constantly remind the powers that be that there are persons like us who are not only on the side of [African Americans and other subjugated people] but are determined

[through resistance and reinterpretation] to stand in their way" (p. 550).

Returning to a central question of her research—Are traditional "scientific" conceptualizations of principal leadership relevant in a time of increased diversity in schools?—Dillard (1995) concluded that Natham's story suggests "it is impossible to create such conceptualizations of teaching or leading—or their 'effectiveness'— without taking issues of culture and community context into account" (p. 558). Natham's caring leadership established a school culture focused on the needs of students. It also provided African American students with a nurturing and caring environment that was similar to what Blacks experienced in all-Black schools before desegregation but that is often missing in urban schools today. Natham's story is illustrative of the effects of race, gender, and culture on principal leadership. She chose to lead in purposeful ways that reflected her own values as an African American and a woman and in ways that she believed would help African American students. This research also provides evidence of the ethno-humanist role identity assumed by African American principals. Natham took ownership of and held herself accountable for the academic and social achievement of her students. Her decision to teach a class, her direct work with parents, and her ritual of making notes on every report card reflected her personal form of cultural management: interpreting, representing, and authenticating the school culture and her relationships with students.

Debbie Pressley, a Black female middle-school principal, was the subject of research conducted by Reitzug and Patterson (1998). The researchers described the caring and empowering practice of Pressley primarily as she interacted with students. Data were collected through interviews, observations, and "shadowing" Pressley as she went about her daily work. Pressley's school was located in an economically depressed area of a large urban city and had a predominantly African American student population. Pressley was selected for the study because of her reputation as an outstanding leader. Her community nomination (Foster, 1997) came from several principals, and her reputation was verified by teachers as well as other educators. Reitzug and Patterson (1998) identified several key themes related to Pressley's leadership practice: her focus on interactions with students, the caring nature of her interactions with students, and the ways in which she empowered students through her interactions with them. Pressley described her role as principal as facilitating learning, empowering others, and developing the healthy child. Using a narrative approach, the researchers told Pressley's story over the course of 2 days, documenting the typical plans, activities, interruptions, and challenges of her workday as well as her interactions with students. Pressley practiced empowerment through caring interactions with students by: (a) establishing and developing a personal connection, (b) honoring their voice, (c) showing concern for the individual well-being of students by setting standards, (d) connecting students to their communities, and (e) helping students consider alternatives to actions and decisions that could jeopardize their social and academic future.

Reitzug and Patterson (1998) observed that Pressley's roles and responsibilities did not differ significantly from those described in the principalship literature. However, Pressley's style of leadership was distinctly different with respect to "*how* she chose to engage in this responsibility and the *amount of time* she chose to devote to it" (p. 178). The "how" of Pressley's caring leadership included *receiving* the perspectives of others through an open-door policy, *responding* to students by caring for them and comforting them, and *remaining* by keeping students with the same teacher for 3 years to build positive relationships. Her focus on the healthy child, academic excellence, and merging individual needs of students and community concerns shaped her caring and empowering style of leadership.

Bloom and Erlandson (2003) conducted in-depth interviews with three middle-aged African American female principals working in urban schools. Each principal "recounted the realities (successes, failures, and limitations) of her actual work, the reconstruction of deeply held leadership belief systems, and the personal resolutions evolving from her leadership experiences within schools" (p. 340). Like Dillard (1995), the researchers sought to listen to the voices of Black female principals as a way to begin to "change minds and social constructs about the 'Others' in America's public school districts" (Bloom & Erlandson, 2003, p. 352). Educated in the segregated schooling of the Midwest and Deep South, the principals drew

on their "cultural consciousness" (Bloom & Erlandson, 2003, p. 359) to guide their leadership decisions. Each woman revealed her experiences with racism, sexism, stereotypes, and assigned identities and her decision to succeed in spite of the barriers she encountered. Each worked in a school where she was challenged with implementing and maintaining policies and programs that were inequitable and impeded student achievement. Despite such challenges, these principals exhibited a personal commitment, based on their cultural affiliation, to educating African American children from low-income backgrounds, many of whom had been subjected to low teacher expectations. Seeking to build schools with a culture of caring, they implemented alternative forms of decision making that not only would benefit students but would also offer alternative definitions of organizational effectiveness in schools.

Claire, one of the principals in the study, was charged with turning around a failing school. In interviews, she discussed the "hopelessness and helplessness" at the school, the poor graduation rates (only 2% to 5%), and other internal and external factors that placed the school in the "failing" category. At the end of Claire's second year as principal, student attendance and test scores had improved, and Claire had increased parental involvement by instituting family partnership nights and had improved relationships with teachers by forming teaching teams. The second principal in the study believed in the power of staff development and devoted a considerable amount of time to planning activities that would "raise the level of consciousness about racist teaching practices" (Bloom & Erlandson, 2003, p. 353). The third principal modeled servant leadership as a way to show teachers how to serve every student. Collectively, the stories of these principals speak of a desire to make a difference in the lives of African American children. Bloom and Erlandson noted that the women's stories reject theories of inferior capabilities based on race or gender. They also acknowledged, however, that the stories do not suggest that "only African American principals know how to effectively operate urban schools" (p. 351). Rather, these stories are illustrative of leadership that is counter to what is generally described in the literature.

According to Loder (2005), "Recent work on African American women principals suggests that motherhood and its associated values of nurturing, caretaking, and helping develop children are salient to how they understand and interpret their roles" (p. 304). This was particularly the case with the principals included in the research conducted by Dillard and by Reitzug and Patterson. Gloria Natham and Debbie Pressley purposely included "othermothering" (interpersonal caring) in their leadership. Both wanted to relate to their students and treated students like their own children or members of their family. They viewed othermothering as consistent with the leadership roles of Black female principals, and their othermothering/interpersonal caring was linked to their identity: Black and female.

The Black female principals in these studies promoted student achievement in both direct and indirect ways. Gloria Natham was the exception among the cases. By choosing to teach a class each semester, she held herself personally accountable for the academic achievement of students in her school. While Dillard did not indicate whether her direct involvement helped raise test scores, Natham chose to model how principal leadership can lead to improved student achievement. Natham is also an exception because in large urban high schools, principals rarely have time to directly participate in teaching, instructional supervision, or curriculum coordination (Mertz & McNeely, 1998). Rather, they typically fulfill bureaucrat/administrator roles focusing on more indirect goals of schooling. Natham's decisions reflected her conscious effort to merge her ethno-humanist and bureaucratic/administrator roles. The cultural perspectives of Black female principals were also a consistent theme in the studies reviewed here. These principals relied on their cultural heritage and their knowledge of the cultural norms of the Black community to motivate students and parents. In addition, their cultural perspectives also included knowing the most appropriate forms of communication, having the ability to talk to students in ways that drew on same-race affiliation, and being part of students' lives. These principals also acknowledged that in the post-*Brown* era, it was their responsibility to address some of the cultural norms that negatively affected students' opportunities for success.

DISCUSSION

The 1954 *Brown v. Board of Education* decision provides a context for the examination of the leadership of Black principals in the periods both before and after the decision. Ideally, the decision would have remedied inequitable educational structures and provided a racially and socially just context for educating Black children. Black principals would have continued to make significant contributions to Black children, their communities, and leadership theory and practice. However, these ideals were not always a reality. The research reviewed here indicates that Black principals often led under extremely adverse circumstances. These Black principal-leaders worked in both segregated and integrated contexts, and in many instances their leadership was defined by oppressed community and educational settings. Yet they were resilient, resourceful, and dedicated, and they remained diligent in their commitment to the education of Black children. They were more than managers—they were also visionaries who adopted a philosophy of agency and prevailed in spite of strong opposition to their efforts.

Evidence suggests that many of these principals embodied the characteristics of Lomotey's (1993) ethno-humanist role identity: commitment to Black students, compassion for these students and their families, and confidence in the intellectual ability of these students. This was particularly evident in the stories of Black principal-leaders in the post-*Brown* era, who were typically assigned to the worst schools in the worst neighborhoods with the lowest-performing students. For example, principals such as Gloria Natham were hired to clean up messes and relate to Black students. Post-*Brown* African American principals also led in the changed contexts of schooling, particularly in urban areas. Urban schools had more racially, ethnically, and economically diverse student bodies, and they underwent complex changes in technological needs, increases in the number and kinds of social support services needed, and decreases in funding (Loder, 2005). Crosby (1999), an African American male principal at a large urban high school, lamented the decline of the urban school context:

> For those of us who work in schools, it is . . . the best of times and the worst of times. Our urban

schools, once the pride of our nation, are now a source of controversy and inequity. We have watched with dismay their descent into confusion and failure. (p. 298)

Clearly, 50 years after *Brown*, Black principal-leaders face different challenges in their efforts to educate Black students.

Collectively, the research reviewed here yielded four consistent themes: (a) resistance to ideologies and individuals opposed to the education of Black students, (b) the academic and social development of Black students as a priority, (c) the importance of the cultural perspectives of Black principals, and (d) leadership based on interpersonal caring. The academic and social development of Black students was a priority for the Black principal-leaders described in this review. They were committed to the academic achievement of Black students, and they fought vigorously for chairs, desks, books, money, well-equipped buildings, and qualified teachers as a way to give Black students every opportunity to experience success. They also believed that schools should be transformational institutions that provide students with various forms of support and that Black students should be given opportunities for their total development. Black students were not "other people's children" (Delpit, 1995); they belonged to their parents and to the school and the community as well. Principals accepted responsibility and held themselves accountable for the well-being of every Black student. Students were nurtured and encouraged in a manner often absent in many urban schools today. Many urban schools, which today have primarily Black populations, often do not provide an atmosphere that is conducive to an ethno-humanist role identity.

Black principal-leaders engaged in both passive and overt acts of resistance in their struggles to educate Black children. They fought against theories of inferiority, funding structures that disadvantaged Black students, an emphasis on vocational over academic preparation, and the displacement of massive numbers of Black teachers and principals. They risked their professional careers and their economic livelihood and stood in the way of opposition to equitable systems of education. Lacking any real power to implement policy, they worked with Black parents who went before White school boards to secure needed resources for schools. In the face of these challenges, they continued to educate Black children, doing more with less.

The importance of the cultural perspectives of Black principal leaders is directly related to the absence of *race* in the discourse on school leadership. Mertz and McNeely (1998) argued that "school administration has been male dominated and male defined (largely White male); that is, explained, conceptualized and seen through the eyes of males" (p. 196). The authors' emphasis on the continuing focus on White males indicates that there is a privileging of one voice over another and a single lens and single authority representing the whole of educational leadership (see also Fenwick, 2001). This privileging of voice also suggests that even while Black principals possess an insider's perspective, their voices have not been considered in debates about the most effective ways to educate Black children. Culture was a constant within this theme. The work of Lomotey (1989a, 1993), Siddle Walker (1993a, 1993b), Dillard (1995), and Bloom and Erlandson (2003) strongly suggests the presence of a distinctly Black perspective in school leadership, a perspective based largely on culture. In the segregated schooling of the South and in many predominantly Black urban schools today, Black principals practice leadership based on their insider status and their membership in the distinct Black culture. Same-race/cultural affiliation appears to influence decision making at the school site, as well as the selection of teachers and interactions with parents.

Because the achievement gap between Black students and their White peers continues to be an important topic in education,[17] it is also important that the perspectives of Black principal-leaders be recognized and included in efforts to close this gap. Siddle Walker's research highlighting the successes of Black principal-leaders provides a critical context for such debates, particularly with respect to their impact on Black student achievement. Morris (2004) concurred with Siddle Walker, asking "In what ways might the kind of agency that was evident among Black educators and institutions in the segregation era become manifest in predominantly African American schools in the post-Civil Rights era?" (p. 72).

Several of the Black principal-leaders in the studies reviewed incorporated interpersonal caring into their leadership. Leadership based on interpersonal caring includes the principal's direct and purposeful attention to meeting the psychological, sociological, and academic needs of students. The purposeful adoption of a leadership style that is intended to address the needs of Black students is contrary to myths about Black educators as uncaring and as unable or unwilling to relate to Black students, particularly those from low socioeconomic backgrounds (Foster, 1997). Interpersonal caring may be a necessary component of leadership in schools with predominantly Black student populations, given that many of these students have been subjected to external factors (poverty, racism, violence) and internal factors (underfunded schools, disproportionate placement in special education, low teacher expectations, below-grade-level achievement) that can contribute to low self-esteem and underachievement. As noted by Lomotey, it is important to encourage students not only to excel academically but to take pride in themselves and their culture. Findings from studies discussed in this review suggest that interpersonal caring in educational leadership is effective in creating school cultures that consider the needs of teachers, students, and parents and are conducive to promoting students' success.

The findings from the studies reviewed suggest that Black-principal leaders rewrote history, redefined theory and practice, and rejected deficit theories about school leadership and the education of Black children. In the spirit in which *Brown* was intended, Black principal-leaders were *transformers*, *translators*, and *cultivators*. These individuals transformed education for Black children from a dream hoped for to a dream realized. They saw the possibilities for enhancing the life chances of Black students and transformed their schools into institutions that promoted Black student achievement, recognized Black culture, and promoted racial pride and self-esteem. They accepted their roles as leaders and held themselves accountable for the uplifting of a race through education, leading schools that were cultural symbols of the development of the whole child. As Black principal-leaders, they transformed the impossible into the possible for many Black children and translated the Black agenda for education to students,

parents, teachers, and the White power structure. Through their models of servant leadership, they used the power of education to change lives. Additionally, they offered teachers and other staff members a vision, provided them with goals and objectives, and showed them the importance of continued professional development. Black principal-leaders cultivated the skills and talents of Black students and teachers. They cultivated the highest ideals of academic achievement and sought to lead "good schools."

The themes articulated in this review are not identified as such in the traditional literature on school leadership, specifically the principalship literature. Contemporary school administration/leadership frameworks typically focus on the various administrative/leadership styles (Bolman & Deal, 1997; Leithwood & Duke, 1999), administrative/leadership functions (Farkas, Johnson, & Duffett, 2003; Leithwood & Riehl, 2003), alternative perspectives on school leadership such as leadership for social justice (Dantley & Tillman, 2005; Marshall, 2004), and diversity in educational administration/leadership (González, 2002; Tillman, 2003).[18] Principals are viewed as instructional leaders who coordinate the curriculum; monitor student progress by assessing and using test data; facilitate teacher competence by providing staff development, resources, and other forms of support; and establish a climate conducive to student success.

Hallinger and Heck (1996), in their review of studies on the principal's role in school effectiveness, found that personal characteristics such as gender, previous teaching experience, and values and beliefs "influence how principals enact their role" (p. 21). There is no evidence to suggest that the race or the cultural perspectives of the principal were factors in these studies. Leithwood and Duke (1999) articulated six models of leadership: instructional, transformational, moral, participative, managerial/strategic, and contingency. Culture as a factor in principal leadership was discussed in only one of the models: transformational leadership. With respect to culture, the authors cited Reitzug and Reeves (1992), who noted that cultural leadership includes "defining, strengthening, and articulating values" but cautioned that "leaders may manipulate culture to further their own ends" (p. 50). Deal and Peterson (2000) discussed culture in educational leadership in the context of the school setting: "Culture arises in response to persisting conditions, novel changes, challenging losses, and enduring ambiguous or paradoxical puzzles" (p. 202). These conceptualizations of culture suggest a different emphasis than those articulated by Lomotey (1989a, 1993), Dillard (1995), Siddle Walker (1993a, 1996), and others.

The descriptions in the contemporary literature do not differ significantly from the descriptions of African American principals who assumed both bureaucrat/administrator and ethno-humanist role identities. As Reitzug and Patterson (1998) found in their study of a Black female principal, differences in leadership philosophy, style, and effectiveness were directly related to "how" the principal practiced leadership and the amount of "time" she invested in her work. The research reviewed here also points to the "why" of principal leadership as an important factor. That is, African American principals, to a great degree, led on the basis of their same-race/cultural affiliation and their desire to positively affect the lives of Black students. In most cases, their "why" was closely linked to their identities: Black and male, and Black and female.

Witziers et al. (2003) noted that the literature on school leadership suggests that principals who are effective instructional leaders positively affect the school climate and student achievement (see also, e.g., Bredeson, 1996; Brookover, Beady, Flood, Schweitzer, & Wisenbaker, 1979; Leithwood & Montgomery, 1982). However, other scholars have questioned the effects of educational leadership on student achievement (e.g., Hallinger & Heck, 1996; Murphy, 1988). Among the reasons given for these opposing viewpoints were the absence of an extensive body of research on the relationship between school leadership and student achievement, the difficulty in measuring the direct effects of such relationships, and the varying ways in which educational leadership is conceptualized and operationalized (Bloom & Erlandson, 2003; Pounder, Ogawa, & Adams, 1995; Witziers et al., 2003).

The research reviewed here suggests that there is a strong relationship between African American principal leadership and African American student achievement. In the pre-*Brown* era of segregated schooling, this relationship was often more subtle; that is, because schools were not driven by state testing mandates and because Black principals worked in a closed system, student achievement was promoted through encouraging students to excel, encouraging them to pursue postsecondary education, and motivating them to become productive citizens. In the immediate post-*Brown* era of schooling, Black principal-leaders (even after they had lost their positions) continued to encourage students to excel in the face of resistance to integration. Later, these principal-leaders established environments, policies, and procedures that would lead to academic success. They hired competent teachers, coordinated curricula, instituted innovative support programs, and began to use test data to assess student achievement.

While the literature provides evidence of a positive relationship between Black principal leadership and Black student achievement, the literature is less clear on the relationship between White principals and African American student achievement (as well as the achievement of other minority and low-income students). Because it is often the case that the race of principals is not revealed in research studies (e.g., Kimball & Sirotnik, 2000; Portin, 2000), there is little conclusive evidence regarding the ways in which this factor affects student achievement. Thus, it may be difficult to determine in what direct and indirect ways cross-race principal-student relationships are a factor in improved student achievement. Several studies have examined the role of White principals in the academic achievement of African American students. Tillman (2005a) found that the White male high school principal in her study attempted to affect student achievement in indirect rather than direct ways. For example, he felt that his personal connection to the Black students in his school allowed him to use informal conversations with students and their parents as one way to encourage students to excel. He did not use more direct approaches such as empowering teachers to implement practices that would lead to student achievement, nor did he use standardized test data to make decisions about improving test scores.

Mertz and McNeely (1998) studied a White female principal of a high school with a student population that was mixed along racial, ethnic, and class lines. The principal wanted her school to be "an academic giant"

(p. 207) and expressed her commitment to "academic excellence, curriculum improvement, and student learning" (p. 212). However, the researchers found that she spent more of her time on managerial tasks than on instructional tasks. While she visited classrooms to evaluate teachers or to check on students, the majority of her time was spent on discipline matters, patrolling the halls, and responding to requests from parents and the central office. As with the principal in Tillman's study, her work was consistent with the literature describing the high school principalship; that is, instructional leadership and curriculum are not among the top five tasks that dominate the work of high school principals. Thus, while this principal professed her commitment to academics, she was constrained by the culture of the traditional high school setting.

Riester, Pursch, and Skrla (2002) examined the roles of six principals in highly successful elementary schools that primarily served minority and low-income students. Each of the schools had achieved "recognized" or "exemplary" status in the state accountability system. Three of the principals were White, and one, a White woman, was placed at her school to raise low test scores. Collectively, these principals shared a common belief system that included (a) promoting a democratic culture, (b) adopting a prescriptive approach to literacy and academic success, and (c) demonstrating a stubborn persistence in "getting there" (p. 292). They believed that it was teachers who did the real work in schools and that principals must empower them to "enact specific practices that lead to learning for all" (p. 283). As noted by a White male principal, "If the children can't learn the way we teach, then we need to learn how to teach to how the children learn" (p. 293). White principals believed that students should not be blamed for poor achievement; rather, after assessing student test scores, teachers used specific prescriptive approaches to developing literacy skills. According to the authors, all of the principals used tools such as benchmarks and assessment of prior performance to guide placement of students. In addition, all held themselves accountable to every student, a characteristic the authors suggested is typically absent in schools. The principals' beliefs that all students could and would be academically successful and a culture of persistence in each

school were instrumental in facilitating academic achievement. A key in the students' academic achievement appeared to be the principal's willingness to allow teachers to make decisions about the most effective curriculum and instructional techniques that would lead to student success. Riester et al.'s findings suggest that White, African American, and Hispanic principals shared similar leadership philosophies and practices with respect to enhancing the academic achievement of minority and low-income students.

RECOMMENDATIONS FOR FUTURE RESEARCH

The majority of the research reviewed here employed the use of qualitative methods. This suggests that qualitative methods represent an effective approach to conducting research about Black principals. These methods allowed researchers to conduct in-depth interviews, observations, and document analyses that yielded thick, rich descriptions of Black principal-leaders. As Tillman (2002) has argued, when research is approached from a cultural perspective, "the individual and collective knowledge of African Americans is placed at the center of the inquiry" (p. 3). However, there is also a need for more research about Blacks in the principalship in which quantitative methods are employed. Survey research based on national samples can yield results that are generalizable to the broader population of Black principals. Such studies are important given that recent large-scale surveys on the principalship have grouped Black principals in the category of women and minorities (e.g., Farkas et al., 2003; Gates, Ringel, Santibañez, Ross, & Chung, 2003) and have failed to illuminate the specific circumstances that affect the leadership of these principals.

Several questions warrant further research. First, what factors affect the leadership of Black principals in urban school contexts in the post-*Brown* era of schooling? Most Black principals are employed in urban school districts; however, the research on urban schools is diffused, and there are a limited number of specific themes evident in the research that has been conducted on Black principals in these schools. The research described here suggests that post-*Brown* Black principals typically lead schools that are underfunded, have shortages of qualified teachers, and have low standardized test scores. There is a need for research that investigates how these factors, as well as others, affect the leadership capacity of Black principals.

Second, what specific leadership styles are exhibited by Black principals? The research reviewed here suggests that culture is an important factor in the leadership styles of African American principals, and some principals adopted both bureaucrat/administrator and ethno-humanist role identities. While findings from the studies that were reviewed indicate that Black principals may employ more than one leadership style, little is known about the specific styles (as articulated in the traditional educational leadership literature) adopted (i.e., transformational, contingency, managerial, participative).

Third, what is the relationship between African American school leadership and African American student achievement? Findings from the studies reviewed here suggest that this relationship is positive. However, there is only limited evidence suggesting the specific ways in which same-race/cultural affiliation is directly linked to African American student achievement, particularly with respect to achievement gaps. While much has been written about the achievement gap between African American students and their White counterparts, there is a shortage of research on the specific ways in which African American leaders directly contribute to African American student achievement.

What are the links between White school leadership and African American student achievement, particularly in urban schools? Fifty years after *Brown*, urban schools are now resegregated. Yet the majority of principals in urban schools with predominantly African American and other minority student populations are White (U.S. Equal Employment Opportunity Commission, 2005). These principals are responsible for facilitating the academic achievement of large numbers of African American students. More research is needed to determine the direct ways in which White principals promote student achievement through their leadership practices.

Research on these as well as other questions regarding the leadership of African American principals in pre-K-12 education would enhance our knowledge of important issues in the field of educational leadership. Moreover, such research is needed to continue the hope, promises, and legacy of *Brown*.

NOTES

1. See, for example, Anderson (2004), Tillman (2004a), Foster (2004), a special issue of the *Journal of Negro Education* on *Brown* at 50 edited by Frank Brown (2004), Ogletree (2004), Orfield and Lee (2004), and a special issue of the *History of Education Quarterly* edited by Michael Fultz (2004b).

2. The terms *Black* and *African American* are used interchangeably in this chapter.

3. The terms *educational leadership* and *educational administration* are used interchangeably here. While it is not within the scope of this chapter to enter into a complete discussion of the similarities and differences between the two terms, much of the focus in the field is on school leadership versus school administration. For a more extensive discussion of the evolution of and increased use of the term *leadership*, see Leithwood and Duke (1999).

4. Leithwood and Duke (1999) reviewed feature-length articles about various types of educational leadership in "four representative English-language educational administration journals" (p. 46). The review included articles published as early as 1988, the year the first edition of the *Handbook of Research on Educational Administration* (Boyan, 1988) was published. According to Leithwood and Duke, two of the journals, *Educational Administration Quarterly* and the *Journal of School Leadership*, publish empirical and theoretical work primarily from North America. The *Journal of Educational Administration* and *Educational Management and Administration* publish work from countries such as Australia, New Zealand, and the United Kingdom as well as from North America. Another journal, not reviewed in Leithwood and Duke's work, is the *International Journal of Leadership in Education*, which also publishes research on educational leadership/administration from other countries as well as North America.

5. There is an emerging body of research on the urban school principalship (see, e.g., Carter & Fenwick, 2001; Cistone & Stevenson, 2000; Gooden, 2005; Mukuria, 2002). In addition, articles published in educational journals such as the *Journal of Negro Education, Urban Review, Urban Education*, and *Education and Urban Society* typically focus on urban schooling. However, no specific lines of research on Blacks in the principalship are evident in the general category of urban school leadership.

6. A recent publication, the *Sage Encyclopedia of Educational Leadership and Administration* (English,

2006), includes a greater diversity of perspectives in the field of educational leadership/administration. This work is intended to be a reference for graduate students, practitioners, and scholars in the field.

7. *Servant leadership* is a term that has been used to describe the leadership of Blacks in leadership positions such as ministers, civil rights activists, and educators. Greenleaf (1977) defined a servant leader as one who is "committed to serving others through a cause, a crusade, a movement, a campaign with humanitarian[,] not materialistic, goals" (p. 13). For more extensive discussions of the concept of African Americans and servant leadership, see Alston and Jones (2002) and Williams (1998).

8. Most of the research conducted on the displacement of Black educators after *Brown* has focused on the massive firing of Black teachers (see, e.g., Ethridge, 1979; Foster, 1997; Fultz, 2004a; Hooker, 1971; Hudson & Holmes, 1994; Lewis, Garrison-Wade, Scott, Douglas, & Middleton, 2004; Milner & Howard, 2004; Orfield, 1969; Tillman, 2004b).

9. For a more extensive discussion about the ways in which Black principals lost their jobs, see Franklin and Collier (1999).

10. For other work on the education of Blacks that also examines the role of the principal, see Jones (1981), Morris (1999, 2004), Savage (2001), and Ward Randolph (1997).

11. Sowell conducted his research at five public schools (Booker T. Washington High School in Atlanta, Georgia; Frederick Douglass High School in Baltimore, Maryland; McDonough 35 High School in New Orleans, Louisiana; P.S. 91 in Brooklyn, New York; and Dunbar High School in Washington, D.C.) and three private Catholic schools (St. Paul of the Cross in Atlanta and St. Augustine and Xavier Prep in New Orleans).

12. Lightfoot conducted her study in two urban high schools (George Washington Carver High School in Atlanta and John F. Kennedy High School in New York City), two suburban high schools (Highland Park High School in Highland Park, Illinois, and Brookline High School in Brookline, Massachusetts), and two elite, private high schools (St. Paul's School in Concord, New Hampshire, and Milton Academy in Boston).

13. Although the participants in this study were female African Americans, their gender was not the focus of the study. Thus, the study is not included in the section that focuses on research about African American female principals.

14. For more extensive discussions on this point, see Dempsey and Noblit (1996) and Edwards (1996).

15. The topic of women in school leadership has also been discussed by Jones (2003), Ortiz and Marshall (1988), and Shakeshaft (1988, 1989, 1999).

16. Loder drew on Collins's (1991) definition of *othermothers* as women "who work on behalf of the Black community by expressing ethics of caring and personal accountability, which embrace conceptions of transformative power and mutuality" (p. 132).

17. See, for example, Anderson (2003), Barton (2004), Caldas and Bankston (1998), Hale (2004), Klein (2002), Kozol (1991), Lomotey (1987, 1989b), Ogbu (2003), Perry (2003), Perry, Steele, and Hilliard (2003), Resnick (2004), and Sizemore (2003).

18. Lomotey, Allen, Canada, Mark, and Rivers (2003) conducted a comprehensive review of the theoretical and empirical literature on African American school leaders. The review covered the years 1972 through 2002 and included dissertations, journal articles, conference papers, books, and bulletins. The authors identified six categories that included work on assistant principals, principals, and superintendents: (a) African American female educational leaders, (b) mobility opportunities for African American educational leaders, (c) roles and role expectations of African American leaders, (d) job satisfaction of African American educational leaders, (e) factors affecting the performance of African American leaders, and (f) management styles of African American leaders.

References

Abney, E. E. (1980). A comparison of the status of Florida's Black public school principals, 1964–65/1975–76. *Journal of Negro Education, 69,* 398–406.

Adkison, J. A. (1981). Women in school administration: A review of the research. *Review of Educational Research, 51,* 311–343.

Allen, K., Jacobson, S., & Lomotey, K. (1995). African American women in educational administration: The importance of mentors and sponsors. *Journal of Negro Education, 64,* 409–420.

Alston, J. A., & Jones, S. N. (2002). Carrying the torch of the Jeanes Supervisors: 21st century African American female superintendents and servant leadership. In B. Cooper & L. Fusarelli (Eds.), *The promises and perils facing today's school superintendent* (pp. 65–75). Lanham, MD: Scarecrow Press.

Anderson, J. D. (1988). *The education of Blacks in the South, 1860–1935.* Chapel Hill: University of North Carolina Press.

Anderson, J. D. (2003). *The historical context for understanding the test score gap.* Unpublished manuscript.

Anderson, J. D. (2004). Crosses to bear and promises to keep: The jubilee anniversary of *Brown v. Board of Education. Urban Education, 39,* 359–373.

Banks, C. M. (1995). Gender and race as factors in educational leadership and administration. In J. A. Banks & C. M. Banks (Eds.), *Handbook of research on multicultural education* (pp. 65–80). New York: Macmillan.

Barton, P. E. (2004). Why does the gap persist? *Educational Leadership, 62*(3), 8–14.

Beck, L. G. (1994a). Cultivating a caring school community: One principal's story. In J. Murphy & K. S. Louis (Eds.), *Reshaping the principalship* (pp. 177–202). Thousand Oaks, CA: Corwin Press.

Beck, L. G. (1994b). *Reclaiming educational administration as a caring profession.* New York: Teachers College Press.

Bell, D. (1992). *Faces at the bottom of the well: The permanence of racism.* New York: Basic Books.

Benham, M. K. P. (1997). Silences and serenades: The journeys of three ethnic minority women school leaders. *Anthropology and Education Quarterly, 28,* 280–307.

Biklen, S. N., & Brannigan, M. B. (1980). *Women and educational leadership.* Lexington, MA: Lexington Books.

Bloom, C. M., & Erlandson, D. A. (2003). African American women principals in urban schools: Realities, (re)constructions, and resolutions. *Educational Administration Quarterly, 39,* 339–369.

Bolman, L. G., & Deal, T. E. (1997). *Reframing organizations: Artistry, choice, and leadership* (2nd ed.). San Francisco: Jossey-Bass.

Boyan, N. (Ed.). (1988). *Handbook of research on educational administration: A project of the American Educational Research Association.* New York: Longman.

Bredeson, P. V. (1996). New directions in the preparation of educational leaders. In K. Leithwood, J. Chapman, D. Corson, P. Hallinger, & A. Hart (Eds.), *International handbook of educational leadership and administration* (pp. 251–277). Dordrecht, The Netherlands: Kluwer Academic.

Brookover, W. B., Beady, C., Flood, P., Schweitzer, J., & Wisenbaker, J. (1979). *School social systems and student achievement: Schools can make a difference.* New York: Praeger.

Brown, F. (Ed.). (2004). *Brown v. Board of Education at 50* [Special issue]. *Journal of Negro Education, 73*(3), 172–378.

Brown, H. V. (1960). *The education of Blacks in the South.* Chapel Hill: University of North Carolina Press.

Brown v. Board of Education, 347 U.S. 483 (1954).

Bullock, H. (1967). *A history of Negro education in the South from 1619 to the present.* Cambridge, MA: Harvard University Press.

Butchart, R. E. (1988). "Outthinking and outflanking the owners of the world": A historiography of the African American struggle for education. *History of Education Quarterly, 28,* 333–366.

Caldas, S. J., & Bankston, C., III. (1998). The inequality of separation: Racial composition of schools and academic achievement. *Educational Administration Quarterly, 34,* 533–557.

Carter, M., & Fenwick, L. (2001). Keeping a close watch: A cultural philosophy of school change. *National Association of Secondary School Principals Bulletin, 85,* 15–21.

Case, K. I. (1997). African American othermothering in the urban elementary school. *Urban Review, 29,* 25–39.

Cecelski, D. S. (1994). *Along freedom road: Hyde County, North Carolina, and the fate of Black schools in the South.* Chapel Hill: University of North Carolina Press.

Cistone, P. J., & Stevenson, J. M. (Eds.). (2000). Perspectives on the urban principalship [Special issue]. *Education and Urban Society, 32*(4).

Clark, K. B. (1963). *Prejudice and your child.* Boston: Beacon Press.

Coffin, G. C. (1972). The Black school administrator and how he's being pushed to extinction. *American School Board Journal, 159,* 33–36.

Collins, P. H. (1991). *Black feminist thought: Knowledge, consciousness, and the politics of empowerment.* New York: Routledge.

Cooper, A. J. (1988). *A voice from the South.* New York: Oxford University Press. (Original work published 1892)

Coursen, D., Mazzarella, J., Jeffress, L., & Hadderman, M. (1989). Two special cases: Women and Blacks. In S. C. Smith & P. K. Piele (Eds.), *School leadership: Handbook for excellence* (pp. 85–106). Eugene, OR: ERIC Clearinghouse on Educational Management.

Crosby, E. A. (1999). Urban schools: Forced to fail. *Phi Delta Kappan, 81,* 298–303.

Crow, G. M., & Glascock, C. (1995). Transformational leadership: Attractions of women and minority recruits to the principalship. *Journal of School Leadership, 5,* 356–378.

Dantley, M. E. (1990). The ineffectiveness of effective schools leadership: An analysis of the effective schools movement from a critical perspective. *Journal of Negro Education, 59,* 585–598.

Dantley, M. E., & Tillman, L. C. (2005). Social justice and moral/transformative leadership. In C. Marshall & M. Oliva (Eds.), *Leadership for social justice: Making revolutions in education* (pp. 16–30). Boston: Allyn & Bacon.

Deal, T. E., & Peterson, K. D. (2000). Eight roles of symbolic leaders. In *Jossey-Bass reader on educational leadership* (pp. 202–214). San Francisco: Jossey-Bass.

Delpit, L. (1995). *Other people's children: Cultural conflict in the classroom.* New York: New Press.

Dempsey, V., & Noblit, G. (1996). Cultural ignorance and school desegregation: A community narrative. In M. Shujaa (Ed.), *Beyond desegregation: The politics of quality in African American schooling* (pp. 115–137). Thousand Oaks, CA: Corwin Press.

Dillard, C. (1995). Leading with her life: An African American feminist (re)interpretation of leadership for an urban high school principal. *Educational Administration Quarterly, 31,* 539–563.

Doughty, R. (1980). The Black female administrator: Woman in a double bind. In S. K. Biklen & M. B. Brannigan (Eds.), *Women and educational leadership* (pp. 165–174). Lexington, MA: Lexington Books.

Edmonds, R. (1979). Effective schools for the urban poor. *Educational Leadership, 37,* 15–24.

Edson, S. K. (1987). Voices from the present: Tracking the female administrative aspirant. *Journal of Educational Equity and Leadership, 7,* 261–277.

Edwards, P. (1996). Before and after school desegregation: African American parents' involvement in schools. In M. Shujaa (Ed.), *Beyond desegregation: The politics of quality in African American schooling* (pp. 138–161). Thousand Oaks, CA: Corwin Press.

English, F. (Ed.). (2006). *Sage encyclopedia of educational leadership and administration.* Thousand Oaks, CA: Sage.

Enomoto, E., Gardiner, M., & Grogan, M. (2000). Notes to Athene: Mentoring relationships for women of color. *Urban Education, 35,* 567–583.

Ethridge, S. (1979). Impact of the 1954 *Brown vs. Topeka Board of Education* decision on Black educators. *Negro Educational Review, 30,* 217–232.

Farkas, S., Johnson, J., & Duffett, A. (2003). *Rolling up their sleeves: Superintendents and principals talk about what's needed to fix public schools.* New York: Wallace Foundation.

Fenwick, L. (2001). *Patterns of excellence: Policy perspectives on diversity in teaching and school leadership.* Atlanta, GA: Southern Education Foundation.

Foster, L. (2004). Administrator and teacher recruitment and selection post-*Brown:* Issues, challenges, and strategies. *Journal of School Public Relations, 25,* 220–232.

Foster, M. (1997). *Black teachers on teaching.* New York: New Press.

Franklin, V. P. (1984). *Black self-determination: A cultural history of the faith of our fathers.* Westport, CT: Lawrence Hill.

Franklin, V. P. (1990). "They rose and fell together": African American educators and community leadership, 1795–1954. *Journal of Education, 172(3),* 39–64.

Franklin, V. P., & Collier, B. T. (1999). *My soul is a witness: A chronology of the Civil Rights era, 1954–1965.* New York: Henry Holt.

Fultz, M. (2004a). The displacement of Black educators post-*Brown:* An overview and analysis. *History of Education Quarterly, 44,* 11–45.

Fultz, M. (Ed.). (2004b). Fiftieth anniversary of the *Brown v. Board of Education* decision [Special issue]. *History of Education Quarterly, 44(1),* 10.

Gardiner, M. E., Enomoto, E., & Grogan, M. (2000). *Coloring outside lines: Mentoring women in school leadership.* Albany: State University of New York Press.

Gates, S. M., Ringel, J. S., Santibañez, L., Ross, K. E., & Chung, C. H. (2003). *Who is leading our schools? An overview of school administrators and their careers.* Arlington, VA: RAND Education.

Georgia Teacher and Education Association. (1970). *Guide to developing an inclusive integration plan.* Atlanta, GA: Author.

Gilligan, C. (1982). *In a different voice: Psychological theory and women's development.* Cambridge, MA: Harvard University Press.

González, M. L. (2002). Professors of educational administration: Learning and leading for the success of ALL children. *University Council for Educational Administration Review, 64,* 4–9.

Gooden, M. A. (2005). The role of an African American principal in an urban information technology high school. *Educational Administration Quarterly, 41(4),* 630–650.

Greenleaf, R. K. (1977). *Servant leadership: A journey into the nature of legitimate power and greatness.* New York: Paulist Press.

Hale, J. (2004). How schools shortchange African American children. *Educational Leadership, 62(3),* 34–39.

Hallinger, P., & Heck, R. H. (1996). Reassessing the principal's role in school effectiveness: A review of empirical research, 1980–1995. *Educational Administration Quarterly, 32,* 5–44.

Hart, A. W., & Bredeson, P. V. (1996). *The principalship.* New York: McGraw-Hill.

Henig, J. R., Hula, R. C., Orr, M., & Pedescleaux, D. S. (1999). *The color of school reform: Race, politics, and the challenge of urban education.* Princeton, NJ: Princeton University Press.

Hine, D. C., & Thompson, K. (1998). *A shining thread of hope: The history of Black women in America.* New York: Broadway Books.

Hobson-Horton, L. D. (2000). *African American women principals: Examples of urban educational leadership.* Unpublished doctoral dissertation, University of Wisconsin.

Hooker, R. (1971). Displacement of Black teachers in the eleven southern states. *Afro-American Studies, 2,* 165–180.

Hudson, M. J., & Holmes, B. J. (1994). Missing teachers, impaired communities: The unanticipated consequences of *Brown v. Board of Education* on the African American teaching force at the precollegiate level. *Journal of Negro Education, 63,* 388–393.

Irvine, J. J. (1999). The education of children whose nightmares come both day and night. *Journal of Negro Education, 68,* 224–253.

James, J. C. (1970). Another vanishing American: The Black principal. *New Republic, September,* 17–20.

Jones, E., & Montenegro, X. (1985). *Women and minorities in school administration.* Washington, DC: Office of Minority Affairs, American Association of School Administrators.

Jones, F. (1981). *A traditional model of educational excellence.* Washington, DC: Howard University Press.

Jones, S. N. (2003). *The praxis of Black female educational leadership from a systems perspective.* Unpublished doctoral dissertation, Bowling Green State University.

Karpinski, C. (2004, April). *Faculty diversity: Brown and the demise of the Black principal.* Paper presented at the annual meeting of the American Educational Research Association, San Diego, CA.

Kimball, K., & Sirotnik, K. (2000). The urban school principalship: Take this job and . . . ! *Education and Urban Society, 32,* 536–543.

Klein, D. W. (2002). Beyond *Brown v. Board of Education:* The need to remedy the achievement gap. *Journal of Law and Education, 31,* 431–457.

Kluger, R. (1977). *Simple justice.* New York: Random House.

Kozol, J. (1991). *Savage inequalities: Children in America's schools.* New York: HarperCollins.

Leithwood, K., & Duke, L. (1999). A century's quest to understand school leadership. In J. Murphy & K. Seashore Louis (Eds.), *The handbook of research on educational administration* (2nd ed., pp. 45–72). San Francisco: Jossey-Bass.

Leithwood, K., & Montgomery, D. (1982). Forms and effects of school-based management: A review. *Educational Policy, 12,* 325–346.

Leithwood, K. A., & Riehl, C. (2003). *What we know about successful school leadership.* Philadelphia: Laboratory for Student Success, Temple University.

Lewis, C., Garrison-Wade, D., Scott, M., Douglas, B., & Middleton, V. (2004). A synthesis of evidence-based research on the status of African American teachers 50 years after *Brown* and its impact on African American student achievement: Implications for teachers and administrators. *E-Journal of Teaching & Learning in Diverse Settings, 2*(1). Retrieved February 10, 2005, from http://subr.edu/coeducation/ejournal

Lightfoot, S. L. (1983). *The good high school: Portraits of character and culture.* New York: Basic Books.

Lightfoot, S. L. (1994). *I've known rivers: Lives of loss and liberation.* New York: Penguin Books.

Loder, T. L. (2002). On women becoming and being principals: Pathways, patterns, and personal accounts. *Dissertation Abstracts International, 63,* 3804.

Loder, T. L. (2005). African American women principals' reflections on social change, community othermothering, and Chicago public school reform. *Urban Education, 40,* 298–320.

Lomotey, K. (1987). Black principals for Black students: Some preliminary observations. *Urban Education, 22,* 173–181.

Lomotey, K. (1989a). *African-American principals: School leadership and success.* Westport, CT: Greenwood Press.

Lomotey, K. (1989b). Cultural diversity in the school: Implications for principals. *NASSP Bulletin,* pp. 81–88.

Lomotey, K. (1993). African-American principals: Bureaucrat/administrators and ethno-humanists. *Urban Education, 27,* 394–412.

Lomotey, K., Allen, K. L., Canada, T. J., Mark, D. L. H., & Rivers, S. (2003). *Research on African American educational leaders: The state of the art.* Unpublished manuscript.

Lyman, L. (2000). *How do they know you care? The principal's challenge.* New York: Teachers College Press.

Mann, H. B. (1970). *The Negro school and professional in America.* Englewood Cliffs, NJ: Prentice Hall.

Marshall, C. (2004). Social justice challenges to educational administration: Introduction to a special issue. *Educational Administration Quarterly, 40,* 3–13.

Mayeroff, M. (1971). *On caring.* New York: Harper & Row.

Mertz, N. T., & McNeely, S. R. (1998). Women on the job: A study of female high school principals. *Educational Administration Quarterly, 34,* 196–222.

Milner, H. R., & Howard, T. C. (2004). Black teachers, Black students, Black communities and *Brown:* Perspectives and insights from experts. *Journal of Negro Education, 73,* 285–297.

Mitchell, D. E., Ortiz, F. I., & Mitchell, T. K. (1987). *Work orientation and job performance: The cultural basis of teaching rewards and incentives.* New York: State University of New York Press.

Morris, J. E. (1999). A pillar of strength: An African American school's communal bonds with families and community since *Brown. Urban Education, 35,* 584–605.

Morris, J. E. (2004). Can anything good come from Nazareth? Race, class, and African American schooling and community in the urban South and Midwest. *American Educational Research Journal, 41,* 69–112.

Mukuria, G. (2002). Disciplinary challenges: How do principals address this dilemma? *Urban Education, 37,* 432–452.

Murphy, J. (1988). Methodological, measurement and conceptual problems in the study of instructional leadership. *Educational Evaluation and Policy Analysis, 4,* 290–310.

Noddings, N. (1984). *Caring: A feminine approach to ethics and moral education.* Berkeley: University of California Press.

Ogbu, J. (2003). *Black American students in an affluent suburb: A study of academic disengagement.* Mahwah, NJ: Erlbaum.

Ogletree, C. J., Jr. (2004). *At deliberate speed: Reflections on the first half century of Brown v. Board of Education.* New York: W. W. Norton.

Orfield, G. (1969). *The reconstruction of southern education: The schools and the 1964 Civil Rights Act.* New York: Wiley.

Orfield, G., & Lee, C. (2004). *Brown at 50: King's dream or Plessy's nightmare?* Retrieved January 26, 2004, from www.civilrightsproject.harvard.edu

Ortiz, F. I. (1982). *Career patterns in education: Women, men and minorities in public school administration.* South Hadley, MA: Bergin.

Ortiz, F. I., & Marshall, C. (1988). Women in educational administration. In N. Boyan (Ed.), *Handbook of research on educational administration* (pp. 123–141). New York: Longman.

Perkins, L. (1987). *Fannie Jackson Coppin and the Institute for Colored Youth, 1865–1902.* New York: Garland.

Perry, T. (2003, January 10). Tackling the myth of Black students' intellectual inferiority. *Chronicle of Higher Education,* p. B10.

Perry, T., Steele, C., & Hilliard, A. (2003). *Young, gifted, and Black: Promoting high achievement among African-American students.* Boston: Beacon Press.

Pollard, D. (1997). Race, gender, and educational leadership: Perspectives from African American principals. *Educational Policy, 11,* 353–374.

Portin, B. S. (2000). The changing urban principalship. *Education and Urban Society, 32,* 492–505.

Pounder, D. G., Ogawa, R. T., & Adams, E. A. (1995). Leadership as an organization-wide phenomenon: Its impact on school performance. *Educational Administration Quarterly, 31,* 564–588.

Reitzug, U. C., & Patterson, J. (1998). "I'm not going to lose you!" Empowerment through caring in an urban principal's practice with students. *Urban Education, 33,* 150–181.

Reitzug, U. C., & Reeves, J. E. (1992). Miss Lincoln doesn't teach here: A descriptive narrative and conceptual analysis of a principal's symbolic leadership behavior. *Educational Administration Quarterly, 28,* 185–219.

Resnick, L. (2004). Closing the gap: High achievement for students of color. *Research Points, 2,* 1–4.

Riester, A. F., Pursch, V., & Skrla, L. (2002). Principals for social justice: Leaders for school success for children from low-income homes. *Journal of School Leadership, 12,* 281–302.

Rodgers, F. A. (1967). *The Black high school and its community.* Lexington, MA: Lexington Books.

Savage, C. G. (2001). "Because we did more with less": The agency of African American teachers in Franklin, Tennessee: 1890–1967. *Peabody Journal of Education, 76,* 170–203.

Scheurich, J. J. (1998). Highly successful and loving, public elementary schools populated mainly by low-SES children of color: Core beliefs and cultural characteristics. *Urban Education, 33,* 451–491.

Shakeshaft, C. (1988). Women in educational administration: Implications for training. In D. E. Griffiths, R. T. Stout, & P. B. Forsyth (Eds.), *Leaders for America's schools: The report and papers of the National Commission on Excellence in Educational Administration* (pp. 403–416). Berkeley, CA: McCutchan.

Shakeshaft, C. (1989). *Women in educational administration.* Newbury Park, CA: Sage.

Shakeshaft, C. (1999). The struggle to create a more gender-inclusive profession. In J. Murphy & K. Seashore Louis (Eds.), *The handbook of research on educational administration* (2nd ed., pp. 99–118). San Francisco: Jossey-Bass.

Shotwell, R. H. (1999). *Leadership theory and context: Black and White principals during desegregation.* Unpublished doctoral dissertation, University of North Carolina at Greensboro.

Siddle Walker, E. V. (1993a). Caswell County Training School, 1933–1969: Relationships between community and school. *Harvard Educational Review, 63,* 161–182.

Siddle Walker, E. V. (1993b). Interpersonal caring in the "good" segregated schooling of African-American children: Evidence from the case of the Caswell County Training School. *Urban Review, 25,* 63–77.

Siddle Walker, E. V. (1996). *Their highest potential: An African American school community in the segregated South.* Chapel Hill: University of North Carolina Press.

Siddle Walker, V. (2000). Value of segregated schools for African American children in the South, 1935–1969: A review of common themes and characteristics. *Review of Educational Research, 70,* 253–285.

Siddle Walker, V. (2001). African American teaching in the South: 1940–1960. *American Educational Research Journal, 38,* 751–779.

Siddle Walker, V. (2003). The architects of Black schooling in the segregated South: The case of one principal leader. *Journal of Curriculum and Supervision, 19,* 54–72.

Siddle Walker, V., & Archung, K. N. (2003). The segregated schooling of Blacks in the southern United States and South Africa. *Comparative Education Review, 47,* 21–40.

Sizemore, B. A. (2003). The imputation of Black inferiority: Does it contribute to the achievement gap? In C. Camp-Yeakey & R. D. Henderson (Eds.), *Surmounting all odds: Education, opportunity and society in the new millennium* (pp. 273–304). Greenwich, CT: Information Age.

Sowell, T. (1976). Patterns of Black excellence. *Public Interest, 43,* 6–58.

Starratt, R. J. (1991). Building an ethical school: A theory for practice in educational leadership. *Educational Administration Quarterly, 27,* 185–202.

Tillman, L. C. (2002). Culturally sensitive research approaches: An African American perspective. *Educational Researcher, 31*(9), 3–12.

Tillman, L. C. (2003). From rhetoric to reality? Educational administration and the lack of racial and ethnic diversity within the profession. *University Council for Educational Administration Review, 45*(3), 1–4.

Tillman, L. C. (2004a). African American parental involvement in a post-*Brown* era: Facilitating the academic achievement of African American students. *Journal of School Public Relations, 25,* 161–176.

Tillman, L. C. (2004b). (Un)intended consequences?: The impact of the *Brown v. Board of Education* decision on the employment status of Black educators. *Education and Urban Society, 36,* 280–303.

Tillman, L. C. (2005a). Mentoring new teachers: Implications for leadership practice in an urban school. *Educational Administration Quarterly, 41*(4), 609–629.

Tillman, L. C. (Ed.). (2005b). Pushing back resistance: African American discourses on school leadership [Special issue]. *Educational Administration Quarterly, 41*(4).

Tillman, L. C. (2007). Bringing the gifts that our ancestors gave: Continuing the legacy of excellence in African American school leadership. In J. Jackson (Ed.), *Strengthening the educational pipeline for African Americans: Informing policy and practice* (pp. 53–69). Albany: State University of New York Press.

Tonnsen, S., & Truesdale, V. (1993). Women and minorities in educational administration: Programs and processes that work. *Journal of School Leadership, 3,* 679–687.

Valverde, L., & Brown, F. (1988). Influences on leadership development of racial and ethnic minorities. In N. Boyan (Ed.), *The handbook on educational administration* (pp. 143–158). New York: Longman.

U.S. Equal Employment Opportunity Commission. (2005). *Job patterns for minorities and women in state and local governments, 2005.* Washington, DC: Author.

Ward Randolph, A. (1997, March). *Champion Avenue School: A historical analysis.* Paper presented at the annual meeting of the American Educational Research Association, Chicago.

Washington, B. T. (1993). *Up from slavery.* New York: Gramercy Books. (Original work published 1901)

Washington, M. H. (1988). *A voice from the South.* New York: Oxford University Press.

Watkins, W. (2001). *The White architects of Black education: Ideology and power in America, 1865–1954.* New York: Teachers College Press.

Wells, G. F. (1991). *A comparison of the role perceptions of Black high school principals.* Unpublished doctoral dissertation, University of North Carolina at Chapel Hill.

White, A. L. (1995). *Factors that affect the professional experiences of African American female principals in the state of Arizona: A case study.* Unpublished doctoral dissertation, Arizona State University.

Williams, L. S. (1998). *Servants of the people: The 1960s legacy of African American leadership.* New York: St. Martin's Griffin.

Witziers, B., Bosker, R. J., & Krüger, M. L. (2003). Educational leadership and student achievement: The elusive search for an association. *Educational Administration Quarterly, 39,* 398–425.

Yeakey, C. C., Johnston, G. S., & Adkison, J. A. (1986). In pursuit of equity: A review of research on minorities and women in educational administration. *Educational Administration Quarterly, 22,* 110–149.

Young, M., & McLeod, S. (2001). Flukes, opportunities, and planned interventions: Factors affecting women's decisions to become school administrators. *Educational Administration Quarterly, 37,* 462–502.

12

LEADERSHIP CHALLENGES IN K-12 URBAN EDUCATION

Prospective African American Administrators' Views on Educating African American Students and Closing the Achievement Gap

ROBERT COOPER

WILL J. JORDAN

A t all levels of the educational system in the United States, African American students continue to lag behind their White and Asian students in academic achievement (Conchas, 2001; Kober, 2001), graduation (Orfield, Losen, Wald, & Swanson, 2004; Rumberger, 1987, 1995; U.S. Department of Education, 1997), and college enrollment (Harvey & Anderson, 2005). Students who underperform in school at an early age disengage from the learning process and often fail to obtain a high school diploma (Bryk, 1994; Cooper & Yamamura, 2005; Lee & Burkam, 2003). Despite the rapid demographic shifts, the vast majority of African American students still attend school in large metropolitan urban centers (Jones-Wilson, 1990; Karpinski, 2006), in school districts that continue to struggle with inadequate funding, ineffective staffing, school violence, and de facto racial and social class segregation (Darling-Hammond, 1999; Jordan & Cooper, 2003; Orfield et al., 2004; Wimberley, 2002). Thus, debates about improving educational outcomes for African American students must involve a discussion about the transformation of urban education. Large city school districts such as New York City, Chicago, Los Angeles, and Miami-Dade County must be at the epicenter of national discourse about ways to improve the educational experience of African American students. With that in mind, this chapter examines the perceptions of a group of aspiring African American school administrators from the greater Los Angeles area about how to transform urban education and improve educational outcomes for African American students.

In light of the fact that the current policy framework for urban school reform is principally driven by NCLB's push for greater accountability for student achievement, which translates to high stakes testing, we examine aspiring administrators' receptiveness toward models of reform commonly referred to as best practices, as a way to improve the educational quality for African American students. We explore the connection between beliefs about reform and the degree of implementation, using what we call "comprehensive" as compared with "process-orientated" strategies as a way to discern divergent beliefs about teaching and learning.

ADDRESSING THE PERSISTENT UNDERACHIEVEMENT OF AFRICAN AMERICAN STUDENTS

Decades of research suggest a variety of reasons why African American students perpetually do not perform as well as students of other races/ethnicities. Frequently cited reasons include disproportionate poverty levels (Baker, 1998; Natriello, McDill, & Pallas, 1990), minority status (Driscoll, 1999; Gordon & Yowell, 1994; Lagerwey & Phillips, 2003; Martinez, DeGarmo, & Eddy, 2004), discontinuity of social values between home and school (Boykin, 1986; Delpit, 1995; Gordon & Yowell, 1994; Taylor, 1991), lack of social capital (Hao & Bonstead-Bruns, 1998), lack of role models (Rouse, 1998), and school policies (Cabrera & Padilla, 2004; Donato, Menchaca, & Valencia, 1991; Mosqueda, 2005). Much of this research takes a deficit perspective, focusing on how growing up African American negatively affects academic achievement. A counter argument, as posited by Noguera (2001), is that urban schools operate as social sorting machines through which inequality is manufactured. That is, the educational system legitimates unfair privileges and reproduces intergenerational disadvantages. According to Noguera, students who we expect to succeed in school—usually children from affluent families—are more likely to succeed, while those whom we expect to fail—usually poor inner-city children—end up failing.

To address the underachievement of poor inner-city children, many urban districts and schools have looked to external change agents for models of effective school practices (Slavin & Fashola, 1998). During the 1990s, much was written about the need for standards-based reform and best practices. In 2002, the U.S. Department of Education invested millions of dollars to establish

the What Works Clearinghouse (WWC) to build a repository of best practices by collecting, screening, and identifying studies of effectiveness of educational interventions. To be catalogued by the WWC, however, such interventions (programs, products, practices, and policies) are required to demonstrate scientific evidence of their effectiveness.

As a result of the national emphasis on evidence-based best practices, many urban schools turned to high-profile education reformers and organizations to adopt comprehensive reform models of curriculum and instruction that would transform entire schools. A theory of action underlying the policies and practices of many of these reforms was the belief that a greater number of students could be better served if traditional notions of teaching and learning were fundamentally altered. In many cases, these comprehensive reform models demanded an unprecedented level of accountability on the part of the classroom teachers and school administrators, requiring a restructuring with the local school as the unit of analysis (Klecker & Loadman, 1999; Slavin & Fashola, 1998). This type of restructuring, among other things, mandates a change in roles, responsibilities, and relationships of site administrators, such as principals (Gainey, 1994; Murphy, 1994). School administrators, with the support of teachers, are expected to create the conditions for reform to be carried out. Some scholars have suggested that because of the multifaceted complex nature of school reform, "leadership" is one of the most critical factors in determining the success and sustainability of the school reform process (Cooper, 1998; Datnow, 2005; Murphy & Datnow, 2003). School leadership has long been recognized as a key element for educational success, and virtually every review of the literature on educational effectiveness cites leadership as a critical element of school reform (Spillane, 1999; Spillane, Halvorson, & Diamond, 2001; York-Barr & Duke, 2004). For example, Spillane (1999) wrote about the importance of leadership, not as an individual enterprise, but as a collective responsibility. His distributed theory of leadership focuses on how leadership is distributed among both positional and informal leaders. Rather than seeing leadership as the responsibility of the site principal, it is best understood as practice distributed and shared among administrators and teachers alike.

Despite the significant influence institutional leadership has on making educational reform happen at the school site level, how current and prospective school site administrators make sense of these reforms, how these reform initiatives affect institutional culture, and what leadership challenges are created when implementing the current wave of reform are largely unanswered questions. Research studies exploring these issues among educators of color are particularly scant.

Thus, the focus of this chapter is to present data from a group of African American educators on their perceptions about commonly used urban school reform models that have emerged in response to the accountability pressures of No Child Left Behind Act of 2001 (NCLB) and are touted as best practices. This group of aspiring school administrators illuminates the complex relationship between ideological orientation of prospective urban school administrators and the approaches being advocated to bring about the transformation of urban education. Additionally, this chapter explores the degree to which this group of prospective administrators believes that this current wave of reforms will be successful in increasing academic achievement among African American students. Embedded in a larger 4-year investigation of how urban educators are affected by the adoption and implementation of externally developed reform, we also discuss the degree to which they feel included in the discourse surrounding reform in schools and classrooms, and how increased accountability pressures have affected their preparation and training for school leadership. Three questions guide this investigation: (1) What perceptions and beliefs does this group of aspiring African American school administrators have regarding the current wave of educational reform? (2) How does this group of African American educators think these reforms will affect the learning process of African American students? (3) What challenges does the implementation of reform models that advocate best practices present for school leaders?

Transforming Urban Schools

This persistent educational gap, which is particularly evident for African American students in high-poverty urban areas, has resulted in policy demands to aggressively restructure urban schools. In response to this call for change, an unprecedented number of researchers, policymakers, and program developers have responded with the development of reform ideas for policy and practice. The passage of the NCLB has enabled an assortment of new and recycled models of reform to surface and to become adopted in urban schools. NCLB, which was the reauthorized Elementary and Secondary Education Act, has been referred to as "the most sweeping change in education policy in three decades" (Malico & Langan, 2003). Of course, there have been numerous aggressive, all-encompassing reforms at the state and local level (such as zero-base staffing), but NCLB represents the greatest federal involvement in education to date. And, in many respects, NCLB is redefining the educational landscape for urban schools. For example, NCLB, through increased school-level rewards and sanctions is requiring schools and districts to disaggregate high stakes tests for all students. As a result, administrators and teachers are responsible for not only raising and maintaining the achievement scores of the whole school, but also the performance of the different subgroup classifications at the school, such as race/ethnicity, English language learners, free and reduced lunch eligibility, and disability status. NCLB is an attempt to ensure both academic excellence and equity by providing new opportunities and challenges for schools to advance the goal of closing the achievement gap, while providing high-quality instruction (Lee, 2006). By design, NCLB relies on high stakes testing to "motivate" schools to make what the legislation refers to as "Adequate Yearly Progress" (AYP) toward the goal of 100% proficiency by the year 2014.

The reform strategies used to bring about change in the schooling process array along a continuum. Datnow, Hubbard, and Mehan (2002) discerned prescriptive models, reforms that are highly specified and provide curriculum, lesson plans, school organization models, implementation plans, and professional development, from those that were process orientated and much less specified. Given that urban schools experience greater instability of teachers and administrators than rural or suburban schools, many urban districts opted for prescriptive reform models as a way to ensure continuity in their instructional program, particularly at the elementary school level. While some of the more prescriptive models experienced early success

(Herman, 1999), the long-term implications have resulted in some educators claiming that urban schools have become giant test prep centers where good teaching is stifled and devalued (Sunderman, Kim, & Orfield, 2005). The extent to which these claims are true must be the focus of ongoing research.

Employing a Micropolitical Framework to Understand Urban School Leadership

School reform is embedded in a context that is neither neutral nor insulated from larger social and political forces (Lipman, 1998). Dominant ideologies and relations of power in the school and the broader society influence the change process. The possibility and pace of educational change depend not only on institutional cultures but also on the relative political power and resources of various groups in the schools and community. As educational change theorists have argued, four conceptual lenses are useful in understanding this line of research: (1) technical, (2) normative, (3) political, and (4) sociocultural (Cooper, Slavin, & Madden, 1998; Oakes & Lipton, 1992). First, the technical lens taps into the dimension that is the most pragmatic. This dimension involves changes in school structures, strategies, and practices. Second, the normative lens exposes the values, ethos, and attitudes that drive policy and practice within urban schools. Furthermore, the normative lens gives insight into the ideological barriers that schools encounter in the reform process and that individuals encounter when asked to alter attitudes, behaviors, and practices. Third, the political lens focuses on the redistribution of decision-making power. It helps researchers to examine how, when, and which individuals participate in reform. This is a particularly important aspect to consider in implementing urban school reform because reform, by definition, is an attempt to alter relationships among educators, administrators, students, and parents. The important issue here is how schools build the capacity to make its structures serve its normative and technical goals. Finally, the sociocultural lens focuses on the social, cultural, and environmental factors that affect school reform, but are seldom given attention. The sociocultural lens gives greater insight to the constraints and challenges educators face

when interacting with school communities. The use of conceptual lenses can provide a fuller picture of the complexities of the structures, strategies, practices, and relationships associated with school reform efforts.

This chapter builds on and extends this theoretical and methodological approach with the use of a micropolitical lens. This approach facilitates the deconstruction and highlighting of the micropolitical processes of implementing school reform designed to increase the achievement of African American students. Using a micropolitical framework to understand this phenomenon gives insight into the political ideologies of the social systems of aspiring African American school leaders, as well as the interaction between these systems. According to Marshall and Scribner (1991), a micropolitical perspective allows the researcher to explicate the "strains and tensions that stem from diverse sources of power, rival interests, and intractable conflicts within and around schools" (p. 350). The study of micropolitics concerns issues of conflict, power, and cooperation, three aspects of educational reform that are often given insufficient attention (High, Scribner, & Clark, 2001). Blasé (1991) argued that micropolitics is

> about power and how people use it to influence others and to protect themselves. It is about conflict and how people compete with each other to get what they want. It is about cooperation and how people build support among themselves to achieve their ends. It is about what people in all social settings think about and have strong feelings about, but what is so often unspoken and not easily observed. (pp. 1–2)

Given the cyclical nature of school reform, where educational strategies and approaches go into and out of fashion, the micropolitical perspective offers researchers an insightful, nonobvious, and provocative way to think about power relationships and human behavior in schools.

Methods

The data presented here were collected as part of a larger 4-year investigation that sought to examine the attitudes and perceptions of educators regarding externally developed reform efforts to transform urban education and close the widening achievement gap. Given that the current wave of reforms is driven by policies emanating from NCLB, the study focused on educators' perceptions of the changes required by this federal legislation. More specifically, the study was designed to gain better understanding of how urban educators think about prescriptive reforms and to investigate how implementation affects the daily operation of teaching and learning in America's schools. Although a theoretical framework was used to guide this study, there was no theory under consideration or hypothesis to test. To avoid biases that might limit data collection, data analysis, or data interpretation, it was important for us to begin our data analysis with as few ideological and philosophical constraints as possible. Our analysis began with a virtually clean theoretical slate. This is not to suggest that this study did not benefit from previous research that explores the role and influence of, and connection between, educator perceptions, attitudes toward school reform, institutional leadership, and instructional practice. In fact, that extant body of literature helped to hone and refine the research questions and gave insight into specific relationships between variables and the implementation process that might be appropriate for further investigation.

Data Collection

Data presented in this chapter come from a series of individual interviews with a group of aspiring African American school administrators. A series of in-depth one-on-one interviews were conducted with each participant between September 2003 and August 2006.These interviews consisted of 60- to 90-minute semistructured discussions guided by open-ended questions that focused on the participant's understanding and conceptions of teaching and learning as well as the challenges faced by administrators as a result of educational reforms emanating from NCLB. Both descriptive and thematic questions guided these exploratory interviews (Bogdan & Biklen, 1992). These interviews were semistructured to ensure that specific topics were covered but included flexibility to allow for the conversation to flow.

Data Analysis

Data from interview transcripts were analyzed in accordance with the principles of inductive research and constant comparative analysis (Taylor & Bogdan, 1998). This procedure allowed us to progressively and inductively develop themes and conceptual constructs from a comparison of each new incident from the data to those coded in emergent categories and subcategories. Data analysis occurred continuously throughout the research and was facilitated by the use of conceptual lenses, which are analytical tools that help to focus our attention on specific structures, policies, and practices of the education process.

Although more than 100 hours of transcribed interview and field note data were collected on both the content and outcome of educational reform as part of the larger investigation, the focus of the data presented in this chapter centers on the qualitative data that illuminates the attitudes and perceptions of the five African American educators who were a part of the larger study. In this chapter, we explore the perceptions of these five African American educators about commonly used urban school reform models that claim to be best practices. Given that four of the five African American educators were enrolled in administrative credentialing programs, this data gives us insight into important questions such as how district, state, and federal policies can affect the perceptions and preparation of school leaders. As aspiring school administrators, these five individuals illuminate the important relationship between the ideological orientation of prospective urban school administrators and the approaches being advocated to bring about the transformation of urban education. Additionally, these case studies highlight the degree to which African American educators believe that this current wave of reforms will be successful in increasing academic achievement among African American students.

Sample

The five African American educators discussed in this chapter are a subset of the stratified sample of 30 urban educators in the larger study. These five educators teach in the greater Los Angeles area. Although the 30 teachers in the larger study were stratified on six important characteristics (gender, race, years of teaching experience, initial support and degree of enthusiasm for educational reform, and grade level taught), the five educators[1] discussed in this chapter were selected because they were African American and aspired to enter the field of school administration.

Mr. Adams

Mr. Adams, a 35-year-old father of one, was educated on the east coast and is considered a very traditional high school social studies teacher. He sees himself as a content expert who is charged with the responsibility of disseminating knowledge. He, like many of his colleagues at the small 4-year comprehensive high school 35 minutes east of downtown Los Angeles, focuses his attention on those students who are interested in obtaining an education. Although Mr. Adams has taught high school social studies for the past 8 years, he has only been at his current teaching assignment for the past 4 years. Mr. Adams began his teaching career on the east coast and moved to California 4 years ago. His current teaching assignment is his first and only assignment in the state of California. The student demographics at his current school mirror that of the state in that almost 70% of the students at the school are Latino. Although Mr. Adams's first teaching assignment was a school with more than 60% African American students, he feels that his professional training and personal experiences serve him well in his new environment.

When Mr. Adams was asked to describe himself, he stated he was a professional student. He holds two master's degrees and is currently enrolled in an administrative credentialing program. Mr. Adams has a love for learning. His rationale for pursuing an administrative credential is to become an administrator at a school where he can create an environment where students can develop a love for learning.

Ms. Brown

Ms. Brown, a 40-year-old mother of two, entered the teaching profession as a second career after a 15-year background in youth and young adult counseling. During the time of the study, Ms. Brown was starting the third year of her first teaching assignment and taught second grade at a small inner-city elementary school about 20 minutes from downtown Los Angeles. For the most part, Ms. Brown's knowledge about

NCLB and reform programs came from her colleagues at school. Ms. Brown taught at a school that had been mandated to use a scripted reading program for the language arts portion of her instruction. Against the widespread resistance on the part of some of the more senior teachers at her school, Ms. Brown was very candid about her support for the structure and scriptedness of the program. Although Ms. Brown indicated that this type of reform initiative goes against everything she was taught in her teacher credentialing program, she could not help but speak positively about how helpful the structure of the program was to her as a new teacher.

Since this was her first teaching assignment, Ms. Brown attributed her positive support for this type of reform to the level of success she was experiencing with her students. She stated, "I like the program. I see where it is making a difference. I'm a new teacher and the structure of the program really helps me to figure out the direction and the pacing. I like the program." Ms. Brown was adamant that "if teachers were faithful to scripted programs, if teachers just gave the program a chance, they could experience academic success with their students." Ms. Brown was particularly supportive of the scripted reforms because she was teaching the same group of students that she taught in the first grade. She stated that this allowed her as a teacher to document that the reading program was having a significant impact on the achievement of her students. Ms. Brown is having a positive experience at her school and has expressed an interest in pursuing an administrative credential in the future. She indicated that she understands the importance of leadership in running an effective school and she believes that she has the commitment and passion to make school a "good place" for all students.

Ms. Collins

Ms. Collins was the veteran of the group. This 35-year-old mother of two has been teaching for 10 years. Ms. Collins began teaching on an emergency credential in the Los Angeles Unified School District right out of college. Although her primary focus has been middle school science, she has taught high school science as well. Her current teaching assignment is at a large middle school about 35 miles northeast of downtown Los Angeles. As a teacher on an emergency credential, Ms. Collins has been enrolled in some type of educational course for the majority of her teaching career that include both teaching and administrative credentialing classes. Ms. Collins is pursuing an administrative credential, not so much because she wants to be an administrator, as much as she wants to continue to move up the salary scale. While she believes that she has the capacity and competence to be a good administrator, she is concerned about the demands of the position given that she is raising her family. She sees herself becoming an administrator later in her career.

Ms. Collins is well-versed on the current wave of reforms that are available to schools to better meet the academic needs of their students. According to Ms. Collins, many of the current reforms advocate the use of instructional strategies and ideas that she used a decade ago. She indicated that while programs that are being touted as best practices are the practices she already employs in her daily pedagogy, she does appreciate how they bring focus to the critical skills that students need to be successful. In the end, the current wave of reforms, according to Ms. Collins, has not resulted in any significant change to her practice. She did indicate that the increased focus on teacher collaboration and thematic teaching has caused her to be more critical of what she teaches and when she teaches it.

Mr. Smith

Mr. Smith is a "youthful" 35-year-old father of two. He has been in the teaching profession for 8 years. Prior to teaching, Mr. Smith was social worker in the Compton/Watts area of Los Angeles. Mr. Smith brings a great deal of empathy and compassion to the teaching profession. Although Mr. Smith has experience teaching at both middle school and high school, his current assignment is at a large middle school located about 35 miles northwest of downtown Los Angeles. The student demographics at the middle school are 88% Latino and 8% African American. As one of six African American educators on the campus, Mr. Smith plays an integral role in ensuring that the campus remains a welcoming place to the African American students.

As an eighth grade English teacher at one of the lowest-performing middle schools in the district, Mr. Smith is directly affected by the current wave of reform initiatives at his school and in the district. With a large number of limited English learners in his school, Mr. Smith's school has been mandated to use a highly scripted language arts program. Overall, Mr. Smith's experience with this language arts program, as well as other reform initiatives adopted or mandated by the district has been positive. His only point of contention was that he did not agree with the strict adherence to the scriptedness of the programs. He believed that he and his colleagues were professionals and did not need the "reform police" monitoring their classroom activities. Mr. Smith was adamant that if teachers were provided with the proper professional development, they would be better able to carry out the reforms as designed. He stated,

> They always talk about "fidelity to the model," well you can have fidelity without policing my every move. I'm a professional and I would appreciate it if they treated me like it. . . . You want to increase student achievement, treat teachers like competent professionals that they are.

Mr. Smith's strong sense of teacher professionalism was one of the factors that motivated him to pursue his administrative credential. He is convinced that if school leadership can create an atmosphere of professionalism among its faculty, many of the issues that schools are facing, including the underperformance of students, could be alleviated. Mr. Smith is pursing his administrative credential so that he can become a school administrator who respects the professionalism of his faculty. Admittedly, Mr. Smith is optimistically cautious about achieving his goal given the high stakes testing climate in the district. According to Mr. Smith, everything is to be driven by the desire to increase AYP scores, including how we treat teachers.

Ms. Soto

Ms. Soto, a relatively young teacher in both age and experience, brings a wealth of information and passion to her classroom. Formally educated at a small liberal arts college on the east coast, she brings an extensive background in the sciences to the classroom. With a chemistry major in college, Ms. Soto serves as a middle school science teacher. While she initially planned to attend medical school, she married and soon began a family.

Initially looking for a job that would allow her to pursue her medical career, Ms. Soto entered the teaching profession on an emergency credential. Given the extreme shortage of qualified math and science teachers, Ms. Soto was quickly offered a teaching position as a science teacher. To Ms. Soto's surprise, teaching was much more involved than she anticipated and required an extensive time commitment. Also to Ms. Soto's surprise, she also greatly enjoyed her students. Her passion for teaching grew over the years so that the combination of enjoying the job and having small children made it almost impossible for her to leave the profession. Ms. Soto is currently teaching at a medium-sized middle school 45 minutes east of downtown Los Angeles. The school is racially diverse with just more than 50% of the students identified as Latino.

Ms. Soto's involvement with reform centers around the push at her school for improved test scores and how this emphasis affected her instructional time and focus. There has been increased attention given to teacher collaboration and thematic teaching. Supportive of this effort, Ms. Soto expressed support for any efforts that ultimately translated into academic achievement and the success of her students. In fact, she attributes her commitment to her students as the catalyst for her return to school to pursue her administrative credential. She indicated that the more time she spends as a teacher, the more she understands the all important relationship between strong administrative leadership and the quality of the schooling experience a student is afforded.

Findings

Three primary questions guided the investigation: (1) What perceptions and beliefs do aspiring African American school administrators have regarding the current wave of educational reform? (2) How does this group of African American educators think these reforms will affect the learning process of African American students? (3) What challenges does the implementation of reform models that advocate best practices present for school leaders?

Not surprising, four of the five educators were very skeptical about whether the current wave of reform could fundamentally transform

urban education and improve the schooling experience for African American students. For example, of the five educators in the study, Mr. Adams was the most skeptical and resistant to the idea that the latest round of reforms would change the schooling experience of African American students. As a teacher leader on campus, and one of the few African American educators on campus, he has been deeply involved in conversations and inquiry about ways to increase student achievement. Mr. Adams indicated that the only way to change the achievement level of the students is to change the expectation level of the teachers. He stated that

teachers have very low expectations for students here [at his school] . . . all students. Teachers here just don't feel like the students are capable of being smart. We only have a handful of African American students here, and very few of them are doing well. It is not about reform, but teacher expectations.

The data suggest that while this group of educators was familiar with the general tenets of NCLB and the types of reforms that are being adopted in response to both state and federal mandates, they question whether these reform initiatives are the best vehicle to bring about student achievement. They argued that the nature of the reforms being driven by NCLB is too focused on teacher accountability and not student learning. Mr. Adams, the high school social studies teacher, suggested that changing the focus of reform from accountability to student learning requires a fundamental shift in institutional culture. For Mr. Adams, changing the school culture meant changing the attitudes, beliefs, norms, and sense of mission that underlie the character of a school. He suggested that school culture is what shapes and influences the ways people think, feel, and interact. When Mr. Adams was asked to expound on what he meant by changing the school culture, he stated,

You know how we think about the kids. We are so quick to point out the fact that the Black kids at the school are doing poorly and are at risk at the school, but we never ask the all important question, why? I'm not saying that the teachers here are racist, but I am saying that many of my colleagues don't understand our Black students. If we are really going to make a difference for Black students we are going to have to change the way we think about them and their families. We are going to have to acknowledge that we might have to do things differently and reach out to them.

Mr. Adams went on to suggest that school culture not only included the climate or atmosphere under which teaching and learning occur but also the nature and quality of relationships between adults and students as well as the curriculum. The relationship between student and teacher as well as the cultural relevancy of the curriculum seemed to be two areas that all five of the participants agreed were areas of concern when addressing the needs of African American students. They suggested that teachers must be culturally sensitive enough to augment the curriculum in ways that acknowledge the sociopolitical nature of schools and address the hidden assumptions, beliefs, and norms undergirding the educational system. They argued that issues of race, prejudice, and inequity in schools must be discussed and confronted. These explicit conversations, these educators would suggest, are a necessary condition for changing the institutional culture of urban schools. The educators in this study argued that to improve the quality of education offered to African American students, we must stop tinkering around the edges of change with limited piecemeal interventions and empower and equip educators with the tools they need to fundamentally change the culture of teaching and learning in schools.

When asked about the ways that NCLB has changed the culture of their school, the educators in this study had varying responses. Ms. Brown and Ms. Soto expressed positive sentiments, suggesting that the reform initiatives that have been adopted as a result of NCLB at their schools have had a positive impact. Ms. Brown stated, "We are implementing Open Court (a reading program). It is providing us with a common curriculum for the school. It is keeping us focused on student achievement." Much of the conversation about the implementation of reform with Ms. Brown was couched in terms of commitment to her students. Although the vast majority of students in her second grade class were not African American, she expressed a deep commitment to their success. Although Ms. Brown indicated that implementing the reading program was not easy because it meant making drastic changes in the way she was

taught to teach, it was acceptable given the academic gains her students were making.

Ms. Soto, echoing Ms. Brown, indicated that in her experience, the reform initiatives at the elementary school grades were easy for her to buy into. She stated,

> You know when I taught in the elementary school I didn't mind that scripted reading program we used, it made my life a lot easier. I knew exactly what I needed to teach. Now I remember I was a new teacher, so that might account for some of my acceptance of it. . . . I find reform very different at the middle school. It seems all about testing and API [2] scores.

Sharing a slightly more critical sentiment, Mr. Smith, a middle school teacher stated,

> I have seen it all. These reforms come and go. Few have any real staying power. It all depends upon what's fashionable. I taught Success for All in the elementary grades, I was an AVID[3] teacher in middle school, and now I am involved in moving towards small learning communities at the high school. It doesn't really matter the reform, its all about our API scores. The focus isn't student achievement . . . its on testing the kids to see if we can increase our scores.

While the opinions about the impact of reform on the schools seemed to vary by experience and grade level, this group of aspiring administrators did feel that the educational lessons that were being learned from NCLB are important for school leaders in discovering the ways to increase student learning and eliminate the achievement gap. One of the biggest lessons that this group of educators seemed to take away from their experiences with NCLB, and the reform initiatives that emanate from it, is the importance of including teacher voice in the shaping of how and when reform is implemented. This finding is very consistent with prior research that suggests that there are a variety of explanations that can account for the attitudes and perceptions educators have toward educational reform, and one of the most important is the role the school leadership plays in its implementation (Cambron-McCabe & McCarthy, 2005; Cooper & Peebles, 2006; Datnow, 2005).

Implementation of reform is often driven by the level of "buy-in" an educator has toward the particular reform idea or initiative. The educators in this study suggested that the notion of buy-in insufficiently captures the necessary commitment and behaviors that lead to successful reform acceptance and implementation. Mr. Adams and Ms. Collins, the two teachers with the greatest number of years in the teaching profession, seemed to suggest that buy-in is only a precursor to a deeper perceptual level of investment that is required. While teachers will voice support for reform based on "best practices," Ms. Collins suggested that this is often more a function of some obligatory reality of their job as opposed to a real commitment. Ms. Collins stated, "Given that educational reform is such an integral part of today's urban educational landscape, teachers feel pressure to buy-in." Ms. Collins suggested that the reforms that work both for teachers and for students are those that give the teacher flexibility to deviate from the model when appropriate. She stated, "The kids at this school are struggling. Sometimes the teachers have to change the pacing plan or supplement the curriculum with materials that students will better understand." She indicated that being able to do this requires an institutional leader who understands both the needs of the students and the need to meet state and federal guidelines. She indicated that strong leadership is the key to changing schools, and elaborated on this point in the following statement:

> I've taught at several different schools and the schools that are good places for kids are the ones with a strong principal. . . . She [the principal] has the responsibility to keep everybody focused on the goals and mission of the school. When I become an administrator my focus will be on professional development; making sure that teachers have the support and training that they need to work with the kids.

For Ms. Brown and Ms. Soto, the rigid structure of the reform initiatives mandated at their schools was viewed very positively. Therefore, the extent to which the program was being used by them, as well as the effectiveness of the program, indicated a deeper level of commitment that went beyond feelings of obligation and necessity. This deeper level of commitment is what we are terming *institutional ownership*.

A MOVE TOWARD COMMUNITY OWNERSHIP

The perception of institutional ownership that we captured in this research is multifaceted. At its root is the notion that institutional ownership comes from a deep vested interest in the success of the institution or the individuals who make up the institution. In the case of educational reform, the interest in the success of the reform need not imply that the reform is drastically altering current instructional practices or institutional culture, but as is more often the case, that it aligns with the ideological orientation of the culture of the school. Data from this study suggest that if current institutional practices and norms are in alignment with the proposed reform initiative, educators are more likely to take ownership of the success of the reform.

The conceptual notion of ownership is a very complex question. Data from this research suggest that the decision to take ownership of a reform idea was driven by two factors: (1) the degree to which the reform benefited the individual, as a member of the school community and (2) the degree to which the educator perceived the reform to benefit the students and/or the greater school community. These two factors led us to distinguish between *individual ownership* and *community ownership*. The data collected for this study fall into both categories. On the one hand, Mr. Adams, Mr. Smith, and Ms. Collins developed feelings of ownership stemming primarily from individualized benefits. For example, when asked about the move toward small learning communities at his school, Mr. Adams stated,

> I mean . . . I have to buy it right? . . . because we have to do it. I think because a lot of the things are dictated to us that we really don't have any sort of choice. . . . Yes, I'll do it. You're going to pay me if I do this, and you won't pay me if I don't. I'll do it, sure fine.

Conversely, Ms. Brown and Ms. Soto voiced motivations primarily associated with what we've called community ownership, where the community interests at stake in the successful implementation of a reform surpass those of the individual. By community interest, we are not referring to a geographic, linguistic, socio-economic, or cultural group. Rather, the type of community we reference is predominantly conceptual; it is those stakeholders that teachers feel responsible to and responsible for serving. Ms. Brown's comments about her second grade class signals a community ownership mentality. She explains,

> It's very important to me that my kids exceed and do well . . . I feel very committed to them [my students], I feel very close to them. They're not just kids that I see everyday, they're like the reason I come to work everyday. . . . It's my obligation as a teacher to prepare them and not to send them to third grade not knowing what's going to happen.

Here, Ms. Brown's first priority is her students. Curriculum is implemented to serve them and her fidelity to the reform model is crucial because of a deep responsibility to adequately prepare students for third grade. Ms. Soto, sharing a similar sentiment, suggests that having a strong stake in the community means more work on the part of the teacher; it means "spending extra time at home, staying after school, getting more involved in committees." Again, this vested interest in the community results in a perceptual level of ownership focused on community benefits above individual benefits.

LEADERSHIP CHALLENGES IN CREATING COMMUNITY OWNERSHIP

Overall, this group of aspiring urban school administrators were familiar with NCLB, its limitations, and the reform options that emanate from it. Each participant was asked to reflect on their experiences in school and talk about the leadership challenges that they anticipate in leading a school in this era of NCLB and creating community ownership. Drawing on a micropolitical perspective, a threefold classification of micropolitical leadership challenges emerged: balancing ideological tensions, leading with a purpose, and developing a culturally diverse and sensitive staff.

BALANCING IDEOLOGICAL TENSIONS

The five aspiring administrators all agreed that the major leadership challenge that they will face as urban school administrators is balancing the tensions between their own beliefs about how best to educate students, particularly African American and other marginalized students with the realities of the urban context. For this group of aspiring administrators, there was a clear tension between the ends and means of reform. Given the climate that has been created by NCLB, a climate of strict accountability and high stakes testing, these educators believed that there was little room for them to infuse the issues that are important to them as school leaders into the discourse on reform. Mr. Smith stated,

> We are so focused on tests and test scores we rarely as a faculty talk about the kids as people. We just focus on those kids that are on the cusp of increasing our AYP. . . . As a principal I would like to focus on student teacher relationships and professional development issues.

When asked to give an example of a reform that had the potential to make a difference for African American students, Mr. Adams stated,

> At the high school, the big thing now is small learning communities. I'm familiar with the research . . . we covered it in my administration program, and in general I think small learning communities are a good idea. But, the real issue is what we are going to do differently than just put these kids in houses and academies. Unless we address the curriculum and how we as teachers are teaching, nothing is going to change for Black students, or any student. I know making the school smaller and more personalized is supposed to increase our AYP score, but nothing is going to happen until we address the real issue . . . how we engage Black kids in school with the curriculum.

When posed with a similar question, Ms. Collins echoed Mr. Adams's sentiments,

> I teach in the Avid program. It is a program aimed at the middle of the road students. I like

the program, but I am not sure it is really making a difference for our students. Our kids are exposed to study skills and strategies that they might not otherwise have been exposed to and they go on field trips, but we have so few African American students selected for the program, I'm not sure it's making a difference. I think we have to find ways to focus on the academic needs of African American students specifically.

These quotes are illustrative of the tension between one's ideological orientation and the realities of the role of urban school administrators. Consistent with the literature on school reform (O'Day, 2002; Ross, Stringfield, Sanders, & Wright, 2003; Timperley, 2005), the data from this study raise the fundamental question of an ongoing debate on how best to achieve fundamental change in urban schools. Public discourse has given rise to two ideologies on the continuum of ideas: (1) local decision making is critical to reform and (2) reform should be standardized and mandated from the top. The first ideology suggests that the transformation of urban education should be organic, bottom-up, and led by the educators in the local context (Fuman & Gruenewald, 2004; Guinier & Torres, 2001; Tillman, 2004). This school of thought is predicated on the idea that education is context driven and that each school community knows how best to meet the needs of its students. This school of thought is principally driven by issues of equality, equity, and social justice. This approach is particularly appealing to school-based educators working in the urban middle and high schools. As Mr. Adams and Ms. Collins suggest, in principle the reforms emanating from NCLB are good ideas, but there must be enough flexibility built into such reforms to meet the specific needs of students across various schooling contexts. Ms. Collins suggested that educating African American students requires the use of pedagogical strategies that teach not only reading, writing, and arithmetic but also how to overcome the doubly marginalized status, in most cases, of being Black and economically disadvantaged. She raises the questions, "Which of the current reforms efforts allow for such training?"

The second school of thought, which none of the aspiring leaders advocated, suggests that reform initiatives should be politically neutral and simply consist of best practices (Slavin & Fashola, 1998). Educational theorists such as Slavin and Stringfield believe that reforms should consist of policies, practices, and pedagogical strategies that are appropriate for all students. While advocates of this school of thought would not suggest that these types of programs are the panacea for urban education, they might argue that they do allow the school to stay focused on teaching and learning in a consistent way. Proponents of this ideology include policymakers and researchers who suggest that the fundamental transformation of urban schools must be facilitated by externally developed reform models. Stringfield and his colleagues argue that externally developed programs and external consultants can be effective in stimulating and supporting local efforts to improve practice (Stringfield, Datnow, Herman, & Berkeley, 1997). While the viability of externally developed whole school reform has been included in the educational policy discourse for several decades, the recent success of several of these reform models has shifted the debate (see Berends, 2000; Bodilly, 1998; Herman, 1999). The debate is no longer about whether or not they are effective, but under what conditions the reforms work best.

LEADING WITH A PURPOSE

The second micropolitical leadership challenge identified by this group of aspiring school administrators is how to lead with a moral purpose. Perhaps one of the strongest commonalities among the participants in this study was an intrinsic desire to make a difference in the lives of the students and communities they serve. Ms. Brown, Ms. Soto, and Mr. Smith all talked about leading with a purpose, seeking to empower their students to be able to take advantage of the educational opportunities afforded them. To a large extent, this was the purpose that all five aspiring administrators gave for desiring to pursue an administrative position.

For the participants in this study, the need to lead with a purpose created a tension because the ideological position that directs and guides their practice is shaped by what Dewey (1909/ 1975) has called "moral ideals." Fullan (2001) contended that moral purpose is about both ends and means. In education, an important end is to make a difference in the lives of the students.

However, the means of obtaining that end is where the aspiring principals in this study and the current reform strategies diverge. While there was a strong ideological commitment to the issues of social justice, the educators in the study also spoke about the difficulties of sustaining such a focus when students continue to underperform on a myriad performance indicators. It is this reality that creates this ongoing tension. There was a strong sentiment among the participants that many of the current reform efforts, because of the explicit absence of a focus on culture, local context, and equity issues, will not be successful in narrowing the achievement gap.

Developing a Culturally Diverse and Sensitive Staff

The third micropolitical challenge identified by this group of educators was the issue of developing a culturally diverse and sensitive staff. Although the United States and its schools are undergoing a dramatic demographic shift where the percentage of students of color is increasing, the nation's teacher corps remains overwhelmingly White (Foster, 2004, 2005), comprising more than 86% of the teacher workforce (Howard, 2000; Sleeter, 2001). Thus, the vast majority of urban schools are staffed by individuals who have different racial, cultural, and socioeconomic backgrounds than the students and the communities in which they teach and lead. While teacher/student racial congruence might improve engagement and achievement of African American students (Cooper & Jordan, 2003; Lomotey, 1993; Mitchell, 1992), the contrast of the teaching force with the level of integration in our public schools underscores the critical role that White educators play in challenging the systemic nature of inequality inherent in the current educational system. Participants in this study felt pressure of being able to create schooling environments where teachers are not only able to connect with and relate to African American students but also able to confront the status quo and advocate social justice for all students. Although many individuals training to be urban school educators have good intentions and a commitment to the students that they serve, they lack exposure to the life experiences of the students and fail to have high, realistic expectations for success. This group of prospective school leaders talked about

making sure that the education of African American students does not become synonymous with low expectations. Ms. Soto captured this sentiment when asked what would be her number one priority when she became a site administrator:

> I want to create a culture in my school where all students, [and particularly African American] have the intellectual capacity to achieve at high academic levels and that school structures, not the children themselves, are reformed to bring about increased achievement.

Conclusion

The implications from this study are clear: The African American educators in the study who were being prepared for urban school leadership believe that the strategies used to enact the transformation of urban schools are largely ineffective ways to positively change the core functions of the institution—teaching and learning. Assisting aspiring administrators in balancing the political realities of urban schools (greater use of externally developed reform models) with their lack of support for the type of reforms being implemented is a difficult but necessary function of principal preparation programs. The tensions that aspiring school administrators experience regarding notions of best practices and their own understandings of effective teaching and learning for urban students should be paramount in the reform debate if we are to improve the schooling experience of African American students.

Enacting a transformative vision for urban education, a vision that demands high-quality educational opportunities for all students, requires school leaders who are open to pushing the boundaries that often constrain fundamental change in large bureaucratic organizations such as schools (Cooper & Peebles, 2006). Ironically, this is supposedly addressed by the mandates of NCLB. There is an obvious contradiction, in that policies aimed at ameliorating such issues end up exacerbating them. Pushing the boundaries first requires the school leader to have a clear vision of what is important and the strategies needed to accomplish the goals. The issue is not how to undermine reform efforts; rather, to find ways to use reform programs to build on the strengths of the students. Oftentimes this necessitates strong collective leadership to create an environment where implementing reforms with a great deal of fidelity is the expectation and norm. Once the classroom teacher understands and internalizes the intent behind the reform and owns it, it can be adapted to the local context.

Understanding the local context is critical to the success of educational reform. Because schools in urban centers remain racially separated, isolated, and underresourced, school leaders must have a vision that pushes beyond the status quo. Research is needed to explore ways to effectively develop an equity agenda. According to Barbra and Krovetz (2005), an equity agenda places at the forefront the goal of achieving equal outcomes for all students and specifically racial minority students such as African Americans. Barbra and Krovetz noted,

> An equity agenda acknowledges that students enter the education system with differing needs and that the way resources are distributed can impact outcomes. It acknowledges that the group performance outcomes achieved within the public education system are indeed unequal and that if resources are distributed equally or evenly, uneven outcomes will only continue and potentially increase. Furthermore, the distribution of resources (money, quality of facilities, and quality of teaching) is seen as a variable within the organization's control. (p. 18)

An equity agenda can be a tool for looking at why and how schools are unjust for some students, imagining the role schools can play in reconstructing a healthy social order and a tool that can facilitate the leadership strategies and practices that will bring about that reconstruction process.

NOTES

1. For the purpose of confidentiality, pseudonyms are used for all participants in the study.

2. The Academic Performance Index (API) is the cornerstone of California's Public Schools Accountability Act of 1999. The purpose of the API is to measure the academic performance and growth of schools. It is a numeric index (or scale) that ranges from a low of 200 to a high of 1,000. A school's score on the API is an indicator of a school's performance level. The statewide API performance target for all schools is 800. A school's growth is measured by how well it is moving toward or past that goal (www.cde.ca.gov/ta/ac/ap/apidescription.asp).

3. AVID stands for advancement via individual determination. This college prep program targets students in the academic middle—B, C, and even D students—who have the desire to go to college and the willingness to work hard. These are students who are capable of completing rigorous curriculum but are falling short of their potential. Typically, they will be the first in their families to attend college, and many are from low-income or minority families. AVID pulls these students out of their unchallenging courses and puts them on the college track: acceleration instead of remediation (www.avidonline.org).

REFERENCES

Baker, J. A. (1998). The social context of school satisfaction among urban, low-income African-American students. *School Psychology Quarterly, 13*, 25–44.

Barbra, M., & Krovetz, M. (2005). Preparing principals to lead the equity agenda. *Educational Leadership Administration, 17*, 11–22.

Berends, M. (2000). Teacher-reported effects of new American School designs: Exploring relationships to teacher background and school context. *Educational Evaluation and Policy Analysis, 22*(1), 65–82.

Blasé, J. (1991). The micropoltical perspective. In J. Blasé (Ed.), *The politics of life in schools: Power, conflict, and cooperation*. Newbury Park, CA: Sage.

Bodilly, S. J. (1998). *Lessons from new American schools' scale-up phase: Prospects for bringing designs to multiple schools*. Santa Monica, CA: Rand.

Bogdan, R. C., & Biklen, S. (1992). *Qualitative research for education: An introduction to theory and methods*. Toronto, Ontario, Canada: Allyn & Bacon.

Boykin, A. W. (1986). The triple quandary and the schooling of Afro-American children. In U. Neisser (Ed.), *School achievement of minority children: New prospective* (pp. 57–92). London: Lawrence Erlbaum.

Bryk, A. S. (1994). More good news that school organization matters. *Issues in restructuring schools*. Madison: University of Wisconsin Press.

Cabrera, N. L., & Padilla, A. M. (2004). Entering and succeeding in the "Culture of College": The story of two Mexican heritage students.

Hispanic Journal of Behavioral Sciences, 26(2), 152–170.

Cambron-McCabe, T., & McCarthy, M. (2005). Educating school leaders for social justice. *Educational Policy, 19*(1), 201–222.

Conchas, G. (2001). Structuring failure and success. Understanding the variability in Latino school engagement. *Harvard Educational Review, 71,* 475–504.

Cooper, R. (1998). *Socio-cultural and within-school factors that affect the quality of implementation of school-wide programs* (Report No. 28). Baltimore: Center for the Social Organization of Schools, Johns Hopkins University.

Cooper, R., & Jordan, W. (2003). Cultural issues in comprehensive school reform. *Urban Education, 38*(4), 380–397.

Cooper, R., & Peebles, L. (2006). *Prospective principals' openness to organizational change driven by NCLB and the education of African American students.* Manuscript submitted for publication.

Cooper, R., Slavin, R. E., & Madden, N. (1998). Improving the quality of implementation of whole-school change through the use of a national reform network. *Education and Urban Society, 30*(3), 385–408.

Cooper, R., & Yamamura, E. (2005, April). *Latino adolescent peer groups: Academic supporters or suppressors?* Paper presented at the annual meeting of the American Educational Research Association, Montreal, Quebec, Canada.

Darling-Hammond, L. (1999). *Teacher quality and student achievement: A review of state policy evidence.* Seattle: Center for the Study of Teaching and Policy, University of Washington.

Datnow, A. (2005). The sustainability of comprehensive school reform models in changing district and state contexts. *Educational Administration Quarterly, 41,* 121–153.

Datnow, A., Hubbard, L., & Mehan, H. (2002). *Extending educational research: One school to many.* New York: Routlege

Delpit, L. (1995). *Other people's children: Cultural conflict in the classroom.* New York: New Press.

Dewey, J. (1975). *Moral principals in education.* Carbondale: Southern Illinois University Press. (Original work published 1909)

Donato, R., Menchaca, M., & Valencia, R. R. (1991). Segregation, desegregation, and the integration of Chicano students: Problems and prospects. In R. R. Valencia (Ed.), *Chicano school failure and success: Research and policy agendas for the 1990's.* New York: Falmer Press.

Driscoll, A. K. (1999). Dropout among immigrant and native Hispanic youth. *Internal Migration Review, 33,* 857–863.

Foster, L. (2004). Administrator and teacher recruitment and selection post-Brown: Issues, challenges, and strategies. *Journal of School Public Relations, 25*(2), 220–232.

Foster, L. (2005). The practice of educational leadership in African American communities of learning, context, scope, and meaning. *Educational Administration Quarterly, 41*(4), 698–700.

Fullan, M. (2001). *Leading in a culture of change.* San Francisco: Jossey-Bass.

Fuman, G., & Gruenewald, D. (2004). Expanding the landscape of social justice: A critical ecological analysis. *Educational Administration Quarterly, 40*(1), 47–76.

Gainey, D. D. (1994). The American high school and change: An unsettling process. *NASSP Bulletin, 78*(506), 26–35.

Gordon, E. W., & Yowell, C. (1994). Educational reforms of students at-risk: Cultural dissonance as a risk factor in the development of students. In R. J. Rossi (Ed.), *Educational reforms and students at-risk* (pp. 51–69). New York: Teachers College Press.

Guinier, L., & Torres, G. (2001). *The miner's canary: Enlisting race, resisting power, transforming democracy.* Cambridge, MA: Harvard University Press.

Hao, L., & Bonstead-Bruns, M. (1998). Parent–child differences in educational expectations and the academic achievement of immigrant and native students. *Sociology of Education, 71*(3), 175–198.

Harvey, W. B., & Anderson, E. L. (2005). *Minorities in higher education 2003–2004: Twenty-first annual status report.* Washington, DC: American Council on Education.

Herman, R. (1999). *An educator's guide to school wide reform.* Arlington, VA: Educational Research Service.

High, C., Scribner, J., & Clark, T. (2001, April). *The micro-politics of a faculty-led school reform.* Paper presented at the Annual Meeting of the American Educational Research Association, Seattle, WA.

Howard, G. (2000). White teachers at the crossroads. *Teaching Tolerance Magazine, 18,* 13–17.

Jones-Wilson, F. C. (1990). The state of African American education. In K. Lomotey (Ed.), *Going to school: The African American experience* (pp. 31–51). Albany: State University of New York Press.

Jordan, W., & Cooper, R. (2003). High school reform and Black male students: Limits and possibilities of policy and practice. *Urban Education, 38*(2), 196–216.

Karpinski, C. (2006). Bearing the burden of desegregation: Black principals and *Brown. Urban Education, 41*(3), 237–276.

Klecker, B., & Loadman, W. E. (1999). Measuring principals' openness to change on three dimensions: Affective, cognitive and behavioral.

Journal of Instructional Psychology, 26(4), 213–225.

Kober, N. (2001). *It takes more than testing: Closing the achievement gap.* Washington, DC: Center on Education Policy.

Lagerwey, M. D., & Phillips, E. (2003). Voices from the pipeline: High school completion among rural Latinos. *Journal of Cultural Diversity, 10,* 42–49.

Lee, J. (2006). *Tracking achievement gaps and assessing the impact of NCLB on the gaps: An in depth look into national and state reading and math outcome trends.* Cambridge, MA: Civil Rights Project at Harvard University.

Lee, V., & Burkam, D. T. (2003). Dropping out of high school: The role of school organization and structure. *American Educational Research Journal, 40*(2), 353–393.

Lipman, P. (1998). *Race, class, and power in school restructuring.* Albany: State University of New York Press.

Lomotey, K. (1993). African American principals: Bureaucrat/administrators and ethnihumanists. *Urban Education, 27,* 395–412.

Malico, M., & Langan, D. (2003, July 9). *Paige focuses on reading during* No Child Left Behind *tour across America.* Retrieved January 10, 2007, from www.ed.gov/news/pressreleases/2002/07/07092002b.html

Marshall, C., & Scribner, J. (1991). It's all political: Inquiry into the micro politics of education. *Education and Urban Society, 23*(4), 347–355.

Martinez, C. R., DeGarmo, D. S., & Eddy, J. M. (2004). Promoting academic success among Latino youth. *Hispanic Journal of Behavioral Science, 26,* 128–151.

Mitchell, V. (1992). African American students in exemplary urban high schools: The interaction of school practices and student actions. In M. Saravia-Shore & S. Arvizu (Eds.), *Cross-cultural literacy: Ethnographies of communication in multiethnic classrooms* (pp. 19–36). New York: Garland.

Mosqueda, E. (2005). *The role of language and institutional arrangements in learning mathematics with understanding for Latino English learners.* Unpublished qualifying paper, Harvard Graduate School of Education.

Murphy, J. (1994). Redefining the principalship in restructuring schools. *NASSP Bulletin, 78*(560), 94–99.

Murphy, J., & Datnow A. (2003). *Leadership lessons from comprehensive school reforms.* Thousand Oaks, CA: Sage.

Natriello, G., McDill, E. L., & Pallas, A. M. (1990). *Schooling disadvantaged children: Racing against catastrophe.* New York: Teachers College Press.

Noguera, P. (2001). Transforming urban schools through investments in social capital. In *Motions Magazine.* Retrieved August 18, 2003, from www.inmotionmagazine.com/pncap1.html

O'Day, J. A. (2002). Complexity, accountability, and school improvement. *Harvard Education Review, 72*(3), 293–327.

Oakes, J., & Lipton, M. (1992). Detracking schools: Early lessons from the field. *Phi Delta Kappan, 73*(6), 317–328.

Orfield, G., Losen, D., Wald, J., & Swanson, C. (2004). Losing our future: How minority youth are being left behind by the graduation rate crisis. *American Educational Research Journal, 40*(2), 353–393.

Ross, S. T., Stringfield, S., Sanders, W. L., & Wright, P. (2003). Inside systemic elementary school reform: Teacher effects and teacher mobility. *School Effectiveness and School Improvement, 14*(1), 73–110.

Rouse, K. G. (1998). Resilience from poverty and stress. *Human Development and Family Life Bulletin, 4*(1), 1–10.

Rumberger, R. W. (1987). High school dropouts: A review of issues and evidence. *Review of Educational Research, 57,* 101–121.

Rumberger, R. W. (1995). Dropping out of middle school: A multilevel analysis of students and schools. *American Educational Research Journal, 32,* 538–625.

Slavin, R. E., & Fashola, O. S. (1998). *Show me the evidence! Proven and promising programs for America's schools.* Thousand Oaks, CA: Corwin Press.

Sleeter, C. E. (2001). Preparing teachers for culturally diverse schools: Research and the overwhelming presence of Whiteness. *Journal of Teacher Education, 52,* 94–103.

Spillane, J. P. (1999). External reform initiatives and teachers' efforts to reconstruct their practice: The mediating role of teachers' zones of enactment. *Journal of Curriculum Studies, 31*(2), 1–33.

Spillane, J. P., Halvorson, R., & Diamond, J. B. (2001). Investigating school leadership practice: A distributed perspective. *Educational Researcher, 30*(3), 23–28.

Stringfield, S., Datnow, A., Herman, R., & Berkeley, C. (1997). Introduction to the Memphis restructuring initiative. *School Effectiveness and School Improvement, 8*(2), 3–35.

Sunderman, G., Kim, J., & Orfield, G. (2005). *2005 NCLB meets school realities: Lessons from the field.* Thousand Oaks, CA: Corwin Press.

Taylor, A. R. (1991). Social competence and the early school transition: Risk and protective factors for African-American children. *Education and Urban Society, 24,* 15–26.

Taylor, S. J., & Bogdan, R. (1998). *Introduction to qualitative research methods* (3rd ed.). New York: Wiley.

Tillman, L. C. (2004). (Un)intended consequences? The impact of the *Brown v. Board of Education* decision on the employment status of Black educators. *Education and Urban Society, 36,* 280–303.

Timperley, H. S. (2005). Distributed leadership: Developing theory from practice. *Journal of Curriculum Studies, 37*(4), 395–420.

U.S. Department of Education. (1997). *The condition of education, 1997.* Washington, DC: National Center for Educational Statistics, Government Printing Office.

Wimberley, G. L. (2002). *School relationships foster success for African American students.* Iowa City, IA: ACT.

York-Barr, J., & Duke, K. (2004). What do we know about teacher leadership? Findings from two decades of scholarship. *Review of Educational Research, 74*(3), 255–316.

13

THE CONFLUENCE OF RACE, GENDER, AND GENERATION IN THE LIVES OF AFRICAN AMERICAN WOMEN PRINCIPALS

TONDRA L. LODER-JACKSON

A frican American women have only recently begun to tap the glass ceiling of the principalship. The typical principal in the United States is a middle-aged White man in a middle-class White suburban school (Doud & Keller, 1999; Strizek, Pittsonberger, Riordan, Lyter, & Orlofsky, 2006). In spite of the spotty popular media images of African American women principals, most notably, the sassy and self-assured "Ms. Regina Clark" of the Steve Harvey Show (Lathan, 1996–2002) and the no-nonsense principals portrayed in the movies *Radio* (Garner, Scanlon, & Robbins, 2003) and *Coach Carter* (Carter, Schwahn, & Gatins, 2005), the reality is that African American men and women combined make up only 10.6% of all U.S. public school principals with the majority leading in urban public schools (Strizek et al., 2006). The educational leadership scholarship mirrors this reality as its portrayal of African American women's advancement to and experiences within the principalship remains sparse and sporadic (Allen, Jacobson, & Lomotey, 1996; Bell & Chase, 1994; Bloom & Erlandson, 2003; McGee Banks, 1995; Nance, 2006). Tillman (2004a) pointed out that the existing body of literature on African American women principals is woefully inadequate because it approaches these principals from a White feminist perspective and obscures their experiences under the catch-all heading of "women and minorities." These limitations result in what Tillman referred to as a "privileging of knowledge that often devalues the leadership theory and practice of African American female principals in the educational leadership discourse" (p. 126).

AUTHOR'S NOTE: The author's current research study cited in this chapter was funded by grants from the Spencer Foundation (#200500140) and the University of Alabama at Birmingham's Office of Equity and Diversity (OED) for a project titled *Bridging the tradition of activism and professionalism within the context of contemporary urban education: Perspectives from Birmingham educators born pre– and post–Civil Rights Movement*. The views expressed here are those of the author only and not necessarily those espoused by the Foundation or the OED.

A small yet emerging body of research on African American women principals indicates that these school leaders have unique leadership styles and orientations grounded in their distinctive history as the descendants of a people oppressed by slavery, Jim Crow, and pervasive discrimination and prejudice (Bloom & Erlandson, 2003; Dillard, 1995). African American women principals are committed to excellence in education and community uplift and are influenced by a strong Black prophetic religious tradition (Jean-Marie, James, & Bynum, 2006). Indeed for many African American women principals, the work of guiding African American children is viewed more as a spiritual calling than as a job (Harris & Ballenger, 2004). Contemporary African American women principals view their work as an extension of the commitment to "uplift the race" pioneered by their predecessors in the 19th and early 20th centuries (Beauboeuf, 2004; Beauboeuf-Lafontant, 2002).

In an effort to augment and bolster the existing literature on African American women principals, in this chapter I examine the leadership capacity of this distinctive cadre of leaders from three perspectives:

1. their emergence to the principalship in the post–Civil Rights Era in the face of institutionalized racism and pervasive discrimination;

2. their struggle to integrate the spheres of work and family in the face of persistent institutionalized sexism and despite the hard-won gains of gender equity post–Civil Rights and women's movements; and

3. their distinctive intergenerational outlook on the role that African American women principals play in carrying forth the tradition of activist leadership in the 21st century.

I address the first two perspectives through an analysis of the historical literature and prior research on African American women principals. I examine the third perspective primarily through the empirical lens of emergent findings from my current life history study of Birmingham educators born during the pre– and post–Civil Rights Era. As a framework for interrogating these three perspectives, in the next section I emphasize the salience of examining *generation*, in confluence with race and gender, in understanding the leadership capacity of multigenerational African American women principals in the 21st century.

THE SALIENCE OF GENERATION IN THE LIVES OF AFRICAN AMERICAN WOMEN PRINCIPALS

Although the emerging literature on African American women principals helps us understand their unique leadership approaches and dilemmas (Allen et al., 1996; Bloom & Erlandson, 2003; Dillard, 1995), this literature typically fails to take into account the important role that generational location plays in shaping African American women principals' opportunities and structural constraints. In particular, we know very little about how the lives of African American women principals are distinguished by being born and coming of age on opposite sides of the latter 20th-century Civil Rights and women's movements. Furthermore, intergenerational life history perspectives on African American women principals are virtually nonexistent in the education scholarship (Loder, 2005a).Very little is known about the juxtaposed self-reported life stories of African American women principals born on opposite sides of the Civil Rights Era. These omissions contribute to an obscure understanding of how efforts to promote racial and gender equity in the principalship have progressed or reversed over time. This gap severely limits our knowledge and understanding of the continuities and discontinuities that underlie the tradition of African American educational leadership across the pre– and post–Civil Rights Eras.

With the exception of a few publications on how the work experiences of African American male and female teachers and African American *male* principals have been affected by the landmark *Brown v. Board of Education* Supreme Court case (Dingus, 2006; Foster, 1990, 1993, 1997; Siddle Walker, 2000; Tillman, 2004b), very little has been published about how the lives and professions of African American women principals have been affected by these social movements. Johnson's (2004, 2006) accounts of African American women activist educators in New York City, which highlights the contributions of Harlem's first African American woman principal, Gertrude Elise McDougald Ayer, is noteworthy but rare. Generational perspectives on African American women principals are critical given that both schools and principals' roles have changed dramatically since the *Brown* era. Principals today confront challenges and problems that did not exist 50 years ago, particularly those who lead in urban schools. Since the *Brown* decision, student bodies have become more diverse and have more needs, and social and technological changes have made the role of principals increasingly complex (Goldring & Rallis, 1993; Loder, 2005c).

An examination of African American women principals born on opposite sides of the Civil Rights and women's movements must be considered in light of Mannheim's (1952) *problem of generations*. Mannheim defined *generation* as "similarly located contemporaries [who] participate in a common destiny and in the ideas and concepts which are in some way bound up with its unfolding" (p. 306). He proposed that the critical link between generational succession and social progress is a shared consciousness among members of a generation. Members of different generations traverse the same lifetime, yet they experience and live in qualitatively different subjective eras. Thus, the critical challenge for scholars at any given point in time is to attempt to sort out the individual voices of multiple generations and to create venues for their fresh contact through intergenerational boundary crossing.

Examining the divergent experiences of African American women principals born prior to and after the Civil Rights and women's movements could prove enlightening and informative given their strikingly different professional opportunities and social realities (Loder, 2005d). African American women born on opposite sides of the Civil Rights Era confronted decidedly different opportunities and constraints for "what a woman could be and do" (Shaw, 1996). African American women principals born pre–Civil Rights were young adults embarking on their first jobs as teachers during the turbulent and rapidly changing policy context of 1960s. Hence, they came of age professionally during the passage of the Civil Rights Act of 1964, the Voting Rights Act of 1965, and Dr. Martin Luther King's and Malcolm X's assassinations. The professional options available to African American women of the Civil Rights generation were woefully restricted, as they were generally channeled into traditionally "female"

careers such as teaching, nursing, and social work (Amott & Matthaei, 1996).

In contrast, African American women principals born after the Civil Rights and women's movements—referred to as the "Generation X" and "Hip Hop" generation—came of age during one of the most conservative political and economic eras in recent history. The birth year bracket for this generation is generally documented between 1965 and 1980 (Bakari, 2002). Coming of age during this era resulted in ambivalent opportunities for young African Americans. The birth of the Hip Hop generation and culture grew out of the early 1970's climate of police brutality, poverty, and unemployment (Dyson, 2007; Ford, 2006). This generation has been defined as the first in the African American historical trajectory to fully partake of the fruits of the Civil Rights and Black power movements (Bakari, 2002). On the one hand, the African American middle class has been growing and rates of college attendance and graduation among African Americans have been increasing; on the other hand, there has been an increasingly impoverished urban and rural African American population, rising crime rates in urban neighborhoods, and increasingly punitive and inequitable political and judicial responses to crime, which have spurred a burgeoning African American prison population (Bositis, 2001; Wilson, 1987). This unique context distinguishes the life experiences, perspectives, and professional opportunities and constraints of post–Civil-Rights-born African American educators (Loder, 2005c; Williams & Evans-Winters, 2005).

With this context in mind, being born on opposite sides of the Civil Rights Era markedly distinguishes how African American women perceive and confront structural barriers and opportunities on their journey to become principals. Since these movements, women's professional options have increased significantly. Yet as underscored by Shakeshaft (1999) almost a decade ago, there is a conspicuous gap in the education scholarship linking U.S. social movements to women's progress in accessing jobs in school leadership and administration.

The next section highlights the emergence of African American women principals in the post–Civil Rights Era, emphasizing how their generational differences distinguish their pathways to school leadership.

The Emergence of African American Women Principals in the Post–Civil Rights Era

Two important public policy legacies of the Civil Rights and women's movements as they relate to the advancement of African American women to the principalship are Title VII of the Civil Rights Act of 1964 and Title IX of the Education Amendments of 1972. Title VII opened up employment and career advancement opportunities in white-collar professions and government jobs for African American women (Amott & Matthaei, 1996). Title IX barred gender discrimination in any education program or activity receiving federal monies, which opened doors for women to move up to the ranks of school leadership (Mertz, 2003).

Although both White and African American women have been traditionally relegated to "female" jobs, being granted opportunities to move into the "professional" sphere, as opposed to domestic work, carried a unique meaning for African American women born prior to the Civil Rights Era. From slavery to Jim Crow, African American women have been traditionally relegated to the lowest-status jobs in U.S. society, which were physically oppressive and emotionally burdensome, often requiring them to work under precarious and substandard conditions (Harley, 2002). Even as recent as 1980, more African American women were concentrated in domestic service than in white- or pink-collar jobs (Amott & Matthaei, 1996). Understandably, African American women privileged enough to attend college and become teachers had a strong sense of personal and community pride, because the teaching profession required higher levels of skill and far less subordination to and control by White employers (Shaw, 1996). Yet even while teaching has been traditionally viewed as a respectable profession and highly valued by the African American community, the pressure to teach diverted many African American women from other vocational pursuits to which they were tabooed at the time such as doctors and lawyers (Etter-Lewis, 1993).

The downside of these civil rights gains, which opened doors for African American women to pursue other professions, has been the decline in their long-standing pursuit of teaching careers that are typically a stepping stone to the principalship (Gordon, 1997; Hudson & Holmes, 1994; Irvine, 2003; King, 1993a, 1993b). Some scholars contend that the landmark *Brown v. Board of Education* Supreme Court decision has had both positive and negative impacts on the livelihood of African American educators. *Brown's* most significant gains are said to have occurred among those Black educators "who were 'ready' to participate, contribute, and play leadership roles in the more-open society wrought by the civil rights movement that followed the 1954 decision" (Hudson & Holmes, 1994). On the other hand, many African American teachers and administrators fared poorly due to the loss of jobs, status, and socioemotional ties to communities with which they closely identified. Some scholars contend that the long-term effects of school desegregation have been to divorce African American teachers and principals from African American students, and to drain a talented pool of African American educators from public schools (Coffin, 1972; Dingus, 2006; Foster, 1990, 1993, 1997; Hudson & Holmes, 1994; Siddle Walker, 2000; Tillman, 2004a, 2004b). According to Wesson (1995), the loss of African American principals "created a leadership vacuum in communities that has not since been recovered" (p. 152). Yet despite this decline, the K-12 education profession continues to be one among a few careers that afford African American women a realizable opportunity to advance into leadership. However, barriers to their advancement continue to persist (Loder, 2005d).

In my previous research of African American women principals and aspiring principals born pre– and post–Civil Rights, being born on opposite sides of the Civil Rights and women's movements markedly distinguishes how African American women perceive and confront structural barriers and opportunities on their journey to become principals (Loder, 2005a, 2005c, 2005d). African American women principals who came of age prior to and during the Civil Rights movement became teachers mainly because this was one among a few professional options open to women during that time. Although these women did not recount stories of blatant racism and sexism, they were quite cognizant of the influence of the "invisible hand" of institutionalized racism and sexism in narrowing and blocking their professional opportunities and aspirations. These women coped with their deferred dreams of not being able to pursue their desired aspirations by later embracing the vocation of teaching as a divine calling from God. Their response is consistent with prior literature on the salience of religion and spirituality in the lives of African American women, particularly recent work citing spirituality as a critical lens through which women school leaders create meaning out of their work and are empowered to confront the daily struggles and challenges associated with leadership (Harris & Ballenger, 2004).

In contrast, the life stories of African American women who were born in the post–Civil Rights Era did not reflect personal experiences with *overt* racism and sexism or even persistent institutionalized and covert racism and sexism. Early grassroots efforts to democratize the principalship paved the way for both older and younger women in this study to become principals. However, because women in the post–Civil Rights generation began embarking on teaching careers 30 odd years after women in the pre–Civil Rights generation, even while both cohorts became principals around the same time, each cohort had been exposed to very different professional opportunity structures early on in their lives. Consequently, younger women's life stories reflected the generational privilege associated with coming of age just as new horizons of professional opportunity in the education profession were beginning to crystallize. These women appeared to know where they wanted to go and how they intended to get there. In marked contrast to their older counterparts, the younger women recounted their early career aspirations in a manner that was self-directed and assured. Contrary to the older women, these younger women had acquired a newly ushered-in language of privilege that encompassed words foreign to their older counterparts such as "aspirations" and "individual choice." However, along with these new choices and relative freedom to advance to leadership arose new dilemmas for younger and older women principals alike. A common concern acknowledged by all women administrators in my previous research, and one that had the potential to drastically limit their capacity to lead once they finally obtained the principalship, was the struggle to integrate the competing demands of work and family.

THE FALL-OUT OF EQUAL RIGHTS: THE STRUGGLE TO INTEGRATE WORK AND FAMILY LIFE

As aforementioned, this chapter attempts to move the lived experiences of African American women principals from the margin to the center of educational leadership discourse. A notable critique of the literature on "women and minorities" in the principalship is that it obscures and omits the distinctive and important experiences and contributions of African American women. Coursen, Mazzarella, Jeffress, and Hadderman (1989) argued that "what is true for blacks is not necessarily true for members of other racial minorities and may have nothing to do with women" (p. 87). Although this statement resonates with my approach to examining the lives of African American women principals, the latter part of this statement runs the risk of perpetuating the very weakness in the educational leadership literature that the authors attempt to redress. A serious examination of the lives of African American women principals must deal squarely with gender, sexuality, and sexism (Collins, 2000, 2004). And while many scholars have purported that the African American women principals are distinctive from their White female and Black male counterparts, there are *some* commonalities they share with these counterparts. The struggle that African American women principals confront as they attempt to integrate the spheres of work and family is an illustrative case in point.

As the demands of the principalship and home life become increasingly complex and taxing, coupled with an inadequate governmental and institutional policy and programmatic response to work-family balance issues, African American women principals must rely on their own resourcefulness and ingenuity to get the job done both at work and at home. Hence, the availability or lack of support from family members, especially from spouses or partners, can make or break a woman's decision to become a principal (Bruckner, 1998; Loder, 2005e; Meyers & Ginsberg, 1994; Nichols, 2002; Young & McLeod, 2001). To frame this dilemma within a broader sociopolitical context, African American women principals in the 21st century confront a "new politics and discourse of gender and race" (Marshall, 1993) unlike any encountered by women prior to the dubious gains of the Civil Rights and women's movement. As scholars have noted, this new politics effectively masks the subtle and detrimental effects of institutionalized sexism (Grogan, 1999; Marshall, 1993). Although they share commonalities of gender, African American women principals experience and manage the new politics of gender and race as it relates to work-family conflicts in different ways. Their diverse strategies for managing gender and race politics are shaped by their unique historical and contemporary experiences.

Key factors that distinguish the lived experiences of African American women and White women principals are the history of slavery, oppression, and discrimination of African Americans and the differential labor market history for these two groups. In other words, the imprint of racism and segregation and the multiplicative effects of race, gender, and class oppression are deeply woven into the lives of African American women (Collins, 2000). Compared with White women, African American women have had higher labor market force participation rates at consistently lower wages and status levels (Malveaux, 1987; Newsome, 2002; Willson & Hardy, 2002). Furthermore, because African American women spend fewer years in marriage than do White women (Lane et al., 2004; Taeuber, 1996; Tucker & Mitchell-Kernan, 1995), gainful employment is more critical for long-term security for African American women compared with White women (Landry, 2000; Willson & Hardy, 2002). Being married *and* employed offers the most optimum chances for economic security (Willson & Hardy, 2002). However, being married may pose marital conflicts for African American women in nontraditional versus traditional women careers (Burlew & Johnson, 1992).

Given the historic role of the Black family in buffering African Americans from the damaging effects of slavery, oppression, and discrimination, African American women principals' upward mobility must be examined in light of kinship bonds (Higginbotham & Weber, 1992; McAdoo, 1997; Miller & Vaughn, 1997; Walker, 1993). Unlike the individualistic model of White male upward mobility, career mobility for African American women principals depends on relationships with immediate family, extended kin, and community members. African American women are more likely than White women to reside in intergenerational families and assume care-giving responsibility for younger successive generations (Burton & Devries, 1992; Burton & Dilworth-Anderson, 1991; Caputo, 1999; Kolb, 2000; Minkler & Fuller-Thomson, 2000).

Both race and generational location uniquely shape women administrators' perspectives about what they are up against and what resources they have available to them as they attempt to negotiate demanding work-family conflicts. African American women administrators are more likely than White women administrators to rely on women kin and extended family for child care and household support (Loder, 2005e). Sometimes they initiate intergenerational living arrangements so that their mothers and grandmothers can care for their children while they pursue their career goals. Similar to their White female counterparts, African American women principals also rely on their spouses for support, particularly those born post–Civil Rights and women's movements. Younger generations of African American women aspiring principals are especially cautious about work-family integration and may opt to remain in what they consider to be lesser demanding roles (e.g., assistant principal) while they give birth to and raise younger children (Loder, 2005e). This may be explained, at least in part, by contemporary African American and White women's unbalanced options for marriage and family. Demographic projections indicate that White women's options for marriage are far more promising than those for Black women (Lane et al., 2004). Therefore, younger African American women may opt to prioritize family over the principalship because delaying family poses more of a personal risk for them than it does for White women. Furthermore, this trade-off is economically rational in light of studies that indicate that being married and employed offer the most stable form of economic security for Black women (Willson & Hardy, 2002).

Even with family support, the overwhelming responsibility for managing work-family conflicts falls largely on African American women principals. Therefore, the possession of expert managerial skills is often an unspoken and latent prerequisite for becoming a principal. This suggests a strong tendency toward self-selection in the principalship of those women who either (a) do not have pressing and competing family obligations or (b) have unusually resilient, flexible, and accommodating systems of family support (Loder, 2005e).

How can the workplace be made more amenable to the needs of African American women principals? There is some encouraging news in the arenas of teachers' unions and higher education. The leadership of the American Teacher's Union has in the recent past called for more emphasis on family policy, noting that child care, elder care, family leave, and flexible schedules are among the topics on which unions should be "setting the standard for the rest of the country" (PSRP Conference: Balancing Work and Home, 2001, May/June). On the higher education front, an increasing number of colleges and universities have been attempting to make it easier for faculty, especially junior members, and graduate students to combine their work, school, and family lives (e.g., child care centers, employee vouchers, graduate stipends, tenure clock flexibility, and counseling; Jaschik, 2007). Some sectors of the corporate world are instituting on-site or subsidized child care and elder care, flexible work hours, job sharing, dependent care spending accounts, easy access to employee assistance programs, and supervisory training on the importance of work-life balance (Hobson, Delunas, & Kesic, 2001). It is hoped that these family-friendly innovations will make their way into the spheres of U.S. K-12 schools.

Few scholars would argue that the great strides made in the Civil Rights and women's movements have not affected the way in which African American women's gender roles and work are viewed in American society. However, there is much more work to be done to level the playing field in the principalship so that when African American women do achieve this position, they do not find themselves hamstrung by the "new politics of gender and race," which masks the subtle yet pernicious effects of institutionalized sexism prevalent in the principalship (Marshall, 1993).

AFRICAN AMERICAN WOMEN PRINCIPALS AND THE TRADITION OF ACTIVIST LEADERSHIP: DILEMMAS, CHALLENGES, AND PROMISES IN THE 21ST CENTURY

In the previous sections, I addressed how the leadership capacity of African American women principals has been augmented, yet at times restricted, by the societal and workplace cultural transformations spurred by the hard-won gains of the Civil Rights and women's movements. It is ironic to note that as desegregation policies opened doors for African American women to become principals, these women now find themselves at the helm of extremely troubled urban schools (Loder, 2005c). Since the *Brown v. Board of Education* Supreme Court decision, urban school districts across the nation have experienced severe economic, fiscal, and social problems caused largely by the loss of middle-class White and African American students and families who were formerly invested in urban schools. These problems have been compounded by a rise in the enrollment of students who are socially and economically disenfranchised, shrinking financial commitments from state and federal governments, and the bombardment of negative press coverage of the so-called urban school crisis. African American women principals confront a starkly different professional context than they would have experienced over 50 years ago had they been afforded the opportunity to become principals during that time. As student bodies become increasingly ethnically and economically diverse, and as social and technological changes render the principal's role more complex, African American women principals today confront problems and crises that did not exist for principals prior to the *Brown* decree.

Although there has been some debate about African American educators' significance in advancing social change during the Civil Rights movement, it is clear that at least some could be deemed *activist* leaders (Fairclough, 2001). But what is the capacity for activist leadership among today's African American women principals? In the face of a rapidly changing urban school leadership context, do contemporary African American women principals (both pre– and post–Civil Rights generation) view themselves as possessing the leadership capacity to carry forth the long-standing tradition to uplift the race? Do younger generations of African American women principals, in particular, who were largely buffered from the overt racism and sexism that prevailed in the profession and American society prior to these watershed movements view it as their professional and social obligation to "uplift the race" as has been widely documented among their predecessors? Do older generations of African American women principals share the same bond of commonality to contemporary Black students and their parents who have been socialized in a Hip Hop culture that they do not understand, do not condone, or are reluctant to embrace?

There is disconcerting evidence of historical *discontinuity* in the activist tradition of African American educational leadership. African American educators in urban schools have been especially criticized for failing to carry forth this tradition (Franklin, 1990). One explanation for this failure is a charge made by some scholars that the *Brown* decision has done more harm than good for African American principals by shrinking their numbers shortly after desegregation decrees and eventually divorcing them from their strong support and power bases in African American communities (Coffin, 1972; Dingus, 2006; Foster, 1990, 1993, 1997; Hudson & Holmes, 1994; Siddle Walker, 2000; Tillman, 2004b).

There is also evidence of the phenomenon of "diverging generations," where an increasing number of post–Civil-Rights-born African Americans are attributing their success and failure in attaining the American Dream to individual efforts versus collective struggle and social and historical influence (Bositis, 2001). Although this is the first generation to significantly reap the rewards of the hard-earned battles for civil rights, some commentators have observed that young African Americans confront persistent institutional and *covert* racism and sexism, poverty, and inequality (Cose, 1993; Dyson, 2007; Tarpley, 1995; West, 1993). The self-reliance and lack of institutional memory about the Civil Rights struggles that exists among some younger African Americans poses a formidable threat to keeping the tradition of activist leadership alive in African American education. Alluding to a rift in this tradition, Collins (2000) cautioned that "large numbers of Black children remain warehoused in inner-city schools, sadly, many of them taught by Black teachers who have little institutional memory of . . . activism" (p. 223). Consequently, today's African American women principals grapple with a sense of alienation from the experiences of the Civil Rights struggle as well as feelings of frustration, incompetence, and despair about their inability to promote meaningful change in contemporary African American schools. With this context in mind, conceivably the new crop of African American women principals assuming the helm of schools in the 21st century might be "unprepared politically to recognize and deal with new forms that racism, sexism, and other kinds of oppression now take" (Collins, 2000, p. 223).

Recent qualitative research on post–Civil-Rights-born African American women principals, at least partially, supports Collins's assessment (Loder, 2005b, 2005d). These "generationally privileged" principals, although committed to serving the needs of African American students, grapple with the symbolic meanings of racial identity and community, and lack historical perspective about the long-standing and unfinished struggles to effect change in African American education. Yet there is some encouraging news about the prospects for activist leadership among post–Civil-Rights-generation principals. A recent study on civic involvement among American youth reports a renewed commitment to civic activism and leadership among younger African Americans (Bullock, 2006).

As an extension of my intergenerational life history research, I am currently investigating how Birmingham educators born pre– and post–Civil Rights view the salience of the activism in enacting their roles as administrators and teachers in contemporary metropolitan school districts (Loder, 2005b). The impetus for this inquiry is both scholarly and personal. As a post–Civil-Rights-born scholar and educator, I am gravely concerned by the scholarly contention that African American educators labeled as the "Generation X/Hip Hop Generation" are ill-equipped to effect social change in education because they lack an experiential knowledge and understanding of their historical place within the activist tradition of African American education. Even in the city of Birmingham, Alabama, a former bastion of segregation and epicenter of the Civil Rights movement, and rich with primary and secondary sources documenting its turbulent history, African American K-12 educators confront a host of problems in carrying forth the tradition of activist education.

It is important to note that this dilemma is historical. Fairclough (2001) underscored the dubious portrayal of southern African American educators in the age of Jim Crow. These educators have been both heralded and vilified for their role or lack thereof in fighting for equity and justice in Black schools. As activists, African American educators reportedly instilled a strong sense of racial pride in a world that denigrated their skin color and culture; led efforts to liberate Blacks through literacy; established self-improvement organizations in response to poverty; and were the backbone of the National Association for the Advancement of Colored People. On the other hand, these educators have been portrayed unflatteringly as accommodationists that bowed to the demands and expectations of racist White-led school districts, some even acting as informants to expose members of Civil Rights organizations. Given this context, where on the continuum of Black progress marked by polarities of activism and accommodationism do contemporary southern African American educators fall?

Emergent findings from my present study suggest that African American women principals and aspiring principals describe activism in relative terms. They distinguish between the activism heralded during the 1960s (e.g., marches, sit-ins, organized protests) and the more subtle and, at times, clandestine activism that took place unassumingly in all-Black schools and classrooms of the 1960s, and continues even today. Retired pre–Civil-Rights-generation principal, "Doris," crystallizes this view:

> I hear people call certain people activists . . . [Does that mean] pulling away from the norm? . . . Is it standing up for a belief that sometimes people don't understand? . . . Does the term change with generations? Does it change with activities [or] with a particular concern and struggle? I do see the word "act" there and it means doing something . . . doing something extraordinary. But to me that's relative . . . I think all of us are activists at some point.

From the perspective of Black feminist thought, it is critical to examine the African American women principals' self-reported perspectives on activism rather than to impose on them a global definition of this phenomenon. Collins (2000) has argued that prevailing conceptions of social and political activism and resistance misunderstand the meaning of activism in African American women's lives. Such conceptions focus on "public, official, visible political activity even though unofficial, private, and seemingly invisible spheres of social life and organization may be equally important" (p. 202). According to Collins,

> It may be more useful to assess Black women's activism less by the ideological content of individual Black women's belief systems— whether they hold conservative, reformist, progressive, or radical ideologies based on some predetermined criteria—and more by Black women's collective actions within everyday life that challenge domination in these multifaceted domains. (p. 203)

Accordingly, the education scholarship bears out that African American women have traditionally expressed their activism through acts of teaching and leading in schools, other-mothering, church work, and keeping their communities and families together (Beauboeuf, 2004; Beauboeuf-Lafontant, 2002). Collins (2000) urged scholars to examine the activism of Black women along two dimensions: daily individual struggles for group or professional survival and collective struggles for institutional transformation.

Consistent with emerging commentary on the cultural orientation of post–Civil–Rights-generation African Americans (Bakari, 2002; Dyson, 2007; Tarpley, 1995), my current research bears out that up and coming educators of the Generation X/Hip Hop Generation in Birmingham see themselves as critical bridge builders between pre–Civil-Rights-born educators and post–Civil-Rights-born African American students. This perspective is consistent with scholars Williams and Evans-Winters's (2005) view that "desegregation babies" are the "hope of the civil rights movement" (Title page). Yet some younger educators report that they feel ill-equipped to teach this younger generation about African American history because they lack an experiential knowledge and understanding of the past. They also feel overwhelmed by the pressing problems confronting urban African American youth such as substandard schools, poverty, rampant violence, drugs, teen pregnancy, and a general disregard for education and African American teachers. Thirty-three-year-old "Wilona," an aspiring principal and history teacher reflected on her bridge-building role:

> Even though I didn't live during that time period, I always try to instill [African American history] into my students. [I say], "You just don't understand how far we've come as a race. Education is here; it's up to you to get it" I tell

them, "I didn't live during that time period but my mother instilled this in me. She taught us this so we could know this. This is a part of our history."

Aspiring young African American women principals feel obligated to build bridges of understanding between educators born pre– and post–Civil Rights as well as with their students. But they articulate a need for seasoned veteran mentors to help them and work alongside them to accomplish this monumental task. African American women principals from different generations have much to share with one another. But the isolating role of the principal, and in turn, the small numbers of African American women principals have stifled possibilities for co-mentoring between older and younger principals (Loder & Spillane, 2005). The transition from teacher to administrator results in a loss of former teacher "friends" whom now view the principal as an evaluator or even an enemy (Loder & Spillane, 2005). By sheer numbers there is typically only one principal per school and maybe one or more assistant principals depending on the school's financial and resource capacity. This means new principals have few, if any, peers to bond with within their school and the hectic schedule of the principal makes it difficult to carve time out to collaborate with principals at neighboring or district schools. This leaves African American women principals, already deprived of same-gender and race mentors, feeling lonely at the top (Loder & Spillane, 2005). Hence, finding opportunities to create the space for or to maximize intergenerational conversations among African American women principals concerning the advancement of Black education in the 21st century is essential to fostering "audacious hope in action" (Generett, 2005, Title page). Recent writings on the shifting contexts of Black women educators' identities will not only fill the empirical and intellectual void in this research area but ideally spark intergenerational conversations (Cozart & Price, 2005).

There may be potential barriers to facilitating intergenerational conversations among African American women principals. For example, some younger participants in my study have expressed concerns that their older colleagues appear to be bitter and angry about the past. These younger educators believe that older educators' unwillingness to yield the bitter past of contentious race relations impedes their effectiveness in developing productive interracial relationships in contemporary integrated school and community settings. In addition, younger participants have noted that their older colleagues are not always willing to try to understand or embrace the culture of their urban students and younger administrator and teacher colleagues—expressly, Hip Hop culture. This sentiment was conveyed by "Wilona" a 33-year-old aspiring principal:

> I tolerate more [than older teachers do]. I'm a little more relaxed. But there are just certain things that [older teachers] are not going to put up with. It wasn't acceptable during their time period and it's still not acceptable. Like [boys wearing] earrings, braids, and pants sagging—but even I have a problem with the [pants sagging]. But the earrings don't bother me.

A noticeable subtext in the narratives of older educators is their tendency to make inferences between a perceived breakdown in Black community values, especially the value for education, and a breakdown in urban school discipline. "Doris," a 63-year-old retired principal, who expressed great pride about being born and raised in a historically Black working-class community and attending a historically Black college, lamented about the changes she perceived in her students' attitudes toward education from the beginning of her career in the late 1960s compared with her retirement in the late 1990s. She was especially critical of what she perceived as an anti-intellectual attitude among her urban Black students. She recounted an incident where students booed high-achieving students who were receiving awards at a school assembly.

Doris:	That was the most depressing thing for me. The top 10% of the class being attacked by the lower 15% of the class.
Interviewer:	And that [behavior] was such a contrast from what you just said [about your peers] when you were growing up.
Doris:	Absolutely . . . because my friends were [my] overseers. [They would chide me saying], "you can't [engage in negative behavior] because you're gonna be our teacher."

Evidently, African American women principals who came of age and began working in schools prior to and during the Civil Rights Era were not experiencing the harmonious authoritarian relationships with their students and local school communities that have been portrayed in previous literature (Siddle Walker, 2000). On the contrary, African American women principals today confront urban students and parents who are younger, poorer, and generationally distant from those students and parents they encountered during earlier decades of their career (Loder, 2005c). This new urban school context is bound to generate feelings of frustration, misunderstanding, and perhaps even resentment between older generations of African American women principals and younger generations of students.

Younger administrators also report being frustrated with their younger, urban Black students, but they appear to be grappling to find creative and constructive responses to this dilemma. "Debbie," a 38-year-old assistant principal at a predominantly upper-middle-class White suburban school and school district also expressed concerns about what she perceived to be an increasing lack of respect for education among her students, a lack of respect that seemed incongruent with her own experiences growing up in 1980s Birmingham. But compared with Doris, the tenor of Debbie's conversation suggested that she was grappling to understand and respond constructively to her students' social reality. For example, Debbie felt obligated to devise positive resolutions to student discipline problems, particularly in a middle-class Whites school where these problems were casually cast as being "Black [male] student problems." As an assistant principal, her role was defined and perceived as being a strict disciplinarian. Yet she opted to address what she perceived to be an increasing discipline problem among Black male students in a positive versus punitive manner. In response to my question about the contributions that she believed African American educators could potentially make to improve the school district, Debbie responded,

> Well, we need to be sure that we secure enough [African Americans] so that we can let our voices be heard. One of the things that we've been able to do here is to address discipline issues. I don't have a lot of [these issues] so I don't want to exaggerate. But they were usually, you know, our African-American children–mostly African-American male children. So we started

to see this pattern emerge and we decided we needed to do something; so we decided to start a mentorship program that we call SAAM: Successful African-American Males. And so we got men from the community to come out and to actually spend time with them, you know, to tell them "I once was where you are. I had a difficult upbringing. I . . . had a single mother."

Perspectives from African American women principals like "Wilona," "Doris," and "Debbie" underscore a pressing need for the creation of new spaces and venues for African American women principals across generations to congregate, share ideas, discuss concerns, and attempt to build bridges of understanding between the past and the present. Perhaps the critical missing link to advancing the aims of African American education in the 21st century is generational in nature. It is hoped that an augmented intergenerational inquiry will generate new ideas, directions, and strategies for bridging the gap of cultural understanding, professional knowledge and wisdom, and lived experiences that exists between older and younger generations of African American women principals.

NOTE

1. Statistical breakdowns by race/gender are not ascertainable from this data source.

REFERENCES

Allen, K., Jacobson, S., & Lomotey, K. (1996). African American women in educational administration: The importance of mentors and sponsors. *Journal of Negro Education, 64*(4), 409–422.

Amott, T., & Matthaei, J. (1996). *Race, gender, and work: A multicultural economic history of women in the United States.* Boston: South End Press.

Bakari, K. (2002). *The Hip Hop generation: Young Blacks and the crisis in African American culture.* New York: Basic Civitas Books.

Beauboeuf, T. (2004, October). *Reinventing teaching: Womanist lessons from Black women teachers.* Paper presented at the Annual Fall conference of the Research on Women and Education SIG of the American Educational Research Association, Cleveland, OH.

Beauboeuf-Lafontant, T. (2002). A womanist experience of caring: Understanding the pedagogy of exemplary Black women teachers. *Urban Review, 34*(1), 71–86.

Bell, C. S., & Chase, S. E. (1994). The underrepresentation of women in school leadership. In C. Marshall (Ed.), *The new politics of race and gender: The 1992 yearbook of the Politics of Education Association* (pp. 141–154). Washington, DC: Falmer.

Bloom, C. M., & Erlandson, D. A. (2003). African American women principals in urban schools: Realities, (re)constructions, and resolutions. *Educational Administration Quarterly, 39*(3), 339–369.

Bositis, D. A. (2001). *Diverging generations: The transformation of African American policy views.* Washington, DC: Joint Center for Political and Economic Studies.

Bruckner, M. (1998). Private lives of public leaders: A spousal perspective. *School Administrator, 55*(6), 24–27.

Bullock, L. (2006, October 16). Young Blacks are the most politically engaged says study. *New America Media.* Retrieved January 12, 2007, from http://news.newamericanmedia .org/news/view_article.html?article_id=

Burlew, K. A., & Johnson, J. L. (1992). Role conflict and career advancement among African American women in nontraditional professions. *Career Development Quarterly, 40*(4), 302–312.

Burton, L., & Devries, C. (1992). Challenges and rewards: African American grandparents as surrogate parents. *Generations, 17*(3), 51–54.

Burton, L., & Dilworth-Anderson, P. (1991). Intergenerational family roles of aged Black Americans. *Marriage & Family Review, 16*(3/4), 311–330.

Caputo, R. K. (1999). Age-condensed and age-gapped families: Coresidency with elderly parents and relatives in a mature women's cohort, 1967–1995. *Marriage & Family Review, 29*(1), 77–95.

Carter, T. (Director), Schwahn, M., & Gatins, J. (Writers). (2005). *Coach Carter* [Motion picture]. United States: Paramount Pictures.

Coffin, G. C. (1972). The black school administrator and how he's being pushed to extinction. *American School Board Journal, 159*(11), 33–36.

Collins, P. H. (2000). *Black feminist thought* (2nd ed.). New York: Routledge.

Collins, P. H. (2004). *Black sexual politics.* New York: Routledge.

Cose, E. (1993). *The rage of a privileged class.* New York: Harper Collins.

Coursen, D., Mazzarella, J., Jeffress, L., & Hadderman, M. (1989). Two special cases: Women and Blacks. In S. C. Smith & P. K. Piele (Eds.), *School leadership: Handbook for excellence*

(pp. 85–106). Eugene, OR: ERIC Clearinghouse on Educational Management.

Cozart, S. C., & Price, P. G. (2005). Black women, identity and schooling: Reclaiming our work in shifting contexts [Special issue]. *Urban Review, 37*(3), 173–179.

Dillard, C. B. (1995). Leading with her life: An African American feminist (re)interpretation of leadership for an urban high school principalship. *Educational Administration Quarterly, 31*(4), 539–563.

Dingus, J. E. (2006). "Doing the best we could": African American teachers' counterstory on school desegregation. *Urban Review, 38*(3), 211–233.

Doud, J. L., & Keller, E. P. (1999). *The K-8 principal in 1998.* Alexandria, VA: National Association of Elementary School Principals.

Dyson, M. E. (2007). *Know what I mean? Reflections on Hip Hop.* New York: Basic Civitas Books.

Etter-Lewis, G. (1993). *My soul is my own: Oral narratives of African-American women in professions* (pp. 155–202). New York: Routledge.

Fairclough, A. (2001). *Teaching equality: Black schools in the age of Jim Crow.* Athens: University of Georgia Press.

Ford, G. (2006, September 19). Bigger than hip-hop. *Witretap: Ideas & action for a new generation.* Retrieved May 30, 2007, from www.wiretapmag .org/stories/41361

Foster, M. (1990). The politics of race: Through the eyes of African-American teachers. *Journal of Education, 172,* 123–141.

Foster, M. (1993). Self-portraits of Black teachers: Narratives of individual and collective struggle against racism. In D. McLaughlin & W. G. Tierney (Eds.), *Naming silenced lives: Personal narratives and processes of educational change* (pp. 155–176). New York: Routledge.

Foster, M. (1997). *Black teachers on teaching.* New York: W. W. Norton.

Franklin, V. P. (1990). They rose and fell together: African American educators and community leadership, 1795–1954. *Journal of Education, 72,* 39–64.

Garner, T., Scanlon, C., & Robbins, B. (Producers). (2003). *Radio* [Motion picture]. United States: Sony Pictures.

Generett, G. G. (2005). Intergenerational discussions as a curriculum strategy: Modeling audacious hope in action [Special issue]. *Urban Review, 37*(3), 267–277.

Goldring, E. B., & Rallis, S. F. (1993). *Principals of dynamic schools: Taking charge of change.* Thousand Oaks, CA: Corwin Press.

Gordon, J. A. (1997). Teachers of color speak to issues of respect and image. *Urban Review, 29,* 44–66.

Grogan, M. (1999). Equity/equality issues of gender, race, and class. *Educational Administration Quarterly, 35*(4), 518–536.

Harley, S. (Ed.). (2002). *Sister circle: Black women and work.* Newark: Rutgers, State University of New Jersey.

Harris, S., & Ballenger, J. (2004, October). *Women leaders and spirituality.* Paper presented at the 29th annual meeting of the Research on Women and Education Conference, Cleveland, OH.

Higginbotham, E., & Weber, L. (1992). Moving up with kin and community: Upward social mobility for Black and White women. *Gender & Society, 6,* 416–440.

Hobson, C. J., Delunas, L., & Kesic, D. (2001). Compelling evidence of the need for corporate work/life balance initiatives: Results from a national survey of stressful life-events. *Journal of Employment Counseling, 38*(1), 38–44.

Hudson, M. J., & Holmes, B. J. (1994). Missing teachers, impaired communities: The unanticipated consequences of *Brown vs. Board of Education* on the African American teaching force at the precollegiate level. *Journal of Negro Education, 63,* 388–393.

Irvine, J. J. (2003). *Educating teachers for diversity: Seeing with a cultural eye.* New York: Teachers College.

Jaschik, S. (2007, April 25). The "family friendly" competition. *Insider Higher Ed.* Retrieved June 27, 2007, from http://insiderhighered.com

Jean-Marie, G., James, C., & Bynum, S. (2006). Black women activists, leaders, and educators: Transforming urban educational practice. In J. Kincheloe, P. Anderson, K. Rose, D. Griffith, & K. Hayes (Eds.), *Urban education: An encyclopedia* (pp. 59–70). Westport, CT: Greenwood.

Johnson, L. (2004, Summer). A generation of women activists: African American female educators in Harlem, 1930–1950. *Journal of African American History, 89,* 223–240.

Johnson, L. (2006). "Making her community a better place to live": Culturally responsive urban school leadership in historical context. *Leadership and Policy in Schools, 5*(1), 19–36.

King, S. H. (1993a). The limited presence of African-American teachers. *Review of Educational Research, 63,* 115–149.

King, S. H. (1993b). Why did we choose teaching careers and what will enable us to stay? Insights from one cohort of the African American teaching pool. *Journal of Negro Education, 62,* 475–492.

Kolb, P. J. (2000). Continuing to care: Black and Latina daughters' assistance to their mothers in nursing homes. *Affilia, 15*(4), 502–525.

Landry, B. (2000). *Black working wives: Pioneers of the American family revolution.* Berkeley: University of California.

Lane, S. D., Keefe, R. H., Rubinstein, R. A., Levandowski, B. A., Freedman, M., Rosenthal, A., et al. (2004). Marriage promotion and missing men: African American women in a demographic double bind. *Medical Anthropology Quarterly, 18*(4), 405–428.

Lathan, S. (Director). (1996–2002). *Steve Harvey show* [Television series]. United States: Brillstein-Grey Entertainment, Stan Lathan TV, Universal TV & Winifred Hervey Productions.

Loder, T. L. (2005a). African-American women principals' reflections on social change, community othermothering, and Chicago public school reform. *Urban Education, 40*(3), 299–320.

Loder, T. L. (2005b, April). *Bridging the tradition of activism and professionalism within the context of contemporary urban education.* Paper presented at the annual meeting of the American Educational Research Association, Montreal, Canada.

Loder, T. L. (2005c). Dilemmas confronting urban principals in the post-civil rights era. In J. Kincheloe, P. Anderson, K. Rose, D. Griffith, & K. Hayes (Eds.), *Urban education: An encyclopedia* (pp. 70–77). Westport, CT: Greenwood.

Loder, T. L. (2005d). On deferred dreams, callings, and revolving doors of opportunity: African American women's reflections on becoming principals [Special issue]. *Urban Review, 37*(3), 243–265.

Loder, T. L. (2005e). Women administrators' negotiate work-family conflicts during changing times: An intergenerational perspective. *Educational Administration Quarterly, 41*(5), 741–776.

Loder, T. L., & Spillane, J. P. (2005). Is a principal still a teacher? U.S. women administrators' accounts of role conflict and role discontinuity. *School Leadership & Management, 25*(3), 263–279.

Malveaux, J. (1987). Comparable worth and its impact on Black women. In M. C. Simms & J. Malveaux (Eds.), *Slipping through the cracks: The status of Black women.* New Brunswick, NY: Transaction Books.

Mannheim, K. (1952). The problem of generations. In K. Mannheim (Ed.), *Essays on the sociology of knowledge* (pp. 276–322). London: Routledge & Kegan Paul. (Original work published 1928)

Marshall, C. (1993). The new politics of race and gender. In C. Marshall (Ed.), *The new politics of race and gender: The 1992 yearbook of the politics of education association* (pp. 1–6). Washington, DC: Falmer Press.

McAdoo, H. P. (1997). Upward mobility across generations in African American families. In H. P. McAdoo (Ed.), *Black families* (pp. 139–162). Thousand Oaks, CA: Sage.

McGee Banks, C. A. (1995). Gender and race factors in educational leadership and administration. In J. A. Banks & C. A. McGee Banks (Eds.), *Handbook of research on multicultural education* (pp. 65–80). New York: Macmillan.

Mertz, N. T. (2003, October). *The promise of Title IX: Longitudinal study of women in administration 1972–2002.* Paper presented at the annual conference of the Research on Women and Education SIG of the American Educational Research Association, Knoxville, TN.

Meyers, S., & Ginsberg, R. (1994). Gender, marital status, and support systems of public school principals. *Urban Review, 26,* 209–223.

Miller, J. R., & Vaughn, G. G. (1997). African American women executives: Themes that bind. In L. Benjamin (Ed.), *Black women in the academy* (pp. 178–188). Gainesville: University of Florida.

Minkler, M., & Fuller-Thomson, E. (2000). Second time around parenting: Factors predictive of grandparents becoming caregivers for their grandchildren. *International Journal of Aging and Human Development, 50*(3), 185–200.

Nance, M. (2006, November 30). ACE Conference: More research needed on experiences of minority women leaders. *Diverse: Issues in Higher Education, 13,* 10, 21.

Newsome, Y. D. (2002). Reversal of fortune: Explaining the decline in Black women's earnings. *Gender and Society, 16*(4), 442–464.

Nichols, J. D. (2002). The first-year principal: A husband's perspective. *Principal, 82*(2), 60–62.

PSRP Conference: Balancing work and home. (2001, May/June). *American Teacher, 85*(8). Retrieved August 28, 2003, from ERIC database.

Shakeshaft, C. (1999). The struggle to create a more gender-inclusive profession. In J. Murphy & K. S. Louis (Eds.), *Handbook of research on educational administration* (pp. 99–118). San Francisco: Jossey-Bass.

Shaw, S. (1996). *What a woman ought to be and to do: Black professional women workers during the Jim Crow era.* Chicago: University of Chicago Press.

Siddle Walker, V. (2000). Valued segregated schools for African American children in the South, 1935–1969: A review of common themes and characteristics. *Review of Educational Research, 70,* 253–285.

Strizek, G. A., Pittsonberger, J. L., Riordan, K. E., Lyter, D. M., & Orlofsky, G. F. (2006). *Characteristics of schools, districts, teachers, principals, and school libraries in the United States: 2003–04 Schools and Staffing Survey* (NCES 2006-313 Revised). U.S. Department of Education, National Center for Education Statistics. Washington, DC: Government Printing Office.

Taeuber, C. M. (1996). *Statistical handbook on women in America* (2nd ed.). Phoenix, AZ: Oryx.

Tarpley, N. (1995). *Testimony: Young African Americans on self-discovery and Black identity.* Boston: Beacon Press.

Tillman, L. C. (2004a). African American principals and the legacy of *Brown. Review of Research in Education, 28,* 101–146.

Tillman, L. C. (2004b). (Un)intended consequences? The impact of *Brown vs. Board of Education* decision on the employment status of Black educators. *Education in Urban Society, 36,* 280–303.

Tucker, M. B., & Mitchell-Kernan, C. (Eds.). (1995). *The decline in marriage among African Americans: Causes, consequences, and policy implications.* Thousand Oaks, CA: Sage.

Walker, C. (1993). Black women in educational management. In J. Ozga, J. (Ed.), *Women in educational management* (pp. 16–24). Buckingham, UK: Open University Press.

Wesson, L. (1995). Equity issues for women and minorities in educational administration. In B. Irby & G. Brown (Eds.), *Women as school executives: Voices and visions* (pp. 149–157). Austin: Texas Association of School Administrators.

West, C. (1993). *Race matters.* Boston: Beacon Press.

Williams, D. G., & Evans-Winters, V. (2005). The burden of teaching teachers: Memoirs of race discourse in teacher education [Special issue]. *Urban Review, 37*(3), 201–219.

Willson, A. E., & Hardy, M. A. (2002). Racial disparities in income security for a cohort of aging American women. *Social Forces, 80*(4), 1283–1306.

Wilson, W. J. (1987). *The truly disadvantaged: The inner city, the underclass, and public policy.* Chicago: University of Chicago Press.

Young, M. D., & McLeod, S. (2001). Flukes, opportunities, and panned interventions: Factors affecting women's decisions to become school administrators. *Educational Administration Quarterly, 37*(4), 462–502.

14

RACE, LAW, AND LEADERSHIP

Exploring the Interest-Convergence Dilemma

MARK A. GOODEN

R ace continues to be a factor in America and in education. Scholars have pointed out how race continues to have an effect on what and who gets taught within schools and the quality of life outside schools and beyond education (Hacker, 1995; Ladson-Billings, 1996; Ladson-Billings & Tate, 1995; Tillman, 2006; West, 2001). For example, an examination of leadership, race, and law in America reveals a phenomenon that has existed since the formative years of this country. That is, White men still hold the majority of all leadership positions in fields ranging from sports to business. This translates into White men having the highest income averages and holding the highest positions of influence and power. This phenomenon is reflected in educational leadership as well (Alston, 2000; Gooden, 2005; Tillman, 2005). While women dominate the education profession, White men dominate the ranks of school leadership (Alston, 2000; Lewis, 2006; Shakeshaft & Nowell, 1992).

In light of the present reality, it is no wonder that educating Black[1] children in an environment dominated by White mainstream culture sets up an intractable dilemma and a set of corollary questions. For instance, given that scholars cogently argue that race is a factor in societal dynamics, how does it apply to school leadership? If race does apply to school leadership, how and to what extent should educational leaders incorporate it into their responsibility to manage American schools? If school leaders are usually rewarded for complying with district edicts, how do they persist in a world that subconsciously rewards leaders who maintain the status quo and punishes and ostracizes those who challenge this process from within? How do the concepts of race, law, and school leadership coincide in such matters to better inform educational leaders?

In this chapter, I present a brief review of the concepts of race, law, and leadership and how they intersect. Throughout this discussion, the distinct lines between these conceptual categories are often blurred and other times intentionally violated as there is much overlap of these concepts in education and society. I then define the construct of interest-convergence and a related concept called the interest-divergence principle. I then demonstrate how these principles apply to educational leadership. As school leaders educate, they must be willing to examine if race affects their leadership style, school culture and climate, curriculum and instruction, family involvement, student organization, accountability, and discipline. This chapter concludes with a set of recommendations for educational leaders.

RACE, LAW, AND EDUCATION

Intersections of race, law, and leadership have existed since African Americans were brought to the country in bondage. Colonists created laws to govern the behavior and define the treatment of the enslaved Africans, who from the very beginning were kept in bondage because of race, the prospect of exploitation of their labor, and White superiority. To establish power and maintain control, Whites enacted stringent laws in the southern states that made it illegal to teach Black people to read (Anderson, 1988; Bell, 1989, 2004b). This was the continuation of a system of robbing the enslaved Africans of language, religion, and other important cultural connections and forbidding them from speaking in their native tongues (Asante, 1999, 2005; Finkelman, 1997). Even worse, this was a deliberate deprivation of educational opportunity. Whites' determination to create and maintain this system was directly related to the reasons they originally brought Blacks to the country—to increase the wealth of individual colonists and the nation in general. Those who could afford slaves would benefit immensely from the financial rewards stemming from this legally sanctioned institution of owning human beings and their offspring for the rest of their lives. The reality of being born to slave-owning parents juxtaposed against that of being born into slavery sets up a stark contrast of an American-created caste system. This system grew into continuous generational financial benefits for wealthy Whites, while it became a legally endorsed generational curse for Blacks.

The system of slavery established the foundation for institutional racism, which I define as a system that promotes discrimination in society at the larger level through historical policies and practices. It is deceptive and inappropriate to argue against institutional racism in person-to-person conflict at the microlevel. Indeed, institutional racism is larger and more pernicious, though not unrelated to one-on-one racism that stems from the actions of those White individuals who discriminate on a personal level through the use of devices such as racial epithets or more mild preconceived notions about Black students' abilities or intelligence. Institutional racism is more related to members of the dominant culture's perceived correct way to do things in America or a lack of cultural proficiency.

Lindsey, Robins, and Terrell (1999) defined culturally proficient leadership as leadership that goes beyond the esteeming of culture, to take every opportunity to increase the awareness level and knowledge base of self and others about culture and the dynamics of difference. Without a movement toward cultural proficiency, assumptions rooted in institutional racism would continue to influence American culture, particularly the ways in which schools are operated. Lindsey, Robins, and Terrell noted that the two barriers leaders face when improving educational opportunities for all children are "(a) the presumption of entitlement or privilege and (b) the use of power which accrues to the privileged" (p. 95). Williams (2001) noted that just as the oppressed are penalized because of their culture, others benefit because of membership in a privileged group. Still, many Whites ignore or overlook this reality and are reluctant to acknowledge White privilege that was generally bestowed on them through an American system that promotes White superiority. Accordingly, these same Whites are even less likely to recognize benefits that extended from years of free slave labor (Delgado & Stefancic, 1997; McIntosh, 1988). Peggy McIntosh (1988), a White scholar, stated, "I was taught to see racism only in individual acts of meanness, not in invisible systems conferring dominance on my group" (p. 31).

The important point here is that it is a mistake to simplify this discussion to one of overt and covert racism, or worse to dismiss the effects of slavery on the education of Blacks in this country with the ahistorical remark, "that was then and this is now," or "that was those racist Whites in the south and I had nothing to do with that." Too often this is an issue in debates in America on race. While at first glance, these arguments seem plausible and appear to make sense, at least ostensibly to Whites and even some Blacks, they must be carefully examined from more than just the perspectives of those who perceive White privilege as perfectly legitimate. First, such viewpoints enforce the broadly held conscious and subconscious belief of "White innocence" in the context of education and society in general. Second, they grossly minimize the inherent power of being a member of the dominant culture. Interestingly, if we imagine a continuum of awareness, Whites range from being unaware of privilege to completely dismissive of it. As members of the dominant culture in America, they are free to choose their level of awareness of this issue on this continuum. Indeed, Whites have tended to dig their heels in when there is even the slightest threat to their privileged position because they are perceived (and perceive themselves) as innocents, and this is exemplified in the law. Affirmative action is a contentious issue in this country that involves among other things, conflicts over who should have access to resources based on race, a need for diversity, and a history of maltreatment of Blacks in this country. A look at text in *Regents of the University of California v. Bakke* (1978) affirmative action case illustrates this point:

> We have never approved a classification that aids persons perceived as members of relatively victimized groups at the expense of other innocent individuals in the absence of judicial, legislative, or administrative findings of constitutional or statutory violations. (p. 307)

The reasoning in the Bakke case is continued 25 years later in *Grutter v. Bollinger* (2003), one of two affirmative actions cases on higher education heard by the Supreme Court recently. The quote below demonstrates how the law keeps alive the notions that Whites are innocent and cannot be expected to bear the burden of slavery. No acknowledgement of White privilege is present here, although within the case the justices admit that there have been societal practices and polices that have wronged Blacks. In the analysis, however, the justices note it would be unfair to deny the present-day Whites access to educational resources by giving "preferential treatment" to Blacks. Note the justices' revival of the *Bakke* language in *Grutter* 25 years later:

> Second, Justice Powell rejected an interest in remedying societal discrimination because such measures would risk placing unnecessary burdens on innocent third parties "who bear no responsibility for whatever harm the beneficiaries of the special admissions program are thought to have suffered." (pp. 323–324)

Dissecting this concept of White innocence is beyond the scope of this chapter but suffice it to say that such thinking reflects the dominant society's belief that remedying racial wrongs in this country must include some benefit or at least the likelihood of insulating Whites (Bell, 1980a). Part of this insulating process conveniently ignores or neglects the institutional benefit that has been conferred on Whites by virtue of their birth. Additionally, it refuses to acknowledge the possibility of a concept of Black innocence. Society has established a number of ways to help Whites remain oblivious to their privilege (Leonardo, 2004; McIntosh, 1988, 1990). McIntosh (1990) listed privileges that Whites take for granted and acknowledged as a White person:

> 1. I can, if I wish, arrange to be in the company of people of my race most of the time.
>
> 2. If I should need to move, I can be pretty sure of renting or purchasing housing in an area that I can afford and in which I would want to live.
>
> 3. I can be pretty sure that my neighbors in such a location will be neutral or pleasant to me.
>
> 4. I can remain oblivious of the language and customs of persons of color, who constitute the world's majority, without feeling in my culture any penalty for such oblivion.
>
> 5. I can criticize our government and talk about how much I fear its policies and behavior without being seen as a cultural outsider.
>
> 6. I can be pretty sure that if I ask to talk to "the person in charge" I will be facing a person of my race. (pp. 32–35)

I have selected these 6 statements out of McIntosh's 25 statements because they illustrate connections to education, law and policy, and school leadership. The first three describe living options and accompanying educational opportunities that tend to be more available for Whites to take advantage of with little or no regard to race. The same is not true for Blacks. Although upwardly mobile Blacks can exercise their choice to live near Whites, there are social consequences that must be considered as these three statements illustrate. Poor Blacks, who compose the majority of major urban school districts, rarely have the choice to move near Whites in upper-class neighborhoods. If few or no Blacks move into White neighborhoods then Whites tend to be oblivious of other customs as Statement

4 indicates. In these cases, the burden, responsibility, and all accompanying risks of teaching about language and customs of people of color are expected to be taken on by those people. The fifth statement touches on the policy issue and how the dominant culture considers those who criticize the government's policies on race outsiders, especially if they are Black. The last statement simply illustrates a phenomenon in America—that the leader will tend to be White and male. As stated earlier, educational leadership is no exception. The average educational leader will most likely be a White man with a master's degree (U.S. Department of Education and the Office of Civil Rights, 2004).

White privilege is the offspring of a culture that was constructed on a system of slavery. Hence, the peculiar institution of slavery and its accompanying effects on education should not go unexamined, even in the context of educational leadership. Although a complete discussion of slavery is beyond the scope of this chapter, the explanation above should establish an adequate foundation to make apparent the accompanying connection of interest-convergence and -divergence principles in the next sections.

The Interest-Convergence Principle

Derrick Bell (1980a) explained how White superiority was the root of challenges facing the implementation of the 1954 *Brown v. Board of Education* decision. Bell set about the task of explaining the theories of two law professors, Wechsler and Black. Wechsler agreed with the *Brown* decision but found the reasoning of the court legally flawed because it was not based on neutral principles. He doubted that the decision was based on the fact that racial segregation caused harm to Black children because evidence was inadequate and conflicting in the view of courts. He also concluded that the *Brown* court must have based its holding on the view that, in principle, racial segregation is a denial of equality for Black people. He eventually dismissed both arguments as not addressing the real state issue.

Instead, Wechsler argues that the legal issue in state-imposed segregation cases is one of associational rights: "the denial by the state of freedom to associate, a denial that impinges in the same way on any groups or races that may be involved" (p. 521). Wechsler reasoned that "if the

freedom of association is denied by segregation, integration forces an association upon those for whom it is unpleasant or repugnant" (p. 521). He concluded his argument with the following question that challenged legal scholars at the time. Wechsler asked,

> Given a situation where the state must practically choose between denying the association to those individuals who wish it or imposing it on those who would avoid it, is there a basis in neutral principles for holding that the Constitution demands that the claims for association should prevail? (p. 521)

Bell (1980a) noted that Professor Black correctly identified racial equality as the neutral principle and in his legal argument Black urged, "[w]hen the directive of equality cannot be followed without displeasing the white[s], then something that can be called a 'freedom' of the white[s] *must* [italics added] be impaired" (p. 522). In other words, the rights of Whites must become subordinate to the neutral principle of racial equality. Bell (1980a) argued that Whites may agree on the surface that Blacks are citizens and entitled to constitutional protection against racial discrimination, but are not willing to remedy racial segregation by altering their status. For instance, Bell (1980a) made his point by noting,

> The extent of this unwillingness is illustrated by the controversy over affirmative action programs, particularly those where identifiable whites must step aside for Blacks they deem less qualified or less deserving. In essence, whites simply cannot envision the personal responsibility and the potential sacrifice inherent in Black's conclusion that true equality for Blacks will require the surrender of racism-granted privileges for whites. (pp. 522–523)

Hence, this brings Bell (1980a) back to Wechsler's point that large segments of the population deem racial equality as not legitimate, at least to the extent that it threatens to impair the societal status of Whites. More clearly, then, Wechsler's argument is that the law is subordinate to interest-group politics. The interest group here is Whites who enjoy special privileges. Bell admits that no such subordination is apparent in *Brown,* but believes that it is possible to discern this principle in school decisions following the landmark case. In studying the implementation of the law decisions since *Brown*, several scholars agree with Bell (Brown, 2004a, 2004b; Gooden, 2004; Harris, Brown, & Russo, 1997; Hunter, 2004). This principle, which relies equally on the political history of America and legal precedent, describes the world in its current state rather than how we might want it to be in terms of race relations. Translated from judicial activity in racial cases both before and after *Brown*, Bell (1980a) referred to this as the principle of "interest convergence" and he noted,

> The interest of blacks in achieving racial equality will be accommodated only when it converges with the interests of whites. However, the fourteenth amendment, standing alone, will not authorize a judicial remedy providing effective racial equality for blacks where the remedy sought threatens the superior societal status of middle and upper class whites. (p. 523)

Bell (1980b, 1989, 2004a) posited that certain legal advancements and policies for Blacks in education and civil rights have moved forward because they primarily benefited or satisfied an interest of the dominant culture. While Bell has made his arguments using a variety of sources, he has used mainly law cases and statutes. Mary Dudziak (2000) has found similar evidence by researching policies and politics of America. Ladson-Billings and Tate (1995) also noted the application of race and property to education. For instance, they pointed out that inequalities can be found in the curriculum when comparing that of suburban schools, which tend to have more academic options, with that of urban schools. They argued that there is a property right found in curriculum. Privilege and property are important parts of interest convergence that Whites hold dearly. Similarly, I argue that these concepts have applications in educational leadership, because while education can provide an opportunity to attain property, educational leaders are responsible for how they provide protection of and access to this valued American resource. Moreover, Black educational leaders who are more aware of race in educating Black youths are challenged by the presence of White supremacy in educating Black children, including inculcating the values of society. On balance,

without the necessary credentialing that schooling affords, Black students face the probability of being subjugated by the dominant culture.

Bell's (1989, 2004b) principle of interest convergence is certainly as apparent in the present-day education as it was 50 years ago. For instance, racial equality in education was promoted at the time of the *Brown* because White policymakers viewed it as a strategy to improve America's international image. Still most Whites disagreed vehemently with *Brown*, even though it would improve policy for the country as a whole. Today, many Whites are not as vocal or openly opposed to segregation. However, many Whites exercise their associational rights and vote with their feet by moving to the suburbs where schools tend to have more resources and the residents are more homogeneous. This mass exodus of Whites from the cities gave rise to the second principle that is discussed below.

THE INTEREST-DIVERGENCE PRINCIPLE

Bell (1980a) presented the interest-divergence principle with the intention of describing the developing relationships between Blacks and Whites in U.S. society and education. Bell pointed out some progress after *Brown* but rightfully cautioned against optimism after examining vigorous dissenting opinions of U.S. Supreme Court Justices in subsequent school desegregation cases. He noted that the decisions and dissenting opinions reflected a growing divergence in the interests of Whites and Blacks. This brings us again to Wechsler's point about associational rights and Bell's fear that White entitlement might eclipse the gains of Blacks precipitated by *Brown*. We are now in a period where the entitlement of Whites not to associate with Blacks in public schools has eclipsed the promises of *Brown*.

Thus, there is an apparent move toward interest divergence manifested first in southern Whites' treatment of Blacks immediately after the *Brown* decision—treatment that continues today. Legally, the present conservative courts endorse this belief by deemphasizing the principles of *Brown* relative to racial equality and school desegregation, thus leading to the resegregation of schools (Orfield, Frankenberg, & Lee, 2003).

We find more interest divergence when we examine urban schools that are racially isolated. The interests of the Whites to exercise their associational rights not to associate with Blacks take precedence over the interests of Blacks to associate with Whites. Whites view this right as a legitimate (real or perceived) indirect mechanism to attain and maintain a property right. Because Whites maintain skin privilege and power, they can support racial equality without ever giving up substantial resources and when they must do so, then they will embrace the notion of White innocence because in their minds, though not expressed, achieving racial equality should always be borne by Blacks primarily since they (Blacks) seek desegregation. Whites can simply argue that they are happy to accommodate diversity and even racial equality up to the point where property and privilege are implicated. In essence, interests diverge where the dominant culture demands that diversity must be based in racially neutral principles or individual choice. One might think that racial equality may be substituted for diversity but evidence shows otherwise. It becomes even more of a challenge to advocate for racial equality with racially neutral principles.

Interest Convergence and Divergence: Applications to Educational Leadership

Bell's (1980a) interest-convergence principle and interest-divergence corollary emerged from an analysis of White privilege and power. They apply to society in general but are pervasive in education and other areas. To be sure, leaders in the private sector face similar issues of power and privilege involving Blacks and Whites (Cobbs & Turnock, 2003; Thomas & Gabarro, 1999). Black educational leaders also face White hegemony as they lead in schools, an issue that sometimes is overlooked or ignored. The positioning of the role of educational leaders may make it more difficult, though necessary, to address issues of race, law, and leadership. Indeed, in American education, any race-based strategies are usually avoided even when diversity is the goal. For instance, after the *Grutter v. Bollinger* decision in 2003, the Bush administration's U.S. Department of Education and The Office of Civil Rights produced a report titled "Achieving Diversity: Race Neutral Alternatives in American Education" (2004). The expressed purpose of the report was

to provide a catalog of both developmental and admissions-oriented race-neutral approaches to achieve diversity. The specific objective was "to improve the educational performance of our nation's students, particularly those in low performing schools so that the admissions process will naturally produce a diverse applicant pool" (U.S. Department of Education and The Office of Civil Rights, 2004, p. 7). Diversity as defined in the report is not the same as racial diversity, but instead includes factors associated with economic disadvantage. As such the report quietly sidesteps racial equality, as the topic of race is neatly kept out of the discussion. In short, these developmental approaches are those designed to develop skills, resources, and abilities of students who might not otherwise apply to and succeed in college. The *Achieving Diversity* report is the second such report produced by the federal government in support of race-neutral principles.

The *Achieving Diversity* report argues that the No Child Left Behind Act of 2001 (NCLB, 2001) has a number of approaches that may be considered developmental including those designed to help schools failing to educate disadvantaged students. Admission approaches are defined as those race-neutral methods used to assign students in postsecondary institutions and include, for example, the subparts of comprehensive review, socioeconomic preferences, class-rank plans, and lottery procedures. Although these parts of the report will not be described here, it is important to note that the comprehensive review should consider a number of factors when admitting students, though race is not listed as one of those in the report. Ironically, the authors of the document note a fact that resonates with Bell's (2004a) interest-convergence principle. That is, on campuses in the University of California system, "as applications increase, the standards at the most competitive campuses rise, and underrepresented minorities are most often found at campuses with relatively fewer applicants" (p. 39). In other words, minority students have been found to apply to less exclusive schools and therefore are smaller in numbers at the exclusive schools. This is a curtailing of opportunity for Black students that the government and many Whites find acceptable, and this illustrates the quandary of using race-neutral policies to address the challenge of achieving racial equality or equal education opportunity. If racial diversity is never achieved, current and future administrations may find this acceptable since other promoted forms of diversity are more palatable.

Additionally, government officials may continue to be reluctant to focus on the central root of the problem as stated by Wechsler (as cited in Bell, 1980a). That is, Whites will cling to associational rights regarding school desegregation. A race-neutral strategy will do little to affect the reality of White power and privilege, but it will do much to appease White consciousness while keeping these tangible resources virtually untouched by minority students. Hence, this strategy is effectively ill equipped to address or achieve racial equality in America.

On a more microcosmic level, educational leaders are faced with the realities of race, law, and leadership. Tillman (2004b) discovered that many Black principals, teachers, and other educational leaders lost their jobs after the 1954 *Brown v. Board of Education* decision. While the *Brown* opinion struck down school segregation, the decision surely carried the presumably (un)intended consequences of firing Black educators and that directly affected their property rights. Tillman (2004b) stated that the "firings threatened the livelihood of Black educators, the structure, values, and cultural norms of the Black community, and ultimately the social, emotional, and academic success of Black children" (p. 281).

Black educators were essentially being denied the benefit of employment, for the greater good of desegregating schools. In reality, they were being punished by southern local governments for a federal mandate to desegregate schools. While segregation was struck down as a part of national policy, Blacks paid for it with loss of employment, a property right. This is consistent with the interest-divergence principle that Blacks should bear the burden of school desegregation. However, such actions confirmed the prevalence and persistence of White superiority. Whites, then as now, cannot be expected to willingly submit those artifacts of authority simply for the benefits of Blacks, including Black educational leaders. Accordingly, they may be challenged by having Black leaders in charge and when given the power to alter this, they will use every possible tool, even the law, to deny Blacks leadership roles. Of course, many Whites follow principles that are morally right, but they are not enough to change society or equalize educational opportunities.

School Leadership

There are alternatives to teaching grounded in White middle-class values. Most notably, these approaches have included culture and/or race as relevant factors in teaching (Delpit, 1988, 2006; Hale, 1986; Milner & Howard, 2004). Accordingly, there are ways of leading in schools that should create an environment conducive for these methods of teaching. Leaders must offer alternatives that challenge the notion that the best way to lead is by protecting the majority position (Gooden, 2002; Shakeshaft, 1987a, 1987b). Leaders must confront White privilege and advocate for curricula that include and value students' positive experiences and prepare them for adulthood. They should opt for ways to lead that support teaching pride in self and academic achievement. Leaders should boldly lead in a way that liberates students to help them understand how society has been constructed to devalue Blacks and their contributions. They must advocate different pedagogical approaches that achieve results.

School leaders may influence these factors with good leadership, school climate and culture, and curriculum and instruction. While Tillman (2004a) has shown that leadership styles of African American principals working in African American urban schools can and do vary, there are important consistencies that suggest a connection to students' achievement. I believe that many successful Black principals have something unique to offer urban schools leaders. First, school leadership does have an effect on all students' learning beyond academics. To enhance learning, an indispensable element in good schools is inspired, strong, and consistent leadership (Lightfoot, 1983). Therefore, leaders, whether Black or White, cannot afford to be silent on issues of White privilege. That does not mean that they should go through the halls preaching Black Power with raised clinched fists, but they must acknowledge and address biased social systems. It means that they must unabashedly advocate on behalf of Black children. School leaders should secure needed resources and encourage teachers to strive to be culturally relevant teachers. Ladson-Billings (1992) noted that the essential elements of this kind of teaching involve

> developing conceptions of self and others that are based on accurate historical and social information; encouraging social relations that

are communal, interdependent, equitable, and just; and developing conceptions of knowledge as socially constructed and open to intellectual challenge. (p. 389)

She also added that teachers must see African American students as capable, intellectual beings who have overcome a history of challenges instead of victims. Leaders must equip teachers and students with tools to address these issues with meaningful professional development. Ladson-Billings (1992) noted that pre-service teachers and teachers in general need "culturally relevant teacher preparation that arms them with accurate self- and historical knowledge, corrects inaccuracies, and provides them with opportunities to develop effective instructional strategies along with learning from and with communities different from their own" (p. 389). Leaders, then, must provide the necessary structure for teachers to feel safe for taking such risks. In light of interest divergence, leaders must demonstrate to teachers and students how to face and successfully negotiate such intellectual challenges.

While most school leaders are White, their race does not necessarily prevent them from advocating for African American children by working to increase personal cultural competence. Accordingly, school leaders must also be prepared to educate staff members on how to relate to African American children. Indeed, it is incumbent on school leaders to understand and address deficit thinking about African American students' achievement and challenge broader viewpoints that consistently fail to value what students bring to the learning environment. If leaders engage in these behaviors, they will be better equipped to change and inspire others to work toward common goals. Ideally, leaders will also need to be compassionate and committed to educating African American children.

School Culture and Climate Issues

Culture is the seemingly subtle stream of norms, values, beliefs, traditions, and rituals that build up over time as people work together, solve problems, and confront challenges (Peterson & Deal, 1998). Leaders must create cultures in their schools that promote learning and value African American students and their culture. Leaders must model behaviors, policies, and procedures while inspiring a shared vision

(Kouzes & Posner, 2002). They also posit that leaders should challenge the process and the system and encourage others to participate in ways that are supportive and affirming. However, establishing a shared vision will be very difficult if the culture of the school is toxic. School leaders must be willing to work collaboratively with teachers, students, and their families in ways that respect them and their culture. Using the backdrop of challenges of association rights and interest-divergence concerns, leaders and teachers can promote a climate that focuses on serving their students without judgment and ill-placed criticism. Williams (2001) noted that productive and positive school cultures should openly support the basic value that the culture of African American students must be understood because their education is guided by their culture, which is likely to appear at odds in many ways with White middle-class values. She went on to note that all aspects of education are cultural.

Reeves (2007) asserted that school leaders must recognize the importance of their actions when trying to change culture. He argued that the greatest impediment to meaningful cultural change is

the gap between what leaders say they value and what they actually do. Staff members are not seduced by a leader's claim of "collaborative culture" when every meeting is a series of lectures, announcements, and warnings. Claims about a "culture of high expectations" are undermined when school policies encourage good grades for poor student work. (p. 94)

The same argument can be applied to working in the interest of Black students. For example, school leaders who advocate that all children can learn but suspend a high percentage of African American males will have little success convincing teachers that they have a culture of high expectations. Leaders must also help their faculty and staff members examine deficit models that keep Black students either heavily referred to special education and/or suspended. To be effective, culture changes must be carefully managed by school leaders.

Curriculum and Instruction Issues

School leaders are often reminded of their roles as instructional leaders. School reform makes this reality more pressing than ever, and leaders must be keenly aware of curricular issues. Curriculum is essentially a course of study that guides how knowledge is conveyed to learners. While it happens within the school building, there are outside forces in play, particularly with respect to alignment with state standards. The curriculum in many schools is dominated by majority culture and as a result African American students will often perceive that their behaviors, ideas, customs, and values are illegitimate or unimportant. Milner (2005) noted,

> Ensuring that various cultural, racial, ethnic, gendered, and linguistic groups of people and their experiences are represented in the curriculum is not the only essential feature in providing access, empowerment, and awareness for students of color. The very nature of this content and how it is actually incorporated into the lessons are also critical. (p. 393)

Students must see themselves in the curriculum and they must feel that they have significantly contributed to society. Milner (2005) went on to state,

> Thus, it is not enough to incorporate the historical, political, and social experiences, events, and challenges of various ethnic groups into the curriculum. Rather, the nature of that curriculum content—what is actually included, how, and why—is very important as students come to understand themselves and others in a pluralistic society. In short, the curriculum needs to be developed in a way that does not reify stereotypes and racism. (p. 393)

These tools help students become more resilient to negative messages from the dominant culture. School leaders must be attentive enough to the curriculum to confidently encourage teachers to balance standardized exams with culture-enhancing aspects of the curriculum.

Williams (2001) suggested that school leaders could ask themselves a set of questions to facilitate self-evaluation of their current practice in curriculum and instruction. In taking the liberty to modify some of the questions slightly with a focus on African American students, I pose the following questions to school leaders:

- Do teachers have an understanding of the cultures of the African American students represented in their respective classrooms?

- Are teachers and supervisors aware of learning styles that tend to be more common to African American students?

- Are conscious efforts made to give equivalent attention and encouragement to African American students?

- Is a variety of approaches used to assess mastery and competencies of African American students?

- How are African American people portrayed in the curriculum?

- What positions of power are represented?

- Who is privileged by the curriculum?

- Are multicultural library and media materials available to support instruction?

- Have all disciplines developed curriculum materials incorporating the histories, perspectives, and contributions of people of color so that an interdisciplinary understanding of all groups is promoted?

In summary, good leadership, school climate and culture, and curriculum and instruction represent three important elements in the addressing issues of White privilege and power in schools. These three areas represent critical starting points to address the many incongruities found in the education of African American children. While this short list of items is not exhaustive, I believe focusing on these items is a priority and change in these areas can affect other areas such as parental involvement.

CONCLUSION

While Whites today did not participate in slavery, they passively benefit from White supremacy and at times recreate it (Leonardo, 2004). These are realities that accrue significant benefits for Whites and serious burdens for Blacks. If this is the reality, then educational leaders must address White skin privilege and power issues and the less than subtle endorsement of White superiority. In preparing African American students for life, school leaders must change what is taught in their schools and how it is taught. By focusing on these challenges school leaders can empower Black children as a defense against White privilege. Indeed, successfully convincing African American students to graduate from school will result in securing a property right, a future job. As interest divergence states, most Whites will not release what has been afforded to them for so long—White privilege.

School leaders should make themselves more aware of issues surrounding race, law, and leadership. They must become culturally proficient leaders. In addition to professional development, leaders should study culturally relevant pedagogy and other strategies that will help them relate to African American students and their cultures. Leaders must also seek to understand the school culture of faculty and staff members. Too often leaders operate under the assumption that they know the culture in their building, but they must make efforts to periodically assess the school culture. These assessments may confirm that the leader's knowledge about the culture is correct, but these should be conducted because they can provide valuable data and insights. What teachers and other staff believe about educating African American students should be assessed, as this is a prerequisite to addressing issues of race. Next, leaders must work with teachers to address curriculum and instruction issues to better learn how teachers relate to African American students.

Bell (1989, 2004a) noted that there is a permanence of racism in America and there is ample evidence to support this premise. Educational leadership is not insulated from racism and White privilege, both of which are rooted in belief systems. To combat these belief systems, educational leaders must share information with their faculty and staff, regardless of the racial composition of the students or the staff. Educational leaders should lead with a social justice focus even in light of the fact that there are costs involved in engaging in this type of leadership. However, the costs of not doing so mean that we continue business as usual, which includes losing large numbers of Black students. Moreover, the rewards of solving this problem greatly outweigh the costs. Indeed, school leaders must work for Black children on the frontlines to bring about real change in the battle to eradicate power and privilege.

NOTE

1. The terms *African American* and *Black* will be used interchangeably in this chapter.

REFERENCES

Alston, J. A. (2000). Missing from action where are the black female school superintendents? *Urban Education, 35*(5), 525–537.

Anderson, J. D. (1988). *The education of blacks in the south, 1860–1935.* Chapel Hill: University of North Carolina Press.

Asante, M. K. (1999). *The painful demise of Eurocentrism: An Afrocentric response to critics.* Trenton, NJ: Africa World Press.

Asante, M. K. (2005). *Race, rhetoric, and identity: The architecton of soul.* Amherst, NY: Humanity Books.

Bell, D. A. (1980a). *Brown v. Board of Education* and the interest-convergence dilemma. *Harvard Law Review, 93,* 518–533.

Bell, D. A. (1980b). *Shades of Brown: New perspectives on school desegregation.* New York: Teachers College Press, Columbia University.

Bell, D. A. (1989). *And we are not saved: The elusive quest for racial justice.* New York: Basic Books.

Bell, D. A. (2004a). *Race, racism, and American law* (5th ed.). New York: Aspen.

Bell, D. A. (2004b). *Silent covenants: Brown v. Board of Education and the unfulfilled hopes for racial reform.* Oxford, UK: Oxford University Press.

Brown, F. (2004a). The first serious implementation of Brown: The 1964 civil rights act and beyond. *Journal of Negro Education, 73*(3), 182–190.

Brown, F. (2004b). The road to *Brown,* its leaders, and the future. *Education and Urban Society, 36*(3), 255–265.

Brown v. Board of Education of Topeka, Kansas, 347 U.S. 483 (1954).

Cobbs, P. M., & Turnock, J. L. (2003). *Cracking the corporate code: The revealing success stories of 32 African American executives.* New York: American Management Association.

Delgado, R., & Stefancic, J. (1997). *Critical white studies: Looking behind the mirror.* Philadelphia: Temple University Press.

Delpit, L. D. (1988). The silenced dialogue: Power and pedagogy in educating other people's children. *Harvard Educational Review, 58*(3), 280–298.

Delpit, L. D. (2006). Lessons from teachers. *Journal of Teacher Education, 57*(3), 220–231.

Dudziak, M. L. (2000). *Cold War civil rights: Race and the image of American democracy.* Princeton, NJ: Princeton University Press.

Finkelman, P. (1997). *Slavery and the law* (1st ed.). Madison, WI: Madison House.

Gooden, M. A. (2002). Stewardship and critical leadership: Sufficient for leadership in urban schools? *Education and Urban Society, 35*(1), 133–143.

Gooden, M. A. (2004). A history of black achievement as impacted by federal court decisions in the last century. *Journal of Negro Education, 73*(3), 230–237.

Gooden, M. A. (2005). The role of an African American principal in an urban information technology high school. *Educational Administration Quarterly, 41*(4), 630–650.

Grutter v. Bollinger, 539 U.S. 306 (2003).

Hacker, A. (1995). *Two nations: Black and white, separate, hostile, unequal* (Expanded and updated ed.). New York: Ballantine Books.

Hale, J. E. (1986). *Black children: Their roots, culture, and learning styles* (Rev. ed.). Baltimore: Johns Hopkins University Press.

Harris, J. J., Brown, F., & Russo, C. J. (1997). The curious case of *Missouri v. Jenkins*: The end of the road for court-ordered desegregation? *Journal of Negro Education, 66*(1), 43–55.

Hunter, R. C. (2004). The administration of court-ordered school desegregation in urban school districts: The law and experience. *Journal of Negro Education, 73*(3), 218–229.

Kouzes, J. M., & Posner, B. Z. (2002). *The leadership challenge* (3rd ed.). San Francisco: Jossey-Bass.

Ladson-Billings, G. (1992). Liberatory consequences of literacy: A case of culturally relevant instruction for African American students. *Journal of Negro Education, 61*(3), 378–391.

Ladson-Billings, G. (1996). "Your blues ain't like mine": Keeping issues of race and racism on the multicultural agenda. *Theory Into Practice, 35*(4), 248–255.

Ladson-Billings, G., & Tate, W. F. (1995). Toward a critical race theory of education. *Teachers College Record, 97*(1), 47–68.

Leonardo, Z. (2004). The color of supremacy: Beyond the discourse of "white privilege." *Educational Philosophy and Theory, 36*(2), 137–152.

Lewis, C. W. (2006). African American male teachers in public schools: An examination of three urban school districts. *Teachers College Record, 108*(2), 224–245.

Lightfoot, S. L. (1983). *The good high school: Portraits of character and culture.* New York: Basic Books.

Lindsey, R. B., Robins, K. N., & Terrell, R. D. (1999). *Cultural proficiency: A manual for school leaders.* Thousand Oaks, CA: Corwin Press.

McIntosh, P. (1988). *White privilege and male privilege: A personal account of coming to see correspondences through work in women's studies.* Wellesley, MA: Wellesley College, Center for Research on Women.

McIntosh, P. (1990). White privilege: Unpacking the invisible knapsack. *Independent School, 49*(2), 31–36.

Milner, H. R. (2005). Developing a multicultural curriculum in a predominantly white teaching context: Lessons from an African American teacher in a suburban English classroom. *Curriculum Inquiry, 35*(4), 391–427.

Milner, H. R., & Howard, T. C. (2004). Black teachers, black students, black communities, and *Brown*: Perspectives and insights from experts. *Journal of Negro Education, 73*(3), 285–297.

No Child Left Behind Act of 2001, Pub. L. No. 107-110, 115 Stat. 1425 (2002).

Orfield, G., Frankenberg, E. D., & Lee, C. (2003). The resurgence of school segregation. *Educational Leadership, 60,* 16–20.

Peterson, K. D., & Deal, T. E. (1998). *The shaping of school culture fieldbook* (1st ed.). San Francisco: Jossey-Bass.

Reeves, D. (2007). How do you change school culture? *Educational Leadership, 64*(4), 94–95.

Regents of the University of California v. Bakke, 438 U.S. 265 (1978).

Shakeshaft, C. (1987a). Training school administrators: The making of the man in the principal's office. *Teacher Education Quarterly, 14*(2), 59–67.

Shakeshaft, C. (1987b). *Women in educational administration.* Newbury Park, CA: Sage.

Shakeshaft, C., & Nowell, I. (1992). Gender and supervision in school personnel. *Education Digest, 57*(6), 14.

Thomas, D. A., & Gabarro, J. J. (1999). *Breaking through: The making of minority executives in corporate America.* Boston: Harvard Business School Press.

Tillman, L. C. (2004a). African American principals and the legacy of Brown. *Review of Research in Education, 28,* 101–146.

Tillman, L. C. (2004b). (Un) intended consequences? *Education and Urban Society, 36*(3), 280–303.

Tillman, L. C. (2005). Mentoring new teachers: Implications for leadership practice in an urban school. *Educational Administration Quarterly, 41*(4), 620–629.

Tillman, L. C. (2006). Researching and writing from an African American perspective: Reflective notes on three research studies. *International Journal of Qualitative Studies in Education, 19*(3), 265–287.

U.S. Department of Education, Office for Civil Rights. (2004). *Achieving diversity: Race neutral alternatives in American Education.* Jessup, MD: Author.

West, C. (2001). *Race matters* (2nd ed.). New York: Vintage Books.

Williams, B. T. (2001). Ethical leadership in schools servicing African American children and youth. *Teacher Education and Special Education, 24*(1), 38–47.

15

AFRICAN AMERICAN[1] SUPERINTENDENTS IN PUBLIC SCHOOL DISTRICTS

KAY LOVELACE TAYLOR

LINDA C. TILLMAN

B efore the *Brown* era, research on African American superintendents was nearly nonexistent, and it was not until the 1970s that African Americans serving in the superintendency came into focus as a particular line of inquiry. According to Tillman (2004), like the research on Black principals, research on Black superintendents is usually grouped in the category of "women and minorities," and information on the specific numbers of Black superintendents, as well as their roles and responsibilities before the 1970s, is sketchy. However, Tillman also noted that as student populations of African Americans and other minorities increased in public schools, so did the demand for African American school superintendents.

Thus, while research on African Americans in the superintendency is not as extensive as that about Black teachers and principals, we do know that Black superintendents have been in the forefront of the struggle to educate African American children (Jackson, 1995, 1999; Simmons, 2005; Tillman, 2004). In this chapter, we provide an overview of African Americans in the superintendency and review their current status. Next, we present perspectives on African Americans in the superintendency based on in-depth interviews with current and former African American superintendents as well as individuals who work in search firms and leadership training organizations and who serve on schools boards. We conclude this chapter with recommendations for the preparation, recruitment, and retention of African American superintendents.

AUTHORS' NOTE: We would like to thank the participants for taking time out of their hectic schedules to participate in this study. We would also like to thank the external reviewers as well as Catherine Lugg and psychologist Karen Conway for their critiques of this chapter. Finally, the first author is humbled by the opportunity to have had rich conversations with Dr. Hugh Scott and Dr. Charles Moody, leading authorities on African American superintendents.

AFRICAN AMERICANS
IN THE SUPERINTENDENCY

Since the 1970s African American school super-intendents have typically served in large, urban cities with majority African American student populations such as Washington, D.C., Philadelphia, Atlanta, and Chicago (Jackson, 1995; Simmons, 2005; Tillman, 2004). Jackson (1995) noted that like big-city mayors, early Black superintendents were called on to "represent the entire race and extraordinary expectations were placed on them" (p. 44). According to Jackson, Black school superintendents "are symbolic leaders and have an influence beyond their cities" (p. 45), and this symbolism is important for Blacks since they have typically been labeled as "inferior and incapable of carrying out high-level responsibilities" (p. 45). A decade later, Hunter and Donahoo (2005) concurred with Jackson's comments and noted that "although it is unrealistic, many expect African American superintendents to be all things to all people" (p. 427).

While national data on the demographics of the superintendency has been collected by the American Association of School Administrators (AASA) since 1953, AASA did not use *race* as a specific category until 1982, and data on Black superintendents were subsumed under the category of "minorities" (Jackson, 1999). Data on Blacks in the superintendency indicate that in 1982 there were 57 Black superintendents, representing 0.7% of the school superintendents nationally (Valverde & Brown, 1988). By the 1989–1990 school year, the number of Black superintendents had increased to 142, or 1.6% of superintendents nationally (Jackson, 1995). Many of these African American superintendents served in large urban districts, and in the 1997 school year 47% of all urban school superintendents were African American (Valverde, 2003).

Over the last half century, the newly found political and educational clout of African Americans has led to an increase in the number of African American superintendents appointed nationwide. The National Alliance of Black School Educators (NABSE) reports that currently of the 14,599 U.S. school superintendents, 323 are African American. Of these 323 superintendents, 222 are males and 101 are females, serving in 36 of the 52 states. According to NABSE, the largest numbers of African American superintendents serve in the states of Mississippi (43), Illinois (27), and Arkansas (25). The states or U.S. territories with three or fewer African American superintendents are Colorado, Idaho, Kansas, Kentucky, Maryland, Massachusetts, Minnesota, Oregon, Rhode Island, the Virgin Islands, and Washington. Twenty states have between 3 and 17 African American superintendents, while 18 states have none (personal communication, NABSE, May 2, 2007). While they are fewer in comparison with their White counterparts, the numbers of African Americans appointed to superintendency positions have increased significantly, particularly in urban districts.

Much of what we know about the current status of African American superintendents is found in reports by organizations concerned with minority issues such as the NABSE and the Education Trust (Robinson, Gault, & Lloyd, 2004) and the Council of the Great City Schools (CGCS, 2006). Theoretical and empirical work on African American superintendents tends to be situated in a limited number of books, articles, and dissertations including work by Scott (1980, 1983, 1990), Alston (1999, 2000), and Dawkins (2004). Most noteworthy is the pioneer work of Dr. Charles Moody, a leading authority on the topic who conducted the first study of African American superintendents. His 1971 dissertation, "Black Superintendents in Public School Districts: Trends and Conditions," focused on conditions of "school districts prior to the appointment of a Black superintendent" (p. 11), and Moody investigated conditions that included trends in financial support and changes in the racial composition of faculty, staff, student population, and school boards. Moody found that the majority of the superintendents in his study worked in districts with severe financial deficits and where the majority of the students, teachers, administrators, and school board members were non-White. While completing his dissertation, Moody, a former school superintendent himself, received a grant from the Metropolitan Applied Research Corporation Foundation to organize a group called the Chief Black School Officers. The group came together to discuss his findings and to strategize ways to address the education of Black children and the roles and responsibilities of Black superintendents. These 16 school superintendents would later become members of what became the NABSE, a group of educators that includes teachers, principals, and superintendents from across the United States and abroad (NABSE Web site). According to Robinson et al. (2004), "NABSE is the nation's premiere education association for Black educators and boasts a total membership of over 6,700 superintendents, public school administrators and teachers" (p. 2).

In 2003, NABSE and the Education Trust formed a partnership to study African Americans in the superintendency. In "Black School Superintendents Progress and Challenges: A Demographic Snapshot of Schools Led by NABSE Superintendents," the two groups indicated that their partnership was intended to "further our mutual goal of providing a high quality education for every Black student in the nation" (Robinson et al., 2004, p. 7). The report provides demographics about 248 African American superintendents who were members of NABSE in the fall of 2003 as well as the districts they served.

Findings from this report included the following:

- Districts headed by Black superintendents in this group varied in size and population. The majority of districts (148) had between 1 and 10 schools; 15 districts in this report had 100 schools or more.

- Black superintendents tended to be concentrated in school districts in the southeastern part of the United States; 137 or 55% of the Black superintendents in this group led districts that were located in states considered to be in the Deep South.

- Superintendents in this group led districts in a variety of settings, but mostly in urban areas; 133 of the 248 districts headed by Black superintendents were in predominantly urban areas. However, Black superintendents were also in charge of 74 districts in rural areas.

- These superintendents educated more than 3 million of the 47.7 million public school students in the country; supervised almost 6,000 schools and more than 193,000 teachers; and, as a group, managed budgets totaling approximately 25.1 billion dollars.

- Of the more than 3 million students in districts led by NABSE superintendents, 1.7 million or 54% were Black; 789,227 were White students, and 481,699 were Latino students.

- Students in these districts came from a variety of economic backgrounds and approximately 1.7 million of the 3 million students in these districts were classified as "low-income."

- A total of 219 schools in districts led by this group scored in the top-quartile on their respective 2002 state tests in reading and mathematics in the fourth and eighth grades. The schools identified in this report help dispel the myth that schools with large populations of minority students cannot achieve at high levels.

According to Robinson et al. (2004), these results show that there are success stories in districts with Black leadership. While the report is focused on a select group of African American superintendents, this group is representative of the majority of African American superintendents in U.S. public schools. Furthermore, this report addresses critical issues about the work of African American superintendents that has been absent in the scholarly literature (Björk, Glass, & Brunner, 2005; Simmons, 2005; Tillman, 2004).

METHODS

Interviews were conducted by the first author in 2006 and 2007 with a purposeful sample of three sitting African American superintendents, two African American former superintendents, the White male president of a search firm that assists school districts in placing superintendents, an African American school board member, two African American educational consultants, and the African American director of public affairs for a leadership training organization. In addition, the first author had conversations with two African Americans who are considered to be pioneers in the study of African Americans in the superintendency. Information gained from these rich conversations helped her to develop questions for this study. Each of the participants was selected because of their theoretical and practical knowledge about the superintendency. Table 15.1 provides an overview of the participants.

Each participant received a written or verbal request to participate in a telephone interview. Each interview lasted approximately 45 minutes,

TABLE 15.1   Participant Profiles

African American Superintendents	District	Tenure	Student Population	Student Ethnicity
Dr. Alice Anderson	Superintendent in Residence and former superintendent of two large urban school districts	2006–present		
Dr. Margaret Gordon	Superintendent of urban school district in the Pacific Northwest	Appointed in 2007	45,800	White, 40%; Black, 33%; Latino, 10%; Asian, 17%
Mr. Warren Madison	Superintendent of a school district in the Midwest	2007–present	15,000	White, 58%; Black, 39%; Hispanic, 1%; other, 2%
Dr. Darrell Samuels	Superintendent of school district in the eastern United States	2000–present	18,000	White, 28%; Black, 28%; Hispanic, 42%; other, 2%
Dr. Georgia Walton	Superintendent of a school district in the southwestern United States	2004–2007	13,000	White, 4%; Black, 17%; Hispanic, 78%; other, 1%
Mr. Garland Rhodes	Search firm president	1976–present		
Mr. Walter Hall	School board president, southwestern United States	1998–2005	24,474	
Corporate and Business				
Mr. Paul Hudson	Educational consultant			
Ms. Janet Warren	Educational consultant			
Ms. Karen Daniels	Director of public relations for a leadership development organization			
Originators				
Hugh Scott, Ed.D.	Pace University			
Charles Moody, Ph.D.	Retired			

and participants were asked to provide their perspectives about topics, which included, but were not limited to

(a) African Americans in the superintendency

(b) The multiple dimensions of the school superintendency

(c) Superintendent–school board relationships

(d) The recruitment of African Americans to the superintendency

(e) Superintendency preparation programs and professional development

(f) Race and gender in the superintendency

Interviews were taped and transcribed, and data were analyzed using the six major topics. In the next section, we present key findings from these interviews.

FINDINGS

There are approximately 14,383 school districts across the United States serving 48.3 million students, 7.7 million of whom are African Americans. As we noted previously, 323 or 2% of these districts are led by African American superintendents. Approximately 14,000 school districts are served by White superintendents, with the remainder of the districts being served by Hispanic, Asian, and other-race superintendents. The ratio of 323 African American superintendents to 7.7 million African American students is one African American superintendent for every 24,000 African American students. For White superintendents, taking into consideration approximations for Hispanic, Asian, and other-race student populations, the ratio is one White superintendent for every 2,200 students. As these data suggest and as Robinson et al. (2004) have noted, "There is an urgent need to increase the number of Black superintendents in the United States" (p. 14).

Respondents identified several issues that contribute to the recruitment, selection, appointment, and retention of African American superintendents. Mr. Walter Hall[2] is past president of a school board in a racially diverse city in the southwestern United States and the first African American to ever serve on this school board. Mr. Hall indicated that while his district received numerous applications from African American candidates who sought the position of superintendent 10 years ago, in recent years African American candidates have become scarce. He attributes the scarcity of African American candidates to three factors. First, he noted that African Americans now have more career opportunities available to them and may not view the superintendency, with all its challenges, as an attractive career. Second, he noted that there is a perception that African Americans can only be appointed to superintendency positions in urban districts. Perhaps most important, Mr. Hall noted that it has been his experience that African American candidates rarely engage in creating a political base or putting support structures in place prior to their interview.

While the lack of a political base or support structure may not apply to all African American candidates, it is likely to be more of a factor for them as a group since they usually do not have the same types of access to social and political networks as their White peers (Hunter & Donahoo, 2005; Simmons, 2005).

Dr. Darrell Samuels serves as a school superintendent in the eastern United States. He suggested that the shortage of African American candidates with superintendency certification could be one reason for the shortage of African American applicants. When he applied for his current position, he held superintendency certification in two different states; however, only one other person in the candidate pool held a superintendent's certificate. Because of the shortage of certified candidates in his district (regardless of race), his state launched a new program to certify superintendents. At the time he was interviewed, at least six individuals in his district would be eligible to apply for a superintendent's position in the state; however, the majority of these individuals were White. Dr. Samuels added that he teaches at a local university where he sees very few, if any, African Americans pursuing superintendent certification. These and other issues are relevant to African Americans in the superintendency. In the sections that follow, we elaborate on some of these issues.

THE MULTIPLE DIMENSIONS OF THE SCHOOL SUPERINTENDENCY

In interviews, participants identified four major areas that they believed were relevant to African Americans in the superintendency: (a) the complexity of the role of the superintendent, (b) the superintendent as Chief Executive Officer (CEO), (c) the superintendent as educational leader, and (d) the superintendent as political leader. Each area is particularly relevant to African Americans who aspire to the superintendency since today's superintendents need a broader array of skills than did their predecessors. These areas are also important because African American superintendents as a group tend to have shorter tenures than do their White counterparts, a factor that contributes to the shortage of African American superintendents (Hunter & Donahoo, 2005).

The Complexity of
the Role of Superintendent

In their book, *Superintendent as CEO: Standards-Based Performance*, Hoyle, Björk, Collier, and Glass (2005) discussed the superintendent's changing role. The authors argued that the superintendency has become so complex that applicants are required to have a set of skills that are much like the skills needed to supervise the day-to-day operations of a major corporation. Dr. Alice Anderson has been a superintendent in two large urban districts and is currently a superintendent in residence at a leadership development organization. She agreed with Hoyle et al.'s (2005) assessment that running a district has become very much like running a corporation. She noted that the business of a corporation is to develop a product for a profit. Similarly, the business of education is the development of children; the profit is student improvement.

Dr. Anderson commented that the superintendency is multifaceted, with three major dynamics: money, power, and politics. According to Dr. Anderson, a superintendent constantly attempts to work within the parameters of who has financial resources and who wants them, where the power rests and who wants it, and who has political clout and who wants it. She asserts that her own success as a superintendent came from understanding these three dynamics while maintaining a focus on the core mission of any district—the academic achievement of all children. Although she views herself as an educational leader, she noted that her job consisted primarily of clearing the way for staff to do what they do best, teach children.

In their book *What We Know About Successful School Leadership*, Leithwood and Riehl (2003) identified the complex environment in which school districts exist. Not only are school districts responsible for curriculum, standards, achievement benchmarks, programmatic requirements, and other policy directives, they must meet the needs of an increasingly diverse student population. The challenges confronting today's superintendents include understanding students' cultural backgrounds and norms, their health and mental status, and their socioeconomic status. Although she was not interviewed for this study, Dr. Beverly Hall, superintendent of the Atlanta Public Schools, discussed the importance of understanding students' cultural backgrounds in her 2006 State of the Schools Address. She emphasized that many of the children in Atlanta live in poverty and this reality brings with it many issues and concerns. Among these issues are the increasing numbers of children who come to school hungry and who live in deplorable living conditions. However, Dr. Hall (2006) indicated that she chooses not to dwell on these factors because they are not an excuse for providing the necessary supports for all children to be successful.

Some of the same issues facing urban districts such as Atlanta are also pervasive in rural schools. O'Hare and Johnson (2004) reported that African Americans represent approximately 4.9 million (9%) of the 14 million children living in rural America. According to O'Hare and Johnson, these children face conditions of extreme poverty, are less educated, and have limited access to social services and health care. Robinson et al. (2004) noted that African American superintendents who were members of NABSE led 74 districts in rural areas. While there is a paucity of literature about factors that affect the work of African American superintendents in rural districts, it appears that these superintendents may face challenges similar to those faced by their counterparts in other types of districts, particularly those in large urban districts (Lamkin, 2006).

The statistics about the poverty levels of millions of children in urban and rural school districts are a part of what makes the superintendency so complex. Many of these issues were prominent in the decision by the Interstate School Leaders Licensure Consortium's (ISLLC) decision to include language in its standards that address the educational needs of all children, while embracing and communicating the importance of understanding issues of poverty, social services, and health concerns as part of the educational process (see also Fusarelli & Fusarelli, 2005). Clearly, the position of school superintendent includes many facets—student achievement, school finance, the social and emotional welfare of students, and issues of diversity—and today's superintendents cannot rely on a "one-size-fits-all" model of leadership to maintain district stability and educate all children.

The Superintendent
as Chief Executive Officer

Over the past decade, several titles have been used to personify the job of the school superintendent. One title that defines the role of a superintendent as having more presence and influence is that of CEO. Mr. Garland Rhodes, the search firm president, suggests that the term *CEO* reflects a multidimensional person with an image comparable to that of a head of a major corporation. Rhodes noted that many large urban school districts are essentially corporations—they require a leader who is visionary and gifted and who has excellent written and verbal skills.

Indeed, the CEO moniker came at a time when U.S. public schools required a more authoritative title for the person responsible for the organizational climate of the district. Yet the title alone cannot convey the expertise needed by the men and women today who straddle the fine line of compromise necessary to appease a governing state or local school board, and a demanding community, while creating change to address more diverse student populations (Hunter & Donahoo, 2005). For example, the Council of the Great City Schools (2006) reported that serving as an urban superintendent is one of the most difficult jobs in America. According to the CGCS, the job requires a unique blend of leadership, management, instructional expertise, and political and operational skills that are needed in few other positions. It is also a position where districts experience superintendency turnover far too frequently, particularly given the need in urban districts to create more stability and momentum for school reform (Hening, Hula, Orr, & Pedescleaux, 2005; Simmons, 2005).

Even so, the requirements of the superintendency have changed in large districts as well as smaller ones (Björk, Glass, & Brunner, 2005; Kowalski, 2005). Educators who were once considered the most likely candidates for the superintendency now find that many communities and school boards are looking for leaders with different skill sets, such as presidents of universities, CEOs of corporations, and high-ranking military officers. These candidates are recruited because many schools, particularly in urban districts, are failing to educate large numbers of students (and particularly African American students), and new leadership is required. In many cases, districts hire noneducators to fill superintendent positions hoping that these individuals will bring unique leadership styles and a different set of skills that can be used to turn failing schools around (Fusarelli, 2005; Usdan & Cronin, 2003).

A close look at one city that hired both traditional and nontraditional leaders reveals that there may be little or no relationship between the professional background and experiences of the superintendent and improved student achievement. From 1987 through 2006, the Detroit (MI) Public Schools system appointed six superintendents to improve the management, leadership, and student achievement of the district. Three of these superintendents were educators with K-12 experience in curriculum and school leadership; two were university presidents nationally known for their effective leadership and management styles; and the last superintendent had an extensive background in finance. During this period, student performance on standardized tests in the Detroit Public Schools remained virtually the same over three reporting periods (1987–1988, 1997–1998, and 2005–2006). Figure 15.1 shows fourth grade reading and math scores: reading scores dropped from 1987 to 1997 and increased slightly from 1997 to 2006; fourth grade math scores remained relatively the same in all three reporting periods (Michigan Department of Education, 2006).

The Detroit example indicates that hiring nontraditional educators as school superintendents does not guarantee that they will have the expertise that can turn failing schools around.

The tenure of superintendents greatly influences the extent to which school districts improve regarding student achievement. The average tenure of a major city school district superintendent is less than 3 years (CGCS, 2003). In a study by Timothy Waters and Robert Marzano (2006), the authors found a direct correlation between student achievement and the length of a superintendent's tenure. Waters and Marzano conducted a meta-analysis of 27 research reports to dispel William Bennett's theory that district leadership is mostly ineffective. Their research revealed a direct relationship between student achievement and district leadership when "the superintendent, district office staff, and school board members do the right work in the right way" (p. 22). Thus, it appears that several factors are important in maintaining the stability of a school district and improving student achievement—who is hired as superintendent or CEO, the skills he or she brings to the position, and the length of his or her tenure in the district.

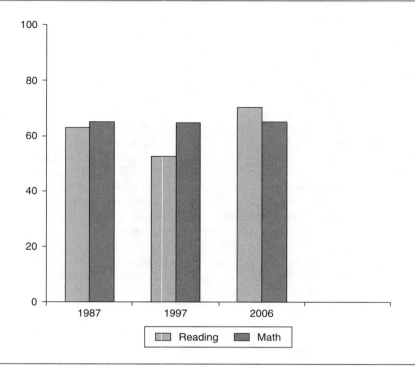

Figure 15.1   Michigan Educational Assessment Program Results for Detroit Public Schools in Reading and Mathematics 1987–1988, 1997–1998, 2005–2006

SOURCE: From "Urban School Superintendents: Characteristics, Tenure, and Salary", June 2006, *Urban Indicator, 8*(1). Reprinted with permission.

The Superintendent as Educational Leader

When asked if the superintendent is *the* educational leader in the school district, the superintendents interviewed for this chapter all answered "yes!" They also indicated that having a broad understanding of education and its various contexts is critical. Clearly, the position of the superintendent as an educational leader has gained new emphasis as a result of the need for effective leadership that addresses the increasing racial/ethnic diversity in schools, the increasing number of socially and economically deprived students, the shortage of highly qualified teachers, and student performance on standardized tests.

A sitting superintendent who participated in this study, Dr. Warren Madison, serves a small midwestern school district. He responded to questions concerning the superintendent as an educational leader (or, as he prefers, instructional leader) by emphasizing that the educational aspect is "why we are all here—it is first and foremost." He suggested that being the

educational leader is really the lynchpin for closing the many different gaps that impede the physical, mental, social, and academic growth of students. According to Dr. Madison, the superintendent must also be cognizant of six essential elements that he himself relies on to create change: (a) effective research-based curriculum, (b) valid and reliable assessments, (c) continuous research-based professional development, (d) development of competent leadership, (e) effective fiscal management, and (f) effective parent and community relations. These elements are consistent with work suggesting that superintendents are also social scientists, instructional leaders, communicators, and politicians (Browne-Ferrigno & Glass, 2005; Kowalski, 2005).

The Superintendent as Political Leader

Hunter and Donahoo (2005) noted that superintendents are accountable to their school boards as well as to local and state-level politicians. Additionally, Simmons (2005), in her discussion of African American and other superintendents of color, noted that

> today's superintendents require a formal political structure to negotiate sustained reform in their districts, especially large urban districts in which reform is most needed. In that many of these districts are where women and superintendents of color are often appointed, it is essential that these minorities gain access to the *political power* needed to develop and sustain reform in their districts. (p. 264)

According to Simmons, this political power is needed to mobilize the entire school community— teachers, parents, students, administrators, and school boards. Indeed, superintendents, and particularly African American superintendents, must understand and respond to the political dynamics in their districts. However, Hunter and Donahoo argue that African American superintendents rarely have the high levels of support from politicians and school boards.

In 2003, the Center on Reinventing Public Education issued a policy brief that discussed the political pressure confronting today's superintendents (Center on Reinventing Public Education Policy Brief, 2003). Superintendents who responded to a survey conducted by the Center reported that it is difficult to address public demands that often shift because of conflicting interests: What is considered a priority one day may be completely forgotten the next. The policy brief also indicated that urban superintendents identified teacher unions, school boards, and central office staff as the "iron triangle" blocking them from working collaboratively to create districtwide improvement. Björk and Gurley (2005) noted that the "politics" of the superintendency is often closely aligned with the agendas of various stakeholders and constituents, and the superintendent must be a political strategist to work effectively with these groups.

In the current study, Dr. Warren Madison described the political role of the superintendency as one requiring a person to multitask while adhering to a calendar of must-keep appointments to ensure that the lines of communication stay open. His experience in a mid-sized midwestern school district included balancing his desire to be a change agent while fighting political battles involving unions and special interest groups. Madison commented that he felt much of his time was spent "pushing through a brick wall" and believes that the political fights were diversions to keep him from focusing on what matters most: the children.

Similarly, Dr. Darrell Samuels, a 12-year veteran superintendent, noted that his first appointment to a large urban school district was a significant learning experience. He commented that he misjudged how important it is to manage political pressures while aggressively working to raise student achievement and promote staff accountability. Dr. Samuels is having success in his current position as superintendent of a smaller district because, according to him, he is cognizant of keeping himself open and receptive to his first allegiance: the school board. Dr. Samuels also recognized what he calls the "Big School Board," the state legislature. He hosts an annual breakfast for state legislators and meets with them individually, particularly during a campaign. He emphasized that this gives politicians an opportunity to hear directly from him about some of the concerns facing schools. From the politician's perspective, this information is invaluable because schools are an important leveraging tool when speaking to potential supporters.

The constant battle being waged in many school districts centers around who will oversee the district. Micromanaging by mayors, state departments of education, and local school boards are signals of dissatisfaction coming from the constituents who elect these governing officials (Björk & Gurley, 2005; Hening et al., 1999; Hunter & Donahoo, 2005; Simmons, 2005). How does a superintendent navigate these political waters to get the job done? Mr. Walter Hall, a former school board president, suggests that the general response to such a question appears to be that it is impossible unless major changes occur. He notes that the changes most likely to produce a climate conducive to children's learning are those that lead to superintendents having authority over programs and staffing, including the central office staff, and when school board members concentrate on creating policies rather than micromanaging districts. Mr. Hall also emphasizes that superintendent preparation programs do play an important role in enabling superintendents to transform educational environments; thus they must include "political astuteness" as a part of the curriculum.

SUPERINTENDENT–SCHOOL BOARD RELATIONSHIPS

A special report by the Education Writers Association (2003), *Effective Superintendents, Effective Boards: Finding the Right Fit*, details the issues facing superintendents and school boards, based on a poll of 175 superintendents and 2,096 school board presidents across the United States. The survey provided anonymous feedback about superintendents' views of their school boards and vice versa. Of the 175 superintendents who responded to the survey, 52% responded that school boards should be restructured, while 16% said they should be completely replaced. Conversely, 75% of school board presidents contended there is no need to change the present model of school board governance. The survey further revealed that nearly 7 out of 10 superintendents indicated that their school boards interfered where they should not, and two thirds of the superintendents believed "too many school boards would rather hire a superintendent they can control" (p. 4). These data indicate that school boards and superintendents do not always agree on the extent of their respective roles and responsibilities with respect to school district governance. Participants in this study had varying experiences in terms of their relationships with school boards.

Dr. Georgia Walton is a former superintendent of a racially diverse district in the southwestern United States. Soon after she was hired, she faced a newly elected school board. Instead of dealing with educational issues, she was completely consumed with political ones. Dr. Walton described her dilemma as trying to fit into the "unwritten rubric" of what her school board expected of her. Soon, she began each day by consulting the board attorney about various issues confronting the district. She usually provided the board members with a legal opinion instead of always agreeing to their demands. Naively, she believed that if board members could consider their requests from a legal standpoint, they would be grateful that she was being thorough in providing the best possible recourse. Dr. Walton believed that she was being a good political leader in her interactions with the board. Instead, the constant battle with the board caused her to take a medical leave. In her absence, the board ended her contract, and at the time of her interview she was in litigation.

Other superintendents in the current study indicated that they have had positive relationships with their school boards. Dr. Margaret Gordon was recently appointed superintendent of a midsized urban school district in the Pacific Northwest. Dr. Gordon suggested that school boards sometimes can become too involved in the day-to-day operations of the district. But, according to Dr. Gordon, her success as a superintendent in another school district came from constantly dialoguing with board members to keep them up-to-date on all matters that affected the district. By doing so, the board members developed more respect for her knowledge and did not become overly involved in the day-to-day district operations. Dr. Gordon indicated that superintendents often have to make tough decisions that are in opposition to the political position of one or more board members. However, she stated, "Ultimately if you feel you have made the right decision for children, you feel vindicated." Additionally, she stated that in her experience when the board is made up of individuals who have similar job-related experiences as the superintendent, members who disagree will come to a consensus once a decision has been made. She also stated that when board members move away from governance of the district to personal issues, relationships become strained and the superintendent may decide to move to another position.

When asked how he relates to his board, Dr. Darrell Samuels noted that he does not make a decision without informing the entire board. If one board member approaches him outside the formal structure, that request is shared with all the school board members. His view is that "you must be careful about the sides you take; so don't take sides—play it straight on every issue with everyone." Dr. Samuels suggested that if superintendents make mistakes when dealing with school boards, the mistakes can usually be traced to the superintendent not appreciating or respecting the board's individual members. He cautioned that the best intentions can be misunderstood and may leave some board members feeling not as respected as others—something than can have a negative impact on the superintendent's tenure. As Hunter and Donahoo (2005) have noted, superintendents are accountable to their school boards, and they must form collaborative working relationships that benefit the district generally and children more specifically.

RECRUITING AFRICAN AMERICANS FOR THE SUPERINTENDENCY: THE ROLE OF SEARCH FIRMS

Bjork, Glass, and Brunner (2005) noted that nearly half of all school districts hire search firms to assist them in identifying candidates for a superintendency position. According to Kowalski, search firms may also "provide in-service training for school board members on how to conduct a superintendent search and selection process" (p. 21). While there are varying perspectives on the effectiveness of search firms and whether they benefit or harm a candidate's chances of being hired (see, e.g., Chion-Kenney, 1994; Tallerico, 2000), search firms can play a key role in identifying African American candidates for superintendent positions.

Mr. Garland Rhodes, a search firm president, provided an in-depth view of the role of search firms in creating a list of viable candidates. He views his job as providing his clients (school districts) with a list of competent candidates so that regardless of who is selected from the list, the individual possesses the skills to potentially do an excellent job. His firm understands that the role of superintendent changes from district to district, "so of course, we look at the educational, political and social demographics of the district to provide the canvas to begin our search." Associates from the firm spend time in the community talking with board members, community leaders, administrators, parents, staff, and other stakeholders to understand the community's cultural, social, and educational norms and to get a feel for the environment. Next, they review the profiles of prospective candidates to determine if there appears to be a match between the needs of the district and a candidate's résumé. Once candidates are identified, the search firm begins to work with the district and the candidate(s) to prepare them for the search process.

When asked to discuss the shortage of African American superintendents, Rhodes stated that his firm understands the imperative to hire more minority superintendents. Rhodes estimated that his firm is responsible for the placement of 60% to 70% of the African American and women superintendents currently serving in the United States. He believes that it is very important to increase the number of minority superintendents for one obvious reason—there is a need to understand there are many talented African Americans across the country who can excel as a superintendent, regardless of the ethnicity of the district. He also emphasized that African American superintendents can serve as positive role models inspiring children simply by their presence, as in "look at me, this is possible." Rhodes continued by noting that all districts have racial issues, and his firm is sensitive to the manner in which those issues are presented in the search process. Sometimes a school district will indirectly indicate the type of candidate it is looking for, which may include a racial preference. But Rhodes stated,

> We stay focused. Our job is to present a good pool of candidates. We make certain that whoever the school board selects, the candidate will be up for the challenge. Sometimes our best thinking backfires. As an example, we presented a very diverse pool of candidates to a school board based on the fact that three-fourths of the student population is African American. However, the school board selected an individual who will be the first white superintendent to lead the district in ten years.

As Kowalski (2005) noted, the reasons a particular individual is hired varies depending on the type of district, and these reasons may include concrete factors such as certification and previous experience or less concrete factors such as personality fit and race.

SUPERINTENDENCY PREPARATION PROGRAMS AND PROFESSIONAL DEVELOPMENT

The complex role of the superintendency suggests that aspiring superintendents must be prepared to excel in politics, finance, curriculum, personnel issues, and teaching and learning while meeting requirements designed to combat the declining achievement of American students (Björk, Kowalski, & Browne-Ferrigno, 2005). Teachers and principals have traditionally participated in certification programs based on professional standards; however, in the past two decades professional standards for superintendents have also been emphasized. Björk et al. (2005) noted that most educational leadership/school administration programs that include preparation for the superintendency offer a core set of courses that include school management, school law, school finance, and other courses that are relevant to the multifaceted job of the superintendency. Today, more than ever before, professional organizations, universities, and state educational agencies are collaborating on the development and implementation of performance standards that are critical to becoming effective in the role of superintendent or CEO (Hoyle et al., 2005), Although many groups were involved in the process of developing professional standards for superintendents, the AASA, the National Council for the Accreditation of Teachers in Education, the National Policy Board for Educational Administration, the Council of Chief State School Officers, and the ISLLC developed the eight performance standards that are widely acknowledged today as the context for the improvement of principals, superintendents, and other school executives (Hoyle et al., 2005).

An analysis of the interview data reveals that for African Americans who aspire to the superintendency, more extensive professional development is needed. Participants suggested that as a complement to required standards, leadership and professional development programs should also include information and course work that is focused on (a) mentoring by successful African Americans who are currently serving as superintendents, (b) learning how to work effectively with school boards and communities to get desired results, (c) understanding the importance of and mastering the art of speaking and writing clearly and persuasively, (d) making certain the district budget is always focused on children, (e) ensuring that the curriculum reflects changing demographics and includes the use of technology, (f) monitoring instructional practices, (g) discussing race and its impact on teaching and learning, and (h) following ethical convictions by making the right decisions the first time. These suggested additions are similar to the ISLLC standards but can also merge theory and the realities of the day-to-day practice of the contemporary superintendency.

African Americans may also participate in alternative superintendency preparation programs. For example, the Broad Academy in Los Angeles, established in 2001, identifies and trains leaders from education, business, the military, nonprofit organizations, and government to become leaders in the largest urban school districts in the country. The intensive 10-month program is designed to provide each candidate with the skills necessary to be effective superintendents in urban schools. The Broad Academy for Superintendents, as well as the Urban Superintendents Program at Harvard University, and the Cooperative Superintendency Program at the University of Texas-Austin are programs that originated from a need to place more African Americans and other minorities in leadership roles. They are designed to provide aspirants with an opportunity to receive an experience that comes as close as possible to the job of superintendent. The programs are tuition-free to the candidates; that is, in most cases fees are paid by the district. Such programs may provide information and training that are not found in traditional superintendency preparation programs, with course work that is more focused on practice than theory. These and other programs provide aspiring superintendents with a variety of options for leadership training and professional development.

RACE AND GENDER IN THE RECRUITMENT OF AFRICAN AMERICAN SUPERINTENDENTS

As noted earlier, African Americans represent only 2% of the superintendents in the nation. Clearly, more African Americans need to pursue and to be appointed to superintendency positions. Yet there are many unanswered questions with respect to the shortage of African Americans in the superintendency pipeline. Among these questions are the following: Is there a shortage of African Americans applying for the position nationally or are the shortages more related to specific regions of the country (north, Pacific Northwest) or types of districts (rural, suburban)? Is there a shortage of African American superintendents with the credentials and experience who can fill vacant positions? Or are race and gender major factors, making the selection of an African American more challenging?

The CGCS conducted a survey in 2006, which included 59 of its 65 member districts. Results of the survey indicate that 46 districts responded to the survey, allowing CGCS to compare race, gender, and tenure statistics of superintendents in urban districts. Results of the survey indicated that 46% of CGCS superintendents identified themselves as White, 45% as Black, 9% as Hispanic, and 2% as other. In contrast, in 1997,

37% of CGCS superintendents identified themselves as White, 47% as Black, and 16% as Hispanic. The 2006 report indicates a 9% increase in White superintendents, a 2% decrease in Black superintendents, and a 7% decrease in Hispanic superintendents. Additionally, in 2006, the number of White female superintendents increased by 12%, and the number of African American female superintendents increased by only 1% (Figure 15.2).

The report by CGCS is based on survey responses and does not provide qualitative data about why some racial/ethnic groups increased their numbers in the superintendency while others did not. However, participants in this study speculated about why the numbers of African American superintendents is not increasing nationally. Paul Hudson, the founder of an executive leadership development program, stated, "Racism is elusive, but if you look at the turnover of African American superintendents versus their white counterparts, therein lies the answer." He indicated that the average African American superintendent holds an appointment for 2.7 years while the average

tenure for White superintendents is 6 years or more. Hudson also contends that the majority of African American superintendents are placed in predominantly African American districts with limited resources and impossible goals such as reducing the achievement gap within 2 years (see also Hunter & Donahoo, 2005). He believes that it is time for search firms and school boards to realize that African Americans are capable of serving in districts that do not have majority African American student populations, just as White superintendents serve in districts that do not have majority White student populations. There are many examples of White superintendents leading districts where a majority of the students are minorities. For example, Joel Klein serves as the chancellor of the New York Public Schools (9% White student population), and Arne Duncan serves as the superintendent of the Chicago Public Schools (14% White student population). However, very few African Americans lead school districts where the majority of the students are White. Two exceptions are Maria Goodloe-Johnson (Seattle Public Schools) and Walter Milton

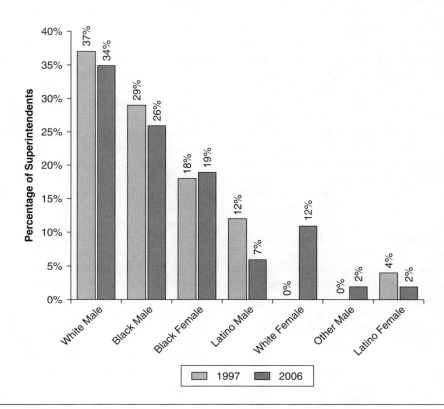

Figure 15.2   Race/Ethnicity and Gender of GCS Superintendents: 1997 and 2006

(Springfield Schools in Illinois), both of whom are African American superintendents in majority White districts.

Hudson continued by indicating that some school boards, regardless of race/ethnicity, do not believe that African American candidates are capable of supervising billion-dollar budgets. But he stressed that in large urban districts, African American superintendents award more multi-million dollar contracts for incidentals such as paint and cleaning supplies than do superintendents in suburban districts. Additionally, he noted that African American superintendents in these districts oversee the purchasing and leasing of buses, the renovating and building of new schools, and the awarding of contracts to food vendors that service urban schools based on poverty index status. According to Hudson, the dollar amounts of these contracts far exceed the dollar amounts for contracts issued by suburban schools. Hudson's comments are consistent with the NABSE/Education Trust report (Robinson et al., 2004), which indicates that the 248 African American superintendents in their study collectively were responsible for budgets totaling 25.1 billion dollars. Hudson further noted that racism is difficult to prove; however, when looking at indicators that include high turnover of African American superintendents, limited human and financial resources, and demands for improvements in a short period of time—all these factors can negatively affect the work of the most effective superintendents. Hudson concluded by noting that another factor is also important: The majority of African American superintendents, unlike White superintendents, receive their appointment by only a small vote margin of the total school board. This fact usually places the African American superintendent in a defensive position from the beginning of his or her tenure.

Mr. Hall, the former school board president, suggests that many African American superintendents face almost impossible odds against being successful, even if they miraculously have all the aforementioned issues under control. Today African American superintendents may face a more difficult issue: simply being African American. Mr. Hall stated that

> most teacher associations are part of the
> interviewing process, and regardless of whether
> this statement is politically correct, the issue is

that many teachers do not believe African American students are capable. How do you think this translates to an African American superintendent.

His view that *race* is a factor is supported by Taylor (2004), who reported that in private conversations educators reveal that not all teachers believe that African American children are capable of achieving at high levels (see also Irvine, 1990; Ladson-Billings, 1994). According to Taylor, teachers mouth the words "all children can learn," but they apologetically give a multitude of reasons why they believe that African American children are such poor achievers. Mr. Hall concluded by noting that the permanence of race as a predictor of student achievement is alive and well in the classroom as well as the board room—that is, African American students as well as superintendents are viewed as less competent based on their race.

When asked if race and gender come into play during the initial selection of candidates by a search firm, Mr. Rhodes, the search firm president, responded that the demographics of the district do play a key role, as do requests by the school board. However, for the initial list of applicants his firm looks first and foremost at the applicant profiles to determine if their skills match the needs of the district. If the applicant's profile matches the district's need, "We have a match, and the candidate's name is submitted regardless of race and gender." While Rhodes appeared to downplay the significance of race and gender, gender may work together with race to particularly disadvantage African American females in the superintendency.

Dr. Gerry House is an African American female and former superintendent of the Memphis, Tennessee, school district. Dr. House, in a discussion about the influence of race and gender in the superintendency stated, "Bias based on race and sex might not be as blatant as it was a decade ago, but that doesn't mean such attitudes don't still exert a powerful influence on how a job unfolds" (Gewertz, 2006, p. 24). Commenting on her tenure as superintendent in Memphis, House also stated, "What I experienced was subtle, but the subtleties are not imagined. Race and gender are always the elephants in the room. To dismiss them as real issues is to put our heads in the sand" (p. 24). Dr. House's comments are similar to Doughty's

(1980) assertion that Black females in administrative positions are in a "double bind"—they are Black and female, a fact that can have negative consequences for their careers (see also Alston, 1999, 2000). Clearly, the issues of race and gender continue to be pervasive as African Americans seek to lead districts and improve the educational achievement of all children.

CONCLUSION

There is a shortage of African American superintendents serving the 48.3 million students in this country, and more must be done to attract, prepare, recruit, and retain African American superintendents—not only in urban school districts—but in all types of school districts across the United States. If indeed we have a commitment to educating all children, we must be more proactive in recruiting and retaining African American superintendents who have the knowledge, skills, dispositions, and vision to improve the educational outcomes for all children.

Participants in this study offered five recommendations for aspiring superintendents, seated superintendents, search firms, and school boards, as well as colleges, universities, and professional development organizations for increasing the number of African Americans who are appointed to school superintendent positions. These recommendations are consistent with the literature on pipeline issues for African Americans in school administration (Simmons, 2005; Tillman, 2004).

First and foremost, aspiring African American superintendents must take a proactive role in seeking the position of superintendent. Dr. Alice Anderson shared that the job of superintendent is not a position that one acquires by chance. Experience, credentials, and personality all come into play. She emphasized that the superintendency is hard work; if done effectively, it can negatively impact one's personal life. African Americans must contend with the pervasiveness of race, as a measure of their competence and African American women must contend with issues of race and gender—there is no getting around these issues. The general consensus of the participants was that African Americans who aspire to the superintendency must be more persistent and devote time to understanding who they are as professionals and what their ultimate goals are before becoming a viable candidate.

Second, given the shortage of African American candidates, search firms can make a greater effort to identify candidates who demonstrate potential but who may not currently have all the desired credentials and experience. Search firms can provide additional information to school boards, include this information in the applicant's package, and discuss with the applicant what credentials and experience he or she will need to be considered a serious candidate. The participants in this study felt strongly that some African American candidates are overlooked for a variety of reasons. If the candidate's profile is a strong match to the needs of the district, search firms can use their influence with the school board to educate members about an African American candidate's skills and qualifications to decrease the likelihood that the candidate will not be treated fairly during the interview process.

Third, participants indicated that school boards must give the power of leading the district to the superintendent. Participants indicated that the role of the school board is to work with the superintendent, rather than working around him or her regarding matters that affect the stability of the district and the education of all children. More important, school boards should assess their perceptions concerning race as a factor in selecting and hiring a superintendent. Participants recommended that all school board members, regardless of race, receive extensive training that focuses on issues of race and race relations to ensure that biased perceptions do not come into play during the search process.

Fourth, African Americans who aspire to the superintendency, as well as seated African American superintendents, need consistent, long-term mentoring. The first author has been a part of two coaching and mentoring projects for educational leaders, including superintendents. In each instance, African Americans indicated they wanted a same-race mentor or coach. As long as race continues to matter in this country, African Americans must be given opportunities to discuss their concerns, without prejudice or bias, with someone who has had similar experiences and who understands the subtle forms of racism and its impact on the day-to-day activities of a school superintendent.

Finally, participants indicated that there is a need for professional development that is responsive to the real-life situations experienced by superintendents. Participants suggested that there is a reason why alternative preparation programs have emerged as viable alternatives to traditional preparation programs—to offer more options for leadership preparation for minority and nontraditional candidates. Although university classes and training programs have progressed over the last decade and are now more closely aligned with professional standards for superintendents and other administrators (Björk, Kowalski, et al., 2005), participants indicated that many course syllabi do not address the complexities and challenges of today's schools. The multidimensional role of the superintendent must be addressed in more substantive ways; that is, university preparation programs must be more aligned with real-world situations that affect the day-to-day practice of superintendents broadly as well as in regional contexts. While these suggestions do not represent the complete range of possibilities for increasing the number of African American superintendents, participants believed that they are necessary to begin to change the face of the superintendency.

African American superintendents can and do play a key role in the education of all students. But some of their most important work has been and will continue to be to enhance the social, emotional, and academic life chances of the many African American students who live in poverty, attend underfunded schools, are taught by underqualified teachers, and whose test scores fall dramatically below those of their White peers. Thus, it is African American superintendents who will continue the legacy of working to educate African American children. To do so, however, will require a focused effort to increase the pipeline of African Americans who are prepared to enter a most important position, the superintendency.

NOTES

1. The terms *Black* and *African American* will be used interchangeably in this chapter.

2. Pseudonyms will be used for participant names as well as the names of school districts and organizations.

REFERENCES

Alston, J. A. (1999). Climbing hills and mountains: Black females making it to the superintendency.

In C. C. Brunner (Ed.), *Sacred dreams: Women and the superintendency* (pp. 79–90). Albany: State University of New York Press.

Alston, J. A. (2000). Missing from action: Where are the Black female school superintendents? *Urban Education, 35*(5), 525–531.

Björk, L. G., Glass, T. E., & Brunner, C. C. (2005). Characteristics of American school superintendents. In L. G. Björk & T. J. Kowalski (Eds.), *The contemporary superintendent: Preparation, practice, and development* (pp. 19–44). Thousand Oaks, CA: Corwin Press.

Björk, L. G., & Gurley, K. D. (2005). Superintendent as educational statesman and political strategist. In L. G. Björk & T. J. Kowalski (Eds.), *The contemporary superintendent: Preparation, practice, and development* (pp. 163–186). Thousand Oaks, CA: Corwin Press.

Björk, L. G., Kowalski, T. J., & Browne-Ferrigno, T. (2005). Learning theory and research: A framework for changing superintendent preparation and development. In L. G. Björk & T. J. Kowalski (Eds.), *The contemporary superintendent: Preparation, practice, and development* (pp. 71–106). Thousand Oaks, CA: Corwin Press.

Browne-Ferrigno, T., & Glass, T. E. (2005). Superintendent as organizational manager. In L. G. Björk & T. J. Kowalski (Eds.), *The contemporary superintendent: Preparation, practice, and development* (pp. 137–162). Thousand Oaks, CA: Corwin Press.

Center on Reinventing Public Education Policy Brief. (2003). *An impossible job: The view from the urban superintendent's chair.* Retrieved August 2, 2007, from www.wallacefunds.org

Chion-Kenney, L. (1994). Boon or bane for non-traditional candidates for the superintendency. *School Administrator, 51*(2), 8–18.

Council of the Great City Schools. (2003). *Urban school superintendents: Characteristics, tenure and salary.* Retrieved August 2, 2007, from www.cgcs.org

Council of the Great City Schools. (2006). *Urban school superintendents: Characteristics, tenure and salary. Fifth survey and report.* Retrieved August 2, 2007, from www.cgcs.org

Dawkins, G. D. (2004). A study of Black superintendents in Michigan. *Dissertation Abstracts International, 65*(04), A. (UMI No. AAT 3130334)

Doughty, R. (1980). The Black female administrator: Woman in a double bind. In S. K. Biklen & M. B. Brannigan (Eds.), *Women and educational leadership* (pp. 165–174). Lexington, MA: Lexington Books.

Education Writers Association. (2003). *Effective superintendents, effective boards: Finding the right fit* (Report). Washington, DC: Author. Retrieved June 27, 2007, from www.wallace foundation.org

Fusarelli, B. C. (2005). When generals (or colonels) become superintendents: Conflict, chaos, and community. In G. J. Petersen & L. D. Fusarelli (Eds.), *The politics of leadership: Superintendents and school boards in changing times* (pp. 117–134). Greenwich, CT: Information Age.

Fusarelli, B. C., & Fusarelli, L. D. (2005). Reconceptualizing the superintendency: Superintendents as applied social scientists and social activists. In L. G. Björk & T. J. Kowalski (Eds.), *The contemporary superintendent: Preparation, practice, and development* (pp. 187–206). Thousand Oaks, CA: Corwin Press.

Gewertz, C. (2006). Race, gender, and the superintendency. *Education Week, 25*(24), 1, 22, 24.

Hall, B. L. (2006). *State of the schools address,* Atlanta, GA. Retrieved August 17, 2006, from www.atlanta.k12.ga.us

Hening, J. R., Hula, R. C., Orr, M., & Pedescleaux, D. S. (1999). *The color of school reform: Race, politics, and the challenge of urban education.* Princeton, NJ: Princeton University Press.

Hoyle, J., Björk, L. G., Collier, V., & Glass, T. E. (2005). *The superintendent as CEO: Standards-based performance.* Thousand Oaks, CA: Corwin Press.

Hunter, R. C., & Donahoo, S. (2005). All things to all people: Special circumstances influencing the performance of African American superintendents. *Education and Urban Society, 37*(4), 419–430.

Irvine, J. J. (1990). *Black students and school failure: Policies, practices, and prescriptions.* Westport, CT: Greenwood Press.

Jackson, B. L. (1995). *Balancing act: The political role of the urban school superintendent.* Lanham, MD: University Press of America, in cooperation with the Joint Center for Political and Economic Studies, Washington, DC.

Jackson, B. L. (1999). Getting inside history— Against all odds: Black women school superintendents. In C. C. Brunner (Ed.), *Sacred dreams: Women and the superintendency* (pp. 141–159). Albany: State University of New York Press.

Kowalski, T. J. (2005). Evolution of the school district superintendent position. In L. G. Björk & T. J. Kowalski (Eds.), *The contemporary superintendent: Preparation, practice, and development* (pp. 1–18). Thousand Oaks, CA: Corwin Press.

Ladson-Billings, G. (1994). *The dreamkeepers: Successful teachers of African American children.* San Francisco: Jossey-Bass.

Lamkin, M. L. (2006). Challenges and changes faced by rural superintendents. *The Rural Educator, 28*(1), 1–12.

Leithwood, K. A., & Riehl, C. (2003). *What we know about successful school leadership* (A Report by Division A of AERA, NCSL). Washington, DC: AERA. Retrieved June 27, 2007, from www.ncsl.org.uk

Michigan Department of Education. (2006). *Michigan educational assessment program 2005–2006.* Retrieved August 2, 2007, from www.michigan.gov

Michigan Department of Education. (n.d.). *Michigan educational assessment program results for Detroit Public Schools in reading and mathematics, 1987-2006.* Retrieved May 2, 2007, from www.detroit.k12.mi.us

Moody, C. D. (1971). Black superintendents in public school districts: Trends and conditions. *Dissertation Abstracts International, 42,* 1413.

O'Hare, W., & Johnson, K. M. (2004). Child poverty in rural America. *Reports on America, 4*(1), 16–18.

Robinson, S., Gault, A., & Lloyd, S. (2004). *Black superintendents: Progress and challenges: A demographic snapshot of school districts led by NABSE superintendents.* Washington, DC: NABSE & The Education Trust. Retrieved June 27, 2007, from www2.edtrust.org

Scott, H. (1980). *The African American superintendent: Messiah or scapegoat?* Washington, DC: Howard University Press.

Scott, H. J. (1983). Views of Black school superintendents on school desegregation. *Journal of Negro Education, 52*(4), 378–382.

Scott, H. J. (1990). Views of Black school superintendents on Black consciousness and professionalism. *Journal of Negro Education, 59*(2), 165–172.

Simmons, J. K. (2005). Superintendents of color: Perspectives on racial and ethnic diversity and implications for professional preparation and practice. In L. G. Björk & T. J. Kowalski (Eds.), *The contemporary superintendent: Preparation, practice, and development* (pp. 251–282). Thousand Oaks, CA: Corwin Press.

Tallerico, M. (2000). Gaining access to the superintendency: Headhunting, gender, and color. *Educational Administration Quarterly, 36*(1), 18–43.

Taylor, K. L. (2004). *Through their eyes: A strategic response to the national achievement gap.* Philadelphia: Research for Better Schools.

Tillman, L. C. (2004). (Un)intended consequences? The impact of the *Brown v. Board of Education* decision on the employment status of Black educators. *Education and Urban Society, 36*(3), 280–303.

Usdan, M. D., & Cronin, J. M. (2003). *Rethinking the urban school superintendency: Nontraditional leaders and new models of leadership.* ERIC Document Reproduction Service No. ED477785.

Valverde, L. (2003). School leadership for 21st century urban communities. In R. Hunter & F. Brown (Eds.), *Challenges of urban education and the efficacy of school reform* (pp. 187–199). London, UK: Elsevier.

Valverde, L., & Brown, F. (1988). Influences on leadership development of racial and ethnic minorities. In N. Boyan (Ed.), *The handbook on educational administration* (pp. 143–158). New York: Longmans.

Waters, J. T., & Marzano, R. J. (2006). *School district leadership that works: The effect of superintendent leadership on student achievement.* Denver, CO: Mid-continent Research for Education and Learning.

SECTION IV

AFRICAN AMERICANS IN HIGHER EDUCATION

INTRODUCTION

KOFI LOMOTEY

Fom one (preferred) perspective, this section is quite comprehensive in that we offer a mere 60+ pages, yet we address (1) undergraduate admissions at predominantly White institutions (Comeaux & Allen), (2) undergraduate curriculum and pedagogy (Yasin), (3) undergraduate campus culture at predominantly Whites institutions (William Smith), (4) a historical analysis of historically Black colleges and universities (HBCUs; Lomotey & Aboh), and (5) graduate school and the professoriate: issues of access (Danley, Land, & Lomotey). Moreover, each discussion is comprehensive, informative, and replete with implications for research, theory, and practice, with widespread generalizability.

From another perspective, the picture that we paint herein of the state of higher education for people of African descent in the United States is dismal—at best. We look at (1) limited access to higher education for students of African descent, leading to limited lifelong economic benefits (Comeaux & Allen); (2) inappropriate practices and attitudes on predominantly White campuses that lead to high levels of physiological and psychological stress for students of African descent (William Smith); (3) the underrepresentation of faculty of African descent at colleges and universities (Danley, Land, & Lomotey); and (4) questionable missions for HBCUs (Lomotey & Aboh). While each of these chapters is, in a sense, upbeat, in that they offer pre-scriptions for change, the chapter by Yasin is upbeat *and* prescriptive, as well—throughout. Yasin offers an effective teaching tool for university faculty that is standing right in front of them in their classes—hip-hop culture (HHC). He offers HHC as a strategy for contributing to the success of students of the hip-hop generation.

Eddie Comeaux and Walter Allen acknowledge a decline in the admission of students of African descent in the University of California system since 1996. Relatedly, the authors indicate that California does not adequately invest in higher education. The authors look at the admission policies and procedures at University of California at Los Angeles and at Berkeley, noting specific procedures on these two campuses as they relate to the campuses' narrowly defined definitions of merit—considering only grade point average and test scores. The discussion is important, in part, because, as Bowen and Bok (1998, cited in the chapter by Comeaux & Allen) indicated, graduates of such selective institutions have significantly higher lifelong economic benefits.

Comeaux and Allen indicate that as the definitions of merit on the two campuses correlate with socioeconomic status, they, by definition, exclude large numbers of students of African descent from their admission pools. Larger issues, they contend, contribute to the underrepresentation of students of African descent in these institutions. They include

- second-class status of students of African descent in K-12 institutions,

- failure of these higher education institutions to use affirmative action practices, and

- insufficient planning for higher education in California.

The authors also point to ambiguity—perhaps intentional—in the selection processes of these two institutions as a factor contributing to the underrepresentation of students of African descent in their admission pools.

In addition, Comeaux and Allen criticize the mechanical nature of the admission processes on these campuses. I would note that some institutions, like Oberlin College, use, as a part of their admission criteria, measures such as "sticktuitiveness" along with traditional admission criteria in considering applicants.

Comeaux and Allen offer specific steps necessary to remedy the challenge of access to higher education for students of African descent. They conclude that these two institutions clearly have flawed selection processes, indicating that to equitably treat applicants for admission, these institutions must reconceptualize the concept of merit. This is necessary, they contend, for us to move forward toward a more democratic society.

Jon Yasin, in an interesting chapter on HHC and higher education, begins with an expansive discussion of the origin of HHC, pointing out that it is global, with its origin in the early 1970s in New York City with youth of African and Latino/Latina descent. The originators of HHC were Deejay Kool Herc, Deejay Afrika Bambaataa, and Deejay Grandmaster Flash. Presently, the elements of HHC are deejayin', emceeing (rapping), b-boyin', and b-girlin' (break dancing), taggin' (graffiti art), and knowledge (studying). HHC, according to Yasin, was, in part, a response to racism, sexism, classism, and other illegitimate forms of exclusion in U.S. society, which manifested themselves in oppression, assassinations, and other violent acts. Yasin refers to this spawning mechanism as knowledge of oppression, injustice, and discrimination in the United States. HHC also grew out of a reaction to the changing African American community as a result of gentrification.

The elements of HHC, most notably b-boyin' and b-girlin', were quickly embraced by mainstream (dance) institutions. This and other forms of acceptance, according to Yasin, have brought about the tolerance (and even acceptance on some levels) of HHC in the larger society and internationally.

Yasin makes the point that HHC is critically important as a teaching tool in that it enables students of the hip-hop generation to relate old knowledge—HHC (often their primary discourse)—with new knowledge. It is used by youth to mediate their travels through higher education. It is, for many youth, a study tool.

Yasin, who has done extensive research on the topic of HHC, indicates that many faculty at a wide cross section of institutions of higher education already use HHC as a pedagogical tool or as the subject matter for courses. These include, but are not limited to, faculty at Clark Atlanta University, Laney College, Minnesota State University, Hofstra University, the College of New Rochelle, New York University, and Syracuse University. He points out that youth already use HHC; therefore, its use in the classroom is critical if large numbers of the youth in the HHC are to be successful.

Yasin's own words best describe the importance of the link between higher education instruction and HHC:

> Because our youth employ aspects of Hip Hop culture as sources of motivation, as tools to assist them in being responsible for studying, learning, and completing homework assignments, educators *must* enable these youth even more by incorporating features of this youth culture into the teaching-learning process in their classrooms.

With the dynamic nature of HHC, Yasin contends that even more strategies will be required in using HHC in college classrooms of the future.

William Smith provides an analysis of the racial climate for students of African descent on predominantly White campuses (PWIs). (He refers to these institutions as historically White institutions.) A major point for Smith is that things have not changed substantially for students of African descent at PWIs since they started attending these institutions in significant numbers in the 1960s. These institutions are, he says, life draining rather than life enhancing for students of African descent. Sadly, Smith adds that neither mental health professionals nor administrators are equipped to address this challenge.

Interestingly, for more than 40 years, researchers have been studying the nature of the support that students of African descent receive at PWIs. Few studies uncover the existence of adequate support. Smith points out that stress is the inverse of support, while arguing that students of African descent are indeed suffering from institutionally induced physiological and psychological stress.

What Smith refers to as reactionary racism (RR) is still perpetuated at PWIs. RR is a view steeped in the belief that students of African descent are (1) focused on too much, (2) too pushy, (3) disproportionately economically advantaged, (4) too demanding, and (5) too influential on desegregation issues. Additionally, there is still a perception on these campuses of students of African descent with an inferior violent culture prone toward a preference for welfare and poverty. Consequently, students of African descent, Smith argues, suffer from racial battle fatigue—which he defines. These students are also, he contends, prone to mundane extreme environmental stress—which he also defines.

Notably, Smith points out that fewer students of African descent are attending HBCUs than was the case in the 1960s, and he ponders what is the effect of these students not receiving the benefits of these culturally affirming institutions.

While acknowledging that people of African descent, including students at PWIs, persevere and even excel at times through the implementation of coping strategies, Smith concludes with the warning that PWIs must change their practices as they relate to students of African descent to derail this viscous, racist, and stress-inducing cycle.

Sessi Aboh and I tackle the topic of HBCUs. We begin with reflections on how many HBCUs began—with the support of Whites. We emphasize the anti-Black intentions of many of these benefactors, while acknowledging that some of these individuals and institutions clearly sought advancement for people of African descent.

We next discuss the attitudes, over the years, of people of African descent toward HBCUs and their benefactors. We talk about the voices of Black intellectuals, Black nationalists, and others.

We consider how far HBCUs have come considering the interplay of the largely White benefactors and the Black elite. We argue that, in spite of the tremendous success of HBCUs over the years, there is a need to "Africanize" the curricula of these institutions—to enable students of African descent to "see themselves in the curriculum." A first step, we argue, in this critically important revamping of the curricula is the establishment and support of the so-called Black studies programs.

Lynette Danley, Roderic R. Land, and I share a perspective on students of African descent in graduate school preparing for careers in academia. While the numbers of students of African descent in higher education have increased, there has been no substantial increase in the number of faculty of African descent, and their numbers are low in comparison to Whites; this is the challenge. We offer an analysis of the graduate student socialization practices, which we argue are race-neutral; all cultures are not given a voice in these programs. We go on to describe some progressive views about the needs of students of African descent as they travel through these graduate programs.

Some of the suggestions that Danley, Land, and I discuss include

- assisting in course development,

- serving as teaching assistants,

- strengthening research skills, and

- preparing curriculum vitae.

Danley, Land, and I also encourage students of African descent in graduate school to

- acknowledge the commitment to teaching students of African descent,

- acknowledge the historical exclusion of people of African descent in the professoriate,

- commit to working to succeed in spite of all odds,

- immerse oneself in the higher education culture,

- help others,

- continue to be yourself,

- network, network, and network,

- strive to understand higher education,

- express your voice in the scholarship arena, and

- contribute to the creation of knowledge.

Danley, Land, and I conclude with several implications for research and practice and with a call for educators to take this challenge—the shortage of faculty of African descent—very seriously. Enjoy!

REFERENCE

Bowen, W., & Bok, D. (1998). *The shape of the river: Long-term consequences of considering race in college and university admissions.* Princeton, NJ: Princeton University Press.

16

EXCLUSIONS AND ILLUSIONS

Rethinking the Mysterious UC Admissions Process That Disadvantages Deserving African American Students

EDDIE COMEAUX

WALTER R. ALLEN

California—and the University of California (UC) system—serves as an instructive case study to understand how Blacks struggle for access to higher education. UC has long been considered one of the most distinguished public universities and a springboard to many tangible benefits and opportunities nationwide for high-achieving degree recipients. In light of this, when voters passed Proposition 209 in 1996 (which outlawed the use of Affirmative Action in California public institutions), several trends became all the more dire. California has the third largest Black population (about 2.4 million) among the states, with Los Angeles County containing the second largest African American population (876,304) of all the nation's counties (U.S. Census Bureau, 2004). Yet African Americans represent a dismal 3.4% of the fall 2006 UC freshman admit offers despite comprising nearly 7% of the state's overall population (California Postsecondary Education Commission, 2004; University of California Office of the President [UCOP], 2006). Indeed, chronic underrepresentation and underenrollment of African Americans on California's most competitive public campuses is cause for grave concern.

Under California's 1960 Master Plan for Higher Education, a major principle was to balance two basic American values—equal opportunity for all students to acquire a UC education, and achievement based on merit. The Master Plan established the UC, California State University, and California Community Colleges as equitable educational options in this tripartite system. Despite the original promise, the reality is that the elite UC tier parallels social and class distinction as more than 60% of UC students are upper income and only 10% to 15% lower income (Hayden, n.d.). Thus, an individual's

AUTHORS' NOTE: The authors gratefully acknowledge Tara Watford, Ophella Dano, and the Ralph J. Bunche Center at UCLA for their contributions to this chapter.

"markers of merit," as defined by each campus, remains closely correlated with socioeconomic status and family background (College Board, 2000). Put another way, students admitted to UC come from an exclusive subset of the state's more affluent high schools and disproportionately from college-educated and privileged families (Martin, Karabel, & Jaquez, 2003). Students admitted to UC are also disproportionately Asian and White because UC admissions criteria penalize Black and Latino students, who are victims of racial inequities in K-12 educational opportunities.

For African Americans in particular, these inequalities are cause for concern, largely because of the fact that admission to California's public selective universities has significant influence on potential earnings and future educational attainment (graduate and professional school attendance). The extensive study by two former college presidents, Bowen and Bok (1998), reported convincing evidence of tremendous economic benefits to all students who attend selective institutions—irrespective of race/ethnicity. For example, the salaries of African American graduates who entered selective institutions in the fall of 1976 were 84% more than the average for all African American male B.A.s nationwide. Black females who graduated from these institutions earned 71% more than their counterparts who received B.A.s from nonselective schools nationwide. Furthermore, Bowen and Bok's analyses revealed African Americans who graduated from selective institutions were typically afforded more opportunities to attend graduate and professional schools than were their counterparts who attended less selective institutions. African Americans in their study also completed graduate school in higher numbers than did their White counterparts at selective institutions. Clearly, the breadth of viable opportunities a selective college education provides African Americans is especially important.

The lessons learned over the past decade tell us that with unsatisfactory efforts to address fairness and individual merit issues, African American admits to our elite UC campuses continue to witness chronic declines. Without efforts to expand opportunities for a UC education to historically underrepresented groups—through such programs and policies as Affirmative Action, the Master Plan, and Eligibility in the Local Context (ELC)—racial disparities persist and expand. While K-12 inequalities and the ban of Affirmative Action are significant issues to be appropriately addressed (requiring long-term strategies and sufficient resources), the most immediate change perhaps could come from the admission practices at UC campuses, which in many regards contribute to these troubling trends. As such, the unacceptably low admits among African Americans to our most competitive UC campuses leave not only scholars and key decision makers scrambling for ways to maintain and improve diversity but also place pressures on university officials to reconsider established admissions procedures. Questions must be raised about inequalities in access and learning opportunities as well as the rationale for admission guidelines and criteria, including the relative weight given to traditional measures of merit in the evaluation of undergraduate applicants from various schooling contexts. We must also ask how these factors reflect the mission and philosophy of the UC system and various campuses.

In an attempt to address these disparities that fall heaviest on African Americans, this case study explores admissions review processes at two selective UC campuses, UC Los Angeles (UCLA) and UC Berkeley (UCB). Specifically, we examine how these campuses operationalize their comprehensive review process in light of concentrated schooling disadvantages in California's public secondary schools. To provide a context for understanding this issue relative to educational access and equity, we highlight inequalities in California secondary schools, the effects of anti–Affirmative Action legislation, and poor state planning in public higher education. Our findings have implications for equal access in California and the nation. Based on this knowledge, we recommend viable strategies to remedy persistent problems surrounding African American college access in California and beyond.

California Schooling Inequalities, Proposition 209, and Inadequate Planning

While access to public higher education has grown, the extent to which all citizens are given equal, equitable educational opportunities to our most selective California campuses continues to gain public attention. At various points, individuals and groups have been denied access to our most prestigious public campuses primarily on the basis of race and social class. In that sense, three factors combine to challenge the maintenance of a democratic society and have contributed to the continual underrepresentation of African Americans on UC campuses: (1) the inequities inherent in California's K-12 educational system; (2) the demise of Affirmative Action through the passing of SB 1 and SB 2 in 1995, and Proposition 209 in 1996; and (3) a failure to extend opportunities to meet the increased demands for public higher education (Allen, Bonous-Hammarth, & Teranishi, 2002).

With dramatic demographic changes in California, the state witnessed nearly 6.3 million students enrolled in the K-12 system during the 2003–2004 school year, with approximate enrollments of 8% African American, 46% Latino, 33% White, 11% Asian, and 1% American Indian (California Department of Education, 2005). California's rich racial/ethnic diversity aside, African Americans, Latinos, and other historically underrepresented minorities have endured an inadequate, underfunded, underresourced K-12 system. Reduced "opportunities to learn" (see Oakes, 1990) have proven to be major constraints to these students' college eligibility and access. For example, California children in urban, public schools study in overcrowded conditions with student-teacher ratios as high as 40 to 1; one quarter of urban school teachers reported not having a textbook for every student and limited access to computers (Hayden, n.d.). Moreover, the recent California Educational Opportunity Report (Rogers, Terriquez, Valladares, & Oakes, 2006) found that almost all California high schools offer students less access to teachers and counselors than other high schools across the nation. Fewer than half of California high schools offer sufficient college preparatory classes for all students to complete a college-preparatory curriculum. For students attending schools severely segregated by race and poverty, conditions worsen. These schools are far more likely to experience overcrowding, receive less funding, and have a shortage of skilled teachers, counselors, and college-preparatory classes (Oakes, Rogers, Siler, Horng, & Goode, 2004; Rogers et al., 2006; Solórzano & Ornelas, 2002).

In this light, *Williams et al. v. State of California et al.* (2004) sought to address the appalling conditions of many public schools. The plaintiffs argued the State failed to provide thousands of public school students, particularly those in low-income communities of color, with the bare minimum necessities required for an education, such as textbooks, trained teachers, and safe and clean facilities (B. Allen, 2005). The huge educational resource gap between suburban and urban schools is exacerbated by troubling trends toward resegregation in secondary and postsecondary education visibly evident in recent years (Orfield & Lee, 2004). These striking conditions underscore the importance in California of understanding the relationships between school contexts (e.g., economic) and racial/ethnic composition of and whether schools provide equitable pathways to college.

Educational inequalities are most apparent in the disproportionate rate at which African American high school graduates gain access to California public higher education, particularly the UC system. Since 1996, the percentage of UC-eligible African American students rose from 2.8% in 1996 to 6.2% in 2003 (California Postsecondary Education Commission, 2004). In comparison, Latinos also made significant gains in UC eligibility, increasing from 3.8% in 1996 to 6.5% in 2003. Asian Pacific Islanders and Whites made modest gains over the period, rising from 30% to 31.4% and 12.7% to 16.2%, respectively. Although in 2003, African Americans constituted nearly 7% of the state's overall population, they constituted only 3.4% of UC undergraduate enrollment compared with Latinos (15.8%), Asians (32.7%), and Whites (37.3%). Furthermore, African Americans at the most selective UC campuses—Los Angeles and Berkeley—were only 2.8% and 3.7%, respectively, of undergraduate enrollment in 2003 (UCOP, n.d.). Indeed, the alarming decline of African Americans attending the state's most competitive public institutions revealed a substantially different reality compared with their other-race peers.

While K-12 schooling inequities are clearly an important factor blocking college access and preventing the full participation of African American students, the policy barring Affirmative Action in public higher education is also critical. California Proposition 209 prohibited the use of racial preferences in college admissions under the guise of preventing discrimination against individuals on the basis of protected attributes such as race or ethnicity. In the wake of Proposition 209, the admission of underrepresented minorities[1] declined dramatically in the UC system. For example, the measure barring Affirmative Action resulted in a noticeable drop (24%) in college enrollments for African American students in the UC system between 1997 and 1998 despite a slight increase in the number of African American applicants. The most significant drop in enrollment that year was seen at UCB where African American freshman enrollment dropped by 51% although the total freshman enrollment increased by 5% (UC Berkeley Office of Student Research, 1998). Moreover, since the demise of affirmation action policies a decade ago, UCB and UCLA experienced the largest drops, plummeting 46% and 57%, respectively. These egregious trends in the aftermath of Affirmative Action battered African American admissions and enrollment. Interestingly, critics of Affirmative Action argue the battle to guarantee equal rights for all citizens has been fought and won—and that Affirmative Action is no longer necessary in our "colorblind" society—while "others suggest that the poor and disenfranchised need simply to take responsibility and pull themselves up by their own bootstraps" (W. R. Allen, 2005, p. 20). Needless to say, these arguments ring hollow as African Americans continue to face unequal access and opportunities at all levels of the educational pipeline up to and including our most prestigious California public institutions.

Beyond the ban on Affirmative Action, the increased demand for public higher education is also, in part, related to the declining presence of African Americans on UC campuses. This problem has been exacerbated by the poor educational planning and decision making by multiple state governments. Over the years, we witnessed dramatic growth coupled with significant funding cuts to education. At UC, the net state-funded operating budget dropped 14% as student enrollments increased 18% (UCOP, 2003). W. R. Allen (2005) wrote,

> The state's population nearly doubled, growing from 19 million in 1970 to 35 million in 2000. For this same thirty-year period, California's Black population grew by roughly 71 percent (1.4 million to 2.5 million), an impressive rate of

population growth under most circumstances. However, this rapid growth was dwarfed alongside the astounding rates of increase for California's Latino/a and Asian American populations. . . . Multiple governors and state administrations failed to anticipate or address the consequences of this population explosion for the California public higher education system, thus contributing to severe demand/supply discrepancies in higher education. Instead of adding beds in college dorms, these administrations chose to invest in exponential increases in the number of prison beds, an investment decision that made neither sound fiscal nor moral sense. (p. 21)

In this context, where education is viewed as the key to upward social and economic mobility, California's insufficient investment in education is painfully apparent. Poor planning and misplaced priorities have created barriers to college access for all students. These patterns are visibly evident and have dire consequences for the state's economic future and future availability of skilled, technical labor.

Limited college access for African Americans is partially influenced by K-12 inequities, the ban on Affirmative Action, and inadequate planning in the state. These persistent barriers require long-term commitments of substantial financial resources and considerable political will to be resolved. Although it is essential that these recuperative efforts occur, the current crisis of African American admissions in the state also calls for an immediate, proactive movement within the UC. A rethinking of UC admissions policies and practices is essential if the UC system is to serve the citizens of California fairly while simultaneously contributing to the creation of a more democratic and egalitarian society.

STATEMENT OF PROBLEM

The central research questions of this study are (a) How do the different UC campuses operationalize their admissions schemes and account for merit in light of concentrated schooling disadvantages in California's public secondary schools? and specifically, (b) How do these conceptions of merit influence California's African American access (or lack thereof) to the UC system?

METHODOLOGY

To appraise the comprehensive review process at each campus, we conducted both formal and informal interviews with various actors within the admissions process. These actors included admission directors, admissions staff members, readers, and faculty representatives at each campus. Interview questions included, but were not limited to, the extent each campus considers academic achievement and supplemental factors within an applicant's schooling context; how formal weights or values are assigned each factor in calculating applicant scores or ranking; whether the selection process considered the full range of the eligibility pool; and the steps taken to recruit prospective and admitted students. We also compiled and analyzed admission documents at each campus, which provided insight into how the comprehensive review discussed was implemented by each school. For the purposes of this review, our findings are limited to UCLA and UCB.

RESULTS

The results of this study are organized as follows. First, we provide an overview of comprehensive review as well as the distinction between eligibility versus selectivity for the UC system. This forms the basis for the subsequent analyses. Next, we present admissions practices employed by UCLA and UCB. Lastly, we offer conclusions and recommendations for change.

Comprehensive Review

For several decades, the UC employed a two-tier admissions system where between 50% and 75% of the entering class were admitted solely on the basis of grades and test scores, with special talents and personal achievements receiving minimal consideration. In fall 2002, UC eliminated the two-tier system and made comprehensive review a systemwide policy to ensure all students received thorough evaluation in the admissions process. This plan aimed to broaden the evaluation criteria for undergraduate applicants to include both scholastic and personal achievement. Most campuses receive more applications from prospective freshman students than they can admit. To select among qualified applicants, comprehensive review permits each campus to draw on 14 criteria such as ELC, grades, special talents, and test scores, among other factors (for a complete list of all criteria, see UCOP, n.d.). For academic achievement, merit is primarily defined by GPA, test scores, and academic subjects completed (known as "a-g" required subjects), whereas personal achievement may include, but not be limited to, employment, community service, demonstration of leadership skills, and other special accomplishments. Although there is considerable variation among UC campuses regarding comprehensive review, each campus claims to view the selectivity[2] process to some degree within the context of the student's opportunities and circumstances. Academic performance, it should be noted, greatly outweighs the other comprehensive review factors in each campus's admissions review process.

Eligibility Versus Selectivity

Eligibility and selectivity are separate stages in the UC admission process; thus, both are the subject of considerable public attention. "UC-eligible" is defined as satisfying the minimum requirements for admission, whereas "selectivity" refers to a set of criteria or standards that each UC campus employs to choose among UC-eligible students who apply. A UC-eligible applicant is guaranteed admission to at least one UC campus, but not necessarily the first-choice campus because of campus selectivity[3] and competition with other applicants who also meet minimum eligibility requirements. In that sense, students' high school GPAs and standardized test scores play a significant role in this evaluation stage to "weed out" applicants using comprehensive review. Factors such as personal achievement and life challenges are used in this process; however, their weight varies considerably by campus. To some degree, we have difficulty understanding and explaining the UC selection process because of the lack of transparency concerning how each campus implements comprehensive review to set its selectivity standards. In short, UC admissions schemes are most mysterious in the ways various factors in comprehensive review are balanced and weighed, particularly at our most selective campuses, UCLA and UCB.

Admissions Schemes

The common thread that runs through the UCLA and UCB admission processes and practices is the notion of selectivity. Each campus attempts to develop selection criteria that clearly indicate its commitment to evaluating and admitting students throughout the full spectrum of the eligibility pool. In addition, the campuses acknowledge that academic merit can be demonstrated in various ways and viewed in several educational contexts. The campuses employ admissions schemes that operationalize these principles in strikingly different ways.

UCLA employs an assembly-line-like scheme in which comprehensive review factors are scored independently, yet viewed together for the final admissions decision—what campus officials refer to as a "balancing approach to selection." That is, two admissions staff members read a given applicant's *academic achievement* profile, while another reader—typically, a high school counselor, retired faculty member, or academic outreach member—reviews the applicant's *personal achievement* and *life challenges* profiles. The applicant is then assigned ranks for each of the three factors discussed, which places him or her in a specific cell, along with other identically ranked applicants, in a three-dimensional admissions matrix. Decisions are then made regarding which *cells* or groups of applicants (as opposed to *individual applicants*) to admit. In contrast, UCB employs a more holistic admissions scheme. For a given applicant's file, a single reader is assigned to evaluate each of the comprehensive review factors, all within the context of one another. A second reader is typically assigned to review files that are considered marginal.

Academic Achievement

Despite the UC campuses' proclamation that they take various factors into account, traditional academic achievement indicators (i.e., standardized test scores and GPA) are the foremost consideration, and indeed appear to be critical measures at these highly selective campuses. UCLA, for example, establishes GPA and Scholastic Aptitude Test (SAT) cutoff points to define standard profiles for a series of achievement ranks to which applicants are assigned. While officials do not set the weights in advance,

it is clear these numbers-driven achievement rankings are overwhelming determinants that trump the other comprehensive review factors considered in the admissions decision. In comparison, UCB also reported that considerable emphasis is placed on academic achievement, but UCB looks more closely at how applicants performed within the context of their high school. During the review, they rely on a "read sheet" that summarizes key statistics about how the student compares with other students in his or her high school and how the high school compares with other high schools. While we know disadvantaged students who lack access to advanced placement courses are not afforded the extra GPA points, it is unclear whether limited schooling opportunities or local context receives much consideration since academic achievement indicators are overwhelming determinants for these campuses (Solórzano & Ornelas, 2002).

Life Challenges

UCLA's review and consideration of life challenges or local context reflect their commitment to serving students from disadvantaged schools. Life challenges consist of three domains: environmental, family, and personal situations. According to UCLA admissions officers, there is no specific emphasis on these factors; rather, a system of "checks and balances" takes into account the sum of schooling experiences and the extent of academic achievement. In contrast, UCB employs a holistic approach that views applicants within the context of the educational circumstances and opportunities or challenges presented, and how they have responded. Thus, UCB, like UCLA, does not clearly show whether the consideration given to the context of applicant educational circumstances substantially lessens the effects of socioeconomic inequalities on selectivity outcomes.

Personal Accomplishments

The review and consideration of personal accomplishment and challenges also resemble schooling context at each campus. UCLA considers personal achievement, including, but not limited to, awards/honors, extracurricular activities, employment, and community service. Most of these items are numerically scored in advance of a given applicant's formal review wherein a volunteer reader consults the applicant's written essays to either to add to or detract from the initial scores. In comparison, UCB's review of personal achievement factors and life challenges are based on a holistic approach; that is, all factors for each applicant are reviewed together by one reader (and sometimes two)[4] within the context of his or her academic and personal circumstances.

It is also worth noting that UCB reported actively recruiting readers each year from various backgrounds in an attempt to achieve a diverse pool while UCLA admissions officials indicated that they have no active recruitment process and preferred minimal readership change each year to maintain consistency. Thus, it appears that while UCB strives to recruit new readers to minimize the chance for reader biases, UCLA has taken a different approach that has serious implications for selectivity outcomes. That is, UCLA recycles the same readers and their biases, which is particularly troubling given the relatively high concentration of volunteers from private and affluent schools in the campus's reader pool.

In sum, equating merit primarily with GPA and test scores appears to be the common practice shared by UCLA and UCB. The extent to which these qualitative—and sometimes quantitative—decisions by UCLA and UCB are determined, justified, and even predict the likelihood of college "competitiveness" and persistence remains a mystery. Moreover, the tacit acceptance of these selection models without a thorough understanding and explanation of the decision-making process is indeed unsatisfactory.

CONCLUSIONS AND IDEAS FOR CHANGE

This chapter examined the UC's selectivity process, given the disastrous effects the elimination of race-conscious policies has had on access to the most selective campuses for many talented, historically excluded minorities. Our findings underscore the magnitude of the access dilemma and systematic flaws in the selection process, which often struggles to mitigate secondary schooling inequalities while relying on dominant, traditional academic achievement indicators. Recently, UC admissions policies changed to emphasize comprehensive review to evaluate applicants within the context of their personal and educational circumstances.

Nevertheless, the proportions of disadvantaged students admitted to UC's more selective campuses continue to spiral downward. While the ideals of the UC emphasize the importance of a diverse student population, we are not convinced that the existing comprehensive review adheres to their mission and philosophy to create equitable educational opportunities for all students and to preserve the quality of educational experience that diversity ensures. Instead, we witness various systematic defects in the selection process that continuously penalize UC-eligible, deserving African Americans and others who experience primary and secondary schooling disadvantages in the state.

Socioeconomic resources (applicants' parents' wealth) are highly correlated with higher GPA and test scores, which in turn increase an applicant's chances of admissions to the most selective UC campuses. Accordingly, affluent parents are afforded numerous opportunities to purchase advantages for their children—private schools, homes in elite school districts, SAT coaches, special tutoring, private college counselors—whereas students from less affluent backgrounds are equally bright, yet resource-starved. As a result, the playing field is far from level (Kozol, 1991, 2005). In other words, these campuses see students as the problem and penalize them because of their lower social positions rather than problematizing how we define merit and confronting systemic racism (Feagin, 2006).

Public higher education is a public good, and to some extent, a major vehicle for upward mobility and increasing equity in society. However, the overreliance on GPA and test scores to narrowly define merit and favor the privileged few ignores the fact that the mission of the UCs extends beyond the needs of the individual student to the greater good of society. The UC is charged to seek students who serve the public good in a broad array of public service settings. Nonetheless, by exclusively equating merit with supposedly objective indicators and neglecting to employ a more inclusive and holistic admissions model that encompasses students from an array of educational contexts who demonstrate academic merit in a variety of ways, we will continue to block the road to a more democratic society. Such a model should seek a "reasonable" balance among the criteria in the admissions scheme, and of course, it should be validated empirically (Laird, 2005).

The existing admissions trends in California public higher education create a sense of urgency to muster the strength to respond to such inequalities and to reverse the momentum. We should take these inequalities as challenges, but understand that these challenges will require intense pressures for the reexamination of definitions of meritocracy. In effect, defining merit primarily by GPA and test scores neglects a host of other factors that contribute to academic achievement (Chang, Witt, Jones, & Hakuta, 2003). While broader and more accurate measures of merit will not necessarily increase African American representation on UC campuses, it will, however, ensure fairness and a more thorough assessment of all students. We must also refine and employ UC policies equal to the task of ensuring equitable representation for all students and that explicitly and sufficiently accounts for the effects of multiple schooling disadvantages on highly selective admissions in light of Proposition 209 constraints. Indeed, ELC was an ambitious step to extend educational opportunities to historically disadvantaged schools; however, African Americans are grossly underrepresented at most public high schools in the state, which make this policy ill-suited for them.[5] Such policies must be vastly improved. Furthermore, we must not only rethink the mission and purpose of California public higher education but also develop proactive policies that ultimately enhance our capacity to serve the public good by advancing diversity and ensuring that all students have equitable educational opportunities. African Americans also want a piece of the American pie—equal access and opportunity to the most competitive graduate schools and lucrative careers—thus creating equitable pathways. Rethinking the mission and purpose of California higher education is imperative. While there are no existing initiatives that replicate race-conscious admission policies, we anticipate these proposed policy changes will effectively remedy the unfavorable course of African American access to our most selective UC campuses and beyond.

Notes

1. Underrepresented minority students include African Americans, Latinas/Latinos, and Native Americans. Although many Asian groups are overrepresented in college admissions in California, it is

important to note that not all Asian nationalities/ethnicities are well represented. For more information on the representation of different Asian nationalities in the UC system, see UCOP (2005).

2. "Selectivity" is synonymous with "admissions."

3. Compared with other UC campuses, UCLA and UCB tend to have admission criteria that are more stringent than the criteria for minimum UC eligibility.

4. Two readers are used for applicants considered in the "margins."

5. There are 11 California public high schools with African American majority student enrollment (Teranishi, Allen, & Solórzano, 2004).

References

Allen, B. (2005). *The Williams v. California settlement: The first year of implementation.* A report by Counsel for the Williams Plaintiffs. Los Angeles: ACLU Foundation of Southern California and Public Advocates.

Allen, W., Bonous-Hammarth, M., & Teranishi, R. (2002). *Stony the road we trod: The Black struggle for higher education in California.* Research report. Los Angeles: CHOICES: Access, Equity and Diversity in Higher Education, UCLA.

Allen, W. R. (2005). A forward glance in a mirror: Diversity challenged—access, equity and success in higher education. *Educational Researcher, 34*(7), 18–23.

Bowen, W., & Bok, D. (1998). *The shape of the river: Long-term consequences of considering race in college and university admissions.* Princeton, NJ: Princeton University Press.

California Department of Education. (2005). *Fact book 2005.* Retrieved May 20, 2006, from www .cde.ca.gov/re/pn/fb/documents/factbook2005 .pdf

California Postsecondary Education Commission. (2004). *University eligibility study for the class of 2003.* Sacramento, CA: Author.

Chang, M., Witt, D., Jones, J., & Hakuta, K. (2003). *Compelling interest: Examining the evidence on racial dynamics in college and universities.* Stanford, CA: Stanford University Press.

College Board. (2000). *Trends in college pricing.* New York: Author.

Feagin, J. R. (2006). *Systemic racism: A theory of oppression.* New York: Routledge.

Hayden, T. (n.d.). *Principles of the 1960 Master Plan.* Unpublished manuscript.

Kozol, J. (1991). *Savage inequalities: Children in America's schools.* New York: Crown.

Kozol, J. (2005). *The shame of the nation: The restoration of apartheid schooling in America.* New York: Crown.

Laird, B. (2005). *The case for affirmative action in university admissions.* Berkeley, CA: Bay Tree.

Martin, I., Karabel, J., & Jaquez, S. W. (2003). High school segregation and access to the University of California. *Educational Policy, 19*(2), 308–330.

Oakes, J. (1990). *Multiplying inequalities: The effects of race, social class, and tracking on opportunities to learn mathematics and science.* Santa Monica, CA: RAND.

Oakes, J., Rogers, J., Siler, D., Horng, E., & Goode, J. (2004). *Separate and unequal—50 years after Brown: California's racial "opportunity gap."* Los Angeles: UCLA Institute for Democracy, Education, and Access.

Orfield, G., & Lee, C. (2004). *Brown at 50: King's dream or Plessy's nightmare?* Cambridge, MA: Civil Rights Movement Project, Harvard University.

Rogers, J., Terriquez, V., Valladares, S., & Oakes, J. (2006). *California educational opportunity report 2006: Roadblocks to college.* Los Angeles: UCLA Institute for Democracy, Education, and Access.

Solórzano, D., & Ornelas, A. (2002). Critical race analysis of AP classes. *Journal of Latinos and Education, 1*(4), 215–229.

Teranishi, R., Allen, W., & Solórzano, D. (2004). Opportunity at the crossroads: Racial inequality, school segregation, and higher education in California. *Teacher College Record, 106*(11), 2224–2245.

UC Berkeley Office of Student Research. (1998). *Undergraduate admissions statistics.* Retrieved May 20, 2006, from https://osr2.berkeley.edu/Public/STAFFWEB/ TC/main1/main1.html at https://osr2.berkeley.edu/Public/STAFFWEB/TC/uas98tables1/uas98menu.html

University of California Office of the President. (2003). *Governor's implementation of mid-year budget cuts.* Retrieved December 22, 2003, from www.ucop.edu/news/archives/2003/dec18art1.htm

University of California Office of the President. (2005). *University of California statistical summary of students and staff, Fall 2005.* Retrieved May 18, 2006, from www.ucop.edu/news/factsheets/2006/fall_2006-admissions_table_c.pdf at www.ucop.edu/news/factsheets/fall2006adm.html

University of California Office of the President. (2006). *Distribution of new California freshman admit offers Fall 1997 through 2006.* Retrieved May 15, 2006, from www.ucop.edu/news/factsheets/2006/fall_2006-admissions_table_c.pdf at www.ucop.edu/news/factsheets/fall2006adm.html

University of California Office of the President. (n.d.). *Comprehensive review.* Retrieved May 20, 2006, from www.ucop.edu/news/comprev/welcome.html

U.S. Census Bureau. (2004). *American community survey: Population projections.* Washington, DC: Author.

Williams et al. v. State of California et al. Superior Court of the State of California (S.F. CA 2004).

17

HIP HOP

A Source of Empowerment for African American Male College Students

JON A. YASIN

Hip Hop is an international youth culture with origins in the Black (African American and African Caribbean) and Brown (Latino, primarily Puerto Rican) communities of New York City during the early 1970s. It was a reaction to the new, but disliked, disco music; a reaction to the large amounts of heroin that appeared on the streets; a reaction to the Counter Intelligence Program (COINTELPRO) of the Federal Bureau of Investigation against the Civil Rights and Black Power Movements; and a reaction to the other negative forces that were beginning to inhabit the local neighborhoods of Black and Brown peoples of New York City. Initially a recreational activity, Hip Hop soon developed into an open culture, a common culture, inviting any willing being to participate. Although the elements of Hip Hop culture were already present in African American culture, they came together in a unique way as Hip Hop, according to Fable, the legendary b-boy, who is the first vice president of the International Rock Steady Crew and Zulu Lord of the Universal Zulu Nation (personal communication, October 15, 2003). Various elements of Hip Hop culture include deejayin', b-boyin' and b-girlin' (breakdancing), taggin' (graffiti art), emceein' (rappin'), and knowledge (studying).

Hip Hop has become a primary Discourse for youth generally, and for African American men, particularly. A primary Discourse, wrote James Gee (1996) in *Social Linguistics and Literacies,* "constitute[s] our first social identity, and something of a base within which we acquire or resist later Discourses" (p. 137). One's primary Discourse shapes a person's initial understanding about who he or she is. African American men, as well as others, socialized with Hip Hop, use it to negotiate and to mediate their contact with other groups and institutions beyond their families, peer groups, and sociocultural settings. Although European American society and other selected societies globally have continuously worked toward impeding the progress of and depowering African Americans, particularly males, because of its origins, Hip Hop culture from its humble beginnings has had an immense empowering effect, so that its elements are regularly appropriated by mainstream society. Such empowerment has allowed those African American males for whom Hip Hop is a primary Discourse to successfully use its cultural elements and traditions in mainstream political, entertainment, government, religious, and educational institutions, including the institutions of higher education.

Because we learn by associating new information with what we already know, it is only natural that Hip Hop, a primary Discourse for so many college students during this period of time in history, is called on as a tool in teaching and learning environments. Many African American male college students use elements of Hip Hop as study tools. Moreover, they draw on its culture in preparing personal homework assignments and projects, while educators collaborate with students active in Hip Hop culture in preparing classroom lessons and presentations. And departments in colleges and universities provide the opportunity for critical analysis of this youth culture through course offerings on Hip Hop.

Before discussing the utilization of Hip Hop culture in the teaching and learning process, it is essential that the history of this movement and its foundation are comprehended; for, in reality, these foundational elements and the various skills acquired by its participants while producing Hip Hop culture are, in fact, called on by African American male college students to negotiate their learning environments. Furthermore, this youth culture "is not just noise," nor did "it drop out of the sky," as many people believe. Built on traditions of the African Diaspora, Hip Hop is a continuation of the struggle for social justice begun by activists in the Civil Rights and Black Power Movements who are parents and grandparents of this Hip Hop generation.

Recognizing the Need for Empowerment

Clive Campbell, known in the Hip Hop community as Deejay Kool Herc, the Father of Hip Hop, migrated with his family from Jamaica to the United States in 1967, settling in the Bronx, one of the five boroughs of New York City. This was a full 13 years after the 1954 decision by the U.S. Supreme Court on the *Brown v. Board of Education of Topeka, Kansas* case, ruling that segregation of children in public schools on the basis of race was unconstitutional. During the following year, 1955, the African American community formally began the Civil Rights Movement in Montgomery, Alabama, after Mrs. Rosa Parks, refusing to give up her seat on a public bus to a European American, was arrested for challenging another segregation law. Moreover, the year

before the migration of Herc's family to the United States, the nonviolent Civil Rights Movement was expanded into the militant Black Power Movement, when Stokely Carmichael (Kwame Ture) and H. Rap Brown (Imam Jamil El-Amin) called for Black Power, which included political and economic unity among African Americans, in Greenwood, Mississippi during a voter registration campaign, spearheaded by African American students and other young peoples. Years before the call for "Black" Power, the Honorable Elijah Muhammad and later, his National Representative, Malcolm X, before his departure from the Nation of Islam, had "redefined" the people of the African Diaspora as "Black" in defiance of the European American community's definitions, "colored," "Negro," and "nigger."

Eventually, with the Civil Rights nonviolent and Black Power Movements' militant challenge to this country's racist standard operating procedure of separation and inequality, members of the European American community launched against them a twofold assault and confrontation, overt actions and covert actions. Overt actions included the political assassinations of leaders, participants, and sympathizers of these Movements *throughout the 1960s, which was the Decade of Terrorist Assassinations.* Early on, in 1962 the Los Angeles Police Department raided Muhammad's Temple, killing one person and injuring more than 30 others. The following year, 1963, the National Association for the Advancement of Colored People Field Representative in Mississippi, Medgar Evers was assassinated, as was the President of the United States, John F. Kennedy. Throughout the decade, other high-profile murders included El Hajj Malik Shabazz, also known as Malcolm X, in 1965. The decade ended with the murder of the leader of the Civil Rights Movement, Nobel Peace Prize recipient, and founder of the Southern Christian Leadership Conference, Dr. Martin Luther King, Jr., in 1968 and that of President Kennedy's brother, Senator Robert F. Kennedy, a candidate for the Democratic Party nomination for the presidency of the United States and former Attorney General of the country (Bergman, 1969). By 2007, the majority of these political assassinations were still unsolved, and few perpetrators had been brought to justice. Children, adolescents, and young adults at that time, who now include many pioneers of the Hip Hop community are aware of this history and have not let the younger Hip Hop youths forget it.

Members of the future Hip Hop community witnessed many other overt actions against African Americans, active and nonactive in these Movements, which included the use of electric shock instruments such as cattle prods, police dogs, and high-powered water hoses by policemen, firemen, and officials representing various levels of governmental departments. On the other hand, Kool Herc and other future pioneers of Hip Hop were not eyewitnesses to the enactment of the covert actions, the second type of assault and confrontation against people struggling for their civil and human rights, but they were witnesses to the effects of these actions. The most infamous of such actions is the COINTELPRO, which was developed and put into action during the tenure of Lyndon Baines Johnson's Presidency of the United States, by J. Edgar Hoover, the Director of the Federal Bureau of Investigation. Johnson, initially the vice president to President Kennedy, ascended to the presidency on Kennedy's assassination to complete Kennedy's term, then was elected to serve from 1965 through 1968, during which time he was working toward the United States becoming the "Great Society" (O'Reilly, 1989, p. 261). While Johnson was forming the Great Society, Hoover was deciding who would and would not be a part of this society.

The struggle put forth by the participants in the Civil Rights and Black Power Movements, in spite of the mistreatment and injustices suffered, resulted in various accomplishments, including the *legal* desegregation of public education institutions; however, these accomplishments came with a harsh penalty of losing control, for example, of many African American children and adolescents to others who knew nothing about the culture of these youths, were not interested in educating them, or hated them because of their skin color. Furthermore, in spite of these accomplishments, nearly a half-century later, still "we are not playing on a level playing field," which youths of the Hip Hop community realize and which was commented on by Hip Hop emcee Kanye West on a televised fund raiser for victims of the 2005 Hurricane Katrina, most of whom were African Americans from the City of New Orleans. This is not surprising, for at the end of the Civil Rights and Black Power Movements,

before the origins of Hip Hop, in 1970 the Police Foundation was founded with a $30-million grant from the Ford Foundation. The Foundation was charged with developing additional policing strategies (Project South, 2005). This led to the development of the Prison-Industrial Complex, which Project South (2005) defined as "neoliberal policies, practices and institutions of all levels of government designed to remove the discarded (those who are unemployed, poor, uneducated, etc.) from society to further the social control of those negatively impacted by globalization" (pp. 4–5). Thirty years later, by the year 2000, there were 2 million people in prison, primarily African Americans. With statistics like these, the realization that this struggle for civil and human rights must continue has mobilized and motivated much of the Hip Hop generation to work toward "leveling this playing field" in all areas of society, especially in education.

EDUCATING THE MASSES IN THE AFRICAN AMERICAN COMMUNITY

Gaining certain basic civil and human rights early on in the Movement empowered African Americans, and other peoples of color began assiduously to assert themselves for control over additional aspects of their personal and public lives. For example, in 1967, the newly formed Black Student Union, and other students at San Francisco State University called for a Black Studies program, which was eventually granted after the University was closed as a result of a 4-month-long student strike. Four decades later, most students benefit from their efforts, as nearly every institution of higher learning in the United States offers courses and programs in African American/Africana/Black Studies, and most offer a majority of other ethnic studies programs. Furthermore, regarding Africa and its diaspora, in addition to the Civil Rights and Black Power Movements, early participants in Hip Hop were privileged to witness citizens of many countries on the African continent and in the Caribbean concurrently fighting for and gaining their independence from the racist colonialism of certain European countries. And so, with the call for Black Power, many more African Americans than in previous years, as well as the future pioneers of Hip Hop, became consciously aware of, acknowledged and embraced, and began to study and to own their African heritage that empowered them with the knowledge and redefinition of themselves.

Embracing their African heritage and maintaining the role of the African traditional griots as entertainers and educators, African American artists—poets, musicians, actors, and playwrights—educated the masses about their heritage in their communities with the cooperation of radio disc jockeys, for example, who over the airwaves played the recordings of Nikki Giovanni reciting poetry over Gospel music, and the Last Poets, a group of African American and Latino young men who recited poetry over drum beats, articulating the political issues of the African American and Latino communities and the struggles of the Movements. In addition to music and poetry played over airwaves, strongly encouraged by community members was the studying of all African American and diasporic writers and scholars, and Kool Herc and young African Americans, the future Hip Hop generation, were exposed to this *national cultural teach-in*. The young people throughout the United States who would become the Hip Hop community were participating in and developing a love for what would become the fifth element of Hip Hop, knowledge.

In addition, the events of the 1960s taught these future pioneers of Hip Hop about oppression, injustice, and discrimination. Their experiences taught them that they had to struggle for social justice and their civil and human rights, that they must define themselves, and that they must do for self. By now, many young African Americans and other youths of color were learning how to empower themselves, a lesson that they would soon *teach* others in their communities and an international community of youths *through the elements of Hip Hop.* As a result,

> Hip Hop culture emerged as a source for youth of alternative identity formation and social status in a community whose . . . local support institutions had been demolished [some by government forces] along with large sectors of its built environment. (Rose, 1994, p. 34)

THE ORIGINS OF HIP HOP

On his arrival in New York City from Jamaica, in addition to being greeted by people in the Civil Rights and Black Power Movements and their resistance by elements of the European American power structure, Kool Herc, the Father of Hip Hop, eventually was greeted by the "tags" of Taki 183 and those of other "writers" as well. Tags, which are like signatures, are one of three types of graffiti art popular in the Hip Hop community; the other two are "throw-ups" or bubble-like letters, which are most often colored in, and "pieces," which are whole scenes. Graffiti artists, who are identified in the Hip Hop community as "taggers" or "writers," must for legal reasons remain anonymous, but legend has it that Taki 183 was a bike messenger in the City, who lived in Washington Heights, also known as the Dominican Heights, which is north of Central Harlem. This young man "habitually wrote his alias, Taki 183, throughout his messenger route. . . . The idea of signaturing caught on like wildfire" (Miller, 2002, p. 6), catching Kool Herc, as well. Jeff Chang (2005) wrote that, according to graffiti experts, "the Black teenager, CORNBREAD, . . . is credited with popularizing the tagging of the Philly subways. . . . CORNBREAD's protégé, TOP CAT, moved to Harlem and brought with him the 'gangster' style of lettering" (p. 74). From his first encounter with it, Kool Herc was fascinated with graffiti art. He developed his tag and maintained this passion until one day when his father went downstairs in the building in which they lived in the West Bronx and saw Herc's moniker on the wall in the hall. Herc (personal communication, February 15, 2006) recalls that a "rival crew got into my building and put my tag on the wall." His father's actions quickly dissuaded him from continuing to tag and persuaded Herc to focus all his attention on playing music, in which he had been engaged already.

Herc's sister Cindy, the Mother of Hip Hop, persuaded him to deejay for a back-to-school party after she had worked for the summer of 1973 in the Neighborhood Youth Corps. By this time, neighborhood youths knew Kool Herc's deejayin' skills from hearing the loud music he played from the family apartment, which had been drawing them to the nearby recreation room to dance. The loud music was the result of Herc's stereo system, Herculoids, which included large amplified speakers and two turntables, similar to those he had experienced in the dance halls in his native Jamaica. In addition to those attending the dance halls, these speaker systems played music for the whole community in Jamaica. The notion of playing music for the entire community had been practiced at the cinemas of bush towns in Senegal, West Africa, as well, so this deejayin' for the community in the Bronx was the maintenance of a tradition among the African Diaspora. The success of the party in 1973, which many consider the birth of Hip Hop, motivated Herc to give additional parties. At his parties, Herc deejayed, using his technique of mixing a record on one turntable into the record playing on the second turntable, while he and his crew member Coke La Rock gave shout-outs and repeated rhymes over the music.

Soon, in addition to playing in clubs, Kool Herc's parties in the streets and in the parks, wherever he could get free electricity, drew a wide sector of the young population of the Bronx, including members of local street gangs. However, spinning records to entertain the community, Herc insisted that they not "rumble" at his events. These were events where members of the community came to dance to the music played by the deejay, to listen to the shout-outs and rhymes by the emcee, and to see the power moves on the dance floor by Herc's b-boys, Kevin and Keith. The gang leaders all agreed, which eventually contributed to a gang truce that is still in existence. Afrika Bambaataa, leader of the Black Spades as well as one of the brokers of the gang truce, and other pioneers in Hip Hop, were studying Kool Herc's performance, and were more interested in developing and honing their skills in the elements of Hip Hop culture than in physically challenging each other. These old gang members and all active participants in Hip Hop culture, however, did and do continue to challenge each other through battles on turntables between deejays, battles on dance floors between b-boys and b-girls, and battles on microphones between emcees rappin' and rhymin'. Deejay Afrika Bambaataa, in fact, called various gang leaders together, and they organized the Zulu Nation, now an *international organization of social activists*. Afrika Bambaataa and other leaders in Hip Hop have become role models for many young adults because of their positive influences in the growth and development of these youths. Identifying their success and positive growth and development with Hip Hop culture, many students participating in this culture, by extension, bring it to their learning experiences and educational institutions. For them, it is a formula for success.

Contemporary Hip Hop society attributes the development of this culture to Deejay Kool Herc,

the Father of Hip Hop; Deejay Afrika Bambaataa, the Godfather of Hip Hop; and a third pioneer, Deejay Grandmaster Flash, who, too, came to Kool Herc's parties, studied Herc's tools, and then introduced additional technology to the element of deejayin'. Grandmaster Flash was a student of electronics at Samuel Gompers Vocational High School in the Bronx, and he used this knowledge to advance the coordination of playing music on two turntables. Cowboy Wiggins, Melle Mel and his brother Kidd Creole Glover, and others, emcees in Grandmaster Flash's crew, known as the Furious Five, took the shout-outs, rhymes and poetry recitations, messages that they communicated over music, an African oral tradition maintained in the communities of the African Diaspora, to another level when they began "to flow," by talking in time to the musical beat produced on the turntables by the deejay (Yasin, 2001). In addition to "flowin'," terms used for this element of Hip Hop include *emceein'*, *rappin'*, *rhymin'*, and *spittin'*. According to Chang (2005), "by 1977, Djs that weren't already rapping . . . were looking to line up rap crews as raw as the Furious" (pp. 113–114).

All these elements of Hip Hop—deejayin', emceein', b-boyin', and b-girlin' (break dancing was a term used by the media)—were in existence in all five boroughs of New York, in southern Connecticut, and in northern New Jersey before mainstream society was introduced to this culture in 1979. Taggin' had been embraced by Hip Hop early on when participants in the culture needed to have signs made to advertise parties and battles, and they employed taggers/writers to design and make them. The other three elements evolved from earlier African and African diasporic traditions. This culture, according to Chuck D (personal communication, November 22, 1993), emcee of Public Enemy, produced about a million dollars in the community yearly before mainstream society was introduced to it. For, before 1979, deejays and their crews/posses, which included their emcees, b-boys and b-girls, and homeboys acting as security, organized dances and battles between deejays and their crews, both of which had admissions fees, while the performances were recorded, reproduced on audiocassette tapes, and sold. Incidentally, the winners of these battles were chosen by those youths who attended, based on the best performances of the competing deejays and their emcees and crews, and those winners were awarded most of the monies collected for admissions after the overhead for the event was paid. Moreover, Hip Hop participants not in the immediate area and not attending a given performance developed entrepreneurial skills, as well. Chuck D explained that he, growing up in Long Island, commissioned the gypsy taxi drivers to bring him new tapes from the deejays and emcees and their parties and battles in New York City, and he duplicated them, selling the copies for 5 dollars each in his 'hood. He and other young men were, in effect, providing employment for themselves and their homies.

In 1979, however, the Fatback Band recorded "King Tut," the first rap record, which was not as successful as a recording released later that year by the Sugar Hill Gang, *Rappers Delight*. *Rapper's Delight*, produced by the rhythm and blues singer, Sylvia Robinson, of the Mickey and Sylvia duo, was widely received internationally, and most of the community entrepreneurs soon were put out of business, for this was when and where the commercial music industry entered. However, participants in this young Hip Hop community, by this time, had gained enough skills "to manipulate factors both internal and external towards meeting [their] own wants and needs," which is power (Atkinson, 1988, p. 7).

Hip Hop's Empowerment of the Collective Self

In addition to the entrepreneurial skills, these young African American men and others in Hip Hop learned certain public relations skills, including all aspects of organizing events that entailed advertising, using positive interpersonal skills for attracting the public, negotiating contractual agreements with deejays and their performance crews of emcees and b-boys and b-girls, securing event sites for dances and battles, eventually talking with the media, and other skills necessary for successfully sponsoring events. The performers had to master a plethora of skills, including being responsible, being disciplined, being accountable to others in the crew, and being dependable. Deejays, for example, had to learn much about electronics and technology. Emcees had to master certain writing skills, the writing process, and other linguistic knowledge necessary to articulate issues about which they rhymed. They had to master certain research skills to gather knowledge on topics about which they wrote and "spit" rhymes. Emcees, also, had to master certain delivery techniques that they had to use when rhyming about issues, including the ability to pronounce word syllables in time to the musical beat, which is the primary uniqueness of Hip Hop lyrics (Yasin, 1997).

The b-boys and b-girls had to learn about the anatomy and physiology of the human body to protect themselves when developing the necessary discipline to learn and to make those power moves on the dance floor. To protect their limbs when they made power moves, according to a pioneer deejay from Brooklyn, Melvin McLauren (personal communication, April 15, 1994), b-boys and b-girls padded their knees and other limbs; then, they bought oversized pants to cover the padding, and used clothesline to hold the pants up, as belts were not strong enough. They then had to wear oversized shirts to cover the pants and the clothesline. When the rest of the world learned about Hip Hop, oversized clothing was one of the first features of this culture appropriated by mainstream society in the United States and around the globe during the early 1980s. While members of the Hip Hop community continued to empower themselves by learning and honing their skills, mainstream society learned about and appropriated elements of this culture.

Appropriation of Hip Hop Culture

Cultural mores, folkways, and traditions of Africans, the only involuntary immigrants coming to what became the United States, and of their offspring, members of the African Diaspora, have been appropriated continuously for any number of reasons, and so it is with the elements of Hip Hop culture. Examples of appropriation of Hip Hop culture can be traced back to the 1990s, to the decade after its commercialization. During the early years of the 1990s, the emcees of the group Naughty by Nature, African American males from East Orange, New Jersey, made a commercial for the Coca-Cola Bottling Company about its product, Sprite. While the raucous rhymes of Hip Hop emcees are used exuberantly to sell the goods and services by and for mainstream society, subtle signatures and other forms of graffiti art by Hip Hop taggers are commissioned and appear throughout mainstream society. When campaigning for the Democratic Party's nomination for presidential candidate in 2004, for instance, Howard Dean commissioned a tagger to prepare the backdrop for the stage on which he gave his political address to the people of New York City in Battery Park. In addition to seeing Hip Hop graffiti art incorporated into a plethora of environments, b-boyin' and b-girlin' and other forms of Hip Hop dancing early on were integrated into institutions of dance in mainstream society. For example, the legendary b-boy Fable who pops and locks, has performed internationally with ballet and other dance companies. Dance companies, such as Alvin Alley, regularly include Hip Hop in their performance repertoire.

Other features of the culture have been introduced to traditional institutions of mainstream society, such as the words from the lexicon of Hip Hop. For instance, not simply borrowing words from African American Vernacular English coined by earlier generations, President Bush, according to a reporter for the Associated Press Wire Service, has taken from the language of Hip Hop as well. Replying to a reporter's question about President Vladimir Putin's comment about some of Vice President Cheney's rhetoric, Bush said "it was pretty clever. Actually, quite humorous—not to *dis* my friend the vice president" ("Clear and Present Diaper," 2006, p. 4). *Dis* was coined by Hip Hop emcees by clipping its root "respect" from the word *disrespect*. Also, words and terms coined or having definitions extended by Hip Hop emcees are quickly becoming entries in the *Oxford English Dictionary* (OED). According to Siemaszko (2004), Jesse Sheidlower, the principal editor of the *OED* stated that "for most of the last century African-American vernacular has been the driving force in [the] American [language]" (p. 6). Dr. G. Mama Geneva Smitherman (2000), University Distinguished Professor at Michigan State University reminded us that

> whatever the motivation for crossover . . . in these postmodern times, there is a multibillion-dollar industry based on Black Language and Culture, while at the same time, there is continued underdevelopment and deterioration among the people who produce this language and culture. (p. 33)

Witnessing the crossover appeal and appropriation of their culture, many males from the African Diaspora and other practitioners revere Hip Hop's values of achievement and personal distinction. These same values—achievement and personal distinction—are taught early on in life to children in the United States. Bernstein and Nash (2005) wrote that such values encourage children to "feel special, to want self-esteem, and to feel good about themselves, partly because these characteristics are associated with superior performance in school" (p. 419). Conscious of their participation in this culture with features that appeal to and are appropriated by mainstream society, it is only natural that youths in Hip Hop culture employ its elements in their interactions with mainstream society, particularly with academic institutions, which consume so much of their daily lives.

THE HIP HOP GENERATION

The appropriation of features of Hip Hop culture by mainstream society and its globalization into an international youth culture have brought widespread tolerance of Hip Hop, if not its acceptance. Mainstream society's appropriation of features of the culture acknowledges and supports the creativity of the pioneers of Hip Hop culture. This creativity had already produced what Bakari Kitwana (2002) identified as the Hip Hop generation, which includes

> those young African Americans born between 1965 and 1984 who came of age in the eighties and nineties and who share a specific set of values and attitudes. At the core are our thoughts about family, relationships, child rearing, careers, racial identity, race relations, and politics. Collectively, these views make up a complex worldview that has not been concretely defined. (p. 5)

However, such views have been discussed in Hip Hop lyrics, in Hip Hop journals such as *XXL*, and other media, such as radio station Hot 97 in New York City. Although there are many, one of the reasons that this worldview has not thus far been concretely defined is because of the double messages being circulated by the society at large. On the one hand, many basic rights have been gained as a result of the Civil Rights and Black Power Movements, which has allowed for many more opportunities available to the Hip Hop generation than were available to their parents; on the other hand, the Hip Hop generation continues to witness and be victimized—as were their parents' generation—by social injustices that abound in institutional practices and racism in the minds of many people. Since the 1970s, in addition to the advent of the Prison-Industrial complex and the advent of Hip Hop, according to Crouch (2006), "there are so many problems that seem to drop like butterfly nets of barbed wire on the lives of black Americans" (p. 29), including higher payments for insurance, the "ghetto tax," police brutality, and denial of employment to residents of the ghetto. The participants of this generation have continuously inspired Hip Hop emcees to rhyme about these social injustices perpetrated against them in their music. When students of this generation write about social injustices, Hip Hop emcees and their lyrics are quoted to support the students' arguments.

Hip Hop is partially filling the void left after the 1970s, when many communities changed as a result of gentrification and when government laws were passed so that middle-class and working-class African Americans had opportunities to move into certain racially heterogeneous communities that provide a better quality of life—although with problems, such as police brutality. As a result, many of the old community support systems have broken down and do not exist for those youth of the Hip Hop generation whose families did not have such opportunities. Kitwana (2002), a member of the Hip Hop generation, explained that "we have turned to ourselves, our peers, global images and products, and the new realities we face for guidance. In the process, the values and attitudes described above anchor our worldview" (p. 7). This worldview defines an alternative social identity for the Hip Hop generation.

Having empowered themselves and an international community of youths through Hip Hop's elements and culture, this alternative social identity for many African American males has its own Discourse, although *aspects of it* are continuously appropriated by others. Gee (1996) defined a Discourse as

a socially accepted association among ways of using language, other symbolic expressions, and "artifacts," of thinking, feeling, believing, valuing, and acting that can be used to identify oneself as

a member of a socially meaningful group or "social network," or to signal (that one is playing) a socially meaningful "role." (p. 131)

After its beginnings in the early 1970s, so strong and determined became the Discourse of Hip Hop, which includes its elements, its worldview, its language, and so forth, that its pioneers influenced the socialization of the Hip Hop generation, which was being conceived, born, or raised during Hip Hop's early days. Thus, Hip Hop is a primary Discourse for the Hip Hop generation, for according to Gee (1996),

Primary Discourses are those to which people are apprenticed early in life during their primary socialization as members of particular families within their sociocultural settings. Primary Discourses constitute our first social identity, and something of a base within which we acquire or resist later Discourses. (p. 137)

Hip Hop has earned the distinction of being the primary Discourse for many African American youths because, in addition to the input of parents and adult members of the family in an individual's socialization, older siblings and their friends, peers, and community members have an influential role. Many young adults from this Hip Hop generation readily comment on being greatly influenced as children by Hip Hop music on hearing it being played in their communities or homes by older brothers and sisters or watching practice sessions of brothers and sisters who were deejays, emcees, or b-boys and b-girls. Yaya Fanusie (personal communication, July 15, 2006), a 32-year-old economist for the federal government and an activist in the African American and Muslim communities, recalled that when he was 14 years old, while at a summer camp in his native California, his camp counselor, an African American college student, continuously played two Hip Hop rhymes by Kris Parker, known as Emcee KRS One (Knowledge Reigns Supreme). These rhymes, "You Must Learn" and "Why Is That?" motivated him to seriously focus on his education, so that Yaya, who is a Hip Hop emcee, studied at the University of California at Berkeley for his B.A., and earned his M.P.A. from the School of International and Public Affairs at Columbia University. Currently, Yaya's 5-year-old son, Ehysan, is rhymin'. Because it is part of the socialization process of a majority of youths, Hip

Hop culture should be used more extensively to assist these youth in acquiring secondary Discourses, which people acquire through using their primary Discourses. "Secondary Discourses are those to which people are apprenticed as part of their socializations within various local, state, and national groups and institutions outside early home and peer-group socialization—for example, churches, gangs, schools, offices" (Gee, 1996, p. 137). Moreover, because of their socialization, because many African American males use Hip Hop elements and culture to empower others and are empowered by these elements themselves, because of mainstream society's appropriation of Hip Hop, and because the Hip Hop generation uses it for certain educational tasks already, educators can aid them in acquiring the secondary Discourse of the educational institution by using Hip Hop as an instructional tool!

HIP HOP AS AN EDUCATIONAL TOOL

African American males as well as other youth of the Hip Hop generation use its culture and elements to negotiate and to mediate secondary Discourses of other institutions, including educational institutions.

Hip Hop is used as a study tool. Wade Colwell, who studied at Stanford University, is now a certified teacher in Tucson, Arizona and cofounder of FunkaMentals, a company that uses Hip Hop culture and elements to teach and to develop Hip Hop–based educational materials. As a student, Wade employed Hip Hop when studying. During his freshman year at Stanford, Wade had to take a calculus course for which he was not prepared. Wade (personal communication, March 15, 2003) recalled that he failed the homework assignments and the tests, so he approached an African American male student who was performing well in the class about studying together for the final examination. During their study session, they wrote a Hip Hop rap with the calculus formulas and equations. After recording the rhyme, they sent a copy to the professor, who called Wade in his dormitory room on receiving the tape. Reminding Wade of his poor performance, the professor informed Wade that if he took the final examination and allowed her to use the taped rhyme with her other students, then

Wade would definitely pass the course. Other youths continuously relate their stories of employing Hip Hop to learn and to study, as well.

Hip Hop is used to complete assignments. As early as 1992, Chris Miles, known as Emcee Tank (personal communication, March 12, 1992) explained how he wrote his rhymes, a procedure that engages the same writing process that instructors of writing introduce to their students throughout the country. Tank stated that many of the same tools that he has at his disposal when he writes rhymes he will later perform, such as certain supporting details and rhetorical devices, are similar to those that were discussed in his writing classes at the college he attended. This realization was serendipitous for Tank! Although Hip Hop raps or rhymes are written in what emcees identify as bars and verses, and academic papers are organized in sentences and paragraphs, both genres of writing require the explanation of and support for a point, main idea, or thesis and both are organized and developed using the steps in the same writing process (Yasin, 2003). Furthermore, in any given classroom, Hip Hop emcees can be easily identified, as they are continually building their vocabularies for their own rhymes and always ask for definitions of unfamiliar words. When an instructor defines a word, the other emcees in a classroom can often be identified, as their heads immediately are lowered to write down the word and its definition.

Because our youth employ aspects of Hip Hop culture as sources of motivation, as tools to assist them in being responsible for studying, learning, and completing homework assignments, educators *must* enable these youths even more by incorporating features of this youth culture into the teaching-learning process in their classrooms. In an NBC Special Report on Race and Poverty 40 years after the Civil Rights Movement, which aired in July 2006, Tom Brokaw, while interviewing African American high school students in Jackson, Mississippi, reported that presently only 45% of the African American males who enter ninth grade actually complete high school. Our youth must be helped by any means necessary. Bringing their culture into the classroom allows them to bring their worldview into the learning situation and relate it to the relevancy of the formal learning process, for as Howard Gardner (1999) said, "there is . . . no royal road to understanding: or, to put it positively, many clues suggest how best to enhance understanding" (p. 126). One of the most affirming clues is to use what the student brings to the learning situation, which for many is Hip Hop.

In various ways, Hip Hop as a teaching tool will allow educators to better assist those students who already call on its elements to negotiate educational institutions.

Collaboration. Because of its status among youth, instructors can most effectively collaborate with students who are participants in Hip Hop by using its elements to teach certain lessons. For example, in our basic writing and our college-level writing courses, students who are Hip Hop emcees are identified during the beginning of the semester and asked to prepare lessons during the semester about writing. When discussing the writing process, emcees in the classroom introduce this topic to the class. This allows the students to bring their knowledge and their interests to the learning experience. It identifies the instructor as "one of us" as opposed to "one of them" and readily commands students to mentally attend to what occurs in the classroom. Other students in the classroom already know the emcees on campus, who by virtue of their skill command a certain respect; thus, students in the class tend to provide their undivided attention. Additionally, the "biting" of another emcee's lyrics—copying and using another emcee's rhymes—is not acceptable within Hip Hop culture; likewise, plagiarism or purloining of another's intellectual property is a serious offense among educators. Students who are emcees can communicate this very effectively to other students. Such discussions lead directly into instruction on documentation. As documentation is essential for research, emcees readily communicate how they research certain topics for accuracy when they compose their rhymes. At the 2004 meeting of the College Language Association at the University of Georgia, Kellie Weiss, a doctoral student at Howard University who teaches the first semester English Composition course, presented her use of the Hip Hop rhyme "Aliens" by Outkast to assist students in understanding the relationship between the thesis and the subsequent paragraphs. Professor Gary Berke at Bergen Community College, in cooperation with his students, writes and presents rhymes to his basic writing

students about grammar, sentence construction, and so forth. Most important, using their popular culture in the classroom assists students in realizing the relationship between what happens in "the isolated classroom" and what happens in "the real world."

Although the above discussion drew illustrations from the writing classroom, instructors in other disciplines are using Hip Hop culture with their students. At Clark Atlanta University, Professor Constance Chapman makes use of Hip Hop lyrics when discussing figurative language in her literature classes. Alan Lawrence Sitomer, a teacher in Los Angeles at Lynwood High School has coauthored *Hip-Hop Poetry and the Classics for the Classroom*, in which he discusses using Hip Hop in literature classes. At Laney College in Oakland, California, Professor Dawn Fisher Banks, now at the Hip Hop Archives at Stanford University, called on Hip Hop culture and its elements to teach anthropology. Professor Sherrise Truesdale at the Minnesota State University uses the rhymes of her students who are emcees in teaching her sociology and criminology courses to impart research skills. Professor Alan Singer at Hofstra University uses rap rhymes to teach about slavery and other topics in history (Eltman, 2006, p. CN2). Other elements of Hip Hop, in addition to emceein,' are used for instruction in the classroom. A "NASA-sponsored science concert uses live performances (Hip Hop dancers), outrageous stunts and music videos to teach students about Newton's laws of motion" (Schapiro, 2005, p. 23). Moreover, Suzy "Stone's Hip Hop Kidz fitness program has over 1,000 students in nearly two dozen locations across four states" (Kesner, 2003, p. 23) dancing to tone their bodies. In addition to Wade Colwell's use of Hip Hop to study mathematics, many instructors are using Hip Hop to teach arithmetic—addition, subtraction, division, and even having students write rhymes incorporating multiplication times tables. H2A, which is an umbrella organization for H2ED and other Hip Hop associations, Cleveland's Rock and Roll Hall of Fame's summer workshop on using Hip Hop in the classroom and other groups throughout the country are now calling for aspects of this youth culture to engage our students in the teaching-learning process.

Critical Analysis. While many instructors collaborate with students to enrich classroom activities by using elements of Hip Hop to explain certain concepts and to assist in development of certain skills, courses specifically on Hip Hop are offered at many institutions, particularly in higher education. For example, in the South Bronx where Hip Hop was born, the John Cardinal O'Connell Campus of the College of New Rochelle, School of New Resources has offered a course on the Sociology of Hip Hop. Dr. Dolores Bost (personal communication, August 5, 2006), an administrator at the campus, stated that the focus of the seminar was to analyze the impact of rap and Hip Hop on the society from different aspects. New York University has offered several courses on Hip Hop to its students and lectures and seminars to participants in its Faculty Resource Network, which is a network of participating institutions of higher education providing various types of resources for their faculties. In its course offerings, Syracuse University has even offered a specific course on Emcee Lil' Kim. Also at Syracuse, Professor Gwendolyn Pough's (2004) courses embrace Hip Hop to bridge gaps in the classroom.

While additional courses for credit are being offered each year by institutions, student conferences on Hip Hop, beginning with the Howard University conference organized by April Silvers and others in 1991, have been offered by various types of institutions of higher education, including the University of Michigan, Rutgers University, Northern Illinois University, Yale University, and Bergen Community College, with roundtables being sponsored by the Hip Hop Archives, in 2002 at Harvard University and in 2006 at Stanford University. Interestingly, organizers of courses and conferences are following the mantra of the Hip Hop community to "keep it real" by inviting scholars as well as participants in Hip Hop culture, including pioneers and performers with college experiences, performers without college experiences, performers from the streets, and community-based programs using Hip Hop in one way or another. While such courses and conferences offer enlightenment to those of us not from the Hip Hop generation, they offer participants in Hip Hop culture, both active and passive participants, the opportunity to network and to resolve certain pertinent issues about which they as well as mainstream society are concerned.

One such pressing issue among pioneers of the culture and the Hip Hop generation is what to do about gangsta rap, which has explicit lyrics and messages about violence, mistreatment of women, glorification of thug life, and other negativity. The emcees of NWA, from Compton, California, are considered the fathers of gangsta rap because of the violence they rhymed about on their album *Straight Outta Compton.* However, according to Dr. Kimberley Ellis, scholar and performer, NWA was following the precedent already set by East Coast emcees, who rhymed about what was occurring in their neighborhoods. Dr. Ellis, at the First Conference of Veterans of the Mississippi Freedom Fighters Civil Rights Movement, at Jackson State University in March 2006, posited that from its beginnings and for about 20 years, Hip Hop emcees were educators and identified as teachers by the Hip Hop Community. They encouraged youth to study, in order to learn about their African roots, history, and leaders from past generations, and they discussed the social injustices in their 'hoods, which is what NWA did, however, using "raw" language. Ellis and others agree that the music industry, for many reasons but primarily financial, seized on the popularity of the NWA recording and used the language and topics emanating from the mouths of those emcees, as the measure by which they gave succeeding emcees recording contracts. From then until now, members of the Hip Hop community have battled about how to control the negativity, if it should be controlled, and what to do about it, while members of the older generations have continuously castigated all Hip Hop music as a result of gangsta rap. This battle received widespread publicity during the spring of 2007, when shock jock Don Imus on public radio used negative phrases first coined by gangsta rappers to describe the nationally acclaimed Rutgers University women's basketball team. These comments cost Imus his job and the discussion rages on!

In an effort to call the Hip Hop generation back to its roots of working toward social justice, Afrika Bambaataa added the fifth element, which is knowledge (studying). The majority of the young adults "living Hip Hop" are not in accord with gangsta rap; they report that for gangsta rap records to go platinum, they must be purchased by European American youth from the suburbs, according to Afrika Bambaataa, because of the required number of records to be sold. Many people without affiliations within the Hip Hop community are not aware of the major controversy going on about gangsta rap. In fact, certain members of the Hip

Hop community have defined Hip Hop music as that with positive, conscious lyrics and rap music as "the bastard child" of Hip Hop with all its negative messages. Of course, while these issues continue to be debated among the Hip Hop generation, the many underground Hip Hop emcees, such as Hassan Salaam, Native Deen, and Iron Triangle continue to sell out of the trunks of their cars their uplifting, enlightening music to those participants in Hip Hop, as the music industry continues to make billions of dollars on the raps with the negative, explicit lyrics. It is hoped that the Imus controversy will bring change to the music industry. Other issues discussed in courses on Hip Hop include topics such as Hip Hop as a political movement, for the Rock the Vote campaigns spearheaded by Hip Hop artists have become a force to be reckoned with. This is vitally important, especially since Bakari Kitwana and others organized the first Hip Hop Political Convention at Rutgers University, Essex County Community College, and several churches in Newark, New Jersey, in July of 2004. The second convention was held in Chicago, Illinois in July of 2006. One of the most important highlights of these conventions is the intergenerational conversations between the Hip Hop generation and the pre–Hip Hop generations. Discussing such issues in courses and at conferences in educational institutions provides a structure for the rigorous work necessary to resolve such issues. Most important in the courses and at these conferences is that students are given the opportunity to discuss, to debate, to decide on courses of action to take, and to develop their critical thinking skills.

Cooperative Education/Course Practicum/ Internships. Various courses of study providing hands-on-experience can be offered to young African American men to assist them in building the necessary skills for negotiation and for mediation in their postcollege lives. While companies sensitive to Hip Hop participants have in recent times offered internships, and students have taken courses that have allowed them to hone skills for success in the world of Hip Hop and beyond, more must be offered to them. It is imperative that most students understand that they will not be offered a lucrative recording contract because they have won several local emcee battles and that having an education is an investment that can be used when and if that

lucrative contract is not forthcoming. Even with the contract, many artists readily admit that the business side of the Hip Hop is important. Artists with college experience understand that other types of knowledge are most vital for success. Professional Hip Hop emcees with college experience include Chuck D, Diddy, Lil Wayne, Guru, D.J. Premier and other members of Gang Starr, Boots Riley, Souls of Mischieve, Mystikal, and Kanye West. Businessmen in Hip Hop with such experience include entrepreneur Russell Simmons; authors Nelson George, Bakari Kitwana, and Adisa Banjoko; the founders of the *Source* magazine, David Mays and Jon Shecter; writer and deejay Davey D; lawyer Navarro Gray; and vice president for Warner Music Group, Kevin Liles. Liles, after college, according to Amy Pan (2005), was

> frustrated by an ensuing struggle for royalties [and] turned to the business side of the music industry. In 1991 he became an unpaid intern at Def Jam, where hard work and perfectionism paid off. In five years, Liles rose through the ranks and became president of Def Jam. While he was president, Def Jam revenues doubled to $400 million. (p. B3)

Hands-on courses, where students work with and are exposed to the realities of production of culture as well as alternative opportunities, are needed more than ever to assist students in understanding that behind the money is hard work!

Additional types of course offerings shall be necessary in the future as this culture continues to evolve. During the spring semester 2007, Howard University began offering additional courses "geared toward engaging undergraduate students in a critical analysis of Hip-Hop using research, policy, and program review, as well as including activist perspectives" (Hip Hop Alerts, 2006). These courses are Hip Hop and the African American Experience, and Black Youth and Hip Hop. Nevertheless, additional courses are needed in the academy to explore why Hip Hop has been so successful in social reform of certain antisocial behaviors, such as the gang truce in the Bronx and why certain hard-core youth decided to pursue skill development in elements of Hip Hop, foregoing earlier criminal activity. Related courses of study should include using Hip Hop to solve social problems, such as prison reform; political problems, such as the uses and abuses of power; and personal problems through participation in arts therapy. Using arts therapy, Licensed Clinical Social Workers Neal Nabil Howard and Maryam Rashada have developed methods using Hip Hop in their group counseling sessions with students and in therapeutic sessions with youth who are clients. At this time, course offerings must be made available for others to be trained to do such work. In addition, course offerings must include an exploration of the relationship between the Hip Hop generation and the generations of the Civil Rights and Black Activists Movements, which sometimes has been tense, in spite of the fact that Hip Hop was born out of the earlier movements. Through formal study, Hip Hop must be placed on the continuum in the struggle for social justice among African Americans and related struggles globally, especially since Hip Hop has been embraced by many international disenfranchised groups. Most important is that this culture has rewarded many of its youth financially; therefore, an exploration of this culture and its resources and how they can be used to build and to develop the African American community is vital for college students, particularly males, who are called on for leadership.

Conclusion

Led by African American males, members of the Hip Hop community have empowered self, learned new skills, and provided jobs for self. Through organizing, they have learned "the ability to survive, 'to make a way outta no way,' and to narrate this experience . . . in such a way that it resonates with [a] primary audience" (Richardson, 2006, p. 12). Elements of Hip Hop have been appropriated by mainstream society, so that today, although not universal, Hip Hop has become an international youth culture acknowledging its origins in African and diasporic traditions. During the early 1980s, it was predicted to have a short life; yet Hip Hop will soon be 50 years old. All of it is not pretty, but the Hip Hop community will continue to grapple with those issues of negativity that plague all of the society through its own forums, conferences, seminars, and courses sponsored by the academy. It has continued to grow with its own

institutions, such as the Hip Hop church in Harlem and other cities under the direction of Emcee Curtis Blow, and with Sister Christie's and Brother Fable's Web site toolsofwar @yahoogroups.com. Because it has permeated the major institutions in society, and because youth successfully use Hip Hop for certain personal educational tasks, other educators must consider its use as well for classroom lectures and presentations. According to Hinckley (2005),

> From the love songs of LL Cool J and Usher to the hard rhymes of Public Enemy to the humor of Snoop Dogg, with a hundred thousand party and road mixes in between, hip hop has survived because it matters to its listeners. When it doesn't, and not before, it will go away. (p. 16)

Peace!

References

Atkinson, L. (1988). *Power and empowerment.* Las Vegas, NV: Falcon Press.

Bergman, P. (1969). *The chronological history of the Negro in America.* New York: Harper & Row.

Bernstein, D. A., & Nash, P. W. (2005). *Essentials of psychology* (3rd ed.). Boston: Houghton Mifflin.

Brown v. Board of Education of Topeka, Kansas, 347 U.S. 483 (1954).

Chang, J. (2005). *Can't stop won't stop: A history of the hip hop generation.* New York: St. Martin's Press.

Clear and present diaper. (2006, July 14). *The New York Daily News,* p. 4.

Crouch, S. (2006, July 24). Time to kill ghetto tax. *The New York Daily News,* p. 29.

Eltman, F. (2006, March 26). Slave lesson hits home for L.I. students. *The New York Daily News,* p. CN2.

Gardner, H. (1999). *The disciplined mind: What all students should understand.* New York: Simon & Schuster.

Gee, J. P. (1996). *Social linguistics and literacies* (2nd ed.). London: Falman Press.

Hinckley, D. (2005, March 27). Give rap a break. *The New York Daily News Now Magazine,* p. 16.

Hip Hop Alerts. (2006, December 10). *Howard University unveils new hip-hop courses.* Retrieved December 11, 2006, from www.allhiphop.com/alerts

Kesner, J. (2003, November 13). Hip hop kidz. *The New York Daily News Now Magazine,* p. 23.

Kitwana, B. (2002). *The hip hop generation: Young blacks and the crisis in African American culture.* New York: Basic Books.

Miller, I. L. (2002). *Aerosol kingdom: Subway painters of New York City.* Jackson: University Press of Mississippi.

O'Reilly, K. (1989). *Racial matters: The FBI files on black America, 1960–1972.* New York: Free Press.

Pan, A. (2005, September 28). Wise words from hip-hop exec. *The Bergen Record,* p. B3.

Pough, G. (2004). *Check it while I wreck it.* Boston: Northeastern University Press.

Project South: Institute for the Elimination of Poverty and Genocide. (2005). *Popular education toolkit: Prison-Industrial Complex.* Atlanta, GA: Author.

Richardson, E. (2006). *Hip hop literacies.* London: Routledge.

Rose, T. (1994). *Black noise: Rap music and black culture in contemporary America.* Hanover, NH: Wesleyan University Press.

Schapiro, R. (2005, November 13). Newton's laws big laughs for school troupe. *The New York Daily News,* p. 23.

Siemaszko, C. (2004, December 16). Crack ho' gains Oxford admissions. *The New York Daily News,* p. 6.

Smitherman, G. (2000). *Black talk: Words and phrases from the hood to the amen corner* (Rev. ed.). Boston: Houghton Mifflin.

Yasin, J. A. (1997). *In yo face! Rappin' beats comin' at you: A study of how language is mapped onto musical beats in rap music.* Unpublished doctoral dissertation, Teachers College, Columbia University, New York.

Yasin, J. A. (2001). Rap in the African American music tradition. In A. K. Spears (Ed.), *Race and ideology: Language symbolism, and popular culture* (pp. 197–223). Detroit, MI: Wayne State University Press.

Yasin, J. A. (2003). Hip hop culture meets the writing classroom. In C. Coriel (Ed.), *Multiple intelligences, Howard Gardner, and new methods of college teaching* (pp. 75–82). Jersey City: New Jersey City University Publication.

18

CAMPUSWIDE CLIMATE

Implications for African American Students

WILLIAM A. SMITH

Every student on a postsecondary campus can claim some degree of stress. Some researchers say that there is no indication of the record levels of stress reported decreasing. According to the former president of the Association of University and College Counseling Center Directors, Dr. Gregory Snodgrass, while postsecondary institutions are reporting increases of student-reported stressors, university counseling centers are already overwhelmed 2 weeks into a new school year. Counseling and educational psychologists are hard at work early in the term attempting to identify the main factors producing stress on campus that continue to place students at risk. While stress can be a factor for many students, there are groups of students who are stressed, exploited, and disadvantaged by sociopolitical, ideological, and behavioral burdens imposed by a controlling population, culture, and climate that extends into and beyond college and university campuses.

Chester Pierce, Felton Earls, and Arthur Kleinman (1999) suggested that "clinicians often fail to realize the significant role that race, culture, and ethnicity play in the etiology, diagnosis, and treatment of mental disease. Consequently, they may subject people of color, especially Blacks, to inappropriate diagnostic and treatment standards" (p. 735). By extension, if campus mental health professionals are incompetent around issues of race and racism, and the standard nomenclature (*Diagnostic and Statistical Manual of Mental Disorders,* American Psychiatric Association, 2000, fourth edition-text revision, better known as the *DSM-IV-TR*) does not address or provide a meaningful understanding on this important issue as a form of mundane and extreme environmental stress (MEES), it is probably unlikely that university and college faculty and administrators are aware of—or have developed—a strategy for eliminating race-related stressors facing African American students.

In this chapter, I discuss the contemporary campus racial climate for African American students who attend historically White institutions of higher education in a post-*Brown,* post–Civil Rights Era. The framers of the *Brown* case were primarily concerned with institutional desegregation and educational equity for Blacks. While some institutions exerted significant proactive efforts, the typical responses were followed by major student-led demonstrations that challenged institutions to change their racist ways. The legal decision of *Brown* had little impact on the persistent negative racial ideologies and reactions about the presence of Blacks that many White students and faculty brought to campus. As a result, today's historically White campus racial culture has continued to nurture, produce, and maintain a particular racial ideology, reactionary racism, toward Black students which feeds a hostile campuswide racial climate.

Reactionary racism is a negative, reactionary sentiment couched in a belief that social changes for Blacks' demands have "gone too far." This racial ideology, in addition to the various racial microaggressions and discrimination that Black students face on- and off-campus, has shaped a campuswide climate that creates racial battle fatigue. This racial battle fatigue—the psychological, emotional, physiological, energy, and time-related cost of fighting against racism—that Black students face daily defending against anti-Black environments is draining and counterproductive as they seek to reach their academic and professional goals. In today's complex racial climate, Black students are not only concerned with White racial animus but are also aware of the growing numbers of Blacks and other people of color who hold similar ideologies about Black people. This chapter will offer the reader a way to understand more fully how a historically White campus climate continues to create racial battle fatigue for many Black students and why these students are spending valuable time and energy fighting back in these environments while trying to earn academic degrees. The terms *African Americans* and *Blacks* are used interchangeably herein. Additionally, any form of the reference to people or students of color refers to Asian Pacific American, American Indian, Black, and Latina/o people as a collective group. Finally, I use historically White institutions (hereafter, HWI) instead of predominantly White institutions to illuminate the fact that the gross numbers or percentages of White students have far less to do with the composition of the majority populations than it does with the historical and contemporary racialized infrastructure that is in place, the current racial campus culture and ecology, and how these modern-day institutions still benefit Whites at the expense of Blacks and other groups of color.

Traditional Explanations of Opposition to Academic and Social Integration

Despite growing opposition to affirmative action efforts, numerous studies (e.g., Chang, 1999; Hurtado, 2002; Villalpando, 2002) refute the racial polarization propagandists who argue that diversity planning and race-targeted policies in the curricula and campus infrastructure are an "illiberal education" (D'Souza, 1991). These propagandists maintain that Blacks' demands have "gone too far" and are now "disuniting" America (Schlesinger, 1992). According to a University of California-Los Angeles law professor and anti-affirmative action propagandist, Richard H. Sander (2004), faulty affirmative action attempts in admissions are adversely affecting African American students, who are being admitted to schools above their intellectual capacity, where they compete against more qualified and intelligent White and Asian American students. In the middle of these debates, a multifaceted racial ideology has emerged on college campuses that has produced a growing ambivalence about affirmative action efforts. Tyrone Forman (2004) maintained that White students and a small but growing number of students of color are placing an emphasis on "color-blindness," allowing Whites to be comforted by the fallacy that all races are now on a level playing field. According to Forman, Whites with this ideology do not recognize the advantages they themselves have reaped from years of inequality. Consequently, they tend to respond apathetically toward others who "erroneously," in their belief, support affirmative action and social justice demands.

In the center of this debate is an alternative position where current research is demonstrating short- and long-term benefits from diversity and multicultural experiences on campuses noted for their proactiveness, and where students take classes from faculty who integrate race, culture, class, gender, sexuality, and/or language issues in their course content (Tatum, Calhoun, Brown, & Ayvazian, 2000; Terenzini, Cabrera, Colbeck, Bjorklund, & Parente, 2001; Villalpando, 2002). Even so, a noteworthy irony still remains. On the one hand, findings from contemporary research studies suggest that the majority of White adults no longer support scientific and biological racism claims forwarded by persons, including the developer of the SAT (Scholastic Aptitude Test), and self-admitted White supremacist, Dr. Carl Campbell Brigham (1923). Findings from other studies maintain that, in theory, the majority of White adults oppose racial and gender discrimination and segregation (cf. Bobo, Kluegel, & Smith, 1997). Whites now show almost universal support for abstract principles of racial equality (Krysan, 2000). Yet resistance to race-targeted efforts aimed at addressing these inequalities persists (Bobo & Kluegel, 1993; Tuch & Sigelman, 1997).

Recent research shows that significant numbers of White adults oppose actions taken to remedy historic wrongdoings and ensure racial equality (Bobo, 2000; Feagin, 2006; Sidanius, Singh, Hetts, & Federico, 2000). Researchers know less about *how* and *why* traditional-aged White college and university students support or oppose affirmative action and diversity initiatives. What researchers do know, from a small number of quantitative and qualitative studies, is that White and Asian American students, in general, tend to be less supportive of campus-directed affirmative action initiatives than African American and Latina/o students (Bonilla-Silva & Forman, 2000; Bowman & Smith, 2002; Inkelas, 2003; Sax & Arredondo, 1999; Smith, 1998). However, there has been some evidence that large numbers of Asian (some student-led) organizations are pro-affirmative action (e.g., Asian American Voices for Affirmative Action, Western Rainbow Coalition Alliance, and Asian Pacific Students for Action). According to a number of polls, 61% of Asian American voters rejected proposition 209[1] in California (1996). Similarly, 75% of Asian American voters voted against Proposition 2[2] in Michigan (against the 58% tide of Michigan voters who approved of it). While it may be true that honorary White Asians (borrowing Bonilla-Silva's term from his Latin Americanization thesis) may be less supportive of affirmative action programs when compared with their African American and Latina/o counterparts, or other darker-skinned Asian groups such as Hmong, Pilipino, and Vietnamese who are likely to overwhelmingly support affirmative action initiatives. These darker-skinned Asians are also more apt to relate to Blacks' plight in the education system as they might face racial microaggressions similar to those experienced by Black students. It is in the face of this complex campus racial climate that Black students must negotiate friends from foes and other race-related stressors that this environment produces. Scholarship that only attends to White students' behaviors and ignores the attitudes and beliefs of Asian American, African American, Latina/o, and other students of color further marginalizes these students' opinions, which are needed for successful educational policy efforts (Bowman & Smith, 2002).

Contemporary Racism

As racial attitudes have changed since the mid-1900s, recent research has shifted in its theoretical foundations and emphases. Today, the most common explanations of racial ideology are found in race-related beliefs referred to as "modern," "symbolic," "aversive," "laissez-faire," "racial resentment," "subtle prejudice," or "color-blind" racism (Bobo et al., 1997; Bonilla-Silva, 2001; Bonilla-Silva & Forman, 2000; Bowman & Smith, 2002; Kinder & Sears, 1981; Krysan, 2000; McConahay, 1986; Sears, 1988; Smith, 1998). Each of these theories emphasizes a move away from old-fashioned racism based on beliefs about biological inferiority to a newer, more subtle racial ideology. As a result, contemporary racism is a complex combination of resentment of Black demands that are viewed as unfair, with feelings that Whites are unjustly losing ground to Blacks, to denial that racism or discrimination remains a significant social problem for Blacks.

Race-Related Attributions

Early research on causal attributions for racial inequality among Black college students and other populations often assigned blame to either the individual or the system in either/or terms within a bipolar framework (e.g., Bowman & Smith, 2002). People tend to believe that *either* individual deficits *or* discriminatory obstacles and barriers in the larger social system should be blamed for persistent Black poverty and other social and economic inequalities (Krysan, 2000; Smith, 2006). In cross-ethnic terms, mainstream socialization may produce greater similarities in beliefs about individual responsibility, while racial/ethnic socialization may produce greater diversity in system attributions. Like Blacks, Latinas/os and Asians more often than Whites experience a "dual consciousness" with a higher correlation between individual-deficit and system-barrier attributions. Hence, in a bicultural sense, people of color more often combine individual-blame beliefs (reflecting to some degree their internalization of mainstream cultural values) with high system-blame beliefs (based on their racial/ethnic socialization). This double consciousness may also reflect a greater recognition among people of color of the complexity and multiplicity of causes for perpetuating poverty and other racial inequalities when assessing contemporary conditions (Bowman & Smith, 2002).

Cultural Pathology Stereotypes

An accepted hypothesis is that Blacks generally do not share the mainstream U.S. values of the so-called Protestant work ethic of hard work, self-reliance, and individualism (Kinder & Sanders, 1996; Kinder & Sears, 1981). Individualism continues to be a central theme in the research literature on aspects of modern racism. Cultural pathology stereotypes, that Blacks in general not only lack mainstream virtues but also hold self-defeating, "ghetto-specific" preferences, may likewise play a significant role in White opposition to race-targeted policies. There is increasing evidence that a significant portion of the U.S. population believes, stereotypically, that African Americans are not so much restricted by structural barriers or individual deficits per se but rather by an inferior culture characterized by a tendency toward violence, a preference for welfare, and a self-perpetuating lifestyle of poverty (Bobo, 2000; Bonilla-Silva, 2002; Peffley, Hurwitz, & Sniderman, 1997; Sears, Henry, & Kosterman, 2000; Smith, 2006).

Conservative Values and Attitudes

An intense debate has emerged in the theoretical and empirical literature on the role of conservative political values and ideology in the growing opposition to race-targeted policies in higher education and other arenas (Sears, Hetts, Sidanius, & Bobo, 2000; Smith, 2006). Proponents of a race-centered model have emphasized the pivotal role of modern racism, racial resentment, race-related attributions, and anti-Black stereotypes in the growing opposition to Civil Rights Era policies. In contrast, Bobo (2000) suggested that proponents of what he considers a politics-centered model undermine the role of race and emphasize the rational choices of the politically informed to reaffirm cherished U.S. values and oppose unfair race-based entitlements. Proponents of this hypothesis argue that the democratic process and intensified political support for a conservative agenda reaffirming core U.S. ideals of individualism, self-reliance, and fair play have increased the opposition to race-targeted policies (Sniderman & Hagen, 1985). As with other race-related beliefs, differences among college students from diverse racial/ethnic groups on conservative policy values, preferences, and attitudes may have important implications for campus discourse, climate, and community.

CONTEMPORARY CAMPUS RACIAL CLIMATE FOR AFRICAN AMERICAN STUDENTS IN HWI OF HIGHER EDUCATION

Mundane and Extreme Environmental Stress

One way of understanding or defining stress is to view it as the inverse of support. From this vantage point, if African American students had ideal biological, cultural, sociological, and psychological support on campus, there would be no stress (Mino, Profit, & Pierce, 2000). Unfortunately, far too many Black students and their personal and/or group's resources are overextended from race-related experiences or events that appear to be uncontrollable, unpredictable, and uncertain. Most of these racial events are subtle, unconscious microaggressive insults or assaults influenced by the racial stereotypes and sentiments that White students, faculty, and administrators add to the ongoing, campuswide racial culture.

Racial microaggressions can range from racial slights, recurrent indignities and irritations, unfair treatment, stigmatization, hypersurveillance, contentious classrooms, to personal threats or attacks on one's well-being. As a result of chronic racial microaggressions, many African American students perceive their environment as extremely stressful, exhausting, and diminishing to their sense of control, comfort, and meaning while eliciting feelings of loss, ambiguity, strain, frustration, and injustice (Brown et al., 1999). For example, consider how a Black male student might feel after entering a computer lab to work on a class assignment and moments later a campus police officer signals for him to step out of the lab for questioning. He is asked what business he has in the lab and that he must show two forms of identification to prove that he is a "legitimate" student on that campus (Smith, Allen, & Danley, 2007). When African Americans and other racially oppressed groups are in situations where they experience environmental stressors as mundane events, the ramifications are as much a psychological and emotional burden as they are a physiological response. Therefore, the campuswide climate for

Black students is one of MEES (see Carroll, 1998; Pierce, 1974).

Of course, there are also racial-gender dynamics that are a part of the racial microaggressions that both Black male and female students experience. Today, we are witnessing the contemporary expressions, practices, and ideologies used to justify slavery and the continued subordination of people of African descent (Anderson, 1993; Ellison, 1952; Jordan, 1968; Wilson, 1990) in the form of Black misandry and Black misogyny. I have defined *Black misandry* as an exaggerated pathological aversion toward and oppression of Black men created and reinforced in societal, institutional, and individual ideologies and practices (Smith, in press-b; Smith, Yosso, & Solórzano, 2007). Along with Black misogyny, these forms of ideological pathology are embedded within scholarly ontologies, axiologies, and epistemologies where Black women and Black men are held under suspicion, marginalized, hated, rendered invisible, put under increased surveillance, or placed into one or more socially acceptable stereotypical categories. According to Yarbrough and Bennett (2000), during the colonial period, White men viewed White women with suspicion, distrust, and also associated them with sexuality. However, as time passed, a racial foil was being created where White women were no longer portrayed as sexual temptresses. Black women were being used as the racial foil where White women could be celebrated as the "nobler half of humanity" and depicted as goddesses rather than sinners—a role assumed by Black women. In this form of racial contract, as Mills (1997) described, White women were thereafter represented as virtuous, pure, and innocent to which African American women have been contrasted and defined as immoral and sinful.

In similar ways, Black misandric meta-narratives and meta-agreements were created about Black men to control, criminalize, and make them appear—without questioning—as less intelligent, lazy, violent, belligerent, mean, and skirters of family responsibilities. As a result, when Black men are seen in places or positions that do not "fit" their Black misandric stereotype, they are viewed as being "out of their place," potentially dangerous, and a threat to "law abiding" citizens. Therefore, the presence of Black men on college campuses is often seen and justified as an example of all the problems that "faulty" affirmative action policies have come to represent—in short, it is an act of "reverse racism" and an undeserved special privilege, unless they are athletes. Consequently, many Black men encounter extreme feelings of reactionary racism on campus. Moreover, many researchers support the view that Black boys are under attack as early as kindergarten.[3]

Reactionary racism is a belief that (a) the government and news media have shown more respect to African Americans than they deserve; (b) African Americans should not push themselves where they are not wanted; (c) African Americans have gotten more economically than they deserve; (d) African Americans are getting too demanding in their push for equal rights; and (e) African Americans have more influence on school desegregation than they ought to have (Bowman & Smith, 2002; Smith, 2006). Together, these beliefs indicate a negative, reactionary sentiment, commonly expressed as the belief that social changes in response to demands from Blacks have "gone too far" (Kinder & Sanders, 1996; Kinder & Sears, 1981; McConahay, 1986; Sears, 1988). Many of the racial microaggressions that Blacks receive are at the expense of the racial ideologies that Whites possess about Blacks and what "their place" should be in society. Consequently, African Americans are spending countless amounts of energy preparing to defend themselves against possible microaggressive assaults. This obligatory steadiness of personal, psychological, and physiological energy mobilization against assaults on historically White campuses contributes, in ways that are still understudied, to racial battle fatigue. In the end, the campus racial contract and the "racial state" it engenders rests in "securing the privileges and advantages of the full white citizens and maintaining the subordination of nonwhites" (Mills, 1997, p. 14).

Racial Battle Fatigue in the Historically White Campus "Racial State"

Racial battle fatigue addresses the emotional, physiological, psychological, behavioral strain exacted on racially marginalized and stigmatized groups and the amount of energy loss dedicated to coping with racism. Racial battle fatigue synthesizes and builds onto the extensive cross-discipline-specific research literature and studies of stress responses to racism and its impact on health and coping strategies (e.g.,

Brown, Parker-Dominguez, & Sorey, 2000; Brown, Wallace, & Williams, 2000; Carroll, 1998; Clark, Anderson, Clark, & Williams, 1999; Feagin & McKinney, 2003; Feagin & Sikes, 1994; Gougis, 1986; James, 1994; Pierce, 1974, 1975, 1995; Prillerman, Myers, & Smedley, 1989; Sapolsky, 1998; Scaer, 2001; Shay, 2002; Shay & Munroe, 1999; Smith, 2004, in press-a, in press-b; Steele, 1997; Steele & Aronson, 1995; Stevenson, 1994a, 1994b, 1997, 1998; Williams, Yu, Jackson, & Anderson, 1997). This theory also uses the literature on combat stress syndrome (also known as combat stress fatigue, combat trauma, combat injury, or posttraumatic stress disorder/injury) for understanding the effects of hostile environments and experiences (Pierce, 1975, 1995; Shay, 2002; Shay & Munroe, 1999; Smith, 2004; U.S. Department of the Army, 1994; Willie & Sanford, 1995).

The historically White campus racial state is one of the many lingering environmental conditions that produce racial battle fatigue for far too many Black students. In this social milieu, where institutional and individual racist practices are present (whether conscious or unconscious, overt or covert, subtle or obvious, or as color-blind acts), Black students must constantly dedicate time and energy to determine if there was a stressor, whether that stressor was motivated by a racist (or gendered racist) purpose, and how or if they should respond. Equipped with several centuries of racial struggle in the United States, most Blacks are racially socialized (e.g., through proactive, protective, or adaptive racial socialization) to employ many forms of coping strategies in combating racial microaggressions (see Bowman & Howard, 1985; Clark et al., 1999; Prillerman et al., 1989; Stevenson, 1994a, 1994b, 1997, 1998). Interestingly, research also suggests that this process has prepared them more effectively for dealing with racial macroaggressions than with microaggressions (Prillerman et al., 1989; Stevenson, 1994a, 1994b, 1997). Depending on the coping responses (i.e., adaptive or maladaptive) and the level of social or institutional support, Blacks will experience racial battle fatigue in varying intervals, amplitudes, duration, and intensity that directly impact their physiological and psychological stress responses and related health outcomes.

Racial battle fatigue has three major responses: (a) psychological stress responses, (b) physiological stress responses, and (c) behavioral responses.

These responses are not separate entities. Researchers now better understand the enormously intricate intertwining of our biology and our emotions, the continuous ways in which our personalities, feelings, and thoughts both reflect and influence the events in our bodies. According to Sapolsky (1998),

> One of the most interesting manifestations of this recognition is understanding that extreme emotional disturbances can adversely affect us. Put in the parlance with which we have grown familiar, *stress can make us sick,* and a critical shift in medicine has been the recognition that many of the damaging diseases of slow accumulation can be either caused by or made far worse by [race-related] stress. (p. 3)

Thus, the psychological stress responses can come from constantly having to react to the mundane, extreme racial microaggressions found in the campuswide racial climate.

The conditions that cause psychological racial battle fatigue for Black students are felt as frustration, shock, anger, disappointment, resentment, anxiety, helplessness, hopelessness, and fear, among many others, known and understudied. Consider a Black female student who feels the need to constantly engage her White sociology professor who persistently and maybe unknowingly uses Black examples in her lectures, readings, and videos as products of a "ghetto-specific" pathological culture. Or, her Black friend who might feel anxious about approaching the professor but has to listen, take notes, and pass a class she is frustrated in every day because of this racial dimension. This might be one explanation as to why recent studies of predominantly Black populations have found an inverse relationship in health outcomes (e.g., rates of hypertension, depression, anxiety, life satisfaction, mortality indicators) between Black men who are college graduates and Black men who are high school graduates (Diez-Roux, Northridge, Morabia, Bassett, & Shea, 1999). The college graduates had higher incomes and presumably better diets and generally improved lifestyles, including lower levels of cigarette smoking, physical inactivity, and being overweight. Yet the chronic race-related stressors associated with historically White spaces are suggested as the cause for the rise in poor health outcomes among these men. In another study, moving up the socioeconomic status ladder for Black women was inversely related to their self-reported stress but positively related to stress for Black men (James, 1994). Researchers in another study found that while suburban residence was associated with lower mortality risk for Whites, it predicted markedly elevated mortality risks for Black men (House et al., 2000). For Black men who seek, or who are trying to maintain, middle-class standing through higher education, the exposure to Black misandric racism and discrimination encountered in historically White spaces are stressors adversely affecting their mental and physical health.

The body responds to insults like it is under a physical attack. Therefore, racial microaggressions found in the campuswide racial climate is physiologically coded as a violent attack, racial terrorism, an act of aggression. For the Black students who are racially unaware, inappropriately racially socialized for a gendered racist world, or the racially fatigued, the psychological and physiological stress responses might be too much for them to bear, and they withdraw. Very few clinicians or campus counselors are trained to appropriately recognize the sources that lead many Black students to display physiological conditions of constant headaches, grinding teeth, clenched jaws, chest pain, shortness of breath, memory loss, a pounding heart, high blood pressure, muscle aches, indigestion, constipation or diarrhea, increased perspiration, fatigue, insomnia, and frequent illness (Smith, in press-a). Consider for a moment what the physiological response of a lone Black male student might be who has to work in a group for a laboratory project where no one ever wants to partner with him. He has to constantly confront a racist stereotype that he does not have the intellectual capacity and might bring down the grades of other students if he is chosen as a partner. The campuswide climate is replete with many microaggressive insults that constantly work at the self-confidence, drain the personal and family coping resources, and deflect important time and energy away from what Black students are really in higher education to do—achieve academically.

Now, reflect back to the definition of stress as being the inverse of support. The stress response is the body's attempt at restoring balance. For African American students, this process is a constant juggling act as there are very few places at HWIs or off campus that are free of racial microaggressions (Bonilla-Silva, Forman, Lewis, & Embrick, 2003). Places and spaces for racial restoration are hard to find or are short lived. In the previous example, the reader was asked to consider the physiological response of the Black male in the classroom. However, a racial stressor can also be the anticipation of the racial microaggressions occurring. The body is engineered to be able to anticipate a stressor and turn on a vigorous stress response as if the event actually occurred. This happens even when a student retells a racist incident she or he witnessed, was a party to, or if she or he recalls it in dreams. In other words, the stress response can be summoned not only when the student is in the moment when physical or psychological racial microaggressions occur but also in expectation of them. In addition, immunity is also hampered because the body is experiencing every day as an emergency whether we psychologically justify it or try to deny that it really is about "race."

Physiological symptoms in the body are the best litmus test for psychologically trying to marginalize the occurrence or impact of racist experiences. Sapolsky (1998) warned us that when the body is under chronic stressful conditions, it constantly mobilizes energy at the cost of energy storage, and it will never store enough surplus energy to fight off typical diseases. This is due to the body fatiguing more rapidly. As a result, the body is weakened and placed at an increased risk of developing diseases, like a form of diabetes (Sapolsky, 1998). Under these conditions, one wonders, if the racist circumstances that cause racial battle fatigue and poor health outcomes for Blacks were appropriately diagnosed, could the increasing racial health disparities be lowered. For example, today, diabetes mellitus is one of the most serious health challenges facing more than 30 million African Americans. National Health Interview Surveys conducted between 1963 and 1990 show that African Americans have a rising prevalence of diabetes. Most African Americans with diabetes have type 2, or noninsulin-dependent diabetes. Type 2 diabetes usually develops after age 40. However, in high-risk populations, susceptible people may develop it at a younger age. A small number of African Americans have type 1 or insulin-dependent diabetes, which usually develops before age 20. What if the chronic racial microaggressions that Blacks experience were the leading contributor to diseases like diabetes mellitus?

As equally problematic as diabetes is among Blacks, so is hypertension. Imagine a professor who states that all papers must be turned in by 3:30 p.m. on Thursday because she does not accept late papers; and late papers will be penalized one letter grade. Now, take a Black student in this class who knows about the "late paper policy." However, she forgot to turn the paper in when she completed it earlier that week. She remembers! It is 3:10 p.m. and she prints her paper in the student computer lab and sprints across campus to her professor's office to turn it in. In this process her blood pressure rises to 180/120 as she arrives to the door with 2 minutes to spare; this is being adaptive and may be an example of memory drain. But the stressor is short lived. However, if her blood pressure rises to 180/120 every time she walks across campus or enters a certain class because she is treated as if she does not belong, then she is headed for sickness and her academics and health (mental and physical) will be compromised.

The good news is that each year Black students persist through HWIs and earn academic degrees. Yet most of these students had similar and unique kinds of behavioral responses to the campuswide racial climate that they personally encountered. While behavioral responses are multifaceted, I focus on the more common but least recognized and understood forms of maladaptive and adaptive coping styles or some combination of both.

Professor Claude Steele has brought to our attention that highly qualified and academically high-performing Black students can be affected by what he calls *Stereotype Threat*. Stereotype threat is "the threat of being viewed through the lens of a negative stereotype, or the fear of doing something that would inadvertently confirm that stereotype" (Steele, 1999, p. 46), such as the stereotype that simply being Black means that they will have the lowest scores in a science class when compared with other racial/ethnic groups. Steele explains that some students try to escape stereotype threat by disidentifying with the part of life in which the stereotype originates, such as race or ethnic identities. In addition to stereotype threat, more common behavioral responses to racial battle fatigue range from overeating or loss of appetite, impatience, quickness to argue,

procrastination, increased use of alcohol or drugs, increased smoking, increased sleeping, withdrawal or isolation from others, neglect of responsibility, poor job performance, poor personal hygiene, change in religious practices, change in close family relationships, hypervigilance, to defensive thinking. If we are to understand more fully what happens to Black students as part of this campuswide climate, then we must realize that racial microaggressions are the most significant, lingering, and inescapable form of racism in HWIs. One microaggressive act can set off a chain reaction that is psychological, physiological, and behavioral. Equally important to understand is how racial microaggressions, these forms of racial slights, recurrent indignities and irritations, unfair treatments, stigmatization, hypersurveillance, often remain as psychopollutants in the campuswide climate. These events are what make up the racial battle fatigue that is felt at the individual and group levels by many African American students and other students of color. Some might say, "But still we rise." But how?

African Americans rise through adaptive coping strategies. Just as the physiological stress response is affected by the psychological, Black students often use psychological factors to alter the physiological. The most successful form of coping appears to be one that is connected to a rich and sophisticated socialization pattern passed down in Black families and communities. For instance, Stevenson and Renard (1993) have found that "racial socialization involves the parental instruction to their children or family members about racism in society, educational struggles, extended family relevance, spiritual and religious awareness, African American culture and pride, and transmission of child-rearing values" (p. 435). African American cultural patterns and expressions have complexities and nuances that are rarely, if ever, understood in counseling textbooks or by counselors themselves. In fact, the coping strategies needed to exist in a racist society could not be readily apparent or visible, especially to the dominant society. Racial socialization does not rely only on a verbal, didactic, or explicit process but can often be transmitted by an indirect, tacit, or behavioral method (Boykin & Toms, 1985; Stevenson & Renard, 1993).

To test the power of coping, Stevenson (1994b) performed a validation study of the Scale of Racial Socialization Attitudes–for Adolescents. Previous studies primarily focused on extending Cross's Nigrescence Theory of Racial Identity Attitude Scales. Stevenson asked African American students to respond to questions with their "people or community in mind." He found four major factors with two underlying themes of proactive and protective racial socialization identity beliefs for adolescents that are more powerful and adaptive than Steele's stereotype threat response. According to Stevenson (1997),

> Protective racial socialization beliefs view the world as racially hostile and worthy of distrust, encourage youth to discern supportive or hostile racial intentions, take on a tone of caution, and encourage youth to succeed despite external oppression. Proactive racial socialization beliefs encourage the individual to succeed as a function of internal talent, cultural heritage, and pay less attention to external oppression. Proactive beliefs are focused more intensively on the respondent's endorsement of parental strategies that instill a sense of cultural empowerment in youth. (p. 40)

The key findings that emerged in Stevenson's (1994b) study were that proactive racial socialization beliefs consisted of three main factors: spiritual and religious coping, cultural pride reinforcement, and extended family caring. Protective racial socialization beliefs, on the one hand, consisted of one factor—racism awareness teaching. Stevenson suggested,

> A robust racial socialization agenda may require discussions about spirituality and religion and how one's identity is not fully shaped by hostile societal influences. It may suggest that children be reinforced to learn about how their cultural heritage is unique and not solely developed out of socially oppressive experiences. Enslavement is a reality of the history of being Black in America, but it does not solely concretize one's cultural identity. Blood and nonblood extended family members play a crucial role in teaching children about their character and in raising children to be responsive to the inner community concerns about racism and cultural pride development . . . Racism awareness teaching may be protective in that it challenges the recipients of the teaching to reject traditional opinions about Black culture that are also influenced by racist, inferior-based rhetoric. (p. 463)

These protective and proactive racial socialization beliefs appear to be successful adaptive coping strategies that aid in the mitigation of persistent physiological and psychological stress responses. When used consistently in the negative campuswide racial climate, these strategies can surely help reduce the troubling effects of racism and racial battle fatigue on the health of African Americans. To be sure, for African American students, as well as Black faculty and staff, HWIs can be life-draining instead of life-enhancing. Certainly, the constant process of having to employ coping strategies just to succeed at HWIs is a battle that Black people have fought for several generations, but with long-term effects. University and college faculty and administrators must become aware of and develop strategies for eliminating race-related microaggresive climates that Black students face on their campus.

Conclusion

In this chapter, I have discussed the contemporary campus racial climate for African American students who attend HWI of higher education in a post-*Brown*, post–Civil Rights Era. The attempt here was to present an explanation about how the racial/racist history of postsecondary institutions is still present and pervasive in the current campuswide racial climate and ideology. Traditional research tends to treat race relations in higher education in two distinct periods, as pre- and post-*Brown*. Conventional color-blind thinking is that Whites have become much more "tolerant" and open to multicultural relationships as a result of the *Brown* legislation, and the distance between current White students' racial ideologies and those of their grandparents are enormous. Here, I agree with Bonilla-Silva (2001) who stated, "This paradigm cannot adequately address—at least in its present form—contemporary ideological constructions, which tend to be subtle, couched in universalistic language, and protected by the mantle of racelessness" (p. 79). As a result, we know far less about how the overt racist practices of the past are manifested in more subtle and institutionalized modern forms within postsecondary settings.

One of the charges of social justice research and researchers must be to develop a resolute focus to uncover the more nuanced racial ideologies and customs imbedded in the campus climate and how they persist from one generation to the next. Unfortunately, Black students are not attending historically Black colleges and universities (HBCUs) in numbers reminiscent of the pre-1960s. Before long, researchers will have to establish, in comprehensive form, the long-term academic, professional, social, economic, and cultural benefits that Black students acquire from attending HBCUs, in addition to the proactive and protective racial socialization it provides. In the meantime, HWIs must be forced to break the current cycle of oppression. The current campus racial climate is a modern form of racial stratification that is just as effective for maintaining White supremacy as it was prior to *Brown.* The Supreme Court has made it much more difficult to establish the *effects* of racist perpetrators or institutions by focusing primarily on the *intentions.* To a significant degree, this has allowed HWIs some flexibility and comfort in not taking institutionalized racism and its responsibility as seriously as it should.

Racial battle fatigue is one method for establishing a more holistic picture of the intentions and effects of racism toward Blacks and other people of color. These racist environments are injurious and the mundane microaggressive assaults inherent in racism or in race-based encounters and experiences speak more to what causes racial battle fatigue. According to Shay (2002),

> As with any injury, the symptoms can range from mild to devastating, depending on the severity of the wound, the robustness of health at the time of the injury, and the conditions—especially nutrition—under which recovery occurred. In the case of a physical wound what counts is physical nutrition; in the case of a psychological [or emotional] injury what counts is social nutrition. (pp. 149–150)

Therefore, it is important to consider the psychological, emotional, physiological, energy, and time-related cost of fighting against racism daily in these anti-Black (misandric and misogynistic) environments and what injuries students have sustained in these battles. In this regard, when Black students' rights have been violated because of psychological, emotional, or physiological injury, the institution should and must be held liable for these violations. Otherwise, the current racially microaggressive campuswide climate will be ready for the next generation of Black students to inherit.

NOTES

1. Proposition 209 was an erroneous proposal to prohibit so-called discrimination or preferential treatment by state and other public entities in California (see http://sshl.ucsd.edu/brown/prop209.htm).

2. Proposition 2 was a proposal to amend the state constitution to ban affirmative action programs that give preferential treatment to groups or individuals based on their race, gender, color, ethnicity, or national origin for public employment, education, or contracting purposes (see www.insidehighered.com/news/2006/11/08/michigan).

3. For example, see the recent book by Mark Chesler, Amanda E. Lewis, and James Crowfoot (2005), *Challenging Racism in Higher Education: Promoting Justice,* or a number of publications by Joe R. Feagin, Amanda E. Lewis, Judith Blau, and Walter R. Allen.

REFERENCES

American Psychiatric Association. (2000). *Diagnostic and statistical manual of mental disorders* (4th ed., text rev.). Washington, DC: Author.

Anderson, J. D. (1993). Race, meritocracy, and the American academy during the immediate post–World War II era. *History of Education Quarterly, 33*(2), 151–175.

Bobo, L. (2000). Race and beliefs about affirmative action. In D. O. Sears, J. Sidanius, & L. Bobo (Eds.), *Racialized politics: The debate about racism in America* (pp. 137–165). Chicago: University of Chicago Press.

Bobo, L., & Kluegel, J. (1993). Opposition to race-targeting: Self-interest, stratification ideology, or prejudice? *American Sociological Review, 58,* 443–464.

Bobo, L., Kluegel, J. R., & Smith, R. A. (1997). Laissez-faire racism: The crystallization of a kinder, gentler, antiblack ideology. In S. A. Tuch & J. K. Martin (Eds.), *Racial attitudes in the 1990s: Continuity and change* (pp. 15–42). Westport, CT: Praeger.

Bonilla-Silva, E. (2001). *White supremacy and racism in the post-civil rights era.* Boulder, CO: Lynne Rienner.

Bonilla-Silva, E. (2002). The linguistics of color blind racism: How to talk nasty about Blacks without sounding 'racist.' *Critical Sociology, 28*(1/2), 41–64.

Bonilla-Silva, E., & Forman, T. A. (2000). "I'm not a racist, but . . .": Mapping White college students' racial ideology in the USA. *Discourse and Society, 11*(1), 51–86.

Bonilla-Silva, E., Forman, T. A., Lewis, A., & Embrick, D. (2003). "It wasn't me!" How will race work in 21st century America. *Research in Political Sociology, 12,* 111–134.

Bowman, P. J., & Howard, C. (1985). Race related socialization, motivation, and academic achievement: A study of Black youths in three generation families. *Journal of American Academy of Child Psychiatry, 24,* 134–141.

Bowman, P. J., & Smith, W. A. (2002). Racial ideology in the campus community: Emerging cross-ethnic differences and challenges. In W. A. Smith, P. G. Altbach, & K. Lomotey (Eds.), *The racial crisis in American higher education: Continuing challenges to the twenty-first century* (pp. 103–120). Albany: State University of New York Press.

Boykin, A. W., & Toms, F. D. (1985). Black child socialization: A conceptual framework. In H. P. McAdoo & J. L. McAdoo (Eds.), *Black children: Social, educational, and parental environments.* Beverly Hills, CA: Sage.

Brigham, C. C. (1923). *A study of American intelligence.* Princeton, NJ: Princeton University Press.

Brown, K., Parker-Dominguez, T., & Sorey, M. (2000). Life stress, social support, and well-being among college-educated African American women. *Journal of Ethnic & Cultural Diversity in Social Work, 9*(1/2), 55–73.

Brown, T. N., Wallace, J. M., & Williams, D. R. (2000). Race-related correlates of young adults' subjective well-being. *Social Indicators Research, 53,* 97–116.

Brown, T. N., Williams, D. R., Jackson, J. S., Neighbors, H. W., Torres, M., Sellers, S. L., et al. (1999). "Being Black and feeling blue": The mental health consequences of racial discrimination. *Race & Society, 2*(2), 117–131.

Carroll, G. (1998). *Environmental stress and African Americans: The other side of the moon.* Westport, CT: Praeger.

Chang, M. J. (1999). Does racial diversity matter? The educational impact of racially diverse undergraduate population. *Journal of College Student Development, 40*(4), 377–395.

Clark, R., Anderson, N. B., Clark, V. R., & Williams, D. R. (1999, October). Racism as a stressor for African Americans: A biopsychosocial model. *American Psychologist, 54*(10), 805–816.

Diez-Roux, A. V., Northridge, M. E., Morabia, A., Bassett, M. T., & Shea, S. (1999). Prevalence and social correlates of cardiovascular disease risk factors in Harlem. *American Journal of Public Health, 89,* 302–307.

D'Souza, D. (1991). *Illiberal education: The politics of race and sex on campus.* New York: Free Press.

Ellison, R. (1952). *Invisible man.* New York: Vintage Books.

Feagin, J. R. (2006). *Systemic racism: A theory of oppression.* New York: Routledge.

Feagin, J. R., & McKinney, K. D. (2003). *The many cost of racism.* New York: Rowman & Littlefield.

Feagin, J. R., & Sikes, M. (1994). *Living with racism: The Black middle class experience.* Boston: Beacon Press.

Forman, T. A. (2004). Color-blind racism and racial indifference: The role of racial apathy in facilitating enduring inequalities. In M. Krysan & A. Lewis (Eds.), *The changing terrain of race and ethnicity* (pp. 43–65). New York: Russell Sage Foundation.

Gougis, R. (1986). The effects of prejudice and stress on the academic performance of Black-Americans. In U. Niesser (Ed.), *The school achievement of minority children: New perspectives* (pp. 145–157). Hillsdale, NJ: Lawrence Erlbaum.

House, J. S., Lepkowski, J. M., Williams, D. R., Mero, R. P., Lantz, P. M., Robert, S. A., et al. (2000). Excess mortality among urban residents: How much, for whom, and why? *American Journal of Public Health, 90,* 1898–1904.

Hurtado, S. (2002). Creating a climate of inclusion: Understanding Latina/o college students. In W. A. Smith, P. G. Altbach, & K. Lomotey (Eds.), *The racial crisis in American higher education: Continuing challenges to the twenty-first century* (pp. 121–137). Albany: State University of New York Press.

Inkelas, K. K. (2003). Diversity's missing minority: Asian Pacific American undergraduates' attitudes toward affirmative action. *Journal of Higher Education, 74*(6), 601–639.

James, S. A. (1994). John Henryism and the health of African-Americans. *Culture, Medicine, and Psychiatry, 18,* 163–182.

Jordan, W. D. (1968). *White over Black: American attitudes toward the Negro, 1550–1812.* New York: W. W. Norton.

Kinder, D. R., & Sanders, L. M. (1996). *Divided by color: Racial politics and democratic ideals.* Chicago: University of Chicago Press.

Kinder, D. R., & Sears, D. O. (1981). Prejudice and politics: Symbolic racism versus racial threats to the good life. *Journal of Personality and Social Psychology, 40,* 414–431.

Krysan, M. (2000). Prejudice, politics, and public opinion: Understanding the sources of racial policy attitudes. *Annual Review of Sociology, 26,* 135–168.

McConahay, J. (1986). Modern racism, ambivalence, and the modern racism scale. In J. F. Dovidio & S. L. Gaertner (Eds.), *Prejudice, discrimination, and racism* (pp. 91–125). Orlando, FL: Academic Press.

Mills, C. (1997). *The racial contract.* Ithaca, NY: Cornell University Press.

Mino, I., Profit, W. E., & Pierce, C. M. (2000). Minorities and stress. In G. Fink (Ed.),

Encyclopedia of stress (Vol. 2, pp. 771–776). San Diego, CA: Academic Press.

Peffley, M., Hurwitz, J., & Sniderman, P. M. (1997). Racial stereotypes and Whites' political views of Blacks in the context of welfare and crime. *American Journal of Political Science, 41,* 30–60.

Pierce, C. (1974). Psychiatric problems of the black minority. In S. Arieti (Ed.), *American handbook of psychiatry* (pp. 512–523). New York: Basic Books.

Pierce, C. (1975). The mundane extreme environment and its effect on learning. In S. G. Brainard (Ed.), *Learning disabilities: Issues and recommendations for research* (pp. 111–119). Washington, DC: National Institute of Education, Department of Health, Education, and Welfare.

Pierce, C. (1995). Stress analogs of racism and sexism: Terrorism, torture, and disaster. In C. V. Willie, P. P. Rieker, B. M. Kramer, & B. S. Brown (Eds.), *Mental health, racism, and sexism* (pp. 277–293). Pittsburgh, PA: University of Pittsburgh Press.

Pierce, C. M., Felton, J. E., & Kleinman, A. (1999). Race and culture in psychiatry. In A. M. Nicholi Jr. (Ed.), *The Harvard guide to psychiatry* (pp. 735–743). Cambridge, MA: Belknap Press of Harvard University Press.

Prillerman, S. L., Myers, H. F., & Smedley, B. D. (1989). Stress, well-being, and academic achievement in college. In G. L. Berry & J. K. Asamen (Eds.), *Black students: Psychological issues and academic achievement* (pp. 198–217). Newbury Park, CA: Sage.

Sander, R. H. (2004, November). A systemic analysis of affirmative action in American law schools. *Stanford Law Review, 57,* 367–483.

Sapolsky, R. M. (1998). *Why zebras don't get ulcers: An updated guide to stress, stress-related disease, and coping.* New York: W. H. Freeman.

Sax, L. J., & Arredondo, M. (1999). Student attitudes toward affirmative action in higher education: Findings from a national study. *Research in Higher Education, 40,* 439–459.

Scaer, R. (2001). *The body bears the burden: Trauma, dissociation and disease.* Binghamton, NY: Haworth Press.

Schlesinger, A. M. (1992). *The disuniting of America: Reflections on a multicultural society.* New York: W. W. Norton.

Sears, D. O. (1988). Symbolic racism. In P. A. Katz & D. A. Taylor (Eds.), *Eliminating racism: Means and controversies* (pp. 53–84). New York: Plenum Press.

Sears, D. O., Henry, P. J., & Kosterman, R. (2000). Egalitarian values and contemporary racial politics. In D. O. Sears, J. Sidanius, & L. Bobo (Eds.), *Racialized politics: The debate about racism in America* (pp. 75–117). Chicago: University of Chicago Press.

Sears, D. O., Hetts, J. J., Sidanius, J., & Bobo, L. (2000). Race in American politics. In D. O. Sears, J. Sidanius, & L. Bobo (Eds.), *Racialized politics: The debate about racism in America* (pp. 1–43). Chicago: University of Chicago Press.

Shay, J. (2002). *Odysseus in America: Combat trauma and the trials of homecoming.* New York: Scribner.

Shay, J., & Munroe, J. (1999). Group and milieu therapy for veterans with complex post-traumatic stress disorder. In P. A. Saigh & J. D. Bremner (Eds.), *Posttraumatic stress disorder: A comprehensive text* (pp. 391–413). Needham Heights, MA: Allyn & Bacon.

Sidanius, J., Singh, P., Hetts, J. J., & Federico, C. (2000). It's not the affirmative action, it's the African Americans: The continuing relevance of race in attitudes toward race-targeted policies. In J. Sidanius, D. Sears, & L. Bobo (Eds.), *Racialized politics: Values, ideology, and prejudice in American public opinion* (pp. 191–235). Chicago: University of Chicago Press.

Smith, W. A. (1998). Gender and racial/ethnic differences in the affirmative action attitudes of U.S. college students. *Journal of Negro Education, 67*(2), 127–141.

Smith, W. A. (2004). Black faculty coping with racial battle fatigue: The campus racial climate in a post-civil rights era. In D. Cleveland (Ed.), *A long way to go: Conversations about race by African American faculty and graduate students* (pp. 171–190). New York: Peter Lang.

Smith, W. A. (2006). Racial ideology and affirmative action support in a diverse college student population. *Journal of Negro Education, 75*(4), 589–605.

Smith, W. A. (in press-a). The relationship between campus race relations, racial ideologies, and racial battle fatigue. In R. T. Schaefer (Ed.), *Encyclopedia of race, ethnicity, and society.* Thousand Oaks, CA: Sage.

Smith, W. A. (in press-b). Toward an understanding of Black misandric microaggressions and racial battle fatigue in Historically White Institutions. In V. C. Polite (Ed.), *The state of the African American male in Michigan: A courageous conversation.* East Lansing: Michigan State University Press.

Smith, W. A., Allen, W. R., & Danley, L. L. (2007). "Assume the position . . . you fit the description": Campus racial climate and the psychoeducational experiences and racial battle fatigue among African American male college students. *American Behavioral Scientist, 51*(4), 551–578.

Smith, W. A., Yosso, T. J., & Solórzano, D. G. (2007). Racial primes and Black misandry on historically White campuses: Toward critical race accountability in educational administration. *Educational Administration Quarterly, 43*(5), 559–585.

Sniderman, P. M., & Hagen, M. G. (1985). *Race and inequality: A study of American values.* Chatham, NJ: Chatham House.

Steele, C. M. (1997). A threat in the air: How stereotypes shape intellectual identity and performance. *American Psychologist, 52*(6), 613–629.

Steele, C. M. (1999, August). Thin ice: "Stereotype threat" and black college students. *The Atlantic Monthly, 284*(2), 44–47, 50–54.

Steele, C. M., & Aronson, J. (1995). Stereotype threat and the intellectual test performance of African Americans. *Journal of Personality and Social Psychology, 69*(5), 797–811.

Stevenson, H. C. (1994a). Racial socialization in African American families: The art of balancing intolerance and survival. *Family Journal: Counseling and Therapy for Couples and Families, 2*(3), 190–198.

Stevenson, H. C. (1994b). Validation of the scale of racial socialization for African American adolescents: Steps toward multidimensionality. *Journal of Black Psychology, 20*(4), 445–468.

Stevenson, H. C. (1997). Managing anger: Protective, proactive, or adaptive racial socialization identity profiles and African-American manhood development. *Journal of Prevention & Intervention in the Community, 16*(1/2), 35–61.

Stevenson, H. C. (1998). Raising safe villages: Cultural-ecological factors that influence the emotional adjustment of adolescents. *Journal of Black Psychology, 24*(1), 44–59.

Stevenson, H. C., & Renard, G. (1993). Trusting ole' wise owls: Therapeutic use of cultural strengths in African American families. *Professional Psychology: Research and Practice, 24*(4), 433–442.

Tatum, B. D., Calhoun, W. R., Brown, S. C., & Ayvazian, A. (2000). Implementation strategies for creating an environment of achievement. *Liberal Education, 86*(2), 18–25.

Terenzini, P. T., Cabrera, A. F., Colbeck, C. L., Bjorklund, S. A., & Parente, J. M. (2001). Racial and ethnic diversity in the classroom: Does it promote student learning? *Journal of Higher Education, 72*(5), 509–531.

Tuch, T., & Sigelman, L. (1997). Race, class, and Black-White differences in social policy views. In B. Norrander & C. Wilcox (Eds.), *Understanding public opinion* (pp. 37–54). Washington, DC: Congressional Quarterly Press.

U.S. Department of the Army. (1994, June). *Battle fatigue GTA 21-3-5 warning signs: Leader actions.* Washington, DC: Author.

Villalpando, O. (2002). The impact of diversity and multiculturalism on *all* students: Findings from a national study. *NASPA Journal: The Journal of Student Affairs Administration, Research, and Practice, 40*(1), 124–144.

Williams, D. R., Yu, Y., Jackson, J. S., & Anderson, N. B. (1997). Racial differences in physical and mental health. *Journal of Health Psychology, 2*(3), 335–351.

Willie, C. V., & Sanford, J. S. (1995). Turbulence on the college campus and the frustration-aggression hypothesis. In C. V. Willie, P. P. Rieker, B. M. Kramer, & B. S. Brown (Eds.), *Mental health, racism, and sexism* (pp. 253–276). Pittsburgh, PA: University of Pittsburgh Press.

Wilson, A. N. (1990). *Black-on-Black violence: The psychodynamics of Black self-annihilation in service of White domination.* Brooklyn, NY: Afrikan World Infosystems.

Yarbrough, M., & Bennett, C. (2000). Cassandra and the "Sistahs": The peculiar treatment of African American women in the myth of women as liars. *Journal of Gender, Race and Justice, 24,* 626–657.

19

HISTORICALLY BLACK COLLEGES AND UNIVERSITIES

Catalysts to Liberation?

KOFI LOMOTEY

SESSI S. F. ABOH

When a human being becomes suddenly conscious of the tremendous powers lying latent within him [sic], when from the puzzled contemplation of a half-known self, he [sic] rises to the powerful assertion of self, conscious of its might, then there is loosed upon the world possibilities of good or of evil that make men [sic] pause. And when this happens in the case of a class or nation or a race, the world fears or rejoices according to the way in which it has been trained to contemplate a change in the conditions of the class or race in question.

—Aptheker (1973, p. 8)

We live in a world where people are often favored or oppressed based on the color of their skin, socioeconomic status, gender, physical appearance, sexual orientation, and many other illegitimate forms of exclusion. Racism—discrimination against a group of people based on a perceived notion of their inferiority, both intellectual and cultural—is an evil that enslaved Africans in the United States endured for centuries. Today, their descendants continue to be discriminated against based on various racist understandings of their origins. In a paradoxical way, educational institutions—preschool through professional—are places where racism is simultaneously perpetuated and/or combated.

The intentions of most of the initial financiers for historically Black colleges and universities (HBCUs)—the U.S. federal government, industrial philanthropists, White benevolent associations, religious denominational entities, various philanthropic foundations, well-to-do individuals, as well as missionary societies—did not always coincide with the interests of people of African descent with regard to their aspirations for freedom, justice, and equality. Apart from a few exceptions, including various missionary societies whose overt intent was to educate the newly freed Africans in the liberal arts tradition, the majority of White financiers of HBCUs were paternalistic by inclination and prone to making unilateral decisions. They supported the racist economic discrimination of the day and attempted in many ways to control the number of people of African descent who would receive a college education. Control strategies were discussed at meetings held by the General Education Board and at other forums where recommendations were made to keep to a minimum the number of HBCUs (Anderson, 1988). In addition, like the higher education institutions that serve African descended people the world over (Fafunwa, 1967; Nyerere, 1964), HBCUs were created to maintain the unfavorable social and economic status quo. These shaky beginnings have not always allowed HBCUs to genuinely serve the interests of people of African descent in the United States.

In this chapter, we focus on HBCUs and the extent to which they, despite their dubious beginnings, have aided and may further help U.S. citizens of African descent in their aspirations for equitable treatment in the political, economical, educational, medical, and social realms of life. Our purpose in writing this chapter is to discuss (1) the critical role of early financiers in constructing higher education for people of African descent in the United States, beginning in the late 19th century; (2) the persistent challenge of Black nationalists[1] to the intentions of these financiers with regard to the education of people of African descent in these new institutions; and (3) a contemporary assessment of what HBCUs should be doing in terms of curricular changes to further help people of African descent in the United States actualize themselves, their dreams, and their destinies.

THE PERSPECTIVE OF THE POWERS THAT BE

Many of the early financiers of HBCUs intended to produce a Black elite, responsible for keeping the masses of people of African descent in the United States as second-class citizens crippled with feelings of inferiority, and as semiskilled and unskilled laborers. They discussed their vision and plans for the "development" of HBCUs at various open forums. These included, but were not limited to, several conferences on

the education of people of African descent beginning in 1915, the deliberations of the General Education Board, and two conferences in 1890 and 1891 at Lake Mohonk in New York. At the two latter conferences, manual labor and morality were established as goals for the education of people of African descent in HBCUs (Carruthers, 1995). Among those in attendance was General Samuel Armstrong, founder of Hampton Institute and teacher/mentor to Booker T. Washington, the celebrated leader of Tuskegee Institute.

Working parallel to this group were religious entities and liberal philanthropists who, instead, saw literacy as a way to enlighten the freed Africans and raise them from abject poverty and barbarism. However, as benevolent and benign as this scheme might appear, it is still undeniable that the overall aim of their planned schooling enterprise was to alienate the Africans from their roots and culture, de-Africanize them so that they may fit—even if marginally—into the social and economic structure of the United States.

While some Black religious organizations helped start a few HBCUs, these institutions facilitated the matriculation of no more than 15% of the total number of enrolled students (Anderson, 1988). Early HBCUs were, therefore, mostly private liberal arts as well as agricultural, mechanical, and technical colleges whose structure and longevity hinged on the influence of White philanthropists. Anderson (1988) recalled the following with regard to one such institution, Fisk University:

> In 1923 the General Education Board generated a memorandum on the Fisk endowment campaign which emphasized the urgent need to train "the right type of colored leaders" who would help make the Negro "a capable workman [sic] and a good citizen." The industrial philanthropists, as the memorandum stated, aimed primarily at "helping the Negro to the sane and responsible leadership that the south wants him [sic] to have." To the white south, "sane" Negro leaders were those who encouraged Blacks to "stay in their place." (p. 267)

While there were slight ideological differences among the various financiers, for the most part, they all supported the Hampton-Tuskegee model. According to Anderson (1988), "Industrial philanthropists believed that Tuskegee was training black leaders to maintain a separate and subordinate Negro society. They were primarily interested in supporting Black institutions committed to this mission" (p. 266).

Anderson (1988) also indicated that the Hampton-Tuskegee program was "A program of interracial harmony predicated on a social foundation of political disenfranchisement, civil inequality, racial segregation and the training of Black youth for certain racially prescribed economic positions" (p. 273).

True to that ideology, Giddings (1901) argued that schooling is intended to constrain, retain the current social order, and bring about uniformity and agreement. Ogden (cited in Watkins, 2001), in turn, contended that HBCUs should prepare teachers in home science skills with the intent of encouraging the masses of people of African descent to accept their second-class status. This is, in part, what Watkins refers to as ideation—putting forth and cementing thoughts and values that reinforce the dominant socioeconomic condition. Watkins offered the following:

> Black education experienced a separate tradition in funding, curriculum administration and teacher training. Black education became a central policy instrument in consolidating the unpredictable newly freed slaves, re-annexing the South, and guaranteeing a pool of cheap semiskilled and unskilled labor. This was as political an undertaking as we have known. (p. 180)

This picture of Black education was further enhanced by the so-called Black elite or Black intellectuals. Because, for the most part, the original mission of HBCUs did not coincide with the interests of the people of African descent, it can be argued that most of the Black elite or Black intellectuals who graduated from these institutions failed the masses. They indeed learned from their schooling to believe in and to perpetuate the worldview of Whites in the United States and a value system that was antithetical to the needs of people of African descent.

THE BLACK PERSPECTIVE

Despite the drudgery of their lives, exhaustion from overwork, and threats of death or separation from loved ones, enslaved Africans managed to design various stratagems to circumvent their enslavers' relentless surveillance to learn to read and write. These tactics attested to their craftiness and resourcefulness. In addition, because discovery undoubtedly meant sale, maiming, or a death sentence, the strategies indicated the Africans' resoluteness toward—and unconditional belief in—the value of literacy. This understanding of the role and value of literacy was, in many ways, contrary to the purpose of schooling put forth by many of the financiers of HBCUs.

The agenda of the financiers was also diametrically opposed to that of many Black nationalists. These individuals, among many others, continuously voiced their concerns and their dissatisfaction about the education of Black people. Blyden (1971) and Woodson (1970) contended that though people of African descent in the United States have been freed from enslavement, their schooling experience facilitates a mental and psychological entrapment that is far more damaging than physical bondage. The schooling experience, they contended, arms people of African descent with a comprehensive arsenal of knowledge regarding the European experience and little with regard to their ability to speak on the history and culture of people of African descent. Thus intellectually crippled, the educated Blacks could do nothing to help their people in their aspirations, in their intellectual and/or economic growth. Even when presented with a position of leadership, schooled Blacks could see nothing wrong with the social system, and therefore, they did not try to question or redress its evils, abuses, and/or contradictions. Woodson (1970) skillfully and convincingly discussed this phenomenon in his masterpiece, *The Mis-Education of the Negro*. He argued,

> With mis-educated Negroes in control, it is doubtful that the system would be very much different from what it is or that it would rapidly undergo change. The Negroes thus placed in charge would be the products of the same system and would show no more conception of the task at hand than do whites who have educated them and shaped their minds as they would have them function. (p. 23)

Carruthers (1995) referred to this social oddity as the *mis-education* of the Black elite that facilitates the *dis-education* of the Black masses.

These social critiques support the notion that the educational parody set up to render Blacks without self-determination and willing to accept menial jobs and second-class citizen status as their manifest destiny was not wholly successful. Indeed, despite being subjected to the damaging schooling and other mental conditioning processes, some individuals did espouse an educational stance geared toward addressing the interests of people of African descent. They saw through the Machiavellian enterprise and formulated other goals and objectives for the education of the masses of their people. Anderson (1988) spoke to the view of some people of African descent with regard to the purposes of Black education in the late 1800s and early 20th century:

> The short-range purpose . . . was to provide the masses of ex-slaves with basic literacy skills plus the rudiments of citizenship training for participation in a democratic society. The long range purpose was the intellectual and moral development of a responsible leadership class that would organize the masses and lead them to freedom and equality. Being educated and literate had an important cultural significance to Afro-Americans, and they pursued these goals in opposition to the economic and ideological interest of the planter-dominated South. (p. 31)

However, the results sometimes fell short of the ideology. Even fair-minded and forward-looking intellectuals, progressive teachers, and some liberal arts colleges shied away from the "Negro problem" in the interest of teaching a "universal" knowledge. This trend, as Du Bois (quoted in Aptheker, 1973) qualified, is a recipe for disaster. He argued that "no system of learning—no university—can be universal before it is German, French, Negro." According to Du Bois,

> A French university is founded in France; it uses the French language and assumes a knowledge of French history. The present problems of the French people are its major problems and it becomes universal only as far as other people of the world comprehend and are at one with France in its might and beautiful history. In the same way, a Negro University in the United States of America begins with Negroes. It uses the variety of the English idiom which they understand; and above all, it is founded, or it should be founded on a knowledge of the history of their people in Africa and in the United States, and their present condition. (Aptheker, 1973, p. 93)

The scholars who, like Du Bois and Woodson, expressed dissatisfaction with the education of people of African descent argued that the schooling of Black people, based on championing a European worldview, detracts significantly from their ability to fit into and serve their own communities. Black people are instead prepared to accept the status quo and to bring their communities to do the same. This, according to Shujaa (1995), is one of the ultimate goals of schooling. He argued that there is a difference between schooling and education and that, unfortunately, people of African descent the world over receive quite a bit of schooling and not enough education. He suggested a deliberate and strategic differentiation between these two processes. He clarified,

> Schooling is a process intended to perpetuate and maintain society's existing power relations and the institutional structures that support those arrangements [. . . .] Education in contrast to schooling is our means of providing for intergenerational transmission of cultural identity through knowledge of the values, beliefs, traditions, customs, rituals and sensibilities that have sustained a people. (Shujaa, 1995, p. 15)

Simply stated, schooling refers to the number of years one spends in an institution of learning, acquiring enough information, skill, and ideology to empathize with specific social arrangements, participate in maintaining the social and economic status quo, and in the case of previously enslaved Africans, to accept a preassigned position in society. Education, in contrast, speaks to the extent to which one is being prepared to assist in addressing the economic, social, political, and cultural challenges facing ones people and humanity at large. Most HBCUs, financiers, and developers obviously believed that it was important to school people of African descent, but saw little need to educate this group.

The curricula at HBCUs were flawed from the beginning because they were not designed to develop an African-centered worldview, which would have led pupils to self-discovery, self-knowledge, and self-determination. The majority of financiers—including most of the plantation owners in the South and the majority of the capitalists in the North—did not have any use for such "enlightened" Blacks. According to Watkins

(2001), what these various groups tacitly agreed on was that the nation needed class peace and race peace. The need for racial and social peace translated into the desire to reduce people of African descent to illiterate plantation workers, training a group of demagogues to propagate the ideology of White supremacy and developing semiliterate, skilled but disenfranchised laborers (Anderson, 1988; Watkins, 2001). Learning to think critically, learning and knowing about self, learning the stories and cultures of one's people, learning to appreciate different worldviews, and learning to work toward self-actualization did not figure into the educational schemes concocted above for the benefit of people of African descent in the United States.

A New Perspective

While most HBCUs were not established to promote the liberatory aspirations of people of African descent in the United States, in many instances they have defied all odds and aided in the advancement of their students and their communities. According to the 2006 U.S. Department of Education/National Center for Education Statistics technical report, HBCUs generate positive economic impacts in terms of output, value-added, labor income, and employment.

From all accounts, HBCUs have been instrumental in training and rendering people of African descent in the United States more marketable. They have indeed trained and graduated more Black teachers, physicians, dentists, lawyers, political leaders, writers, and/or artists than any other institutions of higher learning in the United States. However, while there is no disputing these facts, it is still important to ponder the extent to which HBCUs prepare their graduates to address the interests of people of African descent in their quest for liberation and/or equitable treatment in all areas of life. For example, while various HBCUs rightfully profess to prepare leaders for the Black community, the question, pregnant with relevance, remains: *How and to where* are HBCU graduates leading the masses of people in the United States and in the African world as a whole?

People of African descent in the United States are in a crisis with regard to their education.

Carruthers (1995) argued that "worldview . . . includes the way a people conceive of the fundamental questions of existence and organization of the universe" (p. 53). It is, in a sense, the lens through which one views the world. Too often, students of African descent in the United States receive an educational experience from a European worldview perspective that does not instill in them any desire to develop the communities populated by people of African descent. This miseducation of Black children occurs both in predominantly White institutions and in HBCUs.

To some, this lumping together of predominantly White institutions with HBCUs might seem surprising—or even offensive. However, there is often little, if any, difference in the values, beliefs, and cultural orientation of the curricula in these two types of institutions, for the faculties at HBCUs have, for the most part, learned and become experts in the same educational curricula as faculties at predominantly White institutions. Unfortunately, history has taught us that this kind of "expertise" has not helped, cannot help, and will not help the masses of people of African descent. While Carruthers (1995) convincingly argued that the Black intelligentsia is responsible for the educational crisis in which people of African descent in the United States find themselves, we contend that most college graduates of African descent might be schooled, but they are not all educated.

If people of African descent truly seek freedom, justice, and equality or liberation, then they must address their educational experience and seek to redress social inequality and help their people. Recall our statement in the introduction when we stressed that one of the ways that racism and injustice are perpetuated is through educational institutions. We contend that the self-actualization of people of African descent must be preceded by a redirection of their educational experiences at all institutions of learning and, especially—as far as we are concerned in this chapter—at HBCUs.

The goal, as we see it, is the creation and implementation of an entire curriculum taught from an African-centered perspective. A critical first step, we argue, would be the development and/or reenergizing of Black studies programs taught from an African-centered perspective. Sometimes, these programs already exist; they may be known as Black studies, African American studies, Africana studies, African world studies, or by many other designations. We understand these programs to be transnational in nature and to preoccupy themselves with the studies and interests of all people who can trace their recent origins to the continent of Africa, and most important, people who identify with such origins. As such, we include the study and perspective of communities of people of African descent on all six continents.[2] The call here is for the development and/or amelioration of such programs at all HBCUs, as we believe this has the potential to elevate students' consciousness and to prepare them to address their own communities' plight. We emphasize, however, that it is but a first step, with the ultimate goal being the total transformation of the HBCU curricula; this transformation would enable students of African descent to see the world through the eyes of African people.

Focusing on this first step, African-centered programs, like any other college program, should be flexible in design to allow for a minor and a major. A minor is important because the large majority of students will continue to major in skill areas such as physics, chemistry, biology, and business as well as in the social sciences, the humanities, and the arts. For these students, we suggest a minor because there is an urgent need for these students to develop an African-centered perspective on their chosen disciplines. This type of understanding in a discipline is indispensable if HBCU students are to use their skills, abilities, and expertise in the interest of their communities and their people.

In addition to the minor, these programs should also offer a major because we believe that there is no better place than HBCUs to produce, in large numbers, the African-centered philosophers, researchers, and workers who are needed to foster the development of people of African descent. Brandeis University, Notre Dame University, Niagara University, and/or denominational colleges and other institutions of higher learning are universities/colleges where people enroll to earn academic degrees but also, to a large extent, to experience and/or research a particular culture or worldview. Furthermore, other communities in the United States have developed ways to transmit their cultures and values. When an acquaintance invited her Japanese next-door neighbor's child to a birthday party on a Saturday, she was promptly told that the little girl attends a Japanese cultural school all day every Saturday. Why does a Japanese American girl who will probably always live in the United States need to attend an 8-hour a week course on Japanese language and culture? The answer may be quite simple: No one can be all they were created to be if they do not know who they are, who their people were, what the latter have accomplished or failed to accomplish for that matter, how their people conceptualize life and various inter- and intrarelationships in the world, how they have evolved over time, what experiences they have lived through, and consequently, what as descendents of these people, the individual is supposed to believe in or stand for.

Most cultural communities in the United States understand that a people will survive if, and only if, it reproduces itself and works toward its self-preservation while developing mechanisms to lead productive lives in a culturally diverse world. These communities have designed Saturday schools and/or other formal arrangements through which they perpetuate and transmit to their offspring their people's language(s), worldview, and culture.

Black people happen to have HBCUs readily available. If these institutions are true to their definition, then, they should be in the business of "educating" Black people and, by ricochet, all people. They should be the places where students go to study the culture and life experiences of people of African descent—from an African-centered perspective. Students enrolling at such schools should be confident that they would be receiving the same high-quality education they might receive at any other institution—and much more.

A critical second step will be to infuse African-centered perspective into all curricula whereby the role and history of people of African descent would be used to explore world history and economy. By all accounts, HBCUs accomplish a remarkable feat everyday. They have overcome a multitude of obstacles, financial instability, social ostracism, racism, disparaging news headlines, dilapidated buildings, underpaid faculty, and sometimes, the admission of underprepared students, to prepare responsible citizens. This miracle can only be accomplished through outstanding curricula. Indeed, the vast majority of HBCUs are accredited through national accrediting agencies to grant bachelors, masters, and doctorate degrees that are as valid as any degrees from any other institutions of higher learning. If these schools are able to accomplish all the above, usually with a European-centered curriculum, we can just imagine the potential laying dormant if the curriculum was made to be more culturally relevant and reflective of the students' priorities.

This is not a strange novel idea. Du Bois (1935) advanced a similar view when he argued that the "Negro colleges ought to be studying anthropology, psychology, and the social sciences, from the point of view of the colored races" (p. 333). We add that the natural sciences could also be explored in a more culturally relevant and more comprehensive way. The contention here is not that Du Bois argued for the so-called Black studies programs per se, but that he clearly articulated the necessity for African descended students to be taught from a perspective that is more congruent with their worldview and experiences.

Some may still wonder: Why meddle in the curricula if HBCUs already produce responsible and good citizens? Why fix something that is not broken? We offer that HBCUs have not yet reached their full potential. Recall that our main purpose in writing this chapter is to explore whether or not HBCUs may serve as catalysts to the liberation (economic, social, intellectual, and cultural) of people of African descent in the United States. HBCUs, for the most part, continue to address the interests of those in power. That is, while still very important, HBCUs remain a vehicle for the retention of people of African descent as second-class citizens with inequitable status in politics, economics (i.e., employment, income, and wealth), education, and health. Educated people of African descent need to assume the cultural control of these institutions of higher education.

Some may want to suggest that this is a call for a propagandist agenda, an attempt to promote a romanticized idea of African and African-world realities. Others will decry this proposition as the replacement of a skewed Eurocentric curriculum full of myths and constructed realities with a skewed African-centered curriculum filled with myths and fictitious histories. This is neither. As Du Bois (1935) plainly stated,

> The Negro school and college has an unusual opportunity and role: It does not exist simply to parallel white history with equal boasting regarding the successes of Black and Brown folk, but rather to give an honest evaluation of human effort and accomplishment, without

color blindness, and without transforming history into a record of dynasties and prodigies. (p. 334)

Moreover, what we are proposing would give HBCUs a much needed edge in academia. It would separate these institutions from the larger community of institutions of higher education. It would make HBCUs more of what members of the African community in the United States envisioned for them. Moreover, it would nullify the "competition" for students of African descent that HBCUs find themselves in now, rivaling against better-endowed and better-equipped predominantly White colleges and universities. To be sure, such a rejuvenation could bring about a true selling point for HBCUs enabling them to attract more students of African descent, including international students.

CONCLUSION

We end with a few parting thoughts for further reflection, writing, and research. What we have attempted to suggest herein is that a total revamping of the HBCU educational experience is necessary to bring about a liberatory focus to the experience. This is, we argue, a call for an intellectual revolution of a sort. HBCUs continue to be important because the unique experiences of people of African descent in the United States demand them. In this spirit, Du Bois (1935) said, "American Negroes have, because of their history, group experiences and memories, a distinct entity, whose spirit and reactions demand a certain type of education for its development" (p. 333). It would be unrealistic to expect that predominantly white institutions could (and would) address these unique cultural needs.

Finally, the historical records of HBCUs are replete with pronouncements regarding their rich history as liberatory vehicles for people of African descent. We contend, however, that for these institutions to reach their full potential, there remains a significant piece that must be addressed: the courage to develop and focus on a culturally relevant curriculum. In this regard, Du Bois (1935) said,

> I have become curiously convinced
> that until American Negroes believe in

their own power and ability, they are going to be helpless before the white world, and the white world, realizing this inner paralysis and lack of self-confidence, is going to persist in its insane determination to rule the universe for its own selfish advantage. (p. 333)

Leaders of HBCUs must be willing to acknowledge and have the courage to assert the importance of these institutions as the repositories for the histories and cultures of people of African descent. We suggest, therefore, that an African-centered curriculum is not just a legitimate perspective of study in general; it should be a critical or prevalent perspective on HBCU campuses. When people—anywhere in the world—desire to study the history, culture, and experiences of people of African descent, they should be able to turn to HBCUs with confidence.

NOTES

1. These are social activists of African descent who, frustrated with the economic, political, social, health, and education inequities foisted on their people, articulate Black people's struggle for a more humane, just, and equitable position in the United States.

2. The six continents are North America, South America, Australia, Eurasia, Africa, and Antarctica.

REFERENCES

Anderson, J. A. (1988). *The education of Blacks in the South, 1860–1935.* Chapel Hill: University of North Carolina Press.

Aptheker, H. (Ed.). (1973). *The education of Black people: Ten critiques 1906–1960 by W. E. B. Du Bois.* New York: Monthly Review Press.

Blyden, E. W. (1971). Letter to Governor Hennessey, Freetown (December 11, 1872). In H. R. Lynch (Ed.), *Black spokesperson: Selected published writings of Edward Wilmot Blyden* (pp. 228–229). London: Frank Cass.

Carruthers, J. H. (1995). Black intellectuals and the crisis in Black education. In M. J. Shujaa (Ed.)., *Too much schooling, too little education: A paradox of Black life in White societies* (pp. 35–55). Trenton, NJ: Africa World Press.

Du Bois, W. E. B. (1935). Does the Negro need separate schools? *Journal of Negro Education, 4*(3), 328–335.

Fafunwa, A. B. (1967). *New perspectives in African education.* Lagos, Nigeria: Macmillan.

Giddings, F. H. (1901). Inductive sociology: A syllabus of analysis and classifications and provisionally formulated laws. New York: Macmillan.

Nyerere, J. M. (1964). *Ujamaa: Essays on socialism.* London: Oxford University Press.

Shujaa, M. J. (Ed.). (1995). *Too much schooling, too little education: A paradox of Black life in White societies.* Trenton, NJ: Africa World Press.

Watkins, H. W. (2001). *The White architects of Black education: Ideology and power in America, 1865–1954.* New York: Teachers College, Columbia University.

Woodson, C. G. (1970) *The mis-education of the Negro.* Trenton, NJ: Africa World Press.

20

THE POWER OF PATHWAYS

Strategies for the Preparation of African American Faculty

LYNETTE L. DANLEY

RODERIC R. LAND

KOFI LOMOTEY

While African American faculty continue to make significant contributions in the academy, the underrepresentation of Black faculty members in U.S. higher education is a pervasive and persistent problem (Allen & Epps, 2000; Benjamin, 1997; Butner, Burley, & Marbley, 2000; Danley, 2003; Danley & Green, 2004; Green & Scott, 2003; Moses, 1989). Faculty racial demographics severely lag behind in the race to keep pace with the increasingly diverse student constituency in institutions of higher learning. As more students of color—particularly African Americans—attend colleges and universities, postsecondary institutions are not increasing and diversifying their faculty and administration to reflect the changes in the student body (see Table 20.1; Oliver, 2006). This notion is supported by Turner (2002), who professed that "while we have witnessed steady growth in the racial and ethnic diversity of the student population, we have not seen similar diversification among college faculty" (p. 1).

TABLE 20.1   African American Graduate Students in Science and Engineering Fields at Doctorate-Granting Institutions

	1997	1998	1999	2000	2001	2002	2003	2004
Full-time	10,262	10,223	10,185	10,823	10,722	11,494	12,064	12,658
Part-time	6,025	6,368	7,012	6,771	7,103	7,469	8,157	7,929
Full- and part-time enrollment	16,287	16,591	17,197	17,594	17,825	18,963	20,221	20,587

Recent data indicate that African Americans comprise only 4% of professors and associate professors in higher education, compared with their White counterparts, who make up 87% of tenured faculty. African Americans represent a slightly larger portion of the instructor and lecturer pool at 7%, but this is bleak in comparison with their White peers, who comprise 82% (*Chronicle of Higher Education*, 2000). This under-representation of African American faculty has been attributed to erosions in the pipeline that include deeply rooted racism, institutionalized White power and privilege, the lack of effective mentoring in graduate programs, failure to equip and to expose graduate students to the wide array of faculty responsibilities, faulty hiring practices, and the recruitment and retention policies of these institutions (Bobo, Kluegel, & Smith, 1997; Bonilla-Silvia, 2001; Bowman & Smith, 2002; Tillman, 2001). This issue is about more than quotas; it highlights the continued failure to give different cultures and ideas, and alternative teaching approaches, ideologies, philosophies, and practices a space, place, and voice in a historically culturally homogeneous environment (Collins, 2001; Freire, 1998; Jackson, 2007; Ladson-Billings, 1999, 2000; McKee, 1993; Scheurich & Young, 1997). It is likely that the continued pervasiveness of this issue will escalate to a point that threatens the very existence of the African American professoriate.

Our aim in this chapter is to critique and reassess the traditional "race neutral" and "gendered" socialization practices of African American graduate students in U.S. colleges and universities, particularly at historically and/or predominantly White institutions (Gottlieb, 1961; Green & Scott, 2003; Sedlacek, 2003; Tierney & Rhoads, 1994). In this commentary, we examine the extant literature on the policies and praxis implemented to support African American graduate students as well as the systemic and institutionalized discriminatory mores that have traditionally countered those preparation efforts for Black graduate students interested in faculty appointments (Jackson, 2007; Tierney & Bensimon, 1996). Furthermore, drawing on our experiential knowledge as two junior faculty members, only a few years removed from graduate studies, and a senior-level university administrator, we combine theory with practice to offer strategies, practices, and insight into what leading scholars of race, class, gender,

and other social-science-equitable pedagogical approaches have deemed necessary for the development of future African American faculty (Delgado-Bernal & Villalpando, 2002; Holmes, 1999; Ladson-Billings, 2000; Turner & Myers, 2000).

ACCESS TO THE FIELD

In discussing the movement of African American graduate students into the professoriate, it is important to put the education of Blacks in its proper historical and sociopolitical context. This discussion is by no means exhaustive but will provide a foundational knowledge for understanding a history of White racial antipathy toward Blacks in the United States and the governing ideology—whether conscious or subconscious—that informs policies and practices within the institution of education. When dealing with issues of race relations, Carmichael and Hamilton (1967) asserted that one must address it from factual, sociohistorical perspectives. In short, to better understand the state of African American graduate students today, we need to examine past academic and social experiences related to equity and access for Blacks in society and academia (Bartee & Brown, 2007; Bell, 1993; hooks, 1994; Tillman, 2004).

The founding of Harvard College in 1636 marked the beginning of higher education in the United States (Rudolph, 1990). Similar to the majority of the colleges of this epoch, Harvard College was founded with the intent to train White men to become clergy, lawyers, doctors, and leaders of civic affairs. This experience was inaccessible for most people who did not fit the mold because opportunities were primarily based on race, gender, social class, and property ownership (Solomon, 1986; Tierney & Bensimon, 1996).

The education of Blacks pre– and post–Civil War was illegal, and violations brought about a severe penalty. Because many states prohibited teaching current or formerly enslaved Africans to read and write, they were often taught in secrecy (Anderson, 1988; Cruse, 1984; Lomotey, 1998; Span, 2005; Watkins & Kelley, 2001). Despite the consequences, African Americans continued in their pursuit of education. Anderson (1988) chronicled how slavery limited the rights to formal education of people of

African descent. Nevertheless, enslaved Africans, despite insurmountable odds, continued to yearn with a great fervor for equity and access to education. Scholars of the 20th century, including Clift, Anderson, and Hullfish (1962) discussed how

> Negroes were forcibly prevented from attending schools; teachers were not permitted to teach. Churches that often housed schools were sometimes burned. Some of the teachers, many of whom had lived along the fugitive Underground Railroad, suffered intimidation, insult, scorn and ostracism; a few were killed. (p. 39)

In 1856, the law of the land, as noted by Supreme Court Chief Justice Tanney, asserted both overtly and covertly that the White man did not have to honor or respect the civil rights of Black people. Needless to say, the right to any type of formal education was intricately intertwined with the sociopolitical landscape of the era. Through faith, coalition building, active struggle, and much bloodshed, Blacks would earn their right to a formal education (Bell, 1993; Cruse, 1984; Robinson, 2000).

In efforts to increase the number of African Americans in education, federal laws were later enacted. These laws legally increased access to higher education for women and minorities (Solomon, 1986). The Morrill Federal Land Grant Act of 1862, which granted access for people of modest means to be educated in the areas of agriculture, mechanics, and home economics, was a means of bettering the communities in which people lived. Initially, women and people of color did not have access to these institutions. The Morrill Land Grant Act of 1890 was enacted to increase access for African Americans and other ethnic groups (Rudolph, 1990). Despite such laws, inequity continued to persist in terms of access to education for African Americans in many states across the country. Clift et al. (1962) contended that

> the most decisive words in the history of Negro education in America were spoken on May 17, 1954. . . . To separate [Negro children] from others of similar age and qualifications solely because of their race generates a feeling of inferiority as to their status in the community that may affect their hearts and minds in a way

unlikely ever to be undone. . . . We conclude that in the field of public education the doctrine of "separate but equal" has no place. Separate educational facilities are inherently unequal. (p. 201)

The consistent themes throughout African American history encompass the belief that Black people are rightful citizens, freedom is nonnegotiable, education should be pursued at all costs, sacrifice builds resiliency, and commitment to uplift the community is ultimately the responsibility of the Black community (Span, 2005). Despite the gains made in the Civil Rights era, African Americans continue to fight inequities and injustices in education at every level (Blumer, 1958; *Grutter v. Bollinger*, 2003; Gurin, Dey, Hurtado, & Gurin, 2002). This battle has been complicated by menacing color-blind and patriarchal ideologies that seek to assimilate African Americans into a White cultural paradigm (Delgado, 1995; Hill Collins, 2004; Land, 2006; Thompson & Louque, 2005). Therefore, strategic planning at every step of the educational and professional journey is critical for African Americans who seek faculty appointments.

SOCIALIZING BLACK GRADUATE STUDENTS FOR SURVIVAL IN A HOMOGENEOUS INSTITUTION

Preparing African Americans for the professoriate continues to be a challenge for a number of reasons, which include the historic nature of race, gender, and class exclusivity; ambiguity in criteria; and unpredictability regarding the expectations of internal and external reviewers (Austin, 2002; Battle & Doswell, 2004; Jackson, 2007; Turner & Myers, 2000). Akin to the struggle for position and power that African Americans strategically and politically faced and addressed in the United States during the 1960s, the overt and covert discriminatory practices in the recruitment, retention, promotion, and tenure processes continue to permeate the academy. Thus, the million dollar question becomes, if the academy was not established with the intent to include African Americans, how then do we prepare African American faculty for success in the world of academe, particularly at predominantly White institutions?

Nettles and Millett (2006) asserted,

Socialization is important at every level of education, but given the restricted range of grades that graduate students receive in doctoral programs and the individual tailoring of doctoral student work, the indexes of socialization in graduate school are especially important gauges. (p. 89)

While we look to (re)produce scholars/faculty to join our "elite" status, we have to be careful not to produce an agent that mirrors current standards feeding into the existing social order (Ladson-Billings, 2000; McIntosh, 1988). Instead, we should focus our attention on preparing African American scholars who are critical of the extant literature; able to critique the organization and institutions that they will serve; and downright fearless in their attempts to promote alternative voices, spaces, and contexts. Paraphrasing Carter G. Woodson (2006), when Blacks are taught and/or encouraged to replicate White mores, practices, and ways of knowing, it stifles the construction of new knowledge. Thus, a paradigm shift of the bureaucracies and ideologies that construct and organize current educational institutions is necessary.

Tierney and Bensimon (1996) posited,

The culture of an organization is a contested area in which individuals and groups struggle over the definition of knowledge and what it means to be a knowledgeable individual. . . . Culture is the product of the social relations of the participants within an organization. (p. 15)

The dichotomy within this claim is the assumption being made that there is equal or shared power that allows both sides or all parties to actively engage in the scholarly debate about whose culture influences the scope and direction of research, teaching, and service in academe.

It is important for Black graduate students to be able to maintain a sense of self and not be consumed by a process that wishes to co-opt and homogenize their identity. We have to critically analyze and revamp the "race neutral" systematic approach taken to socialize Black graduate students into a profession historically reserved for White males. This appeal to color blindness, as noted by Crenshaw, Gotanda, Peller, and Thomas (1995), serves as part of an ideological

strategy by which current institutions cloak their active role in maintaining hierarchies of racial power. Furthermore, we have to begin and/or continue to hold institutions accountable when they profess diversity as a cornerstone of their mission. Nettles and Millett (2006) posited that "doctoral students should enter their programs with the expectation that the experience, though demanding, will be a positive one in which they benefit both intellectually and socially" (p. 89). This is as true for traditionally underrepresented students, such as African American students, as it is for other students.

Extant literature indicates that while graduate students of color experience "rites of passage" similar to those of their White peers, their socialization remains quite distinct with regard to disparity, faulty practices, and exclusion (Gaff, Pruitt-Logan, & Weibl, 2000; Jones, 2001a; Mabokela & Green, 2001; Minor, 2003; Tatum, 1992). These differences are systemically evident in terms of the European influence, socialization, culture, and practices that permeate U.S. graduate schools and programs. Tierney and Bensimon (1996) asserted that "in most colleges and universities, the whiteness of the professoriate stands out conspicuously, particularly in comparison to the more racially and ethnically diverse composition of the study body" (p. 103). Unlike their White peers, African American graduate students often experience the burden of having to produce in environments that contradict their Black heritage and lived experiences (e.g., community, family, activism, faith, and working collaboratively to accomplish tasks). Addressing Whiteness, privilege, and its impact on the social construction of race in the United States, Rothenberg (2008) contended,

As for the concern that looking at whiteness and white privilege will deflect our attention from racism, this could not be further from the truth. White privilege is the other side of racism. Unless we name it, we are in danger of wallowing in guilt or moral outrage with no idea of how to move beyond them. It is often easier to deploy racism and its effects than to take responsibility for the privileges that some of us receive as a result of it. (p. 1)

Equally as alarming is the fact that consistent with White privilege, the written and implied policies and practices constantly shift. Carmichael and Hamilton (1967) asserted that "the rules are being changed constantly" (p. viii). Therefore, African American graduate student success or lack thereof is often linked to their ability to observe departmental mores and adapt as necessary to rules and practices—seen and unseen.

Scholarship on African American graduate student socialization, teaching assistants (TAs), preparing of future faculty, life as an academician of color, and many of the complexities and nuances associated with these concerns is plentiful (Diamond & Gray, 1998; Slevin, 1992; Twale, Shannon, & Moore, 1997; Wilkening, 1991; Wise, 2005).

Myers (1995) used scaled instruments to study 64 graduate TAs from several fields to assess students' attitudes toward the communication processes and the impact they had on socialization into the teaching or research arena. Earlier, Gottlieb (1961) looked at disciplines in the arts and sciences to determine whether faculty play a significant role in affecting students' career preferences for research or teaching. Land (2006) examined the experiences of African American TAs in predominantly White classrooms at a historically White institution. He found that the African American TAs faced resistance in the classroom, their authority was constantly challenged, and more than 50% of the participants opted not to pursue faculty appointments as a result of their TA experiences.

The aforementioned studies concluded that assistantships afford graduate students additional opportunities for socialization, both formal and informal, that may or may not have otherwise been available in any other context. However, in some cases (Land, 2006), when race is factored into the equation, the preparation often does not outweigh the microaggressions and cultural taxation for African American graduate students; this is supported by extant literature associated with faculty and graduate students of color (Cole & Barber, 2003; Jones, 2001a; Mabokela & Green, 2001; Smith, Altbach, & Lomotey, 2002; Tate, 1997). Therefore, further inquiry into the experiences of African American graduate students is warranted, particularly their positionality, the influence of race, and students' perceptions of African American graduate students' ability and authority in the classroom (Harlow, 2003; King, 1991; Land, 2006; Myers, 1995; Smith, 2003; Smith & Witt, 1993).

Weidman, Twale, and Stein (2001) coauthored a report on the socialization of graduate and professional students in an effort to fill the gap in the research done by Tierney and Rhoads (1994), in which the researchers looked at faculty socialization using a cultural approach. As noted in Weidman et al. (2001), as a result of the socialization process, students should be able to answer three key questions: (1) What do I do with the skills I have learned? (2) What am I supposed to look like and act like in my professional field? (3) What do I as a professional look like to other professionals as I perform my new roles?

While Weidman et al. (2001) included an extensive analysis and schematic framework for the socialization of graduate students as it relates to the culture of their institutions, they failed to give adequate attention to these experiences from a racialized context. The three questions raised above may elicit very different answers based on the race, gender, and social identity of the graduate student.

From a racialized view, being an African American TA can be seen in and of itself as a gift and a curse. Being a TA provides the teaching experience and training that graduate students need if they plan to join the ranks of the professoriate. It provides a source of funding to defray some of the financial costs of graduate school. Additionally, it affords the opportunity to foster relationships with faculty and administrators, which opens the door for other aspects of identity development, faculty socialization with respect to research, grant writing, developing a curriculum vita or dossier, preparing proposals for conferences, opportunities to present at conferences, understanding the necessity of support groups (internal and external networking), and learning how to prepare manuscripts for publication (Cole & Barber, 2003; Green & Scott, 2003; Lockhart, 2003; Shepherd-Wynn, 2003; Tatum, 1992).

In Turner's (2002) *Diversifying the Faculty: A Guidebook for Search Committees*, it was reported that the Educational Testing Service predicted that by the year 2015, 80% of the projected 2.6 million new college student population will be "African American, Hispanic, Asian/Pacific Islander, or American Indian; an increase from 29.4 percent to 37.2 percent" (p. 1). Unequivocally, the need to strategically prepare African American students at multiple educational levels for the professoriate is critical (Gregory, 1995; Holmes & Terrell, 2004; Jackson & Daniels, 2007).

Despite the fact that U.S. higher education is over 370 years old, racial, ethnic, and gender disparity with regard to student demographics continues to exist. Combating the history of White privilege and exclusion of underrepresented groups such as African Americans, though challenging, is not impossible. The key is purposive and strategic preparation. African American graduate students should be equipped with the necessary skills and tools to strategically navigate the perils and pitfalls often associated with the politics of education at predominantly and/or historically White graduate programs, which include, but are not limited to, deficit discourse, lack of mentoring, racism, and/or a mismatch with institutional culture and individual beliefs and expertise (Hutcheson, 2000; Jones, 2001a, 2001b; Phelps, 1995; Rendon, 2000).

Currently, there are a number of programs, activities, and initiatives from legislative policies (i.e., TRIO, Ronald E. McNair Post Baccalaureate, Summer Research Opportunity Programs, and Preparing Future Faculty) that are designed to prepare students at the undergraduate and graduate levels for life as faculty members or in professional fields such as law, medicine, or business (see Appendix). Similarly, there are preparation programs in the form of fellowships and postdoctoral research positions and visiting professorships at the postgraduate level (e.g., Ford Foundation, Spencer Foundation, American Council on Education, Lumina Foundation, and American Educational Research Association) to better equip individuals for faculty appointments at colleges and universities and/or to assume roles in the professional fields of medicine, law, and business.

The challenge continues to be not the goals and objectives of these initiatives per se. Rather, it is the underlying Western, European tenets that promote the White privilege and entitlement, monolithic values that inform policy, which in turn result in praxis that defines success from an essentialist and constructionalist perspective (Feagin, 2001, 2002; Harris, 1995; Lipsitz, 1998; Scheurich, 1993). Historically, achievement has had to look a certain way, and any deviation from that pattern was and continues to be devalued and/or not accepted in many cases.

STRATEGIC NAVIGATION, NOT ASSIMILATION

Without question, erosions in the pipeline exist for African American graduate students and their aspirations of becoming faculty members. Racism and other interlocking forms of oppression (e.g., gender inequality, classism, religious persecution, literal lynching of African American perspectives, and discriminatory policies and practices) have existed for Black people throughout their history in the United States (Anderson, 1988; *Dred Scott v. Sanford*, 1856). Just recently, Proposition 2 was passed in the state of Michigan banning Affirmative Action. There is no question that this judgment will have a ripple effect on college campuses across the country, making it even more difficult for African American graduate students and other underrepresented, underserved, and marginalized people to gain entrance into and mobility in higher education (Thompson & Louque, 2005; Watson et al., 2002).

It is often said that success occurs when opportunity meets preparation. Therefore, African American graduate students, to the best of their ability, need to proceed with foresight and fortitude. This means being purposive about their pursuit of the professoriate, mapping out a strategic plan to enhance their opportunities for successful navigation, and taking advantage of programs and services that expose them to faculty life and experiences. By researching faculty members whose scholarship aligns with their scholarly agenda, exploring the graduation and placement rates of graduate school programs, and having experiences such as postdoctoral and visiting professorships that allow African Americans to immerse themselves in the institutional and departmental culture, African American graduate students could improve not only their options but also their marketability for the type of institutions they feel best match their expertise and interest (Reay, David, & Ball, 2005).

The need for African Americans to learn the difference between assimilation and strategic navigation within an institution still remains. One way that African American students can learn more about the life of an academician is to observe faculty socialization in a graduate school setting similar to the institution in which they are interested in holding an appointment. This can be done by participating in programs such as the Preparing Future Faculty initiative or in programs such as the Illinois Consortium for Educational Opportunity Program, where graduate students have immersion experiences with faculty members and peers, work as TAs, and participate in conferences where they present and receive feedback on their scholarship. Taking the time to observe the institutional and departmental mores and practices has often meant the difference between success and failure. Once the mores and practices are understood, the next step is to learn the timing of when, how, with whom, and in what spaces to articulate thoughts, differences of opinions, and future career goals. This is where informal and formal mentoring becomes invaluable (Danley & Green, 2004; Holmes, 1999, 2004; Patton & Harper, 2003; Tillman, 2001). In short, one approach to ensuring a more successful navigation of graduate school and, ultimately, life as an academician for African Americans is understanding the dynamics of the institution, college, department, and/or program in which they aspire to hold a faculty appointment.

As is the case with rites of passage, African American graduate students must learn the various stages of faculty development. In this case, department chairs, faculty members, and/or directors of graduate studies could offer graduate students the opportunities to assist in the development of course syllabi with the intent of eventually serving as a TA for the course. It is not uncommon for TAs to be solely responsible for a course, which gives them an excellent chance to demonstrate their leadership abilities and aptitude in their discipline. However, in many cases, assistantships are often given to White students who are groomed from the onset for the professoriate. As a result, many African Americans are overlooked when it comes to teaching assistantships, leaving them ill prepared for the challenges of being the professor of record as a full-time faculty member (Diamond & Gray, 1998; Duesterberg, 1999; Farmer, 2003; King, 1991). Early exposure and experience in classroom settings could alleviate or significantly diminish stress levels surrounding faculty preparation.

Another area where African American students need further development is learning how to conduct research. Graduate programs have the potential to play an instrumental role in the development of solid researchers. For example, faculty members can invite students to participate in research projects, allowing them to collect and analyze data. Equally, if not more important, such research opportunities can develop into conference proposals and presentations and ultimately translate into manuscripts for publication. Scholarship can be intimidating, but when African American graduate students have faculty members and department chairs willing to serve as mentors and guides throughout the process, there is no limit to what they can accomplish.

Successfully navigating the graduate school process entails more than being a consistently strong student, having teaching experience, and understanding how to start and complete a research project. The next step is encapsulating all those experiences in a curriculum vita or dossier. With the exception of networking at professional conferences associated with one's discipline or having an advocate on faculty who can assist with the networking, the letter and curriculum vita are often the first glimpse that prospective institutions have of the African American graduate student. To combat the preconceived notions that cloud the minds of faculty in graduate programs about students of color, an organized, concise, informative, and culturally relevant praxis that projects one's research, teaching, and service expertise is invaluable. The challenge is the limited quality of mentoring. This is so because of a shortage of African American faculty members or other senior scholars who understand the challenges that African American students face regardless of their race/ethnicity. African American graduate students are not privy to critical knowledge on strategic navigation, persistence, and how to acquire the necessary resources for success at the graduate school level and beyond.

Examining what language and action attract support and recognition is important. The goal is not to mimic what peers and/or colleagues who identify with the European culture are doing. Rather, focus should be placed on researching the backgrounds of the faculty who have earned tenure and those who are successfully navigating the retention/reappointment, promotion, and tenure (RPT) processes. Once the expectations associated with granting RPT in that space are identified, it is easier to find ways to incorporate one's own beliefs, practices, and definitions of scholarship, teaching, and service to acquire the desired outcomes, including retention, promotion, and/or mobility (Gordon, 1997; Jackson, 2007; Vargas, 2002).

Life as an academic is a choice. The realization of that very fact often escapes the minds of African American faculty. The thinking behind this statement is simply that the freedom of one's mind is not and should not be compromised because of a faculty appointment. Once one starts to believe or behaves as if one is enslaved to a belief, practice, or vision that drastically takes one further away from one's history, identity, and community, significant parts of one's holistic identity is lost (Cushinberry, 2003; Hill Collins, 2004; Johnson, 2003; Sellers, Smith, Shelton, Rowley, & Chavous, 1998). The desired result for an African American seeking to serve in the capacity of a faculty member is to seek a match between his or her scholarly expertise and ideals and the institutional vision and expectations. Although there is debate over the terms *best, fit,* and *institutional match,* it is naive to assume that one's background; commitment to personal goals; expertise; educational exposure and training; and identifiable strengths related to research, teaching, and service do not play a role in terms of persistence and retention. While there is no road map as to how and why each person succeeds, preparation, access, and understanding organizational culture are all important.

It is important to reiterate the significance of understanding institutional type and campus climate to prospective African American students. For instance, if a student is interested in research, theoretical frameworks, and contextualizing concepts, then a doctoral or research-extensive institution may be more appropriate for that student when seeking a faculty appointment. In contrast, if a student understands her or his strength to lie in applying theory to practice and enjoys exploring various pedagogical approaches, a teaching-intensive college or university may be more applicable. Service can be more of a gray area as institutions vary regarding the weight that is attached to stewardship on and off campus. Moreover, service is multifaceted in that there is an array of ways in which a faculty member can be a change agent, such as in her or his department, at the college and/or university level, as an active member and leader within professional associations and organizations, and/or as a reviewer and member of editorial boards for professional journals. Rhoades (2006) suggested that the mores of higher education in the United States often fall short when it comes to broadening their scope in terms of

valuing the roles that faculty members play both on and off campus. Such scholar-activism, if viewed from an asset rather than deficit perspective contributes to continued growth and development of the academy. Graduate programs, department chairs, and faculty members often fail to realize the significance of service for African American faculty and other faculty members of color regarding their retention and persistence. Baez (2000) discussed how higher education problematizes service when he contended "that conceptualizing service as problematic negates the role of critical agency in resisting and redefining institutional structures" (p. 363). For African Americans, service is historically ingrained by the very nature of their existence in the United States. Giving back to the Black community is one way in which African American faculty are able to survive and sustain their identities and purpose, particularly in predominantly and historically White institutions.

Whether the topic is research, teaching, or service, the key to improving one's opportunity for success in higher education is to understand what institutional values and practices will be valued and rewarded. Equally important, however, is the acknowledgement and acceptance of the talents and strengths that lie within the potential candidate for the faculty position. "To thy own heart be true" becomes more than words when finding the best match between expertise and institutional expectations. The challenges associated with being African American may not diminish, but the obstacles may be more bearable if with a conscious and purposive mind one considers the roles and responsibilities of faculty members at any given institution and whether or not the "fit" is applicable to the interest and goals that one has.

Just as scholars of social justice and equitable pedagogy, regardless of discipline, offer multiple approaches of theoretical, methodological, and praxis to better prepare future faculty of color (Garcia, 2000; Lopez & Parker, 2003; Mabokela & Green, 2001; Nettles & Millett, 2006; Parker, 1998; Tierney & Bensimon, 1996), we too understand the need to discuss a range of developmental strategies to represent the commonalties and unique nuances that shape the African American experience in the United States, capturing the diversity within the Black community.

So how do institutions, faculty, staff, administrators, and communities collectively prepare

African Americans for roles as college professors? There is no blueprint or recommendation that encompasses all the tools needed to guarantee a faculty appointment. However, there are purposive mechanisms that, if employed, can significantly enhance one's access to experiences that lead to the life of an academic (Jackson, 2007; Jones, 2001b; Mabokela & Green, 2001), thus our recommendations for strategic navigation for African American graduate students, department chairs, deans, and faculty members.

ADMINISTRATIVE SUPPORT

It is imperative that African American graduate students observe and feel institutional commitment from the onset of their graduate school recruitment experience from college deans, department chairs, and directors/advisors of graduate studies. High attrition and low retention rates of students of color, along with the need to increase and strengthen the number of African Americans in the professoriate pipeline, should prompt administrators to be more proactive in their approach to create environments conducive to college success for African Americans. For example, nontraditional recruitment efforts (e.g., having current African American graduate students house prospective students as well as host cultural and ethnic receptions at churches and other venues in the local African American community) may need to be explored. Demonstrating a campus-wide commitment to increase the students of color, along with the necessary resources (e.g., mentoring, competitive graduate assistantships, interviews at national conventions that are specifically designed to meet the unique needs of African Americans, interdisciplinary brown bags to demonstrate the interconnectedness of disciplines that speak to the intersectionality of African American students), can make the difference between attracting, retaining, and graduating African American students, particularly at historically and predominantly White institutions. Extant literature has also supported the notion that hiring, retaining, and promoting faculty of color is key for students of color, including African American students, who benefit from having positive images of themselves in leadership roles, such as academicians.

FACULTY SUPPORT

Faculty members play an integral role in the academic, social, and cultural experiences of graduate students. While many scholars would advocate having African American faculty members exclusively teach African American students, the reality is that consistency, respect, and extending oneself as a participant in a mentor-mentee relationship serve both the faculty member and the student. Furthermore, if the professor is White, it is often helpful, regardless of the curriculum, to acknowledge the history of inclusion-exclusion that permeates and continues to inform the mores and practices of higher-education institutions and that has served to impede the progress of African Americans in higher education. The development and/or maintenance of a safe, inclusive, and socially just classroom climate is one way for faculty members to demonstrate their commitment to equity and access for traditionally underrepresented students. Making the commitment to strengthen the pipeline of African Americans who are interested in becoming faculty members by providing African American graduate students exposure to the culture, socialization processes, and varied expectations (e.g., written and implied) of academia is key (e.g., TA opportunities, research and grant-writing opportunities, co-presenting at conferences with their faculty mentors). Seeking ways to reshape and redefine the scope of what constitutes "scholarship" through culturally relevant pedagogy has paved the way for many African American scholars to emerge.

THE PRICE OF PRIVILEGE FOR AFRICAN AMERICAN GRADUATE STUDENTS

African American students bring a plethora of human, social, cultural, economic, and symbolic capital (Bartee & Brown, 2007) to the campus, and this is of great value and importance to institutions, colleges, departments, and/or programs. Learning survival mechanisms such as observing the social norms and tenets that exist at the institutional, college, departmental, and programmatic levels equips African American graduate students with the necessary skills to successfully navigate the challenges of academia.

Understanding the difference between assimilation and strategic navigation is imperative when preparing African American graduate students for the professorate. To strategically negotiate one's voice, space, and context in multiple settings within the world of academe, sometimes it is necessary to be open to experiences that differ from one's cultural experience, making it plausible for some scholars to view such actions as acting "White" or being a "sellout." This misinterpretation is often misguided and fails to recognize the value of networking (formally and informally) and expanding one's view of what it means to be African American in a predominantly and historically White academy. To that end, it is necessary to preserve, respect, and examine, with the intent to challenge and change if and when necessary, the multiple truths associated with being African American in the United States. Reclaiming the right to construct new knowledge in order to develop a more inclusive academy directly relates back to African American heritage, where, as the saying goes, Black people "made a way out of no way." As an African American in academia, one cannot consciously accept the privileges without acknowledging the sacrifices made by other African Americans who accepted the responsibilities, challenges, and unspeakable penalties often associated with the pursuit of academic, social, economic, and cultural mobility for African Americans throughout history. Acknowledging, honoring, and respecting the legacy of sacrifice, resiliency, and commitment to education and the plethora of other survival mechanisms employed by African Americans throughout history to secure access and equity in education is a small price to pay for the privilege to become the next generation of African American scholars in higher education.

IMPLICATIONS FOR FUTURE PRACTICE AND RESEARCH

The challenge for African Americans is not only to resist assimilation but also to reclaim their voice and recognize their distinct contributions to the field (Nettles & Millett, 2006). As a result, historic and contemporary African American faculty members have defied, dispelled, and denounced the notion that the title (term) *scholar* does not apply to them or that knowledge production/construction has adhered to White hegemonic standards. In his theory, Stereotype Threat, Steele (1997) explained how it is "a situational threat—a threat in the air—that, in general form, can affect the members of any group about whom a negative stereotype exists" (p. 614). Steele's theory is applicable to many African American graduate students who experience anxiety in terms of writing, question the validity of their admission, and fear that their academic capabilities are not equal to (or exceed) that of their White peers. To that end, it is imperative that African American scholars pave a steady bridge for others to cross that is maintained by resisting marginalization, debunking White student perceptions about African American intelligence, creating platforms and safe spaces, and reclaiming the power of the Black voice through research, teaching, and service that are indisputably among the greatest contributions to academia.

After exploring the literature and practices associated with the preparation of African Americans for the professorate, we see that there are vast implications for future research and practice. Early identification of Black students who are interested in becoming faculty members is critical. Providing access and exposure to faculty life equips African American graduate students with increased confidence in their abilities to serve in the academy as professors. Understanding the mores, expectations, and practices of faculty and how those roles often differ for African American faculty in comparison with their White peers will better equip students for making informed decisions about their choice to pursue a faculty appointment at the type of institution they believe would be in alignment not only with their research, teaching, and service expertise but with their cultural values (e.g., faith/spirituality, commitment to community, preservation of legacy) as well (Cushinberry, 2003; Johnson & Pichon, 2007; Strange, 2001).

Doctoral students aspiring to the professoriate should not fear the publishing process. They should

- read texts and articles that discuss how to
  - o identify a research topic/hypothesis,
  - o understand and appropriately apply theoretical frameworks, and
  - o develop research questions;
- study methodological approaches to conduct, analyze, and write research in a way that

complements research questions and bodies of literature;

- practice writing and sharing work with others to hone skills; and

- submit work for publication, understanding that rejection is a part of the publishing process.

It is a good idea to request teaching assistantships in order to learn how to develop course syllabi, create reading lists and in-class activities, and facilitate discussions and learn what to look for (i.e., rubric) in terms of grading papers. Most important, exposure to teaching in graduate school helps demystify the role associated with the professor of record so that when the graduate student has the opportunity to teach as a junior faculty member, the anxiety often is not as high.

Additionally, graduate students should ask faculty members and/or researchers for opportunities to assist in the development of conference papers and proposals. The more one writes, the more confident one becomes in her or his ability, bringing about the interdependence and independence needed for graduate student success. In conjunction with this, presenting at conferences (e.g., local, regional, national, international) in one's respective field and discipline is advisable. Networking is essential for graduate students, particularly students of color such as African American graduate students, who represent a small number of people in the pipeline for the professoriate. Working with peers and faculty at various ranks internal and external to your institution provides support through mentoring and mobility based on the connections that one makes.

Doctoral students should familiarize themselves with the financial-aid process, timelines and deadlines for grants, and scholarships and fellowships (e.g., ACE, Ford, Lumina, Spencer, AAUW, and AERA). Such monies assist graduate students with opportunities for their dissertation and postdoctoral research.

CONCLUSION

In this chapter, we drew on extant literature surrounding graduate student socialization, mentorship, and faculty preparation, to problematize

and offer strategies for the development of future African American faculty. We did this in two ways. First, literature from interdisciplinary fields was used to build an argument that African American graduate student experiences of socialization, mentorship, and faculty preparation are different from the experiences of White graduate students. Next, we presented strategies that will enable institutions and mentors to honor the cultural integrity of African American graduate students, particularly at predominantly White institutions that assist them in preparing for faculty positions and in choosing institutions of higher learning that are consistent with these students' career goals.

In summary, there is a fundamental need to redefine and broaden what constitutes "scholarship" and who should and should not be considered "scholars" in the academy. One approach is to draw from alternative epistemologies as well as theoretical and methodological approaches, such as Critical Race Theory and Critical Race Feminism, that challenge dominant ideologies; place race and gender at the center of inquiry; expose racialized power; and allow one to interrogate departmental norms while immersing oneself in empirical research, the conceptualization of ideas, student-centered teaching, and theory-to-praxis service (Berry & Mizelle, 2006; Crenshaw et al., 1995; Solórzano, Ceja, & Yosso, 2000; Wing, 1997, 2003). This immersion process provides the foundation for ascertaining the necessary tools to hone skills and become proficient in one's craft. In doing so, it allows for gaps in the literature to be identified, which, in turn, provides opportunities to construct new knowledge and make unique research contributions. In terms of preparing African American graduate students for the professoriate, Cornel West (1996) summed it up best when he discussed how the Black people used their intellectual capabilities and legacy of activism to serve as a platform or catalyst for social justice.

While academia is not exempt from centuries of institutionalized racism and other discriminatory practices, African Americans continue to persist. There is power in defining pathways of success for African American graduate students. The responsibility for and commitment to the mobility and sustainability of African Americans in higher education and other fields and disciplines lie inherently within the African American community.

REFERENCES

Allen, W., & Epps, E. (2000). The Black academic: Faculty status among African Americans in U.S. higher education. *Journal of Negro Education, 69*(1/2), 112–127.

Anderson, J. D. (1988). *The education of Blacks in the South from 1860–1935.* Chapel Hill: University of North Carolina Press.

Austin, A. E. (2002). Preparing the next generation of faculty: Graduate school as socialization to the academic career. *Journal of Higher Education, 73,* 94–122.

Baez, B. (2000). Race-related service and faculty of color: Conceptualizing critical agency in academe. *Higher Education, 39*(3), 363–391.

Bartee, R. D., & Brown, M. C. (2007). *School matters: Why African American students need multiple forms of capital.* New York: Peter Lang.

Battle, C. Y., & Doswell, C. M. (2004). *Building bridges for women of color in higher education: A practical guide for success.* New York: University Press of America.

Bell, D. A. (1993). Remembrance of racism past: The civil rights decline. In H. Hill & J. E. Jones (Eds.), *Race in America: The struggle for equality* (pp. 73–82). Madison: University of Wisconsin Press.

Benjamin, L. (1997). *Black women in the academy: Promises and perils.* Gainseville: University of Florida Press.

Berry, T. R. B., & Mizelle, N. (2006). *From oppression to grace: Women of color and their dilemmas within the academy.* Sterling, VA: Stylus.

Blumer, H. (1958). Race prejudice as a sense of group position. *Pacific Sociological Review, 1*(1), 3–7.

Bobo, L., Kluegel, J. R., & Smith, R. A. (1997). Laissez-faire racism: The crystallization of a kinder, gentler, antiblack ideology. In S. A. Tuch & J. K. Martin (Eds.), *Racial attitudes in the 1990s: Continuity and change* (pp. 5–13). Westport, CT: Praeger.

Bonilla-Silvia, E. (2001). *White supremacy and racism in the post–Civil Rights era.* Boulder, CO: Lynne Rienner.

Bowman, P. J., & Smith, W. A. (2002). Racial ideology in the campus community: Emerging cross-ethnic differences and challenges. In W. A. Smith, P. G. Altbach, & K. Lomotey (Eds.), *The racial crisis in American higher education: Continuing challenges to the twenty-first century* (pp. 103–120). Albany: State University of New York Press.

Butner, B. K., Burley, H., & Marbley, A. F. (2000). Coping with the unexpected: Black faculty at predominantly White institutions. *Journal of Black Studies, 30*(3), 453–462.

Carmichael, S., & Hamilton, C. V. (1967). *Black power: The politics of liberation in America.* Toronto, Ontario, Canada: Vintage.

Chronicle of Higher Education. (2000). *The Nation: Faculty and staff (2000–2001 Almanac).* Washington, DC: Author.

Clift, V. A., Anderson, A. W., & Hullfish, H. G. (1962). *Negro education in America.* New York: Harper.

Cole, S., & Barber, E. (2003). *Increasing faculty diversity: The occupational choices of high-achieving minority students.* Cambridge, MA: Harvard University Press.

Collins, R. (2001). Ethnic change in macro-historical perspective. In E. Anderson & D. S. Massey (Eds.), *Problem of the century: Racial stratification in the United States* (pp. 13–46). New York: Russell Sage Foundation.

Crenshaw, K., Gotanda, N., Peller, G., & Thomas, K. (Eds.). (1995). Introduction. In *Critical race theory: The key writings that formed the Movement* (p. xiii). New York: New Press.

Cruse, H. (1984). *The crisis of the Negro intellectual.* New York: Quill.

Cushinberry, C. (2003). Maintaining my identity: Enhanced in the system, but not lost in it. In B. Jarmon, A. L. Green, & L. V. Scott (Eds.), *Journey to the Ph.D.* (pp. 90–103). Sterling, VA: Stylus.

Danley, L. D., & Green, D. O. (2004). I know I've been changed: The impact of mentoring on scholarship. In S. L. Holmes & M. C. Terrell (Eds.), *Lifting as we climb: Mentoring the next generation of African American student affairs administrators* (Vol. 7(1), pp. 31–45). National Association of Student Affairs Professionals.

Danley, L. L. (2003). *Truths about sojourner: African American women and the professorship—their struggles and their success on negotiating promotion and tenure at a predominantly White institution.* Ames, IA: Educational Leadership and Policy Studies.

Delgado, R. (1995). Affirmative action as a majoritarian device: Or, do you really want to be a role model? In *Critical race theory: The cutting edge.* Philadelphia: Temple University Press.

Delgado-Bernal, D., & Villalpando, O. (2002). An apartheid of knowledge in academia: The struggle over the legitimate knowledge of faculty of color. *Equity and Excellence in Education, 35*(2), 169–180.

Diamond, R. M., & Gray, P. J. (1998). *1997 National study of teaching assistants.* Syracuse, NY: Syracuse University, Center for Instructional Development.

Dred Scott v. Sanford, 60 U.S. 393 (1856).

Duesterberg, L. M. (1999). Theorizing race in the context of learning to teach. *Teachers College Record, 100*(4), 751–775.

Farmer, V. L. (Ed.). (2003). *The Black student's guide to graduate and professional school success.* Westport, CT: Greenwood Press.

Feagin, J. (2001). *Racist America: Roots, current realities, & future reparations.* New York: Routledge.

Feagin, J. (2002). *The continuing significance of racism: U.S. colleges and universities.* Washington, DC: American Council on Education.

Freire, P. (1998). *Pedagogy of freedom: Ethics, democracy, and civic courage.* Lanham, MD: Rowman & Littlefield.

Gaff, J. G., Pruitt-Logan, A. S., & Weibl, R. A. (2000). *Building the faculty we need.* Washington, DC: Association of American Colleges and Universities and the Council of Graduate Students.

Garcia, M. (2000). Weighing the options: Where do I want to work? In M. Garcia (Ed.), *Succeeding in an academic career: A guide for faculty of color* (pp. 1–26). Westport, CT: Greenwood Press.

Gordon, B. M. (1997). Curriculum, policy, and African American cultural knowledge: Challenges and possibilities for the year 2000 and beyond. *Educational Policy, 11*(2), 227–242.

Gottlieb, D. (1961). Processes of socialization in American graduate schools. *Social Forces, 40*(2), 124–131.

Green, A. L., & Scott, L. V. (Eds.). (2003). *Journey to the Ph.D.* Sterling, VA: Stylus.

Gregory, S. T. (1995). *Black women in the academy: The secrets to success and achievement.* New York: University Press of America.

Grutter v. Bollinger, 539 U.S. 306 (2003).

Gurin, P., Dey, E., Hurtado, S., & Gurin, G. (2002). Diversity and higher education: Theory and impact on educational outcomes. *Harvard Educational Review, 72*(3), 330–366.

Harlow, R. (2003). "Race doesn't matter, but . . .": Management in the undergraduate college classroom. *Social Psychology Quarterly, 66*(4), 348–363.

Harris, C. I. (1995). Whiteness as property. In K. Crenshaw, N. Gotanda, G. Peller, & K. Thomas (Eds.), *Critical race theory* (pp. 276–291). New York: New Press.

Hill Collins, P. (2004). *Black sexual politics: African Americans, gender, and the new racism.* New York: Routledge.

Holmes, S. L. (1999). *Black women academicians speak out: Race, class, and gender in narratives of higher education.* Ames, IA: Educational Leadership and Policy Studies.

Holmes, S. L. (2004). An overview of African American college presidents: A game of two steps forward, one step backward, and standing still. *Journal of Negro Education, 73*, 21–39.

Holmes, S. L., & Terrell, M. C. (Eds.). (2004). *Lifting as we climb: Mentoring the next generation of African American student affairs administrators* (Vol. 7(1)). National Association of Student Affairs Professionals.

hooks, b. (1994). *Teaching to transgress: Education as the practice of freedom.* New York: Routledge.

Hutcheson, P. A. (2000). *A professional professoriate: Unionization, bureaucratization, and the AAUP.* Nashville, TN: Vanderbilt University Press.

Jackson, J. F. L. (Ed.). (2007). *Strengthening the African American educational pipeline: Informing research, policy, and practice.* Albany: State University of New York Press.

Jackson, J. F. L., & Daniels, B. D. (2007). A national progress report of African Americans in the administrative workforce in higher education. In J. F. L. Jackson (Ed.), *Strengthening the African American educational pipeline: Informing research, policy, and practice* (pp. 115–137). Albany: State University of New York Press.

Johnson, B. J., & Pichon, H. (2007). The status of African American faculty in the academy: Where do we go from here? In J. F. L. Jackson (Ed.), *Strengthening the African American educational pipeline: Informing research, policy, and practice* (pp. 97–114). Albany: State University of New York Press.

Johnson, C. (2003). The mask: A survival tool. In A. L. Green & L. V. Scott (Eds.), *Journey to the Ph.D.* (pp. 168–179). Sterling, VA: Stylus.

Jones, L. (Ed.). (2001a). *Brothers of the academy: Up and coming Black scholars earning our way in higher education.* Sterling, VA: Stylus.

Jones, L. (2001b). *Retaining African Americans in higher education: Challenging paradigms for retaining students, faculty and administrators.* Sterling, VA: Stylus.

King, J. (1991). Dysconscious racism: Ideology, identity and the miseducation of teachers. *Journal of Negro Education, 60*(2), 133–146.

Ladson-Billings, G. (1999). Preparing teachers for diverse student populations: A critical race theory perspective. *Review of Research in Education, 24*, 211–247.

Ladson-Billings, G. (2000). Racialized discourses and ethnic epistemologies. In N. K. Denzin & Y. S. Lincoln (Eds.), *Handbook of qualitative research* (pp. 257–277). Thousand Oaks, CA: Sage.

Land, R. R. (2006). *Wounded soul(diers) in the classroom: A study of African American teaching assistants.* Urbana-Champaign, IL: Educational Policy Studies.

Lipsitz, G. (1998). *The possessive investment in whiteness.* Philadelphia: Temple University Press.

Lockhart, K. D. (2003). Psychosocial adjustment to the campus environment. In V. L. Farmer (Ed.),

The Black student's guide to graduate and professional school success (pp. 82–89). Westport, CT: Greenwood Press.

Lomotey, K. (1998). Sailing against the wind: African Americans and women in U.S. education. *Anthropology and Education Quarterly, 29*(2), 257–259.

Lopez, G. R., & Parker, L. (2003). *Interrogating racism in qualitative research methods.* New York: Peter Lang.

Mabokela, R. O., & Green, A. L. (Eds.). (2001). *Sisters of the academy: Emergent Black women scholars in higher education* (pp. 161–173). Sterling, VA: Stylus.

McIntosh, P. (1988). *White privilege and male privilege: A personal account of coming to see correspondences through work in women's studies.* Paper presented at the Wellesley College Center for Research on Women, Wellesley, MA.

McKee, J. (1993). *Sociology and the race problem: The failure of a perspective.* Urbana: University of Illinois Press.

Minor, J. (2003). For better or for worse: Improving advising relationships between faculty and graduate students. In A. L. Green & L. V. Scott (Eds.), *Journey to the Ph.D.* (pp. 238–253). Sterling, VA: Stylus.

Moses, Y. T. (1989). *Black women in academe: Issues and strategies.* Washington, DC: Association of the American Colleges & Universities.

Myers, S. (1995). *Exploring the assimilation stage of GTA socialization: A preliminary investigation.* Paper presented at the Speech Communication Association, San Antonio, TX.

Nettles, M. T., & Millett, C. M. (2006). *Three magic letters: Getting to Ph.D.* Baltimore: Johns Hopkins University Press.

Oliver, J. D. (2006). *Graduate students and postdoctorates in science and engineering: Fall 2004* (NSF 06–325). Washington, DC: National Science Foundation. Retrieved May 29, 2007, from www.nsf.gov/statistics/nsf06325/pdf/nsf06325.pdf

Parker, L. (1998). "Race is . . . race ain't": An exploration of the utility of critical race theory in qualitative research. *Qualitative Studies in Education, 11*(1), 43–55.

Patton, L. D., & Harper, S. R. (2003). Mentoring relationships among African American women in graduate and professional schools. In M. F. Howard-Hamilton (Ed.), *Meeting the needs of African American women* (New Directions for Student Services, No. 104, pp. 67–78). San Francisco: Jossey-Bass.

Phelps, R. (1995). What's in a number? Implications for African American faculty at predominantly White colleges and universities. *Innovative Higher Education, 19,* 255–268.

Reay, D., David, M. E., & Ball, S. (2005). *Degrees of choice: Social class, race and gender in higher education.* Sterling, VA: Trentham Books.

Rendon, L. I. (2000). Academics of the heart: Maintaining body, soul, and spirit. In M. Garcia (Ed.), *Succeeding in an academic career: A guide for faculty of color* (pp. 141–155). Westport, CT: Greenwood Press.

Rhoades, G. (2006). The higher education we choose: A question of balance. *Review of Higher Education, 29*(3), 381–404.

Robinson, R. (2000). *The debt: What America owes to Blacks.* New York: Plume.

Rothenberg, P. S. (2008). *White privilege: Essential readings on the other side of racism* (3rd ed.). New York: Worth.

Rudolph, R. (1990). *The American college and university: A history* (2nd ed.). Athens: University of Georgia Press.

Scheurich, J. (1993). Toward a White discourse on White racism. *Educational Researcher, 22*(8), 5–10.

Scheurich, J. J., & Young, M. D. (1997). Coloring epistemologies: Are our research epistemologies racially biased? *Educational Researcher, 26*(4), 4–16.

Sedlacek, W. E. (2003). Negotiating admission to graduate and professional schools. In V. L. Farmer (Ed.), *The Black student's guide to graduate and professional school success* (pp. 13–22). Westport, CT: Greenwood Press.

Sellers, R. M., Smith, M. A., Shelton, N. J., Rowley, S. A. J., & Chavous, T. M. (1998). Multidimensional model of racial identity: A reconceptualization of African American racial identity. *Personality and Social Psychology Review, 2*(1), 18–39.

Shepherd-Wynn, E. (2003). Promoting scholarly writing and publishing to enhance the scholarship of Black graduate students. In V. L. Farmer (Ed.), *The Black student's guide to graduate and professional school success* (pp. 119–128). Westport, CT: Greenwood Press.

Slevin, J. (1992). *The next generation: Preparing graduate students for the professional responsibilities of college teachers.* Washington, DC: Association of American Colleges.

Smith, E., & Witt, S. (1993). A comparative study of occupational stress among African American and White university faculty: A research note. *Research in Higher Education, 34,* 229–241.

Smith, W. A. (2003). Black faculty coping with racial battle fatigue: The campus racial climate in a post–Civil Rights era. In D. Cleveland (Ed.), *Broken silence: Conversations about race by African Americans at predominantly White institutions* (pp. 171–190). New York: Peter Lang.

Smith, W. A., Altbach, P. G., & Lomotey, K. (Eds.). (2002). *The racial crisis in American higher education: Continuing challenges to the twenty-first century.* Albany: State University of New York Press.

Solomon, B. M. (Ed.). (1986). *In the company of educated women: A history of women and higher education in America.* New Haven, CT: Yale University Press.

Solórzano, D., Ceja, M., & Yosso, T. (2000). Critical race theory, racial microaggressions, and campus racial climate: The experiences of African American college students. *Journal of Negro Education, 69*(1/2), 60–73.

Span, C. (2005). Learning in spite of opposition: African Americans and their history of educational exclusion in antebellum America. In M. C. Brown & R. R. Land (Eds.), *The politics of curricular change: Race, hegemony, and power in education* (pp. 26–53). New York: Peter Lang.

Steele, C. (1997). A threat in the air: How stereotypes shape intellectual identity and performance. *American Psychologist, 52*(6), 613–629.

Strange, C. C. (2001). Spiritual dimensions of graduate preparation in student affairs [Monograph]. *New Directions for Student Affairs, 95,* 57–67.

Tate, W. F. (1997). Critical race theory and education: History, theory, and implications. *Review of Research in Education, 22,* 195–247.

Tatum, B. (1992). Talking about race, learning about racism: The application of racial identity development in the classroom. *Harvard Educational Review, 62*(1), 1–24.

Thompson, G. L., & Louque, A. C. (2005). *Exposing the "culture" of arrogance" in the academy: A blueprint for increasing Black faculty satisfaction in higher education.* Sterling, VA: Stylus.

Tierney, W. G., & Bensimon, E. M. (1996). *Promotion and tenure: Community and socialization in academe.* Albany: State University of New York Press.

Tierney, W. G., & Rhoads, R. A. (1994). *Faculty socialization as cultural processes: A mirror of institutional commitment* (ASHE-ERIC Higher Education Report No. 93–6). Washington, DC: George Washington University, School of Education and Human Development.

Tillman, L. C. (2001). Mentoring African American faculty in predominantly White institutions. *Research in Higher Education, 42*(3), 295–325.

Tillman, L. C. (2004). (Un)intended consequences?: The impact of the *Brown v. Board of Education* decision on the employment status of Black educators. *Education and Urban Society, 36,* 280–303.

Turner, C. S., & Myers, S. L. (2000). *Faculty of color in academe: Bittersweet success.* Needham, MA: Allyn & Bacon.

Turner, C. S. V. (2002). *Diversifying the faculty: A guidebook for search committees.* Washington, DC: Association of American Colleges and Universities.

Twale, D. J., Shannon, D., & Moore, M. (1997). NGTAs and IGTAs training and experience: Comparisons between self-ratings and undergraduate student evaluations. *Innovative Higher Education, 22*(1), 61–77.

Vargas, L. (Ed.). (2002). *Women faculty of color in the White classroom.* New York: Peter Lang.

Watkins, W. H., & Kelley, R. D. J. (2001). *The White architects of Black education: Ideology and power in America, 1865–1954.* New York: Teachers College Press.

Watson, L. W., Terrell, M. C., Wright, D. J., Bonner, F., II, Cuvjet, M., Gold, J., et al. (2002). *How minority students experience college: Implications for planning and policy.* Sterling, VA: Stylus.

Weidman, J. C., Twale, D. J., & Stein, E. L. (2001). *Socialization of graduate and professional students in higher education: A perilous passage?* (ASHE-ERIC Higher Education Report, Vol. 28, No. 3). Washington, DC: George Washington University, School of Education and Human Development.

West, C. (1996). Affirmative action in context. In G. E. Curry (Ed.), *The affirmative action debate* (pp. 31–38). New York: Perseus Books.

Wilkening, L. (1991). Teaching assistants for the professorate. In J. Nyquist, R. Abbott, D. Wulff, & J. Sprague (Eds.), *Preparing the professorate of tomorrow to teach* (pp. 12–16). Dubuque, IA: Kendall/Hunt.

Wing, A. K. (Ed.). (1997). *Critical race feminism: A reader.* New York: New York University Press.

Wing, A. K. (2003). Introduction. In A. K. Wing (Ed.), *Critical race feminism: A reader* (2nd ed., pp. 1–19). New York: New York University Press.

Wise, T. J. (2005). *Affirmative action: Racial preference in Black and White.* New York: Routledge.

Woodson, C. G. (Ed.). (2006). *The mis-education of the Negro.* San Diego, CA: Book Tree.

SECTION V

CURRENT ISSUES

*Theory and Research on the Participation
of African Americans in U.S. Education*

INTRODUCTION

GWENDOLYN CARTLEDGE

This section of the *Handbook* presents chapters that address the practices, policies, and procedures that directly and indirectly affect opportunities for African Americans to gain full participation in our schools. Critical questions include the following: What is the theoretical framework that offers the most promise for educating African American students? What are the important actions of culturally competent direct service school professionals? How are alternative forms of schooling for African Americans perceived by its consumers? How do we rescue African American children from the most debilitating effects within our schools? More specifically, this section intends to analyze issues of race and education, counselor/teacher professionalism, charter schools, special education, and the African American male student.

The first chapter in this section is by Lynn and Bridges who connect critical race theory (CRT) to critical race studies in education (CRSE) as a means for discussing the importance of race in the education of African American children. CRT provides a way to study race relative to certain practices in the larger society. Similarly, CRSE, as stated by the authors, is "about exposing the connections between race and schooling." The authors give the reader an overview of various approaches, traditionalist, postmodernist, Latcrit, and Africana Studies, to CRSE with an emphasis on the latter, Africana Studies. The authors' view of CRSE centers on the work of Carter G. Woodson, contending that the transformation of the African American experience in education resides in heeding Woodson's call. The education for African American students needs to be liberating, enabling students to think for themselves, and needs to be embedded in social justice.

From a less theoretical platform, Moore and Owens also grapple with the schooling issues that encumber the educational outcomes for African American students. Although the authors concentrate on the roles of teachers and counselors, they begin with an overview of the underachievement/poor-outcomes problem, then proceed to contributing factors such as low expectations, negative self-image, social ills, and cultural dissonance. These factors have obvious implications for interventions such as advising teachers and counselors how to become more culturally competent professionals to motivate students to perform rather than further depress them academically and psychologically. According to Moore and Owens, professionals need to recognize their gatekeeping role and adopt the actions needed to promote the advancement of African American students. They offer practical strategies for this purpose.

For more than a decade, charter schools have become an important phenomenon on the U.S. educational landscape and have had a particularly important impact on the schooling of African American children. Since the achievement data for these students has been, at best, equivocal, scholars such as Malloy and Noble are led to ponder why African Americans are disproportionately opting for charter schools over traditional public schools for their children. In pursuit of these understandings, the authors of this chapter systematically examine a variety of factors, including the perceptions of key stakeholders such as parents, students, and school personnel as well as the instructional curriculums in charter schools, their teaching styles, and their stated overarching goals. Data from four charter schools are used to formulate viable assumptions about the attraction of charter schools for African American parents. Their analyses lead the authors to conclude that environmental factors rather than specific academic achievement may be undergirding the parents' decision making.

In the next chapter, Cartledge and Dukes note that special education has long been a contentious and intractable issue in the education of African American children in this society. In nearly every disability area, particularly for mild disabilities, African American children are over-represented relative to their numbers in the general school population. Some authorities argue that this is further representation of the segregation/bias in our schools, while others contend that this condition is largely a function of the subjugated status of African Americans in this society. Special education placement is particularly troublesome when considering that African American students in special education have the poorest outcomes of all the students in our schools. Is this phenomenon simply a matter that African American children, for example, are more likely to be victims of within-child risk factors, teacher/assessment bias, inadequate instruction, or social injustice? As discussed in the chapter, all these conditions are important and contribute, to varying degrees, to special education disproportionality. Understanding causes provides some direction for how to address the problem. Accordingly, the authors identify specific academic and behavioral interventions to prevent and minimize the risk status for African American students. Especially important is the need to intervene early in the child's schooling. Although the problem centers on special education, the interventions to prevent or reduce the effects of disabilities occur largely in general education settings. Thus, the content of this chapter is especially of importance to general educators.

The final chapter in this section limits its discussion to the African American male. The author, James Davis, presents some common features of the African American male culture and analyzes the naturally occurring dissonance between the African American male culture and that of traditional schooling. In this chapter, Davis raises some very important questions such as what are the factors that contribute to the underachievement and disengagement of African American males in the schools and how do African American males "make meaning of their own lives in school." These and other issues are studied within the context of Black masculinity: How is it constructed, perceived, and countered. Promising educational strategies for African American males are those that incorporate heightened awareness, sensitivity, respect, and authenticity. Gender-specific mentoring and schooling are encouraged.

21

CRITICAL RACE STUDIES IN EDUCATION AND THE "ENDARKENED" WISDOM OF CARTER G. WOODSON

MARVIN LYNN

THURMAN L. BRIDGES III

I n this chapter, we use Carter G. Woodson's "endarkened" wisdom as a way to develop an Africana Studies approach to using critical race theory (CRT) to examine African American education. We find that Cynthia Dillard's (2000) use of the term *endarkened* is recognition of the power of words and their potential impact on our consciousness. By using this term, we intend to normalize and center blackness as the central construct through which we formulate our arguments regarding the necessity for developing a liberatory framework to understand Black education. This notion also helps us better situate our perspective on African American education that centers African peoples in the Americas as principled but nevertheless dominated subjects of history who possess a significant degree of agency and will.

OVERVIEW OF CRITICAL RACE THEORY

As we will explain in greater detail later in this chapter, CRT is a framework for analyzing and exploring race and racism in the law and in the broader society (Lynn & Parker, 2006). CRT gives scholars, particularly scholars of color, the theoretical, conceptual, and methodological tools for putting forth arguments, conducting research studies, and developing theories that center race and racism. In particular, some critical race scholars are concerned about uncovering racism where it appears to be

AUTHORS' NOTE: We would like to thank Leshell Hatley for her assistance on the first draft of this chapter.

hidden and illustrating how present racialized conditions are connected to a set of racist historical events. In that sense, CRT puts racism within its proper historical context and shows how history shapes and influences present outcomes (Lynn & Parker, 2006). Next, CRT provides scholars with analytical and methodological tools that they can use to make sense of certain racialized problematics or illustrate the racialized impact of White supremacist policies, practices, or institutional configurations. The interest-convergence principle (Bell, 1980a, 2004; DeCuir & Dixson, 2004; Gillborn, 2006; Taylor, 1998), for example, is widely used by a number of scholars as a way to illustrate why certain policies are promoted or put into practice because they appear to have obvious benefits for Whites. These benefits, of course, incur hidden costs for Blacks at the end of the day. We will discuss more about how education scholars have tended to use this approach. Counternarratives and chronicles have been widely used as a methodological tool for scholars who use storytelling as a method through which to highlight some important concerns about the impact of racist policies and practices in the law, higher education, and K-12 schooling contexts. CRT also provides a space for scholars concerned about race to exercise their agency and articulate their perspectives on racism in the law, higher education, and the K-12 schooling arena. We discuss the contours of the critical race movement within education in greater detail later.

Exploring Various Traditions Within the Critical Race Studies in Education Movement

The term *critical race studies* (CRS) was recently used by Cheryl Harris, Kimberle Crenshaw, and Devon Carbado to describe their efforts to change the curriculum at the University of California at Los Angeles' Law School in order to build an intense focus on "the intersections between race and the law" (Harris, 2002). In a law review article titled "Critical Race Studies: An Introduction," preeminent critical race legal scholar, Cheryl Harris, reflects on the historical evolution of the unique program at the law school. According to Harris (2002), the CRS concentration at UCLA Law School was designed to make

more systematic and comprehensive the study of the interconnections between the American legal system and race, racial inequality, and racialization. . . . The Critical Race Studies concentration also promotes a more comprehensive and comparative approach to the study of race and the law . . . locating as central the intersections of race with other axes of social classification and inequality, including gender, sexual orientation, and social class. (p. 1232)

CRS provides critical race legal scholars with a space to adequately prepare the next generation of critical race scholars in the law to be able to continue the important traditions of uncovering racism where it is normally hidden from view and exposing the subjective nature of legal doctrine in the United States. In a sense, it is the pedagogical companion to CRT and is implicitly focused on the act of teaching. It takes its cue from CRT and is necessarily diverse in its methodological orientations: There is no one pedagogical or legal method promoted by CRS scholars. In that sense, while CRS scholars in the law are very clear about their social and political commitments to expose the radical contradictions in the law around race, they are not wedded to any one pedagogical or doctrinal approach to doing so. CRS then constitutes the effort of the UCLA Law School to help emerging legal minds understand the dynamics and interactions between race and the law. According to Harris, the teaching of race is also indelibly connected to the teaching of racially subordinated students. In that sense, the presence of folks of color is integral to the ongoing study and teaching of race. In other words, CRS is as much about who we teach as it is about what we teach.

The Critical Race Studies in Education (CRSE) movement has followed this path in some ways and has diverted from it in other ways. First, while CRS scholars in education draw much of their inspiration for studying race in education from legal scholars, they are not scholars of the law. We study the link between schools, schooling, and the social context, and we, like scholars of the law, argue that race has been largely unattended to in debates about how the social context influences schools and schooling outcomes (Ladson-Billings & Tate, 1995). In that sense, CRSE is not about exposing the connections between race and the law as much as it is about exposing the connections between race and schooling. In an article published in 2006, Lynn and Parker argued that

> Critical race studies in education questions a range of assumptions and tenets upon which schooling rests like: (1) We live in a fair and just society; (2) Schools are the great equalizer of the races; and that (3) Race can only be used only as a descriptor to merely describe, analyze and examine educational inequalities. Not only do they question these assumptions, they actively seek to create more humane discourses, structures and institutions aimed at creating a society that is free of racism. Critical race scholars in education have transformed the way race is understood and addressed in debates over the links between schooling and inequality. Race is no longer viewed as a secondary or tertiary unit of analysis that gives way to class or gender as explanatory tools of analysis. Even more important, they have relied on the legal scholarship on race in the U.S. to illustrate the important ways in which race acts as a structural phenomenon along side and sometimes in concert with other structures of domination such as class and gender to transform the way in which we understand racism's impact on a number of areas including education policy, teaching and teacher education, qualitative research and lives of racially marginalized students of color. This is important given Ladson-Billings and Tate's important reflection in 1994 that race was "untheorized" in the field of education. Some twelve years later, there exist an abundance of articles, books, special journal issues that illustrate the multiple ways in which race and racism can be understood and used as tools of transformation in education. (p. 279)

As we illustrate, CRSE has significantly changed the terms of the debate on race and education. Moreover, the CRSE literature offers the following:

1. Explanatory work that defines and explains CRT and shows how it might be used in education

2. Research that explores how CRT informs qualitative research methods and the practice of research in communities of color

3. An analysis and formulation of pedagogies of liberation drawn from research with teachers of color

4. An exploration of the schooling experiences of marginalized students of color all along the pipeline from K to graduate school

5. An examination of the efficacy and historical development of and resistance to race-conscious education policy in K-12 and higher education

In the aforementioned article, Lynn and Parker provide a full account of research in the field and explore the possible implications for the schooling of African Americans. However, Lynn and Parker do not address the extent to which there might be different epistemological traditions and ideological orientations within CRSE. In this chapter, we argue that at least four different traditions have begun to emerge in the field of CRSE. We will explain each of those traditions briefly.[1] First, there is the mainstream traditionalist approach promoted by scholars including Tate (2005, 2006) and Dixson and Rousseau (2005a, 2005b). The second approach is the postmodernist approach that is more clearly connected to particular tendencies within the legal movement. Scholars including Garrett Duncan (2002a, 2002b, 2005) and criminologist Christopher Schneider (2003) have written in this tradition. The third emerging tradition, Latcrit or Latino/Latina CRSE, has been employed by Latino/Latina scholars in the fields of law and education (Delgado Bernal, 1998, 2002; Delgado Bernal & Villalpando, 2002; Fernandez, 2002; Solórzano & Yosso, 2000, 2001, 2002a, 2002b, 2002c). The fourth tradition is an Africana Studies tradition, as described by social theorist Reiland Rabaka (2004, 2006). This tradition most closely resembles that which was described and promoted by Carter G. Woodson whose work will be discussed in greater detail. In general, we spend more time describing the first and fourth approaches. We have decided to do this for two reasons. First, the traditionalist approach is more broadly used and accepted by mainstream scholars attempting to explain CRT and its use in education. The fourth approach, the Africana Studies approach, warrants more discussion because it is the tradition from which this chapter emerges. Furthermore, this chapter is, in many ways, exploratory. In that sense, we do not attempt to offer a full treatment of the literature in our explanation of any one tradition. This chapter is an initial attempt to begin the process of drawing some preliminary conceptual boundaries within the emerging field of CRSE as way to begin to explain the wide range of methods, epistemological frames, and conceptual lenses used in the service of examining the links between race, racism, and education. This chapter offers *one* perspective on this issue and does not purport to provide *the* answer to the challenge of setting some conceptual boundaries within this emergent and diverse field of studies.

The Traditionalist Approach in CRSE

Many scholars locate CRT's origins within the law and argue that Derrick Bell, Kimberlé Crenshaw, and Richard Delgado are the chief architects of the movement (Ladson-Billings & Tate, 1995). In one sense, this is true. Derrick Bell (1979, 1980a, 1980b, 1985, 1987, 1988, 1992, 1996, 2004) and Richard Delgado (1984, 1987, 1988a, 1988b, 1989, 1990, 1992, 1993, 1995a, 1995b, 1996, 1999, 2003a, 2003b; see also Delgado & Stefancic, 2000) can be regarded as pioneers in the study of race and racism in the law. Promoting conversations about the impact of racism in the law when it was not popular to do so, they were, in many ways, at the forefront of their fields. Crenshaw (1988) can be credited, of course, with bringing CRT—as a movement—to the attention of the nation with the publication of the important book *Critical Race Theory: The Key Writings That Formed the Movement* (Crenshaw, Gotanda, Peller, & Thomas, 1995). In the book *Crossroads, Directions and a New Critical Race Theory* (Valdes, Culpe, & Harris, 2002), Valdes and colleagues charted the development of the field. They discussed its beginnings at Harvard Law and cited their particular roles in advancing a critical discourse about race and racism in the law through the writing of legal journal articles, the development of course materials and curricula on race and racism, and the establishment of a yearly conference on race and the law. Crenshaw described the night when she sat around a table with others in the movement and came up with the name "Critical Race Theory" as a way to better frame and capture this emergent set of ideas about race and racism in the law. These legal pioneers have done much to shape and influence the direction of the field.

The traditionalist approach to CRSE—which is arguably the most popular and well-respected approach—has two characteristics. First, CRS traditionalists argue for an intense and ongoing engagement with "the legal literature" as a basis for understanding the nature of CRT. They also argue for strict use of legal narratives as a way in which to understand the methodologies embedded within the discourse. In short, they advocate a "back-to-the-legal-roots" approach to examining racism in education. This leads us to our next point about the second tendency within this traditionalist "return to the roots" approach. While traditionalist scholars of CRSE have called for a return to the roots of CRT, there is some question about where the field must go. Tate (2005), for example, proposed that critical race scholars in education "look to moral and spiritual texts" (p. 125) to gain a better understanding of the nature of race and inequality in education. He did not clearly illustrate the ways in which these texts could be used or what they might actually help critical race researchers be able to do or understand. Rather, Tate quoted scriptures from Exodus that point to why racial inequities are wrong. Perhaps this provides the moral and ethical imperative for why racial inequalities in schools must be improved. The challenge, of course, is that the Bible has been historically used by both conservatives and radicals to provide "moral imperatives" for why their way of thinking is correct. The other challenge, of course, for education researchers is the separation between church and state. How can we promote a faith-based moral/ethical political standpoint without being accused of proselytizing those over whom we have some degree of influence—primarily K-12 students? There are no easy answers.

CRT traditionalists have worked hard to make the discourse palatable and even usable to the masses of educational researchers. They have done this in two ways. First, they have consistently and perhaps strategically used Bell's interest-convergence principle—the notion that minorities can make no political, social, or economic gains in a racist society unless the majority is somehow made to believe that these gains will benefit them—as a kind of lynchpin or tool of analysis in their own scholarship (DeCuir & Dixson, 2004; Dixson & Rousseau, 2005a). This traditional approach suggests then that everything that happens to Black people only happens because it is somehow deemed to be in the best interest of Whites. One might suggest that the intense focus on interest-convergence as a principle might also be a roadmap for how Black scholars are to operate within the academy. If, in fact, the intense focus on the interest-convergence principle is a way to help African American critical race scholars navigate the culture of power in the academy, then it would seem to suggest that one develop a "politics of dissemblance and conformity" to White supremacy in all respects while trying to make slow and steady gains for one's own community. Derrick Bell (1994), in his book *Confronting Authority*, discussed the need for critical race theorists to incessantly and vociferously "complain," agitate, and protest against unfair legal, political, and social practices. It could easily be argued that some traditionalists have turned away from Bell's approach, which is based on incessant agitation, protest, and an insistent criticism of White supremacy.

It would appear that within the ranks of traditionalist CRT scholars, there has not been a return to the roots of CRT but a return to social class analyses of education. Tate (2005, 2006) borrowed from the work of L. Scott Miller (1995) to highlight the need for a greater focus on the effects of intergenerational poverty on educational inequality. Critical race scholars in education, he argued, need to understand how the accumulation of "family resources" over time influences the academic achievement of various groups. He also cited Shapiro's (2004) insightful research that examines the gaps in wealth between Black and White members of the middle class. Shapiro emphasized the role of social structures in determining who gets to amass wealth in U.S. society. He pointed to specific policies and laws that directly affected African Americans' ability to obtain resources otherwise made available to Whites. L. Scott Miller also engaged in a rather lengthy discussion about the structure of opportunities for African Americans.

Even when discussions of family resources are tempered by an analysis of the differential opportunities for different groups, these discussions have tended to lead to less informed discussions about the pathological behavior of people in dark ghettos (Clark, 1967; Wilson, 1987). These discussions have also led toward discussions about African American middle-class parents' lack of attention to preparing their children to be successful on standardized tests (Ogbu, 2003). Of course, this discussion is not new. Daniel Patrick Moynihan's extremely controversial report on the "Negro family" published in 1965 addressed similar concerns (U.S. Department of Labor, 1965). The discussion about the intergenerational

effects of widespread poverty on Blacks ignited a firestorm of controversy about the root causes of educational attainment and achievement. In fact, it is Moynihan's report and attendant scholarship (see Oscar Lewis's, 1968, work on the "Culture of Poverty") that also pushed education scholars to develop new ways of looking at educational attainment in public schools (Lynn, Benigno, Williams, Park, & Mitchell, 2006). In short, Tate, a major proponent of the traditionalist approach to CRSE is arguing that critical race scholars must fully explain the moral imperatives that serve to ground their work and must look more deeply at how intergenerational wealth gaps have created significant disparities between groups over time. The challenge that traditionalists must confront is whether the convergence of these approaches can serve as a "magic pill" that solves the problems facing African American children in America's schools. Proposals such as Miller's (1995) that focus on rehabilitating families to make minority children in poor families more competitive unfortunately still views families and their lack of capital as the source of the problem. While critical race theorists do not deny the existence of family, neighborhood, and community factors, they chiefly concern themselves with how racism structures not only opportunities but also our ideas about what constitutes achievement and success. Even more important, critical race theorists adopt Bell's racial realism thesis that suggests that as long we live in a White supremacist society that devalues Blackness and dehumanizes all non-Whites in one way or another—African Americans will never achieve parity with Whites (Bell, 1980a, 1980b; Lynn, 2006). Traditionalists—who tend to look to scholars of European descent for explanations for the Black-White achievement gap—will probably have to decide if CRT is the framework they are employing or if it is something entirely different. Only time will tell. We will briefly address the other traditions before providing a fuller treatment of the fourth tradition.

The Postmodernist Turn and the Latcrit Approach in Critical Race Research

The second and third traditions we have identified are the postmodern and Latcrit approaches within CRSE. We explain these two approaches briefly and turn our attention first to the postmodern approach. It is important to note—as has been discussed elsewhere (Lynn & Parker, 2006)—that there are certain postmodernist tendencies within the CRT that call for a reengagement with notions of racial subjectivity and call for a decentering of materialist analysis that reduces racism to a series of observable, easily discernable events. This tradition is very much in its emergent phase since very little theoretical or empirical work has been done in this tradition. Garrett Duncan (2002a, 2002b, 2005)—quite possibly the sole proponent of this approach in education—typically called on the work of postmodernists such as Lyotard and Derrida to help him explain the subjective dimensions of Black students' experiences in elite schools. He also invoked Friere to help him define what he referred to as "limit situations" that point to Black males' existential condition in racist America. One of the challenges, of course, facing postmodernists is their use of florid and inaccessible (European) language to describe the conditions of everyday people. Duncan typically used terms like *differend*—developed by postmodernist Jean Francis Lyotard—to describe the conditions facing Black boys. While the term is described by Shawver (1998) a postmodernist who specializes in Lyotard's work—as a dispute between two people with different linguistic realities, it is often unclear how Duncan is using the term. Delgado's (2003a) warning about the turn from a more materialist analysis of race toward discourse analysis should be heeded here. In short, Delgado argued that much CRT scholarship has turned away from a sharp critique of White supremacy toward a focus on linguistic codes, symbols, and frames that shape and influence the lives of the oppressed. Despite this, we believe that this emergent area of focus will become a much more widely embraced approach to examining race within the context of urban schools in the United States. It may also serve as an important method through which to help European postmodernist scholars better understand the racial marginality of African diasporic peoples in the United States.

Much of the work in the third tradition—Latcrit—comes out of the Chicano/Chicana or Latino/Latina Studies tradition and is committed to exploring how racism connects to issues of language, social class, culture, and immigrant status. Scholars in this tradition are critical of what Perea (1997) has defined as the Black-White

binary in CRT, and they advocate for an approach that is more inclusive of a more diverse set of perspectives. While they call for CRT to be more responsive to the needs, voices, and perspectives of other groups besides African Americans, this research tends to be Latino-centric because it focuses mostly on subjects who are of Mexican American or Puerto Rican descent—although not always. One of the challenges facing Latcrit scholars is how to call for a more pluralist conception of race without suggesting that the focus on African Americans is wrong or not needed. Latcrit scholars must embrace African Americans' accounting of their own experiences with oppression and help African Americans understand the points of connection and disconnection between their own experiences. Latcrit scholars will also need to examine the extent to which Latinos/Latinas can become "honorary Whites" who often exhibit the qualities and physical characteristics needed for group membership (Bonilla Silva, 2004). We have to be clear about which forms of Latcrit scholarship promote a separatist Anti-Black dialogue that pays more attention to what some define as "Black privilege" in racial discourse than to racism as a system of unearned privileges for Whites.

Latcrit scholarship is undeniably focused on developing and fostering a critique of White supremacist social relations and using CRT as a framework to analyze the experiences of Latino/Latina and African American students. Solórzano and Yosso (2002a), for example, have written chronicles or critical race counternarratives that center African American and Latino/Latina characters. Their work draws on the tradition of chronicles and storytelling in CRT and on the Mexican storias or testimonios (Lynn & Parker, 2006) that uses the story as a key method through which to address issues of race inequality in education (Solórzano & Yosso, 2000, 2001, 2002a, 2002b, 2002c). Delgado Bernal (1998, 2002) and Fernandez (2002) have also used CRT as a method to frame and define the experiences of Latino/Latina students in schools. Delgado Bernal and Villalpando (2002) have also used the framework as a tool to address the "apartheid of knowledge" in higher education that excludes both Latino/Latina and African American scholars from the mainstream meritocratic discourse in the academy. This important work has greatly influenced our conceptions of critical race scholarship in education.

The Africana Studies Approach

The fourth tradition is what might be termed the Africana Studies approach to CRSE. Before we explain the contours of this work, we should explain what we mean by the Africana Studies approach. The term is synonymous in many ways with what is referred to as Africana Thought. Gordon Lewis (2001) defined Africana Thought as "the creative theorizing of grand thought" (p. 27) as it pertains to African people. He went on to state, "oppression [for people of African descent] not only contextualizes the reality of African peoples in the modern but stands as the site of philosophical investigation itself" (p. 27). The Africana Studies approach within CRSE not only examines the impact of racism on schooling but also examines the perspectives, beliefs, and values of African people committed to achieving social justice for African people. This approach looks beyond African people's experience with marginalization to explore how they define, frame, and develop an emancipatory critical praxis in schools and society. African diasporic cultures are viewed as "sites of philosophical investigation" as well as sites of theory construction and development.

The Africana Studies approach forces us to see disciplines and fields as politically constructed boundaries. As a result, it is important to look across these constructed boundaries to draw from the philosophical, sociological, dramatic/creative, legal, and educational research and writing of African peoples to examine the ways in which they have articulated theories of oppression and liberation using a variety of methods, approaches, and theoretical traditions. It is also important to see the Africana Studies tradition as being epistemologically diverse. It represents a range of perspectives from feminist/womanist to Afrocentric to Marxist. This approach also demands that we look across these rigidly constructed barriers as well. We attempt to undertake this approach as a way to look at CRT from a different perspective.

CRT can be clearly linked back to the African American struggle for freedom and equality that began when enslaved Africans first stepped onto the shores of "the new world." In a paper presented at the first conference on CRT in the United Kingdom, Lynn (2006) referred to CRT as "African American protest thought"—borrowing from William Watkins' (2005) important research.

In that regard, he argued that CRT is an important part of the Black radical tradition in the United States (Rabaka, 2006). It is a development of an important set of constructs, philosophies, orientations, beliefs, practices, and methods that are derived from the Black insurgent, intellectual, and activist tradition. In that sense, CRT is both an intellectual and an activist movement because while it is concerned about advancing and fostering a rich intellectual discourse on racism and its effects, it is also committed to ending racism and seeks to foster the kind of scholarship and activist work that will lead toward that end.

Many scholars in the Africana Studies tradition have wed their goals of creating both intellectual and political space for conversations about racism in our society to more specific goals for producing educational scholarship. Rabaka (2006) argued, for example, that

> many, if not all, of the key concerns of contemporary critical race theory are prefigured in Du Bois's discourse on race and racism in ways that makes one wonder whether contemporary critical race theory is simply a continuation, or a contemporary version of Du Bois's classical theory of race. (p. 65)

W. E. B. Du Bois was a leading figure in the movement to (1) conduct research and develop theory that helped us understand the racial conditions of the United States and (2) engage in persistent activist work aimed at transforming structures of racial oppression in our society. Du Bois's work is also important because he articulates a theory of race and analyzes White supremacy as a totalizing and all-encompassing social, political, and economic system of privileges and advantages afforded to Whites based on their skin color (Rabaka, 2006). By the same token, he explained in great detail the ways in which African Americans were denied these privileges and advantages because they did not possess or own White skin. In this regard, Du Bois might very well be the "father of CRT."

Carter G. Woodson—an educator who tried to address the intellectual, political, and social dimensions of the African experience in racist America—is another important figure in the Critical Race Studies in Education movement. We pay particular attention to Woodson's (1990) book *The Mis-Education of the Negro* as we attempt to argue for how and why he could be regarded as a leader of the emerging field of CRSE. The following is a quote from text that captures the heart of Woodson's concerns:

> He [the oppressor] teaches the Negro that he has no worth-while past, that his race has done nothing significant since the beginning of time, and that there is no evidence that he will ever achieve anything great. The education of the Negro then must be carefully directed lest the race may waste time trying to do the impossible. Lead the Negro to believe this and thus control his thinking. If you can thereby determine what he will think, you will not need to worry about what he will do. You will not have to tell him to go to the back door. He will go without being told; and if there is no back door he will have one cut for his special benefit. (p. 192)

In this passage from *The Mis-Education of the Negro*, Woodson highlights the deleterious effects of an inadequate education on the development and advancement of the African American community. This miseducation is not an accidental occurrence, but is the direct result of a White supremacist effort to maintain and perpetuate Black economic, social, and political inferiority. Woodson argues that the "Negro" was created out of social, economic, and political conditioning where White supremacy/Black inferiority prevailed. The idea then is to program Blacks to seek a life of degradation, oppression, and mimicry of their oppressors. This would require that African American children experience the type of education that enslaves the mind and serves to perpetuate the social order that relegates Blacks to positions of servitude. According to Woodson, "the keynote in the education of the negro has been to do what he is told to do" (p. 134).

Woodson goes on to describe the major role teachers play in reinforcing White supremacist ideologies when they ignore the study of Blacks and issues of race within their classrooms by arguing that Black children are too young to be exposed to the harsh realities of racism. Teachers deliberately avoid an intense critical study of the African American experience as they assume that students are too immature and emotionally underdeveloped to handle such topics. He critiques such practices by arguing that Black children, regardless of age, are active participants in a racist society and are fully aware of the inequities they face. Woodson (1990) wrote,

> The misguided teachers ignore the fact that the race question is being brought before black and White children daily in their homes, in the streets, through the press and on the rostrum. How, then, can the school ignore the duty of teaching the truth while these other agencies are playing up falsehood. (p. 135)

Early on, Woodson argued for an early and intense examination of race and class in American schools. In doing so, he attempted to highlight the pervasiveness of racism and the Euro-centric perspectives within school curriculum. He was unapologetic in the assertion that curricular change is essential for the development of the Black child, as he argued for a more African-centered perspective within history, art, literature, economics, and philosophy. Woodson also believed that Black children should be taught the African origins of what they learn in school early in their educational development. He believed that an African-centered curriculum could help diminish the effects of White supremacy on Black identity:

> If the Negro is to be elevated he must be educated in the sense of being developed from what he is, and the public must be so enlightened as to think of the Negro as a man. Furthermore, no one [Negro] can be thoroughly educated until he learns as much about the Negro as he knows about other people. (Woodson, 1990, p. 136)

Woodson advocated for what he called *the new program* for the elevation of Blacks in the United States, which first necessitates a scientific study of the African American community. Under the new program, Blacks would learn to do for themselves what Whites would never do. This program would require Blacks to think, produce, and teach from their own perspectives. He was critical of classical schools of thought or as he put it, "old worn-out theories" (p. 149) that perpetuated ideas of Black inferiority. According to Woodson (1990), "to qualify for certification in the professions Negros must go to other schools, where, although they acquire the fundamentals, they learn much about their 'inferiority' to discourage them in their struggle upward" (p. 149).

Woodson problematizes the traditional study of theology, literature, science, and education and calls for a complete and radical reconstruction of these disciplines. He argues for the replacement of old ways of thinking about theology that has permitted Whites to oppress, degrade, and dehumanize Blacks while maintaining their dominant status in society. For that to occur, a new ideology that promotes true brotherhood and recognizes God as the father of us all is necessary. Woodson also presents a case for a new way of thinking about literature that not only celebrates the work of Shakespeare and the Anglo-Saxon but also critically analyzes African folklore as well. Woodson (1990) asserted, "They [Negro students] should direct their attention also to the folklore of the African, to the philosophy in his proverbs, to the development of the Negro in the use of modern language, and to the works of Negro writers" (p. 150). It is worthless for Blacks to only study of heroism of Alexander the Great, Caesar, and Napoleon, whose greatest contributions have been murder, rape, and destruction, while ignoring the African origins from which most nations evolved. He further posited, "instead of cramming the Negro's mind with what others have shown that they can do, we should develop his latent powers that he may perform in society a part of which others are not capable" (p. 150).

In contrast, Woodson celebrated those who have paved new paths in the fields of education, religion, and economics as he shares stories of Black entrepreneurs who have earned financial independence. These particular Blacks were deemed independent thinkers, free from the "shackles of slavery," as they provided their communities with new and innovative services. Such successes provided evidence of the potential accomplishments that Blacks may achieve if they were to abandon their old ways of thinking for a more progressive program that addresses the needs of the Black community. Woodson (1990) argued, "If you teach the Negro that he has accomplished as much good as any other race he will aspire to equality and justice without regard to race" (p. 192).

At first glance, one could argue that there is no easy connection between the notions Woodson articulates in *The Mis-Education of the Negro* and much of CRSE research. Africana CRS researchers are committed to situating CRT within the larger context of the Black radical tradition in scholarship, teaching, and activism. Africana scholars are deeply invested in illustrating the ways in which critical race scholarship in education comes out of and is closely connected to what Watkins refers to as "Black protest thought." Unlike scholars in the

more traditional area, Africana scholars are deeply concerned about issues of culture as well as race. They call for a critical engagement between critical theories that explore the various cultural, political, social, and economic manifestations of White supremacy. In this way, the work fits more squarely within a Woodsonian tradition because of its commitment to linking culture to race and linking current race theorizing to the Black radical tradition.

The work of David Stovall also fits in this tradition, but in a different way. Like Woodson, Stovall calls for a reexamination of notions of community and puts the African American community at the center of his analysis. Even more so, Parker and Stovall (2004) have reenvisioned CRT as a "call to work" that demands that scholars roll up their sleeves and get busy in and with our communities. CRSE calls for a community-centered approach to studying race and racism in education rather than an academic elitist approach that is separate from the communities we actually hope to serve. This approach calls forth the wisdom of community activists and uses CRT as an approach to more accurately situate this work.

The Africana tradition in CRSE employs Bell's racial realism framework to not only situate Black life in White societies but also is committed to exploring the pragmatics of articulating and practicing a liberatory pedagogy within the context of African American schools and communities (Jennings & Lynn, 2005; Lynn, 1999. In this sense, an Africana perspective follows in the tradition of Woodson who called for African Americans not only to critique White supremacy but also to work to improve their own communities. Woodson called for educators and scholars not only to ground their work within the community context but also to look to the community as a source of theorizing. Critical race pedagogy—for example—is one such approach. It is deeply grounded in the beliefs, experiences, and practices of liberatory African American educators who are committed to the liberation of African peoples.

CONCLUSION

CRT serves as an important paradigm for achieving social justice and social change. These goals were at the very core of Carter G. Woodson's beliefs about transformation in our society. We believe that this ideal presents a major "call to work" for education scholars, teachers, and researchers in the struggle for equality, justice, and freedom. The transformation from the disposition of degradation, oppression, and inferiority to one of achievement, success, and excellence starts with this call to action, and its ultimate response. In conjunction with and perhaps in response to Woodson's earlier critique, critical race scholars in education have illustrated the following:

- Black students experience a raceless curriculum that teaches them to mimic Whites rather than think and create for themselves. It also denies them the opportunity to make sense of and examine the racism they experience daily.

- Racism as an institutional system pervades education, such that education is a powerful means to perpetuate a social order where Blacks remain in positions of service while Whites benefit from their labor.

- Race needs to be reinserted in all the disciplines (theology, literature, science, and education), so that White superiority and Black inferiority may be eradicated.

In short, the Africana Studies tradition in the CRSE calls for a vigorous engagement and interaction between race, culture, and identity. As scholars in this tradition, we are guided by commitments to the broader African community. We are also thoughtful about what is required for success in the academy. However, success in the academy provides Africana Studies scholars with greater opportunities to do informative and transformative research about the conditions of African peoples. This research not only addresses the conditions but also examines the way forward by drawing on the intersection of theory and practice. We are led by Woodson's call to ground ourselves in our own realities and commit ourselves to changing this society for the betterment of people of African descent. Cheryl Harris (2002) captured, we believe, the spirit of the Africana Studies tradition in CRS. She stated,

> Through CRS, we are not seeking or claiming ultimate truth; rather, our intervention is guided by a commitment to investigate, debate, and understand race as a phenomenon that has played a powerful role in our past and has shaped the present.... Through CRS we seek to be self-aware, critical and rigorous in exploring these choices and perspectives, guided by the recognition that at the end of the day, we have a responsibility to make a future in which racial inequality is not an accepted or unfortunate act. (p. 1235)

Note

1. This paper offers an explanation of an emergent concept within the relatively undefined field of Critical Race Studies in Education. As such, the paper offers only a brief explanation of the four traditions that have been identified by the co-authors. It is outside of the scope of the paper to present a fully detailed analysis of all of the literature that might fit within the categories we outline.

References

Bell, D. A. (1979). Bakke, minority admissions, and the usual price of racial remedies. *California Law Review, 76,* 3–19.

Bell, D. A. (1980a). *Brown v. Board of Education* and the interest-convergence dilemma. *Harvard Educational Law Review, 33,* 1–34.

Bell, D. A. (1980b). *Race, racism and the American law* (2nd ed.). Boston: Little, Brown.

Bell, D. A. (1985). The civil rights chronicles. *Harvard Law Review, 99,* 4–83.

Bell, D. A. (1987). Neither separate schools nor mixed schools: The chronicle of the sacrificed Black schoolchildren. In D. Bell (Ed.), *And we are not saved: The elusive quest for racial justice* (pp. 102–122). New York: Basic Books.

Bell, D. A. (1988). White superiority in America: Its legal legacy, its economic costs. *Villanova Law Review, 33,* 767–779.

Bell, D. A. (1992). *Faces at the bottom of the well: The permanence of racism.* New York: Basic Books.

Bell, D.A. (1994). *Confronting authority: Reflections of an ardent protester.* Boston: Beacon Press.

Bell, D. A. (1996). *Gospel choirs: Psalms of survival for an alien land called home.* New York: Basic Books.

Bell, D. A. (2004). *Silent covenants: Brown v. Board of Education and the unfulfilled hopes for racial reform.* New York: Oxford University Press.

Bonilla Silva, E. (2004). *Racism without racists: Color-blind racism and the persistence of racial inequality in the United States.* Lanham, MD: Rowman & Littlefield.

Clark, K. B. (1967). *Dark ghetto: The dilemmas of social power.* New York: Harper & Row.

Crenshaw, K. W. (1988). Race, reform, and retrenchment: Transformation and legitimation in antidiscrimination law. *Harvard Law Review, 101,* 1331–1387.

Crenshaw, K. W., Gotanda, N., Peller, G., & Thomas, K. (Eds.). (1995). *Critical race theory: The key writings that formed the movement.* New York: New Press.

DeCuir, J. T., & Dixson, A. D. (2004). "So when it comes out, they aren't that surprised that it is there": Using critical race theory as a tool of analysis of race and racism in education. *Educational Researcher, 33,* 26–31.

Delgado, R. (1984). The imperial scholar: Reflections on a review of civil rights literature. *University of Pennsylvania Law Review, 132,* 561–578.

Delgado, R. (1987). The ethereal scholar: Does critical legal studies have what minorities want? *Harvard Civil Rights-Civil Liberties Law Review, 22,* 301–322.

Delgado, R. (1988a). Critical legal studies and the realities of race: Does the fundamental contradiction have a corollary? *Harvard Civil Rights-Civil Liberties Law Review, 23,* 407–413.

Delgado, R. (1988b). Derrick Bell and the ideology of racial reform: Will we ever be saved? *Yale Law Review, 97,* 923–947.

Delgado, R. (1989). Storytelling for oppositionists and others: A plea for narrative. *Michigan Law Review, 87,* 2411–2441.

Delgado, R. (1990). When a story is just a story: Does voice really matter? *Virginia Law Review, 76,* 95–111.

Delgado, R. (1992). The imperial scholar revisited: How to marginalize outsider writing, ten years later. *University of Pennsylvania Law Review, 140,* 1349–1372.

Delgado, R. (1993). On telling stories in school: A reply to Farber and Sherry. *Vanderbilt Law Review, 46,* 665–676.

Delgado, R. (Ed.). (1995a). *Critical race theory: The cutting edge.* Philadelphia: Temple University Press.

Delgado, R. (1995b). *The Rodrigo chronicles: Conversations about America and race.* New York: New York University Press.

Delgado, R. (1996). *The coming race war?: And other apocalyptic tales of American after affirmative action and welfare.* New York: New York University Press.

Delgado, R. (1999). *When equality ends: Stories about race and resistance.* Boulder, CO: Westview Press.

Delgado, R. (2003a). Crossroads and blind alleys: A critical examination of recent writing about race. *Texas Law Review, 82,* 121–152.

Delgado, R. (2003b). *Justice at war: Civil liberties and civil rights during times of crisis.* New York: New York University Press.

Delgado, R., & Stefancic, J. (Eds.). (2000). *Critical race theory: The cutting edge second edition.* Philadelphia: Temple University Press.

Delgado Bernal, D. (1998). Using a Chicana feminist epistemology in educational research. *Harvard Educational Review, 68*(4), 555–582.

Delgado Bernal, D. (2002). Critical race theory, Latcrit theory, and critical raced-gendered epistemologies: Recognizing students of color as holders and creators of knowledge. *Qualitative Inquiry, 8*(1), 105–126.

Delgado Bernal, D., & Villalpando, O. (2002). An apartheid of knowledge in academia: The struggle over the "legitimate" knowledge of faculty of color. *Equity & Excellence in Education, 35*(2), 169–180.

Dillard, C. B. (2000). The substance of things hoped for, the evidence of things not seen: Examining an endarkened feminist epistemology in educational research and leadership. *Qualitative Studies in Education, 13*(6), 661–681.

Dixson, A. D., & Rousseau, C. K. (2005a). And we are still not saved: Critical race theory in education ten years later. *Race, Ethnicity and Education, 8*(1), 7–27.

Dixson, A. D., & Rousseau, C. K. (2005b). Editorial. *Race, Ethnicity and Education, 8*(1), 1–5.

Duncan, G. A. (2002a). Beyond love: A critical race ethnography of the schooling of adolescent black males. *Equity & Excellence in Education, 35*(2), 131–143.

Duncan, G. A. (2002b). Critical race theory and method: Rendering race in urban ethnographic research. *Qualitative Inquiry, 8,* 85–104.

Duncan, G. A. (2005). Critical race ethnography in education: Narrative, inequality and the problem of inequality. *Race, Ethnicity and Education, 8*(1), 93–114.

Fernandez, L. (2002). Telling stories about school: Using critical race and Latino critical theories to document Latina/Latino education and resistance. *Qualitative Inquiry, 8*(1), 45–65.

Gillborn, D. (2006). Rethinking white supremacy. *Ethnicities, 6*(3), 318–340.

Harris, C. (2002). Critical Race Studies: An introduction. *UCLA Law Review, 49*(5), 1215–1239.

Jennings, M., & Lynn, M. (2005). The house that race built: African American education and the reconceptualization of a critical race pedagogy. *Educational Foundations, 19*(3/4), 15–32.

Ladson-Billings, G., & Tate, W. F., IV. (1995). Toward a critical race theory of education. *Teachers College Record, 97*(1), 47–68.

Lewis, G. (2001). Africana thought and African diasporic studies. *The Black Scholar, 30*(3/4), 25–30.

Lewis, O. (1968). The culture of poverty. In D. P. Moynihan (Ed.), *On understanding poverty: Perspectives from the social sciences* (pp. 187–199). New York: Basic Books.

Lynn, M. (1999). Toward a critical race pedagogy: a research note. *Urban Education, 33*(6), 606–626.

Lynn, M. (2006, December). *Critical race theory: An African American epistemology with global implications for pedagogy and practice.* Paper presented at "Critical race theory: What it is and how it can inform research and educational practice and pedagogy beyond the US" Conference. Manchester Metropolitan University, Education and Social Research Institute, Manchester, UK.

Lynn, M., Benigno, G., Williams, A., Park, G., & Mitchell, C. (2006). Critical theories of race, class and gender in urban education. *Encounter, 19*(2), 17–25.

Lynn, M., & Parker, L. (2006). Critical Race Studies in education: Examining a decade of research in U.S. schools. *The Urban Review, 38*(4), 257–334.

Miller, L. S. (1995). *An American imperative: Accelerating minority educational advancement.* New Haven, CT: Yale University Press.

Ogbu, J. U. (2003). *Black American students in an affluent suburb: A study of academic disengagement.* Mahwah, NJ: Lawrence Erlbaum.

Parker, L., & Stovall, D. O. (2004). Actions following words: Critical race theory connects to critical pedagogy. *Journal of Educational Philosophy and Theory, 36*(2), 167–183.

Perea, J. F. (1997). The Black/White binary paradigm of race: The "normal science" of American racial thought. *California Law Review, 85,* 1213–1258.

Rabaka, R. (2004). *W. E. B. Du Bois and the problems of the twenty-first century: An essay on Africana critical theory.* Lanham, MD: Lexington Books/Rowman & Littlefield.

Rabaka, R. (2006). W. E. B. Du Bois's "The comet" and contributions to critical race theory: An essay on Black radical politics and anti-racist social ethics. *Ethnic Studies Review: Journal of the National Association for Ethnic Studies, 29*(1), 22–48.

Schneider, C. J. (2003). Integrating critical race theory and postmodernism: Implications for race, class, and gender. *Critical Criminology, 12*(1), 87–103.

Shapiro, T. M. (2004). *The hidden cost of being African American: How wealth perpetuates inequality.* New York: Oxford University Press.

Shawver, L. (1998). On the clinical relevance of selected postmodern ideas: With a focus on

Lyotard's concept of "Differend." *Journal of the American Academy of Psychoanalysis, 26*(4), 599–618.

Solórzano, D., & Yosso, T. J. (2000). Toward a critical race theory of Chicana and Chicano education. In C. Tejeda, C. Martinez, Z. Leonardo, & P. McLaren (Eds.), *Charting new terrains of Chicana(o)/Latina(o) education* (pp. 35–65). Cresskill, NJ: Hampton Press.

Solórzano, D., & Yosso, T. J. (2001). Critical race and LatCrit theory and method: Counter-storytelling Chicana and Chicano graduate school experiences. *International Journal of Qualitative Studies in Education, 14*(4), 471–495.

Solórzano, D., & Yosso, T. J. (2002a). A critical race counter-story of race, racism, and affirmative action. *Equity and Excellence in Education, 35*(2), 155–168.

Solórzano, D., & Yosso, T. J. (2002b). Critical race methodology: Counterstorytelling as an analytical framework for education research. *Qualitative Inquiry, 8*(1), 23–44.

Solórzano, D., & Yosso, T. J. (2002c). Maintaining social justice hopes within academic realities: A Freirean approach to critical race/LatCrit pedagogy. *Denver Law Review, 78*(4), 595–621.

Tate, W. F. (2005). Ethics, engineering and the challenge of racial reform in education. *Race, Ethnicity and Education, 8*(1), 121–127.

Tate, W. F. (2006, April). *A matter of public interest: Schools, neighborhoods and social inequality.* Paper presented at The Spring 2006 Colloquium of the Maryland Institute for Minority Achievement and Urban Education "Embracing Urban Education: Transforming the Future," University of Maryland, College Park.

Taylor, E. (1998). A primer on critical race theory: Who are the critical race theorists and what are they saying? *Journal of Blacks in Higher Education, 19,* 122–124.

U. S. Department of Labor, Office of Planning and Research. (1965, March). *The Negro family: The case for national action.* Retrieved June 10, 2007, from www.blackpast.org/?q=primary/moynihan-report-19650gbu

Valdes, F., Culpe, J. C., & Harris, A. (Eds.). (2002). *Crossroads, directions, and a new critical race theory.* Philadelphia: Temple University Press.

Watkins, W. (Ed.). (2005). *Black protest thought and education.* New York: Peter Lang.

Wilson, W. J. (1987). *The truly disadvantaged: The inner city, the underclass, and public policy.* Chicago: University of Chicago Press.

Woodson, C. G. (1990). *The mis-education of the Negro.* Trenton, NJ: Africa World Press. (Original work published 1933)

22

EDUCATING AND COUNSELING AFRICAN AMERICAN STUDENTS

Recommendations for Teachers and School Counselors

JAMES L. MOORE III

DELILA OWENS

In the United States, a number of neighborhoods are not functioning optimally, and, in these communities, many of the schools are not meeting the educational needs and concerns of students (Barton, 2003; College Board, 1997; Lewis & Moore, 2008; Moore, 2003; U.S. Department of Education, 2000). Such schools, regardless of students' demographic background, are confronted with public outcry to educate *all* students. These concerns are exacerbated when disenfranchised or educationally vulnerable student populations consistently fail to receive a quality education because of their racial heritage, socioeconomic status, English language deficiency, and the location of their neighborhoods (Cooper & Jordan, 2003; Gonzales, George, Fernandez, & Huerta, 2005).

In popular and scientific literature, there is convincing evidence that a number of school districts, around the country, are not meeting state and national standards (Barton, 2003; Moore, 2003). Unfortunately, African Americans are often the students who are not meeting these educational standards (Ford & Moore, 2004; Ogbu, 2003). Although the numbers are more dismal in urban school systems (Cooper & Jordan, 2003; Lewis & Moore, 2008), it is quite evident, when compared with their White counterparts, that African American students are not equaling the performance of their peers in suburban communities (Day-Vines, Patton, & Baytops, 2003; Ferguson, 2002; National Center for Education Statistics [NCES], 2003; Ogbu, 2003). However, it is important to note that African Americans in some school systems do better than their African American counterparts in other school systems (Ogbu, 2003). For example, African American students in Shaker Heights, an affluent suburb outside Cleveland, Ohio, performed considerably better than other African Americans in the state of Ohio and other parts of the country; however, these same students, as a group, did not perform as well as White students in the same Shaker Height's school district (Ogbu, 2003). Based on these findings, it is quite likely that achievement is stratified by race and socioeconomic classifications. Therefore, it is reasonable to believe that race and class dynamics interact to impede academic performance for African American students, as well as contribute to the achievement gap between different groups.

From an education research and policy perspective, the "achievement gap" notion is well documented and widely accepted (Barton, 2003; Ferguson, 2003; Ford & Moore, 2004). This gap is found among racial and ethnic groups and students from low-income, middle-class, and affluent backgrounds. Barton (2003) further asserted: "Achievement differences in school among subgroups of the population have deep roots. They arrive early and stay late—beginning before the cradle and continuing through to graduation, if that happy outcome is obtained" (p. 4). Nevertheless, it is quite evident that differences of students' educational outcomes exist and that the influence of our current public educational system is inadequate. More attention and efforts are needed to rectify these differences.

As a way of addressing continued academic underperformance among low-income students and various racial and ethnic groups, a number of national and state policies have emerged (Moore, 2003; U.S. Department of Education, 2003). Such policies (e.g., No Child Left Behind Act) commonly place a strong emphasis on providing a quality education for *all* students and improving academic outcomes for those student populations traditionally underserved (e.g., African Americans, Hispanics, low-income, and students with disabilities). For example, national educational legislation, such as the No Child Left Behind Act, emphasizes stronger accountability results and more choices for parents (U.S. Department of Education, 2001).

Annually, state and school district report cards are published to inform parents and other community stakeholders about students' academic progress on statewide tests (U.S. Department of Education, 2001). As defined by the states, schools that do not make adequate yearly progress must take corrective actions (i.e., provide free tutoring, after-school programming) to improve the results of their report cards. If a school still fails to make adequate yearly progress after 5 years, the school system's leadership is required to take drastic measures (U.S. Department of Education, 2001). Such actions may include, but are not limited to, changing school administrators, replacing teachers and other educational staff (e.g., school counselors), hiring specialized staff and consultants (i.e., reading specialist, curriculum specialist, school social worker, mental health counselor, parent consultant), revising or

replacing curricula, and developing special programs/initiatives. The No Child Left Behind legislation also gives parents the ability to remove their children from a school that is not making adequate yearly progress. More specifically, after two consecutive years of not making adequate yearly progress,[1] parents can enroll their children in a higher-performing public school or charter school within their district (U.S. Department of Education, 2001). The school district, if necessary, must also provide transportation for the students.

Despite these efforts and many others, African American students are still underperforming at alarming rates (Barton, 2003; Ford & Moore, 2004; Ogbu, 2003; Thernstrom & Thernstrom, 2003). They consistently experience poorer academic outcomes than their White and Asian American counterparts (Barton, 2003; NCES, 2003). African American students also have higher dropout rates and are more likely to attend public schools where racial or ethnic minorities make up the majority of the student body (NCES, 2003). Additionally, many of these students' public schools tend "to be staffed by the least qualified teachers, have high teacher turnover, be under-funded, be under-staffed, have larger class sizes, and have fewer resources, such as books, supplies, etc." (Ford & Moore, 2004, pp. 3–4). Based on national data, many of these students are attending inadequate schools—unparalleled, arguably, with many of the schools in the nation's most affluent school districts (Lewis & Moore, 2008).

Although many measures have been taken to reach parity among public schools, the nation still has "miles to go." Improving access and equity in education remains an important civil rights issue for African Americans. Yet now, more than five decades after *Brown v. Board of Education* (1954), there is still pervasive evidence that the United States remains "separate" and "unequal" (Orfield & Lee, 2006). African Americans, even now, endure numerous challenges in society (Bailey & Moore, 2004; Madison-Colmore & Moore, 2002; Moore & Herndon, 2003; Moore, Madison-Colmore, & Smith, 2003). Many educational researchers have suggested that African American students share a collection of distinct academic, psychological, social, and cultural realities that make them different from their White student counterparts (Bailey & Moore, 2004; Flowers, Milner, &

Moore, 2003; Flowers, Zhang, Moore, & Flowers, 2004). The research literature further suggests that these students are seen as a population at risk (Howard, 2003; Jackson & Moore, 2006; Moore, Flowers, Guion, Zhang, & Staten, 2004; Ogbu, 2003).

By the year 2010, African Americans and other students of color will comprise about 50% of the school-age population across the United States (Haycock, 2001). It is, therefore, critical that public school systems identify the factors that commonly affect these students' school outcomes and work aggressively to reduce, if not eliminate, these factors. With this in mind, this chapter presents factors that have the most profound effect on African American students' school outcomes. Extrapolating from the research literature, these factors are placed in the following broad categories: (a) school, (b) psychological, (c) social, and (d) cultural. This chapter also offers recommendations to teachers and school counselors for improving school outcomes for this student population.

School Factors

To address effectively the school or academic needs of African American students, it is important that educators—teachers and school counselors—are *first* cognizant of the educational trends and patterns of these students. In many states in America (e.g., California, Georgia, New York, and Texas), students of color will represent 70% of the school-age population (U.S. Department of Education, 2003). Educational data, from these states as well as others, indicate a growing achievement gap among African American students and their White and Asian American counterparts (The Education Trust, 1999). For example, by the 10th grade, African American students' reading levels are comparable to their White 6th-grade counterparts. Frequently, these students are overrepresented in special education classes (Thernstrom & Thernstrom, 2003). They also perform significantly lower than their White counterparts on standardized exams (Thernstrom & Thernstrom, 2003). For example, in 2001, African American students scored lower than all other racial groups on both the verbal and math sections of the Scholastic Aptitude Test (SAT). More specifically, these students scored on average 96 points lower

than Whites on verbal and 105 points lower in math (NCES, 2000).

Based on national and state educational data, it is evident that the educational system is experiencing major difficulty with African American students. Countless studies, year after year, indicate that many African American students are underachieving or low achieving (Ferguson, 1998, 2002, 2003; NCES, 2000; Thernstrom & Thernstrom, 2003). According to this body of research literature, there are many explanations as to why African American students are not performing well academically. However, as they relate to school or academic factors, the explanations have primarily focused on "pedagogy, curriculum, quantity issues (such as more course work, longer school days and years, increased graduation requirements, and so forth) rather than the environments in which students learn" (Ford, 1996, p. 135). Thus, it is clear that the school environment—beyond the physical facilities or classroom sizes—has a significant impact on students' learning gains or deficiencies (Flowers et al., 2003; Ford, 1996; Ford & Moore, 2004; Moore, Ford, & Milner, 2005a, 2005b). While we are not suggesting that physical facilities or classroom sizes are not important, this section focuses on the literature related to school climate—the interactions between students and staff and how these interactions can *negatively* influence school outcomes for African American students. In addition to school climate, another hindrance to possible academic achievement and success for African American students is the lack of rigorous and challenging curricula. The lack of access to rigorous curriculum is troubling—given that African American students achieve more academically when given more challenging curriculum (Ford & Harris, 1997).

In American society, public schools have their own set of norms and values. They tend to be a function of students' backgrounds and expectation of the school staff. There is overwhelming evidence that school culture and its many nuisances have a great impact on student achievement (Karpicke & Murphy, 1996; Moore, 2006). They communicate to students the school's attitudes on a range of issues and problems, including how the school views them, and its attitudes toward males, females, gifted students, and ethnic groups (Banks, 2001). Moreover, "[s]chool and classroom environments—their culture, climate, atmosphere, ethos, or ambiance—set the psychological and affective milieu for students learning" (Ford, 1996, p. 196).

When the school's culture is characterized by value conflict and lack of communication, African American students often see themselves as inept and incompetent (Ferguson, 1998; Ford, 1996; Ford & Moore, 2004). On the contrary, when the school environment promotes collegiality, respect, and a schoolwide value system, students' attitudes are much more positive (Ford, 1995, 1996; Moore et al., 2005a, 2005b). In American public schools, the classroom setting for African American students too often represents learning environments of low academic expectations and negative perceptions about their academic ability and potential (Ford & Moore, 2004, 2005, 2006; Moore et al., 2005a, 2005b). Messages—both overt and covert—are communicated about African American intelligence (Jackson & Moore, 2006; Moore et al., 2003). These communications frequently imply intellectual inadequacy and inferiority about the group (Moore et al., 2003). They are communicated "through the projection of stereotyped images, verbal and nonverbal exchanges in daily interaction, and the incessant debate about genetics and intelligence" (Howard & Hammond, 1985, p. 20).

The notion of "Black intellectual inferiority" has deep roots. It is based on centuries of bogus social science research and racist twisted facts (Howard & Hammond, 1985). It is reasonable to believe that this kind of information has pernicious effects on the psyche, particularly in educational settings (Howard & Hammond, 1985; Moore et al., 2003; Steele, 1999). The notion of Black intellectual inferiority dwells in the hallways and classrooms where African American students attend, as well as in the minds and subsequent behaviors of those who teach and educate them. Rumors of Black intellectual inferiority could very well be the lifeline that implants doubt and skepticism, in the minds of teachers and school counselors, about African American students' academic worth and ability.

According to the research literature, many educators (e.g., teachers and school counselors) have lower expectations of African American students than of White students (Ferguson, 1998). This has been discovered to be true for even those African American students who are identified as gifted (Ford, 1996). Low expectations are communicated to African American

students through different means. For example, Ford and Moore (2004) listed the following:

1. Lowering rigor in teaching and instruction while emphasizing the teaching of low-level skills

2. Providing less constructive feedback

3. Viewing low grades as acceptable for students of color

4. Accepting substandard work from diverse students

5. Referring fewer students of color to gifted education screening and placement

6. Using less encouragement and referring fewer students of color to Advanced Placement (AP) classes

7. Placing larger numbers of students in low-ability groups

8. Questioning the high performance of minority students on assignments

9. Providing few opportunities for diverse students to gain higher academic skills (p. 3)

Over the years, a litany of publications has documented the effects of teacher and school counselor expectations on students' achievement (Flowers et al., 2003; Ford & Moore, 2004; Howard, 2003; Moore, Henfield, & Owens, 2008). For example, Hébert (2002) conducted a qualitative study with gifted African American students, and he found that educators' expectations significantly influenced these students' academic motivation and school outcomes. Flowers et al. (2003) also discovered, using a national representative sample, that teachers' expectations had a significant impact on African American students' educational aspirations. Like expectations, student-teacher and student-school relationships are equally important (Ferguson, 1998; Flowers et al., 2003; Howard, 2003; Reid & Moore, 2008). African American students, in Howard's (2003) study, reported that many educators had low expectations of them. For example, Ebony stated,

When I first came here from Hamilton [her middle school] I got good grades and never had detention. But when I came here, it was like these teachers think that just because we're Black kids from the ghetto that we can't learn anything. They don't care. They don't try to teach us anything. After a while you say forget it, I'm not to learn nothing from ya'll [the teachers]. I know that I am smart, but it's like they don't give you the chance to show it. (p. 10)

Reflective of the importance of teacher-student relationships and expectations, Ahmad states,

This year for pre-calculus, I have Mrs. Lord, who is White. She just tells us all the time how smart we are, and she really makes us feel special about what we are learning. If we cannot figure a problem out, she will continue to push us to think harder, analyze the properties, and talk out loud about how we are trying to process. Sometimes I come out of her class feeling like I learned so much information!! I think it's because she believes in ourselves. I know that we are high school students and stuff, but it's still good for us to hear positive stuff about what we can do. (p. 11)

Although this chapter focuses on African American students, it is plausible that *all* students can benefit from supportive, caring, and encouraging educators—teachers and school counselors. Nevertheless, as has been mentioned, African American students may need additional assistance due to those factors that commonly plague their academic performance. Furthermore, it is well documented that many African American students are affected by student-educator interactions and how they perceive educators' attitudes and behaviors toward them.

Psychological Factors

The promotion of academic achievement in African American students is crucial. In public school settings, African American students in particular may experience a host of psychological issues, such as racism, school disengagement, and negotiating numerous identities (Constantine & Gushue, 2003; Howard, 2003; Moore et al., 2005a, 2005b). To this end, many of these students have a keen awareness of the stereotypes associated with their race and implications for being a member of the African American

community (Howard & Hammond, 1985; Moore et al., 2003; Vontress & Epp, 1997). Such awareness can have a negative effect on students' self-concept (Cokley, 2002).

African American students, like any other student population, are motivated to achieve academically if success is encouraged from credible sources (Howard & Hammond, 1985; Moore et al., 2003) and if it fosters a positive self-image or identity (Cokley, 2002). Racial identity development is a way of understanding how African American youth view themselves in relation to their ethnic group. However, African American students may experience additional psychological factors that may impact their academic performance. Racial identity development can also be viewed as an individual's beliefs about the relevance of race in their lives.

African American students who have low or poor self-concept and racial identity development are less likely to achieve than African American students with high or positive self-concept and racial identity development (Ford & Moore, 2006; Moore et al., 2005b). In 1997, Ford and Harris examined the racial identity development and achievement of 44 identified gifted African American students, 67 potentially gifted African American students, and 38 typical African American students. The two educational researchers found that the males and under-achievers had less positive racial identities than the females and achievers. They also found that the gifted students had more positive racial development identities than the others. Such findings further suggest that racial identity development is closely linked to academic achievement.

Those students who possess a positive affiliation and attitude toward one's racial group are also more likely to reject society's negative stereotypes of their racial group (Ward, 1990). Additionally, Chavous et al. (2003) found that African American students who reported lower group affiliation possessed less positive feelings toward their group and held higher negative societal perceptions of themselves. Additionally, Chavous and her colleagues found that these students were among the highest who dropped out of school by Grade 12. On the contrary, the African American youth, who had a positive attitude toward their racial group and held negative attitudes toward societal views of them, showed the lowest number of students out of school by their senior year and had higher rates of postsecondary educational attainment.

It is quite evident that issues of race are central to the African American experience. It is also likely that African American students experience more stress and problems associated to their racial heritages than White students (Henfield, 2006; Moore et al., 2005b). Interactions—viewed as racist, unfair, and inequitable—can also negatively affect the extent that African American students identify with their culture (Gallant & Moore, 2008; Henfield, 2006; Moore et al., 2005b). In turn, it can affect their racial identity development (Moore et al., 2006), as well as their self-concept, self-esteem, motivation, and academics (Ford, 1996; Ford & Moore, 2004). These negative effects are consistent with other studies (Chavous et al., 2003; Cokley, 2002; Ford & Harris, 1997; Ogbu, 2003).

As African American children begin to mature into adolescence, an awareness of race begins to emerge (Ford, 1996; Ford & Harris, 1997). Adolescents are also aware of the societal implications and stereotypes of being from a particular racial or ethnic group. African Americans, particularly at adolescence, may wish to disassociate themselves from African American culture, because of the negative stereotypes associated with their race. Over the years, numerous psychological theories have been given to explain why African American students underachieve or low achieve. Recently, the inability to achieve academically has been attributed to the "stereotype threat" (Steele, 1997; Steele & Aronson, 1995). It refers to the projected image of Black intellectual inferiority (Howard & Hammond, 1985; Moore et al., 2003). It is simply a psychological reaction to this image, which preys on the thoughts and emotions of African Americans in situations where the stereotype may apply (Ford & Moore, 2006; Steele, 1992).

In the 1990s, Dr. Claude Steele devised the stereotype threat theory. It initially focused on the performance of middle-class and academically prepared African American students. Furthermore, Steele (1992, 1997, 1999) and his colleagues (Steele & Aronson, 1995) discovered through countless studies that students' expectations often influenced their academic outcomes. Toward this end, the stereotype threat typically occurs when one is fearful of being judged based on a negative stereotype (Steele, 1999). The stereotype threatens the person's definition of self and disrupts his or her academic outcomes (Steele & Aronson, 1995).

In a variety of settings, the stereotype threat acts on many African Americans (Jackson & Moore, 2006; Moore et al., 2003). It tends to be *most* pronounced in social domains where intellectual ability is regularly assessed or evaluated (Steele, 1997; Steele & Aronson, 1995). Because the prevailing intellectual image of African Americans tends to be negative, self-doubt and fear often seeps in the minds and hearts of African American students (Howard & Hammond, 1985). As a result, many African American students disengage academically or remove themselves from the situation to avoid the psychological pressures of confirming the stereotype threat in the eyes of others or themselves (Ford & Moore, 2006; Steele, 1997, 1999). But the stereotype threat can also generate other alternatives that often lead to more positive results. For example, some students work harder and become more engaged academically to disprove the stereotype threat (Moore et al., 2003).

Aligned with this notion, Mavis Sanders' (1997) qualitative research study indicates that African American students with a high awareness of racial discrimination respond to it in ways more conducive rather than detrimental to academic success. For these students, she found that positive racial socialization was a significant factor for promoting academic achievement. For example, Denise, a 3.75-GPA (grade point average) student, stated,

> I know that being Black and being a woman, I am going to have to work harder to prove what I can do and what I can be. I am willing to work hard, because it is not what you are on the outside, but what you are on the inside. . . . If someone tells me that I can't, I just find a way to do it. (p. 90)

Kenneth, a 3.3-GPA student, asserted: "Racism makes me strive harder. I see Black men everywhere. They are there, making it, regardless of what people say" (p. 90). Patricia, a 3.0-GPA student, stated,

> I know that there will be people to hold me back, there will be people to tell me that I cannot succeed, that I am Black and I am a woman, but I am willing to strive in order to reach my goals. (p. 90)

In essence, students—who have a strong self-concept and racial identity development—are more likely to achieve by working harder to disprove the stereotype (Howard, 2003; Moore et al., 2003). However, these same students might find it psychologically and emotionally taxing to always feel like they need to prove that they are not inferior academically (Moore et al., 2005a, 2005b; Moore et al., 2006). Over the years, many educational researchers have rendered research findings, both at the secondary and postsecondary levels, consistent with this psychological and emotional phenomenon (Howard, 2003; Moore et al. 2003).

Social Factors

Another hypothesis put forth—to explain the lack of academic success in African American students—is related to social context. African American youth frequently encounter social ills (e.g., racism, poverty, violence) in their neighborhoods that often influence their academic development and school engagement. Many of the stressful life events related to African American students are similar for *all* youth (Gonzales et al., 2005). However, for African American students, they commonly endure social pressures that make them educationally vulnerable for underachievement and low achievement (Ford, 1996). They are faced with the challenge to overcome context-defining factors, such as socioeconomic status, integration in mainstream and African American communities, and the location of their communities and schools (Gonzales et al., 2005).

Too often, life stressors experienced by African American students are a function of specific social ills in the African American community and society at-large, including poverty, discrimination, neglect and abuse, poor family involvement and guidance, and drug and mental health problems (Ford, 1996; Gonzales et al., 2005). What is clear is that all these factors have some affect on these students. Toward this end, the worldviews, behaviors, and emotions—produced by these social factors—may explain why some African American students withdraw from academic activities, underachieve and low achieve, and see academic success as "acting White" and academic failure as "acting Black" (Ogbu, 2003; Schultz, 1993). If African American

students view academic achievement as "acting White," what do they see as "acting Black"? Peterson-Lewis and Bratton (2004) decided to investigate this research question with urban, African American high school students. In their study, the two authors discovered, using qualitative interviewing procedures, that these students did not directly associate "acting Black" with specific types of oppositional academic outcomes, such as obtaining poor grades. Instead, the students associated "acting Black" with specific types of behaviors, such as skipping class, not doing school assignments, and emphasizing nonacademic priorities (e.g., being street smart vs. school smart, trying to impress friends over doing well in school). Furthermore, the two authors postulated that "when Black youths have clear and constructive reference group definitions, self-definitions and directives, it is likely that their tendency or need to conceptualize achievement in relationship to whiteness will disappear" (p. 98).

In the practical sense, skipping class, not doing school assignments, and emphasizing nonacademic priorities can be characterized as defense mechanisms against continuous exposure to racial discrimination and inequity in social institutions, such as education (Vontress & Epp, 1997). Students who respond with resentment and anger to racial discrimination may deliberately perform poorly in school or even disobey educators—teachers and school counselors—who are perceived as performers of racial discrimination and inequity (Ford, 1995, 1996; Ogbu, 1988, 2003). Simply stated, achieving in school is seen as an illusion for social mobility. Therefore, some African American students develop an oppositional identity toward learning or achieving. It is a rebellious response used to maintain students' racial and cultural identity (Peterson-Lewis & Bratton, 2004) and to avert disconnection from the group (Ford, 1996; Moore et al., 2006).

Smith (1989) argued that race creates a bond and feelings of connectivity with other members of the group. With this in mind, it is also possible that some African American students view academic achievement as a slight against the group. Because the tag of "acting White" is seen as unacceptable, some African American students are caught between a "rock" and "hard place"—when group expectations differ from the dominant culture (Ford, 1996; Peterson-Lewis &

Bratton, 2004). Among gifted and high achieving students, this social quandary is common. It is also widespread in public school settings, where African American students are represented in large numbers (Ford, 1995, 1996), such as urban school settings (Henfield, 2006; Peterson-Lewis & Bratton, 2004).

Social class variables further exacerbate the academic problems for African American students. Poverty has been associated with school disengagement (Guo, Brooks-Gunn, & Harris, 1996). In America, many public schools lack meaningful relationships with economically disadvantaged students and their parents. There exists an apparent disconnection between school and family. According to Ford (1996), it is "most likely to develop when the values, attitudes, and behaviors espoused in the home and school are incongruent" (p. 82). Toward this end, it is difficult for the school and family to adequately support these students. The school lacks the involvement of the family, and the family lacks the guidance and expertise of the school. As a result, too many of these students are falling between the cracks because of social factors.

CULTURAL FACTORS

Similar to the academic, psychological, and social factors, culture affects African American students' academic performance. Culture provides the rationale for motivation and behavior in African American students. When their values and beliefs mesh with mainstream's viewpoints, African Americans are likely to achieve in school (Flowers et al., 2004; Ford, 1996). However, when the values differ or conflict, these students may underachieve or low achieve (Ford, 1996; Ford & Moore, 2004, 2006). They may also exhibit "acting out" behaviors and other insubordinate gestures (e.g., cool pose). Ford (1996) asserted that theories, such as cultural deficits and cultural conflict, are commonly used to explain the phenomenon of underachievement and low achievement. She further explained that both theories present different implications for the educational outcomes of African American students.

When focusing on cultural needs and issues, it is important that teachers and school counselors understand the harmful effects of deficit thinking (Ford & Moore, 2006; Moore et al.,

2005b). Because these education professionals tend to have the most interactions with these students in public schools, it is critical that they continuously assess and monitor their educational practices with students. Deficit thinking often negatively influences the school outcomes of African American students. Stated differently, cultural deficit theory focuses on students' weaknesses versus strengths (Moore et al., 2005a). Teachers and school counselors who possess this mind set see African Americans culture as flawed. According to the research literature, cultural deficits are cited as a reason why African American youth underachieve or low achieve (Ford, 1996). Aligned with this perspective, Ford (1996) asserted, "If Black students test poorly, they must not be gifted. The fault does not rest with biased or irrelevant tests and related identification practices. This point of view ignores teacher biases and historical and contemporary racism" (p. 84). In another article, Ford, Harris, Tyson, and Frazier Trotman (2002) argued that deficit thinking, by teachers and school counselors, about African American students is a common reason for underachievement and low achievement. Furthermore, Margaret Beale Spencer's (1984, 1985, 1988) work indicates that, although African American children between 3 and 11 years old obtain high scores on personal self-concept measures, educators still show preferences for Caucasian students and a tendency to attribute positive traits to these students, while assigning negative attributes to Blacks. It is, therefore, essential that these educators work to transform their deficit thinking to dynamic/positive thinking (Ford & Moore, 2006; Moore et al., 2005b).

In general, many African Americans embrace values, such as collectivism, kinship and extended families, spirituality, and holistic thinking (Nobles, 1991). Understanding how culture influences educational aspirations is essential. When focusing on these factors, it is also important that teachers and school counselors know how their values conflict with those of African American students, as well as understand how cultural forces shape these students' school experiences and outcomes.

Unlike cultural deficit theory, conflict theory respects and embraces cultural differences (Ford, 1996). It further suggests that "resistance to assimilation is a form of self-protection" (Ford, 1996, p. 86). Because the cultural values of African American students may vary from teachers and school counselors, students are often presented school values that conflict with their own. In turn, this tension can negatively affect the educational experiences and outcomes of African Americans (Ford, 1996; Ford & Moore, 2006; Moore et al., 2005b). Some students are able to adjust accordingly, and others are not. Those students who are unable to make these adjustments are the ones who tend to underachieve and low achieve in school (Ford, 1996). To this end, their failures have a great deal to do with their inability to shift their cultural styles to fit the school culture.

RECOMMENDATIONS

According to the research literature, there are a number of factors that influence the academic achievement of African American students. Based on the books, articles, and reports reviewed, there are a number of promising practices that could be used to reduce, if not eliminate, the factors that impede or hinder school outcomes for African American students. However, there are some effective practices that will assist in supporting African American students (Ford, 1996; Shaffer, Ortman, & Denbo, 2002). Using the research literature (i.e., books, articles, reports), we present recommendations to educators, such as teachers and school counselors. It is believed that teachers and school counselors can play a critical role in helping improve school outcomes for African American students.

Teachers

Teachers are critical in the learning process of educating African American students (Banks, 1997; Gallant & Moore, 2008; Haycock; 2001; Reid & Moore, 2008). To improve the quality of education for African American students, teacher education programs should prepare teachers with an understanding of African American culture and a clear understanding of how culture influences behavior (Ford, Obiakor, & Patton, 1995). Research has documented that African American students tend to be practical, visual, and concrete learners (Hale-Benson, 1986), although this does not apply to *all* African American students. Teachers should practice

culturally relevant practices (Flowers et al., 2003; Shaffer et al., 2002). They should also tailor their instruction to meeting the needs of the students that they are servicing (Banks et al., 2000). Such instruction should complement students' racial, gender, and cultural backgrounds (Ford, 1996). Several recommendations and strategies have been put forth for teachers interested in the academic achievement for African American students. For example, Bartz and Matthews (2001) recommended that teachers do the following:

1. Use vocational, career, and job-related examples in their classroom to demonstrate the relationship between school work and careers.

2. Determine what students' interests are and relate those interests to possible vocations or careers.

3. Discuss the importance of skills needed to master effectively prerequisites for specific careers.

4. Draw a correlation between success at school and on the job success.

5. Assure students that everyone has unique skill sets and with the proper training and preparation it can lead to a successful career.

Instruction in classrooms is certainly one way teachers can assist in improving school outcomes and closing the achievement gap for African American students (Ferguson, 2003). African American students tend to learn best in environments that are both personal and relational (Decker, 2003). The major aim of multicultural education is to use instructional techniques that foster equal opportunities for students, regardless of their race, socioeconomic status, and, most important, preferred learning styles (Banks & Banks, 1995). There are countless implications for inappropriate multicultural teaching and culturally relevant pedagogy. Toward this end, Steele (1999) asserted that the lack of appropriate teaching techniques and strategies often leaves students behind. Such pedagogy—that does not acknowledge differences in learning styles—is commonly detrimental to students' academic development (Steele, 1999). Therefore, it is critical that teachers are multiculturally competent and are able to apply culturally relevant pedagogy in the classroom (Banks, 2001; Moore et al., 2005b). It is also important that teachers are prepared for the culturally diverse needs and challenges that students bring to the classroom. Being multiculturally competent gives teachers the ability to better engage and teach African American students.

Teachers who are multiculturally competent are more likely than those who are not to promote the academic success of African American students (Ford, 1996; Henfield, 2006). They are also likely to provide opportunities for these students to develop affirming racial developmental identities. African American students who develop positive racial development identities are able to create coping strategies that assist in preventing negative academic outcomes (Constantine & Blackmon, 2002). Therefore, it becomes essential that teachers affirm the identities of African American students.

Aligned with this thinking, Ferguson (2003) called for changes in the behavior of teachers. He suggested that teachers generally have the power to help close the achievement gap. As a way of achieving this goal, Ferguson recommended that educators, such as teachers, assume that there are no systematic group-level differences in ability and that all students can be motivated to learn and succeed. Such a belief system could quite possibly reduce the achievement gap. Research shows that there are no systematic group-level differences in potential to put in effort to be motivated (Aronson, Fried, & Good, 2002). However, there may be differences in how successful particular motivational techniques are applied to various racial or ethnic groups (McInerney, Roche, McInerney, & Marsh, 1997). For example, African American students who were told that "intelligence" was not fixed, but adaptable, rendered higher academic outcomes (Aronson et al., 2002).

African American students have a keen awareness of society's stereotypes and perceptions of their abilities (Steele & Aronson, 1995). From the cradle to the grave, they are frequently made aware of this. As a result, many scholars suggest that educators' negative attitudes toward African American students' intellectual ability may pay a role in their underachievement (Steele, 1997, 1999; Steele & Aronson, 1995).

On entering school, many African American students disproportionately enter with weaker academic skills than their White counterparts (Ferguson, 2003). This pattern frequently persists throughout their educational journeys. Even for African American students whose parents hold similar levels of education to White students' parents, this educational trend still exists (Ferguson, 2003; Ogbu, 2003). To remedy this disparity, teachers and students alike should be examined. For teachers, their perceptions, attitudes, and behaviors often affect students' beliefs, behaviors, and task engagement in ways that might perpetuate low achievement or underachievement (Farkas, 2000, 2003; Flowers et al., 2003). Therefore, it is critical that teachers are keenly aware of their personal biases. It is equally as important that teachers are cognizant of resource differences among families and children. The lack of accessibility to resources is why some children enter school lacking basic knowledge and skills. For those African American students who enter school lacking basic knowledge and skills, they may appear less intelligent, when this may not necessarily be the case (Farkas, 2003; Ferguson, 2003). With this in mind, it is essential that teachers do not use deficit teaching models and demeaning communication gestures. Teachers, instead, should use multicultural frameworks and dynamic thinking.

Teachers, who use multicultural frameworks, tend to be more conscientious about how they interact and communicate with students and their parents. They clearly understand the "power" of communication and relationship building. Such teachers frequently offer sincere and authentic praise and support to students. They provide a strong balance of encouragement and rigorous academic standards. In this manner, they use the two to promote performance attributions, enhance competence, and convey attainable expectations (Henderlong & Lepper, 2002). However, when teachers fail to do these things, African American students often become disillusioned about their academic potential, are reluctant to engage their teachers, and eventually disengage academically. Howard (2003) found, using qualitative research procedures, that educators (e.g., teachers) are instrumental in influencing the academic identities of high school, African American students. In a negative way, Kenji, a student in Howard's study, asserted,

> I had this one teacher, and he would just smirk and shake his head whenever I got an answer

wrong. It was like he was thinking to himself "Dumb Black kids, he needs to just stick to sports." It's hard to explain, because teachers don't ever come straight out and say it [that they have low expectations for African American students], but their actions and expressions say a lot. And you can try to ignore that, but when it's your teacher, you can't tell me that it doesn't affect what you think about yourself, and how smart you are. (p. 12)

Based on the aforementioned excerpt, it is clear that teachers' nonverbal and verbal communications can negatively affect African American students. Therefore, as teachers respond and grade student assignments, it is important that they are mindful of their biases and how these biases may negatively affect their feedback and assessment of students' work (Bardine, Schmitz-Bardine, & Deegan, 2000). Because African American students are often subjected to negative stereotypes about their academic abilities in general, they may interpret teacher feedback on class assignments negatively, if it is not presented in an acceptable, nonbiased, and noncondescending manner. Furthermore, it is important that African American students understand the feedback given and perceive it as being constructive rather than demeaning.

School Counselors

School counselors can provide both support and guidance for African American students throughout their educational process. African American students are more likely to work hard and benefit from the student/school counselor process, when the school counselor exhibits genuine respect and authentic concern for the student (Moore, 2006; Moore et al., 2008; Sanchez-Hucles, 2000). It is also important that school counselors communicate "high expectations" of students' academic potential. When school counselors fail to do this, African American students are often negatively affected. As an example of this, Qiana, a student in Howard's (2003) study, asserted,

My uncle told me that I needed to go talk to my counselor at the beginning of the year to tell her all these [college prep] classes that I wanted to take. She [the counselor] was like, "you can't take those classes, they are for college-prep students."

I told her that's why I wanted to take them, and she said those classes would be too hard for me. I was like, how does she know what's too hard for me? What you hear somebody say straight out that you are not college material, it makes you think, "What's the point?" (p. 12)

To assist struggling African American students, like Qiana, it is important that school counselors take appropriate action on behalf of students and focus their efforts on identifying ways to help them succeed academically (Butler, 2003; Flowers et al., 2003). Instead of adopting a negative view of students that focuses on their academic shortcomings, school counselors should focus their attention on school, psychological, social, and cultural factors that commonly inhibit African American students' school outcomes. Toward this end, it is critical that school counselors possess a multicultural understanding of their students and parents. It is also important that they advocate for students and their parents, as well as help them navigate through school bureaucracy so they can advocate for themselves (Martin, 2002; Moore et al., 2008). Clearly, school counselors are in a good position to address an array of school, psychological, social, and cultural factors endured by African American students.

Like teachers, they should address the institutional racism that dwells in many schools, which often impedes the academic success of African American students. School counselors have the ability to improve the school climate for African American students. One important means of enhancing African American students' school outcomes is to create a safe and welcoming school environment. School counselors can do this, by developing programs and initiatives that make the school environment more inviting, serving as an advocate on behalf of students and parents, creating safe spaces of support for students within the school environment, etc. Additionally, Dahir and Stone (2003) suggested that school counselors can lend their support by (a) collaborating with other support staff (e.g., teachers) to ensure and monitor students success; (b) raising student aspirations; (c) partnering with community officials to access student resources for support; (d) introducing students to a wide range of careers and variety of postsecondary opportunities; and (e) helping students develop coping and life skills necessary for success.

School counselors, who are multiculturally conscientious, understand how the school environment influences students' academic development. They also understand themselves and how their attitudes and perceptions may affect the school outcomes of students (Ford & Moore, 2004). Such school counselors tend to communicate passion for "helping others" and compassion for the individuals who they help. They understand "how African American culture interacts, both positively and negatively, with school systems" (Flowers et al., 2003, p. 48). Accordingly, Butler (2003) presented several strategies that school counselors can use to foster academic success for African American students:

1. Include systemic models and emphasize resilience and strength when conceptualizing strategies to improve academic achievement.

2. Include outreach activities such as field trips and be sure that there is a large representation of African Americans at these agencies.

3. Recruit African American college students to assist in developing mentoring and tutoring programs for African American youth.

4. Develop and implement career fairs that expose students to professionals from a wide variety of careers.

In the research literature, it is common knowledge that students bring an array of social and emotional concerns to school (Henfield, 2006; Ockerman, 2006). Nevertheless, school counselors are in a unique position to assist these students. However, it is important that they are multiculturally competent and are keenly aware of the different ways in which culturally diverse students express emotions (Constantine & Gainor, 2001) and value social relationships. This is very important, because relationships and emotions are expressed differently across cultures. It is also well documented that relationships, such as those between peers, can negatively influence achievement for African American students (Ogbu, 2003; Peterson-Lewis & Bratton, 2004). Frequently, in the African American community, African American students are susceptible to teasing and opposition from their peers

(Moore et al., 2005a, 2005b). This is especially the case for those African American students who are doing well academically (Peterson-Lewis & Bratton, 2004). They are often accused of "acting White" (Ford, Grantham, & Whiting, 2008; Moore et al., 2006; Peterson-Lewis & Bratton, 2004). Unfortunately, these kinds of social forces often create psychological and emotional turmoil for African American students. The label "acting White" represents an affront against accused African American students' racial identity, especially the achievers (Peterson-Lewis & Bratton, 2004). Furthermore, the label "leaves them with two primary strategies for resolving the conflict: (a) they must either lower their personal achievement ambitions or; (b) discontinue identification and/or association with other Blacks" (p. 88). To adequately serve these students, it is important that school counselors first understand some of the external and internal challenges African American students may have to endure in school. Second, it is important that school counselors offer responsive counseling services (e.g., individual, group) and guidance lessons (e.g., anger management, conflict resolution) that help African American students cope with negative peer pressure. Responsive counseling includes diverse perspectives (Lee, 2001). Furthermore, school counselors who know how to offer responsive counseling also understand the importance of expanding their roles to include consultation and outreach services that aid the counseling process (Sue & Sue, 2003). These school counselors understand how constructs of identity (e.g., race, class, gender) are embedded within students' concerns (Day-Vines et al., 2003).

CONCLUSION

Both teachers and school counselors are encouraged to use multiculturally relevant strategies to assist African American students in improving their school outcomes. It is important that these educators begin to measure the effectiveness of their work on African American student achievement. Equally, it is imperative that the two professionals have keen awareness of the school, psychological, social, and cultural factors that influence academic achievement for these students.

NOTE

1. The No Child Left Behind Act of 2001 requires states to set annual measurable objectives of proficiency in reading and mathematics, participation in testing, and graduation and attendance rates. Schools and school divisions that meet the annual objectives required by the federal education law are considered to have made adequate yearly progress toward the goal of 100% proficiency of all students in reading and mathematics.

REFERENCES

Aronson, J., Fried, C., & Good, C. (2002). Reducing the effects of stereotype threat on African American college students by shaping theories of intelligence. *Journal of Experimental Social Psychology, 38,* 113–125.

Bailey, D. F., & Moore, J. L., III. (2004). Emotional isolation, depression, and suicide among African American men: Reasons for concern. In C. Rabin (Ed.), *Linking lives across borders: Gender-sensitive practice in international perspective* (pp. 186–207). Pacific Grove, CA: Brooks/Cole.

Banks, C. A., & Banks, J. A. (1995). Equity pedagogy: An essential component of multicultural education. *Theory Into Practice, 34,* 152–158.

Banks, J. A. (1997). *Teaching strategies for ethnic studies* (6th ed.). Boston: Allyn & Bacon.

Banks, J. A. (2001). Multicultural education: Characteristics and goals. In J. A. Banks and C. A. McGee Banks (Eds.), *Multicultural education: Issues and perspectives* (4th ed., pp. 3–30). New York: Wiley.

Banks, J. A., Cookson, P., Gay, G., Hawley, W., Irvine, J. J., Nieto, S., et al. (2000). *Diversity within unity: Essential principles for teaching and learning in a multicultural society.* Seattle, WA: Center for Multicultural Education, College of Education, University of Washington.

Bardine, B. A., Schmitz-Bardine, M., & Deegan, E. F. (2000). Beyond the red pen: Clarifying our role in the response process. *English Journal, 90,* 94–101.

Barton, P. E. (2003). *Parsing the achievement gap: Baselines for tracking progress.* Princeton, NJ: Educational Testing Service.

Bartz, D. E., & Mathews, G. S. (2001). Enhancing students' social and psychological development. *The Education Digest, 66,* 33–36.

Brown v. Board of Education, 347 U.S. 483 (1954).

Butler, K. S. (2003). Helping urban African American high school students to excel academically: The roles of school counselors. *The High School Journal, 87,* 51–57.

Chavous, T. M., Bernat, D. H., Schmeelk-Cone, K., Caldwell, C. H., Kohn-Wood, L., & Zimmerman, M. A. (2003). Racial identity and academic attainment among African American adolescents. *Child Development, 74,* 1076–1090.

Cokley, K. (2002). Ethnicity, gender, and academic self-concept: A preliminary examination of academic disidentification and implications for psychologists. *Cultural Diversity & Ethnic Minority Psychology, 8,* 378–388.

College Board. (1997). *College bound seniors profile of SAT and achievement test-takers: California report.* New York: Author.

Constantine, M. G., & Blackmon, S. M. (2002). Black adolescents' racial socialization experiences: Their relations to home, school and peer self-esteem. *Journal of Black Studies, 32,* 322–335.

Constantine, M. G., & Gainor, K. A. (2001). Emotional intelligence and empathy: Their relation to multicultural counseling knowledge and awareness. *Professional School Counseling, 5,* 131–137.

Constantine, M. G., & Gushue, G. V. (2003). School counselors' attitudes towards ethnic tolerance and racism attitudes as predictors of multicultural case conceptualization ability. *Journal of Counseling and Development, 81,* 185–190.

Cooper, R., & Jordan, W. J. (2003). Cultural issues in comprehensive school reform. *Urban Education, 38,* 380–397.

Dahir, C., & Stone, C. (2003). Accountability: A M.E.A.S.U.R.E. of the impact school counselors have on student achievement. *Professional School Counseling, 6,* 214–221.

Day-Vines, N., Patton, J., & Baytops, J. (2003). Counseling African American adolescents: The impact of race and middle class status. *Professional School Counseling, 7,* 40–51.

Decker, G. (2003). Using data to drive student achievement in the classroom and on high-stakes tests. *T.H.E. Journal, 30,* 44–48.

The Education Trust. (1999). *Dispelling the myth: High poverty schools exceeding expectations.* Retrieved March 3, 2008 from www.eric.ed.gov/ERICDocs/data/ericdocs2sql/content_storage_01/0000019b/80/16/77/61.pdf

Farkas, G. (2000). Teaching low-income children to read at grade level C. *Contemporary Sociology, 29,* 53–62.

Farkas, G. (2003). Racial disparities and discrimination in education: What do we know, how do we know it, and what do we need to know? *Teachers College Record, 105,* 1119–1146.

Ferguson, R. F. (1998). Teachers' perceptions and expectations and the black-white test score gap. In C. Jencks & M. Phillips (Eds.), *The black-white test score gap* (pp. 318–374). Washington, DC: Brookings Institution Press.

Ferguson, R. F. (2002). *Addressing racial disparities in high-achieving suburban schools.* Retrieved February 17, 2005, from http://ww.ncrel.org/policy/pubs/html/piv01113/dec2002b.htm

Ferguson, R. F. (2003). Teachers' perceptions and expectations and the black-white score gap. *Urban Education, 38,* 460–507.

Flowers, L. A., Milner, H. R., & Moore, J. L., III. (2003). Effects of locus of control on African American high school seniors' educational aspirations: Implications for preservice and inservice high school teachers and counselors. *High School Journal, 87,* 39–50.

Flowers, L. A., Zhang, Y., Moore, J. L., III, & Flowers, T. (2004). An exploratory phenomenological study of African American high school students in gifted education programs: Implications for teachers and school counselors. *E-Journal of Teaching & Learning in Diverse Settings, 2,* 39–53. Retrieved August 4, 2006, from www.subr.edu/coeducation/ejournal/v2i1.htm

Ford, B. A., Obiakor, F. E., & Patton, J. M. (1995). *Effective education of African American exceptional learners: New perspectives.* Austin, TX: PRO-Ed.

Ford, D. Y. (1995). *A study of achievement and underachievement among gifted, potentially gifted, and regular education black students:* Storrs: The University of Connecticut, National Research Center on the Gifted and Talented.

Ford, D. Y. (1996). *Reversing underachievement among gifted black students: Promising practices and programs.* New York: Teachers College Press.

Ford, D. Y., Grantham, T. C., & Whiting, G. W. (2008). Another look at the achievement gap: Learning from the experiences of gifted black students. *Urban Education, 43,* 216–239.

Ford, D. Y., & Harris, J. J., III. (1997). A study of the racial identity and achievement of black males and females. *Roeper Review, 20,* 105–110.

Ford, D. Y., Harris, J. J., III, Tyson, C. A., & Frazier Trotman, M. (2002). Beyond deficit thinking: Providing access for gifted African American students. *Roeper Review, 24,* 52–58.

Ford, D. Y., & Moore, J. L., III. (2004). The achievement gap and gifted students of color. *Understanding Our Gifted, 16,* 3–7.

Ford, D. Y., & Moore, J. L., III. (2005). Being gifted and adolescent: Issues and needs of students of color. In F. Dixon & S. M. Moon (Eds.), *The handbook of secondary gifted education* (pp. 113–136). Waco, TX: Prufrock Press.

Ford, D. Y., & Moore, J. L., III. (2006). Eliminating deficit orientations: Creating classrooms and curricula for gifted students from diverse cultural backgrounds. In D. W. Sue & M. Constantine (Eds.), *Racism as a barrier to cultural competence in mental health and educational settings.* Indianapolis, IN: Wiley.

Gallant, D. J., & Moore, J. L., III. (2008). Assessing ethnicity: Equity for first-grade male students on a curriculum-embedded performance assessment. *Urban Education, 43,* 172–188.

Gonzales, N. A., George, P. E., Fernandez, A. C., & Huerta, V. L. (2005). Minority adolescent stress and coping. *The Prevention Researcher, 12,* 7–9.

Guo, G., Brooks-Gunn, J., & Harris, K. M. (1996). Parents' labor force attachment and grade retention among urban black children. *Sociology of Education, 69,* 217–236.

Hale-Benson, J. (1986). *Black children: Their roots, culture, and learning styles* (2nd ed.). Baltimore: Johns Hopkins University Press.

Haycock, K. (2001). Closing the achievement gap. *Educational Leadership, 58,* 6–11.

Hébert, T. P. (2002). Jamison's story: Talent nurtured in troubled times. *Roeper Review, 19,* 142–147.

Henderlong, J., & Lepper, M. R. (2002). The effects of praise on children's intrinsic motivation: A review and synthesis. *Psychological Bulletin, 128,* 774–795.

Henfield, M. S. (2006). *"I am a rarity in my school": Hidden obstacles for African Americans in gifted education.* Unpublished doctoral dissertation, The Ohio State University, Columbus.

Howard, J., & Hammond, R. (1985). Rumors of inferiority: The hidden obstacles to black success. *The New Republic, 193,* 16–21.

Howard, T. C. (2003). "A tug of war for our minds": African American high school students' perceptions of their academic identities and college aspirations. *The High School Journal, 87,* 4–17.

Jackson, J. F. L., & Moore, J. L., III. (2006). African American males in education: Endangered or ignored? *Teachers College Record, 108,* 201–205.

Karpicke, H., & Murphy, M. E. (1996). Productive school culture: Principals working from the inside. *National Association of Secondary School Principals, 80,* 26–32.

Lee, C. (2001). Culturally responsive school counselors and programs: Addressing the needs of all students. *Professional School Counseling, 4,* 257–261.

Lewis, C. W., & Moore, J. L., III. (2008). Editorial: African American students in K-12 urban educational settings. *Urban Education, 43,* 123–126.

Madison-Colmore, O., & Moore, J. L., III. (2002). Using the H.I.S. model in counseling

African-American men. *Journal of Men's Studies, 10,* 197–208.

Martin, P. J. (2002). Transforming school counseling: A national perspective. *Theory Into Practice, 41,* 148–153.

McInerney, D. M., Roche, L. A., McInerney, V., & Marsh, H. W. (1997). Cultural perspectives on school motivation: The relevance and application of Goal Theory. *American Educational Research Journal, 34,* 207–236.

Moore, J. L., III. (2003). Introduction. *The High School Journal, 87,* 1–3.

Moore, J. L., III. (2006). A qualitative investigation of African American males'career trajectory in engineering: Implications for teachers, school counselors, and parents. *Teachers College Record, 108,* 246–266.

Moore, J. L., III, Flowers, L. A., Guion, L. A., Zhang, Y., & Staten, D. L. (2004). Improving the experiences of non-persistent African American males in engineering programs: Implications for success. *National Association of Student Affairs Professionals Journal, 7,* 105–120.

Moore, J. L., III, Ford, D. Y., & Milner, H. R. (2005a). Recruitment is not enough: Retaining African American students in gifted education. *Gifted Child Quarterly, 49,* 51–67.

Moore, J. L., III, Ford, D. Y., & Milner, H. R. (2005b). Underachievement among gifted students of color: Implications for educators. *Theory Into Practice, 44,* 167–177.

Moore, J. L., III, Ford, D. Y., Owens, D., Hall, T., Byrd, M., Henfield, M., et al. (2006). Retention of African-Americans in gifted education: Lessons learned from higher education. *Mid-Western Educational Researcher, 19,* 3–12.

Moore, J. L., III, Henfield, M. S., & Owens, D. (2008). African America males in special education: Their attitudes and perceptions toward high school counselors and school counseling services. *American Behavioral Scientist, 51,* 907–927.

Moore, J. L., III, & Herndon, M. K. (2003). Guest editorial. *Journal of Men's Studies, 12,* 1–2.

Moore, J. L., III, Madison-Colmore, O., & Smith, D. M. (2003). The prove-them-wrong syndrome: Voices from unheard African-American males in engineering disciplines. *Journal of Men's Studies, 12,* 61–73.

National Center for Education Statistics. (2000). *The condition of education, 2000* (NCES 2000–062). Washington, DC: U.S. Department of Education, Government Printing Office.

National Center for Education Statistics. (2003). *Status and trends in the education of Blacks* (NCES 2003–034). Washington, DC: U.S. Department of Education, Government Printing Office.

Nobles, W. (1991). African philosophy: Foundations for Black psychology. In R. Jones (Ed.), *Black psychology* (3rd ed., pp. 47–53). Berkeley, CA: Cobb & Henry.

Ockerman, M. (2006). Unheard voices: Urban students' school experiences and their perceptions of the Ohio State Counseling and Wellness Center. Unpublished doctoral dissertation, The Ohio State University, Columbus.

Ogbu, J. U. (1988). Cultural diversity and human development. In D. Slaughter (Ed.), *Black children and poverty: A developmental perspective* (pp. 11–28). San Francisco: Jossey-Bass.

Ogbu, J. U. (2003). *Black American students in an affluent suburb: A study of academic disengagement.* Mahwah, NJ: Lawrence Erlbaum.

Orfield, G., & Lee, C. (2006). *Racial transformation and the changing nature of segregation.* Cambridge, MA: The Civil Rights Project at Harvard University.

Peterson-Lewis, S., & Bratton, L. M. (2004). Perceptions of "acting black" among African American teens: Implications of racial dramaturgy for academic and social achievement. *Urban Review, 36,* 81–100.

Reid, M. J., & Moore, J. L., III. (2008). College readiness and academic preparation for postsecondary education: Oral histories of first-generation urban college students. *Urban Education, 43,* 240–261.

Sanchez-Hucles, J. C. (2000). *The first session with African Americans: A step-by-step guide.* Indianapolis, IN: Jossey-Bass.

Sanders, M. G. (1997). Overcoming obstacles: Academic achievement as a response to racism and discrimination. *Journal of Negro Education, 66,* 83–93.

Schultz, G. F. (1993). Socioeconomic advantage and achievement motivation: Important mediators of academic performance in minority children in urban schools. *Urban Review, 25,* 221–232.

Shaffer, S., Ortman, P. E., & Denbo, S. J. (2002). The effects of racism, socioeconomic class, and gender on the academic achievement of African American students. In S. J. Denbo & L. Moore Beaulieu (Eds.), *Improving schools for African American students: A reader for educational leaders* (pp. 19–29). Springfield, IL: Charles C Thomas.

Smith, E. M. J. (1989). Black racial identity development. *The Counseling Psychologist, 17,* 277–288.

Spencer, M. B. (1984). Black children's race awareness, racial attitudes, and self-concept: A reinterpretation. *Journal of Child Psychology and Psychiatry, 25,* 433–441.

Spencer, M. B. (1985). Cultural cognition and social cognition as identity correlates on black children's personal-social development. In

M. B. Spencer, G. K. Brookins, & W. R. Allen (Eds.), *Beginnings: The social and affective development of black children* (pp. 215–234). Hillsdale, NJ: Erlbaum.

Spencer, M. B. (1988). Self-concept development. In D. T. Slaughter (Ed.), *Black children and poverty: A developmental perspective* (pp. 103–116). San Francisco: Jossey-Bass.

Steele, C. M. (1992, April). Race and the schooling of black Americans. *The Atlantic Monthly, 269,* 68–78.

Steele, C. M. (1997). A threat in the air. *American Psychologist, 52,* 613–629.

Steele, C. M. (1999). Thin ice: "Stereotype threat" and black college students. *The Atlantic Monthly, 284,* 44–47, 50–54.

Steele, C. M., & Aronson, J. (1995). Stereotype threat and the intellectual test performance of African-Americans. *Journal of Personality and Social Psychology, 69,* 797–811.

Sue, D. W., & Sue, D. (2003). *Counseling the culturally diverse: Theory and practice* (4th ed.). New York: Wiley.

Thernstrom, S., & Thernstrom, A. (2003). *No excuses: Closing the racial gap in learning.* New York: Simon & Schuster.

U.S. Department of Education. (2000). *Twenty-second annual report to Congress on the implementation of the Individuals with Disabilities Education Act.* Washington, DC: Government Printing Office.

U.S. Department of Education. (2001). *No Child Left Behind Act of 2001 (H. R. I.).* Washington, DC: Author.

U.S. Department of Education. (2003). *Overview of public elementary and secondary schools and districts: School year 2001–02: Statistical analysis report* (NCES 2003–411). Retrieved May 3, 2005, from http://nces.ed.gov/pubs2003/2003411.pdf

Vontress, C. E., & Epp, L. R. (1997). Historical hostility in the African American client: Implications for counseling. *Journal of Multicultural Counseling and Development, 25,* 170–184.

Ward, J. V. (1990). Racial identity formation and transformation. In C. Gilligan, N. D. Lyons, & T. J. Hanmer (Eds.), *Making connections: The relational worlds and adolescent girls at Emma Willard School* (pp. 215–238). Cambridge, MA: Harvard University Press.

23

THE EDUCATION OF AFRICAN AMERICAN CHILDREN IN CHARTER SCHOOLS

Four Case Studies

CAROL E. MALLOY

RICHARD NOBLE III

During the 2005–2006 school year, 3,617 charter schools (4% of the nation's public schools) were in operation in the United States with a total enrollment of 1,074,809 students. The number of students in charter schools was approximately equal to the number of students attending public schools in the state of Indiana or Washington (National Center for Educational Statistics [NCES], 2005c). African American students were 31% of this charter school population (NCES, 2005b). Although the actual number of students is not large in comparison with the total number of African American school-age children, the percentage becomes significant to the education of African American students when we observe that 31% of the students in charter schools are African Americans compared with 17% of the students in traditional public schools. Confounding the ratio even more are ratios of charter to traditional public schools for other populations of students—45% to 58% for Caucasian students and 20% to 19% for Hispanic students. Thus, the tendency of African American students to be enrolled in charter schools is greater than all other students. With the approval of an additional 90 charter schools due to open for the 2006–2007 school year (Center for Educational Reform, 2005), it is likely that the proportion of African American students attending charter schools will increase further.

As we reviewed these data, the following questions naturally came to our minds: What is happening in these charter schools? Why are African American parents opting for the charter school education over the traditional public school education? We were aware that national reports on achievement demonstrate that students in traditional public schools outperform students in charter schools on quantitative measures, and that national and local disaggregated achievement reports highlight the lagging academic achievement of African American students. Therefore, we decided to investigate the gravitation of African American parents toward charter schools. The overarching question in this research is why are African American parents opting for the charter school education over the traditional public school education for their children.

THEORETICAL PERSPECTIVES

To understand charter schools' educational programs, their cultural context of the school and educational programs, and their contributions and challenges, we began with the definition of school culture. *School culture* can be described as "the way we do things around here" (Bower, 1996). To present glimpses of school culture, we use "the expressed values and beliefs that were not necessarily observable but can be discerned by how people explain and justify what they do" (Matthews & Crow, 2003, p. 145). We overlaid school culture with Shujaa's (1994) definitions of schooling and education. Shujaa differentiated schooling from education, explaining that education is "the process of transmitting from one generation to the next knowledge of the values, aesthetics, spiritual beliefs, and all things that give a particular cultural orientation its uniqueness" (p. 15). It was a way for students to value and understand their communicative, structural, cultural, and strategic rules and rituals of society. However, Shujaa stated, "Schooling is a process intended to perpetuate and maintain the society's existing power relationships and the institutional structures that support those arrangements" (p. 15).

Our investigation of school culture, education, and schooling required the use of two different lenses. The first lens is pedagogical and is based on research (Dance, 1997; Hale-Benson, 1986; Hilliard, 1976; Shade, 1989; Willis, 1992) that shows students from different ethnic, cultural, and economic groups—students whose achievement, as groups, is below the total population—often approach learning differently. Traditionally, students have been encouraged to focus on detail, use sequential and structured thinking, recall abstract ideas and irrelevant detail, use inanimate materials, learn from formal lecture, achieve individually without group interaction, and value facts and principles. Pedagogy can and should be modified to

provide equitable learning opportunities to many students, including large numbers of African American students who have different preferences for learning.[1] Instruction to these students should encourage them to focus on the whole, use improvisational intuitive thinking, recall relevant verbal ideas, use socially oriented materials, learn from informal class discussion, achieve interdependently, and narrate human concepts (Dance, 1997; Hale-Benson, 1986; Hilliard, 1976; Shade, 1989; Willis, 1992).

The second lens is based on Bowers's (1987) approach to education and the politics of cultural change that argues that students should have access to complex knowledge as seen in the culture of the schools and their educational programs. Complex knowledge affords students the opportunity to (a) experience knowledge through complex language and concepts that is necessary for achievement within our society; (b) use abstraction and symbolic knowledge to help students become independent learners and critical thinkers; and (c) gain insight, knowledge, and understanding through inquiry and creativity. Instead of schools as institutions of cultural authority with total responsibility for student learning, these schools create an instructional culture that makes it possible for students to assume responsibility for learning. The assumption is that complex knowledge and understanding are requisite skills that are within the grasp of students. Development of complex knowledge in schools can result from providing students with a curriculum that not only contains the mandated content but also encourages and empowers students to reach their fullest potential as individuals and as participants in society. For example, a school could establish a learning environment that supports each learner's optimal development and growth in understanding. In such a school, students strengthen their own understandings and problem-solving skills by applying their ideas to real-world situations. Students would be allowed to investigate and challenge issues and relationships rather than being told what they should know. They would assess their own learning and thus understand that goal setting, problem solving, and decision-making skills are the necessary tools for their future success. Specifically, they would be given the opportunity to become responsible for their personal learning.

CONTEXT

Our research took place during the 2005–2006 school year in two cities within the same greater metropolitan area in a southeastern state of the United States. The state defines a *charter school* as a deregulated public school. Charter schools have freedom and flexibility in programs and curriculum, give parents choice, receive public funding, and must meet state achievement goals; however, these schools cannot charge tuition or discriminate. The state limits the number of charter schools to 100 and limits each school district or county to a maximum of 5 charter schools. The first 37 charter schools were approved during the summer of 1997. During the 2005–2006 academic year, there were 97 charter schools statewide causing the state to fall above the national mean for the number of charter schools per state. We used descriptive and interpretive methods to tell the stories of the schools, and a comparative design to synthesize the contributions and challenges to the education of African American students.

Participants

The four schools in this study had been in service at least 8 years and were located in two cities within the same metropolitan area, but in different adjacent counties. To provide a school population context, we present the 2005–2006 demographic information of districts and the four schools. Three schools,[2] Hawley Road, McDaniel, and Westfield, were situated within 3 miles of each other in residential areas of a city with a population of approximately 198,000 people. The county district serving this city had a student population of 31,719 students, 54% African American, 24% Caucasian, and 16% Hispanic. The fourth school, Lakeland, was located in the downtown area of a large city of approximately 320,000 people. The county district serving this city had a student population of 122,072 students, 26% African American, 55% Caucasian, and 9% Hispanic. Hawley Road served 185 students in Grades 6 through 10 who were 60% African American, 30% Caucasian, and 8% Hispanic. Fifty percent of the students, evenly distributed across race, came from low-socioeconomic status (SES) families. McDaniel served 335 students in Grades kindergarten to 8

who were over 99% African American. Eighty percent of students' families were low SES. Westfield served 220 students in Grades kindergarten to 7 who were over 99% African American. Ninety percent of students were from low-SES families. Lakeland Middle served 180 students in sixth to eighth grades who were approximately 78% Caucasian, 19% African American, 3% Latino, and less than 1% Asian. Less than 5% of all students' families, evenly distributed across race, were of low SES.

These schools were selected because they represented a range of charter school reform, had different foci, and had large to small enrollments of African American students. Two schools had always been successful on achievement measures of their students. Two schools fluctuated, but recently have been below state achievement and academic growth expectations.

Board member, teacher, parent, and student participants were recommended by school administrators and recruited by the researchers. A total of 52 school administrators, teachers, board members, and African American students and parents from the four charter schools participated in the study. Specific numbers of participants with available demographic information[3] in each category are presented in Table 23.1.

Procedures

A school's culture creates an environment where students can respond to the instruction afforded them. A charter school's culture—its beliefs, rituals, and common experiences—emanate from the vision of their founders. The construction of a school around beliefs and rituals is formalized when the proposal for the school is written and submitted to the state for approval. The four charter schools presented here used philosophy, mission, and/or structure as the foundation for the construction of their school's cultures. Paramount in these constructions were the beliefs of stakeholders, the enactment of valued rituals, and reactions to those rituals (Malloy, 2005). Therefore, data were gathered from observations of 17 classes (5 at Hawley Road, 4 at McDaniel, 4 at Westfield, 4 at Lakeland), and interviews with school administrators, teachers, students, parents, and board members. Demographic, school resource, and achievement data were gathered from school

TABLE 23.1   Number of Participants and Ethnicity by School

Schools	Students	Parents	Teachers	Board	Principal	Total
Hawley Road						
African American	2	2	1	—	—	5
Caucasian	—	—	4	1	1	6
McDaniel						
African American	3	4	2	—	1	10
Caucasian	—	—	2	2	—	4
Westfield						
African American	2	3	1	1	—	7
Caucasian	—	—	3	—	1	4
Lakeland						
African American	5	5	—	—	—	10
Caucasian	—	—	4	1	1	6
Total	12	14	17	5	4	52

documents and state and school Web pages. We observed classes and interviewed all participants with the exception of one board member and one principal who were interviewed by a colleague. Each school was provided an opportunity to review the second draft of the manuscript for misinterpretation of historical and programmatic information.

Instruments

Observations. We observed both the schools as a structure, student/teacher interactions in the halls, and classroom instruction. The 30- to 40-minute classroom observations were descriptive, not evaluative, using the lenses of complex knowledge and learning preferences of academic program emphasis, student and teacher roles, and students' learning tasks. We looked at the instructional strategies and interaction of students and teachers in the classroom concentrating on pedagogy, content, tasks, assessment, and interaction. Pedagogy included the focus of instruction lesson plans, the resulting flow of the lesson, and how students were given opportunities to learn. Content was seen in the objectives of lesson, including where the student is being led and allowed to advance and the knowledge that students should learn. Tasks represented work that students were engaged in during class and the opportunity students had to internalize

and connect ideas. Assessment included the ways in which the teacher determined what students had learned, specifically, evidence of student performance, the relation of student understanding to content being taught, feedback to students, and student involvement in critique. Interaction was the discourse that resulted from the instruction planned and modified by the teacher and initiated by the students.

Semistructured Interviews. One-hour individual interviews with school administrators and board members were held in schools or restaurants, and 1-hour focus group interviews with teachers, students, and parents were held at the schools. Two initial interviews had a second interviewer and were audiotape recorded to ensure that notes taken by the first researcher during the interviews captured all participant comments. After ensuring the quality of our notes, we discontinued the use of two interviewers and audiotape recorders. Questions asked of participants were modified from protocols used in previous evaluations of charter schools commissioned by the state. Participants in each subgroup were asked the same questions that were designed to obtain their perceptions about factors which included, but were not limited to, the organization, mission, and purpose of the school; academic and extracurricular programming; school success indicators; challenges to school success; challenges to teacher recruitment and retention; and funding and perceptions of charter versus traditional public schools.

Data Analysis

We analyzed data using qualitative methods that include case, comparative, and thematic analysis. Each school was described through cases as a unit using collected qualitative, demographic, school resource, and achievement data gathered from state and school Web pages. We reviewed data through thematic analysis procedures to find themes related to culture, challenges, contributions, and achievements across all the schools. Data were categorized using Miles and Huberman's (1994) matrix approach to qualitative analysis.

Case Summary

These four schools varied in educational program emphases and populations; however, all four schools established functioning schools with educational and extracurricular programs, teaching and support staff, students, and parents. Below we summarize our results by providing information regarding educational structures and programs, cultural contexts, academic achievements, contributions, and challenges of the four schools.

Educational Structures and Programs

Instructional programs in each of the schools were governed by state mandate and structured by school goals. Schools had similar administrative structures, with support staff for student services, testing, and extracurricular activities, and similar extracurricular activities. The schools were different in their use of fully developed philosophies to guide instructional and cultural activities. Lakeland used a Deweyan philosophy, and Hawley Road used a Paideia philosophy. Westfield and McDaniel did not have discernible overarching philosophies. We will address the impact of philosophies in our discussion.

Cultural Contexts

The culture of these schools is presented through the lens of African American students' education. To provide a composite school culture of the schools, we summarize the schools' expressed, demonstrated, and taken-for-granted values, beliefs, and actions and the assumptions that underlie them.

The schools' written goals elucidate their *values*, which included empowering students to become independent learners; providing all students with unlimited opportunities for development of their full potential; providing a positive, individualized learning experience with strong emphasis on academic achievement and community life; and/or helping students develop to their fullest potential. When asked, parents and staff explicitly stated that their schools valued trustworthiness, tolerance, discipline, learning, self-assessment, effort, and parental involvement. Parents added that teachers exhibited care, love of teaching, and love of their students.

The stated *beliefs* of staff were outgrowths of their values, which were grounded in student learning as the most important outcome of schooling. Teachers in each school stated that all students could learn and that their relationship with parents was essential to that learning. Acknowledging that many African American students did not perform well in testing situations, they used entrepreneurial leadership, global understanding, community involvement, character education, public speaking, and/or tolerance of differences as their platforms for knowledge coupled with inquiry-based pedagogy, a state guideline-driven curricula, and/or active group-learning opportunities. Even though instruction varied from school to school and classroom to classroom, teachers challenged students to think deeply and required student productions as an expression of knowledge. Staff of all four schools believed that their students strengthened their own understandings and problem-solving skills in an environment where they were able to apply their ideas to familiar and experienced contexts.

Underlying the values and beliefs were *assumptions* held by school staff, from the inception of the schools. Lakeland was started because the board assumed the global emphasis program was important for students to experience; however, the other three schools were started because parents were dissatisfied with the education their children were receiving and wanted to create an alternative to public schools in the area. The stated assumption of staff in these three schools was the following: *If many of their students were in traditional public schools, the schools would fail to reach and teach them.* Many parents (some from all schools) agreed with this assumption. They viewed their schools as safe places for their children to learn, flourish, and obtain a strong and viable education.

The *transmitted culture* of all the schools was that *no child is lost.* Based on our interviews, one parent who could have spoken for all participating parents stated, "This school exhausts every avenue to help students learn. They do not allow a child to get lost in the system." Parents felt that teachers knew and cared about each and every child and made students more responsible, that staff were responsive and personal, and that communication between the teacher/school and the parents was immediate and thoughtful. Parents believed that teachers felt like family and exemplified the African proverb: It takes a village to raise a child.

The 12 students interviewed understood the transmitted culture and described the schools in similar ways as parents and teachers. They understood that citizenship and the way they carried themselves outside of school, which included respect, sharing, earning good grades, and putting forth effort, were important. Students believed that the smallness of their schools made them safer and afforded them positive social experiences. Individual students spoke positively about the care their teachers had for their learning and safety. All 12 students interviewed said their schools were "very good."

From the comments of board members, principals, and teachers and the responses of parents and students to our questions about the schools, the intended cultures described on school Web pages and in school documents are realized by parents and students in the schools. We believe that these schools were successful in creating the cultures based on their values and beliefs. The schools' academic and social programs addressed some or all the recommendations for the education of African American students. We will provide more information in our discussion.

Academic Achievements

Student achievement is often the tool used by researchers to evaluate the academic success of schools and student groups. This was not our main intention; however, we are reporting achievement data to reveal similarities and differences in schools, populations, and opportunities. The 2004–2005 and 2005–2006 state assessment data for African American students in the charter schools, district schools, and all state schools revealed varied results (State School Report Cards, 2006, 2007). We are reporting 2 years of data to show growth in student achievement in reading. Growth cannot be demonstrated for mathematics because 2005–2006 assessments were revised substantively moving from skills-based to application-based items and because mathematics cutoff scores for at or above grade level were raised. Statewide results in mathematics scores were significantly lower for 2005–2006, causing the state to omit multiyear trends for mathematics on 2005–2006 reports.

The percentage of African American students who were at or above grade level in McDaniel, Hawley Road, and Westfield, City 1 traditional public schools, and in all state public schools are reported in Table 23.2. Data for 2005–2006 reveal that McDaniel and Westfield had lower percentages of African American students at or above grade level in reading and mathematics than City 1 or the state. These findings are consistent with nationally reported achievement differences between charter schools and traditional public schools for all students (Lubienski & Lubienski, 2006; NCES, 2005a). The percentage of Hawley Road African American students at or above grade level in reading and high school mathematics surpasses both City 1 and state. However, the percentage of students at or above grade level in elementary and middle-grade mathematics is lower than City 1 and the state. These findings both confirm and refute prior research. One important observation is the growth of McDaniel's students in reading.

The percentage of African American students who were at or above grade level in Lakeland, City 2 traditional public schools, and in all state public schools are reported in Table 23.3. Data for 2005–2006 reveal that Lakeland had a higher percentage of African American students who were at or above grade level than City 2 and the state in middle grades mathematics.[4] This is inconsistent with reported differences in achievement results between charter schools and traditional public schools. Lakeland and City 2 reading results are almost identical, while the percentage of Lakeland students who are at or above grade level reading is slightly higher than the state percentage.

TABLE 23.2   Percentage of African American Students at or Above Grade Level in Three Charters, City 1, and State Schools

Assessment	Hawley	McDaniel	Westfield	City 1	State
Reading[a]					
2004–2005	72.3	47.6	63.6	73.2	74.7
2005–2006	80.9	57.8	63.9	72.8	75.3
Mathematics[a]					
2004–2005	63.1	53.0	58.3	75.1	77.5
2005–2006	36.2	20.3	25.6	41.8	42.6
High school[b]					
2004–2005	42.9	–	–	52.7	55.8
2005–2006	57.8	–	–	41.8	42.6

NOTES: a. End of grade test in Grades 3 to 8, mathematics and reading; b. End of course tests for high school subjects.

TABLE 23.3   Percentage of African American Students at or Above Grade Level in Lakeland, City 2, and State Schools

Assessment	Lakeland	City 2	State
Reading[a]			
2004–2005	88.9	79.1	74.7
2005–2006	79.5	79.7	75.3
Mathematics[a]			
2004–2005	92.6	80.2	77.5
2005–2006	69.6	48.5	42.6
High school[b]			
2004–2005	>95	64.3	55.8
2005–2006	NA	60.1	52.9

NA = Not available.
NOTES: a. End-of-grade test in Grades 3 to 8, mathematics and reading; b. End-of-course tests for high school subjects taken in middle grades.

From these data, it is clear that two schools were successful in helping students achieve academic success, while two schools—those with 99% African American students—were not successful. To understand differences in achievement may require consideration of the recruited and served populations in the schools. Numerous reports indicate that SES is a stronger predictor of school achievement than race (Dills, 2006; Harman, Bingham, & Hood, 2002; Lubienski & Lubienski, 2006; NCES, 2005a); thus, we include information on the explicitly recruited populations of students in each school. Table 23.4 presents socioeconomic information and availability of transportation to and from school for the four

schools in this study. Qualitative data revealed, and state enrollment data confirmed, that McDaniel and Westfield recruited students who were academically at-risk and from low-SES families. These schools provided free lunch and transportation and had lower percentages of students achieving at grade level. Hawley Road and Lakeland used word-of-mouth as recruitment, employed a lottery system for admittance, did not provide transportation or free lunch, and had higher percentages of students achieving at grade level. Access to transportation and SES could be influencing factors in parents' selection of charter schools and the resulting populations that these charter schools serve.

TABLE 23.4   Population, Ethnicity, and Socioeconomic Information for Four Charter Schools

Schools	Student Population	Population Percentages				Percent Low SES	Free Bus and Lunch
		African American	Caucasian	Hispanic	Other		
Hawley	185	60	30	8	0	50	No
McDaniel	335	>99	<1	0	0	80	Yes
Westfield	220	>99	<1	<1	0	90	Yes
Lakeland	180	19	78	3	<1	<5	No

Contributions

Common themes in contributions from interviews with parents, teachers, administrators, and board members were (a) interactions among parents, teachers, and students; (b) creation of nurturing environments; (c) small class size; and (d) academic programs. Participants from three schools also cited student achievement; and participants from two schools mentioned physical plants and endurance. We briefly summarize each contribution with understanding that some are interrelated.

Interactions. Teachers in all schools implemented positive structures that would allow them to often communicate effectively with students and parents about expectations, accomplishments, and concerns. As a result, parents and students reciprocated with initiated communications with teachers. These interactions promoted student learning.

Nurturing Environment. The environment established in the schools was a result of the culture of the schools. Because of the nurturing and caring environment in the schools, parents in all schools explained that their children felt valued and important in their schools and that their children were better people.

Small Class Size. The four schools implemented an average teacher-student ratio of 1:15, which is 30% lower than the ratio of 1:21 in the traditional school districts in their counties. Small class size can promote a nurturing, caring, open, and safe learning environment.

Academic Programs. Each school had an academic or instructional focus. However, all the schools developed academic programs designed to strengthen students' weaknesses and enrich their strengths. Specific programs mentioned were global awareness, after-school and summer programs, honor societies and academic teams, grants for a reading program, and community service projects. The programs, presented in detail within the cases, were broad and comprehensive.

Student Achievement. Participants in each school, except McDaniel, spoke proudly about the achievements of their students from state testing results to participation on academic teams. It is understandable that participants from Lakeland and Hawley Road would be proud of student achievement because their students performed well on state assessments. Parents from Westfield also were pleased because they could see improvement in their children's learning. Their children had struggled with learning in traditional public schools.

Physical Plants. School facilities were seen as essential in creating a safe environment appropriate for student learning. In the past, all schools felt constrained by limited and inadequate building space. Many space concerns were resolved but with increased debt for most of the schools. Westfield and Lakeland had relatively new buildings, McDaniel moved into an adequate church facility, and Hawley Road was moving to a newly constructed site in the fall of 2006.

Endurance. Even though none of the participants in the four schools spoke of their survival as charter schools as a contribution, they talked about their pride in the fact that they were still functioning and serving students. At the time of this research, the schools had experienced 8 to

10 years as charter schools, and awards of new 10-year charter contracts allowed them to continue trying to educate students who needed a different approach to teaching and learning.

Sports Teams. Whereas participants in only one school mentioned sports teams as a contribution, athletic programs were essential in the development of elementary, middle, and high school students. All the schools had at least one extracurricular sports program, which were budgetary challenges for the schools.

The contributions presented above are important to the education of African American students as they enhance the instructional strategies that help these students thrive. Three schools, Hawley Road, Westfield, and McDaniel, enroll students whom they believe might fall through the cracks in traditional public schools, and these schools try to help their students succeed through educational programs. Hawley Road was successful academically, while Westfield and McDaniel were successful in helping students understand and feel that they were able to learn. Lakeland students have always achieved academically, and African American students contributed to the school's academic success. Academically, two African American students, one at Hawley Road and one at Lakeland, were accepted into and attended the state's specialized high school for gifted students in science and mathematics.

Challenges

Board members, principals, and teachers mentioned challenges associated with charter schools in three main categories—funding, teacher recruitment, and a stable student population. In particular, Westfield and McDaniel experienced significant challenges in each of these categories: funding, teacher recruitment, and a stable student population. Consistent with much of the literature regarding charter schools (Education Commission of the States, 2007), participants in all schools expressed similar funding issues. Moreover, the schools did not receive capital funds, and did not receive money from the state lottery, which was allocated for capital improvements. Board members from all four schools discussed the need for more funding and the unfair educational allotments provided to

charter schools. A board member from McDaniel captured the sentiments of the four boards related to funding in the following manner:

They treat charters schools as though they were orphaned children and thus have to do what the state says. For instance, lottery money was not shared with charter schools. Federal fund allocation goes directly to charter schools, but the county's allocation of local funds was sent to the local school district and the school district gives an allocation to the county schools. This year the county allocation was $2,750, but the charter school only got $2,540 per child. No monies were given for books. Charter schools were not getting their money systemically. As a result, they have to do much more with less.

Because of such disparities in distribution of funds, various aspects of daily school routines were affected, such as transportation, facilities, and services to students with special needs. Westfield and McDaniel had to transport 50% to 75% of the students to maintain enrollment. Because little to no public transportation existed for Lakeland and Hawley Road, transportation was also a challenge. Parents had to transport their children to and from school, causing many to carpool. Three schools had mortgages that had to be paid from the student allotment funds reducing available funding for educational programs. Additionally, Westfield and McDaniel experienced challenges providing funding for services to unidentified students who required special education services.

Westfield and McDaniel experienced challenges in teacher recruitment and professional development. With growing student enrollments, there was a definite need for more qualified teachers. In addition to the recruitment of teachers, professional training programs needed to be established to help teachers not only work with the educational challenges facing many students at these charter schools but also to work with parents.

Finally, there were instructional challenges associated with students centering primarily on student recruitment and students' required meeting academic standards. Many schools felt that they were making good efforts to educate students; however, Westfield and McDaniel experienced academic challenges related to population stability because they served transient populations. The cycle of students entering school below grade level academically, improving in achievement while at their schools, and then moving to other schools made it more difficult to attain the level of school progress desired by the state and stakeholders of the institution.

Summary

These four schools had similar educational structures, cultural contexts, contributions, and challenges. They were different in their use of fully developed philosophies to guide all instructional and cultural activities. The transmitted culture of each school was that *no child is lost.* Two schools were successful in helping students achieve academic success, while two schools, those with 99% African American students, were not successful. Of the four schools, only the two schools that were unsuccessful in achievement experienced significant challenges in each of the identified challenge categories: funding, teacher recruitment, and a stable student population. A discussion of the impact of similarities and differences is presented below.

DISCUSSION

In this section, we first discuss the overriding similarity of the four schools—participants referring to their school communities as "villages" either directly or through descriptions of school values. Next, we discuss how the development of educational philosophies and challenges may contribute to differences in academic success based on state-mandated assessments. Finally, we discuss why African American parents in this study chose charter schools for their children.

CHARTERS BECOME A VILLAGE

The proverb, "It takes a village to raise a child," has as its source a Swahili proverb from East Africa, MKONO MMOJA HAULEI MWANA, translated as "one hand cannot bring up a child (or, cannot nurse a child). Child upbringing was a communal effort" (Scheven, 1981, p. 123, cited in Farsi, 1958). Teachers and parents in this study referred to the village as a way to describe the closeness of the charter schools we investigated.

They spoke of family-like relationships, of nurturing and caring, and of providing character and discipline.

The enactment of the village was overtly seen at Westfield and McDaniel, which had 99% African American student populations. Participants in these schools talked about school values and traditions, and the transmission of values to their students. They also expressed the belief that the staff were committed and sincere in their efforts to foster character development, build self-esteem, and positively motivate the students. Accordingly, the staff engaged the students in frank conversations about life, and helped them understand the contributions of African American people to the world. These were values similar to values and actions of teachers in old segregated schools and community members within the African Village.

African American parents, children, and their teachers had concerns that American society sends messages that African American students cannot achieve the academic success of other ethnic and racial groups. A teacher at McDaniel verbalized this concern, relating her childhood education to the education offered at McDaniel saying,

> I graduated from a school that was all black. And it was just a family. That's what it was. And so teachers, and we're parents too, but the teacher was just an extension of home almost. . . . I think McDaniel was basically doing that same thing for African Americans. Teachers do that for the kids here. . . . I know I do this often, all the time, I'm trying to instill in this kid that it's possible, "you can, you don't give up, keep on, keep at it." And I think that was a piece of the schools before integration, before they became so big, before they stopped being community schools. (Teacher, McDaniel)

Lakeland and Hawley Road schools imparted social and citizenship values similar to the values this teacher expressed. They encouraged young people to respect differences, appreciate similarities, and make connections with the people of the world. Teachers required participation in community service projects, strove to develop the whole child, and instilled in their students the value of citizenship and effort. Parents explained that while the teachers and staff were predominately Caucasian, they worked well with their children. Hawley parents expressed appreciation for two African American male teachers who were role models for their sons and had values similar to their family values.

The goals of these schools were "to create independent learners, critical and creative thinkers, and active and responsible participants in a global society" and "to motivate all students to reach their full potential." Operationalizing school goals through their Deweyan or Paideia philosophies, teachers' messages to all students, including African American students were about life and values, not just instruction. A Hawley Road teacher explained,

> We feel like the kids learn. It was a rare day when we have not taught them something. Kids feel that we care about them. Given the kids we have with their difficulties, I don't always feel successful academically, but the care and conversation about what needs to be done—I know the messages will be a part of who they are. They will remember! This atmosphere will bear fruit. (Teacher, Hawley Road)

Although there were no conversations about neighborhoods as villages, the spirit of the village was apparent. Parents had direct contact with teachers through e-mails, drop-offs and pick-ups, parent meetings, and field trips. As a result, parents felt that their children became accountable for their behavior. Students understood that their teachers and school cared about them, and they became confident.

Our results reveal that the transmitted culture for all four schools was, no child is lost, confirming African American parents' desire for rigorous academic standards, higher expectations, safer environments, and a sense of community (Murrell, 1999; Reid, 2001; Viteritti, 2002). As inspiring as the ideals of old community schools and the African village *are* in helping African American students understand their potential, the implementation of academic instructional programs to help improve student achievement requires more from the community or village. It requires school programs designed to address learning needs and preferences of African American children. The next section discusses how education in these schools attempted to accomplish education of African American students in their schools.

EDUCATIONAL PHILOSOPHIES AND CHALLENGES

The four charter schools created academic programs designed to educate all their students, not just the African American students. The education that was offered to students at Lakeland and Hawley Road used varied methods, varied demonstrations of knowledge, and varied contexts for learning, and supported preferences for African American student learning.[5] The schools expected that students could move beyond just knowledge. Using different words, but with the same meaning, the purpose of these schools was to establish a learning environment that supported each learner's optimal development and growth in understanding. Lakeland used their Deweyan philosophy to develop a curriculum and guide instruction based on Lakeland's "understanding of how young adolescents learn best. With an integrated, interdisciplinary approach in all areas other than mathematics, it strives to create independent learners, critical and creative thinkers, and active and responsible participants in a global society" (School Web page, 2006). Hawley Road's instructional philosophy was based on the Paideia principles that include that (a) all students can learn and (b) the results of the three types of teaching (didactic, coaching, and seminar facilitation) should be the acquisition of organized knowledge, the formation of habits of skill in the use of language and mathematics, and the growth of the mind's understanding of basic ideas and issues (School Web page, 2006).

Recognizing that knowledge existed within the learner, teachers and administrators were permitted time and resources to develop personal schemas for pedagogy and curriculum based on their experiences. For different reasons—population of students, freedom, school programs, new knowledge on learning—Lakeland and Hawley Road teachers were effective in developing pedagogy, curriculum, and norms for interaction that required students to take responsibility for their learning. Students did not always adapt quickly to the instructional norms of these schools. Teachers worked constantly with students to understand classroom norms and to develop instructional behaviors for self-directed and group activities. Students learned to be self-directive, attentive, and focused in their studies. Students said they were used to "sitting down listening to the teacher telling us what not to do instead of what we can do." They had to get used to determining the rules, setting goals, and selecting appropriate activities to learn concepts. Students knew that they were being taught to be independent thinkers and learners, and some students continued to fight against this freedom. Most students understood the instructional cultures that their schools had created. They understood that their schools were about learning complex knowledge, where they experienced knowledge necessary for achievement within our society and became independent learners and critical thinkers (Bowers, 1987). And their teachers were there to help them learn.

The education offered to students at Westfield and McDaniel was similar to that in the traditional public schools in instructional delivery, but not similar in content and process. Westfield students were taught through project-based learning, and teachers concentrated on reading mastery and using a variety of teaching methods, with special emphasis on constructivism. Students participated in junior achievement and career forums with local community groups, and the upper-grade students were taught about entrepreneurial leadership. McDaniel applied and obtained a $2-million grant to train teachers to teach reading scientifically, resulting in improved reading scores during the first year. In recent years, McDaniel made concentrated efforts to move away from teacher-centered instruction to more inquiry-based learning and to incorporate project-based learning through science and math fairs. The teachers described their practice as using whole group and small group instruction that was assessment driven, providing differentiated instruction and focusing on higher-order thinking skills. Both schools had a set of programs that addressed students' learning, but we could not determine the overarching philosophy and learning goals that were driving their instructional programs. Based on state achievement data, the education offered to McDaniel and Westfield was not as successful for all students.

Several organizational challenges existed at Westfield and McDaniel that may contribute to their achievement record. First, both Westfield and McDaniel experienced instability in the most critical areas of funding, administration,

and teacher attrition in their 8 years as charter schools. All schools expressed general funding issues with an emphasis on capital funding for facilities; however, at the time of this research, Lakeland and Hawley Road schools remained in the same location, while Westfield and McDaniel schools had changed locations at least three times. Both Westfield and McDaniel schools had substantial mortgages associated with their physical plants. The administrators in each charter school had changed at least once since the schools opened, but Lakeland and Hawley Road school leaders, at the time of this research, had been teachers in their schools for at least 8 years. Westfield had an interim organizational structure. McDaniel hired a principal who had not been affiliated with the school and had to become familiar with school organization, policy, and culture. During the year prior to our research, Westfield and McDaniel also had higher teacher attrition rates than Lakeland and Hawley Road, which required not only finding new teachers but also enculturating new teachers into the schools. As with all schools (public and private) in transition, it is likely that the instability that Westfield and McDaniel experienced required the schools to expend energies on stabilizing organizational structures rather than on developing instructional programs.

Second, Westfield and McDaniel were not located in areas close to neighborhoods where students lived, thus impeding parent participation in school life. More than 50% of the students in both schools were bused from their neighborhoods to school, which meant that parents did not have transportation available to be involved in the day-to-day education of their children. One school was located at the edge of a middle-to-upper-class neighborhood and the other was located in a commercial/residential area. Even with comprehensive communication opportunities, parents were not visible in the schools.

Third, principals at Westfield and McDaniel schools stated that many children who enrolled in their schools were behind academically when they arrived and that it would take years to help them catch up and then sustain growth, but parents often moved their children through school shopping[6] or the desire for more comprehensive educational or athletic opportunities. Whether enrollment remained fairly constant, increased, or decreased, McDaniel and Westfield had a continuous flow of students in and out of their schools. A McDaniel board member suggested that parents viewed charter schools as a place to send their children "who need to be fixed." When children were repaired, they moved them back to the traditional public school because parents seemed to believe that their children's growth would continue. They did not understand that, for many children, sustained and continued growth required consistency in educational programs. Parents' underlying beliefs seemed to be that charter schools were better; however, some parents were lured to public schools for the more extensive electives and sports programs.

The fourth factor was a recent population shift. Teachers believed that recently their student population had increased to include larger numbers of students with serious social and learning needs. To support their student populations, Westfield and McDaniel schools expanded special education and hired student services staff; however, they were still overwhelmed with student problems associated with behavior and academic achievement.

The challenges discussed in this section were real and cannot be taken lightly; they are acknowledged constraints to the education of African American students in these schools. In our interviews, the leaders of McDaniel and Westfield were open about these challenges. They explained that they worked to stabilize funding, administration, and teaching staff. They also recognized the need to improve social and instructional programs to address the education of their student populations. The combination of a nurturing environment, restructured curriculum, and strong instructional program is certainly promising for these goals.

Why Do Parents Choose Charter Schools?

People choose to leave our traditional public schools and bring their kids somewhere else. . . . That, in itself, says I'm concerned. If my kid was not doing well in traditional public schools, a lot of times for whatever reason—be it academic or behavioral—a parent then decides I'm going to take action because I know my kid was floundering or my child was not being productive. I need to do something. That says

to me that this was a parent who has the best interest of the child at heart. And that's how kids get to public charter schools. Somebody's made a choice to say I don't fit into this particular mold that's been set for everybody else. I have to do something else in order to see that my child was successful and this was what I'm going to do. (Teacher, McDaniel)

In response to the question posed at the start of this chapter, we begin with traditional public schools. Most students in these charter schools or their siblings had spent some time in the traditional public schools. Parents explained that they moved their children from traditional public schools for instructional and learning concerns, including inequitable education afforded their children, low teacher and school expectations for African American students, the failure of schools to address specific learning problems of their children, the size of schools, high student-to-teacher ratios in the classroom, and safety. Parents stated that achievement issues their children experienced at traditional public schools were instrumental in their consideration of charter schools. Hawley Road, McDaniel, and Westfield parents felt that the traditional public schools were not educating their children. Even though students at Westfield and McDaniel, at the time of this research, did not achieve at the level of students in traditional public schools on state-mandated assessments, parents felt that their charter schools were instrumental in teaching their children to read, which helped them learn in other content areas and that traditional public schools did not accomplish this goal. Lakefield parents selected charters to enable their children to maintain their level of achievement as they transitioned into middle school because they were uncomfortable with large middle schools. Because of concerns about traditional public schools, both low- and middle-income parents implied that they were looking for a private education in a public setting. One parent expressed the views of many parents saying, "It [the school] has the feel of a private school without having to pay. It was more like a family in the way that they treat my son. . . . Everyone was responsible for the students." These parents were looking for the best possible education for their children, and they believed that education was in charter schools and not in traditional public schools.

These African American parents choose charter schools because they believed that their children received a better, fairer, and more comprehensive education in charter schools than they received in traditional public schools. Better because their children were safe, had smaller school populations and class sizes, and learned. Fairer because teachers knew, cared about, and understood how their children learned. More comprehensive because the schools' curricular programs fulfilled the requirements of the state guidelines and imparted citizenship and service values that matched the values of their families. These findings support prior research that indicates that parents who are dissatisfied with traditional public schools see charter schools as alternatives for the education of their children (Murrell, 1999; Reid, 2001; Viteritti, 2002). Parents in this study did not compare current achievement data of traditional public schools to their charter schools; they were pleased that their children were learning in their charter schools. They spoke of looking for a school where their children could receive an education that they believed would prepare them for the future. These parents were looking for an *education,* as described by Shujaa (1994), not schooling. Many seemed to have found the school village in these charter schools.

Concluding Comments

Although these four charter schools represented a very small sample of charter schools in the United States, their stories shed light on how parents believed charter schools added value to the education of African American students. Charter schools are not the only schools that have the ability to add value or personify the family/community atmosphere. Schools with strong instructional and organizational structures, small size, less bureaucracy, commitment, passion, and creativity—important components of these schools can also make educational strides with African American students. It was also clear that these schools were not perfect institutions. Some struggled with student achievement, recruitment, funding, parental involvement, and consistent leadership. Nevertheless, parents who selected charter schools for their children were generally pleased with the education their children received, and indicated that they would struggle

to find high schools where their African American children would continue to flourish.

At the start of this research, because of the disparity between traditional public schools and charter school achievement, the first author had mixed feelings about charter school education as a viable means of educating African American students. The second author had not formulated a position on charter schools and African American students. However, we both have learned that these charter schools can add significantly to the education of African American students. These schools attempted to nurture students in ways that would help them to understand that they are capable and can, in fact, achieve their learning and career goals.

Notes

1. For more information on this topic, see Malloy (1997) and Malloy and Malloy (1998).

2. All school names were pseudonyms.

3. SES data were not collected from parents and students.

4. In 2005–2006, there were no reported mathematics percentages for Lakeland students who were enrolled in high school courses.

5. Teachers (a) acknowledged and used individual student preferences in acquisition of knowledge; (b) developed activities that promote discourse within the classroom among students and between the students and teacher; (c) valued student discourse and verbal knowledge; (d) created interdependent learning communities within the classroom; and (e) encouraged, supported, and provided feedback to students as they learned (Malloy, 2004).

6. School shopping, defined by Westfield administrators, was parents' movement of their children from one charter school to another in their search for a more desirable or agreeable school.

References

Bower, M. (1996). *Will to manage.* New York: McGraw-Hill.

Bowers, C. A. (1987). *The promise of theory: Education and the politics of cultural change.* New York: Teachers College Press.

Center for Educational Reform. (2005). *National charter school data.* Retrieved February 17, 2005, from www.edreform.com/index.cfm?fuse Action=stateStats&pSectionID=15&c SectionID=44

Dance, R. (1997, May). *Modeling: Changing the mathematics experience in post-secondary classrooms.* Paper presented at The Nature and Role of Algebra in the K-14 Curriculum: A National Symposium, Washington, DC.

Dills, A. K. (2006). *Trends in the relationship between socioeconomic status and academic achievement.* Retrieved February 24, 2006, from http://ssrn.com/abstract=886110

Education Commission of the States. (2007). *Charter school funding: Inequity's next frontier.* Retrieved August 11, 2007, from www.ecs.org/html/IssueSection.asp?issueid=20&s=Selected+Research+%26+Readings

Farsi, S. S. (1958). *Swahili sayings for Zanzibar, Vol. 1: Proverbs.* Nairobi, Kenya: East African Literature Bureau.

Hale-Benson, J. (1986). *Black children: Their roots, culture, and learning styles.* Baltimore: Johns Hopkins Press.

Harman, P., Bingham, C. S., & Hood, A. (2002). *An exploratory examination of North Carolina charter schools and their impact on Caucasian-minority achievement gap reduction.* Paper presented at the annual meeting of the American Educational Research Association, New Orleans, LA.

Hilliard, A. G. (1976). *Alternatives to IQ testing: An approach to the identification of gifted minority children.* Sacramento: Final Report to California State Department of Education.

Lubienski, C., & Lubienski, S. T. (2006). *Charter, private, public schools and academia achievement: New evidence from NAEP Mathematic data.* New York: National Center for the Study of Privatization in Education.

Malloy, C. E. (1997). Including African-American students in the mathematics community. In J. Trentacosta & M. Kenney (Eds.), *1997 NCTM yearbook: Multicultural and gender equity in the mathematics classroom: The gift of diversity* (pp. 23–33). Reston, VA: NCTM.

Malloy, C. E. (2004). Equity in mathematics education is about access. In R. Rubenstein & G. Bright (Eds.), *2004 NCTM Yearbook: Effective mathematics teaching* (pp. 1–14). Reston, VA: NCTM.

Malloy, C. E. (2005). Contradictions in culture: African American students in two charter schools. In W. T. Pink & G. W. Noblit (Eds.), *Transforming the culture of schools: Lessons learned from field studies of several leading reform strategies.* Cresskill, NJ: Hampton Press.

Malloy, C., & Malloy, W. (1998). Issues of culture in mathematics teaching and learning. *Urban Review, 30*(3), 245–257.

Matthews, L. J., & Crow, G. M. (2003). *Being and becoming a principal.* Boston: Pearson.

Miles, M. B., & Huberman, A. M. (1994). *Qualitative data analysis: A sourcebook of new methods.* Thousand Oaks, CA: Sage.

Murrell, P. C., Jr. (1999). Chartering the village: The making of an African-centered charter school. *Urban Education, 33,* 565–583.

National Center for Educational Statistics. (2005a). *America's charter schools: Results from the NAEP 2003 pilot study.* Retrieved February 24, 2006, from http://nces.ed.gov/nationasrport card/studies/charter/population_table.asp

National Center for Educational Statistics. (2005b). *America's charter schools: Who attends charter schools?* Retrieved February 24, 2006, from http://nces.ed.gov/nationasrportcard/studies/charter/more.asp

National Center for Educational Statistics. (2005c). *State profiles.* Retrieved June 14, 2006, from http://nces.ed.gov/nationasrportcard/states/profile.asp

North Carolina Report Cards. (2006). *Report cards of districts.* Retrieved July 18, 2006, from www.ncreportcards.org/src/search.jsp?pYear=2005-2006

North Carolina Report Cards. (2007). *Report cards of districts.* Retrieved July 7, 2007, from www.ncreportcards.org/src/search.jsp?pYear=2006-2007

Reid, K. S. (2001). Minority parents quietly embrace school choice. *Education Week, 21,* 5–13.

Scheven, A. (1981). *Swahili proverbs.* Washington, DC: University Press of America.

Shade, B. (1989). The influence of perceptual development on cognitive style: Cross ethnic comparisons. *Early Child Development and Care, 15,* 137–155.

Shujaa, M. (1994). *Too much schooling, too little education.* Trenton, NJ: Africa World Press.

Viteritti, J. P. (2002). Coming around on school choice. *Educational Leadership, 59,* 44–48.

Willis, M. G. (1992). Learning styles of African-American children: Review of the literature and interventions. In A. Kathleen, H. Burlew, W. Curtis Banks, H. P. McAdoo, & D. A. Azibo (Eds.), *African-American psychology: Theory, research, practice* (pp. 260–278). Newbury Park, CA: Sage.

24

DISPROPORTIONALITY OF AFRICAN AMERICAN CHILDREN IN SPECIAL EDUCATION

Definition and Dimensions

GWENDOLYN CARTLEDGE

CHARLES DUKES

Discussions and considerations about the disproportionality of students from diverse racial and ethnic backgrounds in special education have persisted for more than four decades. Since the publication of Dunn's groundbreaking paper in 1968, scholars have formulated well-grounded theories, followed by rigorous inquiries into the meaning and impact of disproportionate representation of particular students in special education. The *special education* label suggests that there is some disorder within the child and, accordingly, a need for more resources such as specialized instruction and other therapeutic interventions. Ideally, special education will improve pupil performance; however, positive outcomes have been seriously questioned for many students (e.g., Donovan & Cross, 2002; Dunn, 1968). Some authorities posit that disability diagnoses are likely to result in lowered expectations, thereby reducing special education simply to a place where students are sent when they do not perform (Meyer & Patton, 2001) rather than a service elevating learners to higher levels of performance.

Children with disabilities may be viewed according to two major categories: (1) high incidence and (2) low incidence. High-incidence disabilities are also referred to as mild disabilities and include the subcategories of learning disabilities (LD), emotionally disturbed (ED), mild mental retardation (MMR), and speech and language disorders. Low-incidence disabilities are more severe in nature and include conditions such as sensory disorders (visual and hearing impairments), moderate to severe mental retardation, physical disabilities, and autism. The high- and low-incidence categories might also be distinguished, respectively, by "clinical judgment" and biological factors (Harry & Klinger, 2006). That is, the diagnosis for mild disabilities is relatively subjective, while low-incidence disabilities are based on medical assessments. Harry and Klinger further offered the opinion that high-incidence disabilities are rather arbitrary but often viewed as a permanent state.

Minority students, particularly African, Hispanic, and Native Americans, typically have higher rates of special education identification compared with their European American counterparts (e.g., Valenzuela, Copeland, Qi, & Park, 2006). Donovan and Cross (2002) gave the following special education identification rates according to racial/ethnic groups: 5% Asian/Pacific Islander, 11% Hispanics, 12% Whites, 13% American Indian, and 14% Blacks. Although African Americans have a greater representation in every disability area, the disproportionality is particularly pronounced in the high-incidence areas (Harry & Klingner, 2006).

HIGH-INCIDENCE DISPROPORTIONALITY

Mental retardation is the area of greatest over-representation. African Americans make up 17% of the general pupil population but comprise 33% of all the students assigned to programs for the mentally retarded (Donovan & Cross, 2002). This means that 2.64% of African American students are so diagnosed, compared with 1.18% of European American students, and that African American students are more than twice as likely as European Americans to be labeled *mentally retarded*. Although these are national data, the percentages can vary greatly according to region. In Virginia, for example, African Americans make up 20% of the student population, 28% of the special education population but 51% of the students in programs for MMR (Ladner & Hammons, 2001). Another variation noted by these and other authors (e.g., Oswald, Coutinho, Best, & Singh, 1999; Valenzuela et al., 2006) is that the percentages of African American special education students may be greater in districts where the overall African American population is lower and/or the district is more affluent.

Such findings underscore the subjectivity that enters in the process of identifying students for mild disabilities. Harry and Klingner (2006) cited the National Academy of Sciences (NAS) panel, pointing out the extreme difficulties of attempting to diagnose students with mild disabilities when complex issues of culture and quality schooling enter in. Harry and Klinger used this NAS position as the focus of their book and stated,

> We argue that the process of determining children's eligibility for special education is anything but a science. Rather, it is the result of social forces that intertwine to construct an identity of "disability" for children whom the regular-education system finds too difficult to serve. (p. 9)

Not only are African American students over-represented in special education programs, they also tend to receive the most restrictive educational placements. Documentation from various sources points out that compared with their European American counterparts, African American students with disabilities are much less likely to be educated in settings where they access general education conditions and curriculum (e.g., Fierros & Conroy, 2002; Skiba, Poloni-Staudinger, Gallini, Simmons, & Feggins-Azzis, 2006; Valenzuela et al., 2006). Fierros and Conroy, for example, reported 1998 Office of Civil Rights data showing only 37% of African American students in special education were taught in inclusive settings, while 33% were served in substantially self-contained classes. In contrast, 55% of European American students were taught in inclusive settings, with only 16% restricted to self-contained classes. Similarly, in a review of statewide data in Indiana, Skiba et al. (2006) found that African American students in ED were 1.2 times more likely to be taught in self-contained special classes compared with their European American peers, those in MMR 1.5 times more likely, and those in LD 3.2 times more likely. Stated differently, African Americans made up 13% of the students in special education but only represented 8.4% of those in general education settings, while they made up 27% of those in separate classes. In their analyses of these data, the authors highlighted the finding that the greatest discrepancies and restrictiveness were in categories that typically provide services in less restrictive settings (e.g., LD). According to Skiba et al. (2006), this outcome argues against the notion espoused by the Office of Special Education Programs that the greater restrictiveness of African American students is likely due to their tendency to fall in disability categories that tend to provide services in more restrictive categories. In every disability category, African American students are found disproportionately in the most restrictive settings (Skiba et al., 2006).

Beyond classroom restrictiveness, other researchers note that compared with their European American counterparts, African American students with ED were found to receive fewer appropriate services such as counseling (Osher, Woodruff, & Sims, 2002) and more likely to be referred to the juvenile justice system (Parrish, 2002). These findings relative to restrictiveness appear to be in violation of IDEA 2004, which is predicated on the principle of least restrictive environments for students with disabilities. Ferri and Connor (2005) asserted that because the least restrictive environment provisions of IDEA are interpreted on a case-by-case basis, they offer a loophole to avoid integrated placements. They also viewed this as a civil rights issue and equated the lack of inclusion of African American students with the lack of progress for desegregation. The basis for this restrictiveness is unclear but needs to be explored along with the reasons for special education disproportionality.

DISPROPORTIONALITY AND GENDER

Researchers consistently point out that males are more likely to be identified for special education compared with females (Coutinho & Oswald, 2005; Wehmeyer & Schwartz, 2001), with African American males being the most vulnerable. Ferri and Connor (2005) reported that African American males are two times as likely to be labeled MR in 38 states, ED in 29 states, and LD in 8 states. Although the ratios vary by region and state, the data generally show males are 1.5 times, 2 times, and 3 times more likely to be placed in MR, LD, and ED programs, respectively, compared with females (Coutinho & Oswald, 2005). The greater representation of males in special education is often explained according to (1) biological factors, considering that males are more prone than females to certain physical conditions (e.g., birth defects) that are likely to lead to disabilities; (2) externalizing behaviors where males tend to be more active and disruptive in the classroom; and (3) referral bias in that referring teachers may have unrealistic expectations of males (Wehmeyer & Schwartz, 2001). The empirical data on gender differences in special education are limited, but some of the existing research suggests irregularities related more to females than to males

(Coutinho & Oswald, 2005; DuPaul et al., 2006; Wehmeyer & Schwartz, 2001).

Wehmeyer and Schwartz (2001) examined the special education placement records in three school districts to determine gender differences in admission decisions. Findings indicated that girls displayed more significant deficits in terms of IQ scores, were admitted at a slightly older age than males, and were placed in more restrictive settings, leading the researchers to conclude that males were not overidentified but rather females were being underserved. Concern for underserved females is expressed as well by other researchers who advise that male preponderance may be due to dual disabilities, especially accompanied by attention deficit/hyperactivity disorder, which is more common among males. These researchers surmise that since externalizing behavior problems are found less among girls, school personnel are reluctant to identify and address girls' more common internalizing emotional problems. Nevertheless, underidentification of females does not necessarily rule out the legitimate concern for the tremendous risk status of African American males. Not only are they the number one candidate for special education, but, compared with their European American male peers, African American males are more likely to be suspended at a younger age, receive lengthier suspensions, be tracked into low-ability classes, be retained in their grade levels, programmed into punishment facilities, and given more pathological labels than warranted (e.g., Coutinho, Oswald, & Forness, 2002; Irvine, 1990; Oakes, 1994).

Discipline or punishment appears to be a key factor related to African American males and special education disproportionality. Skiba and colleagues (e.g., Skiba, Michael, Nardo, & Peterson, 2002; Skiba, Poloni-Staudinger, Simmons, Feggins-Azzis, & Chung, 2005) found school suspension to be related more consistently than other factors to special education disproportionality and found that African American males are disproportionately referred for disciplinary actions. On a smaller scale, Lo and Cartledge (2007), for instance, studied the disciplinary referral patterns for one urban elementary school and noted that African American males (compared with African American females and European American males and females) emerged with the greatest disciplinary risk. Another observation was that over a 2-year period, disciplinary referrals for students at the greatest risk systematically escalated. That is, students did not evidence expected improvements, but, rather, their social behaviors (based on disciplinary referrals) progressively deteriorated. These findings suggest that these excessively punitive procedures are most likely exacerbating problem behaviors and increasing the African American males' risk for exclusion and special education placement. Research is needed to more clearly establish these relationships and, more important, identify interventions effective in bringing about more successful school adjustments for African American males.

DISPROPORTIONALITY AND POVERTY

Poverty, which disproportionately affects African American children, is considered to be a major factor in the overrepresentation of African American children in special education (Osher et al., 2004). Nearly half of African American children are reported to live below the poverty line (Watkins & Kurtz, 2001). Donovan and Cross (2002) offered the idea that poverty creates stress factors that suppress cognitive development. Typical stressors include a higher incidence of lead toxins, low birth weight births, and maternal health issues such as hypertension and diabetes. They also noted that impoverished children are more likely to attend poverty schools that often provide less adequate teachers and fewer resources. Additionally, as noted by Blanchett, Mumford, and Beachum (2005), schools of the poor are characterized by a high teacher turnover, limited technology, fewer specialists, and fewer advanced courses. An obvious implication is that children of poverty, affected by various environmental/physical factors that minimize their social and intellectual potential, enter inadequate schools that further aggravate their deficiencies rather than enhance their abilities. There is an assumption of a relationship between poverty and special education because there is a relationship between poverty and school failure (Skiba et al., 2005). Despite the obvious logic of this position, the role that poverty plays in the overrepresentation of African American children in special education is not entirely clear.

Oswald et al. (1999), for example, found that disproportionality within the category of ED was greater for African American students in more affluent districts than in low-income ones. These researchers found a direct relationship between poverty and MMR (i.e., MMR increased with poverty), but, conversely, levels of SED did not increase with poverty. Along the same lines, Ladner and Hammons (2001) documented greater disproportionality in counties with lower numbers of minority students.

In an effort to determine the relative contributions of race and poverty to disproportionality, Skiba et al. (2005) similarly found some influence of poverty in that levels of MMR were found to increase proportionately as poverty increased. On the other hand, there was an inverse relationship between poverty and LD, with the levels of LD decreasing as poverty increased. Poverty was not found to relate to either ED or moderate mental retardation. The only factor that consistently related to disproportionality in these categories was district suspension-expulsion rates. The weak influence of poverty in this and other studies underscores the complexity of race, poverty, and special education referral, making it nearly impossible to ferret out any one contributing factor. Nevertheless, race consistently remains powerful and salient, so that Skiba et al. concluded that

> the continued significance of race as a predictor of special education disability identification regardless of controls for a variety of other variables leads us to agree with those who contend that the process of special education referral and identification remains to some extent discriminatory. (p. 142)

The work of Skiba and other researchers (e.g., Ladner & Hammons, 2001) underscores the influence of poverty in disability. However, the equivocal nature of this research means that we cannot rule out other factors such as systemic and cultural biases (Osher et al., 2004).

FACTORS CONTRIBUTING TO DISPROPORTIONALITY

In discussing factors contributing to disproportionality, issues of racial bias and institutional racism come to the forefront. These racial tones cannot be ignored, but at the same time, there is a need for reasoned analysis to determine why one condition (in this case special education placement) would disproportionately impact one particular race. Accordingly, we must examine variables that uniquely confront African American children, factors that may be within a child, within the school, or within the larger society. For the purpose of this chapter, we organize this discussion as follows: (a) factors placing students at-risk, (b) assessment, (c) teacher attitudes and expectations, and (d) social justice.

Factors Placing Students at Risk

For the past two decades, school reform has been one of the most critical issues facing society in general and educators in particular. Since the publication of *A Nation at Risk* (National Commission on Excellence in Education, 1983), there has been a heightened awareness of certain sects of the general student population that do not meet academic standards. Students of color are particularly vulnerable to this charge (e.g., African American) and are often targeted for special education referral. Almost immediately after the publication of the report, the term *at risk* became synonymous with urban dwelling, poor, low-achieving students in a number of the most populous school districts in the largest American cities (Winfield, 1991). At issue here is the etiology of underachievement. Is it possible that students themselves have innate deficits that are at best difficult to remediate or at worst impossible? One of the earliest notions about "within"-student deficits is expressed through the *cultural disadvantage theory.* Allen and Boykin (1992) stated that the advocates of this theory hold that African American students are subject to school failure because their home environments (i.e., parents) do not engage in the necessary intellectual interactions leading to the development of cognitive skills appropriate for academic achievement. Gardner and Miranda (2001) highlighted similar and extended notions held about African American children. The proposed shortcomings of African American students do not stop with parents but extend beyond the individual home to the entire community. Thus, African American communities are alleged to function as ineffective networks for facilitating the knowledge and skills necessary for school. As noted previously in this chapter, African Americans are more vulnerable to poorer birthing, health, and economic conditions than are their European American peers (Donovan & Cross, 2002). However, "finger pointing" and placing blame on students, parents, and entire communities is nonproductive and possibly contributes to the problem of overrepresentation (Arnold & Lassmann, 2003; Patton, 1998).

The previously noted conditions are considered to lead to the most commonly identified within-child factors of cognitive deficits as manifested in academic underachievement. Academic achievement is one of the most reliable predictors of referral to special education (Hosp & Reschly, 2004). In a meta-analysis of the relevant literature, Hosp and Reschley (2003) not only found academic underachievement to influence special education considerations most but also that African American students were the number one candidates for placement, followed by Latino students. They found European American students were the least likely to be deemed in need of services even after initial referral. Since academic achievement is a function of many factors, one questions how much of the poor achievement of African American students is due to deficits within the child or to poor schooling. One also questions the role of bias—that is, why referrals are more likely to lead to placements for African American students than for other groups.

Assessment

One of the foundations of special education is assessment. The positivist tradition in science assumes the existence of an objective "truth" that can be determined based on the scientific method. A number of scholars have questioned the "objective" measures of intelligence and behavior that lead to the overwhelming number of African American students in special education. Thus, the role of assessment must be examined to gain further insight into the disproportionality issue.

Teaching and learning are fundamental to the educational process. Educators responsible for instructing students in content and skill development must continuously evaluate the progress of their students. In short, assessment is a necessary component of the teaching and learning process. Measured gains or failure to learn content knowledge and appropriately utilize skills are two of the most cited reasons for initial referral to special education. Referral for special education services involves two different phases of the entire special education process, but these are inextricably linked nonetheless. A large part of the disproportionality issue begins with the initial referral and the assessment associated with the referral. Educators are faced with a sizeable challenge. If students do not make adequate academic progress, then several critical questions must be posed. First, educators must question the root cause of the deficiency in progress. Can the lack of progress be attributed to an innate deficit (e.g., low intelligence)? Can the lack of progress be attributed to environmental factors (e.g., lack of parental support or conditions associated with poverty)? Often, one question not asked, but still plausible, is, can the lack of progress be attributed to the absence of a rich educational experience (e.g., ineffective instruction)? The sparse availability of quality educational services in large urban school districts has been well documented (Roderick, 2003; Waxman & Huang, 1997), and quite often educators fail to question the integrity or quality of educational interventions as a possible determining factor for special education referral. This lack of self-evaluation has led some to question the influence of bias in the assessment process to yield a disproportionate number of African American students in special education.

Schools rely heavily on testing, and standardized tests are often the basis for most special education placements. Over the years, there has been much controversy over IQ tests, with many advocates arguing that these tests are biased and not valid for culturally and linguistically diverse (CLD) learners (e.g., de la Cruz, 1996). Some other authorities contend, however, that the issue is not bias but rather cultural loading (Flanagan & Ortiz, 2001). That is, intelligence tests are technologically sound and appropriately normed, but the items are developed and normed on one cultural group and given to children in another culture. They offer the explanation that simple differences in a child's cultural background can result in a lowered score. Skiba, Knesting, and Bush (2002) similarly argued that the problem is not with the psychometrics of the tests but that the tests are conducted under conditions of social inequities that consistently undermine the performance of minority students. They contended that "cultural competence in assessment

is based on awareness of the social and historical forces that continue to depress the academic performance of minorities" (p. 75). Working toward educational equity is one means for reducing assessment bias and discrepancies.

Multidisciplinary teams (MDTs) were mandated in the Education for All Handicapped Education Act of 1975 (EHA) as a means to reduce inappropriate and discriminatory referral and placement in special education (Friend & Bursuck, 2006). MDTs were intended to circumvent the potentially unfair and biased use of one test and one decision maker for special education placements. Although they are an improvement over pre-EHA conditions, a biasing effect is still evident. An ethnographic study of MDT meetings by Knotek (2003), for instance, revealed that teachers' concerns were generally more negative than those of any of the other team members, perhaps due to the close contact teachers share with students. Another interesting finding was the apparent linking of demographic variables to expectations of academic performance. For example, the study was conducted in a rural area where many families lived in modular or "trailer" homes. Children from families who lived in "single-wide trailer" homes were thought to be beyond intervention. One of the most interesting findings also has support from previous work, *confirmatory bias.* This is the apparent strong correlation between a teacher's initial judgment and later eligibility decisions. The phenomenon has been cited as a solid indicator of reliable teacher professional judgment or a clear sign of the inadequacy of the current system (Hosp & Reschly, 2004; Oswald & Coutinho, 1999; Warner, Dede, Garvan, & Conway, 2002).

In the wake of large-scale school reform efforts, assessment has also been discussed as a means of ensuring that students who are referred for special education services can be offered assistance in the general education setting, thereby reducing the overall numbers of children served under the "umbrella" of special education services. Traditional assessment practices have been called into question as a means to accomplish this goal. Some have proposed instead the creation of culturally responsive performance-based assessment procedures to include authentic measures leading to valid and reliable measures of student performance (Gordon, 1999; Harry & Klingner, 2006; Hood, 1998; Lee, 1998).

Teacher Attitudes and Expectations

Educators and administrators play a vital role in determining students' academic success or failure (Jacobson, 2000). The attitudes and expectations these professionals maintain about their students' current performance, motivation, and future potential is another factor contributing to the disproportionate representation of African American students in special education. The relationship between student and teacher is a vital one for many students of color. For a number of children, learning is a collective process, characterized by a genuine need to view learning experiences from a broad context, enabling them to make connections between content and the environment (Gay, 2004). If teachers espouse a tentative or negative attitude about a student's potential, it is possible that students sense this and underperform. The combined factors of bias, attitude, and expectations can actually cloud the decision-making process in regard to objective measures of genuine learning needs. Several scholars have highlighted the manifestation of expectations and attitudes by documenting the following: (a) *movement styles* or the way in which students of color use body language to communicate is often misunderstood by educators and administrators from the dominant culture (Neal, McCray, & Webb-Johnson, 2001); (b) *differentiated expectations* or simply expecting that students from diverse backgrounds will not perform based solely on demographic features (e.g., race or ethnicity; Warren, 2002); and (c) *negative teacher-student interactions*, characterized by less time spent on students' questions (Casteel, 2000), less positive verbal press bestowed on African American students (Casteel, 1998), and less satisfaction with overall school experiences as early as the third grade (Baker, 1999). The lowered expectations based on demographic variables alone indicate that the referral process is not based on sound professional judgment but rather preconceived notions about race.

Social Justice

It is almost impossible to overstate the impact and importance of the disproportionate issue of African American students in special education (Arnold & Lassmann, 2003). The current state of educational affairs would seem to suggest that one sect of the student population is incapable of learning and making acceptable academic progress. This notion is clearly counter to the basic premise of the American educational system, "all students can learn." Even the more liberal notion of "all students can learn something" seems to be challenged by the alarming number of African American students who do not complete 12 years of formal education. The impact of culture on teaching and learning must be brought to the front and center of education (Nieto, 2000). Patton and Townsend (1999) encouraged educators to come to terms with the very real presence of "power and privilege," influencing the selection of curriculum, development and implementation of school-wide programming, and instructional methods used in individual classrooms. The presence and promotion of dominant cultural beliefs about the nature of schooling often comes into direct conflict with the learning, movement, and cognitive styles of African American students (Parsons, 2003).

A large portion of this nation's teaching force is made up of European American females. Much of this population lacks the direct experience as well as the technical knowledge of effective instructional methodology for CLD student populations (Voltz, Brazil, & Scott, 2003). Although there is no evidence to support educators of one particular race or ethnicity as being incapable of teaching a student from a different race or ethnicity, there is a distinct knowledge that is required to teach all children, especially those from diverse cultural and linguistic backgrounds (Howard, 2001).

The organization of schools must also be examined as a contributing factor to the overall state of education for African American students in special education. One of the concerns is the convenient practice existing in schools that may benefit adults and undermine the education and civil rights of children. For example, debates continue about the effectiveness of tracking (see Grossman, Utley, & Obiakor, 2003, for pros and cons of tracking), and yet there is no clear consensus whether the practice should remain or be jettisoned from educational practice altogether. Some authorities speculate that tracking and special education are used to avoid the mandates of *Brown vs. Board of Education* (Ferri & Connor, 2005) and that designations such as *LD* and *dyslexia* were long used by European American parents as a way to explain the poor performance of their children but also to avoid mixing their children with minorities (Ferri & Connor, 2005; Harry & Klingner, 2006). Early in her public school career the first author directly experienced this type of integration resistance on the part of many European American parents in a large urban district. Several classrooms for students with LD had been constructed in the basement of one predominately White elementary school. The parents strongly protested against the addition of these classes and did not relent until they learned that most of the special education students were White and that few, if any, of the Black children would be integrated into the all-White general education classes. Another, not uncommon, incident was when a school psychologist argued against the placement of a European American middle-class student into the program for students with MMR because this child came from a more sophisticated background compared with most of the children placed in such programs. The school psychologist felt that these classes would not permit this youngster to grow, as would be the case if he remained in the programs for children with LD, who were predominately European American. The clear implication was that programs for children with MMR were the domains of the poor and the minority, where the expectations for progress were minimal.

Another related example is that many administrators will assign teachers to classes based on an attempt to reward or even punish educators for past deeds. This practice neglects the needs of children, especially those with the greatest needs, who are quite often paired with the least qualified of the teaching staff (Stringfield, 1997). Borderline students exposed to inadequate teaching conditions will be further marginalized and placed at an even greater risk for special education programming. The social injustice found in the educational system for African American students requires a fundamental change. The inequities need to be recognized and greater effort put forth to provide early and effective instruction for all students.

ADDRESSING DISPROPORTIONALITY

Legislative Interventions and Disproportionality

The latest reauthorization of the Individuals with Disabilities Education Improvement Act (IDEA/IDEIA—previously known as the Education of the Handicapped Act, 94–142) of 2004 includes some provisions that specifically target the disproportionality of minority students. The latest bill permits schools to determine LD eligibility without relying on the IQ discrepancy model. As noted previously in this chapter, IQ testing has long been considered discriminatory against minorities, particularly African Americans. One alternative and potentially promising model that has received much attention is response to intervention. Within this model, interventionists systematically use a series of interventions with learners who evidence risk markers for LD. Over a period of time, learners who fail to respond to these interventions and do not make substantial academic progress may be viewed as having specific LD and are programmed accordingly. Additionally, the 2004 authorization provides for professional development funds so that school personnel may acquire skills relative to effective instruction and positive behavioral interventions to limit the overidentification of students. Ostensibly, this provision is aimed at general educators who need to become more skilled in teaching and managing the behaviors of low-performing students, whose problem behaviors are aggravated by inadequate schooling and poor classroom management. Disability designations for many African American students may well be a function of the instructional failure of the school.

A third provision of IDEA 2004 is that school districts with significant rates of disproportionality are expected to implement pre-referral programs that could minimize the overidentification problem. Such programs are expected to provide well-designed effective interventions that will enable at-risk learners to be maintained in general education programs. Although these specifications are made through special education legislation, the professional implications are mainly for general rather than special educators. The goal is not simply to reduce the numbers of children placed in special education but, more important, to ensure school programs that result in academic and social competence.

Another legislative act that includes provisions for disproportionality is No Child Left Behind (NCLB), formerly the Elementary and Secondary Education Act of 1965. The law attempts to reduce racial achievement disparities and disproportionality by educational accountability. The principal tool of account-ability is through statewide tests where all students in Grades 3 through 8 are tested annu-ally in reading and math. This testing includes minorities, students with disabilities, and students who are English language learners, who are expected to make adequate yearly progress until they display competence in year 2014. Districts are expected to disaggregate their test data so the progress of these subgroups can be monitored. Prior to NCLB, students with disabilities typi-cally were excluded from large-scale testing. This policy often led to placing low-performing students in special education to avoid including their poor test scores in the school's test data. If these children's skills are not assessed, there is little pressure to enhance their performance—thus, there is little accountability. NCLB is intended to remove the incentive to either over-or misidentify students with disabilities as well as to ignore the lack of progress of students with disabilities. Despite these laudable goals, NCLB has been severely criticized (e.g., Meier & Wood, 2004). One of the most common criticisms by both educators and policymakers is the lack of funds allocated by the law to fund these man-dates. Meier and Wood pointed out that the law failed to equalize the funding. Some of the wealthiest districts in the country spend at least 10 times more than the poorest districts on edu-cation. It is not realistic to expect poor and minority students to progress commensurately with their more affluent peers when they are being taught in inadequate schools.

Another concern pertains to "high-stakes" testing intended to increase accountability. These tests are labeled *high stakes* because they have contingencies attached to them. Some of the contingencies are placed on students so that students are not permitted to matriculate through school or to graduate if they do not pass state tests. Several authorities complain that these conditions unfairly punish students for the failures of schools and the larger society in that students are held accountable for material that they have not been taught (La Roche & Shriberg, 2004). A related issue is that NCLB causes schools and teachers to focus on test-taking skills rather than addressing individual learning needs. The data on the beneficial effects of high stakes testing are equivocal (Rosenshine, 2003). There is no question that accountability is important to curbing the problems of overiden-tification for African American students;

whether the current testing procedures will help achieve that goal is yet to be determined.

Early Interventions

For children at the greatest risk, early inter-vention needs to parallel, if not exceed, those services that are currently available to families of infants with low-incidence disorders such as sensory disabilities, Down syndrome, and autism. CLD children born into families with specific markers associated with severe school failure (e.g., extreme poverty, premature parenting, parent criminality, family disorganization) need to be targeted, as well, for early intervention. These interventions should include family support/education, health services, sustained high-quality care, and cognitive stimulation. Preschool children from this population need access to high-quality preschool programs. Recent scientific reports indicate that quality early childhood child care has lasting effects. Campbell, Pungello, Miller-Johnson, Burchinal, and Ramey (2001) found high-quality early childhood child care to have a lasting effect on cognitive and academic devel-opment even into adulthood. Similarly, for slightly older children, Conyers, Reynolds, and Ou (2003) reported that 4- and 5-year-olds who participated in half-day preschool had 32% fewer special education placements than did their nonparticipating peers. Discrepancies between the two groups were noted as early as first grade, and treatment students who did experience special education had fewer years of placement than did those without preschool experience. An important emphasis needs to be placed on high-quality early learning programs. In some cases the school programs for many low-income children are of such poor quality that its developmental impact is questionable (Horm, 2003).

Teachers of young at-risk children need to be able to provide explicit, systematic, and intensive instruction to reduce or eliminate learning problems. Teachers need to be able to identify children at the greatest risk, to assess their learn-ing needs, and to implement empirically validated curricula effectively to remedy or min-imize potential learning problems. There is a real need to upgrade teacher preparation pro-grams of young children so that teachers can skillfully apply valid early interventions before learning and behavior problems take root. Stress needs to be placed not only on remediation for those at risk for school failure but also on stimulating the cognitive abilities of youngsters who show promise of giftedness.

Intervening in the Referral Process

An important step in addressing the overidentification of African American children in special education is intervening at the point of referral. If prevention strategies in the form of early childhood intervention have not been employed, school personnel need to pursue high-quality interventions at the point of referral considerations. There is evidence that nearly 90% of referred children will be placed and that the teacher's decision greatly influences whether a child will eventually be removed from the general education classroom (Harry, Klingner, Sturges, & Moore, 2002). Prior to assessing the child, an assessment of environmental and instructional factors needs to take place. Influential environmental factors include (a) working conditions within the school system; (b) pressures within the school; and (c) the ecology of the classroom. Quality assessments need to be comprehensive and thorough, taking into consideration the ecology of the child as well as behavioral and cognitive factors. Loe and Miranda (2002) pointed out that in urban areas, partly due to large caseloads, thorough evaluations are often sacrificed in the interest of expediency. Information about the student's classroom is extremely important. For example, behaviorally vulnerable boys enrolled in disorderly first grade classrooms show trajectories of increasingly aggressive behavior (Harry et al., 2002). Classroom discipline needs to enter into the referral intervention because the classroom decorum indicates the degree to which classroom disruption may be contributing to the target child's behavior or cognitive problems. It is also important to note the quality and quantity of instruction the student receives.

There is legitimate concern regarding the perceptions and skills of teachers of urban students. Some studies show that teachers are more likely to refer minority students to special education (e.g., Riccio, Ochoa, Garza, & Nero, 2003). Other researchers point out that urban teachers are more likely than their suburban counterparts to have questionable qualifications, experience, preparation, commitments, and pupil expectations (Kozleski, Sobel, &

Taylor, 2003; Pang & Sablan, 1998; Skiba, Simmons, Ritter, Kohler, & Wu, 2003). These concerns justify the scrutiny of school and teacher factors before labeling and placing African American students in special education. After assessing the teacher's experience, instructional skill, management skill, and pupil perceptions, and the quality of the instruction provided the student previously by this teacher, in some cases, the most appropriate steps might be first to place the student in another general education classroom with a highly qualified teacher.

Once the teacher's qualifications are ascertained, the next step would be to proceed with instructional interventions within the general education classroom. Gravois and Rosenfield (2006) discussed the importance of instructional consultation teams in reducing the disproportionate referrals of minority students. The teams in their study focused on how to solve problems and structure interventions to help students become successful in the classroom. Teachers in 13 schools were trained and coached in interventions for their referred students. The results showed that minority students in the treatment schools, as compared with the controls, were much less likely to be referred or placed in special education. Longitudinal research would be of interest in such studies to determine if students who are maintained in general education continue to make progress and if they outperform their peers in nonintervention schools.

Effective Instruction

Too often African American children, especially poor children, enter the schooling process with one half of the language and academic readiness of their more affluent peers (Hart & Risley, 1995, 1999). Their unreadiness sets the occasion for a path of increasingly greater failure. After a sufficient period of failure, the schools will initiate the process of labeling and special education placement. Schools are challenged to interrupt this cycle and redirect these students onto a more productive path through effective instruction. The importance of challenging curricula, effective teaching, and robust learning cannot be overemphasized. Rosenshine (1987, 2002) identified seven components shown to be effective in the existing research. He noted that good instruction consisted of *clear academic focus* and *clear learning goals* (called pinpoints). Instructors need to know exactly what they are trying to accomplish and how the learner will exhibit the targeted behavior. A clear goal, for example, would be to know that you expect the learner to read 60 correct words per minute with comprehension at the end of first grade. *Comprehensive content coverage* requires that students are taught all the relevant curriculum material and there is *ongoing monitoring of student performance.* The fifth and sixth components are *high rates of overt responding* and *immediate student feedback.* The *immediate and complete correlation of errors* are important to make sure that students have high rates of correct responding and the instruction is *fast paced.*

An important research finding in recent years is that poor instruction in urban classrooms is characterized by few opportunities for students to respond to the instructional material (Arreaga-Mayer & Greenwood, 1986). Arreaga-Mayer and Greenwood proposed that for urban students to receive the same number of opportunities as students in the suburbs they would have to remain in school for the entire summer. Active student responses that can be produced in various forms (e.g., choral responding, response cards, peer tutoring, repeated readings, and direct instruction) have been shown to be effective in increasing academic performance as well as student attendance (Heward, 2006; Lambert, Cartledge, Lo, & Heward, 2006).

The lessons of good, active student responding are characterized by high rates of oral and written student responses and are so tightly structured that students are constantly engaged in academic responding with limited opportunities to act otherwise. For primary-aged children, a good model of these principles can be seen in the Early Reading Intervention (Simmons & Kame'enui, 2003) program. This scripted curriculum has been used successfully to reduce the reading risk of kindergarten and first-grade children (e.g., Musti-Rao & Cartledge, 2007; Simmons et al., 2002). Since a combination of reading and behavior problems is the number one reason for referral to special education, it is imperative that school personnel be able to intervene effectively in these areas. Another model that employs these features for a broader age range is Direct Instruction (DI; e.g., Engelmann, Becker, Carnine, & Gersten, 1988). DI has been researched over several decades with consistently positive reports, particularly

with low-income African American students. Many reports from DI schools evidence high academic achievement, good discipline, eager learning, and purposeful academic responding in African American students (Lindsay, 2004; Nadler, 1998; Raspberry, 1998).

An extremely important outcome noted in many of these DI schools is a reduced reliance on special education in restrictive, self-contained classes/schools. As noted in a previous publication (Cartledge, 1999), the first author was greatly encouraged when she observed urban African American males identified with behavior problems fully integrated into general education DI classes. The classes were so highly structured and well taught that the typical uninformed observer could not easily pick out the students diagnosed with behavior disorders.

Behavior Management

A major factor in improving the schooling and overall success of African American students is to empower school personnel to be *proactive* rather than reactive. This means that school personnel must become skilled in behavior management strategies that enable them to create school environments that motivate students to act according to school and classroom rules, as well as foster positive interpersonal interactions with peers and authority figures. A promising model that has emerged in recent years is Positive Behavior Interventions Supports (PBIS; e.g., Lewis & Sugai, 1999). In contrast to the zero-tolerance policies that emphasize punishing instead of positive consequences, PBIS is designed to stress positive incentives to motivate students to be socially appropriate. PBIS is designed to provide (1) *primary interventions,* where all students are taught school rules and positively reinforced for compliance; (2) *secondary interventions,* where students who fail to respond sufficiently to primary interventions receive more direct instruction and support through small group interventions; and (3) *tertiary interventions* for students who fail to respond to the first two levels. These are the students at the greatest risk, and individualized interventions may be effective in preventing or minimizing special education placements.

Lo and Cartledge (2006) employed tertiary interventions in the form of functional behavior assessments (FBAs) and behavior intervention plans (BIPs) to reduce and prevent the special education risk for four African American males. A functional assessment indicated that the function of the disruptive behavior for all four students was to gain teacher attention. Intervention involved teaching the students how to solicit teacher attention appropriately and how to monitor their own behavior. Reductions in classroom disruptive behaviors were observed for all students. Furthermore, students were either maintained in general education settings or were not referred for more restrictive special education settings. Behavioral interventions are extremely important for young children, before maladaptive behavior patterns are permitted to metastasize. Many teachers are unskilled in behavior management strategies and tend to resort only to punishing or exclusion practices, which are often counterproductive. Yurick and Cartledge (2006), for example, coached a kindergarten teacher to use a token economy combined with precision requests (Rhode, Jenson, & Reavis, 1992) to reduce the total disruptive behaviors of eight males (seven African American and one European American). The children were first taught the expected behaviors and then rewarded when they complied. The data from this intervention showed that disruptive behaviors declined when the token economy was introduced but declined even further when the teacher began using precision requests. That is, the teacher learned firm and precise ways to deliver directions to noncompliant children through a systematic procedure that resulted in reductive measures for nonresponding. A critical understanding with these findings is the importance of teachers developing key management skills that help African American children, particularly males, become more adaptive in their behavior and more successful in the classroom.

Parental Advocacy

Parents of African American students need to be vigilant about the schooling of their children. Parents need to become familiar with the developmental milestones from infancy to determine if their children are developing in an age-appropriate manner. If delays are noted, parents should not hesitate to seek professional assistance because early interventions are key to ameliorating disabilities. Even if a child appears to be developing typically, parents need to make sure their children are making satisfactory progress in all school programs, including preschool. For instance, on entering kindergarten the parent should request a readiness assessment (e.g., Dynamic Indicators of Basic Early Literacy; Good & Kaminsky, 2002) to make sure the child is performing at benchmark. If not, interventions need to be implemented immediately and monitored closely. Even if at benchmark, the parent needs to request a midyear assessment to make certain the child is making expected progress. If not, intensive interventions are in order. The interventions are to be delivered by the school with reinforcement at home. Parents need to insist on interventions and should not be made to feel guilty for their child's lack of progress. Nor should they have to assume full responsibility for remedying their child's learning problems. African American parents need to build alliances with other parents and parent organizations that will help them identify resources and advocate for their children. In addition to parent organizations for all children with special needs (e.g., Pacer Center; www.pacer .org/about .htm), there are national organizations that focus exclusively on African American children (e.g., National Association for the Education of African American Children with Learning Disabilities; www.charityadvantage .com/aacld/HomePage.asp). These organizations encourage parents to utilize the legal process to obtain the services needed to promote their children's success.

Professional Development

Children are labeled and placed in special education programs only after an extended period of failure in general education classrooms. For many children improvements in school performance can be brought about through increased teacher support and effective instruction/behavior management practices. Preservice and in-service training for general education teachers needs to be designed to equip personnel with critical competencies in teaching reading and social skills. The emphasis is on these abilities because deficits in these areas are most predictive of special education referrals/ placements for African American students.

Cultural Competence

School personnel need to acquire an understanding of children's backgrounds so that they accurately and effectively perceive children's behaviors, display respect for children and their culture, design strategies effective in helping children become most adaptive in their behavior, and acquire skill in recruiting and involving CLD families in the schooling process. Teachers who are able to incorporate cultural understanding into effective instruction strategies are best equipped to ward off disproportionate special education for African American learners.

Conclusions

The disproportionate placement of African American students in special education is a long-standing complex issue. It is also part of a larger problem related to the disparity in academic achievement between African American and European American students. Many factors including inadequate instruction, inappropriate assessments, low expectations, poverty, and racism seem to help account for this phenomenon, but delineating exact causes may be an extremely time-consuming, futile exercise. Efforts aimed at prevention and early intervention are probably most meaningful and productive. The research literature is replete with good evidence of effective instructional and behavior interventions that greatly reduce the need for special placements. The focus needs to be placed on educators who resist acquiring the cultural, instructional, and management competencies needed to remedy this problem.

References

Allen, B. A., & Boykin, A. W. (1992). African-American children and the educational process: Alleviating cultural discontinuity through prescriptive pedagogy. *School Psychology Review, 21*(4), 586–596.

Arnold, M., & Lassmann, M. E. (2003). Overrepresentation of minority students in special education. *Education, 124*(2), 230–236.

Arreaga-Mayer, C., & Greenwood, C. R. (1986). Environmental variables affecting the school achievement of culturally and linguistically different learners: An instructional perspective. *NABE: The Journal for the National Association for Bilingual Education, 10*(2), 113–135.

Baker, J. A. (1999). Teacher-student interaction in urban at-risk classrooms: Differential behavior, relationship quality, and student satisfaction with school. *The Elementary School Journal, 100*(1), 57–70.

Blanchett, W. J., Mumford, V., & Beachum, F. (2005). Urban school failure and disproportionality in a post-Brown era. *Remedial and Special Education, 26*, 70–81.

Campbell, F. A., Pungello, E. P., Miller-Johnson, S., Burchinal, M., & Ramey, C. T. (2001). The development of cognitive and academic abilities: Growth curves from an early childhood educational experiment. *Developmental Psychology, 37*, 231–242.

Cartledge, G. (1999). African-American males and serious emotional disturbance: Some personal perspectives. *Behavioral Disorders, 25*(1), 76–79.

Casteel, C. A. (1998). Teacher-student interactions and race in integrated classrooms. *Journal of Educational Research, 92*(2), 115–120.

Casteel, C. A. (2000). African American students' perceptions of their treatment by Caucasian teachers. *Journal of Instructional Psychology, 27*(3), 143–148.

Conyers, L. M., Reynolds, A. J., & Ou, S.-R. (2003). The effect of early childhood intervention and subsequent special education services: Findings from the Chicago Child-Parent Centers. *Educational Evaluation and Policy Analysis, 25*, 75–95.

Coutinho, M. J., & Oswald, D. P. (2005). State variation in gender disproportionality in special education: Findings and recommendations. *Remedial and Special Education, 26*, 7–15.

Coutinho, M. J., Oswald, D. P., & Forness, S. R. (2002). Gender and sociodemographic factors and the disproportionate identification of culturally and linguistically diverse students with emotional disturbance. *Behavioral Disorders, 27*(2), 109–125.

de la Cruz, R. E. (1996). *Assessment-bias issues in special education: A review of literature* (ERIC Document Reproduction Service No. ED390246).

Donovan, M. S., & Cross, C. T. (Eds.). (2002). *Minority students in special and gifted education.* Washington, DC: National Academy Press.

Dunn, L. M. (1968). Special education for the mildly retarded—Is much of it justifiable? *Exceptional Children, 35*, 5–22.

DuPaul, G. J., Jitendra, A. K., Tresco, K. E., Junod, R. E. V., Volpe, R. J., & Lutz, J. G. (2006). Children with attention deficit hyperactivity disorder:

Are there gender differences in school functioning? *School Psychology Review, 35,* 292–308.

Englemann, S., Becker, W. C., Carnine, D., & Gersten, R. (1988). The Direct Instruction follow through model: Design and outcomes. *Education and Treatment of Children, 11,* 303–317.

Ferri, B. A., & Connor, D. J. (2005). Tools of exclusion: Race, disability, and (re)segregated education. *Teachers College Record, 107,* 453–474.

Fierros, E. G., & Conroy, J. W. (2002). Double jeopardy: An exploration of restrictiveness and race in special education. In D. J. Losen & G. Orfield (Eds.), *Racial inequity in special education* (pp. 39–70). Cambridge, MA: Harvard Education Press.

Flanagan, D. P., & Ortiz, S. (2001). *Essentials of cross-battery assessment.* New York: Wiley.

Friend, M., & Bursuck, W. D. (2006). *Including students with special needs: A practical guide for classroom teachers* (4th ed.). Boston: Allyn & Bacon.

Gardner, R., & Miranda, A. H. (2001). Improving outcomes for urban African American students. *Journal of Negro Education, 70*(4), 255–263.

Gay, G. (2004). The importance of multicultural education. *Educational Leadership, 61*(4), 30–35.

Good, R. H., & Kaminski, R. A. (Eds.). (2002). *Dynamic indicators of basic early literacy skills* (6th ed.). Eugene, OR: Institute for the Development of Educational Achievement. Retrieved February 27, 2008, from http://dibels.uoregon.edu

Gordon, E. W. (1999). *Education and justice: A view from the back of the bus.* New York: Teacher College Press.

Gravois, T. A., & Rosenfield, S. A. (2006). Impact of instructional consultation teams on the disproportionate referral and placement of minority students in special education. *Remedial and Special Education, 27,* 42–52.

Grossman, H., Utley, C. A., & Obiakor, F. E. (2003). Multicultural learners with exceptionalities in general and special education settings. In F. E. Obiakor, C. A. Utley, & A. Rotatori (Eds.), *Advances in special education: Effective education for learners with exceptionalities* (pp. 445–463). Stamford, CT: JAI Press.

Harry, B., & Klingner, J. (2006). *Why are so many minority students in special education? Understanding race and disability in schools.* New York: Teachers College Press.

Harry, B., Klingner, J. K., Sturges, K. M., & Moore, R. F. (2002). Of rocks and soft places: Using qualitative methods to investigate disproportionality. In D. J. Losen, & G. Orfield (Eds.), *Racial inequity in special education* (pp. 71–92). Cambridge, MA: Harvard Education Press.

Hart, B., & Risley, T. R. (1995). *Meaningful differences in the everyday experience of young American children.* Baltimore: Brookes.

Hart, B., & Risley, T. R. (1999). *The social world of children learning to talk.* Baltimore: Brookes.

Heward, W. L. (2006). *Exceptional children: An introduction to special education* (7th ed.). Upper Saddle River, NJ: Merrill/Prentice Hall.

Hood, S. (1998). Culturally responsive performance-based assessment: Conceptual and psychometric considerations. *Journal of Negro Education, 67*(3), 187–196.

Horm, D. M. (2003). Preparing early childhood educators to work in diverse urban settings. *Teachers College Record, 105,* 226–244.

Hosp, J. L., & Reschly, D. L. (2003). Referral rates for intervention or assessment: A meta-analysis of racial differences. *Journal of Special Education, 37*(2), 67–80.

Hosp, J. L., & Reschly, D. J. (2004). Disproportionate representation of minority students in special education: Academic, demographic, and economic predictors. *Exceptional Children, 70*(2), 185–199.

Howard, T. C. (2001). Powerful pedagogy for African American students: A case of four teachers. *Urban Education, 36*(2), 179–202.

Irvine, J. J. (1990). *Black students and school failure: Policies, practices, and prescriptions.* New York: Greenwood.

Jacobson, L. O. (2000). Valuing diversity-students teacher relationships that enhance achievement. *Community College Review, 28*(1), 49–66.

Knotek, S. (2003). Bias in problem solving and the social process of student study teams: A qualitative investigation. *Journal of Special Education, 37*(1), 2–14.

Kozleski, E. B., Sobel, D., & Taylor, S. V. (2003) Embracing and building culturally responsive practices. *Multiple Voices, 6,* 73–87.

La Roche, M. J., & Shriberg, D. (2004). High stakes exams and Latino students: Toward a culturally sensitive education for Latino children in the United States. *Journal of Educational and Psychological Consultation, 15,* 205–223.

Ladner, M., & Hammons, C. (2001). Special but unequal: Race and special education. In C. Finn, A. J. Rotherham, & C. R. Hokanson (Eds.), *Rethinking special education for a new century.* Washington, DC: Thomas B. Fordham Foundation, Progressive Policy Institute.

Lambert, M. C., Cartledge, G., Lo, Y., & Heward, W. L. (2006). Effects of response cards on disruptive behavior and academic responding during math lessons by fourth-grade students in an urban school. *Journal of Positive Behavior Interventions, 8,* 88–99.

Lee, C. D. (1998). Culturally responsive pedagogy and performance-based assessment. *Journal of Negro Education, 67*(3), 268–279.

Lewis, T. J., & Sugai, G. (1999). Effective behavior support: A systems approach to proactive schoolwide management. *Focus on Exceptional Children, 31,* 1–24.

Lindsay, J. (2004). Direct instruction: The most successful teaching model. Retrieved August 13, 2006, from www.jefflindsay.com/EducData .shtml

Lo, Y., & Cartledge, G. (2006). FBA and BIP: Increasing the behavior adjustment of African American boys in schools. *Behavioral Disorders, 31,* 147–161.

Lo, Y., & Cartledge, G. (2007). Office disciplinary referrals in an urban elementary school. *Multicultural Learning and Teaching, 2*(1), 20–38.

Loe, S. A., & Miranda, A. H. (2002). Assessment of culturally and linguistically diverse learners with behavioral disorders. In G. Cartledge, K. Y. Tam, S. A. Loe, A. H. Miranda, M. C. Lambert, C. D. Kea, & E. Simmons-Reed (Eds.), *Culturally and linguistically diverse students with behavioral disorders* (pp. 25–36). Arlington, VA: Council for Behavioral Disorders.

Meier, D., & Wood, G. (Eds.). (2004). *Many children left behind.* Boston: Beacon Press.

Meyer, G., & Patton, J. M. (2001). *On the nexus of race, disability, and overrepresentation: What do we know? Where do we go? IDEAs that work.* Washington, DC: National Institute for Urban School Improvement, Office of Special Education Programs (OSEP).

Musti-Rao, S., & Cartledge, G. (2007). Effects of a supplemental early reading intervention with at-risk urban learners. *Topics in Early Childhood Special Education, 27*(2), 70–85.

Nadler, R. (1998). Failing grade. *National Review, June,* 38–39.

National Commission on Excellence in Education. (1983). *A nation at risk: The imperative for educational reform.* Washington, DC: Government Printing Office.

Neal, L. I., McCray, A. D., & Webb-Johnson, G. (2001). Teachers' reactions to African American students' movement styles. *Intervention in School and Clinic, 36*(3), 168–174.

Nieto, S. (2000). Placing equity front and center: Some thoughts on transforming teacher education for a new century. *Journal of Teacher Education, 51*(3), 180–187.

Oakes, J. (1994). Tracking, inequality, and the rhetoric of reform: Why schools don't change. In J. Kretovics & E. J. Nussel (Eds.), *Transforming urban education* (pp. 146–164). Needham, MA: Allyn & Bacon.

Osher, D., Cartledge, G., Oswald, D., Sutherland, K. S., Artiles, A. J., & Coutinho, M. (2004). Cultural and linguistic competency and disproportionate representation. In R. B. Rutherford Jr., M. M. Quinn, & S. R. Mathur (Eds.), *Handbook of research in emotional and behavioral disorders* (pp. 54–77). New York: Guilford Press.

Osher, D., Woodruff, D., & Sims, A. E. (2002). Schools make a difference: The overrepresentation of African American youth in special education and the juvenile justice system. In D. J. Losen & G. Orfield (Eds.), *Racial inequity in special education* (pp. 93–126). Cambridge, MA: Harvard Education Press.

Oswald, D. P., & Coutinho, M. J. (1999). Trends in disproportionate representation: Implications for multicultural education. In C. A. Utley & F. E. Obiakor (Eds.), *Special education, multicultural education, and school reform: Components of quality education for learners with mild disabilities* (pp. 53–73). Springfield, IL: Charles C Thomas.

Oswald, D. P., Coutinho, M. J., Best, A. M., & Singh, N. N. (1999). Ethnic representation in special education: The influence of school-related economic demographic variables. *Journal of Special Education, 32,* 194–206.

Pang, V. O., & Sablan, V. A. (1998). Teacher efficacy: How do teachers feel about their abilities to teach African American students? In M. E. Dilworth (Eds.), *In being responsive to cultural differences: How teachers learn* (pp. 39–58). Thousand Oaks, CA: Corwin Press.

Parrish, T. (2002). Racial disparities in the identification, funding, and provision of special education. In D. J. Losen & G. Orfield (Eds.), *Racial inequity in special education* (pp. 15–37). Cambridge, MA: Harvard Education Press.

Parsons, E. C. (2003). Culturalizing instruction: Creating a more inclusive context for learning for African American students. *The High School Journal, 86*(4), 23–31.

Patton, J. M. (1998). The disproportionate representation of African Americans in special education: Looking behind the curtain for understanding and solutions. *Journal of Special Education, 32*(1), 25–31.

Patton, J. M., & Townsend, B. L. (1999). Ethics, power, and privilege: Neglected considerations in the education of African American learners with special needs. *Teacher Education and Special Education, 22*(4), 276–286.

Raspberry, W. (1998, March 30). Direct system really teaches. *Columbus Dispatch,* p. 7A.

Rhode, G., Jenson, W. R., & Reavis, H. K. (1992). *The tough kid book: Practical classroom management strategies.* Longmont, CO: Sopris West.

Riccio, C. A., Ochoa, S. H., Garza, S. G., & Nero, C. L. (2003). Referral of African American children for evaluation of emotional or behavioral concerns. *Multiple Voices, 6,* 1–12.

Roderick, M. (2003). What's happening to the boys? Early high school experiences and school outcomes among African American male adolescents in Chicago. *Urban Education, 38*(5), 538–607.

Rosenshine, B. (1987). Explicit teaching. In D. C. Berliner & B. Rosenshine (Eds.), *Talks to teachers* (pp. 75–92). New York: Random House.

Rosenshine, B. (2002). *Converging findings on classroom instruction: Executive summary.* Retrieved July 3, 2007, from www.asu.edu/educ/epsl/EPRU/documents/EPRU%202002–101/Chapter%2009-Rosenshine-Final.pdf

Rosenshine, B. (2003, August 4). High-stakes testing: Another analysis. *Education Policy Analysis Archives, 11*(24). Retrieved February 6, 2006, from http://epaa.asu.edu/epaa/v11n24

Simmons, D. C., & Kame'enui, E. J. (2003). *Scott Foresman Early Reading Intervention.* Glenview, IL: Scott Foresman. Retrieved February 27, 2008, from www.scottforesman.com/eri/index.cfm

Simmons, D. C., Kame'euni, E. J., Harn, B. A., Thomas-Beck, C., Edwards, L. L., & Coyne, M. D. (2002). *A summary of the research findings of Project Optimize: Improving the early literacy skills of kindergarteners at-risk for reading difficulties using effective design and delivery principles.* Retrieved May 6, 2004, from reading.uoregon.edu/curricula/opt_research.pdf

Skiba, R. J., Knesting, K., & Bush, L. D. (2002). Culturally competent assessment: More than nonbiased tests. *Journal of Child and Family Studies, 11*(1), 61–78.

Skiba, R. J., Michael, R. S., Nardo, A. C., & Peterson, R. (2002). The color of discipline: Sources of racial and gender disproportionality in school punishment. *Urban Review, 34*(4), 317–342.

Skiba, R. J., Poloni-Staudinger, L., Gallini, S., Simmons, A. B., & Feggins-Azziz, R. (2006). Disparate access: The disproportionality of African American students with disabilities across educational environments. *Exceptional Children, 72,* 411–424.

Skiba, R. J., Poloni-Staudinger, L., Simmons, A. B., Feggins-Azziz, R., & Chung, C.-G. (2005).

Unproven links: Can poverty explain ethnic disproportionality in special education? *Journal of Special Education, 39,* 130–144.

Skiba, R. J., Simmons, A. B., Ritter, S., Kohler, K. R., & Wu, T. C. (2003). The psychology of disproportionality: Minority placement in context. *Multiple Voices, 6,* 27–40.

Stringfield, S. (1997). Research on effective instruction for at-risk students: Implications for the St. Louis public schools. *Journal of Negro Education, 66*(3), 258–288.

Valenzuela, J. S., Copeland, S. R., Qi, C. H., & Park, M. (2006). Examining educational equity: Revisiting the disproportionate representation of minority students in special education. *Exceptional Children, 72,* 425–441.

Voltz, D. L., Brazil, N., & Scott, R. (2003). Professional development for culturally responsive instruction: A promising practice for addressing the disproportionate representation of students of color in special education. *Teacher Education and Special Education, 26*(1), 63–73.

Warner, T. D., Dede, D. E., Garvan, C. W., & Conway, T. W. (2002). One size does not fit all in specific learning disability assessment across ethnic groups. *Journal of Learning Disabilities, 35*(6), 500–508.

Warren, S. R. (2002). Stories from the classrooms: How expectations and efficacy of diverse teachers affect the academic performance of children in poor urban schools. *Educational Horizons, 80*(3), 109–116.

Watkins, A. M., & Kurtz, D. (2001). Using solution-focused intervention to address African American male overrepresentation in special education: A case study. *Children & Schools, 23,* 223–234.

Waxman, H. C., & Huang, S. L. (1997). Classroom instruction and learning environment differences between effective and ineffective urban elementary schools for African American students. *Urban Education, 32*(1), 7–44.

Wehmeyer, M. L., & Schwartz, M. (2001). Disproportionate representation of males in special education services: Biology behavior or bias? *Education and Treatment of Children, 24,* 28–45.

Winfield, L. F. (1991). Resilience, schooling, and development in African-American youth. *Education and Urban Society, 24*(1), 5–14.

Yurick, A., & Cartledge, G. (2006). *The effects of a token economy system and precision requests on kindergarten students' disruptive behavior.* Unpublished manuscript, The Ohio State University, Columbus.

25

TOWARD UNDERSTANDING AFRICAN AMERICAN MALES AND K-12 EDUCATION

JAMES EARL DAVIS

Interest in the education of African American males has increased over the past two decades among researchers, practitioners, policymakers, and among the general public. The interest has manifested itself in at least two ways. For example, while the nation's focus on educating African American males during this time has been rather consistent, more recent attention by philanthropic, advocacy, and policy groups such as the Schott Foundation for Public Education (Holzman, 2006), the Children's Aid Society (Morgan & Bhola, 2006), and the Joint Center for Political and Economic Studies (Dellums Commission, 2006) has created a heightened sense of urgency. At the same time, community and school-based efforts that do not receive much national visibility are also pushing issues about academic performance and achievement to the center of their work. These national and local efforts are uncovering and attempting to attend to complex problems faced by African American boys and young men in and out of school. Clearly, this interest builds on several broadscale efforts during the 1970s when we saw an emergence of programs for young Black males (Rainwater, 1970) as well as current research efforts that are underway across the country (Dancy & Brown, 2008; Mincy, 2006). Despite this attention and renewed interest in African American males, particularly those of school age, there are still overarching concerns about the sources of the problems undermining the educational and life changes of African American males.

Large gaps, both in theory and in practice, persist between how African American males are represented in popular culture and how they are faring in their actual lives in school. The disconnect between the socially constructed "Black male crisis" and what is known about these students' schools experiences and academic attitudes provides an opening for a much-needed discussion that crosses the boundaries of school, work, and community life. In the absence of such a discussion, school engagement and achievement of African American males will continue to be considered in policy and practice without the benefit of a full range of perspectives or data. The field is unfortunately stuck in the "problem" without clear directions and paths to solutions.

In addition, the array of strategies and interventions that have captured the attention of school administrators, teachers, parents, and local communities (Davis, 2006; Hudley, 1995; Jackson &

Moore, 2006) unsurprisingly fail to take into account the challenge of educating students whose experiences, identity, and desires are complicated by both broader societal forces and more personal decisions. The strategies and interventions rely on problem-centered research and analyses. However, contemporary problem-centered research and analyses may inadvertently obscure insightful models of success, persistence, and resilience that also captures the educational experiences of many African American males and denies opportunities to understand the diversity among these students. This chapter aims, in part, to move beyond a problem-centered approach and makes use of what we generally know about these students to invigorate conversations and policy discussions about the critical importance of educational uplift for this group.

While it is true that African American males often pose a challenge to schools, the question of whether school leaders, teachers, and educational institutions themselves provide meaningful opportunities for effectively understanding these students remains unanswered. In this chapter, I try to unravel some of the issues related to African American males and education. Specifically, I call attention to the ways in which African American males complicate schools for themselves and for their teachers and peers, thus highlighting the ongoing tensions African American males create for education. I also balance the discussion against the failures of schools as well, noting how stereotypes and social constructions of these students as problems have resulted in differential, and sometimes inappropriate, responses that may put these males at further risk. The next part of the chapter describes the unique social locations of race and gender and how they shape identity for African American males in school. The significant place of teachers and teaching African American males is also examined with coverage of practical strategies that are content-based as well as those informed by teacher-student relationships. I conclude with additional perspectives that offer possibilities for the effective education of African American males. What ideally emerges from this treatment of African American males and education are insights that inform how the field conceptualizes the conditions of these students as well as how policy and practice can reflect these new understandings.

AFRICAN AMERICAN MALES AND THE CHALLENGE OF SCHOOLS

Focusing exclusively on African American males in K-12 education may appear too narrow for some, given the difficult circumstances that African American girls experience in school. My intention is not to diminish the need to address the educational conditions of African American females (O'Connor, 1999). Instead, my intention is to locate a discussion of education at this critical intersection of race and gender for African American males, in a way that not only targets the very vulnerable population but also points to broader issues of educational and human capacity for all African American students.

Public concern over the precarious state of African American youth, particularly males, tends to be episodic. During periods of concern about limited employment opportunities, crime and drug involvement, HIV infection, incarceration, and parental and family relationships, for example, attention of the media and that of the public that follows is heightened, but rarely sustained over time (Jackson & Moore, 2008; Rome, 2004). Notwithstanding, issues surrounding problems in education and participation in economic life consistently hold the public's attention. This is due, in part, to the link between educational opportunities, work force participation, and broader consequences for social and community well-being. Challenges facing African American males have gained prominence in consideration about their mainstream existence, their stability in various communities, and their social development (Noguera, 2003). Recently, reports and studies have highlighted the endangerment of African American males in mainstream American life with the goal of refocusing civic and political attention to a central concern for the nation's general welfare instead of a problem with Black men (Edelman, Holzer, & Offner, 2006; Mincy, 2006). New questions are being asked about the best strategies to engage and support African American males to increase their educational success and economic position. Clearly, "one size does not fit all" and thus, understanding the particular needs of African American males is a significant undertaking but with potentially tremendous social benefits.

The role of education in the lives of African American males has been cited as an essential element in improving their life chances as well as the communities in which they live (Reese, 2004). The importance of education to African American males is not disputed; however, how their educational experiences are organized, experienced, and delivered are points of disagreement among academics and among those in the general public. For instance, the disproportionate placement of African American males in special education continues to tarnish American education and frustrate those concerned about equity and opportunity for all students (Harry & Klinger, 2006). Unfortunately, these sporadic attempts to disentangle the complexities of the Black male "problem" may be futile unless more is known about how and why education is important to and understood by those who are often marginalized by schools that offer both barriers and hope for their futures. For those who are committed to the social development and uplift of African American males and their communities, understanding schools as sites where both problems and solutions are located is a key consideration.

Contextualizing Gender Disparities in Education

The alarming statistics that describe a growing achievement gap, increasing behavioral problems, and decreasing motivation have captured the attention of American educators, researchers, and the public (Graham & Hudley, 2005; Graham, Taylor, & Hudley, 1998; Holzman, 2006). It is easily argued that African American males in America are placed at risk for all types of negative schooling outcomes. Issues such as grade retention, special education assignment, disciplinary actions, and relatively low test performance are ongoing areas of concern for African American males (Irving & Hudley, 2005; Roderick, 2003). Explanations by researchers for these experiences and outcomes usually range from personal decisions and attributes to broader structural reasons such as the social organization of schools (Davis, 2003). For example, African American males' inability or disinterest in conforming to traditional learning roles in school (Polite & Davis, 1999) and the kind of learning opportunities and access to quality instruction and educational services (Patterson, 2005) are frequently cited as areas of concern. As the negative consequences of the achievement

disparities become more widely known and accepted, researchers are motivated to discover precursors and effects of these achievement gaps (Cunningham & Meunier, 2004; Osborne, 1997). In general, lower levels of achievement for these students appear to have the most significant consequences for the development of social identity, cognitive ability, emotional capacity, and social competence. These developmental outcomes are negatively affected by poor schooling experiences. Similarly, the inherent social and economic limitations associated with underachievement are also supported by research among social scientists (Entwisle, Alexander, & Olson, 2007). Rather than forming a question about the negative effects of achievement disparities for African American males relative to other students, I might pose the following question: What are the processes at work that create the impetus for school disengagement and underachievement?

The social processes that belie the social, academic, and cognitive interests of African American males are often traced in the sociohistoric nature of schooling in America that is rooted in privilege and exclusion (Brown, Dancy, & Davis, 2007). At their origin, powerful autonomous status groups provide an exclusive education to their own children or strengthen respect for their cultural values founded in schools. The public school system in America was founded mainly by White, Anglo-Saxon, and Protestant elites with the purpose of teaching respect for Protestant and middle-class standards of cultural and religious propriety, especially in the face of Catholic, working-class immigration from Europe (Collins, 2004). This conflict gave rise to school systems that deemed public school education as fundamentally White and middle class in its orientation and tolerance.

Today, schools are somewhat more diverse in their orientation, but they engage in the intentional work of silencing disadvantaged culturally marginalized groups, such as African American males, whose backgrounds can be very different. In a postindustrial global economy, where most schools are still likely to be segregated by race and class because of residential housing patterns, students are implicitly disadvantaged by racial and class-based segregation—the lack of meaningful diversity (Nembhard, 2005). The experiences of students in many of these schools are characterized by limited access to the most qualified teachers, the best learning materials and equipment, and students and parents who are highly engaged and achievement motivated. Another area of concern is the disproportionate exposure to high levels of violence and interpersonal conflict these students experience at school and in their communities. Strategies and reforms to increase students' opportunity to learn and to address achievement and performance lags due to current school climate and resources are being proposed. However, how these strategies and reforms should be shaped to address particular needs of African American males are often missing (Dimitriadis, 2003; Gadsden & Trent, 1995; Young, 2003).

BLACK AND MALE:
IDENTITY AND EDUCATION

One important issue that often gets lost in the contemporary research and scholarly treatment of African American males and education is gender. For sure, gender is an important lens to understand schooling experience, but discussions in the field are at times disparate and conflicting. While I acknowledge the tension between focusing on sex differences in learning and issues of sex equity and outcomes (Gurian, 2002; Sax, 2005), I refer to gender as the social and cultural categories that define and distinguish meanings of being a boy or girl and how these meanings are manifested in school. Socially constructed understandings and realities of these categories inform the core of my work where gender, specifically qualities of masculinity are culturally attributed and defined (Browne & Fletcher, 1995; Connell, 1996). Furthermore, a working definition of masculinity is how these constructed meanings and definitions are attributed to being male. In other words, what does it mean to be male (boy, young man, man) as operationalized by specific behavior, attitude, affect, style, disposition, and belief? We should think about masculinity in plurality—masculinities as a more precise way to conceptualize this idea (Connell, 1995). Here, the emphasis is on the multiple ways of being male. Understanding the intersection of race and gender is also complicated by the inclusion of class. Differences in special education placement highlight the importance of class and race in the education experience of African American males. For example,

the percentage of African American males identified as having emotional and behavioral disorders, those who are suspended, expelled, or removed from schools (Monroe, 2006), and those who will eventually end up in the criminal justice system, is far greater than for low-income students. And regardless of class, African American males are also five times as likely as White females to be labeled as emotionally disturbed and then subject to negative consequences of this designation (Oswald, Countinho, & Best, 2002).

This discussion situates the social construction of gender in school by presenting what we currently know about gender and Black masculine identity and provides some useful ways to reimagine the roles of schools in promoting gender diversity and the development of African American males. To uncover understandings of gendered and racial identities connected to educational experiences and outcomes for African American males is the objective here. Factors such as masculinity are important to consider, particularly the role that the schools play in the formation of masculine identities as well as the ways in which they respond to them (Wiens, 2005).

At the center of this discussion is not only concerns about how African American males in school are perceived and related to by teachers, school leaders, and their peers, but also how they make meaning of their own lives in school. The actions of federal, state, and local education departments aimed at addressing identity issues have minimally shifted the discussion about educational equity and quality schooling for African American males (Hopkins, 1997; Sadker, 2000). The relaxation of Title IX and the implementation of single-sex schools and classrooms serve as an illuminating example of structuring schooling experiences based on gender identity (Hubbard & Datnow, 2005). With the exception of single-sex schooling, very few options exist that consciously focuses on gender identity. These limited attempts to inaction, or minimal reaction, highlight long-standing tensions about the role that public schools should assume in the racial and gender development of its students. Additional efforts to understand African American male experiences in schools are increasingly drawing the attention of those who work and advocate for these students and their communities (Polite & Davis, 1999). Questions about the uncomfortable shared spaces of race and gender are raised by the current situation of African American males in schools. These questions end with stories steeped in uneasiness about the perceived competition between the roles of race versus gender identity in education.

Identity and School Outcomes

The ways in which students identify with schooling and its various components are related to successful outcomes (Osborne, 1995; Spencer, Cunningham, & Swanson, 1995). Some have argued that at the core of African American male underachievement is an identity mismatch or a disidentification with schooling and its processes (Murrell, 1999; Osborne, 1995, 1997). This battle between how African American males feel about school and how they feel about themselves is waged in the classrooms, hallways, and in the principal's office as students attempt to remain authentic to who they are and who they perceive themselves to be. Albeit all students are experiencing some identity disconnection with school, African American males have shown higher levels of identity incongruence with school than their peers (Davis, 2003).

The interaction of school context, masculine identities, and socialization is an untapped entry of intervention. Generally, masculinity centers on the ways that males "perform" or act out their conceptions of what it means to be a man. The source of these definitions comes from their immediate social environments coupled with the reinforcement by peers who hold similar conceptions (Seidler, 2006). The distinctions between masculinity and manhood are often minimized in research, but these differences have unique implications for educational work. Ideas and conceptions of what it means to be an African American boy or man are at the core of the definition of manhood, whereas an actual set of behaviors and dispositions connected to being a boy/man is masculinity (Ferguson, 2000; Hunter & Davis, 1994). The relationship between these two is intertwined and complimentary. For instance, the idea of manhood provides a ready-made script that usually dictates behaviors and attitudes. African American males tend to understand and embrace traditional conceptions of masculinity that typically honor the traditional economic provider role, power, and as a player of women—constructions of manhood

(Hunter & Davis, 1994). In turn, a responsive culture of African American masculinity is constructed that informs and directs specific masculine expectations and acceptable behavior (Ginwright, 2004). It does seem that the issues of manhood are so prominent in the lives of Black boys that they are struggling to be boys, without the benefit of time to be boys. Often family, communities, and schools have expectations for them to adultify, leaving them with few options except to assert the significance of masculinity in school. The conflicting and ambivalent use of the concept Black males versus Black boys points to an inherent complexity of capturing them in developmentally appropriate ways.

Black Masculinity at School

Not necessarily masculinity, but how teachers and other adults interpret masculinity is linked to troubles for African American males in schools (Ferguson, 2000). African American males tend to behave in accordance with ideas that reflect who they are and how they want to be seen as African American males. These conceptions of Black masculinity are a means of challenging a school climate that excludes and labels them as at-risk and problematic. African American males create a very distinctive culture for themselves shaped by a unique gender position in school (Davis, 2001). The culture that these African American males develop functions as a vehicle where a hypermasculine style serves as a form of protest and defiance. Sadly, the resulting behaviors only confirm negative opinions that teachers and peers already hold (Ferguson, 2003). Subsequently, African American males react to these negative opinions through maladaptive responses, which only further distance these students from the mainstream of teaching and learning at school (Harry & Anderson, 1999).

The masculine culture in which African American males engage is focused on collectively producing and reproducing what they consider an authentic identity of Black masculinity (Davis, 1999). To be sure, these students are well aware of their marginalized academic and social status by the time they enter middle school, and in turn, create their own rules for resisting and engaging schooling (Ferguson, 2000). This space that results from this identity dance is where their version of masculinity becomes protest and defiance in the face of negative expectations of teachers and peers. It seems that these students are both victimized and liberated by their self-constructed identity in schools. They enjoy the power and social benefits of social agency and self-expression; however, they are stymied by gender stereotypes, particularly related to academic achievement. Again, the interpretations of these masculine expressions are at the source of many of the problems faced by African American males at school (Sewell, 1997).

Controlling/Disciplining Black Males at School

African American males unfortunately carry a heavy load of expectations from fellow students and teachers. For instance, they endure gender stereotyping surrounding issues of achievement coupled with the "troublemaker" label both in and out of class. Unfortunately and unknowingly, they reinforce these gender stereotypes by asserting their masculinity, which, in turn, negatively affects their performance and increases the likelihood of discipline and punishment. The decision to reject these conceptions presents a dilemma for African American males as the potential social benefits of their hypermasculine status make it difficult for most of them to counter these notions. Issues of discipline pose a significant barrier to educational attainment of many African American males. Monroe (2006) noted that young African American males are twice as likely to be at risk for dropping out when compared with young African American females and are suspended more often than Whites in elementary schools, and twice as often in high school. Throughout K-12 schooling, African American males have the highest suspension and dropout rates. The convergence of African American male identity and discipline codes of schools creates an inevitable disaster for persistence and engagement.

Although troublemakers experience the most acute forms of punishment and persecution in schools (i.e., detention, suspension, "time out"), these Black males also contribute to how punishments are constructed, given their behavioral responses to a schooling environment perceived as hostile and disruptive. By defying teachers' authority, for instance, they risk being punished but delight in the pleasure of asserting some control over teacher expectations and school rules that they find unacceptable.

The social construction of African American males as troublesome bodies is tied to the idea that they are violent, threatening, and menacing. This is a way of understanding the behaviors of males in school and justifying their punishment and control. African American males, however, differ from other troublemakers who bring varied social resources—family and behavioral strategies—to bear on their likelihood of not being punished by the school and by society.

Countering Imposed Definitions of Masculinity

The restrictive masculine culture of African American males also serves as a policing agent for normative masculine enforcement. African American males enforce their meanings of masculinity by sanctioning other African American males who do not adhere to their definitions. What can be said of the few African American males who do not always conform to the prescribed masculine orthodoxy? I refer to these students as transgressors because they decline accepted notions of appropriate peer-approved masculinity at school. Often, severe social punishment is directed toward these African American males who act counter to the strict behavioral code of peers. Shaming, shunning, and ridiculing African American males who transgress the masculine standard frequently accomplish this objective. One area of notable transgression is presentation style and school engagement. African American males make it very clear what is accepted masculine presentational behavior, including how African American males walk and talk, dress, and their interaction style with girls and other African American males (Davis, 1999).

African American males who go against the traditional masculine value system and are considered out of the masculine mainstream by their peers are severely stigmatized because of the weight of gender norms (Connell, 1995; Martino & Meyenn, 2001). African American males who do not meet the standards of an acceptable masculinity are treated as masculine outcast, including students who dare to verbalize alternative views on masculinity. Additionally, African American males who transgress occupy a very complicated and vulnerable social position in school. Since they defy gender regulations, these African American males are constantly juggling and negotiating their multiple identities.

Usually, their efforts for legitimacy and recognition fall short among their peers.

Learning Masculinity at School

K-12 schools are places in which African American males make sense about what it means to be a male. In the process, a space is created that feeds on traditional masculine behavior and attitude. The development of African American males' social identity is complicated by the heavy dosages of social instruction they receive from sources, such as family, peers, community, church, and the media. Indeed, these identity messages and interpretations provide African American males with information about their place and purpose. Similarly, schools are sites where African American males learn to endorse and participate in masculinity activities that restrict their possibilities. Unfortunately, a very narrow conception of masculinity is readily available for most African American males at school, and thus, broader and more diverse definitions of masculinity, although needed, are generally not available or encouraged in typical schools. Any thought, action, or response counter to the normative expectations of males at school is considered inappropriate and subject to peer-group punishment (Davis, 2001). This regulation of masculinity requires a level of gender "know-how" by African American males to socially survive at school.

The dynamic nature of negotiating coexisting gender and race identity categories can be a challenge for many students and a barrier to taking full advantage of learning opportunities and support from teachers and other school personnel. Nonconformity to these valued behaviors and roles not only increase the level of anxiety about being ostracized by peers but also control access to a full and healthy complement of social, emotional, and academic experiences in school. For African American males, the inability to explore and embrace other possibilities of what it means to be a man reduces the kinds of options and opportunities they may have and desperately need at school. The development of a school culture that acknowledges and nurtures real diversity among male students will go untried and untested until normative definitions of masculinity are confronted by educators, parents, communities, and students themselves.

Therefore, it is important for educators to understand how African American males make sense and construct meanings of masculinity. These constructions usually are a source of power among peers. Insight into African American male identity development and the behavior it informs in schools emerge from this understanding. The ways in which teachers learn about identity constructions need not be burdensome or separate from their classroom practice. As suggested by Tatum (2005), specific questions about what it means to be a Black male and other questions about race/gender stereotypes (e.g., "How does it feel to be feared?") are appropriate in teaching literacy and literature. Likewise, examining students' personal feelings about their experiences as Black males could contextualize social studies content. The active voices and experiences of these students serve as new understandings about their role in school and problems that affect them. These perspectives not only frame conditions confronting African American males as learners and resisters but also inform teachers and administrators about potential interventions. Implications for teacher practice, both at curricula and relational levels, are numerous (Hudley, 1997; Patterson, 2005). Toward this end, knowing diverse constructions of masculinity and how identity shapes the teaching and learning process for African American males is essential for teachers and other school personnel.

TEACHING AND LEARNING AFRICAN AMERICAN MALES

Without a doubt, teachers play a very significant role in the school lives of students. Most of the school day for African American males is spent in classrooms where teachers' responsibilities for academic guidance and supervision should never be discounted. Teachers are blamed for many problems such as the low levels of performance and disengagement African American males face, yet they tend to be excluded from serious discussions about remedies (Lewis, 2006). The influence of teachers on African American males' academic and social well-being is too important for them to be absent from policy conversations and contributions.

Studies by Davis (2001) and Roderick (2003) reveal that young African American males generally share a desire for a more personal connection with their teachers. They feel that they are often misunderstood and wrongly judged because of how they look and act. Teachers bear a disproportionate role in creating learning environments that support students both academically and socially. Traditionally, teachers have felt less prepared to support students' personal development and connect with them in ways that are more social and affirming. While teachers are held accountable for structuring students' learning opportunities, so must teachers take a more active role in understanding African American males and intervening when necessary with social lessons that cultivate an appreciation for a variety of ways that African American males can behave at school.

Negative images of African American males prematurely inform teachers' beliefs about students' abilities and interests in the classroom. Influenced by these generalizations and inadequate understanding of Black masculine differences, teachers misinterpret language, demeanors, and dispositions as defiant, aggressive, and intimidating. One such performance style is the "cool pose" (Majors & Billson, 1992), a ritualized form of masculinity that is expressed through scripted behaviors and posturing to communicate power and control over their environment. However, general responses from African American males at school are encouraging (Lewis, 2006; Tatum, 2005). According to Roderick (2003), Black males tend to recognize teachers' potential in effectively educating them and develop the capacity to reach out to teachers. These personal relationships allow teachers to see African American males as individuals and to uniquely understand their behaviors and beliefs.

Teaching for Manhood

Teaching strategies need to be refocused and centered on the lives created and lived by African American males in schools. For instance, when teachers take a personal and sincere interest in the lives of African American males in their classrooms, teaching opportunities are created where mutual respect and learning about manhood can be developed. Likewise, awareness of these students' desire for authenticity about what it means to be a man creates potential segues to introduce relevant classroom and learning activities. Understanding how African American males make sense of who they are in school and their relation to a school culture of masculinity offers new points of entry for

teachers. While it is true that school is an important site of critical, social, and cultural intervention (Fashola, 2005), teachers need to be able to map where African American males are positioned. These multifaceted and complicated school lives of males are too often ignored, misunderstood, and thought to be unimportant. Teaching should represent a meaningful intervention to promote positive portrayals that highlight the possible selves of school-aged African American males—new images that link masculinity to the importance of schooling, academic achievement, and a diversity of relational styles. The consistent message should be that African American males can be men, and also learn to love reading, writing, and mathematics.

To effectively teach African American males to transgress boundaries imposed by intense peer culture, teachers are encouraged to become full partners in promoting positive interventions that broaden the range of identity options, talents, and other social resources available to African American males. This work must include nontraditional gender projects in curricular and noncurricular activities. Rethinking current subject material in schools that relates to new masculine objectives, particularly in literature and social studies is essential. In music, art, physical education, and other subject areas, teachers are responsible for creating a safe academic and physical space where African American males are encouraged to explore nontraditional gender activities without the ridicule and threats of other students (Ginsberg, Shapiro, & Brown, 2004). The work will be difficult at times, but the responsibility for cultivating healthy zones for masculine nurturing and self-discovery where African American males are not deprived of imagining their whole selves falls where it should—with educators.

The idea of African American males as victims of female teachers continue to create a ground swell of activity directed toward improving educational outcomes. Most will argue that traditional notions of masculinity inform African American males about what success in school means as opposed to a school experience that feminizes African American males (Polite & Davis, 1999). Programs and activities should be in place across schools where there are significant numbers of males who are underachieving. The use of men as role models continues to grow in popularity in schools. Interestingly, these efforts emerge out of concern for African

American males' relative lack of exposure to educational success.

The current political context of instructional and outcome accountability has increased the pressure on schools and teachers to focus on their most vulnerable students. African American males in particular and other under-performing students have been targeted for test score improvements. It is not surprising that there is no consensus on the best strategies for accomplishing these objectives. However, the inclusion of cultural- and gender-relevant learning activities into classroom practice is an area that holds some promise for students (Tatum, 2005). In some schools, the task of increasing African American male students' engagement and achievement is difficult for teachers, but connecting notions of gender and racial identity to classroom academics provides a potential link to academic outcomes.

While there is no utopian solution for teachers, increased sensibilities and awareness of African American male students is a promising start. For instance, when teachers take a personal and sincere interest in the lives of Black males in their classrooms, an opportunity is created for developing mutual respect and admiration. Likewise, awareness of these students' desire for authenticity—"keeping it real"—creates potential segues to introduce relevant classroom and learning activities. For intervention strategies to be effective, it is important for teachers to recognize that multiple strategies are potentially greater than any single one.

Gender-Specific Teaching and Learning

The influence of teaching strategies in creating classrooms that connect with learning outcomes is crucial. Teachers who authentically endeavor to connect instructional content to African American males' prior knowledge and shared history facilitate student learning (Murrell, 1994). This alignment of culture and context encourages the modeling of practices within classrooms that make explicit the linkages between cultural knowledge and expectations of content learning. Another benefit of this gender-specific alignment is that African American male students' personal and social locations are centered in the curriculum and classroom that they previously resisted due to feelings of alienation and neglect. The social interactions of African American males with each other, other peers, and teachers, when paired with the gender-based materials and effective pedagogical practices, provide guidance about how these students can be motivated in classrooms that they generally perceived boring and irrelevant to their experiences.

School should be an intentional space where African American males are free to attempt to make sense about their various identities. One common critique of young African American males is the narrow way they define their manhood, often connected to media-induced expectations of economic and sexual prowess. The opportunities to hold other identities, such as those based on academic interests, are often limited by peers and popular culture. Schools and teachers in particular are uniquely positioned to provide the options and support for young Black males to think about themselves and self-define in ways that go far beyond their current circumstance. Identities can be created and explored in school with the help of caring teachers who are not afraid to challenge students to see themselves differently.

The development of African American males' social identities at school will surely be challenged by identity development outside school. Indeed, these broader messages provide African American males concrete information about their place, purpose, and perspective. Schools, however, are powerful in their potential to become counter spaces where various identities are wrestled with and experienced. African American males have to be supported in their negotiation of these possible gendered identities just as they are supported in academic concerns. Unfortunately, the schooling experiences of most African American males represent limits and constraints rather than options and opportunities. There is a pressing need for development of alternative identities in school. By not being able to live out other identities within the classroom, curricula, and peer culture, very little hope is generated about a world and one's place in that world that exists beyond the current lives of these students.

Promises of Early Education

The early schooling experiences of young African American males, while not perfect, are contrary to popular versions of these students as resistant, defiant, and disengaged in school. In general, young African American males have very positive experiences in early schooling.

Almost all these students look forward to going to kindergarten, have positive things to say about school, and like their teachers (Davis, 2001). They also have high levels of achievement orientation and are very actively engaged in classroom learning activities. According to Tyson (2002), negative attitudes about school begin to surface in the elementary grades for African American males when they start to experience academic problems. The apparent disconnect between how young males are experiencing school and the broader social construction of African American males as academically disengaged is based on the power of stereotypes to privilege the negative experiences and attitudes of all African American males regardless of age and developmental stage.

Ability grouping of African American males in elementary school appears to have negative effects on their later academic achievement. Simmons and Grady (1992) found that African American males, if tracked, are more likely to be placed in lower-level subjects and classes. Declines in test-score performance follow and are linked to limited access to higher levels of instruction. Access to the best instruction and the most qualified teachers is important for all students, but particularly for African American males who appear more susceptible to negative educational outcomes.

The need for early school-based interventions for African American males who are placed at risk for school disengagement is supported by findings from research on schooling success (Entwisle et al., 2007). To ensure good academic progress from the start, curriculum improvement, instruction, and support for teachers should begin in preschool and earlier, before these students begin to fall behind. It is clear that program interventions are less effective if they are implemented after African American males have started experiencing lags in performance. The real problem with early education, I assert, is less a matter of the background and social capital that African American males bring to educational settings than the will and resources to keep these students eager and excited about schooling.

PERSPECTIVES ON AFRICAN AMERICAN MALES AND EDUCATION

Recent policy and programmatic strategies aimed at improving the educational status of Black males have centered on some innovative

and potentially new directions in the ongoing struggle. Alternatives in the structure of schools such as same-sex schools and classrooms, gender-specific and relevant curriculum and learning materials, and job-training and occupational-focused schools are being explored in school districts around the country. Traditional education can be very rigid with formal expectations of progression and passage. Alternative educational routes and programs such as "second-chance schools" for high school dropouts and those that provide employment training and workforce development often mirror nonlinear life and personal development of young people (Davis, 2006). Like the real families and supportive communities that many of these young people never had, these educational programs provide structured opportunities for success as well as care, nurturance, and acceptance of the young people. To actualize relevant and responsive schooling in a postindustrial technology-based economy, alternative schooling programs connect academic studies with real-world experience where students learn by doing and are given chances to engage in leadership development and community service (Horvat & Traore, 2001). As alternatives to traditional schools continue to expand, African American males will be provided options for developing literacy skills, job training, and pursuits of nontraditional learning outcomes.

African American male academies and all-male classrooms take a more nontraditional approach to the current gender achievement disparities (Hudley, 1995). Given the severity of performance problems associated with African American males in schools in many school districts, gender-specific schooling offers an approach that centers on the experience of African American males. These learning environments are but one part of a series of interventions aimed at changing educational outcomes for African American males. While they are showing potential for supporting African American males through embracing the diversity of male roles at school, they can also reinforce normative expectations and attitude about gender roles. Much more attention will have to be paid to assessing the effectiveness of all-male schools and classrooms as well as other gender-based interventions.

While the problems facing African American males in schools are often described as insurmountable, too often little attention is given to success among this population. For instance, high-achieving African American males represent useful models of success, resistance, and resilience. High-achieving African American males tend to be proactive in seeking help from and making connections with teachers (Roderick, 2003). These students display resilience as they struggle through academic difficulties and peer pressures. The strong relationships that high-achieving, African American male students develop with teachers help these students navigate the curriculum and academic expectations. Notwithstanding, much of the attention paid to highlighting and understanding African American male underachievement has ironically hindered our understanding of why some of these students actually achieve and perform well in school. Too often, our efforts have focused on their failure instead of profiling African American males who are high achievers in K-12 schools. Studying high achievers also acknowledges teaching strategies, school structures, and student attitudes that are effective in producing achievement results. Additionally, resilient high-achieving African American males reveal different ways in which they persevere and succeed despite schools being uninviting and they being misunderstood (Hrabowski, Maton, & Greif, 1998).

Another explanation for African American males' underachievement focuses on gender and masculine identity development and socialization. One reason commonly mentioned for the alienation and poor academic performance of African American males is that they perceive schooling activities foreign from their personal conceptions of what it means to be a man (Hunter & Davis, 1994). In other words, they have little or no exposure to models of what academic success looks like for men they admire. The presence of committed and successful professional male adults in schools can enhance African American males' academic and social identity development (Barker, 2005; Hunter et al., 2003). This positive male presence diffuses some traditional conceptions and makes room for the development of ideals and expressions of masculinity that are congruent with positive behaviors in and out of school.

There is also need to rethink how African American males with similar demographic backgrounds and shared schooling environments have differential achievement outcomes. Ultimately, African American males will be disadvantaged by restrictive social and learning contexts. Conformity to strict gender norms and behaviors has a "cooling-out" effect on all students, but African American males may be even more vulnerable to limitations on the range of social, emotional, and academic experiences to which they are exposed. The inability of these students to explore and embrace other possibilities beyond the maleness of their families, neighborhoods, and communities reduces the kinds of academic and intellectual options available to them. The development and support of a school and learning culture that acknowledges and honors multidimensional ways in which African American males can be men rests with those who believe in diversity and dignity for all students.

Media coverage of violence, unemployment, and relatively low literacy and school completion rates has spawned a public discussion insisting that something is terribly awry with African American males. However, the predominant perspective on understanding African American males calls for solutions without much attention to the active role that African American males play in creating their own school experiences and outcomes. A critical understanding of African American males' own agency in their schooling experience is largely ignored. This perspective can play a significant role in drawing a more complex portrait of these students and exposing the dual role of victims and victor that African American males play in school contexts.

Conclusions

What has gone unexplored in the era of contemporary schooling is the significant role of education as a source of empowerment for African American males. However, empowerment only occurs when educational settings provide students with a sense of ownership and belonging. African American males do not by and large feel a sense of ownership and/or belonging to schools and their purposes. As African American students proceed through the K-12 academic pipeline, public school settings must seek to accommodate their diverse educational and developmental needs (Spencer, 2001). Educational differences often embodied in the experiences and dispositions that young Black men bring to school must not be treated as educational deficits. Failure to acknowledge the importance of self-affirmation through the imposition and claims of identity in schools creates educational environments that disempower rather than greet African American males with acceptance where they enter. The experience of and response to gender and its variation in school provides an insightful commentary on the current state and future of educational opportunities. For instance, the interplay between education and a variety of social and personal identities of African American boys and young men should be considered in light of current educational reform efforts aimed at increasing achievement outcomes.

Access to high-quality academic programs, curricula, and teachers is extremely important for African American males who bring to school background experiences and dispositions that make them targets for marginalization (Brown & Davis, 2000). To continue seeing African American males as only victims of their schooling and environments denies them agency in how they make meaning of who they are at school. New gender-relevant teaching and learning activities focused on the experience and desires of African American males describe possible solutions to disengagement and disinterest. By attempting to capture their unique voices, schools and teachers become co-constructors with African American males. Understanding the role of peers, in addition to teachers and families, in the social construction of masculinity for African American males beginning with early education would also constitute a major effort in addressing later issues of disengagement and achievement. For instance, understanding African American males' constructions of masculinity and framing how these constructions are relevant to academic achievement and motivation could be useful to identify strategies to positively influence African American males.

In this chapter, I have provided some context on the current state of African American males in education with highlights on practice and policy directions. From the onset, I wanted this chapter to be a sensitive, yet discerning, analysis about the problems, potentials, and possibilities of educating African American males. In doing so, I attempted to keep focus on an important goal for this population—providing education with decency, respect, and a commitment to the betterment of their personal and collective development. This chapter also sought to overcome a major limitation in the field by providing a more meaningful and balanced discussion about issues confronting African American males in school. By unraveling some of the complexities of the precarious positions of Black males in school, an opportunity to rethink and reimagine education for African American males ideally becomes apparent from this effort. Understanding how the connections between the everyday significance of race and gender identities play out in schools, classrooms, and in relationship with school personnel are important for improving the educational status of African American males. It is hoped that what surfaces from this treatment of African American males are new insights and perspectives that inform not only how the field conceptualizes the conditions of these students but also how policy and practice, in turn, reflect these new understandings.

REFERENCES

Barker, G. T. (2005). *Dying to be men: Youth, masculinity and social exclusion.* New York: Routledge.

Brown, M. C., & Davis, J. E. (2000). *Black sons to mothers: Compliments, critiques, and challenges for cultural workers in education.* New York: Peter Lang.

Brown, M. C., II, Dancy, T. E., & Davis, J. E. (2007). Drowning beneath a rising tide: How America leaves its disadvantaged students behind. In S. P. Robinson & M. C. Brown (Eds.), *The children hurricane Katrina left behind: Schooling contexts, professional preparation, and community politics* (pp. 54–72). New York: Peter Lang.

Browne, R., & Fletcher, R. (1995). *Boys in schools: Addressing the real issues—behavior, values and relationships.* Sydney: Finch.

Collins, R. (2004). Conflict theory of educational stratification. In J. H. Ballentine & J. Z. Spade (Eds.), *Schools and society: A sociological approach to education* (pp. 41–49). Belmont, CA: Thomson Wadsworth.

Connell, R. W. (1995). *Masculinities.* Berkeley: University of California Press.

Connell, R. W. (1996). Teaching the boys: New research on masculinity, and gender strategies for schools. *Teacher College Record, 98*(2), 206–235.

Cunningham, M., & Meunier, L. N. (2004). The influence of peer experiences on bravado among African American males. In N. Way & J. Chu (Eds.), *Adolescents boys in context:*

Exploring diverse cultures of boyhood (pp. 219–234). New York: New York University Press.

Dancy, T. E., & Brown, M. C., II. (2008). Unintended consequences: African American male educational attainment and collegiate perceptions after Brown v. Board of Education. *American Behavioral Scientist, 51*(7), 984–1003.

Davis, J. E. (1999). Forbidden fruit: Black males' constructions of transgressive sexualities in middle school. In W. J. Letts & J. T. Sears (Eds.), *Queering elementary education: Advancing the dialogue about sexualities and schooling* (pp. 49–59). Lanham, MD: Rowman & Littlefield.

Davis, J. E. (2001). Black boys at school: Negotiating masculinities and race. In R. Majors (Ed.), *Educating our Black children: New directions and radical approaches* (pp. 169–182). London: Routledge-Falmer.

Davis, J. E. (2003). Early school and academic achievement of African American males. *Urban Education, 38*(5), 515–537.

Davis, J. E. (2006). Research at the margin: Mapping masculinity and mobility of African American high school dropouts. *International Journal of Qualitative Studies in Education, 19*(3), 289–304.

Dellums Commission. (2006). *A way out: Creating partners for our nation's prosperity by expanding life paths of youth men of color: Final report.* Washington, DC: Joint Center for Political and Economic Studies.

Dimitriadis, G. (2003). *Friendship, cliques, and gangs: Young Black men coming of age in urban America.* New York: Teachers College Press.

Edelman, P., Holzer, H. J., & Offner, P. (2006). *Reconnecting disadvantaged young men.* Washington, DC: Urban Institute Press.

Entwisle, D. R., Alexander, K. L., & Olson, L. S. (2007). Early schooling: The handicap of being poor and male. *Sociology of Education 2007, 2*(80), 114–138.

Fashola, O. S. (2005). Developing the talents of African American male students during the nonschool hours. In O. S. Fashola (Ed.), *Educating African American males: Voices from the field* (pp. 19–49). Thousand Oaks, CA: Corwin Press.

Ferguson, A. A. (2000). *Bad boys: Public schools and the making of Black masculinity (law meaning and violence).* Ann Arbor: University of Michigan Press.

Ferguson, R. F. (2003). Teachers' perceptions and expectations and the Black-White test score gap. In O. S. Fashola (Ed.), *Educating African American males: Voices from the field* (pp. 79–128). Thousand Oaks, CA: Corwin Press.

Gadsden, V. L., & Trent, W. (Eds.). (1995). *Transitions in the life course of African American males: Issues of schooling, adulthood, fatherhood, and families.* Philadelphia: National Center on Fathers and Families.

Ginsberg, A. E., Shapiro, J. P., & Brown, S. P. (2004). *Gender in urban education: Strategies for student achievement.* Portsmouth, NH: Heinemann.

Ginwright, S. A. (2004). *Black in school: Afrocentric reform, urban youth, and the promise of hip-hop culture.* New York: Teachers College Press.

Graham, S., & Hudley, C. (2005). Race and ethnicity in the study of motivation and competence. In C. Dwick & A. Elliott (Eds.), *Handbook of motivation and competence* (pp. 392–413). New York: Guilford Press.

Graham, S., Taylor, A., & Hudley, C. (1998). Exploring achievement values among ethnic minority early adolescents. *Journal of Educational Psychology, 90,* 606–620.

Gurian, M. (2002). *Boys and girls learn differently: A guide for teacher and parents.* San Francisco: Jossey-Bass.

Harry, B., & Anderson, M. G. (1999). The social construction of high-incidence disabilities: The effects on African American males. In V. C. Polite & J. E. Davis (Eds.), *African American males in school and society: Policy and practice for effective education* (pp. 34–50). New York: Teachers College Press.

Harry, B., & Klinger, J. (2006). *Why are so many minority students in special education? Understanding race and disability in schools.* New York: Teachers College Press.

Holzman, M. (2006). *Public education and Black male students: The 2006 state report card.* Schott Educational Inequity Index, Cambridge, MA: Schott Foundation for Public Education.

Hopkins, R. (1997). *Educating Black males: Critical lessons in schooling, community and power.* Albany: State University of New York Press.

Horvat, E. M., & Traore, R. (2001). Rebuilding the lives of high school dropouts: Lessons from a successful program. *Journal of Research in Education, 11*(1), 88–95.

Hrabowski, F. A., Maton, K. I., & Greif, G. L. (1998). *Beating the odds: Raising academically successful African American males.* New York: Oxford University Press.

Hubbard, L., & Datnow, A. (2005). Do single sex schools improve the education of low-income and minority students? *Anthropology and Education, 36*(2), 115–131.

Hudley, C. A. (1995). Assessing the impact of separate schooling for African American male adolescents. *Journal of Early Adolescence, 15,* 38–57.

Hudley, C. A. (1997). Teacher practices and student motivation in middle school program for African American males. *Urban Education, 32,* 304–319.

Hunter, A. G., & Davis, J. E. (1994). Hidden voices of Black men: The meaning, structure and complexity of Black manhood. *Journal of Black Studies, 25*(1), 20–40.

Hunter, A. G., Friend, C., Murphy, S. Y., Rollins, A., Williams-Wheeler, M., & Laughinghouse, J. (2003). Loss, survival, and redemption: African American male youth's reflections on life without fathers, manhood, and coming of age. *Youth & Society, 37*(4), 423–452.

Irving, M. A., & Hudley, C. (2005). Cultural mistrust, academic outcome expectation, and outcome value among African American adolescent men. *Urban Education, 40*(5), 476–496.

Jackson, J. F. L., & Moore, J. L. (2006). African American males in education: Endangered or ignored? *Teachers College Record, 108*(2), 201–205.

Jackson, J. F. L., & Moore, J. L. (2008). The African American males crisis in education: A popular media infatuation or needed public policy responses? *American Behavioral Scientist, 51*(7), 847–853.

Lewis, C. W. (2006). African American teachers in public schools: An examination of three urban districts. *Teachers College Record, 108*(2), 224–245.

Majors, R., & Billson, J. M. (1992). *Cool pose: The dilemmas of Black manhood in America.* New York: Simon & Schuster.

Martino, W., & Meyenn, B. (Eds.). (2001). *What about the boys? Issues of masculinity in schools.* Buckingham, UK: Open University Press.

Mincy, R. B. (Ed.). (2006). *Black males left behind.* Washington, DC: Urban Institute Press.

Monroe, C. R. (2006). African American boys and the discipline gap: Balancing educators' uneven hand. *Educational Horizon, 2,* 84.

Morgan, L. P., & Bhola, S. (2006). *Creating a culture of success: Black men—Steps toward success.* New York: Children's Aid Society.

Murrell, P. C. (1994). In search of responsive teaching for African American males: An investigation of students' experiences of middle school mathematics curriculum. *Journal of Negro Education, 63*(4), 556–569.

Murrell, P. C. (1999). Responsive teaching for African American male adolescents. In V. C. Polite & J. E. Davis (Eds.), *African American males in school and society: Practices and polices for effective education* (pp. 82–96). New York: Teachers College Press.

Nembhard, G. J. (2005). On the road to democratic economic participation: Educating African American youth in the postindustrial global economy. In J. King (Ed.), *Black education: A transformative research and action agenda for the*

new century (pp. 225–240). Mahwah, NJ: Lawrence Erlbaum.

Noguera, P. (2003). The trouble with Black boys: The role and influence of environment and cultural status on the academic performance of African American males. *Urban Education, 38,* 431–459.

O'Connor, G. (1999). Race, class, and gender in America: Narratives of opportunity among low-income African American youth. *Sociology of Education, 72,* 137–157.

Osborne, J. (1995). Academic, self esteem and race. A look at the underlying assumptions of the disidentification hypotheses. *Personality and Social Psychology Bulletin, 21,* 449–455.

Osborne, J. (1997). Race and academic misidentification. *Journal of Educational Psychology, 89,* 728–735.

Oswald, D. P., Coutinho, M. J., & Best, A. M. (2002). Community and school predictors of overrepresentation of minority children in special education. In D. L. Losen & G. Orfield (Eds.), *Racial inequity in special education* (pp. 1–13). Cambridge, MA: Harvard Education Press.

Patterson, K. B. (2005). Increasing positive outcomes for African American males in special education with the use of guided notes. *Journal of Negro Education, 74*(4), 311–320.

Polite, V., & Davis, J. E. (Eds.). (1999). *African American males in school and society: Policy and practice for effective education.* New York: Teachers' College Press.

Rainwater, L. (1970). *Behind ghetto walls: Black families in a federal slum.* Chicago: Aldine.

Reese, R. (2004). *American paradox: Young Black men.* Durham, NC: Carolina Academic Press.

Roderick, M. (2003). What's happening to the boys? Early high school experience and school outcomes among African American male adolescents in Chicago. *Urban Education, 38,* 538–607.

Rome, D. (2004). *Black demons: The media's depiction of the African American male criminal stereotype.* Westport, CT: Preager.

Sadker, D. (2000). Gender equity: Still knocking at the door. *Equity & Excellence in Education, 33*(1), 80–83.

Sax, L. (2005). *Why gender matters: What parents and teacher need to know about the emerging science of sex differences.* New York: Double Day.

Seidler, V. J. (2006). *Young men & masculinities: Global culture and intimate lives.* London: Zed Books.

Sewell, T. (1997). *Black masculinities and schooling: How Black boys survive modern schooling.* Stoke-on-Trent, UK: Trentham.

Simmons, W., & Grady, M. (1992). *Black male achievement: From peril to promise.* Report of the Superintendent's Advisory Committee on Black Male Achievement. Prince George's County Public Schools, Upper Marlboro, MD.

Spencer, M. B. (2001). Resiliency and fragility factors associated with the contextual experiences of low-resources urban African American male youth and families. In A. Booth & A. C. Crouter (Eds.), *Does it take a village? Community effects on children, adolescents, and families* (pp. 51–78). Mahwah, NJ: Lawrence Erlbaum.

Spencer, M. B., Cunningham, M., & Swanson, D. P. (1995). Identity as coping: Adolescent African-American males' adaptive responses to high-response environments. In H. W. Harris, H. C. Blue, & E. H. Griffith (Eds.), *Racial and ethnic identity: Psychological development and creative expression* (pp. 31–52). New York: Routledge.

Tatum, A. (2005). *Teaching reading to Black adolescent males: Closing the achievement gap.* Portland, ME: Stenhouse.

Tyson, K. (2002). Weighing in: Elementary age students and the debate on attitudes toward schools and Black students. *Social Forces, 80*(4), 1157–1189.

Wiens, K. (2005). The new gender gap: What went wrong? *Journal of Education, 186*(3), 11–27.

Young, A. (2003). *The minds of marginalized Black men: Making sense of mobility, opportunity, and future life chances.* Princeton, NJ: Princeton University Press.

SECTION VI

AFRICAN AMERICANS SHAPING EDUCATIONAL POLICY

INTRODUCTION

JENNIFER BEAUMONT

The education of African Americans is an unresolved dilemma of continuing moral, political, legal, economic, and psychological issues for the nation (Jones-Wilson, 1996). The statement begs the question, "Who has the responsibility for resolving the dilemma?" Both Carter G. Woodson (1972) in *The Mis-Education of the Negro* and Paulo Freire (1973) in his theories on the relationship between pedagogy and the liberation of an individual and/or a peoples' consciousness offered positions for African American policymakers to consider. Woodson advocated taking responsibility for self. Freire's "We cannot enter the struggle as objects in order to later become subjects" (as cited in hooks, 1994, p. 46) requires that the actors advocating for the African American students enter the policy arena with a clarity of the issues on the agenda, the contributing factors to the issues, the opposing viewpoints, optimal outcomes, and the resources required for the implementation of those outcomes.

Historically, education reforms, particularly those affecting African Americans, have been rooted in significant social and political changes resulting from activism emanating from communities. For many readers, landmark cases associated with the desegregation of schools will come to mind. Equally significant, however, are lesser-known examples such as the Brownsville, New York City, experience where African American families organized and mobilized community support for more parental and community control of schools (Levine, 1969). This mobilization led to an organizational change in the New York City Board of Education to the creation of Community School Boards and an increased presence of African American teachers in the school system. While reforms such as this one have evolved from movements of a critical mass of people in the African American community using the judiciary, the legislature, and community policy arenas, there are also many examples of individuals or smaller groups who have effected changes in the system.

Theories on policy making focus on determining whose values are important and which group/groups of actors have the power to influence the direction of the policy being made (Bell & Stevenson, 2006; Gertson, 1997; Lindbloom & Woodhouse, 1993; Marshall & Gerstl-Pepin, 2005). Within this arena, functional stages of activity for the development of policy—issue definition, proposal formulation, support mobilization, and decision enactment—have been identified (Campbell & Mazzoni, 1976) to demystify and allow for a linear analysis of the process. At each stage, the confluence of dominant actors, their values, available resources, and the influences of interested parties play an integral part in winnowing the issues on the policy agenda. It is important to note that items on the menu of competing issues are often wide ranging and disconnected. Ultimately, at the fourth stage, decision enactment, the policy that evolves usually reflects the interests of a narrow spectrum of the population, clearly that of the groups wielding the most power and influence.

To be active participants in education policy making and to resolve this dilemma defined by Jones-Wilson requires that more African Americans who are policymakers, and members of interest groups, exert political, financial, and/or other resources to experience what hooks (1994) described as that "historical moment when one begins to think critically about the self and identity in relation to one's political circumstance" (p. 47). This epiphany lends credence to Bob Marley's (1980) "Emancipate yourself from mental slavery, none but ourselves can free our minds" and propels the movement forward to responsibility for self.

Responsibility for self and changes within self and community speak to the unearthing of strategies "used to keep power and exclude challengers . . . [and] strategies used by challengers to raise often-silenced and ignored voices and needs" (Marshall & Gerstl-Pepin 2005, p. 5). Effecting and sustaining the changes in the policy-making arenas and in the policies made require a "coming of age" among African Americans. As community members, we are all so familiar with measures and evaluation tools such as district, school, and student report cards. Annually, in most communities, the performance of all schools is reported, compared, and analyzed in the local media, research communities, and policy think tanks. Very few of these scenarios delve beneath the commonly measured factors such as test scores, attendance rates, teacher qualifications, connectivity, and student-to-teacher ratios. Very few of these scenarios explore the policies that guide the decisions determining what factors are measured, why those factors are measured, and the impact of these measures on students, families, and communities. Understanding these issues requires a "behind-the-scenes" look at the policy-making process, the policymaker, and the agents/forces influencing both the process and the policymakers. A policymaker, intent on shaping effective and pertinent policies to benefit African American students must constantly reflect on and evaluate the values being espoused and the significance and long-term impact on the African American community at large.

The chapters in this section present five slices of education policy making having an impact on African American students and evolving in different policy-making arenas. The first chapter by Beaumont helps us understand the personal histories of four African American policymakers. Their narratives show that there are individuals who have built on the results of the activism of the critical mass and have assumed the responsibility for personal and community changes. Essentially therefore, they represent the possibilities for professional practices that are linked to the consciousness described by hooks, Freire, and Woodson. In the next chapter, Eric Cooper examines the outcomes of a school reform model that uses student strengths as a launching point for movement toward high intellectual performance within a crucible of that student's culture. In their chapter, Sabrina Hope King and Nancy Cardwell present an analysis of collaborations among a range of stakeholders internal and external to public schools in one community. Next, Sheila Vance addresses the impact of equity in school finance in communities of schools serving predominantly African American student populations. In this chapter, the challenges to the status quo and the resulting policies are made in the judicial arena. The expansion of the role of African American Studies Departments in helping college level students to have a deeper understanding of the economic power within their communities and developing entrepreneurism is the question of interest to Jessica Gordon Nembhard.

Commitment and courage to effect change, deep caring for the students and their families, promoting changes within self and community, clarity of purpose, and focused outcomes are threaded throughout all the chapters. The magnitude of the challenge was presented by the Commerce Department's Census Bureau in a February 2001 report, which indicates that "79 percent of African Americans age 25 and over had earned at least a high school diploma and 17 percent had attained at least a bachelor's degree by March 2000. Both percentages represented record levels of educational attainment" (Commerce Department, Census Bureau, 2001, para. 1). While the Census Bureau's assessment that 17% of students aged 25 years and above earning a college degree is a record high, the National Urban League's (2006) *The State of Black America 2006: The Opportunity Impact* presents a different interpretation. There is a dearth of both quality of education received and the number of degrees earned as only 39% of all African American college students were completing 4-year programs (pp. 25–29). The awareness that something needs to be done at many levels, with many actors, and using multiple strategies if the data on educational access, attainment, and participation are to change, is evident across the chapters. Effective education policy making for African American students is underscored, therefore, by the creation and sustaining of policies guaranteeing substantially equal educational opportunities.

REFERENCES

Bell, L., & Stevenson, H. (2006). *Education policy: Process, themes and impact*. London: Routledge.

Campbell, R. F., & Mazzoni, T. L. (1976). *State policy making for the public schools*. Richmond, CA: McCutchan.

Commerce Department, Census Bureau. (2001). *Census bureau releases update on country's African American population*. Retrieved April 25, 2007, from www.census.gov/Press-Release/www/2001/cb01–34.html

Freire, P. (1973). *Education for critical consciousness*. New York: Seabury Press.

Gertson, L. N. (1997). *Public policy making: Process and principles*. New York: M. E. Sharpe.

hooks, b. (1994). *Teaching to transgress: Education as the practice of freedom*. New York: Routledge.

Jones-Wilson, F. C. (1996). *Encyclopedia of African-American education*. Westport, CT: Greenwood Press.

Levine, N. B. (1969). *Ocean Hill-Brownsville: A case history of schools in crisis*. New York: Popular Library.

Lindbloom, C. E., & Woodhouse, E. J. (1993). *The policy making process* (3rd ed.). Englewood Cliffs, NJ: Prentice Hall.

Marley, R. N. (1980). *Redemption song on Uprising* [CD]. New York: Island Records.

Marshall, C., & Gerstl-Pepin, C. (2005). *Re-framing educational politics for social justice*. Boston: Pearson.

National Urban League. (2006). *The state of Black America 2006: The opportunity impact*. New York: Image Partners Custom.

Woodson, C. G. (1972). *The mis-education of the Negro*. New York: AMS Press.

26

CREATING OPPORTUNITIES FOR EDUCATIONAL SUCCESS

Oral Histories of Four African Americans Shaping Education Policy

JENNIFER BEAUMONT

School report cards are as familiar to the average citizen as student report cards. Annually in most communities the performance of all schools are reported, compared, and analyzed in the local media, research communities, and by policy think tanks. Very few of these scenarios delve beneath the commonly measured factors such as test scores, attendance rates, teacher qualifications, connectivity, and student-to-teacher ratios. Very few of these scenarios explore the policies that guide the decisions determining what factors are measured, why those factors are measured, and the impact of these measures on students, families, and communities. Understanding these issues requires a "behind-the-scenes" look at the policy-making process, the policymaker, and the agents/forces influencing both the process and the policymakers.

To facilitate the understanding of the policy process, Brewer and deLeon (1983) developed linear stages for what is clearly neither a linear nor a simple process. The six stages listed below are cyclical and interwoven, and activities in any stage can be prompts for initiating a new policy. While participants in the policy-making process can be involved at more than one of the stages, it is extremely rare for participation in all six stages:

1. *Policy initiation*—how a policy need is articulated and alternatives proposed

2. *Estimation*—during which the proposed alternatives are assessed

3. *Policy selection*—how a specific policy alternative is chosen

4. *Policy implementation*—how a newly chosen program is executed

5. *Evaluation*—how policies and programs' merits/shortcomings are judged, so that future iterations can be more effective in reaching their goals

6. *Termination or change*—how a policy/program is ended or modified

Recognizing that policy does not take place in a vacuum and that there are as many alternatives to an identified problem as there are perspectives on the problem, Lindblom and Woodhouse (1993) found that the people, the general public, want policy to be informed and well analyzed, but they also want policy making to be democratic and hence an exercise of power. That is, there is the assumption that policy making is the domain of politicians where decisions can be determined by special deals and barters rather than rational and logically derived cost-benefit analyses. In tandem with the linear cost-benefit analyses, there is the need to know that the democratic process, the voice of the people, is well represented in the decisions.

The question that surfaces for many policy analysts and policymakers centers on what are the ideological and philosophical foundations for policy making. Marshall, Mitchell, and Wirt (1989) stated that the foundations are choice/liberty, quality, efficiency, and equity. As policy analysts like most policymakers place a greater emphasis on policies for social justice, issues of equity gain more prominence. Marshall et al. see equity as a matter of redressing problems through the creation of new, different laws and social programs that relieve the effects of inequity. These laws and social programs reflect social justice, not mere political expediency or symbolic policy actions that appear as rituals, ceremonies, and words. To determine if a policy represents social justice, analysts need to examine the overt and covert strategies used to maintain power among the dominant group as well as the overt and covert strategies used to exclude those who challenge both the existing policies and the values they represent. Conversely, policies for social justice will reflect the often-silenced and ignored voices and examine the type or content of the policy to determine how/whether it is working as intended (Marshall & Gerstl-Pepin, 2005).

Policy making occurs in many settings and contexts such as the legislative, executive, and judicial branches of national government; state and local legislatures; communities and municipalities; and institutions such as colleges and universities, think tanks, and philanthropic organizations. Several questions emerge about policy making, including "Whose interests are being examined?" "What inequities are being redressed?" "How are the concerns of the often-silenced and ignored voices represented?"

Historically, the educational needs and values of the African American students, families, and communities have not always been represented at the policy table or within the education policy communities. Defined by Campbell and Mazzoni (1976) as a network of policy professionals and advocates clustering around a specific area, policy communities tend to collude to make policy with little or no outside input. What are the political values that must therefore be challenged to create and ensure that all African American students have opportunities to learn? What are the community values that must be advocated for so that the education policies meet the needs of all African American students?

This chapter examines the policy work of four African Americans through their oral histories to reveal the complexities of policy making and to better understand how their lives and work experiences have prepared them for service benefiting African American students, their families, and their communities. These policymakers, with known track records for effecting change in public service through education policy, who expressed a willingness to participate, and whose schedules actually allowed for their participation were selected using the community nomination process. According to Michele Foster (1997), community nomination is a process of selecting appropriate persons for a community-based study by soliciting names through direct contact with members of the community. All the participants in this study serve the city and/or state in which they were raised. With more than 25 years of involvement in policy-making arenas, each person's history, though not mutually exclusive, tells a story from a different context for policy making. Each person's work falls within at least one of the six stages of policy making identified by Brewer and deLeon (1983). Rather than allowing for generalization of theories about their effectiveness, these personal stories offer the opportunity to explore and understand the symbiotic relationships between individuals and their communities.

At the national level, Congressman Chaka Fattah (D-PA) has spearheaded GEAR-UP (Gaining Early Awareness and Readiness for Undergraduate Programs), the only educational policy encompassing supports and opening doors for low-income students from middle through high school into postsecondary educational opportunities. Both Augusta Kappner, President, Bank Street College of Education, and

Fern Kahn, Dean, Division of Continuing Education, Bank Street College of Education have opened doors to success for African Americans through higher education systems. Helen Marshall (D-NY), Borough President, Queens, New York, began her advocacy for equity in educational opportunities in the public schools as a young mother of preschool children in The Bronx, New York. Collectively these stories, their oral histories, create a tapestry for seeing and understanding the complexities of policy making around education issues and the changes that can be made at any stage within the process.

Oral history was selected as a research tool to record and understand events that have taken place within the lived experiences of participants. According to Studs Terkel (1956), the oral history interview allows participants to talk about themselves and what they do best. It provides an insider account of pivotal historical events and complex social issues. It is important to note, however, that predetermined questions serve only as a guide to the interview as in many instances what ultimately become the salient factors, the flow of the conversation, as well as the storytelling that shapes the information shared were all determined by the interviewees. Triangulation took place through primary documents and secondary sources. Primary documents pertaining to the work of Congressman Fattah and Borough President Marshall are archived and available, respectively, at the Charles L. Blockson African American Collection at Temple University and at the LaGuardia Community College Wagner Archives. Additional information for all persons was found in secondary sources such as books, newspaper articles, and Web sites. Videotaped interviews were conducted during the summer and fall of 2006 at each person's office. Each person was asked to focus on the following five questions:

(1) Tell me about yourself and how you arrived at this position.

(2) How would you describe the policy-making process in public education?

(3) How would you describe yourself as a policymaker in public education?

(4) With a focus on your city/state what is your assessment of the needs of African American students?

(5) How does your area of expertise/interest address these issues?

As the videotapes were transcribed, the need for additional information and/or for clarification of information was addressed through telephone calls and e-mail messages. What follows are the voices of the policymakers describing their lived experiences. Their stories are presented, alphabetically and within the policy-making context where they function.

NATIONAL LEGISLATIVE CONTEXT: CHAKA FATTAH

Working as a policymaker within the national legislative context means Chaka Fattah was elected from a congressional district. As a representative of the Second Congressional District in Pennsylvania, he works in a bicameral congress of 435 members in the House of Representatives and 100 members of the Senate. Any bill he initiates, and/or supports, will only become a law if identical versions are agreed to by both chambers. Effectiveness in this context requires responding to constituent needs and demands so that the benefits of the legislation accrue not only to citizens within his specific congressional district but to citizens across the nation. His success as a policymaker means he must build coalitions and get buy-in from both sides of the aisle. As a legislator, his effectiveness is measured by the number of bills he sponsors and cosponsors that become laws.

It is rhetorical to ask Congressman Chaka Fattah about his impact on education policy. In 1998, the GEAR-UP legislation he sponsored as an amendment to the 1965 Higher Education Act was approved by Congress. Since its enactment, 577 State and partnership (with institutions of higher education) GEAR UP grants have been awarded; more than 6 million students in 48 states, the District of Columbia, and three territories have been or are being served, and almost $2 billion in federal funds have been appropriated to the GEAR UP program (U.S. Department of Education, 2007). Independent researchers have shown that schools with GEAR UP programs make a difference when compared with non–GEAR UP schools with respect to academic readiness and college intent. GEAR UP students were more likely to be on track as college-ready, more likely to be taking the necessary core curriculum, and more likely to have plans for college by 10th grade (National Council for Community and Education Partnerships [NCCEP], 2007; U.S. Department of Education, 2007). "GEAR UP is one of the most promising educational strategies for decreasing the academic achievement gap and increasing this country's global competitiveness" states Hector Garza, President of NCCEP (2007).

Coming from a home and a community that worked at identifying and implementing strategies to sustain African Americans in stable and positive environments, it is no surprise that Fattah has a strong track record in promoting and supporting educational programs at all levels for students from economically depressed communities. As a teen, his parents Falaka Brown Fattah and David Fattah raised him in the commitment-driven environment of the House of Umoja (Unity), one of the only urban boy's homes in the country (*The HistoryMakers*, 2005). The home was founded as a vehicle to claim one of his older brothers, a loved son, from the streets of Philadelphia. In the course of reporting a story about gang warfare in her self-published magazine *Umoja*, Falaka discovered that one of Chaka's older brothers, Robin, was in a gang. Rather than throw Robin out of the house, Sister Falaka did the only thing she could think of: She took everybody else in, inviting the gang to move into her home. By replacing the boys' dysfunctional home lives with an entirely new sort of family, she reasoned, she might be able to turn them around and save her son. The shelter would come to be called the House of Umoja, and Chaka would become as much a child of it as he was of his parents (Putz, 2007).

This childhood immersed in community service, African American history, and the Civil Rights Movement fostered an adult who recognizes his responsibility to challenge the status quo that would restrict optimal growth experiences for African American students and their families. His policies demonstrate that these constituents require not only access, but the financial and other ancillary supports necessary for success at all levels of the educational process. Interventions from his policies include

- 1986—The annual Pennsylvania Graduate Opportunities Conference later renamed the Fattah Conference on Higher Education, to

respond to the lack of minority candidates applying for graduate and professional schools. In 1990, 400 Black and Hispanic students were presented with full-scholarships, totaling $8 million.

- 1986—"Read to Lead" a free summer reading program that provides books and classroom teaching for 5,000 children at 50 sites in Philadelphia.

- 1988—The Child Literacy Initiative, a model for community-based delivery of children, youth, and family services in Philadelphia.

- 1990—The Educational Advancement Alliance, Inc., with a mission to provide educational information and opportunities to members of underrepresented groups in the Philadelphia area. It has provided services to more than 8,000 prekindergarten through graduate school students.

- 1999—The William H. Gray III College Completion Challenge Grant Program of 1999, which became a $35 million program as part of the Clinton administration's fiscal 2001 budget proposal to support college retention.

- 2003—The CORE Philly programs, in collaboration with Mayor John Street, which gives students money to cover college costs not covered by financial aid.

- 2005—The Fattah Learning Lab opens, under the auspices of the Educational Advancement Alliance, Inc., as a high-tech "'state of the art" science lab for Philadelphia public school students.

- 2005—Distributed $17.5 million in federal grant money to the School District of Philadelphia national and state senators, congressional representatives, the Mayor, and city council members.

As a policymaker, Congressman Fattah is proactive, initiating bills addressing the needs of his constituents and African Americans across the country (Fenno, 2003). Supporters of Lu Blackwell, who lost his Congressional seat to Fattah in 1994, with 58% of the vote—the largest margin in the country—always said that he voted the right way on everything. Fattah believes that a congressman should do more than vote the right way, a congressman should be initiating legislation and authoring his own proposals, rather than having others propose solutions that he has to spend time arguing against (Putz, 2007). Therefore, he believes that African Americans must decide to carry their own buckets, that is, accept and act on Carter G. Woodson's (1972) counsel of being responsible for self.

Fattah approaches educational policy making from a place of strength, warning that marginalizing oneself is definitely self-defeating, offering alternative solutions to ones on the table so that upward movement of the race is promoted, and focusing on creating and sustaining an African American middle class. The policies that he supports and authors all focus on educational attainment, and his emphasis is on creating the safety net for all students within a cohort, not offering escape routes for a selected group of students. His goals around policy development are twofold—the programs must be able to be adopted as legislation; that is, he needs to be able to get the votes needed for passage, *and* they must make a difference for the targeted population. He attributes this approach of bringing political competency to bear on growing small/localized programs to scale to two of his mentors. First, the late Dr. Ruth Wright Hayre, an African American educator in the Philadelphia School District, used a portion of her retirement annuity and solicited contributions to create a scholarship program for teenagers so that they could complete the last 6 years of school while being prepared for college. This program was named after her popular statement, "Tell them we are rising." The second mentor, Leroy Irvis, the first African American speaker of any state legislature since Reconstruction, created the Pennsylvania Higher Education Assistance Agency in 1956 and the state's community college system. Their mentorship taught Fattah that the tripod for self and community change are self-efficacy, self-guidance, and careful planning.

In retrospect Congressman Fattah attributes his effectiveness to several ways of seeing and moving through the world. First, effectiveness with education policy is partly a result of making the connections between education and the other aspects of life that support success in education such as job development (he played a key role in the development and negotiation of the 1998 Workforce Investment Partnership Act) and housing (he sponsored the 2003 Homeowners'

Emergency Mortgage Assistance Act to assist homeowners experiencing unavoidable, temporary difficulty making payments on mortgages insured under the National Housing Act). Second, his effectiveness can also be attributed to understanding the big picture. He shared statistics that reveal that Pennsylvania ranks 49th of 50 states in the number of students going to college; less than 15% of students from low-income families get a geometry and algebra course on time in middle and/or high school to be well prepared for success in mathematics and the sciences in college; and the state of Pennsylvania has lost 240,000 jobs over the past 20 years. Third, his effectiveness can be attributed to perseverance—in each congress since 2005, he has introduced his Student Bill of Rights that requires states to certify that their public school systems provide students with equal access to qualified teachers, up-to-date textbooks, and access to school facilities. Finally, his effectiveness can be attributed to his pride in African American history—in 2005, he commissioned an official portrait of the first African American Congressman, Joseph H. Rainey, to hang in the U.S. Capitol.

Fattah's political career presents a record of enacting policies at the national level within his local constituency. He has developed an expertise in education and uses that expertise to create the laws and social programs that relieve the effects of inequity in the public schools and in access to higher education (Marshall et al., 1989).

INSTITUTIONAL CONTEXT: FERN KAHN

Colleges and universities, like other institutions, have cultural norms unique to themselves. Policy making within an institution must be aligned with its vision and mission. The decisions being made are just as important as the process used in making those decisions and the person(s) guiding the decision-making process. Perceptions of the impact of the decisions made, by internal and external stakeholders, are critical to the culture and climate of the institution within which the decisions are made as well as to the relationships between and among other like institutions. Common policy issues in institutions of higher education include access and success, accountability, diversity, finance, and global impact.

Fern Kahn functions within the established context of institutions of higher education for developing and implementing education policy. "I'm lucky, I've worked with men and women who have allowed me to take risks," says Kahn as she reflected on the professional milestones leading up to her current position as Dean, Division of Continuing Education, Bank Street College of Education. Trained as a social worker, she was exposed to the cutting edge of practice by Kenneth and Mamie Clark at their Northside Center for Child Development in Harlem (Maimin, 2004). The Clarks's work demonstrating the negative impact of race relations on the self-esteem of young African American children was an important step in Kahn's decision to use race, class, and culture as lenses from which to view and shape her work.

After several years of providing one-to-one counseling services, the opportunity to broaden her reach in the community came through a discrimination suit against Hunter College Elementary School (HCES). Founded in 1940 as an experimental and demonstration center for intellectually gifted students, the student population of HCES in the 1960s lacked diversity. A discrimination suit brought by parents led to the order that the Hunter College Educational Clinic identify a diverse student body. As a member of the team of two social workers and six psychologists, Kahn visited day care centers, Head Start programs, and early childhood programs in settlement houses to find eligible 3-year-olds to enter HCES' nursery school. From 1968 through 1971, when New York City's fiscal deficit closed the clinic, the team identified incoming classes that were one third African American, one third Hispanic American, and one third European American. Her work at the Clinic reinforced the knowledge that providing information about, and access to, opportunities to improve a person's life chances and a family's quality of life were critical elements in serving one's community.

When asked how her path of service to the community evolved, she said it was through a unique mixture of solid academic and professional preparation, meaningful work, along with having a broad network of colleagues and carefully selected mentors. When the Hunter College Educational Clinic closed, a former colleague encouraged her to accept a position at the newly created LaGuardia Community College (LGC) within the City University of New York (CUNY)

system. Created to specifically meet the needs of its community and led by 30-year-old Joseph Shenker, LGC partnered with the United Federation of Teachers to offer a career ladder program for paraprofessionals within the New York City Board of Education to earn teaching credentials through the Department of Continuing Education. According to archivist Ken Riccardi (1998), the Department of Continuing Education was created with a three-pronged purpose to (a) provide credit bearing courses for adult learners, (b) offer courses and programs of study that meet specific needs of employers, and (c) address the academic needs of specific groups such as the deaf population. After teaching and leading the career ladder program for 3 years, Kahn was called on to develop the program for the deaf population.

Drawing on the seminal research on the state of education for the deaf population, convening planning meetings with the experts on education and other needs of the deaf, and study visits to Gallaudet University, Kahn and her team designed a program for the deaf population of New York City. In reflecting on the lessons learned from this experience, Kahn revealed that although the deaf population came together around the common need for better educational supports, the stereotypes about race and class within the general population were still evident. There was that constant reminder that a strident voice would always be needed to ensure that the specific supports and structures needed to bring about the changes in access and equity were in place. Among the strategies she used to widen the windows of opportunity was the staffing of the program. As associate dean in the Division of Adult and Continuing Education, Kahn hired Glenn Anderson, the first deaf African American male to earn a doctoral degree in rehabilitation research for persons who are deaf and hard of hearing. Strategically, having Dr. Anderson manage the program from 1975 through 1982 met administrative, academic, and symbolic goals.

Leadership, policy development, and implementation coalesced in the years at Bank Street College of Education. Demonstrating his confidence in her leadership, vision, and commitment to making a difference, Joe Shenker asked Kahn to accompany him to Bank Street College of Education; he as president, she as Dean of the Division of Continuing Education. This position has given Kahn a wide berth for initiating programs, disseminating information, influencing policy development and interpreting policy for implementation targeting students and families most in need of educational interventions and supplemental resources. This work is done primarily through afterschool programs for students and professional development for teachers. Through a network of partnerships, grants, and tuition-based programs serving students of all ages, family and community members, teachers, and female inmates, there is a focus on students generally underrepresented in the annals of success. And the outcomes are changing. Among the many after school options is the Liberty Program Partnership. Funded by New York State to provide a holistic program for students at risk for academic failure, it served 220 adolescents in the 2004–2005 academic year, offering opportunities such as 3-week residential programs in environmental science at Vassar and Bard Colleges, scholarships for summer travel, and opportunities for exploring the city. Specific examples of success include a young lady who participated in the program for underrepresented students in Catholic schools and who is now working toward a Ph.D. in neurosciences from the University of Chicago.

What are the elements present in these programs that promote success within students who were considered at risk for academic failure? What are the education policies in place that support and facilitate success not only in their public school settings but in other arenas and long after they have completed the intervention programs? Dean Kahn believes that all students, at all ages, must be encouraged to recognize and accept their personal stories about themselves, their families, and their past histories. These personal stories are necessary for the development of a strong positive sense of self and positive identities. An important part of the history of the Bank Street College of Education was the Long Trip begun by founder Lucy Sprague Mitchell to allow teachers to learn first-hand about the issues of a specific time period by experiencing how other people lived—not as tourists, but as eyewitnesses and participants. In 1996, Kahn revived this tradition to allow more teachers, administrators, community members, and students to delve deeper into personal and family histories.

Citing experiences of limited information, and miseducation, Kahn stated that the history of many African American families has been neutralized by the absence of connections to positive achievements in their families and histories. The family histories that are shared are usually about pain; however, on one of the Long Trips, she and the other participants also learned about the wealth of contributions made by free African American families living in the Savannah, Georgia, area in the years after the Civil War. The Long Trip was to the Penn Center, St. Helena Island, South Carolina. Built to educate the freed Sea Island slaves, the Penn Center was only one of the educational institutions serving free Blacks. Schools that were established to educate the children of wealthy African Americans and which offered challenging and nontraditional courses such as Latin, are rarely discussed in the history books. The Penn Center is the principal repository of primary written, audio, and photographic documentation of the history and culture of African Americans of the Sea Islands. Participants on this Long Trip had the opportunity to become immersed in experiences prompting personal, professional, and community self-reflection that led to critical epiphanies about race, class, and gender and their impact—both intended and unintended—on interactions among and between all members of the school community. The experience at the Penn Center was a process of demystifying and questioning long held beliefs that high levels of achievements in academic and other areas is a rarity among African American students. Experiences such as these foster the understandings that high levels of achievements are normal and expected across the African American population.

Kahn, like many of the proponents of the after school movement, sees the programs offered through the Division of Continuing Education as enrichment and an extension of experiences, not solely as the remediation of deficits experienced in the school settings. This advocacy for after school programs as enrichment creates a tension with many of the legislators who support funding for remediation. Her work continues in concert with others, to inform the policymakers so that the decisions are in the best interest of the students. Kahn stipulates that her influence in education policy making is evident in agenda setting, policy implementation, and policy evaluation.

INSTITUTIONAL AND GOVERNMENTAL CONTEXTS: AUGUSTA SOUZA KAPPNER

Augusta Kappner, like Fern Kahn, functions within the established contexts of institutions of higher education for developing and implementing educational policy. She has also functioned at the national governmental level as a member of the executive branch of the federal government. Members of the executive branch are participants in the agenda-setting process as agents of the President. They are often also responsible for policy implementation and evaluation once Congress has passed legislation.

We are all familiar with the adage, "The journey begins with the first step." For Augusta Souza Kappner, the step she remembers first making on this journey that has taken her from social worker to Dean of Students, to Assistant Secretary for Vocational and Adult Education in the first Clinton Administration, to the presidency of two colleges began with the support and encouragement of her sixth-grade teacher, Mrs. Sherman. Growing up in the South Bronx, the child of immigrant parents, her first time out of the neighborhood was shepherded by Mrs. Sherman who recommended and guided her application to, and enrollment in, Hunter College Junior and High Schools.

Kappner's story of how she developed into the person we now know is studded with the knowledge, experiences, and belief systems molded by (a) interactions with students and adults she would not have met in the "neighborhood," (b) the guidance of mentors steeped in the values of social justice, (c) active involvement in connecting community organization and policy, and (d) being inspired by proponents of advocacy planning in urban affairs. Advocacy planning in urban affairs involves residents in thinking about what the communities in which they live would look like and then assisting in their design. She related the importance of her multiple meaningful and mind-expanding internships such as the experiences with the Model Cities Housing program in East Harlem and the South Bronx as well as working as a field advisor in the Urban Social Work Program sponsored by Columbia University's School of Social Work. These experiences exposed her to the possibilities available for social change, while academic and professional preparation combined with an understanding of how

to access the resources, cemented her commitment to activism. Mentors mediated her understanding of the worlds she could function in. From Dr. Gladys Meyer at Barnard College, she realized that studying and learning how society works is not synonymous with accepting the status quo. Simultaneously, she also realized that colleges and universities as institutions could be used for the social good (Bank Street College of Education, 2002).

Within the institutions of higher education and as a member of President Clinton's cabinet, Kappner's advocacy is for the creation of access into higher education and the elimination of barriers to retention in college and success in the workforce. From 1993 to 1995, she guided development of the School-to-Work legislation resulting in national and international relationships around vocational and continuing education. This legislation, an integral component of President Clinton's plan for education supporting and enabling seamless connections between school and work, had implications for schools, employers, and postsecondary institutions. Kappner's partners in this process represented national and international states with a common focus on the options available for preparing students to enter the world of work and providing activities as early as kindergarten to expose students to potential future careers. Equally important during her service to the executive branch was the work on Literacy Behind Walls, an assessment of the literacy levels of federal and state prisoners. The assessment had strong implications for those who administered, worked, or volunteered in programs that directly affect prisoners' learning.

While the arena within which Kappner works has changed over the years, the emphasis on providing access to higher education and removing barriers to retention and completion of degree programs has been nonnegotiable. Joan Baum (2003) described Kappner's priorities as "an activist sense of education and a belief that education is essential for children and teachers in breaking down societal barriers and enhancing potential, personally and professionally" (p. 1). The effective use of these components required the building and sustaining of relationships that are internal and external to the institution. As the coordinator of Human Services at LGC with the responsibility to facilitate a career ladder through academia for adult students in the field of social work, she nurtured relationships among students, faculty, and potential employers. As the president of the Borough of Manhattan Community College (BMCC), she brought the importance of mentors to the student population. Without much experience in being mentors or being mentored themselves, the need to demystify the role and value of mentors for the predominantly African American and Hispanic American student population was paramount. As the first African American female president in the CUNY system at BMCC, the largest community college in New York City, the prospects could have been daunting, but Kappner had clarity about the critical issues. What does access to higher education mean? And, now that access is offered, how do we ensure that those students are retained in the institution, leaving as successful graduates with earned degrees?

Partnerships, the external relationships, had to be purposeful and meet a range of needs. There were the partnerships with the P-12 systems to develop and advocate for strong alignment and articulation. There were the national networks such as the American Council on Education and women's groups to build alliances for the work that was being done and to gain/provide support for women in similar positions. As policymaker, Kappner identified the factors contributing to the declining enrollment of African Americans in higher education. In delivering the keynote address at the 1989 Annual Convention of the American Association of Community and Junior Colleges, she shared influencing factors such as the effects of institutional policies, leadership, and mentoring. She also shared specific actions such as the institution of the largest Freshman Immersion program to provide intensive tutoring and counseling to BMCC's entering class of 1988 and each entering class after that. Supported by alternative funding through partnerships with the business sector, these student supports led to stronger articulation agreements with 4-year colleges (Kappner, 1989).

When asked what she sees as her impact on educational policy, her assessment is that her role is usually one of advisor influencing and educating those actors in the formal process to make good policy. Advisors sit on governing boards, chancellor searches, and task forces, and are appointed to Boards of Education. Advisors are the links to expert knowledge and have the courage to make moral decisions that can be in opposition to the politicians who ask for that advice, as was the case in 2005 when she publicly opposed New York City's Mayor Bloomberg on his policy for social promotion. She advocates for schools being held accountable for the progress for all students, with the advice that data be used to determine the interventions needed as well as the effectiveness of the interventions used. To her, the interventions would be more effective if provided to students during the early years of school so that strong foundations for learning are created, rather than being provided during the high school and college years when more extensive and more costly remediation is needed.

Kappner's work incorporates all six of Brewer and deLeon's (1983) stages for policy making. As Assistant Secretary of Vocational and Adult Education with the responsibility for administering programs with a budget of $1.7 billion, she was actively involved in estimation, selection, and implementation of policy. As president of BMCC from 1986 to 1992, her capacity to set the policy agenda resulted in increased student enrollment, an increased number of academic programs, more grants available to the school and its students, and stronger partnerships with the college's external communities.

COMMUNITY CONTEXT: HELEN MARSHALL

Community members often share sets of values, experiences, concerns, and needs. Participation in the policy-making process as a representative of the community can occur at any one of the six stages delineated by Brewer and deLeon (1983). The prompt for participation might have been catalyzed merely by the need to have a voice in a problem that is being discussed or debated within the community, without any declared overt design or desire to be a part of a process. A participant, individually, as a part of a loosely configured group or as a member of a well-organized special interest group, can help define a problem; get that problem on the local, state, or national legislative agenda; and participate in shaping the remedy to that problem and/or assessing the implementation and/or impact of the policy created to redress the inequity that prompted the problem. Recognition of an individual as a part of the policy-making process within a community means that person has proven to be an effective communicator, is easily accessible, has demonstrated influence, and most often evolves into a dynamic leader from ongoing participation in the policy process. This is the story of how Helen Marshall became an active member of the policy-making process in New York City.

> Why are you doing this? You spent all this money to come to Queens to get a house here for a better life for your children, and now you're going to have to get money together to pay tuition at private and parochial schools when you have brand new schools here?

These were the questions that Helen Marshall asked the African American parents whom she met in the Corona and East Elmhurst sections of Queens in the early 1960s. She had just moved from the Bronx with her husband and young children with the belief that she was now among New York City's solidly middle-class African Americans. She would learn that while the African American families had accumulated the funds to purchase the homes, their children were still in segregated schools, and they were not willing to insist on getting the quality of education associated with living in a middle-class neighborhood. Instead, they struggled to raise the tuition for private and/or parochial schools.

Gregory (1998) reported that the East Elmhurst/Corona section of Queens was one of the few neighborhoods in New York City where African Americans could buy homes in the early 1940s. Ditmars Boulevard, a main street, was considered the "black gold coast." Yet as respectable as the residents thought the schools to be, their children were not afforded the same educational opportunities as the White children. By the 1960s, Marshall and three other parents spearheaded the integration and improvement of the schools. She tells of moving to Queens with her son and daughter. Her son was beginning second grade and her daughter was in nursery school. Active in the schools while living in the Bronx, she began attending the Parent Teacher Association meetings and was very vocal about the changes that were needed. Invited to chair the legislative committee, Marshall immersed herself in learning the rules and regulations and quickly found out that most of the schools in Queens were unfinished because construction began during the War and

all the metal was targeted for the War needs. Efforts had to be made to have the schools completed. As the schools were being completed, school district personnel, school staff, and members of the community realized that there were no libraries. Using funds available through the Library Services and Construction Act (LSCA), they helped create the Langston Hughes Community Library, now a repository of 45,000 books and videos on Black heritage. First legislated in 1957, and reauthorized with different priorities in subsequent years, the LSCA provided funding for the building and supporting of libraries in underserved and disadvantaged communities. What prepared Helen Marshall for this level of activism? How did she learn to navigate the system to make things happen?

There were several pivotal changes in Marshall's life that prepared her for advocacy. At the age of 7, her family moved from Harlem to an apartment in the Bronx. Her father, a house painter, got a job painting apartments for a man who owned two apartment buildings that were rented to "coloreds." This move made her 1 of approximately 5 African American children on the block and 1 of about 10 African American children in her new school. Close to her home was Claremont House, an annex to the Bronx Settlement House. This settlement house provided the opportunities for sleep away camp as a child, family camp later with her husband and children, and most important, the germination of activism. Growing up in an integrated community, and having a history of participating in the activities of the settlement house, Marshall had a sense of the broader possibilities available. Additionally, her involvement in the Inter Group Committee—comprising social workers who had conducted a study of the New York City Public Schools showing that the least effective schools were in the communities where African American children lived—exposed her to the processes that resulted in creating new schools, building coalitions, reviewing school board budgets, and advocating for change.

Enrolling her son in kindergarten brought her face-to-face with a problem. There was a new school built on Fulton Avenue in the Bronx that was intended to replace the existing school on Third Avenue, under the El (the elevated sections of the subway tracks). As quickly as the schools were built they were filled, and there was huge overcrowding. Instead of moving to the new Fulton Avenue School, the third- and fourth-grade students remained in the old school. The conditions there were deplorable, and it was hard to imagine instruction taking place there with the constant rumbling of the trains coming and going in and out of the station. At a loss as to what to do, Marshall shared her concerns with the other parents at the Bronx House nursery school her daughter attended. Many of them were her friends from the Bronx Settlement House. Like her, they had gone to summer camp, nursery school, and after school classes there, and while living in other areas of the Bronx, still brought their children to the nursery school.

One of the parents, living in the area where the Cross Bronx Expressway was being built, shared that there was a huge displacement of families that left more than 10 classrooms empty in the school her children attended. They coalesced into a group petitioning the Board of Education for 12 months to provide transportation for the children from the Third Avenue school to this underused school. This yearlong process to gain approval taught Marshall the importance of building alliances and forced her to develop a knowledge base about the budgeting and funding of different aspects of providing education to communities. Her efforts did not go unnoticed, and in 1956 she was the first non-Jewish person to receive the Bronx House award.

Her activism within the community led to her involvement in the Democratic Party. Service within the party led to her being voted district leader in 1974, member of the New York State Assembly for 9 years (1982–1991), member of the New York City Council for 10 years (1991–2001), and then Queens Borough President in 2001. Consistent across her political career has been concern about education and ensuring that students receive all available services. Within the P-12 education system she shepherded the implementation of the Princeton Plan as a vehicle for integrating the schools. First used in the Princeton, New Jersey, township and borough public schools in 1949, the plan paired schools so that students of all races attended one building from K through fifth grade and another building from sixth through ninth grade (Handelman, 1999). Adopted in Queens as a pilot program, it paired schools #69 and #92 that were six blocks apart. Resistance from the White community was immediate with many

families sending their children to private schools. Years later, when the New York Public Schools removed ninth grade from the junior high schools and assigned the students to a school where racial hostility was rampant, the African American parents partnered with the First Baptist Church to create a Freedom School for the 64 students.

Efforts to fully integrate the public schools in Queens and ensure high-quality education for all students kept Marshall active in the community. The focus this time was on securing a location for a junior high/intermediate school that would be easily accessible for students of all racial and ethnic groups across the borough. It was envisioned that this school would provide a well-rounded education to students of all academic abilities. Collaborative endeavors with two of the community school districts were encouraged, but did not materialize. Eventually Marshall and her group, counseled by the civil rights attorney Paul Zuber, appealed to the Frank J. Macchiarola, Chancellor of the New York City public schools. In 1979, he agreed to the founding of IS 227, making a Chancellor's school, therefore, not belonging to any of the Community School Districts in Queens. Renamed the Louis Armstrong school, IS 227 has become one of the most sought-after schools because of its academic programs, organizational structure, and strong special education component.

As representative for the 35th Assembly district and then for the 21st Councilmanic district, Marshall's focus moved toward higher education, creating and being the founding chair of the Committee on Higher Education in New York City. She noted that less than 17% of all graduating seniors from New York City were admitted to the CUNY system before the advent of Open Admissions. Her mission here was to ensure that students in need of remediation as well as students in need of enrichment received services.

The trajectory of Marshall's public life also reflects all six stages of the policy-making process. Moving from the role of a private citizen working within a group to influence a specific policy selection that would benefit themselves and fellow parents of young students, Marshall participated in policy implementation and even influenced the termination of policies supporting segregated schools in Queens. As an influential policymaker within the state, city, and borough political arenas, she set the agenda and developed many educational policies that will continue to accrue benefits to residents of Queens, New York City, and New York State.

Conclusion

Educational opportunities to learn and succeed require much more than the macro view of performance on standardized tests, quality of teacher preparation, and access to technology. Without denying the importance of these factors, the oral histories of these four African American policymakers provide a basis for an understanding of how the policy-making process can make a difference for the educational opportunities of African American students. A checklist of the factors contributing to their effectiveness as policymakers would reveal a deep understanding of the political, social, and financial systems as the number one item. Each person has spent at least 25 years in his or her policy arena totally immersed in, and passionate about, the work of improving the life chances for students and their families. In so doing, their spheres of influence are strong, and their reputations for getting things done in ways that are beneficial to African American communities are well-known. Vying for top billing on the checklist also would be their credibility among peers, colleagues, and external partners. Each of these policymakers was very clear in stating that tasks accomplished are never done solely by the leadership. Each of the policymakers is also recognized as a courageous and committed person, but integral to the attainment of goals is the willingness to support others in their courageous steps. Exemplified in their personal lives and in the policies they have championed are their consistent commitment to providing opportunities that broaden the geographical, mental, and visionary boundaries of the young African American students living in economically depressed communities and having a limited number of role models who have access to and are functioning in the professional and work worlds.

The success that each of these policymakers has experienced in generating change was shaped by personal histories, a willingness to challenge public values incongruent with their understanding of the needs of African American

students, and their commitment and courage to effect change. In so doing, they are ensuring that through education, African Americans acquire a voice in society and in history, which ultimately allows them to alter the collective reality (Freire, 1985). In so doing, they exemplify the words of well-known African American singer Nina Simone, "Those of us who are lucky leave a legacy so that when we are dead, we also live on" (Garland, 1969).

References

Bank Street College of Education. (2002, March). Augusta Kappner, Bank Street College of Education. *Education Update*. Retrieved May 25, 2007, from www.educationupdate.com/archives/2002/mar02/htmls/cover_kappner.html

Baum, J. (2003, March). Augusta Souza Kappner, President, Bank Street, leader and champion for children everywhere. *Education Update*. Retrieved May 25, 2007, from www.education update.com/archives/2003/march03/issue/cov_augusta.html

Brewer, G. D., & deLeon, P. (1983). *The foundations of policy analysis*. Monterey, CA: Brooks/Cole.

Campbell, R. F., & Mazzoni, T. L. (1976). *State policymaking for the public schools in 12 states and a treatment of state governance models*. Berkeley, CA: McCutchan.

Fenno, R. F. (2003). *Coming home: Black representatives and their constituents*. Chicago: University of Chicago Press.

Foster, M. (1997). *Black teachers on teaching*. New York: New Press.

Freire, P. (1985). *The politics of education: Culture, power and liberation* (D. Macedo, Trans.). South Hadley, MA: Bergin & Garvey.

Garland, P. (1969). *The sound of soul: The story of Black music*. Raleigh, NC: Contemporary.

Gregory, S. (1998). *Black Corona: Race and the politics of place in an urban community*. Princeton, NJ: Princeton University Press.

Handelman, L. (1999, June 8). The Princeton plan: Fifty years of school desegregation. *Princeton Packet*. Retrieved May 25, 2007, from www.pacpubserver.com/new/news/6-9-99/princetonplan.html

The HistoryMakers. (2005, May 5). Retrieved May 25, 2007, from http://thehistorymakers.com/biography/biography.asp?bioindex=1075

Kappner, A. S. (1989). *Leadership toward empowerment: The national agenda for blacks in the 21st century*. Remarks made at the 1989 Annual Convention of the American

Association of Community and Junior Colleges, Washington, DC.

Lindblom, C. E., & Woodhouse, E. J. (1993). *The policy-making process* (3rd ed.). Englewood Cliffs, NJ: Prentice Hall.

Maimin, S. (2004, February). Fern Khan: Bank Street Dean forges social work, community outreach & continuing education into powerful force for change. *Education Update, 9*(6). Retrieved May 25, 2007, from www.educationupdate.com/archives/2004/Feb04/issue/col_kahn.html

Marshall, C., & Gerstl-Pepin, C. (2005). *Reframing educational politics for social justice.* Boston: Pearson.

Marshall, C., Mitchell, D., & Wirt, F. (1989). *Culture and education policy in the American States.* New York: Falmer Press.

National Council for Community and Education Partnerships. (2007, March). *Using EXPLORE and PLAN data to evaluate GEAR UP programs.* Iowa City, IA: Author.

Putz, A. (2007, March). Chaka Fattah: Just your average politician. *Philadelphia Magazine, 98,* 100–103, 161–167.

Riccardi, K. (1998, April 23). *Laguardia Community College, Division of adult and continuing education collection: 1971 to the present.* Retrieved June 12, 2007, from www.lagcc.cuny.edu/library/archives/cont_edu/intro.htm

Terkel, S. (1956). *Division Street: America.* New York: New Press.

U.S. Department of Education. (2007). *GEAR-UP 2008 program performance plan.* Retrieved July 30, 2007, from www.ed.gov/about/reports/annual/2008plan/g2heagaining.doc

Woodson, C. G. (1972). *The mis-education of the Negro.* New York: AMS Press.

27

REALITIES AND RESPONSIBILITIES IN THE EDUCATION VILLAGE

ERIC J. COOPER

I t is popular today to declare that education policy should be "data driven." I hold that policy should be driven by values and by vision, informed by data. For example, the policy that America "doesn't give up on people" isn't data driven; it's a statement of values. Policy should begin with values that are formed into a vision of how the world should be. Data should inform the development of policy that guides action, and plans to carry out the policy. Data must inform the "how" of our plans; values must shape the substance of our vision and our mission to make that vision real. Beliefs unite values and information.

I believe that virtually no child, including no African American child, is so compromised by his or her family or community circumstances that he or she cannot be successful in school. I say "virtually" because there are some children who have conditions that impair their ability to fulfill this goal, but they are fewer than are institutionally classified in this way. Here, I am writing about the vast majority of our children. The experience of the National Urban Alliance for Effective Education (NUA) is that strenuous, continuous efforts of students within, and adults within and around a school, can have almost magical effects on the seemingly intractable factors that compromise cumulative learning.

The National Urban Alliance for Effective Education (NUA) was founded in 1989 with a vision of school reform based on three beliefs: All children are capable of attaining high educational standards; intelligence is modifiable, not fixed; and all stakeholders in the community must be involved in addressing the social, cultural, and intellectual needs of our youth. The mission of the NUA is to substantiate in the public schools of urban America an irrefutable belief in the capacity of all children to reach the high levels of learning and thinking demanded by our ever-changing global community. The NUA's work is focused on learning and teaching. The NUA's network of more than 50 mentors are highly skilled and exemplary professionals in the field of education; many of whom have doctoral degrees in education. They come from all areas of the country and provide ongoing professional development activities for teachers to improve classroom instruction. NUA mentors are current or

---

AUTHOR'S NOTE: This chapter is dedicated to the life and legacy of Dr. Asa G. Hilliard III (1933–2007). He championed and mentored many, not the least of which is the leadership of the National Urban Alliance for Effective Education (NUA). He will be deeply missed for his advocacy, knowledge, counsel, and love that he brought to the world.

retired teachers, administrators, and university faculty who promote instructional strategies based on the latest research on concept and cognitive development, reasoning, thinking, and higher-order comprehension skills.

Under contract with school districts, NUA mentors work in schools demonstrating lessons in math, science, reading, and writing with groups of students. NUA coaches the administrative and instructional staff in best practices to accelerate learning for all students. With guidance, assistance, and coaching from the NUA mentor, teachers learn how to work together to unleash their knowledge, skills, and creativity in a supportive environment. Because the NUA mentors understand the challenges faced by educators today, their work is as much about lifting morale and giving people hope as it is about providing educators with the latest knowledge, tools, and techniques.

The National Study Group for the Affirmative Development of Academic Ability (2004), organized under the leadership of Dr. Edmund Gordon, concluded from its review of research that "academic ability is a developed ability— the quality of which is not primarily a function of one's biological endowment or fixed aptitudes" (p. 7). The group further concluded that "affirmative development of academic ability is nurtured and developed through (1) high-quality teaching and instruction in the classroom; (2) trusting relationships in school; and (3) supports for pro-academic behavior in the school and community" (p. 7). Schools are at the heart of the group's findings, but are not alone in their responsibility to live out the promise of our nation to all our children, or to develop their ability to fashion their own good life. In this chapter, based on, but ranging beyond, the NUA experience, I will focus on the first of this trinity. Good teaching and good schools attend to trust and to creating a web of support for proacademic behavior.

The Record on Equity and Excellence: How Is It Going?

What is the current record of success to achieve educational equity and excellence? There is neither space nor patience to review all the data or analyses about various approaches, various factors, and vagaries of many efforts to achieving both equity and excellence in the same place, for all the students. The following are some indicators of how things are going that suggest a path for greater, more rapid, and more sustainable success.

Combinations of education policy and education practices are raising the achievement of African American students above historic averages, not just in individual exceptions but in whole classes, in whole schools. Michael Casserly (2006), in *Beating the Odds VI*, published by the Council of the Great City Schools (CGCS)[1] (CGCS membership includes 66 of the nation's largest urban school districts) in March 2006, reported that

- Ninety-four percent of CGCS districts showed gains in fourth-grade math scores on their respective state tests.

- Seventy percent of CGCS districts showed math gains in both fourth and eighth grade that were greater than overall gains in their respective states.

- The percentage of students in CGCS districts scoring at or above the proficient level on their respective state math tests rose from 45% in 2001–2002 to 59% in 2004–2005.

- Ninety percent of the CGCS districts increased their fourth-grade reading scores on state assessments between 1999–2000 and 2004–2005, and 59% did so at a rate equal to or greater than their respective states.

- Eighty-eight percent of the districts increased their eighth-grade reading scores in the same period, 73% at the same or faster rate than their state.

- In 2005, 54% of fourth-grade students in CGCS schools scored at or above state-defined "proficiency" levels in reading, up 4 points from 2004 and 11 points from 2002; 40% of eighth graders were scored "proficient," up 1 and 4 points from 2004 and 2002, respectively.

- While 85% of all fourth graders tested narrowed the gap between African American and White students on their state reading test from 2002 to 2005, 63% of eighth graders who were tested did so. Seventy-six percent of students in both grades narrowed the gap between White and Hispanic students.

- Fifty-eight percent of fourth graders and 43% of eighth graders tested in CGCS schools narrowed that gap at rates equal to or faster than their respective states. A smaller percentage narrowed the gap between White and Hispanic students in fourth grade, but a larger percentage narrowed that gap in eighth grade.

Perie, Grigg, and Donahue (2005) reported in the National Center for Educational Statistics (NCES) Reading Report 2005 that more progress was made in fourth-grade reading between 2000 and 2005 (10 points for African American students, 5 points for White students) than was made between 1992 and 2000 (−2 points for African American students).

Should We Be Encouraged?

The gains reported by the CGCS and National Assessment of Educational Progress (NAEP) are encouraging, but they are not comforting. One cannot be comfortable when facing the following data from the 2003 NAEP—the nation's report card—presented by Poliokaff (2006) in *Closing the Gap: An Overview* issued by the Association for Supervision and Curriculum Development (ASCD) in January 2006:

- On the 2003 reading assessment, 84% of students eligible for free or reduced-price lunches scored at or below the basic level (55% below that line defined as "partially mastering" the knowledge and skills in reading for that grade). This compared with 54% and 24%, respectively, for students not qualifying for federal meal subsidies.

- Fifty-eight percent of Black fourth graders were below the basic level, compared with 54% of Hispanic students and 24% of White students.

- On the 2004–2005 NAEP reading test, 20% of urban fourth- and eighth-grade students reached or surpassed the "proficient" level compared with the national rates of 30% and 29%, respectively. The fourth-grade scores were up 3 points for the urban students, flat nationally, since 2002. For eighth graders it was flat for urban students, down 2 points nationally over the same period.

Beating the Odds VI reported that 24% of fourth-grade students in 67 city school districts (a sample of NAEP called the Trial Urban District Assessment) scored at or above the "proficient" level in 2005 compared with 20% in 2002 while an equal gain of 4 points brought the overall national level to 34%. We cannot be satisfied with such performance in our great nation, in our great cities, or in our growing urban populations.

The Academic Achievement Gap: Facts and Figures

We cannot be comfortable or complacent in light of the following reported by Teachers College (TC), Columbia University *News* (June 9, 2005). The educational achievement gap in the United States exists in and out of the classroom, and extends from the earliest years of childhood across the life span. The wealth of information documenting the gap is vast, but the following are some of the more telling statistics reported by the TC *News*:

- By age 3, children of professionals have vocabularies that are nearly 50% greater than those of working-class children and twice as large as those of children whose families are on welfare.

- By the end of fourth grade, African American, Latino, and poor students of all races are 2 years behind their wealthier, predominantly White peers in reading and math. By eighth grade, they have slipped 3 years behind, and by twelfth grade, 4 years behind.

- Only 1 in 50 Hispanic and Black 17-year-olds can read and gain information from specialized text (such as the science section of a newspaper) compared with about 1 in 12 White students.

- By the end of high school, Black and Hispanic students' reading and mathematics skills are roughly the same as those of White students in the eighth grade.

- African American students are three times more likely than White students to be placed in special education programs and are half as likely to be in gifted programs in elementary and secondary schools.

- "Among 18- to 24-year olds, about 90 percent of whites have either completed high school or earned a GED [graduate equivalent degree]. Among blacks, the rate is 81 percent; among Hispanics, 63 percent. However, a much larger share of blacks earn GEDs than whites, and only about 50 percent of black students earn regular diplomas, compared with about 75 percent of whites."

- Black students are only about half as likely (and Hispanics about one third as likely) as White students to earn a bachelor's degree by age 29.

- One in three African American males will be incarcerated in state or federal prison at some point during their lives, and the rate is significantly higher for Black men who do not finish high school. For Hispanic males, the rate is 1 in 6; for White males, 1 in 17.

- Homicide has been the leading cause of death among African Americans aged 15 to 34 since 1978. The lifetime risk of violent death for young Black males is 1 in 27, and for Black females, 1 in 17. In contrast, 1 in 205 young White males and 1 in 496 young White females are murdered.

Even good news brings with it sobering measures of how far there is to go. A study by the Center for Strengthening the Teaching Profession (2005) in Washington State reported that the percentage of African American students who met or exceeded the standard for "proficiency" on the state reading test for fourth grade jumped from 35% to 69% from 1996–1997 to 2004–2005. That 34-point increase narrowed the achievement gap between African American and Caucasian students who gained 22 points in the same period. But the absolute gap was significant: Only 69% of African American students achieved the "proficient" mark compared with 84% of Caucasian students (p. 8).

The experience of the NUA is consistent with the findings above, both the encouraging and the cautionary. Data reported in December 2002 show that in the Seattle Public Schools, African American students who spent 2 years with teachers who completed the district's literacy training conducted by NUA had twice the pass rate on the Washington Assessment of Student Learning (WASL) of students whose teachers

did not have that training. On the WASL Writing Test for the 10th grade, the pass rate for African American students doubled to 34% from 2001 to 2004 across the entire district. Data for the school year 2006 also indicate that Seattle Public School's 4th- and 10th-grade students improved from 67% to 81% meeting the WASL (Washington State Report Card, 2005/2006).

Similarly, the Indianapolis Public Schools (IPS), while near the very bottom of the state rankings for students passing both reading and math sections of the Indiana State Test of Educational Progress, narrowed the gap between Black and White students in English/Language Arts by more than 35% in Grade 3 between 1999–2000 and 2005–2006 (Annual Report Card, Indianapolis Public Schools, 2006). NUA's analysis of Indiana data shows that elementary schools of IPS that showed high-fidelity implementation of the IPS/NUA Vanguard initiative for literacy instruction outstripped statewide gains from 1999 to 2005. Data sent to NUA from the Newark Public Schools (NPS) for the High School Proficiency Assessment growth in 2005 indicated that the four high schools participating in NUA training between 2002 and 2003 showed an average increase in their student pass rate on the state test of 13.5 percentage points (a gain of 31%) compared with eight other schools listed by NPS that averaged 1 point of growth during the same period. From 2004 to 2005, these four schools experienced a 10.5 percentage point gain while the other eight schools were essentially flat, decreasing by 0.54%. In Minneapolis, it was reported by Steve Brandt under his byline on the *Star-Tribune* Web site, April 5, 2006, that students who participated in the West Metro Education Program integration initiative, which allowed low-income city residents to choose suburban schools supported by NUA's comprehensive instructional coaching, tripled the gains of eligible students who did not choose those suburban schools.

Should We Look Outside or Inside the Schools for Causes and Cures?

Across the country, we are confronted by variation in student achievement within a single grade level among schools in the same school district, often in the same neighborhood. We are also confronted by variation in student achievement among classes of the same grade within the same school. I say confronted because these variations challenge explanations of low (or high) student achievement that rely on external factors, whether home conditions (e.g., single parent or low income) or community conditions (e.g., crime or widespread unemployment). Discouraging or distracting circumstances surely do not help kids learn their school lessons, but they are not—except in extreme situation—insurmountable barriers to school success. Intraschool and intradistrict successes call for identification of factors within schools to account for variation in student performance.

Beating the Odds VI, in sum, shows that many districts, schools, and classrooms are making progress not only in terms of meeting state standards but also in closing the persistent gap in achievement rates between African American students and White students. These advances suggest strongly that schools can blunt and, yes, overcome the gaps faced by many African American children outside the school—substandard housing, dangerous streets, unemployment in their family and community, poor nutrition, peer culture that dampens rather than celebrates ambition to succeed in school. Much of the story is related to the effects of economics, but poverty per se is not the key; important effects of poverty can be ameliorated by the family, by the community, and by school. For example, if economic stress leads the single parent in a household to work two jobs, the children need alternatives for supervision and support of homework to supplement the time that the parent can provide.

Stanford University Professor Linda Darling-Hammond reported in Education Policy Analysis Archives (January, 2000) that

> while student demographic characteristics are strongly related to student outcomes at the state level, they are less influential in predicting achievement levels than variables assessing the quality of the teaching force. . . . When aggregated at the state level, teacher quality variables appear to be more strongly related to student achievement than class sizes, overall spending levels, teacher salaries (at least when unadjusted for cost of living differentials), or such factors as the statewide proportion of staff who are teachers. (p. 40)

She adds that "substantial evidence from prior reform efforts indicates that changes in course taking, curriculum content, testing, or textbooks make little difference if teachers do not know how to use these tools well and how to diagnose their students' learning needs" (p. 41). It stands to reason that student learning should be enhanced by the efforts of teachers who are more knowledgeable about their academic field *and* are skillful in teaching it to others. Thus, in this chapter, I concentrate on policy and programs that raise the quality of teaching.

Why Aren't Successes Far More Widespread?

A key to the question raised in the title of this section is the will to do the right thing. The oft-cited statement of Ron Edmonds offers one perspective on this fundamental question: In the book *Young, Gifted and Black* (Perry, Steele, & Hilliard, 2003), the late and sorely missed Asa Hilliard III, a professor at Georgia State University and long-time friend of NUA, quoted Ronald Edmonds, who stated, "We can, whenever and wherever we wish, teach successfully all children whose education is of interest to us. Whether we do or do not do it depends in the final analysis on how we feel about the fact that we have not done so thus far" (p. 165). Edmonds often stressed that, in my words, the existence of one success is proof that success can be achieved in all similar circumstances. He was asserting that the nation, the states, school districts, schools, educators—and those at home and in the community—lack the will to bring the achievement distribution of African American students in line with the achievement distribution of White students.

Many years after the *Brown* decision, we all must recognize that not only are there no separate but equal tables, ultimately there are no separate tables at all. The education of all children is "of interest" to all of us in the general sense that all in the American economy, policy, and society have a stake—an interest—in all children growing into contributing members of those elements of America. To be indifferent to this is shortsighted, wasteful, and wrong in a society—one still shedding the burdens of pernicious practices and suffering the stains of private prejudices (from all directions)—that is the keeper of the American dream held up by Martin Luther King, Jr. in his speech at the Lincoln

Memorial on August 28, 1963. We need to hold his dream both in our dreams and in our waking hours.

The need to close the achievement gap is great, national, and urgent. It is also personal and practical. An article by Paul Barton in *Education Leadership* (February, 2006) cited National Center for Educational Statistics data when reporting that for 25- to 34-year-old (high school) dropouts who manage to work full-time, the average annual salary of males dropped from $35,087 (in 2002 constant dollars) in 1971 to $22,903 in 2002, a decline of 35%. The comparable annual earnings for females without a diploma were $19,888 in 1971, declining to $17,114 in 2002. Even when they work full-time, the average earnings of this age group of dropouts are not far above the poverty line for a family with children— and most dropouts do not even reach this level of earnings. The earnings of high school graduates also have declined since 1971, but not as steeply as those of dropouts (NCES, 2004, tables 14–1, 14–2, and 14–3). High school graduates are four times more likely to be unemployed than college graduates, and even when high school graduates are working, college graduates earn 80% more (Olson, 2006). Surely, everyone on a stoop or on the street can understand that a seat in class is a ticket to ride the American train, or it will leave the station without them.

The shift of demographics in America to so-called minority-majority, as with school enrollments in which non-White students are the majority, should not give false comfort that power or success will follow. In our world, many growing economies and political systems are non-White, but they control their own infrastructures. We need look no farther than the "Asian tiger" economies, such as India and China, much of Latin American, or the Middle East. And although the proportion of U.S. population that is African American is not rising above the 12% to 13% range held for some time, the African American teaching force is one half that proportion. Additionally, although the proportion of students who are African American is dropping nationally, it remains high in concentrated areas and schools within systems. As a CGCS snapshot of urban schools, *Beating the Odds VI* reports, 78% of the students in its 66 member districts are African American, Hispanic, Asian American, or other students of color compared with 41% in all schools nationwide. The designation "Black" has broader meaning than what it had at the time of the *Brown* decision. For example, Broward County, Florida, had the largest numerical increase in Black population of any county in the nation from 2000 to 2005, mainly by in-migration of Caribbean peoples.[2] But in-migration is not a testimony to educational success. The Schott Foundation (2006) report, *Public Education and Black Male Students: The 2006 State Report Card,* puts Florida last in the nation in its rate of graduating Black males—31%—"on time."

Despite shifts toward a "minority-majority" population in many communities and their schools, and racial/ethnic concentrations in neighborhoods and neighborhood schools, African American children will be taught by teachers who are mostly White and middle class. And although we work toward more schools with first-rate teachers of diverse backgrounds, we recognize the importance of students meeting and learning with people of different backgrounds. Too often, students' experiences in school—in the social and cultural curriculum that is embedded in the institutional experience— do not prepare them sufficiently for work and life in the wider world. Thus, even when "minority" students perform adequately in their academics, schools can fall short of their broader mission to nurture a complete person ready to manage his or her way in the real world.

Current education performance of some populations that are expanding may grow into a threat to those communities and thus to the prosperity and social unity of America. This is everybody's business, literally as members of a national economy and figuratively as members of a diverse but intertwined society. It must be observed that making the education of African American child "everybody's business" cuts at least two ways. It imposes on the larger society and polity an obligation to provide resources and policy that presses for, and provides for, virtually universal achievement above basic thresholds for participation in America's prosperity and society. But it also invites everyone whose business it is to examine the factors that contribute to student success—school, community, and home factors.

Given the realities of family circumstances in America—more families with two wage earners, high proportions of African American children living with one parent, relative, or caregiver— and an acknowledgment that many African American children are "school dependent" for their learning of basic as well as advanced subject matter, skills, and behaviors that are advantageous in the world, does not shield families and communities from challenges to do more and to do better by our children. And before we castigate the conveyers of that message, about dependence on school, let's reflect on it. Was Bill Cosby wrong to tell students to strive to exercise self-discipline? Were Black American leaders wrong to generally agree with Dr. Cosby that individuals have responsibility and that youth and adults in a community have responsibilities to one another? (Williams, 2006). Can we distinguish between responsibility and blame? Can we honor the efforts of people in tough situations yet spur them to greater individual and collective action? I think so. Can we spur folks on without the spur insulting their pride and humanity? We must take the risk, seeking to balance responsibilities of institutions and individuals. The world economy is changing rapidly, and those behind or beneath the curve of those changes will just lose more ground, unless we act on the genius that is America—our ability to absorb all citizens on "common ground" and toward the "common good."

As we work toward a unified vision of America in terms of providing equal opportunity to all citizens, we recognize, as expressed by W. E. B. Du Bois (1996), that an African American "ever feels his two-ness—an American, a Negro; two souls, two thoughts, two unreconciled strivings" (p. 3). For many African American students, there is a "two-ness" of cultural norms—those of the neighborhood and those of the school. This does not mean that African American youth must "act White"; we need not deny who we are or our affiliations with one another and our roots. It does mean that students should learn to channel their energy, intellect, and imagination into getting the content and codes of power that schools offer so that African American students, families, and communities are ready to earn prosperity and a position in the nation. This is not "acting White" nor does it accept cultural imperialism by schools insisting that students present themselves as Oreos. It means that schools should demonstrate, every day, respect for the dignity of each student, providing opportunity commensurate with the policy that no American is expendable, that all of America has a stake in the success of all Americans, and that accountability is institutional as well as individual, for adults and students. Additionally, it means that American society should examine the data on opportunity and accountability, making sure that individuals have a fair opportunity to meet high standards. And it means that the African American community of America should embrace and encourage its children to strive in school and should celebrate their success.

Student Achievement Gaps

Two achievement gaps demand attention in relation to African American students: The gap between student performance and established targets for achievement, such as "cut scores" for passing or grade averages for promotion; and the gap between African American students and students of other racial/ethnic groups. The first gap is criterion referenced, using an "absolute" standard that does not examine whether one group, or anyone at all, meets the standard. The second gap uses a relative standard that does not examine the level of achievement in relation to a standard of learning or performance. Everyone and every group must attend to both gaps.

It is vital for effective policy, advocacy, and practice to understand that to close one or both of these gaps is not to deny that there may well be a distribution of performance—some students will be assessed as "higher or lower" than others against the standard. We want *all* students to have an education that launches their life fairly and with the potential for them to apply themselves in ways of their choosing. Because individuals vary in the development of their minds, in their preferences and personalities, and in the effort they apply to a particular goal, they will create a continuum of performance against various standards. With fair opportunity, that distribution should not be correlated with race, class, or gender. However, there are several barriers to achieving this goal.

SOCIAL AND POLITICAL FACTORS

In July 2006, I participated in The Ideas Festival of the Aspen Institute, discussing "family capital" in terms that go beyond, yet can come before, financial wealth. The National Study Group (2004) developed a similar list of what they call "education-relevant capital." They cited Bourdieu (1986), Coleman et al. (1966), Gordon (1999), and Miller (1995) as background for this useful construct that ranges from networks of social relationships to cultural norms that emphasize education, to institutional access, to confidence in new circumstances, to nutrition and healthful physical conditions. Just looking at health indicators one worries about the future. The June 2005 Teachers College report noted the following health-related disparities that contribute to— and reflect—the educational achievement gap:

- *Vision:* Poor children have severe vision impairment at twice the general rate. Fifty percent or more of minority and low-income children have vision problems that interfere with their academic work.

- *Medical Care:* Black preschoolers are one third less likely than Whites to get standard vaccinations—probably, one reason why poor children lose 30% more days from school than nonpoor children.

- *Nutrition:* Poor children have higher rates of anemia (20% of Black children, 8% of all children) and more frequently fall below national averages in height and weight due to inferior nutrition.

- *Exposure to Lead:* Low-income children have dangerously high levels of lead in their blood, five times the rate of middle-class children. High lead levels harm cognitive functioning and contribute to hearing loss.

EDUCATIONAL FACTORS

Too often teacher perceptions of students are based on race or class prejudice, on first impressions of a youngster, or on reputation with an earlier teacher, or from the playground. Expectations may follow those perceptions. School curricula and general school programs are not "teacher proof." The manner of a teacher's engagement with his or her students, a teacher's ability to engage each student in learning content and skills, and a teacher's ability to assess student progress so that teaching can be

adjusted to better engage each student—all these factors are important to student success, particularly for school-dependent students who do not have opportunities to learn school material at home. Stanford University Professor Linda Darling-Hammond (2000) summed up a broad range of research on factors contributing or inhibiting student achievement in this way (some of which was cited earlier):

> First, while student demographic characteristics are strongly related to student outcomes at the state level, they are less influential in predicting achievement levels than variables assessing the quality of the teaching force. Second, when aggregated at the state level, teacher quality variables appear to be more strongly related to student achievement than class sizes, overall spending levels, teacher salaries (at least when unadjusted for cost of living differentials), or such factors as the statewide proportion of staff who are teachers. Among these variables assessing teacher "quality," the percentage of teachers with full certification and a major in the subject they teach is a more powerful predictor of student achievement than teachers' education levels. Like other studies cited earlier, this research indicates that the effects of well-prepared teachers on student achievement can be stronger than the influences of student background factors, as poverty, language background and minority status. And while smaller class sizes appear to contribute to student learning, particularly in fields like elementary reading, the gains occasioned by smaller classes are most likely to be realized, as they were in the Tennessee experiment, when they are accompanied by the hiring of well-qualified teachers. The large-scale hiring of unqualified teachers, as was the case in the California's recent class size reduction initiative, would likely offset any achievement gains that could be realized by smaller class sizes. (pp. 40–41)

The Center for Strengthening the Teaching Profession, based in Washington State, found in a 2004–2005 survey of teachers that although 92% of new teachers said they received training in how to teach all students of diverse backgrounds, only 25% felt confident they could do so (p. 4). For their students to succeed, both their confidence and underlying competence will have to improve markedly.

Finally, I cite the need for students' practice of school-taught skills. The National Study Group (2004) illustrated the importance of practice and pitfalls for children—particularly school-dependent children—in whom the nation has, a la Edmonds, a special interest and who are the focus of this chapter. (The practice called for should come through applications to creative and interesting tasks, not just from repetition of an exercise.)

> Practice is the best strategy for developing improved comprehension. With practice, comprehending complex processes becomes less effortful and more automatic. Practice can be formal or not. For example, some parents may sit down very purposely with their children and go over the day's school lessons or listen to their child read aloud. Or, they may pay for tutors to do such activities. Others may simply provide an opportunity for practicing some skills during routine activities, such as bedtime reading. Some children, however, may not get any opportunities for practice outside the classroom. (p. 11)

DISTORTED PERCEPTIONS OF ANALYSTS AND ADVOCATES

Three classic problems of individual's perception of a situation plague analysis of educational issues, advocacy about how to address them, and assessments of progress to resolve them. They distort research designs and undermine research findings and conclusions:

I won't see it if I don't believe it. Some analysts see the limits of nature in low test scores of African American students. They believe that nature has put a limit—breached by the rare exception, or perhaps by a person with what one might call a "mixed background"—on those students' potential for learning and intellectual achievement. Firm in this belief, they examine persistent low performance on standardized tests and find confirmation of their belief that there is a natural limit on a group of people that accounts for their achievement gap. Exceptions are just anomalies, not Edmond's proof that things need not be the way they are.

I won't see it unless I believe it. Other analysts have difficulty looking at data with clear eyes. Urban

success stories? Folks who believe urban school districts are hopeless, or (worse) are a danger to the more capable and motivated children, may well say that any successes are an artifact of data manipulation or low standards and tricky reporting or special circumstances. If, on the other hand, they believe that charter schools are the next worse thing to education vouchers, then they may well declare that any charter successes are only a function of selecting the best and expelling the rest of their students, particularly just before test time. Some community advocates believe that only institutional policy and practices, not individual choices as well, are accountable for violence or achievement gaps. They only see discrimination denying achievement and miss seeing opportunities to foster individual and family determination to achieve. In all these cases, beliefs overpower a fair reading of relevant data. Ideology trumps research.

I only see what I believe. Teachers often look at reports about a student and establish expectations of them. What then happens has been called Sustaining Expectation Effects (Good & Brophy, 1984)—the teachers pitch their instruction and guidance to their expectations and they filter out any new information, from others or the student, that do not sustain that expectation. The Pygmalion Effect reported by Rosenthal and Jacobson in 1968 emphasized the power of suggestion—projections of high student potential that exceeded the linear projections of past performance that seemed to induce teachers to treat those students in positive ways that they would not have employed for a cross-section of students, and the students performed at levels above predictions based on their actual record. In various forms, this Effect is carried forward today in the call for high expectations for all students. But high expectations, like beliefs, are only the beginning (see Cooper, 2005).

FEARS THAT CHILL AMBITION AND CONSTRAIN EFFORT

Students often fear tests they must take that have consequences for themselves, their teachers, and their school. It is often a fine line between getting students' attention for a test by highlighting potential positive and negative consequences, on the one hand, and traumatizing them to the point of being unable to show at test time what they know. In this context, students also fear the not-so-subtle "stereotype threat" about which Claude Steele and his colleagues have written "that corrosive feeling among students that they are not good enough to succeed [on tests and assessments of learning] solely because of their gender, race, ethnicity, or background" (Froning, 2006, p. 72). Students are also often set up for this form of self-fulfilling prophecy by the policies of academic tracking, where schools organize instruction based on student testing, and parent lobbying for placement of their child in talented and gifted programs or the honors track (Cooper, 2005).

Teachers too evidence fears by word and action. I am sure many of us can recall encountering these in discussions with teachers or when observing their practice. Space prohibits more than mention of them here:

> Teachers fear that tests are so insensitive to cultural differences that their minority students cannot succeed on them.

> Teachers fear their teaching abilities are inadequate to reach and relate to their students, engaging them in learning before they are in a spiral of compound failure.

> Teachers fear that they are alone in the community fighting for their students.

Again, the views of the National Study Group (2004) are relevant:

> The social-psychological literature points to a clear message that feelings of trust in the institution, and in those who are seen to represent the interests of those institutions (e.g., teachers, professors, administrators), are a fundamental building block in the affirmative development of high minority achievement. (p. 19)

(The National Study Group cites Bryk & Schneider, 2002; Mendoza-Denton & Aronson, in press; Steele & Aronson, 1995, 2000.) Yet successful African American students are likely, as they move up the achievement ladder, to encounter contexts and situations in which their group has been historically excluded and underrepresented. Trust is challenged again and again.

The past decade in particular has witnessed an explosion of research on the experience of being stigmatized, attributable in large part to research on two separate but related phenomena: One is attributional ambiguity (Crocker & Major, 1989) and the other is referenced above as the stereotype threat (Steele & Aronson, 1995; Steele & Aronson, 2000, cited in National Study Group, 2004). Attributional ambiguity involves the challenge that a student of color may face, when receiving feedback about his or her performance, in determining whether it is accurate and particular to his or her performance, or is reflective of general racial bias on the part of the one giving the feedback.

CONDITIONS FACILITATING STUDENT EFFORTS AND SUCCESS ARE PRESENT OR KNOWN

Schools will not succeed with as many students as they might if schools are not organized for those administrative and organizational arrangements that provide prerequisites for enabling all students to learn. These include differentiated instruction for diverse student populations; detracked instructional groupings; access to rigorous and honors courses for all students; improved teacher quality; educator advocacy for all students; access to tutors and instructional interventions that extend the school day through after-school programs.

Good schooling can lift students above the limits of physical poverty and even above a social environment that is indifferent to striving and success in school. Good schooling is sorely and unreasonably challenged by active resistance encountered when student peer culture undercuts ambition to succeed in school (Ogbu, 2003; Steinberg, 1996) or when circumstances disrupt student attention to schooling. When an African American child lives in a low-income environment or with family members who have minimal literacy skills, or in a community that has high unemployment—that child's intelligence can be nurtured by the school, that child's spirit can be inspired by their teacher. Indeed, these children need rigor in school as much or more than the advantaged child. Too often they do not get it. With misplaced compassion, or a lack of belief in the capacity of African American students to succeed academically with rigorous and challenging content, their curriculum is "thinned," the pace of instruction slowed, and they get more hours of that regimen mistaken for rigor, or avoided entirely.

Paul Barton (2003), in *Parsing the Achievement Gap* (ETS Policy Information Report), reported on the differential treatment of students as an indicator of rigor. For example, although 17% of high school students nationwide in 2002 were African Americans, those students took just 4% of the advanced placement exams that year. Hispanic students were 16% of the student body and took 10% of the exams. In addition to teacher support and a focus on engagement, studies have shown that combining academic rigor with career or technical learning, work-based learning, and specific guidance or mentoring designed to help the student move toward postsecondary goals, not only improves graduation rates but also helps boost scores in reading, math, and science—outcomes that will help all graduates, whether they go on to college or go directly to work (Aratoni, 2006; Bottoms, 2003).

In "*Parsing*," Barton reported that in the year 2000 only 57% of Black fourth-grade students attended schools where the same teachers started and ended the school year, compared with 82% for White students and 73% for Hispanic students (p. 14). He also reported that in 1998 schools with "high" proportions of students from low-income families or who are "minorities" have twice the proportion of teachers with 3 years or less experience in the profession (p. 14). In 2000, Black and Hispanic high school students were twice as likely as White students to have 6% to 10% (or more) of their teachers absent. All these findings work against school success. But schools can and do improve.

Beating the Odds VI cites nine factors that, in combination, are features of unusually successful schools: (1) working harder and working smarter, (2) squeezing inefficiencies out of every scare dollar, (3) high standards, (4) strong and stable leadership, (5) better teaching, (6) more instructional time, (7) regular assessments, (8) stronger accountability, and (9) efficient management.

Beating the Odds VI then concludes with the following observation: The data suggest that improvement is possible on a large scale—not just school-by-school. It is now time to determine how the pace of improvement can be accelerated. Those who advocate and partner in the NUA agree and support those allies in the struggle.

What Is Needed Now for Reform Action to Be Effective?

To address the factors cited by *Beating the Odd VI*, to redress the imbalances in the correlates of student achievement cited by Barton, to gain traction on the factors that can lift the promising "upward tilt" in African American student achievement reported by NAEP, and to institutionalize moments of success that reduce—toward the goal of elimination—gaps in opportunity for students to learn, both schools and districts must give sustained attention to the following:

(1) *Instruction:* High standards in content and pedagogy, delivered in a culturally relevant and respectful manner that allows differentiated student interventions

(2) *Leadership:* For some a cliché but nevertheless important, this holds beliefs together with mission and creates an organizational culture and environment that guides and supports people within and around the school to apply their will and skill to the success of every student

(3) *Organization:* School-based policies and procedures that determine grouping, tracking, class and school size, administrative and organizational arrangements that serve or constrain accelerated and enriched instruction for all students

(4) *Professional Development:* Providing teachers access to the tools of effective practices, particularly instruction, so that they can tailor them to their community, classroom, and kids, and providing principals insight and skills to guide and support the teachers in their building

(5) *Community Engagement:* Including parental and stakeholder involvement and advocacy that enables improvements in and across the schools to occur and to be sustained

Attention to each is necessary if we are to help African American students accelerate their learning. In the remainder of this chapter, I will focus on professional development, a key itself to student success and instrumental as well to other factors of student success, such as policies encouraging greater enrollment in Advanced Placement courses or systematically fostering a schoolwide culture of respect for property, people, determination, and achievements.

Professional Development

Sustained and cohesive professional development provides the threads that bind, within each teacher and within a faculty, the complex weaving of effective school factors. It strengthens individuals while creating appreciation of and networks for collegiality that enables continuing development. This requires that districts rethink how they organize professional development. Traditional staff development for teachers by districts include one-shot workshops, sporadic in-service training highlighted by a "superintendent's day," workshop-type presentations conducted during stolen moments of a faculty meeting, staff retreats with cluttered agendas, and after-school training that encounters but often is unable to overcome the fatigue of a long work day. Even the establishment of a district-based professional development center is often more a river of separate programs rather than a well of cumulative and coherent ideas, strategies, and assistance. Widespread or long-term success does not come from chipping away at problems; the attack must be comprehensive and integrative.

Traditional approaches to professional development and the education change process in use today are doomed to continue the treadmill of new initiatives and the swinging pendulum that often defines the so-called reform. Sustained and compelling educational change must involve a dialogue about and a careful review of the status quo and of various reform practices chosen by central and school-based educators. There must be attention to the consistency and cumulative effects of the broad theoretical and pedagogical principles under consideration. "Change overload" should be avoided. All too often, I have observed educators who act as "change junkies," moving from reform to reform, using a checklist approach to school change and mistaking any action for constructive action. And all too often, with shifts in the office of the superintendents, the new leader decides to remove successful programs so that

distance is established between and among administrations. Improvement will come from more disciplined work.

To offset what to some might seem to be immutable obstacles to sustained improvements, educators and community stakeholders must do the following:

1. Develop and maintain an irrefutable belief in the capacity of all students to succeed at high levels; create collaborations with universities, community-based organizations, faith-based institutions, parent groups, businesses, the media, and outside advocacy groups to build a critical mass in support of a renewed belief in student capacity; and build these coalitions and belief systems with exuberance and deep commitment.

2. Conduct assessments of instructional practice to ascertain a school's climate for learning and how it prepares and conducts differentiated instruction tailored to each student while attending to common local and state standards. For example, districts might add to their agenda what might be termed an "Instructional Impact Assessment" when budgeting, structuring, and staffing the district and each school; when creating policy and operating procedures; and when designing systems for assessing learning so that instruction can be informed in time for constructive action.

3. Provide cohesive and continuing districtwide professional development that models effective interventions with students, so that the skeptics among teachers and administrators can see that indeed ALL students can succeed with rigorous content. For example, to deepen, individualize, and sustain professional development for the critical subject of literacy across the grades, trained literacy coaches should be hired for each school that has been certified as part of the districtwide professional development process. Additionally, the use of informative data to adjust instruction should be modeled.

4. Put instruction at the center of continuous improvement. Develop a coherent and articulated, if not centralized, curriculum and instruction plan across a district so that the deleterious effects of student mobility are reduced while maintaining the value of teacher creativity and professional judgment. Embed the use of

cognitive strategies into the curriculum so that essential skills become skills-in-use by the students. Use universal themes in instruction so that students activate their prior knowledge, enabling them to bridge the gap between what they know and do not know, and between their lives and the necessarily larger world of the curriculum. For example,

    a. use instructional tools such as "thinking maps" that help students organize what they know and what they are learning (Hyerle, 2005);

    b. avoid piling on "best practices" that do not fit together, fit the standards and curriculum, or fit the situation—effectiveness should be the watchword;

    c. coordinate classroom, district, and outside assessments so that to the degree possible, teachers are informed in ways and at times that help them do a better job without delay.

5. Provide extra support for the lowest-performing schools, support that is tuned to specific needs and is disciplined to get results.

6. Create parent workshops that provide participants with strategies for learning at home, after school, and in the summers (use entertainment, food, and community advocacy with partners as outreach to motivate parents to attend).

The NUA works with school districts on a 10-point approach to sustainable reform, keeping instruction at the center. NUA works with the district and staff at all levels toward the following goals:

1. *Advocating for children:* All personnel must affirm that all students have the ability to achieve in school and deserve the opportunity to strive for the highest levels of achievement. All personnel recognize that by their continued access to parents and urban youth they have a special opportunity to engage residents and youth in sustained conversations and activities that foster the dispositions and conditions contributing to success in school.

2. *Assessing the situation with insight and imagination:* This begins with an on-location look at instruction.

3. Developing an action plan tailored to the specifics of the instructional assessment, standards, and aspirations.

4. Motivating teachers with systemic support and respect.

5. *Using proven products, programs, and tools:* Careful selection and knitting them together into practical strategies for use are keys to success.

6. Aligning instruction with standards.

7. Engaging the community to animate belief in the potential of every student.

8. Eliminating achievement gaps related to students' race or ethnicity, socioeconomic status, or gender while recognizing that there will continue to be differences among students.

9. *Succeeding with the federal No Child Left Behind law:* Testing should not get in the way of good instruction or of students' enthusiasm for learning and showing what they know and are able to do in a variety of ways.

10. Building sustainable capacity to succeed, with strong individuals, teams, and organizations.

Intervention strategies will not have their potential effect on student learning and achievement without four qualities embraced by educators and community leaders that adhere and animate the effective practices by applying knowledge and skill. These four important qualities are belief, hope, determination, and confidence.

Educators and leaders must believe in the potential of their students—all their students—to achieve at levels that will advance them to the next school grade, that will prepare them to tackle postsecondary education or a job that will require postsecondary literacy and thinking—this belief should apply to students whether they desire to be an auto mechanic or a technology engineer. Educators must believe in their ability to engage and educate their students, and educators must believe in their ability to gain the professional knowledge and skills to do so. Communities must believe in the ability and willingness of their schools to engage and educate all the students. *Hope* is a bridge between belief and action. We are sustained not by taking cover when times are hard or challenges great, but by taking courage from both historical figures of our struggles and also from the innocent yet strong hopes of our children. But hope is not a strategy; hope begets strategy. *Determination* is the expression of belief and hope in action. *Confidence* must be rooted in competence and high expectations for all students (Groopman, 2004).

CONCLUSION

The NUA experience, driven and deepened by district-led partnerships (i.e., superintendents, educators, union leaders, community stakeholders, parents, students, business and faith-based leaders) is clear: All partners must embrace a comprehensive and coordinated effort that engages the many parts of a school, of a school system, and of the surrounding social/political/economic system. As Jean Anyon (2005) has written, "educators are in an excellent position to build a constituency for [sustained] economic and education change in urban communities" (p. 178).

In 2002, NUA issued a statement, which also was published as an "advertorial" in *Quality Counts 2003* by *Education Week* (January 9, 2003), that declared,

> Neither shortsighted simplicity in programs nor unsustainable complexity in process hit the mark. Coaching not catcalls, and detailed demonstrations not shrill demands, mark the way. Educators, and the communities and systems that support them, must examine their driving beliefs; they must reinforce their skills and will to reach every student; they must recognize that high expectations, an enriched curriculum and challenging instruction are not rewards for past achievement by a few, but are resources for future achievements of all students. (NUA, 2003)

Teaching is that center of the combination of policies, programs, practices, and beliefs that lifts and accelerates student achievement. Educators are the professionals who craft and deliver that teaching. Their professional skills and professional behavior, their beliefs that undergird and guide that behavior are targeted and tuned by professional development activities, before and during their service. Because most of the teachers who will be in classrooms over the coming 15 to 20 years are already teaching, in-service professional development

has a great mission and is the binding agent for most reforms (Jackson, 2005).

It is a truism that learning occurs one person at a time, for learning is within each of us. And school change takes place one classroom at a time, for our schools are organized so that the primary "unit of production" is the classroom. And teaching only improves one teacher at a time, for no public policy, outrage, or outcry can force teachers to do what they will not do, certainly not for as long as it will take for their students to overcome external deficiencies, to gather external supports, and to build internal strengths. Thus, progress must occur one teacher, one classroom, one student at a time. Yet there is nothing in this formulation or in nature that denies that this can take place *simultaneously* with many places and people. This combination of efforts is demanding, but it is doable and long overdue.

NOTES

1. The Council of Great City Schools' membership includes 66 of the nation's largest urban school Districts.

2. Despite this information, the Schott Foundation report, *Public Education and Black Male Students: The 2006 State Report Card*, puts Florida last in the nation in its rate of graduating Black males—31%—on time.

REFERENCES

Anyon, J. (2005). *Radical possibilities.* New York: Routledge.

Aratoni, L. (2006, March 12). Vo-tech as a door to college. *The Washington Post,* p. C11. Retrieved August 20, 2006, from www.washington poast.com/wp-dyn/content/article/2006/03/11/AR2006031101158.html

Barton, P. E. (2003, October). *Parsing the achievement gap: Baselines for tracking progress* (ETS Policy Information Report). Princeton, NJ: Educational Testing Service.

Barton, P. E. (2006, February). The dropout problem: Losing ground. *Education Leadership, 63*(5), 14–18. Retrieved September 8, 2006, from www.ascd.org

Bottoms, G. (2003). *Closing the achievement gap: A "high schools that work" design for challenged schools.* Atlanta, GA: Southern Regional Education Board.

Brandt, S. (2006, April 5). *Poor Minneapolis students bussed to suburbs do better in school.* Startribune.com

Casserly, M. (2006). *Beating the Odds VI.* Washington, DC: Council of the Great City Schools. Retrieved August 1, 2006, from www.cgcs.org/pdgs/BTOVI%20Final%2054%20pages.pdf

Center for Strengthening the Teaching Profession. (2005). *Making gains: With an eye on the gap.* Silverdale, WA: Author.

Cooper, E. (2005, September). It begins with belief: Social demography is not destiny. *Voices from the Middle, 13*(1), 25–33. Urbana, IL: National Council of Teachers of English.

Crocker, J., & Major, B. (1989). Social stigma and self-esteem: The self-protective properties of stigma. *Psychological Review, 26*, 608–630.

Darling-Hammond, L. (2000). Teacher quality and student achievement: A review of state policy evidence. *Education Policy Analysis Archives, 8*(1). Retrieved August 2, 2006, from http://epaa.asu.edu/epaa/v8n1

Du Bois, W. E. B. (1996). *Of our spiritual strivings in the souls of Black folk* [Electronic version]. Charlottesville, VA: Electronic Text Center, University of Virginia Library. (Original published 1903)

Froning, M. F. (2006). Recruiting, preparing, and retaining urban teachers: One person's view from many angles. In K. R. Howey, M. L. Post, & N. L. Zimpher (Eds.), *Recruiting, preparing, and retaining teachers for urban schools* (pp. 67–82). New York: AACTE.

Good, T. L., & Brophy, J. E. (1984). *Looking in classrooms* (3rd ed., p. 13). New York: Harper & Row.

Groopman, J. (2004). *The anatomy of hope: How people prevail in the face of illness.* New York: Random House.

Hyerle, D. (Ed.). (2004). *Student successes with thinking maps: School-based research, results, and models for achievement using visual tools.* Thousand Oaks, CA: Corwin Press.

Indiana Accountability System for Academic Progress 2006 for Indianapolis Public Schools. (2006). Retrieved March 5, 2008, from http://mustang.doe.state.in.us/SEARCH/snapcorp.cfm?corp=5385

Jackson, Y. (2005). Unlocking the potential of African American students: Keys to reversing underachievement. *Theory Into Practice, 44*(3), 203–210. Retrieved March 5, 2008, from www.nuatc.org/articles/pdf/Jackson_article.pdf

National Assessment of Educational Progress. (2005). *The Nation's report card: Reading 2005.* Washington, DC: National Center for Education Statistics.

National Center for Education Statistics. (2004). *The condition of education 2004* (NCES 2004–077, p. 54). Washington, DC: U.S. Department of Education, Government Printing Office.

National Study Group for the Affirmative Development of Academic Ability. (2004). *All students reaching the top.* Naperville, IL: Learning Point.

National Urban Alliance for Effective Education. (2003). *Quality counts, but just counting doesn't reveal all the qualities that count* (On NUA Web site and published as an "advertorial" in *Quality Counts 2003* [January 9, 2003]). Arlington, VA: Education Week.

Ogbu, J. U. (2003). *Black Americans in an affluent suburb: A study of academic disengagement.* Mahwah, NJ: Lawrence Erlbaum.

Olson, L. (2006). Economic trends fuel push to retool schooling. *Education Week, 25*(28), 1, 20, 22, 24.

Perie, M., Grigg, W., & Donahue, P. (2005). *The Nation's report card: Reading 2005* (NCES 2006–451). Washington, DC: U.S. Department of Education, Government Printing Office.

Perry, T., Steele, C., & Hilliard, A. (2003). *Young, gifted, and Black: Promoting high achievement among African-American students.* Boston: Beacon Press.

Poliakoff, A. (2006, January). *Closing the gap: An overview* (Infobrief No. 44). Alexandria, VA: ASCD.

Rosenthal, R., & Jacobson, L. (1968). *Pygmalion in the classroom: Teacher expectation and pupils' intellectual development.* New York: Rinehart & Winston.

Schott Foundation. (2006). *Public education and Black male students: The 2006 state report card.* Cambridge, MA: Author.

Steele, C. M., & Aronson, J. (1995). Stereotype threat and the intellectual test performance of African Americans. *Journal of Personality and Social Psychology, 69*, 797–811.

Steinberg, L. (1996). *Beyond the classroom: Why school reform has failed and what parents need to do.* New York: Simon & Schuster.

Teachers College, Columbia University. (2005, June 9). The academic achievement gap: Facts and figures. *News.* Retrieved August 2, 2006, from www.tc.edu/news/article.htm?id=5183

Washington State Report Card. (2005/2006). Retrieved from http://reportcard.ospi.k12.wa.us

Williams, J. (2006). *Enough: The phony leaders, dead-end movements, and culture of failure that are undermining Black America: And what we can do about it.* New York: Crown.

28

CREATING A NEW MODEL OF EDUCATION FOR AFRICAN AMERICAN CHILDREN

Mobilizing Stakeholder Partners in Service to Sustained Academic Success

SABRINA HOPE KING

NANCY M. CARDWELL

If you think the struggle is over, think again.

—NAACP Legal Defense and Education Fund (2005)

I f the challenge of the 20th century was creating a system of schools that could provide minimal education and basic socialization for masses of previously uneducated citizens, the challenge of the 21st century is creating schools that ensure—for all students in all communities—a genuine right to learn. Meeting this new challenge is not an incremental undertaking. It requires a fundamentally different enterprise (Darling-Hammond, 2001).

There have been multiple efforts and approaches to improve the quality of education and the educational achievement of African American children. Throughout the history of African Americans' time in the United States, there has been a diversity of philosophies, approaches, and practices developed to educate and, some would argue, miseducate African American children. In the wake of the Civil Rights struggle and the *Brown v. Board of Education* decision in 1954, the U.S. public school system has made significant strides toward providing an excellent education for African American children, but more remains to be done to achieve this goal.

At the beginning of the 21st century, the United States faced significant problems with respect to educating African American children, including overcrowding, harsh disciplinary practices, the lack of intellectually rich curricula, and low expectations that converge to create the very real school-to-prison pipeline (NAACP Legal and Education Defense Fund, 2005; Wald & Losen, 2003). This *Handbook* confirms the need to address African American education in its own right, and for our part, we envision a new model of education for African American children that ultimately emerges from a renewed collective effort to improve the education of African American children and, by extension, all children in the United States. Our proposed effort does not rest on improved test scores alone, although improved test scores will be an intentional by-product of this work. We envision rigorous curriculum content that is intellectually challenging and culturally affirming, to create a rich academic experience for African American children, ushering them into an economically productive, socially active adulthood. To be effective and successful, we think this approach needs to be coordinated, collaborative, and comprehensive. Our chapter focuses on developing such an approach to mobilize stakeholder partners who will ultimately engage and mobilize the general public to create and sustain an excellent system of education for African American children.

We begin by offering a brief examination of the historical and current contexts of African American education that have shaped and continue to shape African American children's life outcomes in the United States. As a result, our approach to this chapter will be informed by, but not tethered to, the enduring challenges African Americans have faced and continue to face. Here, we contend that the current crisis affecting African American children and youth demands the attention and support of our nation. We conclude with a vision and plan to establish and sustain a stellar system of education for African American children in service to strengthened economic and social opportunities with policy suggestions for school districts nationwide to adopt to reverse the troubling trends for African American children.

Given the fraught history of education in America, particularly for African Americans, partnerships and coalitions to improve African American education need to be recreated, supported, and sustained. In light of the school-to-prison pipeline facing too many African American children (Wald & Losen, 2003) and drawing on the authors' collective experiences as African American female students and educators in a variety of educational settings, we offer this new model to realign the trajectory of African American children's lives with the unlimited possibilities of America, improving the economic, social, and political standing of African Americans and in doing so, improve the economic, social, and political fortunes of the United States.

HISTORICAL INFLUENCES SHAPING AFRICAN AMERICAN EDUCATION IN THE UNITED STATES

Since the United States was founded on the idea of democracy and religious freedom, universal, free public education is a necessity to sustain this nation. As such, U.S. public schools are a quintessential American institution in that it is in this location that people from all walks of life come together to learn about and discover their role in this society (Wilentz, 2005). From the nation's inception, education has always been a contentious issue with the debates between Thomas Jefferson and Alexander Hamilton over what type of publicly funded education would best serve the new nation, liberal education for citizenship or vocational education for economic development (Darling-Hammond, 2001, 2006; Wilentz, 2005). This debate was never fully resolved and resurfaced in the wake of the emancipation proclamation in the debates between W. E. B. Du Bois and Booker T. Washington between liberal education and industrial education (Anderson, 1988).

In large part, the education of African Americans in the South was decided by a coalition of Whites from the North and South. In a series of annual conferences held between 1898 and 1915, this coalition, the Southern Education Movement, was the South's third and last campaign for universal education. In all, there were three major campaigns for universal education for African Americans, determining how the newly freed enslaved Africans would be educated. The first campaign took place during the Reconstruction era when the newly freed enslaved Africans advocated for universal public education for all children. The second campaign took place in the late 1880s when White farmers belonging to the Farmers' Alliance and Populist

Party gained control of the state legislature and local governments, instituting measures to establish universal public education for all children in the South, including African American children. These campaigns failed because they threatened the existing southern social power structure. Universal public education for African Americans did not succeed until the third campaign, begun in 1898, which advanced universal education for Blacks without challenging White supremacy. The legacy of this final successful campaign remains today in the form of underresourced public schools that many African American children attend.

A major actor in this campaign was Robert C. Ogden, a New York City merchant capitalist. Ogden was largely responsible for bringing the northern philanthropists together with the southern White educational reformers. Ogden advocated for industrial training as the appropriate form of schooling to bring racial order, political stability, and material prosperity to the American South. Another influential figure in this effort was George Foster Peabody, Jr., a wealthy *Wall Street* investment banker, who became actively involved in the Southern Education Movement by visiting Hampton Institute. Peabody saw Hampton as the solution to the southern race problem and worked successfully to place Hampton and Tuskegee on firm financial footing (Anderson, 1988).

In 1898, the first conference for Southern Education Movement was held for the fragile coalition of northern philanthropists and southern education reformers could identify and solidify their shared beliefs about "Negro" education. Ogden and Peabody made sure they included all concerned constituencies, with the exception of barring African American participation. This coalition coalesced to advocate for publicly funded universal education for African Americans with a curriculum that focused on teaching domestic work and all kinds of menial labor, thereby educating African Americans for the place Whites held open for them—perpetual servitude (Anderson, 1988; Cremin, 1972).

At the conclusion of the third conference in 1900, the northern philanthropists and their southern education reformer partners solidified and refined their shared beliefs about universal education, White supremacy, Black industrial training, public welfare, training laboring classes, industrialization, and the efficient organization

of society that perpetually locates African Americans at the bottom of American society. Specifically, Charles Dabney, president of the University of Tennessee, advocated for universal education for Black children, cautioning, "We must use common sense in all the education of the Negro. . . . We must recognize . . . that momentous fact that the Negro is a child race at least two thousand years behind the Anglo-Saxon in its development" (Anderson, 1988, p. 85).

At the fourth conference for education in the South in 1901, Ogden believed that the coalition's views were ready to be disseminated and implemented. To this end, Ogden invited John D. Rockefeller, Jr. to attend and took him to see Hampton and Tuskegee. Rockefeller was so impressed by the Hampton-Tuskegee model of industrial education that he petitioned his father, John D. Rockefeller, for monetary support to fund the institutionalization of the coalition's shared beliefs.

By 1921, Rockefeller had contributed $129 million to the General Education Board, the institution created to implement the universal public education designed to train African Americans. As a result of the Rockefeller support, the General Education Board gained a virtual monopoly over the administration of educational philanthropic funding for southern education for African Americans. Despite the accord reached within the coalition that formed the General Education Board, the majority of White southerners saw any system of universal education for African Americans as a prelude to universal suffrage. However, the efforts of the coalition organized by Ogden and Peabody was an organized attempt to offer African Americans minimal basic skills to make them useful workers but without the information necessary to ensure full participation of African Americans in U.S. democracy (Anderson, 1988; Cremin, 1972; Talbot, 1904).

More Recent Developments in African American Education

The bureaucratized public school mission, created at the turn of the 20th century, was designed to process a large number of students efficiently, supporting only a select few for "thinking work." This shift allowed greater routinization of teaching and less reliance on professional judgment, resulting in the decision to structure teaching as semiskilled work (Darling-Hammond, 1997). This bureaucratized design has its roots in the coalition organized by Ogden and Peabody that led to the General Education Board in the South to preserve White supremacy offering the patina of education. It is from these fraught contexts of the 19th and 20th centuries that gave rise to Schwebel's (2004) school typology as outlined in the table.

Table 28.1   School Typology

Types of School Systems	Description
Elite leadership school system	Provides high skills and rigorous content to encourage imaginative thinking and creativity found in public exam schools and elite private schools preparing society's future leaders in industry, commerce, government, education, health, journalism, and the arts.
Workforce school system	Provides basic skills and knowledge, discouraging creative and independent thought to cultivate efficiency and dependability found in good public schools and parochial schools charged with preparing the large work force necessary to perform the everyday tasks that keep society moving.
Custodial school system	Exposure to rudimentary skills designed to cultivate punctuality, obedience, and passivity found in urban public schools serving children from low-income families to satisfy society's need for minimum wage workers.

Meeting society's economic need for workers in this way comes at an enormous cost to individual potential, human development, and national growth. The individual cost to the many children in Custodial School Systems, many of whom are African American, whose development is stunted by sustained inferior educational opportunity is incalculable (Cardwell, 2007). The societal cost is considerable because of the many prisons that must be built and maintained to house so many children who emerge, undereducated, from the third system (Schwebel, 2004).

Current Context

Our contemplation of the historical influences and the different conceptions of schooling that have influenced the trajectory of African American education is exacerbated by current statistics that illuminate the precarious position of African American children and youth despite the gains made as a result of the *Brown v. Board of Education* decision. In fact, none of the three systems Schwebel (2004) identified have served African American children well overall. Granted, while select African Americans have experienced educational, financial, personal, and societal success, the vast majority of African American children live in a world of constrained resources and limited opportunities, which is a legacy of the early decisions to undereducate, and miseducate African Americans, excluding many from the resources necessary to regularly access health care, career advancement, and home ownership.

In 2000, the African American population was 33.5 million and in 2002, over one half of all African Americans lived in a central city within a metropolitan area (McKinnon, 2003). African Americans accounted for about one quarter of the U.S. population in poverty in 2001 and while the overall population decreased since 1959, the African American infant mortality rate was twice that of the White population (McKinnon, 2003; National Center for Health Statistics, 2006). Forty-two percent of U.S. public school students are children of color, with African American students representing 16% of the student population. The average African American student attends a segregated, high-poverty elementary school and secondary school with fewer certified teachers, fewer up-to-date textbooks, and fewer advanced placement courses (National Center for Education Statistics, 2007).

Many school systems move a disproportionate number of African American students out of regular schools and classrooms into suspension centers, alternative schools, and juvenile prisons where educational opportunities are minimal. African American students are overrepresented in special education and underrepresented in gifted programs (Noguera, 2005). Only 50% of all African American ninth graders will graduate with their class in 4 years and 55% of those African American students who graduate from high school enroll in college immediately after high school. This means that just over 25% of

African American ninth graders enroll in college immediately following high school. African Americans above age 25 are more likely to be high school dropouts than college graduates.

African American males are far more likely than their White peers to be suspended, expelled, or arrested for the same kind of conduct in school, which is attributed to the stereotyping and degradation of African American boys but also to the disparities in the quality of education available to African Americans (Noguera, 2005). "Districts in which African American students are concentrated tend to have racially segregated schools, do worse on the National Assessment of Educational Progress, suspend and expel more African American boys than White boys and assign more African American boys than White boys to special education using procedures open to abuse and effectively preventing those students from receiving a high school diploma with their peers" (Holzman, 2006, p. ii). In 2003, African American youths made up 16% of the nation's overall juvenile population but accounted for 45% of juvenile arrests.

Zero tolerance policies adversely affect African American student learning related to drugs, violence, and/or bad language, for example, prematurely criminalize sporadic, childish mistakes and behavior, making it easier for a young Black person to stay in jail than to stay in school. Furthermore, there are myriad policies at all levels of our education system that place disadvantaged and special needs students in remedial learning environments as opposed to accelerated and intellectually stimulating environments.

These are a few examples of punitive policies that have served to limit African American children's potential. Unfortunately, the failure of our nation and our nation's schools to address the challenges that African American children face has resulted in the National Criminal Justice Commission's projection that by the year 2020, 63% of all African American men between 18 and 34 years old would be in prison (Burton-Rose & Wright, 1998; Wimsatt, 1999). These dire realities provide a detailed window on the dilemmas of individual teachers in a variety of predominantly African American urban public schools. Collectively, these policies and statistics sketch a troubling picture of African American children's unanswered needs and teachers'

thwarted desire to provide necessary support within the confines of the structure of custodial urban public schools (Schwebel, 2004). These statistics further illustrate the consequences of misguided policies, intellectual waste, and emotional turmoil of sustained denial of access to educational opportunity (Ladson-Billings, 1994). Meaningful education has been elusive to many African American children and has had dire consequences on their success and survival and on our country as a whole.

Entering the 21st century, we are in the precarious position of no longer debating how to educate but whether to educate at all. At this important moment, we propose a new model of public education, replete with empowering policies, for all children and African American children, in particular, in service to democratic citizenship and full economic participation (Cardwell, 2007). The significance of these structured and purposeful strategies of social exclusion from the public education African Americans paid for, wanted, and were denied must be considered in light of the current state of public education for African American children and point to the potential and productive role stakeholder partnerships might play (Cardwell, 2007).

A New Model for African American Education

We have an opportunity to create a new model of African American education and learn from the paradoxes on which this nation was founded and on which our urban public schools currently rest. The time is ripe to imagine a new, excellent model of education for African American children. This new model needs to be conceptualized by stakeholder partners of all backgrounds committed to an academically rigorous, culturally affirming education for all children and African American children in particular.

What if we imagined a nation where we looked to all our citizens as partners? What if we looked to each citizen for the cure for cancer, AIDS, Alzheimer's disease, and Parkinson's disease to name only a few? What if we looked to each citizen for creativity, artistry, invention, leadership, entrepreneurship? What if we looked to each citizen for advances in mathematics and science? What might the public school system look like if we prepared all students to fulfill these roles? Specifically, what would a system of public education look like if we supported all African American children with abundant educational resources? What if policies could be developed to support myriad efforts to successfully educate African American children? In the sections that follow, we will begin to address these queries as we create a new model for an abundantly resourced system of public education for African American children.

Broad Tenets

We begin with the premise that in a free democratic society, all children should have free and equitable access to all of society's knowledge for their benefit as human beings and for society's benefit as contributing members. We believe that all African American children are entitled to attend excellent public schools. Schools should be structured and policies need to be developed to guarantee that no resource or support system is overlooked to support academic excellence. Public schools should become safe harbors, full of physical and human resources, vehicles for engagement with intellectually rigorous and culturally affirming curriculum and places where learning, experimentation, exploration, and mistakes can be made and learned from. An excellent public school for African American children would be abundantly resourced, not wasteful, with a pervasive culture of generosity and largesse.

An excellent public school for African American students will rest on a web of policies designed to educate and support the whole child—his or her academic needs, home life, and encounters with societal challenges. Every child who enters these model public schools would have full and easy access to all the books, materials, and school supplies that they need to succeed. Breakfast, lunch, and dinner would be provided for every child who desires it. Our school system would have a family health clinic to serve the health needs of the children and their parents because we know that healthy, academically successful children need the support of healthy families. In keeping with existing models of public education serving children who are homeless, our school system would make clothing available for any child who needs it, particularly those children whose families are

homeless. Schools would be designed physically and conceptually to feel welcoming and comfortable for all students—those from supportive, happy families as well as for students who face challenging family and life circumstances.

African American children need to experience a rich, rigorous education in a school building that is inviting, stimulating, and welcoming on the outside and on the inside, making it a place they are excited to enter. These schools should have fully-equipped science labs, computer labs, art rooms, music rooms, performance spaces, smart board and wireless Internet access in each classroom, laptops, a library, athletic facilities, and an inviting cafeteria and lunchroom. Teachers and students should have school and home copies of all necessary materials promoting a smooth transition between home and school.

Schools serving African American children must be amply staffed with a range of faculty and staff who are eminently qualified. Regardless of their role, each faculty and staff member must be personally invested in every child's academic and life success. The faculty and staff must want to work in a collaborative educational community, designing and teaching curricula that are interesting, rigorous, and multidisciplinary with clear connections to the children's lives (Dewey, 1916/1966; Vygotsky, 1978). African American children need to see African American adults in a variety of roles—teaching, leadership, and support. One way to address this need would be to productively blur the home/school boundary and offer paid and volunteer positions to children's family members and community members.

Every child needs an advocate and African American children are no different (Erikson, 1950). Ideally, children would have multiple advocates, parents, teachers, and neighbors, who can partner with each other in a coordinated, focused effort to support children's ongoing academic and life success. However, for those children whose parents cannot or do not take care of them on a daily basis, children need to know that their success in school is not tethered to their parents' capacity to take care of them. They also need to know that there are enough resources available to help them succeed in school and in life because they are respected, valuable individuals inside the school, their community, and society.

These broad tenets translate into social policies that serve as a safety net ensuring that no child has to do without the support they need to succeed in school and in life. Furthermore, these broad tenets can be enacted by using a culturally responsive approach to teaching where student's questions, opinions, and interests are taken seriously and woven into the curriculum. African American students need to know with concrete examples that their participation in education can transform their own lives and by extension, the world. African American children need to know, understand, and appreciate the world in all its diversity by being understood, appreciated, and taught in caring, understanding, and intellectually challenging environments.

A part of this education must include attention to learning about the depth and breadth of African American experiences to develop a strong, affirmative cultural consciousness that provides a sense of self, purpose, pride, and potential. African American children are entitled to a school experience that supports their learning growth and development as human beings and African Americans with valuable contributions to offer. The planned course of study would be developmentally appropriate, culturally affirming, and intellectually rigorous to stimulate children in the present while preparing them for the following year and beyond. Their school experiences should provide the necessary constellation of educative experiences for school success and in life, constructing an unimagined future for themselves, the African American community, America, and by extension, the world (Dewey, 1916/1966). This is in stark contrast to the custodial schools that so many African American children attend.

In light of these broad tenets, we anticipate that African American children will learn about their homes, families, and neighborhoods. A look at the lives students lead in their neighborhoods, states, and nation, for example, is an important base of study from which children would learn about the larger African American community as well as the ancient civilizations of Egypt, Greece, and Rome (Daiute, Buteau, & Rawlins, 2001). To promote flexibility of thought and openness, African American children would become fluent in at least three languages, one of which could be Latin, to conceptualize the world in multiple ways and on a functional level to converse with their neighbors, in their native languages. The curriculum for older students would include a more analytic look at diversity in the African American community and in the other cultures represented in their lived reality as connected to the dilemmas and struggles around the world. This would include educational projects involving problem solving, community service, advocacy, and political activism. These experiences could translate into children developing programs, organizations, or fundraising initiatives to engage in activism to make life better for others and themselves in service to social justice.

In our new model of education for African American children, "classical" literature would be broadly defined to include the traditionally acknowledged "canon" and expanded to include literature from around the world so that all children could find themselves reflected in the literature they read whether it is a cultural connection, an emotional connection, or a connection rooted in a shared intellectual interest. Math, science, art, and music would hold prominent roles in this school system as part of a liberal education that prepares students for full citizenship in the United States, for employment in adulthood, and for life enjoyment without neglecting the intrinsic value of learning in the present. Music, as a site of innovation, beauty, and science, would occupy a significant role in the academic curriculum as music has been and continues to be a vehicle for African American culture, survival, and connection.

We do not assume that the curriculum would reside solely within the school. An integral dimension of mining children's lived experiences is to provide numerous educational experiences beyond the school walls, breathing life and passion into the lessons learned in school (Dewey, 1916/1966). Providing students with a wide variety of trips to museums, libraries, gardens, scientific events, sports events, neighborhood walks, studies of the transportation system and important landmarks such as the Statue of Liberty, the African burial ground, and the Schomburg Center for Research on Black Culture in New York City would be opportunities to experience the world as a dynamic, interesting place they can shape. Specifically, these trips would be a vehicle for children to conduct research, learn about and experience firsthand, the diversity of their own culture as part of the African Diaspora and the larger human family.

To achieve and sustain academic excellence, the expectations for African American children must be set at a high, but not unattainable, level. Our model would offer after-school, evening, and Saturday programs, providing additional support for struggling students and increased challenges for gifted students. These programs would offer a rich array of extracurricular activities such as classical dance, African American dance, sports, visual arts, and music classes. It is critical that an excellent model of schooling for African American students attends to students' health, weight, physical fitness, spiritual, and emotional well-being.

The Role of Government

Our new model for successfully educating African American students should be abundantly funded by the government of the United States. As a nation-state, the United States depends on an educated citizenry for its survival. We envision public schools preparing children for the demands of citizenship and work. All children, and African American children in particular, should not have to seek out special schools to receive the best possible education because every public school in the United States would be excellent. Our school system can become the balm to right past injustices endured by African Americans. Policies need to be developed to positively affect the possibilities for the education of African American students. Our stance is one that focuses on the needs of African American children first without the constraints of which political party is in power. At the same time, it is important to be cognizant of the politics swirling around education without being swept away by them. Making note of successful movements in the past, it would be important to develop educational policies with stakeholder partners. Given the trajectory of our current political system, we believe that instituting our new model of African American education will require the sustained and dedicated support of the stakeholder partners.

Mobilizing Stakeholder Partnerships to Support a New Model of African American Education

While in Africa it may have required a village to raise a child, African American children now require the full backing of our nation. As we consider the current context of African Americans, education can play a pivotal role to improve this current reality. Specifically, we believe that it is critical to engage in dialogue, partnership, and collaboration with all the stakeholders in high-quality public education for all children and particularly African American children. Enough challenges persist to warrant continued, focused, sustained, and aligned attention from those within and outside the African American community.

Organizations in partnership with the public school system have been critical in the work to improve African American education and have the potential to play a much larger role. Examples of such partners include foundations, private schools, nonprofit organizations, universities, and civil rights organizations, some with an explicit focus on improving the education of African Americans. Given the role that the southern philanthropists played at the turn of the century in the design of the oppressive purpose and content of education for African Americans, it is critical that current efforts attend to, and include the perspectives and the expertise of, those who support unfettered academic and life opportunities for African Americans.

Partnerships can serve as significant resources in the work to conceptualize the problem, contribute ideas and financial capital, serving as critical friends for the work of educators. Given the controversial nature of race and ethnicity inspired work and the constricting nature of urban public school bureaucracies serving so many African American children, stakeholder partners have the potential to play an inspirational role. We have taken the lessons from these efforts to transform the quality of African American education and provide a larger, collaborative role to play in this coordinated effort. Examples of the types of stakeholder partnerships we envision include foundations supporting the collaborative and design process; private schools serving as sites of innovation such as the City and Country School's pioneering after-school program in the 1960s that was later adopted by the then New York City Board of Education; nonprofit organizations such as Goddard Riverside's efforts to support children and families to improve children's school attendance; university schools of arts and sciences supplying cutting-edge information for educators to sustain the rigorous curriculum.

Organizations such as the Harlem Children's Zone, the Wallace Foundation, the NAACP Legal and Education Defense Fund, the Schott Foundation, the New World Foundation, and the Annie E. Casey Foundation that have created or supported academically rigorous, culturally responsive approaches to diverse groups of African American children are a few examples of possible stakeholder partners. We will offer the example of Manhattan Country School (MCS) as an innovative private school, which can provide support by example, of a rigorous examination of history through the study of protest movements anchored in social justice. This school provides a view of the possibilities and struggles attached to partnering with families, children, and teachers in intellectually rigorous and personally meaningful ways.

Manhattan Country School

MCS was founded in the 1960s as an educational response to the goals of the Civil Rights Movement. It is a progressive private school founded on the principles of the civil rights movement with an explicitly stated public mission to create a model of Martin Luther King's beloved community. The founders purposefully located the school on East 96th in Manhattan, New York, an informal but clear dividing line between the predominantly White Upper East Side and the largely African American and Latino East Harlem, as a way to be accessible to the diverse student body they wanted to attract.

In their 40th year, MCS is a school that is truly committed to social justice in theory and in practice. As part of this theory and practice, MCS has remained committed to ensuring that all children have equal access to an excellent and progressive education that will provide them with the will and the skills to make a difference in this society. Importantly, MCS created itself as a private school with a public mission. To that end, MCS developed a sliding scale tuition plan to try to mute the economic privilege of wealth so that all parents could speak their minds freely. Although it was funded with private funds and tuition, MCS saw itself as an instrument not only to provide for the excellent education of MCS students but also as an instrument in the nations' struggle to improve public schools by sharing materials and resources with partner public schools. MCS serves an ethnically, culturally, and economically diverse student population.

As such, navigating the boundaries of race, class, ethnicity, and culture became a significant part of the social and academic work of the students, the teachers, and the parental committee to improve the educational opportunities and, subsequently, the life opportunities of the underserved. The lessons from this small-scale experience provide invaluable frames of reference for large-scale public schools.

MCS provided an opportunity for African American parents to have a positive and meaningful education for their children in a racially diverse school. It provided an opportunity for all parents to think about the world that they wanted their children to grow up in and live in and to contribute to that dream ideologically, pedagogically, and financially. As such, MCS instills in their students and alumnae a sense of purpose and commitment to education.

MCS as a private institution, external to and in dialogue with the public education system provides an example of possibility. A common assumption about the work of private schools is that they can do it because they have the money and they have the freedom. In many ways, this is true. However, MCS's efforts provide an important reservoir of innovation and insight for successful curriculum development and practices with African American children.

ENGAGING IN DIALOGUE

MCS has engaged in dialogues with a variety of individuals and institutions to share their work, insights, and practices, ensuring their work appropriately represents Dr. Martin Luther King's vision. These dialogues take place within the school community, the broader educational community, at conferences, during school visits, and through writings that have been generated by MCS's work. By hosting and participating in conferences, MCS leaders and faculty have shared their work with others who share a similar vision and mission in both public and private school settings. Dialogue is not always easy and does represent a critical engagement strategy that is often overlooked. For example, there was a long dialogue over the course of years between the school administration and a parent group, the Black Caucus, to discuss the representation of African Americans in the administration and ways to shape the curriculum as it related to African American and Puerto Rican Studies.

On a global level, MCS partnered with public schools in South Africa and Vietnam to exchange ideas and share resources as a way to learn from their colleagues, without assuming that they are the ones who have the expertise. This stance is enacted in the MCS curriculum.

One of the most compelling aspects of MCS is the curriculum. MCS personnel work to create a curriculum that feeds children's intellectual curiosity while leaving spaces for children's questions and interests to influence the curriculum. Furthermore, the MCS curriculum strives to help children value themselves and where they are from so that they can value the heritages of others.

Stakeholder Partnerships

It is necessary to mobilize stakeholder partnerships to create, implement, and sustain the new model of African American education. These reenvisioned stakeholder partnerships can serve as significant resources in the work to conceptualize problems, contribute intellectual and financial capital, and serve as "critical friends" in the partnership work with educators. These partnerships ensure an inclusive, collaborative design reflective of the schools we envision for African American children. We envision four stakeholder partnerships critical to the work of improving African American education.

Facilitating Partners

We imagine that schools of education can serve as facilitating partners to gather all stakeholder partners at the table because in preparing classroom teachers, school building leaders, and district leaders, these educators cross numerous boundaries, ideally sharing information across those boundaries, and interact with all the following stakeholder partners already. We envision small and large schools of education serving as partners of practical, curricular, and pedagogical innovation, facilitating conversations across the boundaries of field, institution, and practice; and civil rights and social justice partners, making sure that we "walk our talk" and create excellent public schools for African American children.

Funding Partners

These include foundations, corporations, and individuals who are engaged with schools, school districts, and universities to provide financial resources in the service of the ideal model. While the work of the Southern Education Movement and the philanthropists at the turn of the century point to the influence funding partners can have, it will be critical for these partners to work as part of a coalition committed to improving African American education so that all African Americans have choices in terms of the type of life they plan to lead. A recent example of productive partnerships in service to improving African American education would be the DeWitt Wallace Foundation's funding for the Pathways Program at Bank Street College of Education designed to establish a model of certification to diversify teachers and school leaders, which served to inform the design of alternate pathways for teachers and leaders.

Cultural Partners

Including museums, libraries, cultural institutions, as well as arts organizations and schools of arts and sciences in universities will be a pivotal part of establishing and sustaining the rigorous, diverse, and most current content for the curricula we propose. In particular, institutions that represent the African American community are particularly important supports for schools establishing and/or expanding their school libraries. An ideal cultural partner in this work would be the Schomberg Center for Research on Black Culture because it is an invaluable resource to the New York City and worldwide communities.

Social Justice and Equity Advocacy Partners

These include individuals, schools, and organizations committed to and actively working for social justice and equity in U.S. education. Examples of organizations dedicated to this work would be National Association for the Advancement of Colored People (NAACP), the National Urban League, Mothers on the Move, and Educators for Social Responsibility.

GETTING STARTED

Drawing on the lessons from the successful Southern Education Movement (Anderson, 1988), there is a clear need to engage in a coalition-wide conversation with the four stakeholder partners to develop explicitly shared goals, purposes, and practices in service to a rigorous education for African American children. To begin, the first phase in developing an exemplary public school experience for African American students would involve gathering stakeholder partners to elicit and establish shared goals, purposes, practices, and meanings as well as to develop a strategic plan that involves a plan for sustained funding. A series of three conferences open to the stakeholder partners would be convened in New York City, Detroit, and Los Angeles, cities that are geographically diverse and with large African American communities. During this process of establishing shared meanings, purposes, and practices, we will need significant funds to support and sustain this early work before it can be implemented inside public schools and supported by federal, state, and local governments.

The second phase will be to establish communication and funding strategies to disseminate the shared meanings, purposes, practices, and vision as a series of platforms open for public discussion serving to transform the platforms into policies to promote intellectually rigorous, culturally affirming education for African American children.

The third stage will be for stakeholder partners, public supporters, and local and federal legislators to advocate for the educational policies designed to advocate for school- and district-level policies that are intentionally designed to support African American students and educational achievement. Such policies need to be amply funded to provide unlimited opportunities for success. In an excellent school system, there is always room for second chances. Providing children with the appropriate academic, social, and emotional supports necessary to ensure academic success prior to failure are more effective than the more common public school approach, remediation. Similarly, early, preventative interventions to keep children from failing and committing infractions that lead to lengthy absences from school are more effective and cost effective than remediation and rehabilitation. Such policies would focus on possibility as opposed to zero tolerance. Examples of policies that can have an empowering effect on African American education include in-school alternatives to suspension, homework policies that are directly related to meaningful class work, policies that provide for increased salaries

for teachers who work in schools with students who need the best and who need more education, mandatory collaboration between public schools and juvenile detention facilities, and the provision of accelerated course work as opposed to remedial coursework.

Meaningful in-school alternatives to suspension and detention need to be crafted to provide the opportunity for students to receive consequences for their infractions and to learn from them. Once removed from school through suspension or expulsion, students who return are at high risk for dropping out because there are few, if any, supports to smooth their return to school from long suspensions, expulsion, residential placements, or incarceration. Often, in-school detention and out-of-school suspension become opportunities for students to do nothing. It is a fact that for many African American students simply being out of school is a dangerous endeavor. For others, a week out of school is an opportunity to watch TV or to engage in inappropriate behaviors. Possibilities include suspending a student for a week in school, engaging in a meaningful project that provides a way for students to reflect on their inappropriate behavior, while keeping up with their school work.

Homework policies can be created to ensure that homework is directly related to the rigorous and intellectually stimulating course content in the ideal African American school. Homework should be designed to provide the opportunity for students to reflect on what they have learned and to extend that learning. Students could be responsible for answering three simple questions: (a) What did I learn today? (b) How did I learn today? and (c) What can I do this evening or tomorrow to ensure that I will learn even more? This type of assignment serves to develop the skill of reflection, learning from experience that can lead to higher-order thinking skills, while building students' self-confidence about what they learned and to motivate sustained learning. Importantly, this exercise, performed on a consistent basis, can help students become invested in their own learning by taking ownership of their own learning.

Linda Darling-Hammond calls for a Marshall Plan for teaching to include federal support for the recruitment, preparation, and retention of teachers for our highest-needs schools. In the meantime, individual districts could develop programs and policies to recruit teachers intentionally for schools that serve large numbers of

African American students. With intention, schools could seek teachers with a particular commitment to the improved educational opportunities for African American children, providing whatever it takes—academic, social, cultural, and recreational services—to ensure children's needs are met. Such a policy needs to include financial incentives. If funding were provided to amply prepare the best school leaders and teachers for these schools, the school faculty could then be relied on to exercise discretion to create meaningful consequences to bad behavior without separating children from school, a major risk factor for dropping out.

Given that the school-to-prison pipeline is real, policies need to be created to value and ensure productive collaboration between public schools and juvenile detention facilities to keep children in school (Osher, Quinn, Poirier, & Rutherford, 2003). Collaborations between the two entities could facilitate a more synchronous curriculum as well as an expanded repertoire of strategies to reach young people, which may, in the long-term, keep students in school. Specifically, many detention facilities currently mandate a full state-approved curriculum. A policy requiring collaboration would help ensure that the detention curriculum is fully aligned with that of the ideal public school so that students can leave detention and successfully return to public school.

In sum, the effective mobilization of stakeholder partnerships and the federal, state, and local government will transform the public education system we have into the new model of education we have begun to describe for African American children. Collectively, this work will focus on the improved and sustained educational achievement of African American students in the United States and the need to address African American education in its own right with the understanding that such a focus will serve to improve the education of all students. All stakeholder partners will aid the involvement of committed entities within and outside the African American community and public school system. A communication strategy will be developed to facilitate sharing successful practices and possibilities in service to the ideal model of education for African American students, and by extension all students. Funding streams will be coordinated and aligned to sustain ongoing curricular, pedagogical, practical innovation so that this model of excellence can grow and evolve for generations.

Educating all children inside excellent public schools is truly this nation's gift to the world and especially, all those who reside within the borders of the United States. The question is not "Can we afford it?" The real question is, "In a climate of increasing disenfranchisement and disaffection, can the United States, a diverse nation of many joined by shared beliefs (Wilentz, 2005), afford to continue excluding large groups of people from educational and economic opportunity, many of whom are African Americans?" As eternal optimists and educators, we think continuing to exclude large numbers of African Americans from excellent public schools undermines the stability of the United States and that we can dramatically shift this trajectory with the investment of time, money, and goodwill. There is urgency to our proposal because there are millions of African American children sitting inside classrooms right now unable to achieve their full academic potential due to lack of all kinds of resources. The time is ripe for the infusion of intellectual, financial, pedagogical, and material resources into the public school system. In service to this goal, we offer the beginnings of our new model as an invitation to mobilize stakeholder partners to bring their funds of knowledge and resources to create generations of academic achievement for African American children, and by extension, all children.

REFERENCES

Anderson, J. (1988). *The education of Blacks in the South 1860—1935.* Chapel Hill: University of North Carolina Press.

Burton-Rose, D., & Wright, P. (Eds.). (1998). *The celling of America: An inside look at the U.S. prison industry.* Monroe, ME: Common Courage Press.

Cardwell, N. M. (2007). *Hope feeds development: Re-creating urban public schools in service to personal and national growth.* Unpublished second doctoral examination, the Graduate Center, City University of New York, New York.

Cremin, L. (1972). *American education: The colonial experience 1607—1783.* New York: HarperCollins.

Daiute, C., Buteau, E., & Rawlins, C. (2001). Social-relational wisdom: Developmental diversity in children's written narratives about social conflict. *Narrative Inquiry, 11*(2), 1–30.

Darling-Hammond, L. (1997). Education equity and the right to learn. In J. I. Goodlad & T. J. McMannon (Eds.), *The public purpose of education and schooling.* San Francisco: Jossey-Bass.

Darling-Hammond, L. (2001). *The right to learn: A blueprint for creating schools that work.* Hoboken, NJ: Wiley.

Darling-Hammond, L. (2006). *Powerful teacher education.* Hoboken, NJ: Jossey-Bass.

Dewey, J. (1966). *Democracy and education.* New York: Free Press. (Original work published 1916)

Erikson, E. (1950). *Childhood and society.* New York: W. W. Norton.

Holzman, M. (2006). *Public education and Black male students: The 2006 state report card.* Cambridge, MA: Schott Foundation for Public Education.

Ladson-Billings, G. (1994). *The dreamkeepers: Successful teachers of African American children.* San Francisco: Jossey-Bass.

McKinnon, J. (2003). *The Black population in the United States: March 2002* (Current Population Reports, Series P20–541). Washington, DC: U.S. Census Bureau.

NAACP Legal Defense and Education Fund, Inc. (2005). *Annual report 2004/2005.* New York: Author.

National Center for Education Statistics. (2007). *The condition of education, 2007* (NCES, 2007–064). Washington, DC: U.S. Department of Education.

National Center for Health Statistics. (2006). *Health, United States, 2006 with chart book on trends in the health of Americans.* Washington, DC: U.S. Department of Health and Human Services.

Noguera, P. (2005, August). School reform and second generation discrimination: Toward development of bias-free and equitable schools. *SAGE Race Relations Abstracts, 30*(3), 30–33.

Osher, D. M., Quinn, M. M., Poirier, J. M., & Rutherford, R. B. (2003). Deconstructing the pipeline: Using efficacy, effectiveness, and cost-benefit data to reduce minority youth incarceration. In J. Wald & D. Losen (Eds.), *Deconstructing the school-to-prison pipeline, New Directions for Youth Development.* Cambridge, MA: Jossey-Bass.

Schwebel, M. (2004). *Remaking America's three school systems: Now separate and unequal.* Lanham, MD: Scarecrow Education Book.

Talbot, E. (1904). *Samuel Chapman Armstrong: A biographical study.* New York: Doubleday.

Vygotsky, L. S. (1978). *Mind in society.* Cambridge, MA: Harvard University Press.

Wald, J., & Losen, D. J. (2003). Defining and redirecting a school-to-prison pipeline. In J. Wald & D. Losen (Eds.), *Deconstructing the school-to-prison pipeline. New Directions for Youth Development.* Cambridge, MA: Jossey-Bass.

Wilentz, S. (2005). *The rise of American democracy: Jefferson to Lincoln.* New York: W. W. Norton.

Wimsatt, W. (1999). *No more prisons.* New York: Subway & Elevated Books.

29

BEYOND SEGREGATION

The Continuing Struggle for Educational Equity
50 Years After Brown v. Board of Education

SHEILAH D. VANCE

> *It is doubtful that any child may reasonably be expected to succeed in life if he is denied the*
> *opportunity of an education.* Such an opportunity where the state has undertaken to pro-
> vide it, *is a* right *which must be made available to all on* equal *[emphasis added] terms.*
>
> —Brown v. Board of Education (1954, p. 493)

The evening of May 17, 1954, was a night of jubilant celebration for African Americans across
the country, who hailed the landmark decision of *Brown v. Board of Education* earlier that day
by the nation's high court, the U.S. Supreme Court, as a remedy for dashed hopes that sprung
"out from the gloomy past" (Bell, 2004, p. 14). Thurgood Marshall, one of the chief architects of the
Brown litigation, stumbled upon one such celebration among the staff of the National Association for
the Advancement of Colored People (NAACP), frowned, and said, "You fools go ahead and have your
fun, but we ain't begun to work yet" (Bell, 2004, p. 14). Marshall's words proved prophetic when considering that educational equity for African American children 50 years after *Brown v. Board of
Education* is still an elusive goal.

The nation's education and civil rights laws are providing little recourse for those who seek to guarantee equal educational opportunity, or some semblance thereof, for African American children in
this country, as well as other students of color, the vast majority of whom attend underfunded urban
school systems. Post-*Brown* desegregation resulted in some improvements in the quality of education
for African American children (Ryan, 1999). However, desegregation was not a panacea, and many
schools resegregated after White flight from the desegregated schools and from urban areas, leaving
some schools more segregated than ever.

Educational activists then turned toward fixing the inequities in the schools themselves rather than
just sitting African American children next to White children. The essence of the inequities was that
schools in high-income areas had a higher quantity and a better quality of what the U.S. Supreme

Court called "tangible resources" (buildings, curricula, qualifications and salaries of teachers, etc.) than schools in low-income areas (Ryan, 1999). Advocates realized that the state systems of funding public education primarily by relying on local property taxes were the culprits (Hurst, Tan, Meek, & Sellers, 2003). The result of this movement to remedy these inequities has been mixed, and the legal recourses that activists have used have been varied. Therefore, this chapter will demonstrate that when it comes to achieving educational equity for African American school children, the struggle still continues.

This chapter is organized into five sections: (1) an examination of the history of desegregation, (2) an overview of school finance litigation from federal and state law perspectives, (3) an examination of the link between the judicial approach to school finance litigation and student achievement, (4) an examination of the impact of No Child Left Behind Act (NCLB) of 2001 on educational equity issues, and (5) a discussion of the future of the intersection between school finance and educational equity issues.

THE HISTORY OF *BROWN V. BOARD OF EDUCATION*

In *Brown*, plaintiffs argued that state laws that separated public school children based on race were a violation of the Equal Protection Clause (EPC) of the Fourteenth Amendment of the U.S. Constitution. Plaintiffs sought to overturn the U.S. Supreme Court's decision in *Plessy v. Ferguson*, which held that state laws requiring "separate but equal" facilities were permissible under the federal constitution (*Brown v. Board of Education*, 1954). The *Brown* plaintiffs argued that separate public schools were not equal and could not be made equal. The U.S. Supreme Court largely disagreed with the plaintiffs and accepted the findings of the lower courts and the assertions of the states that physical facilities and other tangible factors in the educational system were equal, they were being equalized, or the states would spend the money to make them equal (*Brown v. Board of Education*, 1954). The Court then proclaimed that its decision could not turn on "merely a comparison of these tangible factors [among them, buildings, curricula, qualifications and salaries of teachers] in the Negro and white schools" (p. 492). The Court continued

that "we must look instead to the effect of segregation itself on public education" (p. 492).

In the Court's ruling, it looked at the psychological impact of segregation on African American children and used this as a basis for its decision. The court held that segregating students based on race "generates a feeling of inferiority as to their status in the community that may affect their hearts and minds in a way unlikely to ever be undone" (p. 494). The result of this "feeling of inferiority," the Court held, was the retardation of the educational and mental development that the children could attain in racially integrated schools. In holding that "separate educational facilities are inherently unequal," the Supreme Court held that segregated schools violated the EPC of the Fourteenth Amendment.

THE EDUCATIONAL AND MENTAL DEVELOPMENT OF AFRICAN AMERICAN CHILDREN POST-*BROWN*

After the *Brown* decision, the nation began a long, tortured history of desegregating public education. Despite the U.S. Supreme Court order that public schools be desegregated "with all deliberate speed" (p. 301) in 1955, many states and school districts defiantly refused to desegregate. In 1964, Congress passed the Civil Rights Act, which prohibited any legally segregated institution, including schools, from receiving federal funds. At the same time, the Civil Rights Movement was picking up speed. Civil rights activists worked for desegregation of all public facilities and criticized the federal government for allowing its funds to support segregated institutions.

The massive successful 1963 March on Washington called for an end to segregation and the passage of the Civil Rights Act. The Bill was met with staunch opposition by many southern legislators. After the assassination of President John F. Kennedy, President Lyndon Johnson became a reluctant supporter of the Civil Rights Act. In 1964, advocates for integration strengthened the Bill, and Congress passed this Act, which was the first major civil rights act in 90 years.

Advocates of desegregation believed then that the real changes envisioned by *Brown* were possible. The U.S. Attorney General was authorized to sue officials who perpetuated systems of de jure segregation[1] and began to do so vigorously.

Because the "all deliberate speed" instruction was an unknown and never clearly defined legal standard, those committed to segregation routinely interpreted the Court's instructions as they chose—which typically meant that school districts disregarded the Court's order with little to no recourse prior to the implementation of the Civil Rights Act (Bell, 2004). Regulations implementing the Civil Rights Act became effective in 1965, and Justice Department lawyers began suing school districts that refused to desegregate. The U.S. Supreme Court, furious that school districts had ignored its order in *Brown II* to desegregate "with all deliberate speed," stepped back into the fray and ordered schools to desegregate "at once" (*Brown v. Board of Education*, 1955, p. 301). Federal courts required school districts to undertake action to remedy the historical discrimination against African American students and other students of color attending de facto[2] or de jure segregated schools. Busing became widespread as a form of desegregation. Schools were ordered to make improvements in the "tangible factors" referenced in *Brown*. However, the educational achievement of African American children did improve to some degree in integrated schools (Ryan, 1999).

Desegregation did not prove to be a panacea. For a host of reasons, the educational achievement of African American children still lagged. First, many desegregated schools became resegregated due to "White flight" to private schools or suburban areas. Second, the U.S. Supreme Court refused to use interdistrict transfers of African American students to suburban, predominantly White school districts, which were better financed to desegregate than were urban, predominantly minority school districts. Third, African American students in desegregated schools suffered psychologically in ways that retarded their educational and mental development. For years, advocates for racial equality and educational equity firmly cleaved to the belief that integration, on its own, would improve the educational prospects of African American children (Bell, 2004, p. 161); however, by the 1970s, African Americans, joined by other minority groups who had begun their own movements to improve public education, started to view the remedies for educational achievement of minority and poor children in a different way. These advocates shifted their focus to "desegregating the money" after observing the difficulty of integrating African American and Latino American students with their "swiftly fleeing white counterparts" (Bell, 2004, p. 161).

AN OVERVIEW OF SCHOOL FINANCE LITIGATION

The free public education that students in the United States enjoy is a state responsibility that can be found in the Constitutions of all 50 states. Basically, to establish a system of free public education, states provide a designated amount of money from the state budget to local school districts to fund the basic education program. States also have a large dependence on local funds and expect school districts to levy local property owners to provide such funds in order to supplement the state subsidy. School districts that are located in communities with more expensive property can raise more money through school taxes than districts that are located in communities where the majority of the property values are low. The federal government also provides funds, but only to support specific categories of programs and to supplement the basic educational program, not to supplant the state and local funds.

Advocates began legal challenges to state education funding systems based on two key themes: (1) that education is a fundamental right and (2) that state laws that rely on the existence of local property taxes as supplemental funding discriminated against children based on wealth, in violation of the EPC of the Fourteenth Amendment of the U.S. Constitution.

THE U.S. CONSTITUTION CHALLENGE: *SAN ANTONIO V. RODRIGUEZ*

The first school equity financing case to reach the U.S. Supreme Court was *San Antonio Independent School District v. Rodriguez* (1973). *San Antonio* was a class action lawsuit brought on behalf of school children from poor families who resided in school districts that had a low property tax rate and, therefore, could not raise as much local money to fund their school systems as districts with higher property tax rates (*San Antonio Independent School District v. Rodriguez*). Plaintiffs argued that the Texas school financing scheme, which relied on an ad valorem tax on property within a district to supplement the funds that the state provided to the local education agency, violated the EPC.

Educators soon learned that the federal EPC was not going to provide relief for children in inadequately funded school districts, which was a crushing blow. The U.S. Supreme Court held that the Texas school financing law did not violate the EPC. Two holdings from this case shaped the future of educational equity law. First, the Court held that education was not a fundamental right under the U.S. Constitution. Second, the Court held that "wealth" was not a suspect class[3] and that the state education finance law would be subject to rational basis review.[4] The Supreme Court reiterated that public education was a state function and essentially directed advocates to look to their state constitutions, state courts, and state legislatures to solve their educational equity problems—unless they involved desegregation or other disparities based on a recognized suspect class.

The Waves of School Finance Litigation

After *San Antonio*, advocates began bringing lawsuits in state court based on two theories: first, the enforcement of the education clause in the state constitution and, second, the enforcement of the state constitution EPC, if the state was one of the 27 states that had such a clause. Lawsuits are typically based on both clauses if they are both found in the state constitution. From 1973 to 1993, educational equity/school finance cases were filed in 45 states (Thro, 1993).

State Education Clause Litigation

The state education clauses require the state to fund and maintain an education system of varying types and quality (Thro, 1993). State constitutions typically require the maintenance of a "uniform" system of schools, an "efficient" system, a "thorough" system, or some combination thereof. Equity cases seek to define quality terms such as *uniform*, *thorough*, and *efficient*. It was argued that children in underfunded districts are not provided the quality of education that their state constitution guarantees. Cases based solely on this clause have met with varying success.

State Equal Protection Clause Litigation

Many of the state EPCs are identical or similar to the federal EPC. State EPC litigation has been the decisive factor in most lawsuits where a state school financing scheme was found to be unconstitutional. Of the 31 lawsuits involving a state EPC, 5 state courts have found that the financing scheme violated the clause; 21 found that it did not, and 5 based their decision on other factors.

The reasons for these decisions vary. Some courts have relied on the Supreme Court's analysis in *San Antonio*. Other courts have relied on their own jurisprudence, with some courts stating specifically that even though their EPC may be similar to the federal EPC, they are not bound by federal EPC jurisprudence and their interpretation of similar language may exceed the U.S. Supreme Court's interpretation of such language. However, the analysis in a successful challenge is almost always the same: The court applies some type of strict scrutiny analysis[4] after finding that (1) education is a fundamental right under its state constitution or (2) wealth is a suspect class.

Specific Equal Protection Cases

An analysis of selected state cases applying an equal protection analysis leads to further insights linking state legislative policies on education expenditures to the provision of substantial educational opportunities for students, especially African American students in low-income districts. Several of these cases will be discussed here.

Serrano v. Priest

In *Serrano v. Priest* (1971; hereinafter *Serrano I*), the California Supreme Court held that under its state constitution, education was a fundamental right and, more important, that wealth was a suspect class. In *Serrano v. Priest* (1976; hereinafter *Serrano II*), the California court found that because of the fully developed trial record in the *Serrano I* case, it did indeed have the "'expertise' and familiarity with local problems of school financing and educational policy" that the U.S. Supreme Court found to "[counsel] against premature interference with informed judgments made at the state and local levels" (pp. 951–952).

The Court reaffirmed its decision in *Serrano II* and held that the system allowed "the availability of educational opportunity to vary as a function of the assessed valuation per ADA [average daily attendance] of taxable property within a given district" (p. 953). The Court rejected the state's argument that the system was justified because of "local control," stating that interest was "chimerical from the standpoint of those districts which are less favored in terms of taxable wealth per pupil" (p. 953).

The California court's opinion contains strong language on the impact of property taxes and why wealth should be considered a suspect class:

> Substantial disparities in expenditures per pupil among school districts cause and perpetuate substantial disparities in the quality and extent of availability of educational opportunities. For this reason the school financing system before the court fails to provide equality of treatment to all the pupils in the state. Although an equal expenditure level per pupil in every district is not educationally sound or desirable because of differing educational needs, *equality of educational opportunity requires that all school districts possess an equal ability in terms of revenue to provide students with substantially equal opportunities for learning* [italics added]. The system before the court fails in this respect, for it gives high-wealth districts a substantial advantage in obtaining higher quality staff, program expansion and variety, beneficial teacher-pupil ratios and class sizes, modern equipment and materials, and high-quality buildings. *There is a distinct relationship between cost and the quality of educational opportunities afforded* [italics added]. Quality cannot be defined wholly in terms of performance on statewide achievement tests because such tests do not measure all the benefits and detriments that a child may receive from his educational experience. However, even using pupil outputs as a measure of the quality of a district's educational program, differences in dollars do *produce differences in pupil achievement* [italics added]. (*Serrano II*, 1976, p. 939)

California, then, was required to overhaul its school financing system. A decade later, education advocates were still dissatisfied with the overhaul and reinstituted a suit alleging continued disparities based on wealth (*Serrano v. Priest*, 1986; hereinafter *Serrano III*). In *Serrano III*, the Court disagreed and upheld the financing system.

Lake View School District No. 25 v. Huckabee (2002)

In *Lake View School District No. 25 v. Huckabee* (2002), a more recent case, a school district along with three other school districts that entered the litigation as intervenors challenged the state financing laws. The Arkansas Supreme Court found that the school funding system was unconstitutional under its state constitution. In its equal protection analysis, the Court found that there was a discriminatory classification based on wealth between poor and rich districts and that the state, with its school funding formula, fostered this discrimination. It found that the system violated the state EPC because the students were not being afforded equal educational opportunity and there was no legitimate government purpose warranting the discrepancies in curriculum, facilities, equipment, and teacher pay among the school districts.

Bismarck Public School District No.1 v. North Dakota (1994)

In the *Bismarck Public School District* case, the plaintiff was a school district that alleged that the statutory method for funding education as a whole failed to equalize local property tax disparities and resulted in substantial inequities in educational opportunities in violation of the state equal protection provisions. At the retrial level, a state district court in North Dakota held that the statutory method violated the state EPC and retained jurisdiction to monitor the implementation of a constitutional method for distributing funding.

The defendants appealed. The North Dakota Supreme Court declared that the fundamental right to education is a substantive right,[5] which is subject to an intermediate level of scrutiny that requires "the distribution of funding to bear a close correspondence to legislative goals" (*Bismarck Public School District No. 1 v. North Dakota*, 1994, p. 259). The court held that the statutory method of school funding did not bear a close correspondence to the legislative goals of providing equal education based on the wide disparities in educational cost per pupil.

Tennessee Small School Systems v. McWherter (2002)

In Tennessee, the school finance challenge took a different approach. At issue in *Tennessee Small School Systems v. McWherter* (2002) was whether the state's method of funding salaries for teachers equalized teachers' salaries and, if it failed to do so, whether it violated the state EPC by denying students substantially equal educational opportunities. Plaintiffs contended that the plan violated the EPC because it did not provide for cost determination or annual cost review of salaries and that large disparities in teachers' salaries still existed. The plaintiffs sought an order from the Supreme Court of Tennessee that would direct the legislature to make teachers' salaries a component of a new plan, subjecting the salaries to annual cost determination and review.

In its analysis, the Tennessee Supreme Court used the rational basis test, which normally would have caused the law to be upheld. However, here the Court found no rational basis for structuring a basic education program where all its components were cost-driven except for the cost of providing teachers. It declared that teacher salaries are an integral part of any constitutional funding plan and that the integrity and effectiveness of the entire plan would be destroyed if this part were compromised. The court further held that teachers' salaries are a significant factor in determining where teachers choose to work, and it determined that the lack of cost determination and periodic cost review of teachers' salaries was a constitutional problem. Thus, the Court held that the lack of teacher salary equalization according to the plan formula was a significant constitutional defect in the funding scheme. It held that the plan failed to "comply with the state's constitutional obligation to formulate and maintain a system of public education that affords a substantially equal educational opportunity to all students" (*Tennessee Small School Systems v. McWherter*, 2002, p. 234).

Brigham v. Vermont (1997)

In Vermont, plaintiffs alleged that the state constitution provided a guarantee of the fundamental right to education leading to the right to equal educational opportunities. Plaintiffs contended that such a guarantee required the

funding system to be reviewed with strict scrutiny under the Common Benefits Clause, which is similar to the EPC.

The Supreme Court of Vermont found that whether under rational basis or strict scrutiny, it could not find a legitimate governmental purpose "to justify the gross inequities in educational opportunities evident from the record" (*Brigham v. Vermont*, 1997, p. 396). As a result, the Court concluded that the financing system failed to achieve "reasonable educational equality of opportunity" (p. 397) and violated the Common Benefits Clause. The court stated that it did not profess that there should be *absolute* equality, only that the state ensure *substantial* equality, of educational opportunity throughout the state.

CASES WHERE COURTS FOUND NO STATE EQUAL PROTECTION CLAUSE VIOLATION

In 21 cases, the state courts found that the state school financing laws did not violate the state EPC. While these cases are more numerous, the analysis is quite similar. In just about every case, the court found that education was not a fundamental right or the rational basis level of scrutiny, or something similar, was applied. In applying the rational basis analysis, many state courts have refused to remedy acknowledged school financing inequities, citing separation of powers and finding that all matters as to the operation of the public education system are constitutionally under the autonomy of the state legislature. One such case is *Hornbeck v. Somerset County Board of Education* (1983). In that case, the Court of Appeals of Maryland, under the "deferential" rational basis standard of review, held that Maryland's school financing law did not violate Maryland's equal protection provision because there was at least some reasonable explanation for the law, it did not violate fundamental personal rights, and it did not involve inherently suspect distinctions (p. 782).

BEYOND EQUAL PROTECTION: TITLE VI OF THE CIVIL RIGHTS ACT

As the above analysis of state EPCs shows, the state EPCs have not resulted in rectifying or diminishing school financing inequities in most states. When the state courts were closed as an avenue of relief, advocates sought out another federal civil rights law—Title VI of the Civil Rights Act (2003). Advocates began lawsuits alleging that the state school financing laws had a disparate impact on predominately minority school districts in violation of Title VI. There had been some successes under this theory in a few states, so desperate plaintiffs in Pennsylvania pursued it.

In *Powell v. Ridge* (1999), plaintiffs included parents of Philadelphia School District students; advocacy organizations such as NAACP and the Parents United for Public Schools; the Philadelphia School Superintendent; the president of the teachers' union; and the Mayor of Philadelphia, who brought suit against various state officials. The plaintiffs alleged that even where the levels of poverty in various school districts were the same, school districts with more White students received more state funds than districts with more non-White students. They alleged that the state's school financing law, which seemed racially neutral on its face, resulted in a disparate impact on school districts with high percentages of minority students. One of the most descriptive allegations in the *Powell v. Ridge* complaint was that "school districts with a higher non-white enrollment received $52.88 less per pupil for each increase of 1% in non-white enrollment" (pp. 394–395) when both districts are faced with the *same level of poverty*. Thus, the system was not just rife with disparities between high-income and low-income school districts. The system was also rife with disparities between poor White school districts and poor non-White school districts.

The plaintiffs stated that the result of the funding policy was, naturally, the "serious impairment of the educational opportunities of the students in the School District" (*Powell v. Ridge*, 1999, pp. 394–395). They contended that

lack of sufficient resources in the School District results, *inter alia*, in larger class sizes and higher pupil-to-teacher ratios than in surrounding school districts; reduced curricula; cuts in and elimination of programs and electives and advanced placement courses, shortages of textbooks and use of outdated textbooks, shortages of equipment, supplies and technology; spartan physical education and extracurricular programs; lack of librarians and library services; insufficient numbers of counselors and psychologists; and many inadequate and crumbling physical facilities. (*Powell v. Ridge*, 1999, pp. 394–395)

The District Court sustained the defendants' motion to dismiss for failure to state a claim and concluded that the plaintiffs' complaint pled that the funding disparity was based on wealth or economic status. This depiction may have led the District Court to its decision since the U.S. Supreme Court, in *San Antonio Independent School District v. Rodriguez* (1973), held that wealth was not a suspect class. The Third Circuit Court of Appeals reversed, holding that the plaintiffs met their burden to overcome a motion to dismiss by providing "more than sufficient notice to meet the pleading standard" (*Powell v. Ridge,* 1999, p. 395). The Court of Appeals disagreed with the lower court's determination of the plaintiffs' allegations. It found that the plaintiffs clearly alleged that the disparity could not be explained by references to wealth "because the disparities are present when districts of the same poverty level are compared" (*Powell v. Ridge,* 1999, p. 395). For a moment, the plaintiffs rejoiced and thought that, finally, a judicial avenue to an equitably funded Philadelphia school system was open. Such joy was short-lived, however.

In *Alexander v. Sandoval* (2001), the U.S. Supreme Court held that there is no implied private right of action under the disparate impact regulations that implement Title VI. Basically, the Court held that a private individual could not sue to enforce the Title VI disparate impact regulations. After *Sandoval*, commentators expected all the Title VI educational equity cases to be dismissed. Most of them were.

While *Sandoval* left open the possibility of private suits under Section 1983 of the Civil Rights Act to enforce Title VI, the Third Circuit closed the door on this possibility. It held in *South Camden Citizens in Action v. New Jersey Department of Environmental Protection* (2001) that no private right of action existed under Section 1983 to enforce disparate impact discrimination regulation under Title VI. Again, advocates lost another civil rights law as a means to achieve educational equity.

LINKING JUDICIAL APPROACHES TO SCHOOL FINANCE LITIGATION TO STUDENT ACHIEVEMENT

Data-Based Analysis of the Relationship Between Student Achievement and Judicial Decisions

Given the prevalence of school finance litigation in ensuring that at least substantially equal educational opportunities are being provided for African American students, the natural question is "What has been the impact of the judicial decisions?" Plaintiffs claim that better and more equitably financed schools lead to greater student achievement. Defendants and detractors often claim that spending more money on the schools will not solve the student achievement problems.

Judges have taken different approaches in resolving school finance disputes, from being quite proactive in ordering school restructuring and reform to taking a minimalist approach and deferring to the state legislature's decisions. The question could again be asked as to which judicial approach has the most impact on student achievement.

School financing decisions have generally taken one of five approaches: (1) the court determining that the school finance issue is nonjusticiable, giving complete deference to the legislature, (2) the court determining that the issue is justiciable but still giving great deference to the legislature and declaring that the current school financing system that the legislature passed is constitutional, (3) the court determining that the school finance system is unconstitutional yet providing no guidance to the legislature as to how to rectify the system, (4) the court holding the school finance system unconstitutional and suggesting to the legislature the implementation of certain characteristics for a new constitutional funding scheme, and (5) the court holding the school finance system unconstitutional and ordering specific programs to be implemented.

The effectiveness of these approaches will be weighed by examining cases in five states and relating those to student performance on standardized achievement and aptitude tests.

Court Determined School Finance Issue Nonjusticiable and Completely Deferred to the Legislature

In *Coalition for Adequacy and Fairness in School Funding v. Chiles* (1996), the judiciary took the first approach—deferring completely to the state legislature. In that case, the appellants sought a declaration that an adequate education is a fundamental right under the state constitution and that the state has failed to provide students with this right by failing to provide adequate resources. The Supreme Court of Florida reviewed the education article of the state's constitution and sought to define the duty placed on the state legislature to provide a certain level of education. In making this determination, the Court concluded that it would overstep its boundaries if it decided whether the legislature's appropriation of funds was adequate. It noted that the separation-of-powers doctrine prevented judicial intrusion into this matter because "the power to appropriate state funds is assigned to the legislature" (p. 408).

Court Determined Issue Justiciable yet Gave Greater Deference to Legislature and Held Finance System Constitutional

An example of the second approach, where the court determined the school finance action justiciable but still provided the legislature with some degree of deference while finding the school financing system constitutional, is *Vincent v. Voight* (2000). In this case, the petitioners in Wisconsin challenged the state's school finance system under the education article and the EPC of the state constitution. The court contended that the system failed to provide equal access to financial resources across school districts. The Supreme Court of Wisconsin held that the petitioners did not prove beyond a reasonable doubt that the school finance system violated the state constitution. With that holding, the Court did find that children of the state had a "fundamental right to an equal opportunity for a sound basic education" (p. 396). In making this observation, the Court found that the legislature articulated a standard for this fundamental right and was providing sufficient resources so that school districts could offer students this opportunity. Accordingly, the Court held that the state school finance system passed "constitutional muster" (p. 397). As the Court made its determination on whether the state EPC was violated, it employed the rational basis standard of review. It determined that it must give great deference to the state legislature and found the classifications within the school finance system rationally related to the purpose of educating the state's children. Thus, the system was declared constitutional.

Court Determined System Unconstitutional, Implementation of New Constitutional School Finance System Left to Legislature

An example of the third approach, where the court determined the school financing system unconstitutional but left implementation of a new constitutional system to the legislature is *DeRolph v. Ohio* (2002). In that case, the Supreme Court of Ohio revisited the issue of the constitutionality of the state's school finance system four times. In the first and second decisions, the Court determined that the financing system was unconstitutional but provided no guidance to the legislature on how to implement a constitutional school finance system. The third decision was an attempt by the Court to provide some guidance to the legislature. In the fourth decision, the Court vacated the third decision and held that the first two decisions were the "law of the case" (p. 530). The Court directed the legislature to enact a constitutional funding scheme but provided no guidance on its implementation. The Court also acknowledged the difficulties of the state's duty to implement but concluded that the constitution places such a duty on the legislature and it cannot be trumped.

Court Determined System Unconstitutional, Suggested Implementation of Certain Characteristics for New System

An example of the fourth approach, where the court declared a financing system unconstitutional and provided limited guidance to the legislature by noting certain characteristics that should be implemented for a constitutional system, is *McDuffy v. Secretary of the Executive Office of Education* (1993). In that case, plaintiffs in Massachusetts sought a declaration that the school financing system denied them the opportunity to receive an adequate education as mandated by the state constitution. The plaintiffs contended that the system violated both the education clause and the EPC of the state constitution. The court researched the history of public education and the state's legislative history and concluded that the state had a duty to provide an education to both rich and poor children in order to serve their interests

and prepare them as citizens of the state. The court held that the state had failed to fulfill its duty.

The court articulated broad guidelines in an attempt to help the legislature remedy the constitutional violations within its school finance system (*McDuffy v. Secretary of the Executive Office of Education,* 1993, p. 554). Accordingly, "an educated child must possess at least the seven following capabilities:

   (i) Sufficient oral and written communication skills to enable students to function in a complex and rapidly changing civilization

  (ii) Sufficient knowledge of economic, social, and political systems to enable students to make informed choices

 (iii) Sufficient understanding of governmental processes to enable the student to understand the issues that affect his or her community, state, and nation

 (iv) Sufficient self-knowledge and knowledge of his or her mental and physical wellness

  (v) Sufficient grounding in the arts to enable each student to appreciate his or her cultural heritage

 (vi) Sufficient training or preparation for advanced training in either academic or vocational fields so as to enable each child to choose and pursue life work intelligently; and

(vii) Sufficient level of academic or vocational skills to enable public school students to compete favorably with their counterparts in surrounding states, in academics or in the job market." (*McDuffy v. Secretary of the Executive Office of Education,* 1993, p. 544)

Although the Court provided such guidelines, it left the task of fulfilling this constitutional duty to the magistrates and the legislature.

Court Determined System Unconstitutional, Ordered Implementation of Specific Programs

An example of the final approach, where the court determined a school finance system unconstitutional and ordered specific programs and characteristics implemented before the financing system can be deemed constitutional is *Abbott v. Burke* (1998). This case involved an ongoing action by public school students in New Jersey alleging that the state's school financing system was unconstitutional. The Supreme Court of New Jersey held that the system was facially constitutional, but unconstitutional as applied to special needs districts. The court then remanded the decision to the New Jersey Superior Court for fact-finding hearings to determine the proper remedy.

In this decision, the New Jersey Supreme Court affirmed and further specified the reform that the lower court set forth. The court directed the implementation of specific programs such as whole-school reform, full-day kindergarten, technology, and school-to-work and school-to-college transition. It also directed the implementation of a facilities plan, the securing of funds for the cost of infrastructure deficiencies in the school buildings and other costs that are associated with school construction. The court noted that the success of these measures will depend on whether "there is a top-to-bottom commitment to ensuring that the reforms are conscientiously undertaken and vigorously carried forward" (*Abbott v. Burke*, 1998, p. 474).

Relationship Between Jurisprudential Approach and School Funding and Student Achievement Disparities

In an attempt to draw some conclusions as to the relationship between the jurisprudential approach in the five cases discussed and school funding and student achievement disparities, the following unique, albeit unscientific, examination is presented. Table 29.1 presents a summary of these relationships.

It appears that the greater the degree of judicial involvement, the greater the amount of expenditures per pupil for students in high-poverty districts. For example, in Florida, where the court determined that the issue was nonjusticiable and gave complete deference to the legislature, Carey (2004) noted that the cost-per-student differential between districts with the lowest rates of poverty and those with the highest was $248. In Wisconsin, where the court held that the issue was justiciable but still deferred to the legislature and held the system constitutional, the cost-per-student differential was $337. Similarly, in Ohio, where the court determined that the system was unconstitutional

but provided no guidance to the legislature, the differential was $347 per student. In Massachusetts, where the court determined that the system was unconstitutional and suggested the implementation of certain characteristics for a new system, the differential was $774 *more* per student in the high-poverty districts. In New Jersey, where the court determined that the system was unconstitutional and very specifically ordered the state to implement certain programs, the differential was $566 *more* per student.

These results may be explained by theorizing that where the court does not see as significant a variation in initial per-pupil spending, it sees little reason or justification for intervention. However, when the court does intervene and judges believe that they must be more specific and targeted in intervening to rectify the unconstitutional system, expenditures per pupil rise beyond negative numbers and more funds are actually directed toward the poorer school districts.

The relationship between student achievement and judicial intervention is not as clear when it relates to student academic improvement. In Florida, where the court found the challenge nonjusticiable, fourth-grade students' National Assessment of Educational Progress (NAEP) reading scores increased by 12 points from 1998 to 2003 (National Center for Education Statistics [NCES], 2005). However, in Massachusetts, where the court held the funding system unconstitutional and suggested certain characteristics to implement a valid system, student NAEP reading scores increased by only 5 points during that time period (NCES, 2005). In contrast, students' NAEP reading scores in Wisconsin, where the court held the challenge justiciable and constitutional, decreased by 1 point (NCES, 2005).

The academic achievement statistics paint a mixed picture. Information from the Education Trust (2004) regarding student achievement in Wisconsin, New Jersey, Florida, Massachusetts, and Ohio is instructive. On statewide testing, the highest percentage of fourth graders from the states examined who scored at proficient or advanced was 80% in Wisconsin, where the court upheld the school financing system. In New Jersey, where the court orders were very specific, students achieved similarly, with 79% of the fourth graders at proficient or above. At the other end of the spectrum, in Florida, where the issue was held nonjusticiable, only 60% of

TABLE 29.1   Judicial Analysis Compared Against National and State Reading Test Scores

Judicial Analysis	Court determined issue non-justiciable and completely deferred to legislature	Court determined issue justiciable but provided great deference to legislature, holding system constitutional	Court determined system unconstitutional but provided no guidance to legislature	Court determined system unconstitutional and suggested implementation of certain characteristics for new system	Court determined system unconstitutional and ordered specific programs
Cases	Coalition for Adequacy and Fairness in School Funding v. Chiles (Fla. 1996)	Vincent v. Voight (Wis. 2000)	DeRolph v. Ohio (Ohio 2002)	McDuffy v. Secretary of the Executive Office of Education (Mass. 1993)	Abbott v. Burke (N.J. 1998)
Funding for Districts With Highest Child Poverty Rates Compared With Those With Lowest Rates in 2002	$248 fewer per student, total $6,200 less for a class of 25 students	$337 fewer per student, total $8,425 less for a class of 25 students	$347 fewer per student, total $8,675 less for a class of 25 students	$774 more per student, total $19,350 more for a class of 25 students	$566 more dollars per student, total $14,150 more for a class of 25 students
Academic Achievement in Reading	State: 60% at Level 3 or higher NAEP: 32% proficient or above; 63% basic or above	State: 80% proficient and advanced NAEP: 33% proficient or above; 68% basic or above	State: 66% at or above proficient NAEP: 34% proficient or above; 69% basic or above	State: 56% proficient or advanced NAEP: 40% proficient or advanced; 73% basic or above	State: 79% proficient and advanced NAEP: 39% proficient or above; 70% basic or above
Improvement in Reading Scores From 1998 to 2003	Increased by 12 points	Decreased by 1 point	Increased by 5 points	Increased by 5 points	Increased by 2 points

fourth graders performed at or above grade level. Massachusetts has produced a slightly worse result, in that the court only suggested the implementation of certain characteristics for a new system, only 56% of students scored at proficient level or above. In Ohio, where the court determined the system to be unconstitutional but provided no guidance to the legislature, there was middle ground—66% of all fourth graders scored at the passing level.

Fourth-grade student percentage scores on the NAEP statistics are no clearer. Of the five states, only three have given their students the NAEP exam on a regular basis (NCES, 2005). Of those three, the highest level of students' state reading scores at proficient level was in Massachusetts, with 40%, compared with the scores in the two states with the constitutional system, Wisconsin at 33% and Florida at 32% (Education Trust, 2004). Slightly more students are scoring at proficient levels in the states where the court ordered changes in the school financing system.

However, the other side of the NAEP story is that more students (73%) scored at basic or above in Massachusetts than in Florida (63%) or Wisconsin (68%; Education Trust, 2004). So, despite the mixed picture that statewide testing shows when compared with particular judicial analysis, more students scored at basic or above when the court took a more active judicial approach to the school funding challenge presented.

THE IMPACT OF THE NO CHILD LEFT BEHIND ACT OF 2001

The education centerpiece of George W. Bush's presidency, NCLB, may turn out to be the most significant law in achieving enhanced educational achievement for children of color, if it is true to one of its stated purposes—to improve academic achievement for disadvantaged and minority students. NCLB was passed in 2001 as the reauthorization of the Elementary and Secondary Education Act, the federal law that provides a certain percentage of federal funds to public schools with low-income students in a variety of categorical programs (U.S. Department of Education, n.d.).

Traditionally, through the Elementary and Secondary Education Act, the federal government simply provided funds to qualifying school districts. NCLB now sets the "tone, direction and priorities of public education in every school in the United States" (Wenkart, 2003). NCLB establishes standards for accountability and educational progress at every level. Each student must make "adequate yearly progress" (AYP) in academic achievement according to the state's definition of that term. According to the U.S. Department of Education, NCLB is an equal-opportunity law because it requires AYP for *each* child, no matter the status of the child. This includes students in the category of special education and limited English proficient students, who are frequently left out of educational achievement, even in otherwise high-performing school districts. Each school must meet achievement goals set by the state that require a percentage of that school's students to reach a certain level of mastery, meaning a passing or proficient score, on statewide achievement tests in reading and math by 2014. By the 2007–2008 school year, assessments in science will be added.

Beginning in 2002, NCLB provided remedies to students who attended schools that failed to demonstrate that the requisite levels were met. The remedies stipulated that (1) students in noncompliant schools qualify for a tutor at the school's expense, (2) they have the right to transfer to "achieving" schools within their district, and (3) if there is no "achieving" school in the district, the district can ask other districts in the state if they will enroll its students (U.S. Department of Education Web site).

But is NCLB a Trojan horse? Despite the positive items in NCLB, some commentators believe that the real goal of NCLB is to support vouchers and reduce funds to public schools. Others contend that NCLB is setting public schools up for failure—more ammunition for vouchers—by requiring schools to meet high standards yet not providing funds to help them in doing so, thus creating yet another unfunded federal mandate. For now, however, NCLB has much to offer in the area of educational opportunity.

NCLB has been criticized as unprecedented federal involvement in traditional state and local control of education—in its requirements that states set certain achievement standards for students, teachers, and schools and in establishing sanctions for failure to meet them. NCLB's tentacles have reached into every area of the schools.

Similarly, NCLB is beginning to have an impact on school finance litigation. Some courts have looked to NCLB to set or influence the standards of an adequate or quality education. Others, in essence, are using NCLB's standard-setting and sanctioning provisions as justifications for little or no judicial involvement in restructuring school financing or educational offerings. What follows is an analysis of some key cases in which the implementation of NCLB triggered school finance litigation.

CASE ANALYSIS

Cranston School Committee v. City of Cranston (2004)

In this case, the plaintiff, Cranston School Committee in Cranston, Rhode Island, argued that NCLB created an increased need for funding to meet its mandate and that additional funding was needed to run a quality school system (*Cranston School Committee v. City of Cranston*, 2004). It brought suit against the defendant, the City of Cranston, seeking additional appropriations for the 2003–2004 fiscal year. The Rhode Island Superior Court made numerous findings of fact and ultimately concluded that the public school system was adequately funded by the City.

Campaign for Fiscal Equity, Inc. v. New York (2003)

In *Campaign for Fiscal Equity, Inc. v. New York* (2003), NCLB has surfaced several times. In one opinion in the case, the court held that NCLB does not define a sound basic education but helps the state determine schools that have the greatest need and sets goals for improvement. As the case continued, the measurement of school districts that met performance targets under NCLB was considered as one of the standards to be used to evaluate whether the New York City schools provided students with an adequate education. However, the court decided against using that standard and instead used the state's own Regents Criteria.

Flores v. Arizona (2005)

In this opinion, the court refused the defendants' request for an advisory opinion on the role of federal funding made available through NCLB and on the adequacy of state funding for

its English Language Learners (ELL) program (*Flores v. Arizona,* 2005). Besides acknowledging that issuing an advisory opinion would just delay the court issuing a final opinion in the case, the court agreed with plaintiffs' arguments that such an opinion was largely irrelevant because federal funds should supplement, not substitute for, the state's obligation to provide a constitutional school funding system, part of which was to fund the state's ELL programs (*Flores v. Arizona,* 2005, pp. 1118–1119).

Save Our Schools—Southeast & Northeast v. District of Columbia Board of Education (2006)

In this case, plaintiffs' suit alleged various deficiencies in the District of Columbia public schools (*Save Our Schools-Southeast & Northeast v. District of Columbia Board of Education,* 2006). The plaintiffs sued the defendant Margaret Spellings, U.S. Secretary of Education, under the premise that NCLB deprived students of much-needed funding by requiring schools to meet the Act's unfunded mandates. The plaintiffs further claimed that the provision of NCLB that allows students in low-performing schools to transfer to better schools fails because many students are unable to transfer due to lack of space. The court held that Spellings and the other defendants were immune from suit. The court dismissed the claims against Spellings because the plaintiffs failed to state a claim against the Secretary of Education under Sections 1981 and 1983 of the Civil Rights Act. The court found that neither statute included actions against Spellings because her actions were "taken under color of federal law, not state law" (*Save Our Schools-Southeast & Northeast v. District of Columbia Board of Education,* 2006, p. 6). As for the other defendants, the court held that they were entities immune from suit.

ADDITIONAL DEVELOPMENTS IN LITIGATION INVOLVING THE NO CHILD LEFT BEHIND ACT

In 2005, the National Education Association and eight school districts in Michigan, Texas, and Vermont filed suit against the U.S. Department of Education in the case of *School District of City of Pontiac v. Spellings,* seeking declaratory and injunctive relief from NCLB (*Pontiac v. Spellings*, 2005). Plaintiffs alleged that the Department violated a provision in the Act that asserted that states could not be forced to comply with this federal mandate if it was not funded by the federal government. They contended that the federal government was forcing states and school districts to follow an unfunded federal mandate that has caused states and school districts to use non-NCLB funds earmarked for other important educational programs in order to comply with NCLB. They further alleged that many schools were unable to fully comply with the Act because of its underfunding (*Pontiac v. Spellings*, 2005).

The plaintiffs argued that for the fiscal year 2005, NCLB was underfunded in the amount of $9.8 billion less than the funding authorization levels approved by Congress. As a result of these "multibillion-dollar shortfalls," states and school districts were struggling to meet many of the requirements of the Act, including, but not limited to, achieving AYP, implementing and administering standards and assessments, compiling data tracking student performance, reporting progress to state and federal authorities, and implementing various strategies for school improvement. The plaintiffs projected that this problem would worsen for the fiscal year 2006 due to President Bush's proposed budget, which increased NCLB funding by only 1.3%. As a result of this, plaintiffs sought an order from the U.S. District Court in Michigan declaring that states and school districts are not required to follow NCLB mandates by using non-NCLB funds and that failure to comply with those mandates because of underfunding by the federal government is not a basis to withhold federal funds. The plaintiffs also requested that the Court enjoin the department from withholding funds from states and school districts for noncompliance with NCLB directly attributable to their refusal to use any non-NCLB funds for this mandate.

At first, the plaintiffs were disappointed. In November 2005, The District Court dismissed the complaint after determining that Congress did not intend federal funding to pay for all the requirements under the Act, nor was it prohibited from requiring compliance with the Act to receive federal funding (*Pontiac v. Spellings*, 2005). However, in January 2008, the Court of Appeals reversed the District Court's decision, holding that the plaintiffs could proceed with their case. The Court of Appeals sent the case back to the District Court, where the case is now pending. Its outcome is being closely watched by all parties, and the case may have a major impact on future compliance with and funding of No Child Left Behind (*Pontiac v. Spellings*, 2005).

CONCLUSION

In the area of educational equity, the federal civil rights laws now provide little equality or protection. State constitutional EPCs have provided much sought after remedies in some states but not in others. NCLB, which may provide the greatest hope for educational advancement for African American children, at least in the short term, is also influencing school finance litigation. NCLB basically requires states to establish standards as to what constitutes a constitutionally sufficient education under the state constitution. NCLB allows each state to establish its own standards for adequate or proficient student performance for students in every grade. Education activists are beginning to use the reporting data required by NCLB to bolster state equal protection arguments. Due to NCLB, federal and state law must be examined in concert with educational equity cases.

The jury is still out as to which approach to school finance cases generates the highest levels of student achievement for African Americans. Current analysis shows that prior to NCLB, a court was more likely to intervene and order remedies reflecting the increasingly high disparity in the per-pupil spending between low- and high-poverty districts. The high-performing schools examined have been influenced by the restructuring of the school finance laws in their states in varying degrees. The more specific the court order, particularly as to capital improvements, the more visible the school improvement. School finance litigation has been a multilayered area of the law that has been affected by the intersection of federal and state law and changing curricular focus. Educational equity for the masses of minority children, particularly African Americans, has never been easy to achieve, and current school finance jurisprudence bears that out.

Now, compliance with NCLB looms over it all. Therefore, the struggle still continues.

Notes

1. *De jure* is a Latin legal term that literally means "a matter of law." In the law, the term means "existing by right or according to law." De jure segregation then is segregation that is permitted by law (Garner, 2004).

2. *De facto* is a Latin legal term that literally means "in point of fact." De facto segregation is segregation that occurs without state authority, usually on the basis of socioeconomic factors (Garner, 2004).

3. A suspect class is a statutory classification based on race, national origin, or lineage and thereby subject to strict scrutiny under equal protection analysis (Garner, 2004).

4. Strict scrutiny is the standard applied to suspect classifications (such as race) in equal protection analysis and to the fundamental rights (such as voting rights) in due process analysis. Under strict scrutiny, the state must establish that it has a compelling interest that justifies and necessitates the law in question. "Equal protection analysis requires strict scrutiny of a legislative classification only when the classification impermissibly interferes with the exercise of a fundamental right or operates to the peculiar disadvantage of a suspect class" (*Massachusetts Board of Retirement et al. v. Murgia*, 1976, pp. 307, 312). A rational basis review is the criterion for judicial analysis of a statute that does not implicate a fundamental right or a suspect or quasi-suspect classification under the Due Process Clause or the EPC, whereby the court will uphold a law if it bears a reasonable relationship to the attainment of a legitimate governmental objective. "[The rational basis standard] employs a relatively relaxed standard reflecting the Court's awareness that the drawing of lines that create distinctions is peculiarly a legislative task and an unavoidable one" (*Massachusetts Board of Retirement et al. v. Murgia*, 1976, pp. 307, 314; see also Garner, 2004).

5. A substantive right is a right that can be protected or enforced by law; a right of substance rather than form (Garner, 2004).

References

Abbott v. Burke, 710 A.2d 450 (N.J. 1998).

Alexander v. Sandoval, 532 U.S. 275 (2001).

Bell, D. (2004). *Silent covenants: Brown v. Board of Education and the unfulfilled hopes for racial reform.* Oxford, UK: Oxford University Press.

Bismarck Public School District No. 1 v. North Dakota, 511 N.W.2d 247 (N.D. 1994).

Brigham v. Vermont, 692 A.2d 384 (Vt. 1997).

Brown v. Board of Education, 347 U.S. 483 (1954).

Brown v. Board of Education, 349 U.S. 294 (1955).

Campaign for Fiscal Equity, Inc. v. New York, 801 N.E.2d 326 (N.Y. 2003).

Carey, K. (2004). *The funding gap 2004: Many states still shortchange low-income and minority students.* Retrieved May 16, 2005, from www2.edtrust.org/NR/rdonlyres/30B3C1B3-3DA6-4809-AFB9-2DAACF11CF88/0/funding2004.pdf

Coalition for Adequacy and Fairness in School Funding v. Chiles, 680 So.2d 400 (Fla. 1996).

Cranston School Committee v. City of Cranston, No. PC/03–5110, 2004 R.I. Super. LEXIS 52 (R.I. Super. Ct. March 8, 2004).

DeRolph v. Ohio, 780 N.E.2d 529 (Ohio 2002).

Education Trust. (2004). *Education watch 2004 state summary reports.* Retrieved May 16, 2005, from www2.edtrust.org/edtrust/summaries2004/states.html

Flores v. Arizona, 405 F. Supp.2d 1112 (D. Ariz. 2005).

Garner, B. A. (Ed.). (2004). *Black's law dictionary* (8th ed.). St. Paul, MN: Thomas West.

Hornbeck v. Somerset County Board of Education, 295 Md. 597, 458 A.2d 758 (1983).

Hurst, D., Tan, A., Meek, A., & Sellers, J. (2003). *Overview and inventory of state education reforms—1990 to 2000: Sources of revenue.* Retrieved May 16, 2005, from http://nces.ed.gov/pubs2003/2003020.pdf

Lake View School District No. 25 v. Huckabee, 91 S.W.3d 472 (Ark. 2002).

Massachusetts Board of Retirement et al. v. Murgia, 427 U.S. 307 (1976).

McDuffy v. Secretary of the Executive Office of Education, 615 N.E.2d 516 (Mass. 1993).

National Center for Education Statistics. (2005). *The nation's report card, state profiles.* Retrieved May 16, 2005, from http://nces.ed.gov/nationsreportcard/states/profile.asp

Powell v. Ridge, 189 F.3d 387 (3d Cir. 1999).

Ryan, J. E. (1999). School, race, and money. *Yale Law Journal, 109,* 249–316.

San Antonio Independent School District v. Rodriguez, 411 U.S. 1 (1973).

Save Our Schools—Southeast & Northeast v. District of Columbia Board of Education, No. 04–01500, 2006 U.S. Dist. LEXIS 45073 (D. D.C. July 3, 2006).

School District of City of Pontiac v. Spellings, 2005 WL 3149545 (E.D. Mich. 2005); rev'd, 512 F.3d 252 (6th Cir. 2008) (Complaint for Declaratory and Injunctive Relief).

Serrano v. Priest, 487 P.2d 1241 (Cal. 1971) (Serrano I).

Serrano v. Priest, 557 P.2d 929 (Cal. 1976) (Serrano II).

Serrano v. Priest, 226 Cal. Rptr. 584 (Cal. Ct. App. 1986) (Serrano III).

South Camden Citizens in Action v. New Jersey Department of Environmental Protection, 274 F.3d 771 (3d Cir. 2001).

Tennessee Small School Systems v. McWherter, 91 S.W.3d 232 (Tenn. 2002).

Thro, W. E. (1993). The role of language of the state education clauses in school finance litigation. *Education Law Reporter, 79,* 19–31.

U.S. Department of Education. (n.d.). No Child Left Behind Act. Retrieved May 16, 2005, from www.ed.gov/nclb/landing.jhtml?src=ln

Vincent v. Voight, 614 N.W.2d 388 (Wis. 2000).

Wenkart, R. D. (2003). The No Child Left Behind Act and Congress' power to regulate under the spending clause. *Education Law Reporter, 174,* 589–597.

30

EDUCATING BLACK YOUTH FOR ECONOMIC EMPOWERMENT

Democratic Economic Participation and School Reform Practices and Policies

JESSICA GORDON NEMBHARD

School reform is complex and multidimensional. Much attention has been given to urban school reform, particularly regarding equitable school financing, increasing teacher training and credentials, smaller classroom size, curriculum reform (either for more prescribed directed teaching, or for more arts and culture in the curriculum), enhancing school-community partnerships, improving parent and family resources, and increasing supplemental education. Most of those reforms are found to have had impact over time (see, e.g., Danielson, 2003; Gardner & Miranda, 2001; Glasser, 1989; Gordon, Bridglall, & Meroe, 2005). One focus, however, that is continually neglected in curricular reform is economic content, and the connections not just between the political economy of schooling and school achievement but between the ways economic theory and practice are taught (or not taught) in schools, as well as the connections between economics education, educational achievement, and motivation.

In the 21st century, economic inequality remains a blight on our society as well as a societal challenge. The systemic challenges to democratic economic participation for African American students are daunting and belie the myth of achievement through hard work alone. It is crucial, therefore, to understand not only what skills and mastery our current economic system requires schools to develop but also the possible economic experiences our schools could make available if the curricula were relevantly transformed (see Gordon Nembhard, 2005; Skilton-Sylvester, 2003). Teaching African American students the "inspiring" economics of alternative development strategies and the cooperative model increases their academic skills, helps them to think more innovatively, and empowers them to be change makers in their communities.

AUTHOR'S NOTE: The author thanks Joyce King for helpful references and thoughtful comments, Carol Lee for rigorous editing and feedback on a previous version of this chapter, and Linda Tillman for her expert editing. She also thanks T. J. Lehman and Walker J. Foster for invaluable research assistance at various stages. Remaining shortcomings or mistakes are of course the author's responsibility.

My exploration into teaching democratic economic participation at both the high school and college levels leads me to investigate innovative economic practices in primary and secondary schools as well as strategies for teaching alternative economics at the postsecondary school level as examples of how the use of transformative economics curricula enhance both schooling and community development in African American communities. Anecdotal evidence suggests that Black students increase academic confidence, motivation, and sometimes achievement as they learn certain economic content and practice alternative economic development in a school setting (Gordon Nembhard, 2005; Skilton-Sylvester, 1994).[1] They learn about economics as a transformative body of knowledge and experience entrepreneurship and working with alternative economic structures so that they have more options when they leave high school and/or college. At the very least, these experiences enhance their credentials in the larger world, often leading to greater personal and community well-being and deeper school-community partnerships. The potential for increasing school achievement is high.

In my preliminary investigation into this relationship, I note that African American students who are involved in cooperative businesses and alternative economic activities in high schools and middle schools, for example, often better apply what they have been learning in a variety of subjects, learn entrepreneurship and team work, may stay in school longer, and often go on to college having earned some of their own money to attend college (Gordon Nembhard, 2005; Pang, Gordon Nembhard, & Holowach, 2006). In addition, these student entrepreneurs often provide needed services to their community through their businesses, contribute to the development of their communities, develop leadership skills, and train other students (Gordon Nembhard & Pang, 2003). Therefore, expanding the type of economics education also expands the purpose of education beyond being just for individual achievement and preparation for future employment and higher education. A school's larger purposes can now include meaningful school-community partnerships, community and economic development, and social change through economic transformation. African American students learn how to create economic opportunities for themselves and their communities by engaging in democratic economic activity, at the same time that they continue their education.

Implications for education policy include the promotion of entrepreneurship, economics and cooperative economics education, and cooperative business experiences in curriculum development and teacher training; and the allocation of adequate funds for these activities.[2]

In the first section of this chapter, I offer four major reasons why adding more economics and alternative economic analyses and experiences to the school curriculum is a strategy that may increase African American students' school achievement, facilitate genuine school-community partnerships, and enhance community economic development. The second section of the chapter is an exploration of the economic content in high school social studies and economics classes, with a focus on the lack of education about alternative and cooperative economics. In the next sections, I summarize the kinds of experiences African American students have practicing cooperative economics in their schools and in school-related programs and introduce a discussion about teaching alternative economics in college courses, particularly in African American Studies' departments and for schools of education. I conclude this chapter with a discussion of some implications for school reform policy and societal economic benefits.

ECONOMIC CHALLENGES AND OPPORTUNITIES FOR TEACHING ALTERNATIVE ECONOMICS AND ENGAGING AFRICAN AMERICAN YOUTH IN COLLECTIVE ENTREPRENEURSHIP

Expanding the economic content and rigor of the school curriculum by including alternative economic theories and practices is important to African American students for several reasons: (1) additional and often different kinds of skills are needed to prepare students to function in the current (and future) deindustrialized economy; (2) the number and type of economic inequalities are increasing, which limits the effectiveness of academic achievement; (3) local economic and community building challenges also reduce the effectiveness of academic achievement but provide pedagogic opportunities; and (4) participatory democracy in the 21st century requires economic literacy.

First, the requirements of the "new economy" (a deindustrial global information-based network) suggest that what we teach and what students experience in school should correspond better to their economic needs. Specifically, in terms of African American students, it is important that the curriculum be aligned with the needs of marginalized communities for the purposes of both social mobility and social change.[3] While many interpret this to mean that curricula should focus on more technical skills,[4] or more vocational education, "cooperative education" (matching students with business internships), and junior achievement programs aligned with the corporate agenda,[5] my research suggests that schools include political economic analyses and alternative economic experiences for their students as part of a transformative curriculum. The curriculum can better prepare African American students to be more proactive economic actors in a very competitive and ever-changing economic milieu if it includes the study of the current economic system and the economic conditions students experience, and engages students in creating economic development opportunities in their communities.

What is this changing economic milieu? Over the past 30 years or more, the U.S. economy has been shifting from being based on manufacturing to one based on service; from production dependent on craft to a dependency on technology and information; and from being domestically centered to an expanding international, multinational, and global transnational focus. This has changed both the nature and the requirements of work in the United States, yet school curricula have not changed commensurately. The consequences have been particularly severe for African American youth (Darity & Mason, 1998; Gordon Nembhard, 2000; Skilton-Sylvester, 2003; Williams, 2000). African Americans continue to be left behind both academically and economically. Skilton-Sylvester (2003) noted,

> The question of whether the information economy and the "new work order" will leave behind the urban ghetto poor is really no longer a matter of speculation. It has happened, and the question for educators is whether we will find ways to push back the growing inequality. (p. 3)

Current conditions in industry suggest that students now need to be trained more flexibly, to "think on their feet," apply knowledge in a variety of contexts, use technology, communicate well, and be team players who can also be leaders (Haynes & Gordon Nembhard, 1999), and to "do the thinking between the tasks" (Skilton-Sylvester, 2003). Many public and inner-city school districts, however, are embracing directed learning and standards-based reforms that give "lip service" to some of these skills, but do not actually facilitate problem solving or democratic decision making. Too often, the high-level skills are not being taught.

While opportunities to participate in democratic economic decision making may be limited, the returns of having such a skill are relatively high for both employees and employers, when appreciated. For example, occupations that require more autonomy and decision-making opportunities pay higher salaries (U.S. Bureau of Labor Statistics, 2004; Wright & Dwyer, 2000/2001), and businesses prosper when such skills and relationships are nurtured among employees (Case, 2003; Fenton, 2002; Krimerman & Lindenfeld, 1992; Levine & Tyson, 1990). In addition, deindustrialization and the decline in steady well-paying jobs means that young people must be prepared to take their careers into their own hands, create their own opportunities, and rely less on finding that one good long-term employer, who no longer exists.

Second, our economic system is becoming more unequal as the wealthy become wealthier and the poor, poorer (Davies, Sanstrom, Shorrock, & Wolff, 2006). In the United States, the net worth of African American families, for example, is only about 15.7% of the average wealth of White families (Gordon Nembhard & Chiteji, 2006), and income inequality persists. Economics education in high school and college is important if we want to empower African American students to understand the system and how to make change in it.

Third, with increasing globalization and the movement of industry and finance across national borders, local economies struggle to maintain their residents' standards of living. Many of the localities in the United States where African Americans are concentrated, for example, are experiencing decreased economic activity and a loss of resources. Many central city areas have few jobs, little formal official economic activity, and even fewer financial services. Those that are revitalizing are doing it by gentrifying—moving out the long-term low-income residents and small businesses of color and replacing them with middle- and upper-income Whites and large corporations or their franchises. Our young people can be encouraged to fill the resource void in their neighborhoods by becoming involved in community building and community-based economic development during their school years and once they graduate (Gordon Nembhard & Pang, 2003). This will help them economically and can also help their families remain in their neighborhoods.

Schutz (2006) suggested that urban schools not only use community collaborations "to participate in struggles against the exclusionary dynamics of the market, governments, industry, and the like, that prevent even accomplished students from advancing," but also help their students to find "other paths for survival and success" (p. 727). I am finding that early involvement in entrepreneurship, business development, and democratic management in their communities gives African American students more options as they face a shrinking traditional economy and persistent racial, class, gender, and regional economic inequality. This is one way that schools can help African American students create other paths for survival and success. Cotton (1992) addressed the importance of collective economic action:

> Interdependent Black utilities or material well-being is . . . better realized as Black inter- and intra-community cooperation or "Black community help" [rather than "Black self help"]. For if each Black person's material well-being is dependent on that of all other Blacks then community cooperation rather than individualistic competition should prevail as an economic behavioral norm in the Black community. (p. 24)

Involving African American students in cooperative economic enterprises thus help develop such an economic behavioral norm.

Such involvement also engages African American students in community building and community development that benefits their families and neighborhoods as well as their schools and themselves. While some African American students come to school with a community orientation, interested in bettering or being involved in their community, others need opportunities to become more involved in their communities. The development of a school or community business can provide outlets that allow them to become involved. Helping students to organize democratic workplaces and own and manage their businesses cooperatively involves them in their communities and gives them experience with democratic participation and collective decision making. This is a strategy that addresses the need for a "collective sense of community and shared destiny" that Schutz (2006) concluded is crucial for inner-city schools to develop in their students. He argued that "only by establishing roots and making commitments to their communities can youth begin to envision long-term membership in the local as a concrete option for them" (p. 727). Similarly Gordon (2005) recommended that "the supplemental educator can utilize the impulse to resistance that is a stumbling block to academic achievement within schools to motivate students to take part in and learn from these programs of instruction" (p. 99). He found that

> through these programs, students will develop, in the service of resistance, critical thinking, literacy, and other skills and knowledge that can also be utilized to achieve academic success. Programs such as these [with political goals] will demonstrate to students that many of the skills taught in schools do have potential for use on the behalf of their communities and themselves. (pp. 99–100)

Moreover, educators are finding a correlation between vibrant school-community partnerships and student achievement. Schutz (2006) found, for example, that

> a growing collection of scholars, often from very different corners of the field, have increasingly come to understand that without robust community participation there is little hope that most comprehensive school reform efforts can be sustained over the long term. (p. 726)

Forging genuine partnerships, however, is difficult to achieve. Schutz (2006) contended that

> despite limited research, participation in a range of community development efforts seems to be a

critical method of rooting schools more deeply in their local environments. Scholars, educators, and community leaders must give more attention, however, to efforts that harness the myriad resources of youth. In general, community-based efforts seem much more promising than those dependent on the altruism of schools for fostering more "authentic" forms of participation. (p. 725)

Involving students directly in their communities—problem solving, developing relationships, and creating businesses—harnesses the resources of youth and contributes to building more authentic school-community partnerships.

Fourth, participatory democracy requires some level of economic sophistication, if only for the training of productive citizens. Campaign finance inequities and the power of wealth to control lobbyists and candidates undermine grassroots political participation. In addition, as more companies practice workplace democracy, and many jobs require flexible thinking and employee participation, there is growing agreement that economics is an important general prerequisite subject matter in high school and college (Rosenzweig, 2000; Skilton-Sylvester, 2003). With increasing calls for government, nonprofit, and even corporate transparency and accountability, economic literacy becomes increasingly important.

These points suggest that students, and particularly African American students, who gain some facility in economics and learn to be proactive economic agents (for themselves and their neighborhoods), work collectively, and think "out of the box," are better prepared in and out of school for a variety of contingencies. This is important because changes in our economic system have not eliminated economic discrimination and inequality, although the nature and manifestation of these disparities may be different. If education is to be one of the solutions, then educating African American students about the nature of the economic system and about alternative economic strategies, and providing them with opportunities to develop and experience innovative practices, are crucial pedagogic tools. Such innovations will contribute to the overall development of Black youth as well as to social change in African American communities.

HIGH SCHOOL ECONOMICS AND A MISSING COMPONENT: COOPERATIVE ECONOMICS

Economics education appears to be a growing field in public education. Over a decade ago, Grimes (1994) wrote,

> The results suggest that students in public schools may learn more economics than students in private schools (holding everything else constant, including student ability, aptitude, and prior exposure to economic concepts.) Thus, public schools appear to be doing a better job in the teaching of economics than private schools do. (p. 27)

Moreover, Walstad and Rebeck (2000) noted an increase in economic education for students of color:

> In 1994, a significantly higher percentage of high school graduates who were black, Hispanic, or Asian/Pacific Islanders took economics relative to those who were white. These percentages increased dramatically over the years, especially for Hispanic students. A likely reason for this increase is that the states that have mandated economics (such as New York or California) have higher proportions of these racial or ethnic groups relative to states that have not mandated economics courses. (p. 98)

In sum, students of color as well as public school and urban students, and those in the college track, are more likely to take an economics course in high school. The question is what kind of economics is being taught?

Forty-six percent of all high school graduates take a course titled "economics" before they receive their diplomas (National Center for Education Statistics, 2001). While there are no basic national or even statewide standards for what to include in an economics curriculum, the National Council on Economics Education (NCEE) delineates 20 "voluntary content standards" for economics courses from the 4th to 12th grades. The growing scholarship portraying economics as an analysis and decision-making tool is reflected in each of the principals (Siegfried & Meszaros, 1998). The standards reflect mainstream economic thought and highlight issues of scarcity, marginal analysis, competition, rationality, trade specialization, investment strategies, and the role of government.

Traditional economic content in school curricula, however, ignores information about labor market discrimination (racial and gender discrimination in the workplace) and its consequences. Therefore, Black students may not learn to recognize current signs of economic discrimination or to develop strategies to combat the discrimination. This handicaps Black students' knowledge about structural racism and how to address it. Black students may believe that if they do not succeed, especially once they achieve the academic credential, it is their own fault. This lack of knowledge may result in a failed opportunity to provide Black students with tools such as political economic analysis to help them uncover, understand, and navigate through structural inequalities and institutional discrimination and to introduce them to concepts such as cooperative economics, community ownership, and collective action that direct them to achievable solutions.

Additionally, typical economics curricula tend to ignore the subtle as well as obvious interdependencies, supports, and collaborations involved in economic activity and focus on individual action—the single entrepreneur or the single consumer. Economics education students rarely learn about different ownership structures and alternative community economic development strategies, whether in high school or college, even though they are widely used and have an impressive success rate. Economics education tends to ignore social and community entrepreneurship, and the alternative business structures that arise from such entrepreneurship, although attention is paid to a traditional perspective on entrepreneurship.

Left out of the equation, for example, are the cooperative enterprise, the social entrepreneur—those businesses and entrepreneurship activities that are created and produced through the joint efforts of partners and teams for the benefit of the group and the community.[6] These alternative structures are entrepreneurial, innovative, creative, and viable.[7] The bias against cooperatives is reflected in the most commonly used textbooks. Hill's (2000) survey of 19 leading Canadian and American introductory economics textbooks finds that nine, or about half of them, mention cooperatives. Eight include some analysis of cooperatives, but not one of the textbooks include more than a page describing or analyzing cooperatives. This is despite the fact that the "[r]esearch about co-ops has expanded considerably in the last few decades [and] ... the example of co-operative firms raise a variety of interesting positive and normative questions" (Hill, 2000, p. 287).

Cooperatives are often a response to market failure (affordable goods or services are not readily available or provided by private companies or public enterprises) and economic marginalization (certain populations or communities lack access to certain markets or are discriminated against in certain markets). The cooperative model helps address market failure and equitable development in urban and rural areas, asset building among low-resource people, greater worker participation, and control at the workplace (Gordon Nembhard, 2004b). African American students and their communities can use cooperative business ownership as an alternative economic development strategy in the face of economic discrimination, lack of employment, and urban decline. This is empowering and motivating. Few African Americans, however, are exposed to the model or know the history of African American cooperative ownership (Gordon Nembhard, 2004a). Learning about cooperative businesses and their potential benefits increases the relevance of the economics curriculum and can be exciting to African American students. This omission is therefore glaring and shortsighted.

Also missing in economics education is the economic agency of African Americans. Too often entrepreneurship is viewed as something African Americans do not or cannot practice; and economic innovation is only recognized as something that can be accomplished by Whites. Broadening the purview of economics education to include African American students, therefore, expands their vision of what they can accomplish as economic agents.

I study cooperative enterprise development and community-based economic development based on democratic economic participation.[8] I examine ways that entrepreneurship training and the experience of running cooperative businesses help African American students gain important knowledge and skills for participation in the economy as well as their academic achievement and their leadership in economic transformation. There is increasing evidence that Black students who engage in entrepreneurial projects, especially cooperative businesses, gain benefits such as more confidence, increased general and technical skills, more motivation to learn, and incentive (and sometimes funding) to go on to college (Brooks & Lynch, 1944; Dorson, 2003; Food From the 'Hood, 2005; Gordon Nembhard, 2005; Nagel, Shahyd, & Weisner, 2005; Skilton-Sylvester, 1994). Participation in and creation of cooperative business endeavors teach students business, math, research and communication skills, resourcefulness and problem solving, teamwork, and facilitation skills needed to participate in democratic enterprises. At the same time, participation in cooperative businesses also fosters concern for community and facilitates community-building strategies among youth (Gordon Nembhard & Pang, 2003; Pang et al., 2006).

Curriculum development sensitive to the needs of democratic businesses can combine teaching critical thinking, problem solving, and team building, along with the necessary technical and business skills (Skilton-Sylvester, 2003).[9] Schools can facilitate experiences that develop good learning habits and creative, flexible thinking by teaching cooperative economics and providing cooperative entrepreneurship experiences. Through school-based cooperative economic experiences, African American youth can also become active participants in democratic enterprises and civil society.

As the number of democratic businesses increase, primary and secondary schools continue to lag behind in teaching students how to participate and operate in such a climate (see Skilton-Sylvester, 2003), and teacher education programs still do not adequately prepare teachers to prepare their students for democratic economic participation. Cooperation is included as an eighth-grade-level benchmark, for example, in the NCEE guidelines pertaining to collective bargaining and labor unions, but not as a business organizing principle, an entrepreneurial response to a business problem, or a community economic development strategy. In addition, cooperative economics is taught in some farming communities in schools and during the summer, usually through or with the help of cooperative associations and farmer's unions. Wisconsin's law that teachers take a course in cooperatives is an important first step but appears not yet to translate into significant co-op education in that state's public schools. In Canada, particularly in Quebec Province, public

schools are increasingly teaching cooperation and cooperative economics from preschool to high school (I. St. Pierre, personal interview, October 23, 2003). These are still limited and isolated cases. The norm is to ignore cooperatives and democratically run businesses in economics education and in school curricula.

The next section provides several examples of programs that help youth of color incorporate cooperative business development into their school experience to enhance the curriculum, gain skills, raise money to attend college, and contribute to the revitalization of their communities.

PRACTICING COOPERATIVE ECONOMICS AMONG BLACK YOUTH

The lack of cooperative education in the high school curriculum may be a significant oversight particularly for youth of color. Inner-city youth of color, for example, are likely to experience a lack of capital, and a lack of access to capital (loans), to experience racial discrimination in the workplaces, and to live in an economically underserved or underdeveloped community. At the same time, they may have strong bonds with their peers and interest in helping their communities. Cooperative business development is a viable strategy to help Black students creatively bring capital to a demand, to produce a good or service on their own terms. Educating inner-city youth not only in economic decision making and firm structure but also about cooperatives can help them to use peer bonds in legitimate businesses. These businesses allow them to work together, share ideas, learn skills, earn money, and minimize financial risks. Cooperatives facilitate entrepreneurial activity as the engine of economic growth and originality. There are tremendous barriers to entry in starting businesses in inner cities such as raising the necessary start-up money, finding space and affording a good location, training employees and managers, and securing clients. A strong, creative economics education curriculum that includes the study of cooperatives and a practicum in business development can help students expand their economic potential by exposing them to a variety of economic business options, increasing their skill sets, and reducing barriers to entry. School-based cooperative businesses also face fewer barriers since space is usually provided by the school, and sometimes funding and clientele are secured by the school.

School-based cooperative businesses range from in-class role playing and model city experiments such as "Sweet Cakes Town" described by Skilton-Sylvester (1994), to schoolwide credit unions and school stores, to school-based and established farmers markets and buying clubs, and other businesses and projects that operate on school grounds during the school day, after school, and during summer programs. In addition, I include youth development programs initiated outside schools using students from a particular school or class or that provide services, workshops, or training to school-age children, sometimes in a school setting, during or after school, or in summer programs. The examples in this section focus on school-based programs serving predominantly African American students in low-income urban areas.

Incorporating entrepreneurial education in inner-city schools is not new. One study finds that inner-city youths have been quite receptive to this education. Kourilsky and Esfandiari (1997) conducted an empirical study on entrepreneurship education and lower socioeconomic Black high school sophomores. The study was based on the survey conducted by Gallup (1996) on Black high school students' attitudes and knowledge with respect to entrepreneurship education. The study confirmed that Black lower-income students know little about entrepreneurship, recognize their knowledge gap, and, by an 84% positive response, want more entrepreneurship education in schools. The results of their study confirm that "appropriate curricular innovation can significantly affect the acquisition of entrepreneurship concepts and skills by lower socioeconomic black students" (Kourilsky & Esfandiari, 1997, p. 212).

There are also historical examples. The young people's branch of the Consumers' Cooperative Trading Company, for example, a Black-owned cooperative enterprise in Gary, Indiana, operated its own ice-cream parlor and candy store in the 1930s. In addition, members of Consumers' Cooperative held weekly educational meetings for 18 months before opening any of their businesses. In 1933, they instituted a cooperative economics course in Roosevelt High School's evening school. By 1936, it had the largest enrollment of any academic class offered by the night school (Hope, 1940).

At the national level, in the early 1930s the Young People's Cooperative League connected Black cooperative movements from around the country and helped young people start cooperatives (Schuyler, 1932). Ella Jo Baker was the League's first Executive Director and was a champion of youth development and cooperative education for youth. During the 1930s and 1940s, some African American–run schools and several "Negro colleges and universities" were experimenting with cooperative business ventures and teaching cooperative economics (Brooks & Lynch, 1944; Pitts, 1950).

More recently, cooperative entrepreneurship is being fostered in some schools as part of the school gardening experience. In the Fall of 1992, students from Crenshaw High School in South Central Los Angeles revitalized the school garden to help rebuild their community after the 1992 uprising and, in particular, to donate the food to the homeless. After turning a profit from selling in a farmer's market the produce they grew in the school gardens, they focused on the economic potential of their project. They developed a business plan to produce salad dressing. Their business, "Food From the 'Hood" began selling salad dressing made from what they grew in the school garden. Food From the 'Hood is managed by the students and run similarly to a cooperative business. At least 50% of the profits are saved to award scholarships to students who wish to attend college. Over the past 10 years, 77 student managers have graduated and were awarded more than $180,000 in college scholarships (Dorson, 2003; Food from the 'Hood, 2005).

So Fresh and So Clean is a student-owned company out of The Learning Tree Cultural Preparatory School in Bronx, New York (Nagel et al., 2005). Students began with a school garden and later decided to make soap out of the excess herbs from the garden. They farm during the summer school session, receive entrepreneurship training in the fall, and produce the soap. They also began to make shampoo and insect repellent. While students from a variety of grades participate in the gardening, the eighth graders use the business development, production, and sale of the product for their senior project before graduating to high school. They are assisted by a business advisor who helps each eighth grade class plan and execute a business.

Similarly, the University of Pennsylvania has partnered with the West Philadelphia Partnership and Philadelphia Public Schools on a school-based community health promotion collaboration, the Urban Nutrition Initiative (UNI, www.urbannutrition.org). The interdisciplinary program uses college students who are learning horticulture and nutrition to teach high school students horticulture and nutrition. High school students teach middle school students, who teach elementary school students about health, nutrition, and business development. This is a learning-by-doing experience for all involved, at every level. It is a "dynamic educational process based on experiential learning and community problem-solving" integrated with public service (UNI, 2002, p. 3). The program combines a community health curriculum, school-based urban gardens, and entrepreneurial and business development.

The students, the majority of whom are African American, combine learning about nutrition, teaching nutrition to others, growing healthy food, and creating businesses to sell and market the food. The businesses they create are cooperative purchasing clubs, food co-ops, and farmer's markets. As part of the Center for Community Partnerships' summer jobs program (using school district funds) in 2003, for example, six students from University City High School Eco Tech learning community worked with UNI to develop plans for a food cooperative in the neighborhood (Rossi, 2003). The purpose was to supplement the Saturday farmer's market that the UNI had already established. Students and the community wanted to provide affordable healthy food for the neighborhood on a daily basis, as well as jobs for the students using an empowering ownership structure. Through such projects, the young participants develop entrepreneurship and many related skills (math, science, marketing, and communication). Students engage in school and community service through a "democratic collaborative process" (UNI, 2002, pp. 3, 8).

Another project combines youth entrepreneurship and sustainable transportation. Chain Reaction is a project of the EcoDesign Corps of Shaw EcoVillage in Washington, D.C., founded in 1997. Youth in the EcoDesign Corps participate by creating educational workshops and creating and implementing their own community development and urban planning projects (Shaw EcoVillage, 2005). High school students work with college-aged leaders and professional mentors.

The youth corps created Chain Reaction to educate youth about bicycle transportation; equip youth with bicycle repair skills; and to repair, recycle, and resell bicycles in the Shaw neighborhood (Shaw EcoVillage, 2005; Varney, 2003). The EcoDesign Corps used as a model a New York City youth bike repair program. Since 2001, when the full-service bicycle shop opened, about 120 youth have become active members and mechanics, cooperatively managing the business. They also run bicycle repair training workshops in schools around Washington, D.C. and sponsor in-school bike safety clubs and vocational training camps, in addition to community Bike Festivals (Varney, 2003). By 2005, six youth mechanics (each in the program for at least 2 years) had graduated to careers in the bicycle industry. More than 50 young people have been trained in basic bike repairs and safe riding techniques (Shaw EcoVillage, 2005). All revenues are reinvested to support the work of the youth mechanics and for inventory and educational workshops. Chain Reaction won the Washington Area Bicyclists Association award in 2003.

Toxic Soil Busters Co-op is a lead abatement business created and owned by youth in Worcester, Massachusetts (www.WorcesterRoots .org). As part of an extracurricular project sponsored by the nonprofit Worcester Roots, students learn about environmental hazards and environmental racism and learn to be proactive about environmental sustainability—helping to detoxify their communities and advocating for environmental policies. They produce skits that they present to other students and at community events to advertise their services, communicate their message, and educate their audiences about lead poisoning and other toxic wastes in their homes and backyards. The students first research the issue, receive training in soil cleansing, and hone their communication skills. The cooperative is a lead abatement business owned and run by the young people themselves. They provide consultation and detoxification services. While not explicitly school based, Toxic Soil Busters is part of a youth development program that combines study, policy advocacy, and economic action, with self education and public education.

These examples illustrate the range of activities available to schools and after-school programs to involve African American students more in their own economic development as well as their community's well-being. In these examples, the students use cooperative economic principles to set up and manage their businesses that enable them to benefit materially as well as academically and personally. Preliminary analyses of these programs show that students increase academic confidence; gain academic, communication, and business skills; sustain viable businesses; and educate other students and residents about their business and their goals and mission.

Alternative Economics in the College Curriculum

It is usually the case that only a limited number of African American high school students receive economics education and a very few have experience forming and managing their own businesses. Therefore, they typically enter college with some exposure to economics as a field of study, but very few receive exposure to alternative economic theories, cooperative economics or Black political economy, or experience with setting up their own business. Once in college, most economics departments do not teach alternative economics or cooperative economics courses, though some departments do teach political economy. I conducted a cursory investigation into economics and alternative economics courses taught to undergraduates in African American Studies departments (Gordon Nembhard, 2008), particularly looking for discussion of alternative economic paradigms and cooperative economics.

Some African American Studies programs teach courses about "race, class and gender," or "caste and class," mainly addressing labor conditions and class differences. One or two courses in a few of the departments cover economic development, mostly in Africa in relation to decolonization, and U.S. urban development. Three departments sponsor internships, placing students in community organizations. I found no courses that specifically mention cooperative economics or cooperative enterprise ownership. Many courses focus on Black intellectual history, political thought, and social change, particularly in relation to the Civil Rights Movement, without much economic analysis. I found two departments in addition to my own department that offer public policy courses.

Examining titles and course descriptions on the Web may not be the most effective method for determining course coverage and content, however. In my own example, I do teach cooperative enterprise ownership in the courses I have taught at the University of Maryland, College Park. However, in only one course—community economic development—does the course description specifically identify cooperatives. I am familiar with more than 90% of the Black economists and social scientists who study or teach cooperative economics in the United States,[10] and therefore without recourse to a formal survey, I have a fairly accurate picture of what is available to students. Few campuses offer such study at all and fewer still provide in a course devoted to the topic, particularly for undergraduates—and none in courses for teacher training.

Interestingly, however, during the 1940s some Black colleges were teaching about cooperatives. Brooks and Lynch (1944) surveyed 75 "Universities, Colleges, and Junior Colleges for Negroes in the Southern States" in the fall of 1943 about courses taught on "consumer problems" and the "cooperative movement." Of the 57 institutions that responded, 37 indicated that the study of cooperatives was currently included in their curriculum. There was some overlap with respondents who considered discussion of consumer problems to be similar to teaching about cooperatives. It became clear that at least 25 or so different institutions did teach about cooperatives, with eight indicating that they taught an entire course on "the cooperative movement." Twenty-three responded that there was a cooperative organization now functioning on their campus. In addition, about twice as many of the accredited colleges as nonaccredited devoted "the equivalent of half a course or more to each of these subjects"—consumer problems and cooperatives (p. 435). The faculty was very conscious that teaching about cooperatives helped students to be more economically literate and to address problems in their communities, while developing leadership and agency. The authors conclude that the cooperative "movement does offer possibilities for the up-building of the Negro" (p. 436).

In terms of African American students, many mainstream economics departments discourage African American students from studying economics. Anecdotally, we are finding that this is because most economics teaching and course content overemphasize mathematic analyses and use sterile theoretical models whose assumptions often ignore issues of concern to communities of color. The implications of these traditional models often lay the blame on the victims' behavior, and offer no viable solutions for suffering communities. In addition, many of the intermediate-level economics courses are designed to weed out a certain number of students—and Black students often end up among that group, without help or support to make it through.[11] Ijere (1972) also found that dissatisfaction with the teaching, difficulty grasping the topic, and lack of mathematics preparation explained much of why Black students were not majoring in economics in the early 1970s. Mason and wa Githinji (2008) suggested that African American Studies programs as well as economics departments house too few Black economists; thus, many Black students do not have the role models or mentors they need. As a result, many Black students lose interest in economics and/or are discouraged from taking economics courses and, therefore, miss important opportunities to engage in the national discourse on economic issues and think proactively about economic development. Even when Black economists are present in higher education, there are few opportunities to train Black students in economics, help them to earn economics degrees, or teach them about alternative economics and creative ways to address economic development. African American Studies students receive very little training in economics, political economy, or alternative economic development strategies, even if they may have been exposed to the topic.[12] Additionally, education departments do not train students in this area.

One of the first challenges, then, is to help African American students overcome their reluctance to study economics and/or think mathematically and to make certain that they enter college with the mathematics training that they need. Because they cannot avoid some mastery of statistics and mathematical concepts, it is also important that we provide African American students with extra help in mathematics and economics courses, so that these are accessible. A close second challenge is to offer innovative ways to teach economics, such as teaching political economy. A focus on political economy helps students to understand economics as a discipline that is more than just mathematics. In addition, we can provide pedagogical

experiences that help them to learn about economic innovations, as well as design and experience economic transformation that is similar to the types of innovative economics/business curricula some high schools have begun to offer.

I teach alternative economic development strategies and cooperative ownership as solutions to wealth inequality, underdevelopment, and inner-city urban redevelopment in the public policy undergraduate courses I teach in African American Studies. I challenge my students to think creatively about alternative strategies after exposing them to some examples. I ask them to review the existing strategies and the policy history and then devise a nontraditional approach. I also expect them to explain why they think their approach could work. Many of my students have difficulty with this assignment (probably because they are not asked often enough to think "out of the box"), but a few are quite thoughtful and creative. Even those who do not master the assignment well end up learning from it and thinking differently afterward.

When I teach African American public policy or community development courses, I begin with an alternative definition of economics. I also provide them with a working definition of political economy and Black political economy. Black political economy, for example, focuses on the study of the political and economic relationships relative to African American existence and applied economic strategies relative to Black communities. According to Conrad, Whitehead, Mason, and Stewart (2005), the definition of Black political economy begins with

> the premise that race matters—and then proceed with an analysis of the implications of race and racism for the economic status of African Americans and for the operation of the American economy. This approach challenges the adequacy of neoclassical mainstream economic analysis as a useful paradigm in explaining the persistence of racial inequality. . . . The intellectual origins of this approach lie in the last three decades of scholarship generated by black political economists in the African Diaspora. (p. 1)

I also provide my students with an overview of how Black communities have used alternative economic development strategies throughout history. I give a short history of African American cooperative business and agricultural ownership and provide examples of how Blacks have used cooperative ownership to provide the economic independence needed both to support their families and engage in civil rights activity in the face of racial economic, social, and political discrimination. Freedom Quilting Bee, in Alabama, for example, was started in 1966 by women in sharecropping families who needed to supplement the meager sharecropping earnings (when there were any). They sold their quilts through the cooperative that was able to buy land and build a small sewing "factory," and a day care center. By the early 1990s, the co-op was the largest employer in their town. In the 1960s and early 1970s, the income from the cooperative enabled many of the sharecropping families to transition to their own farms. Many of the families were evicted from the leased farms by White landlords who were angry that they had registered to vote or participated in civil rights activities. The cooperative provided a safe haven and the independence needed for these families and some of their neighbors to start new—no longer dependent on the "plantation bloc." The co-op sold or leased land to evicted sharecroppers so they could buy their own farms. At its height, Freedom Quilting Bee sold quilts around the country through the Sears catalogue and in department stores such as Bloomingdale's (Federation of Southern Cooperatives, 1992; Freedom Quilting Bee, n.d.).

An additional strategy would be to provide students with opportunities to apply their knowledge, to work with communities on economic alternatives and community-based economic development, and to start their own cooperatives. There are examples of cooperative businesses on college campuses owned and run by the students, though few among students of color. While cooperative housing is more prevalent on college campuses, some students also own restaurants, grocery/health food stores, book stores, ticket sales, and other enterprises such as a media collective.

Conclusion and Policy Implications: Transforming Schools for African American Students Through Transformative Economics

Thinking like an economist involves problem solving to take the raw materials of human need and productivity, supply and demand of goods and services, natural resource preservation, and the creation of stores of value and means of exchange, to design sustainable systems that use diverse inputs and balance competing needs. Students proficient in this special form of problem solving may become adept at entrepreneurship. Entrepreneurs, acting on the principles that economics teachers espouse, are prized for their ability to combine demand, capital, and innovative thinking to add value to their own and the lives of others. Entrepreneurs are often thought of as the driving force of the U.S. economy.

African American students are not often provided the opportunity to be economic problem solvers. Too often, they are not taught entrepreneurship or encouraged to be community change makers, but rather are taught how to be good workers and follow the rules, even when it is not clear that doing so will increase their economic or personal well-being. Persistent and in some cases increasing economic inequality requires that our education of Black youth be more innovative and proactive. Teaching African American students the "inspiring" economics of alternative development strategies and the cooperative model increases their academic skills, helps them to think more innovatively, and empowers them to be change makers in their communities. Schutz (2006) predicted that

> only through collective struggle on the local level (and more broadly) will the "dumping grounds" of global society [central cities] be able to develop even the minimal resources necessary to provide for human development. This is a radical challenge for schools, because nearly all levels of education focus on the empowerment of relatively isolated individuals. (p. 727)

Educating African American youth about the values not just of entrepreneurship, but of collective and social entrepreneurship, and about how cooperatives can facilitate entrepreneurial activity within areas that current market forces neglect or exploit, gives them new perspectives and increases their opportunities to help themselves, their families, and their communities. With innovative economics training, African American students can increase their options to creatively solve complex problems. Economic experiences with democratic economic participation provide high school students with skills for employment, future entrepreneurship, and college—and often with earnings that help pay the costs of higher education. Similarly, college students benefit from an economics education that encourages them to think "out of the box" as they gain economic knowledge and entrepreneurial skills.

That few economics curricula identify or expose students to the cooperative model, and the ways co-ops address current issues in economic development is perhaps understandable but shortsighted. The lack of such content in most economics curricula suggests missed opportunities both for how we train our youth and for prospects in community economic development (see Gordon Nembhard, 2005). Studying cooperative economics and democratic business structures provides an expanded analysis of the many ways that capital, management, and labor can interact, that profits or surplus can be generated and distributed, and that businesses and communities can work together. Educating African American students to think critically and innovatively, and about alternative economic development strategies, can empower them to be proactive about democratizing our economic system and transforming their neighborhoods. Skilton-Sylvester's work (1994, 2003) also addresses these issues. He articulated a similar notion to theories that I have articulated:

> The challenge facing teachers has at least two parts. First is the challenge of social change: preparing students to be active agents in changing the social structures of society. Second is the challenge of social mobility: preparing students to be successful in the *existing* social structures in the meantime. (Skilton-Sylvester, 2003, p. 5)

Teaching cooperative economics and facilitating students' experiences developing cooperatively owned and community-based democratic businesses has the potential to achieve both goals. So far, we have anecdotal evidence in support of this theory. More empirical research is needed. There is limited research about the benefits of an education in cooperative economics for African American youth. More research is needed to gain an understanding of if and how student involvement in cooperative business ownership increases educational achievement, transition to adulthood, job acquisition, and college enrollment, as well as innovations in community economic development, for example. Education policy can promote and support more programs in schools that teach students

about economic alternatives and aid students in forming and managing their own cooperative businesses. This would also require that more teachers be trained in cooperative economics, business development, and experiential learning. In addition, monies would need to be allocated to teacher training and to cover minor start-up costs to initiate the school-based businesses.

Giving African American youth opportunities to build their communities, be involved in leadership development, and study and practice economic democracy in action involves them early in economic activity and may motivate them to be academic achievers. While it is important for all students, it is particularly important for African American students to have more technical skills and advanced credentials to compete in the "new" economy. These skills and credentials, however, will not be enough. Success in the new economy rewards a wide variety of skills and often requires participants to create their own opportunities. Moreover, economic discrimination still exists, so that being proactive about one's place in the economy and attaining some level of economic independence are important goals. The more economic knowledge that African American students possess, the more this knowledge will benefit them. This carries over into higher education. Important goals then for higher education are to teach more African American students economics and alternative economic theories and practices, and to teach teachers how to teach alternative economics and learn how to provide economic experiences for their students. Not only does this make sense from the perspective of providing economic education to enhance their careers and generate entrepreneurship, but it is also good pedagogy. Teaching African American students to be proactive "movers and shakers" in the economy can increase their engagement in academics, keep them in school, and help them to help their own communities. Such economic engagement develops critical thinking, uses interdisciplinary methodologies, combines experiential and theoretical learning, promotes intellectual as well as social engagement, and emphasizes guided and self-directed research and retrieval, organization of information, and persuasive presentation of arguments. While more research demonstrating and evaluating these achievements is needed, it is clear that there are myriad benefits from teaching African American students about alternative economics and providing them with collective entrepreneurial experiences.

NOTES

1. Gordon (2005) similarly found that involving Black students in political goals, particularly through supplementary educational programs, motivates them for academic success and develops critical thinking, literacy, and other academic skills and knowledge.

2. While funding is needed, especially to start some of these projects, successful programs are often self-financing or generate income, such as Food From the 'Hood described in Section 3 where students earn money from the sale of their product and that revenue is used both to support the continuing business and for college scholarships.

3. Skilton-Sylvester (2003) provided a thoughtful discussion of this dichotomy—both in terms of how to teach inner-city students better and more meaningfully and in terms of the tensions between teaching for social mobility versus for social change—that is, using practices associated with "progressive education" or aligning the curriculum to the needs of business (and what happens when they overlap).

4. In Gordon Nembhard (2005), I noted that the necessary new skills include both highly technical skills, particularly in computer sciences and mathematics, along with communication skills, critical thinking, flexibility, and ability to work in teams. Skilton-Sylvester (2003, p. 9, note 7) referred to the abilities delineated by R. J. Murnane and F. Levy (*Teaching the New Basic Skills: Principles for Educating Children to Thrive in a Changing Economy*, 1996), which include a 9th-grade level in reading and mathematics; effective oral and written communication skills; and the ability to solve semistructured problems where hypotheses must be formed and tested, to work in groups with people of various backgrounds, and to use a personal computer at least for word processing.

5. In the 1930s and 1940s, members of the Ladies' Auxiliary of the Brotherhood of Pullman Car Porters (the first Black labor union) opposed Junior Achievement business programs for teaching Black youth "how to circumvent existing labor laws and how to oppose organized labor" (Chateauvert, 1998, p. 151). These African American women leaders promoted and formed consumer cooperatives to recirculate union/labor dollars and help union families better control access to and the quality and price of the goods and services they needed. They also developed a youth program (the Junior Economic Council) to work with young people to promote consumer education and cooperatives.

6. Cooperative businesses are enterprises owned by their members (consumers, producers, or employees) who organize the business around the production of a needed good or service, jointly own the business, and govern it democratically. Cooperative businesses operate according to a set of principles that include

open membership, "one person one vote," returns based on use, continuous education, and concern for community (see the International Cooperative Alliance, 2007; the National Cooperative Business Association, 2006). "Co-operatives are based on the values of self-help, self-responsibility, democracy, equality, equity and solidarity" (International Cooperative Alliance, 2007). Cooperatives are community-based businesses that anchor and increase economic activity in a local community.

7. Approximately 120 million people in the United States are members of more than 47,000 cooperatives that operate in almost every kind of industry and range in size from a Fortune 500 company to a single store front (www.ncba.coop).

8. I identify this field as Democratic Community Economics, which focuses on the study of people-centered local economic development that is community based and controlled, collaborative, democratically or at least broadly owned and governed, through a variety of structures. These structures include worker, producer, and consumer cooperatives and credit unions; community land trusts; and democratic ESOPs (Employee Stock Ownership Programs) and other forms of worker ownership and self-management. Other structures include collective not-for-profit organizations involved in social entrepreneurship; community-controlled community development corporations, and community-controlled development planning and community development financial institutions.

9. More and more companies worldwide use democratic organizational structures and management-labor cooperation in operating their businesses to address increasing competition. Today's successful industries, for example, are changing from

> a management system of 'command and control' to a system that can be described as 'high-involvement management'—a term used to describe organizations that aspire to give employees more meaningful involvement in the organization and a stake in its performance. (Skilton-Sylvester, 2003, p. 6, partially quotes E. E. Lawler III in *High Involvement Management*, 1986)

There is increasing documentation that democratic firms, which practice flexibility, teamwork, decentralized control, and participatory governance, are more effective and competitive (Levine & Tyson, 1990; see also Case, 2003; Fenton, 2002; Krimerman & Lindenfeld, 1992).

10. I am an officer on the board of directors of the National Economic Association whose members are African American economists and economists who study the African diaspora; and I have convened

the only public gathering of African American economists who study cooperative economics at a session sponsored by the NEA and one sponsored by the Cleveland Urban League in Ohio.

11. While this is anecdotal data, I cannot ignore the many students (on my campus and at other universities) who tell me that they have dropped economics or will not even pursue economic training for those reasons.

12. See the articles in the special issue of the *Journal of Black Studies, 38*(5), May 2008. on "Black Political Economy in the 21st Century: Exploring the Interface of Economics and Black Studies."

REFERENCES

Brooks, L. M., & Lynch, R. G. (1944). Consumer problems and the cooperative movement in the curricula of southern Negro colleges. *Social Forces, 22*(4), 429–436.

Case, J. (2003, March). The power of listening: How does an old-line manufacturer in a stagnant industry manage to grow 25% a year for 10 years? By taking its employees seriously. *Inc Magazine, 25*(3), 77–84, 110.

Chateauvert, M. (1998). *Marching together: Women of the brotherhood of sleeping car porters.* Urbana: University of Illinois Press.

Conrad, C., Whitehead, J., Mason, P., & Stewart, J. (2005). *African Americans in the United States economy.* New York: Rowman & Littlefield.

Cotton, J. (1992). Towards a theory and strategy for Black economic development. In J. Jennings (Ed.), *Race politics and economic development* (pp. 11–32). New York: Verso Press.

Danielson, C. (2003). *Enhancing student achievement: A framework for school improvement.* Alexandria, VA: Association for Supervisions and Curriculum Development.

Darity, W. A., Jr., & Mason, P. L. (1998). Evidence on discrimination in employment: Codes of color, codes of gender. *Journal of Economic Perspectives, 12*(2), 63–90.

Davies, J. B., Sanstrom, S., Shorrock, A., & Wolff, E. N. (2006). *The world distribution of household wealth.* United Nations University—World Institute for Development Economics Research, Helsinki, Finland, December 5. Retrieved January 26, 2007, from www.wider.unu.edu

Dorson, C. (2003). *Essay: Grounds for learning: Hope for America's derelict schoolyards.* Retrieved March 2, 2008, from www.learningbydesign.biz/2003/grounds.html

Federation of Southern Cooperatives/Land Assistance Fund. (1992). *25th Anniversary, Annual Report 1967–1992.* Atlanta, GA: Author.

Fenton, T. L. (2002). *The democratic company: Four organizations transforming our workplace and our world.* Arlington, VA: World Dynamics.

Food From the 'Hood. (2005). *About us 2004–2005.* Retrieved May 28, 2005, from www.foodfromthehood.com

Freedom Quilting Bee. (n.d.). *History.* Retrieved May 28, 2005, from www.ruraldevelopment.org/FQB.html

Gallup Organization and National Center for Research in Economic Education. (1996). *Entrepreneurship and small business in the United States: A survey report on minority and gender attitudes and opinions among high school youth.* Kansas City, MO: Center for Entrepreneurial Leadership.

Gardner, R., & Miranda, A. H. (2001). Improving outcomes for Urban African American students. *Journal of Negro Education, 70*(4), 255–263.

Glasser, C. (1989). *The quality school.* Chatsworth, CA: William Glasser Institute.

Gordon, E. T. (2005). Academic politicalization: Supplementary education from Black resistance. In E. W. Gordon, B. L. Bridglall, & A. S. Meroe (Eds.), *Supplementary education* (pp. 88–103). Lanham, MD: Rowman & Littlefield.

Gordon, E. W., Bridglall, B. L., & Meroe, A. S. (2005). *Supplementary education: The hidden curriculum of high academic achievement.* Lanham, MD: Rowman & Littlefield.

Gordon Nembhard, J. (2000). Post-industrial economic experiences of African American men, 1973–1993. In C. C. Yeakey (Ed.), *Advances in research, policy and praxis in diverse communities series: Vol. 1. Edmund W. Gordon: Producer of knowledge, pursuer of understanding* (pp. 241–262). London: Elsevier.

Gordon Nembhard, J. (2004a). Cooperative ownership in the struggle for African American economic empowerment. *Humanity & Society, 28*(3), 298–321.

Gordon Nembhard, J. (2004b). Non-traditional analyses of cooperative economic impacts: Preliminary indicators and a case study. *Review of International Co-Operation, 97*(1), 6–21.

Gordon Nembhard, J. (2005). On the road to democratic economic participation: Educating African American youth in the post-industrial global economy. In J. King (Ed.), *Black education: A transformative research and action agenda for the new century* (pp. 225–239) (Commission on Research in Black Education, American Educational Research Association). Fairfax, VA: Tech Books.

Gordon Nembhard, J. (2008). Alternative economics—a missing component in the African American studies curriculum: Teaching public policy and democratic community economics to Black undergraduate students. In Black political economy in the 21st century: Exploring the interface of economics and Black studies [Special issue]. *Journal of Black Studies, 38*(5), 758–782.

Gordon Nembhard, J., & Chiteji, N. (2006). *Wealth accumulation and communities of color in the United States: Current issues.* Ann Arbor: University of Michigan Press.

Gordon Nembhard, J., & Pang, V. A. (2003). Ethnic youth programs: Teaching about caring economic communities and self-empowered leadership. In G. Ladson-Billings (Ed.), *Critical race theory perspectives on social studies: The profession, policies, and curriculum* (pp. 171–197) (A volume in Research in Social Education). Greenwich, CT: Information Age.

Grimes, P. W. (1994). Public versus private secondary school and the production of economics education. *Journal of Economic Education, 25*(Winter), 17–30.

Haynes, C., Jr., & Gordon Nembhard, J. (1999). Cooperative economics: A community revitalization strategy. *Review of Black Political Economy, 27*, 47–71.

Hill, R. (2000). The case of the missing organizations: Cooperatives and the textbooks. *Journal of Economic Education, 31*, 281–295.

Hope, J., II. (1940). Rochdale cooperation among Negroes. *Phylon, 1*(1), 39–52.

Ijere, M. O. (1972). Whither economics in a Black studies program? *Journal of Black Studies, 3*(2), 149–165.

International Cooperative Alliance. (2007). *What is a co-operative? and co-operative identity, principles, and values.* Retrieved February 2, 2007, from www.ica.coop/coop/principles.html

Kourilsky, M. L., & Esfandiari, M. (1997). Entrepreneurship education and lower socioeconomic Black youth: An empirical investigation. *Urban Review, 29*(3), 205–215.

Krimerman, L., & Lindenfeld, F. (1992). *When workers decide: Workplace democracy takes root in North America.* Philadelphia: New Society.

Levine, D., & Tyson, L. D. (1990). Participation, productivity, and the firm's environment. In A. Blinder (Ed.), *Paying for productivity: A look at the evidence* (pp. 183–237). Washington, DC: Brookings Institute.

Mason, P. L., & wa Githinji, M. (2008). Excavating for economics in Africana Studies. In Black political economy in the 21st century: Exploring the interface of economics and Black studies [Special issue]. *Journal of Black Studies, 38*(5), 731–757.

Nagel, K, Shahyd, K., & Weisner, M. (2005). *Youth cooperative toolkit.* Cambridge, MA: MIT, Department of Urban Studies and Planning.

National Center for Education Statistics. (2001). *The 1998 high school transcript study tabulations: Comparative data on credits earned and demographics for1998, 1994, 1990, 1987, and 1982 high school graduates, revised* (NCES 2001–498). Washington, DC: Government Printing Office.

National Cooperative Business Association. (2006). *Co-op statistics.* Retrieved February 2, 2007, from www.ncba.coop

Pang, V. O., Gordon Nembhard, J., & Holowach, K. (2006). What is multicultural education? Principles and new directions. In V. Ooka (Ed.), *Multicultural education: Principles and practices* (pp. 23–43). Westport, CT: Praeger.

Pitts, N. A. (1950). *Studies in sociology: Vol. 33. The cooperative movement in Negro communities of North Carolina: A dissertation.* Washington, DC: Catholic University of America Press.

Rosenzweig, M. R. (2000). Schooling, learning, and economic growth. In R. Marshall (Ed.), *Back to shared prosperity: The growing inequality of wealth and income in America* (pp. 229–237). Armonk, NY: M. E. Sharpe.

Rossi, E. (2003, October 20). Local students join to create food co-operatives. *The Daily Pennsylvanian.* Retrieved March 2, 2008, from http://media.www.dailypennsylvanian.com/media/storage/paper882/news/2003/10/20/News/Local.Students.Join.To.Create.Food.CoOperative-2153609.shtml

Schutz, A. (2006). Home is a prison in the global economy: The tragic failure of school-based community engagement strategies. *Review of Educational Research, 76*(4), 691–743.

Schuyler, G. S. (1932). The Young Negro Co-operative League. *The Crisis, 41*(1), 456–472.

Shaw EcoVillage. (2005). *Our mission, chain reaction, success stories.* Retrieved May 28, 2005, from www.shawecovillage.com

Siegfried, J. J., & Meszaros, B. T. (1998). Voluntary economics content standards for America's schools: Rationale and development. *Journal of Economic Education, 29*(Spring), 139–149.

Skilton-Sylvester, P. (1994). Elementary school curricula and urban transformation. *Harvard Educational Review, 64*(3), 309–331.

Skilton-Sylvester, P. (2003). Less like a robot: A comparison of change in an inner-city school and a Fortune 500 company. *American Educational Research Journal, 40*(1), 3–41.

Urban Nutrition Initiative. (2002). *Annual Report May 2001–May 2002.* Philadelphia: University of Pennsylvania, Center for Community

Partnerships. Retrieved March 2, 2008, from www.urbannutrition.org/UNI/documents/reports/report02-03.pdf

U.S. Bureau of Labor Statistics. (2004). BLS releases 2002–12 employment projections. *News* [Press Release USDL 04–148]. Washington, DC: U.S. Department of Labor. Retrieved February 11, 2004, from www.bls.gov/emp/home.htm

Varney, D. (2003). Shaw EcoVillage: Starting a positive chain reaction [Electronic version]. *Children, Youth and Environments, 13*(1). Retrieved May 28, 2005, from www.colorado.edu/journals/cye

Walstad, W. B., & Rebeck, K. (2000). The status of economics in the curriculum. *Journal of Economic Education, 31*(Winter), 95–101.

Williams, R. (2000). *If you're Black, get back, if you're brown, stick around, if you're White, hang tight: Race, gender and work in the global economy.* Working Paper for the Preamble Center, Washington, DC.

Wright, E. O., & Dwyer, R. (2000/2001). The American jobs machine. Is the new economy creating good jobs. *Boston Review, 25*(6), 21–26.

FURTHER READINGS

Adams, F. T., & Hansen, G. B. (1992). *Putting democracy to work: A practical guide for starting and managing worker-owned businesses.* San Francisco: Berrett-Koehler.

Barone, C. A. (1991). Contending perspectives: Curricular reform in economics. *Journal of Economic Education, 22*(Winter), 15–26.

Baumol, W. J., Panzar, J. C., & Willig, R. D. (1982). *Contestable markets and the theory of industry structure.* New York: Harcourt Brace Jovanovich.

Birchall, J. (2003). *Rediscovering the cooperative advantage: Poverty reduction through self-help.* Geneva, Switzerland: Cooperative Branch, International Labour Office.

Browne, R. S. (1974). Wealth distribution and its impact on minorities. *Review of Black Political Economy, 4*(4), 27–37.

Churchill, N. C. (1995). Analysis, overview, and application to pedagogy. In I. Bull, H. Thomas, & G. Willard (Eds.), *Entrepreneurship: Perspectives on theory building.* Tarrytown, NY: Pergamon Press.

Cobbs, J. L. (1976). A job that badly needs doing: A business editor looks at economics education. *Journal of Economic Education, 8*(Winter), 5–8.

Conrad, C. A. (1998). National standards or economic imperialism. *Journal of Economic Education, 29*(2), 167–169.

Fitzgerald, J., & Green Leigh, N. (2002). *Economic revitalization: Cases and strategies for city and suburb.* Thousand Oaks, CA: Sage.

Frey, B. (2001). *Inspiring economics, human motivation in political economy.* Cheltenham, UK: Edward Elgar.

Gibb, A. (1998). Growing an entrepreneurial economy [Electronic version]. *Economic Reform Today, 4.* Retrieved May 28, 2005, from www.cipe.org

Gijselaers, W., Tempelaar, D., Keizer, P., Blammaert, J., Bernanrd, E., & Kasper, H. (1995). *Educational innovation in economics and business administration.* Dordrecht, The Netherlands: Springer.

Giloth, R. (1998). Jobs and economic development. In R. Giloth (Ed.), *Jobs and economic development.* Thousand Oaks, CA: Sage.

Gordon Nembhard, J. (2002a). Cooperatives and wealth accumulation: Preliminary analysis. *American Economic Review, 92*(2), 325–329.

Gordon Nembhard, J. (2002b). Education for a people-centered democratic economy. *GEO Newsletter, 53–54*(July–October), 8–9.

Gordon Nembhard, J. (2006). Entering the new city as men and women, not mules. In L. Randolph & G. Tate (Eds.), *The black urban community* (pp. 75–100). New York: Palgrave Macmillan.

Gordon Nembhard, J., & Blasingame, A. (2002, December). *Economic dimensions of civic engagement and political efficacy.* Working Paper, Democracy Collaborative-Knight Foundation Civic Engagement Project, University of Maryland, College Park.

Hansen, W. L. (1998). Principles-based standards: On the voluntary national content standards in economics. *Journal of Economic Education, 29*(2), 150–156.

International Labour Conference. (2002). *Recommendation 193: Recommendation concerning the promotion of cooperatives.* Retrieved August 23, 2006, from www.ilo.org/coop

James, E. J. (1899). *Educational value—economics as a school study. Economic studies 4.* Ithaca, NY: Andrus & Church Press.

Nadeau, E. G., & Thompson, D. J. (1996). *Cooperation works!* Rochester, MN: Lone Oak Press.

National Consumers Union. (2003). *Captive kids: A report on commercial pressures on kids at school.* Retrieved May 28, 2005, from www.consumers union.org/other/captivekids/index.htm

National Council for the Social Studies. (1994). *Expectations of excellence: Curriculum standards for social studies.* Silver Spring, MD: National Council for the Social Studies.

Nelson, J. L., Palonsky, S. B., & Carlson, K. (2000). *Critical issues in education.* Boston: McGraw-Hill.

Rhodes, V. J. (1987, July). *Cooperatives and contestable/sustainable markets. Cooperative theory: New approaches* (Service Report No. 18). Washington, DC: U.S. Department of Agriculture. Retrieved May 28, 2005, from www.rurdev.usda .gov/rbs/pub/sr18/contents.htm

Schur, L. (1985). What economics is worth teaching? In M. Schug (Ed.), *Economics in the school curriculum, K-12.* Washington, DC: Joint Council on Economics Education.

Sexton, R. J., & Sexton, T. A. (1987). Cooperatives as entrants. *RAND Journal of Economics, 18*(Winter), 581–595.

Shaffer, J. D. (1987, July). *Thinking about farmers' cooperatives, contracts, and economic coordination. Cooperative theory: New approaches* (Service Report No. 18). Washington, DC: U.S. Department of Agriculture. Retrieved May 28, 2005, from www.rurdev.usda.gov/rbs/pub/sr18/contents.htm

Stigler, G. (1983). The case, if any, for economic literacy. *Journal of Economic Education, 14*(Summer), 60–66.

Wagner, F. W., Joder, T., & Mumphrey, A., Jr. (1995). *Urban revitalization: Policies and programs.* Thousand Oaks, CA: Sage.

Black Education Post-Katrina:
And All Us We Are Not Saved[1]

Joyce Elaine King

Remember the Kongo saying, "It hurts to lose certain traditions." The more a society moves away from its traditions, the more its people and system become physically and spiritually weak and disoriented. To lose one's cultural traditional values is not only to terrorize oneself but to ridicule oneself in the eyes of the world.

—K. Kia Bunseki Fu-Kiau, Kindezi: The Kongo Art of Babysitting

How can we be successful if we have no idea or, worse, the wrong idea of who we were and, therefore are? . . . Our minds can be trained for individual career success, but our group morale, the very soul of us has been devastated by the assumption that what has not been told about ourselves does not exist to be told.

—Randall Robinson, The Debt

The Maafa gave rise to a single world-wide strategy among our oppressors: prevent African families and communities from educating their children.

—The Millions More Movement Education Task Force Report, 2006[2]

Katrina accomplished in a day . . . what Louisiana school reformers couldn't do after years of trying.

—American Enterprise Institute[3]

All that is public, including schools, is under attack.

—Erica Meiners (2007)

The lower classes are worth more to private corporations when they are in prison than when they are free.

—Dedon Kemanthi[4]

This Epilogue asks, What is the state of Black education "post-Katrina"? What is at stake? What is to be done? The dire condition of public education in New Orleans in the aftermath of the 2005 Gulf coast storm serves not as metaphor but as context for framing the complexities of Black education as a *civilizational* crisis.[5] This crisis includes mass Black criminalization and incarceration and the school-to-prison track (e.g., prison industrial complex) as well as the dismantling of public education. What has appeared simply to be the government's abandonment of the most impoverished Black people in New Orleans is a pattern of systematic neglect in jobless urban ghettos across the nation that is better understood as the racialized privatization of public spheres—notably schools and prisons. Moreover, as Meiners (2007) observed, "All that is public is under attack."

Wynter (2006) argued that fundamentally this is a crisis of knowledge: Western civilization's best minds and academic disciplines are deeply implicated in the belief structure and ways of (not) knowing that systematically jeopardize Black lives. However, this destruction of Black life ("as life unworthy of life") also diminishes White America's humanity (Rimstead, 2001). And while democracy, human rights, justice, and our planetary environment are at stake, civilization also hangs in the balance (King, 2005). Following are indications of this civilizational knowledge crisis.

BEYOND RESCUE

First, Black people in America have been "beyond rescue" in the nation's schools, cities, and prisons long before Hurricane Katrina—a marginalization that has been justified in part by the neglect and distortion of African descent people's history. The current state of Black education, for example, differs drastically from the historical record of Black accomplishments and educational excellence—from the specialized knowledge of the African ancestors who built the pyramids in ancient Kemet and the Songhay Empire's universities at Sankoré, Gao, and D'jenné in West Africa, to clandestine "slave schools" and African Free Schools in early America, Citizenship schools and Freedom schools during the Civil Rights Movement as well as independent Black institutions (Anderson, 1988; Butchart, 1980; Dannett, 1964; Hilliard, 1997).

Second, "rescue" via prevailing education policy, practice, theory, and research is doubtful if the *systemic* causes of this racially rooted civilizational crisis are not addressed. Instead, as the crisis is normalized and those who suffer are blamed, the true nature of the crisis is denied, distorted, and hidden in mystification and euphemism. For example, Black people's poverty is the focus of analysis instead of systemic White supremacy/oppression; success and inclusion actually require some form of complicity and self/group abnegation; dismantling public education is called "restructuring" locally and "structural adjustment" globally and "a new national model of a market-based system of education" obfuscates the transfer of public resources into the hands of private entities.

Third, the condition of education in New Orleans and the mass incarceration of African Americans provide interrelated vantage points from which to grasp the relationship between Black education "post-Katrina" and the public good, that is, what is at stake for "all us we." Tate's (2007) analysis of the need for societal investments in education and employment opportunities—opportunity expansion—for urban youth identifies concrete material benefits that would accrue to the entire society, but which remain unrecognized and "hypothetical" (Belfield & Levin, 2007; Day & Newberger, 2002). Thus, the larger policy context and arena for action must include the knowledge crisis and the need for transformative possibilities that address the systemic connection between education, racialized domination, and real democracy and freedom.

INCLUSION/COMPLICITY AND NEGATION/NIHILATION AT WHAT COST?

Part of what often remains just beyond recognition, understanding, analysis, and action is Black nihilation (or nonbeing) as a requirement of White America's supposed well-being.[6] In his description of "White America's sense of self," for example, Wacquant (2002) captured part of this dialectical interconnection in terms of how social class interacts with race. That is, White America senses itself as "profoundly unlike and distinct from the Black and unworthy poor." This complex racialized "alter-ego" relationship between "White" being and "Black" negation appears now to be associated with the unworthiness/unfitness of "the Black poor" (in mostly Black "failing schools," failing "ghetto" cities such as New Orleans, and their "extensions in the prisons"). But it also extends to the entire continent of Africa and is a condition of (the idea/ideal of) "Whiteness" as a privileged mode of being (more human).[7]

One cost of this privileged ("White") sense of self is the attenuation of White America's humanity (King, 2006). The benefits of privileged (and "honorary") "Whiteness" and the associated worthiness of (White) middle-class acceptability lull the rest of us into a false sense of security, success, and well-being:

> In every era, Blacks have been viewed as apart, inferior and unworthy, as fringe players in the American narrative. But in the last 35 years the Black communities have been stripped of jobs, seen their poor isolated, resegregated, and redefined as unworthy and inherently dangerous. Government, the state itself has been refashioned into a punitive and carceral machine whose main function is to contain and control this unworthy, dishonored and dangerous poor and black population. (Dixon, 2007, online text)[8]

"All us we are not saved," however, if people of African ancestry anywhere remain culturally and spiritually dislocated, economically dispossessed, and politically marginalized by the mythology of race and its economic, cultural, and political inequities/iniquities.

The standpoint, that Black Americans "exist as an African people, an ethnic family," is not usually considered in prevailing education policy, research, theory, and practice (King, 2005, p. 20).[9] Ironically, Black academics and opinion leaders who publicly castigate the (Black) "lower socioeconomic people" (Bill Cosby's phrase) and exhort them to do better and be better tacitly acknowledge Black people's shared identity and community-family connections (Cosby & Poussaint, 2007).[10]

Yet in the arenas of public policy and education, transformative possibilities that address the racialized roots of our predicament and that build on our collective legacy of democratizing and humanizing public spheres long dominated

by White supremacy racism are curtailed. The need for group-based solutions for African Americans is typically unacknowledged, even by the most progressive observers. Certainly, this is the case with respect to the "shocking" and "awful" state of Black education in "post-Katrina" New Orleans, where nihilating academic knowledge has also played a pernicious role.

SHOCKING AND AWFUL: ERASING PUBLIC EDUCATION IN NEW ORLEANS

In *The Shock Doctrine*, award-winning investigative journalist Naomi Klein (2007) documented how governments, following economic strategies devised by the renowned economics professor Milton Friedman and his Chicago School of "fundamentalist capitalism," have used disasters as a pretext to experiment with drastic "free market" reforms at the expense of the public good. Klein began her analysis of this "disaster capitalism" with the example of the near-total "erasure" of public education in New Orleans and its almost complete replacement by a system of privately run but publicly funded for-profit charter schools in the aftermath of Hurricane Katrina.

In the turmoil and panic of natural and government instigated disasters such as the lack of adequate response to the floodwaters of Hurricane Katrina, various populations have been "shocked" and "awed" into acquiescing to large-scale (and profitable) emergency economic, political, and social "reforms" that are rapidly implemented and then quickly made permanent.

Professor Friedman, also an advisor to presidents (and dictators like Pinochet) and "grand guru of unfettered capitalism" in the "hypermobile" global economy, was an ardent and influential supporter of school vouchers. He advanced the notion that Katrina's devastation in New Orleans represented a fortuitous opportunity. In an op-ed in the *New York Times* 3 months after the hurricane, Friedman wrote,

> Most New Orleans schools are in ruins . . . as are the homes of the children who have attended them. The children are now scattered all over the country. This is a tragedy. It is also an opportunity to radically reform the educational system. (Klein, 2007, pp. 4–5)

A Nobel laureate, Friedman's ideas have exerted enormous influence on public policy in the United States and the foreign policy elites who studied with him at the University of Chicago. Primarily, he emphasized the "preservation and extension of individual freedom."[11] Klein noted that for Freidman a "state-run school system reeked of socialism." He passed away on November 16, 2006, less than a year after advancing his proposal for privatizing schooling in New Orleans but not before his scheme was seized by the George W. Bush administration and "a network of right-wing think tanks ... that descended upon the city after the storm" (Klein, 2007, p. 5).

> Freidman's radical idea was that instead of spending a portion of the billions of dollars in reconstruction on rebuilding and improving New Orleans' existing public school system, the government should provide families with vouchers, which they could spend at private institutions, many run at a profit, that would be subsidized by the state. (p. 5)

Before the storm, the New Orleans public school system, like other resource-starved urban districts, was chronically ineffective in serving the mostly poor African American students who attended the city's 123 schools. (It is worth noting, however, that White students were relatively well served.)

UNFIT/UNWORTHY: NARRATIVES OF BLACKNESS

In 2003, in accord with the accountability requirements of the federal No Child Left Behind Act, the Louisiana Department of Education created the "Recovery School District" (RSD) to take over its "failing schools," which at the time of the storm in 2005 numbered 23.[12] As the online *Parents' Guide to Public Schools* (2007) in New Orleans states, "The Recovery School District is a state-wide, intermediate school district created by the state Board of Elementary and Secondary Education to take over and operate failed schools." These are "low-performing schools that do not meet state-set goals for academic improvement for four or more consecutive years."[13] Within a

neoliberal business model, such school "takeovers" are portrayed as rescue and reform to "save" mostly Black and Latino/Latina children from "failing" urban schools. To the extent that this federally prescribed top-down school "restructuring" effectively ends democratic governance in urban schools and communities, these accountability maneuvers mean a loss of liberty for the society. For another example, the teachers' union contract was dissolved after the storm and all 4,700 professional educators in New Orleans were summarily fired.

After the storm, the number of charter schools, which are mostly managed by the RSD, jumped from 7 to 31. The locally elected New Orleans Public School board currently serves more than 20,000 students. It coexists with this parallel "governance" structure and operates only five public schools but oversees 12 charters operating in buildings that were previously public schools. The "sale" of public lands and property, forced relocation of working class and poor/inner city families, and gentrification are all part of a pattern of economic and political dynamics that are at stake in urban school "reform."[14] Elites have allowed urban schools to atrophy in deteriorating ecological environments, while the lifeblood is drained from their surrounding jobless communities.

However, mismanagement by "unfit," "incompetent," and "corrupt" leadership is suggested as justification for the transfer of public wealth to private interests. For example, Ralph Adamo (2006), a New Orleans journalist (who is also a parent), concluded at the end of the second school year since the hurricane (2006–2007) that the "mismanaged and undersupplied" RSD that was responsible for 22 schools and about 9,500 mostly African American students was "nothing as much as a failed experiment."[15] His news report decries privatization running "amok" in New Orleans:

> The story of the RSD is, in part, a story of how the idea that public entities (either systems or individuals) that were not fit or competent to run public schools came to dominate the reconfiguration of public education in New Orleans. That narrative was combined, of course, with the narrative that only private, market-driven forces can effectively improve school

performance and carry on the tasks of public education. (Adamo, 2006)

However, locals can read a racialized subtext in this narrative. Prior to Hurricane Katrina New Orleans schools served 63,000 students: 93% were African American and 75% were "low-income" (see Note 11). Therefore, "low-performing" (mostly Black) schools are in "New Orleans," which is also mostly Black, in contrast to "*metropolitan* New Orleans," which consists of six other "Whiter" parishes. Thus, a decoded narrative reads,

> The idea that public entities *where Black people were predominate* were not fit or competent to run public schools came to dominate in the reconfiguration of public education in New Orleans.

Similarly unspoken, spatially coded language operates in the racial discourse in other locales. In Atlanta, Georgia, for another example, when some Whites say "the city of Atlanta" or "Fulton County," they really mean "Black people" as opposed to references to surrounding ("Whiter") "Gwinnett" or "Henry" counties. (On an airport bus, I overheard one non-Atlanta resident say to another: "Whenever I need documents from the court in Atlanta, I know it's going to be hassle. They are so disorganized, I just go to Gwinnett where I don't have any problem.") Likewise, "urban" and "inner city" (as compared with "rural") are erstwhile spatial markers that connote racially coded meanings making them "near-synonymous with black in policy making as well as everyday parlance" (Wacquant, 2002).

In these racialized reconfigurations, the interests of Black middle-class educators and homeowners, as well as White people are expendable "collateral damage" given the larger goal of controlling/relocating/exploiting the dangerous/unworthy/unfit "Black poor," who frequently occupy prime urban real estate or school property (Tate, 2007). The economics and politics of urban school reform involve discourses and disparities of power that are evident not only in the "achievement gap" but also the wealth gap, the health gap, and the incarceration gap. In fact, Meiners (2007) cited the complicity of educators as a cost of the link between schools, prisons, and the normalization of mass incarceration, that is, the "making of public enemies."

MASS BLACK CRIMINALIZATION AND INCARCERATION

Before Hurricane Katrina, New Orleans was like no other American city; even with its "exotic" blend of French, Spanish, African, and Anglo-American cultures, it was acknowledged to be America's "most African city" city as well. In fact, the major contours of the Black Experience in the Americas can be observed in the history of New Orleans, from the depredations of market-driven African enslavement, the deceptions of freedom and Reconstruction, the shortfall of integration, and current Black dispossession from their homes and schools by 21st century "market-driven forces." New Orleans has been a crucible of Black educational excellence and resistance. However, mass Black criminalization and incarceration—which the Children's Defense Fund has dubbed a "cradle-to-prison pipeline"[SM]—has eclipsed mass mobilizations for justice. The online Black newspaper *BlackCommentator .com* (2004) observed, "Mass incarceration is by far the greatest crisis facing Black America, ultimately eclipsing all others."

WHO BENEFITS?

Today, almost 2.25 million Americans are incarcerated in local, state, and federal prisons—more than any other nation and more than seven times the international average. African Americans and Latino/Latinas are disastrously overrepresented in this number. As a result of the national policy of mass criminalization and incarceration of Black Americans, liberty and democracy for all are also called into question. Virginia Senator Jim Webb chaired a recent Joint Economic Committee (JEC) of the U.S. Senate hearing on October 4, 2007, that examined this question: "Mass Incarceration in the United States: At What Cost?" Shockingly absent is any societal debate in the nation today concerning what Senator Webb described as "one of the largest public policy experiments" in the nation's history and the "alarming" numbers of incarcerated African Americans. The JEC hearing testimony addressed reasons why

- the incarceration rate has continued to rise despite falling crime rates;

- institutionalization rates have skyrocketed for Black men;

- Black male high school drop-outs have much greater risk of ending up in prison than other demographics;

- the U.S. incarceration rate is the highest in the world; and

- the incarceration rate for Black males remains much higher than other demographic groups.[16]

Economist Glenn C. Loury's testimony made the racialized interconnection between criminal (in)justice policy and the skyrocketing incarceration of African Americans explicit:

What all this comes to is that, to save "our" middle class kids from the threat of their being engulfed by a drug epidemic that might not have even existed by the time drug incarceration began rapidly rising in the 1980s, we criminalized "our" underclass kids.[17]

Privatization, Profits, and Disparities of Power

A study by Roberts (2004) describes the social impact of this policy on young Black men and their communities:

The extraordinary prison expansion involved young black men in grossly disproportionate numbers. Achieving another historic record, most of the people sentenced to time in prison today are black. On any given day, nearly one-third of black men in their twenties are under the supervision of the criminal justice system—either behind bars, on probation, or on parole . . . African Americans experience a uniquely astronomical rate of imprisonment, and the social effects of imprisonment are concentrated in their communities. Thus, the transformation of prison policy at the turn of the twenty-first century is most accurately characterized as the mass incarceration of African Americans. (pp. 1271)

While the public and educators are led to focus on the "behavior" of Black youth and to speculate about the deficiencies of Black culture, Wacquant (2002) argued that "Physical isolation of the Black poor enables racially selective policing, prosecution and imprisonment without the need of special laws explicitly targeting blacks." As Wilder (2000) has also concluded, racism continues in other institutionalized structures:

Social relations can undergo revolutionary change without impacting the power dynamics of the society. . . . Racism continues to reflect a disparity of power and it is as egregious today as it was in the eighteenth century because the advent of less dramatic forms of dominance is *not* progress. More insidious in modern social relations is the fact that white people do not have to expressly target black people in order to exploit them. They only have to locate their interests in private and public policies that have disparate impact. Freed from involvement in color-specific political decisions and specific acts of racial oppression, white Americans can more easily imagine the injustices of their society to be natural or irrational. (pp. 240–241)

Therefore, we should not be deceived because segregation is no longer the law of the land. The policy of unprecedented prison proliferation and mass incarceration coalesced in the 1980s with a shift to private for-profit prisons that have replaced state-run institutions—just as private for-profit schools have begun to replace public schools in New Orleans and other urban districts. Similar nonracial but racially coded narratives normalize both.

Private prison corporations are a multibillion dollar business; they are involved with other providers of "health care, phone, food, and other services in correctional facilities" as well as economic development in rural, mostly White communities. These "free market" forces aggressively recruit new prison construction and work "actively to increase the number of citizens being locked up."[18] In a well-documented essay titled "Prison Profit and Slave Labor," blogger "NdicaBud" examines ways in which privatization is again "encroaching ever further on what had been state responsibilities, and prison systems are the target of private interests." This analysis, which illustrates how corporations and service-related businesses benefit from the prison industry, is worth quoting at length:

The shift to privatization coalesced in the mid-1980s when three trends converged: The ideological imperatives of the free market; the huge increase in the number of prisoners; and the concomitant increase in imprisonment costs. In the giddy atmosphere of the Reagan years, the argument for the superiority of free enterprise resonated profoundly. Only the fire departments seemed safe, as everything from municipal garbage services to Third World state enterprises went on sale. Proponents of privatized prisons put forward a simple case: The private sector can do it cheaper and more efficiently. This assortment of entrepreneurs, free market ideologues, cash-strapped public officials, and academics promised design and management innovations without reducing costs or sacrificing "quality of service." In any case, they noted correctly, public sector corrections systems are in a state of chronic failure by any measure, and no other politically or economically feasible solution is on the table.[19]

Data compiled by the Children's Defense Fund (2007) offers additional insight regarding the interconnection between education "failure" and incarceration:

- Black Americans constitute 13% of the population but half the nation's prisoners.

- Black youth are almost five times as likely to be incarcerated as White youth for drug offenses.

- Government data show Black students face much harsher discipline and are put out of school more often than any other ethnic group for similar offenses.

- Some 70% of Black children are born to single mothers, a major cause of youth delinquency.[20]

It is also important to note that women are now the fastest growing prison population and many are young mothers with children (Talvi, 2007).

EDUCATION AND SOCIALIZATION FOR CULTURAL WELL-BEING

The above statistics suggest that the condition of our youth as well as the state of Black education are far removed from the traditional culture of achievement of people of African ancestry. After the defeat of the Songhay Empire in 1591, the European Transatlantic enslavement enterprise interrupted this legacy of educational and cultural excellence. For instance, when it was illegal to teach our ancestors to read, they hid their counterknowledge and societal critique in the words of "sorrow songs" such as "everybody talking 'bout heaven ain't going there," songs that document their refusal to acquiesce to the inhumanity and ideology of enslavement.

During Reconstruction, "free people of color" in Louisiana and other Black leaders who had obtained some schooling participated in rewriting state constitutions in the South to provide free public schools for all children (Anderson, 1988). Such educational provisions constituted a watershed in the Black freedom movement that benefited the society as a whole. However, the reestablishment of plantation power with northern complicity meant disenfranchisement, Jim Crow terror, lynching and segregated, unequal education—for nearly a century—but not without continuing resistance that is part of our cultural excellence tradition.

The African American legacy of cultural excellence and resistance to oppression includes the Harlem Renaissance, the Black Arts Movement, the modern Civil Rights Movement, the Ocean Hill-Brownsville community control movement, the Black Studies movement, and the establishment of African-centered schools and curricula, as well as independent Muslim and Christian schools (Lee, Lomotey, & Shujaa, 1991; Lee & Slaughter-Defoe, 2004; Muhammad, 2005), to cite a few examples. It remains to be seen whether the education system's current gambit—school takeovers, high stakes testing, and dismantling public schools with the promotion of vouchers and charters as the only viable alternative to chronically failing schools—will permit Black people to continue to carve out enough "liberated space" for authentic Black education and socialization for our cultural well-being (King, 2008).

WHAT REALLY HAPPENED IN NEW ORLEANS?

In 1960, four Black girls braved hysterical crowds of "angry white women in pin curlers and toreador pants" during what has been called "the Second Battle of New Orleans"—the

100-year struggle to integrate the public schools (Baker, 1996). A Norman Rockwell painting shows one of them, six-year-old Ruby Bridges, walking alone past armed Federal marshals on her way to "integrate" Frantz Elementary School. At another school, McDonough 19, Tessie Prevost, Gaile Etienne, and Leona Tate were also "protected" by Federal marshals. This movement to integrate the schools in New Orleans was a sustained collective action on behalf of the entire Black community-family.

There is no hint of this heritage of collective action and "community capacity" (Roberts, 2004) in the images and news reports that were broadcast in the aftermath of Hurricane Katrina. Rather, the media vilified and dehumanized those who were left stranded in New Orleans in grotesque tales of wanton savagery, supposedly inflicted by young Black males (e.g., raping babies and elderly women). While the authorities later denied the veracity of these widely circulated tales, no one reported *why* the elderly and mothers with babies were gathered together outside at the front of the Morial Convention Center. Anecdotal "Word" from the community and evacuees, on the other hand, indicates that traditional Black cultural values prevailed during this crisis: The young men gave the elders and women the utmost respect. They *organized the people* at the Convention Center; they directed the elders and mothers with children to the front *so they could be rescued first* when the buses they had been told to wait for finally arrived.

WHAT IS TO BE DONE?

Research documents that mass incarceration destroys "social citizenship" (Roberts, 2004). At this time of crisis in Black education and the society, what do students, teachers, and community educators have to know if Black youth are to learn in ways that enable them to care about their communities and to contribute to community-building rather than the pursuit of education only as a one-way ticket out? Post-Katrina Black education challenges include what educators are learning (or not learning) about Black students, about our culture, and about our African heritage, which contributes to educational inequity and policies and practices implicated in the "school-to-prison

pipeline" (Dance, 2002; Davis, 2003; Duncan, 2000; Ferguson, 2000; Meiners, 2007).

One possibility discussed in this *Handbook*, Black economic literacy, can also incorporate Black-community-family consciousness (Gordon Nembhard, 2008). Questions that should inform such literacy include Why are Black communities so poor and why is Africa poor/ underdeveloped? What have African people given to the world? How can we restore community capacity and make a living in this era of deindustrialization, other global changes in the economy, and prevailing "market forces"? These are the kinds of questions Black youth (and their teachers) should be able to answer and they should be able to develop solutions for such systemic problems. In teacher education, curriculum development, and community outreach, there is a critical role for Black Studies in addressing the crisis of knowledge that undermines Black educational excellence (Gordon Nembhard & Forstater, in press; Ward & Marable, 2003).

Systemic and historical thinking is rare regarding social issues such as the legacy of slavery, poverty *and* oppression, African American group identity, consciousness and identification with our African heritage as well as the mechanisms of White supremacy racism. Cosby's widely publicized criticisms (and concern about) poor Black people fail to link the systemic impoverishment of Black communities to the institutionalized privilege and advantages of White-middle-classness. In response, for example, Dyson asks, *Is Bill Cosby Right? Or Has the Black Middle Class Lost Its Mind?* (Dyson, 2006).[21]

The failure of public education to serve Black youth is a form of human rights abuse—the 21st century *Maafa*. While the "terrible consequences" of racialized disparities are life threatening for the Black community-family, they actually call into question the values of the society, including democracy, freedom, and justice for all. Education professionals and policymakers focus on high stakes testing and "teacher quality and accountability" to the exclusion of other possibilities that engage youth in active learning and doing for democratic citizenship (Lipman, 2003; McLaughlin, Irby, & Langman, 2001) and cultural well-being (King, 2008). Lipman's (2003) research links accountability to "racialized social control" and needed community-based strategies for social change. As Lipman argued, "Policy responses are conditioned by the relative strength and mobilization of social forces (e.g., organizations of civil society, working-class organizations, popular social movements)" (p. 12). Our ability to address the challenges of this era depends on opportunities that we create to educate, to socialize, and to mobilize the next generation.

In conclusion, the state of Black education "post-Katrina" challenges us to educate all children, including "other people's children," to build a world in which "all god's chillun got shoes." That is to say, our humanity places certain obligations on us—to be responsible for ourselves—for our own spiritual, intellectual, and economic integrity and cultural well-being and to understand how our society *really* works. The education "reform" that has been engineered in New Orleans faster than the broken levees could be repaired has been lauded in the press as "the nation's preeminent laboratory for the widespread use of charter schools" (Klein, 2007, p. 6). However, public school teachers there have described this massive experiment with the futures of our children as a "land grab" (Klein, 2007, pp. 6–7). After visiting New Orleans recently, the President of the United Federation of Teachers, Randi Weingarten, concluded that "A major part of the reshaping of the city's ethnic face has been played out on the stage of New Orleans public schools."[22]

Our obligation is to be proactive especially on behalf of those who suffer. Safeguarding public education would seem to be an important part of that obligation. Saving our children requires both quality education and appropriate community-family socialization. We require creative community-based solutions for this responsibility (King, 2005). For example, the study of African language to access core values and African social practice and organization—before European values intruded—is one possible venue for the recovery of valuable traditions and the reunification of the African family. In Songhoy-senni (language) and classical Songhoy society there was no word for "prison" because other social institutions worked to harmonize society (Maiga, 2007).

In response to mass Black incarceration and criminalization we need a mass movement for educational, social, and economic justice that includes investment in our communities and in people. The future of public education and livable communities is what is at stake for African Americans, the nation, and the world when Black children in a public education system in a major American city become pawns in a massive experiment in "crisis exploitation" to persuade an unsuspecting nation to accept privatized, for-profit rather than public education at our expense.

NOTES

1. In Trinidad and Jamaica, "all ah we" means "all of us," so "all ah we" is one. "We are all one people." Personal communications, Janice B. Fournillier, Annette Henry, and Ashley Hamilton-Taylor, November 10, 2007. In Jamaica, one might also hear: "All ah we no save." Personal communication, Sylvia Wynter, November 11, 2007. "All us we" incorporates a Black American inflection and includes humanity in general.

2. Marimba Ani introduced this Kiswahili term, *Maafa*, which means "disaster" or "terrible consequence," to describe the disconnection, displacement, and dislocation that African people have suffered through 500 years of enslavement, imperialism, colonialism, invasions, and exploitation. See Richards (1989) and Ani (1994).

3. Cited in Klein (2007).

4. "Prison profit and slave labor." See www.yahooka.com/forum/politics-current-affairs/22956-prison-profit-slave-labor.html.

5. The concept "civilizational" is adapted from Munford's (2001) definition of "civilizational historicism": a system of thought, a philosophy, an explanatory model with a specific purpose—"a world view of use to Black folk" (p. 1).

6. Annihilation and nihilation are related but distinct social processes. Wynter (1989) described the concept of nihilation (from the French word *néantisé*) as the total negation of being. See also King (2005).

7. Sylvia Wynter (2006) explored the interconnections between our "unbearable wrongness of being," "the epistemology of knowledge", and the "liberation of people" (p. 113).

8. Dixon summarizes Wacquant's (2002) analysis.

9. This is the first of "Ten Vital Principles of Black Education and Socialization" advanced by the Commission on Research in Black Education established by the American Educational Research Association (www.coribe.org).

10. A rash of hate crimes, including events that recently occurred in Jena, Louisiana, have invigorated mass mobilizing—spurred by Black radio commentators who address listeners as "family."

11. Hoover Institution, Stanford University press release, November 16, 2006, "Milton Friedman noted

economist, Nobel laureate, and Hoover senior research fellow, dies at 94." Retrieved November 9, 2006, from www.hooveSr.org/pubaffairs/releases/4667846.html.

12. See Steiner (2005).

13. The *Parents' Guide* states, "In New Orleans, the RSD operates 24 schools and oversees 20 charter schools. RSD is run by a superintendent who is appointed by the state Superintendent of Education. An advisory board was established to advise the superintendent on matters pertaining to the RSD." See www.nolaparentsguide.org/Parents'%20Guide%20Aug07.pdf.

14. It can also be argued that the provisions of NCLB permit local and national "effective school" models and charters, including African-centered schools, to provide community-designed, if not controlled, alternatives. The issue of disenfranchisement and dismantling of public education remains, however. The sale of public lands and buildings when school enrollments in deteriorating areas are allowed to drop and threaten public schools' economic viability is another example. See "Chronology of California School District Takeovers, Youth Strategy Project." www.datacenter.org/research/oaklandtakeover.pdf. "Dismantling a Community" provides a New Orleans privatization timeline. www.soros.org/resources/articles_publications/publications/dismantling_20061026/dismantling_20061026.pdf.

15. That parents have chided the new RSD superintendent for using the word "experiment" when describing educational conditions in New Orleans (Adamo, 2006), perhaps illustrates the community's understandable sensitivity given the historical legacy of nefarious "experimentation" on Black lives in other contexts. See, for example, the history of medical experimentation documented by Washington (2008).

16. Testimony before the JEC of the U.S. Congress, Washington, D.C., October 4, 2007. See http://jec.senate.gov/Hearings/10.04.07EconomicCostofIncarceration.htm. Data presented included these statistics: Although African Americans constitute 14% of regular drug users, they are 37% of those arrested for drug offenses and 56% of persons in state prisons for drug crimes. African Americans serve nearly as much time in federal prisons for drug offenses as Whites do for violent crimes. A Black male who does not finish high school now has a 60% chance of going to jail. One who has finished high school has a 30% chance.

17. *Mass Incarceration and American Values*, JEC Testimony, October 4, 2007.

18. See www.motherjones.com/news/special_reports/prisons/print_overview.html. See also Blankenship and Yanarell (2004).

19. See http://www.yahooka.com/forum/politics-current-affairs/22956-prison-profit-slave-labor.html.

20. Children's Defense Fund, reported in Powell (2007).

21. It is worth noting that Dr. Cosby's attention has shifted away from a compelling research, policy, and government agenda that he cogently advanced in his book with Dwight Allen, titled *American Schools: The 100 Billion Dollar Challenge*, in which he called for a massive federal investment in research. Retrieved June 30, 2001, from ipublish.com www.bn.com.

22. See Weingarten (2007).

REFERENCES

Adamo, R. (2006, August 15). NOLA's Failed Education Experiment: Privatization runs amok in the post-Katrina New Orleans school system. *The American Prospect.* Retrieved October 30, 2007, from www.prospect.org/cs/articles?article=nolas_failed_education_experiment_

Anderson, J. (1988). *The education of Blacks in the south, 1860–1935.* Chapel Hill: University of North Carolina Press.

Ani, M. (1994). *Yurugu: An African-centered critique of European cultural thought and behavior.* Trenton, NJ: Africa World Press.

Baker, L. (1996). *The second battle of New Orleans: The hundred-year struggle to integrate the schools.* New York: HarperCollins.

Belfield, C. R., & Levin, H. M. (2007, August). *The economic losses from high school dropouts in California* (Policy Brief 1). Santa Barbara: California Dropout Research Project, University of California at Santa Barbara Gevirtz Graduate School of Education.

BlackCommentator.com. (2004, June 17). Mass incarceration and rape: The savaging of Black America. No. 95. www.blackcommentator.com/95/95_cover_prisons.html

Blankenship, S., & Yanarell, E. (2004, June). Prison recruitment as a policy tool of local economic development: A critical evaluation. *Contemporary Justice Review, 7*(2), 183–198.

Butchart, R. E. (1980). *Northern schools, Southern Blacks, and Reconstruction: Freedmen's education, 1862–1875.* Westport, CT: Greenwood Press.

Children's Defense Fund. (2007). *America's cradle to prison pipeline.* Washington, DC: Author.

Cosby, B., & Poussaint, A. L. (2007). *Come on people: On the path from victims to victors.* Nashville, TN: Thomas Nelson.

Dance, L. J. (2002). *Tough fronts: The impact of street culture on schooling.* New York: Routledge/Falmer.

Dannett, S. L. (1964). Profile of Negro womanhood. *Negro Heritage Library.* Vol. I 1619–1900. Yonkers, NY: Educational Heritage.

Davis, A. Y. (2003). *Are prisons obsolete?* New York: Seven Stories Press.

Day, J. C., & Newberger, E. (2002, July). *The big payoff: Educational attainment and synthetic estimates of work-life earnings* (Population Division No. P23–210). Washington, DC: U.S. Census Bureau.

Dixon, B. (2007, October 13). *Black mass incarceration is now a political issue.* Dissident. Retrieved November 1, 2007, from www.dissidentvoice .org/2007/10/black-mass-incarceration-is-now-a-political-issue

Duncan, G. A. (2000). Urban pedagogues and the celling of adolescents of color. *Social Justice: A Journal of Crime, Conflict, and World Order, 27,* 29–42.

Dyson, M. E. (2006). *Is Bill Cosby right? Or has the Black middle class lost its mind?* New York: Basic Civitas Books.

Ferguson, A. A. (2000). *Bad boys: Public schools in the making of Black masculinity.* Ann Arbor: University of Michigan Press.

Gordon Nembhard, J. (2008). Alternative economics, a missing component in the African American studies curriculum: Teaching public policy and democratic community economics to Black students. *Journal of Black Studies, 38* (doi: 10.1177/0021934707310294).

Gordon Nembhard, J., & Forstater, M. (in press). Guest editors. Special Issue: Black political economy in the 21st century: Exploring the interface of economics and Black studies. *Journal of Black Studies, 38.*

Hilliard, A. G. (1997). *SBA: Reawakening the African mind.* Gainesville, FL: Makare Press.

King, J. (2008). Critical and qualitative research in teacher education: A blues epistemology for cultural well-being and reason for knowing. In M. Cochran-Smith, S. Feiman-Nemser, & J. McIntyre (Ed.), *Handbook of research on teacher education: Enduring questions in changing contexts,* (3rd ed., pp. 1094–1136). New York: Routledge.

King, J. E. (Ed). (2005). *Black education: A transformative research and action agenda for the new century.* Mahwah, NJ: Erlbaum.

Klein, N. (2007). *The shock doctrine: The rise of disaster capitalism.* New York: Henry Holt.

Lee, C. D., Lomotey, K., & Shujaa, M. (1991). How shall we sing the Lord's song in a strange land? The dilemma of double consciousness and the complexities of African centered pedagogy. *Journal of Education, 172*(2), 45–61.

Lipman, P. (2003). *High stakes education: Inequality, globalization, and urban school reform.* New York: Routledge.

Maiga, H. O. (2007). *La contribution socio-culturelle du people Songhoy en Afrique.* Algiers, Algeria: Magreb Press.

McLaughlin, M. W., Irby, L. A., & Langman, J. (2001). *Urban sanctuaries: Neighborhood organizations in the lives and futures of inner-city youth.* San Francisco: Jossey-Bass.

Meiners, E. R. (2007). *Right to be hostile: Schools, prisons, and the making of public enemies.* New York: Routledge.

Muhammad, Z. (2005). Faith and courage to educate our own: Reflections on Islamic schools in the African American community. In J. E. King (Ed.), *Black education: A transformative research and action agenda for the new century* (pp. 261–280). Mahwah, NJ: Erlbaum.

Munford, C. J. (2001). *Race and civilization: Rebirth of Black centrality.* Trenton, NJ: Red Sea Press.

Parents' guide to public schools. (2007). Retrieved November 1, 2007, from www.nolaparentsguide.org/Parents'%20Guide% 20Aug07.pdf

Powell, T. (2007, November 1). Prioritizing education over the penal system. *Diverse,* p. 11.

Richards, D. M. (1989). *Let the circle be un-broken: The implications of African spirituality in the Diaspora.* Trenton, NJ: Red Sea Press.

Rimstead, R. (2001). *Remnants of nation: On poverty narratives by women.* Toronto, Ontario, Canada: University of Toronto Press.

Roberts, D. E. (2004). The social and moral costs of mass incarceration in African American communities. *Stanford Law Review, 56*(5), 1271–1305.

Steiner, L. M. (2005). *School restructuring options under no child left behind: What works when: State takeovers of individual schools.* Washington, DC: Center for Comprehensive School Reform and Improvement. Retrieved November 1, 2007, from www.centerforcsri.org/pubs/restructuring/Kno wledgeIssues1StateTakeovers.pdf

Talvi, S. J. A. (2007). Incarceration nation. *The Nation.* Retrieved November 1, 2007, from www.thenation.com/doc/20070122/incarceratio n_nation

Tate, W. F. (2007, October). *Knowledge workers and the need for opportunity expansion regimes in urban America.* Brief Report prepared for the National Education Association. Washington, DC: Author.

Wacquant, L. (2002). From slavery to mass incarceration: Rethinking the "race question" in the US. *New Left Review, 13,* 41–60.

Ward, G. K., & Marable, M. (2003). Toward a new civic leadership: The Africana Criminal Justice Project. *Social Justice, 30*(2), 89–97.

Washington, H. A. (2008). *Medical apartheid: The dark history of medical experimentation on Black Americans from colonial times to the present.* New York: Harlem Moon Press.

Weingarten, R. (2007, August 27). *New Orleans and the future of American Education.* Retrieved

November 1, 2007, from http://edwize.org/new-orleans-and-the-future-of-american-education

Wilder, C. S. (2000). *A covenant with color: Race and social power in Brooklyn.* New York: Columbia University Press.

Wynter, S. (1989, May). Beyond the word of man: Glissant and the new discourse of the Antilles. *World Literature Today, 63*(4), 637–647.

Wynter, S. (2006). On how we mistook the map for the territory and re-imprisoned ourselves in our unbearable Wrongness of Being, of Désêtre: Black Studies toward the Human Project. In L. Gordon & A. Gordon (Eds.), *Not only the master's tools: African-American Studies in theory and practice* (pp. 107–169). Boulder, CO: Paradigm.

Graduate School Programs to Prepare Future Faculty of Color

LYNETTE L. DANLEY, RODERIC R. LAND, AND KOFI LOMOTEY

Following is a list of various programs and contacts that have played and continue to be an integral part in the process of preparing future faculty of color and strengthening the pipeline. Attached to each program is a brief description of the contribution/service they provide as well as a link to the Web site where more information is available. The maintenance and success of these programs are vital to the growth of a "seemingly diminutive" pipeline of "qualified" applicants of color.

The Western Name Exchange

The Western Name Exchange is a consortium of 24 universities located in the western and southwestern United States, which annually collects and exchanges names of talented under-represented ethnic minority students who are in their junior or senior year of their undergraduate education. The purpose of the Exchange is to ensure that participating universities continue to identify a pool of qualified students who could be recruited to the graduate programs at these "name-exchanging" institutions. The consortium of universities conducts other activities consistent with the national efforts to increase the enrollment of traditionally under-represented peoples in graduate education.

www.grad.washington.edu/nameexch/western
John P. Drew
Graduate School
Box 353770
University of Washington
Seattle, WA 98195
e-mail: jdrew@u.washington.edu

Ronald E. McNair Post-Baccalaureate Achievement Program

This program prepares participants for doctoral studies through involvement in research and other scholarly activities. Participants are from disadvantaged backgrounds and have demonstrated strong academic potential. Institutions work closely with participants as they complete their undergraduate requirements. Institutions encourage participants to enroll in graduate programs and then track their progress through to the successful completion of advanced degrees. The goal is to increase the attainment of Ph.D. degrees by students from under-represented segments of society.

www.ed.gov/programs/triomcnair/index.html
Federal TRIO Programs
U.S. Department of Education, OPE
Higher Education Programs
1990 K Street, N.W., Suite 7000
Washington, DC 20006-8510
e-mail: OPE_TRIO@ed.gov
Tel.: (202) 502-7600
Fax: (202) 502-7857 or (202) 219-7074

Summer Research Opportunity Program (SROP)

This is a program to expose talented undergraduates to professional and educational opportunities in the academy. The goal of the program is to increase the number of underrepresented students who pursue academic careers by enhancing their preparation for graduate study through intensive research experiences with faculty mentors. The SROP was initiated in 1986 by the CIC Graduate Deans to encourage talented undergraduate students to pursue graduate study and subsequently academic careers. That first year 99 students participated; 529 students majoring in more than 100 fields of study are participating this year. Since this program began, some 7,000 students have participated. The major activity of the SROP is an in-depth research experience with students working one-on-one with faculty mentors. SROP students are required to write a paper and an abstract describing their projects and to present the results of their work at a campus symposium.

www.cic.uiuc.edu/programs/SROP/SROPProgramDescription.shtml
Yolanda Zepeda
Assistant Director for Graduate Education and Diversity Committee on
    Institutional Cooperation
08K Bricker Hall
190 North Oval Mall
Columbus, OH 43210-1366
Tel.: (614) 247-5068
e-mail: cicsropcoord@staff.cic.net

Undergraduate Research Opportunity Program

The Undergraduate Research Opportunity Program (UROP) creates research partnerships between first- and second-year students and University of Michigan faculty. All schools and colleges of the University of Michigan are active participants in UROP, thereby providing a wealth of research topics from which a student can choose. Begun in 1989 with 14 student/faculty partnerships the program continues to grow, offering more first- and second-year students the opportunity to be part of an exciting research community. Today, approximately 900 students and more than 600 faculty researchers are engaged in research partnerships.

www.lsa.umich.edu/urop
Undergraduate Research Opportunity Program
University of Michigan
1190 Undergraduate Science Building
204 Washtenaw Avenue
Ann Arbor, MI 48109-2215

Preparing Future Faculty

The Preparing Future Faculty (PFF) program is a national movement to transform the way aspiring faculty members are prepared for their careers. PFF programs provide doctoral students, as well as some master's and postdoctoral students, with opportunities to observe and experience faculty responsibilities at a variety of academic institutions with varying missions, diverse student bodies, and different expectations for faculty. The PFF initiative was launched in 1993 as a partnership between the Council of Graduate Schools and the Association of American Colleges and Universities. During a decade of grant activity, from 1993 to 2003, PFF evolved into four distinct program phases, with support from the Pew Charitable Trusts, the National Science Foundation, and the Atlantic Philanthropies. During this time, PFF programs were implemented at more than 45 doctoral degree-granting institutions and nearly 300 "partner" institutions in the United States. While the grant periods have expired, the Council of Graduate Schools continues to provide administrative support to existing programs and to those wishing to develop new PFF programs. Since the PFF initiative began, a number of institutions and programs have developed PFF programs without external funding. These programs incorporate many or all the activities and components of grant-funded programs, and have been significant contributors to the PFF community.

www.preparing-faculty.org
Council of Graduate Schools
One Dupont Circle, N.W.
Suite 430
Washington, DC 20036-1173
Tel.: (202) 223-3791
Fax: (202) 331-7157
e-mail: pff@cgs.nche.edu

Washington State University (WSU) Summer Doctoral Fellows Program

This program provides select doctoral students with the opportunity to work closely with faculty mentors at WSU in preparing for academic careers as future faculty members. During the program, research fellows work on completing dissertations; engage in seminars on the changing roles and expectations of faculty, the future of the professoriate, the changing nature of higher education, and the issues facing faculty of color and women; and design individualized programs for enhancing their ability to teach, conduct research, and other scholarship.

www.wsu.edu/~gradsch/summerfellow.htm
Dr. Howard Grimes
Dean of the Graduate School
c/o Joe Merrill
P.O. Box 641030
Washington State University
Graduate School
Pullman, WA 99164-1030
e-mail: gsdean@wsu.edu

Institute for the Recruitment of Teachers

The Institute for Recruitment of Teachers aims to reduce over time the critical underrepresentation on the faculties of certain minority groups, as well as to address the attendant educational consequences of these disparities. Providing positive role models to youth, the institute serves the related goals of supporting school and campus environments.

Each year, the institute supports throughout the graduate school application process outstanding college students and graduates from diverse backgrounds who are committed to these ideals.

www.andover.edu/irt/home.htm
Institute for Recruitment of Teachers
Phillips Academy
180 Main Street
Andover, MA 01810
e-mail: irt@andover.edu

Sisters of the Academy Research Boot Camp

As Sisters of the Academy, our mission is to create a network of Black women in higher education committed to fostering continuous scholarship and academic achievement. Through this commitment, members of the organization will reinforce the idea of excellence in access to higher education for Black people, schools, and communities. The Research Boot Camp is an intense, 1-week program designed to assist doctoral students and junior faculty members in the development of skills necessary for success in the academy. Senior scholars, statisticians, and theorists will facilitate workshops intended to help doctoral students conceptualize and design key components of their dissertations including: Research Question and hypothesis development, Literature Review, Conceptual Framework development, Instrumentation, Methodology, and Data analysis. These senior scholars will also assist junior scholars in the development of manuscripts for publication and clarification of a future research agenda. In addition to the research component, each participant will be linked with a mentor, either a junior or senior scholar, to help cultivate a mentoring relationship.

www.sistersoftheacademy.org
Sisters of the Academy Institute
4036 Haley Center
Auburn University
Auburn, AL 36849-5221
Tel.: (334) 844-3087
Fax: (334) 844-3072 fax
e-mail: sotains@auburn.edu

Florida A&M Graduate School Feeder Program

The Graduate Feeder Scholars Program (GFSP) in the School of Graduate Studies and Research is an official partnership agreement arranged by Florida A&M University (FAMU) with more than 40 participating universities located throughout the United States. The GFSP affords FAMU students the opportunity to receive advanced study in graduate programs not available at FAMU. The feeder arrangement was conceptualized and created in response to the national need to increase the number of African Americans participating in advanced graduate education. The GFSP was designed with FAMU as the lead university in this consortium. As the lead institution, FAMU acts as the hub of the consortium with a committed role of providing a pool of qualified African American students motivated to pursue the master's or Ph.D. degree.

www.famu.edu/index.cfm?a=graduatestudies&p=GraduateFeeder#9
School of Graduate Studies & Research
Florida A&M University
400 Tucker Hall
Tallahassee, FL 32307
Tel.: (850) 599-3505

Ford Foundation Diversity Fellowships for Achieving Excellence in College and University Teaching

This program is designed to increase the diversity of the nation's college and university faculties by increasing their ethnic and racial diversity, to maximize the educational benefits of diversity, and to increase the number of professors who can and will use diversity as a resource for enriching the education of all students. Predoctoral fellowships support study toward a Ph.D. or Sc.D.; dissertation fellowships offer support in the final year of writing the Ph.D. or Sc.D. thesis; postdoctoral fellowships offer 1-year awards for Ph.D. recipients. Applicants must be U.S. citizens in research-based fields of study.

www.nationalacademies.org/gateway/pga/3366.html
Policy and Global Affairs
500 Fifth St., NW
Washington, DC 20001
Tel.: (202) 334-2425

AUTHOR INDEX

SUBJECT INDEX

ABOUT THE EDITOR

Linda C. Tillman is professor and program coordinator in the Educational Leadership Program at the University of North Carolina at Chapel Hill. She is Vice President of Division A (Administration, Organization, and Leadership) of the American Educational Research Association and Associate Director of Graduate Student Development for the University Council for Educational Administration. She has teaching and administrative experience in an urban school district and has held faculty positions at the University of New Orleans (Louisiana) and Wayne State University (Michigan). Her research interests include leadership theory; the education of *all* children, particularly African Americans in K-12 and postsecondary education; mentoring African American teachers, administrators, and faculty; and the use of racially and culturally sensitive qualitative research approaches. Based on her article *Culturally Sensitive Research Approaches: An African American Perspective,* she uses a culturally sensitive research framework to investigate factors that affect African Americans in K-12 and higher education. Recent publications include *Boston Public as Public Pedagogy* (with James Trier) in the *Peabody Journal of Education.* She was also the guest editor of special issues of *The International Journal of Qualitative Studies in Education,* titled *Research on the Color Line: Perspectives on Race, Culture and Qualitative Research* and *Educational Administration Quarterly,* titled *Pushing Back Resistance: African American Perspectives on School Leadership.* She is also the co-editor (with Lenoar Foster) of a forthcoming book titled *African American Perspectives on Schools: Building a Culture of Empowerment.* She is the 2004 recipient of the Early Career Contribution Award from the American Educational Research Association Committee on Scholars of Color in Education.

ABOUT THE SECTION EDITORS

Derrick P. Alridge is director and associate professor in the Institute for African American Studies and Associate Professor of Education at the University of Georgia. He is the author of *W. E. B. Du Bois: An Intellectual History*. He is currently writing *The Hip Hop Mind: An Intellectual History of the Social Consciousness of a Generation*.

Jennifer Beaumont works in the Office of Innovative Programs, New Jersey Department of Education. Her responsibilities include coordinating Advanced Placement programs across the state, supporting school districts in the use of Federal Title V funds, and developing special programs that deepen the awareness and understanding of equity and diversity issues. She also assists state departments of education, local education agencies, and individual schools in the formulation of policy and the development of strategies for implementing comprehensive changes in schools. Her research interests include the political and policy context of educational leadership and education in urban settings. She has taught in the New York City public schools and at the University of Buffalo.

Gwendolyn Cartledge, Ph.D., is a professor at The Ohio State University (OSU), School of Physical Activity and Educational Services, special education programs. She documents an extensive teaching career in both the public schools and higher education. A faculty member at OSU since 1986, her professional teaching, research, and writings have centered on students with mild disabilities, the development of social skills, and early intervention and prevention of learning and behavior problems through effective instruction. Currently, her research and writing interests have concentrated on early reading intervention with a particular emphasis on urban and culturally/linguistically diverse learners. She has coauthored four books: *Teaching Social Skills to Children and Youth* (1995, 3rd ed.), *Cultural Diversity and Social Skills Teaching: Understanding Ethnic and Gender Differences* (1996), *Teaching Urban Learners* (2006), and *Diverse Learners With Exceptionalities: Culturally Responsive Teaching in the Inclusive Classroom* (2008). She has also coauthored two social skills curricula and numerous articles in professional journals.

V. P. Franklin, Ph.D., holds a University of California Presidential Chair and is Distinguished Professor of history and education at the University of California, Riverside. He also serves as Editor of *The Journal of African American History* (formerly *The Journal of Negro History*). He is the author of numerous articles and books on African American history and education, including *The Education of Black Philadelphia* (1979), *Black Self-Determination: A Cultural History of African American Resistance* (1984, 1992), and *Living Our Stories, Telling Our Truths: Autobiography and the Making of the African American Intellectual Tradition* (1995); and is the coeditor of *New Perspectives on Black Educational History* (1978), *Sisters in the Struggle: African American Women in the Civil Rights-Black Power Movement* (2001), *Cultural Capital and Black Education: Black Communities and the Finding of Black Schooling, 1860 to the Present* (2004), and other works.

Jacqueline Jordan Irvine is the Charles Howard Candler Professor Emeritus in the Division of Educational Studies at Emory University and visiting professor at the University of Maryland

College Park. Her specialization is in multicultural education and urban teacher education, particularly the education of African Americans. Her books include, *Black Students and School Failure, Growing Up African American in Catholic Schools, Critical Knowledge for Diverse Students, Culturally Responsive Lesson Planning for Elementary and Middle Grades, In Search of Wholeness: African American Teachers and Their Culturally Specific Pedagogy,* and *Seeing With the Cultural Eye.* In addition to these books, she has published numerous articles and book chapters and presented hundreds of papers to professional education and community organizations. Some of her awards and recognitions include *American Educational Research Association (AERA)*'s Outstanding Achievement Award—Research Focus on Black Education (RFBE) SIG; Distinguished Career Award from Committee on the Role and Status of Minorities; Dewitt-Wallace/AERA Lecture Award; President's Distinguished Service Award from the SIG: RFBE; AERA Social Justice Award; Division G's award for Outstanding Service in the Preparation of the Next Generation. The American Association of Colleges of Teacher Education has recognized her work with the Outstanding Writing Award; Hunt Lecture; and the Lindsay Award for Distinguished Research in Teacher Education. Emory University noted her accomplishments with The Distinguished Emory University Faculty Lecture and Award; Thomas Jefferson Award, an award given at Commencement to a faculty for their contributions in research and service; and Emory University's Crystal Apple Award for Excellence in Teaching Graduate Education. Finally, she was elected to the National Academy of Education in 2007. She received her B.A. and M.A. degrees from Howard University and her Ph.D. from Georgia State University in educational leadership.

Kofi Lomotey is presently the executive vice president and provost at Fisk University in Nashville, Tennessee. He has published several books, articles in professional journals, and book chapters. His research interests include urban schools, students of African descent in higher education, principals of African descent in elementary schools, and independent African-centered schools. He serves as Editor of *Urban Education*, and of the SAGE *Encyclopedia of African American Education*. He has served as President of Fort Valley State University, Senior Vice President, Provost, and Professor of Education at Medgar Evers College (City University of New York) and as a member of the faculties at Louisiana State University and the State University of New York (Buffalo).

ABOUT THE CONTRIBUTORS

Sessi S. F. Aboh is assistant provost at Fisk University. Before joining Fisk University, she served as an assistant professor and the Associate Director of the African World Studies Institute (AWSI) at Fort Valley State University. She formerly served as the Associate Director of the Center for Diopian Inquiry of Research on Education as Culture Transmission (DIRECT Center) at Medgar Evers College of the City University of New York. She is the Managing Editor for the *Journal of Culture and its Transmission in the African World* (JCTAW), a reviewer for the *Urban Education,* and a reviewer and editorial board member for the *Journal of Negro Education* (JNE).

Walter R. Allen is Allan Murray Cartter Professor in Higher Education, Graduate School of Education and Information Studies at the University of California, Los Angeles. He is also professor of sociology and codirector of CHOICES, a longitudinal study of college attendance among African Americans and Latinos in California. His research interests include higher education, race and ethnicity, family patterns, and social inequality. He has worked as a consultant to courts, communities, foundations, business, and government.

Sana Ansari is currently completing her Ph.D. in curriculum studies at the University of Illinois, Chicago. Her professional experience began as a high school teacher. Consequently, as a researcher, her area of inquiry is secondary literacy and urban education with a focus on adolescent identity development. She is currently examining the ways in which institutions shape identity within urban school contexts through the lens of critical race theory, postcolonial theory, and identity theory.

Thurman L. Bridges III is a doctoral student in the Minority & Urban Education Unit at the University of Maryland, College Park, in the College of Education. He worked as a classroom teacher for 4 years in Richmond, Virginia. As a doctoral student, his areas of concentration are in urban education, Black male teacher beliefs, social and ecological contexts of urban schools, critical race theory, and emancipatory pedagogies. More specifically, his work will examine which factors (extrinsic and intrinsic) influence the motivation, beliefs, and persistence of post–Civil Rights Era African American male teachers in urban public schools. With this work, he hopes to influence the admissions and hiring practices of colleges of education and school districts as they work to recruit and retain African American male classroom teachers in urban public schools. He plans to pursue an assistant professor position at a research institution upon graduation.

Nancy M. Cardwell is a member of the graduate faculty at Bank Street College of Education where she teaches child development, research methods, and foundations of educational leadership. She is the recipient of a multiyear Spencer Foundation Discipline Based Studies in Education grant to critically examine social development through the prism of social justice. Her research, informed by 20 years of graduate-level study and teaching experience in higher education and in central Harlem public elementary schools, has focused on identity development in cultural contexts, narrative teaching practices, as well as issues of race, gender, and power in urban public schools. Her dissertation will examine novice teachers' beliefs about child development theory and how these beliefs shape classroom practice.

Eddie Comeaux is currently a lecturer at the University of California, Los Angeles. His research interests include the sociology of education, critical race theory, college access issues regarding underrepresented minorities, and critical pedagogical strategies that translate into personal and academic intervention for underrepresented minorities and college student athletes. The meta-objective of his research has been to examine the ways in which the interaction patterns between personal characteristics (e.g., race/ethnic and culture) and characteristics of the social environment influence subsequent educational experiences and outcomes.

Eric J. Cooper is the President of the National Urban Alliance for Effective Education (NUA). His extensive career in education policy includes vice president for Inservice Training & Telecommunications, Simon & Schuster Education Group; associate director of Program Development, The College Board; administrative assistant, Office of Curriculum, Boston Public Schools; researcher; and advocate. As a MacArthur Foundation Fellow, he received a $500,000 award to produce prime-time documentaries and training programs for television, on improving the literacy skills of students. He is currently working with the University of Alabama/Birmingham to improve education in the Birmingham Public Schools and led the "Eleanor & Brown" project partnership that commemorates the *Brown v. the Board of Education* decision while viewing education not just as a civil right but as a human justice right. He received the 2008 Martin Luther King, Jr. award from the Israeli Consulate of New York City and the Jewish National Fund. He maintains an irrefutable belief in the capacity of all school children and youth to succeed at the highest academic levels.

Robert Cooper is an assistant professor at the University of California-Los Angeles. He conducts research on the implementation and scale up of school reform models. His research focuses on the politics and policies of school reform, particularly as they relate to issues of race and equity for African American and Latino students. Specializing in the use of a mixed methods approach, he has published and presented numerous papers on the varying aspects of school reform and school change, including recent articles in *Urban Education, Journal of Negro Education, Education and Urban Society,* and *Journal of Education for Students Placed at Risk.*

Lynette L. Danley is an assistant professor in the Department of Educational Leadership and Policy and Ethnic Studies Program at the University of Utah. Her research interests include college preparation, mentoring, and erosions in the PK-20 pipeline that impede the academic and social mobility for women and people of color in higher education, particularly Black women who are university faculty members, undergraduate and graduate students, and girls who identify as Black/African American high school students. As she investigates strategies for successful navigation of the academy and the PK-12 educational systems, her current scholarship applies critical race feminism epistemologies and methodological approaches by using story telling, narratives, and counter stories to shed light on how the intersections of race, class, and gender shape the diverse experiences of their lives. She is a native of Chicago, Illinois, first-generation college student, and a product of the Chicago Public School System. She is the proud mother of an 8-year-old son, Julian, and the founder of Black Butterflies, a college preparation program that empowers Black girls to live their legacy.

James Earl Davis is professor in the Department of Educational Leadership and Policy Studies at Temple University with affiliate appointments in African American Studies and Women Studies. His research focuses on the academic and social experiences of African American boys and young men placed at risk for underachievement and school disengagement. His work has appeared in numerous journals, including *Gender & Society, Urban Education, American Journal of Evaluation,* and *Educational Researcher.* He is coauthor of *African American Males in School and Society: Policies and Practices for Effective Education* (with Vernon Polite) and *Black Sons to Mothers: Compliments, Critiques, and Challenges for Cultural Workers in Education* (with M. Christopher Brown). He has taught at the University of Delaware and Cornell University. His work has been funded by the Spencer Foundation, the National Science Foundation, Marcus Foundation, and the U.S. Center for Substance Abuse Prevention.

Charles Dukes is an assistant professor in the Department of Exceptional Student Education at Florida Atlantic University. His research interests include positive behavioral support, inclusive education for individuals with significant disabilities in high schools, sexuality, and cultural issues for individuals with disabilities.

Cheryl Fields-Smith is currently a member of the faculty in the Department of Elementary and Social Studies Education at the University of Georgia. Her research agenda focuses on the areas of African American parental participation and issues of diversity in teacher education. In March 2006, she was awarded a Spencer Foundation research grant to conduct a 2-year study of home schooling among African American families. She earned her master's degree in elementary education from the University of Bridgeport and taught elementary school in Connecticut Public Schools. Before she began her public school teaching career, she received her B.A. in economics from Hampton University and worked for Xerox Corporation in Stamford, Connecticut. She received her doctorate from Emory University in Atlanta, Georgia.

Michael Fultz is Professor and Chair of the Department of Educational Policy Studies at the University of Wisconsin-Madison, where he teaches courses in the history of American education, the history of African American education, and urban education. His research interests focus on the history of African American teachers in the South and the organizational infrastructure African Americans developed from the post–Civil War period through the 1960s. He holds master's and doctoral degrees from Harvard Graduate School of Education.

Mark A. Gooden is an associate professor in the departments of Educational Leadership and Urban Educational Leadership (UEL) and Director of the UEL program. His research interests include educational technology and its use by administrators; legal issues related to the connection between the Internet, students' rights, and school violence; and issues in urban educational leadership. He taught mathematics and served as the Departmental Chairperson at the high school and middle school levels in the Columbus Public Schools district. His most recent publications appear in *Education and Urban Society, School Business Affairs, Education Law Association Case Citations 2002: Violence and Safety, The Journal of Negro Education,* and *Educational Administration Quarterly.* He served as one of the editors for the Education Law Association's *Principal Legal Handbook* and also completed a chapter for that volume on legal issues associated with students' use of technology and the Internet.

Jessica Gordon Nembhard is an assistant professor and economist in the African American Studies Department, and cofounder of The Democracy Collaborative at the University of Maryland, College Park. Her research focuses on community- and asset-based economic development and democratic community economics, cooperative economics and worker ownership, alternative urban economic and educational development strategies, racial wealth inequality and wealth accumulation in communities of color, and popular economic literacy. Her recent publications include "Cooperatives and Wealth Accumulation," in the *American Economic Review;* "Non Traditional Analyses of Cooperative Economic Impacts," in the *Review of International Co-Operation;* and "On the Road to Democratic Economic Participation: Educating African American Youth in the Post-Industrial Global Economy," in *Black Education: A Transformative Research and Action Agenda for the New Century.* She and Ngina Chiteji are editors of *Wealth Accumulation and Communities of Color: Current Issues* (2006). She was a visiting scholar and senior urban fellow of the Annenberg Institue for School Reform at Brown University. She is the recipient of a Henry C. Welcome Fellowship Grant from the Maryland Higher Education Commission. She has been a member of the Black Enterprise Board of Economists since October 1999.

Will J. Jordan is an associate professor of educational leadership and policy studies at Temple University. His scholarly interests, informed by his background in sociology of education, include school reform, educational policy, and social stratification in school and society. His work focuses on empirical research to broaden understandings of educational inequality and, more practically, to enhance program and policy development for improving the overall quality and conditions of education. With an emphasis on urban schools, his works are aimed at fostering social justice. He has conducted impact evaluation research, which employs experimental design (randomized control trials) and quasi-experimental designs. Prior to joining the faculty at Temple University, he was a senior analyst at The CNA Corporation, a Washington-based, research and consulting firm, and was Research Scientist and Associate Director of the *Center for Social Organization of Schools* at Johns Hopkins University.

Joyce Elaine King holds the Benjamin E. Mays Endowed Chair for Urban Teaching, Learning and Leadership at Georgia State University where she is also Professor of educational policy studies. She is recognized in the United States and abroad for her contributions to the field of education. Her publications include four books—*Preparing Teachers for Diversity, Teaching Diverse Populations, Black Mothers to Sons: Juxtaposing African American Literature With Social Practice,* and *Black Education: A Transformative Research and Action Agenda for the New Century.* Numerous other publications also address the role of cultural knowledge in effective teaching and teacher preparation, Black teachers' emancipatory pedagogy, Black Studies epistemology and curriculum change. One of her most recent publications is, "If Justice Is Our Objective": Diaspora Literacy, Heritage Knowledge, and the Praxis of Critical Studyin' in the *National Society for the Study of Education Yearbook.* In 2001, she founded the Academy for Diaspora Literacy to enable educators and families to use community cultural resources and heritage knowledge to support excellence in education. She is the coeditor of the top-ranked journal, the *Review of Educational Research.*

Sabrina Hope King has devoted her career to improving the educational opportunities and outcomes of those students who are most in need of an excellent education. She spent the first 9 years of her career in the field of urban education as a teacher of ESL and high school equivalency (GED), and as a high school history teacher and dean in the New York City Public School System. For the next 9 years, she was on the curriculum and teaching faculty at University of Illinois at Chicago and Hofstra University. She has also worked as an assistant superintendent of curriculum and instruction and a senior program officer at the Wallace Foundation where she comanaged a national educational leadership policy and practice initiative. A strong understanding of urban school leadership, diversity, culturally relevant practice, and educational equity inform her practice and scholarship. She now directs the Leadership Preparation Institute at Bank Street College where she is able to use all her experiences and expertise in the service of improved school leadership preparation and practice.

Gloria Ladson-Billings is the Kellner Family Chair of Urban Education in the Department of Curriculum & Instruction and Faculty Affiliate in the Department of Educational Policy Studies at the University of Wisconsin-Madison. She is a member of the National Academy of Education and a former president of the American Educational Research Association.

Roderic R. Land is an assistant professor in the Department of Education, Culture, & Society and the Ethnic Studies Program at the University of Utah.

Tondra L. Loder-Jackson is currently an assistant professor in the educational foundations program in the School of Education at the University of Alabama at Birmingham (UAB). Her credentials and training are grounded in interdisciplinary programs of education, human development, and urban policy. Her research and teaching interests include urban education, life course perspectives on education, intergenerational life histories of educators, and the influence of U.S. social movements on education, especially the Birmingham Civil Rights Movement. She is the principal investigator of a Spencer Foundation–funded study examining the salience of activism among Birmingham educators born pre– and post–Civil Rights Movement. As an inaugural member of the UAB Commission on the Status of Women, she chairs the Campus Climate & Environment and Child Care committees.

Marvin Lynn is associate professor and director of Elementary Education at the University of Illinois at Chicago. He was previously Associate Professor and Founder/Director of the

Minority & Urban Education Program at the University of Maryland, College Park. He an emerging leader in the area of studies he identifies as Critical Race Studies in Education. He has published articles in *Teachers College Record, Qualitative Studies in Education,* and *Review of Research in Education.* He also serves on the editorial boards of several education journals. Prior to coming to the university, he taught in public and private elementary schools in New York City (Harlem) and Chicago.

Yolanda J. Majors is an assistant professor of curriculum design in the College of Education, University of Illinois at Chicago (UIC), where she focuses her research on adult/adolescent literacy, curriculum instruction, and multicultural education. She has been with the University since 2004. Prior to joining the faculty at UIC, she was assistant professor of language education at the University of Georgia (2001–2003).

Carol E. Malloy is associate professor in mathematics education in the School of Education at the University of North Carolina at Chapel Hill. Her major research interests are mathematics learning, the influence of culture on the cognitive development of African American students as it relates to mathematics learning, and teacher/student interactions that lead to achievement and understanding in mathematics. She and two other colleagues have just completed data collection for a major 3-year study, funded by the National Science Foundation, investigating students' development as mathematical learners in reform-oriented classrooms. She has research experience related to school reform, including the capacity and successes of the Comer School Development Program and an investigation of two charter schools.

H. Richard Milner IV is the Betts Associate Professor of Education and Human Development in the Department of Teaching and Learning at Peabody College of Vanderbilt University. In 2006, he was awarded the Scholars of Color in Education Early Career Contribution Award of the American Educational Research Association. His research, teaching, and policy interests are (a) urban education, (b) race and equity in education, and (c) teacher education. He is the coeditor (with E. W. Ross) of the book, *Race, Ethnicity, and Education: The Influences of Racial and Ethnic Identity in Education.* His research has appeared in numerous refereed journals including *Educational Researcher; Journal of Negro Education; Urban Education; Education and Urban Society; Teaching and Teacher Education; Race, Ethnicity and Education;* and *Curriculum Inquiry.* He earned the M.A. and Ph.D. from The Ohio State University in Educational Policy and Leadership and the B.A. (in English) and M.A. (in the Teaching of English) from South Carolina State University.

James L. Moore III is an associate professor in counselor education in the College of Education and Human Ecology and coordinator of the school counseling program at The Ohio State University (OSU). He also has a faculty appointment at the Kirwan Institute for the Study of Race and Ethnicity and is the inaugural director of the Todd Anthony Bell National Resource Center on the African American Male at OSU. He has made significant contributions in the fields of (a) school counseling, (b) urban education, (c) gifted education, and (d) multicultural education. On these broad topical areas, he has published more than 70 publications. Additionally, he has received numerous professional honors and awards, such as the Academic Key's Who's Who in Education (2003), Brothers of the Academy's National Junior Scholar Award (2003), OSU College of Education's Distinguished Scholar Award (2004), Ohio School Counselor Association's Research Award (2004), North Central Association for Counselor Education and Supervision's Research Award (2004), Ohio School Counseling Association's George E. Hill Counselor Educators Award (2005), American Education Research Association's Early Career Award in Counseling-Division E Award (2005), North Central Association for Counselor Education and Supervision's Deanna Hawes Outstanding Mentor Award (2005), Manchester Who's Who Among Professionals in Counseling and Development (2005), Counselors for Social Justice's Ohana Award (2006), and Phi Delta Kappa International's Emerging Leader Award (2007) and American Education Research Association's Distinguished Scholar Award in Counseling—Division E (2008).

Peter C. Murrell Jr. is the Founding Dean of the School of Education at Loyola College in Maryland. Prior to that he served as professor of urban education at Northeastern University in Boston, director of its Center for Innovation in Urban Education, and as chair of the Education Department. As a steering committee member of the Institute on Race and Justice, Dr. Murrell was a 2006 corecipient of the University Aspiration Award for extraordinary contributions in social justice and diversity in education. He has taught graduate and undergraduate courses in cognitive learning theory, educational psychology, instructional theory, and the sociocultural contexts of teaching and learning. Dr. Murrell's research focuses upon the development academic identity and racial identity as a joint process of learner achievement and teacher effectiveness. He has authored numerous articles and book chapters on a number of areas in urban education. He is the author of several books, including *The Community Teacher: A New Framework for Effective Urban Teaching, African Centered Pedagogy: Developing Schools of Achievement for African American Children,* and *Like Stone Soup: The Role of the Professional Development School in the Renewal of Urban Schools.* His most recent book addresses this dynamic of identity, learning and teaching: *Race, Culture and Schooling: Identities of Achievement in Multicultural Urban Schools.*

Richard Noble III is a doctoral student in the School of Education at the University of North Carolina at Chapel Hill. He is also a high school mathematics teacher. For the past years, he has taught mathematics (ranging from algebra to calculus) at several colleges and universities and two high schools. Through these experiences, he has seen a need for enhanced pedagogical techniques and enhanced educational techniques to fully develop all students, but specifically African American males. The focus of his research interests is identifying some of the factors that assist African American males to successfully perform in collegiate level mathematics courses. He is interested in developing a program that would assist Black males in successfully completing their collegiate program.

Delila Owens, L.P.C., is an assistant professor in counselor education in the College of Education, Theoretical and Behavioral Foundations Division at Wayne State University. She currently serves on the Michigan Board of Counseling and is president-elect of North Central Associations of Counselor Educators and Supervisors. Her research interests focus on urban school counseling, schooling practices of students of color (particularly urban African American girls), and the career development of underserved populations.

Linda M. Perkins is University Associate Professor and Director of Applied Women's Studies at the Claremont Graduate University. She holds an interdisciplinary university appointment in the departments of Applied Women's Studies, Educational Studies and History. Perkins is a historian of women's and African American higher education. Her primary areas of research are the history of African American women's higher education, the education of African Americans in elite institutions, and the history of talent identification programs for African Americans students. She has served as Fellow and Assistant Director of the Mary Ingraham Bunting Institute of Radcliffe College (1979–1983) and on the faculties of Women's Studies Programs at Barnard College, Hunter College, and the William Paterson College of New Jersey.

Mari Ann Roberts, a former high school English teacher, is a doctoral student in the Division of Educational Studies at Emory University. Her research interests include multicultural education, African American secondary teachers and students, and teacher care. Her current work, *African American Secondary Teachers and Their Definitions of Care for African American Students,* examines teacher care by applying care theory and critical race epistemologies and methodological approaches to African American high school teacher narratives and counter stories.

William A. Smith is an associate professor in the Department of Education, Culture & Society and the Ethnic Studies Program at the University of Utah. In July 2007, he accepted two administrative appointments as the Associate Dean for Diversity, Access, & Equity in the College of Education as well as the Special Assistant to the President & Faculty Athletics Representative. He has held administrative and faculty positions at Eastern Illinois University, Governors State

University in University Park, Illinois, Western Illinois University, and, in 1997, he was awarded a 2-year postdoctoral fellowship with the Center for Urban Educational Research and Development at the University of Illinois at Chicago. Since his arrival in Salt Lake City in 1999, he published his highly regarded coedited book (Philip Altbach and Kofi Lomotey), *The Racial Crisis in American Higher Education: The Continuing Challenges for the 21st Century* (2002). In 2003, he was awarded the Ford Foundation Postdoctoral Research Fellowship to further develop his theoretical concept of Racial Battle Fatigue.

Kay Lovelace Taylor is president of KLT & Associates. She has served as Executive Director for Professional Development for Detroit Public Schools; Associate Superintendent for Philadelphia Public Schools; and Associate Professor in the College of Education at Temple University in Philadelphia. She is president of the board of directors for the George Washington Carver Museum and serves on the national advisory boards for Michigan State University' College of Education and "The Learning Classroom" presented by Mort Crim Communications and Stanford University. She is a founding member of the National Staff Development Council's *Coaching for Results*. She is the author of *Through Their Eyes: A Strategic Response to the National Achievement Gap* and has received numerous awards for her work on behalf of African American children.

Sheilah D. Vance, Esquire, is executive director of the Institute for Educational Equity and Opportunity in Washington, D.C., a research, education, and training organization that focuses on K-12 public school finance issues, and she maintains a private law practice in Philadelphia, Pennsylvania. She is an adjunct professor at Villanova University School of Law, where she teaches education law. She has published and presented extensively in the areas of public education and legal education. She has a J.D. from the Georgetown University Law Center and a B.A. in communications, magna cum laude, from Howard University.

Adah Ward Randolph is associate professor and program coordinator of the Educational Research and Evaluation Program in the Department of Educational Studies at Ohio University. Her research has been published in *Urban Education,* the *Journal of African American History, Howard University Archives.net,* and *Journal of Critical Inquiry Into Curriculum and Instruction.* Her research has primarily focused on the late-19th and early-20th century educational experiences and contributions of African American teachers and principals, particularly in the urban North and South and rural North. She is currently on the editorial board for the *History of Education Quarterly.* She recently received a Spencer Grant to support her research on the life of Ethel Thompson Overby, the first African American woman principal in Richmond, Virginia.

Jon A. Yasin is professor of English, linguistics, and religion at Bergen Community College in Paramus, New Jersey. He taught linguistics for 8 years at the University of the United Arab Emirates in Abu Dhabi. In addition, he was invited by Teachers Across Borders to organize seminars and to lecture at Yangoon University in Myanmaar (Burma) and Pannasastras University in Phenom Penn, Cambodia. He was also the director of Le Centre du Amimation Rurale in N'Gabou, Senegal, for 2 years. On hearing Hip Hop emcees in 1979, he equated their performances with the indigenous griots in Senegal and other countries in West Africa. He has published various articles on emceeing and other styles of talk in African American music, on using Hip Hop to educate millennial students, and on Hip Hop culture.